Marketing
Planning
& Strategy

Subhash C. Jain
School of Business Administration
University of Connecticut

SOUTH-WESTERN College Publishing

An International Thomson Publishing Company

Acquisitions Editor: Dreis E. Van Landuyt
Production Editor: Judith O'Neill
Internal Design: Rick Moore
Cover Design: Tin Box Studio/Sandy Weinstein
Cover Photos: Images provided by ©1994 Photo Disc, Inc.
Production House: DPS Associates, Inc.
Marketing Manager: Stephen E. Momper

Copyright © 1997
by SOUTH-WESTERN COLLEGE PUBLISHING
Cincinnati, Ohio

Library of Congress Cataloging-in-Publication Data
Jain, Subhash C., 1942-
    Marketing planning & strategy / Subhash C. Jain, --5th ed.
        p.   cm.
    Includes bibliographical references and index.
    ISBN 0-538-85283-6
    1. Marketing--Management. I. Title
HF5415.13.J35   1996
658.8'02--dc20   95-51292
                                                 CIP

Printed in the United States of America

    5 6 MT 10 9 8

I(T)P

International Thomson Publishing
South-Western College Publishing is an ITP Company. The ITP trademark is used under license.

With love to
my wife, Sadhna

Contents in Brief

Contents

Preface

In an era marked by the challenges of global competition, rapidly changing technology, new consumer needs, and shifting demographics, the development of strategic marketing skills is essential if companies are to survive, let alone prosper. Because unique strategic marketing moves are not often transparent to competitors and are nearly always difficult and time-consuming to copy, a focus on marketing strategy often yields significant advantage.

Marketing Planning and strategy is a primer on strategic marketing. The book is intended for use in capstone marketing courses. The fifth edition contains two principle parts: text and cases. The text reviews the state of the art in marketing strategy, focusing on both research and concepts. The cases are comprehensive and integrative, most dealing with a broad range of marketing issues across varying strategic circumstances.

Today each company shares with all other companies the challenge of identifying and understanding the markets unfolding around it. Success will depend on the ability to perceive and understand these markets in all their subtlety, inconsistency, and rationality—in other words, in all their complexity. By choice, Marketing Planning and Strategy tries to illustrate and enrich this complexity so that students will approach the subject with the sophistication it deserves.

The book offers new ideas, new insights, and a reliable perspective on marketing strategy formulation. Topics of special interest include:

- Determining what marketing strategy can realistically accomplish for a business
- Determining when a business needs to reformulate its marketing strategy
- Distinguishing marketing strategy from marketing management
- Identifying underlying factors that must be considered in developing marketing strategy
- Analyzing corporate perspective and measuring strengths and weaknesses

- Examining basic changes in America's social and industrial environments that have led to the new emphasis on marketing strategy
- Developing a mission statement that can advance marketing efforts
- Setting realistic marketing objectives
- Determining roles for different products of a business unit
- Employing portfolio techniques in strategy determination and resource allocation
- Organizing for successful strategy implementation
- Identifying the latest techniques for gathering information, undertaking strategic analysis, and formulating strategies

In recent years, to clearly delineate the role of marketing in strategy development, a new term, strategic marketing, has been coined. Marketing may be viewed in three ways: as marketing management, as marketing strategy or strategic marketing, and as corporate marketing. Marketing management deals with strategy implementation, usually at the product/market or brand level. Strategic marketing focuses on strategy formulation, whereas corporate marketing provides inputs for corporatewide strategy.

Strategy is commonly considered at the business unit level. At the heart of business unit strategy is marketing strategy, which becomes the basis of strategy in other functional areas. Integration of all functional strategies represents the business unit strategy. Marketing Planning and Strategy focuses on marketing strategy from the viewpoint of the business unit. The principles and concepts discussed in the book are universally applicable to organizations of all types: manufacturing and service, profit and nonprofit, domestic and foreign, small and large, low- and high-tech, and consumer and industrial products organizations. The book is analytical in approach and managerial in orientation.

HALLMARKS OF THE FIFTH EDITION

This fifth edition presents a much more comprehensive treatment of the subject than previous editions. Developments in the field as evidenced by numerous journal articles, reports, and books on strategic marketing and the extension of my own thinking on the subject have enabled me to provide state-of-the-art coverage of the discipline.

Preparation of this new edition was guided by the following objectives:

- To provide emerging perspectives on strategic marketing
- To add material on global market strategies
- To bring in the international focus in developing marketing strategy
- To examine such emerging topics as product quality and service
- To strengthen the discussion on strategy implementation
- To include new cases reflecting a variety of strategic marketing situations
- To update concepts, illustrations, and statistics throughout

Accomplishment of these objectives led to a number of this edition's distinguishing features.

THE TEXT

Like the previous editions, the fifth edition is based on current conceptual and research literature. The text follows a basic model to explain marketing strategy formulation. The text is organized according to this model, which focuses on company, competition, customer, environment, strengths and weaknesses, objectives and goals, strategy development, and strategy implementation. The fifth edition also contains several significant improvements:

- Current thoughts and concepts in marketing strategy formulation, based on constructs that have taken place in the field
- Incorporation of global focus throughout the book
- Discussion of problems and their solution for successful marketing strategy implementation
- Substantial revision of the chapters on market, product, pricing, distribution, and promotion strategies as well as those on strategic marketing, competitive analysis, environmental scanning, customer analysis, and strategy implementation
- Updating of references to provide the most current perspectives on the subject
- Emphasis on the importance of emerging technologies in formulating marketing strategy
- Importance of ethical and social issues

THE CASES

This edition includes 25 cases, of which 16 are new. The cases have been used at such schools as Harvard Business School, Stanford University, University of Western Ontario, and the University of Connecticut. The cases included involve companies with which students will be familiar—Anheuser-Bush, Gillette, Lever Brothers', American Greetings, Kmart/Wal-Mart, Motorola, Proctor & Gamble, Playboy, and Johnson Controls. Cases to illustrate each aspect of marketing strategy are included. Important improvements in cases include the following:

- An increased emphasis has been placed on including comprehensive and integrative cases that involve as many major strategy components as possible
- New cases have been included, although the total number of cases has been kept to a manageable size
- A concentrated effort has been made to include cases that cover the full spectrum of organizational size
- The number international cases has been increased to 14
- One new case, Mr. Jax Fashion, Inc., deals with NAFTA
- Two cases about service organizations—one about insurance, and one about entertainment—have been included
- Four cases focus on distribution sector

INSTRUCTOR'S MANUAL

The instructor's manual has been completely revised to provide in-depth analysis with a variety of new pedagogical aids: answers to the end-of-chapter discussion questions in the text; true/false, multiple-choice, and fill-in exam questions; suggested syllabi, solutions to cases, suggestions for further reading; and a list of additional cases. Significant improvements in the manual include the following:

- Careful revision of fourth edition test bank questions and the addition of new questions for each chapter
- Transparency masters
- Chapter outlines providing quick chapter reviews
- Comprehensive case notes

Assumptions about the audience significantly affect the style and content of a book. This book is intended primarily for advanced undergraduates and graduate students. Thus, the material has been developed from a classroom-tested conceptual framework. Many of the conceptual schemes included in the book have been reshaped and modified, based on feedback provided by many distinguished marketers. The experiences of a large number of companies have been drawn upon and are cited throughout the book as illustrations.

This book concentrates on areas of strategic importance only, especially those having significant implications and particular relevance for the making of policy decisions in competitive situations. Discussion of routine day-to-day decisions is intentionally avoided to keep focus intact. The overall approach of this book is analytic rather than normative. This approach is necessary because strategy development is more an art than a science. In addition, strategy formulation is a highly complex process for which neat models and econometric equations, no matter how diligently worked out, do not suffice.

ACKNOWLEDGMENTS

A project of this nature cannot be completed without active support from different sources. I have been lucky in this respect to have received advice and assistance from many directions. I acknowledge the valuable feedback provided by students at the University of Connecticut and Graduate School of Business Administration Zurich, who read early drafts of the text as part of their assignments during 1994.

A special mention of appreciation must go to Martha Bory, Assistant Director of the University of Connecticut Center for International Business Education and Research (CIBER), for her editorial assistance; to my doctoral student B. J. Moon for his research help; to departmental secretary Mary Palmer and student helpers Suzette Riley, Marcus Giles, and Michelle Dempsey for their administrative support; and to Melissa Pember in the school's word processing center for typing portions of the manuscript. I am indebted to many writers and publishers for granting permission to include excerpts from their works or their cases, especially Harvard Business School; University of Western Ontario; North American Case Research Association; and the Planning Forum.

I wish to express gratitude to the following individuals for their permission to include cases written by them or under their supervision: Professor Frank V.

Cespedes, Harvard Business School; Professor C. Patrick Woodcock, University of Western Ontario; Professor J. Michael Geringer, University of Western Ontario; Professor Gordon H. G. McDougall, Wilfrid Laurier University; Professor Douglas Snetsinger, Wilfrid Laurier University; Professor Adrian B. Ryans, University of Western Ontario; V. Kasturi Rangan, Harvard Business School; Professor C. P. Rao, Old Dominion University; Professor D. Michael Fields, Southwest Missouri State University; Professor Neil C. Herndon Jr., Southwest Missouri State University; Professor Dan Kopp, Southwest Missouri State University; Professor Louis Shufeldt, Southwest Missouri State University; Professor Fred W. Kniffin, University of Connecticut; Professor Natalie Tabb Taylor, Babson College; Professor C. B. Johnston, University of Western Ontario; Professor Robert T Davis, Stanford Graduate School of Business; Professor Shreekant G. Joag, St. John's University; Juan M. Florin, University of Connecticut; Dean Aluzio, University of Connecticut; Professor Michael Lubatkin, University of Connecticut; Professor J. B. Wilkinson, Youngstown State University; Professor Gary B. Frank, University of Akron; Professor Franklin Ramsoomair, Wilfrid Laurier University; Tracy K. Short, Johnson Controls, Inc.

Throughout the development of this fifth edition, a number of reviewers made important contributions, and at the same time, many colleagues provided insightful suggestions. All these individuals had an important influence on my thinking:

John K. Rayans, Jr., *Kent State University;*

Roberto Friedman, *University of Georgia;*

P. Rajan Varadarajan, *Texas A&M University;*

Lewis R. Tucker, *University of Hartford;*

Ronald J. Patten, *DePaul University;*

Rajan Chandran, *Temple University;*

Hugh E. Kramer, *University of Hawaii;*

William E. Rice, *California State University-Fresno;*

Suresh Subramanian, *University of South Dakota;*

Lee Pickler, *Baldwin-Wallace College;*

David M. Pressner, *Tampa College;*

I owe a special word of gratitude to my former teacher, Professor Stuart U. Rich of the University of Oregon, who taught me what I know about marketing strategy, and to my dean, Thomas G. Gutteridge, who encouraged me to undertake this project.

I am indebted to the talented staff at South-Western Publishing Co., for their role in shaping the fifth edition. My editor, Dreis Van Landuyt, furnished excellent advice on the structure of the fifth edition. My production editor Judy O'Neill, did a super job of seeing the book to completion. I also want to thank DPS Associates, Inc., for the fine job of editing and publishing.

Finally, my gratitude must go to my wife and our children, who not only made it possible for me to live through the experience but gave me their support and inspiration in countless ways. This book belongs more to them than to me.

S C J
Storrs, Connecticut
March 7, 1996

Introduction

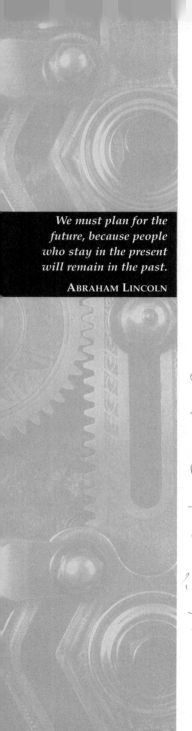

Marketing and the Concept of Planning and Strategy

Over the years marketers have been presented with a series of philosophical approaches to marketing decision making. One widely used approach is the *marketing concept approach*, which directs the marketer to develop the product offering, and indeed the entire marketing program, to meet the needs of the customer base. A key element in this approach is the need for information flow from the market to the decision maker. Another approach is the *systems approach*, which instructs the marketer to view the product not as an individual entity but as just one aspect of the customer's total need-satisfaction system. A third approach, the *environmental approach*, portrays the marketing decision maker as the focal point of numerous environments within which the firm operates and that affect the success of the firm's marketing program. These environments frequently bear such labels as legal-political, economic, competitive, consumer, market structure, social, technological, and international.

Indeed, these and other philosophical approaches to marketing decision making are merely descriptive frameworks that stress certain aspects of the firm's role vis-a-vis the strategic planning process. No matter what approach a firm follows, it needs a reference point for its decisions that is provided by the strategy and the planning process involved in designing the strategy. Thus, the strategic planning process is the guiding force behind decision making, regardless of the approach one adopts. This relationship between the strategic planning process and approaches to marketing decision making is depicted in Exhibit 1-1.

Planning perspectives develop in response to needs that arise internally or that impinge on the organization from outside. During the 1950s and 1960s, growth was the dominant fact of the economic environment, and the planning processes developed during that time were typically geared to the discovery and exploitation of entrepreneurial opportunities. Decentralized planning was the order of the day. Top management focused on reviewing major investment proposals and approving annual operating budgets. Long-range corporate plans

EXHIBIT 1-1

Relationship between the Strategic Planning Process and Approaches to Marketing Decision Making

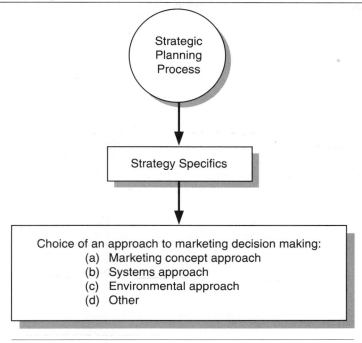

were occasionally put together, but they were primarily extrapolations and were rarely used for strategic decision making.

Planning perspectives changed in the 1970s. With the quadrupling of energy costs and the emergence of competition from new quarters, followed by a recession and reports of an impending capital crisis, companies found themselves surrounded by new needs. Reflecting these new management needs and concerns, a process aimed at more centralized control over resources soon pervaded planning efforts. Sorting out winners and losers, setting priorities, and conserving capital became the name of the game. A new era of strategic planning dawned over corporate America.

The value of effective strategic planning is virtually unchallenged in today's business world. A majority of the *Fortune* 1000 firms in the United States, for instance, now have senior executives responsible for spearheading strategic planning efforts.

Strategic planning requires that company assets (i.e., resources) be managed to maximize financial return through the selection of a viable business in accordance with the changing environment. One very important component of strategic planning is the establishment of the product/market scope of a business. It is within this scope that strategic planning becomes relevant for marketers.[1] Thus, as companies adopted and made progress in their strategic planning capabilities, a new strategic role for marketing emerged. In this strategic role, marketing concentrates on the markets to serve, the competition to be tackled, and the timing of market entry/exit.

CONCEPT OF PLANNING

Throughout human history, people have tried to achieve specific purposes, and in this effort some sort of planning has always found a place. In modern times, the former Soviet Union was the first nation to devise an economic plan for growth and development. After World War II, national economic planning became a popular activity, particularly among developing countries, with the goal of systematic and organized action designed to achieve stated objectives within a given period. Among market economies, France has gone the furthest in planning its economic affairs. In the business world, Henri Fayol, the French industrialist, is credited with the first successful attempts at formal planning.

Accomplishments attributed to planning can be summarized as follows:

1. Planning leads to a better position, or standing, for the organization.
2. Planning helps the organization progress in ways that its management considers most suitable.
3. Planning helps every manager think, decide, and act more effectively and progress in the desired direction.
4. Planning helps keep the organization flexible.
5. Planning stimulates a cooperative, integrated, enthusiastic approach to organizational problems.
6. Planning indicates to management how to evaluate and check up on progress toward planned objectives.
7. Planning leads to socially and economically useful results.

Planning in corporations emerged as an important activity in the 1960s. Several studies undertaken during that time showed that companies attached significant importance to planning. A Conference Board survey of 420 firms, for example, revealed that 85 percent had formalized corporate planning activity.[2] A 1983 survey by Coopers & Lybrand and Yankelovich, Skelly, and White confirmed the central role played by the planning function and the planner in running most large businesses.[3] Although the importance of planning had been acknowledged for some time, the executives interviewed in 1983 indicated that planning was becoming more important and was receiving greater attention. A 1991 study by McDonald's noted that marketing planning is commonly practiced by companies of all sizes, and there is wide agreement on the benefits to be gained from such planning.[4]

Some companies that use formal planning believe that it improves profits and growth, finding it particularly useful in explicit objective setting and in monitoring results.[5] Certainly, the current business climate is generating a new posture among executives, with the planning process being identified by eight out of ten respondents as a key to implementing the chief executive officer's (CEO) chosen strategy.[6] Today most companies insist on some sort of planning exercise to meet the rapidly changing environment. For many, however, the exercise is cathartic rather than creative.

Growth is an accepted expectation of a firm; however, growth does not happen by itself. Growth must be carefully planned: questions such as how much, when, in which areas, where to grow, and who will be responsible for different tasks must be answered. Unplanned growth will be haphazard and may fail to provide desired levels of profit. Therefore, for a company to realize orderly growth, to maintain a high level of operating efficiency, and to achieve its goals fully, it must plan for the future systematically. Products, markets, facilities, personnel, and financial resources must be evaluated and selected wisely.

Today's business environment is more complex than ever. In addition to the keen competition that firms face from both domestic and overseas companies, a variety of other concerns, including environmental protection, employee welfare, consumerism, and antitrust action, impinge on business moves. Thus, it is desirable for a firm to be cautious in undertaking risks, which again calls for a planned effort.

Many firms pursue growth internally through research and development. This route to growth is not only time-consuming but also requires a heavy commitment of resources with a high degree of risk. In such a context, planning is needed to choose the right type of risk.

Since World War II, technology has had a major impact on markets and marketers. Presumably, the trend of accelerating technological change will continue in the future. The impact of technological innovations may be felt in any industry or in any firm. Therefore, such changes need to be anticipated as far in advance as possible in order for a firm to take advantage of new opportunities and to avoid the harmful consequences of not anticipating major new developments. Here again, planning is significant.

Finally, planning is required in making a choice among the many equally attractive alternative investment opportunities a firm may have. No firm can afford to invest in each and every "good" opportunity. Planning, thus, is essential in making the right selection.

Planning for future action has been called by many different names: long-range planning, corporate planning, comprehensive planning, and formal planning. Whatever its name, the reference is obviously to the future.

| *Definition of Planning* | Warren defines **planning** as |

> essentially a process directed toward making today's decisions with tomorrow in mind and a means of preparing for future decisions so that they may be made rapidly, economically, and with as little disruption to the business as possible.[7]

Though there are as many definitions of planning as there are writers on the subject, Warren's emphasis on the future is the common thread underlying all planning theory. In practice, however, different meanings are attached to planning. A distinction is often made between a *budget* (a yearly program of operations) and a *long-range plan.* Some people consider planning as something done by staff specialists, whereas budgeting is seen to fall within the purview of line managers.

It is necessary for a company to be clear about the nature and scope of the planning that it intends to adopt. A definition of planning should then be based on what planning is supposed to be in an organization. It is not necessary for every company to engage in the same style of comprehensive planning. The basis of all planning should be to design courses of action to be pursued for achieving stated objectives such that opportunities are seized and threats are guarded against, but the exact planning posture must be custom-made (i.e., based on the decision-making needs of the organization).

Operations management, which emphasizes the current programs of an organization, and planning, which essentially deals with the future, are two intimately related activities. Operations management or budgeted programs should emerge as the result of planning. In the outline of a five-year plan, for example, years two through five may be described in general terms, but the activities of the first year should be budgeted and accompanied by detailed operational programs.

A distinction should also be made between planning and forecasting. Forecasting considers future changes in areas of importance to a company and tries to assess the impact of these changes on company operations. Planning takes over from there to set objectives and goals and develop strategy.

Briefly, no business, however small or poorly managed, can do without planning. Although planning per se may be nothing new for an organization, the current emphasis on it is indeed different. No longer just one of several important functions of the organization, planning's new role demands linkage of various parts of an organization into an integrated system. The emphasis has shifted from planning as an aspect of the organization to planning as the basis of all efforts and decisions, the building of an entire organization toward the achievement of designated objectives.

There is little doubt about the importance of planning. Planning departments are key in critiquing strategies, crystallizing goals, setting priorities, and maintaining control;[8] but to be useful, planning should be done properly. Planning just for the sake of it can be injurious; half-hearted planning can cause more problems than it solves. In practice, however, many business executives simply pay lip service to planning, partly because they find it difficult to incorporate planning into the decision-making process and partly because they are uncertain how to adopt it.

| *Requisites for Successful Planning* | If planning is to succeed, proper arrangements must be made to put it into operation. The Boston Consulting Group suggests the following concerns for effective planning: |

- There is the matter of outlook, which can affect the degree to which functional and professional viewpoints, versus corporate needs, dominate the work of planning.
- There is the question of the extent of involvement for members of the management. Who should participate, and to what extent?
- There is the problem of determining what part of the work of planning should be accomplished through joint effort and how to achieve effective collaboration among participants in the planning process.

- There is the matter of incentive, of making planning an appropriately empha-sized and rewarded kind of managerial work.
- There is the question of how to provide staff coordination for planning, which raises the issue of how a planning unit should be used in the organization.
- And there is the role of the chief executive in the planning process. What should it be? [9]

Though planning is conceptually rather simple, implementing it is far from easy. Successful planning requires a blend of many forces in different areas, not the least of which are behavioral, intellectual, structural, philosophical, and managerial. Achieving the proper blend of these forces requires making difficult decisions, as the Boston Consulting Group has suggested. Although planning is indeed complex, successful planning systems do have common fundamental characteristics despite differing operational details. First, it is essential that the CEO be completely supportive. Second, planning must be kept simple, in agree-ment with the managerial style, and unencumbered by detailed numbers and fancy equations. Third, planning is a shared responsibility, and it would be wrong to assume that the president or vice president of planning, staff special-ists, or line managers can do it single-handedly. Fourth, the managerial incen-tive system should give due recognition to the fact that decisions made with long-term implications may not appear good in the short run. Fifth, the goals of planning should be achievable without excessive frustration and work load and with widespread understanding and acceptance of the process. Sixth, overall flexibility should be encouraged to accommodate changing conditions.

Initiating Planning Activities

There is no one best time for initiating planning activities in an organization; however, before developing a formal planning system, the organization should be prepared to establish a strong planning foundation. The CEO should be a central participant, spearheading the planning job. A planning framework should be developed to match the company's perspective and should be generally accepted by its executives. A manual outlining the work flow, information links, format of various documents, and schedules for completing various activities should be prepared by the planner. Once these foundations are completed, the company can initiate the planning process anytime.

Planning should not be put off until bad times prevail; it is not just a cure for poor performance. Although planning is probably the best way to avoid bad times, planning efforts that are begun when operational performance is at an ebb (i.e., at low or no profitability) will only make things worse, since planning efforts tend initially to create an upheaval by challenging the traditional patterns of deci-sion making. The company facing the question of survival should concentrate on alleviating the current crisis.

Planning should evolve gradually. It is wishful thinking to expect full-scale planning to be instituted in a few weeks or months. Initial planning may be for-malized in one or more functional areas; then, as experience is gained, a company-wide planning system may be designed. IBM, a pioneer in formalized planning, followed this pattern. First, financial planning and product planning were attempted in the post-World War II period. Gradual changes toward increased formality were made over the years. In the later half of 1960s, increased attention was given to planning contents, and a compatible network of planning data systems was initiated. Corporate-wide planning, which was introduced in the 1970s, forms the backbone of IBM's current global planning endeavors. Beginning in 1986, the company made several changes in its planning perspectives in response to the contingencies created by deteriorating performance. In the 1990s, planning at IBM became more centralized to fully seek resource control and coordination.

Philosophies of Planning

In an analysis of three different philosophies of planning, Ackoff established the labels satisfying, optimizing, and adaptivizing.[10] Planning on the basis of the **satisfying** philosophy aims at easily achievable goals and molds planning efforts accordingly. This type of planning requires setting objectives and goals that are "high enough" but not as "high as possible." The satisfying planner, therefore, devises only one feasible and acceptable way of achieving goals, which may not necessarily be the best possible way. Under a satisfying philosophy, confrontations that might be caused by conflicts in programs are diffused through politicking, underplaying change, and accepting a fall in performance as unavoidable.

The philosophy of **optimizing** planning has its foundation in operations research. The optimizing planner seeks to model various aspects of the organization and define them as objective functions. Efforts are then directed so that an objective function is maximized (or minimized), subject to the constraints imposed by management or forced by the environment. For example, an objective may be to obtain the highest feasible market share; planning then amounts to searching for different variables that affect market share: price elasticity, plant capacity, competitive behavior, the product's stage in the life cycle, and so on. The effect of each variable is reduced to constraints on the market share. Then an analysis is undertaken to find out the optimum market share to target.

Unlike the satisfying planner, the optimizer endeavors, with the use of mathematical models, to find the best available course to realize objectives and goals. The success of an optimizing planner depends on how completely and accurately the model depicts the underlying situation and how well the planner can figure out solutions from the model once it has been built.

Ackoff considers the philosophy of **adaptivizing** planning as an innovative approach not yet popular in practice. To understand the nature of this type of planning, let us compare it to optimizing planning. In optimization, the significant variables and their effects are taken for granted. Given these, an effort is made to achieve the optimal result. With an adaptivizing approach, on the other hand, planning may be undertaken to produce changes in the underlying relationships themselves and thereby create a desired future. Underlying relationships refer to an organization's internal and external environment and the dynamics of the values of the actors in these environments (i.e., how values relate to needs and to the satisfaction of needs, how changes in needs produce changes in values, and how changes in needs are produced).

CONCEPT OF STRATEGY

Strategy in a firm is

the pattern of major objectives, purposes, or goals and essential policies and plans for achieving those goals, stated in such a way as to define what business the company is in or is to be in and the kind of company it is or is to be. [11]

Any organization needs strategy (a) when resources are finite, (b) when there is uncertainty about competitive strengths and behavior, (c) when commitment of resources is irreversible, (d) when decisions must be coordinated between far-flung places and over time, and (e) when there is uncertainty about control of the initiative.

An explicit statement of strategy is the key to success in a changing business environment. Strategy provides a unified sense of direction to which all members of the organization can relate. Where there is no clear concept of strategy, decisions rest on either subjective or intuitive assessment and are made without regard to other decisions.[12] Such decisions become increasingly unreliable as the pace of change accelerates or decelerates rapidly. Without a strategy, an organization is like a ship without a rudder going around in circles.[13]

Strategy is concerned with the deployment of potential for results and the development of a reaction capability to adapt to environmental changes. Quite naturally, we find that there are hierarchies of strategies: corporate strategy and business strategy. At the corporate level, strategy is mainly concerned with defining the set of businesses that should form the company's overall profile. **Corporate strategy** seeks to unify all the business lines of a company and point them toward an overall goal. At the business level, strategy focuses on defining the manner of competition in a given industry or product/market segment. A **business strategy** usually covers a plan for a single product or a group of related products. Today, most strategic action takes place at the business unit level, where sophisticated tools and techniques permit the analysis of a business; the forecasting of such variables as market growth, pricing, and the impact of government regulation; and the establishment of a plan that can sidestep threats in an erratic environment from competitors, economic cycles, and social, political, and consumer changes.

Each functional area of a business (e.g., marketing) makes its own unique contribution to strategy formulation at different levels. In many firms, the marketing function represents the greatest degree of contact with the external environment, the environment least controllable by the firm. In such firms, marketing plays a pivotal role in strategy development.

In its strategic role, marketing consists of establishing a match between the firm and its environment. It seeks solutions to problems of deciding (a) what business the firm is in and what kinds of business it may enter in the future and (b) how the chosen field(s) of endeavor may be successfully run in a competitive environment by pursuing product, price, promotion, and distribution perspectives to serve target markets. In the context of strategy formulation, marketing has two dimensions: present and future. The present dimension deals with the existing relationships of the firm to its environments. The future dimension encompasses intended future relationships (in the form of a set of objectives) and the action programs necessary to reach those objectives. The following example illustrates the point.

McDonald's, the hamburger chain, has among its corporate objectives the goal of increasing the productivity of its operating units. Given the high proportion of costs in fixed facilities, McDonald's decided to increase facility utilization during off-peak hours, particularly during the morning hours. The program developed to accomplish these goals, the Egg McMuffin, was followed by a breakfast menu consistent with the limited product line strategy of McDonald's regular fare. In this example, the corporate goal of increased productivity led to the marketing perspective of breakfast fare (intended relationship), which was built over favorable customer attitudes toward the chain (existing relationship). Similarly, a new marketing strategy in the form of McDonald's Pizza (intended relationship) was pursued over the company's ability to serve food fast (existing relationship) to meet the corporate goal of growth.

Generally, organizations have identifiable existing strategic perspectives; however, not many organizations have an explicit strategy for the intended future. The absence of an explicit strategy is frequently the result of a lack of top management involvement and commitment required for the development of proper perspectives of the future within the scope of current corporate activities.

Marketing provides the core element for future relationships between the firm and its environment. It specifies inputs for defining objectives and helps formulate plans to achieve them.

CONCEPT OF STRATEGIC PLANNING

Strategy specifies direction. Its intent is to influence the behavior of competitors and the evolution of the market to the advantage of the strategist. It seeks to change the competitive environment. Thus, a strategy statement includes a description of the new competitive equilibrium to be created, the cause-and-effect relationships that will bring it about, and the logic to support the course of action. Planning articulates the means of implementing strategy. A strategic plan specifies the sequence and the timing of steps that will alter competitive relationships.

The strategy and the strategic plan are quite different things. The strategy may be brilliant in content and logic, but the sequence and timing of the plan, inadequate. The plan may be the laudable implementation of a worthless strategy. Put together, strategic planning concerns the relationship of an organization to its environment. Conceptually, the organization monitors its environment, incorporates the effects of environmental changes into corporate decision making, and formulates new strategies. Exhibit 1-2 provides a scorecard to evaluate the viability of a company's strategic planning effort.

Companies that do well in strategic planning define their goals clearly and develop rational plans to implement them. In addition, they take the following steps to make their strategic planning effective:

EXHIBIT 1-2
A Strategic Planning Scorecard

- Is our planning really strategic?

  Do we try to anticipate change or only project from the past?

- Do our plans leave room to explore strategic alternatives?

  Or do they confine us to conventional thinking?

- Do we have time and incentive to investigate truly important things?

  Or do we spend excessive planning time on trivia?

- Have we ever seriously evaluated a new approach to an old market?

  Or are we locked into the status quo?

- Do our plans critically document and examine strategic assumptions?

  Or do we not really understand the implications of the plans we review?

- Do we consistently make an attempt to examine consumer, competitor, and distributor responses to our programs?

  Or do we assume the changes will not affect the relationships we have seen in the past?

Source: Thomas P. Justad and Ted J. Mitchell, "Creative Market Planning in a Partisan Environment," *Business Horizons* (March–April 1982): 64, copyright 1982 by the Foundation for the School of Business at Indiana University. Reprinted by permission.

- They shape the company into logical business units that can identify markets, customers, competitors, and the external threats to their business. These business units are managed semi-autonomously by executives who operate under corporate financial guidelines and with an understanding of the unit's assigned role in the corporate plan.
- They demonstrate a willingness at the corporate level to compensate line managers on long-term achievements, not just the yearly bottom line; to fund research programs that could give the unit a long-term competitive edge; and to offer the unit the type of planning support that provides data on key issues and encourages and teaches sophisticated planning techniques.
- They develop at the corporate level the capacity to evaluate and balance competing requests from business units for corporate funds, based on the degree of risk and reward.
- They match shorter-term business unit goals to a long-term concept of the company's evolution over the next 15 to 20 years. Exclusively the CEO's function, effectiveness in matching business unit goals to the firm's evolution may be tested by the board of directors.

Strategic Planning: An Example	The importance of strategic planning for a company may be illustrated by the example of the Mead Corporation. The Mead Corporation is basically in the forest products business. More than 75 percent of its earnings are derived from trees, from the manufacture of pulp and paper, to the conversion of paperboard to beverage carriers, to the distribution of paper supplies to schools. Mead also has an array of businesses outside the forest products industry and is developing new

technologies and businesses for its future, primarily in storing, retrieving, and reproducing data electronically. In short, Mead is a company growing in the industries in which it started as well as expanding into areas that fit the capabilities and style of its management.

Although Mead was founded in 1846, it did not begin to grow rapidly until around 1955, reaching the $1 billion mark in sales in the late 1960s. Unfortunately, its competitive position did not keep pace with this expansion. In 1972 the company ranked 12th among 15 forest products companies. Clearly, if Mead was to become a leading company, its philosophy, its management style and focus, and its sense of urgency—its whole corporate culture—had to change. The vehicle for that change was the company's strategic planning process.

When top managers began to discuss ways to improve Mead, they quickly arrived at the key question: What kind of performing company should Mead be? They decided that Mead should be in the top quartile of those companies with which it was normally compared. Articulation of such a clear and simple objective provided all levels of management with a sense of direction and with a frame of reference within which to make and test their own decisions. This objective was translated into specific long-term financial goals.

In 1972 a rigorous assessment of Mead's businesses was made. The results of this assessment were not comforting—several small units were in very weak competitive positions. They were substantial users of cash that was needed elsewhere in businesses where Mead had opportunities for significant growth. Mead's board decided that by 1977 the company should get out of certain businesses, even though some of those high cash users were profitable.

Setting goals and assessing Mead's mix of businesses were only the first steps. Strategic planning had to become a way of life if the corporate culture was going to be changed. Five major changes were instituted. First, the corporate goals were articulated throughout the company—over and over and over again.

Second, the management system was restructured. This restructuring was much easier said than done. In Mead's pulp and paper businesses, the culture expected top management to be heavily involved in the day-to-day operation of major facilities and intimately involved in major construction projects, a style that had served the company well when it was simply a producer of paper. By the early 1970s, however, Mead was simply too large and too diverse for such a hands-on approach. The nonpulp and paper businesses, which were managed with a variety of styles, needed to be integrated into a more balanced management system. Therefore, it was essential for top management to stay out of day-to-day operations. This decision allowed division managers to become stronger and to develop a greater sense of personal responsibility for their operations. By staying away from major construction projects, top managers allowed on-site managers to complete under budget and ahead of schedule the largest and most complex programs in the company's history.

Third, simultaneously with the restructuring of its management system, seminars were used to teach strategic planning concepts and techniques. These seminars, sometimes week-long sessions, were held off the premises with groups of

5 to 20 people at a time. Eventually, the top 300 managers in the company became graduates of Mead's approach to strategic planning.

4   Fourth, specific and distinctly different goals were developed and agreed upon for each of Mead's two dozen or so business units. Whereas the earlier Mead culture had charged each operation to grow in any way it could, each business unit now had to achieve a leadership position in its markets or, if a leadership position was not practical, to generate cash.

5   Finally, the board began to fund agreed-upon strategies instead of approving capital projects piecemeal or yielding to emotional pleas from favorite managers.

The first phase of change was the easiest to accomplish. Between 1973 and 1976, Mead disposed of 11 units that offered neither growth nor significant cash flow. Over $100 million was obtained from these divestitures, and that money was promptly reinvested in Mead's stronger businesses. As a result, Mead's mix of businesses showed substantial improvement by 1977. In fact, Mead achieved its portfolio goals one year ahead of schedule.

For the remaining businesses, developing better strategies and obtaining better operating performance were much harder to achieve. After all, on a relative basis, the company was performing well. With the exception of 1975, 1984, 1989, and 1992, the years from 1973 to 1993 set all-time records for performance. The evolution of Mead's strategic planning system and the role it played in helping the good businesses of the company improve their relative performance are public knowledge. The financial results speak for themselves. In spite of the divestitures of businesses with sales of over $500 million, Mead's sales grew at a compound rate of 9 percent from 1973 to reach $4.8 billion in 1993. In addition, by the end of 1993, Mead's return on total capital (ROTC) reached 11.2 percent. More important, among 15 forest products companies with which Mead is normally compared, it had moved from twelfth place in 1972 to second place in 1983, a position it continued to maintain in 1994. These were the results of using a strategic planning system as the vehicle for improving financial performance.

During the period from 1988 to 1993, Mead took additional measures to increase its focus in two areas: (a) its coated paper and board business and (b) its value-added, less capital-intensive businesses (the distribution and conversion of paper and related supplies and electronic publishing). Today Mead is a well-managed, highly focused, aggressive company. It is well positioned to be exceptionally successful in the rest of 1990s, and beyond.

Strategic Planning:
Emerging
Perspectives

Many forces affected the way strategic planning developed in the 1970s and early 1980s. These forces included slower growth worldwide, intense global competition, burgeoning automation, obsolescence due to technological change, deregulation, an explosion in information availability, more rapid shifts in raw material prices, chaotic money markets, and major changes in macroeconomic and sociopolitical systems. As a result, destabilization and fluidity have become the norm in world business.

Today there are many, many strategic alternatives for all types of industries. Firms are constantly coming up with new ways of making products and getting them to market. Comfortable positions in industry after industry (e.g., in banking, telecommunications, airlines, automobiles) are disappearing, and barriers to entry are much more difficult to maintain. Markets are open, and new competitors are coming from unexpected directions.

To steadily prosper in such an environment, companies need new strategic planning perspectives. First, top management must assume a more explicit role in strategic planning, dedicating a large amount of time to deciding how things ought to be instead of listening to analyses of how they are. Second, strategic planning must become an exercise in creativity instead of an exercise in forecasting. Third, strategic planning processes and tools that assume that the future will be similar to the past must be replaced by a mindset obsessed with being first to recognize change and turn it into competitive advantage. Fourth, the role of the planner must change from being a purveyor of incrementalism to that of a crusader for action. Finally, strategic planning must be restored to the core of line management responsibilities.

These perspectives can be described along five action-oriented dimensions: managing a business for competitive advantage, viewing change as an opportunity, managing through people, shaping the strategically managed organization, and managing for focus and flexibility. Considering these dimensions can make strategic planning more relevant and effective.

Managing for Competitive Advantage.   Organizations in a market economy are concerned with delivering a service or product in the most profitable way. The key to profitability is to achieve a sustainable competitive advantage based on superior performance relative to the competition. Superior performance requires doing three things better than the competition. First, the firm must clearly designate the product/market, based on marketplace realities and a true understanding of its strengths and weaknesses. Second, it must design a winning business system or structure that enables the company to outperform competitors in producing and delivering the product or service. Third, management must do a better job of managing the overall business system, by managing not only relationships within the corporation but also critical external relationships with suppliers, customers, and competitors.[14]

Viewing Change as an Opportunity.   A new culture should be created within the organization such that managers look to change as an opportunity and adapt their business system to continuously emerging conditions. In other words, change should not be viewed as a problem but as a source of opportunity, providing the potential for creativity and innovation.

Managing through People.   Management's first task is to create a vision of the organization that includes (a) where the organization should be going, again based on a clear examination of the company's strengths and weaknesses; (b) what markets it should compete in; (c) how it will compete; and (d) major action programs required. The next task is to convert vision to reality—to develop the capabilities of the organization, to expedite change and remove obstacles, and to shape the environment. Central to both the establishment and execution of a corporate vision is the effective recruitment, development, and deployment of human resources. "In the end, management is measured by the skill and sensitivity with which it manages and develops people, for it is only through the quality of their people that organizations can change effectively."[15]

Shaping the Strategically Managed Organization.[16]   Management should work toward developing an innovative, self-renewing organization that the future will demand. Organizational change depends on such factors as structure, strategy, systems, style, skills, staff, and shared values. Organizations that take an externally focused, forward-looking approach to the design of these factors have a much better chance of self-renewal than those whose perspective is predominantly internal and historical.

Managing for Focus and Flexibility.   Today, strategic planning should be viewed differently than it was viewed in the past. A five-year plan, updated annually, should be replaced by an ongoing concern for the direction the organization is taking. Many scholars describe an ongoing concern for the direction of the firm, that is, concern with what a company must do to become smart, targeted, and nimble enough to prosper in an era of constant change, as strategic thinking.[17] The key words in this pursuit are focus and flexibility.

Focus means figuring out and building on what the company does best. It involves identifying the evolving needs of customers, then developing the key skills—often called the *core competencies*—making sure that everyone in the company understands them. Flexibility means sketching rough scenarios of the future (i.e., bands of possibilities) and being ready to pounce on opportunities as they arise.

STRATEGIC BUSINESS UNITS (SBUs)

Frequent reference has been made in this chapter to the business unit, a unit comprising one or more products having a common market base whose manager has complete responsibility for integrating all functions into a strategy against an identifiable competitor. Usually referred to as a **strategic business unit (SBU)**, business units have also been called strategy centers, strategic planning units, or independent business units. The philosophy behind the SBU concept has been described this way:

> The diversified firm should be managed as a "portfolio" of businesses, with each business unit serving a clearly defined product-market segment with a clearly defined strategy.
>
> Each business unit in the portfolio should develop a strategy tailored to its capabilities and competitive needs, but consistent with the overall corporate capabilities and needs.
>
> The total portfolio of businesses should be managed by allocating capital and managerial resources to serve the interests of the firm as a whole—to achieve balanced growth in sales, earnings, and assets mix at an acceptable and controlled level of risk. In essence, the portfolio should be designed and managed to achieve an overall corporate strategy.[18]

Since formal strategic planning began to make inroads in corporations in the 1970s, a variety of new concepts have been developed for identifying a corporation's opportunities and for speeding up the process of strategy development. These newer concepts create problems of internal organization. In a dynamic economy, all functions of a corporation (e.g., research and development, finance, and marketing) are related. Optimizing certain functions instead of the company as a whole is far from adequate for achieving superior corporate performance. Such an organizational perspective leaves only the CEO in a position to think in terms of the corporation as a whole. Large corporations have tried many different structural designs to broaden the scope of the CEO in dealing with complexities. One such design is the profit center concept. Unfortunately, the profit center concept emphasizes short-term consequences; also, its emphasis is on optimizing the profit center instead of the corporation as a whole.

The SBU concept was developed to overcome the difficulties posed by the profit center type of organization. Thus, the first step in integrating product/market strategies is to identify the firm's SBUs. This amounts to identifying natural businesses in which the corporation is involved. SBUs are not necessarily synonymous with existing divisions or profit centers. An SBU is composed of a product or product lines having identifiable independence from other products or product lines in terms of competition, prices, substitutability of product, style/quality, and impact of product withdrawal. It is around this configuration of products that a business strategy should be designed. In today's organizations, this strategy may encompass products found in more than one division. By the same token, some managers may find themselves managing two or more natural businesses. This does not necessarily mean that divisional boundaries need to be redefined; an SBU can often overlap divisions, and a division can include more than one SBU.

SBUs may be created by applying a set of criteria consisting of price, competitors, customer groups, and shared experience. To the extent that changes in a product's price entail a review of the pricing policy of other products may imply that these products have a natural alliance. If various products/markets of a company share the same group of competitors, they may be amalgamated into an SBU for the purpose of strategic planning. Likewise, products/markets sharing a common set of customers belong together. Finally, products/markets in different parts of the company having common research and development, manufacturing, and marketing components may be included in the same SBU. For purposes of illustration, consider the case of a large, diversified company, one division of which manufactures car radios. The following possibilities exist: the car radio division, as it stands, may represent a viable SBU; alternatively, luxury car radios with automatic tuning may constitute an SBU different from the SBU for standard models; or other areas of the company, such as the television division, may be combined with all or part of the car radio division to create an SBU.

Overall, an SBU should be established at a level where it can rather freely address (a) all key segments of the customer group having similar objectives; (b) all key functions of the corporation so that it can deploy whatever functional expertise is needed to establish positive differentiation from the competition in the eyes of the customer; and (c) all key aspects of the competition so that the corporation can seize the advantage when opportunity presents itself and, conversely, so that competitors will not be able to catch the corporation off-balance by exploiting unsuspected sources of strength.

A conceptual question becomes relevant in identifying SBUs: How much aggregation is desirable? Higher levels of aggregation produce a relatively smaller and more manageable number of SBUs. Besides, the existing management information system may not need to be modified since a higher level of aggregation yields SBUs of the size and scope of present divisions or product groups. However, higher levels of aggregation at the SBU level permit only general notions of strategy that may lack relevance for promoting action at the operating level. For example, an SBU for medical care is probably too broad. It could embrace equipment, service, hospitals, education, self-discipline, and even social welfare.

On the other hand, lower levels of aggregation make SBUs identical to product/market segments that may lack "strategic autonomy." An SBU for farm tractor engines would be ineffective because it is at too low a level in the organization to (a) consider product applications and customer groups other than farmers or (b) cope with new competitors who might enter the farm tractor market at almost any time with a totally different product set of "boundary conditions." Further, at such a low organizational level, one SBU may compete with another, thereby shifting to higher levels of management the strategic issue of which SBU should formulate what strategy.

The optimum level of aggregation, one that is neither too broad nor too narrow, can be determined by applying the criteria discussed above, then further refining it by using managerial judgment. Briefly stated, an SBU must look and act like a freestanding business, satisfying the following conditions:

1. Have a unique business mission, independent of other SBUs.
2. Have a clearly definable set of competitors.
3. Be able to carry out integrative planning relatively independently of other SBUs.
4. Be able to manage resources in other areas.
5. Be large enough to justify senior management attention but small enough to serve as a useful focus for resource allocation.

The definition of an SBU always contains gray areas that may lead to dispute. It is helpful, therefore, to review the creation of an SBU, halfway into the strategy development process, by raising the following questions:

- Are customers' wants well defined and understood by the industry and is the market segmented so that differences in these wants are treated differently?
- Is the business unit equipped to respond functionally to the basic wants and needs of customers in the defined segments?
- Do competitors have different sets of operating conditions that could give them an unfair advantage over the business unit in question?

If the answers give reason to doubt the SBU's ability to compete in the market, it is better to redefine the SBU with a view to increasing its strategic freedom in meeting customer needs and competitive threats.

The SBU concept may be illustrated with an example from Procter & Gamble.[19] For more than 50 years the company's various brands were pitted against each other. The Camay soap manager competed against the Ivory soap manager as fiercely as if each were in different companies. The brand management system that grew out of this notion has been used by almost every consumer-products company.

In the fall of 1987, however, Procter & Gamble reorganized according to the SBU concept (what the company called "along the category lines"). The reorganization did not abolish brand managers, but it did make them accountable to a new corps of mini-general managers who were responsible for an entire product line—all laundry detergents, for example. By fostering internal competition among brand managers, the classic brand management system established strong incentives to excel. It also created conflicts and inefficiencies as brand managers squabbled over corporate resources, from ad spending to plant capacity. The system often meant that not enough thought was given to how brands could work together. Despite these shortcomings, brand management worked fine when markets were growing and money was available. But now, most packaged-goods businesses are growing slowly (if at all), brands are proliferating, the retail trade is accumulating more clout, and the consumer market is fragmenting. Procter & Gamble reorganized along SBU lines to cope with this bewildering array of pressures.

Under Procter & Gamble's SBU scheme, each of its 39 categories of U.S. businesses, from diapers to cake mixes, is run by a category manager with direct responsibility. Advertising, sales, manufacturing, research, engineering, and other disciplines all report to the category manager. The idea is to devise marketing strategies by looking at categories and by fitting brands together rather than by coming up with competing brand strategies and then dividing up resources among them. The paragraphs that follow discuss how Procter & Gamble's reorganization impacted select functions.

Advertising.   Procter & Gamble advertises Tide as the best detergent for tough dirt. But when the brand manager for Cheer started making the same claim, Cheer's ads were pulled after the Tide group protested. Now the category manager decides how to position Tide and Cheer to avoid such conflicts.

Budgeting.   Brand managers for Puritan and Crisco oils competed for a share of the same ad budget. Now a category manager decides when Puritan can benefit from stepped-up ad spending and when Crisco can coast on its strong market position.

Packaging.   Brand managers for various detergents often demanded packages at the same time. Because of these conflicting demands, managers complained that projects were delayed and nobody got a first-rate job. Now the category manager decides which brand gets a new package first.

Manufacturing.   Under the old system, a minor detergent, such as Dreft, had the same claim on plant resources as Tide—even if Tide was in the midst of a big promotion and needed more supplies. Now a manufacturing staff person who helps to coordinate production reports to the category manager.

Problems in Creating SBUs

The notion behind the SBU concept is that a company's activities in a marketplace ought to be understood and segmented strategically so that resources can be allocated for competitive advantage. That is, a company ought to be able to answer three questions: What business am I in? Who is my competition? What is my position relative to that competition? Getting an adequate answer to the first question is often difficult. (Answers to the other two questions can be relatively easy.) In addition, identifying SBUs is enormously difficult in organizations that share resources (e.g., research and development or sales).

There is no simple, definitive methodology for isolating SBUs. Although the criteria for designating SBUs are clear-cut, their application is judgmental and problematic. For example, in certain situations, real advantages can accrue to businesses sharing resources at the research and development, manufacturing, or distribution level. If autonomy and accountability are pursued as ends in themselves, these advantages may be overlooked or unnecessarily sacrificed.

SUMMARY

This chapter focused on the concepts of planning and strategy. Planning is the ongoing management process of choosing the objectives to be achieved during a certain period, setting up a plan of action, and maintaining continuous surveillance of results so as to make regular evaluations and, if necessary, to modify the objectives and plan of action. Also described were the requisites for successful planning, the time frame for initiating planning activities, and various philosophies of planning (i.e., satisfying, optimizing, and adaptivizing). Strategy, the course of action selected from possible alternatives as the optimum way to attain objectives, should be consistent with current policies and viewed in light of anticipated competitive actions.

The concept of strategic planning was also examined. Most large companies have made significant progress in the last 10 or 15 years in improving their strategic planning capabilities. Two levels of strategic planning were discussed: corporate and business unit level. Corporate strategic planning is concerned with the management of a firm's portfolio of businesses and with issues of firm-wide impact, such as resource allocation, cash flow management, government regulation, and capital market access. Business strategy focuses more narrowly on the SBU level and involves the design of plans of action and objectives based on analysis of both internal and external factors that affect each business unit's performance. An SBU is defined as a standalone business within a corporation that faces (an) identifiable competitor(s) in a given market.

For strategic planning to be effective and relevant, the CEO must play a central role, not simply as the apex of a multilayered planning effort, but as a strategic thinker and corporate culture leader.

DISCUSSION QUESTIONS

1. Why is planning significant?
2. Is the concept of strategic planning relevant only to profit-making organizations? Can nonprofit organizations or the federal government also embrace planning?
3. Planning has always been considered an important function of management. How is strategic planning different from traditional planning?
4. What is an SBU? What criteria may be used to divide businesses into SBUs?
5. What are the requisites for successful strategic planning?
6. Differentiate between the planning philosophies of satisfying, optimizing, and adaptivizing.

NOTES

[1] Gordon E. Greenley, "Perceptions of Marketing Strategy and Strategic Marketing in UK Companies," *Journal of Strategic Marketing* (September 1993): 189–210.
[2] James Brown, Saul S. Sands, and G. Clark Thompson, "The Status of Long Range Planning," *Conference Board Record* (September 1966): 11.
[3] *Business Planning in the Eighties: The New Competitiveness of American Corporations* (New York: Coopers & Lybrand, 1984).
[4] Malcolm McDonald, *The Marketing Audit: Translating Marketing Theory Into Practice* (Oxford, U.K.: Butterworth-Heinemann, 1991).
[5] J. Scott Armstrong, "The Value of Formal Planning for Strategic Decisions: Review of Empirical Research," *Strategic Management Journal* 3 (1982): 197–211.
[6] C. Don Burnett, Dennis P. Yeskey, and David Richardson, "New Roles for Corporate Planners in the 1980's," *Journal of Business Strategy* (Spring 1984): 64–68.
[7] Kirby E. Warren, *Long Range Planning: The Executive Viewpoint* (Englewood Cliffs, NJ: Prentice-Hall, 1966), 5.
[8] See Lawrence C. Rhyne, "The Relationship of Strategic Planning to Financial Performance," *Strategic Management Journal* (1986): 423–36.
[9] *Perspectives on Corporate Planning* (Boston: Boston Consulting Group, 1968), 48.
[10] Russell L. Ackoff, *A Concept of Corporate Planning* (New York: John Wiley & Sons, 1970), 13.
[11] Kenneth R. Andrews, *The Concept of Corporate Strategy* (Homewood, IL: Dow Jones-Irwin, 1971), 28.
[12] Andrea Dunham and Barry Marcus, *Unique Value: The Secret of All Great Business Strategies* (New York: Macmillan, 1993).
[13] Bruce D. Henderson, "The Origin of Strategy," *Harvard Business Review* (November–December 1989): 139–45.
[14] Henry Mintzberg, "The Fall and Rise of Strategic Planning," *Harvard Business Review* (January–February 1994): 107.
[15] Fred Gluck, "A Fresh Look at Strategic Management," *Journal of Business Strategy* (Fall 1985): 18–21.
[16] For a detailed discussion on this topic, see Chapter 11.
[17] Frederick E. Webster, Jr., "The Changing Role of Marketing in the Corporation," *Journal of Marketing* (October 1992): 1–17.
[18] William K. Hall, "SBU: Hot New Topic in the Management of Diversification," *Business Horizons* (February 1978): 17.
[19] "The Marketing Revolution at Procter & Gamble," *Business Week* (25 July 1988): 72.

Strategic Marketing

In its strategic role, marketing focuses on a business's intentions in a market and the means and timing of realizing those intentions. The strategic role of marketing is quite different from marketing management, which deals with developing, implementing, and directing programs to achieve designated intentions. To clearly differentiate between marketing management and marketing in its new role, a new term—*strategic marketing*—has been coined to represent the latter. This chapter discusses different aspects of strategic marketing and examines how it differs from marketing management. Also noted are the trends pointing to the continued importance of strategic marketing. The chapter ends with a plan for the rest of the book.

> *Marketing is merely a civilized form of warfare in which most battles are won with words, ideas, and disciplined thinking.*
>
> ALBERT W. EMERY

CONCEPT OF STRATEGIC MARKETING

Exhibit 2-1 shows the role that the marketing function plays at different levels in the organization. At the corporate level, marketing inputs (e.g., competitive analysis, market dynamics, environmental shifts) are essential for formulating a corporate strategic plan. Marketing represents the boundary between the marketplace and the company, and knowledge of current and emerging happenings in the marketplace is extremely important in any strategic planning exercise. At the other end of the scale, marketing management deals with the formulation and implementation of marketing programs to support the perspectives of strategic marketing, referring to marketing strategy of a product/market. Marketing strategy is developed at the business unit level.

Within a given environment, marketing strategy deals essentially with the interplay of three forces known as the **strategic three Cs:** the customer, the competition, and the corporation. Marketing strategies focus on ways in which the corporation can differentiate itself effectively from its competitors, capitalizing on its distinctive strengths to deliver better value to its customers. A good marketing strategy should be characterized by (a) a clear market definition; (b) a good match between corporate strengths and the needs of the market; and (c) superior performance, relative to the competition, in the key success factors of the business.

Together, the strategic three Cs form the marketing strategy triangle (see Exhibit 2-2). All three Cs—customer, corporation, and competition—are dynamic, living creatures with their own objectives to pursue. If what the customer wants does not match the needs of the corporation, the latter's long-term viability may be at stake. Positive matching of the needs and objectives of customer and corporation is required for a lasting good relationship. But such matching is

EXHIBIT 2-1
Marketing's Role in the Organization

Organizational Level	Role of Marketing*	Formal Name
Corporate	Provide customer and competitive perspective for corporate strategic planning.	Corporate marketing
Business unit	Assist in the development of strategic perspective of the business unit to direct its future course.	Strategic marketing
Product/market	Formulate and implement marketing programs.	Marketing management

*Like marketing, other functions (finance, research and development, production, accounting, and personnel) plan their own unique roles at each organizational level. The business unit strategy emerges from the interaction of marketing with other disciplines.

relative, and if the competition is able to offer a better match, the corporation will be at a disadvantage over time. In other words, the matching of needs between customer and corporation must not only be positive, it must be better or stronger than the match between the customer and the competitor. When the corporation's approach to the customer is identical to that of the competition, the customer cannot differentiate between them. The result could be a price war that may satisfy the customer's but not the corporation's needs. **Marketing strategy**, in terms of these three key constituents, must be defined as an endeavor by a corporation to differentiate itself positively from its competitors, using its relative corporate strengths to better satisfy customer needs in a given environmental setting.

Based on the interplay of the strategic three Cs, formation of marketing strategy requires the following three decisions:

1. *Where* to compete; that is, it requires a definition of the market (for example, competing across an entire market or in one or more segments).
2. *How* to compete; that is, it requires a means for competing (for example, introducing a new product to meet a customer need or establishing a new image for an existing product).
3. *When* to compete; that is, it requires timing of market entry (for example, being first in the market or waiting until primary demand is established).

The concept of strategic marketing may be illustrated with reference to the establishment by General Mills of a chain of Italian restaurants, the Olive Garden.[1] In 1980, faced with unsteady performance of its restaurant division (mainly the Red Lobster chain), General Mills looked around for new opportunities. A chain of Italian restaurants looked attractive. Because of the long-accelerating trend toward eating out, restaurants' share of the total food market had been increasing, from $2.50 of every $10 spent on food in 1955 to $4 in 1980. Further, the company's

EXHIBIT 2-2
Key Elements of Marketing Strategy Formulation

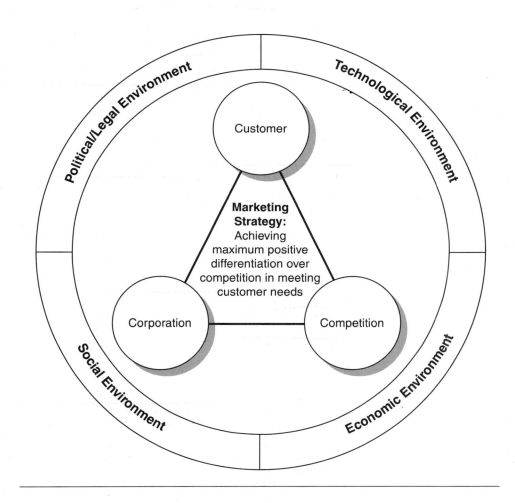

research showed that consumers ranked Italian food as the most popular ethnic cuisine and indicated that it was in short supply. In 1980, compared with 17,000 oriental restaurants and 14,000 Mexican restaurants, the United States had only 11,800 Italian restaurants. General Mills delineated the following marketing strategy:

- *Market* (where to compete)—open 10 to 12 restaurants annually for the next five years in areas popular for vacations.
- *Means* (how to compete)—cater to the mass market by offering an "Americanized" Italian fare for a price of about $10 for both food and wine.
- *Timing* (when to compete)—be cautious because starting a restaurant is risky.

According to the National Restaurant Association, about 50 percent of new restaurants fail in their first year; 65 percent within two years. General Mills itself had earlier failed in its attempt to run a Betty Crocker Treehouse chain, which served pie on elevated tables to the sound of tape-recorded bird chirping. Consequently, General Mills canvassed more than 1,000 restaurants for recipes, interviewed 5,000 consumers, and concocted more than 80 pots of spaghetti sauce before it settled on its final version, after three years of testing recipes.

General Mills based its marketing strategy decisions on extensive consumer research involving 5,000 interviews. These interviews revealed that most consumers seemed to have only vague impressions of Italy. For example, men often mentioned gladiators, fountains, and Sophia Loren; women brought up hillside picnics and vineyards. People described Italian food as tasty and healthy but with too much basil and garlic; chocolate mousse (a French dessert) was ranked by consumers as the best Italian dessert. Based on these inputs, it became clear that authentic Italian food would not satisfy the American appetite. Therefore, the company's choice of an ethnic motif did not mean that eating at the Olive Garden would be a culinary adventure. General Mills lavished its time and money on creating an ambiance and a cuisine that was "sort of" Italian: people should think they are eating Italian food, but in reality, the food would be fully adapted to American taste.

General Mills's strategy emerged from a thorough consideration of the strategic three Cs. First, market entry was dictated by growing customer demand for restaurants. Second, the decision to enter the market was based on full knowledge of the competition, which included different types of ethnic and nonethnic restaurants. General Mills knew that the idea of a nationwide chain of Italian restaurants was hardly revolutionary. What was important and what would provide Olive Garden a differential advantage that competitors would find difficult to copy quickly was the creation of a real vision of Italian food being served in an Italian atmosphere. Third, the corporation's strength as an aggressive, successful marketer of packaged goods with experience in the restaurant business and adequate financial resources (initial start-up costs of $100 million) properly equipped it to seek entry into new fields. Finally, the environment (in this case, a trend toward eating out and a preference for fancy Italian food) substantiated the opportunity.

This strategy seems to have worked well for General Mills. In 1993 the typical Olive Garden had annual pretax earnings of at least $415,000 on sales of more than $3.2 million. Most of the 326 Olive Garden restaurants became profitable within six months of start-up.

ASPECTS OF STRATEGIC MARKETING

Strategic thinking represents a new perspective in the area of marketing. In this section we will examine the importance, characteristics, origin, and future of strategic marketing.

Importance of Strategic Marketing

Marketing plays a vital role in the strategic management process of a firm. The experience of companies well versed in strategic planning indicates that failure in marketing can block the way to goals established by the strategic plan. A prime example is provided by Texas Instruments, a pioneer in developing a system of strategic planning called the OST system. Marketing negligence forced Texas Instruments to withdraw from the digital watch business. When the external environment is stable, a company can successfully ride on its technological lead, manufacturing efficiency, and financial acumen. As the environment shifts, however, lack of marketing perspective makes the best-planned strategies treacherous. With the intensification of competition in the watch business and the loss of uniqueness of the digital watch, Texas Instruments began to lose ground. Its experience can be summarized as follows:

> The lack of marketing skills certainly was a major factor in the . . . demise of its watch business. T.I. did not try to understand the consumer, nor would it listen to the marketplace. They had the engineer's attitude.[2]

Philip Morris's success with Miller Beer illustrates how marketing's elevated strategic status can help in outperforming competitors. If Philip Morris had accepted the conventional marketing wisdom of the beer industry by basing its strategy on cost efficiencies of large breweries and competitive pricing, its Miller Beer subsidiary might still be in seventh place or lower. Instead, Miller Beer leapfrogged all competitors but Anheuser-Busch by emphasizing market and customer segmentation supported with large advertising and promotion budgets. A case of true strategic marketing, with the marketing function playing a crucial role in overall corporate strategy, Philip Morris relied on its corporate strengths and exploited its competitors' weaknesses to gain a leadership position in the brewing industry.

Indeed, marketing strategy is the most significant challenge that companies of all types and sizes face. As a study by Coopers & Lybrand and Yankelovich, Skelly, and White notes, "American corporations are beginning to answer a 'new call to strategic marketing,' as many of them shift their business planning priorities more toward strategic marketing and the market planning function."[3]

Characteristics of Strategic Marketing

Strategic marketing holds different perspectives from those of marketing management. Its salient features are described in the paragraphs that follow.

Emphasis on Long-Term Implications. Strategic marketing decisions usually have far-reaching implications. In the words of one marketing strategist, strategic marketing is a commitment, not an act. For example, a strategic marketing decision would not be a matter of simply providing an immediate delivery to a favorite customer but of offering 24-hour delivery service to all customers.

In 1980 the Goodyear Tire Company made a strategic decision to continue its focus on the tire business. At a time when other members of the industry were deemphasizing tires, Goodyear opted for the opposite route.[4] This decision had wide-ranging implications for the company over the years. Looking back, Goodyear's strategy worked. In the 1990s, it continues to a globally dominant force in the tire industry.

The long-term orientation of strategic marketing requires greater concern for the environment. Environmental changes are more probable in the long run than in the short run. In other words, in the short run, one may assume that the environment will remain stable, but this assumption is not at all likely in the long run.

Proper monitoring of the environment requires strategic intelligence inputs. Strategic intelligence differs from traditional marketing research in requiring much deeper probing. For example, simply knowing that a competitor has a cost advantage is not enough. Strategically, one ought to find out how much flexibility the competitor has in further reducing price.

2 → *Corporate Inputs.*   Strategic marketing decisions require inputs from three corporate aspects: corporate culture, corporate publics, and corporate resources. **Corporate culture** refers to the style, whims, fancies, traits, taboos, customs, and rituals of top management that over time have come to be accepted as intrinsic to the corporation. **Corporate publics** are the various stakeholders with an interest in the organization. Customers, employees, vendors, governments, and society typically constitute an organization's stakeholders. **Corporate resources** include the human, financial, physical, and technological assets/experience of the company. Corporate inputs set the degree of freedom a marketing strategist has in deciding which market to enter, which business to divest, which business to invest in, etc. The use of corporate-wide inputs in formulating marketing strategy also helps to maximize overall benefits for the organization.

3 → *Varying Roles for Different Products/Markets.*   Traditionally it has been held that all products exert effort to maximize profitability. Strategic marketing starts from the premise that different products have varying roles in the company. For example, some products may be in the growth stage of the product life cycle, some in the maturity stage, others in the introduction stage. Each position in the life cycle requires a different strategy and affords different expectations. Products in the growth stage need extra investment; those in the maturity stage should generate a cash surplus. Although conceptually this concept—different products serving different purposes—has been understood for many years, it has been articulated for real-world application only in recent years. The lead in this regard was provided by the Boston Consulting Group, which developed a portfolio matrix in which products are positioned on a two-dimensional matrix of market share and growth rate, both measured on a continuous scale from high to low.

The portfolio matrix essentially has two properties: (a) it ranks diverse businesses according to uniform criteria, and (b) it provides a tool to balance a company's resources by showing which businesses are likely to be resource providers and which are resource users.[5]

The practice of strategic marketing seeks first to examine each product/market before determining its appropriate role. Further, different products/markets are synergistically related to maximize total marketing effort. Finally, each product/market is paired with a manager who has the proper background and experience to direct it.

4 →   *Organizational Level.*   Strategic marketing is conducted primarily at the business unit level in the organization. At General Electric, for example, major appliances are organized into separate business units for which strategy is separately formulated. At Gillette Company, strategy for the Sensor razor is developed at the razor business unit level.

5 →   *Relationship to Finance.*   Strategic marketing decision making is closely related to the finance function.[6] The importance of maintaining a close relationship between marketing and finance and, for that matter, with other functional areas of a business is nothing new. But in recent years, frameworks have been developed that make it convenient to simultaneously relate marketing to finance in making strategic decisions.[7]

Origin of Strategic Marketing

Strategic marketing did not originate systematically. As already noted, the difficult environment of the early 1970s forced managers to develop strategic plans for more centralized control of resources. It happened that these pioneering efforts at strategic planning had a financial focus. Certainly, it was recognized that marketing inputs were required, but they were gathered as needed or were simply assumed. For example, most strategic planning approaches emphasized cash flow and return on investment, which of course must be examined in relation to market share. Perspectives on such marketing matters as market share, however, were either obtained on an ad hoc basis or assumed as constant. Consequently, marketing inputs, such as market share, became the result instead of the cause: a typical conclusion that was drawn was that market share must be increased to meet cash flow targets. The financial bias of strategic planning systems demoted marketing to a necessary but not important role in the long-term perspective of the corporation.

In a few years' time, as strategic planning became more firmly established, corporations began to realize that there was a missing link in the planning process. Without properly relating the strategic planning effort to marketing, the whole process tended to be static. Business exists in a dynamic setting, and by and large, it is only through marketing inputs that perspectives of changing social, economic, political, and technological environments can be brought into the strategic planning process.

In brief, while marketing initially got lost in the emphasis on strategic planning, currently the role of marketing is better understood and has emerged in the form of strategic marketing.

Future of Strategic Marketing

A variety of factors point to an increasingly important role for strategic marketing in future years.[8] First, the battle for market share is intensifying in many industries as a result of declining growth rates. Faced with insignificant growth, companies have no choice but to grasp for new weapons to increase their share, and strategic marketing can provide extra leverage in share battles.

Second, deregulation in many industries is mandating a move to strategic marketing. For example, take the case of the airline, trucking, banking, and telecommunications industries. In the past, with territories protected and prices regulated, the need for strategic marketing was limited. With deregulation, it is an entirely different story. The prospect of Sears, Roebuck and Merrill Lynch as direct competitors would have been laughable as recently as eight years ago. Thus, emphasis on strategic marketing is no longer a matter of choice if these companies are to perform well.

Third, many packaged-goods companies are acquiring companies in hitherto nonmarketing-oriented industries and are attempting to gain market share through strategic marketing. For example, apparel makers, with few exceptions, have traditionally depended on production excellence to gain competitive advantage. But when marketing-oriented consumer-products companies purchased apparel companies, the picture changed. General Mills, through marketing strategy, turned Izod (the alligator shirt) into a highly successful business. Chesebrough-Pond's has done much the same with Health-Tex, making it the leading marketer of children's apparel. On acquiring Columbia Pictures in 1982, the Coca-Cola Company successfully tested the proposition that it could sell movies like soft drinks. By using Coke's marketing prowess and a host of innovative financing packages, Columbia emerged as a dominant force in the motion picture business. It almost doubled its market share between 1982 and 1987 and increased profits by 20 percent annually.[9] Although in the last few years Izod, Health-Tex, and Columbia Pictures have been sold, they fetched these marketing powerhouses huge prices for their efforts in turning them around.

Fourth, shifts in the channel structure of many industries have posed new problems. Traditional channels of distribution have become scrambled, and manufacturers find themselves using a mixture of wholesalers, retailers, chains, buying groups, and even captive outlets. In some cases, distributors and manufacturers' representatives are playing more important roles. In others, buying groups, chains, and cooperatives are becoming more significant. Because these groups bring greatly increased sophistication to the buying process, especially as the computer gives them access to more and better information, buying clout is being concentrated in fewer hands.

Fifth, competition from overseas companies operating both in the United States and abroad is intensifying. More and more countries around the world are developing the capacity to compete aggressively in world markets. Businesspeople in both developed and developing countries are aware of world market trends and are confident that they can reach new markets. Eager to improve their economic conditions and their living standards, they are willing to learn, adapt, and innovate. Thirty years ago, most American companies were confident that they could beat foreign competitors with relative ease. After all, they reasoned, we have the best technology, the best management skills, and the famous

American "can do" attitude. Today competition from Europe, Japan, and elsewhere is seemingly insurmountable. To cope with worldwide competition, renewed emphasis on marketing strategy achieves significance.

Sixth, the fragmentation of markets—the result of higher per capita incomes and more sophisticated consumers—is another factor driving the increased importance of strategic marketing. In the United States, for example, the number of segments in the automobile market increased by one-third, from 18 to 24, during the period from 1978 to 1985 (i.e., two subcompact, two compact, two intermediate, four full size, two luxury, three truck, two van, and one station wagon in 1978 to two minicompact, two subcompact, two compact, two midsized, two intermediate, two luxury, six truck, five van, and one station wagon in 1985).[10] Many of these segments remain unserved until a company introduces a product offering that is tailored to that niche. The competitive realities of fragmented markets require strategic marketing capability to identify untapped market segments and to develop and introduce products to meet their requirements.

Seventh, in the wake of easy availability of base technologies and shortening product life cycles, getting to market quickly is a prerequisite for success in the marketplace. Early entrants not only can command premium prices, but they also achieve volume break points in purchasing, manufacturing, and marketing earlier than followers and, thus, gain market share. For example, in the European market, the first company to market car radios can typically charge 20 percent more for the product than a competitor who enters the market a year later.[11] In planning an early entry in the marketplace, strategic marketing achieves significance.

Eighth, the days are gone when companies could win market share by achieving cost and quality advantages in existing, well-defined markets. In the rest of 1990s and beyond, companies will need to conceive and create new and largely uncontested competitive market space. Corporate imagination and expeditionary policies are the keys that unlock new markets.[12] Corporate imagination involves going beyond served markets; that is, thinking about needs and functionalities instead of conventional customer-product grids; overturning traditional price/performance assumptions; and leading customers rather than following them.[13] Creating new markets is a risky business; however, through expeditionary policies, companies can minimize the risk not by being fast followers but by the process of low-cost, fast-paced market incursions designed to reach the target market. To successfully develop corporate imagination and expeditionary policies, companies need strategic marketing. Consider this lesson in auto industry economics. Today it takes about 20 worker-hours to assemble a Ford Taurus with a retail price of, say, $18,000. Since labor costs about $42 an hour, the direct-assembly expense is $840, about 5% of the sticker price. By comparison, the cost of marketing and distributing the car can reach 30%.[14] The costs include advertising, promotions (such as cash rebates and lease incentives), and dealer rent and mortgage payments plus inventory financing. Controlling marketing costs begin even before the vehicle leaves the drawing board or computer screen. By ensuring that a design meets the needs and desires of its customers—

size, features, performance, and so on—a manufacturer can sell a new automobile for a higher price and avoid expensive rebates and other promotional gimmicks.

Finally, demographic shifts in American society have created a new customer environment that makes strategic marketing an imperative.[15] In years past, the typical American family consisted of a working dad, a homemaker mom, and two kids. But the 1990 census revealed that only 26 percent of the 93.3 million households then surveyed fit that description. Of those families reporting children under the age of 18, 63 percent of the mothers worked full or part time outside the home, up from 51 percent in 1985 and 42 percent in 1980. Smaller households now predominate: more than 55 percent of all households comprise only one or two persons. Even more startling, and frequently overlooked, is the fact that 9.7 million households are now headed by singles. This fastest-growing segment of all—up some 60 percent over the previous decade—expanded mainly because of an increase in the number of men living alone. Further, about 1 in 8 Americans is 65 years or older today. This group is expected to grow rapidly such that by 2030, 1 in 5 Americans will be elderly.[16] And senior citizens are around for a lot longer as life expectancy has risen. These statistics have strategic significance. The mass market has splintered, and companies can't sell their products the way they used to. The largest number of households may fall into the two-wage-earner grouping, but that group includes everyone from manicurists to Wall Street brokers, a group whose lifestyles and incomes are too diverse to qualify as a mass market. We may see every market breaking into smaller and smaller units, with unique products being aimed at defined segments.

STRATEGIC MARKETING AND MARKETING MANAGEMENT

Strategic marketing focuses on choosing the right products for the right growth markets at the right time. It may be argued that these decisions are no different from those emphasized in marketing management. However, the two disciplines approach these decisions from different angles. For example, in marketing management, market segments are defined by grouping customers according to marketing mix variables. In the strategic marketing approach, market segments are formed to identify the group(s) that can provide the company with a sustainable economic advantage over the competition. To clarify the matter, Henderson labels the latter grouping a **strategic sector**. Henderson notes:

> A strategic sector is one in which you can obtain a competitive advantage and exploit it. . . . Strategic sectors are the key to strategy because each sector's frame of reference is competition. The largest competitor in an industry can be unprofitable in that the individual strategic sectors are dominated by smaller competitors.[17]

A further difference between strategic marketing and marketing management is that in marketing management the resources and objectives of the firm, however defined, are viewed as uncontrollable variables in developing a marketing mix. In strategic marketing, objectives are systematically defined at different levels after a thorough examination of necessary inputs. Resources are allocated to maximize overall corporate performance, and the resulting strategies are formulated with a more inclusive view. As Abell and Hammond have stated:

> A strategic market plan is not the same . . . as a marketing plan; it is a plan of all aspects of an organization's strategy in the market place. A marketing plan, in contrast, deals primarily with the delineation of target segments and the product, communication, channel, and pricing policies for reaching and servicing those segments—the so-called marketing mix.[18]

Marketing management deals with developing a marketing mix to serve designated markets. The development of a marketing mix should be preceded by a definition of the market. Traditionally, however, market has been loosely defined. In an environment of expansion, even marginal operations could be profitable; therefore, there was no reason to be precise, especially when considering that the task of defining a market is at best difficult. Besides, corporate culture emphasized short-term orientation, which by implication stressed a winning marketing mix rather than an accurate definition of the market.

To illustrate how problematic it can be to define a market, consider the laundry product Wisk. The market for Wisk can be defined in many different ways: the laundry detergent market, the liquid laundry detergent market, or the prewash-treatment detergent market. In each market, the product would have a different market share and would be challenged by a different set of competitors. Which definition of the market is most viable for long-term healthy performance is a question that strategic marketing addresses.

> A market can be viewed in many different ways, and a product can be used in many different ways. Each time the product-marketing pairing is varied, the relative competitive strength is varied, too. Many businesspeople do not recognize that a key element in strategy is choosing the competitor whom you wish to challenge, as well as choosing the marketing segment and product characteristics with which you will compete.[19]

Exhibit 2-3 summarizes the differences between strategic marketing and marketing management. Strategic marketing differs from marketing management in many respects: orientation, philosophy, approach, relationship with the environment and other parts of the organization, and the management style required. For example, strategic marketing requires a manager to forgo short-term performance in the interest of long-term results. Strategic marketing deals with the business to be in; marketing management stresses running a delineated business.

For a marketing manager, the question is: Given the array of environmental forces affecting my business, the past and the projected performance of the industry or market, and my current position in it, which kind of investments am I justified in making in this business? In strategic marketing, on the other hand, the question is rather: What are my options for upsetting the equilibrium of the marketplace and reestablishing it in my favor? Marketing management takes

EXHIBIT 2-3

1. Major Differences between Strategic Marketing and Marketing Management*

Point of Difference	Strategic Marketing	Marketing Management
Time frame	Long range; i.e., decisions have long-term implications	Day-to-day; i.e., decisions have relevance in a given financial year
Orientation	Inductive and intuitive	Deductive and analytical
Decision process	Primarily bottom-up	Mainly top-down
Relationship with environment	Environment considered ever-changing and dynamic	Environment considered constant with occasional disturbances
Opportunity sensitivity	Ongoing to seek new opportunities	Ad hoc search for a new opportunity
Organizational behavior	Achieve synergy between different components of the organization, both horizontally and vertically	Pursue interests of the de-centralized unit
Nature of job	Requires high degree of creativity and originality	Requires maturity, experience, and control orientation
Leadership style	Requires proactive perspective	Requires reactive perspective
Mission	Deals with what business to emphasize	Deals with running a delineated business

*These differences are relative, not opposite ends of a continuum.

market projections and competitive position as a given and seeks to optimize within those constraints. Strategic marketing, by contrast, seeks to throw off those constraints wherever possible. Marketing management is deterministic; strategic marketing is opportunistic. Marketing management is deductive and analytical; strategic marketing is inductive and intuitive.

THE PROCESS OF STRATEGIC MARKETING: AN EXAMPLE

The process of strategic marketing planning, charted in Exhibit 2-4, may be illustrated with an SBU (health-related remedies) of the New England Products

EXHIBIT 2-4
Process of Strategic Marketing

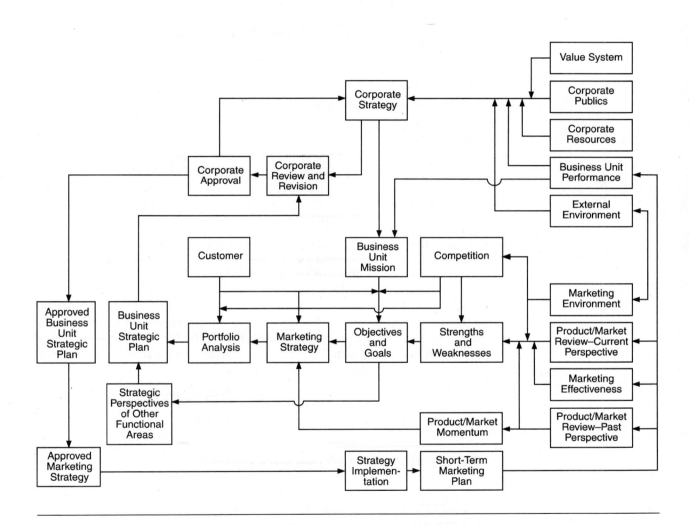

Company (a fictional name). Headquartered in Hartford, Connecticut, NEPC is a worldwide manufacturer and marketer of a variety of food and nonfood products, including coffee, orange juice, cake mixes, toothpaste, diapers, detergents, and health-related remedies. The company conducts its business in more than 100 countries, employs approximately 56,000 people, operates more than 147 manufacturing facilities, and maintains three major research centers. In 1993, the company's worldwide sales amounted to $31.2 billion.

Corporate Strategy | In 1986, the company's strategic plan established the following goals:

- To strengthen significantly the company's core businesses (i.e., toothpaste, diapers, and detergents).
- To view health care products as a critical engine of growth.
- To boost the share of profits from health-related products from 20 percent to 30 percent over the next decade.
- To divest those businesses not meeting the company's criteria for profitability and growth, thus providing additional resources to achieve other objectives.
- To make an 18 percent return on total capital invested.
- To a great extent, to depend on retained earnings for financing growth.

This above strategy rested on the five factors, shown in Exhibit 2-4, that feed into corporate strategy:

- *Value system*—always to be strong and influential in marketing, achieving growth through developing and acquiring new products for specific niches.
- *Corporate publics*—the willingness of NEPC stockholders to forgo short-term profits and dividends in the interest of long-term growth and profitability.
- *Corporate resources*—strong financial position, high brand recognition, marketing powerhouse.
- *Business unit performance*—health-related remedies sales, for example, were higher worldwide despite recessionary conditions.
- *External environment*—increased health consciousness among consumers.

Business Unit Mission | The mission for one of NEPC's 36 business units, health-related remedies, emerged from a simultaneous review of corporate strategy, competitive conditions, customers' perspectives, past performance of the business unit, and marketing environment, as charted in Exhibit 2-4. The business unit mission for health-related remedies was delineated as follows:

- To consolidate operations by combining recent acquisitions and newly developed products and by revamping old products.
- To accelerate business by proper positioning of products.
- To expand the product line to cover the entire human anatomy.

The mission for the business unit was translated into the following objectives and goals:

- To invest heavily to achieve $11.1 billion in sales by 1998, an increase of 110 percent over $5.3 billion in 1993.
- To achieve a leadership position in the United States.
- To introduce new products overseas as early as possible to preempt competition.

Marketing objectives for different products/markets emerged from these overall business unit objectives. For example, the marketing objectives for a product to combat indigestion were identified as follows:

- To accelerate research to seek new uses for the product.
- To develop new improvements in the product.

Marketing Strategy Marketing objectives, customer and competitive perspectives, and product/market momentum (i.e., extrapolation of past performance to the future) form the basis of marketing strategy. In the case of NEPC, the major emphasis of marketing strategy for health-related remedies was on positioning through advertising and on new product development. Thus, the company decided to increase advertising support throughout the planning period and to broaden research and development efforts.

NEPC's strategy was based on the following rationale. Consumers are extremely loyal to health products that deliver, as shown by their willingness to resume buying Johnson & Johnson's Tylenol after two poisoning episodes. But while brand loyalty makes consumers harder to lure away, it also makes them easier to keep, and good marketing can go a long way in this endeavor. The company was able to enlarge the market for its indigestion remedy, which experts thought had hit maturity, through savvy marketing. NEPC used television advertising to sell it as a cure for overindulgence, which led to a 30 percent increase in business during 1988–93.

As NEPC pushes further into health products, its vast research and technological resources will be a major asset. NEPC spends nearly $750 million a year on research, and product improvements have always been an important key to the company's marketing prowess.

The overall strategy of the health-related remedies business unit was determined by industry maturity and the unit's competitive position. The industry was found to be growing, while the competitive position was deemed strong.

With insurers and the government trying to drive health care costs down, consumers are buying more and more over-the-counter nostrums. Advertisers are making health claims for products from cereal to chewing gum. As the fitness craze exemplifies, interest in health is higher than ever, and the aging of the population will accentuate these trends: people are going to be older, but they are not going to want to feel older. Thus the health-related remedies industry has a significant potential for growth. NEPC is the largest over-the-counter remedies marketer. As shown in the list below, it has products for different ailments. The company's combined strength in marketing and research puts it in an enviable position in the market.

- *Skin*—NEPC produces the leading facial moisturizer. NEPC also leads the teenage acne treatment market. Work is now underway on a possible breakthrough anti-aging product.
- *Mouth*—After being on the market for 28 years, NEPC's mouthwash is the market leader. Another NEPC product, a prescription plaque-fighting mouthwash, may go over the counter, or it may become an important ingredient in other NEPC oral hygiene products.
- *Head*—An NEPC weak spot, its aspirin holds an insignificant share of the analgesic market. NEPC may decide to compete with an ibuprofen-caffeine combination painkiller.
- *Chest*—NEPC's medicated chest rub is an original brand in a stable that now includes cough syrup, cough drops, a nighttime cold remedy, and nasal spray. Other line extensions and new products are coming, but at a fairly slow pace.

- *Abdomen*—The market share for NEPC's indigestion remedy is up 22 percent in the last three years. Already being sold to prevent traveler's diarrhea, it may be marketed as an ulcer treatment. NEPC also dominates the over-the-counter bulk laxative market. New clinical research shows that its laxative may reduce serum cholesterol.
- *Bones*—NEPC orange juice has a 10 percent share of the market. Orange juice with calcium is now being expanded nationwide and could be combined with a low-calorie version.

Briefly, these inputs, along with the business unit's goals, led to the following business unit strategy: to attempt to improve position, to push for share.

Portfolio Analysis.   The marketing strategy for each product/market was reviewed using the portfolio technique (see Chapter 10). By positioning different products/markets on a multifactor portfolio matrix (high/medium/low business strength and high/medium/low industry attractiveness), strategy for each product/market was examined and approved from the viewpoint of meeting business unit missions and goals. Following the portfolio analysis, the approved marketing strategy became a part of the business unit's strategic plan, which, when approved by top management, was ready to be implemented. As a part of implementation, an annual marketing plan was formulated and became the basis for operations managers to pursue their objectives.

Implementation of the Strategic Plan.   A few highlights of the activities of the health-related remedies business unit during 1993–95 show how the strategic plan was implemented.

- Steps were taken to sell its laxative as an anticholesterol agent.
- The company won FDA permission to promote its indigestion remedy to doctors as a preventive for traveler's diarrhea.
- Company research has shown that its indigestion remedy helps treat ulcers. Although some researchers have disputed this claim, the prospect of cracking the multibillion dollar ulcer treatment market is tantalizing.
- The company introduced its orange juice brand with calcium. The company sought and won the approval of the American Medical Women's Association for the product and put the group's seal on its containers.

STRATEGIC MARKETING IMPLEMENTATION

Strategic marketing has evolved by trial and error. In the 1980s, companies developed unique strategic marketing procedures, processes, systems, and models. Experience shows, however, that most companies' marketing strategies are burdened with undue complexity. They are bogged down in principles that produce similar responses to competition. Changes are needed to put speed and freshness into marketing strategy.

Failings in Strategic Marketing

The following are the common problems associated with marketing strategy formulation and implementation.

1. **Too much emphasis on "where" to compete and not enough on "how" to compete.** Experience shows that companies have devoted much more attention to identifying markets in which to compete than to the means to compete in these markets. Information on where to compete is easy to obtain but seldom brings about sustainable competitive advantage. Further, "where" information is usually easy for competitors to copy. "How" information, on the other hand, is tough to get and tough to copy. It concerns the fundamental workings of the business and the company. For example, McDonald's motto, QSC & V, is a how-to-compete strategy—it translates into *quality* food products; fast, friendly *service*; restaurant *cleanliness*; and a menu that provides *value*. It is much more difficult to copy the "how" of McDonald's strategy than the "where."[20]

   In the next era of marketing strategy, companies will need to focus on how to compete in entirely new ways. In this endeavor, creativity will play a crucial role. For example, a large insurance company substantially improved its business by making improvements in underwriting, claim processing, and customer service, a "how" strategy that could not be replicated by competitors forthwith.

2. **Too little focus on uniqueness and adaptability in strategy.** Most marketing strategies lack uniqueness. For example, specialty stores increasingly look alike because they use the same layout and stock the same merchandise. In the 1970s, when market information was scarce, companies pursued new and different approaches. But today's easy access to information often leads companies to follow identical strategies to the detriment of all.

   Ideas for uniqueness and adaptability may flow from unknown sources. Companies should, therefore, be sensitive and explore all possibilities. The point may be illustrated with reference to Arm and Hammer's advertising campaign that encouraged people to place baking soda in their refrigerators to reduce odors. The idea was suggested in a letter from a consumer. The introduction of that *unique* application for the product in the early 1970s caused sales of Arm and Hammer baking soda to double within two years.

3. **Inadequate emphasis on "when" to compete.** Because of the heavy emphasis on where and how to compete, many marketing strategies give inadequate attention to "when" to compete. Any move in the marketplace should be adequately timed. The optimum time is one that minimizes or eliminates competition and creates the desired impact on the market; in other words, the optimum time makes it easier for the firm to achieve its objectives. Timing also has strategy implementation significance. It serves as a guide for different managers in the firm to schedule their activities to meet the timing requirement.

   Decisions on timing should be guided by the following:

   a. *Market knowledge.* If you have adequate information, it is desirable to market readily; otherwise you must wait until additional information has been gathered.

   b. *Competition.* A firm may decide on an early entry to beat minor competition. If you face major competition, you may delay entry if necessary; for example, to seek additional information.

   c. *Company readiness.* For a variety of reasons, the company may not be ready to compete. These reasons could be lack of financial resources, labor problems, inability to meet existing commitments, and others.

Addressing the
Problems of
Strategic Marketing

Having the ability to do all the right things, however, is no guarantee that planned objectives will be realized. Any number of pitfalls may render the best strategies inappropriate. To counter the pitfalls, the following concerns should be addressed:

1. Develop attainable goals and objectives.
2. Involve key operating personnel.
3. Avoid becoming so engrossed in current problems that strategic marketing is neglected and thus becomes discredited in the eyes of others.
4. Don't keep marketing strategy separate from the rest of the management process.
5. Avoid formality in marketing strategy formulation that restrains flexibility and inhibits creativity.
6. Avoid creating a climate that is resistant to strategic marketing.
7. Don't assume that marketing strategy development can be delegated to a planner.
8. Don't overturn the strategy formulation mechanism with intuitive, conflicting decisions.

PLAN OF THE BOOK

Today's business and marketing managers are faced with a continuous stream of decisions, each with its own degree of risk, uncertainty, and payoff. These decisions may be categorized into two broad classes: operating and strategic. With reference to marketing, operating decisions are the domain of marketing management. Strategic decisions constitute the field of strategic marketing.

Operating decisions are those dealing with current operations of the business. The typical objective of these decisions in a business firm is profit maximization. During times of business stagnation or recession, as experienced in the early 1990s, efforts at profit maximization have typically encompassed a cost minimization perspective. Under these conditions, managers are pressured into shorter and shorter time horizons. All too frequently, decisions are made regarding pricing, discounts, promotional expenditures, collection of marketing research information, inventory levels, delivery schedules, and a host of other areas with far too little regard for the long-term impact of the decision. As might be expected, a decision that may be optimal for one time period may not be optimal in the long run.

The second category of decision making, **strategic decisions**, deals with the determination of strategy: the selection of the proper markets and the products that best suit the needs of those markets. Although strategic decisions may represent a very small fraction of the multitude of management decisions, they are truly the most important as they provide the definition of the business and the general relationship between the firm and its environment. Despite their importance, however, the need to make strategic decisions is not always as apparent as the need (sometimes urgency) for successfully completing operating decisions.

Strategic decisions are characterized by the following distinctions:

1. They are likely to effect a significant departure from the established product market mix. (This departure might involve branching out technologically or innovating in other ways.)

2. They are likely to hold provisions for undertaking programs with an unusually high degree of risk relative to previous experience (e.g., using untried resources or entering uncertain markets and competitive situations where predictability of success is noticeably limited).

3. They are likely to include a wide range of available alternatives to cope with a major competitive problem, the scope of these alternatives providing for significant differences in both the results and resources required.

4. They are likely to involve important timing options, both for starting development work and for deciding when to make the actual market commitment.

5. They are likely to call for major changes in the competitive "equilibrium," creating a new operating and customer acceptance pattern.

6. They are likely to resolve the choice of either leading or following certain market or competitive advances, based on a trade-off between the costs and risks of innovating and the timing vulnerability of letting others pioneer (in the expectation of catching up and moving ahead at a later date on the strength of a superior marketing force).

This book deals with strategic decisions in the area of marketing. Chapter 1 dealt with planning and strategy concepts, and this chapter examined various aspects of strategic marketing. Chapters 3 through 6 deal with analysis of strategic information relative to company (e.g., corporate appraisal), competition, customer, and external environment. Chapter 7 focuses on the measurement of strategic capabilities, and Chapter 8 concentrates on strategic direction via goals and objectives.

Chapters 9 and 10 are devoted to strategy formulation. Organization for strategy implementation and control is examined in Chapter 11. Chapter 12 discusses strategic techniques and models. The next five chapters, Chapters 13 through 17, review major market, product, price, distribution, and promotion strategies. The final chapter, Chapter 18, focuses on global market strategy.

SUMMARY

This chapter introduced the concept of strategic marketing and differentiated it from marketing management. Strategic marketing focuses on marketing strategy, which is achieved by identifying markets to serve, competition to be tackled, and the timing of market entry/exit. Marketing management deals with developing a marketing mix to serve a designated market.

The complex process of marketing strategy formulation was described. Marketing strategy, which is developed at the SBU level, essentially emerges from the interplay of three forces—customer, competition, and corporation—in a given environment.

A variety of internal and external information is needed to formulate marketing strategy. Internal information flows both down from top management (e.g., corporate strategy) and up from operations management (e.g., past performance of products/markets). External information pertains to social, economic, political, and technological trends and product/market environment. The effectiveness of marketing perspectives of the company is another input in strategy formulation. This information is analyzed to identify the SBU's strengths and weaknesses, which together with competition and customer, define SBU objectives. SBU objectives lead to marketing objectives and strategy formulation. The process of marketing strategy development was illustrated with an example of a health-related product.

Finally, this chapter articulated the plan of this book. Of the two types of business decisions, operating and strategic, this book will concentrate on strategic decision making with reference to marketing.

DISCUSSION QUESTIONS

1. Define strategic marketing. Differentiate it from marketing management.
2. What are the distinguishing characteristics of strategic marketing?
3. What emerging trends support the continuation of strategic marketing as an important area of business endeavor?
4. Differentiate between operating and strategic decisions. Suggest three examples of each type of decision from the viewpoint of a food processor.
5. How might the finance function have an impact on marketing strategy? Explain.
6. Adapt to a small business the process of marketing strategy formulation as presented in Exhibit 2-4.
7. Specify the corporate inputs needed to formulate marketing strategy.

NOTES

[1] Robert Johnson, "General Mills Risks Millions Starting Chain of Italian Restaurants," *Wall Street Journal* (21 September 1987): 1.
[2] "When Marketing Failed at Texas Instruments," *Business Week* (22 June 1981): 91. See also Bro Uttal, "Texas Instruments Regroups," *Fortune* (9 August 1982): 40.
[3] *Business Planning in the Eighties: The New Competitiveness of American Corporations* (New York: Coopers & Lybrand, 1984).
[4] "Goodyear Feels the Heat," *Business Week* (7 March 1988): 26. Also see 1993 Annual Report of Goodyear Tire Company.
[5] For further discussion of the portfolio matrix, see Chapter 10.
[6] See Robert W. Ruekert and Orville C. Walker, Jr., "Marketing's Interaction with Other Functional Units: A Conceptual Framework and Empirical Evidence," *Journal of Marketing* (January 1987): 1–19.
[7] See Chapter 12.
[8] See David W. Cravens, "Strategic Forces Affecting Marketing Strategy," *Business Horizons* (September-October 1986): 77–86; and Frederick E. Webster, Jr., "Marketing Strategy in a Slow Growth Economy," *California Management Review* (Spring 1986): 93–105.
[9] Laura Landro, "Parent and Partners Help Columbia Have Fun at the Movies," *Wall Street Journal* (7 December 1984): 1.
[10] T. Michael Nevens, Gregory L. Summe, and Bro Uttal, "Commercializing Technology: What the Best Companies Do," *Harvard Business Review* (May–June 1990): 154–63.
[11] Don G. Reinertsen, "Whodunit? The Search for New Product Killers," *Electronic Business* (July 1983): 62–66.
[12] Gary Hamel and C. K. Prahalad, "Corporate Imagination and Expeditionary Marketing," *Harvard Business Review* (July–August 1991): 81–92.

[13] John Brady and Ian Davis, "Marketing's Mid-Life Crisis," *The Mckinsey Quarterly* 2 (1993): 17–28. Also see Adrian J. Slywotzky and Benson P. Shapiro, "Leveraging to Beat the Odds: The New Marketing Mind-Set," *Harvard Business Review* (September–October 1993): 97–107.

[14] *Fortune* (4 April 1994): 61.

[15] Ken Dychtwald and Grey Gable, "American Diversity," *American Demographics* (July 1991): 75–77.

[16] "The Economics of Aging," *Business Week* (12 September 1994): 60.

[17] Bruce D. Henderson, *Henderson on Corporate Strategy* (Cambridge, MA: Abt Books, 1981), 38.

[18] Derek F. Abell and John S. Hammond, *Strategic Market Planning* (Englewood Cliffs, NJ: Prentice-Hall, 1979), 9.

[19] Henderson, *Henderson on Corporate Strategy*, 4.

[20] Joel A. Bleeke, "Peak Strategies," *Across the Board* (February 1988): 45–80.

Strategic Analysis

Corporate Appraisal

One important reason for formulating marketing strategy is to prepare the company to interact with the changing environment in which it operates. Implicit here is the significance of predicting the shape the environment is likely to take in the future. Then, with a perspective of the company's present position, the task ahead can be determined. Study of the environment is reserved for a later chapter. This chapter is devoted to corporate appraisal.

An analogy to corporate appraisal is provided by a career counselor's job. Just as it is relatively easy to make a list of the jobs available to a young person, it is simple to produce a superficial list of investment opportunities open to a company. With the career counselor, the real skill comes in taking stock of each applicant; examining the applicant's qualifications, personality, and temperament; defining the areas in which some sort of further development or training may be required; and matching these characteristics and the applicant's aspirations against various options. Well-established techniques can be used to find out most of the necessary information about an individual. Digging deep into the psyche of a company is more complex but no less important. Failure by the company in the area of appraisal can be as stunting to future development in the corporate sense as the misplacement of a young graduate in the personal sense.

How should the strategist approach the task of appraising corporate perspectives? What needs to be discovered? These and other similar questions are explored in this chapter.

MEANING OF CORPORATE APPRAISAL

Broadly, **corporate appraisal** refers to an examination of the entire organization from different angles. It is a measurement of the readiness of the internal culture of the corporation to interact with the external environment. Marketing strategists are concerned with those aspects of the corporation that have a direct bearing on corporate-wide strategy because that must be referred in defining the business unit mission, the level at which marketing strategy is formulated. As shown in Exhibit 3-1, corporate strategy is affected by such factors as value orientation to top management, corporate publics, corporate resources, past performance of the business units, and the external environment. Of these, the first four factors are examined in this chapter.

Two important characteristics of strategic marketing are its concern with issues having far-reaching effects on the entire organization and change as an essential ingredient in its conduct. These characteristics make the process of marketing strategy formulation a difficult job and demand creativity and adaptability on the part of the organization. Creativity, however, is not common among all organizations. By the same token, adaptation to changing conditions is not easy. As has been said:

> Success in the past always becomes enshrined in the present by the over-valuation of the policies and attitudes which accompanied that success. . . . With time these attitudes become embedded in a system of beliefs, traditions, taboos, habits, customs, and inhibitions which constitute the distinctive culture of that firm. Such cultures are as distinctive as the cultural differences between nationalities or the personality differences between individuals. They do not adapt to change very easily.[1]

Human history is full of instances of communities and cultures being wiped out over time for the apparent reason of failing to change with the times. In the context of business, why is it that organizations such as Xerox, R.J. Reynolds, Hewlett-Packard, and Microsoft, comparative newcomers among large organizations, are considered blue-chip companies? Why should United States Rubber, American Tobacco, and Sears lag behind? Why are General Electric, Walt Disney, Citicorp, Du Pont, and 3M continually ranked as "successful" companies? The outstanding common denominator in the success of companies is the element of change. When time demands that the perspective of an organization undergo a change, success is the outcome.

EXHIBIT 3-1
Scope of Corporate Appraisal

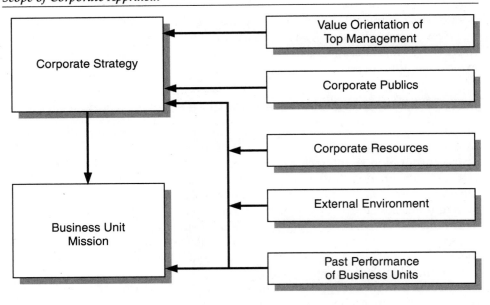

Obviously, marketing strategists must take a close look at the perspectives of the organization before formulating future strategy. Strategies must bear a close relationship to the internal culture of the corporation if they are to be successfully implemented.

FACTORS IN APPRAISAL: CORPORATE PUBLICS

Business exists for people. Thus, the first consideration in the strategic process is to recognize the individuals and groups who have an interest in the fate of the corporation and the extent and nature of their expectations.

Meaning of Corporate Publics | The following groups generally constitute the interest-holders in business organizations:

1. Owners
2. Employees
3. Customers
4. Suppliers
5. Banking community and other lenders
6. Government
7. Community in which the company does business
8. Society at large

For the healthy growth of the organization, all eight groups must be served adequately.[2] Of all the stakeholders, in the past corporations paid little attention to the communities in which they operated; today, however, the importance of service to community and to society is widely acknowledged. The community may force a company to refrain from activities that are detrimental to the environment. For example, the Boise Cascade Company was once denounced as harsh, stingy, socially insensitive, and considerably short of the highest ethical standards because of its unplanned land development. Community interests ultimately prevailed, forcing the company to either give up its land development activities or make proper arrangements for the disposal of waste and to introduce other environmental safeguards. Similarly, social concern may prevent a company from becoming involved in certain types of business. A publishing company responsive to community standards may refuse to publish pornographic material.

Johnson & Johnson exemplified responsible corporate behavior when it resolved the contingency created by the deaths of seven individuals who had consumed contaminated Tylenol capsules.[3] Within a few days, the company instituted a total product recall at a cost of $50 million after taxes, despite the fact that the problem did not occur because of negligence on the part of the company. Subsequently, the company took the initiative to develop more effective packaging to prevent tampering in the future. The company's commitment to socially responsible behavior was reaffirmed when it quit producing capsules entirely after the tampering occurred again. Johnson & Johnson put the well-being of the customer ahead of profitability in resolving this tampering problem. In brief, the requirements and expectations of today's society must serve as basic ingredients in the development of strategy:

> Though profit and efficiency must remain central values within the culture, they must be balanced by other values that help define the limits of activities designed to achieve those objectives and by values describing other important ethical and socially responsible behaviors. Without the integration of concerns about ethics and social responsibility at the very beginning of the marketing planning process, as well as throughout the process, the organizational culture may not provide the checks and balances needed to develop ethical and socially responsible marketing programs.[4]

Corporate Response to Different Publics

Historically, a business organization considered its sole purpose to be economic gain, concerning itself with other spheres of society only when required by law or self-interest or when motivated by philanthropy or charity. Charity was merely a celebration of a corporation's good fortune that it desired to share with "outsiders" or a display of pity for the unfortunate.[5] Indirectly, of course, even this rather uninspired notion of charity gave the company a good name and thus served a public relations function.[6] In slack times, a company reduced its activities in all areas, instituting both inside cost-cutting measures and the lowering of commitments to all publics other than stockholders. Such a perspective worked well until the mid-1960s; however, with economic prosperity almost assured, different stakeholders have begun to demand a more equitable deal from corporations.

Concern over environmental pollution by corporations, for example, has become a major issue in both the public and the private sector. Similarly, customers expect products to be wholesome; employees want opportunities for advancement and self-improvement; and the community hopes that a corporation would assume some of its concerns, such as unemployment among minorities. Society now expects business corporations to help in resolving social problems. In brief, the role of the corporation has shifted from that of an economic institution solely responsible to its stockholders to that of a multifaceted force owing its existence to different stakeholders to whom it must be accountable. As one of the most progressive institutions in the society, the corporation is expected to provide balanced prosperity in all fields. Two generations ago, the idea of a business being a party to a contract with society would have provoked an indignant snort from most businesspeople. Even 10 years ago, a business's contract with society was more likely material for a corporate president's speech to the stockholders than a basis for policy. It is a measure of how much the attitudes of middle-of-the-road businesspeople have changed that the notion of a social contract is now the basic assumption for their statements on the social responsibilities of a business. This new outlook extends the mission of the business beyond its primary obligation to owners.[7]

In today's environment, corporate strategy must be developed not simply to enhance financial performance, but also to maximize performance across the board, delivering the highest gains to all stakeholders, or corporate publics. And companies are responding to changing times. As former chairman Waldron of Avon Products noted, "We have 40,000 employees and 1.3 million representatives. . . . They have much deeper and more important stakes in our company than shareholders."[8]

The "concept of stakeholders" is really an extension of the marketing concept, the central doctrine in marketing.

> Marketing concept and the stakeholder concept are strongly related with a common root or core. Clearly, one commonality is that the stakeholder concept recognizes the consumer as a public with concerns central to the organization's purpose. Perhaps a further element of this common core is a realization of the importance of cooperative exchange with the consumer. In fact, all publics of an organization can be viewed in a cooperative vs. adversarial perspective. Cooperative strategies with labor, marketing channel members, etc., may result in eventual but not mutual symbiosis. For example, if a manufacturer cooperates with wholesalers, then these wholesalers may be more likely to cooperate with retailers. Similarly, retailers may then be more likely to treat the customer well. Consequently, the customer will be more loyal to certain brands, and this catalyzes the manufacturer to continue to be cooperative with channel members. This eventual, but not necessarily mutual, symbiosis may result in more long-run stability and evolutionary potential within the business system.[9]

One company that systematically and continuously examines and serves the interests of its stakeholders is Corning. It cooperates with labor, promotes diversity, and goes out of its way to improve the community. For example, the company's partnership with the glass workers' union promotes joint decision making. Worker teams determine job schedules and even factory design. All U.S. workers share a bonus based on point performance. All managers and salaried workers attend seminars to build sensitivity and support for women and African-American coworkers. A network of mentors helps minorities (i.e., African-Americans, Asians, Hispanics, and women) with career planning. Corning acquires and rehabilitates commercial properties, then finds tenants (some minority-owned) at market rates to locate their business there. It works to attract new business to the region and has invested in the local infrastructure by building a Hilton hotel, a museum, and a city library.

> More than the biggest employer in town, Corning plays benefactor, landlord, and social engineer. The company is half-owner of a racetrack and sponsors a professional golf tournament. Affordable housing, day care, new business development—it's doing all that, too. Corning is more directly involved in its community than most big U.S. corporations. . . . When a flood in 1972 put the town under 10 feet of water, the company paid area teenagers to rehabilitate damaged homes and appliances, then spent millions to build a new library and skating rink. But Corning's recent efforts have been more focused: They aim to turn a remote, insular town into a place that will appeal to the smart professionals Corning wants to attract—a place that offers social options for young singles, support for new families, and cultural diversity for minorities.
>
> It's a strategy that often borders on corporate socialism. Corning bought the run-down bars—which "didn't fit with our objective," says one executive—as part of a block-long redevelopment of Market Street, the town's main commercial strip.

More important, Corning is working to create a region less dependent on its headquarters and 15 factories. . . . To help support the flagging local economy, Corning bought the Watkins Glen auto-racing track, which had slipped into bankruptcy. It rebuilt the facility, took in a managing partner, and last summer, saw the track host 200,000 visitors. Similarly, the company lobbied a supermarket chain to build an enormous new store. It persuaded United Parcel Service to locate a regional hub nearby.

In all, Corning expects its Corning Enterprises subsidiary, which spearheads community investments, to bring 200 new jobs to the Chemung River valley each year. It also wants to boost the number of tourists by 2% annually and attract four new businesses to town. Corning Enterprises funds its activities largely with rental income from real estate that it has purchased and rehabilitated.[10]

Corporate Publics: Analysis of Expectations

Although the expectations of different groups vary, in our society growth and improvement are the common expectations of any institution. But this broad view does not take into account the stakes of different groups within a business. For planning purposes, a clearer definition of each group's hopes is needed.

Exhibit 3-2 summarizes the factors against which the expectations of different groups can be measured. The broad categories shown here should be broken down into subcategories as far as possible. For example, in a community where juvenile delinquency is rampant, youth programs become an important area of corporate concern. One must be careful, however, not to make unrealistic or false assumptions about the expectations of different groups. Take owners, for example. Typically, 50 percent of earnings after taxes must be reinvested in the business to sustain normal growth, but the payout desired by the owners may render it difficult to finance growth. Thus, a balance must be struck between the payment of dividends and the plowing back of earnings. A vice president of finance for a chemical company with yearly sales over $100 million said in a conversation with the author:

> While we do recognize the significance of retaining more money, we must consider the desires of our stockholders. They happen to be people who actually live on dividend payments. Thus, a part of long-term growth must be given up in order to maintain their short-term needs for regular dividend payments.

Apparently this company would not be correct in assuming that growth alone is the objective of its stockholders. Thus, it behooves the marketing strategist to gain clear insight into the demands of different corporate publics.

Who in the company should study stakeholders' expectations? This task constitutes a project in itself and should be assigned either to someone inside the company (such as a strategic planner, an assistant to the president, a director of public affairs, or a marketing researcher) or to a consultant hired for this purpose. When this analysis is first undertaken, it will be fairly difficult to specify stakeholders, designate their areas of concern, and make their expectations explicit. After the initial study is made, updating it from year to year should be fairly routine.

The groups that constitute the stakeholders of a business organization are usually the same from one business to another. Mainly they are the owners,

EXHIBIT 3-2
Corporate Publics and their Concerns

Publics	Areas of Concern
Owners	Payout
	Equity
	Stock price
	Nonmonetary desires
Customers	Business reliability
	Product reliability
	Product improvement
	Product price
	Product service
	Continuity
	Marketing efficiency
Employees of all ranks	Monetary reward
	Reward of recognition
	Reward of pride
	Environment
	Challenge
	Continuity
	Advancement
Suppliers	Price
	Stability
	Continuity
	Growth
Banking community and other lenders	Sound risk
	Interest payment
	Repayment of principal
Government (federal, state, and local)	Taxes
	Security and law enforcement
	Management expertise
	Democratic government
	Capitalistic system
	Implementation of programs
Immediate community	Economic growth and efficiency
	Education
	Employment and training
Society at large	Civil rights
	Urban renewal and development
	Pollution abatement
	Conservation and recreation
	Culture and arts
	Medical care

employees, customers, suppliers, the banking community and other lenders, government, the immediate community, and society at large. The areas of concern of each group and their expectations, however, require surveying. As with any other survey, this amounts to seeking information from an appropriate sample within each group. A structured questionnaire is preferable for obtaining objective answers. Before surveying the sample, however, it is desirable to obtain in-depth interviews with a few members of each group. The information provided by these interviews is helpful in developing the questionnaire. While overall areas of concern may not vary from one period to another, expectations certainly do. For example, during a recession stockholders may desire a higher payout in dividends than at other times. Besides, in a given period, the public may not articulate expectations in all of its areas of concern. During inflationary periods, for example, customers may emphasize stable prices only, while product improvement and marketing efficiency may figure prominently in times of prosperity.

Corporate Publics and Corporate Strategy

The expectations of different publics provide the corporation with a focus for working out its objectives and goals. However, a company may not be able to satisfy the expectations of all stakeholders for two reasons: limited resources and conflicting expectations among stakeholders. For example, customers may want low prices and simultaneously ask for product improvements. Likewise, to meet exactly the expectations of the community, the company may be obliged to reduce dividends. Thus, a balance must be struck between the expectations of different stakeholders and the company's ability to honor them.

The corporate response to stakeholders' expectations emerges in the form of its objectives and goals, which in turn determine corporate strategy. While objectives and goals are discussed in detail in Chapter 8, a sample of corporate objectives with reference to customers is given here.

Assume the following customer expectations for a food-processing company:

1. The company should provide wholesome products.
2. The company should clearly state the ingredients of different products in words that are easily comprehensible to an ordinary consumer.
3. The company should make all efforts to keep prices down.

The company, based on these expectations, may set the following goals:

Wholesome Products

1. Create a new position—vice president, product quality. No new products will be introduced into the market until they are approved for wholesomeness by this vice president. The vice president's decision will be upheld no matter how bright a picture of consumer acceptance of a product is painted by marketing research and marketing planning.
2. Create a panel of nutrient testers to analyze and judge different products for their wholesomeness.
3. Communicate with consumers about the wholesomeness of the company's products, suggesting that they deal directly with the vice president of product quality should there be any questions. (Incidentally, a position similar to vice president of

product quality was created at Gillette a few years ago. This executive's decisions overruled the market introduction of products despite numerous other reasons for early introduction.)

Information on Ingredients

1. Create a new position—director, consumer information. The person in this position will decide what information about product ingredients, nutritive value, etc., should be included on each package.
2. Seek feedback every other year from a sample of consumers concerning the effectiveness and clarity of the information provided.
3. Encourage customers, through various forms of promotions, to communicate with the director of consumer information on a toll-free phone line to clarify information that may be unclear.
4. Revise information contents based on numbers 2 and 3.

Keeping Prices Low

1. Communicate with customers on what leads the company to raise different prices (e.g., cost of labor is up, cost of ingredients is up, etc.).
2. Design various ways to reduce price pressure on consumers. For example, develop family packs.
3. Let customers know how much they can save by buying family packs. Assure them that the quality of the product will remain intact for a specified period.
4. Work on new ways to reduce costs. For example, a substitute may be found for a product ingredient whose cost has gone up tremendously.

By using this illustration, the expectations of each group of stakeholders can be translated into specific goals. Some firms, Adolph Coors Company, for example, define their commitment to stakeholders more broadly (see Exhibit 3-3). However, this company is not alone in articulating its concern for stakeholders. A whole corporate culture has sprung up that argues for the essential commonality of labor-management community-shareholder interests.

FACTORS IN APPRAISAL: VALUE ORIENTATION OF TOP MANAGEMENT

The ideologies and philosophies of top management as a team and of the CEO as the leader of the team have a profound effect on managerial policy and the strategic development process. According to Steiner:

> [The CEO's] aspirations about his personal life, the life of his company as an institution, and the lives of those involved in his business are major determinants of choice of strategy. His mores, habits, and ways of doing things determine how he behaves and decides. His sense of obligation to his company will decide his devotion and choice of subject matter to think about.[11]

Rene McPherson, former CEO of Dana Corporation, incessantly emphasized cost reduction and productivity improvement: the company doubled its productivity in seven years. IBM chairmen have always preached the importance of calling on customers—to the point of stressing the proper dress for a call. Over time, a certain way of dressing became an accepted norm of behavior for the

EXHIBIT 3-3
Coors' Commitment to its Stakeholders

Our corporate philosophy can be summed up by the statement, "Quality in all we are and all we do." This statement reflects our total commitment to quality relationships with customers, suppliers, community, stockholders and each other. Quality relationships are honorable, just, truthful, genuine, unselfish, and reputable.

We are committed first to our customers for whom we must provide products and services of recognizably superior quality. Our customers are essential to our existence. Every effort must be made to provide them with the highest quality products and services at fair and competitive prices.

We are committed to build quality relationships with suppliers because we require the highest quality goods and services. Contracts and prices should be mutually beneficial for the Company and the supplier and be honorably adhered to by both.

We are committed to improve the quality of life within our community. Our policy is to comply strictly with all local, state and federal laws, with our Corporate Code of Conduct and to promote the responsible use of our products. We strive to conserve our natural resources and minimize our impact on the environment. We pay our fair tax share and contribute resources to enhance community life. We boldly and visibly support the free enterprise system and individual freedom within a framework which also promotes personal responsibility and caring for others.

We are committed to the long-term financial success of our stockholders through consistent dividends and appreciation in the value of the capital they have put at risk. Reinvestment in facilities, research and development, marketing and new business opportunities which provide long-term earnings growth take precedence over short-term financial optimization.

These values can only be fulfilled by quality people dedicated to quality relationships within our Company. We are committed to provide fair compensation and a quality work environment that is safe and friendly. We value personal dignity. We recognize individual accomplishment and the success of the team. Quality relationships are built upon mutual respect, compassion and open communication among all employees. We foster personal and professional growth and development without bias or prejudice and encourage wellness in body, mind and spirit for all employees.

Source: Adolph Coors Company.

entire corporation. Texas Instruments' ex-chairman Patrick Haggerty made it a point to drop in at a development laboratory on his way home each night when he was in Dallas to emphasize his view of the importance of new products for the company. Such single-minded focus on a value becomes an integral part of a company's culture. As employees steeped in the corporate culture move up the ladder, they become role models for newcomers, and the process continues.[12]

How companies in essentially the same business move in different strategic directions because of different top management values can be illustrated with an example from American Can Company and Continental Group. Throughout the 1970s, both Robert S. Hatfield, then Continental's chairman, and William F. May, his counterpart at American Can, made deep changes in their companies' product portfolios. Both closed numerous aged can-making plants. Both divested tangential businesses they deemed to have lackluster growth prospects. And both sought either to hire or promote executives who would steer their companies in profitable directions.

But similar as their overall strategies might seem, their concepts of their companies diverged markedly. May envisioned American Can as a corporate think tank, serving as both a trend spotter and a trendsetter. He put his trust in the advice of financial experts who, although lean on operating experience, were knowledgeable about business theory. They took American Can into such diverse fields as aluminum recycling, record distribution, and mail-order consumer products. By contrast, Hatfield sought executives with proven records in spotting new potential in old areas. The company acquired Richmond Corporation, an insurance holding company, and Florida Gas Company.[13]

Importance of Value Orientation in the Corporate Environment

It would be wrong to assume that every firm wants to grow. There are companies that probably could grow faster than their current rates indicate. But when top management is averse to expansion, sluggishness prevails throughout the organization, inhibiting growth. A large number of companies start small, perhaps with a family managing the organization. Some entrepreneurs at the helm of such companies are quite satisfied with what they are able to achieve. They would rather not grow than give up complete control of the organization. Obviously, if managerial values promote stability rather than growth, strategy will form accordingly. Of course, if the owners find that their expectations are in conflict with the value system of top management, they may seek to replace the company's management with a more philosophically compatible team. As an example, a flamboyant CEO who emphasizes growth and introduces changes in the organization to the extent of creating suspicion among owners, board members, and colleagues may lead to the CEO's exit from the organization. An unconventionally high debt-to-equity ratio can be sufficient cause for a CEO to be dismissed.

In brief, the value systems of the individual members of top management serve as important inputs in strategy development. If people at the top hold conflicting values, the chosen strategy will lack the willing cooperation and commitment of all executives. Generally, differing values are reflected in conflicts over policies, objectives, strategies, and structure.

This point may be illustrated with reference to Johnson & Johnson, a solidly profitable company. Its core businesses are entering market maturity and offer limited long-term growth potential. In the mid-1980s, therefore, the company embarked on a program to manufacture sophisticated technology products. But the development and marketing of high-tech products require a markedly different culture than that needed for Johnson & Johnson's traditional products. High-tech products require greater cooperation among corporate units, which is sometimes hard to obtain. Traditionally, Johnson & Johnson's various businesses have been run as completely decentralized units with total autonomy. To successfully achieve the shift to technology products, the CEO of the company, James E. Burke, is tinkering in subtle but important ways with a management style and corporate culture that have long been central to the company's success.[14] Similar efforts are at work at Procter & Gamble: "Pressed by competitors and aided by new technology, P&G is, in fact, remodeling its corporate culture—a process bringing pain to some, relief to others and wonderment to most."[15]

Top Management Values and Corporate Culture

Over time, top management values come to characterize the culture of the entire organization. Corporate culture in turn affects the entire perspective of the organization. It influences its product and service quality, advertising content, pricing policies, treatment of employees, and relationships with customers, suppliers, and the community.[16]

Corporate culture gives employees a sense of direction, a sense of how to behave and what they ought to be doing. Employees who fail to live up to the cultural norms of the organization find the going tough. This point may be illustrated with reference to PepsiCo and J.C. Penney Company. At PepsiCo, beating the competition is the surest path to success. In its soft drink operation, Pepsi takes on Coke directly, asking consumers to compare the taste of the two colas. This kind of direct confrontation is reflected inside the company as well. Managers are pitted against each other to grab more market share, to work harder, and to wring more profits out of their businesses. Because winning is the key value at PepsiCo, losing has its penalties. Consistent runners-up find their jobs gone. Employees know they must win merely to stay in place and must devastate the competition to get ahead.[17]

But the aggressive manager who succeeds at Pepsi would be sorely out of place at J.C. Penney Company, where a quick victory is far less important than building long-term loyalty.

> Indeed, a Penney store manager once was severely rebuked by the company's president for making too much profit. That was considered unfair to customers, whose trust Penney seeks to win. The business style set by the company's founder—which one competitor describes as avoiding "taking unfair advantage of anyone the company did business with"—still prevails today. Customers know they can return merchandise with no questions asked; suppliers know that Penney will not haggle over terms; and employees are comfortable in their jobs, knowing that Penney will avoid layoffs at all costs and will find easier jobs for those who cannot handle more demanding ones. Not surprisingly, Penney's average executive tenure is 33 years while Pepsi's is 10.[18]

These vastly different methods of doing business are just two examples of corporate culture. People who work at PepsiCo and at Penney sense that corporate values constitute the yardstick by which they will be measured. Just as tribal cultures have totems and taboos that dictate how each member should act toward fellow members and outsiders, a corporation's culture influences employees' actions toward customers, competitors, suppliers, and one another. Sometimes the rules are written, but more often they are tacit. Most often they are laid down by a strong founder and hardened by success into custom.

One authority describes four categories of corporate culture—academies, clubs, baseball teams, and fortresses.[19] Each category attracts certain personalities.

The following are some of the traits among managers who gravitate to a particular corporate culture.

Academies

— Have parents who value self-reliance but put less emphasis on honesty and consideration.
— Tend to be less religious.
— Graduate from business school with high grades.
— Have more problems with subordinates in their first ten years of work.

Clubs

— Have parents who emphasize honesty and consideration.
— Have a lower regard for hard work and self-reliance.
— Tend to be more religious.
— Care more about health, family, and security and less about future income and autonomy.
— Are less likely to have substantial equity in their companies.

Baseball Teams

— Describe their fathers as unpredictable.
— Generally have more problems planning their careers in the first ten years after business school and work for more companies during that period than classmates do.
— Include personal growth and future income among their priorities.
— Value security less than others.

Fortresses

— Have parents who value curiosity.
— Were helped strongly by mentors in the first year out of school.
— Are less concerned than others with feelings of belonging, professional growth, and future income.
— Experience problems in career planning, on-the-job decisions, and job implementation.

An example of an academy is IBM, where managers spend at least 40 hours each year in training being carefully groomed to become experts in a particular function. United Parcel Service represents a club culture, which emphasizes grooming managers as generalists, with initiation beginning at the entry level. Generally speaking, accounting firms, law firms, and consulting, advertising, and software development companies exhibit baseball team cultures. Entrepreneurial in style, they seek out talent of all ages and experience and value inventiveness. Fortress companies are concerned with survival and are usually best represented by companies in a perpetual boom-and-bust cycle (e.g., retailers and natural resource companies).

Many companies cannot be neatly categorized in any one way. Many exhibit a blend of corporate cultures. For example, within General Electric, the NBC unit has baseball team qualities, whereas the aerospace division operates like a club, the electronics division like an academy, and the home appliance unit like a fortress. Companies may move from one category to another as they mature or as forced by the environment. For example, Apple started out as a baseball team but now appears to be emerging as an academy. Banks have traditionally exhibited a club culture, but with deregulation, they are evolving into baseball teams.

In the current environment, the changes that businesses are being forced to make merely to stay competitive—improving quality, increasing speed, becoming customer oriented—are so fundamental that they must take root in a company's very essence; that is, its culture. Cultural change, while difficult and time-consuming to achieve, is nevertheless feasible if approached properly. The CEO must direct change to make sure that it happens coherently. He or she must live the new culture, become the walking embodiment of it, and spot and celebrate subordinates who exemplify the values that are to be inculcated. The following are keys to cultural change:

— **Understand your old culture first.** You can't chart a course until you know where you are.
— **Encourage those employees** who are bucking the old culture and have ideas for a better one.
— **Find the best subculture** in your organization, and hold it up as an example from which others can learn.
— **Don't attack culture head on.** Help employees find their own new ways to accomplish their tasks, and a better culture will follow.
— **Don't count on a vision** to work miracles. At best, a vision acts as a guiding principle for change.
— **Figure on five to ten years** for significant, organization-wide improvement.
— **Live the culture you want.** As always, actions speak louder than words.[20]

Trying to change an institution's culture is certain to be frustrating. Most people resist change, and when the change goes to the basic character of the place where they earn a living, many people become upset. A company trying to improve its culture is like a person trying to improve his or her character. The process is long, difficult, often agonizing. The only reason that people put themselves through such difficulty is that it is correspondingly satisfying and valuable. As AT&T's CEO Robert Allen comments:

> It's not easy to change a culture that was very control oriented and top down. We're trying to create an atmosphere of turning the organization chart upside down, putting the customers on top. The people close to the customer should be doing the key decision-making.[21]

Measurement of Values

In emphasizing the significance of the value system in strategic planning, several questions become pertinent. Should the corporation attempt to formally establish values for important members of management? If so, who should do it? What measures or techniques should be used? If the values of senior executives are in conflict, what should be done? Can values be changed?

It is desirable that the values of top management should be measured. If nothing else, such measurement will familiarize the CEO with the orientation of top executives and will help the CEO to better appreciate their viewpoints. Opinions differ, however, on who should do the measuring. Although a good case can be made for giving the assignment to a staff person, a strategic planner or a human resources planner, for example, hiring an outside consultant is probably the most effective way to gain an objective perspective on management values. If a consultant's findings appear to create conflict in the organization, they can be scrapped. With help from the consultant, the human resources planner in the company, working closely with the strategic planner, can design a system for the measurement of values once the initial effort is made.

Values can be measured in various ways. A popular technique is the self-evaluating scale developed by Allport, Vernon, and Lindzey.[22] This scale divides values into six classes: religious, political, theoretical, economic, aesthetic, and social. A manual is available that lists the average scores of different groups. Executives can complete the test in about 30 minutes and determine the structure of their values individually. Difficulties with using this scale lie in relating the executives' values to their jobs and in determining the impact of these values on corporate strategy.

A more specific way is to pinpoint those aspects of human values likely to affect strategy development and to measure one's score in relation to these values on a simple five- or seven-point scale. For example, we can measure an executive's orientation toward leadership image, performance standards and evaluation, decision-making techniques, use of authority, attitude about change, and nature of involvement. Exhibit 3-4 shows a sample scale for measuring these values.

As a matter of fact, a formal value orientation profile of each executive may not be entirely necessary. By raising questions such as the following about each top executive, one can gather insight into value orientations. Does the executive:

- Seem efficiency-minded?
- Like repetition?
- Like to be first in a new field instead of second?
- Revel in detail work?
- Seem willing to pay the price of keeping in personal touch with the customer, etc.?

Can the value system of an individual be changed? Traditionally, it has been held that a person's behavior is determined mainly by the inner self reacting within a given environment. In line with this thinking, major shifts in values should be difficult to achieve. In recent years, however, a new school of behaviorists has emerged that assigns a more significant role to the environment. These new behaviorists challenge the concept of "self" as the underlying force in determining behavior.[23] If their "environmental" thesis is accepted, it should be possible to bring about a change in individual values so that senior executives can become more unified. However, the science of human behavior has yet to discover the tools that can be used to change values. Thus, it would be appropriate to say that minor changes in personal values can be produced through manipulation of the environment; but where the values of an individual executive differ significantly from those of a colleague, an attempt to alter an individual's values would be difficult.

EXHIBIT 3-4
Measuring Value Orientation

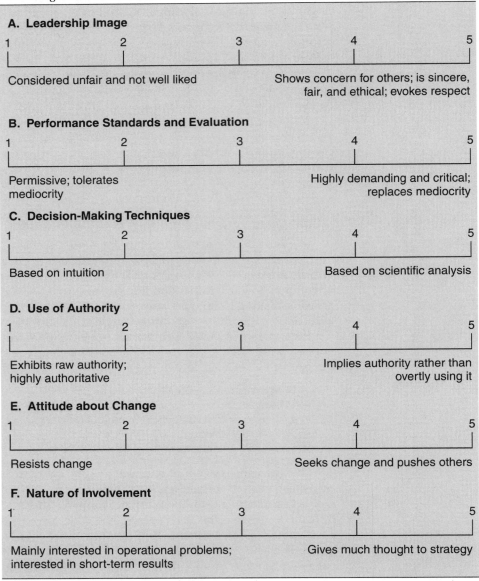

A. **Leadership Image**

| 1 | 2 | 3 | 4 | 5 |

Considered unfair and not well liked   Shows concern for others; is sincere,
                                              fair, and ethical; evokes respect

B. **Performance Standards and Evaluation**

| 1 | 2 | 3 | 4 | 5 |

Permissive; tolerates   Highly demanding and critical;
mediocrity   replaces mediocrity

C. **Decision-Making Techniques**

| 1 | 2 | 3 | 4 | 5 |

Based on intuition   Based on scientific analysis

D. **Use of Authority**

| 1 | 2 | 3 | 4 | 5 |

Exhibits raw authority;   Implies authority rather than
highly authoritative   overtly using it

E. **Attitude about Change**

| 1 | 2 | 3 | 4 | 5 |

Resists change   Seeks change and pushes others

F. **Nature of Involvement**

| 1 | 2 | 3 | 4 | 5 |

Mainly interested in operational problems;   Gives much thought to strategy
interested in short-term results

Several years ago, differing values caused a key executive at Procter & Gamble, John W. Hanley, to leave the company for the CEO position at Monsanto. Other members of the Procter & Gamble management team found him too aggressive, too eager to experiment and change practices, and too quick to challenge his superior. Because he could not be brought around to the conservative style of the company's other executives, he was passed over for the presidency and eventually left the company.[24]

Value Orientation and Corporate Strategy

The influence of the value orientation of top management on the perspectives of the business has already been emphasized. This section examines how a particular type of value orientation may lead to certain objectives and strategy perspectives. Two examples of this influence are presented below. In the first example, the president is rated high on social and aesthetic values, which seems to indicate a greater emphasis on the quality of a single product than on growth per se. In the second example, again, the theoretical and social orientation of top management appears to stress truth and honesty rather than strictly growth. If the strategic plans of these two companies were to emphasize growth as a major goal, they would undoubtedly fail. Planned perspectives may not be implemented if they are constrained by top management's value system.

Example A

Values

The president of a small manufacturer of office duplicating equipment ranked relatively high on social values, giving particular attention to the security, welfare, and happiness of the employees. Second in order of importance to the president were aesthetic values.

Objectives and Strategies

1. Slow-to-moderate company growth.
2. Emphasis on a single product.
3. An independent-agent form of sales organization.
4. Very high-quality products with aesthetic appeal.
5. Refusal to compete on a price basis.

Example B

Values

The top-management team members of a high-fidelity loudspeaker systems manufacturer placed greater emphasis on theoretical and social values than on other values.

Objectives and Strategies

1. Scientific truth and integrity in advertising.
2. Lower margins to dealers than competitors were paying.
3. Maintenance of "truth and honesty" in relationships with suppliers, dealers, and employees.

A corporation's culture can be its major strength when it is consistent with its strategies, as demonstrated by the following examples:

- At IBM, marketing drives a service philosophy that is almost unparalleled. The company keeps a hot line open 24 hours a day, seven days a week, to service IBM products.
- At International Telephone and Telegraph Corporation, financial discipline demands total dedication. To beat out the competition in a merger, an executive once called former chairman Harold S. Geneen at 3 a.m. to get his approval.
- At Digital Equipment Corporation, an emphasis on innovation creates freedom with responsibility. Employees can set their own hours and working style, but they are expected to articulate and support their activities with evidence of progress.
- At Delta Air Lines Inc., a focus on customer service produces a high degree of teamwork. Employees switch jobs to keep planes flying and baggage moving.
- At Atlantic Richfield Company, an emphasis on entrepreneurship encourages action. Managers have the autonomy to bid on promising fields without hierarchical approval.[25]

In summary, an organization in the process of strategy formulation must study the values of its executives. While exact measurement of values may not be possible, some awareness of the values held by top management is helpful to planners. Care should be taken not to threaten or alienate executives by challenging their beliefs, traits, or outlooks. In the strategy formulation, the value package of the management team should be duly considered even if it means compromising on growth and profitability. Where no such compromise is feasible, it is better to transfer or change the assignment of a dissenting executive.

The experience of Interpace Corporation's CEO is relevant here. After moving from International Telephone and Telegraph Corporation (ITT) in the early 1980s, he drew on his ITT background to manage Interpace, a miniconglomerate with interests in such diverse products as teacups and concrete pipes. He used a formula that had worked well at ITT, which consisted of viewing assets primarily as financial pawns to be shifted around at the CEO's will, of compelling managers to abide by financial dicta, and of focusing on financial results. The approach seemed reasonable, but its implementation at Interpace was fraught with problems. ITT's management style did not fit the Interpace culture, despite the fact that the CEO replaced 35 members of a 51-person team.[26] Culture that prevents a company from meeting competitive threats or from adapting to changing economic or social environments can lead to stagnation and the company's ultimate demise unless the company makes a conscious effort to change.

FACTORS IN APPRAISAL: CORPORATE RESOURCES

The resources of a firm are its distinctive capabilities and strengths. Resources are relative in nature and must always be measured with reference to the competition.

Resources can be categorized as financial strength, human resources, raw material reserve, engineering and production, overall management, and marketing strength. The marketing strategist needs to consider not only marketing resources but also resources of the company across the board. For example, price setting is a part of marketing strategy, yet it must be considered in the context of the financial strength of the company if the firm is to grow as rapidly as it should. It is obvious that profit margins on sales, combined with dividend policy, determine the amount of funds that a firm can generate internally. It is less well understood, but equally true, that if a firm uses more debt than its competitors or pays lower dividends, it can generate more funds for growth by decreasing profit margins. Thus, it is important in strategy development that all of the firm's resources are fully utilized in a truly integrated way. The firm that does not use its resources fully is a target for the firm that will—even if the latter has fewer resources. Full and skillful utilization of resources can give a firm a distinct competitive edge.

Resources and Marketing Strategy

Consider the following resources of a company:

1. Has ample cash on hand (financial strength).
2. Average age of key management personnel is 42 years (human resources).
3. Has a superior raw material ingredient in reserve (raw material reserve).
4. Manufactures parts and components that go into the final product using the company's own facilities (plant and equipment).
5. The products of the company, if properly installed and serviced regularly, never stop while being used (technical competence).
6. Has knowledge of, a close relationship with, and expertise in doing business with grocery chains (marketing strength).

How do these resources affect marketing strategy? The cash-rich company, unlike the cash-tight company, is in a position to provide liberal credit accommodation to customers. General Electric, for example, established the General Electric Credit Corporation (now called GE Capital Corporation) to help its dealers and ultimate customers to obtain credit. In the case of a manufacturer of durable goods whose products are usually bought on credit, the availability of easy credit can itself be the difference between success and failure in the marketplace.

If a company has a raw material reserve, it does not need to depend on outside suppliers when there are shortages. In the mid-1980s, there was a shortage of high-grade paper. A magazine publisher with its own forests and paper manufacturing facilities did not need to depend on paper companies to acquire paper. Thus, even when a shortage forced its competitors to reduce the sizes of their magazines, the company not dependent on outsiders was able to provide the same pre-shortage product to its customers.

In the initial stages of the development of color television, RCA was the only company that manufactured color picture tubes. In addition to using these tubes in its own television sets, RCA also sold them to other manufacturers/competitors such as GE. When the market for color television began to grow, RCA was in a strong position to obtain a larger share of the growth partly because of its easy access to picture tubes. GE, on the other hand, was weaker in this respect.

IBM's technical capabilities, among other things, helped it to be an innovator in developing data processing equipment and in introducing it to the market. IBM's excellent after-sale service facilities in themselves promoted the company's products. After-sale servicing put a promotional tool in the hands of salespeople to push the company's products.

Procter & Gamble is noted for its superior strength in dealing with grocery channels. The fact that this strength has served Procter & Gamble well hardly needs to be mentioned. More than anything else, marketing strength has helped Procter & Gamble to compete successfully with established companies, such as Coca-Cola and Seagram, in the frozen orange juice market. In brief, the resources of a company help it to establish and maintain itself in the marketplace. It is, of course, necessary for resources to be appraised objectively.

Measurement of Resources

A firm is a conglomerate of different entities, each having a number of variables that affects performance. How far should a strategist probe into these variables to designate the resources of the firm? Exhibit 3-5 is a list of possible strategic factors. Not all of these factors are important for every business; attention should be focused on those that could play a critical role in the success or failure of the particular firm. Therefore, the first step in designating resources is to have executives in different areas of the business go through the list and identify those variables that they deem strategic for success. Then each strategic factor may be evaluated either qualitatively or quantitatively. One way of conducting the evaluation is to frame relevant questions around each strategic factor, which may be rated on either a dichotomous or a continuous scale. As an example, the paragraphs that follow discuss questions relevant to a men's sportswear manufacturer.

Top Management.   Which executives form the top management? Which manager can be held responsible for the firm's performance during the past few years? Is each manager capable of undertaking future challenges as successfully as past challenges were undertaken? Is something needed to boost the morale of top management? What are the distinguishing characteristics of each top executive? Are there any conflicts, such as personality conflicts, among them? If so, between whom and for what reasons? What has been done and is being done for organizational development? What are the reasons for the company's performance during the past few years? Are the old ways of managing obsolete? What more can be done to enhance the company's capabilities?

Marketing.   What are the company's major products/services? What are the basic facts about each product (e.g., market share, profitability, position in the life cycle, major competitors and their strengths and weaknesses, etc.)? In which field can the firm be considered a leader? Why? What can be said about the firm's pricing policies (i.e., compared with value and with the prices of competitors)? What is the nature of new product development efforts, the coordination between

EXHIBIT 3-5
Strategic Factors in Business

A. *General Managerial*

1. Ability to attract and maintain high-quality top management
2. Ability to develop future managers for overseas operations
3. Ability to develop future managers for domestic operations
4. Ability to develop a better organizational structure
5. Ability to develop a better strategic planning program
6. Ability to achieve better overall control of company operations
7. Ability to use more new quantitative tools and techniques in decision making at
   a. Top management levels
   b. Lower management levels
8. Ability to assure better judgment, creativity, and imagination in decision making at
   a. Top management levels
   b. Lower management levels
9. Ability to use computers for problem solving and planning
10. Ability to use computers for information handling and financial control
11. Ability to divest nonprofitable enterprises
12 Ability to perceive new needs and opportunities for products
13. Ability to motivate sufficient managerial drive for profits

B. *Financial*

1. Ability to raise long-term capital at low cost
   a. Debt
   b. Equity
2. Ability to raise short-term capital
3. Ability to maximize value of stockholder investment
4. Ability to provide a competitive return to stockholders
5. Willingness to take risks with commensurate returns in what appear to be excellent new business opportunities in order to achieve growth objectives
6. Ability to apply return on investment criteria to research and development investments
7. Ability to finance diversification by means of
   a. Acquisitions
   b. In-house research and development

C. *Marketing*

1. Ability to accumulate better knowledge about markets
2. Ability to establish a wide customer base
3. Ability to establish a selective consumer base
4. Ability to establish an efficient product distribution system
5. Ability to get good business contracts (government and others)
6. Ability to assure imaginative advertising and sales promotion campaigns
7. Ability to use pricing more effectively (including discounts, customer credit, product service, guarantees, delivery, etc.)
8. Ability to develop better relationships between marketing and new product engineering and production
9. Ability to produce vigor in sales organization

EXHIBIT 3-5
Continued

D. *Engineering and Production*

1. Ability to develop effective machinery and equipment replacement policies
2. Ability to provide more efficient plant layout
3. Ability to develop sufficient capacity for expansion
4. Ability to develop better materials and inventory control
5. Ability to improve product quality control
6. Ability to improve in-house product engineering
7. Ability to improve in-house basic product research capabilities
8. Ability to develop more effective profit improvement (cost reduction) programs
9. Ability to develop better ability to mass produce at low per-unit cost
10. Ability to relocate present production facilities
11. Ability to automate production facilities
12. Ability to inspire better management of and better results from research and development expenditures
13. Ability to establish foreign production facilities
14. Ability to develop more flexibility in using facilities for different products
15. Ability to be in the forefront of technology and be extremely scientifically creative

E. *Products*

1. Ability to improve present products
2. Ability to develop more efficient and effective product line selection
3. Ability to develop new products to replace old ones
4. Ability to develop new products in new markets
5. Ability to develop sales for present products in new markets
6. Ability to diversify products by acquisition
7. Ability to attract more subcontracting
8. Ability to get bigger share of product market

F. *Personnel*

1. Ability to attract scientists and highly qualified technical employees
2. Ability to establish better relationships with employees
3. Ability to get along with labor unions
4. Ability to better utilize the skills of employees
5. Ability to motivate more employees to remain abreast of developments in their fields
6. Ability to level peaks and valleys of employment requirements
7. Ability to stimulate creativity in employees
8. Ability to optimize employee turnover (not too much and not too little)

G. *Materials*

1. Ability to get geographically closer to raw material sources
2. Ability to assure continuity of raw material supplies
3. Ability to find new sources of raw materials
4. Ability to own and control sources of raw materials
5. Ability to bring in house presently purchased materials and components
6. Ability to reduce raw material costs

research and development and manufacturing? How does the market look in the future for the planning period? What steps are being taken or proposed to meet future challenges? What can be said about the company's channel arrangements, physical distribution, and promotional efforts? What is the behavior of marketing costs? What new products are expected to be launched, when, and with what expectations? What has been done about consumer satisfaction?

Production.   Are people capable of working on new machines, new processes, new designs, etc., which may be developed in the future? What new plant, equipment, and facilities are needed? What are the basic facts about each product (e.g., cost structure, quality control, work stoppages)? What is the nature of labor relations? Are any problems anticipated? What steps have been proposed or taken to avert strikes, work stoppages, and so forth? Does production perform its part effectively in the manufacturing of new products? How flexible are operations? Can they be made suitable for future competition and new products well on the way to being produced and marketed commercially? What steps have been proposed or taken to control pollution? What are the important raw materials being used or likely to be used? What are the important sources for each raw material? How reliable are these sources?

Finance.   What is the financial standing of the company as a whole and of its different products/divisions in terms of earnings, sales, tangible net worth, working capital, earnings per share, liquidity, inventory, cash flow position, and capital structure? What is the cost of capital? Can money be used more productively? What is the reputation of the company in the financial community? How does the company's performance compare with that of competitors and other similarly sized corporations? What steps have been proposed or taken to line up new sources of capital, to increase return on investment through more productive use of resources, and to lower break-even points? Has the company managed tax matters aggressively? What contingency steps are proposed to avert threats of capital shortage or a takeover?

Research and Development.   What is the research and development reputation of the company? What percentage of sales and profits in the past can be directly attributed to research and development efforts? Are there any conflicts or personality clashes in the department? If so, what has been proposed and what is being done? What is the status of current major projects? When are they expected to be completed? In what way will they help the company's performance? What kind of relationships does research and development have with marketing and manufacturing? What steps have been proposed and are being taken to cut overhead and improve quality? Are all scientists/researchers adequately used? If not, why not? Can we expect any breakthroughs from research and development? Are there any resentments? If so, what are they and for what reason do they exist?

Miscellaneous.   What has been proposed or done to serve minorities, the community, the cause of education, and other such concerns? What is the nature of productivity gains for the company as a whole and for each part of the company? How does the company stand in comparison to industry trends and national goals? How well does the company compete in the world market? Which countries/companies constitute tough competitors? What are their strengths and weaknesses? What is the nature and scope of the company's public relations function? Is it adequate? How does it compare with that of competitors and other companies of similar size and character? Which government agencies—federal, state, or local—does the company deal with most often? Are the company's relationships with various levels of government satisfactory? Who are the company's stockholders? Do a few individuals/institutions hold majority stock? What are their corporate expectations? Do they prefer capital gains or dividend income?

Ratings on these questions may be added up to compute the total resource score in each area. It must be understood that not all questions can be evaluated using the same scale. In many cases, quantitative measurement may be difficult and subjective evaluation must be accepted. Further, measurement of resources should be done for current effectiveness and for future perspectives.

Strategic factors for success lie in different functional areas, the distribution network, for example, and they vary by industry. As shown in Exhibit 3-6, the success factors for different industries fall at different points along a continuum of functional activities that begins with raw materials sourcing and ends with

EXHIBIT 3-6
Success Factors for Different Industries

Key Factor or Function	Specimen Industries	
	To Increase Profit	*To Gain Share*
Raw materials sourcing	Uranium	Petroleum
Product facilities (economies of scale)	Shipbuilding, steelmaking	Shipbuilding, steelmaking
Design	Aircraft	Aircraft, hi-fi
Production technology	Soda, semiconductors	Semiconductors
Product range/variety	Department stores	Components
Application engineering /engineers	Minicomputers	Large-scale integration (LSI), microprocessors
Sales force (quality × quantity)	Electronic code recorders (ECR)	Automobiles
Distribution network	Beer	Films, home appliances
Servicing	Elevators	Commercial vehicles (e.g., taxis)

Source: Kenichi Ohmae, *The Mind of the Strategist* (New York: McGraw-Hill Book Co., 1982), 47.

servicing. In the uranium industry, raw materials sourcing is the key to success because low-quality ore requires much more complicated and costly processing. Inasmuch as the price of uranium does not vary among producers, the choice of the source of uranium supply is the crucial determinant of profitability. In contrast, the critical factor in the soda industry is production technology. Because the mercury process is more than twice as efficient as the semipermeable membrane method of obtaining soda of similar quality, a company using the latter process is at a disadvantage no matter what else it might do to reduce extra cost. In other words, the use of mercury technology is a strategic resource for a soda company if its competitors have chosen not to go to the expense and difficulty of changing over from the semipermeable membrane method.[27]

PAST PERFORMANCE OF BUSINESS UNITS

The past performance of business units serves as an important input in formulating corporate-wide strategy. It helps in the assessment of the current situation and possible developments in the future. For example, if the profitability of an SBU has been declining over the past five years, an appraisal of current performance as satisfactory cannot be justified, assuming the trend continues. In addition, any projected rise in profitability must be thoroughly justified in the light of this trend. The perspectives of different SBUs over time, vis-a-vis other factors (top management values, concerns of stakeholders, corporate resources, and the socioeconomic-political-technological environment), show which have the potential for profitable growth.

SBU performance is based on such measures as financial strength (sales—dollar or volume—operating profit before taxes, cash flow, depreciation, sales per employee, profits per employee, investment per employee, return on investment/sales/assets, and asset turnover); human resources (use of employee skills, productivity, turnover, and ethnic and racial composition); facilities (rated capacity, capacity utilization, and modernization); inventories (raw materials, finished products, and obsolete inventory); marketing (research and development expenditures, new product introductions, number of salespersons, sales per salesperson, independent distributors, exclusive distributors, and promotion expenditures); international business (growth rate and geographic coverage); and managerial performance (leadership capabilities, planning, development of personnel, and delegation).

Usually the volume of data that the above information would generate is much greater than required. It is desirable, therefore, for management to specify what measures it considers important in appraising the performance of SBUs. From the viewpoint of corporate management, the following three measures are frequently the principal measures of performance:

1. **Effectiveness** measures the success of a business's products and programs in relation to those of its competitors in the market. Effectiveness commonly is measured by such items as sales growth in comparison with that of competitors or by changes in market share.

2. **Efficiency** is the outcome of a business's programs in relation to the resources employed in implementing them. Common measures of efficiency are profitability as a percentage of sales and return on investment.

3. **Adaptability** is the business's success in responding over time to changing conditions and opportunities in the environment. Adaptability can be measured in a variety of ways, but common measures are the number of successful new product introductions in relation to those of competitors and the percentage of sales accounted for by products introduced within some recent time period.[28]

To ensure consistency in information received from different SBUs, it is worthwhile to develop a pro forma sheet listing the categories of information that corporate management desires. The general profile produced from the evaluation of information obtained through pro forma sheets provides a quick picture of how well things are going.

SUMMARY

Corporate appraisal constitutes an important ingredient in the strategy development process because it lays the foundation for the company to interact with the future environment. Corporate publics, value orientation of top management, and corporate resources were the three principal factors in appraisal discussed in this chapter. Appraisal of the past performance of business units, which also affects formulation of corporate strategy for the future, was covered briefly.

Corporate publics are all those groups having a stake in the organization; that is, owners, employees, customers, suppliers, the banking community and other lenders, government, the community in which the company does business, and society at large. Expectations of all stakeholders should be considered in formulating corporate strategy. Corporate strategy is also deeply influenced by the value orientation of the corporation's top management. Thus, the values of top management should be studied and duly assessed in setting objectives. Finally, the company's resources in different areas should be carefully evaluated. They serve as major criteria for the formulation of future perspectives.

DISCUSSION QUESTIONS

1. How often should a company undertake corporate appraisal? What are the arguments for and against yearly corporate appraisal?
2. Discuss the pros and cons of having a consultant conduct the appraisal.
3. Identify five companies that in your opinion have failed to change with time and have either pulled out of the marketplace or continue in it as laggards.
4. Identify five companies that in your opinion have kept pace with time as evidenced by their performance.
5. What expectations does a community have of (a) a bank, (b) a medical group, and (c) a manufacturer of cyclical goods?
6. What top management values are most likely to lead to a growth orientation?
7. Is growth orientation necessarily good? Discuss.
8. In your opinion, what marketing resources are the most critical for success in the cosmetics industry?

NOTES

1 *Perspectives on Corporate Strategy* (Boston: Boston Consulting Group, 1968), 93.

2 See James Collins and Jerry Porras, *Built to Last* (New York: Harper Business, 1994).

3 Donald P. Robin and R. Eric Reidenback, "Social Responsibility Ethics and Marketing Strategy: Closing the Gap between Concept and Application," *Journal of Marketing* (January 1987): 55.

4 Robin and Reidenback, "Social Responsibility," 52.

5 See Peter F. Drucker, "A New Look at Corporate Social Responsibility," in *Public-Private Partnership*, ed. H. Brooks, L. Liebman, and C. Schelling (Lexington, MA: Ballinger Publishing Co., 1984).

6 "Are Good Causes Good Marketing," *Business Week* (21 March 1994): 64.

7 See Mark Dowie, "Mother Jones Goes Searching for Excellence," *Wall Street Journal* (6 May 1985): 34.

8 "The Battle for Corporate Control," *Business Week* (18 May 1987): 102.

9 Robert F. Lusch and Gene R. Laczniak, "The Evolving Marketing Concept, Competitive Intensity and Organizational Performance," *Journal of the Academy of Marketing Science* (Fall 1987): 10.

10 "Corning's Class Act," *Business Week* (13 May 1991): 76.

11 George A. Steiner, *Top Management Planning* (New York: Macmillan Co., 1969), 241.

12 Thomas J. Peters, "Putting Excellence into Management," *McKinsey Quarterly* (Autumn 1980): 37.

13 "Where Different Styles Have Led Two Canmakers," *Business Week* (27 July 1981): 81–82. See also Bernard Wysocki, Jr., "The Chief's Personality Can Have a Big Impact For Better or Worse," *Wall Street Journal* (11 September 1984): 1.

14 "Changing a Corporate Culture," *Business Week* (14 May 1984): 130.

15 Brian Dumaine, "P&G Rewrites the Marketing Rules," *Fortune* (6 November 1989): 34.

16 Shelby D. Hunt, Van R. Wood, and Lawrence B. Chonko, "Corporate Ethical Values and Organizational Commitment in Marketing," *Journal of Marketing* (July 1989): 79–90.

17 Mayron Magnet, "Let's Go for Growth," *Fortune* (7 March 1994): 70.

18 "Corporate Culture," 34. See also Bro Uttal, "The Corporate Culture Vultures," *Fortune* (17 October 1983): 66–73; Trish Hall, "Demanding Pepsi Company Is Attempting to Make Work Nicer for Managers," *Wall Street Journal* (23 October 1984): 31.

19 Carol Hymowitz, "Which Corporate Culture Fits You?" *Wall Street Journal* (17 July 1989): B1.

20 Brian Dumaine, "Creating a New Company Culture," *Fortune* (15 January 1990): 128.

21 David Kirpatrick, "Could AT&T Rule the World," *Fortune* (17 May 1993): 57.

22 Gordon W. Allport, Philip E. Vernon, and Gardner Lindzey, *Study of Values and the Manual of Study of Values* (Boston: Houghton Mifflin Co., 1960).

23 B. F. Skinner, *Beyond Freedom and Dignity* (New York: Alfred A. Knopf, 1971).

24 Aimee L. Horner, "Jack Hanley Got There by Selling Harder," *Fortune* (November 1976): 162.

25 "Corporate Culture," 34.

26 "How a Winning Formula Can Fail," *Business Week* (25 May 1981): 119–20.

27 Kenichi Ohmae, *The Mind of the Strategist* (New York: McGraw-Hill Book Co., 1982), 46–47.

28 Orville C. Walker, Jr. and Robert W. Ruekert, "Marketing's Role in the Implementation of Business Strategies: A Critical Review and Conceptual Framework," *Journal of Marketing* (July 1987): 19.

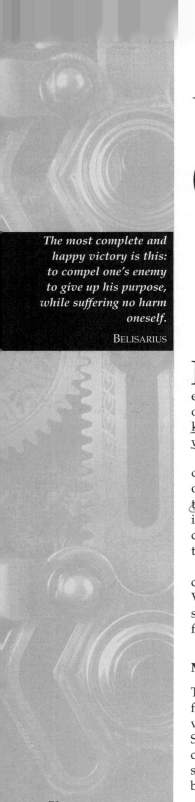

Understanding Competition

> *The most complete and happy victory is this: to compel one's enemy to give up his purpose, while suffering no harm oneself.*
>
> BELISARIUS

In a free market economy, each company tries to outperform its competitors. A competitor is a rival. A company must know, therefore, how it stands up against each competitor with regard to "arms and ammunition"—skill in maneuvering opportunities, preparedness in reacting to threats, and so on. To obtain adequate knowledge about the competition, a company needs an excellent intelligence network.

Typically, whenever one talks about competition, emphasis is placed on price, quality of product, delivery time, and other marketing variables. For the purposes of strategy development, however, one needs to go far beyond these marketing tactics. Simply knowing that a competitor has been lowering prices, for example, is not sufficient. Over and above that, one must know how much flexibility the competitor has in further reducing the price. Implicit here is the need for information about the competitor's cost structure.

This chapter begins by examining the meaning of competition. The theory of competition is reviewed, and a scheme for classifying competitors is advanced. Various sources of competitive intelligence are mentioned, and models for understanding competitive behavior are discussed. Finally, the impact of competition in formulating marketing strategy is analyzed.

MEANING OF COMPETITION

The term *competition* defies definition because the view of competition held by different groups (e.g., lawyers, economists, government officials, and businesspeople) varies. Most firms define competition in crude, simplistic, and unrealistic terms. Some firms fail to identify the true sources of competition; others underestimate the capabilities and reactions of their competitors. When the business climate is stable, a shallow outlook toward the competition might work, but in the current environment, business strategies must be competitively oriented.

Natural and Strategic Competition

A useful way to define competition is to differentiate between natural and strategic competition. Natural competition refers to the survival of the fittest in a given environment. It is an evolutionary process that weeds out the weaker of two rivals. Applied to the business world, it means that no two firms doing business across the board the same way in the same market can coexist forever. To survive, each firm must have something uniquely superior to the other.

Natural competition is an extension of the biological phenomenon of Darwinian natural selection. Characteristically, this type of competition—evolution by adaptation—occurs by trial and error; is wildly opportunistic day to day; pursues growth for its own sake; and is very conservative, because growth from successful trials must prevail over death (i.e., bankruptcy) by random mistake.

Strategic competition, on the other hand, tries to leave nothing to chance. In Bruce Henderson's definition, **strategic competition** is the studied deployment of resources based on a high degree of insight into the systematic cause and effect in the business ecological system. Strategic competition is a new phenomenon in the business world that may well have the same impact upon business productivity that the industrial revolution had upon individual productivity. Strategic competition requires (a) an adequate amount of information about the situation, (b) development of a framework to understand the dynamic interactive system, (c) postponement of current consumption to provide investment capital, (d) commitment to invest major resources to an irreversible outcome, and (e) an ability to predict the output consequences even with incomplete knowledge of inputs. Henderson identifies the basic elements of strategic competition as follows:

- The ability to understand competitive interaction as a complete dynamic system that includes the interaction of competitors, customers, money, people, and resources.
- The ability to use this understanding to predict the consequences of a given intervention in the system and how that intervention will result in new patterns of equilibrium.
- The availability of uncommitted resources that can be dedicated to different uses and purposes in the present even though the dedication is permanent and the benefits will be deferred.
- The ability to predict risk and return with sufficient accuracy and confidence to justify the commitment of such resources.
- The willingness to deliberately act to make the commitment.[1]

Japan's emergence as a major industrial power over a short span of time illustrates the practical application of strategic competition.

The differences between Japan and the U.S. deserve some comparative analysis. There are lessons to be learned. These two leading industrial powers came from different directions, developed different methods, and followed different strategies.

Japan is a small group of islands whose total land area is smaller than a number of our 50 states. The U.S., by comparison, is a vast land.

Japan is mountainous with very little arable land. The U.S. is the world's largest and most fertile agricultural area in a single country.

Japan has virtually no energy or natural resources. The U.S. is richly endowed with energy, minerals, and other vital resources.

Japan has one of the oldest, most homogenous, most stable cultures. For 2,000 years or more, there was virtually no immigration, no dilution of culture, or any foreign invasion. The U.S. has been a melting pot of immigrants from many cultures and many languages over one-tenth the time span. For most of its history, the U.S. has been an agrarian society and a frontier society.

The Japanese developed a high order of skill in living together in cooperation over many centuries. Americans developed a frontier mentality of self-reliance and individuality.

The evolution of the U.S. into a vast industrial society was a classic example of natural competition in a rich environment with no constraints or artificial barriers.

This option was not open to Japan. It had been in self-imposed isolation from the rest of the world for several hundred years until Commodore Perry sailed into Tokyo harbor and forced the signing of a navigation and trade treaty. Japan had been unaware of the industrial revolution already well underway in the West. It decided to compete in that world. But it had no resources.

To rise above a medieval economy, Japan had to obtain foreign materials. To obtain foreign materials, it had to buy them. To buy abroad required foreign exchange. To obtain foreign exchange, exports were required. Exports became Japan's lifeline. But effective exports meant the maximum value added, first with minimum material and then with minimum direct labor. Eventually this led Japan from labor intensive to capital intensive and then to technology intensive businesses. Japan was forced to develop strategic business competition as part of national policy.[2]

THEORY OF COMPETITION

Competition is basic to the free enterprise system. It is involved in all observable phenomena of the market—the prices at which products are exchanged, the kinds and qualities of products produced, the quantities exchanged, the methods of distribution employed, and the emphasis placed on promotion. Over many decades, economists have contributed to the theory of competition. A well-recognized body of theoretical knowledge about competition has emerged and can be grouped broadly into two categories: (a) economic theory and (b) industrial organization perspective. These and certain other hypotheses on competition from the viewpoint of businesspeople will now be introduced.

Economic Theory of Competition

Economists have worked with many different models of competition. Still central to much of their work is the model of *perfect competition*, which is based on the premise that, when a large number of buyers and sellers in the market are dealing in homogeneous products, there is complete freedom to enter or exit the market and everyone has complete and accurate knowledge about everyone else.

Industrial Organization Perspective

The essence of the industrial organization (IO) perspective is that a firm's position in the marketplace depends critically on the characteristics of the industry environment in which it competes. The industry environment comprises structure, conduct, and performance. This structure refers to the economic and technical perspectives of the industry in the context in which firms compete. It includes (a) concentration in the industry (i.e., the number and size distribution of firms), (b) barriers to entry in the industry, and (c) product differentiation among the offerings of different firms that make up the industry. Conduct, which is essentially strategy, refers to firms' behavior in such matters as pricing, advertising, and distribution. Performance includes social performance, measured in terms of allocative efficiency (profitability), technical efficiency (cost minimization), and innovativeness.

Following the IO thesis, the structure of each industry vis-à-vis concentration, product differentiation, and entry barriers varies. Structure plays an important role in the competitive behavior of different firms in the market.

> Businesspeople must be continually aware of the structure of the markets they are presently in or of those they seek to enter. Their appraisal of their present and future competitive posture will be influenced substantially by the size and concentration of existing firms as well as by the extent of product differentiation and the presence or absence of significant barriers to entry.
>
> If a manager has already introduced the firm's products into a market, the existence of certain structural features may provide the manager with a degree of insulation from the intrusion of firms not presently in that market. The absence, or relative unimportance, of one or more entry barriers, for example, supplies the manager with insights into the direction from which potential competition might come. Conversely, the presence or absence of entry barriers indicates the relative degree of effort required and the success that might be enjoyed if the manager attempted to enter a specific market. In short, a fundamental purpose of marketing strategy involves the building of entry barriers to protect present markets and the overcoming of existing entry barriers around markets that have an attractive potential.[3]

Business Viewpoint | From the businessperson's perspective, competition refers to rivalry among firms operating in a market to fill the same customer need. The businessperson's major interest is to keep the market to himself or herself by adopting appropriate strategies. How and why competition occurs, its intensity, and what escape routes are feasible have not been conceptualized.[4] In other words, there does not exist a theory of competition from the business viewpoint.

In recent years, however, Henderson has developed the theory of strategic competition discussed above. Some of the hypotheses on which his theory rests derive from military warfare:

- Competitors who persist and survive have a unique advantage over all others. If they did not have this advantage, then others would crowd them out of the market.
- If competitors are different and coexist, then each must have a distinct advantage over the other. Such an advantage can only exist if differences in a competitor's characteristics match differences in the environment that give those characteristics their relative value.
- Any change in the environment changes the factor weighting of environmental characteristics and, therefore, shifts the boundaries of competitive equilibrium and "competitive segments." Competitors who adapt best or fastest gain an advantage from change in the environment.[5]

Henderson presents an interesting new way of looking at the marketplace: as a battleground where opposing forces (competitors) devise ways (strategies) to outperform each other. According to Henderson, some of his hypotheses can be readily observed, tested, and validated and could lead to a general theory of business competition. However, many of his interlocking hypotheses must still be revised and tested, with the science of sociobiology playing a big role. As Henderson observes:

> To understand competition and its homeostasis, we must be able to integrate its entire system. The quantification of sociobiology has demonstrated the power of analysis when competition is viewed as a dynamic, ever-changing system.
>
> If competition is fully understood as a system, the benefits in rationalization of public policy with respect to antitrust regulation and international trade can be far-reaching.
>
> I believe that insight into strategic competition has the promise of quantum increase in our productivity and our ability to both control and expand the potential of our own future.[6]

CLASSIFYING COMPETITORS

A business may face competition from various sources either within or outside its industry. Competition may come from essentially similar products or from substitutes. The competitor may be a small firm or a large multinational corporation. To gain an adequate perspective on the competition, a firm needs to identify all current and potential sources of competition.

Competition is triggered when different industries try to serve the same customer needs and demands. For example, a customer's entertainment needs may be filled by television, sports, publishing, or travel. New industries may also enter the arena to satisfy entertainment needs. In the early 1980s, for example, the computer industry entered the entertainment field with video games.

Different industries position themselves to serve different customer demands—existing, latent, and incipient. Existing demand occurs when a product is bought to satisfy a recognized need. An example is Swatch Watch to determine time. Latent demand refers to a situation where a particular need has been recognized, but no products have yet been offered to satisfy the need. Sony tapped the latent demand through Walkman for the attraction of "music on the move." Incipient demand occurs when certain trends lead to the emergence of a need of which the customer is not yet aware. A product that makes it feasible to read books while sleeping would illustrate the incipient demand.

A competitor may be an existing firm or a new entrant. The new entrant may enter the market with a product developed through research and development or through acquisition. For example, Texas Instruments entered the educational toy business through research and development that led to the manufacture of their Speak and Spell product. Philip Morris entered the beer market by acquiring Miller Brewing Company.

Often an industry competes by producing different product lines. General Foods Corporation, for example, offers ground, regular instant, freeze-dried, decaffeinated, and "international" coffee to the coffee market. Product lines can be grouped into three categories: a me-too product, an improved product, or a breakthrough product. A **me-too product** is similar to current offerings. One of many brands currently available in the market, it offers no special advantage over competing products. An **improved product** is one that, while not unique, is generally superior to many existing brands. A **breakthrough product** is an innovation and is usually technical in nature. The digital watch and the color television set were once breakthrough products.

In the watch business, companies have traditionally competed by offering me-too products. Occasionally, a competitor comes out with an improved product, as Seiko did in the 1970s by introducing quartz watches. Quartz watches were a little fancier and supposedly more accurate than other watches. Texas Instruments, however, entered the watch business via a breakthrough product, the digital watch.

Finally, the scope of a competing firm's activities may be limited or extensive. For example, PepsiCo may not worry if a regional chain of pizza parlors is established to compete against its Pizza Hut subsidiary. However, if Procter & Gamble were to enter the pizza restaurant business, PepsiCo would be concerned at the entry of such a strong and seasoned competitor.

Exhibit 4-1 illustrates various sources of competition available to fulfill the liquid requirements of the human body. Let us analyze the competition here for a company that maintains an interest in this field. Currently, the thrust of the market is to satisfy existing demand. An example of a product to satisfy latent demand would be a liquid that promises weight loss; a liquid to prevent aging would be an example of a product to satisfy incipient demand.

The industries that currently offer products to quench customer thirst are the liquor, beer, wine, soft drink, milk, coffee, tea, drinking water, and fruit juice industries. A relatively new entrant is mineral and sparkling water. Looking just at the soft drink industry, assuming that this is the field that most interests our company, we see that the majority of competitors offer me-too products (e.g., regular cola, diet cola, lemonade, and other fruit-based drinks). However, caffeine-free cola has been introduced by two major competitors, Coca-Cola Company and PepsiCo. There has been a breakthrough in the form of low-calorie, caffeine-free drinks. A beverage containing a day's nutritional requirements is feasible in the future.

The companies that currently compete in the regular cola market are Coca-Cola, PepsiCo, Seven-Up, Dr. Pepper, and a few others. Among these, however, the first two have a major share of the cola market. Among new industry entrants, General Foods Corporation and Nestle Company are likely candidates (an assumption). The two principal competitors, Coca-Cola Company and PepsiCo, are large multinational, multibusiness firms. This is the competitive arena where our company will have to fight if it enters the soft drink business.

EXHIBIT 4-1

Source of Competition

Customer Need: Liquid for the Body	
Existing need	Thirst
Latent need	Liquid to reduce weight
Incipient need	Liquid to prevent aging

Industry Competition (How Can I Quench My Thirst?)	
Existing industries	Hard liquor
	Beer
	Wine
	Soft drink
	Milk
	Coffee
	Tea
	Water
New industry	Mineral water

Product Line Competition (What Form of Product Do I Want?)	
Me-too products	Regular cola
	Diet cola
	Lemonade
	Fruit-based drink
Improved product	Caffeine-free cola
Breakthrough product	Diet and caffeine-free cola providing full nutrition

Organizational Competition (What Brand Do I Want?)	
Type of Firm	
Existing firms	Coca-Cola
	PepsiCo
	Seven-Up
	Dr. Pepper
New entrants	General Foods
	Nestle
Scope of Business	
Geographic	Regional, national, multinational
Product/market	Single versus multiproduct industry

INTENSITY, OR DEGREE, OF COMPETITION

The degree of competition in a market depends on the moves and countermoves of various firms active in the market. It usually starts with one firm trying to achieve a favorable position by pursuing appropriate strategies. Because what is good for one firm may be harmful to rival firms, rival firms respond with counter strategies to protect their interests.

Intense competitive activity may or may not be injurious to the industry as a whole. For example, while a price war may result in lower profits for all members of an industry, an advertising battle may increase demand and actually be mutually beneficial. Exhibit 4-2 lists the factors that affect the intensity of competition in the marketplace. In a given situation, a combination of factors determines the degree of competition.

Opportunity Potential | A promising market is likely to attract firms seeking to capitalize on an available opportunity. As the number of firms interested in sharing the pie increases, the degree of rivalry increases. Take, for example, the home computer market. In the early 1980s, everyone from mighty IBM to such unknowns in the field as Timex Watch Company wanted a piece of the personal computer pie. As firms started jockeying for position, the intensity of competition increased manifold. A number of firms, for example, Texas Instruments and Atari, were forced to quit the market.

Ease of Entry | When entry into an industry is relatively easy, many firms, including some marginal ones, are attracted to it. The long-standing, committed members of the industry, however, do not want "outsiders" to break into their territory. Therefore, existing firms discourage potential entrants by adopting strategies that enhance competition.

Nature of Product | When the products offered by different competitors are perceived by customers to be more or less similar, firms are forced into price and, to a lesser degree, service competition. In such situations, competition can be really severe.

Exit Barriers | For a variety of reasons, it may be difficult for a firm to get out of a particular business. Possible reasons include the relationship of the business to other businesses of the firm, high investment in assets for which there may not be an advantageous

EXHIBIT 4-2
Factors Contributing to Competitive Rivalry

Opportunity potential
Ease of entry
Nature of product
Exit barriers
Homogeneity of market
Industry structure or competitive position of firms
Commitment to the industry
Feasibility of technological innovations
Scale economies
Economic climate
Diversity of firms

alternative use, high cost of discharging commitments (e.g., fixed labor contracts and future purchasing agreements), top management's emotional attachment to the business, and government regulations prohibiting exit (e.g., the legal requirement that a utility must serve all customers).

Homogeneity of the Market	When the entire market represents one large homogeneous unit, the intensity of competition is much greater than when the market is segmented. Even if the product sold is a commodity, segmentation of the market is possible. It is possible, for example, to identify frequent buyers of the commodity as one segment; and occasional buyers as another. But if a market is not suited to segmentation, firms must compete to serve it homogeneously, thus intensifying competition.
Industry Structure	When the number of firms active in a market is large, there is a good chance that one of the firms may aggressively seek an advantageous position. Such aggression leads to intense competitive activity as firms retaliate. On the other hand, if only a few firms constitute an industry, there is usually little doubt about industry leadership. In situations where there is a clear industry leader, care is often taken not to irritate the leader since a resulting fight could be very costly.
Commitment to the Industry	When a firm has wholeheartedly committed itself to a business, it will do everything to hang on, even becoming a maverick that fearlessly makes moves without worrying about the impact on either the industry or its own resources. Polaroid Corporation, for example, with its strong commitment to instant photography, must maintain its position in the field at any cost. Such an attachment to an industry enhances competitive activity.
Feasibility of Technological Innovations	In industries where technological innovations are frequent, each firm likes to do its best to cash in while the technology lasts, thus triggering greater competitive activity.
Scale Economies	Where economies realizable through large-scale operations are substantial, a firm will do all it can to achieve scale economies. Attempts to capture scale economies may lead a firm to aggressively compete for market share, escalating pressures on other firms. A similar situation occurs when a business's fixed costs are high and the firm must spread them over a large volume. If capacity can only be added in large increments, the resulting excess capacity will also intensify competition.
Economic Climate	During depressed economic conditions and otherwise slow growth, competition is much more volatile as each firm tries to make the best of a bad situation.
Diversity of Firms	Firms active in a field over a long period come to acquire a kind of industry standard of behavior. But new participants invading an industry do not necessarily like to play the old game. Forsaking industry patterns, newcomers may have different strategic perspectives and may be willing to go to any lengths to achieve

their goals. The Miller Brewing Company's unconventional marketing practices are a case in point. Miller, nurtured and guided by its parent, Philip Morris, segmented the market by introducing a light beer to an industry that had hitherto considered beer a commodity-type product. When different cultures meet in the marketplace, competition can be fierce.

COMPETITIVE INTELLIGENCE

Competitive intelligence is the publicly available information on competitors, current and potential, that serves as an important input in formulating marketing strategy. No general would order an army to march without first fully knowing the enemy's position and intentions. Likewise, before deciding which competitive moves to make, a firm must be aware of the perspectives of its competitors. Competitive intelligence includes information beyond industry statistics and trade gossip. It involves close observation of competitors to learn what they do best and why and where they are weak. No self-respecting business admits to not doing an adequate job of scanning the competitive environment, but what sets the outstanding companies apart from the merely self-respecting ones is that they watch their competition in such depth and with such dedication that, as a marketing executive once remarked to the author, "The information on competitive moves reaches them before even the management of the competing company learns about it."

Three types of competitive intelligence may be distinguished: defensive, passive, and offensive intelligence. **Defensive intelligence**, as the name suggests, is gathered to avoid being caught off-balance. A deliberate attempt is made to gather information on the competition in a structured fashion and to keep track of moves that are relevant to the firm's business. **Passive** intelligence is ad hoc information gathered for a specific decision. A company may, for example, seek information on a competitor's sales compensation plan when devising its own compensation plan. Finally, **offensive intelligence** is undertaken to identify new opportunities. From a strategic perspective, offensive intelligence is the most relevant.

Strategic Usefulness of Competitive Intelligence

Such information as how competitors make, test, distribute, price, and promote their products can go a long way in developing a viable marketing strategy. The Ford Motor Company, for example, has an ongoing program for tearing down competitors' products to learn about their cost structure. Exhibit 4-3 summarizes the process followed at Ford. This competitive knowledge has helped Ford in its strategic moves in Europe. For example, from regularly tearing down the Leyland Mini (a small truck), the company concluded that (a) Leyland was not making money on the Mini at its current price and (b) Ford should not enter the small truck market at current price levels. Based on these conclusions, Ford was able to arrive at a firm strategic decision not to assemble a "Mini."

The following example compares two companies that decided to enter the automatic dishwasher market at about the same time. One of the companies

EXHIBIT 4-3
Ford Motor Company's Competitive Product Tear-Down Process

1. **Purchase the product.** The high cost of product teardown, particularly for a car-maker, gives some indication of the value successful competitors place on the knowledge they gain.
2. **Tear the product down—literally.** First, every removable component is unscrewed or unbolted; the rivets are undone; finally, individual spot welds are broken.
3. **Reverse-engineer the product.** While the competitor's car is being dismantled, detailed drawings of parts are made and parts lists are assembled, together with analyses of the production processes that were evidently involved.
4. **Build up costs.** Parts are costed out in terms of make-or-buy, the variety of parts used in a single product, and the extent of common assemblies across model ranges. Among the important facts to be established in a product teardown, obviously, are the number and variety of components and the number of assembly operations. The costs of the processes are then built up from both direct labor requirements and overheads (often vital to an understanding of competitor cost structures).
5. **Establish economies of scale.** Once individual cost elements are known, they can be put together with the volume of cars produced by the competitor and the total number of people employed to develop some fairly reliable guides to the competitor's economies of scale. Having done this, Ford can calculate model-run lengths and volumes needed to achieve, first, break even and then profit.

Source: Robin Leaf, "How to Pick Up Tips from Your Competitors," *Director* (February 1978): 60.

ignored the competition, floundered, and eventually abandoned the field; the other did a superior job of learning from the competition and came out on top. When the CEO of the first company, a British company, learned from his marketing department about the market growth potential for dishwashers and about current competitors' shares, he lost no time setting out to develop a suitable machine.

Finding little useful information available on dishwasher design, the director of research and development decided to begin by investigating the basic mechanics of the dishwashing process. Accordingly, she set up a series of pilot projects to evaluate the cleaning performance of different jet configurations, the merits of alternative washing-arm designs, and the varying results obtained with different types and quantities of detergent on different washing loads. At the end of a year she had amassed a great deal of useful knowledge. She also had a pilot machine running that cleaned dishes well and a design concept for a production version. But considerable development work was still needed before the prototype could be declared a satisfactory basis for manufacture.

To complicate matters, management had neglected to establish effective linkages among the company's three main functions—marketing, technology, and production. So it was not until the technologists had produced the prototype and design concepts that marketing and production began asking for revisions and suggesting new ideas, further delaying the development of a marketable product.

So much for the first company, with its fairly typical traditional response to market opportunities. The second company, which happened to be Japanese, started with the same marketing intelligence but responded in a very different fashion.

First, it bought three units of every available competitive dishwasher. Next, management formed four special teams: (a) a product test group of marketing and technical staff, (b) a design team of technologists and production people, (c) a distribution team of marketing and production staff, and (d) a field team of production staff.

The product test group was given one of each competitive model and asked to evaluate performance: dishwashing effectiveness, ease of use, and reliability (frequency and cause of breakdown). The remaining two units of each competitive model were given to the design team, who stripped down one of each pair to determine the number and variety of parts, the cost of each part, and the ease of assembly. The remaining units were stripped down to "life-test" each component, to identify design improvements and potential sources of supply, and to develop a comprehensive picture of each competitor's technology. Meanwhile, the distribution team was evaluating each competitor's sales and distribution system (numbers of outlets, product availability, and service offered), and the field team was investigating competitors' factories and evaluating their production facilities in terms of cost of labor, cost of supplies, and plant productivity.

All this investigating took a little less than a year. At the end of that time, the Japanese still knew a lot less about the physics and chemistry of dish washing than their British rivals, but the knowledge developed by their business teams had put them far ahead. In two more months they had designed a product that outperformed the best of the competition, yet would cost 30 percent less to build, based on a preproduction prototype and production process design. They also had a marketing plan for introducing the new dishwasher to the Japanese domestic market before taking it overseas. This plan positioned the product relative to the competition and defined distribution system requirements in terms of stocking and service levels needed to meet the expected production rate. Finally, the Japanese had prepared detailed plans for building a new factory, establishing supply contracts, and training the labor force.

The denouement of this story is what one might expect: The competitive Japanese manufacturer brought its new product to market two years ahead of the more traditionally minded British manufacturer and achieved its planned market share 10 weeks later. The traditional company steadily lost money and eventually dropped out of the market.

As the above anecdote shows, competitive analysis has three major objectives:

1. It allows you to understand your position of comparative advantage and your competitors' positions of comparative advantage.
2. It allows you to understand your competitors' strategies—past, present, and as they are likely to be in the future.
3. is a key criterion of strategy selection, the element that makes your strategies come alive in the real world.

Gathering Competitive Intelligence

Knowledge about the competition may be gained by raising the following questions. To answer each question requires systematic probing and data gathering on different aspects of competition.

- Who is the competition? now? five years from now?
- What are the strategies, objectives, and goals of each major competitor?
- How important is a specific market to each competitor and what is the level of its commitment?
- What are the relative strengths and limitations of each competitor?
- What weaknesses make competitors vulnerable?
- What changes are competitors likely to make in their future strategies?
- So what? What will be the effects of all competitors' strategies, on the industry, the market, and our strategy?

The following procedure may be adopted to gather competitive intelligence:

1. **Recognize key competitors** in market segments in which the company is active. Presumably a product will be positioned to serve one or more market segments. In each segment there may be different competitors to reckon with; an attempt should be made to recognize all important competitors in each segment. If the number of competitors is excessive, it is sufficient to limit consideration to the first three competitors. Each competitor should be briefly profiled to indicate total corporate proportion.

2. **Analyze the performance record** of each competitor. The performance of a competitor can be measured with reference to a number of criteria. As far as marketing is concerned, sales growth, market share, and profitability are the important measures of success. Thus, a review of each competitor's sales growth, market share, and profitability for the past several years is desirable. In addition, any ad hoc reasons that bear upon a competitor's performance should be noted. For example, a competitor may have lined up some business, in the nature of a windfall from Kuwait, without making any strategic moves to secure the business. Similar missteps that may limit performance should be duly pointed out. Occasionally a competitor may intentionally pad results to reflect good performance at year end. Such tactics should be noted, too. Rothschild advises the following:

   > To make it really useful, you must probe how each participant keeps its books and records its profits. Some companies stress earnings; others report their condition in such a way as to delay the payment of taxes; still other bookkeep to increase cash availability.
   >
   > These measurements are important because they may affect the company's ability to procure financing and attract people as well as influence stockholders' and investors' satisfaction with current management.[7]

3. **Study how satisfied each competitor** appears to be with its performance. Refer to each competitor's objective(s) for the product. If results are in concert with the expectations of the firm's management and stakeholders, the competitor will be satisfied. A satisfied competitor is most likely to follow its current successful strategy. On the other hand, if results are at odds with management expectations, the competitor is most likely to come out with a new strategy.

4. **Probe each competitor's marketing strategy.** The strategy of each competitor can be inferred from game plans (i.e., different moves in the area of product, price, promotion, and distribution) that are pursued to achieve objectives. Information on game plans is available partly from published stories on the competitor and partly from the salespeople in contact with the competitor's customers and salespeople.

To clarify the point, consider a competitor in the small appliances business who spends heavily for consumer advertising and sells products mainly through discount stores. From this brief description, it is safe to conclude that, as a matter of strategy, the competitor wants to establish the brand in the mass market through discounters. In other words, the competitor is trying to reach customers who want to buy a reputable brand at discount prices and hopes to make money by creating a large sales base.

5. **Analyze current and future resources and competencies of each competitor.** In order to study a competitor's resources and competencies, first designate broad areas of concern: facilities and equipment, personnel skills, organizational capabilities, and management capabilities, for example. Refer to the checklist in Exhibit 4-4. Each area may then be examined with reference to different functional areas (general management, finance, research and development, operations, and especially marketing). In the area of finance, the availability of a large credit line would be listed as a strength under management capabilities. Owning a warehouse and refrigerated trucks is a marketing strength listed under facilities and equipment. A checklist should be developed to specifically pinpoint those strengths that a competitor can use to pursue goals against your firm as well as other firms in the market. Simultaneously, areas in which competitors look particularly vulnerable should also be noted. The purpose here is not to get involved in a ritualistic, detailed account of each competitor but to demarcate those aspects of a competitor's resources and competencies that may account for a substantial difference in performance.

6. **Predict the future marketing strategy of each competitor.** The above competitive analysis provides enough information to make predictions about future strategic directions that each competitor may pursue. Predictions, however, must be made qualitatively, using management consensus. The use of management consensus as the basic means for developing forecasts is based on the presumption that, by virtue of their experience in gauging market trends, executives should be able to make some credible predictions about each competitor's behavior in the future. A senior member of the marketing research staff may be assigned the task of soliciting executive opinions and consolidating the information into specific predictions on the moves competitors are likely to make.

7. **Assess the impact of competitive strategy on the company's product/market.** The *delphi technique,* examined in Chapter 12, can be used to specify the impact of competitive strategy. The impact should be analyzed by a senior marketing personnel, using competitive information and personal experiences on the job as a basis. Thereafter, the consensus of a larger group of executives can be obtained on the impact analysis performed previously.

Sources of Competitive Information

Essentially, three sources of competitive intelligence can be distinguished: (a) what competitors say about themselves, (b) what others say about them, and (c) what employees of the firm engaged in competitive analysis have observed and

EXHIBIT 4-4
Sources of Economic Leverage in the Business System

	Facilities and Equipment	Personnel Skills	Organizational Capabilities	Management Capabilities
1. General Mgmt.				
2. Finance				Large credit line
3. R&D				
4. Operations				
5. Marketing	Warehousing	Door-to-door selling	Direct sales	Industrial marketing
	Retail outlets	Retail selling	Distributor chain	Customer purchasing
	Sales offices	Wholesale selling	Retail chain	Department of Defense marketing
	Service offices	Direct industry selling	Consumer service organization	State and municipality marketing
	Transportation equipment	Department of Defense selling	Industrial service organization	Well-informed and receptive management
	Training facilities for sales staff	Cross-industry selling	Department of Defense product support	Large customer base
	Data processing equipment	Applications engineering	Inventory distribution and control	Decentralized control
		Advertising	Ability to make quick response to customer requirements	Favorable public image
		Sales promotion	Ability to adapt to sociopolitical upheavals in the marketplace	Future orientation
		Servicing	Loyal set of customers	Ethical standards
		Contract administration	Cordial relations with media and channels	
		Sales analysis	Flexibility in all phases of corporate life	
		Data analysis	Consumer financing	
		Forecasting	Discount policy	
		Computer modeling	Teamwork	
		Product planning	Product quality	
		Background of people		
		Corporate culture		

learned about competitors. Information from the first two sources, as shown in Exhibit 4-5, is available through public documents, trade associations, government, and investors. Take, for example, information from government sources. Under the Freedom of Information Act, a great amount of information can be obtained at low cost.

As far as information from its own sources is concerned, the company should develop a structured program to gather competitive information. First, a tear-down program like Ford's (Exhibit 4-3) may be undertaken. Second, salespeople may be trained to carefully gather and provide information on the competition, using such sources as customers, distributors, dealers, and former salespeople. Third, senior marketing people should be encouraged to call on customers and speak to them in-depth. These contacts should provide valuable information on competitors' products and services. Fourth, other people in the company who happen to have some knowledge of competitors should be encouraged to channel this information to an appropriate office.

themselves, others

EXHIBIT 4-5
Sources of Competitive Intelligence

	Public	Trade Professionals	Government	Investors
What competitors say about themselves	• Advertising • Promotional materials • Press releases • Speeches • Books • Articles • Personnel changes • Want ads	• Manuals • Technical papers • Licenses • Patents • Courses • Seminars	• SEC reports • FIC • Testimony • Lawsuits • Antitrust	• Annual meetings • Annual reports • Prospectors • Stock/bond issues
What others say about them	• Books • Articles • Case studies • Consultants • Newspaper reporters • Environmental groups • Consumer groups • "Who's Who" • Recruiting firms	• Suppliers/ vendors • Trade press • Industry study • Customers • Subcontractors	• Lawsuits • Antitrust • State/federal agencies • National plans • Government programs	• Security analyst reports • Industry studies • Credit reports

Information gathering on the competition has grown dramatically in recent years. Almost all large companies designate someone specially to seek competitive intelligence. A *Fortune* article has identified more than 20 techniques to keep tabs on the competition.[8] These techniques, summarized below, fall into seven groups. Virtually all of them can be legally used to gain competitive insights, although some may involve questionable ethics. A responsible company should carefully review each technique before using it to avoid practices that might be considered illegal or unethical.

1. **Gathering information from recruits and employees of competing companies.** Firms can collect data about their competitors through interviews with new recruits or by speaking with employees of competing companies. According to the *Fortune* article:

   When they interview students for jobs, some companies pay special attention to those who have worked for competitors, even temporarily. Job seekers are eager to impress and often have not been warned about divulging what is proprietary. They sometimes volunteer valuable information. . . . Several companies now send teams of highly trained technicians instead of personnel executives to recruit on campus.

   Companies send engineers to conferences and trade shows to question competitors' technical people. Often conversations start innocently—just a few fellow technicians discussing processes and problems . . . [yet competitors'] engineers and scientists often brag about surmounting technical challenges, in the process divulging sensitive information.

   Companies sometimes advertise and hold interviews for jobs that don't exist in order to entice competitors' employees to spill the beans. . . . Often applicants have toiled in obscurity or feel that their careers have stalled. They're dying to impress somebody.

   In probably the hoariest tactic in corporate intelligence gathering, companies hire key executives from competitors to find out what they know.

2. **Gathering information from competitors' customers.** Some customers may give out information on competitors' products. For example, a while back Gillette told a large Canadian account the date on which it planned to begin selling its new Good News disposable razor in the United States. The Canadian distributor promptly called Bic about Gillette's impending product launch. Bic put on a crash program and was able to start selling its razor shortly after Gillette introduced its own.

3. **Gathering information by infiltrating customers' business operations.** Companies may provide their engineers free of charge to customers. The close, cooperative relationship that engineers on loan cultivate with the customer's staff often enables them to learn what new products competitors are pitching.

4. **Gathering information from published materials and public documents.** What may seem insignificant, a help wanted ad, for example, may provide information about a competitor's intentions or planned strategies. The types of people sought in help wanted ads can indicate something about a competitor's technological thrusts and new product development. Government agencies are another good source of information.

5. **Gathering information from government agencies under the Freedom of Information Act.** Some companies hire others to get this information more discreetly.
6. **Gathering information by observing competitors or by analyzing physical evidence.** Companies can get to know competitors better by buying their products or by examining other physical evidence. Companies increasingly buy competitors' products and take them apart to determine costs of production and even manufacturing methods.

   In the absence of better information on market share and the volume of product being shipped, companies have measured the rust on the rails of railroad sidings to their competitors' plants and have counted tractor-trailers leaving loading bays.
7. **Gathering information from competitors' garbage.** Some firms actually purchase such garbage. Once it has left a competitor's premises, refuse is legally considered abandoned property. Although some companies shred paper generated by their design labs, they often neglect to shred almost-as-revealing refuse from marketing and public relations departments.

Organization for Competitive Intelligence

Competitive, or business, intelligence is a powerful new management tool that enhances a corporation's ability to succeed in today's highly competitive global markets. It provides early warning intelligence and a framework for better understanding and countering competitors' initiatives. Competitive activities can be monitored in-house or assigned to an outside firm. A recent survey indicates that over 300 U.S. firms are involved or interested in running their own competitive intelligence activities.[9] Usually, companies depend partly on their own people and partly on external help to scan the competitive environment.

Within the organization, competitive information should be acquired both at the corporate level and at the SBU level. At the corporate level, competitive intelligence is concerned with competitors' investment strengths and priorities. At the SBU level, the major interest is in marketing strategy, that is, product, pricing, distribution, and promotion strategies that a competitor is likely to pursue. The true payoff of competitive intelligence comes from the SBU review.

Organizationally, the competitive intelligence task can be assigned to an SBU strategic planner, to a marketing person within the SBU who may be a marketing research or a product/market manager, or to a staff person. Whoever is given the task of gathering competitive intelligence should be allowed adequate time and money to do a thorough job.

As far as outside help is concerned, three main types of organizations may be hired to gather competitive information. First, many marketing research firms (e.g., A.C. Nielsen, Frost and Sullivan, SRI International, Predicasts) provide different types of competitive information, some on a regular basis and others on an ad hoc arrangement. Second, clipping services scan newspapers, financial journals, trade journals, and business publications for articles concerning designated competitors and make copies of relevant clippings for their clients. Third, different brokerage firms specialize in gathering information on various industries. Arrangements may be made with brokerage firms to have regular access to their information on a particular industry.

SEEKING COMPETITIVE ADVANTAGE

To outperform competitors and to grow despite them, a company must understand why competition prevails, why firms attack, and how firms respond. Insights into competitors' perspectives can be gained by undertaking two types of analysis: industry and comparative analysis. Industry analysis assesses the attractiveness of a market based on its economic structure. Comparative analysis indicates how every firm in a particular market is likely to perform, given the structure of the industry.

Industry Analysis

Every industry has a few peculiar characteristics. These characteristics are bound by time and thus are subject to change. We may call them the dynamics of the industry. No matter how hard a company tries, if it fails to fit into the dynamics of the industry, ultimate success may be difficult to achieve.

An example of how the perspectives of an entire industry may change over time is provided by the cosmetics industry. The cosmetics business was traditionally run according to personal experience and judgment, by the seat-of-the-pants, so to speak, with ultimate dependence on the marketing genius of inventors. In the 1980s, a variety of pressures began to engulf the industry. The regulatory climate became tougher. Consumers have become more demanding and are fewer in number. Although the number of working women is expected to continue rising until the year 2000, this increase will not offset another more significant demographic change: The population of teenagers—traditionally the heaviest and most experimental makeup users—has been declining. In 1990, there were 15 percent fewer 18- to 24-year-olds than in 1980. As a result, sales of cosmetics are projected to increase only about 2.5 percent per year to the year 2000. These shifts, along with unstable economic conditions and rising costs, have made profits smaller. In the 1980s, several pharmaceutical and packaged-goods companies, including Colgate-Palmolive Co., Eli Lilly and Co., Pfizer, and Schering Plough, acquired cosmetics companies. Among these, only Schering Plough, which makes the mass market Maybelline, has maintained a meaningful business. Colgate, which acquired Helena Rubenstein, sold the brand seven years later after it languished. At the start of the 1990s, the industry began to change again. New mass marketers Procter & Gamble and Unilever entered the arena, bringing with them their great experience producing mundane products such as soap and toilet paper, sparking disdain in the glamorous cosmetics trade. However, the mammoth marketing clout of these giant packaged-goods companies also sparked fear. Procter & Gamble bought Noxell Corporation, producer of Cover Girl and Clarion makeup, making it the top marketer of cosmetics in mass market outlets. Unilever acquired Faberge and Elizabeth Arden.[10]

These changes made competition in the industry fierce. Although capital investment in the industry is small, inventory and distribution costs are extremely high, partly because of the number of shades and textures required in each product line. For example, nail polish and lipstick must be available in more than 50 different shades.

The cosmetics industry has gone through a tremendous change since the 1980s. In those days, success in the industry depended on having a glamorous product. As has been observed, Revlon was manufacturing lipstick in its factories, but it was selling beautiful lips. Today, however, success rests on such nuts-and-bolts matters as sharp positioning to serve a neatly defined segment and securing distribution to achieve specific objectives in sales, profit, and market share.[11] Basic inventory and financial controls, budgeting, and planning are now utilized to the fullest extent to cut costs and waste: "In contrast to the glitzy, intuitive world of cosmetics, Unilever and P&G are the habitats of organization men in grey-flannel suits. Both companies rely on extensive market research."[12] This type of shift in direction and style in an industry has important ramifications for marketing strategy.

The dynamics of an industry may be understood by considering the following factors:

1. Scope of competitors' businesses (i.e., location and number of industries).
2. New entrants in the industry.
3. Other current and potential offerings that appear to serve similar functions or satisfy the same need.
4. Industry's ability to raise capital, attract people, avoid government probing, and compete effectively for consumer dollars.
5. Industry's current practices (price setting, warranties, distribution structure, after-sales service, etc.).
6. Trends in volume, costs, prices, and return on investment, compared with other industries.
7. Industry profit economics (the key factors determining profits: volume, materials, labor, capital investment, market penetration, and dealer strength).
8. Ease of entry into the industry, including capital investment.
9. Relationship between current and future demand and manufacturing capacity and its probable effects on prices and profits.
10. Effect of integration, both forward and backward.
11. Effect of cyclical swings in the relationship between supply and demand.

To formulate marketing strategy, a company should determine the relevance of each of these factors in its industry and the position it occupies with respect to competitors. An attempt should be made to highlight the dynamics of the company in the industry environment.

Porter's Model of Industry Structure Analysis

Conceptual framework for industry analysis has been provided by Porter. He developed a five-factor model for industry analysis, as shown in Exhibit 4-6. The model identifies five key structural features that determine the strength of the competitive forces within an industry and hence industry profitability.

As shown in this model, the degree of rivalry among different firms is a function of the number of competitors, industry growth, asset intensity, product differentiation, and exit barriers. Among these variables, the number of competitors and industry growth are the most influential. Further, industries with high fixed costs tend to be more competitive because competing firms are forced to cut price

EXHIBIT 4-6
Porter's Model of Industry Competition

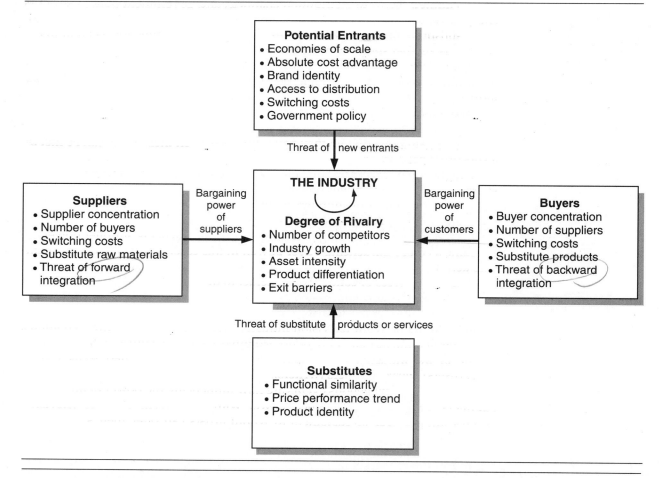

Source: Michael E. Porter, "Industry Structure and Competitive Strategy: Keys to Profitability," *Financial Analysis Journal* (July–August 1980): 33.

to enable them to operate at capacity. Differentiation, both real and perceived, among competing offerings, however, lessens rivalry. Finally, difficulty of exit from an industry intensifies competition.

Threat of entry into the industry by new firms is likely to enhance competition. Several barriers, however, make it difficult to enter an industry. Two cost-related entry barriers are economies of scale and absolute cost advantage. Economies of scale require potential entrants either to establish high levels of production or to accept a cost disadvantage. Absolute cost advantage is enjoyed by firms with proprietary technology or favorable access to raw materials and by firms with production experience. In addition, high capital requirements, high switching costs (i.e., the cost to a buyer of changing suppliers), product differentiation, limited access to distribution channels, and government policy can act as entry barriers.

A substitute product that serves essentially the same function as an industry product is another source of competition. Since a substitute places a ceiling on the price that firms can charge, it affects industry potential. The threat posed by a substitute also depends on its long-term price/performance trend relative to the industry's product.

Bargaining power of buyers refers to the ability of the industry's customers to force the industry to reduce prices or increase features, thus bidding away profits. Buyers gain power when they have choices—when their needs can be met by a substitute product or by the same product offered by another supplier. In addition, high buyer concentration, the threat of backward integration, and low switching costs add to buyer power.

Bargaining power of suppliers is the degree to which suppliers of the industry's raw materials have the ability to force the industry to accept higher prices or reduced service, thus affecting profits. The factors influencing supplier power are the same as those influencing buyer power. In this case, however, industry members act as buyers.

These five forces of competition interact to determine the attractiveness of an industry. The strongest forces become the dominant factors in determining industry profitability and the focal points of strategy formulation, as the following example of the network television industry illustrates. Government regulations, which limited the number of networks to three, have had a great influence on the profile of the industry. This impenetrable entry barrier created weak buyers (advertisers), weak suppliers (writers, actors, etc.), and a very profitable industry. However, several exogenous events are now influencing the power of buyers and suppliers. Suppliers have gained power with the advent of cable television because the number of customers to whom artists can offer their services has increased rapidly. In addition, as cable television firms reduce the size of the network market, advertisers may find substitute advertising media more cost-effective. In conclusion, while the industry is still very attractive and profitable, the changes in its structure imply that future profitability may be reduced.

A firm should first diagnose the forces affecting competition in its industry and their underlying causes and then identify its own strengths and weaknesses relative to the industry. Only then should a firm formulate its strategy, which amounts to taking offensive or defensive action in order to achieve a secure position against each of the five competitive forces.[13] According to Porter, this involves

- Positioning the firm so that its capabilities provide the best defense against the existing array of competitive forces.
- Influencing the balance of forces through strategic moves, thereby improving the firm's relative position.
- Anticipating shifts in the factors underlying the forces and responding to them, hopefully exploiting change by choosing a strategy appropriate to the new competitive balance before rivals recognize it.[14]

Take, for example, the U.S. blue jeans industry. In the 1970s most firms except for Levi Strauss and Blue Bell, maker of Wrangler Jeans, took low profits. The situation can be explained with reference to industry structure (see Exhibit 4-7). The extremely low entry barriers allowed almost 100 small jeans manufacturers to join the competitive ranks; all that was needed to enter the industry was some equipment, an empty warehouse, and some relatively low-skilled labor. All such firms competed on price.

Further, these small firms had little control over raw materials pricing. The production of denim is in the hands of about four major textile companies. No one small blue jeans manufacturer was important enough to affect supplier prices or output; consequently, jeans makers had to take the price of denim or leave it. Suppliers of denim had strong bargaining power. Store buyers also were in a strong bargaining position. Most of the jeans sold in the United States were handled by relatively few buyers in major store chains. As a result, a small manufacturer basically had to sell at the price the buyers wanted to pay, or the buyers could easily find someone else who would sell at their price.

But then along came Jordache. Creating designer jeans with heavy up-front advertising, Jordache designed a new way to compete that changed industry

EXHIBIT 4-7
Structure of Blue Jeans Industry

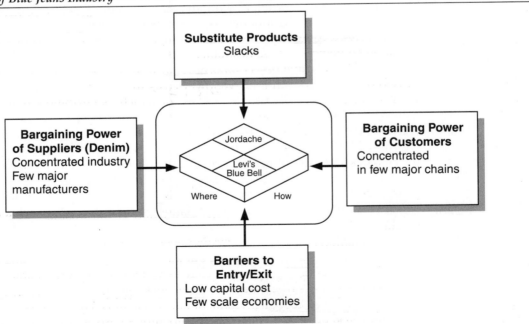

Source: Ennlus E. Bergsma, "In Strategic Phase, Line Management Needs 'business's Research, Not Market Research," *Marketing News* (21 January 1983): 22.

forces. First, it significantly lowered the bargaining power of its customers (i.e., store buyers) by creating strong consumer preference. The buyer had to meet Jordache's price rather than the other way around. Second, emphasis on the designer's name created significant entry barriers. In summary, Jordache formulated a strategy that neutralized many of the structural forces surrounding the industry and gave itself a competitive advantage.

Comparative Analysis

Comparative analysis examines the specific advantages of competitors within a given market. Two types of comparative advantage may be distinguished: structural and response. Structural advantages are those advantages built into the business. For example, a manufacturing plant in South Korea may, because of low labor costs, have a built-in advantage over another firm. Responsive advantages refer to positions of comparative advantage that have accrued to a business over time as a result of certain decisions. This type of advantage is based on leveraging the strategic phenomena at work in the business.

Every business is a unique mixture of strategic phenomena. For example, in the soft drink industry a unit of investment in advertising may lead to a unit of market share. In contrast, the highest-volume producer in the electronics industry is usually the lowest-cost producer. In industrial product businesses, up to a point, sales and distribution costs tend to decline as the density of sales coverage (the number of salespeople in the field) increases. Beyond this optimum point, costs tend to rise dramatically. However, cost is only one way of achieving a competitive advantage. A firm may explore issues beyond cost to score over competition. For example, a company may find that distribution through authorized dealers gives it competitive leverage. Another company may find product differentiation strategically more desirable.

In order to survive, any company, regardless of size, must be different in one of two dimensions. It must have lower costs than its direct head-to-head competitors, or it must have unique values for which its customers will pay more. Competitive distinctiveness is essential to survival. Competitive distinctiveness can be achieved in different ways: (a) by concentrating on particular market segments, (b) by offering products that differ from rather than mirror competing products, (c) by using alternative distribution channels and manufacturing processes, and (d) by employing selective pricing and fundamentally different cost structures. An analytical tool that may be used by a company seeking a position of competitive advantage/distinction is the business-system framework.

Examination of the business system operating in an industry is useful in analyzing competitors and in searching out innovative options for gaining a sustainable competitive advantage. The business-system framework enables a firm to discover the sources of greatest economic leverage, that is, stages in the system where it may build cost or investment barriers against competitors.[15] The framework may also be used to analyze a competitor's costs and to gain insights into the sources of a competitor's current advantage in either cost or economic value to the customer.

Exhibit 4-8 depicts the business system of a manufacturing company. At each stage of the system—technology, product design, manufacturing, and so on—a company may have several options. These options are often interdependent. For example, product design will partially constrain the choice of raw materials. Likewise, the perspectives of physical distribution will affect manufacturing capacity and location and vice versa. At each stage, a variety of questions may by raised, the answers to which provide insights into the strategic alternatives a company may consider: How are we doing this now? How are our competitors doing it? What is better about their way? About ours? How else might it be done? How would these options affect our competitive position? If we change what we are doing at this stage, how would other stages be affected? Answers to these questions reveal the sources of leverage a business may employ to gain competitive advantage (see Exhibit 4-9).

The use of the business-system framework can be illustrated with reference to Savin Business Machines Corporation.[16] In 1975, this company with revenues of $63 million was a minor factor in the U.S. office copier market. The market was obviously dominated by Xerox, whose domestic copier revenues were approaching $2 billion. At that time, Xerox accounted for almost 80 percent of plain-paper copiers in the United States. In November 1975, Savin introduced a plain-paper copier to serve customers who wanted low- and medium-speed machines (i.e., those producing fewer than 40 copies per minute). Two years later, Savin's annual

EXHIBIT 4-8
Business System of a Manufacturing Company

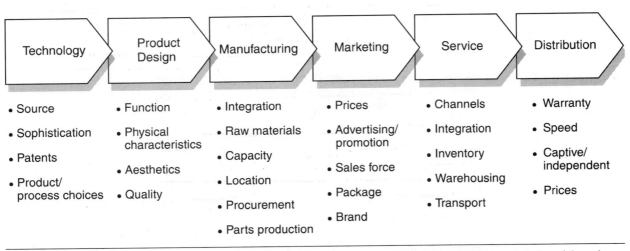

Source: Roberto Buaron, "New-Game Strategies," *The McKinsey Quarterly* (Spring 1981): 34. Reprinted by permission of the publisher. Also, "How to Win the Market-Share Game? Try Changing the Rules." Reprinted by permission of publisher, from *Management Review* (January 1981) © 1981. American Management Association, New York. All rights reserved.

EXHIBIT 4-9
Sources of Economic Leverage in the Business System

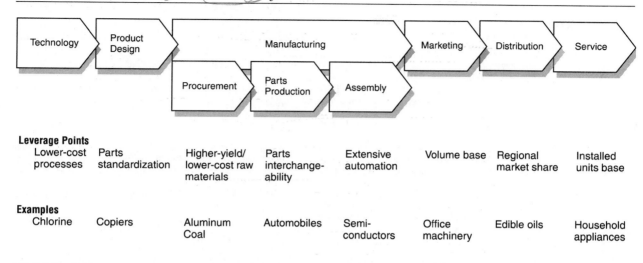

Leverage Points

Lower-cost processes	Parts standardization	Higher-yield/ lower-cost raw materials	Parts interchange-ability	Extensive automation	Volume base	Regional market share	Installed units base

Examples

Chlorine	Copiers	Aluminum Coal	Automobiles	Semi-conductors	Office machinery	Edible oils	Household appliances

Source: Roberto Buaron, "New-Game Strategies," *The McKinsey Quarterly* (Spring 1981): 35. Reprinted by permission of the publisher. Also, "How to Win the Market-Share Game? Try Changing the Rules." Reprinted by permission of publisher, from *Management Review* (January 1981) © 1981. American Management Association, New York. All rights reserved.

revenues passed $200 million; the company had captured 40 percent of all new units installed in the low-end plain-paper copier market in the United States. Savin managed to earn a 64 percent return on equity while maintaining a conservative 27 percent debt ratio. In early 1980s, its sales surpassed $470 million, selling more copiers in the U.S. than any other company.[17] Meanwhile Xerox, which in 1974 had accounted for more than half of the low-end market, saw its share shrink to 10 percent in 1978. What reasons may be ascribed to Savin's success against mighty Xerox? Through careful analysis of the plain-paper copier business system, Savin combined various options at different stages of the system to develop a competitive advantage to successfully confront Xerox. As shown in Exhibit 4-10, by combining a different technology with different manufacturing, distribution, and service approaches, Savin was able to offer business customers, at some sacrifice in copy quality, a much cheaper machine. The option of installing several cheaper machines in key office locations in lieu of a single large, costly, centrally located unit proved attractive to many large customers.

At virtually every stage of the business system, Savin took a radically different approach. First, it used a low-cost technology that had been avoided by the industry because it produced a lower quality copy. Next, its product design was based on low-cost standardized parts available in volume from Japanese suppliers. Further, the company opted for low-cost assembly in Japan. These business-system innovations permitted Savin to offer a copier of comparable reliability and

EXHIBIT 4-10
Plain-Paper Copier Strategy: Xerox versus Savin

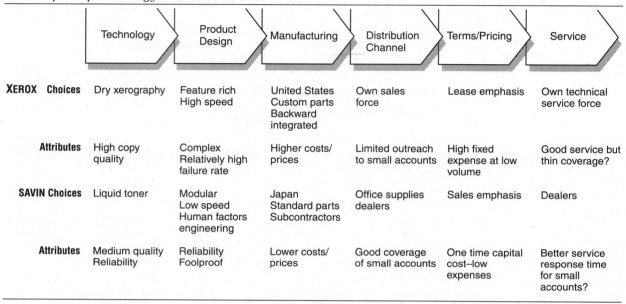

	Technology	Product Design	Manufacturing	Distribution Channel	Terms/Pricing	Service
XEROX Choices	Dry xerography	Feature rich High speed	United States Custom parts Backward integrated	Own sales force	Lease emphasis	Own technical service force
Attributes	High copy quality	Complex Relatively high failure rate	Higher costs/ prices	Limited outreach to small accounts	High fixed expense at low volume	Good service but thin coverage?
SAVIN Choices	Liquid toner	Modular Low speed Human factors engineering	Japan Standard parts Subcontractors	Office supplies dealers	Sales emphasis	Dealers
Attributes	Medium quality Reliability	Reliability Foolproof	Lower costs/ prices	Good coverage of small accounts	One time capital cost–low expenses	Better service response time for small accounts?

Source: Peter R. Sawers, "How to Apply Competitive Analysis to Strategic Planning," *Marketing News* (18 March 1983): 11. Reprinted by permission of the American Marketing Association.

acceptable quality for half the price of Xerox's equivalent model. (Note: Starting from the mid-1980s, the Savin Corp. ran into all sorts of managerial problems. In 1993, it went into bankruptcy.)

SUSTAINING COMPETITIVE ADVANTAGE

A good strategist seeks not only to "win the hill, but hold on to it." In other words, a business should not only seek competitive advantage but also sustain it over the long haul. Sustaining competitive advantage requires erecting barriers against the competition.

A barrier may be erected based on size in the targeted market, superior access to resources or customers, and restrictions on competitors' options.[18] Scale economies, for example, may equip a firm with an unbeatable cost advantage that competitors cannot match. Preferred access to resources or to customers enables a company to secure a sustainable advantage if (a) the access is secured under better terms than competitors have and (b) the access can be maintained over the long run. Finally, a sustainable advantage can be gained if, for various reasons, competitors are restricted in their moves (e.g., pending antitrust action or given past investments or existing commitments).

In financial terms, barriers are based on competitive cost differentials or on price or service differentials. In all cases, a successful barrier returns higher margins than the competition earns. Further, a successful barrier must be sustainable and, in a practical sense, unbreachable by the competition; that is, it must cost the competition more to surmount than it costs the protected competitor to defend.

The nature of the feasible barrier depends on the competitive economics of the business. A heavily advertised consumer product with a leading market share enjoys a significant cost barrier and perhaps a price-realization barrier against its competition. If a consumer product has, for example, twice the market share of its competition, it need spend only one-half the advertising dollar per unit to produce the same impact in the marketplace. It will always cost the competition more, per unit, to attack than it costs the leader to defend.

On the other hand, barriers cost money to erect and defend. The expense of the barrier may become an umbrella under which new forms of competition can grow. For example, while advertising is a barrier that protects a leading consumer brand from other branded competitors, the cost of maintaining the barrier is an umbrella under which a private-label product may hide and grow.

A wide product line, large sales and service forces, and systems capabilities are all examples of major barriers. Each of these has a cost to erect and maintain. Each is effective against smaller competitors who are attempting to copy the leader but have less volume over which to amortize barrier costs.

Each barrier, however, holds a protective umbrella over focused competitors. The competitor with a narrow product line faces fewer costs than the wide-line leader. The mail-order house may live under the umbrella of costs associated with the large sales and service force of the leader. The "cherry picker" may produce components compatible with the systems of the leader without bearing the systems engineering costs.

Exhibit 4-11 shows the relationship between barrier and umbrella strategies in sustaining competitive advantage. The best position in the system is high

EXHIBIT 4-11
Strategies for Sustaining Competitive Advantage

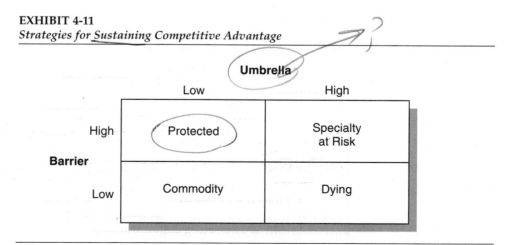

Source: Sandra O. Moose, "Barriers and Umbrellas," *Perspectives* (Boston: Boston Consulting Group, 1980). Reprinted by permission.

barrier and low umbrella. A product or business with a position strong enough that the costs of maintaining the barrier are, on a per unit basis, insignificant is in a high-barrier, low-umbrella position. The low-barrier, low-umbrella quadrant is, by definition, a commodity without high profitability.

Most interesting is the high-barrier, high-umbrella quadrant. The business is protected by the existence of the barrier. At the same time, it is at risk because the cost of supporting the barrier is high. Profitability may be high, but the risk of competitive erosion, too, may be substantial. The marketplace issue is the trade-off between consumer preferences for more service, quality, choice, or "image" and lower prices from more narrowly focused competitors.

These businesses face profound decisions. Making no change in direction means continual threats from focused competition. Yet any change in spending to lower the umbrella means changing the nature of the competitive protection; that is, eroding the barrier.

Successful marketing strategy requires being aware of the size of the umbrella and continually testing whether to maintain investment to preserve or heighten the barrier or to withdraw investment to "cash out" as the barrier erodes.

A sustainable advantage is meaningful in marketing strategy only when the following conditions are met: (a) customers perceive a consistent difference in important attributes between the firm's product or service and those of its competitors, (b) the difference is the direct result of a capability gap between the firm and its competitors, and (c) both the difference in important attributes and the capability gap can be expected to endure over time.

SUMMARY | Competition is a strategic factor that affects marketing strategy formulation. Traditionally, marketers have considered competition as one of the uncontrollable variables to be reckoned with in developing the marketing mix. It is only in the last few years that the focus of business strategy has shifted to the competition. It is becoming more and more evident that a chosen marketing strategy should be based on competitive advantage to achieve sustained business success. To implement such a perspective, resources should be concentrated in those areas of competitive activity that offer the best opportunity for continuing profitability and sound investment returns.

There are two very different forms of competition: natural and strategic. Natural competition implies survival of the fittest in a given environment. In business terms, it means firms compete from very similar strategic positions, relying on operating differences to separate the successful from the unsuccessful. With strategic competition, on the other hand, underlying strategy differences vis-à-vis market segments, product offerings, distribution channels, and manufacturing processes become paramount considerations.

Conceptually, competition may be examined from the viewpoint of economists, industrial organization theorists, and businesspeople. The major thrust of economic theories has centered on the model of perfect competition. Industrial organization emphasizes the industry environment (i.e., industry structure, conduct, and performance) as the key determinant of a firm's performance. A theoretical framework of competition from the viewpoint of the businessperson, other than the pioneering efforts of Bruce Henderson, hardly exists.

Firms compete to satisfy customer needs, which may be classified as existing, latent, or incipient. A firm may face competition from different sources, which may be categorized as industry competition, product line competition, or organizational competition. The intensity of competition is determined by a combination of factors.

A firm needs a competitive intelligence system to keep track of various facets of its rivals' businesses. The system should include proper data gathering and analysis of each major competitor's current and future perspectives. This chapter identified various sources of competitive information, including what competitors say about themselves, what others say about them, and what a firm's own people have observed. To gain competitive advantage, that is, to choose those product/market positions where victories are clearly attainable, two forms of analysis may be undertaken: industry analysis and comparative analysis. Porter's five-factor model is useful in industry analysis. Business-system framework can be gainfully employed for comparative analysis.

DISCUSSION QUESTIONS

1. Differentiate between natural and strategic competition. Give examples.
2. What are the basic elements of strategic competition? Are there any prerequisites to pursuing strategic competition?
3. How do economists approach competition? Does this approach suffice for businesspeople?
4. What is the industrial organization viewpoint of competition?
5. Identify, with examples, different sources of competition.
6. How does industry structure affect intensity of competition?
7. What are the major sources of competitive intelligence?
8. Briefly explain Porter's five-factor model of industry structure analysis.

NOTES

[1] Bruce D. Henderson, "Understanding the Forces of Strategic and Natural Competition," *Journal of Business Strategy* (Winter 1981): 11.
[2] Bruce D. Henderson, "New Strategies for the Global Competition," *A Special Commentary* (Boston: Boston Consulting Group, 1981), 5–6.
[3] Louis W. Stern and John R. Grabner, Jr., *Competition in the Marketplace* (Glenview, IL: Scott, Foresman and Company, 1970), 29.
[4] See Michael E. Porter, *Competitive Strategy* (New York: The Free Press, 1980), Chapter 1. See also E. T. Grether, *Marketing and Public Policy* (Englewood Cliffs, NJ: Prentice-Hall, 1960), 25; and George Fisk, *Marketing Systems: An Introductory Analysis* (New York: Harper & Row, 1967), 622.
[5] Bruce D. Henderson, "The Anatomy of Competition," *Journal of Marketing* (Spring 1983): 8–9.
[6] Henderson, "Understanding the Forces of Strategic and Natural Competition," 15.
[7] William E. Rothschild, *Putting It All Together* (New York: AMACOM, 1976), 85.

[8] Steven Flax, "How to Snoop on Your Competitors," *Fortune* (14 May 1984): 29–33. Also see Richard Teitelbaum, "The New Race for Intelligence," *Fortune* (2 November 1992): 104.

[9] Fahri Karakaya and Michael J. Stahl, "Barriers to Entry and Market Entry Decisions in Consumer and Industrial Goods Market," *Journal of Marketing* (April 1989): 80–91.

[10] "Unilever is All Made Up with Everywhere to Go," *Business Week* (31 July 1989): 33–34.

[11] "L'Oreal Aiming at High and Low Markets," *Fortune* (22 March 1993): 89.

[12] Kathleen Deveny and Alecia Swasy, "In Cosmetics, Marketing Cultures Clash," *Wall Street Journal* (31 October 1989): B1.

[13] See George S. Day and Prakash Nedungadi, "Managerial Representations of Competetive Strategy," *Journal of Marketing* (April 1994): 31–44.

[14] Michael E. Porter, "Note on the Structural Analysis of Industries," *Harvard Business School Case Service* (1975): 22.

[15] Richard Normann and Rafael Ramirez,"From Value Chain to Value Constellation: Designing Interactive Strategy," *Harvard Business Review* (July–August 1993): 65–77.

[16] Roberto Buaron, "New-Game Strategies," *McKinsey Quarterly* (Spring 1981): 24–40.

[17] Tom Giordano, "From Riches to Rags," *The Hartford Courant* (12 December 1993): 61.

[18] Pankaj Ghemawat, "Sustainable Advantage," *Harvard Business Review* (September–October 1986): 53–58. See also Kevin P. Coyne, "The Anatomy of Sustainable Competitive Advantage," *Business Horizons* (January–February 1986): 16–17.

Focusing on the Customer

Consumption is the sole end and purpose of production; and the interest of the producer ought to be attended to only so far as it may be necessary for promoting that of the consumer.

ADAM SMITH

Businesses compete to serve customer needs. Not only are there different types of customers, but their needs vary, too. Thus, most markets are not homogeneous. Further, the markets that are homogeneous today may not remain so in the future. In brief, a market represents a dynamic phenomenon that, influenced by customer needs, evolves over time.

In a free economy, each customer group tends to want a slightly different service or product. But a business unit cannot reach out to all customers with equal effectiveness; it must distinguish easily accessible customer groups from hard-to-reach customer groups. Moreover, a business unit faces competitors whose ability to respond to customer needs and cover customer groups differs from its own. To establish a strategic edge over its competition with a viable marketing strategy, it is important for the business unit to clearly define the market it intends to serve. It must segment the market, identifying one or more subsets of customers within the total market, and concentrate its efforts on meeting their needs. Fine targeting of the customer group to serve offers the opportunity to establish competitive leverage.

This chapter introduces a framework for identifying markets to serve. Various underlying concepts of market definition are examined. The chapter ends with a discussion of alternative ways of segmenting a market.

IDENTIFYING MARKETS

Contemporary approaches to strategic planning require proper definition of the market; however, questions about how to properly characterize a market make it difficult to arrive at an acceptable definition. Depending on how the market is defined, the relative market positions of two companies and their two products can be reversed, as shown on the page 102.

	Percentage Market Share	
Brands	Unsegmented (Mass)	Segmented
S	32	40
T	24	30
U	16	20
V	8	10
X	12	60
Y	6	30
Z	2	10

Though brand X has a low share in the unsegmented, or mass, market (12 percent), it has a much higher share within its own segment of the mass market (60 percent) than does brand S (40 percent). Which of the two shares shown is better for the business: the total mass market for the product category or some segmented portion of that market? The arguments go both ways, some pointing out the merits of having a larger share of industry volume and others noting the favorable profit consequences of holding a larger share within a smaller market niche. Does Sanka compete in the total mass market for coffee with Maxwell House and Folgers or in a decaffeinated market segment against Brim and Nescafe? Does the market for personal computers include intelligent and dumb terminals as well as word processors, desktop and laptop computers, and intelligent telephones? Grape Nuts has 100 percent of the Grape Nuts market, a smaller percentage of the breakfast cereal market, an even smaller percentage of the packaged-foods market, a still smaller percentage of the packaged-goods market, a tiny percentage of the U.S. food market, a minuscule percentage of the world food market, and a microscopic percentage of total consumer expenditures. All descriptions of market share are meaningless, however, unless a company defines the market in terms of the boundaries separating it from its rivals.

Considering the importance of adequately defining the market, it is desirable to systematically develop a conceptual framework for that purpose. Exhibit 5-1 presents such a framework.

The first logical step in defining the market is to determine customer need. Based on need, the market emerges. Because customer need provides a broad perspective of the market, it is desirable to establish market boundaries. Traditionally, market boundaries have been defined in terms of product/market scope, but recent work suggests that markets should be defined multidimensionally.

The market boundary delineates the total limits of the market. An individual business must select and serve those parts, or segments, of the total market in which it is best equipped to compete over the long run. Consider Polaroid. It started as an instant photography firm. As such, it had only a 7 percent stake in the $15 billion photography industry. Over the years, it carried out a multi-billion dollar market for itself. But in the 1990s, the company realized it had little chance of any further growth. The developed world was already saturated with cameras, and photography itself was beginning to lose out to home videomaking. By

EXHIBIT 5-1
Identifying Markets to Serve

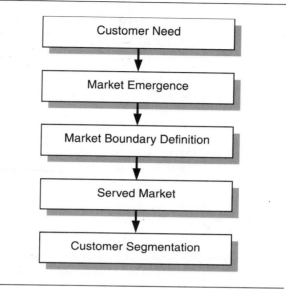

aiming instead at the entire imaging industry—from photocopying to printing and video as well as photography—Polaroid saw a chance to compete in a rapidly growing, $150 billion global business.[1]

CUSTOMER NEED

Satisfaction of customer need is the ultimate test of a business unit's success. Thus, an effective marketing strategy should aim at serving customer needs and wants better than competitors do. Focus on customers is the essence of marketing strategy. As Robertson and Wind have said:

> Marketing performs a boundary role function between the company and its markets. It guides the allocation of resources to product and service offerings designed to satisfy market needs while achieving corporate objectives. This boundary role function of marketing is critical to strategy development. Before marshaling a company's resources to acquire a new business, or to introduce a new product, or to reposition an existing product, management must use marketing research to cross the company-consumer boundary and to assess the likely market response.
>
> The logic and value of consumer needs assessment is generally beyond dispute, yet frequently ignored. It is estimated, for example, that a majority of new products fail. Yet, there is most often nothing wrong with the product itself; that is, it works. The problem is simply that consumers do not want the product.

AT&T's Picture Phone is a classic example of a technology-driven product that works; but people do not want to see each other on a telephone. It transforms a comfortable, low involvement communication transaction into a demanding, high involvement one. The benefit is not obvious to consumers. Of course, the benefit could become obvious if transportation costs continue to outpace communication costs, and if consumers could be "taught" the benefits of using a Picture Phone.

Marketing's boundary role function is similarly important in maintaining a viable competitive positioning in the marketplace. The passing of Korvette from the American retail scene, for example, can be attributed to consumer confusion as to what Korvette represented—how it was positioned relative to competition. Korvette's strength was as a discount chain—high turnover and low margin. This basic mission of the business was violated, however, as Korvette traded-up in soft goods and fashion items and even opened a store on Manhattan's Fifth Avenue. The result was that Korvette became neither a discount store nor a department store and lost its previous customer base. Sears has encountered a similar phenomenon as it opted for higher margins in the 1970s and lost its reputation for "value" in the marketplace. The penalty has been declining sales and profitability for its retail store operation, which it is now trying valiantly to arrest by reestablishing its "middle America" value orientation. Nevertheless, consumer research could have indicated the beginning of the problem long before the crisis in sales and profits occurred.[2]

Concept of Need

Customer need has always formed the basis of sound marketing. Yet, as Ohmae points out, it is often neglected or ignored:

> Think for a moment about aching heads. Is my headache the same as yours? My cold? My shoulder pain? My stomach discomfort? Of course not. Yet when a pharmaceutical company asked for help . . . [it] asked 50 employees in the company to fill out a questionnaire—throughout a full year—about how they felt physically at all times of the day every day of the year. Then [it] pulled together a list of the symptoms described, sat down with the company's scientists, and asked them, item by item: Do you know why people feel this way? Do you have a drug for this kind of symptom? It turned out that there were no drugs for about 80 percent of the symptoms, these physical awarenesses of discomfort. For many of them, some combination of existing drugs worked just fine. For others, no one had ever thought to seek a particular remedy. The scientists were ignoring tons of profit.
>
> Without understanding customers' needs—the specific types of discomfort they were feeling—the company found it all too easy to say, "Headache? Fine, here's a medicine, an aspirin, for headache. Case closed." It was easy not to take the next step and ask, "What does the headache feel like? Where does it come from? What is the underlying cause? How can we treat the cause, not just the symptom?" Many of these symptoms, for example, are psychological and culture-specific. Just look at television commercials. In the United States, the most common complaint is headache; in the United Kingdom, backache; in Japan, stomach ache. In the United States, people say that they have a splitting headache; in Japan it is an ulcer. How can we truly understand what these people are feeling and why?[3]

Looking closely at needs is the first step in delivering value to customers. Traditionally, needs have been classified according to Maslow's hierarchy of human needs. From lowest to highest, Maslow's hierarchy identifies five levels of needs: physiological, safety, belongingness, self-esteem, and self-actualization. Needs at each level of the hierarchy can be satisfied only after needs at the levels below it have been satisfied. A need unsatisfied becomes a source of frustration. When the frustration is sufficiently intense, it motivates a relief action—the purchase of a product, for example. Once a need is satisfied, it is forgotten, creating space for the awareness of other needs. In a marketing context, this suggests that customers need periodic reminders of their association with a product, particularly when satisfied.

Business strategy can be based on the certainty that needs exist. As we move up Maslow's hierarchy, needs become less and less obvious. The challenge in marketing is to expose non-obvious needs, to fill needs at all levels of the hierarchy.

Maslow's first two levels can be called survival levels. Most businesses operate at Level 2 (safety), with occasional spikes into higher levels. A business must satisfy a safety need to have a viable operation. The customer must feel both physically and economically safe in buying the product. The next higher levels—belongingness and self-esteem—are customer reward levels, where benefits of consuming a product accrue to the customer personally, enhancing his or her sense of worth. At the highest level, self-actualization, the customer feels a close identification with the product. Of course, not all needs can be filled, nor would it be economically feasible to attempt to do so. But a business can move further toward satisfaction of customer needs by utilizing the insights of the Maslow hierarchy.

MARKET EMERGENCE

Customer need gives rise to a market opportunity, and a market emerges. To judge the worth of this market, an estimate of market potential is important. If the market appears attractive, the strategist takes the next step of delineating the market boundary. This section examines the potential of the market.

Simply stated, **market potential** is the total demand for a product in a given environment. Market potential is measured to gain insights into five elements: market size, market growth, profitability, type of buying decision, and customer market structure. Exhibit 5-2 summarizes these elements and shows a pro forma scheme for measuring market potential.

The first element, *market size*, is best expressed in both units and dollars. Dollar expression in isolation is inadequate because of distortion by inflation and international currency fluctuations. Also, because of inflationary distortion, the screening criteria for new product concepts and product line extensions should separately specify both units and dollars. Market size can be expressed as total market sales potential or company market share, although most companies through custom utilize market share figures.

The second element, *market growth*, is meant to reflect the secular trend of the industry. Again, the screening criteria should be specified for new product concepts and product line extensions. The criteria and projections should be based on percentage growth in units. Projections in industrial settings often are heavily dependent on retrofit possibilities and plans for equipment replacement.

EXHIBIT 5-2
Measurement of Market Potential

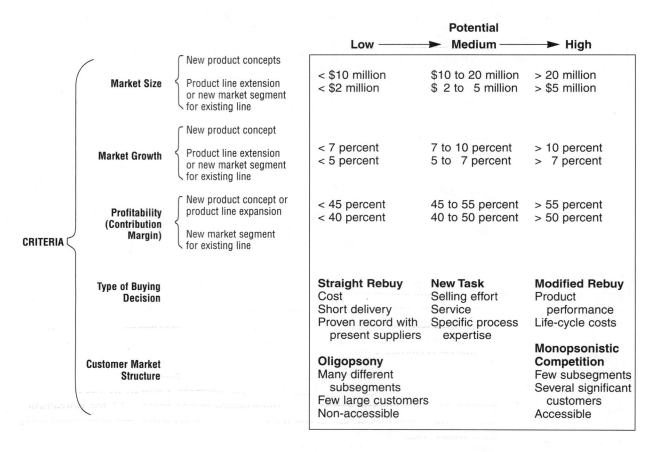

Criteria	Low		Medium		High		Data Source	Comments/Additional Data Needed
Market								
Market Growth								
Profitability								
Type of Buying Decision								
Customer Market Structure								
Overall Rating								

Source: Reprinted by permission of Terry C. Wilson, West Virginia University.

The third element in this evaluation of strategic potential is _profitability_. It usually is expressed in terms of contribution margin or in one of the family of return calculations. Most U.S. companies view profitability in terms of return on investment (ROI), return on sales (ROS), or return on net assets (RONA). Return on capital employed (ROCE) is often calculated in multinational companies. For measuring market potential, no one of these calculations appears to function better than another.

The fourth element is the _type of buying decision_. The basis for a buying decision must be predicated on whether the decision is a straight rebuy, a modified rebuy, or a new task.

The fifth and final element is the _customer market structure_. Based on the same criteria as competitive structure, the market can be classified as monopsony, oligopsony, differentiated competition (monopsonistic competition), or pure competition.

DEFINING MARKET BOUNDARIES

The crux of any strategy formulation effort is market definition:

> The problem of identifying competitive product-market boundaries pervades all levels of marketing decisions. Such strategic issues as the basic definition of a business, the assessment of opportunities presented by gaps in the market, the reaction to threats posed by competitive actions, and the decisions on major resource allocations are strongly influenced by the breadth or narrowness of the definition of competitive boundaries. The importance of share of market for evaluating performance and for guiding territorial advertising, sales force, and other budget allocations and the growing number of antitrust prosecutions also call for defensible definitions of product-market boundaries.[4]

Defining the market is difficult, however, since market can be defined in many ways. Consider the cooking appliance business. Overall in 1993 about 16 million gas and electric ranges and microwave ovens were sold for household use. All these appliances serve the basic function of cooking, but their similarity ends there. They differ in many ways: (a) with reference to fuels—primarily gas versus electricity; (b) in cooking method—heat versus radiation; (c) with reference to type of cooking function—surface heating, baking, roasting, broiling, etc.; (d) in design—freestanding ranges, built-in countertop ranges, wall ovens, countertop microwave ovens, combinations of microwave units, and conventional ranges, etc.; and (e) in price and product features.

These differences raise an important question: Should all household cooking appliances be considered a single market or do they represent several distinct markets? If they represent several distinct markets, how should these markets be defined? There are different possibilities for defining the market: (a) with reference to product characteristics; (b) in terms of private brand sales versus manufacturers' brand sales; (c) with reference to sales in specific regions; and (d) in terms of sales target, for example, sales to building contractors for installation in new houses versus replacement sales for existing homes.

Depending on the criteria adopted to define the market, the size of a market varies considerably. The strategic question of how the marketer of home cooking appliances should define the market is explored below.

Dimensions of
Market Boundaries

Traditionally, market boundaries have been defined in terms of product/market space. Consider the following:

> A market is sometimes defined as a group of firms producing identical or closely related products. . . . A preferable approach is to define the markets in terms of products. . . . [What is meant by] a close relationship among products? Goods and services may be closely related in the sense that they are regarded as substitutes by consumers, or they may be close in that the factors of production used in each are similar.[5]

Some identify a market with a generic class of products. One hears of the beer market, the cake mix market, or the cigarette market. According to others, product markets refer to individuals who have purchased a given class of products.

These two definitions of the market—the market as a class of closely related products versus the market as a class of people who purchase a certain kind of product—view it from one of two perspectives: who are the buyers and what are the products. In the first definition, buyers are implicitly assumed to be homogeneous in their behavior. The second definition suggests that the products and brands within a category are easily identified and interchangeable and that the problem is to search for market segments.

In recent years, it has been considered inadequate to perceive market definition as simply a choice of products for chosen markets. Instead, the product may be considered a physical manifestation of a particular technology to a particular customer function for a particular customer group. Market boundaries should then be determined by choices along these three dimensions.[6]

Technology. A particular customer function can be performed by different technologies. In other words, alternative technologies can be applied to satisfy a particular customer need. To illustrate, consider home cooking appliances again. In terms of fuel, the traditional alternative technologies have been gas and electricity. In recent years, a new form of technology, microwave radiation, has also been used. In another industry, alternative technologies may be based on the use of different materials. For example, containers may be made from metal, glass, or plastic. In defining market boundaries, a decision must be made whether the products of all relevant technologies or only those of a particular technology are to be included.

Customer Function. Products can be considered in terms of the functions they serve or in terms of the ways in which they are used. Some cooking appliances bake and roast, others fry and boil; some perform all these functions and perhaps more. Different functions provide varying customer benefits. In establishing market boundaries, customer benefits to be served should be spelled out.

Customer Group. A group refers to a homogeneous set of customers with similar needs and characteristics. The market for cooking appliances, for example, can be split into different groups: building contractors, individual households buying through retail stores, and so on. The retail stores segment can be further broken down into traditional appliance specialty stores, mass merchandisers, and so on. Decisions about market boundaries should indicate which types of customers are to be served.

In addition to these three dimensions for determining market boundaries, Buzzell recommends a fourth—level of production/distribution.[7] A business has the option of operating at one or more levels of the production/distribution process. For example, producers of raw materials (e.g., aluminum) or component products (e.g., semiconductors, motors, compressors) may limit their business to selling only to other producers, they may produce finished products themselves, or they may do both. Decisions about production/distribution levels have a direct impact on the market boundary definition. This point may be illustrated with reference to Texas Instruments:

> The impact that a business unit's vertical integration strategy can have on competition in a market is dramatically illustrated by Texas Instruments' decision, in 1972, to enter the calculator business. At the time, it was a principal supplier of calculator components (integrated circuits) to the earlier entrants into the market, including the initial market leader, Bowmar Instruments. As most readers undoubtedly know, TI quickly took over a leadership position in calculators through a combination of "pricing down the experience curve" and aggressive promotion. For purposes of this discussion, the important point is one of a finished product. Some other component suppliers also entered the calculator business, while others continued to supply OEMs. In light of these varying strategies, is there a "calculator component market" and "calculator market," or do these constitute a single market?[8]

Exhibit 5-3 depicts the three dimensions of the market boundary definition from the viewpoint of the personal financial transactions industry. Market boundaries are defined in terms of customer groups, customer functions, and technologies. The fourth dimension, level of production/distribution, is not included in the diagram because it is not possible to show four dimensions in a single chart. The exhibit shows a matrix developed around customer groups on the vertical axis, customer functions on the right axis, and technologies on the left axis. Any three-dimensional cell in the matrix constitutes an elementary "building block" of market definition. An automatic teller machine (ATM) for cash withdrawals at a commercial bank is an example of such a cell.

Redefining Market Boundaries | As markets evolve, boundaries may need to be restated. Five sets of "environmental influences" affect product/market boundaries. These influences are technological change (displacement by a new technology); market-oriented product development (e.g., combining the features of several products into one multipurpose offering); price changes and supply constraints (which influence the perceived set of substitutes); social, legal, or government trends (which influence patterns of competition); and international trade competition (which changes geographic boundaries).[9] For example, when management introduces a new product, markets an existing product to new customers, diversifies the business

EXHIBIT 5-3
Dimensions of Market Boundary Definition for Personal Financial Transactions

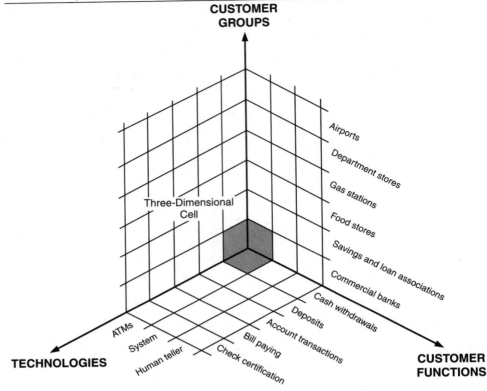

through acquisition, or liquidates a part of the business, the market undergoes a process of evolution. Redefinition of market boundaries may be based on any one or a combination of the three basic dimensions. The market may be extended through the penetration of new customer groups, the addition of products serving related customer functions, or the development of products based on new technologies. As shown in Exhibit 5-4, these changes are caused by three fundamentally different phenomena: "The adoption and diffusion process underlies the penetration of new customer groups, a process of systemization results in the operation of products to serve combinations of functions, and the technology substitution process underlies change on a technology dimension."

SERVED MARKET

Earlier in this chapter, it was concluded that the task of market boundary definition amounts to grouping together a set of market cells (see Exhibit 5-3), each

EXHIBIT 5-4
Market Evolution in Three Dimensions

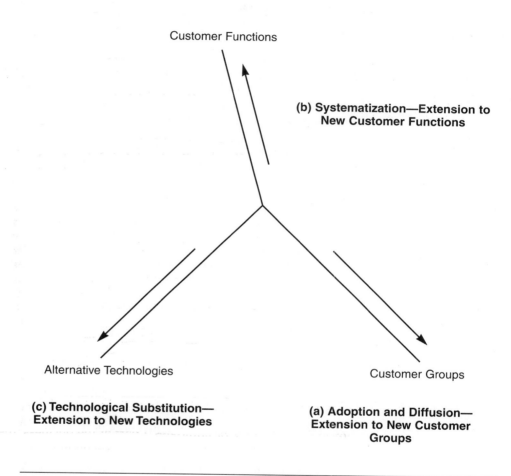

Source: Derek F. Abell, *Defining the Business: The Starting Point of Strategic Planning,* © 1980, p. 207. Reprinted by permission of Prentice-Hall, Inc., Englewood Cliffs, N.J.

defined in terms of three dimensions: customer groups, customer functions, and technologies. In other words, a market may comprise any combination of these cells. An additional question must now be answered. Should a business unit serve the entire market or limit itself to serving just a part of it? While it is conceivable that a business unit may decide to serve the total market, usually the served market is considerably narrower in scope and smaller in size than the total market. The decision about what market to serve is based on such factors as the following:

1. Perceptions of which product function and technology groupings can best be protected and dominated.
2. Internal resource limitations that force a narrow focus.
3. Cumulative trial-and-error experience in reacting to threats and opportunities.
4. Unusual competencies stemming from access to scarce resources or protected markets.[10]

In practice, the choice of served market is not based on conscious, deliberate effort. Rather, circumstances and perceptions surrounding the business unit dictate the decision. For some businesses, lack of adequate resources limits the range of possibilities. Dell Computer, for example, would be naive to consider competing against IBM across the board. Further, as a business unit gains experience through trial and error, it may extend the scope of its served market. For example, the U.S. Post Office entered the overnight package delivery market to participate in an opportunity established by the Federal Express Company. The task of delineating the served market, however, is full of complications. As Day has noted:

> In practice, the task of grouping market cells to define a market is complicated. First, there is usually no one defensible criterion for grouping cells. There may be many ways to achieve the same function. Thus, boxed chocolates compete to some degree with flowers, records, and books as semicasual gifts. Do all of these products belong in the total market? To confound this problem, the available statistical and accounting data are often aggregated to a level where important distinctions between cells are completely obscured. Second, there are many products which evolve by adding new combinations of functions and technologies. Thus, radios are multifunctional products which include clocks, alarms, appearance options. To what extent do these variants dictate new market cells? Third, different competitors may choose different combinations of market cells to serve or to include in their total market definitions. In these situations there will be few direct competitors; instead, businesses will encounter each other in different but overlapping markets, and, as a result, may employ different strategies.[11]

Strategically, the choice of a business unit's served market may be based on the following approaches:

I. Breadth of Product Line

  A. Specialized in terms of technology, broad range of product uses
  B. Specialized in terms of product uses, multiple technologies
  C. Specialized in a single technology, narrow range of product uses
  D. Broad range of (related) technologies and uses
  E. Broad versus narrow range of quality/price levels

II. Types of Customers

  A. Single customer segment
  B. Multiple customer segments

    1. Undifferentiated treatment
    2. Differentiated treatment

III.   Geographic Scope

    A.   Local or regional
    B.   National
    C.   Multinational

IV.   Level of Production/Distribution

    A.   Raw or semifinished materials or components
    B.   Finished products
    C.   Wholesale or retail distribution

An Example of a Served Market

The choice of served market may be illustrated with reference to one company's entry into the snowmobile business. The management of this company considered snowmobiles an attractive market in terms of sales potential. The boundaries of this market are extensive. For example, in terms of technology, a snowmobile may be powered by gas, diesel fuel, or electricity. A snowmobile may fulfill such customer functions as delivery, recreation, and emergency transportation. Customer groups include household consumers, industrial buyers, and the military.

Since the company could not cover the total market, it had to define the market it would serve. To accomplish this task, the company developed a product/market matrix (see Exhibit 5-5a). The company could use any technology—gasoline, diesel, or electric—and it could design a snowmobile for any one of three customer groups: consumer, industrial, or military. The matrix in Exhibit 5-5a furnished nine possibilities for the company. Considering market potential and its competencies to compete, the part of the market that looked best was the diesel-powered snowmobile for the industrial market segment, the shaded area in Exhibit 5-5a.

But further narrowing of the market to be served was necessary. A second matrix (see Exhibit 5-5b) laid out the dimensions of customer use (function) and customer size. Thus, as shown in Exhibit 5-5b, snowmobiles could be designed for use as delivery vehicles (e.g., used by business firms and the post office), as recreation vehicles (e.g., rented at resort hotel sites), or as emergency vehicles (e.g., used by hospitals and police forces). Further, the design of the snowmobile would be affected by whether the company would sell to large, medium, or small customers. After evaluating the nine alternatives in Exhibit 5-5b, the company found the large customer, delivery use market attractive, defining its served market as diesel-driven snowmobiles for use as delivery vehicles by large industrial customers.

Served Market Alternatives

In the preceding example, the company settled on a rather narrow definition of the served market. It could, however, expand the scope of the served market as it gains experience and as opportunities elsewhere in the market appear attractive. The following is a summary of the served market alternatives available to a business similar to this one.

EXHIBIT 5-5
Defining the Served Market

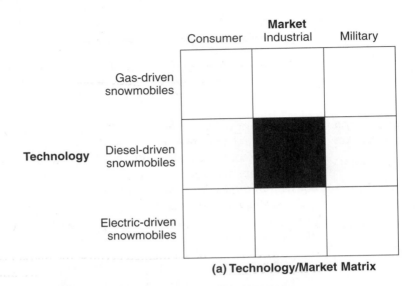

(a) Technology/Market Matrix

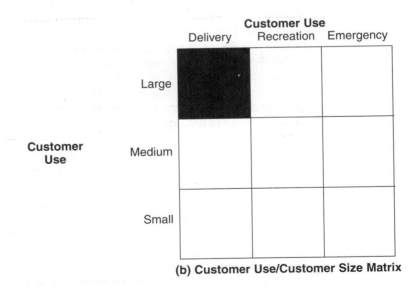

(b) Customer Use/Customer Size Matrix

Source: Philip Kotler, "Strategic Planning and the Marketing Process," *Business* (May–June 1980):
6–7. Reprinted by permission of the author.

1. Product/market concentration consists of the company's niching itself in only one part of the market. In the above example, the company's niche was making only diesel-driven snowmobiles for industrial buyers.
2. Product specialization consists of the company's deciding to produce only diesel-driven snowmobiles for all customer groups.
3. Market specialization consists of the company's deciding to make a variety of snowmobiles that serve the varied needs of a particular customer group, such as industrial buyers.
4. Selective specialization consists of the company's entering several product markets that have no relation to each other except that each provides an individually attractive opportunity.
5. Full coverage consists of the company's making a full range of snowmobiles to serve all market segments.

CUSTOMER SEGMENTATION

In the snowmobile example, the served market consisted of one segment. But conceivably, the served market could be much broader in scope. For example, the company could decide to serve all industrial customers (large, medium, small) by offering diesel-driven snowmobiles for delivery use. The "broader" served market, however, must be segmented because the market is not homogeneous; that is, it cannot be served by one type of product/service offering.

Currently, the United States represents the largest market in the world for most products; it is not a homogeneous market, however. Not all customers want the same thing. Particularly in well-supplied markets, customers generally prefer products or services that are tailored to their needs. Differences can be expressed in terms of product or service features, service levels, quality levels, or something else. In other words, the large market has a variety of submarkets, or segments, that vary substantially. One of the crucial elements of marketing strategy is to choose the segment or segments that are to be served. This, however, is not always easy because different methods for dissecting a market may be employed and deciding which method to use may pose a problem.[12]

Virtually all strategists segment their markets. Typically, they use SIC codes, annual purchase volume, age, and income as differentiating variables. Categories based on these variables, however, may not suffice as far as the development of strategy is concerned.

RCA, for example, initially classified potential customers for color television sets according to age, income, and social class. The company soon realized that these segments were not crucial for continued growth because potential buyers were not confined to those groups. Later analysis discovered that there were "innovators" and "followers" in each of the above groups. This finding led the company to tailor its marketing strategy to various segments according to their "innovativeness." Mass acceptance of color television might have been delayed substantially if RCA had followed a more traditional approach.[13]

An American food processor achieved rapid success in the French market after discovering that "modern" Frenchwomen liked processed foods while "traditional" French housewives looked upon them as a threat.

A leading industrial manufacturer discovered that its critical variable was the amount of annual usage per item, not per order or per any other conventional variable. This proved to be critical since heavy users can be expected to be more sensitive to price and may be more aware of and responsive to promotional perspectives.[14]

Segmentation aims at increasing the scope of business by closely aligning a product or brand with an identifiable customer group. Take, for example, cigarettes. Thirty years ago, most cigarette smokers chose from among three brands: Camel, Chesterfield, and Lucky Strike. Today more than 160 brands adorn retail shelves. In order to sell more cigarettes, tobacco companies have been dividing the smoking public into relatively tiny sociological groups and then aiming one or more brands at each group. Vantage and Merit, for example, are aimed at young women; Camel and Winston are aimed mostly at rural smokers. Cigarette marketing success hinges on how effectively a company can design a brand to appeal to a particular type of smoker and then on how well it can reach that smoker with sharply focused packaging, product design, and advertising.

What is true of cigarettes applies to many, many products; it applies even to services. Banks, for example, have been vying with one another for important customers by offering innovative services that set each bank apart from its competition.

These illustrations underscore not only the significance of segmenting the market but also the importance of carefully choosing segmentation criteria.

Segmentation
Criteria
Q 6

Segmentation criteria vary depending on the nature of the market. In consumer-goods marketing, one may use simple demographic and socioeconomic variables, personality and lifestyle variables, or situation-specific events (such as use intensity, brand loyalty, and attitudes) as the bases of segmentation. In industrial marketing, segmentation is achieved by forming end use segments, product segments, geographic segments, common buying factor segments, and customer size segments. Exhibit 5-6 provides an inventory of different bases for segmentation. Most of these bases are self-explanatory. For a detailed account, however, reference may be made to a textbook on marketing management.

In addition to these criteria, creative analysts may well identify others. For example, a shipbuilding company dissects its tanker market into large, medium, and small markets; similarly, its cargo ship market is classified into high-, medium-, and low-grade markets. A forklift manufacturer divides its market on the basis of product performance requirements. Many consumer-goods companies, General Foods, Procter & Gamble, and Coca-Cola among them, base their segments on lifestyle analysis.[15]

Data for forming customer segments may be analyzed with the use of simple statistical techniques (e.g., averages) or multivariate methods. Conceptually, the following procedure may be adopted to choose a criterion for segmentation:

1. Identify potential customers and the nature of their needs.
2. Segment all customers into groups having
   a. Common requirements.
   b. The same value system with respect to the importance of these requirements.

Handwritten margin notes (left):
4. criteria for segament.

1. homogeneous w/in

2. heterogeneous b/t

3. substantial (market potential
   to make money)

4. operational

EXHIBIT 5-6   *→ Characteristics.*
Bases for Customer Segmentation

A.   Consumer Markets
  1. Demographic factors (age, income, sex, etc.)
  2. Socioeconomic factors (social class, stage in the family life cycle)
  3. Geographic factors
  4. Psychological factors (lifestyle, personality traits)
  5. Consumption patterns (heavy, moderate, and light users)
  6. Perceptual factors (benefit segmentation, perceptual mapping)
  7. Brand loyalty patterns

B.   Industrial Markets
  1. End use segments (identified by SIC code)
  2. Product segments (based on technological differences or production economics)
  3. Geographic segments (defined by boundaries between countries or by regional differences within them)
  4. Common buying factor segments (cut across product/market and geographic segments)
  5. Customer size segments

3. Determine the theoretically most efficient means of serving each market segment, making sure that the distribution system selected differentiates each segment with respect to cost and price.
4. Adjust this ideal system to the constraints of the real world: existing commitments, legal restrictions, practicality, and so forth.

Handwritten margin notes (left):
future. SIC, comp.

→ VALS

→

A market can also be segmented by level of customer service, stage of production, price/performance characteristics, credit arrangements with customers, location of plants, characteristics of manufacturing equipment, channels of distribution, and financial policies. The key is to choose a variable or variables that so divide the market that customers in a segment respond similarly to some aspect of the marketer's strategy.[16] The variable should be measurable; that is, it should represent an objective value, such as income, rate of consumption, or frequency of buying, not simply a qualitative viewpoint, such as the degree of customer happiness. Also, the variable should create segments that may be accessible through promotion. Even if it is feasible to measure happiness, segments based on the happiness variable cannot be reached by a specific promotional medium. Finally, segments should be substantial in size; that is, they should be sufficiently large to warrant a separate marketing effort.

Once segments have been formed, the next strategic issue is deciding which segment should be selected. The selected segment should comply with the following conditions:

1. It should be one in which the maximum differential in competitive strategy can be developed.
2. It must be capable of being isolated so that competitive advantage can be preserved.

3. It must be valid even though imitated.

The success of Volkswagen in the United States in 1960 can be attributed to its fit into a market segment that had two unique characteristics. First, the segment served by VW could not be adequately served by a modification to conventional U.S. cars. Second, U.S. manufacturers' economies of scale could not be brought to bear to the disadvantage of VW. In contrast, American Motors was equally successful in identifying a special segment to serve with its compact car, the Rambler. The critical difference was that American Motors could not protect that segment from the superior scale of manufacturing volume of the other three U.S. automobile producers.

The choice of strategically critical segments is not straightforward. It requires careful evaluation of business strengths as compared with the competition. It also requires analytical marketing research to uncover market segments in which these competitive strengths can be significant.[17]

In consumer markets, rarely do market segments conveniently coincide with such obvious categories as religion, age, profession, or family income; in the industrial sector, with the size of company. For this reason, market segmentation is emphatically not a job for statisticians. Rather, it is a task that can be mastered only by the creative strategist. For example, an industrial company found that the key to segmenting customers is by the phase of the purchase decision process that they experienced. Accordingly, three segments were identified: (a) first-time prospects, (b) novices, and (c) sophisticates.[18] These three segments valued different benefits, bought from different channels, and carried varying impressions of providers.

Micromarketing, or Segment-Of-One Marketing

An interesting development in the past few years has been the emergence of a new segmentation concept called micromarketing, or segment-of-one marketing. Forced by competitive pressures, mass marketers have discovered that a segment can be trimmed down to smaller subsegments, even to an individual. Micromarketing combines two independent concepts: information retrieval and service delivery. On one side is a proprietary database of customers' preferences and purchase behaviors; on the other is a disciplined, tightly engineered approach to service delivery that uses the database to tailor a service package for individual customers or a group of customers. Of course, such custom-designed service is nothing new, but until recently, only the very wealthy could afford it. Information technology has brought the level of service associated with the old carriage trade within reach of the middle class.

Micromarketing requires

1. **Knowing the customers**—Using high-tech techniques, find out who the customers are and aren't. By linking that knowledge with data about ads and coupons, fine-tune marketing strategy.
2. **Making what customers want**—Tailor products to individual tastes. Where once there were just Oreos, now there are Fudge Covered Oreos, Oreo Double Stufs, and Oreo Big Stufs.
3. **Using targeted and new media**—Advertising on cable television and in magazines can be used to reach special audiences. In addition, develop new ways to

reach customers. For example, messages on walls in high-school lunchrooms, on videocassettes, and even on blood pressure monitors may be considered.

4. **Using nonmedia**—Sponsor sports, festivals, and other events to reach local or ethnic markets.

5. **Reaching customers in the store**—Consumers make most buying decisions while they are shopping, so put ads on supermarket loudspeakers, shopping carts, and in-store monitors.

6. **Sharpening promotions**—Couponing and price promotions are expensive and often harmful to a brand's image. Thanks to better data, some companies are using fewer, more effective promotions. One promising approach: aiming coupons at a competitor's customers.

7. **Working with retailers**—Consumer-goods manufacturers must learn to "micro market" to the retail trade, too. Some are linking their computers to retailers' computers, and some are tailoring their marketing and promotions to an individual retailer's needs.

An example of micromarketing is provided by a North Carolina bank, First Wachovia.[19] The bank's staff serves all customers the way it used to serve its best customer. The staff greets each customer by name and provides personalized information about her or his finances and how they relate to long-term objectives. Based on this knowledge, the staff suggests new products. In this way, the commodity retail banking has been turned into a customized, personalized service. This marketing strategy has resulted in more sales at lower marketing costs and powerful switching barriers relative to the competition. Three major investments are behind this seemingly effortless new level of service: a comprehensive customer database, accessible wherever the customer makes contact with the bank; an extensive training program that teaches a personalized service approach; and an ongoing personal communications program with each customer. Similarly, Noxell's Clarion line illustrates how micromarketing can be implemented. When the company introduced its line of mass market cosmetics in drugstores, it looked for a way to differentiate it in a crowded market. The answer was the Clarion computer. Customers type in the characteristics of their skin and receive a regimen selected from the Clarion line, thus providing department store-type personal advice without sales pressure in the much more convenient drug channel.

SUMMARY

This chapter examined the role of the third strategic C—the customer—in formulating marketing strategy. One strategic consideration in determining marketing strategy is the definition of the market. A conceptual framework for defining the market was outlined.

The underlying factor in the formation of a market is customer need. The concept of need was discussed with reference to Maslow's hierarchy of needs. Once a market emerges, its worth must be determined through examining its potential. Different methods may be employed to study market potential.

Based on its potential, if a market appears worth tapping, its boundaries must be identified. Traditionally, market boundaries have been defined on the basis of product/market scope. Recent work on the subject recommends that market boundaries be established around the following dimensions: technology, customer function, and customer group. Level of production/distribution was suggested as a fourth dimension. The task of market boundary definition amounts to grouping together a set of market cells, each defined in terms of these dimensions.

Market boundaries set the limits of the market. Should a business unit serve a total market or just a part of it? Although it is conceivable to serve an entire market, usually the served market is considerably narrower in scope and smaller in size than the total market. Factors that influence the choice of served market were examined.

The served market may be too broad to be served by a single marketing program. If so, then the served market must be segmented. The rationale for segmentation was given, and a procedure for segmenting the market was outlined.

DISCUSSION QUESTIONS

1. Elaborate on marketing's boundary role function. How is it related to customer needs?
2. Identify the elements determined by market potential.
3. What dimensions may be used to define market boundaries?
4. Illustrate the use of these dimensions with a practical example.
5. What is meant by served market? What factors determine the served market?
6. How may a business unit choose the criteria for segmenting the market?
7. Describe the concept of micromarketing. How may a durable goods company adopt it to its business?

NOTES

[1] "Polariod: Sharper Focus," *The Economist* (24 April 1993): 72.

[2] Thomas S. Robertson and Yoram Wind, "Marketing Strategy," in *Handbook of Business Strategy* (New York: McGraw-Hill Book Co., 1982). See also Yoram Wind and Thomas S. Robertson, "Marketing Strategy: New Directions for Theory and Research," *Journal of Marketing* (Spring 1983): 12–25.

[3] Kenichi Ohmae, "Getting Back to Strategy," *Harvard Business Review* (November–December 1988): 155–56.

[4] George S. Day and Allan D. Shocker, *Identifying Competitive Product-Market Boundaries: Strategic and Analytical Issues* (Cambridge, MA: Marketing Science Institute, 1976), 1.

[5] Peter Asch, *Economic Theory and the Antitrust Dilemma* (New York: John Wiley & Sons, 1970), 168. See also George S. Day, Allan D. Shocker, and Rajendra K. Srivastava, "Customer-Oriented Approaches to Identifying Product Markets," *Journal of Marketing* (Fall 1979): 8–19; and Rajendra K. Srivastava, Robert P. Leone, and Allan D. Shocker, "Market Structure Analysis: Hierarchical Clustering of Products Based on Substitution-in-Use," *Journal of Marketing* (Summer 1981): 38–48.

[6] Derek F. Abell, *Defining the Business: The Starting Point of Strategic Planning* (Englewood Cliffs, NJ: Prentice-Hall, 1980).

[7] Robert D. Buzzell, "Note on Market Definition and Segmentation," A Harvard Business School Note, 1978, distributed by HBS Case Services.

[8] Buzzell, "Note on Market Definition and Segmentation," 6.

[9] Day and Shocker, *Identifying Competitive Product-Market Boundaries*.

[10] George S. Day, "Strategic Market Analysis and Definition: An Integrated Approach," *Strategic Management Journal* 2 (1981): 284.

[11] Day, "Strategic Market Analysis and Definition," 288.

[12] Peter R. Dickson and James L. Ginter, "Market Segmentation, Product Differentiation, and Marketing Strategy," *Journal of Marketing* (April 1987): 1–10

[13] "Strategy and Market Segment Research," an informal statement issued by the Boston Consulting Group, 1968.

[14] See V. Kasturi Rangan, Rowland T. Moriarty, and Gordon S. Swartz, "Segmenting Customers in Mature Industrial Markets," *Journal of Marketing* (October 1992): 72–82.

[15] See Jack A. Lesser and Marie Adele Hughes, "The Generalizability of Psychographic Market Segments across Geographic Locations," *Journal of Marketing* (January 1986): 18–27. See also "Stalking the New Consumer," *Business Week* (28 August 1989).

[16] See Nigel F. Piercy and Neil A. Morgan, "Strategic and Operational Market Segmentation: A Managerial Analysis," *Journal of Strategic Marketing* (June 1993): 123–140.

[17] Brian E. Kardon, "Customer Schizophrenia: Extremism in the Marketplace," *Planning Review* (July/August 1992): 18–23.

[18] Thomas S. Robertson and Howard Barich, "A Successful Approach to Segmenting Industrial Markets," *Planning Review* (November/December 1992): 4–11.

[19] Kathleen Deveny, "Segments of One," *Wall Street Journal* (22 March 1991): B4. See also "Segment-of-One Marketing," *Perspectives* (Boston: Boston Consulting Group, 1989). Also see: Howard Schlossberg, "Packaged-goods Experts: Micromarketing the only way to Go," *Marketing News* (6 July 1992): 8.

Scanning the Environment

An organization is a creature of its environment. Its very survival and all of its perspectives, resources, problems, and opportunities are generated and conditioned by the environment. Thus, it is important for an organization to monitor the relevant changes taking place in its environment and formulate strategies to adapt to these changes. In other words, for an organization to survive and prosper, the strategist must master the challenges of the profoundly changing political, economic, technological, social, and regulatory environment. To achieve this broad perspective, the strategist needs to develop and implement a systematic approach to environmental scanning. As the rate and magnitude of change increase, this scanning activity must be intensified and directed by explicit definitions of purpose, scope, and focus. The efforts of businesses to cope with these problems are contributing to the development of systems for exploring alternatives with greater sensitivity to long-run implications. This emerging science has the promise of providing a better framework for maximizing opportunities and allocating resources in anticipation of environmental changes.

This chapter reviews the state of the art of environmental scanning and suggests a general approach that may be used by a marketing strategist. Specifically, the chapter discusses the criteria for determining the scope and focus of scanning, the procedure for examining the relevance of environmental trends, the techniques for evaluating the impact of an environmental trend on a particular product/market, and the linking of environmental trends and other "early warning signals" to strategic planning processes.

IMPORTANCE OF ENVIRONMENTAL SCANNING

Without taking into account relevant environmental influences, a company cannot expect to develop its strategy. It was the environmental influences emerging out of the energy crisis that were responsible for the popularity of smaller, more fuel-efficient automobiles and that brought about the demise of less efficient rotary engines. It was the environmental influence of a coffee bean shortage and geometric price increases that spawned the "coffee-saver" modification in Mr. Coffee automatic drip coffee makers. Shopper and merchant complaints from an earlier era contributed to the virtual elimination of deposit bottles; recent pressures from environmental groups, however, have forced their return and have prompted companies to develop low-cost recyclable plastic bottles.

Another environmental trend, Americans' insatiable appetite for eating out (in 1990, restaurant sales accounted for $0.44 of every $1 spent on food; this number is expected to reach $0.63 by the year 2000), worries food companies such as Kraft. In response, Kraft is trying to make cooking as convenient as eating out (e.g., by providing high-quality convenience foods) to win back food dollars.[1]

The sad tales of companies that seemingly did everything right and yet lost competitive leadership as a result of technological change abound. Du Pont was beaten by Celanese when bias-ply tire cords changed from nylon to polyester. B.F. Goodrich was beaten by Michelin when the radial overtook the bias-ply tire. NCR wrote off $139 million in electro-mechanical inventory and the equipment to make it when solid-state point-of-sale terminals entered the market. Xerox let Canon create the small-copier market. Bucyrus-Erie allowed Caterpillar and Deere to take over the mechanical excavator market. These companies lost even though they were low-cost producers. They lost even though they were close to their customers. They lost even though they were market leaders. They lost because they failed to make an effective transition from old to new technology.[2]

In brief, business derives its existence from the environment. Thus, it should monitor its environment constructively. Business should scan the environment and incorporate the impact of environmental trends on the organization by continually reviewing the corporate strategy.[3]

The underlying importance of environmental scanning is captured in Darwinian laws: (a) the environment is ever-changing, (b) organisms have the ability to adapt to a changing environment, and (c) organisms that do not adapt do not survive. We are indeed living in a rapidly changing world. Many things that we take for granted today were not even imagined in the 1960s. Before the end of this century, many more "wonders" will come to exist.

To survive and prosper in the midst of a changing environment, companies must stay at the forefront of changes affecting their industries. First, it must be recognized that all products and processes have performance limits and that the closer one comes to these limits the more expensive it becomes to squeeze out the next generation of performance improvements. Second, one must take all competition seriously. Normally, competitor analyses seem to implicitly assume that the most serious competitors are the ones with the largest resources. But in the context of taking advantage of environmental shifts, this assumption is frequently not adequate. Texas Instruments was a $5- to $10-million company in 1955 when it took on the mighty vacuum tube manufacturers—RCA, GE, Sylvania, and Westinghouse—and beat them with its semiconductor technology. Boeing was nearly bankrupt when it successfully introduced the commercial jet plane, vanquishing larger and more financially secure Lockheed, McDonnell, and Douglas corporations.

Third, if the environmental change promises potential advantage, one must attack to win and attack even to play the game. Attack means gaining access to new technology, training people in its use, investing in capacity to use it, devising strategies to protect the position, and holding off on investments in mature lines. For example, IBM capitalized on the emerging personal computer market created by its competitor, Apple Computer. By becoming the low-cost producer, distributor, seller, and servicer of personal computers for business use, IBM took command of the marketplace in less than two years.

Fourth, the attack must begin early. The substitution of one product or process for another proceeds slowly and then rarely predictably explodes. One cannot wait for the explosion to occur to react. There is simply not enough time. B.F. Goodrich lost 25 percentage points of market share to Michelin in four years. Texas Instruments passed RCA in sales of active electronic devices in five to six years.

Fifth, a close tie is needed between the CEO and the operating managers. Facing change means incorporating the environmental shifts in all aspects of the company's strategy.

WHAT SCANNING CAN ACCOMPLISH

Scanning improves an organization's abilities to deal with a rapidly changing environment in a number of ways:

1. It helps an organization capitalize on early opportunities rather than lose these to competitors.
2. It provides an early signal of impending problems, which can be defused if recognized well in advance.
3. It sensitizes an organization to the changing needs and wishes of its customers.
4. It provides a base of objective qualitative information about the environment that strategists can utilize.
5. It provides intellectual stimulation to strategists in their decision making.
6. It improves the image of the organization with its publics by showing that it is sensitive to its environment and responsive to it.
7. It is a means of continuing broad-based education for executives, especially for strategy developers.

THE CONCEPT OF ENVIRONMENT

Operationally, five different types of environments may be identified—technological, political, economic, regulatory, and social—and the environment may be scanned at three different levels in the organization—corporate, SBU, and product/market level (see Exhibit 6-1). Perspectives of environmental scanning vary from level to level. Corporate scanning broadly examines happenings in different environments and focuses on trends with corporate-wide implications. For example, at the corporate level IBM may review the impact of competition above and below in the telephone industry on the availability and rates of long-distance telephone lines to its customers. Emphasis at the SBU level focuses on those changes in the environment that may influence the future direction of the business. At IBM, the SBU concerned with personal computers may study such environmental perspectives as diffusion rate of personal computers, new developments in integrated circuit technology, and the political debates in progress on

EXHIBIT 6-1
Constituents of Environment

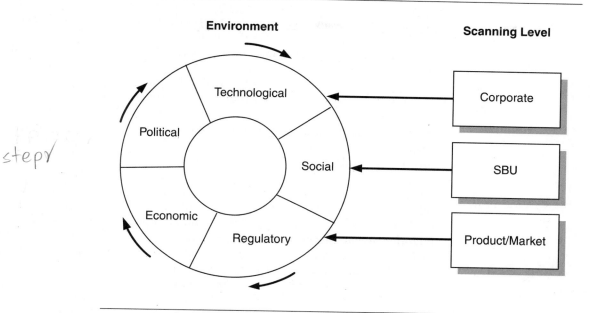

step

the registration (similar to automobile registration) of personal computers. At the product/market level, scanning is limited to day-to-day aspects. For example, an IBM personal computer marketing manager may review the significance of rebates, a popular practice among IBM's competitors.

The emphasis in this chapter is on environmental scanning from the viewpoint of the SBU. The primary purpose is to gain a comprehensive view of the future business world as a foundation on which to base major strategic decisions.

STATE OF THE ART

Scanning serves as an early warning system for the environmental forces that may impact a company's products and markets in the future. Environmental scanning is a comparatively new development. Traditionally, corporations evaluated themselves mainly on the basis of financial performance. In general, the environment was studied only for the purpose of making economic forecasts. Other environmental factors were brought in haphazardly, if at all, and intuitively. In recent years, however, most large corporations have started doing systematic work in this area.

A pioneering study on environmental scanning was done by Francis Aguilar. In his investigation of selected chemical companies in the United States and Europe, he found no systematic approach to environmental scanning. Aguilar's different types of information about the environment that the companies found interesting have been consolidated into five groups: *market tidings* (market potential, structural change, competitors and industry, pricing, sales negotiations, customers); *acquisition leads* (leads for mergers, joint ventures); *technical tidings* (new products, processes, and technology; product problems; costs; licensing and patents); *broad issues* (general conditions relative to political, demographic, national issues; government actions and policies); *other tidings* (suppliers and raw materials, resources available, other). Among these groups, market tidings was found to be the dominant category and was of most interest to managers across the board.

Aguilar also identified four patterns for viewing information: *undirected viewing* (exposure without a specific purpose), *conditioned viewing* (directed exposure but without undertaking an active search), *informal search* (collection of purpose-oriented information in an informal manner), and *formal search* (a structured process for collection of specific information for a designated purpose). Both internal and external sources were used in seeking this information. The external comprised both personal sources (customers, suppliers, bankers, consultants, and other knowledgeable individuals) and impersonal sources (various publications, conferences, trade shows, exhibitions, and so on). The internal personal sources included peers, superiors, and subordinates. The internal impersonal sources included regular and general reports and scheduled meetings. Aguilar's study concluded that while the process is not simple, a company can systematize its environmental scanning activities for strategy development.[4]

Aguilar's framework may be illustrated with reference to the Coca-Cola Company. The company looks at its environment through a series of analyses. At the corporate level, considerable information is gathered on economic, social, and political factors affecting the business and on competition both in the United States and overseas. The corporate office also becomes involved in special studies when it feels that some aspect of the environment requires special attention. For example, in the 1980s, to address itself to a top management concern about Pepsi's claim that the taste of its cola was superior to Coke's, the company undertook a study to understand what was going on in the minds of their consumers and what they were looking for. How was the consumption of Coca-Cola related to their consumers' lifestyle, to their set of values, to their needs? This study spearheaded the work toward the introduction of New Coke.

In the mid-1980s, the corporate office also made a study of the impact of antipollution trends on government regulations concerning packaging. At the corporate level, environment was scanned rather broadly. Mostly market tidings, technical tidings, and broad issues were dealt with. Whenever necessary, in-depth studies were done on a particular area of concern, and corporate information was made available to different divisions of the company.

At the division level (e.g., Coca-Cola, USA), considerable attention is given to the market situation, acquisition leads, and new business ventures. The division also studies general economic conditions (trends in GNP, consumption, income), government regulation (especially antitrust actions), social factors, and even the political situation. Part of this division-level scanning duplicates the efforts of the corporate office, but the divisional planning staff felt that it was in a position to do a better job for its own purpose than could the corporate office, which had to serve the needs of other divisions as well. The division also undertakes special studies. For example, in the early 1980s, it wondered whether a caffeine-free drink should be introduced and, if so, when.

The information received from the corporate office and that which the division had collected itself was analyzed for events and happenings that could affect the company's current and potential business. Analysis was done mostly through meetings and discussions rather than through the use of any statistical model. At the Coca-Cola Company, environmental analysis is a sort of forum. There is relatively little cohesion among managers; the meetings, therefore, respond to a need for exchange of information between people.

A recent study of environmental scanning identifies four evolutionary phases of activity, from primitive to proactive (see Exhibit 6-2). The scanning activities in most corporations can be characterized by one of these four phases.[5]

In Phase 1, the primitive phase, the environment is taken as something inevitable and random about which nothing can be done other than to accept each impact as it occurs. Management is exposed to information, both strategic and nonstrategic, without making any effort to distinguish the difference. No discrimination is used to discern strategic information, and the information is rarely related to strategic decision making. As a matter of fact, scanning takes place without management devoting any effort to it.

Phase 2, the ad hoc phase, is an improvement over Phase 1 in that management identifies a few areas that need to be watched carefully; however, there is no

EXHIBIT 6-2
Four Phases in the Evolution of Environmental Scanning

PHASE 1	PHASE 2	PHASE 3	PHASE 4
Primitive	**Ad Hoc**	**Reactive**	**Proactive**
Face the environment as it appears	*Watch out for a likely impact on the environment*	*Deal with the environment to protect the future*	*Predict the environment for a desired future*
• Exposure to information without purpose and effort.	• No active search	• Unstructured and random effort	• Structured and deliberate effort
	• Be sensitive to information on specific issues	• Less specific information collection	• Specific information collection
			• Preestablished methodology
Scanning without an Impetus	Scanning to Enhance Understanding of a Specific Event	Scanning to Make an Appropriate Response to Markets and Competition	Strategic Scanning to Be on the Lookout for Competitive Advantage

formal system for scanning and no initiative is taken to scan the environment. In addition, that management is sensitive to information about specific areas does not imply that this information is subsequently related to strategy formulation. This phase is characterized by such statements as this: All reports seem to indicate that rates of interest will not increase substantially to the year 2000, but our management will never sit down to seriously consider what we might do or not do as a company to capitalize on this trend in the pursuit of our goals. Typically, the ad hoc phase characterizes companies that have traditionally done well and whose management, which is intimately tied to day-to-day operations, recently happened to hire a young M.B.A. to do strategic planning.

In Phase 3, the reactive phase, environmental scanning begins to be viewed as important, and efforts are made to monitor the environment to seek information in different areas. In other words, management fully recognizes the significance of the environment and dabbles in scanning but in an unplanned, unstructured fashion. Everything in the environment appears to be important, and the company is swamped with information. Some of the scanned information may never be looked into; some is analyzed, understood, and stored. As soon as the leading firm in the industry makes a strategic move in a particular matter, presumably in response to an environmental shift, the company in Phase 3 is quick to react, following the footsteps of the leader. For example, if the use of cardboard bottles for soft drinks appears uncertain, the Phase 3 company will understand the problem on the horizon but hesitate to take a strategic lead. If the leading firm decides to experiment with cardboard bottles, the Phase 3 firm will quickly respond in kind. In other words, the Phase 3 firm understands the problems and opportunities that the future holds, but its management is unwilling to be the first to take steps to avoid problems or to capitalize on opportunities. A Phase 3 company waits for a leading competitor to pave the way.

The firm in Phase 4, the proactive phase, practices environmental scanning with vigor and zeal, employing a structured effort. Careful screening focuses the scanning effort on specified areas considered crucial. Time is taken to establish proper methodology, disseminate scanned information, and incorporate it into strategy. A hallmark of scanning in Phase 4 is the distinction between macro and micro scanning. **Macro scanning** refers to scanning of interest to the entire corporation and is undertaken at the corporate level. **Micro scanning** is often practiced at the product/market or SBU level. A corporate-wide scanning system is created to ensure that macro and micro scanning complement each other. The system is designed to provide open communication between different micro scanners to avoid duplication of effort and information.

A multinational study on the subject concluded that environmental scanning is on its way to becoming a full-fledged formalized step in the strategic planning process. This commitment to environmental scanning has been triggered in part by the recognition of environmental turbulence and a willingness to confront relevant changes within the planning process. Commitment aside, there is yet no accepted, effective methodology for environmental scanning.[6]

TYPES OF ENVIRONMENT

Corporations today, more than ever before, are profoundly sensitive to technological, political, economic, social, and regulatory changes. Although environmental changes may be felt throughout an organization, the impact most affects strategic perspectives. To cope with a changing and shifting environment, the marketing strategist must find new ways to forecast the shape of things to come and to analyze strategic alternatives and, at the same time, develop greater sensitivity to long-term implications. Various techniques that are especially relevant for projecting long-range trends are discussed in the appendix at the end of this chapter. Suffice it to say here that environmental scanning necessarily implies a forecasting perspective.

Technological Environment

Technological developments come out of the research effort. Two types of research can be distinguished: basic and applied. A company may engage in applied research only or may undertake both basic and applied research. In either case, a start must be made at the basic level, and from there the specific effect on a company's product or process must be derived. A company may choose not to undertake any research on its own, accepting a secondary role as an imitator. The research efforts of imitators will be limited mainly to the adaptation of a particular technological change to its business.

There are three different aspects of technology: type of technology, its process, and the impetus for its development. Technology itself can be grouped into five categories: energy, materials, transportation, communications and information, and genetic (includes agronomic and biomedical). The original impetus for technological breakthroughs can come from any or all of three sources: meeting defense needs, seeking the welfare of the masses, and making a mark commercially. The three stages in the process of technological development are invention, the creation of a new product or process; innovation, the introduction of that product or process into use; and diffusion, the spread of the product or process beyond first use.

The type of technology a company prefers is dictated, of course, by the company's interests. Impetus points to the market for technological development, and the process of development shows the state of technological development and whether the company is in a position to interface with the technology in any stage. For example, the invention and innovation stages may call for basic research beyond the resources of a company. Diffusion, however, may require adaptation, which may not be as difficult as the other two stages.

To illustrate the point, let us look at personal computers. In the 1960s, as computers made inroads in the business world, a number of data processing bureaus were born to service small companies that could not afford computers. Over the years, these bureaus have rendered a very useful service by processing such information as payroll, accounts receivable, and accounts payable. Developments in the field of computer technology made it feasible in the late 1970s to build and market small computers at a price within the reach of small businesses. While a typical computer in the 1960s sold for more than $100,000, in 1991 a personal computer could be purchased for as little as $500.

The personal computer has become a threat to the data processing service bureaus because small businesses can now choose between buying their own computers and hiring the services of a data processing bureau.

Consider another example: Startling things have been happening to the television set in the last few years. For example, Panasonic now offers a color-projection system with a 60-inch screen. Toshiba Corp. of Japan has developed large, flat screen television sets that are so slim that they can hang on the wall like paintings. Even traditional 19-inch sets aren't just for looking at anymore; they are basic equipment on which to play video games, to learn how to spell, or to practice math. Videodisc players produce television images from discs; videocassette recorders tape television shows and play prerecorded videotapes. With two-way television, the viewer can respond to questions flashed on the screen. Teleprint enables the conversion of television sets into video-display tubes so that viewers can scan the contents of newspapers, magazines, catalogs, and the like and call up any sections of interest.[7] Finally, cable television permits the viewer to call on the system's library for a game, movie, or even a French lesson.

The 1990s are almost certain to be a period of technological change and true innovation. One of the areas of greatest impact is going to be communications. Until now, electronic communication has largely been confined to the traditional definition of voice (telephone), pictures (television), and graphics (computer), three distinct kinds of communication devices. From now on, electronics will increasingly produce total communications.[8] Today it is possible to make simultaneous and instantaneous electronic transmission of voice, pictures, and graphics. People scattered over the face of the globe can now talk to each other directly, see each other, and, if need be, share the same reports, documents, and graphs without leaving their own offices or homes.[9] Consider the impact of this innovation on the airline industry. Business travel should diminish in importance, though its place may well be taken by travel for vacations and learning.

To analyze technological changes and capitalize on them, marketing strategists may utilize the technology management matrix shown in Exhibit 6-3. The matrix should aid in choosing appropriate strategic options based on a business's technological position. The matrix has two dimensions: technology and product. The technology dimension describes technologies in terms of their relationships to one another; the product dimension establishes competitive position. The interaction of these two dimensions suggests desirable strategic action. For example, if a business's technology is superior to anything else on the market, the company should enhance its leadership by identifying and introducing new applications for the technology. On the other hand, if a business's technology lags behind the competition, it should either make a technological leap to the competitive process, abandon the market, or identify and pursue those elements that are laggards in terms of adopting new technologies.[10]

Briefly, the rapid development and exploitation of new technologies are causing serious strategic headaches for companies in almost every type of industry. It

EXHIBIT 6-3
Technology Management Matrix

	TECHNOLOGY POSITION		
		Different Technology	
Product Position	Same Technology	Older Technology	Newer Technology
Behind competitors	Take traditional strategic actions — Assess marketing strategy and target markets — Enhance product features — Improve operational efficiency	Evaluate viability of your technology — Implement newer technology — Divest products based on older technology	Evaluate availability of resources to sustain technology development and full market acceptance — Continue to define new applications and product enhancements — Scale back operations
Ahead of competitors	Define new applications for the technology and enhance products accordingly	Take advantage of all possible profit	Define new applications for the technology and enhance products accordingly

Source: Susan J. Levine, "Marketers Need to Adopt a Technological Focus to Safeguard Against Obsolescence," *Marketing News* (28 October 1988): 16. Reprinted by permission of the American Marketing Association.

has become vital for strategists to be able to recognize the limits of their core technologies, know which new technologies are emerging, and decide when to incorporate new technology in their products.

Political Environment

In stable governments, political trends may not be as important as in countries where governments are weak. Yet even in stable countries, political trends may have a significant impact on business. For example, in the United States one can typically expect greater emphasis on social programs and an increase in government spending when Democrats are in power in the White House. Therefore, companies in the business of providing social services may expect greater opportunities during Democratic administrations.

More important, however, are political trends overseas because the U.S. economy is intimately connected with the global economy. Therefore, what goes on in the political spheres of other countries may be significant for U.S. corporations, particularly multinational corporations.

The following are examples of political trends and events that could affect business planning and strategy:

1. An increase in geopolitical federations.
   a. Economic interests: resource countries versus consumer countries.
   b. Political interests: Third World versus the rest.

2. Rising nationalism versus world federalism.
   a. Failure of the United Nations.
   b. Trend toward world government or world law system.
3. Limited wars: Middle East, Serbia-Croatia.
4. Increase in political terrorism; revolutions.
5. Third-party gains in the United States; rise of socialism.
6. Decline of the major powers; rise of emerging nations (e.g., China, India, Brazil).
7. Minority (female) president.
8. Rise in senior citizen power in developed nations.
9. Political turmoil in Saudi Arabia that threatens world oil supplies and peace in the Middle East.
10. Revolutionary change in Indonesia, jeopardizing Japanese oil supplies.
11. Revolutionary change in South Africa, limiting Western access to important minerals and threatening huge capital losses to the economies of Great Britain, the United States, and Germany.
12. Instability in other places where the economic consequences could be important, including Mexico, Turkey, Zaire, Nigeria, South Korea, Brazil, Chile, and the People's Republic of China.

Already in the 1990s we have seen the overwhelming impact that political shocks can have on the world economy. The value of the Mexican peso is the perfect illustration: it was not just the product of an arbitrary monetary policy that was temporarily out of control but a rational response to problems that were fundamentally political. The Mexican government in the 1990s continued to incur huge budget deficits and kept on borrowing, making itself dangerously dependent on the inflows of foreign capital. As the new government took over in 1994, inflation was high and the country became vulnerable to capital flight, leaving no choice for the government but to devalue the peso. The weakened Mexican economy, staggered by the deep devaluation of the peso, is expected to have strong reverberations for the U.S., with hundreds of thousands of jobs and billions of dollars of export business lost.

Marketing strategy is deeply affected by political perspectives. For example, government decisions have significantly affected the U.S. automotive industry. Stringent requirements, such as fuel efficiency standards, have burdened the industry in several ways.[11] The marketing strategist needs to study both domestic and foreign political happenings, reviewing selected published information to keep in touch with political trends and interpret the information as it relates to the particular company.

Governments around the world help their domestic industries strengthen their competitiveness through various fiscal and monetary measures. Political support can play a key role in an industry's search for markets abroad. Without it, an industry may face a difficult situation. For instance, the U.S. auto industry would benefit from a U.S. government concession favoring U.S. automotive exports. European countries rely on value-added taxes to help their industries. Value-added taxes are applied to all levels of manufacturing transactions up to and including the final sale to the end user. However, if the final sale is for export, the value-added tax is rebated, thus effectively reducing the price of European goods in international commerce. Japan imposes a commodity tax on selected lines of products, including automobiles. In the event of export, the commodity tax is waived. The United States has no corresponding arrangement. Thus, when a new automobile is shipped from the United States to Japan, its U.S. taxes upon export are not rebated and the auto also must bear the cost of the Japanese commodity tax (15 or 20 percent, depending on the size of the vehicle) when it is sold in Japan. This illustrates how political decisions affect marketing strategy.

Economic Environment

Economic trends and events affecting businesses include the following possibilities:

- Depression; worldwide economic collapse.
- Increasing foreign ownership of the U.S. economy.
- Increasing regulation and management of national economies.
- Several developing nations become superpowers (e.g., Brazil, India, China).
- World food production: famine relief versus holistic management.
- Decline in real world growth or stable growth.
- Collapse of world monetary system.
- High inflation.
- Significant employee-union ownership of U.S. businesses.
- Worldwide free trade.

It is not unrealistic to say that all companies, small or large, that are engaged in strategic planning examine the economic environment. Relevant published information is usually gathered, analyzed, and interpreted for use in planning. In some corporations, the entire process of dealing with economic information may be manual and intuitive. The large corporations, however, not only buy specific and detailed economic information from private sources, over and above what may be available from government sources, but they analyze the information for meaningful conclusions by constructing econometric models. For example, one large corporation with nine divisions has developed 26 econometric models of its different businesses. The data used for these models are stored in a database and are regularly updated. The information is available on-line to all divisions for further analysis at any time. Other companies may occasionally buy information from outside and selectively undertake modeling.

Usually the economic environment is analyzed with reference to the following key economic indicators: employment, consumer price index, housing starts, auto sales, weekly unemployment claims, real GNP, industrial production, personal income, savings rate, capacity utilization, productivity, money supply (weekly M1: currency and checking accounts), retail sales, inventories, and durable goods orders. Information on these indicators is available from government sources. These indicators are adequate for short-run analysis and decision making because, by and large, they track developments over the business cycle reasonably well. However, companies that try to base strategic plans on these indicators alone can run into serious trouble. Deficiencies in the data prove most dangerous when the government moves to take a more interventionist role in the economy. Further, when the ability of statistical agencies to respond has been hampered by unprecedented budget stringency, rapid changes in the structure of the economy cause a gradual deterioration in the quality of many of the economic statistics that the government publishes.

The problem of government-supplied data begins with a recondite document called the *Standard Industrial Classification (SIC) Manual*, which divides all economic activity into 12 divisions and 84 major groups of industries. The SIC Manual dictates the organization of and the amount of data available about production, income, employment, and other vital economic indicators. Each major group has a two-digit numerical code. The economy is then subdivided into hundreds of secondary groups, each with a three-digit code, and is further subdivided into thousands of industries, each with four-digit codes. But detail in most government statistical series is available only at the major group level; data at the three-digit level are scarce; at the four-digit level, almost nonexistent. Thus, information available from public sources may not suffice.

To illustrate the effect of economic climate on strategy, consider the following trends. In the more elderly capitalist countries, it is expected that old markets will become saturated much faster than new markets will take their place. Staple consumer goods, such as cars, radios, and television sets, already outnumber households in North America and in much of Western Europe; other products are fast approaching the same fate. The slow growth of populations in most of these countries means that the number of households is likely to grow at only about 2 percent annually to the year 2000 and that demand for consumer goods is unlikely to grow any faster. Furthermore, while demand in these markets decreases, supply will increase, leading to intensified price competition and pressure on profit margins.

For example, in the second half of the 1990s the auto industry is likely to suffer from overcapacity. It is expected that there will be three buyers for every four cars.[12] Already the market concentration in many consumer sectors has fallen significantly, mainly because of increased foreign competition. And the expansion of production capacity in such primary industries as metals and chemicals, especially in developing countries, may bring some kind of increased competition to producer goods.

These trends indicate the kind of economic issues that marketing strategists must take into account to determine their strategies.

Social Environment

The ultimate test of a business is its social relevance. This is particularly true in a society where survival needs are already being met. It therefore behooves the strategic planner to be familiar with emerging social trends and concerns. The relevance of the social environment to a particular business will, of course, vary depending on the nature of the business. For a technology-oriented business, scanning the social environment may be limited to aspects of pollution control and environmental safety. For a consumer-products company, however, the impact of the social environment may go much further.

An important aspect of the social environment concerns the values consumers hold. Observers have noted many value shifts that directly or indirectly influence business. Values mainly revolve around a number of fundamental concerns regarding time, quality, health, environment, home, personal finance, and diversity.[13]

Orientation Toward Time. Given the scarcity of time and/or money to have products repaired or to buy new ones, consumers look for offerings that endure. Time has become the scarce resource of the 1990s as the result of the prevalence of dual income-earning households. Convenience is a critical source of differential advantage, particularly in foods and services. In addition, youth are making or influencing more household purchasing decisions than ever before. Moreover, as the population ages, time pressures become more widespread and acute. Consumers are going to need innovative and, in some cases, almost customized solutions. With time generally scarcer than money, offerings that ease time pressures will garner higher margins.

Quality. Given the standards set by the influx of imported products, American consumers have developed a new set of expectations regarding quality; hence, they assign high priorities to those offerings that provide optimal price/quality. We are witnessing a move toward the adoption of a greater price/quality orientation in mass markets. There will continue to be a strong general desire for authenticity and lasting quality. Consumers will require fewer and more durable products rather than more ephemeral, novelty products. Heightened consumer expectations will translate into trying a manufacturer once. If the value, the quality, or the intrinsic characteristics that the consumer demands are not found, the consumer will not return to that manufacturer.

Health. A large and growing segment of the American population has become increasingly preoccupied with health. Health concerns are a function of both an aging population and changing predispositions. America is hungry for health and is impatient for its achievement. Industry experts are predicting that nutritional tags, such as "low in fat," will probably be the newest food fad to sweep the United States. There is some consensus that a diet rich in soluble fiber and low in fat and a lifestyle that includes plenty of regular exercise reduce cholesterol. As an aging population strives to maintain its youth and vitality, alcohol and tobacco consumption and other unhealthy dietary habits will continue to decline. In short, American consumers have become highly health conscious. The impact of this trend will not only be felt in the grocery store but in the travel and hospitality sectors of the economy, as well as in an array of services that contribute to lifelong wellness.

Environment. Perhaps the 1990s has become the "earth decade." A growing number of Americans consider themselves "environmentalists." Outdoor activities, such as rock-climbing expeditions and whitewater rafting, are superseding more vicarious, passive ways of spending time. This heightened appreciation of the outdoors is being translated in choice criteria in the marketplace. Hence, more and more marketers are pressured into adopting "green" strategies; that is, offering products and services that are beneficial to the environment.[14]

Home. In a more domesticated society, the many technological innovations of the 1990s are making staying at home more fun. Some of the most beneficial advances of this home-centered decade are in the design and construction of houses that resemble self-contained entertainment/educational activity centers. The recent slump in the housing market has rebounded, and opportunities for marketers to provide creative, more personalized, high-value offerings in home furnishings are evolving.[15]

Personal Finance. Most experts on consumer behavior expect that in the remainder of 1990s, people will be more frugal than they were in the past. The slow-and-steady consumer approach spawned by an attitude for upscale products that may outstrip finances makes every purchase especially important. We are witnessing several important consumer finance trends. First, consumers continue to seek out the best price/value before buying and accordingly place downward pressure on seller profit margins. Second, American consumers may have the income to spend freely, but recent economic difficulties nonetheless have caused them to remain cautious. Finally, quality is insisted upon, and a competitive premium price is willingly paid for performance and durability.

Diversity of Lifestyles. The predominance of diverse lifestyles is reflected by the significant increase in the number and the stature of women in the labor market. The increased presence of women in the labor force has dramatically influenced how men and women relate to one another and the personal and professional roles assumed by each. With 70 percent of women holding jobs outside the home, millions of men are doing chores their fathers would never have dreamed of. For example, men bought 25 percent of the groceries in the U.S. in 1991, up from 17 percent five years earlier.[16] There has also been a dramatic change in racial integration and improved race relations. The United States has also witnessed the development of openly gay and lesbian lifestyles as well as an increase in the number of unmarried, cohabiting relationships. Significant changes in attitudes toward work and careers have also resulted in a new sense of independence and individuality. Accordingly, there has been an upsurge in the number of people who are self-employed. Experts hold that this pattern of social diversity will likely continue into the future. Social diversity creates opportunities for marketers to develop personalized offerings that allow individuals to derive satisfaction in the pursuit of different living alternatives.

In conclusion, American consumers will continue to search for basic values and will experience heightened ethical awareness.[17] Consumers will still care about what things cost, but they will value only things that will endure—family, community, earth, faith.

Information on social trends may be derived from published sources. The impact of social trends on a particular business can be studied in-house or with the help of outside consultants. A number of consulting firms specialize in studying social trends.

Let us examine the strategic impact of two of the value shifts mentioned above: orientation toward time and concern for health. Consider the retail industry. Little is being done to support consumers in their quest to reduce shopping stress, although stress is a major consumer concern. Fast service has been the basis for growth for a number of well-known firms, among them American

Express, McDonald's, and Federal Express; however, only a small but significant number of businesses have recognized and responded to the consumer's lack of free time for shopping and service transactions:

- Dayton-Hudson has moved away from a maze-like floor design to a center aisle design, making it easier for customers to find their way through the store. At Childworld, toys are coordinated in learning centers so that buyers can examine and play with products. Management feels that this arrangement enables buyers to shop more quickly.
- A new firm, Shopper's Express, is assisting large chains such as A&P and Safeway by taking telephone orders and delivering merchandise.
- Rather than forcing the consumer to sit at home for an entire day awaiting a service call, GE, for years, has been making specific service appointments.
- Sears now offers six-day-a-week and evening repair service. In addition, in specifying when a repair person will arrive, Sears assigns a two-hour window.
- Montgomery Ward authorizes 7,700 sales clerks to approve sales checks and handle merchandise returns on their own, eliminating the time needed to get a floor manager's approval.
- Burger King uses television monitors that enable drive-up customers to see the waiter and the order.
- A&P, Shop Rite, and Publix are experimenting with automated grocery checkout systems that reduce waiting time in checkout lines.
- Wegman's, a supermarket chain in Rochester, New York, has a computer available for entering deli orders so that the customer does not have to wait to be served. The customer simply enters the order and picks it up on the way out of the store.[18]

More and more companies need to focus on developing shopping support systems and environments that help customers move through the buying process quickly. For firms that pride themselves for providing customers with a leisurely shopping environment, this will be a radical departure. Firms accepting this challenge will be able to support and stay closer to their customers through such changes. In addition, firms that help customers reduce shopping time will be able to differentiate themselves from competitors more easily.

For health reasons, salads and fish are replacing the traditional American dinner of meat and potatoes. Vegetarianism is on the rise. According to *Time*, about 8 million Americans call themselves vegetarians.[19] Increasing varieties of decaffeinated coffee and tea and substitutes for sugar and salt are crowding supermarket shelves. Shoppers are reading the small print to check for artificial ingredients in foods and beverages that they once bought without a thought. Smoking is finally declining. Manufacturers and retailers of natural foods are building a healthy "health industry." Even products that do not easily accommodate healthier choices are being redeveloped in response to consumer concerns. For example, Dunkin Donuts has yanked the egg yolks from all but four of its 52 varieties to make its donuts cholesterol-free.[20] Fast food firms—McDonald's Corporation and Hardee's Food Systems, for example—have introduced low-fat foods into their menus.[21]

The nation's dramatic new awareness of health is prompting these changes. The desire to feel better, look younger, and live longer exerts a powerful influence on what people put into their bodies. This strong force is now moving against a well-entrenched habit that affects millions and dates back to biblical times—the consumption of too much alcohol.[22]

Health substitutes for alcoholic beverages, labeled "dealcoholized" beverages, are now being offered to American consumers. For some time, gourmet food shops have stocked champagne-like bottles of carbonated grape juice and cans containing a not-fully-brewed mixture of water, malt, corn, yeast, and hops. Except for their packaging, these alcohol-free imitations failed to resemble wine and beer, especially in the crucial area of taste. New dealcoholized beverages, however, are fully fermented, or brewed, before their alcohol is separated out—either by pressure or heat—to below an unnoticeable 0.5 percent, the federal maximum before classifying a drink as alcoholic. The taste and body of the new beverages match that of their former alcoholized selves.

This 0.5 percent level is so low that a drinker would need to consume 24 glasses of dealcoholized wine or 8 cans of dealcoholized beer to obtain the amount of alcohol in one 4-ounce glass of regular wine or one 12-ounce can of regular beer. Thus, the drinker avoids not only intoxication but also worthless calories. A regular glass of wine or beer has about 150 calories, while their dealcoholized copies contain about 40 to 60 calories, respectively. And their prices are the same.[23] Introduced in Europe about five years ago, dealcoholized wines are slowly making headway in the United States.

Regulatory Environment

Government influence on business appears to be increasing. It is estimated that businesses spend, on the average, twice as much time fulfilling government requirements today as they did 10 years ago.[24] Even a cautious company such as Procter & Gamble can get into problems for not heeding the regulatory environment. The Food and Drug Administration (FDA) has been complaining that Procter & Gamble has been misleading consumers through its advertising claims. Although initially the company denied any improprieties, ultimately it had to reform a number of products:

- **Ultra Protection Crest**—Halted national launch after FDA said new toothpaste with antibacterial agent required new drug approval.
- **Citrus Hill Fresh Choice**—Agreed to drop "fresh" from product name after FDA seized some of the orange juice and said the labeling was false and misleading.
- **Crisco Corn Oil**—Dropped "no cholesterol" labels from all food products after FDA told vegetable oil marketers to stop using the claim.
- **Metamucil**—Increased clinical research to support cholesterol-reduction claims for this fiber laxative after FDA asked for more data.
- **Didronel**—Sought FDA approval to market this prescription drug as an osteoporosis treatment, but an advisory panel has questioned some of the company's data. Still awaiting approval.
- **Olestra**—Has not won FDA's go-ahead four years after company's initial petition to sell this fat substitute.[25]

Interestingly, government in recent years has changed its emphasis from regulating specific industries to focusing on problem areas of national interest, including environmental cleanup, elimination of job discrimination, establishment of safe working conditions, and reduction of product hazards. A number of steps have been taken toward deregulation of various industries.

This shift in focus in the regulatory environment deeply affects the internal operations of business. To win or even survive in the competitive free-for-all environment that follows deregulation, companies in once-regulated industries must make some hard choices. Astute management can avoid some of the trauma by developing an explicit strategy to operate in a deregulated environment well in advance of the event, rethinking relationships with customers, considering new roles to play in the market, and realigning their organizations accordingly.

To study the impact of the regulatory environment, that is, of laws already on the books and of pending legislation, legal assistance is required. Small firms may seek legal assistance on an ad hoc basis. Large firms may maintain offices in Washington staffed by people with legal backgrounds who are well versed in the company's business, who know important government agencies from the point of view of their companies, who maintain a close liaison with them, and who pass on relevant information to planners in different departments of their companies.

ENVIRONMENTAL SCANNING AND MARKETING STRATEGY

The impact of environmental scanning on marketing strategy can be illustrated with reference to videotex technology.[26] Videotex technology—the merging of computer and communications technologies—delivers information directly to the consumer. The consumer may instantly view desired textual and visual information from on-line databases on television screens or other video receivers by pushing the appropriate buttons or typing the proper commands.

Possibilities for business and personal use of videotex are as endless as the imagination. Consumers are already utilizing videotex for shopping, travel, personal protection, financial transactions, and entertainment, in greater privacy and autonomy than ever before.

With the mechanism for getting things done most efficiently and cost effectively, marketing strategists have begun to explore the implications of videotex on marketing decisions. Videotex will alter the demand for certain kinds of goods and services and the ways in which consumers interact with marketing activities. For the first time, the average consumer, not just the affluent consumer, can interact directly with the production process, dictating final product specifications as the product is being manufactured. As small-batch production becomes more cost-effective, this type of consumer-producer interaction will become more common.

Product selection might also be enhanced by videotex, as sellers stock a more complete inventory at fewer, more central locations rather than dealing with many retail outlets. Because packages will no longer serve as the communications vehicle for selling the product, less money will be spent on packaging. Product changes can also be kept up-to-date. Information on videotex will be current, synthesized, and comprehensive. The user will have the power to access only desired information at the time it is desired. Advertising messages and articles will be available in index form.

Direct consumer interaction with manufacturers will eliminate distribution channels. Reduced or zero-based inventory will reduce obsolescence and turnover costs. Centrally located warehouses and new delivery routes will become increasingly cost-effective. The remaining retail stores will be transformed into showrooms with direct-order possibilities via viewdatalike terminals.

Promotional material will become more educational and information-based, including the provision of product specifications and independent product evaluations. Interactive video channels will provide advertisers and interested shoppers with prepackaged commercials and live shopping programs.

With more accurate price and product information, more perfect competition will result. Price discrepancies will be reduced. Consumers will engage in more preshopping planning, price-comparison shopping, and in-home shopping.

The market segment concept will be more important than ever before. The individualizing possibilities of videotex will enable the seller to measure and reach segments with unparalleled accuracy and will also enable consumers to effectively self-segment. Advertisers and consumers will benefit from 24-hour, 7-day-a-week salespeople. Everyone will be better prepared through videotex to satisfy customers.

ENVIRONMENTAL SCANNING PROCEDURE

Like any other new program, the scanning activity in a corporation evolves over time. There is no way to introduce a foolproof system from the beginning. If conditions are favorable—if there is an established system of strategic planning in place and the CEO is interested in a structured effort at scanning—the evolutionary period shortens, of course, but the state of the art may not permit the introduction of a fully developed system at the outset. Besides, behavioral and organizational constraints require that things be done over a period of time. The level and type of scanning that a corporation undertakes should be custom designed, and a customized system takes time to emerge into a viable system.

Exhibit 6-4 shows the process by which environmental scanning is linked to marketing strategy. Listed below and on the next pages are the procedural steps that explain this relationship.

1. **Keep a tab on broad trends appearing in the environment**—Once the scope of environmental scanning is determined, broad trends in chosen areas may be reviewed from time to time. For example, in the area of technology, trends in energy utilization, material science, transportation capability, mechanization and automation, communications and information processing, and control over natural life may be studied.

2. **Determine the relevance of an environmental trend**—Not everything happening in the environment may be relevant for a company. Therefore, attempts must be made to select those trends that have significance for the company. There cannot be any hard-and-fast rules for making a distinction between relevant and irrelevant. Consider, for example, the demise of the steam locomotive industry. Management's creativity and farsightedness would play an important role in a

company's ability to pinpoint relevant areas of concern. Described below is one way (for a large corporation) of identifying relevant trends in the environment:

- Place a senior person in charge of scanning.
- Identify a core list of about 100 relevant publications worldwide.
- Assign these publications to volunteers within the company, one per person. Selected publications considered extremely important should be scanned by the scanning manager.
- Each scanner reviews stories/articles/news items in the assigned publication that meet predetermined criteria based on the company's aims. Scanners might also review books, conference proceedings, lectures, and presentations.
- The scanned information is given a predetermined code. For example, a worldwide consumer-goods company used the following codes: subject (e.g., politics); geography (e.g., Middle East); function (e.g., marketing); application (e.g., promotion, distribution); and "uniterm," or keyword, for organizing the information. An abstract is then prepared on the story.
- The abstract, along with the codes, is submitted to a scanning committee, consisting of several managers, to determine its relevance in terms of effect on

EXHIBIT 6-4
Linking Environmental Scanning to Corporate Strategy

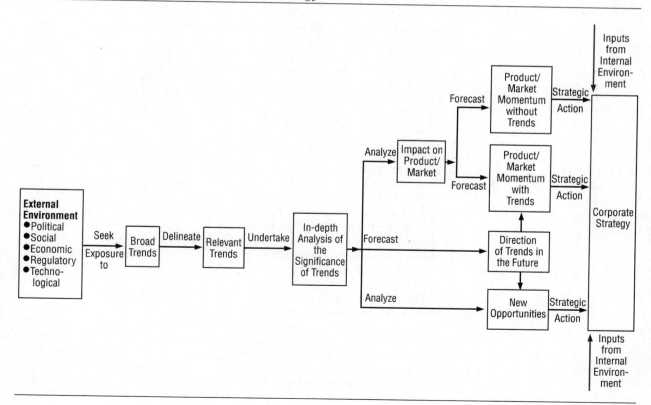

corporate, SBU, and product/market strategy. An additional relevance code is added at this time.

- The codes and the abstract are computerized.
- A newsletter is prepared to disseminate the information companywide. Managers whose areas are directly affected by the information are encouraged to contact the scanning department for further analysis.

3. **Study the impact of an environmental trend on a product/market**—An environmental trend can pose either a threat or an opportunity for a company's product/market; which one it turns out to be must be studied. The task of determining the impact of a change is the responsibility of the SBU manager. Alternatively, the determination may be assigned to another executive who is familiar with the product/market. If the whole subject appears controversial, it may be safer to have an ad hoc committee look into it; or consultants, either internal or external, may be approached. There is a good chance that a manager who has been involved with a product or service for many years will look at any change as a threat. That manager may, therefore, avoid the issue by declaring the impact to be irrelevant at the outset. If such nearsightedness is feared, perhaps it would be better to rely on a committee or a consultant.

4. **Forecast the direction of an environmental trend into the future**—If an environmental trend does appear to have significance for a product/market, it is desirable to determine the course that the trend is likely to adopt. In other words, attempts must be made at environmental forecasting.

5. **Analyze the momentum of the product/market business in the face of the environmental trend**—Assuming that the company takes no action, what will be the shape of the product/market performance in the midst of the environmental trend and its future direction? The impact of an environmental trend is usually gradual. While it is helpful to be the "first" to recognize a trend and take action, all is not lost if a company waits to see which way the trend proceeds. But how long one waits depends on the diffusion process, the rate at which the change necessitated by the trend is adopted. People did not jump to replace their black-and-white television sets overnight. Similar examples abound. A variety of reasons may prohibit an overnight shift in markets due to an environmental trend that may deliver a new product or process. High prices, religious taboos, legal restrictions, and unfamiliarity with the product or service would restrict changeover. In brief, the diffusion process should be predicted before arriving at a conclusion.

6. **Study the new opportunities that an environmental trend appears to provide**—An environmental trend may not be relevant for a company's current product/market, but it may indicate promising new business opportunities. For example, the energy crisis provided an easy entry point for fuel-efficient Hondas into the United States. Such opportunities should be duly pinpointed and analyzed for action.

7. **Relate the outcome of an environmental trend to corporate strategy**—Based on environmental trends and their impacts, a company needs to review its strategy on two counts: changes that may be introduced in current products/markets and feasible opportunities that the company may embrace for action. Even if an environmental trend poses a threat to a company's product/market, it is not necessary for the company to come out with a new product to replace an existing one. Neither is it necessary for every competitor to embrace the "change." Even without developing a new product, a company may find a niche in the market to

which it could cater despite the introduction of a new product by a competitor. The electric razor did not make safety razor blades obsolete. Automatic transmissions did not throw the standard shift out of vogue. New markets and new uses can be found to give an existing product an advantage despite the overall popularity of a new product.

Although procedural steps for scanning the environment exist, scanning is nevertheless an art in which creativity plays an important role. Thus, to adequately study the changing environment and relate it to corporate strategy, companies should inculcate a habit of creative thinking on the part of its managers. The experience of one insurance company illustrates the point: in order to "open up" line managers to new ideas and to encourage innovation in their plans, they are, for a while, withdrawn from the line organization to serve as staff people. In staff positions, they are granted considerable freedom of action, which enhances their ability to manage creatively when they return to their management positions.

CONDUCTING ENVIRONMENTAL SCANNING: AN EXAMPLE

Following the steps in Exhibit 6-5, an attempt is made here to illustrate how specific trends in the environment may be systematically scanned.

A search of the literature in the area of politics shows that the following federal laws were considered during the 1990s:

1. Requiring that all ad claims be substantiated.
2. Publishing corporate actions that endanger the environment.
3. Disclosing lobbying efforts in detail.
4. Reducing a company's right to fire workers at will.
5. Eliminating inside directors.

The marketing strategist of a consumer-goods company may want to determine if any of these trends has any relevance for the company. To do so, the strategist may undertake trend-impact analysis. Trend-impact analysis requires the formation of a delphi panel (see Chapter 12) to determine the desirability (0-1), technical feasibility (0-1), probability of occurrence (0-1), and probable time of occurrence (2000, 2005, and beyond 2005) of each event listed. The panel may also be asked to suggest the area(s) that may be affected by each event (i.e., production, labor, markets [household, business, government, export], finance, or research and development).

Information about an event may be studied by managers in areas that, according to the delphi panel, are likely to be affected by the event. If their consensus is that the event is indeed important, scanning may continue (see Exhibit 6-6).

Next, cross-impact analysis may be undertaken. This type of analysis studies the impact of an event on other events. Where events are mutually exclusive, such analysis may not be necessary. But where an event seems to reinforce or inhibit other events, cross-impact analysis is highly desirable for uncovering the true strength of an event.

EXHIBIT 6-5
Systematic Approach to Environmental Scanning

1. Pick up events in different environments (via literature search).
2. Delineate events of interest to the SBU in one or more of the following areas: production, labor, markets (household, business, government, foreign), finance, or research and development. This could be achieved via trend-impact analysis of the events.
3. Undertake cross-impact analysis of the events of interest.
4. Relate the trends of the noted events to current SBU strategies in different areas.
5. Select the trends that appear either to provide new opportunities or to pose threats.
6. Undertake forecasts of each trend
   —wild card prediction
   —most probable occurrence
   —conservative estimate
7. Develop three scenarios for each trend based on three types of forecasts.
8. Pass on the information to strategists.
9. Repeat Steps 4 to 7 and develop more specific scenarios vis-à-vis different products/markets. Incorporate these scenarios in the SBU strategy.

Cross-impact analysis amounts to studying the impact of an event (given its probability of occurrence) upon other events. The impact may be delineated either in qualitative terms (such as critical, major, significant, slight, or none) or in quantitative terms in the form of probabilities.

Exhibit 6-7 shows how cross-impact analysis may be undertaken. Cross-impact ratings, or probabilities, can best be determined with the help of another delphi panel. To further sharpen the analysis, whether the impact of an event on

EXHIBIT 6-6
Trend-Impact Analysis: An Example

Event	Requiring That All Ad Claims Be Substantiated	Reducing a Company's Right to Fire Workers at Will
Desirability	0.8	0.5
Feasibility	0.6	0.3
Probability of occurrence	0.5	0.1
Probable time of occurrence	1995	Beyond 2000
Area(s) impacted	Household markets Business markets Government markets Finance Research and development Production	Labor Finance
Decision	Carry on scanning	Drop from further consideration

Note: Two to three rounds of delphi would be needed to arrive at the above probabilities.

EXHIBIT 6-7

Cross-Impact Analysis: An Example

Event	Probability of Occurrence	Impact				
		a	b	c	d	e
a. Requiring that all ad claims be sub-stantiated	0.5				0.1*	
b. Publishing corporate actions that endanger workers or environment	0.4	0.7**				
c. Disclosing lobbying efforts in detail	0.4					
d. Reducing a company's right to fire workers at will	0.1					
e. Eliminating inside directors	0.6					

*This means that requiring that all claims be substantiated has no effect on the probability of Event d.

**This means that if publishing corporate actions that endanger workers or the environment occurs (probability 0.4), the probability of requiring that all ad claims be substantiated increases from 0.5 to 0.7.

other events will be felt immediately or after a certain number of years may also be determined.

Cross-impact analysis provides the "time" probability of the occurrence of an event and indicates other key events that may be monitored to keep track of the first event. Cross-impact analysis is more useful for project-level scanning than for general scanning.

To relate environmental trends to strategy, consider the following environmental trends and strategies of a cigarette manufacturer:

Trends

T1: Requiring that all ad claims be substantiated.
T2: Publishing corporate actions that endanger workers or the environment.
T3: Disclosing lobbying efforts in detail.
T4: Reducing a company's right to fire workers at will.
T5: Eliminating inside directors.

Strategies

S1: Heavy emphasis on advertising, using emotional appeals.
S2: Seasonal adjustments in labor force for agricultural operations of the company.
S3: Regular lobbying effort in Washington against further legislation imposing restrictions on the cigarette industry.
S4: Minimum number of outside directors on the board.

The analysis in Exhibit 6-8 shows that Strategy S_1, heavy emphasis on advertising, is most susceptible and requires immediate management action. Among the trends, Trend T_5, eliminating inside directors, will have the most positive overall impact. Trends T_1 and T_2, requiring that all ad claims be substantiated and publishing corporate actions that endanger the environment, will have a devastating impact. This type of analysis indicates where management concern

EXHIBIT 6-8
Matrix to Determine the Impact of Selected Trends on Different Corporate Strategies

Trends	Strategies				Impact (I_1)	
	S_1	S_2	S_3	S_4	+	−
T_1	− 8	0	+ 2	− 2		8
T_2	− 4	− 2	− 6	0		12
T_3	0	+ 4	− 4	+ 2	2	
T_4	0	− 4	0	+ 6	2	
T_5	− 2	+6	+ 4	+ 2	10	
+	−	4	−	8		
−	14	−	4	−		

Scale

+ 8	*Enhance the*	Critical
+ 6	*implementation*	Major
+ 2	*of strategy*	Significant
+ 2		Slight
0		**No effect**
− 2	*Inhibit the*	Slight
− 4	*implementation*	Significant
− 6	*of strategy*	Major
− 8		Critical

and action should be directed. Thus, it will be desirable to undertake forecasts of Trends T_1 and T_2. The forecasts may predict when the legislation will be passed, what will be the major provisions of the legislation, and so on. Three different forecasts may be obtained:

1. Extremely unfavorable legislation.
2. Most probable legislation.
3. Most favorable legislation.

Three different scenarios (using three types of forecasts) may be developed to indicate the impact of each trend. This information may then be passed on to product/market managers for action. Product/market managers may repeat Steps 4 through 7 (see Exhibit 6-5), studying selected trend(s) in depth.

ORGANIZATIONAL ARRANGEMENTS AND PROBLEMS

Corporations organize scanning activity in three different ways: (a) line managers undertake environmental scanning in addition to their other work, (b) scanning is made a part of the strategic planner's job, (c) scanning responsibility is instituted in a new office of environmental scanning.

*Structuring
Responsibility for
Scanning*

Most companies use a combination of the first two types of arrangements. The strategic planner may scan the corporate-wide environment while line managers concentrate on the product/market environment. In some companies, a new office of environmental scanning has been established with a responsibility for all types of scanning.[27] The scanning office undertakes scanning both regularly and on an ad hoc basis (at the request of one of the groups in the company). Information scanned on a regular basis is passed on to all in the organization for whom it may have relevance. For example, General Electric is organized into sectors, groups, and SBUs. The SBU is the level at which product/market planning takes place. Thus, scanned information is channeled to those SBUs, groups, and sectors for which it has relevance. Ad hoc scanning may be undertaken at the request of one or more SBUs. These SBUs then share the cost of scanning and are the principal recipients of the information.

The environmental scanner serves to split the work of the planner. If the planner already has many responsibilities and if the environment of a corporation is complex, it is desirable to have a person specifically responsible for scanning. Further, it is desirable that both planners (and/or scanners) and line managers undertake scanning because managers usually limit their scanning perceptions to their own industry; that is, they may limit their scanning to the environment with which they are most familiar. At the corporate level, scanning should go beyond the industry.

Whoever is assigned to scan the environment should undertake the following six tasks:

1. **Trend monitoring**—Systematically and continuously monitoring trends in the external environments of the company and studying their impact upon the firm and its various constituencies.
2. **Forecast preparation**—Periodically developing alternative scenarios, forecasts, and other analyses that serve as inputs to various types of planning and issue management functions in the organization.
3. **Internal consulting**—Providing a consulting resource on long-term environmental matters and conducting special future research studies as needed to support decision-making and planning activities.
4. **Information center**—Providing a center to which intelligence and forecasts about the external environment from all over the organization can be sent for interpretation, analysis, and storage in a basic library on long-range environmental matters.
5. **Communications**—Communicating information on the external environment to interested decision makers through a variety of media, including newsletters, special reports, internal lectures, and periodic analyses of the environment.
6. **Process improvement**—Continually improving the process of environmental analysis by developing new tools and techniques, designing forecasting systems, applying methodologies developed elsewhere, and engaging in a continuing process of self-evaluation and self-correction.

Successful implementation of these tasks should provide increased awareness and understanding of long-term environments and improve the strategic planning capabilities of the firm. More specifically, environmental inputs are helpful in product design, formulation of marketing strategies, determination of marketing mix, and research and development strategies.

In addition, the scanner should train and motivate line managers to become sensitive to environmental trends, encouraging them to identify strategic versus tactical information and to understand the strategic problems of the firm as opposed to short-term sales policy and tactics.

Time Horizon of | Scanning may be for a short term or a long term. Short-term scanning is useful for
Scanning | programming various operations, and the term may last up to two years. Long-term scanning is needed for strategic planning, and the term may vary from three to twenty-five years. Rarely does the term of scanning go beyond twenty-five years. The actual time horizon is determined by the nature of the product. Forest products, for example, require a longer time horizon because the company must make decisions about tree planting almost twenty-five years ahead of harvesting those trees for lumber. Fashion designers, however, may not extend scanning beyond four years. As a rule of thumb, the appropriate time horizon for environmental scanning is twice as long as the duration of the company's strategic plan. For example, if a company's strategic plan extends eight years into the future, the environmental scanning time horizon should be sixteen years. Likewise, a company with a five-year planning horizon should scan the environment for ten years. Presumably, then, a multiproduct, multimarket company should have different time horizons for environmental scanning. Using this rule of thumb, a company can be sure not only of discovering relevant trends and their impact on its products/markets but also of implementing necessary changes in its strategy to marshal opportunities provided by the environment and to avert environmental threats.

Discussed below are the major problems companies face in the context of environmental scanning. Many of these problems are, in fact, dilemmas that may be attributed to a lack of theoretical frameworks on the subject.

1. The environment per se is too broad to be tracked by an organization; thus, it is necessary to separate the relevant from the irrelevant environment. Separating the relevant from the irrelevant may not be easy since, in terms of perceptible realities, the environment of all large corporations is as broad as the world itself. Therefore, a company needs to determine what criteria to develop to select information on a practical basis.
2. Another problem is concerned with determining the impact of an environmental trend, that is, with determining its meaning for business. For example, what does the feminist movement mean for a company's sales and new business opportunities?
3. Even if the relevance of a trend and its impact are determined, making forecasts of the trend poses another problem. For example, how many women will be in managerial positions ten years from now?
4. A variety of organizational problems hinder environmental scanning. Presumably, managers are the company's ears and eyes and therefore should be good sources for perceiving, studying, and channeling pertinent information within the organization. But managers are usually so tied up mentally and

physically within their specific roles that they simply ignore happenings in the environment. The structuring of organizations by specialized functions can be blamed for this problem to a certain extent. In addition, organizations often lack a formal system for receiving, analyzing, and finally disseminating environmental information to decision points.

5. Environmental scanning requires "blue sky" thinking and "ivory tower" working patterns to encourage creativity, but such work perspectives are often not justifiable in the midst of corporate culture.

6. Frequently top managers, because of their own values, consider dabbling in the future a waste of resources; therefore, they adopt unkind attitudes toward such projects.

7. Many companies, as a matter of corporate strategy, like to wait and see; therefore, they let industry leaders, the ones who want to be first in the field, act on their behalf.

8. Lack of normative approaches on environmental scanning is another problem.

9. Often, a change is too out of the way. It may be perceived, but its relationship to the company is not conceivable.

10. It is also problematic to decide what department of the organization should be responsible for environmental scanning. Should marketing research undertake environmental scanning? How about the strategic planning office? Who else should participate? Is it possible to divide the work? For example, the SBUs may concentrate on their products, product lines, markets, and industry. The corporate level may deal with the rest of the information.

11. Often, information is gathered that is overlapping, leading to a waste of resources. There are frequently informational gaps that require duplication of effort.

SUMMARY

The environment is ever-changing and complex; thus firms must constantly scan and monitor it. Environmental scanning may be undertaken at three levels in the organization: corporate level, SBU level, and product/market level. This chapter approaches scanning primarily from the SBU viewpoint. The environments discussed are technological, political, economic, social, and regulatory.

Environmental scanning evolves over a long haul. It is sufficient, therefore, to make a humble beginning rather than designing a fully structured system.

The impact of different environments on marketing strategy was illustrated by numerous examples. A step-by-step procedure for scanning the environment was outlined. A systematic approach to environmental scanning, using such techniques as trend-impact analysis, cross-impact analysis, and the delphi method, was illustrated. Feasible organizational arrangements for environmental scanning were examined, and problems that companies face in their scanning endeavors were discussed.

DISCUSSION QUESTIONS

1. Explain the meaning of environmental scanning. Which constituents of the environment, from the viewpoint of a corporation, require scanning? /05

2. Illustrate with examples the relevance of technological, political, economic, social, and regulatory environments in the context of marketing strategy.

3. Who in the organization should be responsible for scanning the environment? What role may consultants play in helping corporations in their environmental scanning activity?

4. Explain the use of trend-impact analysis and cross-impact analysis with reference to environmental scanning.

5. How may the delphi technique be useful in the context of environmental scanning? Give an example.

6. What types of responsibilities should be assigned to the person in charge of environmental scanning?

7. How may managers be involved in environmental scanning?

NOTES

[1] Richard Gibson, "Super-Cheap and Midpriced Eateries Bite Fast-Food Chains from Both Sides," *Wall Street Journal* (22 June 1990): B1.

[2] Joseph L. Bower and Clayton M. Christensen, "Disruptive Technologies: Catching the Wave," *Harvard Business Review* (January–February 1995): 43–53.

[3] George S. Day, "Continuous Learning About Markets," *California Management Review* (Summer 1994): 9–31.

[4] Francis Joseph Aguilar, *Scanning the Business Environment* (New York: Macmillan Co., 1967): 40.

[5] Subhash C. Jain, "Environmental Scanning: How the Best Companies Do It," *Long Range Planning* (April 1984): 117–28.

[6] Harold E. Klein and Robert E. Linneman, "Environmental Assessment: An International Study of Corporate Practice," *Journal of Business Strategy* (Summer 1984): 66–92. Also see Anil Menon and P. Rajan Varadarajan, "A Model of Marketing Knowledge Use Within Firms," *Journal of Marketing* (October 1992): 53–71.

[7] "Shop-Till-You-Drop at the Touch Of a Button," *Financial Times* (9 June 1994): 11.

[8] "Gambling on the Air," *The Economist* (21 August 1993): 49.

[9] Alan Deutschman, "Scramble on the Information Highway," *Fortune* (7 February 1994): 129.

[10] Richard N. Foster, *Innovation: The Attacker's Advantage* (New York: Summit Books, 1986).

[11] "Electric Cars in California," *Business Week* (1 October 1990): 40.

[12] "Will the Auto Glut Choke Detroit?" *Business Week* (7 March 1988): 54.

[13] Anne B. Fisher, "What Consumers Want in the 1990s," *Fortune* (29 January 1990): 108.

[14] Howard Schlossberg, "Report Says Environmental Marketing Claims Level Off," *Marketing News* (May 24, 1993): 12.

[15] J. Brooke Aker and Cornelia Hanbury, "The Changing Concept of Home," *The Futures Group Outlook* (December 1994): 2.

[16] "Real Men Buy Paper Towels, Too," *Business Week* (9 November 1992): 75.

[17] See Stan Rapp and Thomas L. Collins, *Beyond Maxi-Marketing: The New Power of Caring And Daring* (New York: McGraw-Hill, Inc., 1994), 10–11.

[18] "The Time Compressed Shopper," *Marketing Insights* (Summer 1991): 36.

[19] *Time* (7 March 1988): 84.

[20] "Yolkless Dunkin Donuts," *Business Week* (8 April 1991): 70.

[21] Richard Gibson, "Lean and Mean: Hardee's Joins Low-Fat Fray," *Wall Street Journal* (15 July 1991): B1. Also see Eleena De Lisser, "Taco Bell, Low-Price King, Will Offer Low-Fat Line," *Wall Street Journal* (6 February 1995): B1.

[22] John B. Hinge, "Some Companies Serve Up Lighter Liquor," *Wall Street Journal* (25 April 1991): B1. See also "Changing the Game," *Marketing Insights* (Summer 1990): 68–81.

[23] Trish Hall, "Americans Drink Less, and Makers of Alcohol Feel a Little Woozy," *Wall Street Journal* (14 March 1984): 1; and Allan Luks, "Dealcoholized Beverages: Changing the Way Americans Drink," *The Futurist* (October 1982): 44–49. See also "The Spirited Battle for Those Who Want to Drink Light," *Business Week* (16 June 1986): 84; and Michael Rogers, "A Sales Kick from Beer without the Buzz," *Fortune* (23 June 1986): 89.

[24] Murray L. Weidenbaum, "The Future of Business/Government Relations in the United States," in *The Future of Business*, ed. Max Ways (New York: Pergamon Press, 1978), 50. See also Robert Reich, "The Fourth Wave of Regulation," *Across the Board* (May 1982).

[25] "Procter & Gamble: On a Short Leash," *Business Week* (22 July 1991): 76.

[26] Paul B. Carroll, "Computer-Ordering Method Helps Newcomer Blossom," *Wall Street Journal* (22 January 1991): B2. See also Bill Saportio, "Are IBM and Sears Crazy? or Canny?" *Fortune* (28 September 1987): 74.

[27] See R. T. Lenz and Jack L. Engledow, "Environmental Analysis Units and Strategic Decision-Making: A Field Study of Selected Leading-Edge Corporations," *Strategic Management Journal* 7 (1986): 69–89. See also *TFG Reports* (November 1990).

APPENDIX | *Scanning Techniques*

Traditionally, environmental scanning has been implemented mainly with the use of conventional methods, including marketing research, economic indicators, demand forecasting, and industry studies. But the use of such conventional techniques for environmental scanning is not without pitfalls. These techniques have failed to provide reliable insights into the future. Discussed below are a variety of new techniques that have been adapted for use in environmental scanning.

Extrapolation Procedures

These procedures require the use of information from the past to explore the future. Obviously, their use assumes that the future is some function of the past. There are a variety of extrapolation procedures that range from a simple estimate of the future (based on past information) to regression analysis.

Historical Analogy

Where past data cannot be used to scan an environmental phenomenon, the phenomenon may be studied by establishing historical parallels with other phenomena. Assumed here is the availability of sufficient information on other phenomena. Turning points in the progression of these phenomena become guideposts for predicting the behavior of the phenomenon under study.

Intuitive Reasoning

This technique bases the future on the "rational feel" of the scanner. Intuitive reasoning requires free thinking unconstrained by past experience and personal biases. This technique, therefore, may provide better results when used by free-lance think tanks than when used by managers on the job.

Scenario Building	This technique calls for developing a time-ordered sequence of events bearing a logical cause-and-effect relationship to one another. The ultimate forecast is based on multiple contingencies, each with its respective probability of occurrence.
Cross-Impact Matrices	When two different trends in the environment point toward conflicting futures, this technique may be used to study these trends simultaneously for their effect. As the name implies, this technique uses a two-dimensional matrix, arraying one trend along the rows and the other along the columns. Some of the features of cross-impact analyses that make them attractive for strategic planning are (a) they can accommodate all types of eventualities (social or technological, quantitative or qualitative, and binary events or continuous functions), (b) they rapidly discriminate important from unimportant sequences of developments, and (c) their underlying rationale is fully retraceable from the analysis.
Morphological Analysis	This technique requires identification of all possible ways to achieve an objective. For example, the technique can be employed to anticipate innovations and to develop optimum configurations for a particular mission or task.
Network Models	There are two types of network methods: contingency trees and relevance trees. A contingency tree is simply a graphical display of logical relationships among environmental trends that focuses on branch-points where several alternative outcomes are possible. A relevance tree is a logical network similar to a contingency tree but is drawn in a way that assigns degrees of importance to various environmental trends with reference to an outcome.
Missing-Link Approach	The missing-link approach combines morphological analysis and the network method. Many developments and innovations that appear promising and marketable may be held back because something is missing. Under these circumstances, this technique may be used to scan new trends to see if they provide answers to any missing links.
Model Building	This technique emphasizes the construction of models following deductive or inductive procedures. Two types of models may be constructed: phenomenological models and analytic models. Phenomenological models identify trends as a basis for prediction but make no attempt to explain underlying causes. Analytic models seek to identify underlying causes of change so that future developments may be forecast on the basis of a knowledge of their causes.
Delphi Technique	The delphi technique is the systematic solicitation of expert opinion. Based on reiteration and feedback, this technique gathers opinions of a panel of experts on happenings in the environment.

Strategic Capabilities and Direction

Measuring Strengths and Weaknesses

A business does not perform well by accident. Good performances occur because the people directing the affairs of the business interact well with the environment, capitalizing on its strengths and eliminating underlying weaknesses. In other words, to operate successfully in a changing environment, the business should plan its future objectives and strategies around its strengths and downplay moves that bear on its weaknesses. Thus, assessment of strengths and weaknesses becomes an essential task in the strategic process.

In this chapter, a framework will be presented for identifying and describing a business's strengths and weaknesses. The framework also provides a systematic scheme for an objective appraisal of the performance and strategic moves of the marketing side of business.

The appraisal of the marketing function has traditionally been pursued in the form of a marketing audit that stresses the review of current problems. From the strategic point of view, the review should go further to include the future as well.

Strengths and weaknesses in the context of marketing are relative phenomena. Strengths today may become weaknesses tomorrow and vice versa. This is why a penetrating look at the different aspects of a business's marketing program is essential. This chapter is directed toward these ends—searching for opportunities and the means for exploiting them and identifying weaknesses and the ways in which they may be eliminated.

MEANING OF STRENGTHS AND WEAKNESSES

Strengths refer to the competitive advantages and other distinctive competencies that a company can exert in the marketplace. Andrews notes that "the distinctive competence of an organization is more than what it can do; it is what it can do particularly well."[1] **Weaknesses** are constraints that hinder movements in certain directions. For example, a business short of cash cannot afford to undertake a large-scale promotional offensive. In developing marketing strategy, the business should, among other things, dig deeply into its skills and competencies and chart its future in accordance with these competencies.

As an example, in many businesses, service—speed, efficiency, personal attention—makes a crucial difference in gaining leverage in the marketplace.

Companies that score higher than their rivals in the category of service have a real competitive strength. McDonald's may not be everyone's idea of the best place in town to dine, but at its level, McDonald's provides a quality of service that is the envy of the industry. Whether at a McDonald's in a rural community or in the downtown area of a large city, the customer gets exactly the same service. Every McDonald's employee is supposed to strictly follow the rules. Cooks must turn, never flip, hamburgers one, never two, at a time. If they haven't been purchased, Big Macs must be discarded ten minutes after being cooked; french fries after seven minutes. Cashiers must make eye contact with and smile at every customer.

Similarly, visitors to Disney World come home impressed with its cleanliness and with the courtesy and competence of the staff. The Disney World management works hard to make sure that the 14,200 employees are, as described in a *Fortune* article, "people who fulfill an expectation of wholesomeness, always smiling, always warm, forever positive in their approach."[2]

STUDYING STRENGTHS AND WEAKNESSES: STATE OF THE ART

A systematic scheme for analyzing strengths and weaknesses is still in embryonic form.[3] One finds few scholarly works on the subject of strengths and weaknesses. An interesting study on the subject was done by Stevenson, who examined six companies.[4] He was interested in the process of defining strengths and weaknesses in the context of strategic planning. He was concerned with the company attributes examined, the organizational scope of the strengths and weaknesses identified, the measurement employed in the process of definition, the criteria used for distinguishing a strength from a weakness, and the sources of information used. Exhibit 7-1 illustrates the process in detail.

Companies should make targeted efforts to identify their competitive strengths and weaknesses. This is a far from easy process, however. Many companies, especially the large ones, have only the vaguest notion of the nature and degree of the competencies that they may possess. The sheer multiplicity of production stages and the overlapping among product lines hinder clear-cut assessment of the competitive strength of a single product line. Despite such problems, development of competitive strategy depends on having a complete perspective on strengths and weaknesses. Success requires putting the best foot forward.

Unique strengths may lie in different areas of the business and may impact the entire company. Stevenson found a general lack of agreement on suitable definitions, criteria, and information used to measure strengths and weaknesses. In addition to the procedural difficulties faced by managers in their attempts to measure strengths and weaknesses, the need for situational analysis, the need for self-protection, the desire to preserve the status quo, and the problems of definition and computational capacity complicated the process. Stevenson makes the following suggestions for improvement of the process of defining strengths and weaknesses. The manager should

- Recognize that the process of defining strengths and weaknesses is primarily an aid to the individual manager in the accomplishment of his or her task.

EXHIBIT 7-1
Steps in the Process of Assessing Strengths and Weaknesses

Which Attributes Can Be Examined?	With What Organizational Entity Is the Manager Concerned?	What Types of Measurements Can the Manager Make?	What Criteria Are Applicable to Judge a Strength or a Weakness?	How Can the Manager Get the Information to Make These Assessments?
Organizational structure	The corporation	Measure the existence of an attribute	Historical experience of the company	Personal observation
Major policies	Groups	Measure an attribute's efficiency	Intracompany competition	Customer contacts
Top manager's skills	Division	Measure an attribute's effectiveness	Direct competitors	Experience
Information system	Departments		Other companies	Control system documents
Operation procedures	Individual employees		Consultant's opinions	Meetings
Planning system			Normative judgments based on management's understanding of literature	Planning system documents
Employee attitudes			Personal opinions	Employees
Manager's attitudes			Specific targets of accomplishment, such as budgets, etc.	Subordinate managers
Union agreements				Superordinate managers
Technical skills				Peers
Research skills				Published documents
New product ideas				Competitive intelligence
Production facilities				Board members
Demographic characteristics of personnel				Consultants
Distribution network				Journals
Sales force's skill				Books
Breadth of product line				Magazines
Quality control procedures				Professional meetings
Stock market reputation				Government economic indicators
Knowledge of consumer's needs				
Market domination				

Source: Reprinted from "Defining Corporate Strengths and Weaknesses," by Howard H. Stevenson, *Sloan Management Review*, Vol. 17, No. 3 (Spring, 1976), p. 54, by permission of the publisher. Copyright © 1976 by Sloan Management Review Association. All rights reserved.

- Develop lists of critical areas for examination that are tailored to the responsibility and authority of each individual manager.
- Make the measures and the criteria to be used in evaluation of strengths and weaknesses explicit so that managers can make their evaluations against a common framework.
- Recognize the important strategic role of defining attributes as opposed to efficiency or effectiveness.
- Understand the difference in the use of identified strengths and identified weaknesses.[5]

Despite the primitive state of the art, today many more companies review their strengths and weaknesses in the process of developing strategic plans than did 10 years ago. Strengths and weaknesses may be found in the functional areas of the business, or they may result from some unusual interaction of functions. The following example illustrates how a study of strengths and weaknesses may uncover opportunities that might otherwise have not been conceived. A national distiller and marketer of whiskeys may possess such strengths as sophistication in natural commodity trading associated with its grain purchasing procedures; knowledge of complex warehousing procedures and inventory control; ability and connections associated with dealing in state political structures (i.e., state liquor stores, licensing agencies, and so on); marketing experience associated with diverse wholesale and retail outlets; and advertising experience in creating brand images. If these strengths are properly analyzed with a view to seeking diversification opportunities, it appears that the distiller has unique abilities for successfully entering the business of selling building products, such as wood flooring or siding and composition board. The distiller's experience in commodity trading can be transferred to trading in lumber; its experience in dealing with political groups can be used to gain building code acceptances; and its experience in marketing can apply to wholesalers (e.g., hardware stores and do-it-yourself centers) of building products.

The case of XYZ Corporation, on the other hand, illustrates how a company can get into trouble if it does not carefully consider its strengths and weaknesses. XYZ was a Northfield, Illinois, company with a penchant for diversifying into businesses that were in vogue in the stock market. Until it was reorganized as the Lori Corporation in 1985, it had been in the following businesses: office copying machines, mobile homes, jewelry, speedboats and cabin cruisers, computers, video recording systems, and small buses. Despite entry into some glamorous fields, XYZ did not share the growth and profits that other companies in some of these fields achieved. This is because XYZ entered new and diverse businesses without relating its moves to its basic skills and competencies. For example, despite the fact that it was the first company to develop a photocopy process, developing its process even before Xerox, its total market share for all types of copier machines and supplies in 1984 was well under 3 percent. XYZ Corporation could not keep pace with technological improvements nor with service on installed machines, an essential competency in the copier business. In addition, it overextended itself so much so that managerial controls were rendered inadequate. The company finally got out of all its. *trendy* businesses and was reorganized in 1985 to design, manufacture, and distribute costume jewelry, fashion jewelry, and fashion accessories.[6]

SYSTEMATIC MEASUREMENT OF STRENGTHS AND WEAKNESSES

The strengths and weaknesses of a business can be measured at different levels in the organization: corporate, SBU, and product/market level. The thrust of this chapter is on the measurement of strengths and weaknesses at the SBU level. However, as the strengths and weaknesses of the SBU are a composite of the strengths and weaknesses of different products/markets, the major portion of the discussion will be devoted to the measurement of the marketing strengths and weaknesses of a product/market.

Exhibit 7-2 illustrates the factors that require examination in order to delineate the strengths and weaknesses of a product/market. These factors, along with competitive perspectives, describe the strengths and weaknesses of the product.

Current Strategic Posture

Current strategic posture constitutes a very important variable in developing future strategy. Although it is difficult and painful to try to understand current strategy if formal planning has not been done in the past, it is worth the effort to probe current strategy to achieve a good beginning in strategic planning.

The emphasis here is on the study of the current strategy of a product/market. Before undertaking such a study, however, it is desirable to assess company-wide perspectives by raising such questions as

1. What underlies our company's success, given competitor's patterns of doing business?
2. Are there any characteristics and traits that have been followed regularly?
3. To what strategic posture do these characteristics and traits lead?
4. What are the critical factors that could make a difference in the success of the strategy?
5. To what extent are critical factors likely to undergo a change? What may be the direction of change?

These questions cannot be answered entirely objectively; they call for creative responses. Managers often disagree on various issues. For example, the vice president of marketing of a company that had recently made a heavy investment in sales training considered this investment to be a critical success factor. He thought a well-trained sales staff was crucial for developing new business. On the other hand, the vice president of finance saw only that the investment in training had increased overhead. Though disagreements of this sort are inevitable, a review of current strategy is very important. The operational scheme for studying current strategy from the point of view of the entire corporation outlined below has been found useful.

1. Begin with an identification of the actual current scope of the company's activities. The delineation of customer/product/market emphasis and concentration will give an indication of what kind of a company the company is currently.

EXHIBIT 7-2
Measurement of Product Strengths and Weaknesses

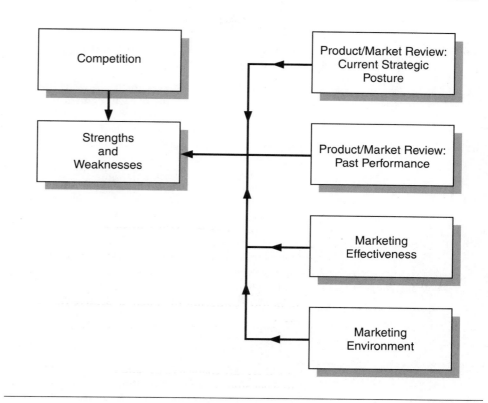

2. An analysis of current scope should be followed by identification of the pattern of actual past and existing resource deployments. This description will show which functions and activities receive the greatest management emphasis and where the greatest sources of strength currently lie.
3. Given the identification of scope and deployment patterns, an attempt should be made to deduce the actual basis on which the company has been competing. Such <u>competitive advantages or distinctive competencies represent the central core of present performance and future opportunities.</u>
4. Next, on the basis of observation of key management personnel, the actual performance criteria (specifications), emphasis, and priorities that have governed strategic choices in the past should be determined.

Current Strategy of a Product/Market   As far as marketing is concerned, the strategy for a product is formulated around one or more marketing mix variables. In examining present strategy, the purpose is to pinpoint those perspectives of the marketing mix that currently dominate strategy. The current strategy of a product may be examined by seeking answers to the following two questions:

1. What markets do we have?
2. How is each market served?

What Markets Do We Have? Answering this question involves consideration of several aspects of the market:

1. Recognize different market segments in which the product is sold.
2. Build a demographic profile of each segment.
3. Identify important customers in each segment.
4. Identify those customers who, while important, also do business with competitors.
5. Identify reasons each important customer may have for buying the product from us. These reasons may be economic (e.g., lower prices), functional (e.g., product features not available in competing products), and psychological (e.g., "this perfume matches my individual chemistry").
6. Analyze the strategic perspective of each important customer as it concerns the purchase of our product. This analysis is relevant primarily for business customers. For example, an aluminum company should attempt to study the strategy of a can manufacturer as far as its aluminum can business is concerned. Suppose that the price of aluminum is consistently rising and more and more can manufacturers are replacing all-aluminum cans with cans of a new alloy of plastic and paper. Such strategic perspectives of an important customer should be examined.
7. Consider changes in each customer's perspectives that may occur in the next few years. These changes may become necessary because of shifts in the customer's environment (both internal and external), abilities, and resources.

If properly analyzed, information concerning what markets a company has should provide insight into why customers buy the company's products and how likely it is that they will do business with the company in the future. For example, a paper manufacturer discovered that most of his customers did business with him because, in their opinion, his delivery schedules were more flexible than those of other suppliers. The quality of his paper might have been superior, too, but this was not strategically important to his customers.

How Is Each Market Served? The means the company employs to serve different customers may be studied by analyzing the information contained in Exhibit 7-3. A careful examination of this information will reveal the current strategy the company utilizes to serve its main markets. For example, analysis of the information in Exhibit 7-3 may reveal the following facts pertaining to a breakfast cereal: Of the seven different segments in the market, the product is extremely popular in two segments. Customers buy the product mainly for health reasons or because of a desire to consume "natural" foods. This desire is strong enough for customers to pay a premium price for the product. Further, customers are willing to make a trip to another store (other than their regular grocery store) to buy this product. Different promotional devices keep customers conscious of the "natural" ingredients in the product. This analysis may point toward the following strategy for the product:

EXHIBIT 7-3
Information for Recognizing Present Market Strategy

1. Basis for segmenting the market.
2. Definition of the markets for the product.
3. Profile of customers in each segment: age, income level, occupation, geographical location, etc.
4. Scope and dimensions of each market: size, profitability, etc.
5. Expected rate of growth of each segment.
6. Requirements for success in each market.
7. Market standing with established customers in each segment: market share, pattern of repeat business, expansion of customer's product use.
8. Benefits that customers in different segments derive from the product: economics, better performance, displaceable costs, etc.
9. Reasons for buying the product in different segments: product features, awareness, price, advertising, promotion, packaging, display, sales assistance, etc.
10. Customer attitudes in different segments: brand awareness, brand image (mapping), etc.
11. Overall reputation of the product in each segment.
12. Purchase or use habits that contribute to these attitudes.
13. Reasons that reinforce customer's faith in the company and product.
14. Reasons that force customers to turn elsewhere for help in using the product.
15. Life-cycle status of the product.
16. Story of the product line: quality development, delivery, service.
17. Product research and improvements planned.
18. Market share: overall and in different segments.
19. Deficiencies in serving or assisting customers in using the product.
20. Possibility of reducing services in areas where customers are becoming more self-sufficient.
21. Resource base: nature of emerging and developing resources—technical, marketing, financial—that could expand or open new markets for the product.
22. Geographic coverage of the product market.
23. Identification of principal channels: dealer or class of trade.
24. Buying habits and attitudes of these channels.
25. Sales history through each type of channel.
26. Industry sales by type of outlet: retail, wholesale, institutional; and by major types of outlets within each area: department store, chain store, specialty store, etc.
27. Overall price structure for the product.
28. Trade discount policy.
29. Variations in price in different segments.
30. Frequency of price changes.
31. Promotional deals offered for the product.
32. Emphasis on different advertising media.
33. Major thrust of advertising copy.
34. Sales tips or promotional devices used by salespeople.

1. Concentrate on limited segments.
2. Emphasize the naturalness of the product as its unique attribute.
3. Keep the price high.
4. Pull the product through with heavy doses of consumer advertising.

Where strategy in the past has not been systematically formulated, recognition of current strategy will be more difficult. In this case, strategy must be inferred from the perspectives of different marketing decisions.

Past Performance   Evaluation of past performance is invaluable in measuring strengths and weaknesses because it provides historical insights into a company's marketing strategy and its success. Historical examination should not be limited to simply noting the directions that the company adopted and the results it achieved but should also include a search for reasons for these results. Exhibit 7-4 shows the type of information that is helpful in measuring past performance.

Strategically, the following three types of analysis should be undertaken to measure past performance: product performance profile, market performance profile, and financial performance profile. Information used for developing a product performance profile is shown in Exhibit 7-5. A product may contribute to company performance in six different ways: through profitability, image of product leadership, furnishing a base for further technological growth, support of total product line, utilization of company resources (e.g., utilization of excess plant capacity), and provision of customer benefits (vis-à-vis the price paid). An example of this last type of contribution is a product that is a small but indispensable part of another product or process with low cost relative to the value of the finished product. Tektronics, a manufacturer of oscilloscopes, is an example. An oscilloscope is sold along with a computer. It is used to help install the computer, to test it, and to monitor its performance. The cost of the oscilloscope is small when one considers the essential role it plays in the use of the much more expensive computer.

A market performance profile is illustrated in Exhibit 7-6. In analyzing how well a company is doing in the segments it serves, a good place to begin is with the marginal profit contribution of each customer or customer group. Other measures used are market share, growth of end user markets, size of customer base, distribution strength, and degree of customer loyalty. Of all these, only distribution strength requires some explanation. Distribution and dealer networks can greatly influence a company's performance because it takes an enormous effort to cultivate dealers' loyalty and get repeat business from them. Distribution strength, therefore, can make a significant difference in overall performance.

The real value of a strategy must be reflected in financial gains and market achievements. To measure financial performance, four standards may be employed for comparison: (a) the company's performance, (b) competitor's performance, (c) management expectations, and (d) performance in terms of resources committed. With these standards, for the purposes of marketing strategy, financial performance can be measured with respect to the following variables:

EXHIBIT 7-4
Information for Measuring Past Performance

The Consumer

Identify if possible the current "light," "moderate," and "heavy" users of the product in terms of

1. Recent trends in percentage of brand's volume accounted for by each group.
2. The characteristics of each group as to sex, age, income, occupation, income group, and geographical location.
3. Attitudes toward the product and category and copy appeals most persuasive to each group.

The Product

Identify the current consumer preference of the brand versus primary competition (and secondary competition, if available), according to

1. Light, moderate, and heavy usage (if available).
2. The characteristics of each group as to sex, age, income, occupation, income group, geographical location, size of family, etc.

Shipment History

Identify the recent shipment trends of the brand by total units and units/M population (brand development), according to districts, regions, and nation.

Spending History

Identify the recent spending trends on the brand by total dollars, dollar/M population, and per unit sold for advertising, for promotion, and for total advertising and promotion by districts, regions, and nation.

Profitability History

Identify the recent trends of list price, average retail price (by sales areas), gross profit margins, and profit before taxes (PBT), *in addition* to trends in

1. Gross profit as a percentage of net sales.
2. Total marketing as percentage of gross profit and per unit sold.
3. PBT as a percentage of net sales and per unit sold.
4. ROFE (Return of Funds Employed) for each recent fiscal year.

Share of Market History

Identify recent trends of

1. The brand's share of market nationally, regionally, and district-wide.
2. Consumption by total units and percentage gain/loss versus year ago nationally, regionally, and district-wide.
3. Distribution by pack size nationally, regionally, and district-wide.

Where applicable, trends in all of the above data should also be identified by store classification: chain versus independent (large, medium, and small).

Total Market History

Identify recent trends of the total market in terms of units and percentage gain/loss versus year ago nationally, regionally, and district-wide per M population, store type, county size, type of user (exclusive versus partial user), retail price trends, and by user characteristics (age, income, etc.).

EXHIBIT 7-4
continued

Competitive History (Major Brands), Where Available
Identify significant competitive trends in share; consumption levels by sales areas and store types; media and promotion expenditures; types of media and promotion; retail price differentials; etc

---

1. Growth rate (percentage).
2. Profitability (percentage), that is, rate of return on investment.
3. Market share (percentage as compared with that of principal competitors).
4. Cash flow.

It is desirable to analyze financial performance for a number of years to determine the historical trend of performance. To show how financial performance analysis may figure in formulating marketing strategy, consider the following excerpt from a study on the subject:

> A maker of confectioneries that offers more than one hundred brands, flavors and packagings, prunes its lines—regularly and routinely—of those items having the lowest profit contribution, sales volume, and vitality for future growth. . . .
>
> Each individual product has been ranked on these three factors, and an "index of gross profitability" has been prepared for each in conjunction with annual marketing plans. These plans take into account longer-term objectives for the business, trends in consumer wants and expectations, competitive factors in the marketplace and, lastly, a deliberately ordered "prioritization" of the company's resources. Sales and profit performance are then checked against projected targets at regular intervals through the year, and the indexes of gross profitability are adjusted when necessary.
>
> The firm's chief executive emphasizes that even individual items whose indexes of profitability are ranked at the very bottom are nonetheless profitable and paying their way by any customary standard of return on sales and investment. But the very lowest-ranking items are regularly reviewed; and, on a judgmental basis, some are marked for pruning at the next convenient opportunity. This opportunity is most likely to arrive when stocks of special ingredients and packaging labels for the items have been exhausted.

EXHIBIT 7-5
Product Performance Profile Contribution to Company Performance

Product Line	Profit-ability	Product Leader-ship	Techno-logical Growth	Support of Total Product Line	Utiliza-tion of Company Resources	Provision of Customer Benefits
- - - -						
- - - -						
- - - -						
- - - -						

EXHIBIT 7-6
Market Performance Profile Contribution to Company Performance

Market Segments	Profit-ability	Market Share	Growth of End User Markets	Size of Customer Base	Distribu-tion Strength	Degree of Customer Loyalty
- - - -						
- - - -						
- - - -						
- - - -						

In a recent year, the company dropped 16 items that were judged to be too low on its index of gross profitability. Calculated and selective pruning is regarded within the company as a healthy means of working toward the best possible mix of products at all times. It has the reported advantages of increasing efficiencies in manufacturing as a result of cutting the "down time" between small runs, reducing inventories, and freeing resources for the expansion of the most promising items—or the development of new ones—without having to expand productive capacity. Another important benefit is that the sales force concentrates on a smaller line containing only the most profitable products with the largest volumes. On the negative side, however, it is acknowledged that pruning, as the company practices it, may result in near-term loss of sales for a line until growth of the rest of the items can compensate.[7]

Appraising Marketing Excellence

Marketing is concerned with the activities required to facilitate the exchange process toward managing demand. The perspectives of these activities are founded on marketing strategy. To develop a strategy, a company needs a philosophical orientation. Four different types of orientation may be considered: manufacturing, sales, technology, and marketing. Manufacturing orientation emphasizes a physical product or a service and assumes that the customer will be pleased with it if it has been well conceived and developed. Sales orientation focuses on promoting the product to make the customer want it. The thrust of technology orientation is on reaching the customer through new and varied products made feasible through technological innovations. Under marketing orientation, first the customer group that the firm wishes to serve is designated. Then the requirements of the target group are carefully examined. These requirements become the basis of product or service conception and development, pricing, promotion, and distribution. Exhibit 7-7 contrasts marketing-oriented companies with manufacturing-, sales-, and technology-oriented firms.

An examination of Exhibit 7-7 shows that good marketers should think like general managers. Their approach should be unconstrained by functional boundaries. Without neglecting either near- or medium-term profitability, they should concentrate on building a position for tomorrow.[8]

Despite the lip service that has been paid to marketing for more than 30 years, it remains one of the most misunderstood functions of a business. According to Canning, only a few corporations, Procter & Gamble, Citibank, Avon, McDonald's, Emerson Electric, and Merck, for example, really understand

EXHIBIT 7-7
Comparison of Four Kinds of Companies

	Orientation			
	Manufacturing	*Sales*	*Technology*	*Marketing*
Typical strategy	Lower cost	Increase	Push research	Build share profitability
Normal structure	Functional	Functional or profit centers	Profit centers	Market or product or brand; decentralized profit responsibility
Key systems	Plant P&L's Budgets	Sales forecasts Results vs. plan	Performance tests R&D plans	Marketing plans
Traditional skills	Engineering	Sales	Science and engineering	Analysis
Normal focus	Internal efficiencies	Distribution channels; short-term sales results	Product performance	Consumers Market share
Typical response to competitive pressure	Cut costs	Cut price Sell harder	Improve product	Consumer research, planning, resting, refining
Overall mental set	"What we need to do in this company is get our costs down and our quality up."	"Where can I sell what we make?"	"The best product wins the day."	"What will the consumer buy that we profitably make?"

Source: Edward G. Michaels, "Marketing Muscle: Who Needs It?" *Business Horizons*, May–June, 1982, p. 72. © 1982 by the foundation for the School of Business at Indiana University. Reprinted by permission.

and practice true marketing.[9] Inasmuch as marketing orientation is a prerequisite for developing a successful marketing strategy, it behooves a company to thoroughly examine its marketing orientation. The following checklist of 10 questions provides a quick self-test for a company that wants a rough measure of its marketing capabilities.

- Has your company carefully segmented the various segments of the consumer market that it serves?
- Do you routinely measure the profitability of your key products or services in each of these consumer market segments?
- Do you use market research to keep abreast of the needs, preferences, and buying habits of consumers in each segment?

- Have you identified the key buying factors in each segment, and do you know how your company compares with its competitors on these factors?
- Is the impact of environmental trends (demographic, competitive, lifestyle, governmental) on your business carefully gauged?
- Does your company prepare and use an annual marketing plan?
- Is the concept of "marketing investment" understood—and practiced—in your company?
- Is profit responsibility for a product line pushed below the senior management level?
- Does your organization "talk" marketing?
- Did one of the top five executives in your company come up through marketing?

The number of yes answers to these questions determines the marketing orientation of a company. For example, a score of nine or ten yes answers would mean that the company has a strong marketing capability; six to eight would indicate that the firm is on the way; and fewer than six yes answers would stress that the firm is vulnerable to marketing-minded competitors. Essentially, truly marketing-oriented firms are consumer oriented, take an integrated approach to planning, look further ahead, and have highly developed marketing systems. In such firms, marketing dominates the corporate culture. A marketing-oriented culture is beneficial in creating sustainable competitive advantage. It becomes one of the internal strengths an organization possesses that is hard to imitate, is more durable, not transparent nor transferable.[10]

This analysis reveals the overall marketing effectiveness of the company and highlights the areas that are weak and require management action. Management may take appropriate action—management training, reorganization, or installation of measures designed to yield improvements with or without the help of consultants. If weaknesses cannot be addressed, the company must live with them, and the marketing strategist should take note of them in the process of outlining the business's future direction. A marketing orientation perspective of a firm largely reflects its marketing excellence.

Marketing Environment

Chapter 6 was devoted to scanning the environment at the macro level. This section looks at the environment from the product/market perspective. Environmental scanning at the macro level is the job of a staff person positioned at the corporate, division, group, or business unit level. The person concerned may go by any of these titles: corporate planner, environmental analyst, environmental scanner, strategic planner, or marketing researcher.

Monitoring the environment from the viewpoint of products/markets is a line function that should be carried out by those involved in making marketing decisions because product/market managers, being in close touch with various marketing aspects of the product/market, are in a better position to read between the lines and make meaningful interpretations of the environment. The constituents of the product/market environment are social and cultural effects, political influences, ethical considerations, legal requirements, competition, economic climate, technological changes, institutional evolution, consumerism, population, location of consumers, income, expenditure patterns, and education. Not all aspects of the environment are relevant for every product/market. The scanner, therefore, should first choose which parts of the environment influence the product/market before attempting to monitor them.

The strategic significance of the product/market environment is well illustrated by the experience of Fanny Farmer Candy Shops, a familiar name in the candy industry. Review of the environment in the mid-1980s showed that Americans were watching their waistlines but that they were also indulging in chocolate. In 1983, the average American ate nearly 18 pounds of confections—up from a low of 16 pounds in 1975. Since the mid-1980s, the market for upscale chocolates has been growing rapidly. Chocolates are again popular gifts for dinner parties, providing a new opportunity for candy makers, who traditionally relied on Valentine's Day, Easter, and Christmas for over half of their annual sales.

Equipped with this analysis of the environment, Fanny Farmer decided to become a dominant competitor in the upscale segment. It introduced rich new specialty chocolates at $14 to $20 per pound, just below $25-per-pound designer chocolates (a market dominated by Godiva, a subsidiary of Campbell Soup Co., and imports such as Perugina of Italy) and above Russell Stover and Fannie May candies, whose chocolates averaged $10 per pound. The company thinks that its new strategic thrust will advance its position in the candy market, though implementing this strategy will require overcoming a variety of problems.[11]

ANALYZING STRENGTHS AND WEAKNESSES

The study of competition, current strategic perspectives, past performance, marketing effectiveness, and marketing environment provides insights into information necessary for designating strengths and weaknesses. Exhibit 7-8 provides a rundown of areas of strength as far as marketing is concerned. Where feasible, strengths should be stated in objective terms. Exhibit 7-8 is not an all-inclusive list, but it indicates the kind of strength a company may have over its competitors. It should be noted that most areas of strength relate to the excellence of personnel or are resource based. Not all factors have the same significance for every product/market; therefore, it is desirable to first recognize the critical factors that could directly or indirectly bear on a product's performance. For example, the development of an improved product may be strategic for drug companies. On the other hand, in the case of cosmetics, where image building is usually important, advertising may be a critical factor. After-sale service may have significance for products such as copying machines, computers, and elevators. Critical factors may be chosen with reference to Exhibit 3-6. From among the critical factors, an attempt should be made to sort out strengths. It is also desirable to rate different strengths for a more objective analysis.

An example from the personal computer business illustrates the measurement of strengths and weaknesses. In 1987, Apple, IBM, Tandy, and imports from Taiwan and South Korea were the major competitors. In 1990, the major firms in the industry included Apple, IBM, Tandy, Compaq Computers, Zenith

EXHIBIT 7-8
Areas of Strength

1. Excellence in product design and/or performance (engineering ingenuity).
2. Low-cost, high-efficiency operating skill in manufacturing and/or in distribution.
3. Leadership in product innovation.
4. Efficiency in customer service.
5. Personal relationships with customers.
6. Efficiency in transportation and logistics.
7. Effectiveness in sales promotion.
8. Merchandising efficiency—high turnover of inventories and/or of capital.
9. Skillful trading in volatile price movement commodities.
10. Ability to influence legislation.
11. Highly efficient, low-cost facilities.
12. Ownership or control of low-cost or scarce raw materials.
13. Control of intermediate distribution or processing units.
14. Massive availability of capital.
15. Widespread customer acceptance of company brand name (reputation).
16. Product availability, convenience.
17. Customer loyalty.
18. Dominant market share position, deal from a position of strength.
19. Effectiveness of advertising.
20. Quality sales force.
21. Make and sell products of highest quality.
22. High integrity as a company

Electronics, and imports from Taiwan and South Korea. In 1995, the front-runners in the business were IBM, Compaq, Apple, Dell, and Packard-Bell. Among these, Compaq Computer Corp. was the leader in worldwide PC shipments, followed by IBM. As a matter of fact, in the important U.S. market IBM ranked fourth, trailing even the late-entrant Packard Bell Electronics Inc. Exhibit 7-9 lists the relative strengths of these firms in 1994.

Success in the personal computer business depends on mastery of the following three critical areas:

- **Low-cost production**—As personal computer hardware becomes increasingly standardized, the ability to provide the most value for the dollar greatly influences sales. The most vertically integrated companies have the edge.
- **Distribution**—Retailers have shelf space for just two or three brands; only those makers that are able to keep their products in the customer's line of sight are likely to survive.
- **Software**—Computer sales suffer unless a wide choice of software packages is offered to increase the number of applications.

Without these three strengths in place, a company cannot make it in the personal computer business. Thus, Texas Instruments withdrew from the field in 1983 because it did not have enough applications software. Fortune Systems dropped out in 1984. Zenith Electronics left the field in the early 1990s; Tandy became an insignificant contestant. Even imports from Taiwan and South Korea

EXHIBIT 7-9
Relative Strengths of Personal Computer Firms in 1994

Companies	Current Strengths	Applications software	Brand image	Depth of management	Financial muscle	Low-cost production	National sales force	Retail distribution	Service support
Apple Computer	●	●	●					●	●
Compaq Computer		●	●		●			●	●
Packard-Bell	●			●	●	●			●
IBM	●	●	●	●	●	●		●	●
Dell Computer	●		●	●	●			●	●

could not cope with changes in the fast-moving PC business, in which prices fall more than 20 percent a year, and product life cycles have shortened to as little as six months. Introducing a new generation of PCs just three months behind schedule can cost a company 40 percent to 50 percent of the gross profit it had planned to make on the new line.[12]

Both IBM and Apple appear to be in trouble in 1995. IBM had been working to overcome its weaknesses in logistics, manufacturing, and research and development. The company has reorganized the PC division and hired seasoned executives to fix the problems. In addition, the company has shifted the focus to push for market share instead of profit to realize production efficiencies and lower parts costs. IBM hopes that with these measures, and the company's unrivaled assets— the IBM name and the brand equity built over many years—in its favor, it can create a solid turnaround fairly quickly. IBM's example illustrates the importance of analyzing strengths and weaknesses to define objectives and strategies for the future.

Strengths should be further examined to undertake what may be called opportunity analysis (matching strengths, or competencies, to opportunity). Opportunity analysis serves as an input in establishing a company's economic mission. Opportunity analysis is also useful in developing an individual product's objectives. In Exhibit 7-10 the objectives for a food product are shown as they emerged from a study of its strengths. The objectives were to produce a premium product for an unscored segment and to develop a new channel outlet. In other words, at the product level, the opportunity analysis seeks to answer such questions as: What opportunity does the company have to capitalize on a competitor's weaknesses? Modify or improve the product line or add new products? Serve the needs of more customers in existing markets or develop new markets? Improve the efficiency of current marketing operations?

Opportunities emerge from the changing environment. Thus, environmental analysis is an important factor in identifying opportunities. Exhibit 7-11 suggests a simple format for analyzing the impact of the environment.

The concept of opportunity analysis may be illustrated with Procter & Gamble's moves in the over-the-counter (OTC) drug business. There is an increasing sense in the drug industry that the OTC side of the drug business will grow faster than prescription sales will grow. Consumers and insurers are becoming more

EXHIBIT 7-10
Matching Strengths with Opportunities

Strength	Likely Impact	Opportunity Furnished by the Environment	Objectives and Goals
Customer loyalty	Incremental product volume increases	A trend of changing taste	Develop a premium product
	Price increases for premium quality/service	An identified geographic shift of part of the market	Introduce the existing product in a segment hitherto not served
	New product introductions	A market segment neglected by the industry	
			Develop a new channel for the product, etc.
Cordial relationships with channels	New product introductions	A product-related subconscious need not solicited by the competition	
	Point-of-purchase advertising	A product weakness of the competition	
	Reduction of delivered costs through distribution innovations	A distribution weakness of the competition	
	Tied-in products	Technical feasibility for improving existing package design	
	Merchandising differentiation	A discovered new use for the product or container	

EXHIBIT 7-11
Impact of Environmental Trends

Trends	Impact	Timing of Impact	Response Time	Urgency	Threats	Opportunities

interested in OTC medications, partly because of the steep cost of prescription drugs. Further, with the patents of many major medicines expiring, generic drugs will pose an even greater threat to prescription products. Consequently, drugmakers are taking another look at the OTC business, where a well-marketed brand can keep a franchise alive long after exclusive rights have expired. A case in point is the success of Advil, an ibuprofen-based painkiller.

To participate in the growing OTC market, Procter & Gamble has been making inroads into the industry. As a matter of fact, Procter & Gamble is already one of the largest marketers of OTC drugs. But to expand its position in the field, Procter & Gamble decided to speed things up by entering into partnerships with drugmakers and technology companies. By linking its formidable marketing strength with emerging technological advances in medicine, Procter & Gamble hopes to propel itself to the forefront of the health market.

Thus, the company is working on new formulations for minoxidil, a baldness remedy, and other new products promoting hair growth with UpJohn. It joined with Syntex to market Aleve, a nonprescription version of Anaprox, an anti-inflammatory drug that is popular with arthritis sufferers. It hopes to sell De-Nol, a gastrointestinal medicine made by Dutch drugmaker Gist-Brocades, as an ulcer treatment. It may use technology from Alcide, a Connecticut maker of disinfectants, in its toothpaste or mouthwash business. Finally, Procter & Gamble has an agreement with Triton Biosciences and Cetus to use Betaseron, a synthetic interferon, that it hopes will fight the common cold.[13]

In this case, it was Procter & Gamble's marketing strength that led it to enter the OTC drug industry. The opportunity was furnished by the environment—a concern for increasing health care costs—and many drug companies were glad to form alliances with this established OTC marketer.

An interesting observation with regard to opportunity analysis, made by Andrews, is relevant here:

> The match is designed to minimize organizational weakness and to maximize strength. In any case, risk attends it. And when opportunity seems to outrun present

distinctive competence, the willingness to gamble that the latter can be built up to the required level is almost indispensable to a strategy that challenges the organization and the people in it. It appears to be true, in any case, that the potential capability of a company tends to be underestimated. Organizations, like individuals, rise to occasions, particularly when the latter provide attractive reward for the effort required.[14]

In the process of analyzing strengths, underlying weaknesses should also be noted. Exhibit 7-12 is a list of typical marketing weaknesses. Appropriate action must be taken to correct weaknesses. Some weaknesses have SBU-wide bearing; others may be weaknesses of a specific product. SBU weaknesses must be examined, and necessary corrective action must be incorporated into the overall marketing strategy. For example, weaknesses 3, 5, and 6 in Exhibit 7-12 could have SBU-wide ramifications. These must be addressed by the chief marketing strategist. The remaining three weaknesses can be corrected by the person in charge of the product/market with which these weaknesses are associated.

CONCEPT OF SYNERGY

Before concluding the discussion of strengths and weaknesses, it will be desirable to briefly introduce the concept of synergy. **Synergy**, simply stated, is the concept that the combined effect of certain parts is greater than the sum of their individual effects. Let us say, for example, that product 1 contributes X and product 2 contributes Y. If they are produced together, they may contribute X+Y+Z. We can say that Z is the synergistic effect of X and Y being brought together and that Z represents positive synergy. There can be negative synergy as well. The study of synergy helps in analyzing new growth opportunities. A new product, for instance, may have such a high synergistic effect on a company's existing product(s) that it may be an extremely desirable addition.

Quantitative analysis of synergy is far from easy. Conceptually, however, synergy may be evaluated following the framework illustrated in Exhibit 7-13. This framework refers to a new product/market entry synergy measurement.

A new product/market entry contribution could take place at three levels: contribution to the parent company (from the entry), contribution to the new entry (from the parent), and joint opportunities (benefits that accrue to both as a result of consolidation). As far as it is feasible, entries in Exhibit 7-13 should be assigned a numerical value, such as increase in unit sales by 20 percent, time saving by two

EXHIBIT 7-12
Typical Marketing Weaknesses

1. Inadequate definition of customer for product/market development.
2. Ambiguous service policies.
3. Too many levels of reporting in the organizational setup.
4. Overlapping channels.
5. Lack of top management involvement in new product development.
6. Lack of quantitative goals.

EXHIBIT 7-13
Measurement of the Synergy of a New Product/Market Entry

	SYNERGY MEASURES							
	Startup Economies			Operating Economies				
Synergistic Contribution to:	*Investment*	*Operating*	*Timing*	*Investment*	*Operating*	*Expansion of Present Sales*	*New Product and Market Areas*	*Overall Synergy*
Parent								
New entry								
Joint opportunities								

months, reduction in investment requirements by 10 percent, and so on. Finally, various numerical values may be given a common value in the form of return on investment or cash flow.

SUMMARY

This chapter outlined a scheme for the objective measurement of strengths and weaknesses of a product/market, which then become the basis of identifying SBU strengths and weaknesses. Strengths and weaknesses are tangible and intangible resources that may be utilized for seeking growth of the product. Factors that need to be studied in order to designate strengths and weaknesses are competition, current strategic perspectives, past performance, marketing effectiveness, and marketing environment. Present strategy may be examined with reference to the markets being served and the means used to serve these markets.

Past performance was considered in the form of financial analysis, ranging from simple measurements, such as market share and profitability, to developing product and market performance profiles. Marketing effectiveness was related to marketing orientation, which may be determined with reference to questions raised in the chapter. Finally, various aspects of the product/market marketing environment were analyzed.

These five factors were brought together to delineate strengths and weaknesses. An operational framework was introduced to conduct opportunity analysis. Also discussed was the concept of synergy. The analysis of strengths and weaknesses sets the stage for developing marketing objectives and goals, which will be discussed in the next chapter.

DISCUSSION | 1. Why is it necessary to measure strengths and weaknesses?
QUESTIONS | 2. Because it is natural for managers and other employees to want to justify their actions and decisions, is it possible for a company to make a truly objective appraisal of its strengths and weaknesses?

3. Evaluate the current strategy of IBM related to personal computers and compare it with the strategy being pursued by Apple Computer.

4. Develop a conceptual scheme to evaluate the current strategy of a bank.

5. Is it necessary for a firm to be marketing oriented to succeed? What may a firm do to overcome its lack of marketing orientation?

6. Making necessary assumptions, perform an opportunity analysis for a packaged-goods manufacturer.

7. Explain the meaning of synergy. Examine what sort of synergy Procter & Gamble achieved by going into the frozen orange juice business.

NOTES

[1] Kenneth R. Andrews, *The Concept of Corporate Strategy* (Homewood, IL: Dow Jones-Irwin, 1971), 97.

[2] Jeremy Main, "Toward Service without a Snare," *Fortune* (23 March 1981): 64–66.

[3] Philip Kotler, William T. Gregor, and William H. Rodgers III, "The Marketing Audit Comes of Age," *Sloan Management Review* (Winter 1989): 49–62.

[4] Howard H. Stevenson, "Defining Corporate Strengths and Weaknesses: An Exploratory Study," (Ph.D. diss., Harvard Business School, 1969).

[5] Howard H. Stevenson, "Defining Corporate Strengths and Weaknesses," *Sloan Management Review* (Spring 1976): 66.

[6] *Moody's Industrial Manual* (1991), 5872–73.

[7] David S. Hopkins, *Business Strategies for Problem Products* (New York: Conference Board, 1987), 29.

[8] Benson P. Shapiro, "What the Hell Is 'Market Oriented'?" *Harvard Business Review* (November–December 1988): 119–25.

[9] Gordon Canning, Jr., "Is Your Company Marketing Oriented?" *Journal of Business Strategy* (May–June 1988): 34–36.

[10] Hans Kasper, "Corporate Culture, Market Orientation and Marketing Strategy: Results of Two Case Studies in the Dutch Service Sector," *Working Paper*, Limburg University, Netherland, 1993.

[11] David Tuller, "Repackaging Chocolates," *Working Women* (January 1987): 45–46; updated based on interview with a company executive.

[12] Bart Ziegler, "IBM Tries, And Fails, to Fix PC Business," *Wall Street Journal*, (22 February 1995): B1. Also see "It Just May Be The Year of the Apple," *Business Week* (16 January 1995): 4.

[13] "Can Procter & Gamble Commandeer More Shelves in the Medicine Chest?" *Business Week* (10 April 1989): 64. Also see "Painkillers are about to O.D.," *Business Week* (11 April 1994): 54.

[14] Andrews, *The Concept of Corporate Strategy*, 100.

Developing
Marketing Objectives
and Goals

An organization must have an objective to guide its destiny. Although the objective in itself cannot guarantee the success of a business, its presence will certainly mean more efficient and financially less wasteful management of operations.

Objectives form a specific expression of purpose, thus helping to remove any uncertainty about the company's policy or about the intended purpose of any effort. To be effective, objectives must present startling challenges to managers, jolting them away from traditional in-a-rut thinking. If properly designed, objectives permit the measurement of progress. Without some form of progress measurement, it may not be possible to know whether adequate resources are being applied or whether these resources are being managed effectively. Finally, objectives facilitate relationships between units, especially in a diversified corporation, where the separate goals of different units may not be consistent with some higher corporate purpose.

Despite its overriding importance, defining objectives is far from easy: there is no mechanical or expert instant-answer method. Rather, defining goals as the future becomes the present is a long, time-consuming, and continuous process. In practice, many businesses run either without any commonly accepted objectives and goals or with conflicting objectives and goals. In some cases, objectives may be understood in different ways by different executives. At times, objectives may be defined in such general terms that their significance for the job is not understood. For example, a product manager of a large company once observed that "our objective is to satisfy the customer and increase sales." After cross-checking with the vice president of sales, however, she found that the company's goal was making a minimum 6 percent after-tax profit even when it meant losing market share. "Our objective, or whatever you choose to call it, is to grow," the vice president of finance of another company said. "This is a profit-oriented company, and thus we must earn a minimum profit of 10 percent on everything we do. You may call this our objective." Different companies define their objectives differently. It is the task of the CEO to set the company's objectives and goals and to obtain for them the support of his or her senior colleagues, thus paving the way for other parts of the organization to do the same.

The purpose of this chapter is to provide a framework for goal setting in a large, complex organization. A first step in planning is usually to state objectives so that, knowing where you are trying to go, you can figure out how to get there. However, objectives cannot be stated in isolation; that is, objectives cannot be formed without the perspectives of the company's current business, its past performance, resources, and environment. Thus, the subject matter discussed in previous chapters becomes the background material for defining objectives and goals.

FRAMEWORK FOR DEFINING OBJECTIVES

This chapter deals with defining objectives and goals at the SBU level. Because SBU objectives should bear a close relationship to corporate strategic direction, this chapter will start with a discussion of corporate direction and will then examine SBU objectives and goals. Product/market objectives will also be discussed, as they are usually defined at the SBU level and derived from SBU objectives.

The framework discussed here assumes the perspectives of a large corporation. In a small company that manufactures a limited line of related products, corporate and SBU objectives may be identical. Likewise, in a company with a few unrelated products, an SBU's objectives may be no different from those of the product/market.

It is desirable to define a few terms one often confronts in the context of objective setting: mission, policy, objective, goal, and strategic direction. A **mission** (also referred to as corporate concept, vision, or aim) is the CEO's conception of the organization's raison d'être, or what it should work toward, in the light of long-range opportunity. A **policy** is a written definition of general intent or company position designed to guide and regulate certain actions and decisions, especially those of major significance or of a recurring nature. An **objective** is a long-range purpose that is not quantified or limited to a time period (e.g., increasing the return on stockholders' equity). A **goal** is a measurable objective of the business, judged by management to be attainable at some specific future date through planned actions. An example of a goal is to achieve 10 percent growth in sales within the next two years. **Strategic direction** is an all-inclusive term that refers to the network of mission, objectives, and goals. Although we recognize the distinction between an objective and a goal, we will consider these terms simultaneously in order to give the discussion more depth.

The following are frequently cited types of frustrations, disappointments, or troubling uncertainties that should be avoided when dealing with objectives:

1. Lack of credibility, motivation, or practicality.
2. Poor information inputs.
3. Defining objectives without considering different options.
4. Lack of consensus regarding corporate values.
5. Disappointing committee effort to define objectives.
6. Sterility (lack of uniqueness and competitive advantage).

Briefly, if objectives and goals are to serve their purpose well, they should represent a careful weighing of the balance between the performance desired and the probability of its being realized:

> Strategic objectives which are too ambitious result in the dissipation of assets and the destruction of morale, and create the risk of losing past gains as well as future opportunities. Strategic objectives which are not ambitious enough represent lost opportunity and open the door to complacency.[1]

CORPORATE STRATEGIC DIRECTION

Corporate strategic direction is defined in different ways. In some corporations, it takes the form of a corporate creed, or code of conduct, that defines perspectives from the viewpoint of different stakeholders. At other corporations, policy statements provide guidelines for implementing strategy. In still others, corporate direction is outlined in terms of objective statements. However expressed, corporate direction consists of broad statements that represent a company's position on various matters and serve as an input in defining objectives and in formulating strategy at lower echelons in the organization.

A company can reasonably expect to achieve a leadership position or superior financial results only when it has purposefully laid out its strategic direction. Every outstanding corporate success is based on a direction that differentiates the firm's approach from that of others. Specifically, strategic direction helps in

1. Identifying what "fits" and what needs the company is well suited to meet.
2. Analyzing potential synergies.
3. Undertaking risks that simply cannot be justified on a project basis (e.g., willingness to pay for what might appear, on a purely financial basis, to be a premium for acquisition).
4. Providing the ability to act fast (presence of strategic direction not only helps in adequately and quickly scanning opportunities in the environment but capitalizing on them without waiting).
5. Focusing the search for opportunities and options more clearly.

Corporate Strategic Direction: An Example

To illustrate the point, consider the corporate direction of Dow Chemical Company, which has persisted for more than 60 years.[2] Herbert Dow founded and built Dow Chemical on one fundamental and energizing idea: start with a cheap and basic raw material; then develop the soundest, lowest-cost process possible. This idea, or direction, defined certain imperatives Dow has pursued consistently over time:

1. First, don't copy or license anyone else's process. In other words, as Dow himself put it, "Don't make a product unless you can find a better way to do it."
2. Second, build large, vertically integrated complexes to achieve maximum economies of scale; that is, maintain cost leadership by building the most technologically advanced facilities in the industry.
3. Third, locate near and tie up abundant sources of cheap raw materials.
4. Fourth, build in bad times as well as good. In other words, become the large-volume supplier for the long pull and preempt competitors from coming in. Be there, in place, when the demand develops.
5. Fifth, maintain a strong cash flow so that the corporation can pursue its vision.

Over the years, Dow has consistently acted in concert with this direction, or vision. It has built enormous, vertically integrated complexes at Midland, Michigan; Freeport, Texas; Rotterdam, Holland; and the Louisiana Gulf Coast. And it has pursued with almost fanatical consistency the obtaining of secure, low-cost sources of raw materials.

Strategic Direction and Organizational Perspectives. Pursuing this direction has, in turn, mandated certain human and organizational characteristics of the company and its leadership. For example, Dow has been characterized as a company whose management shows "exceptional willingness to take sweeping but carefully thought out gambles."[3] The company has had to make leaps of faith about the pace and direction of future market and technological developments. Sometimes, as in the case of shale oil, these have taken a very long time to materialize. Other times, these leaps of faith have resulted in failure. But as Ben Branch, a top Dow executive for many years, was fond of saying, "Dow encourages well-intentioned failure."

To balance this willingness to take large risks, the company has had to maintain an extraordinary degree of organizational flexibility to give it the ability to respond quickly to unexpected changes. For example, "Dow places little emphasis on, and does not publish, organization charts, preferring to define areas of broad responsibility without rigid compartments. Its informal style has given the company the flexibility to react quickly to change."[4]

Changing the Strategic Direction. Over the years, Dow's direction has had to expand to accommodate a changing world, its own growth, and expanding horizons of opportunity. The expansion of its direction, or vision, has included, for example:

1. Recognition of the opportunities and the need to diversify downstream into higher-value-added, technologically more sophisticated intermediate and end-use products, with the concomitant requirement for greater technical selling capability after World War II.
2. The opportunity and the imperative to expand abroad. In fact, Herbert Dow's core vision may have initially been retarded expansion abroad, since raw material availability was not as good in Europe or in Japan as it was in the United States and since it was harder to achieve comparable economies of scale.
3. The need to reorganize and decentralize foreign operations, setting them up on a semiautonomous basis to give them room for growth and flexibility.

But throughout its history, Dow's leadership has consistently held to a guiding concept that perhaps has been best articulated as this: "In this business, it's who's there with the vision, the money, and the guts to seize an opportunity."[5]

In the 1980s, Xerox Corporation faced the task of redefining its strategic direction in response to a new technological era. There were three different schools of thought within the company. One school believed it should stick to its core competency—copying—and that paper would be there for a long time. Another view, held by a smaller group, felt Xerox ought to quickly transform itself into a systems company. Based on its leading-edge technology at Palo Alto Research Center, this view suggested getting out of the paper world as quickly as possible. A third school of thought said that the company should finesse the differences and focus on being "the" office company. After all, it was reasoned, the company had a worldwide direct sales force that reached into almost every office around the world; it could sell anything through that direct sales force.

Looking carefully at the future, the company concluded that paper would not go away, but that its use would change. The creation, storage, and communication of documents will increasingly be in electronic form; however, for many years, people will prefer the paper document display to the electronic document display. They will print out their electronic documents closer to their end use and then throw them away, thereby making paper a transient display medium. Xerox chose to bridge the gap between the paper and electronic world. The strategic direction was defined to not remain the *copier* company, but to become the *document* company.[6]

Corporate Strategic Direction and Strategy Development. What can be concluded from this brief history of Dow Chemical's corporate direction? First, it seems clear that, for more than 50 years, all of Dow's major strategic and operating decisions have been amazingly consistent. They have been consistent because they have been firmly grounded in some basic beliefs about where and how to compete. The direction has evidently made it easier to make the always difficult and risky long-term/short-term decisions, such as investing in research for the long haul or aggressively tying up sources of raw materials.

This direction, or vision, has also driven Dow to be aggressive in generating the cash required to make risky investments possible. Most important, top management seems never to have eschewed its leadership role in favor of becoming merely stewards of a highly successful enterprise. They have been constantly aware of the need to question and reshape Dow's direction, while maintaining those elements that have been instrumental in achieving the company's long-term competitive success. Dow illustrates that corporate direction gives coherence to a wide range of apparently unrelated decisions, serving as the crucial link among them.

Corporate Strategic Direction and Marketing Strategy

Without exception, the corporate direction of all successful companies is based not only on a clear notion of the markets in which they compete but also on specific concepts of how they can sustain an economically attractive position in those markets. Their direction is grounded in deep understanding of industry and competitive dynamics and company capabilities and potential. Corporate direction should focus in general on continually strengthening the company's economic or market position, or both, in some substantial way. For example, Dow was not immobilized by existing industry relationships, current market shares, or its past shortcomings. It sought and found new ways to influence industry dynamics in its favor. Corporate direction should foster creative thinking about realistic and achievable options, driving product, service and new business decisions. Its impact can actually be measured in the marketplace. In other words, in addition to having thought through the questions of where and how to compete, top management should also make realistic judgments about (a) the capital and human resources that are required to compete and where they should come from, (b) the changes in the corporation's functional and cultural biases that must be accomplished, (c) the unique contributions that are required of the corporation (top management and staff) to support pursuit of the new direction by the SBUs, and (d) a guiding notion of the timing or pace of change within which the corporation should realistically move toward the new vision.

In summary, strategic direction is not an abstruse construct based on the inspiration of a solitary genius. It is a hard-nosed, practical concept based on the thorough understanding of the dynamics of industries, markets, and competition and of the potential of the corporation for influencing and exploiting these dynamics. It is only rarely the result of a flash of insight; much more often it is the product of deep and disciplined analysis.

Formulating Corporate Strategic Direction

Strategic direction frequently starts out fuzzy and is refined through a messy process of trial and error. It generally emerges in its full clarity only when it is well on its way to being realized. Likewise, changes in corporate direction occur by a long process and in stages.

Changing an established direction is much more difficult than starting from scratch, because one must overcome inherited biases and set norms of behavior. According to Quinn, change is effected through a sequence of steps.[7] First, a need for change is recognized. Second, awareness of the need for change is built throughout the organization by commissioning study groups, staff, or consultants to examine problems, options, contingencies, or opportunities posed by the sensed need. Third, broad support for the change is sought through unstructured discussions, probing of positions, definition of differences of opinion, and so on, among executives. Fourth, pockets of commitment are created by building necessary skills or technologies within the organization, testing options, and taking opportunities to make decisions to build support. Fifth, a clear focus is established, either by creating an ad hoc committee to formulate a position or by expressing in written form the specific direction that the CEO desires. Sixth, a definite commitment to change is obtained by designating someone to champion the goal and be accountable for its accomplishment. Finally, after the organization arrives at the new direction, efforts are made to be sensitive to the need for further change in direction, if necessary.

Specific Statements about Corporate Strategic Direction

Many companies make specific statements to designate their direction. Usually these statements are made around such aspects as target customers and markets, principal products or services, geographic domain, core technologies, concern for survival, growth and profitability, company philosophy, company self-concept, and desired public image. Some companies make only brief statements of strategic direction (sometimes labeled corporate objectives); others elaborate on each aspect in detail. Avon products expressed its strategic direction rather briefly: "to be the company that best understands and satisfies the product, service and self-fulfillment needs of women globally."[8] IBM defines its direction, which it calls principles, separately for each functional area. For example, in the area of marketing, the IBM principle is: "The marketplace is the driving force behind everything we do." In technology, it is "at our core, we are a technology company with an overriding commitment to quality."[9] Apple Computer states its direction five years into the future with detailed statements under the following headings: corporate concept, internal growth, external growth, sales goal, financial, planning for growth and performance, management and personnel, corporate citizenship, and stockholders and financial community. Exhibit 8-1 shows the strategic direction of the Hewlett-Packard Corporation. As can be noted, this company defines its strategic perspective through brief statements.

No matter how corporate strategic direction is defined, it should meet the following criteria. First, it should present the firm's perspectives in a way that enables progress to be measured. Second, the strategic direction should differentiate the company from others. Third, strategic direction should define the business that the company wants to be in, not necessarily the business that it is in. Fourth, it should be relevant to all the firm's stakeholders. Finally, strategic direction should be exciting and inspiring, motivating people at the helm.[10]

SBU OBJECTIVES

An SBU was defined in Chapter 1 as a unit comprising one or more products having a common market base whose manager has complete responsibility for integrating all functions into a strategy against an identifiable external competitor. We will examine the development and meaning of SBUs again in this chapter to make it clear why objectives must be defined at this level. Abell's explanation is as follows:

> The development of marketing planning has paralleled the growing complexity of business organizations themselves. The first change to take place was the shift from functionally organized companies with relatively narrow product lines and served-market focus to large diversified firms serving multiple markets with multiple product lines. Such firms are usually divided into product or market divisions, divisions may be divided into departments, and these in turn are often further divided into product lines or market segments. As this change gradually took place over the last two decades, "sales planning" was gradually replaced by "marketing planning" in most of these organizations. Each product manager or market manager drew up a marketing plan for his product line or market segment. These were aggregated together into an

EXHIBIT 8-1
Hewlett-Packard's Corporate Direction

Profit

To achieve sufficient profit to finance our company growth and to provide the resources we need to achieve our other corporate objectives.

Customers

To provide products and services of the greatest possible value to our customers, thereby gaining and holding their respect and loyalty.

Field of Interest

To enter new fields only when the ideas we have, together with our technical, manufacturing and marketing skills, assure that we can make a needed and profitable contribution in the field.

Growth

To let our growth be limited only by our profits and our ability to develop and produce technical products that satisfy real customer needs.

People

To help our own people share in the company's success, which they make possible: to provide job security based on their performance, to recognize their individual achievements, and to help them gain a sense of satisfaction and accomplishment from their work.

Management

To foster initiative and creativity by allowing the individual great freedom of action in attaining well-defined objectives.

Citizenship

To honor our obligations to society by being an economic, intellectual and social asset to each nation and each community in which we operate.

Source: Company records.

overall divisional "marketing plan." Divisional plans in turn were aggregated into the overall corporate plan.

But a further important change is now taking place. There has been over the last decade a growing acceptance of the fact that individual units or subunits within a corporation, e.g., divisions, product departments, or even product lines or market segments, may play different roles in achieving overall corporate objectives. Not all units and subunits need to produce the same level of profitability; not all units and subunits have to contribute equally to cash flow objectives.

This concept of the organization as a "portfolio" of units and subunits having different objectives is at the very root of contemporary approaches to strategic marketing planning. It is commonplace today to hear businesses defined as "cash cows," "stars," "question marks," "dogs," etc.* It is in sharp contrast to practice in the 1960s and earlier which emphasized primarily sales and earnings (or return on investment) as a major measure of performance. Although different divisions or departments were intuitively believed to have different capabilities to meet sales and earning goals, these

---

* These items are defined in Chapter 10.

differences were seldom made explicit. Instead, each unit was expected to "pull its weight" in the overall quest for growth and profits.

With the recognition that organizational entities may differ in their objectives and roles, a new organizational concept has also emerged. This is the concept of a "business unit." A business unit may be a division, a product department, or even a product line or major market, depending on the circumstances. It is, however, usually regarded by corporate management as a reasonably autonomous profit center. Usually it has its own "general manager" (even though he may not have that title, he has general managerial responsibilities). Often it has its own manufacturing, sales, research and development, and procurement functions although in some cases some of these may be shared with other businesses (e.g., pooled sales). A business unit usually has a clear market focus. In particular it usually has an identifiable strategy and an identifiable set of competitors. In some organizations (the General Electric Company, for example), business units are clearly identified and defined. In other organizations, divisions or product departments are treated as relatively autonomous business units although they are not explicitly defined as such.

A business unit will usually comprise several "program" units. These may be product lines, geographic market segments, end-user industries to which the company sells, or units defined on the basis of any other relevant segmentation dimension. Program units may also sometimes differ in their objectives. In such cases, the concept of a portfolio exists both in terms of business units within a corporate structure (or substructure, such as a group) or in terms of programs within a business unit. Usually, however, the business unit is a major focus of strategic attention, and strategic market plans are of prime importance at this level.[11]

As Abell notes, a large, complex organization may have a number of SBUs, each playing its unique role in the organization. Obviously, then, at the corporate level, objectives can be defined only in generalities. It is only at each SBU level that more specific statements of objectives can be made. Actually, it is the SBU mission and its objectives and goals that product/market managers need to consider in their strategic plans.

BUSINESS MISSION

Defining the
Business Mission:
The Traditional
Viewpoint

Mission is a broad term that refers to the total perspectives or purpose of a business. The mission of a corporation was traditionally framed around its product line and expressed in mottoes: "Our business is textiles," "We manufacture cameras," and so on. With the advent of marketing orientation and technological innovations, this method of defining the business mission has been decried. It has been held that building the perspectives of a business around its product limits the scope of management to enter new fields and thus to make use of growth opportunities. In a key article published in 1960, Levitt observed:

The railroads did not stop growing because the need for passengers and freight transportation declined. That grew. The railroads are in trouble today not because the need was filled by others (cars, trucks, airplanes, even telephones), but because it was not filled by the railroads themselves. They let others take customers away from them because they assumed themselves to be in the railroad business rather than in the transportation business. The reason they defined their industry wrong was because they were railroad-oriented instead of transportation-oriented; they were product-oriented instead of customer-oriented.[12]

According to Levitt's thesis, the mission of a business should be defined broadly: an airline might consider itself in the vacation business, a publisher in the education industry, an appliance manufacturer in the business of preparing nourishment.

Recently, Levitt's proposition has been criticized, and the question has been raised as to whether simply extending the scope of a business leads far enough. The Boston Consulting Group, for example, has pointed out that the railroads could not have protected themselves by defining their business as transportation:

> Unfortunately, there is a prevalent notion that if one merely defines one's business in increasingly general terms such as transportation rather than railroading the road to successful competitive strategy will be clear. Actually, that is hardly ever the case. More often, the opposite is true. For example, in the case of the railroads, passengers and freight represent very different problems, and short haul vs. longer haul are completely different strategic issues. Indeed, as the unit train demonstrates, just coal handling is a meaningful strategic issue.[13]

In the early 1980s, Coca-Cola extended its business mission from being a soft drink marketer to a beverage company. Subsequently, the company bought three wine companies. A few years later, the company decided to leave the wine business. What happened is simply this: Although soft drinks and wine both are parts of the beverage industry, the management skills required to run a soft drink business are quite different from those required for the wine business. Coca-Cola overlooked some basics. For example, because wine must be aged, inventory costs run much higher than for soft drinks. Further, grapes must be bought ahead of time. Coke added to its work by vastly overestimating the amount of grapes it needed. Another key characteristic of the wine business is a requirement for heavy capital investment; Coke did not want to make that investment.[14]

As the Coca-Cola example illustrates, the problem with Levitt's thesis is that it is too broad and does not provide a common thread: a relationship between a firm's past and future that indicates where the firm is headed and that helps management to institute directional perspectives. The common thread may be found in marketing, production technology, finance, or management. ITT took advantage of its managerial abilities when it ventured into such diverse businesses as hotels and bakeries. Merrill Lynch found a common thread via finance in entering the real estate business. Bic Pen Company used its marketing strength to involve itself in the razor blade business. Thus, the mission cannot be defined by making abstract statements that one hopes will pave the way for entry into new fields.

It would appear that the mission of a business is neither a statement of current business nor a random extension of current involvements. It signifies the scope and nature of business, not as it is today, but as it could be in the future. The mission plays an important role in designating opportunities for diversification, either through research and development or through acquisitions. To be meaningful, the mission should be based on a comprehensive analysis of the business's technology and customer mission. Examples of technology-based definitions are computer companies and aerospace companies. Customer mission refers to the fulfillment of a particular type of customer need, such as the need for basic nutrition, household maintenance, or entertainment.

Whether the company has a written business mission statement or not is immaterial. What is important, however, is that due consideration is given to technological and marketing factors (as related to particular segments and their needs) in defining the mission. Ideally, business definitions should be based on a combination of technology and market mission variables, but some companies venture into new fields on the basis of one variable only. For example, Texas Instruments entered the digital watch market on the basis of its lead in integrated circuits technology. Procter & Gamble added over-the-counter remedies to its business out of its experience in fulfilling the ordinary daily needs of customers.

To sum up, the mission deals with these questions: What type of business do we want to be in at some future time? What do we want to become? At any given point, most of the resources of a business are frozen or locked into current uses, and the outputs in services or products are for the most part defined by current operations. Over an interval of a few years, however, environmental changes place demands on the business for new types of resources. Further, because of personnel attrition and depreciation of capital resources, management has the option of choosing the environment in which the company will operate and acquiring commensurate new resources rather than replacing the old ones in kind. This explains the importance of defining the business's mission. The mission should be so defined that it has a bearing on the business's strengths and weaknesses.

Defining the Business Mission: A New Approach

In his pioneering work on the subject, Abell has argued against defining a business as simply a choice of products or markets.[15] He proposes that a business be defined in terms of three measures: (a) scope; (b) differentiation of the company's offerings, one from another, across segments; and (c) differentiation of the company's offerings from those of competitors. The scope pertains to the breadth of a business. For example, do life insurance companies consider themselves to be in the business of underwriting insurance only or do they provide complete family financial planning services? Likewise, should a manufacturer of toothpaste define the scope of its business as preventing tooth decay or as providing complete oral hygiene? There are two separate contexts in which differentiation can occur: differentiation across segments and across competitors. Differentiation across segments measures the degree to which business segments are treated differently. An example is personal computers marketed to young children as educational aids and to older people as financial planning aids. Differentiation across competitors measures the degree to which competitors' offerings differ.

These three measures, according to Abell, should be viewed in three dimensions: (a) customer groups served, (b) customer functions served, and (c) technologies used. These three dimensions (and a fourth one, level of production/distribution) were examined at length in Chapter 5 in the context of defining market boundaries and will not be elaborated further here. An example will illustrate how a business may be defined using Abell's thesis.

Customer groups describe who is being satisfied; customer functions describe what needs are being satisfied; technologies describe how needs are being satisfied. Consider a thermometer manufacturer. Depending on which measure is used, the business can be defined as follows:

Customer Groups	Customer Functions	Technologies Used
Households	Body temperature	Mercury-base
Restaurants	Cooking temperature	Alcohol-base
Health care facilities	Atmospheric temperature	Electronic-digital

The manufacturer can confine the business to just health care facilities or broaden the scope to include restaurants and households. Thermometers can be provided only for measurement of body temperature or the line can be extended to offer cooking or atmospheric thermometers. The manufacturer could decide to produce only mercury-base thermometers or could also produce alcohol-base or electronic-digital thermometers. The decisions that the manufacturer makes about customer groups, customer functions, and technologies ultimately affects the definition of the business in terms of both scope and differentiation. Exhibits 8-2 and 8-3 graphically show how business can be defined narrowly or broadly around these three dimensions. In Exhibit 8-2, the manufacturer limits the business to service health care facilities only, offering just mercury-base thermometers for measuring body temperatures. In Exhibit 8-3, however, the definition has been broadened to serve three customer groups: households, restaurants, and health care facilities; two types of thermometers: mercury-base and alcohol-base; and three customer functions. The manufacturer could further expand the definition of the business in all three directions. Physicians could be added as a customer group. A line of electronic-digital thermometers could be offered. Finally, thermometers could be produced to measure temperatures of industrial processes.

An adequate business definition requires proper consideration of the strategic three Cs: customer (e.g., buying behavior), competition (e.g., competitive definitions of the business), and company (e.g., cost behavior, such as efficiencies via economies of scale; resources/skills, such as financial strength, managerial talent, engineering/manufacturing capability, physical distribution system, etc.; and differences in marketing, manufacturing, and research and development requirements and so on, resulting from market segmentation).

Typology of Business Definitions

Abell proposed defining business in terms of three measures: scope, differentiation across segments, and differentiation across competitors. According to Abell, scope and both kinds of differentiation are related to one another in complex ways. One way to conceptualize these interrelationships is in terms of a typology of business definitions. Three alternative strategies for defining a business are recommended: (a) a focused strategy, (b) a differentiated strategy, and (c) an undifferentiated strategy.

EXHIBIT 8-2
Defining Business Mission—Narrow Scope

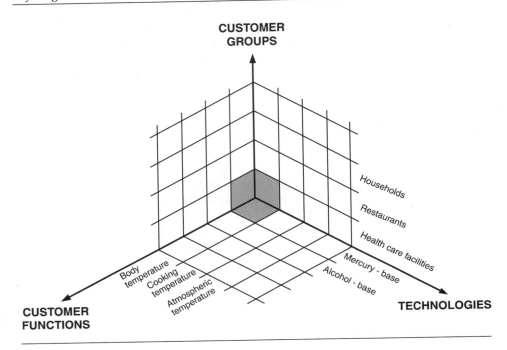

- *Focused strategy*—A business may choose to focus on a particular customer group, customer function, or technology segment. Focus implies a certain basis for segmentation along one or more of these dimensions, narrow scope involving only one or a few chosen segments, and differentiation from competitors through careful tailoring of the offering to the specific need of the segment(s) targeted.
- *Differentiated strategy*—When a business combines broad scope with differentiation across any or all of the three dimensions, it may be said to follow a differentiated strategy. Differentiation across segments may also be related to competitive differentiation. By tailoring the offering to the specific needs of each segment, a company automatically increases the chance for competitive superiority. Whether or not competitive differentiation also results is purely a function of the extent to which competitors have also tailored their offerings to the same specific segments. If they have, segment differentiation may be substantial, yet competitive differentiation may be small.
- *Undifferentiated strategy*—When a company combines broad scope across any or all of the three dimensions with an undifferentiated approach to customer group, customer function, or technology segments, it is said to follow an undifferentiated strategy.[16]

   Each of these strategies can be applied to the three dimensions (customer groups, customer functions, and technologies) separately. In other words, 27 different combinations are possible: (a) focused, differentiated, or undifferentiated across customer groups; (b) focused, differentiated, or undifferentiated across

EXHIBIT 8-3
Defining Business Mission—Broader Scope

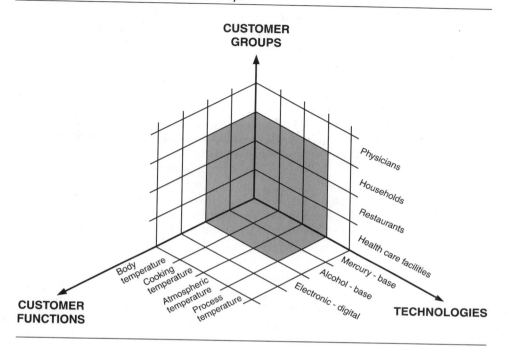

customer functions; (c) focused, differentiated, or undifferentiated across technologies, and so on.

A focused strategy serves a specific customer group, customer function, or technology segment. It has a narrow scope. Docutel Corporation's strategy in the late 1960s exemplified a focused strategy relative to customer function. When Docutel first pioneered the development of the automated teller machine (ATM), it defined customer function very narrowly, concentrating on one function only—cash dispensing.

A differentiated strategy combines broad scope with differentiation across one or more of the three dimensions. A differentiated strategy serves several customer groups, functions, or technologies while tailoring the product offered to each segment's specific needs. An example of a differentiated strategy applied to customer groups is athletic footwear. Athletic footwear serves a broad range of customer groups and is differentiated across those groups. Tennis shoes are tailored to meet the needs of one specific customer group; basketball shoes, another.

An undifferentiated strategy combines a broad scope across one or more of the three dimensions. This strategy is applied to customer groups in a business that serves a wide range of customer groups but does not differentiate its offerings among those groups. Docutel's strategy was focused with respect to customer function but not with respect to customer groups: they offered exactly the same product to commercial banks, savings and loans, mutual savings banks, and credit unions. To sum up, the strategy that a business chooses to follow, based on the amount of scope and differentiation applied to the three dimensions, determines the definition of the business.

SBU OBJECTIVES AND GOALS

The objectives and goals of the SBU may be stated in terms of activities (manufacturing a specific product, selling in a particular market); financial indicators (achieving targeted return on investment); desired positions (market share, quality leadership); and combinations of these factors. Generally, an SBU has a series of objectives to cater to the interests of different stakeholders. One way of organizing objectives is to split them into the following classes: measurement objectives, growth/survival objectives, and constraint objectives. It must be emphasized that objectives and goals should not be based just on facts but on values and feelings as well. What facts should one look at? How should they be weighed and related to one another? It is in seeking answers to such questions that value judgments become crucial.

The perspectives of an SBU determine how far an objective can be broken down into minute details. If the objective applies to a number of products, only broad statements of objectives that specify the role of each product/market from the vantage point of the SBU are feasible. On the other hand, when an SBU is created around one or two products, objectives may be stated in detail.

Exhibit 8-4 illustrates how SBU objectives and goals can be identified and split into three groups: measurement, growth/survival, and constraint. Measurement objectives and goals define an SBU's aims from the point of view of the stockholders. The word *profit* has been traditionally used instead of measurement. But, as is widely recognized today, a corporation has several corporate publics besides stockholders; therefore, it is erroneous to use the word profit. On the other hand, the company's very existence and its ability to serve different stakeholders depend on financial viability. Thus, profit constitutes an important measurement objective. To emphasize the real significance of profit, it is more appropriate to label it as a measurement tool.

It will be useful here to draw a distinction between corporate objectives and measurement objectives and goals at the level of an SBU. Corporate objectives define the company's outlook for various stakeholders as a general concept, but the SBU's objectives and goals are specific statements. For example, keeping the environment clean may be a corporate objective. Using this corporate objective as a basis, in a particular time frame an SBU may define prevention of water pollution as one of its objectives. In other words, it is not necessary to repeat the company's obligation to various stakeholders in defining an SBU's objectives as this is already covered in the corporate objectives. Objectives and goals should underline the areas that need to be covered during the time horizon of planning.

EXHIBIT 8-4
Illustration of an SBU's Objectives

I. SBU
   Cooking Appliances

II. Mission
   To market to individual homes cooking appliances that perform such functions as baking, boiling, and roasting, using electric fuel technology.

III. Objectives (general statements in the following areas):
   A. Measurement
      1. Profitability
      2. Cash flow
   B. Growth/Survival
      1. Market standing
      2. Productivity
      3. Innovation
   C. Constraint
      1. Capitalize on our research in certain technologies
      2. Avoid style businesses with seasonal obsolescence
      3. Avoid antitrust problems
      4. Assume responsibility to public

IV. Goals
   Specific targets and time frame for achievement of each objective listed above.

Growth objectives and goals, with their implicit references to getting ahead, are accepted as normal goals in a capitalistic system. Thus, companies often aim at growth. Although measurements are usually stated in financial terms, growth is described with reference to the market. Constraint objectives and goals depend on the internal environment of the company and how it wishes to interact with the outside world.

An orderly description of objectives may not always work out, and the three types of objectives and goals may overlap. It is important, however, that the final draft of objectives be based on investigation, analysis, and contemplation.

PRODUCT/MARKET OBJECTIVES

Product/market objectives may be defined in terms of profitability, market share, or growth. Most businesses state their product/market purpose through a combination of these terms. Some companies, especially very small ones, may use just one of these terms to communicate product/market objectives. Usually, product/market objectives are stated at the SBU level.

Profitability | Profits in one form or another constitute a desirable goal for a product/market venture. As objectives, they may be expressed either in absolute monetary terms or as a percentage of capital employed or of total assets.

At the corporate level, emphasis on profit in a statement of objectives is sometimes avoided because it seems to convey a limited perspective of the corporate purpose. But at the product/market level, an objective stated in terms of profitability provides a measurable criterion with which management can evaluate performance. Because product/market objectives are an internal matter, the corporation is not constrained by any ethical questions in its emphasis on profits.

An ardent user of the profitability objective is Georgia-Pacific Company. The company aims at achieving a return of 20 percent on stockholders' equity. The orthodox view has been that, in an industry where product differentiation is not feasible, the goal of profitability is irrelevant. But Georgia-Pacific's CEO, Marshall Hahn, insists on the profit goal, and the outcome has been very satisfactory. Georgia-Pacific's overall performance has been twice as good as any other competitor in the industry.[17] Similarly, Chrysler Corporation shuns market share in favor of profits. In 1993, for example, Chrysler earned more from the auto business than GM and Ford combined, or the nine Japanese automakers.[18]

How can the profitability goal be realized in practice? First, the corporate management determines the desired profitability, that is, the desired rate of return on investment. There may be a single goal set for the entire corporation, or goals may vary for different businesses. Using the given rate of return, the SBU may compute the percentage of markup on cost for its product(s). To do so, the normal rate of production, averaged over the business cycle, is computed. The total cost of normal production then becomes the standard cost. Next, the ratio of invested capital (in the SBU) to a year's standard cost (i.e., capital turnover) is computed. The capital turnover multiplied by the rate of return gives the markup percentage to be applied to standard cost. This markup is an average figure that may be adjusted both among products and over time.

Market Share

In many industries, the cigarette industry, for example, gaining a few percentage points in market share has a positive effect on profits. Thus, market share has traditionally been considered a desirable goal to pursue. In recent years, extensive research on the subject has uncovered new evidence on the positive impact of market share on profitability.[19]

The importance of market share is explainable by the fact that it is related to cost. Cost is a function of scale or experience. Thus, the market leader may have a lower cost than other competitors because superior market share permits the accumulation of more experience. Prices, however, are determined by the cost structure of the least effective competitor. The high-cost competitor must generate enough cash to hold market share and meet expenses. If this is not accomplished, the high-cost competitor drops out and is replaced by a more effective, lower-cost competitor. The profitability of the market leader is ascertained by the same price level that determines the profit of even the least effective competitor. Thus, higher market share may give a competitive edge to a firm.

One strong proponent of market share goal is Eastman Kodak Co. The company takes a long-term view and commits itself to obtaining a big share of growth markets. It keeps building new plants even though its first plant for a product has yet to run at full capacity. It does so hoping large-scale operations will provide a cost advantage that it can utilize in the form of lower prices to customers. Lower prices in turn lead to a higher market share.

Kodak has 80 percent of the U.S. consumer film market and 50 percent of the global business. Yet even with such a high share, the company does not believe in simply maintaining market share. For Kodak, there are only two alternatives: grow the share or it will decline. After all, in the film business, one point of global market share amounts to $40 million in revenues.[20]

While market share is a viable goal, tremendous foresight and effort are needed to achieve and maintain market share positions. A company aspiring toward a large share of the market should carefully consider two aspects: (1) its ability to finance the market share and (2) its ability to effectively defend itself against antitrust action that may be instigated by large increases in market share. For example, when General Electric considered entering the computer business, it found that to meet its corporate profitability objective it had to achieve a specific market share position. To realize its targeted market share position required huge investment. The question, then, was whether General Electric should gamble in an industry dominated by one large competitor (IBM) or invest its monies in fields where there was the probability of earning a return equal to or higher than returns in the computer field. General Electric decided to get out of the computer field.

Fear of antitrust suits also prohibits the seeking of higher market shares. A number of corporations—Kodak, Gillette, Xerox, and IBM, for example—have been the target of such action.

These reasons suggest that, although market share should be pursued as a desirable goal, companies should opt not for share maximization but for an optimal market share. Optimal market share can be determined in the following manner:

1. Estimate the relationship between market share and profitability.
2. Estimate the amount of risk associated with each share level.
3. Determine the point at which an increase in market share can no longer be expected to earn enough profit to compensate the company for the added risks to which it would expose itself.

The advantages of higher market share do not mean that a company with a lower share may not have a chance in the industry. There are companies that earn a respectable return on equity despite low market shares. Examples of such corporations are Crown Cork and Seal, Union Camp, and Inland Steel. The following characteristics explain the success of low-share companies: (a) they compete only in those market segments where their strengths have the greatest impact, (b) they make efficient use of their modest research and development budgets, (c) they shun growth for growth's sake, and (d) they have innovative leaders.[21]

Briefly, market share goals should not be taken lightly. Rather, a firm should aim at a market share after careful examination.

The following example illustrates the importance of market share. Exhibit 8-5 shows the experience of the industry leader in an industrial product. With an initially high share of a growing and competitive market, management shifted its

EXHIBIT 8-5
Relationship Between Market Share and After-Tax Profit

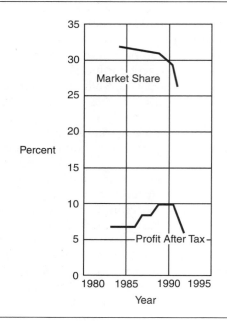

emphasis from market share to high earnings. A manager with proven skills was put in charge of the business. Earnings increased for six years at the expense of some slow erosion in market share. In the seventh year, however, market share fell so rapidly that, though efforts to hold profits were redoubled, they dropped sharply. Share was never regained. The manager had been highly praised and richly rewarded for his profit results up to 1990. These results, however, were achieved in exchange for a certain unreported damage to the firm's long-term competitiveness. Only by knowing both and by weighing the gain in current income against the degree of market share liquidation that entailed could the true value of performance be judged. In other words, reported earnings do not tell the true story unless market share is constant. Loss of market share is liquidation of an unbooked asset upon which the value of all other assets depends. Gain in market share is like an addition to cost potential, just as real an asset as credit rating, brand image, organization resources, or technology. In brief, market share guarantees the long-term survival of the business. Liquidation of market share to realize short-term earnings should be avoided. High earnings make sense only when market share is stable.

Growth   Growth is an accepted phenomenon of a modern corporation. All institutions should progress and grow. Those that do not grow invite extinction. Static corporations are often subject to proxy fights.

There are a variety of reasons that make growth a viable objective: (a) growth expectations of the stockholders, (b) growth orientation of top management, (c) employees' enthusiasm, (d) growth opportunities furnished by the environment, (e) corporate need to compete effectively in the marketplace, and (f) corporate strengths and competencies that make it easy to grow. Exhibit 8-6 amplifies these reasons under the following categories: customer reasons; competitive reasons; company reasons; and distributor, dealer, and agent reasons.

EXHIBIT 8-6
Reasons for Growth

Customer Reasons

The product line or sizes too limited for customer convenience.
Related products needed to serve a specific market.
Purchasing economies: one source, one order, one bill.
Service economies: one receiving and processing; one source of parts, service, and other assistance.
Ability to give more and better services.
Production capacity not enough to fill needs of important customers who may themselves be growing.

Competitive Reasons

To maintain or better industry position; growth is necessary in any but a declining industry.
To counter or better chief competitors on new offerings.
To maintain or better position in specific product or market areas where competition is making strong moves.
To permit more competitive pricing ability through greater volume.
To possess greater survival strength in price wars, product competition, and economic slumps by greater size.

Company Reasons

To fulfill the growth expectations of stockholders, directors, executives, and employees.
To utilize available management, selling, distribution, research, or production capacity.
To supplement existing products and services that are not growth markets or are on downgrade of the profit cycle.
To stabilize seasonal or cyclical fluctuations.
To add flexibility by broadening the market and product base of opportunities.
To attain greater borrowing and financial influence with size.
To be able to attract and pay for better management personnel.
To attain the stability of size and move to management by planning.

Distributor, Dealer, and Agent Reasons

To add products, sizes, and ranges necessary to attract interest of better distributors, dealers, and agents.
To make additions necessary to obtain needed attention and selling effort from existing distributors, dealers, and agents.

An example of growth encouraged by corporate strength is provided by R.J. Reynolds Industries. In the early 1980s, the company was in an extremely strong cash position, which helped it to acquire Heublein, Del Monte Corp., and Nabisco. H. S. Geneen's passion for growth led ITT into different industries (bakeries, car rental agencies, hotels, insurance firms, parking lots) in addition to its traditional communications business. Any field that promised growth was acceptable to him. Thus, the CEO's growth orientation is the most valuable prerequisite for growth. Similarly, growth ambitions led Procter & Gamble to venture into cosmetics and over-the-counter health remedies.

Other Objectives | In addition to the commonly held objectives of profitability, market share, and growth (discussed above), a company may sometimes pursue a unique objective. Such an objective might be technological leadership, social contribution, the strengthening of national security, or international economic development.

Technological Leadership. A company may consider technological leadership a worthwhile goal. In order to accomplish this, it may develop new products or processes or adopt innovations ahead of the competition, even when economics may not justify doing so. The underlying purpose in seeking this objective is to keep the name of the company in the forefront as a technological leader among security analysts, customers, distributors, and other stakeholders. To continue to be in the forefront of computer technology, in 1987 IBM entered the field of supercomputers, an area that it had previously shunned because the market was limited.[22]

Social Contribution. A company may pursue as an objective something that will make a social contribution. Ultimately, that something may lead to higher profitability, but initially it is intended to provide a solution to a social problem. A beverage company, for example, may attack the problem of litter by not offering its product in throwaway bottles. As another example, a pharmaceutical company may set its objective to develop and market an AIDS-preventive medicine.

Strengthening of National Security. In the interest of strengthening national defense, a company may undertake activities not otherwise justifiable. For example, concern for national security may lead a company to deploy resources to develop a new fighter plane. The company may do so despite little encouragement from the air force, if only because the company sincerely feels that the country will need the plane in the coming years.

International Economic Development. Improvement in human welfare, the economic progress of less-developed countries, or the promotion of a worldwide free enterprise system may also serve as objectives. For example, a company may undertake the development of a foolproof method of birth control that can be easily afforded and conveniently used.

PROCESS OF SETTING OBJECTIVES

At the very beginning of the process of setting objectives, an SBU should attempt to take an inventory of objectives as they are currently understood. For example, the SBU head and senior executives may state the current objectives of the SBU and the type of SBU they want it to be in the future. Various executives perceive current objectives differently; and, of course, they will have varying ambitions for the SBU's future. It will take several top-level meetings and a good deal of effort on the part of the SBU head to settle on final objectives.

Each executive may be asked to make a presentation on the objectives and goals he or she would like the SBU to adopt for the future. Executives should be asked to justify the significance of each objective in terms of measuring performance, satisfying environmental conditions, and achieving growth. It is foreseeable that executives will have different objectives; they may express the same objectives in terms that make them appear different, but there should emerge, on analysis, a desire for a common destiny for the SBU. Disharmony of objectives may sometimes be based on diverse perceptions of a business's resource potential and corporate strategy. Thus, before embarking on setting SBU objectives, it is helpful if information on resource potential and corporate strategy is circulated.

Before finalizing the objectives, it is necessary that the executive team show a consensus; that is, each one should believe in the viability of the set objectives and willingly agree to work toward their achievement. A way must be found to persuade a dissenting executive to cooperate. For example, if a very ambitious executive works with stability-oriented people, in the absence of an opportunity to be creative, the executive may fail to perform routine matters adequately, thus becoming a liability to the organization. In such a situation, it may be better to encourage the executive to look for another job. This option is useful for the organization as well as for the dissenting executive. This type of situation occurs when most of the executives have risen through the ranks and an "outsider" joins them. The dynamism of the latter is perceived as a threat, which may result in conflict. The author is familiar with a $100 million company where the vice president of finance, an "outsider," in his insistence on strategic planning came to be perceived as such a danger by the old-timers that they made it necessary for him to quit.

To sum up, objectives should be set through a series of executive meetings. The organizational head plays the role of mediator in the process of screening varying viewpoints and perceptions and developing consensus from them.

Once broad objectives have been worked out, they should be translated into specific goals, an equally challenging task. Should goals be set so high that only an outstanding manager can achieve them, or should they be set so that they are attainable by the average manager? At what level does frustration inhibit a manager's best efforts? Does an attainable budget lead to complacency? Presumably a company should start with three levels of goals: (a) easily attainable, (b) most desirable, and (c) optimistic. Thereafter, the company may choose a position somewhere between the most desirable goals and the optimistic goals, depending on the organization's resources and the value orientation of management. In no case, however, should performance fall below easily attainable levels, even if everything goes wrong. Attempts should be made to make the goals realistic and achievable. Overly elusive goals can discourage and affect motivation. As a matter of fact, realistic goals may provide higher rewards. In 1992, Eastman Kodak lowered its 6 percent annual revenue growth from the core film and photographic paper business to 3 percent. Subsequently, its stock price went up from $40 to $50.[23]

There are no universally accepted standards, procedures, or measures for defining objectives. Each organization must work out its own definitions of objectives and goals—what constitutes growth, what measures to adopt for their evaluation, and so on. For example, consider the concept of return on investment, which for decades has been considered a good measure of corporate performance. A large number of corporations consider a specified return on investment as the most sacrosanct of goals. But ponder its limitations. In a large, complex organization, ROI tends to optimize divisional performance at the cost of total corporate performance. Further, its orientation is short-term. Investment refers to assets. Different projects require a varying amount of assets before beginning to yield results, and the return may be slow or fast, depending on the nature of the project. Thus, the value of assets may lose significance as an element in performance measurement. As the president of a large company remarked, "Profits are often the result of expenses incurred several years previously." The president suggested that the current amount of net cash flow serves as a better measure of performance than the potential amount of net cash flow: "The net cash contribution budget is a precise measure of expectations with given resources."

The following six sources may be used to generate objectives and goals:

1. Focus on material resources (e.g., oil, minerals, forest).
2. Concern with fabricated objects (e.g., paper, nylon).
3. Major interest in events and activities requiring certain products or services, such as handling deliveries (Federal Express).
4. Emphasis on the kind of person whose needs are to be met: "Babies Are Our Business" (Gerber).
5. Catering to specific parts of the body: eyes (Maybelline), teeth (Dr. West), feet (Florsheim), skin (Noxzema), hair (Clairol), beard (Gillette), and legs (Hanes).
6. Examination of wants and needs and seeking to adapt to them: generic use to be satisfied (nutrition, comfort, energy, self-expression, development, conformity, etc.) and consumption systems (for satisfying nutritional needs, e.g.).

Whichever procedure is utilized for finally coming out with a set of objectives and goals, the following serve as basic inputs in the process. At the corporate level, objectives are influenced by corporate publics, the value system of top management, corporate resources, the performance of business units, and the external environment. SBU objectives are based on the strategic three Cs of customer, competition, and corporation. Product/market objectives are dictated by product/market strengths and weaknesses and by momentum. Strengths and weaknesses are determined on the basis of current strategy, past performance, marketing excellence, and marketing environment. Momentum refers to future trends—extrapolation of past performance with the assumption that no major changes will occur either in the product/market environment or in its marketing mix.

Identified above are the conceptual framework and underlying information useful in defining objectives at different levels. Unfortunately, there is no computer model to neatly relate all available information to produce a set of acceptable objectives. Thus, whichever conceptual scheme is followed and no matter how much information is available, in the final analysis objective-setting remains a creative exercise.

Once an objective has been set, it may be tested for validity using the following criteria:

1. Is it, generally speaking, a guide to action? Does it facilitate decision making by helping management select the most desirable alternative courses of action?
2. Is it explicit enough to suggest certain types of action? In this sense, "to make profits" does not represent a particularly meaningful guide to action, but "to carry on a profitable business in electrical goods" does.
3. Is it suggestive of tools to measure and control effectiveness? "To be a leader in the insurance business" and "to be an innovator in child care services" are suggestive of measuring tools in a helpful way; but statements of desires merely to participate in the insurance field or child care field are not.
4. Is it ambitious enough to be challenging? The action called for should in most cases be something in addition to resting on one's laurels. Unless the enterprise sets objectives that involve reaching, there is the threat that the end of the road may be at hand.

> Canon illustrates this point clearly. In 1975, Canon was a mediocre Japanese camera company. It was scarcely growing and had recently turned unprofitable for the first time since 1949. It set a few enormously aggressive goals, most of them quantitative. Its key goals were to increase sales *fivefold* over the next decade, to achieve 3 percent productivity improvement per *month*, to cut in half the time required to develop new products, and to build the premier manufacturing organization.
>
> To achieve these goals, Canon established policies that focused on continuous improvement through the elimination of waste, broadly defined. Among other new policies, Canon put in place a number of organizational measures to promote active employee cooperation. A prime objective was to increase the number of suggestions per employee to 30 per year by 1982, up from one in 1975. This goal was achieved and then surpassed: by 1986, each employee was contributing, on average, 50 suggestions annually.
>
> Planning within the company was refocused on methods to reach targets and, more importantly, on identifying internal capabilities required to achieve targets. Another policy was to make every performance measure visual, so employees could see at a glance where they were in relation to goals. In each factory, for example, there are visual representations of ongoing improvement activity in relation to goals.
>
> By 1982, Canon had achieved each of its goals. It is now a significant and vigorous competitor in cameras, copiers, and computers.[24]

5. Does it suggest cognizance of external and internal constraints? Most enterprises operate within a framework of external constraints (e.g., legal and competitive restrictions) and internal constraints (e.g., limitations in financial resources).

> In the late 1970s, Toyota set as its goal to defeat General Motors. It realized that to do so, it needed scale. To achieve scale, it needed first to defeat Nissan. Toyota initiated a battle against Nissan in which it rapidly introduced a vast array of new autos, capturing market share from Nissan. That battle won, Toyota could turn its attention to its long-term goal—besting General Motors. Targeting the leader is a great way to build momentum and create an organizational challenge.

6. Can it be related to both the broader and the more specific objectives at higher and lower levels in the organization? For example, can SBU objectives be related to corporate objectives, and in turn, do they also relate to the objectives of one of its products/markets?

SUMMARY

The thrust of this chapter was on defining objectives and goals at the SBU level. Objectives may be defined as general statements of the long-term purpose the business wants to pursue. Goals are specific targets the corporation would like to achieve within a given time frame. Because SBU objectives should bear a close relationship to overall corporate direction, the chapter first examined the networks of mission, objectives, and goals that make up a company's corporate direction. The example of the Dow Chemical Company was given.

The discussion of SBU objectives began with the business mission, which defines the total perspectives or purpose of a business. In addition to presenting the traditional viewpoint on business mission, a new framework for defining the business was introduced. SBU objectives and goals were defined in terms of either financial indicators or desired positions or combinations of these factors. Also considered were product/market objectives. Usually set at the SBU level, product/market objectives were defined in terms of profitability, market share, growth, and several other aspects. Finally, the process of setting objectives was outlined.

DISCUSSION QUESTIONS

1. Define the terms *policy*, *objective*, and *goal*.
2. What is meant by corporate direction? Why is it necessary to set corporate direction?
3. Does corporate direction undergo change? Discuss.
4. How does the traditional view of the business mission differ from the new approach?
5. Examine the perspectives of the new approach to defining the business mission.
6. Using the new approach, how may an airline define its business mission?
7. In what way is the market share objective viable?
8. Give examples of product/market objectives in terms of technological leadership, social contribution, and strengthening of national security.

NOTES

[1] *Perspectives on Corporate Strategy* (Boston: Boston Consulting Group, 1970), 44.

[2] The discussion on Dow Chemical Company draws heavily on information provided by the company.

[3] "The Right Move Early," *Forbes* (8 January 1990): 130–31.

[4] Lee Smith, "Dow vs. Du Pont: Rival Formulas for Leadership," *Fortune* (10 September 1979): 74.

[5] "Dow Chemical's Drive to Change Its Market and Its Image," *Business Week* (9 June 1986): 92.

[6] Roger E. Levien, "Technological Transformation at Xerox," in *Strategic Management: Bridging Strategy and Performance* (New York: The Conference Board, Inc., 1992): 21–22.

[7] James Brian Quinn, "Strategic Goals: Process and Politics," *Sloan Management Review* (Fall 1977): 34–36.

[8] Robert F. McCracken, "Bringing Vision to Avon," in *Strategic Management: Bridging Strategy and Performance* (New York: The Conference Board, Inc., 1993): 25.

[9] "IBM: A Work in Progress—Its Strategic Direction Remains Unclear," *Business Week* (9 August 1993): 24.

[10] "The Vision Thing," *The Economist* (9 November 1991): 81.

[11] Derek F. Abell, "Metamorphosis in Marketing Planning," in *Research Frontiers in Marketing: Dialogues and Directions,* ed. Subhash C. Jain (Chicago: American Marketing Association, 1978): 257.

[12] Theodore Levitt, "Marketing Myopia," *Harvard Business Review* (July–August 1960): 46.

[13] *Perspectives on Corporate Strategy*, 42.

[14] "Coca-Cola: A Sobering Lesson from Its Journey into Wine," *Business Week* (3 June 1985): 96.

[15] Derek F. Abell, *Defining the Business: The Starting Point of Strategic Planning* (Englewood Cliffs, NJ: Prentice Hall, 1980).

[16] Abell, *Defining the Business*, 174–75.

[17] Erik Calonius, "America's Toughest Papermaker," *Fortune* (26 February 1990): 80.

[18] Alex Taylor III, "Will Success Spoil Chrysler?" *Fortune* (10 January 1994): 88.

[19] See Robert D. Buzzell and Bradley T. Gale, *The PIMS Principles* (New York: The Free Press, 1987).

[20] Bill Saporito, "Companies That Compete Best," *Fortune* (22 May 1989): 36.

[21] Carolyn Y. Woo and Arnold C. Cooper, "The Surprising Case for Low Market Share," *Harvard Business Review* (November–December 1982): 106–13.

[22] *Time* (28 March 1988): 36.

[23] "Higher Rewards in Lowered Goals," *Fortune* (8 March 1993): 75.

[24] Robert Reiner, "Goal Setting," in *Perspectives* (Boston: Boston Consulting Group, Inc., 1988).

Strategy Formulation

Strategy Selection

Two things were achieved in the previous chapters. First, the internal and external information required for formulating marketing strategy was identified, and the methods for analyzing information were examined. Second, using the available information, the formulation of objectives was covered. This chapter takes us to the next step toward strategy formulation by establishing a framework for it.

Our principal concern in this chapter is with business unit strategy. Among several inputs required to formulate business unit strategy, one basic input is the strategic perspective of different products/markets that constitute the business unit. Therefore, as a first step toward formulating business unit strategy, a scheme for developing product/market strategies is introduced.

Bringing product/market strategies within a framework of business unit strategy formulation emphasizes the importance of inputs from both the top down and the bottom up. As a matter of fact, it can be said that strategic decisions in a diversified company are best made at three different levels: jointly by product/market managers and the SBU manager when questions of implementation are involved, jointly by the CEO and the SBU manager when formulation of strategy is the concern, and by the CEO when the mission of the business is at issue.

CONCEPTUAL SCHEME

Exhibit 9-1 depicts the framework for developing marketing strategy. As delineated earlier, marketing strategy is based on three key factors: corporation, customer, and competition. The interaction between these three factors is rather complex. For example, the corporation factor impacts marketing strategy formulation through (a) business unit mission and its goals and objectives, (b) perspectives of strengths and weaknesses in different functional areas of the business at different levels, and (c) perspectives of different products/markets that constitute the business unit. Competition affects the business unit mission as well as the measurement of strengths and weaknesses. The customer factor is omnipresent, affecting the formation of goals and objectives to support the business unit mission and directly affecting marketing strategy.

PRODUCT/MARKET STRATEGY

The following step-by-step procedure is used for formulating product/market strategy:

EXHIBIT 9-1
Framework for Formulating Marketing Strategy

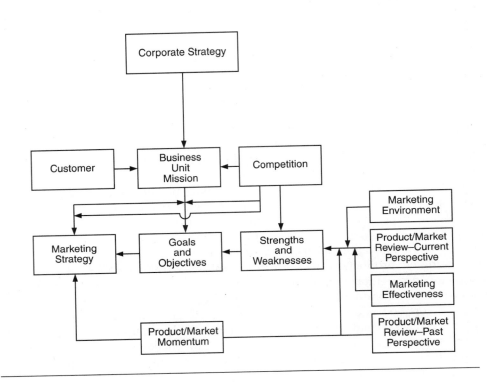

1. Start with the present business. Predict what the momentum of the business will be over the planning period if no significant changes are made in the policies or methods of operation. The prediction should be based on historical performance.
2. Forecast what will happen to the environment over the planning period. This forecast will include overall marketing environment and product/market environment.
3. Modify the prediction in Step 1 in light of forecasted shifts in the environment in Step 2.
4. Stop if predicted performance is fully satisfactory vis-à-vis objectives. Continue if the prediction is not fully satisfying.
5. Appraise the significant strengths and weaknesses of the business in comparison with those of important competitors. This appraisal should include any factors that may become important both in marketing (market, product, price, promotion, and distribution) and in other functional areas (finance, research and development, costs, organization, morale, reputation, management depth, etc.).
6. Evaluate the differences between your marketing strategies and those of your major competitors.
7. Undertake an analysis to discover some variation in marketing strategy that would produce a more favorable relationship in your competitive posture in the future.

8. Evaluate the proposed alternate strategy in terms of possible risks, competitive response, and potential payout.
9. Stop if the alternate strategy appears satisfactory in terms of objectives.
10. Broaden the definition of the present business and repeat Steps 7, 8, and 9 if there is still a gap between the objective and the alternative strategy. Here, redefining the business means looking at other products that can be supplied to a market that is known and understood. Sometimes this means supplying existing products to a different market. It may also mean applying technical or financial abilities to new products and new markets simultaneously.
11. The process of broadening the definition of the business to provide a wider horizon can be continued until one of the following occurs:

    a. The knowledge of the new area becomes so thin that a choice of the sector to be studied is determined by intuition or by obviously inadequate judgment.
    b. The cost of studying the new area becomes prohibitively expensive because of lack of related experience.
    c. It becomes clear that the prospects of finding a competitive opportunity are remote.

12. Lower the objectives if the existing business is not satisfactory and if broadening the definition of the business offers unsatisfactory prospects.

There are three tasks involved in this strategy procedure: information analysis, strategy formulation, and implementation. At the product/market level, these tasks are performed by either the product/market manager or an SBU executive. In practice, analysis and implementation are usually handled entirely by the product/market manager; strategy formulation is done jointly by the product/market manager and the SBU executive.

Essentially, all firms have some kind of strategy and plans to carry on their operations. In the past, both plans and strategy were made intuitively. However, the increasing pace of change is forcing businesses to make their strategies explicit and often to change them. Strategy per se is getting more and more attention.

Any approach to strategy formulation leads to a conflict between objectives and capabilities. Attempting the impossible is not a good strategy; it is just a waste of resources. On the other hand, setting inadequate objectives is obviously self-defeating. Setting the proper objectives depends upon prejudgment of the potential success of the strategy; however, you cannot determine the strategy until you know the objectives. Strategy development is a reiterative process requiring art as well as science. This dilemma may explain why many strategies are intuitively made rather than logically and tightly reasoned. But there are concepts that can be usefully applied in approximating opportunities and in speeding up the process of strategy development. The above procedure is designed not only to analyze information systematically but also to formulate or change strategy in an explicit fashion and implement it.

Measuring the Momentum

The first phase in developing product/market plans is to predict the future state of affairs, assuming that the environment and the strategy remain the same. This future state of affairs may be called *momentum*. If the momentum projects a desirable future, no change in strategy is needed. More often, however, the future implied by the momentum may not be the desired future.

The momentum may be predicted using modeling, forecasting, and simulation techniques. Let us describe how these techniques were applied at a bank. This bank grew by opening two to three new branches per year in its trading area. The measurement of momentum consisted of projecting income statement and balance sheet figures for new branches and merging them with the projected income statement and balance sheet of the original bank. A model was constructed to project the bank's future performance. The first step in construction of the model was the prediction of B_{ijt}, that is, balances for an account of type i in area j and in time period t. Account types included checking, savings, and certificates of deposit; areas were chosen to coincide with counties in the state. County areas were desirable because most data at the state level were available by county and because current branching areas were defined by counties. Balances were projected using multiple linear regression. County per capita income and rate of population growth were found to be important variables for predicting total checking account balances, and these variables, along with the last period's savings balance, were shown to be important in describing savings account balances.

The next step was to predict M_{jt} (i.e., the market share of the bank being considered in area j and time period t). This was done using a combination of data of past performances and managerial judgment. The total expected deposit level for the branch being considered, D_{it}, was then calculated as:

$$D_{it} = \sum_{jb} (B_{ijt} M_{jt})$$

For the existing operations of the bank, past data were utilized to produce a 10-year set of deposit balances. These deposit projections were added to those of new branches. Turning to other figures, certain line items on the income statement could be attributed directly to checking accounts, others to savings accounts. The remaining figures were related to the total of account balances.

For this model, ratios of income and expense items to appropriate deposit balances were predicted by a least-squares regression on historical data. This was not considered the most satisfactory method because some changing patterns of incurring income and expenses were not taken into account. However, more sophisticated forecasting techniques, such as exponential smoothing and Box-Jenkins, were rejected because of the potential management misunderstanding they could generate.

Once the ratio matrix was developed, income statements could be generated by simply multiplying the ratios by the proper account balance projection to arrive at the 10-year projection for income statement line items. These income statements, in conjunction with the bank's policy on dividends and capitalization, were then used to generate a 10-year balance sheet projection. The net results were presented to the bank's senior executive committee to be reviewed and modified. After incorporating executive judgment, final 10-year income statements and balance sheets were obtained, indicating the bank's momentum into the future.

Gap Analysis

In the banking example, momentum was extrapolated from historical data. Little attention was given to either internal or external environmental considerations in developing the momentum. However, for a realistic projection of future outcomes, careful analysis of the overall marketing environment as well as the product/market environment is necessary.

As a part of gap analysis, therefore, the momentum should be examined and adjusted with reference to environmental assumptions. The industry, the market, and the competitive environment should be analyzed to identify important threats and opportunities. This analysis should be combined with a careful evaluation of product/market competitive strengths and weaknesses. On the basis of this information, the momentum should be evaluated and refined.

For example, in the midst of continued concern about inflation in 1994, the chairman of the Federal Reserve System, Alan Greenspan, decided to limit the money supply. To do so, the prime and short-term interest rates were increased. For instance, the rate of interest on many 30-month certificates of deposit went up from 4.5 percent in 1993 to 7.0 percent in 1994. This increase led many depositors to choose certificates of deposit over other forms of investment. In the illustration discussed in the last section, the impact of such a increase in interest rates was not considered in arriving at the momentum (i.e., in making forecasts of deposit balances). As a part of gap analysis, this shift in the environment would be duly taken into account and the momentum would be adequately adjusted.

The "new" momentum should then be measured against objectives to see if there is a gap between expectation and potential realization. More often than not, there will be a gap between desired objectives and what the projected momentum, as revised with reference to environmental assumptions, can deliver. How this gap may be filled is discussed next.

Filling the Gap

The gap must be filled to bring planned results as close to objectives as possible. Essentially, gap filling amounts to reformulating product/market strategy.[1] A three-step procedure may be used for examining current strategy and coming up with a new one to fill the gap. These steps are issue assessment, identification of key variables, and strategy selection. The experience of some companies suggests that gap filling should be assigned to a multifunctional team. Nonmarketing people often provide fresh inputs; their objectivity and healthy skepticism are generally of great help in sharpening focus and in maintaining businesswide perspectives. The process the team follows should be carefully structured and the analytical work punctuated with regular review meetings to synthesize findings, check progress, and refocus work when desirable. The SBU staff should be deeply involved in the evaluation and approval of the strategies.

Issue Assessment. The primary purpose of this step is to raise issues about the status quo to evaluate the business's competitive standing in view of present and expected market conditions. To begin, a team would typically work through a series of general questions about the industry to identify those few issues that will most crucially affect the future of the business. The following questions might be included: How mature is the product/market segment under review? What new avenues of market growth are conceivable? Is the industry becoming more cyclical? Are competitive factors changing (e.g., Is product line elaboration declining and cost control gaining in importance?)? Is our industry as a whole likely to be hurt by continuing inflation? Are new regulatory restrictions pending?

Next, the company should evaluate its own competitive position, for which the following questions may be raised: How mature is our product line? How do our products perform compared with those of leading competitors? How does our marketing capability compare? What about our cost position? What are our customers' most common criticisms? Where are we most vulnerable to competitors? How strong are we in our distribution channels? How productive is our technology? How good is our record in new product introduction?

Some critical issues are immediately apparent in many companies. For example, a company in a highly concentrated industry might find it difficult to hold on to its market share if a stronger, larger competitor were to launch a new low-priced product with intensive promotional support. Also, in a capital-intensive industry, the cyclical pattern and possible pressures on pricing are usually critical. If a product's transport costs are high, preemptive investments in regional manufacturing facilities may be desirable. Other important issues may be concerned with threats of backward integration by customers or forward integration by suppliers, technological upset, new regulatory action, or the entry of foreign competition into the home market. Most strategy teams supplement this brainstorming exercise with certain basic analyses that often lead to fresh insights and a more focused list of critical business issues. Three such issues that may be mentioned here are profit economics analysis, market segmentation analysis, and competitor profiling.

Profit Economics Analysis. Profit economics analysis indicates how product costs are physically generated and where economic leverage lies. The contribution of the product to fixed costs and profits may be calculated by classifying the elements of cost as fixed, variable, or semivariable and by subtracting variable cost from product price to yield contribution per item sold. It is then possible to test the sensitivity of profits to possible variations in volume, price, and cost elements. Similar computations may be made for manufacturing facilities, distribution channels, and customers.

Market Segmentation Analysis. Market segmentation analysis shows alternate methods of segmentation and whether there are any segments not being properly cultivated. Once the appropriate segment is determined, efforts should be made to project the determinants of demand (including cyclical factors and any constraints on market size or growth rate) and to explain pricing patterns, relative market shares, and other determinants of profitability.

Competitor Profiling. Profiling competitors may involve examining their sales literature, talking with experts or representatives of industry associations, and interviewing shared customers and any known former employees of competitors. If more information is needed, the team may acquire and analyze competing products and perhaps even arrange to have competitors interviewed by a third party. With these data, competitors may be compared in terms of product features and performance, pricing, likely product costs and profitability, marketing and service efforts, manufacturing facilities and efficiency, and technology and product development capabilities. Finally, each competitor's basic strategy may be inferred from these comparisons.

Identification of Key Variables. The information on issues described above should be analyzed to isolate the critical factors on which success in the industry depends.[2] In any business, there are usually about five to ten factors with a decisive effect on performance. As a matter of fact, in some industries one single factor may be the key to success. For example, in the airline industry, with its high fixed costs, a high load factor is critical to success. In the automobile industry, a strong dealer network is a key success factor because the manufacturer's sales crucially depend on the dealer's ability to finance a wide range of model choices and offer competitive prices to the customer. In a commodity component market, such as switches, timers, and relays, both market share and profitability are heavily influenced by product range. An engineer who is designing circuitry normally reaches for the thickest catalog with the richest product selection. In this industry, therefore, the manufacturer with a wide selection can collect more share points with only a meager sales force.

Key factors may vary from industry to industry. Even within a single company, factors may vary according to shifts in industry position, product superiority, distribution methods, economic conditions, availability of raw materials, and the like.[3] Therefore, suggested here is a set of questions that may be raised to identify the key success factors in any given situation:

1. What things must be done exceptionally well to win in this industry? In particular, what must we do well today to lead the industry in profit results and competitive vitality in the years ahead?
2. What factors have caused or could cause companies in this industry to fail?
3. What are the unique strengths of our principal competitors?
4. What are the risks of product or process obsolescence? How likely are they to occur and how critical could they be?
5. What things must be done to increase sales volume? How does a company in this industry go about increasing its share of the market? How could each of these ways of growing affect profits?
6. What are our major elements of cost? In what ways might each of them be reduced?
7. What are the big profit leverage points in this industry (i.e., What would be the comparative impact on profits of equal management efforts expended on each of a whole series of possible improvement opportunities?)?
8. What key recurring decisions must be made in each major functional segment of the business? What impact on profits could a good or bad decision in each of these categories have?
9. How, if at all, could the performance of this function give the company a competitive advantage?

Once these key factors have been identified, they should be examined with reference to the current status of the product/market to define alternative strategies that may be pursued to gain competitive advantage over the long term. Each alternative strategy should be evaluated for profit payoff, investment costs, feasibility, and risk.

It is important that strategy alternatives be described as specifically as possible. Simply stating "maintain product quality," "provide high-quality service," or "expand market overseas" is not enough. Precise and concrete descriptions, such as "extend the warranty period from one year to two years," "enter U.K., French, and German markets by appointing agents in these countries," and "provide a $100 cash rebate to every buyer to be handed over by the company directly," are essential before alternatives can be adequately evaluated.

Initially, the strategy group may generate a long list of alternatives, but informal discussion with management can soon pare these down to a handful. Each surviving alternative should be weighted in terms of projected financial consequences (sales, fixed and variable costs, profitability, investment, and cash flow) and relevant nonfinancial measures (market shares, product quality and reliability indices, channel efficiency, and so on) over the planning period.

At this time, due attention should be paid to examining any contingencies and to making appropriate responses to them. For example, if market share increases by only half of what was planned, what pricing and promotional actions might be undertaken? If customer demand instantly shoots up, how can orders be filled? What ought to be done if the Consumer Product Safety Commission should promulgate new product usage controls? In addition, if the business is in a cyclical industry, each alternative should also be tested against several market-size scenarios, simultaneously incorporating varying assumptions about competitive pricing pressures. In industries dominated by a few competitors, an evaluation should be made of the ability of the business to adapt each strategy to competitive actions—pricing moves, shifts in advertising strategy, or attempts to dominate a distribution channel, for example.

Strategy Selection. After information on trade-offs between alternative strategies has been gathered as discussed above, a preferred strategy should be chosen for recommendation to management. Usually, there are three core marketing strategies that a company may use: (a) operational excellence, (b) product leadership, and (c) customer intimacy. Operational excellence strategy amounts to offering middle-of-the-market products at the best price with the least inconvenience. Under this strategy, the proposition to the customer is simple: low price or hassle-free service or both. Wal-Mart, Price/Costco, and Dell Computer epitomize this kind of strategy. The product leadership strategy concentrates on offering products that push performance boundaries. In other words, the basic premise of this strategy is that customers receive the best product. Moreover, product leaders don't build their propositions with just one innovation: they continue to innovate year after year. Johnson & Johnson, for instance, is a product leader in the medical equipment field. With Nike, the superior value does not reside just in its athletic footwear, but also in the comfort customers can take from knowing that whatever product they buy from Nike will represent the hottest style and technology on the market.

For product leaders, competition is not about price or customer service, it is about product performance. The customer intimacy strategy focuses not on what the market wants but on what specific customers want. Businesses following this strategy do not pursue one-time transactions; they cultivate relationships. They specialize in satisfying unique needs, which often only they recognize, through a close relationship with and intimate knowledge of the customer. The underlying proposition of this strategy is: we have the best solution for you, and provide all the support you need to achieve optimum results. Long-distance telephone carrier Cable and Wireless, for example, follows this strategy with a vengeance, achieving success in a highly competitive market by consistently going the extra mile for its selectively chosen, small business customers. Exhibit 9-2 summarizes the differentiating aspects of the three core strategies examined above.

The core strategy combines one or more areas of the marketing mix.[4] For example, the preferred strategy may be product leadership. Here the emphasis of the strategy is on product, the area of primary concern. However, in order to make an integrated marketing decision, appropriate changes may have to be made in price, promotion, and distribution areas.[5] The strategic perspectives in these areas may be called *supporting strategies*. Thus, once strategy selection has been undertaken, core and supporting strategy areas should be delineated. Core

EXHIBIT 9-2
Distinguishing Aspects of Different Core Marketing Strategies

	Core Strategy		
Managerial Attributes	*Operational Excellence*	*Product Leadership*	*Customer Intimacy*
Strategic Direction	Sharpen distribution systems and provide no-hassle service	Nurture ideas, translate them into products, and market them skillfully	Provide solutions and help customers run their businesses
Organizational Arrangement	Has strong, central authority and a finite level of empowerment	Acts in an ad hoc, organic, loosely knit, and ever-changing way	Pushes empowerment close to customer contact
Systems Support	Maintain standard operating procedures	Reward individuals' innovative capacity and new product success	Measure the cost of providing service and of maintaining customer loyalty
Corporate Culture	Acts predictably and believes "one size fits all"	Experiments and thinks "out-of-the-box"	Is flexible and thinks "have it your way"

and supporting strategies should fit the needs of the marketplace, the skills of the company, and the vagaries of the competition.

The concept of core and supporting strategies may be examined with reference to the Ikea furniture chain.[6] Ikea, the giant Swedish home-furnishings business, has done well in the U.S. market by pursuing operational excellence as its core strategy. Where other Scandinavian furniture stores have faltered in the United States, Ikea keeps growing. Despite its poor service, customers keep coming to buy trendy furniture at bargain basement prices. The company has well aligned its supporting strategies of product, promotion, and distribution with its core strategy. For example, it selects highly visible sites easily accessible from major highways to generate traffic. Few competitors can match the selection offered by its cavernous 200,000-square-foot branches, which on average are five times larger than full-line competitors. The products are stylish and durable as well as functional; the quality is good. Advertising attempts to mold Ikea's image as hip and appealing. Ikea's enticing in-store models, easy-to-find price tags, and attractive displays create instant interest in the merchandise. But all these supporting strategies are fully price relevant. The company is so price conscious that it has used components from as many as four different manufacturers to make a single chair. Briefly, Ikea follows a strategy to satisfy the desire for contemporary furniture at moderate prices.

It is rather common for firms competing in the same industry to choose different core and supporting strategies through which to compete. The chosen strategy reflects the particular strength of the firm, the specific demands of the market, and the competitive thrust. As has been noted:

> Coca-Cola was born a winner, but Pepsi had to fight to survive by distinguishing itself from the leader. For most of its history, Pepsi differentiated itself purely on price: "Twice as much for a nickel, too." Only in the early 1970s did Pepsi start to believe that its product actually may be as good as if not better than Coke's. The resulting strategy was: "The Pepsi challenge."
>
> The first belief of Coca-Cola was that its product was sacred. The resulting strategy was simple: "Don't touch the recipe" and "don't put lesser products under the same brand name" (call them "Tab"). Coca-Cola's second belief was that anyone should be able to buy Coke within a few steps of anywhere on earth. This belief drove the company to make its product available in every conceivable outlet and required a distribution strategy that allowed all outlets a reasonable profit at competitive prices.
>
> While Coca-Cola was driven by a product focus, Pepsi developed a more market-oriented perspective. Pepsi was the first to offer new sizes and packages. When consumer trends toward health, fitness and sweeter taste emerged, Pepsi again was the innovator: It was the first to market diet and light varieties and it quickly sweetened its formula. Unencumbered by reverence for its base brand, it introduced the new varieties as extensions of the Pepsi signature. Where Coca-Cola feared a dilution of its brand name, Pepsi saw an opportunity to exploit the cost advantages and advertising of an umbrella brand.[7]

It is important to remember that the core strategy is formulated around the critical variable(s) that may differ from one segment to another for the same product. This is well supported by the following quotation taken from a case study of the petroloids business. Petroloids, a family of such unique materials as oils, petro-rubbers, foams, adhesives, and sealants, are manufactured substances based on the synthesis of organic hydrocarbons:

> Major producers competed with one another on a variety of dimensions. Among the most important were price, technical assistance, advertising and promotion, and product availability. Price was used as a competitive weapon primarily in those segments of the market where products and applications had become standardized. However, where products had been developed for highly specialized purposes and represented only a small fraction of a customer's total material cost, the market was often less price sensitive. Here customers were chiefly concerned with the physical properties of the product and operating performance.
>
> Technical assistance was an important means of obtaining business. A sizable percentage of total petroloid sales were accounted for by products developed to meet the unique needs of particular customers. Products for the aerospace industry were a primary example. Research engineers of petroloid producers were expected to work closely with customers to define performance requirements and to insure the development of acceptable products.
>
> Advertising and promotional activities were important marketing tools in those segments which utilized distribution channels and/or which reached end users as opposed to OEM's. This was particularly true of foams, adhesives, and sealants which were sold both to industrial and consumer markets. A variety of packaged consumer products were sold to hardware, supermarkets, and "do-it-yourself" outlets by our company as well as other competitors. Advertising increased awareness and stimulated interest among the general public while promotional activities improved the effectiveness of distribution networks. Since speciality petroloid products accounted for only a small percentage of a distributor's total sales, product promotion insured that specific products received adequate attention.
>
> Product availability was a fourth dimension on which producers competed. With manufacturing cycles from 2–16 weeks in length and thousands of different products, no supplier could afford to keep all his items in stock. In periods of heavy demand, many products were often in short supply. Those competitors with adequate supplies and quick deliveries could readily attract new business.[8]

Apparently, strategy development is difficult because different emphases may be needed in different product/market situations. Emphasis is built around critical variables that may themselves be difficult to identify. Luck plays a part in making the right move; occasionally, sheer intuition suffices. Despite all this, a careful review of past performance, current perspectives, and environmental changes should go a long way in choosing the right areas on which to concentrate.

Reformulation of current strategy may range from making slight modifications in existing perspectives to coming out with an entirely different strategy. For example, in the area of pricing, one alternative for an automobile manufacturer may be to keep prices stable from year to year (i.e., no yearly price increases). A different alternative is to lease cars directly to consumers instead of selling them. The decision on the first alternative may be made by the SBU executive. But the second alternative, being far-reaching in nature, may require the review and approval of top management. In other words, how much examination and review a product/market strategy requires depends on the nature of the strategy (in terms of the change it seeks from existing perspectives) and the resource commitment required.

Another point to remember in developing core strategy is that the emphasis should always be placed on searching for new ways to compete. The marketing strategist should develop strategy around those key factors in which the business has more freedom than its competitors have. The point may be illustrated with reference to Body Shop International, a cosmetic company that spends nothing on advertising, even though it is in one of the most image-conscious industries in the business world.[9] Based in England, this company operates in 37 nations. Unlike typical cosmetic manufacturers, which sell through drugstores and department stores, Body Shop sells its own franchise stores. Further, in a business in which packaging costs often outstrip product costs, the Body Shop offers its products in plain, identical rows of bottles and gives discounts to customers who bring Body Shop bottles in for refills. The company has succeeded because it is so different from its rivals. Instead of assailing its customers with promotions and ads, it educates them. A great deal of Body Shop's budget is spent on training store personnel on the detailed nature of how its products are made and how they ought to be used. Training, which is accomplished through newsletters, videotapes, and classroom study, enables salesclerks to educate consumers on hair care, problem skin treatments, and the ecological benefits of such exotic products as rhassoul and mud shampoo, white grape skin tonic, and peppermint foot lotion. Consumers have also responded to Body Shop's environmental policies: the company uses only natural ingredients in its products, doesn't use animals for lab testing, and publicly supports saving whales and Brazilian rain forest preservation.

In the final analysis, companies with the following characteristics are most likely to develop successful strategies:[10]

1. **Informed opportunism**—Information is the main strategic advantage, and flexibility is the main strategic weapon. Management assumes that opportunity will keep knocking but that it will knock softly and in unpredictable ways.
2. **Direction and empowerment**—Managers at renewing companies define the boundaries, and their subordinates figure out the best way to do the job within them. Managers give up some control to gain results.
3. **Friendly facts, congenial controls**—Renewing companies love information that provides context and removes decision making from the realm of mere opinion. Managers regard financial controls as the benign checks and balances that allow them to be creative and free.
4. **A different mirror**—Leaders are open and inquisitive. They get ideas from almost anyone in and out of the hierarchy: customers, competitors, even next-door neighbors.
5. **Teamwork, trust, politics, and power**—Renewers stress the value of teamwork and trust their employees to do the job. Relentless at fighting office politics, they acknowledge that politics are inevitable in the workplace.

6. **Stability in motion**—Renewing companies are constantly changing but have a base of underlying stability. They understand the need for consistency and norms, but they also realize that the only way to respond to change is to deliberately break the rules.
7. **Attitudes and attention**—Visible management attention, rather than exhortation, gets things done. Action may start with words, but it must be backed by symbolic behavior that makes those words come alive.
8. **Causes and commitment**—Commitment results from management's ability to turn grand causes into small actions so that everyone can contribute to the central purpose.

DETERMINING SBU STRATEGY

SBU strategy concerns how to create competitive advantage in each of the products/markets it competes with. The business unit-level strategy is determined by the three Cs (customer, competition, and company). The experience of different companies shows that, for the purposes of strategy formulation, the strategic three Cs can be articulated by placing SBUs on a two-by-two matrix with industry maturity or attractiveness as one dimension and strategic competitive position as the other.

Industry attractiveness may be studied with reference to the life-cycle stage of the industry (i.e., embryonic, growth, mature, or aging). Such factors as growth rate, industry potential, breadth of product line, number of competitors, market share perspectives, purchasing patterns of customers, ease of entry, and technology development determine the maturity of the industry. As illustrated in Exhibit 9-3, these factors behave in different ways according to the stage of industry maturity. For example, in the embryonic stage, the product line is generally narrow, and frequent changes to tailor the line to customer needs are common. In the growth stage, product lines undergo rapid proliferation. In the mature stage, attempts are made to orient products to specific segments. During the aging stage, the product line begins to shrink.

Going through the four stages of the industry life cycle can take decades or a few years. The different stages are generally of unequal duration. To cite a few examples, personal computers and solar energy devices are in the embryonic category. Home smoke alarms and sporting goods in general fall into the growth category. Golf equipment and steel represent mature industries. Men's hats and rail cars are in the aging category. It is important to remember that industries can experience reversals in the aging processes. For example, roller skates have experienced a tremendous resurgence (i.e., moving from the aging stage back to the growth stage) because of the introduction of polyurethane wheels. It should also be emphasized that there is no "good" or "bad" life-cycle position. A particular stage of maturity becomes "bad" only if the expectations or strategies adopted by an industry participant are inappropriate for its stage of maturity. The particular characteristics of the four different stages in the life cycle are discussed in the following paragraphs.

EXHIBIT 9-3
Industry Maturity Guide

| | Stages of Industry Maturity | | | |
Descriptors	Embryonic	Growth	Mature	Aging
Growth rate	Accelerating; meaningful rate cannot be calculated because base is too small	Substantially faster than GNP; industry sales expanding significantly	Growth at rate equal to or slower than GNP; more subject to cyclicality	Industry volume declining
Industry potential	Usually difficult to determine	Demand exceeds current industry volume but is subject to unforeseen developments	Well known; primary markets approach saturation	Saturation is reached; supply capability exceeds demand
Product line	Line generally narrow; frequent changes tailored to customer needs	Product lines undergo rapid proliferation; some evidence of products oriented toward multiple industry segments	Product line turnover but little or no change in breadth; products frequently oriented toward narrow industry segments	Product line shrinking but tailored to major customer needs
Number of competitors	Few competing at first but number increasing rapidly	Number and types are unstable; increase to peak followed by shakeout and consolidation	Generally stable or declining slightly	Declines or industry may break up into many small regional suppliers
Market share stability	Volatile; share difficult to measure; share frequently concentrated	Rankings can change; a few firms have major shares	Little share volatility; firms with major shares are entrenched; significant niche competition; firms with minor shares are unlikely to gain major shares	Some change as marginal firms drop out; as market share declines, market share generally becomes more concentrated
Purchasing patterns	Varies; some customers have strong loyalties; others have none	Some customer loyalty; buyers are aggressive but show evidence of repeat or add-on purchases; some price sensitivity	Suppliers are well known; buying patterns are established; customers generally loyal to acceptable suppliers; increasing price sensitivity	Strong customer loyalty as number of alternatives decreases; customers and suppliers may be tied to each other
Ease of entry (exclusive of capital considerations)	Usually easy; opportunity may not be apparent	Usually easy; presence of competitors is offset by growth	Difficult; competitors are entrenched; growth slowing	Little incentive
Technology	Important to match performance to market needs; industries started on technological breakthrough or application; multiple technologies	Fewer competing technologies; significant product line refinements or extensions likely; performance enhancement is important	Process and materials refinement; technologies developed outside this industry are used in seeking efficiencies	Minimal role in ongoing products; new technology sought to renew growth

Embryonic industries usually experience rapid sales growth, frequent changes in technology, and fragmented, shifting market shares. The cash deployment to these businesses is often high relative to sales as investment is made in market development, facilities, and technology. Embryonic businesses are generally not profitable, but investment is usually warranted in anticipation of gaining position in a developing market.

The growth stage is generally characterized by a rapid expansion of sales as the market develops. Customers, shares, and technology are better known than in the embryonic stage, and entry into the industry can be more difficult. Growth businesses are usually capital borrowers from the corporation, producing low-to-good earnings.

In mature industries, competitors, technology, and customers are all known and there is little volatility in market shares. The growth rate of these industries is usually about equal to GNP. Businesses in mature industries tend to provide cash for the corporation through high earnings.

The aging stage of maturity is characterized by

1. Falling demand for the product and limited growth potential.
2. A shrinking number of competitors (survivors gain market share through attrition).
3. Little product line variety.
4. Little, if any, investment in research and development or plant and equipment.

The competitive position of an SBU should depend not only on market share but also on such factors as capacity utilization, current profitability, degree of integration (forward or backward), distinctive product advantages (e.g., patent protection), and management strength (e.g., willingness to take risks). These factors may be studied for classifying a given SBU in one of the following competitive positions: dominant, strong, favorable, tenable, or weak.

Exhibit 9-4 summarizes the typical characteristics of firms in different competitive positions. An example of a dominant firm is IBM in the computer field; its competitors pattern their behavior and strategies on what IBM does. In the beer industry, Anheuser-Busch exemplifies a strong firm, a firm able to make an independent move without being punished by the major competitor.

Determining strategic competitive position is one of the most complex elements of business analysis and one of the least researched. With little state-of-the-art guidance available, the temptation is to fall back on the single criterion of market share, but the experiences of successful companies make it clear that determining competitive position is a multifaceted problem embracing, for example, technology, breadth of product line, market share, share movement, and special market relationships. Such factors change in relative importance as industry maturity changes.

Choice of Strategy | Once the position of an SBU is located on the industry maturity/competitive position matrix, the guide shown in Exhibit 9-5 may be used to determine what strategy the SBU should pursue. Actually, the strategies shown in the exhibit are

EXHIBIT 9-4
Classification of Competitive Strategic Positions

Dominant	• Controls behavior and/or strategies of other competitors.
	• Can choose from widest range of strategic options, independent of competitor's actions.
Strong	• Can take independent stance or action without endangering long-term position.
	• Can generally maintain long-term position in the face of competitor's actions.
Favorable	• Has strengths that are exploitable with certain strategies if industry conditions are favorable.
	• Has more than average ability to improve position.
	• If in a niche, holds a commanding position relatively secure from attack.
Tenable	• Has sufficient potential and/or strengths to warrant continuation in business.
	• May maintain position with tacit consent of dominant company or of the industry in general but is unlikely to significantly improve position.
	• Tends to be only marginally profitable.
	• If in a niche, is profitable but clearly vulnerable to competitors' actions.
Weak	• Has currently unsatisfactory performance but has strengths that may lead to improvement.
	• Has many characteristics of a better position but suffers from past mistakes or current weaknesses.
	• Inherently short-term position; must change (up or out).
Nonviable	• Has currently unsatisfactory performance and few, if any, strengths that may lead to improvement (may take years to die).

guides to strategic thrust rather than strategies per se. They show the normal strategic path a business unit may adopt, given its industry maturity and competitive position. The Appendix at the end of this chapter further examines the strategic thrusts identified in Exhibit 9-5. Each strategic thrust is defined, and its objective, requirements, and expected results are noted.

To bridge the gap between broad guidelines and specific strategies for implementation, further analysis is required. A three-stage process is suggested here. First, using broad guidelines, the SBU management may be asked to state strategies pursued during previous years. Second, these strategies may be reviewed by using selected performance ratios to analyze the extent to which strategies were successfully implemented. Similarly, current strategies may be identified and their link to past strategies established. Third, having identified and analyzed past and current strategy with the help of strategic guidelines, the management, using the same guidelines, selects the strategy it proposes to pursue in the future. The future perspective may call for the continuation of current strategies or the development

EXHIBIT 9-5
Guide to Strategic Thrust Options

Competitive Position	Stages of Industry Maturity			
	Embryonic	*Growth*	*Mature*	*Aging*
Dominant	Grow fast Start up	Grow fast Attain cost leadership Renew Defend position	Defend position Focus Renew Grow fast	Defend position Renew Grow into maturity
Strong	Start up Differentiate Grow fast	Grow fast Catch up Attain cost leadership Differentiate	Attain cost leadership Renew, focus Differentiate Grow with industry	Find niche Hold niche Hang in Grow with industry Harvest
Favorable	Start up Differentiate Catch up Focus Grow fast	Differentiate, focus Find niche, hold niche Grow with industry	Harvest, hang in Turn around Renew, turn around Differentiate, focus Grow with industry	Retrench
Tenable	Start up Grow with industry Focus	Harvest, catch up Hold niche, hang in Find niche Turn around Focus Grow with industry	Harvest Turn around Find niche Retrench	Divest Retrench
Weak	Find niche Catch up Grow with industry	Turn around Retrench	Withdraw Divest	Withdraw

of new ones. Before accepting the future strategic course, however, it is desirable to measure its cash consequences or internal deployment (i.e., percentage of funds generated that are reinvested). Exhibit 9-6 illustrates an SBU earning 22 percent on assets with an internal deployment of 80 percent. Such an SBU would normally be considered in the mature stage. However, if the previous analysis showed that the SBU was in fact operating in a growth industry, the corporation would need to rethink its investment policy. All quantitative information pertaining to an SBU may be summarized on one form, as shown in Exhibit 9-7.

Different product/market plans are reviewed at the SBU level. The purpose of this review is twofold: (a) to consider product/market strategies in finalizing SBU strategies and (b) to approve product/market strategies. The underlying criterion for evaluation is a balanced achievement of SBU goals, which may be specified in terms of profitability and cash consequences. If there is a conflict of interest between two product/market groups in the way the strategy is either articulated

EXHIBIT 9-6
Profitability and Cash Position of a Business

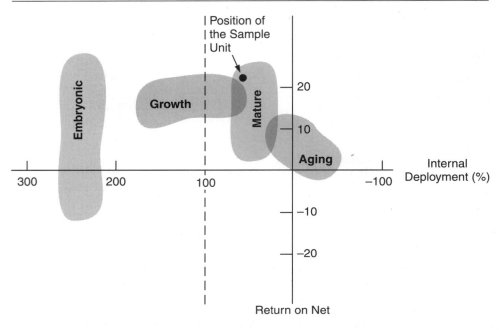

or implemented, the conflict should be resolved so that SBU goals are maximized. Assume that both product/market groups seek additional investments during the next two years. Of these, the first product/market will start delivering positive cash flow in the third year. The second one is not likely to generate positive cash flow until the fourth year, but it will provide a higher overall return on capital. If the SBU's need for cash is urgent and if it desires additional cash for its goals during the third year, the first product/market group will appear more attractive. Thus, despite higher profit expectations from the second product/market group, the SBU may approve investment in the first product/market group with a view to maximizing the realization of its own goals.

At times, the SBU may require a product/market group to make additional changes in its strategic perspective before giving its final approval. On the other hand, a product/market plan may be totally rejected and the group instructed to pursue its current perspective.

Industry maturity and competitive position analysis may also be used in further refining the SBU itself. In other words, after an SBU has been created and is analyzed for industry maturity and competitive position, it may be found that it has not been properly constituted. This would require redefining the SBU and undertaking the analysis again. Drawing an example from the car radio industry,

EXHIBIT 9-7

Sources of Competitive Information

PERFORMANCE

	Indices of:					Return					
							Investment (per $ sales)				
Year	Industry Capacity (A)	Business Unit's Product Capacity (B)	Business Unit's Sales (C)	Profits after Taxes (D)	New Assets (E)	Receivables (F)	Inventories (G)	New Current Liabilities (H)	Working Capital (I)	Other Assets (J)	Total Net Assets (K)

INVESTMENT

	Return (continued)								Funds Generation and Deployment			
	Cost and Earnings (per $ sales)								(per $ sales)			(%)
Year	Cost of Goods Sold (L)	Research and Development (M)	Sales and Marketing (N)	General and Administrative (O)	Other Income and Expenses (P)	Profit before Taxes (Q)	Profit after Taxes (R)	Return on Net Assets (S)	Operating Funds Flow (T)	Changes in Assets (U)	Net Cash Flow to Corporation (V)	Internal Development (U ÷ T) (W)

Source: Arthur D. Little, Inc. Reprinted by permission.

considerable differences in industry maturity may become apparent between car radios with built-in cassette players and traditional car radios. Differences in industry maturity or competitive position may also exist with regard to regional markets, consumer groups, and distribution channels. For example, the market for cheap car radios sold by discount stores to end users doing their own installations may be growing faster than the market served by specialty retail stores providing installation services. Such revelations may require further refinement in formulating SBUs. This may continue until the SBUs represent the highest possible level of aggregation consistent with the need for clear-cut analyses of industry maturity and competitive position.

STRATEGY EVALUATION

"The time required to develop resources is so extended, and the timescale of opportunities is so brief and fleeting, that a company which has not carefully delineated and appraised its strategy is adrift in white water." This quotation from an article by Seymour Tilles underlines the importance of strategy evaluation.[11] The adequacy of a strategy may be evaluated using the following criteria:[12]

1. **Suitability**—Is there a sustainable advantage?
2. **Validity**—Are the assumptions realistic?
3. **Feasibility**—Do we have the skills, resources, and commitments?
4. **Internal consistency**—Does the strategy hang together?
5. **Vulnerability**—What are the risks and contingencies?
6. **Workability**—Can we retain our flexibility?
7. **Appropriate time horizon**.

Suitability | Strategy should offer some sort of competitive advantage. In other words, strategy should lead to a future advantage or an adaptation to forces eroding current competitive advantage. The following steps may be followed to judge the competitive advantage a strategy may provide: (a) review the potential threats and opportunities to the business, (b) assess each option in light of the capabilities of the business, (c) anticipate the likely competitive response to each option, and (d) modify or eliminate unsuitable options.

Validity (Consistency with the Environment) | Strategy should be consistent with the assumptions about the external product/market environment. At a time when more and more women are seeking jobs, a strategy assuming traditional roles for women (i.e., raising children and staying home) would be inconsistent with the environment.

Feasibility (Appropriateness in Light of Available Resources) | Money, competence, and physical facilities are the critical resources a manager should be aware of in finalizing strategy. A resource may be examined in two different ways: as a constraint limiting the achievement of goals and as an opportunity to be exploited as the basis for strategy. It is desirable for a strategist to make correct estimates of resources available without being excessively optimistic about them. Further, even if resources are available in the corporation, a particular product/market group may not be able to lay claim to them. Alternatively, resources currently available to a product/market group may be transferred to another group if the SBU strategy deems it necessary.

Internal Consistency | Strategy should be in tune with the different policies of the corporation, the SBU, and the product/market arena. For example, if the corporation decided to limit the government business of any unit to 40 percent of total sales, a product/market strategy emphasizing greater than 40 percent reliance on the government market would be internally inconsistent.

Vulnerability (Satisfactory Degree of Risk) | The degree of risk may be determined on the basis of the perspectives of the strategy and available resources. A pertinent question here is: Will the resources be available as planned in appropriate quantities and for as long as it is necessary to implement the strategy? The overall proportion of resources committed to a venture becomes a factor to be reckoned with: the greater these quantities, the greater the degree of risk.

Workability | The workability of a strategy should be realistically evaluated with quantitative data. Sometimes, however, it may be difficult to undertake such objective analysis. In that case, other indications may be used to assess the contributions of a strategy. One such indication could be the degree of consensus among key executives about the viability of the strategy. Identifying ahead of time alternate strategies for achieving the goal is another indication of the workability of a strategy. Finally, establishing resource requirements in advance, which eliminates the need to institute crash programs of cost reduction or to seek reduction in planned programs, also substantiates the workability of the strategy.

Appropriate Time Horizon | A viable strategy has a time frame for its realization. The time horizon of a strategy should allow implementation without creating havoc in the organization or missing market availability. For example, in introducing a new product to the market, enough time should be allotted for market testing, training of salespeople, and so on. But the time frame should not be so long that a competitor can enter the market first and skim the cream off the top.

SUMMARY | This chapter was devoted to strategy formulation for the SBU. A conceptual framework for developing SBU strategy was outlined. Strategy formulation at the SBU level requires, among different inputs, the perspectives of product/market strategies. For this reason, a procedure for developing product/market strategy was discussed first.

Product/market strategy development requires predicting the momentum of current operations into the future (assuming constant conditions), modifying the momentum in the light of environmental changes, and reviewing the adjusted momentum against goals. If there is no gap between the set goal and the prediction, the present strategy may well be continued. Usually, however, there is a gap between the goal and expectations from current operations. Thus, the gap must be filled.

The following three-step process was suggested for filling the gap: (a) issue assessment (i.e., raising issues with the status quo vis-à-vis the future), (b) identification of key variables (i.e., isolating the key variables on which success in the industry depends) and development of alternative strategies, and (c) strategy selection (i.e., choosing the preferred strategy). The thrust of the preferred strategy is on one or more of the four variables in the marketing mix—product, price, promotion, or distribution. The major emphasis of marketing strategy, the core strategy, is on this chosen variable. Strategies for the remaining variables are supporting strategies.

The SBU strategy is based on the three Cs (customer, competition, and company). SBUs were placed on a two-by-two matrix with industry maturity or attractiveness as one dimension and strategic competitive position as the other. Stages of industry maturity—embryonic, growth, mature, and aging—were identified. Competitive position can be classified as dominant, strong, favorable, tenable, or weak. Classification by industry maturity and competitive position generates 20 different quadrants in the matrix. In each quadrant, an SBU requires a different strategic perspective. A compendium of strategies was provided to figure out the appropriate strategy in a particular case.

The chapter concluded with a procedure for evaluating the selected strategy. This procedure consists of examining the following aspects of the strategy: suitability, validity, feasibility, internal consistency, vulnerability, workability, and appropriateness of time horizon.

DISCUSSION QUESTIONS

1. Describe how a manufacturer of washing machines may measure the momentum of the business for the next five years.
2. List five issues Sears may raise to review its strategy for large appliances.
3. List five key variables on which success in the home construction industry depends.
4. In what industry state would you position (a) light beer and (b) color television?
5. Based on your knowledge of the company, what would you consider to be Miller's competitive position in the light beer business and GE's position in the appliance business?
6. Discuss how strategy evaluation criteria may be employed to review the strategy of an industrial goods manufacturer.

NOTES

[1] Gary Hamel and C.K. Prahalad, "Strategy as Stretch and Leverage," *Harvard Business Review* (March–April 1993): 75–85.

[2] Alistair Hanna, "Evaluating Strategies," *The McKinsley Quarterly* 3 (1991): 158–77.

[3] See George S. Day and Robin Wensley, "Assessing Advantage: A Framework for Diagnosing Competitive Superiority," *Journal of Marketing* (April 1988): 1–20.

[4] Peter R. Dickson and James L. Ginter, "Market Segmentation, Product Differentiation, and Marketing Strategy," *Journal of Marketing* 51 (April 1987): 1–10.

[5] Benson P. Shapiro, "Rejuvenating the Marketing Mix," *Harvard Business Review* (September–October 1985): 28–34.

[6] Jeffrey A. Trachtenberg, "Ikea Furniture Chain Pleases with Its Prices, Not with Its Service," *Wall Street Journal* (17 September 1991): 1.

[7] Michael Norkus, "Soft Drink Wars: A Lot More Than Just Good Taste," *Wall Street Journal* (8 July 1985): 12.

[8] "Tex-Fiber Industries Petroloid Products Division (A)," a case developed by John Craig under the supervision of Derek F. Abell, copyrighted by the President and Fellows of Harvard College, 1970, 7.

[9] Allan J. Magrath, "Contrarian Marketing," *Across the Board* (October 1990): 46–50.

[10] Adapted from Robert H. Waterman, Jr., *The Renewal Factor: How the Best Get and Keep the Competitive Edge* (New York: Bantam Books, 1987).

[11] Seymour Tilles, "How to Evaluate Corporate Strategy," *Harvard Business Review* (July–August 1963): 111–21.

[12] See George S. Day, "Tough Questions for Developing Strategies," *Journal of Business* (Winter 1986): 60–68.

APPENDIX | *Perspectives on Strategic Thrusts*

A. Start Up

Definition: Introduction of new product or service with clear, significant technology breakthrough.

Objective: To develop a totally new industry to create and satisfy new demand where none existed before.

Requirements: Risk-taking attitude of management; capital expenditures; expense.

Expected Results: Negative cash flow; low-to-negative returns; a leadership position in new industry.

B. Grow with Industry

Definition: To limit efforts to those necessary to maintain market share.

Objective: To free resources to correct market, product, management, or production weaknesses.

Requirements: Management restraint; market intelligence; some capital and expense investments; time-limited strategy.

Expected Results: Stable market share; profit, cash flow, and RONA not significantly worse than recent history, fluctuating only as do industry averages.

C. Grow Fast

Definition: To pursue aggressively larger share and/or stronger position relative to competition.

Objective: To grow volume and share faster than competition and faster than general industry growth rate.

Requirements: Available resources for investment and follow-up; risk-taking management attitude; and appropriate investment strategy.

Expected Results: Higher market share; in the short term, perhaps lower returns; above average returns in the longer term; competitive retaliation.

D. Attain Cost Leadership

Definition: To achieve lowest delivered costs relative to competition with acceptable quality levels.

Objective: To increase freedom to defend against powerful entries, strong customer blocks, vigorous competitors, or potential substitute products.

Requirements: Relatively high market share; disciplined, persistent management efforts; favorable access to raw materials; substantial capital expenditures; aggressive pricing.

Expected Results: In early stages, may result in start-up losses to build share; ultimately, high margins; relatively low capital turnover rates.

E. Differentiate

Definition: To achieve the highest degree of product/quality/service difference (as perceived by customers) in the industry with acceptable costs.

Objective: To insulate the company from switching, substitution, price competition, and strong blocks of customers or suppliers.

Requirements: Willingness to sacrifice high market share; careful target marketing; focused technological and market research; strong brand loyalty.

Expected Results: Possibly lowered market share; high margins; above-average earnings; highly defensible position.

F. Focus

Definition: To select a particular segment of the market/product line more narrow in scope than competing firms.

Objective: To serve the strategic target area (geographic, product, or market) more efficiently, fully, and profitably than it can be served by broad line competitors.

Requirements: Disciplined management; persistent pursuit of well-defined scope and mission; premium pricing; careful target selection.

Expected Results: Above-average earnings; may be low-cost producer in its area; may attain high differentiation.

G. Renew

Definition: To restore the competitiveness of a product line in anticipation of future industry sales.

Objective: To overcome weakness in product/market mix in order to improve share or to prepare for a new generation of demand, competition, or substitute products.

Requirements: Strong enough competitive position to generate necessary resources for renewal efforts; capital and expense investments; management capable of taking risk; recognition of potential threats to existing line.

Expected Results: Short-term decline in sales, then sudden or gradual breakout of old volume/profit patterns.

H. Defend Position

Definition: To ensure that relative competitive position is stable or improved.

Objective: To create barriers that make it difficult, costly, and risky for competitors, suppliers, customer blocks, or new entries to erode your firm's market share, profitability, and growth.

Requirements: Establishment of one or more of the following: proprietary technology, strong brand, protected sourcing, favorable locations, economies of scale, government protection, exclusive distribution, or customer loyalty.

Expected Results: Stable or increasing market share.

I. Harvest

Definition: To convert market share or competitive position into higher returns.

Objective: To bring returns up to industry averages by trading, leasing, or selling technology, distribution rights, patents, brands, production capacity, locations, or exclusive sources to competitors.

Requirements: A better-than-average market share; rights to entry or mobility barriers that the industry values; alternative investment opportunities.

Expected Results: Sudden surge in profitability and return; a gradual decline of position, perhaps leading to withdrawal strategy.

J. Find Niche

Definition: To opt for retaining a small, defensible portion of the available market rather than withdraw.

Objective: To define the opportunity so narrowly that large competitors with broad lines do not find it attractive enough to dislodge you.

Requirements: "Think small" management style; alternative uses for excess production capacity; reliable sources for supplies and materials; superior quality and/or service with selected sector.

Expected Results: Pronounced decline in volume and share; improved return in medium to longer term.

K. Hold Niche

Definition: To protect a narrow position in the larger product/market arena from larger competitors.

Objective: To create barriers (real or imagined) that make it unattractive for competitors, suppliers, or customer blocks to enter your segment or switch to alternative products.

Requirements: Designing, building, and promoting "switching costs" into your product.

Expected Results: Lower-than-industry average but steady and acceptable returns.

L. Catch Up

Definition: To make up for poor or late entry into an industry by aggressive product/market activities.

Objective: To overcome early gains made by first entrants into the market by careful choice of optimum product, production, distribution, promotion, and marketing tactics.

Requirements: Management capable of taking risk in flexible environment; resources to make high investments of capital and expense; corporate understanding of short-term low returns; probably necessary to dislodge weak competitors.

Expected Results: Low-to-negative returns in near term; should result in favorable to strong position by late growth stage of industry.

M. Hang In

Definition: To prolong existence of the unit in anticipation of some specific favorable change in the environment.

Objective: To continue funding a tenable (or better) unit only long enough to take advantage of unusual opportunity known to be at hand; this might take the form of patent expiration, management change, government action, technology breakthrough, or socioeconomic shift.

Requirements: Clear view of expected environmental shift; a management willing and able to sustain poor performance; opportunity and resources to capitalize on new environment; a time limit.

Expected Results: Poorer-than-average performance, perhaps losses; later, substantial growth and high returns.

N. Turn Around | *Definition*: To overcome inherent, severe weaknesses in performance in a limited time.

Objective: To halt further declines in share and/or volume; to bring about at least stability or, preferably, a small improvement in position; to protect the line from competitive and substitute products.

Requirements: Fast action to prevent disaster; reductions or redirection to reduce losses; change in morale.

Expected Results: Stable condition and average performance.

O. Retrench | *Definition*: To cut back investment in the business and reduce level of risk and exposure to losses.

Objective: To stop unacceptable losses or risks; to prepare the business for divestment or withdrawal; to strip away loss operations in hopes of exposing a "little jewel."

Requirements: Highly disciplined management system; good communication with employees to prevent wholesale departures; clear strategic objective and timetable.

Expected Results: Reduced losses or modestly improved performance.

P. Divest | *Definition*: To strip the business of some or all of its assets through sale of the product line, brands, distribution facilities, or production capacity.

Objective: To recover losses sustained through earlier strategic errors; to free up funds for alternative corporate investments; to abandon part or all of a business to competition.

Requirements: Assets desirable to others competing or desiring to compete in the industry; a recognition of the futility of further investments.

Expected Results: Increase in cash flow; reduction of asset base; probable reduction in performance levels and/or losses.

Q. Withdraw | *Definition*: To remove the business from competition.

Objective: To take back from the business whatever corporate assets or expenses can be recovered through shutdown, sale, auction, or scrapping of operations.

Requirements: A decision to abandon; a caretaker management; a phased timetable; a public relations plan.

Expected Results: Losses and write-offs.

Portfolio Analysis

The previous chapters dealt with strategy development for individual SBUs. Different SBU strategies must ultimately be judged from the viewpoint of the total organization before being implemented. In today's environment, most companies operate with a variety of businesses. Even if a company is primarily involved in a single broad business area, it may actually be operating in multiple product/market segments. From a strategy angle, different products/markets may constitute different businesses of a company because they have different roles to play. This chapter is devoted to the analysis of the different businesses of an organization so that each may be assigned the unique role for which it is suited, thus maximizing long-term growth and earnings of the company.

Years ago, Peter Drucker suggested classifying products into six categories that reveal the potential for future sales growth: tomorrow's breadwinners, today's breadwinners, products capable of becoming net contributors if something drastic is done, yesterday's breadwinners, the "also rans," and the failures. Drucker's classification provides an interesting scheme for determining whether a company is developing enough new products to ensure future growth and profits.

In the past few years, the emphasis has shifted from product to business. Usually a company discovers that some of its business units are competitively well placed, whereas others are not. Because resources, particularly cash resources, are limited, not all SBUs can be treated alike. In this chapter, three different frameworks are presented to enable management to select the optimum combination of individual SBU strategies from a spectrum of possible alternatives and opportunities open to the company, still satisfying the resource limitations within which the company must operate. The frameworks may also be used at the SBU level to review the strategic perspective of its different product/market segments.

The first framework to be discussed, the **product life cycle**, is a tool many marketers have traditionally used to formulate marketing strategies for different products. The second framework was developed by the Boston Consulting Group and is commonly called the product portfolio approach. The third, the multifactor portfolio approach, owes its development to the General Electric Company. The chapter concludes with the Porter's generic strategies framework.

PRODUCT LIFE CYCLE

Products tend to go through different stages, each stage being affected by different competitive conditions. These stages require different marketing strategies at different times if sales and profits are to be efficiently realized. The length of a product's life cycle is in no way a fixed period of time. It can last from weeks to years, depending on the type of product. In most texts, the discussion of the product life cycle portrays the sales history of a typical product as following an S-shaped curve. The curve is divided into four stages: introduction, growth, maturity, and decline. (Some authors include a fifth stage, saturation.)

However, not all products follow an S-shaped curve. Marketing scholars have identified varying product life-cycle patterns. For example, Tellis and Crawford[1] identify 17 product life-cycle patterns, while Swan and Rink name 10.[2] Exhibit 10-1 conceptualizes a typical product life-cycle curve, which shows the relationship between profits and corresponding sales throughout a product's life.

Introduction is the period during which initial market acceptance is in doubt; thus, it is a period of slow growth. Profits are almost nonexistent because of high marketing and other expenses. Setbacks in the product's development, manufacture, and market introduction exact a heavy toll. Marketing strategy during this stage is based on different combinations of product, price, promotion, and distribution. For example, price and promotion variables may be combined to generate the following strategy alternatives: (a) high price/high promotion, (b) high price/low promotion, (c) low price/heavy promotion, and (d) low price/low promotion.

Survivors of the introduction stage enjoy a period of rapid growth. During this **growth** period, there is substantial profit improvement. Strategy in this stage takes the following shape: (a) product improvement, addition of new features and models; (b) development of new market segments; (c) addition of new channels; (d) selective demand stimulation; and (e) price reductions to vie for new customers.

EXHIBIT 10-1
Product Life Cycle

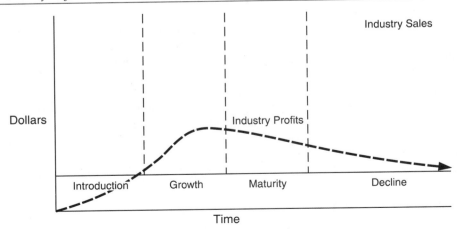

During the next stage, **maturity**, there is intense rivalry for a mature market. Efforts may be limited to attracting a new population, leading to a proliferation of sizes, colors, attachments, and other product variants. Battling to retain the company's share, each marketer steps up persuasive advertising, opens new channels of distribution, and grants price concessions. Unless new competitors are obstructed by patents or other barriers, entry is easy. Thus, maturity is a period when sales growth slows down and profits peak and then start to decline.

Strategy in the maturity stage comprises the following steps: (a) search for new markets and new and varied uses for the product, (b) improvement of product quality through changes in features and style, and (c) new marketing mix perspectives. For the leader firm, Step c may mean introducing an innovative product, fortifying the market through multibrand strategy, or engaging in a price-promotion war against the weaker members of the industry; the nonleader may seek a differential advantage, finding a niche in the market through either product or promotional variables.

Finally, there is the **decline** period. Though sales and profits continue their downward trend, the declining product is not necessarily unprofitable. Some of the competition may have left the market by this stage. Customers who remain committed to the product may be willing to use standard models, pay higher prices, and buy at selected outlets. Promotional expenses can also be reduced.

An important consideration in strategy determination in the decline stage is exit barrier. Even when it appears appropriate to leave the industry, there may be one or more barriers to prevent easy exit. For example, there may be durable and specialized assets peculiar to the business that have little value outside the business; the cost of exit may be prohibitive because of labor settlement costs or contingent liabilities for land use; there may be managerial resistance; the business may be important in gaining access to financial markets; quitting the business may have a negative impact on other businesses in the company; or there may be government pressure to continue in the business, a situation that a multinational corporation may face, particularly in developing countries.

Overall, in the decline stage, the choice of a specific alternative strategy is based on the business's strengths and weaknesses and the attractiveness of the industry to the company. The following alternative strategies appear appropriate:

1. Increasing the firm's investment (to dominate or get a good competitive position).
2. Holding the firm's investment level until the uncertainties about the industry are resolved.
3. Decreasing the firm's investment posture selectively by sloughing off unpromising customer groups, while simultaneously strengthening the firm's investment posture within the lucrative niches of enduring customer demand.
4. Harvesting (or milking) the firm's investment to recover cash quickly, regardless of the resulting investment posture.
5. Divesting the business quickly by disposing of its assets as advantageously as possible.[3]

In summary, in the introduction stage, the choices are primarily with what force to enter the market and whether to target a relatively narrow segment of customers or a broader customer group. In the growth stage, the choices appear to be to fortify and consolidate previously established market positions or to develop new primary demand. Developing new primary demand may be accomplished by a variety of means, including developing new applications, extending geographic coverage, trading down to previously untapped consumer groups, or adding related products. In the late growth and early maturity stages, the choices lie among various alternatives for achieving a larger share of the existing market. This may involve product improvement, product line extension, finer positioning of the product line, a shift from breadth of offering to in-depth focus, invading the market of a competitor that has invaded one's own market, or cutting out some of the "frills" associated with the product to appeal better to certain classes of customers. In the maturity stage, market positions have become established and the primary emphasis is on nose-to-nose competition in various segments of the market. This type of close competition may take the form of price competition, minor feature competition, or promotional competition. In the decline stage, the choices are to continue current product/market perspectives as is, to continue selectively, or to divest.

Exhibit 10-2 identifies the characteristics, marketing objectives, and marketing strategies of each stage of the S-shaped product life cycle. The characteristics help locate products on the curve. The objectives and strategies indicate what marketing perspective is relevant in each stage. Actual choice of strategies rests on the objective set for the product, the nature of the product, and environmental influences operating at the time. For example, in the introductory stage, if a new product is launched without any competition and the firm has spent huge amounts of money on research and development, the firm may pursue a high price/low promotion strategy (i.e., skim the cream off the top of the market). As the product becomes established and enters the growth stage, the price may be cut to bring new segments into the fold—the strategic perspective Texas Instruments used for its digital watches.

On the other hand, if a product is introduced into a market where there is already a well-established brand, the firm may follow a high price/high promotion strategy. Seiko, for example, introduced its digital watch among well-to-do buyers with a high price and heavy promotion without any intention of competing against Texas Instruments head on.

Of the four stages, the maturity stage of the life cycle offers the greatest opportunity to shape the duration of a product's life cycle. These critical questions must be answered: Why have sales tapered off? Has the product approached obsolescence because of a superior substitute or because of a fundamental change in consumer needs? Can obsolescence be attributed to management's failure to identify and reach the right consumer needs or has a competitor done a better marketing job? Answers to these questions are crucial if an appropriate strategy is to be employed to strengthen the product's position. For example, the product may be redirected on a growth path through repackaging, physical modification, repricing, appeals to new users, the addition of new distribution channels, or the use of some combination of marketing strategy changes. The choice of a right

EXHIBIT 10-2
Perspectives of the Product Life Cycle

	Introduction	Growth	Maturity	Decline
Characteristics				
Sales	Low sales	Rapidly rising sales	Peak sales	Declining sales
Costs	High cost per customer	Average cost per customer	Low cost per customer	Low cost per customer
Profits	Negative	Rising profits	High profits	Declining profits
Customers	Innovators	Early adopters	Middle majority	Laggards
Competitors	Few	Growing number	Stable number beginning to decline	Declining number
Marketing Objectives				
	Create a product awareness and trial	Maximize market share	Maximize profit while defending market share	Reduce expenditure and milk the brand
Strategies				
Product	Offer a basic product	Offer product extensions, service warranty	Diversify brands and models	Phase out weak items
Price	Use cost-plus	Price to penetrate market	Price to match or beat competitors	Cut price
Distribution	Build selective distribution	Build intensive distribution	Build more intensive distribution	Go selective; phase out unprofitable outlets
Advertising	Build product awareness among early adopters and dealers	Build awareness and interest in the mass market	Stress brand differences and benefits	Reduce to level needed to retain hardcore loyals
Sales Promotion	Use heavy sales promotion to entice trial	Reduce to take advantage of heavy consumer demand	Increase to encourage brand switching	Reduce to minimal level

Source: Philip Kotler, *Marketing Management: Analysis, Planning and Control,* 8th Ed., © 1994, p. 373. Reprinted by permission of Prentice-Hall, Inc., Englewood Cliffs, N.J.

strategy at the maturity stage can be extremely beneficial, since a successfully revitalized product offers a higher return on management time and funds invested than does a new product.

This point may be illustrated with reference to a Du Pont product, Lycra, a superstretching polymer invented in its labs in 1959. A little more than 30 years after its humble start as an ingredient for girdles, demand for Lycra is exploding so fast that the company must allocate sales of the fiber. The product's success may be directly attributed to a shrewd marketing strategy, initiated during the maturity stage, that allowed Lycra's use to expand steadily, from bathing suits in the 1970s to cycling pants and aerobic outfits in the 1980s. Teenagers were lured to it and use it in their everyday fashion wardrobes. Avant-garde designers picked up on the trend, using Lycra in new, body-hugging designs. Now, this distinctly unnatural fiber is part of the fashion mainstream. Du Pont's marketing strategy has paid off well. A recent study showed that consumers would pay 20 percent more for a wool-Lycra skirt than for an all-wool version.[4]

Product Life-Cycle Controversy

The product life cycle is a useful concept that may be an important aid in marketing planning and strategy. A concept familiar to most marketers, it is given a prominent place in every marketing textbook. Its use in practice remains limited, however, partly because of the lack of normative models available for its application and partly because of the vast amount of data needed for and the level of subjectivity involved in its use. As a matter of fact, the product life-cycle concept has many times been criticized for its lack of relevance to businesspeople. Years ago, Buzzell remarked: "There is very little empirical evidence to show how the life cycles operate and how they are related to competition and marketing strategy."[5] A few years ago, Dhalla and Yuspeh challenged the whole concept of the product life cycle. They contended that the product life cycle has led many companies to make costly mistakes and pass up promising opportunities.[6] Such criticism of the product life cycle may be attributed to the lack of a research base on the subject. As Levitt has observed:

> Most alert and thoughtful senior marketing executives are by now familiar with the concept of the product life cycle. Even a handful of uniquely cosmopolitan and up-to-date corporate presidents have familiarized themselves with this tantalizing concept. Yet a recent survey I took of such executives found none who used the concept in any strategic way whatever and pitifully few who used it in any kind of tactical way. It has remained—as have so many fascinating theories in economics, physics, and sex—a remarkably durable but almost totally unemployed and seemingly unemployable piece of professional baggage whose presence in the rhetoric of professional discussions adds a much-coveted but apparently unattainable legitimacy to the idea that marketing management is somehow a profession. The concept of the product life cycle is today at about the stage that the Copernican view of the universe was 300 years ago: A lot of people know about it, but hardly anybody seems to use it in any effective or productive way.[7]

While Levitt's criticism is very penetrating, many academicians and practitioners feel that, even in its present stage of development, the product life cycle has proved to be remarkably durable because it has been valuable to those who know how to use it. Smallwood claims that

> the product life cycle is a useful concept. It is the equivalent of the periodic table of the elements in the physical sciences. The maturation of production technology and product configuration along with marketing programs proceeds in an orderly, somewhat predictable course over time with the merchandising nature and marketing environment noticeably similar between products that are in the same stage of their life cycles. Its use as a concept in forecasting, pricing, advertising, product planning, and other aspects of marketing management can make it a valuable concept, although considerable amounts of judgment must be used in its application.[8]

One caution that is in order when using the product life cycle is to keep in mind that not all products follow the typical life-cycle pattern. The same product may be viewed in different ways: as a brand (Pepsi Light), as a product form (diet cola), and as a product category (cola drink), for example. Among these, the product life-cycle concept is most relevant for product forms. Further, in recent years, research on the subject has provided new and interesting insights that should help in its continued refinement. For example, Tellis and Crawford suggest that products, influenced by market dynamics, managerial creativity, and government intervention, are in a state of constant evolution in the direction of greater efficiency, greater complexity, and greater diversity. The five stages in this evolutionary process, which the authors call the **product evolutionary cycle (PEC)**, are as follows:

1. Divergence . . . is the start of a new product type (e.g., TV). This term is suggested because most often a product is not an entirely new concept but a modification or combination of existing products and technologies. It is a divergence from a line of product evolution. Thus TV may be considered an evolutionary divergence from the radio and the motion picture.
2. Development . . . is the pattern where a new product's sales increase rapidly and the product is increasingly adapted to suit consumer needs best. Thus in the '50s, TV sales increased rapidly accompanied by frequent product improvements.
3. Differentiation . . . is the pattern that occurs when a highly successful product is differentiated to suit varying consumer interests. More recently TV's are available as black and white, color, portable, and console sets, and variation has extended to CRTs, rear-projection screens, home computers, and videodiscs.
4. Stabilization . . . is a pattern characterized by few and minor changes in the product category, but numerous changes in packaging, service deals, product accessories, and stable or fluctuating sales. Black and white television was in stabilization for years prior to differentiation into portable sets and the other uses mentioned above.
5. Demise . . . occurs when a product fails to meet consumer expectations or can no longer satisfy changes in consumer demand. Sales decline and the product is ultimately discontinued.[9]

Following this framework, the growth of a product is to some extent a function of the strategy being pursued. Thus, a product is not necessarily predestined to mature, as propounded by the traditional concept of product life cycle, but can be kept profitable by proper adaptation to the evolving market environment.

Locating Products in
Their Life Cycles

The easiest way to locate a product in its life cycle is to study its past performance, competitive history, and current position and to match this information with the characteristics of a particular stage of the life cycle. Analysis of past performance of the product includes examination of the following:

1. Sales growth progression since introduction.
2. Any design problems and technical bugs that need to be sorted out.
3. Sales and profit history of allied products (those similar in general character or function as well as directly competitive products).
4. Number of years the product has been on the market.
5. Casualty history of similar products in the past.

The review of competition focuses on

1. Profit history.
2. Ease with which other firms can get into the business.
3. Extent of initial investment needed to enter the business.
4. Number of competitors and their strength.
5. Number of competitors that have left the industry.
6. Life cycle of the industry.
7. Critical factors for success in the business.

In addition, current perspectives may be reviewed to gauge whether sales are on the upswing, have leveled out for the last couple of years, or are heading down; whether any competitive products are moving up to replace the product under consideration; whether customers are becoming more demanding vis-à-vis price, service, or special features; whether additional sales efforts are necessary to keep the sales going up; and whether it is becoming harder to sign up dealers and distributors.

This information on the product may be related to the characteristics of different stages of the product life cycle as discussed above; the product perspectives that match the product life cycle indicate the position of the product in its life cycle. Needless to say, the whole process is highly qualitative in nature, and managerial intuition and judgment bear heavily on the final placement of the product in its life cycle. As a matter of fact, making the appropriate assumptions about the types of information described here can be used to construct a model to predict the industry volume of a newly introduced product through each stage of the product life cycle.[10]

A slightly different approach for locating a product in its life cycle is to use past accounting information for the purpose. Listed below are the steps that may be followed to position a product in its life cycle:

1. Develop historical trend information for a period of three to five years (longer for some products). Data included should be unit and dollar sales, profit margins, total profit contribution, return on invested capital, market share, and prices.
2. Check recent trends in the number and nature of competitors, number and market share rankings of competing products and their quality and performance advantages, shifts in distribution channels, and relative advantages enjoyed by products in each channel.

3. Analyze developments in short-term competitive tactics, such as competitors' recent announcements of new products or plans for expanding production capacity.

4. Obtain (or update) historical information on the life cycle of similar or related products.

5. Project sales for the product over the next three to five years, based on all information gathered, and estimate an incremental profit ratio for the product during each of these years (the ratio of total direct costs—manufacturing, advertising, product development, sales, distribution, etc.—to pretax profits). Expressed as a ratio (e.g., 4.8 to 1 or 6.3 to 1), this measure indicates the number of dollars required to generate each additional dollar of profit. The ratio typically improves (becomes lower) as the product enters its growth period, begins to deteriorate (rise) as the product approaches maturity, and climbs more sharply as it reaches obsolescence.

6. Estimate the number of profitable years remaining in the product's life cycle and, based on all information at hand, fix the product's position on its life-cycle curve: (a) introduction, (b) early or late growth, (c) early or late maturity, or (d) early or late decline.

Developing a Product Life Cycle Portfolio

The current positions of different products in the product life cycle may be determined by following the procedure described above, and the net results (i.e., the cash flow and profitability) of these positions may be computed. Similar analyses may be performed for a future period. The difference between current and future positions indicates what results management may expect if no strategic changes are made. These results may be compared with corporate expectations to determine the gap. The gap can be filled either by making strategic changes to extend the life cycle of a product or by bringing in new products through research and development or acquisition. This procedure may be put into operation by following these steps:

1. Determine what percentage of the company's sales and profits fall within each phase of the product life cycle. These percentages indicate the present life-cycle (sales) profile and the present profit profile of the company's current line.

2. Calculate changes in life-cycle and profit profiles over the past five years and project these profiles over the next five years.

3. Develop a target life-cycle profile for the company and measure the company's present life-cycle profile against it. The target profile, established by marketing management, specifies the desirable share of company sales that should fall within each phase of the product life cycle. It can be determined by industry obsolescence trends, the pace of new product introductions in the field, the average length of product life cycles in the company's line, and top management's objectives for growth and profitability. As a rule, the target profile for growth-minded companies whose life cycles tend to be short calls for a high proportion of sales in introductory and growth phases.

With these steps completed, management can assign priorities to such functions as new product development, acquisition, and product line pruning, based on the discrepancies between the company's target profile and its present life-cycle profile. Once corporate effort has been broadly allocated in this way among products at various stages of their life cycles, marketing plans can be detailed for individual product lines.

PORTFOLIO MATRIX

A good planning system must guide the development of strategic alternatives for each of the company's current businesses and new business possibilities. It must also provide for management's review of these strategic alternatives and for corresponding resource allocation decisions. The result is a set of approved business plans that, taken as a whole, represent the direction of the firm. This process starts with, and its success is largely determined by, the creation of sound strategic alternatives.

The top management of a multibusiness firm cannot generate these strategic alternatives. It must rely on the managers of its business ventures and on its corporate development personnel. However, top management can and should establish a conceptual framework within which these alternatives can be developed. One such framework is the portfolio matrix associated with the Boston Consulting Group (BCG). Briefly, the **portfolio matrix** is used to establish the best mix of businesses in order to maximize the long-term earnings growth of the firm. The portfolio matrix represents a real advance in strategic planning in several ways:

- It encourages top management to evaluate the prospects of each of the company's businesses individually and to set tailored objectives for each business based on the contribution it can realistically make to corporate goals.
- It stimulates the use of externally focused empirical data to supplement managerial judgment in evaluating the potential of a particular business.
- It explicitly raises the issue of cash flow balancing as management plans for expansion and growth.
- It gives managers a potent new tool for analyzing competitors and for predicting competitive responses to strategic moves.
- It provides not just a financial but a strategic context for evaluating acquisitions and divestitures.[11]

As a consequence of these benefits, the widespread application of the portfolio matrix approach to corporate planning has sounded the death knell for planning by exhortation, the kind of strategic planning that sets uniform financial performance goals across an entire company—15 percent growth in earnings or 15 percent return on equity—and then expects each business to meet those goals year in and year out. The portfolio matrix approach has given top management the tools to evaluate each business in the context of both its environment and its unique contribution to the goals of the company as a whole and to weigh the entire array of business opportunities available to the company against the financial resources required to support them.

The portfolio matrix concept addresses the issue of the potential value of a particular business for the firm. This value has two variables: first, the potential for generating attractive earnings levels now; second, the potential for growth or, in other words, for significantly increased earnings levels in the future. The portfolio matrix concept holds that these two variables can be quantified. Current earnings potential is measured by comparing the market position of the business to that of its competitors. Empirical studies have shown that profitability is directly determined by relative market share.

Growth potential is measured by the growth rate of the market segment in which the business competes. Clearly, if the segment is in the decline stage of its life cycle, the only way the business can increase its market share is by taking volume away from competitors. Although this is sometimes possible and economically desirable, it is usually expensive, leads to destructive pricing and erosion of profitability for all competitors, and ultimately results in a market that is ill served. On the other hand, if a market is in its rapid growth stage, the business can gain share by preempting the incremental growth in the market. So if these two dimensions of value are arrayed in matrix form, we have the basis for a business classification scheme. This is essentially what the Boston Consulting Group portfolio matrix is. Each of the four business categories tends to have specific characteristics associated with it. The two quadrants corresponding to high market leadership have current earnings potential, and the two corresponding to high market growth have growth potential.

Exhibit 10-3 shows a matrix with its two sides labeled *product sales growth rate* and *relative market share.* The area of each circle represents dollar sales. The market share position of each circle is determined by its horizontal position. Each circle's product sales growth rate (corrected for inflation) in the market in which it competes is shown by its vertical position.

With regard to the two axes of the matrix, relative market share is plotted on a logarithmic scale in order to be consistent with the experience curve effect, which implies that profit margin or rate of cash generation differences between two competitors tends to be proportionate to the ratio of their competitive positions. A linear axis is used for growth, for which the most generally useful measure is volume growth of the business concerned; in general, rates of cash use should be directly proportional to growth.

The lines dividing the matrix into four quadrants are arbitrary. Usually, high growth is taken to include all businesses growing in excess of 10 percent annually in volume. The line separating areas of high and low relative competitive position is set at 1.0.

The importance of growth variables for strategy development is based on two factors. First, growth is a major influence in reducing cost because it is easier to gain experience or build market share in a growth market than in a low-growth situation. Second, growth provides opportunity for investment. The relative market share affects the rate at which a business will generate cash. The stronger the relative market share position of a product, the higher the margins it will have because of the scale effect.

Classification of Businesses | Using the two dimensions discussed here in Exhibit 10-4, one can classify businesses and products into four categories. Businesses in each category exhibit different financial characteristics and offer different strategic choices.

EXHIBIT 10-3
Product Portfolio Matrix

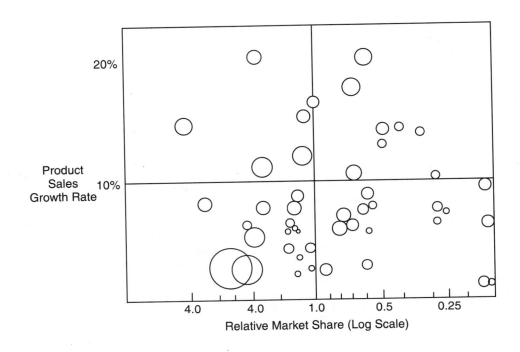

Stars. High-growth market leaders are called *stars.* They generate large amounts of cash, but the cash they generate from earnings and depreciation is more than offset by the cash that must be put back in the form of capital expenditures and increased working capital. Such heavy reinvestment is necessary to fund the capacity increases and inventory and receivable investment that go along with market share gains. Thus, star products represent probably the best profit opportunity available to a company, and their competitive position must be maintained. If a star's share is allowed to slip because the star has been used to provide large amounts of cash in the short run or because of cutbacks in investment and rising prices (creating an umbrella for competitors), the star will ultimately become a dog.

The ultimate value of any product or service is reflected in the stream of cash it generates net of its own reinvestment. For a star, this stream of cash lies in the future—sometimes in the distant future. To obtain real value, the stream of cash must be discounted back to the present at a rate equal to the return on alternative opportunities. It is the future payoff of the star that counts, not the present reported profit. For GE, the plastics business is a star in which it keeps investing.

EXHIBIT 10-4
Matrix Quadrants

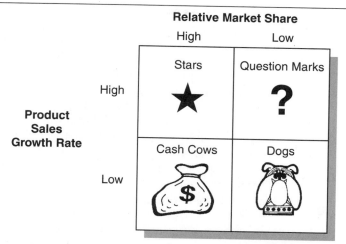

As a matter of fact, the company even acquired Thomson's plastics operations (a French company) to further strengthen its position in the business.

Cash Cows. *Cash cows* are characterized by low growth and high market share. They are net providers of cash. Their high earnings, coupled with their depreciation, represent high cash inflows, and they need very little in the way of reinvestment. Thus, these businesses generate large cash surpluses that help to pay dividends and interest, provide debt capacity, supply funds for research and development, meet overheads, and also make cash available for investment in other products. Thus, cash cows are the foundation on which everything else depends. These products must be protected. Technically speaking, a cash cow has a return on assets that exceeds its growth rate. Only if this is true will the cash cow generate more cash than it uses. For NCR Company, the mechanical cash register business is a cash cow. The company still maintains a dominant share of this business even though growth has slowed down since the introduction of electronic cash registers. The company uses the surplus cash from its mechanical cash registers to develop electronic machines with a view to creating a new star. Likewise, the tire business can be categorized as a cash cow for Goodyear Tire and Rubber Company. The tire industry is characterized by slow market growth, and Goodyear has a major share of the market.

Question Marks. Products in a growth market with a low share are categorized as *question marks*. Because of growth, these products require more cash than they are able to generate on their own. If nothing is done to increase market share, a question mark will simply absorb large amounts of cash in the short run and later, as the growth slows down, become a dog. Thus, unless something is done to change its perspective, a question mark remains a cash loser throughout its existence and ultimately becomes a cash trap.

What can be done to make a question mark more viable? One alternative is to gain share increases for it. Because the business is growing, it can be funded to dominance. It may then become a star and later, when growth slows down, a cash cow. This strategy is a costly one in the short run. An abundance of cash must be poured into a question mark in order for it to win a major share of the market, but in the long run, this strategy is the only way to develop a sound business from the question mark stage. Another strategy is to divest the business. Outright sale is the most desirable alternative. But if this does not work out, a firm decision must be made not to invest further in the business. The business must simply be allowed to generate whatever cash it can while none is reinvested.

When Joseph E. Seagram and Sons bought Tropicana from Beatrice Co. in 1988, it was a question mark. The product had been trailing behind Coke's Minute Maid and was losing ground to Procter & Gamble's new entry in the field, Citrus Hill. Since then, Seagram has invested heavily in Tropicana to develop it into a star product. After just two years, Tropicana has emerged as a leader in the not-from-concentrate orange juice market, far ahead of Minute Maid, and has been trying to make inroads into other segments.[12]

Dogs. Products with low market share positioned in low-growth situations are called *dogs.* Their poor competitive position condemns them to poor profits. Because growth is low, dogs have little potential for gaining sufficient share to achieve viable cost positions. Usually they are net users of cash. Their earnings are low, and the reinvestment required just to keep the business together eats cash inflow. The business, therefore, becomes a cash trap that is likely to regularly absorb cash unless further investment is rigorously avoided. An alternative is to convert dogs into cash, if there is an opportunity to do so. GE's consumer electronics business had been in the dog category, maintaining only a small percentage of the available market in a period of slow growth, when the company decided to unload the business (including the RCA brand acquired in late 1985) to Thomson, France's state-owned leading electronics manufacturer.

Exhibit 10-5 summarizes the investment, earning, and cash flow characteristics of stars, cash cows, question marks, and dogs. Also shown are viable strategy alternatives for products in each category.

Strategy Implications

In a typical company, products could be scattered in all four quadrants of the portfolio matrix. The appropriate strategy for products in each cell is given briefly in Exhibit 10-5. The first goal of a company should be to secure a position with cash cows but to guard against the frequent temptation to reinvest in them excessively. The cash generated from cash cows should first be used to support those stars that are not self-sustaining. Surplus cash may then be used to finance selected question marks to dominance. Any question mark that cannot be funded should be divested. A dog may be restored to a position of viability by shrewdly segmenting the market; that is, by rationalizing and specializing the business into

EXHIBIT 10-5

Characteristics and Strategy Implications of Products in the Strategy Quadrants

Quadrant	Investment Characteristics	Earning Characteristics	Cash Flow Characteristics	Strategy Implication
Stars	—Continual expenditures for capacity expansion —Pipeline filling with cash	Low to high	Negative cash flow (net cash user)	Continue to increase market share, if necessary at the expense of short-term earnings
Cash cows	—Capacity maintenance expenditures	High	Positive cash flow (net cash contributor)	Maintain share and leadership until further investment becomes marginal
Question marks	—Heavy initial capacity expenditures —High research and development costs	Negative to low	Negative cash flow (net cash user)	Assess chances of dominating segment: if good, go after share; if bad, redefine business or withdraw
Dogs	—Gradually deplete capacity	High to low	Positive cash flow (net cash contributor)	Plan an orderly withdrawal so as to maximize cash flow

a small niche that the product may dominate. If this is not practical, a firm should manage the dog for cash; it should cut off all investment in the business and liquidate it when an opportunity develops.

Exhibit 10-6 shows the consequences of a correct/incorrect strategic move. If a question mark is given adequate support, it may become a star and ultimately a cash cow (success sequence). On the other hand, if a star is not appropriately funded, it may become a question mark and finally a dog (disaster sequence).

Top management needs to answer two strategic questions: (a) How promising is the current set of businesses with respect to long-term return and growth? (b) Which businesses should be developed? maintained as is? liquidated? Following the portfolio matrix approach, a company needs a cash-balanced portfolio of businesses; that is, it needs cash cows and dogs to throw off sufficient cash to fund stars and question marks. It needs an ample supply of question marks to ensure long-term growth and businesses with return levels appropriate to their matrix position. In response to the second question, capital budgeting theory requires the lining up of capital project proposals, assessment of incremental cash flows attributable to each project, computation of discounted rate of return on each, and approval of the project with the highest rate of return until available funds are exhausted. But the capital budgeting approach misses the strategic content; that is, it ignores questions of how to validate assumptions about volume, price, cost, and investment and how to eliminate natural biases. This problem is solved by the portfolio matrix approach.

EXHIBIT 10-6
Product Portfolio Matrix: Strategic Consequences

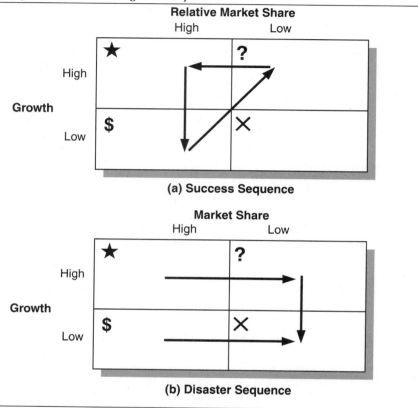

(a) Success Sequence

(b) Disaster Sequence

Source: Bruce D. Henderson, "The Product Portfolio" (Boston: The Boston Consulting Group, Inc., 1970). *Perspectives* No. 66. Reprinted by permission.

Portfolio Matrix and Product Life Cycle

The product portfolio matrix approach propounded by the Boston Consulting Group may be related to the product life cycle by letting the introduction stage begin in the question mark quadrant; growth starts toward the end of this quadrant and continues well into the star quadrant. Going down from the star to the cash cow quadrant, the maturity stage begins. Decline is positioned between the cash cow and the dog quadrants (see Exhibit 10-7). Ideally, a company should enter the product/market segment in its introduction stage, gain market share in the growth stage, attain a position of dominance when the product/market segment enters its maturity stage, maintain this dominant position until the product/market segment enters its decline stage, and then determine the optimum point for liquidation.

EXHIBIT 10-7

Relationship Between Product Portfolio Matrix and Product Life Cycle

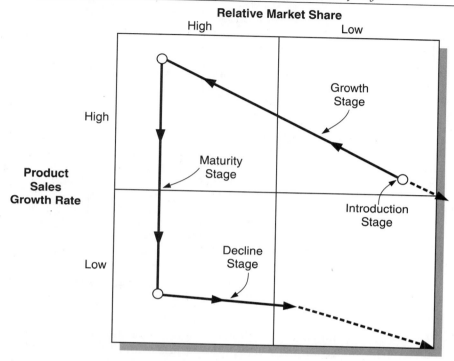

Balanced and Unbalanced Portfolios

Exhibit 10-8 is an example of a balanced portfolio. With three cash cows, this company is well positioned with stars to provide growth and to yield high cash returns in the future when they mature. The company has four question marks, two of which present good opportunities to emerge as stars at an investment level that the cash cows should be able to support (based on the area of the circles). The company does have dogs, but they can be managed to avoid drain on cash resources.

Unbalanced portfolios may be classified into four types:

1. Too many losers (due to inadequate cash flow, inadequate profits, and inadequate growth).
2. Too many question marks (due to inadequate cash flow and inadequate profits).
3. Too many profit producers (due to inadequate growth and excessive cash flow).
4. Too many developing winners (due to excessive cash demands, excessive demands on management, and unstable growth and profits).

Exhibit 10-9 illustrates an unbalanced portfolio. The company has just one cash cow, three question marks, and no stars. Thus, the cash base of the company is inadequate and cannot support the question marks. The company may allocate available cash among all question marks in equal proportion. Dogs may also be given occasional cash nourishment. If the company continues its current strategy,

EXHIBIT 10-8
Illustration of a Balanced Portfolio

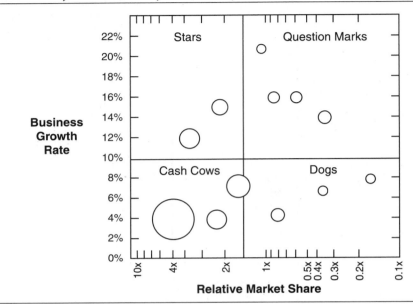

it may find itself in a dangerous position in five years, particularly when the cash cow moves closer to becoming a dog. To take corrective action, the company must face the fact that it cannot support all its question marks. It must choose one or maybe two of its three question marks and fund them adequately to make them stars. In addition, disbursement of cash in dogs should be totally prohibited. In brief, the strategic choice for the company, considered in portfolio terms, is obvious. It cannot fund all question marks and dogs equally.

The portfolio matrix focuses on the real fundamentals of businesses and their relationships to each other within the portfolio. It is not possible to develop effective strategy in a multiproduct, multimarket company without considering the mutual relationships of different businesses.

Conclusion | The portfolio matrix approach provides for the simultaneous comparison of different products. It also underlines the importance of cash flow as a strategic variable. Thus, when continuous long-term growth in earnings is the objective, it is necessary to identify high-growth product/market segments early, develop businesses, and preempt the growth in these segments. If necessary, short-term profitability in these segments may be forgone to ensure achievement of the dominant share. Costs must be managed to meet scale-effect standards. The appropriate point at which to shift from an earnings focus to a cash flow focus must be determined and a liquidation plan for cash flow maximization established. A cash-balanced mix of businesses should be maintained.

EXHIBIT 10-9
Illustration of an Unbalanced Portfolio

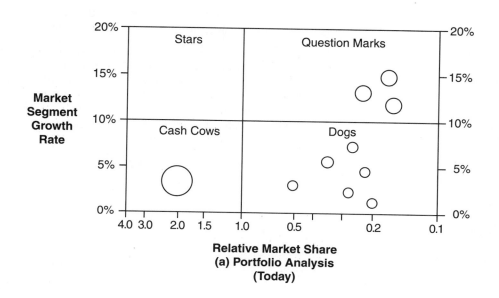

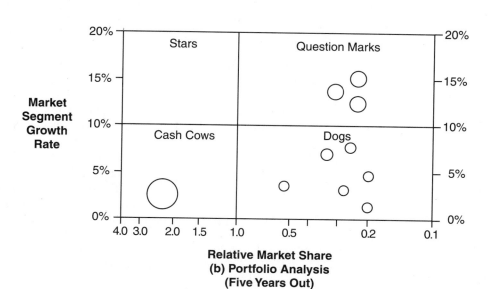

Many companies worldwide have used the portfolio matrix approach in their strategic planning. The first companies to use this approach were the Norton Company, Mead, Borg-Warner, Eaton, and Monsanto. Since then, virtually all large corporations have reported following it.

The portfolio matrix approach, however, is not a panacea for strategy development. In reality, many difficulties limit the workability of this approach. Some potential mistakes associated with the portfolio matrix concept are

1. Overinvesting in low-growth segments (lack of objectivity and "hard" analysis).
2. Underinvesting in high-growth segments (lack of guts).
3. Misjudging the segment growth rate (poor market research).
4. Not achieving market share (because of improper market strategy, sales capabilities, or promotion).
5. Losing cost effectiveness (lack of operating talent and control system).
6. Not uncovering emerging high-growth segments (lack of corporate development effort).
7. Unbalanced business mix (lack of planning and financial resources).

Thus, the portfolio matrix approach should be used with great care.

MULTIFACTOR PORTFOLIO MATRIX

The two-factor portfolio matrix discussed above provides a useful approach for reviewing the roles of different products in a company. However, the growth rate-relative market share matrix approach leads to many difficulties. At times, factors other than market share and growth rate bear heavily on cash flow, the mainstay of this approach. Some managers may consider return on investment a more suitable criterion than cash flow for making investment decisions. Further, the two-factor portfolio matrix approach does not address major investment decisions between dissimilar businesses. These difficulties can lead a company into too many traps and errors. For this reason, many companies (such as GE and the Shell Group) have developed the multifactor portfolio approach.

Exhibit 10-10 illustrates the GE matrix. Its two dimensions, industry attractiveness and business strengths, are based on a variety of factors. It is this multifactor characteristic that differentiates this approach from the one discussed in the previous section. In its early attempts with the portfolio matrix, GE used the criteria and measures shown in Exhibit 10-11 to determine industry attractiveness and business strengths. These criteria and measures are only suggestions; another company may adopt a different list. For example, GE later added cyclicality as a criterion under industry attractiveness. The measure of relative profitability, as shown in the exhibit, was used for the first time in 1985.

Exhibits 10-12 and 10-13 illustrate how the factors may be weighed and how a final industry attractiveness and business strengths score may be computed. Management may establish cutoff points for high, medium, and low industry attractiveness and competitive position scores.

It is worthwhile to mention that the development of a multifactor matrix may not be as easy as it appears. The actual analysis required may take a considerable

EXHIBIT 10-10
Multifactor Portfolio Matrix

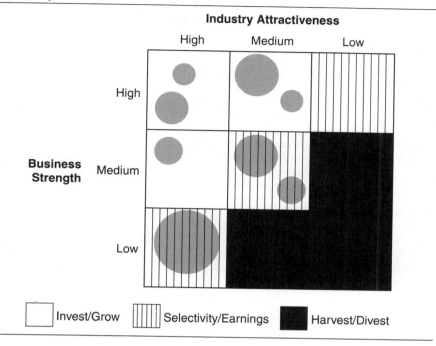

amount of foresight and experience and many, many days of work. The major difficulties lie in identifying relevant factors, relating factors to industry attractiveness and business strengths, and weighing factors.

Strategy Development

The overall strategy for a business in a particular position is illustrated in Exhibit 10-10. The area of the circle refers to the business's sales. Investment priority is given to products in the high area (upper left), where a stronger position is supported by the attractiveness of an industry. Along the diagonal, selectivity is desired to achieve a balanced earnings performance. The businesses in the low area (lower right) are the candidates for harvesting and divestment.

A company may position its products or businesses on the matrix to study its present standing. Forecasts may be made to examine the directions different businesses may go in the future, assuming no changes are made in strategy. Future perspectives may be compared to the corporate mission to identify gaps between what is desired and what may be expected if no measures are taken now. Filling the gap requires making strategic moves for different businesses. Once strategic alternatives for an individual business have been identified, the final choice of a strategy should be based on the scope of the overall corporation vis-à-vis the matrix. For example, the prospects for a business along the diagonal may appear good, but this business cannot be funded in preference to a business in the high-

EXHIBIT 10-11
Portfolio Considerations and Measures Used by GE in 1980

Industry Attractiveness		Business Strengths	
Criterion	*Measure*	*Criterion*	*Measure*
1. Market size	• Three-year average served industry market dollars	1. Market position	• Three-year average market share (total dollars) • Three-year average international market share • Two-year average relative market share (SBU/Big Three competitors)
2. Market growth	• Ten-year constant dollar average market growth rate		
3. Industry profitability	• Three-year average ROS, SBU and Big Three competitors: • Nominal • Inflation adjusted	2. Competitive position	Superior, equal, or inferior to competition in 1980: • Product quality • Technological leadership • Manufacturing/cost leadership • Distribution/marketing leadership
4. Cyclicality	• Average annual percent variation of sales from trend		
5. Inflation recovery	• Five-year average ratio of combined selling price and productivity change to change in cost due to inflation	3. Relative profitability	Three-year average SBU ROS less average ROS, Big Three competitors: • Nominal • Inflation adjusted
6. Importance of non-U.S. markets	• Ten-year average ratio of international to total market		

☐ Indicates measure used for first time in 1980

Source: General Electric Co. Reprinted by permission. The measurements do not reflect current GE practice.

high cell. In devising future strategy, a company generally likes to have a few businesses on the left to provide growth and to furnish potential for investment and a few on the right to generate cash for investment in the former. The businesses along the diagonal may be selectively supported (based on resources) for relocation on the left. If this is not feasible, they may be slowly harvested or divested. Exhibit 10-14 summarizes desired strategic perspective in different cell positions.

For an individual business, there can be four strategy options: investing to maintain, investing to grow, investing to regain, and investing to exit. The choice of a strategy depends on the current position of the business in the matrix (i.e., toward the high side, along the diagonal, or toward the low side) and its future direction, assuming the current strategic perspective continues to be followed. If the future appears unpromising, a new strategy for the business is called for.

Analysis of present position on the matrix may not pose any problem. At GE, for example, there was little disagreement on the position of the business.[13] The mapping of future direction, however, may not be easy. A rigorous analysis must

EXHIBIT 10-12
Assessing Industry Attractiveness

Criteria	Weights*×Ratings** = Values		
Market size	.15	4	.60
Growth rate	.12	3	.36
Profit margin	.05	3	.15
Market diversity	.05	2	.10
Demand cyclicality	.05	2	.10
Expert opportunities	.05	5	.25
Competitive structure	.05	3	.15
Industry profitability	.20	3	.60
Inflation vulnerability	.05	2	.10
Value added	.10	5	.50
Capital intensity	GO	4	—
Raw material availability	GO	4	—
Technological role	.05	4	.20
Energy impact	.08	4	.32
Social	GO	4	—
Environmental impact	GO	4	—
Legal	GO	4	—
Human	GO	4	—
	1.00	1 to 5	3.43

*Some criteria may be of a GO/NO GO type. For example, many *Fortune* 500 firms would probably not invest in industries viewed negatively by society even if it were legal and profitable to do so.
** "1" denotes very unattractive; "5" denotes very attractive.

be performed, taking into account environmental shifts, competitors' perspectives, and internal strengths and weaknesses.

The four strategy options are shown in Exhibit 10-15. Strategy to maintain the current position (Strategy 1 in the exhibit) may be adopted if, in the absence of a new strategy, erosion is expected in the future. Investment will be sought to hold the position; hence, the name invest-to-maintain strategy. The second option is the invest-to-grow strategy. Here, the product's current position is perceived as less than optimum vis-à-vis industry attractiveness and business strengths. In other words, considering the opportunities furnished by the industry and the strengths exhibited by the business, the current position is considered inadequate. A growth strategy is adopted with the aim of shifting the product position upward or toward the left. Movement in both directions is an expensive option with high risk.

The invest-to-regain strategy (Strategy 3 in Exhibit 10-15) is an attempt to rebuild the product or business to its previous position. Usually, when the environment (i.e., industry) continues to be relatively attractive but the business position has slipped because of some strategic past mistake (e.g., premature

EXHIBIT 10-13
Assessing Business Strengths

Criteria	Weights*	×Ratings**	= Values
Market share	.10	5	.50
SBU growth rate	X	3	—
Breadth of product line	.05	4	.20
Sales/distribution effectiveness	.20	4	.80
Proprietary and key account effectiveness	X	3	—
Price competitiveness	X	4	—
Advertising and promotion effectiveness	.05	4	.20
Facilities location and newness	.05	5	—
Capacity and productivity	X	3	.10
Experience curve effects	.15	4	.60
Value added	X	4	—
Investment utilization	.05	5	.25
Raw materials cost	.05	4	.20
Relative product quality	.15	4	.60
R&D advantage/position	.05	4	.20
Cash throwoff	.10	5	.50
Organizational synergies	X	5	—
General image	X	5	—
	1.00	1 to 5	4.30

*For any particular industry, there will be some factors that, while important in general, will have little or no effect on the relative competitive position of firms within that industry.

** "1" denotes very weak competitive position; "5" denotes a very strong competitive position.

harvesting), the company may decide to revitalize the business through new investments. The fourth and final option, the invest-to-exit strategy, is directed toward leaving the market through harvesting or divesting. Harvesting amounts to making very low investments in the business so that in the short run the business will secure positive cash flow and in a few years die out. (With no new investments, the position will continue to deteriorate.) Alternatively, the whole business may be divested, that is, sold to another party in a one-time deal. Sometimes small investments may be made to maintain the viability of business if divestment is desired but there is no immediate suitor. In this way the business can eventually be sold at a higher price than would have been possible right away.

Unit of Analysis | The framework discussed here may be applied to either a product/market or an SBU. As a matter of fact, it may be equally applicable to a much higher level of aggregation in the organization, such as a division or a group. Of course, at the

EXHIBIT 10-14

Prescriptive Strategies for Businesses in Different Cells

		Competitive Position		
		Strong	Medium	Weak
Market Attractive-ness	High	**Protect Position** • Invest to grow at maximum digestible rate • Concentrate effort on maintaining strength	**Invest to Build** • Challenge for leadership • Build selectively on strengths • Reinforce vulnerable areas	**Build Selectively** • Specialize around limited strengths • Seek ways to overcome weaknesses • Withdraw if indications of sustainable growth are lacking
	Medium	**Build Selectively** • Invest heavily in most attractive segments • Build up ability to counter competition • Emphasize profitability by raising productivity	**Selectivity/Manage for Earnings** • Protect existing program • Concentrate investments in segments where profitability is good and risk is relatively low	**Limited Expansion or Harvest** • Look for ways to expand without high risk; otherwise, minimize investment and rationalize investment
	Low	**Protect and Refocus** • Manage for current earnings • Concentrate on attractive strengths • Defend strengths	**Manage for Earnings** • Protect position in most profitable segments • Upgrade product line • Minimize investment	**Divest** • Sell at time that will maximize cash value • Cut fixed costs and avoid investment meanwhile

group or division level, it may be very difficult to measure industry attractiveness and business strengths unless the group or division happens to be in one business.

In the scheme followed in this book, the analysis may be performed first at the SBU level to determine the strategic perspective of different products/markets. Finally, all SBUs may be simultaneously positioned on the matrix to determine a corporate-wide portfolio.

EXHIBIT 10-15
Strategy Options

Industry Attractiveness

	Current Position Strategy (to maintain this position)	

Business Strength

(a) Invest to Maintain

Industry Attractiveness

Strategy	Current Position	
	Current Position	

Business Strength

(b) Invest to Grow

Industry Attractiveness

Strategy		
Current Position		

Business Strength

(c) Invest to Regain

Industry Attractiveness

	Current Position	Strategy

Business Strength

(d) Invest to Exit

Directional Policy Matrix | A slightly different technique, the directional policy matrix, is popularly used in Europe. It was initially worked out at the Shell Group but later caught the fancy of many businesses across the Atlantic. Exhibit 10-16 illustrates a directional policy matrix. The two sides of the matrix are labeled business sector prospects

EXHIBIT 10-16
Directional Policy Matrix

		Business Sector Prospects		
		Unattractive	Average	Attractive
	Weak	Disinvest	Phased withdrawal	Double or quit
			Proceed with care	
Company's Competitive Capabilities	**Average**	Phased withdrawal	Proceed with care	Try
	Strong	Cash generator	Growth	Leader
			Leader	

(industry attractiveness) and company's competitive capabilities (business strengths). *Business sector prospects* are categorized as unattractive, average, and attractive; and the *company's competitive capabilities* are categorized as weak, average, and strong. Within each cell is the overall strategy direction for a business depicted by the cell. The consideration of factors used to measure business sector prospects and a company's competitive capabilities follows the same logic and analyses discussed above.

PORTFOLIO MATRIX: CRITICAL ANALYSIS

In recent years, a variety of criticisms have been leveled at the portfolio framework. Most of the criticism has centered on the Boston Consulting Group matrix.

1. A question has been raised about the use of market share as the most important influence on marketing strategy. The BCG matrix is derived from an application of the learning curve to manufacturing and other costs. It was observed that, as a firm's product output (and thus market share) increases, total cost declines by a fixed percentage. This may be true for commodities; however, in most product/market situations, products are differentiated, new products and brands are continually introduced, and the pace of technological changes keeps increasing. As a result, one may move from learning curve to learning curve or encounter a discontinuity. More concrete evidence is needed before the validity of market share as a dimension in strategy formulation is established or rejected.
2. Another criticism, closely related to the first, is how product/market boundaries are defined. Market share varies depending on the definition of the corresponding

product/market. Hence, a product may be classified in different cells, depending on the market boundaries used.

3. The stability of product life cycles is implicitly assumed in some portfolio models. However, as in the case of the learning curve, it is possible for the product life cycle to change during the life of the product. For example, recycling can extend the life cycle of a product, sparking a second growth stage after maturity. A related subissue concerns the assumption that investment is more desirable in high-growth markets than in low-growth ones. There is insufficient evidence to support this proposition.[14] This overall issue becomes more problematic for international firms because a given product may be in different stages of its life cycle in different countries.

4. The BCG portfolio framework was developed for balancing cash flows. It ignores the existence of capital markets. Cash balancing is not always an important consideration.

5. The portfolio framework assumes that investments in all products/markets are equally risky, but this is not the case. In fact, financial portfolio management theory does take risk into account. The more risky an investment, the higher the return expected of it. The portfolio matrix does not consider the risk factor.

6. The BCG portfolio model assumes that there is no interdependency between products/markets. This assumption can be questioned on various grounds. For instance, different products/markets might share technology or costs.[15] These interdependencies should be accounted for in a portfolio framework.

7. There is no consensus on the level at which portfolio models are appropriately used. Five levels can be identified: product, product line, market segment, SBU, and business sector. The most frequent application has been at the SBU level; however, it has been suggested that the framework is equally applicable at other levels. Because it is unlikely that any one model could have such wide application, the suggestion that it does casts doubt on the model itself.

8. Most portfolio approaches are retrospective and overly dependent on conventional wisdom in the way in which they treat both market attractiveness and business strengths.[16] For example, despite evidence to the contrary, conventional wisdom suggests the following:

   a. Dominant market share endows companies with sufficient power to maintain price above a competitive level or to obtain massive cost advantages through economies of scale and the experience curve. However, the returns for such companies as Goodyear and Maytag show that this is not always the case.

Market Situation	Conventional Wisdom	Examples	Return on Total Capital Employed 1975–79
Dominant market	Market leader gains — Premium prices — Cost advantages due to scale and experience curve	Goodyear: 40% of U.S. tire market; market leader	7.0%
		Maytag: 5% of U.S. appliance industry; niche competitor	26.7%

b. High market growth means that rivals can expand output and show profits without having to take demand out of each other's plants and provoking price warfare. But the experience of industries as different as the European tungsten carbide industry and the U.S. airline industry suggests that it is not always true.

Market Situation	Conventional Wisdom	Examples	Return on Total Capital Employed 1975–79
High market growth	High market growth allows companies to expand output without provoking price competition and leads to higher profits	European tungsten carbide industry: 1% annual growth	15.0%
		U.S. airline industry: 13.6% annual growth	5.7%

c. High barriers to entry allow existing competitors to keep prices high and earn high profits. But the experience of the U.S. brewing industry seems to refute conventional wisdom.

Market Situation	Conventional Wisdom	Examples	Return on Total Capital Employed 1975–79
High barriers to entry	High barriers prevent new entrants from competing away previously excess profits	U.S. brewing industry is highly concentrated with very high barriers to entry	8.6%

9. There are also issues of measurement and weighting. Different measures have been proposed and used for the dimensions of portfolio models; however, a product's position on a matrix may vary depending on the measures used.[17] In addition, the weights used for models having composite dimensions may impact the results, and the position of a business on the matrix may change with the weighting scheme used.

10. Portfolio models ignore the impact of both the external and internal environments of a company. Because a firm's strategic decisions are made within its environments, their potential impact must be taken into account. Day highlights a few situational factors that might affect a firm's strategic plan. As examples of internal factors, he cites rate of capacity utilization, union pressures, barriers to entry, and extent of captive business. GNP, interest rates, and social, legal, and regulatory environment are cited as examples of external factors.[18] No systematic treatment has been accorded to such environmental influences in the portfolio models. These influences are always unique to a company, so the importance of customizing a portfolio approach becomes clear.

11. The relevance of a particular strategy for a business depends on its correct categorization on the matrix. If a mistake is made in locating a business in a particular cell of the matrix, the failure of the prescribed strategy cannot be blamed on the framework. In other words, superficial and uncritical application of the portfolio framework can misdirect a business's strategy. As Gluck has observed:

Portfolio approaches have their limitations, of course. First, it's just not all that easy to define the businesses or product/market units appropriately before you begin to analyze them. Second, some attractive strategic opportunities can be overlooked if management treats its businesses as independent entities when there may be real advantages in their sharing resources at the research or manufacturing or distribution level. And third, like more sophisticated models, when it's used uncritically the portfolio can give its users the illusion that they're being rigorous and scientific when in fact they've fallen prey to the old garbage-in, garbage-out syndrome.[19]

12. Most portfolio approaches suggest standard or generic strategies based on the portfolio position of individual SBUs. But these kinds of responses can often result in lost opportunities, turn out to be impractical or unrealistic, and stifle creativity. For example, the standard strategy for managing dogs (SBUs that have a low share of a mature market) is to treat them as candidates for divestment or liquidation. New evidence demonstrates, however, that, with proper management, dogs can be assets to a diversified corporation. One recent study of the performance of more than a thousand industrial-product businesses slotted into the four cells of the BCG matrix found that the average dog had a positive cash flow even greater than the cash needs of the average question mark. Moreover, in a slow-growth economy, more than half of a company's businesses might qualify as dogs. Disposing of them all would be neither feasible nor desirable. Yet the portfolio approach provides no help in suggesting how to improve the performance of such businesses.[20]

13. Portfolio models fail to answer such questions as (a) how a company may determine whether its strategic goals are consistent with its financial objectives, (b) how a company may relate strategic goals to its affordable growth, and (c) how relevant the designated strategies are vis-à-vis competition from overseas companies. In addition, many marketers have raised other questions about the viability of portfolio approaches as a strategy development tool. For example, it has been claimed that the BCG matrix approach is relevant only for positioning existing businesses and fails to prescribe how a question mark may be reared to emerge as a star, how new stars can be located, and so on. Empirical support for the limitations of portfolio planning methods come from the work of Armstrong and Brodie. According to them, the limitations are so serious that portfolio matrices are detrimental since they produce poorer decisions.[21]

    In response to these criticisms, it should be pointed out that the BCG portfolio framework was developed as an aid in formulating business strategies in complex environments. Its aim was not to prescribe strategy, though many executives and academicians have misused it in this way. As one writer has noted:

> No simple, monolithic set of rules or strategy imperatives will point automatically to the right course. No planning system guarantees the development of successful strategies. Nor does any technique. The Business Portfolio (the growth/share matrix) made a major contribution to strategic thought. Today it is misused and overexposed. It can be a helpful tool, but it can also be misleading or, worse, a straitjacket.[22]

A NEW PRODUCT PORTFOLIO APPROACH: PORTER'S GENERIC STRATEGIES FRAMEWORK

Porter has identified three generic strategies: (a) overall cost leadership (i.e., making units of a fairly standardized product and underpricing everybody else); (b) differentiation (i.e., turning out something customers perceive as unique—an item whose quality, design, brand name, or reputation for service commands higher-than-average prices); and (c) focus (i.e., concentrating on a particular group of customers, geographic market, channel of distribution, or distinct segment of the product line).[23]

Porter's choice of strategy is based on two factors: the **strategic target** at which the business aims and the **strategic advantage** that the business has in aiming at that target. According to Porter, forging successful strategy begins with understanding of what is happening in one's industry and deciding which of the available competitive niches one should attempt to dominate. For example, a firm may discover that the largest competitor in an industry is aggressively pursuing cost leadership, that others are trying the differentiation route, and that no one is attempting to focus on some small specialty market. On the basis of this information, the firm might sharpen its efforts to distinguish its product from others or switch to a focus game plan. As Porter says, the idea is to position the firm "so it won't be slugging it out with everybody else in the industry; if it does it right, it won't be directly toe-to-toe with anyone." The objective is to mark out a defensible competitive position—defensible not just against rival companies but also against the forces driving industry competition (discussed in Chapter 4).

What it means is that the give-and-take between firms already in the business represents only one such force. Others are the bargaining power of suppliers, the bargaining power of buyers, the threat of substitute products or services, and the threat of new entrants. In conclusion, Porter's framework emphasizes not only that certain characteristics of the industry must be considered in choosing a generic strategy, but that they in fact dictate the proper choice.

PORTFOLIO ANALYSIS CONCLUSION

Portfolio approaches provide a useful tool for strategists. Granted, these approaches have limitations, but all these limitations can be overcome with a little imagination and foresight. The real concern about the portfolio approach is that its elegant simplicity often tempts managers to believe that it can solve all problems of corporate choices and resource allocation. The truth is that it addresses only half of the problem: the back half. The portfolio approach is a powerful tool for helping the strategist select from a menu of available opportunities, but it does not put the menu into his or her hands. That is the front half of the problem. The other critical dimension in making strategic choices is the need to generate a rich array of business options from which to choose. No simple tool is available that can provide this option-generating capability. Here only creative thinking about one's environment, one's business, one's customers, and one's competitors can help.

For a successful introduction of the portfolio framework, the strategist should heed the following advice:

1. Once introduced, move quickly to establish the legitimacy of portfolio analysis.
2. Educate line managers in its relevance and use.
3. Redefine SBUs explicitly because their definition is the "genesis and nemesis" of adequately using the portfolio framework.
4. Use the portfolio framework to seek the strategic direction for different businesses without haggling over the fancy labels by which to call them.
5. Make top management acknowledge SBUs as portfolios to be managed.
6. Seek top management time for reviewing different businesses using the portfolio framework.
7. Rely on a flexible, informal management process to differentiate influence patterns at the SBU level.
8. Tie resource allocation to the business plan.
9. Consider strategic expenses and human resources as explicitly as capital investment.
10. Plan explicitly for new business development.
11. Make a clear strategic commitment to a few selected technologies or markets early.

SUMMARY

A diversified organization needs to examine its widely different businesses at the corporate level to see how each business fits within the overall corporate purpose and to come to grips with the resource allocation problem. The portfolio approaches described in this chapter help management determine the role that each business plays in the corporation and allocate resources accordingly.

Three portfolio approaches were introduced: product life cycle, growth rate-relative market share matrix, and multifactor portfolio matrix. The product life-cycle approach determines the life status of different products and whether the company has enough viable products to provide desired growth in the future. If the company lacks new products with which to generate growth in coming years, investments may be made in new products. If growth is hurt by the early maturity of promising products, the strategic effort may be directed toward extension of their life cycles.

The second approach, the growth rate-relative market share matrix, suggests locating products or businesses on a matrix with relative market share and growth rate as its dimensions. The four cells in the matrix, whose positions are based on whether growth is high or low and whether relative market share is high or low, are labeled stars, cash cows, question marks, and dogs. The strategy for a product or business in each cell, which is primarily based on the business's cash flow implications, was outlined.

The third approach, the multifactor portfolio matrix, again uses two variables (industry attractiveness and business strengths), but these two variables are based on a variety of factors. Here, again, a desired strategy for a product/business in each cell was recommended. The focus of the multifactor matrix approach is on the return-on-investment implications of strategy alternatives rather than on cash flow, as in the growth rate-relative market share matrix approach.

Various portfolio approaches were critically examined. The criticisms relate mainly to operational definitions of dimensions used, weighting of variables, and product/market boundary determination. The chapter concluded with a discussion of Porter's generic strategies framework.

DISCUSSION QUESTIONS

1. What purpose may a product portfolio serve in the context of marketing strategy?
2. How can the position of a product in its life cycle be located?
3. What is the strategic significance of products in the maturity stage of the product life cycle?
4. What is the meaning of relative market share?
5. What sequence should products follow for success? What may management do to ensure this sequence?
6. What factors may a company consider when measuring industry attractiveness and business strengths? Should these factors vary from one business to another in a company?
7. What is the basic difference between the growth rate-relative market share matrix approach and the multifactor portfolio matrix approach?
8. What major problems with portfolio approaches have critics identified?
9. What generic strategies does Porter recommend? Discuss.

NOTES

[1] Gerald J. Tellis and C. Merle Crawford, "An Evolutionary Approach to Product Growth Theory," *Journal of Marketing* (Fall 1981): 125–34.

[2] John E. Swan and David R. Rink, "Fitting Market Strategy to Varying Product Life Cycles," *Business Horizons* (January–February 1982): 72–76; and Yoram J. Wind, *Product Policy: Concepts, Methods, and Strategy* (Reading, MA: Addison-Wesley Publishing Co., 1982).

[3] Kathryn Rudie Harrigan, "Strategies for Declining Industries," *Journal of Business Strategy* (Fall 1980): 27.

[4] "How Du Pont Keeps Them Coming Back for More," *Business Week* (20 August 1990): 80.

[5] Robert D. Buzzell, "Competitive Behavior and Product Life Cycles," in *New Ideas for Successful Marketing*, ed. John S. Wright and Jac L. Goldstrucker (Chicago: American Marketing Association, 1966), 47.

[6] Nariman K. Dhalla and Sonia Yuspeh, "Forget the Product Life-Cycle Concept," *Harvard Business Review* (January–February 1976): 102–09.

[7] Theodore Levitt, "Exploit the Product Life Cycle," *Harvard Business Review* (November–December 1965): 81.

[8] John E. Smallwood, "The Product Life Cycle: A Key to Strategic Market Planning," *MSU Business Topics* (Winter 1973): 35. See also George S. Day, "The Product Life Cycle: Analysis and Applications Issues," *Journal of Marketing* (Fall 1981): 60–67.

[9] Tellis and Crawford, "An Evolutionary Approach."

[10] Stephen G. Harrell and Elmer D. Taylor, "Modeling the Product Life Cycle for Consumer Durables," *Journal of Marketing* (Fall 1981): 68–75.

[11] See Philippe Haspeslagh, "Portfolio Planning: Uses and Limits," *Harvard Business Review* (January–February 1982): 60, 73.

[12] "They're All Juiced Up at Tropicana," *Business Week* (13 May 1991). Information updated through company sources.

[13] *Organizing and Managing the Planning Function* (Fairfield, CT: GE Company, n.d.).

[14] Robin Wensley, "Strategic Marketing: Betas, Boxes, or Basics," *Journal of Marketing* (Summer 1981): 173–82.

[15] Michael E. Porter, *Competitive Strategy* (New York: The Free Press, 1981).

[16] Fred Gluck, "A Fresh Look at Strategic Management," *Journal of Business Strategy* (Fall 1985): 23.

[17] Yoram Wind, Vijay Mahajan, and Donald J. Swire, "An Empirical Comparison of Standardized Portfolio Models," *Journal of Marketing* (Spring 1983): 89–99.

[18] George Day, "Diagnosing the Product Portfolio," *Journal of Marketing* (April 1977): 29–38.

[19] Frederick W. Gluck, "Strategic Choice and Resource Allocation," *McKinsey Quarterly* (Winter 1980): 24.

[20] Donald Hambrick and Ian MacMillan, "The Product Portfolio and Man's Best Friend," *California Management Review* (Fall 1982): 16–23.

[21] J. Scott Armstrong and Roderick J. Brodie, "Effects of Portfolio Planning Methods on Decision Making: Experimental Results," *International Journal of Research in Marketing* 11 (1994): 73–84.

[22] *The Boston Consulting Group Annual Perspective* (Boston: Boston Consulting Group, 1981).

[23] Porter, *Competitive Strategy*.

Strategy Implementation and Control

Organizational Structure

A strategic planning system should provide answers to two basic questions: what to do and how to do it. The first question refers to selection of a strategy; the second, to organizational arrangements. An organization must have not only a winning strategy to pursue but also a matching structure to facilitate its implementation. The emphasis in the preceding chapters has been on strategy formulation. This chapter is devoted to building a viable organizational structure to administer the strategy.

As we move further into the 1990s, principles of strategic analysis and planning have been fully integrated into corporate decision making at all levels. Yet, although these precepts now enjoy global acceptance, the need to translate strategic guidelines into long-term results and adapt them to rapidly changing market conditions continues to rank among the major challenges confronting today's companies. Essentially, there are three aspects of implementation that, if properly organized, can lead to superior corporate performance and competitive advantage: organization planning, management systems, and executive reward programs.

Fitting these aspects to the underlying strategy requires strategic reorganization. There is no magic formula to ensure successful reorganization and, generally, no "perfect" prototype to follow. Reorganization is a delicate process that above all requires a finely tuned management sense.

The discussion in this chapter focuses on five dimensions: (a) the creation of market-responsive organizations, (b) the role of systems in implementing strategy, (c) executive reward systems, (d) leadership style (i.e., the establishment of an internal environment conducive to strategy implementation), and (e) the measurement of strategic performance (i.e., the development of a network of control and communication to monitor and evaluate progress in achieving strategic goals). In addition, the impact of strategic planning on marketing organization is studied.

THE TRADITIONAL ORGANIZATION

Corporations have traditionally been organized with a strong emphasis on pursuing and achieving established objectives. Such organizations adapt well to growing internal complexities and provide adequate incentive mechanisms and systems of accountability to support objectives. However, they fail to provide a congenial environment for strategic planning. For example, one of the organizational capabilities needed for strategic planning is that of modifying, or redefining, the objectives themselves so that the corporation is prepared to meet future competition. The traditional organizational structure, based on "command and control" principles, resists change, which is why a new type of structure is needed for strategic planning:

> The forces shaping organization today are dramatically different from those facing Frederick Taylor and Alfred Sloan. End-use markets are fragmenting, requiring faster and more targeted responses. Advances in the ability to capture, manipulate, and transmit information electronically make it possible to distribute decision making ("command") without losing "control." Gone is the abundant, primarily male, blue-collar workforce. Workers today are better educated, in short supply, and demanding greater participation and variety in their jobs.
>
> Individually all these changes are dramatic; collectively they shape a new era in organization and strategy. Strategies are increasingly shifting from cost- and volume-based sources of competitive advantage to those focusing on increased value to the customer. Competitive strength is derived from the skills, speed, specificity, and service levels provided to customers. The Command and Control organization is under strain. Indeed, many businesses are finding that C&C principles now result in competitive disadvantage.[1]

Exhibit 11-1 differentiates the characteristics of command and control structure (i.e., traditional organization with emphasis on the achievement of established objectives) and strategic planning. By and large, command and control structure works in known territory and is concerned with immediate issues. Strategic planning stresses unfamiliar perspectives and is oriented toward the future.[2]

CREATING MARKET-RESPONSIVE ORGANIZATIONS

As markets and technologies change more and more rapidly, organizations must respond quickly and frequently to strategic moves if they are to sustain competitive advantage. Although corporations have learned to make changes in strategy quickly, their organizations may lack parallel market responsiveness. One major reason for this failure is the conflict between scale economics, which is geared to the expansion and aggregation of resources, and the economics of vertical integration, which links differentiated functions and resources for maximum efficiency in responding to market changes.

The opposing pressures fueling this conflict are both subtle and complex. On one side of the equation are all the forces contributing to the need to reap maximum scale advantage. On the other side of the equation, the accelerated pace of change—environmental, competitive, and technological—drives corporations toward increased flexibility, high levels of internal integration, and smaller operating units.

EXHIBIT 11-1
Organizational Characteristics

Command and Control Structure	Strategic Planning
1. Concerned with goals derived from established objectives.	1. Concerned with the identification and evaluation of new objectives and strategies.
2. Goals usually have been validated through extensive experience.	2. New objectives and strategies can be highly debatable; experience within the organization or in other companies may be minimal.
3. Goals are reduced to specific subgoals for functional units.	3. Objectives usually are evaluated primarily for corporate significance.
4. Managers tend to identify with functions or professions and to be preoccupied with means.	4. Managers need a corporate point of view oriented to the environment.
5. Managers obtain relatively prompt evidence of their performance against goals.	5. Evidence of the merit of new objectives or strategies is often available only after several years.
6. Incentives, formal and social, are tied to operating goals.	6. Incentives are at best only loosely associated with planning.
7. The "rules of the game" become well understood. Experienced individuals feel competent and secure.	7. New fields of endeavor may be considered. Past experience may not provide competence in a "new game."
8. The issues are immediate, concrete, and familiar.	8. Issues are abstract, deferrable (to some extent), and may be unfamiliar.

Although scale advantage has traditionally held high ground, evidence is mounting that highly integrated organizations can increase productive capacity through the efficient coordination of functions and resources while remaining highly adaptive and market sensitive. Such organizations respond to the strategic need for change more quickly, smoothly, and successfully than centralized, large-unit organizations oriented toward scale aggregation.[3]

Management has basically three options for resolving the conflict between scale and integration. First, a company can choose to centralize its functions in order to achieve scale at the expense of market responsiveness. Second, it can opt for market responsiveness over scale; that is, it can emphasize small, independent units. Third, it can adopt another, more difficult approach, exploiting the strengths associated with both large and small organizational units to achieve benefits of scale and market responsiveness simultaneously. The key to sustainable competitive advantage lies in successful pursuit of the third alternative.

Exploiting the benefits of both large and small organizational structures involves creating market-responsive units within a framework of shared resources. Such units can combine the strengths of a small company (lean, entrepreneurial management; sharp focus on the business; immediacy of the relationship with the customer; dedication to growth; and action-oriented viewpoint) with those of the large company (extensive financial information and resources;

availability of multiple technologies; recognition as an established business; people with diverse skills to draw on; and an intimate knowledge of markets and functions).

The creation of such units demands that planners determine, as precisely as possible, in what form and to what degree resources must be integrated to ensure the level of market responsiveness dictated by their business strategy. This process can be successful only when it is undertaken in the context of a rigorous analytical framework that links strategy to organization.

Procedure for Creating a Market-Responsive Organization

To create a market-responsive organization, management can use a three-phase process: (a) determine corporate strategic boundaries, (b) balance the demands of scale and market responsiveness, and (c) organize for strategic effectiveness.

Determine Corporate Strategic Boundaries. How successfully a corporation aligns its structure with its strategic objectives depends on its success in making a number of key decisions: determining the stage of the value-added process at which it will compete, identifying those activities in which it has a competitive edge, selecting the functions it should execute internally, and developing a plan of action for integrating those functions most productively. These decisions determine how resources should be allocated and how external and internal boundaries should be drawn. They define the company's business—its products, services, customers, and markets—and determine both long- and short-term strategic potential. How well the company exploits its assets and the degree to which each division's performance supports strategic objectives determine how close it will come to achieving that potential.

How strategic boundary setting reflects the trade-offs between scale and integration becomes clearer when one considers the case of an assembler facing a typical make-or-buy decision for components. As long as the components manufacturer is able to produce common components for several customers, the assembler among them, the components manufacturer enjoys scale advantage. As the products ordered by the assembler become more specialized in response to market demands or increased competitive pressures, however, the benefits the components manufacturer gains from scale begin to decline. At the same time, the cost of integrating operations with those of the assembler increases as technical specifications become more complex and as manufacturing operations become more interdependent. To continue their relationship and sustain their respective advantages, the components manufacturer and the assembler are required to make additional investments: the components manufacturer in capital equipment outlays and product design; the assembler in negotiating terms, research and development planning, quality control, and related areas. As a result, a substantial "disruption cost" is incurred if the components manufacturer and the assembler decide to end their business relationship. Both parties attempt to guard against this potential loss through longer-term contracts, whether explicit or implicit. As interdependence increases, prices and contract negotiations become cumbersome and unresponsive. At some point, the economies of scale may decline enough and the integration costs climb high enough that the assembler finds it more cost effective to produce components internally—to bring that particular function inside the assembler's corporate boundaries.

In this classic make-or-buy example, economic trade-offs between scale and integration costs are direct and relatively clear-cut. As we move from simple make-or-buy decisions to issues of full-scale vertical integration, the economic impact can be far more subtle and far-reaching. Scale advantage is not expressed solely in terms of lower unit manufacturing costs but may also flow from the critical mass of skills gained or from the transferability of new product or process technologies. Valuable integration benefits, on the other hand, may be gained from the willingness to undertake more profitable research and development investments because vertical integration ensures a "market" in downstream operations.

Balance the Demands of Scale and Market Responsiveness. The balancing of scale and market responsiveness demands may be illustrated with reference to a large insurance company. The company faced a complex set of internal and market-based organizational trade-offs in its core business—property and casualty insurance. Lagging market growth, increased price sensitivity, new forms of product distribution, new information technology, and escalating competition were all placing enormous pressures on the company's traditional mode of operation. Top management realized that fundamental changes in organization were needed in both its home office and in its field network if the company was to remain competitive and meet aggressive new growth and profit goals.

In responding to these pressures, the company found itself facing a familiar dilemma. On the one hand, it was vital that its organizational structure become more responsive to local market demand, particularly in terms of regional product pricing and agent deployment. This need pointed to decentralization as the logical method for restructuring operations, with the field divided into smaller sales and marketing regions and more responsibility assigned to local management. On the other hand, however, management was determined to reduce the costs of transaction processing. Meeting this need for administrative streamlining appeared to require that field offices around the country be reorganized into larger regional centers to exploit fully the scale economies offered by improvements in automated processing capacity.

Initially, these strategic requirements seemed to set large centers against locally responsive marketing and sales units. Yet, by carefully analyzing and "rewiring" its structure, the company was able to resolve the apparent conflict cost-effectively and efficiently. Here is the approach it pursued. The company's field operations consisted of essentially self-sufficient regional centers; each center included all functional departments under its umbrella, ranging from sales, claims, and underwriting to operations and personnel. Two of these functions dominated field operations: customer interaction through sales and marketing and transaction processing. Originally, the field organization was designed around exploiting administrative scale in the processing function and balancing the need to locate sales and marketing functions to serve the customer base effectively.

The underlying basis for the organizational design was the need to coordinate sales and processing functions because of the high volume of transactions and interactions between them. A layer of management between the home office and the regional centers coordinated programs and enforced company policies.

In line with its new strategic objectives (greater market responsiveness and increased productivity), the company instituted major organizational changes. First, the layer of management between the home office and regional centers was eliminated to improve communications and to facilitate more market-responsive decision making. Second, to achieve scale economies and contain costs, the reporting relationships of the processing centers were shifted from the regional level directly to the home office. New information technology allowed the company to "unhook" processing centers from sales functions and still remain adequately integrated. As a result, the number of regions of independent sale organizations was no longer tied to the number of processing centers. The number of processing centers was reduced as information-technology innovations allowed additional processing capacity, whereas the number of marketing and sales regions was increased as market requirements demanded, allowing the entire sales organization to move closer to its local client base. The needs for both market responsiveness and scale economies in processing was fully satisfied.

Organize for Strategic Effectiveness. To organize for strategic effectiveness, it is important to recognize that the ultimate goal of a business organization is competitive advantage, and the drive for competitive advantage must be expressed in economic terms and pursued through the use of economic tools. Only by placing organizational decisions in an economic context can the value of alternative forms of structure, incentive, and management process be determined. It is only in the light of these assessments that the steps needed to strike the proper balance between scale and market responsiveness can be taken. Needless complexity, excessive layers of management, and nonessential integration of channels must all be eliminated.[4] The design phase is easy when compared to the difficulties of execution (i.e., implementing organizational change). It requires strong leadership, consistent signals and actions, and strategically driven incentive programs.

Managing a Market-Responsive Organization

Designing and managing a market-responsive organization requires overturning old assumptions. First, the linearity from strategy to structure and on to systems, staff, etc., cannot be reasoned. The process is instead iterative: a team is formed to meet a strategic need; it sizes up the situation, develops a specific strategy, and reorganizes itself as necessary. What's more, the structure is temporary. The organization needs to be ready to change its configuration quickly to respond to new needs and circumstances. Second, the organization's purpose is not to control from the top; it is to empower a group of people to get a job done. Management occurs through training, incentives, and strongly articulated goals, strategies, and standards.

Market-responsive organizations are found most often in businesses that are driven by product development and customer service—electronics and software companies, for example—and are often smaller, younger organizations where traditional boundaries are weaker. Some large-scale models include parts of Honda and Panasonic, 3M, and also, in some ways, GE, which has developed extraordinary flexibility in recent years in reshaping its organization and pushing authority down to front-line managers.

Market-responsive organizations have obvious drawbacks: they lack tight controls, they are ill-suited to exploit scale or to accomplish massive tasks, and they depend on capable and motivated people at the working level. However, companies that cannot use the full market-responsive model can appropriate aspects of it—new product development teams, for instance.

Some large companies, such as IBM, Digital Equipment, and Dow Chemical, with the need for both innovation and coordination of resources among markets, product lines, and technologies, often use the concept in modified form. They frequently change the focus of resources and control by reshuffling product groups—shifting power among parts of the organization or by using ad hoc teams.

Experience suggests that people are quite willing and able to change as long as they have a clear understanding of what's expected of them, know why it is important to change, and have latitude in designing the new organization. Five key elements that companies should carefully consider in seeking strategic effectiveness are discussed below:[5]

1. **Forge a clear link between strategy and skills**—A company's strategy, which should embody the value it proposes to deliver to its customers, determines the skills it needs. Many companies, however, are not sufficiently clear or rigorous about this linkage. Because Frank Perdue promises to deliver more tender chickens, his organization must excel at the breeding and logistics skills necessary to deliver them. Because Volvo promises to deliver more reliable, tougher, and safer station wagons, it must be skilled in designing and manufacturing them. Because Domino's Pizza says it will deliver fresh pizza hot to your door within 30 minutes, each of its 5,000 outlets needs to be skilled at making a good pizza quickly and at customer order processing and delivery. Strategy drives skills, but if this linkage is missed, a company may end up doing some things right but not the right things right.

2. **Be specific and selective about core skills**—Managers often describe the core skills their companies need in terms that are too general. Saying that you need to be first rate at customer service or marketing is not good enough. For example, the employees of a department store committed to being better at customer service will not know what to do differently because the term *customer service* doesn't paint a specific enough picture of the behavior desired of them. In fact, a department store needs to be good in at least three different types of customer services: with hard goods such as refrigerators or furniture, customer service must have a high component of product and technical knowledge; with fine apparel, what counts is expertise in fashion counseling; with basics and sundries, the need is for friendly, efficient self-service. Each of these service goals translates into a different set of day-to-day behaviors expected of employees. Unless these behaviors are precisely defined, even willing employees won't change their behavior very much because they won't know how.

3. **Clarify the implications for pivotal jobs**—Consider the department store again. The definition of different types of customer services drives through to the identification of several specific jobs whose performance determines whether customers think the store is good at customer service: the product salesperson for refrigerators, the fashion counselor for fine apparel, and the cashier for sundries. Pushing the skill definition to these specific jobs, which may be called pivotal jobs, allows the company to describe in specific terms what the holders of these jobs should do or not do, which kind of people to hire, which kind of training and coaching to give them, which rewards motivate them, and which kind of information they need. For example, at Nordstrom, the excellent Seattle-based fashion specialty retailer, the pivotal job is the front-line sales associate. Because Nordstrom is clear about the type of person it wants for this job—someone interested in a career, not just a summer position—it looks more for a service orientation than prior experience. It pays better than the industry average and offers incentives that allow top sales associates to make over $80,000 a year. Nordstrom stresses customer service above all else. The company philosophy is to offer the customer, in this order, "the best service, selection, quality, and value."

   This clarity about priorities helps sales associates determine appropriate service behavior. So does the excellent product and service training they receive. And so does the customer information system that provides sales associates with up-to-date sales and service records on their customers. Nordstrom recognizes that its business success depends on the success of pivotal jobholders in delivering value to customers, and the company has geared its entire organization to support these front-line associates.

4. **Provide leadership from the top**—The key ingredients that have been found workable in this task include

   - Appeal to the pride of the organization. Most people want to do a superior job, especially for a company that expresses its mission with an idea bigger than just making money. Providing them with a single noble purpose—be it "quality, service, cleanliness, value" or "innovation"—will unleash energy but keep it focused.
   - Clarify the importance and value of building core skills. Provide the organization with a good economic understanding of the value as well as a clear picture of the consequences of not paying attention to core skills.
   - Be willing to do the tough things that break bottlenecks and establish credibility for the belief that "this change is for real." Usually, the toughest things involve replacing people who are change blockers, committing key managers to the skill-building effort, and spending money on it.
   - Treat the program to build skills as something special, not as business as usual. Reflect this in the leader's own time allocation, in the questions he or she asks subordinates, in the special assignments he or she gives people, in the choice of the special measurements he or she looks at, and so on.
   - Over-communicate to superiors, subordinates, customers, and especially to pivotal jobholders. Talk and write incessantly about the skill-building program—about the skills the company is trying to build and about why they are critical; about early wins, heroes, and lessons learned from failures; about milestones achieved.

5. **Empower the organization to learn**—Organizations, like individuals, learn best by doing. Building new core skills is preeminently a learning process. Sketch out for employees the boundaries of their playing field by defining the strategy, the skills the company is trying to build, the pivotal job behaviors required, and the convictions they must hold about what is right. But within these boundaries, give them a lot of room to run—to try things, succeed, fail and to learn for themselves exactly what works and what doesn't. They will figure out for themselves details that could never be prescribed from above.

To illustrate the point, take, for example, the 10,000 route salespeople of Frito-Lay. Michael Jordan, the company's president, says that these people with their "store to door service" control the destiny of Frito-Lay. Wayne Calloway, PepsiCo president and past CEO of Frito-Lay, describes this pivotal job as follows: "Our sales people are entrepreneurs of the first order. Over 100,000 times a day they encounter customers who are making buying decisions on the spot. How in the world could an old-fashioned sort of management deal with those kinds of conditions? Our approach is to find good people and to give them as much responsibility as possible because they're closest to the customer, they know what's going on."[6]

ROLE OF SYSTEMS IN IMPLEMENTING STRATEGY

The term *systems* refers to management systems, which include any of the formally organized procedures that pervade a business. Three types of systems may be distinguished: execution systems, monitoring systems, and control systems.

1. **Execution systems** focus directly on the basic processes for conducting the firm's business. They include systems that enable products to be designed, supplies to be ordered, production to be scheduled, goods to be shipped, cash to be applied, and employees to be paid.
2. **Monitoring systems** are any procedures that measure and assess basic processes. They can be designed to gather information in different ways to serve a number of internal or external reporting purposes: to meet SEC or other regulatory requirements, to control budgets, to pay taxes, and to serve the strategic and organizational intent of the company.
3. **Control systems** are the means through which processes are made to conform or are kept within tolerable limits. At the broadest level, they include separation of duties, authority limits, product inspection, and plan submittals.

As can be seen from this brief description, systems pervade the conduct of business. For that very reason, systems provide ample opportunity for strategies to fail. In most companies, the major emphasis is on execution systems. But creating systems that support strategies and organizational intent requires top management to include monitoring and control systems in addition to executing systems in strategic thinking and to focus on systems in strategy implementation. It means, as part of the strategic planning, answering such key questions as: What are the critical success factors? How do they translate into operational performance? How should that operational performance be measured and motivated?

How should information about financial performance be derived? What business cycles are important? How should systems support them? What is the role of financial controls and measures? Where should control of information reside? How should strategic objectives and organizational performance be monitored and modified? How should internal and external information be linked?

In short, integrating all systems with strategy requires great vision—the ability to see the firm as an organic whole. Unfortunately, too many systems managers lack vision or clout and too many executives lack the understanding or the inclination to make this integration happen.

Techniques for Systems Design

To create systems that support strategic and organizational intent, top management must include systems in strategic thinking and focus on systems in strategy implementation. Once critical success factors have been identified and translated into operational measurements, good systems design techniques are needed to ensure that those factors and measurements are appropriately accommodated by all systems. Following are some guidelines for good systems design:

1. **Design an effective information-capturing procedure**—Data should be captured close to the source, and source documents should be linked. For example, at one company, data processing personnel collected information on raw materials from receiving reports two days after delivery and entered that information into purchasing control and inventory management systems. Two days later, accounting gathered information on the same delivery from invoices, this time entering it into accounting systems. The failure to link source documents led to apparent inventory discrepancies. Purchasing and inventory processes focused on inventory codes and quantities; accounting processes dealt with accounting codes and monetary amounts, which were available only at the end of the month.[7]

   These problems required a three-part solution: placing terminals at the receiving dock, where receiving clerks could enter operating information; using internal links to accounting codes; and creating a reconciliation proof on which quantities and amounts were entered as invoices were received.

2. **Manage commonly used data elements for firmwide accessibility and control**—If a multidivisional firm allows each unit to code inventory discretely, stock that is commonly used cannot be traded and rebalanced. Traditionally, auto dealers maintained independent inventory controls. By contrast, Ford Motor Company has worked to keep its inventory records consistent and thus accessible to dealers so that imbalances at one lead to opportunities for another.

3. **Decide which applications are common and which tolerate distributed processing**—Typical considerations here include pinpointing the need to share data, determining the availability of hardware and software offerings that make a distributed approach feasible, and investigating the effect of geographical distance. Once a particular application or function is judged appropriate for a distributed approach, it must be integrated into an information network.

4. **Manage information, not reports**—Systems are often developed with end reports in mind, focusing on output, not content. If needs change or if developers and users misunderstand each other, the results can lead to frustration at best or the inability to modify output at worst. When the development focus is on content, on information that has been strategically identified as critical to success, users

can tailor the presentation of output to their purposes. For example, in one company with a well-constructed receivables database, one manager chose to compare cash collections to target amounts, another used days outstanding, and a third used turnover ratios.

5. **Examine cost-effectiveness**—Questioning the value of a system and of the work required to support it is healthy. But such questioning must be handled properly. As an example, to escape merely chipping away at existing processes through cost reduction, Procter & Gamble developed its elimination approach, which is based on the key "if" question: If it were not for this [reason], this [cost] would be eliminated.[8]

Designing and maintaining systems that focus on strategic intent and that assess performance in terms of that intent is crucial to the success of a strategy. In fact, a lack of integration between systems and strategy is an important reason why sound strategic and organizational concepts get bogged down in implementation and do not achieve the results their creators intended. Soundly designed and managed systems do not happen casually: they emerge only with top management involvement and with a clear vision of the importance of systems to strategic outcomes.

EXECUTIVE REWARD SYSTEMS

Executive compensation and strategy are mutually dependent and reinforcing. A good reward system should have three characteristics:[9] (a) it should optimize value to all key stakeholders, including both shareholders and management alike (the so-called agency problem); (b) it should properly measure and recapture value; and (c) it should integrate compensation signals with those implicit in strategy and structure. Although these issues are generally addressed from the perspective of plan implementation, they also have an important but rarely noted strategic dimension. And that strategic dimension actually has a make-or-break impact on plan effectiveness.

The Agency Problem

The agency problem refers to the potential conflict of interest between shareholders and their agents, the executives charged with implementing corporate strategy. The executives of a corporation serve as agents of the corporation's shareholders. Yet, though both executives and shareholders are stakeholders in a corporation, their interests do not coincide. In fact, they naturally diverge on three counts: risk position (e.g., shareholders stand last in line among claimants to the resources of the corporation, whereas executives have the right to payment of salaries and benefits before the claims of shareholders are met); ability to redeploy (e.g., shareholders can freely redeploy their investments; the executives' human capital invested in the course of a career may not be easily redeployable at full value); time horizon (e.g., shareholders embrace long time horizons to earn competitive returns; time horizons of executives are usually shorter). These differences lead to differences in the ways each group measures the risks and rewards of any corporate action. In general, the differences in risk evaluation make a company's executives more averse to risk than are its shareholders.

Resolving the agency problem requires bridging the gap between the inherently divergent interests of shareholders and the executives entrusted with the responsibility of safeguarding and increasing shareholder investments. Though executive compensation plans can and should help resolve this problem, they often compound it. Most incentive plans, for example, are based on improvements in short-term earnings; therefore, they actually inhibit the very risk decisions required to provide highly competitive returns to shareholders.

New and creative ways of compensating executives must be developed to synchronize their interests with those of shareholders.

The Value Problem | From the company's viewpoint, the value issue is twofold. One aspect revolves around the need to reward executive performance in a way that is systematically related to the market value of the corporation. The other is the need to create incentive plans for managers of individual business units.

In this book, our major concern is with creating incentive plans for managers of individual business units. Compensation planning for individual business units is illustrated with reference to a hypothetical company, Hellenic Corporation.[10]

Hellenic Corporation consists of four businesses: Alpha, Beta, Gamma, and Delta. Alpha operates in a promising market but needs to increase market share rapidly. Beta is an efficient, well-run business that already has the largest share of a mature market. Gamma, once a top performer, has suffered recently from serious management mistakes; nevertheless, it has the potential to be a winner again. Delta is a mediocre performer in a mediocre market; moreover, its business is largely unrelated to the other businesses of the corporation.

Hellenic's strategic plan calls for Alpha to grow rapidly, for Beta to capitalize on its well-established position, for Gamma to turn itself around, and for Delta to be divested. This plan maximizes the value of the corporation as a whole. Each division is vital to the corporation's success; however, the management objectives of the chiefs at Alpha, Beta, Gamma, and Delta differ from one another and influence the market value of the firm in distinct ways. This conflict, however, does not mean that shareholder value is an impractical standard for determining executive reward. Even when a manager's performance is related only indirectly to shareholder value, increasing shareholder value need not be abandoned as the aim of executive compensation planning. The challenge is to craft a plan that links performance to value in a way that is consistent with the corporation's long-term strategy. To do this requires tailoring a specific compensation package for the manager of each business unit. The determinants of compensation at Alpha must be different from those at Beta, which again must be different from those at Gamma and at Delta.

This overall plan can be created by analyzing how risk and time horizons in executive pay plans suit the strategic objectives of each business unit. For example, the top manager at Alpha is engaged in a very long-term project. Exceptional growth and profitability are planned, and the risks incurred in executing the plan are considerable. These circumstances call for a pay package geared to the entrepreneurial challenges facing Alpha. Accordingly, the time horizon is very long and the risk posture is high. At Beta, where the prime objective is to maximize returns from a well-established market position, the time horizon and risk posture are moderate. At Gamma, the turnaround candidate, the time horizon is short and the risk posture is very high. At Delta, being managed for window dressing, the time horizon is short and the risk posture is low. In addition, other special sell-off compensation arrangements (e.g., a percentage of the sale price) may be needed.

The Signaling Problem

A *signal* is simply an inducement to action. Because pay is clearly a powerful inducement to action, compensation systems are powerful signaling devices. Other signaling devices include financial controls, the planning process, and the top management succession plan. All these factors convey messages about what a corporation expects and what it values. Collectively, these signals shape the corporation's culture and determine the actions it takes in given situations.

When management sends consistent signals through all channels, it adheres to a clear strategic track. Unfortunately, conflicting internal signals are common, and compensation is frequently the area of greatest dissonance. Companies must tackle the signaling problem directly. Winners should be paid like winners, and poor performers must not be rewarded. Briefly, executive compensation plans require more risk taking based on real value.

Incentive plans should be designed to induce risk taking. They should make executives think like owners. That is, the plan must bring the interests of executives in line with the interests of shareholders. By resolving the problems of agency and value, by ensuring that high levels of risk taking reap commensurate rewards, and by eliminating conflicting signals, companies can put in place the kinds of incentives required to create exceptional value for owners and agents alike.

LEADERSHIP STYLE

However strategic plans are arrived at, only one person, the CEO, can ensure that energies and efforts throughout the organization are orchestrated to attain desired objectives. What the Chinese general and philosopher Sun-tzu said in 514 B.C. is still true today: "Weak leadership can wreck the soundest strategy; forceful execution of even a poor plan can often bring victory." This section examines the key role of the CEO in shaping the organization for strategy implementation. Also discussed is the role of the strategic planner, whose activities also have a major impact on the organization and its attitude toward strategic change.

Role of the CEO

The CEO of a company is the chief strategist. He or she communicates the importance of strategic planning to the organization. Personal commitment on the part of the CEO to the significance of planning must not only be highly visible—it must also be consistent with all other decisions that the CEO makes to influence the work of the organization. To be accepted within the organization, the strategic planning process needs the CEO's support. People accustomed to a short-term orientation may resist the strategic planning process, which requires different methods. But the CEO can set an example for them by adhering to the planning process. Essentially, the CEO is responsible for creating a corporate climate conducive to strategic planning. The CEO can also set a future perspective for the organization. One CEO remarked:

> My people cannot plan or work beyond the distance of my own vision. If I focus on next year, I'll force them to become preoccupied with next year. If I can try to look five to ten years ahead, at least I'll make it possible for the rest of the organization to raise their eyes off the ground immediately in front of them.[11]

The CEO should focus attention on the corporate purpose and approve strategic decisions accordingly. To perform these tasks well, the CEO should support the staff work and analysis upon which his or her decisions are based. Along the same lines, the CEO should ensure the establishment of a noise-free communications network in the organization. Communications should flow downward from the CEO with respect to organizational goals and aspirations and the values of top management. Similarly, information about risks, results, plans, concepts, capabilities, competition, and the environment should flow upward. The CEO should avoid seeking false uniformity, trying to eliminate risk, trusting tradition, dominating discussion, and delegating strategy development.[12] A CEO who does these things could inadvertently discourage strategy implementation.

Concern for the future may require a change in organizational perspectives, as discussed above. The CEO should not only perceive the need for a change but should also be instrumental in making it happen. Change is not easy, however, because past success provides a strong motive for preserving the status quo. As long as the environment and competitive behavior do not change, past perspectives are fine. However, as the environment shifts, changes in policies and attitudes become essential. The CEO must rise to the occasion and not only initiate change but encourage others to accept it and adapt to it. The timing of a change may be more important than the change itself. The need for change must be realized before the optimum time for it has passed so that competitive advantage and flexibility are not lost.

Zaleznink makes a distinction between the CEO who is a manager and the CEO who is a leader. Managers keep things running smoothly; leaders provide longer-term direction and thrust.[13] Successful strategic planning requires that the CEO be a good leader. In this capacity, the CEO should

1. Gain complete and willing acceptance of his or her leadership.
2. Determine those business goals, objectives, and standards of behavior that are as ambitious as the potential abilities of the organization will permit.
3. Introduce these objectives and motivate the organization to accept them as their own. The rate of introduction should be the maximum that is consistent with continued acceptance of the CEO's leadership. Because of this need for acceptance, the new manager must always go slowly, except in emergencies. In emergencies, the boss must not go slowly if he or she is to maintain leadership.

4. Change the organizational relationships internally as necessary to facilitate both the acceptance and attainment of the new objectives.[14]

A coordinated program of change in pursuit of a sound and relevant strategy under the active direction of the chief executive and the chief planner can lead to significant progress. Although this may only begin a long-term program, it should yield benefits far beyond the time and effort invested. Although pace and effectiveness of strategic change cannot be judged in quantitative terms, there are useful criteria by which they may be assessed. Some of the more important hallmarks of progress are listed here:

- Strategies are principally developed by line managers, with direct, constructive support by the staff.
- Real strategic alternatives are openly discussed at all levels within the corporation.
- Corporate priorities are relatively clear to senior management, but they permit flexible response to new opportunities and threats.
- Corporate resources are allocated based on these priorities and in view of future potential as well as historical performance.
- The strategic roles of business units are clearly differentiated as are the performance measures applied to their managers.
- Realistic responses to likely future events are worked out well in advance.
- The corporate staff adds real value to the consideration of strategic issues and receives cooperation from most divisions.[15]

Role of the Strategic Planner

A strategic planner is a staff person who helps line executives in their planning efforts. Thus, there may be a corporate strategic planner working closely with the CEO. A strategic planner may also be attached to an SBU. This section examines the role of a strategic planner at the SBU level.

The planner conceptualizes the planning process and helps translate it for line executives who actually do the planning. As part of this function, the planner works out a planning schedule and may develop a planning manual. He or she may also design a variety of forms, charts, and tables that may be used to collect, analyze, and communicate planning-oriented information. The planner may also serve as a trainer in orienting line managers to strategic planning.

The planner generates innovative ways of performing difficult tasks and educates line managers in new techniques and tools needed for an efficient job of strategic planning. The planner also coordinates the efforts of other specialists (i.e., marketing researchers, systems persons, econometricians, environmental monitors, and management scientists) with those of line management. In this role, the planner exposes managers to the newest and most sophisticated concepts and techniques in planning.

The planner serves as an adviser to the head of the SBU. In matters of concern, the SBU head may ask the planner to undertake a study. For example, the SBU head may seek the advice of the SBU strategic planner in deciding whether private branding should be accepted so as to increase market share or whether it should be rejected for eroding the quality image of the brand.

Another key role the planner plays is that of evaluator of strategic plans. For example, strategic plans relative to various products/markets are submitted to the SBU head. The latter may ask the planner to develop an evaluation system for products/markets. In addition, the planner may also be asked to express an opinion on strategic issues.

The planner may be involved in integrating different plans. For example, the planner may integrate different product/market plans into an SBU strategic plan. Similarly, an SBU's plans may be integrated by the corporate strategic planner from the perspectives of the entire corporation. For example, if a company uses the growth rate-relative market share matrix (see Exhibit 10-4) to judge plans submitted by different businesses, the planner may be asked not only to establish the position of these businesses on the matrix but also to furnish a recommendation on such matters as which of two question marks (businesses in the high-growth-rate, low-market-share quadrant of the matrix) should be selected for additional funding. The planner's recommendation on such strategic issues helps crystallize executive thinking.

Matters of a nonroutine nature may be assigned to the planner for study and recommendation. For example, the planner may head a committee to recommend structural changes in the organization.

Obviously, the job of strategic planner is not an easy one. The strategic planner must

1. Be well versed in theoretical frameworks relevant to planning and, at the same time, realize their limitations as far as practical applications are concerned.
2. Be capable of making a point with conviction and firmness and, at the same time, be a practical politician who can avoid creating conflict in the organization.
3. Maintain a working alliance with other units in the organization.
4. Command the respect of other executives and managers.
5. Be a salesperson who can help managers accept new and difficult tools and techniques.

In short, a planner needs to be a jack-of-all-trades.

MEASURING STRATEGIC PERFORMANCE

Tracking strategy, or evaluating progress toward established objectives, is an important task in strategy implementation. There are three basic considerations in putting together a performance measurement system: (a) selecting performance measures, (b) setting performance standards, and (c) designing reports. A strategic performance measurement system requires reporting not by profit center or cost center but by SBU. It may require allocation or restatement of financial results based on the new type of reporting center. Most management reporting is geared to SEC and FASB requirements and focuses on the bottom line. For many business units, however, profit is not the pertinent measure of a unit's strategic performance.

In selecting performance measures, only those measures that are relevant to the strategies adopted by each SBU should be chosen. Further, when setting performance standards, the targets, or expected values, should be established so that they are consistent with both the strategic position of business units and the strategies selected. Finally, reports should focus management attention on key performance measures. Exhibit 11-2 summarizes significant issues in measuring strategic performance.

ACHIEVING STRATEGIC PLANNING EFFECTIVENESS

As mentioned above, most companies have made significant progress in the last 10 to 15 years in improving their strategic planning capabilities. Clear, concise methods have been developed for analyzing and evaluating market segments,

---

EXHIBIT 11-2
Strategic Performance Measurements

1. To be effective, strategic performance measures must be tailored to the particular strategy of each individual business unit. While there is a basket of generic strategic measurement tools, selection and application is highly dependent on detailed understanding of the particular business strategy and situation.

2. Strategic performance measurements have two dimensions:

   - **Monitoring key program implementation** to ensure that the necessary elements of strategy are being provided.
   - **Monitoring results** to ensure that the programs are having the desired effects.

3. Strategy performance necessarily involves trade-offs—costs and benefits. Both must be recognized in any useful strategic performance measurement system:

   - **Objectives**—assessing progress toward primary goals.
   - **Constraints**—monitoring other dimensions of performance that may be sacrificed, to some degree and for some period, in order to achieve strategic objectives.

4. Strategic performance measurements do not replace, but rather supplement, short-term financial measurements. They do provide management with a view of long-term progress in contrast to short-term performance. They may indicate that fundamental objectives are being met in spite of short-term problems, and that strategic programs should be sustained despite adversity. They may also show that fundamentals are not being met although short-term performance is satisfactory, and, therefore, strategy needs to be changed.

5. Strategic-performance measurement is linked to competitive analysis. Performance measurements should be stated in competitive terms (share, relative profitability, relative growth). While quantitative goals must be established, evaluating performance against them should include an assessment of what competition has been able to attain.

6. Strategic-performance measurement is linked to environmental monitoring. Reasonable goals cannot always be met by dint of effort if the external world turns against us. Strategic-performance measurement systems must attempt to filter uncontrollable from controllable performance, and provide signals when the measures themselves may be the problem, rather than performance against them.

Source: Rochelle O'Connor, *Tracking the Strategic Plan* (New York: The Conference Board, Inc., no date), p. 11. Reprinted by permission of the publisher.

business performance, and pricing and cost structures. Creative, even elegant, methods have been devised for displaying the results of these strategic analyses to top management.

Few today would argue the value—in theory at least—of the strategic approach to business planning. RJR Nabisco's former CEO, Lou Gerstner (now CEO at IBM), describes that value in the following words: "It is my absolute conviction that you can out-manage your competition by having brilliant strategies."[16] Unfortunately, RJR Nabisco's successful experience appears to be more the exception than the rule. Much more typical are reports of dissatisfaction with the results of strategic planning.

Why the achievement gap between strategic planning and strategic performance? Reasons undoubtedly will vary from corporation to corporation, but certain ones appear to be critical. First, many companies have found that top-down strategic planning produces resistance on the part of operating managers. Second, strategic planning efforts have failed to encourage innovative ideas, techniques, and products and to create an innovative business strategy to implement them. Third, even in companies known for excellence in strategic planning, lack of adequate emphasis on marketing has led to poor implementation of strategic plans.

Strategy Implementation and Management Behavior

Strategic planning as currently practiced has produced resistance on the part of operating managers. One observer has identified three types of resistance: measurement myopia (i.e., managers behave in ways that show good short-term performance), measurement invalidation (i.e., managers supply top management with distorted or selected biased data), and measurement justification (i.e., managers justify their behavior excessively and become excessively cautious about specific factors identified as critical cash flow or ROI determinants).[17]

To solve this resistance problem, it is important to remember that, although sophisticated management tools and the up-to-the-minute techniques of business schools may help identify a desirable strategic course, implementation of a strategy requires time-honored simple and straightforward approaches. As a matter of fact, the latter are still vital prerequisites for success. Experience shows the following specific steps are helpful in effective implementation.[18]

- **Benchmark using world standards.** Find the world champions in every process you measure, from inventory turns to customer service, and try to exceed them.
- **Use process mapping.** Break down your organization's activities to their component parts. Identify the inefficiencies, then redesign each process as if from scratch. For each step, ask whether customers would pay for it if they knew about it.
- **Communicate with employees to encourage them to focus on external reality— customers and competitors.** Define a clear vision that creates a sense of urgency. Help them understand the impact of their own behavior.
- **Distinguish what needs to be done from how hard it is to do it.** The difficulty of doing is irrelevant; real emphasis should be on what is to be done.
- **Set stretch targets.** There is nothing wrong with asking employees to perform as well as the best in the world. But don't tell them how to do it. They will come out with ideas to accomplish what has to be done.

- **Never stop.** When you get ahead of the pack, don't relax. That is just when your competitors are getting energized by benchmarking against you.

Effective Innovative Planning

Effective strategic planning should eliminate organizational restraints, not multiply them; it should contribute to innovation, not inhibit it. In the coming years, strategic planners face a unique challenge because innovation and new product development must be stimulated within the structure of large, multinational corporate enterprises. A number of companies have proved that innovation and entrepreneurial drive can be institutionalized and fostered by a responsive organizational structure. Celanese and IBM, for example, have established technology review boards to ensure that promising product ideas and new technologies receive adequate start-up support. Adopting another approach, Dow Chemical has instituted an "innovation department" to streamline technology commercialization.

To encourage perpetuation of new ideas and innovation, management should:[19]

1. Focus attention on the goals of strategic planning rather than on process; that is, concentrate on substance, not form.
2. Integrate into its business strategy the analysis of emerging technologies and technology management, consumer trends and demographic shifts, regulatory impact, and global economics.
3. Design totally new planning processes and review standards and acceptance criteria for technological advances and new business "thrusts" that may not conform completely to the current corporate base.
4. Adopt a longer planning horizon to ensure that a promising business or technological development will not be cut off prematurely.
5. Ensure that overly stringent financial requirements aren't imposed during the start-up phase of a promising project.
6. Create special organizational "satellites," such as new venture groups, whose mission is to pursue new ideas free from the pressures of day-to-day operations.
7. Institute financial and career reward systems that encourage bold, innovative development programs.

STRATEGIC PLANNING AND MARKETING ORGANIZATION

Strategic planning deals with the relationship of the organization to its environment and thus relates to all areas of a business. Among all these areas, however, marketing is the most susceptible to outside influences. Thus, marketing concerns are pivotal to strategic planning. Initially, however, the role of marketing in the organization declined with the advent of strategic planning. As Kotler noted in 1978:

Strategic planning threatens to demote marketing from a strategic to an operational function. Instead of marketing being in the driver's seat, strategic planning has moved into the driver's seat. Marketing has moved into the passenger seat and in some companies into the back seat.[20]

It has generally been believed that the only marketing decision that has strategic content is the one concerned with product/market perspectives. As far as other marketing decisions are concerned, they are mainly operational in nature; that is, they deal with short-term performance, although they may occasionally have strategic marketing significance. Product/market decisions, however, being the most far-reaching in nature as far as strategy is concerned, are frequently made by top management; the marketing organization is relegated to making operating decisions. In brief, the inroads of strategic planning have tended to lower marketing's status in the organization.

Many marketers have opined that marketing would continue to be important, but mainly for day-to-day operations. For example, Kotler predicted that

1. The marketer's job would be harder than ever in the 1980s because of the tough environment.
2. The strategic planner would provide the directive force to the company's growth, not the marketer.
3. The marketer would be relied on to contribute a great deal of data and appraisal of corporate purposes, objectives and goals, growth decisions, and portfolio decisions.
4. The marketer would assume more of an operational and less of a strategic role in the company.
5. The marketer would still need to champion the customer concept because companies tend to forget it.[21]

Experience has shown, however, that marketing definitely has an important strategic role to play. How neglect of marketing can affect strategy implementation and performance can be illustrated by Atari's problems. This company had been a pioneer in developing video games. Because of negligence in marketing, however, Atari failed to realize how quickly the market for video games would mature. Atari based earnings projections on the assumption that demand would grow at the same rate as in the past and that the company would hold its share of the market. But its assumption proved to be wrong. The market for video games grew at a much lower rate than anticipated.

Continuous close contact with the marketplace is an important prerequisite to excellent performance that no firm can ignore:

> Stay close to the customer. No company, high tech or low, can afford to ignore it. Successful companies always ask what the customer needs. Even if they have strong technology, they do their marketing homework.[22]

More businesses today than during the establishment years of strategic planning are making organizational arrangements to bring in marketing perspectives—an understandable development because, with the emergence of strategic planning (particularly in organizations that have adopted the SBU concept), marketing has become a more pervasive function. Thus, although marketing positions at the corporate level may have vanished, the marketing function still plays a key strategic role at the SBU level.[23]

Businesses, by and large, have recognized that an important link is missing in their strategic planning processes: inadequate attention to marketing. Without properly relating the strategic planning effort to marketing, the whole process tends to become static. Business exists in a dynamic setting. It is only through marketing inputs that perspectives of changing social, economic, political, and technological environments can be brought into the strategic planning process.

Overall, marketing is once again assuming prominence. Businesses are finding that marketing is not just an operations function relevant to day-to-day decision making. It has strategic content as well.

As has been mentioned before, strategic planning emerged largely as an outgrowth of the budgeting and financial planning process, which demoted marketing to a secondary role. However, things are different now. In some companies, of course, concern with broad strategy considerations has long forced routine, high-level attention to issues closely related to markets and marketing. There is abundant evidence, however, of renewed emphasis on such issues on the part of senior management and hence of staff planners in a growing number of other companies as well. Moreover, both marketers and planners are drawing increasingly from the same growing body of analytical techniques for futurist studies, market forecasts, competitive appraisals, and the like. Such overlapping in orientation, resources, and methods no doubt helps to reinstate the crucial importance of marketing in the strategic planning effort.

Accumulating forces have caused most firms to reassess their marketing perspectives at both the corporate and the SBU level. Although initially marketing got lost in the midst of the emphasis on strategic planning, now the role of marketing is better understood and is reemerging in the form of strategic marketing.[24] The decade of the 1990s will indeed be considered as a period of marketing renaissance.

SUMMARY | The chapter examined five dimensions of strategy implementation and control: creation of a market-responsive organization, the role of systems in implementing strategy, executive reward systems, leadership style, and measurement of strategic performance. It is not enough for an organization to develop a sound strategy. It must, at the same time, structure the organization in a manner that ensures the implementation of the strategy. This chapter examined how to accomplish this task, that is, to match organizational structure to strategy.

Inasmuch as strategic planning is a recent activity in most corporations, no basic principles have been developed on the subject. As a matter of fact, little academic research has been reported in this area. However, it is clear that one fundamental aspect that deeply impacts strategy implementation is the proper linking of organization, systems, and compensation. This chapter examined how to ensure maximum market responsiveness, how to fully exploit management systems as a strategic tool, and how to tie the reward system to the strategic mission.

Strategy implementation requires establishing an appropriate climate in the organization. The CEO plays a key role in adapting the organization for strategic planning. Also examined was the role of the strategic planner in the context of strategic planning and its implementation.

Many companies have not been satisfied with their strategic planning experiences. Three reasons were given for the gap between strategic planning and strategic performance: (a) resistance on the part of operating managers, (b) lack of emphasis on innovations, and (c) neglect of marketing. Suggestions were made for eliminating dysfunctional behavior among managers and for improving innovation planning.

As far as the strategic role of marketing is concerned, with the advent of strategic planning, marketing appears to have lost ground. Lately, however, marketing is reemerging as an important force in strategy formulation and implementation.

DISCUSSION QUESTIONS

1. What is the meaning of scale integration in the context of creating a market-responsive organization?
2. Discuss the three broad principles of establishing a market-responsive organization.
3. Define the term *systems*. Discuss the three categories of systems examined in this chapter.
4. Discuss the three problems that affect the establishment of a sound executive reward system.
5. What is the significance of the office of the CEO in strategic planning?
6. How does the role of a strategic planner at the corporate level differ from the role of a planner within the SBU?

NOTES

[1] Steven F. Dichter, "The Organization of the '90s," *McKinsey Quarterly* (Fall 1991): 146–47.
[2] "Paradigms for Postmodern Managers," *Business Week*, Reinventing America Issue (1992): 62.
[3] Michael Treacy and Fred Wiersema, "How Market Leaders Keep Their Edge," *Fortune* (6 February 1995): 88.
[4] See "The Horizontal Corporation," *Business Week*, (20 December 1993): 76.
[5] See Robert A. Irwin and Edward G. Michaels III, "Core Skills: Doing the Right Things Right," *McKinsey Quarterly* (Summer 1989): 4–19.
[6] Ron Zemke and Dick Schaaf, *The Service Edge* (New York: New American Library, 1989), 342.
[7] Raymond G. Ernst, "How to Streamline Operations," *Journal of Business Strategy* (Fall 1987): 32–36.
[8] "The New Breed of Strategic Planner," *Business Week* (17 September 1984): 62.
[9] Paul F. Anderson, "Integrating Strategy and Executive Rewards: Solving the Agency, Value and Signaling Problems" (Speech delivered at the Strategic Financial Planning Seminar at Northwestern University, Evanston, IL, March 1985).

[10] Louis J. Brindisi, Jr., "Paying for Strategic Performance: A New Executive Compensation Imperative," *Strategic Management* (1981): 31–39. See also Joel A. Bleeke, "Peak Strategies," *McKinsey Quarterly* (Spring 1989): 19–27.

[11] Frederick G. Hilmer, "Real Jobs for Real Managers," *McKinsey Quarterly* (Summer 1989): 24.

[12] Thomas A. Stewart, "New Ways to Exercise Power," *Fortune* (6 November 1989): 52.

[13] See Abraham Zaleznink, "Managers and Leaders: Are They Different?" *Harvard Business Review* (May–June 1977): 67–68.

[14] Bruce D. Henderson, *Henderson on Corporate Strategy* (Cambridge, MA: Abt Associates, 1979), 54. See also Thomas J. Peters, "A Style for All Seasons," *Best of Business* (Spring 1981): 23–27.

[15] Robert D. Paulson, "Making It Happen: The Real Strategic Challenge," *McKinsey Quarterly* (Winter 1982): 65.

[16] Irwin and Michaels, "Core Skills," 5.

[17] Thomas V. Bonoma and Victoria L. Crittenden, "Managing Marketing Implementation," *Sloan Management Review* (Winter 1988): 7–14.

[18] Stratford Sherman, "Are You As Good As the Best in the World," *Fortune* (13 December 1993): 95. Also see: "What Is So Effective About Stephen Covey," *Fortune* (12 December 1994): 116.

[19] See Ray Stata, "Organizational Learning: The Key to Management Innovation," *Sloan Management Review* (Spring 1989): 63–74.

[20] Philip Kotler, "The Future Marketing Manager," in *Marketing Expansion in a Shrinking World: 1978 Business Proceedings*, ed. Betsy D. Gelb (Chicago: American Marketing Association, 1978), 3.

[21] Kotler, "The Future Marketing Manager," 5.

[22] Susan Fraker, "High-Speed Management for the High-Tech Age," *Fortune* (5 March 1984): 62.

[23] See Stewart, "New Ways to Exercise Power," 52.

[24] Ravi S. Achrol, "Evolution of the Marketing Organization: New Forms for Turbulent Environments," *Journal of Marketing* (October 1991): 77–93.

CHAPTER TWELVE

Strategic Tools

The Red Queen said: "Now, here, it takes all the running you can do to keep in the same place. If you want to get somewhere else, you must run twice as fast as that."

LEWIS CARROLL
(ALICE IN
WONDERLAND)

Strategy development is by no means an easy job. Not only must decision makers review a variety of inside factors, they must also incorporate the impact of environmental changes in order to design viable strategies. Strategists have become increasingly aware that the old way of "muddling through" is not adequate when confronted by the complexities involved in designing a future for a corporation.

Economic uncertainty, leveling off of productivity, international competition, and environmental problems pose new challenges with which corporations must cope when planning their strategies. There is, therefore, a need for systematic procedures for formulating strategy. This chapter discusses selected tools and models that serve as aids in strategy development.

A **model** may be defined as an instrument that serves as an aid in searching, screening, analyzing, selecting, and implementing a course of action. Because marketing strategy interfaces with and affects the perspectives of an entire corporation, the tools and models of the entire science of management can be considered relevant here. In this chapter, however, we deal with eight models that exhibit direct application to marketing strategies: the experience curve concept, PIMS model, value-based planning and game theory, the delphi technique, trend-impact analysis, cross-impact analysis, and scenario building.

EXPERIENCE CURVE CONCEPT

Experience shows that practice makes perfect. It is common knowledge that beginners are slow and clumsy and that with practice they generally improve to the point where they reach their own permanent level of skill. Anyone with business experience knows that the initial period of a new venture or expansion into a new area is frequently not immediately profitable. Many factors, such as making a product name known to potential customers, are often cited as reasons for this nonprofitability. In brief, even the most unsophisticated businessperson acknowledges that experience and learning lead to improvement. Unfortunately, the significance of experience is realized only in abstract terms. For example, managers in a new and unprofitable situation tend to think of experience in vague terms without ever analyzing it in terms of cost. This statement applies to all functions of a business where cost improvements are commonly sought—except for production management.

As growth continues, we anticipate greater efficiency and more productive output. But how much improvement can one reasonably expect? Generally, management makes an arbitrary decision to ascertain what level of output reflects the optimum level. Obviously, in the great majority of situations, this decision is primarily based on pure conjecture. Ideally, however, one should be able to use historical data to predict cost/volume relationships and learning patterns. Many companies have, in fact, developed their own learning curves—but only in the areas of production or manufacturing where tangible data are readily available and most variables can be quantified.

Several years ago the Boston Consulting Group observed that the concept of experience is not limited to production alone. The experience curve concept embraces almost all cost areas of business.

> Unlike the well-known "learning curve" and "progress function," the experience curve effect is observed to encompass all costs—capital, administrative, research and marketing—and to have transferred impact from technological displacements and product evolution.[1]

In the rest of this section, the application of the experience curve concept to marketing is examined.

Historical Perspective

The experience effect was first observed in the aircraft industry. Because the expense incurred in building the first unit is exceptionally high in this industry, any reduction in the cost of manufacturing succeeding units is readily apparent and becomes extremely pertinent in any management decision regarding future production. For example, it has been observed that an "80 percent air frame curve" could be developed for the manufacture of airplanes. This curve depicts a 20 percent improvement every time production doubles (i.e., to produce the fourth unit requires 80 percent of the time needed to produce the second unit, and so on).[2] Studies of the aircraft industry suggest that this rate of improvement seems to prevail consistently over the range of production under study; hence, the label *experience* is applied to the curve.

Implications

Although the significance of the experience curve concept is corporate-wide, it bears most heavily on the setting of marketing objectives and the pricing decision. As already mentioned, according to the experience curve concept, all costs go down as experience increases. Thus, if a company acquired a higher market share, its costs would decline, enabling it to reduce prices. The lowering of prices would enable the company to acquire a still higher market share. This process is unending as long as the market continues to grow. But as a matter of strategy, while aiming at a dominant position in the industry, the company may be wise to stop short of raising the eyebrows of the Antitrust Division of the U.S. Department of Justice.

During the growth phase, a company keeps making the desired level of profit, but in order to provide for its growth, a company needs to reinvest profits. In fact, further resources might need to be diverted from elsewhere to support such growth. Once the growth comes to an end, the product makes available huge cash throw-offs that can be invested in a new product.

The Boston Consulting Group claims that, in the case of a second product, the accumulated experience of the first product should provide an extra advantage to the firm in reducing costs. However, experience is transferable only imperfectly. There is a transfer effect between identical products in different locations, but the transfer effect between different products occurs only if the products are somewhat the same (i.e., in the same family). This is true, for instance, in the case of the marketing cost component of two products distributed through the same trade channel. Even in this case, however, the loss of buyer "franchise" can result in some lack of experience transferability. Exhibit 12-1 is a diagram of the implications of the experience curve concept.

Some of the Boston Consulting Group's claims about the experience effect are hard to substantiate. In fact, until enough empirical studies have been done on the subject, many claims may even be disputed.[3] But even in its simplest form, the concept adds new importance to the market share strategy.

To summarize, the experience curve concept leads to the conclusion that all producers must achieve and maintain the full cost-reduction potential of their experience gains if they hope to survive. Furthermore, the experience framework has implications for strategy development, as shown in Exhibit 12-2. The appendix at the end of this chapter describes construction of experience curves, showing how the relationship between costs and accumulated experience can be empirically developed.

Application to Marketing

The application of the experience curve concept to marketing requires sorting out various marketing costs and projecting their behavior for different sales volumes. It is hoped that the analyses will show a close relationship between increases in cumulative sales volume and declines in costs. The widening gap between volume and costs establishes the company's flexibility in cutting prices in order to gain higher market share.

Declines in costs are logical and occur for reasons such as the following:

1. Economies of scale (e.g., lower advertising media costs).
2. Increase in efficiency across the board (e.g., ability of salespersons to reduce time per call).
3. Technological advances.

Conceivably, four different techniques could be used to project costs at different levels of volume: regression, simulation, analogy, and intuition. Because historical information on growing products may be lacking, the regression technique may not work. Simulation is a possibility, but it continues to be rarely practiced because it is strenuous. Drawing an analogy between the subject product and the one that has matured perhaps provides the most feasible means of projecting various marketing costs as a function of cumulative sales. But analogy alone may not suffice. As with any other managerial decision, analogy may need to be combined with intuition.

The cost characteristics of experience curves can be observed in all types of costs: labor costs, advertising costs, overhead costs, distribution costs, development

EXHIBIT 12-1
Schematic Presentation of Implications of the Experience Concept

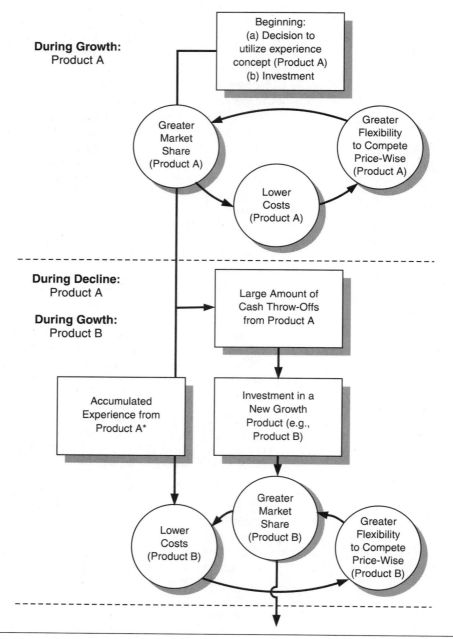

*An assumption is made here that Product B is closely related to Product A.

EXHIBIT 12-2
Experience Curves Strategy Implications

		Market Power	
		High	Low
Industry Growth Rate	High	Continue to invest increased market share up to "target" level	Assess competition; then either invest heavily in increased share, segment market, or withdraw
	Low	Obtain highest possible earnings consistent with maintaining market share	Assess competition; then either challenge, segment market, or withdraw

costs, or manufacturing costs. Thus, marketing costs as well as those for production, research and development, accounting, service, etc., should be combined to see how total cost varies with volume. Further, total costs over different ranges of volume should be projected while considering the company's ability to finance an increased volume of business, to undertake an increased level of risk, and to maintain cordial relations with the Antitrust Division.

Each element of cost included in total cost may have a different slope on a graph. The aggregation of these elements does not necessarily produce a straight line on logarithmic coordinates. Thus, the relationship between cost and volume is necessarily an approximation of a trend line. Also, the cost derivatives of the curve are not based on accounting costs but on accumulated cash input divided by accumulated end-product output. The cost decline of the experience curve is the rate of change in that ratio.

Management should establish a market share objective that projects well into the future. Estimates should be made of the timing of price cuts in order to achieve designated market share. If at any time a competitor happens to challenge a firm's market share position, the firm should go all out to protect its market share and never surrender it without an awareness of its value. Needless to say, the perspective of the entire corporation must change if the gains expected from a particular market share strategy are to become reality. Thus, proper coordination among different functions becomes essential for the timely implementation of related tasks.

Although the experience effect is independent of the life cycle, of growth rate, and of initial market share, as a matter of strategy it is safer to base one's actions on experience when the following conditions are operating: (a) the product is in the early stages of growth in its life cycle, (b) no one competitor holds a dominant position in the market, and (c) the product is not amenable to nonprice competition (e.g., emotional appeals, packaging). Because the concept demands undertaking a big offensive in a battle that might last many years, a well-drawn long-range plan should be in existence. Top management should be capable of undertaking risks and going through the initial period of fast activity involved in sudden moves to enlarge the company's operations; the company should also have enough resources to support the enlargement of operations.

The experience effect has been widely accepted as a basis for strategy in a number of industries, the aircraft, petroleum, consumer electronics, and a variety of durable and maintenance-related industries among them. The application of this concept to marketing has been minimal for the following reasons:

1. Skepticism that improvement can continue.
2. Difficulty with the exact quantification of different relationships in marketing.
3. Inability to recognize experience patterns even though they are already occurring.
4. Lack of awareness that the improvement pattern can be subjectively approximated and that the concept can apply to groups of employees as well as to individual performance across the board in different functions of the business.
5. Inability to predict the effect of future technological advances, which can badly distort any historical data.
6. Accounting practices that may make it difficult to segregate costs adequately.

Despite these obstacles, the concept is too exciting for one to give up striving for its smooth application to marketing.

PROFIT IMPACT OF MARKETING STRATEGY (PIMS)

In 1960, the vice president of marketing services at GE authorized a large-scale project (called PROM, for profitability optimization model) to examine the profit impact of marketing strategies. Several years of effort produced a computer-based model that identified the major factors responsible for a great deal of the variation in return on investment. Because the data used to support the model came from diverse markets and industries, the PROM model is often referred to as a cross-sectional model. Even today, cross-sectional models are popularly used at GE.

In 1972, the PROM program, henceforth called PIMS, was moved to the Marketing Science Institute, a nonprofit organization associated with the Harvard Business School. The scope of the PIMS program has increased so much and its popularity has gained such momentum that a few years ago its administration moved to the Strategic Planning Institute, a new organization established for PIMS.

The PIMS program is based on the experience of more than 500 companies in nearly 3,800 "businesses" for periods that range from two to twelve years. "Business" is synonymous with "SBU" and is defined as an operative unit that sells a distinct set of products to an identifiable group of customers in competition with a well-defined set of competitors. Essentially, PIMS is a cross-sectional study of the strategic experience of profit organizations. The information gathered from participating businesses is supplied to the PIMS program in a standardized format in the form of about 200 pieces of data. The PIMS database covers large and small companies; markets in North America, Europe, and elsewhere; and a wide variety of products and services, ranging from candy to heavy capital goods to financial services. The information deals with such items as

- A description of the market conditions in which the business operates, including such things as the distribution channels used by the SBU, the number and size of its customers, and rates of market growth and inflation.
- The business unit's competitive position in its marketplace, including market share, relative quality, prices and costs relative to the competition, and degree of vertical integration relative to the competition.
- Annual measures of the SBU's financial and operating performance over periods ranging from two to twelve years.

Overall Results

The PIMS project indicated that the profitability of a business is affected by 37 basic factors, explaining the more than 80 percent profitability variation among businesses studied. Of the 37 basic factors, seven proved to be of primary importance (see Exhibit 12-3).

Based on analysis of information available in the PIMS database, Buzzell and Gale have hypothesized the following strategy principles, or links between strategy and performance:

1. In the long run, the most important single factor affecting a business unit's performance is the quality of its products and services relative to those of competitors. A quality edge boosts performance in two ways. In the short run, superior quality yields increased profits via premium prices. In the longer term, superior or improving relative quality is the more effective way for a business to grow, leading to both market expansion and gains in market share.
2. Market share and profitability are strongly related. Business units with very large shares—over 50 percent of their served markets—enjoy rates of return more than three times greater than small-share SBUs (those that serve under 10 percent of their markets). The primary reason for the market share-profitability link, apart from the connection with relative quality, is that large-share businesses benefit from scale economies. They simply have lower per-unit costs than their smaller competitors.
3. High-investment intensity acts as a powerful drag on profitability. Investment-intensive businesses are those that employ a great deal of capital per dollar of sales, per dollar of value added, or per employee.
4. Many so-called "dog" and "question mark" businesses generate cash, while many "cash cows" are dry. The guiding principle of the growth-share matrix approach to planning (see Chapter 10) is that cash flows largely depend on market growth and competitive position (your share relative to that of your largest competitor). However, the PIMS-based research shows that, while market growth and relative share are linked to cash flows, many other factors also influence this dimension of performance. As a result, forecasts of cash flow based solely on the growth-share matrix are often misleading.
5. Vertical integration is a profitable strategy for some kinds of businesses, but not for others. Whether increased vertical integration helps or hurts depends on the situation, quite apart from the question of the cost of achieving it.
6. Most of the strategic factors that boost ROI also contribute to long-term value.[4]

EXHIBIT 12-3
Return on Investment and Key Profit Issues

Return on Investment (ROI):

The ratio of net pretax operating income to average investment. Operating income is what is available after deduction of allocated corporate overhead expenses but before deduction of any financial charges on assets employed. "Investment" equals equity plus long-term debt, or, equivalently, total assets employed minus current liabilities attributed to the business.

Market Share:

The ratio of dollar sales by a business, in a given time period, to total sales by all competitors in the same market. The "market" includes all of the products or services, customer types, and geographic areas that are directly related to the activities of the business. For example, it includes all products and services that are competitive with those sold by the business.

Product (Service) Quality:

The quality of each participating company's offerings, appraised in the following terms: What was the percentage of sales of products or services from each business in each year that were superior to those of competitors? What was the percentage of equivalent products? Inferior products?

Marketing Expenditures:

Total costs for sales force, advertising, sales promotion, marketing research, and marketing administration. The figures do not include costs of physical distribution.

R&D Expenditures:

Total costs of product development and process improvement, including those costs incurred by corporate-level units that can be directly attributed to the individual business.

Investment Intensity:

Ratio of total investment to sales.

Corporate Diversity:

An index that reflects (1) the number of different 4-digit Standard Industrial Classification industries in which a corporation operates, (2) the percentage of total corporate employment in each industry, and (3) the degree of similarity or difference among the industries in which it participates.

Source: Reprinted by permission of the Harvard Business Review. Exhibit from Impact of Strategic Planning on Profit Performance by Sidney Schoeffler, Robert D. Buzzell, and Donald F. Heany (March–April 1974): 140. Copyright © 1974 by the President and Fellows of Harvard College, all rights reserved.

These principles are derived from the premise that business performance depends on three major kinds of factors: the characteristics of the market (i.e., market differentiation, market growth rate, entry conditions, unionization, capital intensity, and purchase amount), the business's competitive position in that market (i.e., relative perceived quality, relative market share, relative capital intensity, and relative cost), and the strategy it follows (i.e., pricing, research and development spending, new product introductions, change in relative quality, variety of products/services, marketing expenses, distribution channels, and relative vertical integration). Performance refers to such measures as profitability (ROS, ROI, etc.), growth, cash flow, value enhancement, and stock prices.

Managerial Applications

The PIMS approach is to gather data on as many actual business experiences as possible and to search for relationships that appear to have the most significant effect on performance. A model of these relationships is then developed so that an estimate of a business's return on investment can be made from the structural competitive/strategy factors associated with the business. Obviously, the PIMS conceptual framework must be modified on occasion. For example, repositioning structural factors may be impossible and the costs of doing so prohibitive. Besides, actual performance may reflect some element of luck or some unusual event.[5] In addition, results may be influenced by the transitional effect of a conscious change in strategic direction.[6] Despite these reservations, the PIMS framework can be beneficial in the following ways:

1. It provides a realistic and consistent method for establishing potential return levels for individual businesses.
2. It stimulates managerial thinking on the reasons for deviations from par performance.
3. It provides insight into strategic moves that will improve the par return on investment.
4. It encourages a more discerning appraisal of business unit performance.

Since the mid-1970s, the PIMS database has been used by managers and planning specialists in many ways. Applications include developing business plans, evaluating forecasts submitted by divisional managers, and appraising possible strategies. The data suggests that[7]

- For followers, current profitability is adversely affected by a high level of product innovation, measured either by the ratio of new product sales to total sales or by research and development spending. The penalty paid for innovation is especially heavy for businesses ranked fourth or lower in their served markets. The market leader's profitability, on the other hand, is not hurt by new product activity or research and development spending.
- High rates of marketing expenditure depress return on investment for followers, not for leaders.
- Low-ranking market followers benefit from high inflation. For businesses ranked first, second, and third, inflation has no relation to return on investment.

MEASURING THE VALUE OF MARKETING STRATEGIES

In the last few years, a new yardstick for measuring the worth of marketing strategies has been suggested. This new approach, called **value-based planning**, judges marketing strategies by their ability to enhance shareholders' value. It emphasizes the impact a strategic move has on the *value* investors place on the equity portion of a firm's assets.[8] The principal feature of value-based planning is that managers should be evaluated on their ability to make strategic investments that produce returns greater than their cost of capital.

Value-based planning draws ideas from contemporary financial theory. For example, a company's primary obligation is to maximize returns from capital appreciation. Similarly, the market value of a stock depends on investors' expectations of the ability of each business unit in the firm to generate cash.[9]

Value is created when the financial benefits of a strategic activity exceed costs. To account for differences in the timing and riskiness of the costs and benefits, value-based planning estimates overall value by discounting all relevant cash flows.

A company that has been using the value-based approach for some time is the Connecticut-based Dexter Corporation. Its value-based planning uses four subsystems:[10]

- The Dexter financial decision support system (DSS), which provides strategic business segments (SBS) with financial data. The DSS provides a monthly profit and loss and balance sheet statement of each strategic business segment. All divisional expenses, assets, and current liabilities are allocated to the SBSs.
- A microcomputer-based system, which transforms this data for use in the two following subsystems: corporate financial reports system and value planner system. The financial data generated by DSS must be transformed to fit the input specifications of these two subsystems.
- The corporate financial reports system, which estimates the cost of capital of an SBS. For estimating cost of capital, Dexter uses two models. The first is the bond-rating simulation model. This model is used to estimate the capital structure appropriate to each of its SBSs, given its six-year financial history. Each SBS is assigned the highest debt-to-total capital ratio that would allow it to receive an A bond rating. The second model used to compute cost of capital is the business risk index estimation model. This model allows cost of equity to be estimated for business segments that are not publicly traded.
- The value planner system, which estimates a business's future cash flows. The basic premise of the value planner system is that business decisions should be based on a rigorous consideration of expected future cash flows. Dexter uses the 12 most recent quarters of SBS data to produce a first-cut projection of future cash flows. As information on a new quarter becomes available, the oldest quarter in the model is deleted. These historical trends are used for projecting financial ratios into the future. The following assumptions are made to compute future cash flows:

  Sales growth—Based on the expectation that each SBS will maintain market share.
  Net plant investment—Based on the growth rate in unit volume deemed necessary to maintain Dexter's market share.
  Unallocated divisional expenses—Projected for each SBS using the same percentage of sales used for the division as a whole.
  The appropriate time horizon for cash flow projections—Based on the expected number of years that a business can reinvest at an expected rate of return.

These assumptions are controversial because they do not allow cash flow projections to be tailored to each SBS. Dexter management terms its historical forecast a *naive* projection and uses it to challenge its managers to explain why the future will be different from the recent past.

The next step in the value-based planning process is to compute the value of projected future cash flows and to discount them by the cost of capital for an SBS. If the estimated value of an SBS is in excess of its book value, the SBS contributes positively to the wealth of Dexter's stockholders, which means it makes sense to reinvest in it.

The major strengths of Dexter's SBS value planner system have been articulated as follows:

- **Its emphasis on being intelligible to line managers**—A value-based planning model can indicate which SBSs are not creating value for the firm's stockholders. However, it is the SBS manager who must initiate action to rectify problems that the analysis uncovers.
- **Its degree of accuracy**—The real dilemma in designing models for value-based planning is to make them easy to use while improving the accuracy with which they reflect or predict the firm's market value.
- **Its integration with existing systems and databases**—By developing a system that works with existing systems, costs are reduced and upgrades are easier to implement. Also, it is easier to gain the acceptance of line managers if the value-based planning system is presented as an extension of the decision support system they are currently using.

In the four years that Dexter has used the value-based approach, it has made important contributions to the decision-making process. Using this approach, Dexter managers made the following decisions:

- Not to invest further in an SBS with high-growth prospects until its valuation, based on actual performance, increases significantly.
- To harvest and downsize an SBS with a negative value.
- To sell an SBS with negative value to its employees for book value.
- To sell an SBS with a value higher than book value but for which an offer was received that was significantly greater than any valuation that could be reasonably modeled in Dexter's hands.

The interesting characteristic of these decisions is that they can run somewhat counter to the prescriptions that flow out of a typical portfolio-planning approach. The first decision, for example, refers to a star business, presumably worthy of further investment. Unlike portfolio planning, in which growth is desirable in and of itself, under value-based planning, growth is healthy only if the business is creating value.

Dexter uses value-based planning as a guideline for decision making, not as an absolute rule. The approach is, in general, understood and accepted, but many managers question its relevance. They now know whether their divisions create value for the company, but they do not understand how they can use that information to make or change important business decisions. Top management understands that value-added planning needs more time before it is completely accepted.

GAME THEORY

Game theory is a useful technique for companies to rapidly respond to changes in products, technologies, and prices. It helps companies pay attention to interactions with competitors, customers, and suppliers, and induces companies to focus on the end-game so that their near-term actions promote their long-term interest by influencing what these players do.

The theory is reasonably straightforward to use. There are two competitors, Ace and Smith. Ace expects Smith to enter the market and is trying to understand Smith's likely pricing strategy. To do so, Ace uses something called a *payoff matrix* (see Exhibit 12-4). Each quadrant in the matrix contains the payoffs—or financial impact—to each player for each possible strategy. If both players maintain prices at current levels, they will both be better off: Ace will earn $100 million and Smith will earn $60 million (Quadrant A). Unfortunately for both Ace and Smith, however, they have perverse incentives to cut prices.

Ace calculates that if he maintains prices, Smith will cut prices to increase earnings to $70 million from $60 million. (See the arrow moving from Quadrant A to Quadrant B.) Smith makes a similar calculation that if she maintains prices, Ace will cut. The logic eventually drives them both to Quadrant D, with both cutting prices and both earning lower returns than they would with current prices in place. This equilibrium is unattractive for both parties. If each party perceives this, then there is some prospect that each will separately determine to try to compete largely on other factors, such as product features, service levels, sales force deployment, or advertising.

But it is necessary to have in-depth knowledge of the industry before game theory is truly valuable. Whether the goal is to implement by fully quantifying the outcomes of a payoff matrix or by more qualitatively assessing the outcome of the matrix, it is necessary to understand entry costs, exit costs, demand functions, revenue structures, cost curves, etc. Without that understanding, the game theory may not provide correct answers.

The following are the rules to observe to make the best use of the theory:

- **Examine the number, concentration, and size distribution of the players.** Industries with four or fewer significant competitors have the greatest potential for using game theory to gain an edge because (a) the competitors will usually be large enough to benefit more from an improvement in general industry conditions than they would from improving their position at the expense of others, and (b) with smaller numbers of competitors it is possible for managers to think through the different combinations of moves and countermoves. Similarly, the number of customers, suppliers, etc. affects the usefulness of game theory.
- **Keep an eye out for strategies inherent in one's market share.** Small players can use "judo economics" to take advantage of larger companies that may be more concerned with maintaining the status quo than with retaliating against a small

EXHIBIT 12-4
Game Theory: An Illustration of the Pricing Game

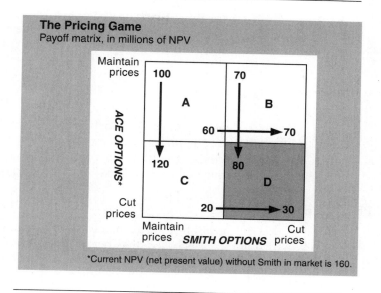

The Pricing Game
Payoff matrix, in millions of NPV

*Current NPV (net present value) without Smith in market is 160.

entrant. In 1992, for instance, Kiwi Airlines got away with undercutting Delta's and Continental's prices between Atlanta and Newark by as much as 75 percent. The reason: When Kiwi first entered the market it represented less then 7 percent of that route's capacity, and the cost of a significant pricing response by the incumbents would have likely exceeded the benefits.[11] Conversely, large players can create economies of scale or scope. Companies such as United and American have used frequent-flier programs to create switching barriers, whereas most small airlines would not have the route structure required to make their frequent-flier programs very attractive.

- **Understand the nature of the buying decision.** If there are only a few deals signed in an industry each year, it will be hard to avoid aggressive competition. In the jet engine industry, for example, three manufacturers (GE, Pratt & Whitney, and Rolls Royce) compete ruthlessly for scarce orders. If a producer loses several large bids in a row, layoffs will be likely, and it might even go out of business. In this kind of situation, the challenge for game theory is to improve the bidding process to shift the power balance between the industry and its customers.

- **Scrutinize the competitors' cost and revenue structures.** Industries where competitors have a high proportion of fixed-to-variable cost will probably behave more aggressively than those where production costs are more variable. In the paper, steel, and refining industries, for example, high profit contributions on extra volume give most producers strong incentives to cut prices to get volume.

- **Examine the similarity of firms.** Industries where competitors have similar cost and revenue structures often exhibit independently determined but similar behavior. Consider the U.S. cellular telephone industry: The two providers in each market share similar technologies, and have similar cost structures. Given their similar economic incentives, the challenge is to find prices that create the largest markets and then to compete largely on factors such as distribution and service quality.

- **Analyze the nature of demand.** The best chances to create value with less aggressive strategies are in markets where demand is stable or growing at a moderate rate. For example, even in oil-field services in the early 1980s after drilling activity had plummeted, declining demand did not lead to lower prices in all sectors. In those more-technology-demanding parts of the industry where there were only a limited number of competitors (e.g. open-hole logging and well-pressure control), prices were more stable than in other sectors.

Done right, game theory can turn conventional strategies on their heads and dramatically improve a company's ability to create economic value. Sometimes it can increase the size of the pie; on other occasions it can make a company's slice of the pie bigger, and it may even help do both.

DELPHI TECHNIQUE

The **delphi technique**, named after Apollo's oracle at Delphi, is a method of making forecasts based on expert opinion. Traditionally, expert opinions were pooled in committee. The delphi technique was developed to overcome the weaknesses of the committee method. Some of the problems that occur when issues are discussed in committee include:

1. The influence of a dominant individual.
2. The introduction of a lot of redundant or irrelevant material into committee workings.
3. Group pressure that places a premium on compromise.
4. Reaching decisions is slow, expensive, and sometimes painful.
5. Holding members accountable for the actions of a group.

All of these factors provide certain psychological drawbacks to people in face-to-face communication. Because people often feel pressure to conform, the most popular solution, instead of the best one, prevails. With the delphi technique, a staff coordinator questions selected individuals on various issues. The following is a sample of questions asked:

1. What is the probability of a future event occurring? (E.g., By what year do you think there will be widespread use of robot services for refuse collection, as household slaves, as sewer inspectors, etc.?)

   a. 2000
   b. 2010
   c. 2020
   d. 2030

2. How desirable is the event in Question 1?

   a. needed desperately
   b. desirable
   c. undesirable but possible

3. What is the feasibility of the event in Question 1?

    a. highly feasible
    b. likely
    c. unlikely but possible

4. What is your familiarity with the material in Question 1?

    a. fair
    b. good
    c. excellent

The coordinator compiles the responses, splitting them into three groups: lower, upper, and inner. The division into groups may vary from one investigation to another. Frequently, however, the lower and upper groups each represent 10 percent, whereas the inner group takes the remaining 80 percent. When a person makes a response in either the upper or lower group, it is customary to ask about the reasons for his or her extreme opinion.

In the next round, the respondents are given the same questionnaire, along with a summary of the results from the first round. The data feedback includes the consensus and the minority opinion. During the second round, the respondents are asked to specify by what year the particular product or service will come to exist with 50 percent probability and with 90 percent probability. Results are once again compiled and fed back. This process of repeating rounds can be continued indefinitely; however, rarely has any research been conducted past the sixth round. In recent years, the delphi technique has been refined by the use of interactive computer programs to obtain inputs from experts, to present summary estimates, and to store revised judgments in data files that are retrievable at user terminals.

The delphi technique is gradually becoming important for predicting future events objectively. Most large corporations use this technique for long-range forecasting. Some of the advantages of the delphi technique are listed below:

1. It is a rapid and efficient way to gain objective information from a group of experts.
2. It involves less effort for a respondent to answer a well-designed questionnaire than to participate in a conference or write a paper.
3. It can be highly motivating for a group of experts to see the responses of knowledgeable persons.
4. The use of systematic procedures applies an air of objectivity to the outcomes.
5. The results of delphi exercises are subject to greater acceptance on the part of the group than are the consequences arrived at by more direct forms of interaction.

Delphi Application

Change is an accepted phenomenon in the modern world. Change coupled with competition forces a corporation to pick up the trends in the environment and to determine their significance for company operations. In light of the changing environment, the corporation must evaluate and define strategic posture to be able to face the future boldly. Two types of changes can be distinguished: cyclical and developmental. A **cyclical change** is repetitive in nature; managers usually develop routine procedures to meet cyclical changes. A **developmental change** is innovative and irregular; having no use for the "good" old ways, managers abandon them. Developmental change appears on the horizon so slowly that it may go unrecognized or ignored until it becomes an accomplished fact with drastic consequences. It is this latter category of change that assumes importance in the context of strategy development. The delphi technique can be fruitfully used to analyze developmental changes. Functionally, a change may fall into one of the following categories: social, economic, political, regulatory, or technological. The delphi technique has been used by organizations to study emerging perspectives in all these areas.

One drawback of the delphi technique is that each trend is given unilateral consideration on its own merits. Thus, one may end up with conflicting forecasts; that is, one trend may suggest that something will happen, whereas another may lead in the opposite direction. To resolve this problem, another forecasting technique, the cross-impact matrix (discussed later) has been used by some researchers. With this technique, the effect of potential interactions among items in a forecasted set of occurrences can be investigated. If the behavior of an individual item is predictable (i.e., if it varies positively or negatively with the occurrence or nonoccurrence of other items), the cross-impact effect is present. It is thus possible to determine whether a predicted event will have an enhancing or inhibiting influence upon each of the other events under study by using a cross-impact matrix.

Recent research shows that the use of the delphi technique has undergone quite a change. The salient features of the revised delphi technique are (a) identifying recognized experts in the field of interest; (b) seeking their cooperation and sending them a summary paper on the topic being examined (based on a literature search); and (c) conducting personal interviews with each expert based on a structured questionnaire, usually by two interviewers. Feedback and repeated rounds of responding to written questionnaires are no longer considered necessary.

TREND-IMPACT ANALYSIS

Trend-impact analysis is a technique for projecting future trends from information gathered on past behavior. The uniqueness of this method lies in its combination of statistical method and human judgment. If predictions are based on quantitative data alone, they will fail to reflect the impact of unprecedented future events. On the other hand, human judgment provides only subjective insights into the future. Therefore, because both human judgment and statistical extrapolation have their shortcomings, both should be taken into consideration when predicting future trends.

In trend-impact analysis (TIA), past history is first extrapolated with the help of a computer. Then the judgment of experts is sought (usually by means of the delphi technique) to specify a set of unique future events that may have a bearing on the phenomenon under study and to indicate how the trend extrapolation may be affected by the occurrence of each of these events. The computer then uses these judgments to modify its trend extrapolation. Finally, the experts review the adjusted extrapolation and modify the inputs in those cases in which an input appears unreasonable.[12]

To illustrate TIA methods, let us consider the case of the average price of a new prescription drug to the year 2005. As shown in Exhibit 12-5, statistical extrapolation of historical data shows that price will rise to $13 by the year 2000 and to $14.23 by the year 2005. The events considered relevant include (a) generic dispensing increases 20 percent of all prescriptions filled, (b) Medicaid and Medicare prescription reimbursement is based on a fixed monthly fee per covered patient ("capitation plan"), and (c) 50 percent decrease in the average rate of growth in prescription size. Consider the first event, i.e., 20 percent increase in generic dispensing. Expert judgment may show that this event has a 75 percent chance of occurring by 1997. If this event does occur, it is expected that its first impact on the average price of a new prescription will begin right away. The maximum impact, a 3 percent reduction in the average price, will occur after five years.

The combination of these events, probabilities, and impacts with the baseline extrapolation leads to a forecast markedly different from the baseline extrapolation (see Exhibit 12-5). The curve even begins to taper off in the year 2005. The level of uncertainty is indicated by quartiles above and below the mean forecast. (The quartiles indicate the middle 50 percent of future values of the curve, with 25 percent lying on each side of the forecast curve.) The uncertainty shown by these quartiles results from the fact that many of the events that have large impacts also have relatively low probabilities.

At this juncture, it is desirable to determine the sensitivity of these results to the individual estimates upon which they are based. For example, one might raise valid questions about the estimates of event probability, the magnitude of the impacts used, and the lag time associated with these impacts. Having prepared these data in a disaggregated fashion, one can very easily vary such estimates and view the change in results. It may also be observed that intervention policies, whether they are institutional (such as lobbying, advertising, or new marketing approaches) or technological (such as increased research and development expenditures), can be viewed as a means of influencing event probabilities or impacts.

TIA can be used not only to improve forecasts of time series variables but also to study the sensitivity of these forecasts to policy. Of course, any policy under consideration should attempt to influence as many events as possible rather than one, as in this example. Corporate actions often have both beneficial and detrimental effects because they may increase both desirable and undesirable possibilities. The use of TIA can make such uncertainties more clearly visible than can traditional methods.

CROSS-IMPACT ANALYSIS

Cross-impact analysis, as mentioned earlier, is a technique used for examining the impacts of potential future events upon each other. It indicates the relative

EXHIBIT 12-5
Average Retail Price of a New Prescription

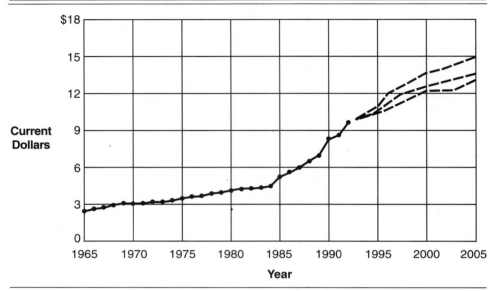

Historical Data					Forecast		
					Lower Quartile	*Mean*	*Upper Quartile*
1962	2.17	1979	3.86	1993	10.65	10.70	10.75
1964	2.41	1980	4.02	1994	10.92	11.03	11.14
1966	2.78	1981	4.19	1995	11.21	11.40	11.61
1967	2.92	1982	4.32	1996	11.54	11.79	12.10
1968	2.99	1983	4.45	1997	11.83	12.15	12.54
1969	3.15	1984	4.70	1998	12.08	12.45	12.92
1970	3.22	1985	5.20	1999	12.30	12.74	13.25
1971	3.27	1986	5.60	2000	12.52	13.00	13.55
1972	3.26	1987	5.98	2001	12.74	13.25	13.83
1973	3.35	1988	6.44	2002	12.95	13.50	14.10
1974	3.42	1989	7.03	2003	13.17	13.75	14.38
1975	3.48	1990	7.66	2004	13.39	13.99	14.64
1976	3.56	1991	8.63	2005	13.60	14.23	14.90
1977	3.63	1992	10.37				
1978	3.70						

importance of specific events, identifies groups of reinforcing or inhibiting events, and reveals relationships between events that appear unrelated. In brief, cross-impact analysis provides a future forecast, making due allowance for the effect of interacting forces on the shape of things to come.

Essentially, this technique consists of selecting a group of five to ten project participants who are asked to specify critical events having any relationship with the subject of the analysis. For example, in an analysis of a marketing project, events may fall into any of the following categories:

1. Corporate objectives and goals.
2. Corporate strategy.
3. Markets or customers (potential volume, market share, possible strategies of key customers, etc.).
4. Competitors (product, price, promotion, and distribution strategies).
5. Overall competitive strategic posture, whether aggressive or defensive.
6. Internally or externally developed strategies that might affect the project.
7. Legal or regulatory activities having favorable or unfavorable effects.
8. Other social, demographic, or economic events.

The initial attempt at specifying critical events presumably will generate a long list of alternatives that should be consolidated into a manageable size (e.g., 25 to 30 events) by means of group discussion, concentrated thinking, elimination of duplications, and refinement of the problem. It is desirable for each event to contain one and only one variable, thus avoiding double counting. Selected events are represented in an $n \times n$ matrix for developing the estimated impact of each event on every other event. This is done by assuming that each specific event has already occurred and that it will have an enhancing, an inhibiting, or no effect on other events. If desired, impacts may be weighted. The project coordinator seeks impact estimates from each project participant individually and consolidates the estimates in the matrix form. Individual results, in summary form, are presented to the group. Project participants vote on the impact of each event. If the spread of votes is too wide, the coordinator asks those persons voting at the extremes to justify their positions. The participants are encouraged to discuss differences in the hope of clarifying problems. Another round of voting takes place. During this second round, opinions usually converge, and the median value of the votes is entered in the appropriate cell in the matrix. This procedure is repeated until the entire matrix is complete.

In the process of completing the matrix, a review of occurrences and interactions identifies events that are strong actors and significant reactors and provides a subjective opinion of their relative strengths. This information then serves as an important input in formulating strategy.

The use of cross-impact analysis may be illustrated with reference to a study concerning the future of U.S. automobile component suppliers. The following events were set forth in the study:

1. Motor vehicle safety standards that come into effect between 1992 and 1996 will result in an additional 150 pounds of weight for the average-sized U.S. car.
2. The 1993 NO_x emissions regulations will be relaxed by the EPA.
3. The retail price of gasoline (regular grade) will be $2 per gallon.
4. U.S. automakers will introduce passenger cars that will achieve at least 40 mpg under average summer driving conditions.

These events are arranged in matrix form in Exhibit 12-6. The arrows show the direction of the analysis. For example, the occurrence of Event A would be likely to bring more pressure to bear upon regulatory officials; consequently, Event B would be more likely to occur. An enhancing arrow is therefore placed in the cell where Row A and Column B intersect. Moving to Column C, it is not expected that the occurrence of Event A will have any effect on Event C, so a horizontal line is placed in this cell. It is judged that the occurrence of Event A would make Event D less likely to occur, and an inhibiting arrow is placed in this cell. If Event B were to occur, the consensus is that Event A would be more likely; hence the enhancing arrow. Event B is not expected to affect Event C but would make Event D more likely. Cells are completed in accordance with these judgments. Similar analyses for Events C and D complete the matrix.

The completed matrix shows the direction of the impact of rows (actors) upon columns (reactors). An analysis of the matrix at this point reveals that Reactor C has only one actor (Event D) because there is only one reaction in Column C. If interest is primarily focused on Event D, Column D should be studied for actor events. Then each actor should be examined to determine what degree of influence, if any, it is likely to have on other actors in order to bring about Event D.

Next, impacts should be quantified to show linkage strengths (i.e., to determine how strongly the occurrence or nonoccurrence of one event would influence the occurrence of every other event). To assist in quantifying interactions, a subjective rating scale, such as the one shown on page 307, may be used.

EXHIBIT 12-6
Basic Format for Cross-Impact Matrix

If This Event Were to Occur — Then the Impact upon This Event Would Be

	If This Event Were to Occur	A	B	C	D
A	MVSS (1992 through 1996) requires 150 pounds additional weight for average-sized U.S. autos		↑	—	↓
B	1993 NO$_x$ emissions requirements are relaxed by EPA	↑		—	↑
C	Retail price of gasoline is $2/gallon	↓	↑		↑
D	U.S. automakers introduce cars capable of 40 mpg in average summer driving	↑	↓	↓	

↑ = enhancing
— = no effect
↓ = inhibiting

Voting Scale	Subjective Scale	
+ 8	Critical: essential for success	**Enhancing**
+ 6	Major: major item for success	
+ 4	Significant: positive and helpful but not essential	
+ 2	Slight: noticeable enhancing effect	
0	**No effect**	
− 2	Slight: noticeable inhibiting effect	**Inhibiting**
− 4	Significant: retarding effect	
− 6	Major: major obstacle to success	
− 8	Critical: almost insurmountable hurdle	

Consider the impact of Event A upon Event B. It is felt that the occurrence of Event A would significantly improve the likelihood of the occurrence of Event B. Both the direction and the degree of enhancing impact are shown in Exhibit 12-7 by the + 4 rating in the appropriate cell. Event A's occurrence would make Event D less likely; therefore, the consensus rating is − 4. This process continues until all interactions have been evaluated and the matrix is complete.

There are a number of variations for quantifying interactions. For example, the subjective scale could be 0 to 10 rather than − 8 to + 8, as shown in the example above.

Another technique for quantifying interactions involves the use of probabilities. If the probability of the occurrence of each event is assessed before the construction of the matrix, then the change in that probability can be assessed for each interaction. As shown in Exhibit 12-8, the probabilities of occurrence can be entered in a column preceding the matrix, and the matrix is constructed in the conventional manner. Consider the impact of Event A on the probable occurrence of Event B. It is judged to be an enhancing effect, and the consensus is that the probability of Event B occurring will change from 0.8 to 0.9. The new probability is therefore entered in the appropriate cell. Event A is judged to have no effect upon Event C; therefore, the original probability, 0.5, is unchanged. Event D is inhibited by the occurrence of Event A, and the resulting probability of occurrence is lowered from 0.5 to 0.4. The occurrence of Event B increases the probability of Event A occurring from 0.7 to 0.8. Event B has no impact upon Event C (0.5, unchanged) and increases the probability of Event D to 0.7. This procedure is followed until all cells are completed.

An examination of the matrix at this stage reveals several important relationships. For example, if we wanted Event D to occur, then the most likely actors are Events B and C. We would then examine Columns B and C to determine what actors might be influenced. Influences that bring about desired results at a critical moment are often secondary, tertiary, or beyond. In many instances, the degree of impact is not the only important information to be gathered from a consideration of interactions. Time relationships are often very important and can be shown in a number of ways. For example, in Exhibit 12-8 information about time has been added in parentheses. It shows that if Event A were to occur, it would have an enhancing effect upon Event B, raising B's

EXHIBIT 12-7
Cross-Impact Matrix Showing Degrees of Impact

If This Event Were to Occur		Then the Impact upon This Event Would Be			
		A	B	C	D
A	MVSS (1992 through 1996) requires 150 pounds additional weight for average-sized U.S. autos		+4	0	−4
B	1993 NO$_x$ emissions requirements are relaxed by EPA	+2		0	+4
C	Retail price of gasoline is $2/gallon	−4	+4		+2
D	U.S. automakers introduce cars capable of 40 mpg in average summer driving	+2	−2	−2	

probability of occurrence from 0.8 to 0.9, and that this enhancement would occur immediately. If Event B were to occur, it would raise the probability of the occurrence of Event D from 0.5 to 0.7. It would also take two years to reach the probable time of occurrence of Event D.

SCENARIO BUILDING

Plans for the future were traditionally developed on a single set of assumptions. Restricting one's assumptions may have been acceptable during times of relative stability, but as we enter the new century experience has shown that it may not be desirable to commit an organization to the most probable future alone. It is equally important to make allowances for unexpected or less probable future trends that may seriously jeopardize strategy. One way to focus on different future outcomes within the planning process is to develop scenarios and to design strategy so that it has enough flexibility to accommodate whatever outcome occurs. In other words, by developing multiple scenarios of the shape of things to come, a company can make a better strategic response to the future environment. Scenario building in this sense is a synopsis that depicts potential actions and events in a likely order of development, beginning with a set of conditions that describe a current situation or set of circumstances. In addition, scenarios depict a possible course of evolution in a given field. Identification of changes and evolution of programs are two stages in scenario building.

Changes in the environment can be grouped into two classes: (a) scientific and technological changes and (b) socioeconomic-political changes. Chapter 6 dealt with environmental scanning and the identification of these changes. Identification

EXHIBIT 12-8

Cross-Impact Matrix Showing Interactive Probabilities of Occurrence

If This Event Were to Occur		Probability of Occurrence	Then the Impact upon This Event Would Be			
			A	B	C	D
A	MVSS (1992 through 1996) requires 150 pounds additional weight for average-sized U.S. autos	0.7		0.9 (immed.)	0.5	0.4 (immed.)
B	1993 NO$_x$ emissions requirements are relaxed by EPA	0.8	0.8 (immed.)		0.5	0.7 (+2 yrs.)
C	Retail price of gasoline is $2/gallon	0.5	0.6 (+1 yr.)	0.9 (+1 yr.)		0.7 (+2 yrs.)
D	U.S. automakers introduce cars capable of 40 mpg in average summer driving	0.5	0.8 (immed.)	0.6 (immed.)	0.4 (+1 yr.)	

should take into consideration the total environment and its possibilities: What changes are taking place? What shape will change take in the future? How are other areas related to environmental change? What effect will change have on other related fields? What opportunities and threats are likely?[13]

A scenario should be developed without any intention of predicting the future. It should be a time-ordered sequence of events that reflects logical cause-and-effect relationships among events. The objective of a scenario building should be to clarify certain phenomena or to study the key points in a series of developments in order to evolve new programs. One can follow an inductive or a deductive approach in building a scenario. The deductive approach, which is predictive in nature, studies broad changes, analyzes the impact of each change on a company's existing lines, and at the same time generates ideas about new areas of potential exploitation. Under the inductive approach, the future of each product line is simulated by exposing its current environment to various foreseen changes. Through a process of elimination, those changes that have relevance for one's business can be studied more deeply for possible action. Both approaches have their merits and limitations. The deductive approach is much more demanding, however, because it calls for proceeding from the unknown to the specific.

Exhibit 12-9 summarizes how scenarios may be constructed. Scenarios are not a set of random thoughts: they are logical conclusions based on past behaviors, future expectations, and the likely interactions of the two. As a matter of fact, a variety of analytical techniques (e.g., the delphi technique, trend impact analysis, and cross-impact analysis) may be used to formulate scenarios.

EXHIBIT 12-9
Scenario-Building Method at GE

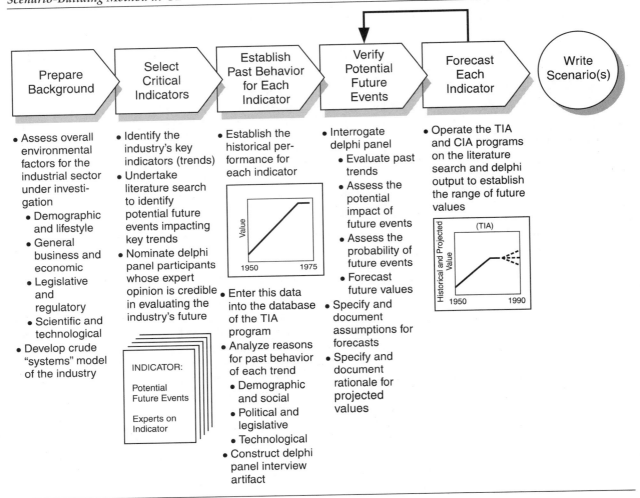

Note: TIA = trend-impact analysis.

The following procedure may be utilized to analyze the scenarios:

- Identify and make explicit your company's mission, basic objective, and policies.
- Determine how far into the future you wish to plan.
- Develop a good understanding of your company's points of leverage and vulnerability.
- Determine factors that you think will definitely occur within your planning time frame.
- Make a list of key variables that will have make-or-break consequences for your company.

- Assign reasonable values to each key variable.
- Build scenarios in which your company may operate.
- Develop a strategy for each scenario that will most likely achieve your company's objectives.
- Check the flexibility of each strategy in each scenario by testing its effectiveness in the other scenarios.
- Select or develop an "optimum response" strategy.

SUMMARY

This chapter presented a variety of tools and techniques that are helpful in different aspects of strategy formulation and implementation. These tools and techniques include experience curves, the PIMS model, a model for measuring the value of marketing strategies, the delphi technique, trend-impact analysis, cross-impact analysis, and scenario building. Most of these techniques require data inputs both from within the organization and from outside. Each tool or technique was examined for its application and usefulness. In some cases, procedural details for using a technique were illustrated with examples from the field.

DISCUSSION QUESTIONS

1. Explain the relevance of experience curves in formulating pricing strategy.
2. Discuss how the delphi technique may be used to generate innovative ideas for new types of distribution channels for automobiles.
3. Explain how PIMS judgments can be useful in developing marketing strategy.
4. Experience curves and the PIMS model both seem to imply that market share is an essential ingredient of a winning strategy. Does that mean that a company with a low market share has no way of running a profitable business?
5. One of the PIMS principles states that quality is the most important single factor affecting an SBU's performance. Comment on the link between quality and business performance.

NOTES

[1] *Perspective on Experience* (Boston: Boston Consulting Group, 1970), 1.

[2] See also John Dutton and Annie Thomas, "Treating Progress Functions as a Managerial Opportunity," *Academy of Management Review* (April 1984).

[3] George S. Day and David B. Montgomery, "Diagnosing the Experience Curve," *Journal of Marketing* (Spring 1983): 44–58. See also William W. Alberts, "The Experience Curve Doctrine Reconsidered," *Journal of Marketing* (July 1989): 36–49; and Robert Jacobson, "Distinguishing among Competing Theories of the Market Share Effect," *Journal of Marketing* (October 1988): 68–80.

[4] Robert D. Buzzell and Robert T. Gale, *The PIMS Principles: Linking Strategy to Performance* (New York: The Free Press, 1987), 2.

[5] Robert Jacobson and David A. Aaker, "Is Market Share All It's Cracked Up to Be?" *Journal of Marketing* (Fall 1985): 11–22. See also John E. Prescott, Ajay K. Kohli, and N. Venkatraman, "The Market Share-Profitability Relationship: An Empirical Assessment of Major Assertions and Contradictions," *Strategic Management Journal* 7 (1986): 377–94.

6 See Cheri T. Marshall and Robert D. Buzzell, "PIMS and the FTC Line-of-Business Data: A Comparison," *Strategic Management Journal* 11 (1990): 269–82.

7 Buzzell and Gale, *PIMS Principles*, 192–93. Also see V. Ramanujan and N. Venkatraman, "An Inventory and Critique of Strategy Research Using the PIMS Data Base," *Academy of Management Review* (January 1984): 138–51.

8 George S. Day and Liam Fahey, "Valuing Market Strategies," *Journal of Marketing* (July 1988): 45–57.

9 Sharon Tully, "The Real Key to Creating Wealth," *Fortune* (20 September 1993): 38. Also see Laura Walbert, "America's Best Wealth Creators," *Fortune* (27 December 1993): 64.

10 See Bala Chakravarthy and Worth Loomis, "Dexter Corporation's Value-Based Strategic Planning System," *Planning Review* (January–February 1988): 34–41.

11 F. William Barnett, "Making Game Theory Work in Practice," *Wall Street Journal* (13 February 1995): B8.

12 See "Trend Impact Analysis," a reference paper of the Futures Group, Glastonbury, CT, 1978.

13 Frank Rutolo, "Scenarios: Moving Beyond Survival Toward Prosperity," *Outlook* (November 1994).

APPENDIX | *Experience Curve Construction*

The experience curve concept can be used as an aid in developing marketing strategy. The procedure for constructing curves discussed below describes how the relationship between costs and accumulated experience can be empirically developed.

The first step in the process of constructing the experience curve is to compute experience and accumulated cost information. Experience for a particular year is the accumulation of all volume up to and including that year. It is computed by adding the year's volume to the experience of previous years. Accumulated cost (constant dollars) is the total of all constant costs incurred for the product up to and including that year. It is computed by adding the year's constant dollar cost to the accumulated costs of previous years. A year's constant dollar cost is the real dollar cost for that year, corrected by inflation. It is computed by dividing cost (actual dollars) by the appropriate deflator.

The second step is to plot the initial and annual experience/accumulated cost (constant dollars) data on log-log graph paper (see Exhibit 12-A). It is important that the experience axis of this graph be calibrated so that its point of intersection with the accumulated cost axis is at one unit of experience. The accumulated cost axis may be calibrated in any convenient manner.

The next step is to fit a straight line to the points on the graph, which may be accomplished by using the least-squares method (Exhibit 12-A).

It is useful at this point to stop and analyze the accumulated cost diagram. In general, the closer the data points are to the accumulated cost curve, the stronger the evidence that the experience effect is present. Deviations of the data points from the curve, however, do not necessarily disprove the presence of the experience effect. If the deviations can be attributed to heavy investment in

EXHIBIT 12-A
Accumulated Cost Diagram

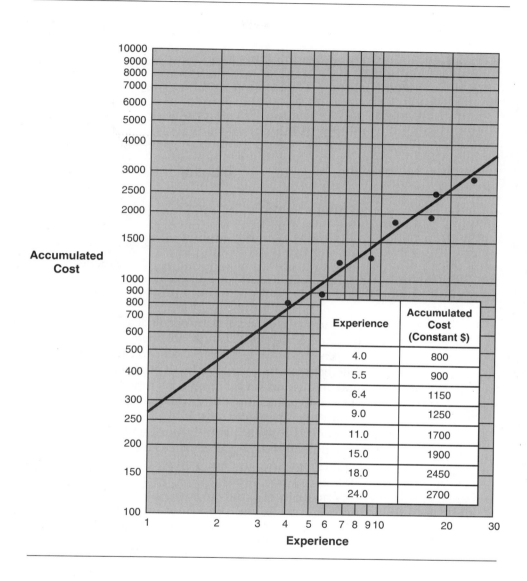

Experience	Accumulated Cost (Constant $)
4.0	800
5.5	900
6.4	1150
9.0	1250
11.0	1700
15.0	1900
18.0	2450
24.0	2700

plant, equipment, etc. (as is common in very capital-intensive industries), the experience effect still holds, but only in the long run because, in the long run, the fluctuations are averaged out. If, on the other hand, significant deviations from the line cannot be explained as necessary periodic changes in the rate of investment, then the presence of the experience effect, or at least its consistency, is open to question. In Exhibit 12-B there is one deviation (see Point *X*) that stands out as

EXHIBIT 12-B
Interpretation of Deviations from Accumulated Cost Curve

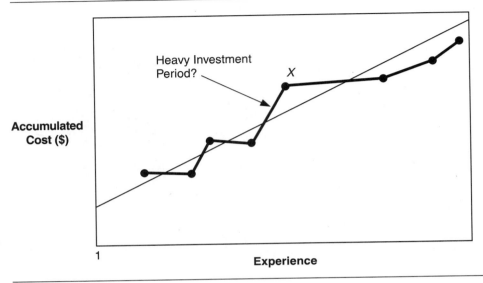

significant. If this can be ascribed to heavy investment (in plant, equipment, etc.), the experience effect is still viable here.

The next step in the process of constructing the experience curve is to calculate the intensity of the product's experience effect. Intensity is the percentage in unit cost reduction achieved each time the product's experience is doubled. As such, it determines the slope of the experience curve. To compute the intensity from the accumulated cost curve, arbitrarily select an experience level on the experience axis (e.g., Point E_1 in Exhibit 12-C). Draw a line vertically up from E_1 until it intersects the accumulated cost curve. From that point on the curve, draw a horizontal line left until it intersects the accumulated cost axis. Read the corresponding accumulated cost (A_1) from the scale. Follow the same procedure for experience level E_2, where E_2 equals $E_1 \times 2$, to obtain A_2. Divide A_2 by A_1, divide the result by 2, and subtract the second result from the number 1. The final answer is the product's intensity. With the information given in Exhibit 12-C, the intensity equals 16.7 percent:

$$1 - \frac{2500}{1500} \times \frac{1}{2} = 0.167 = 16.7\%$$

When the intensity has been computed, the slope of the experience curve is determined. However, as shown in Exhibit 12-D, this information in itself is not sufficient for constructing the curve. Because all of the lines in Exhibit 12-D are parallel, they have the same slope and represent the same intensity. To construct the experience curve, it is necessary to find a point (C_1) on the unit cost axis. This

EXHIBIT 12-C
Product Intensity Computation

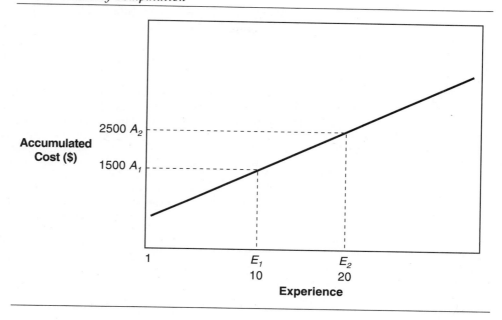

EXHIBIT 12-D
Slopes of Parallel Lines

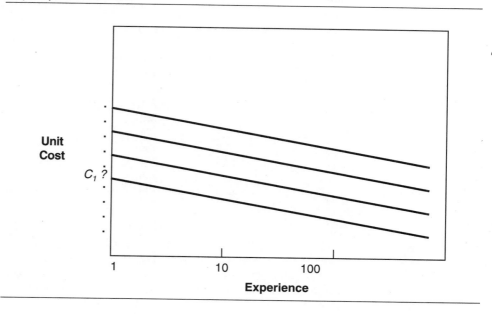

can be achieved in the following manner: Find the *intensity multiplier* corresponding to the product's intensity from the table specially prepared for the purpose (Exhibit 12-E). If the intensity falls between two values in Exhibit 12-E, the appropriate intensity multiplier should be determined by implementation and control interpolation. Read the value on the accumulated cost axis where the curve intersects that axis. Multiply this value by the intensity multiplier. The result is C_1.

The intensity was calculated above as 16.7 percent. By using Exhibit 12-E, the corresponding intensity multiplier can be interpolated as approximately 0.736. As shown in Exhibit 12-A, the accumulated cost at the point of intersection can be

EXHIBIT 12-E
Intensity Multipliers

Intensity	Intensity Multiplier	Intensity	Intensity Multiplier
5.0%	.926	20.5%	.669
5.5	.918	21.0	.660
6.0	.911	21.5	.651
6.5	.903	22.0	.642
7.0	.895	22.5	.632
7.5	.888	23.0	.623
8.0	.880	23.5	.614
8.5	.872	24.0	.604
9.0	.864	24.5	.595
9.5	.856	25.0	.585
10.0	.848	25.5	.575
10.5	.840	26.0	.566
11.0	.832	26.5	.556
11.5	.824	27.0	.546
12.0	.816	27.5	.536
12.5	.807	28.0	.526
13.0	.799	28.5	.516
13.5	.791	29.0	.506
14.0	.782	29.5	.496
14.5	.774	30.0	.485
15.0	.766	30.5	.475
15.5	.757	31.0	.465
16.0	.748	31.5	.454
16.5	.740	32.0	.444
17.0	.731	32.5	.433
17.5	.722	33.0	.422
18.0	.714	33.5	.411
18.5	.705	34.0	.401
19.0	.696	34.5	.390
19.5	.687	35.0	.379
20.0	.678	35.5	.367

read as approximately $260. Multiplying $260 by 0.736 yields a C_1 of $191. The experience curve can now be plotted on log-log graph paper. Position C_1 on the unit cost axis. Multiply C_1 by the quantity (1 – intensity) to obtain C_2:

$$\$191 \times (1 - 0.167) = \$159$$

Locate C_2 on the unit cost axis. Find the point of intersection (y) of a line drawn vertically up from 2 on the experience axis and a line drawn horizontally right from C_2 on the unit cost axis. Draw a straight line through the points C_1 and y. The result is the product's experience curve (Exhibit 12-F).

The application of the experience curve concept to marketing strategy requires the forecasting of costs. This can be achieved by using the curve. Determine the current cumulative experience of the product. Add to this value the planned cumulative volume from the present to the future time point. The result is the planned experience level at that point. Locate the planned experience level on the experience axis of the graph. Move vertically up from that point until the line extension of the experience curve is reached. Move horizontally left from the line to the unit cost axis. Read the estimated unit cost value from the scale. The unit cost obtained is expressed in constant dollars, but it can be converted to an actual dollar cost by multiplying it by the projected inflator for the future year.

Cost forecasts can also be used to determine the minimum rate of volume growth necessary to offset an assumed rate of inflation. For example, with an assumed inflation rate of 3.8 percent, a producer having an intensity of 20 percent must realize a volume growth of approximately 13 percent per year just to maintain unit cost in real dollars. Should growth be slower or should full cost-reduction potential not be realized, the producer's unit cost would rise.

EXHIBIT 12-F
Experience Curve Estimation

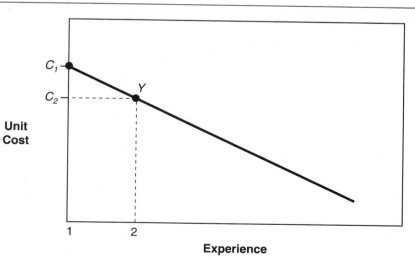

Competitor cost is one of the most fundamental yet elusive information needs of the producer attempting to develop marketing strategy. The experience curve concept provides a sound basis for estimating the cost positions of competitors as well. With certain assumptions, competitors' curves can be estimated.

Marketing Strategies

Market Strategies

In the final analysis, all business strategies must be justified by the availability of a viable market. When there is no viable market, even the best strategy will flop. In addition, the development of marketing strategies for each business should be realistically tied to the target market. Because the market should be the focus of successful marketing, strategies aligned to the market point the way for each present business, serve as underpinnings for overall corporate-wide strategy, and provide direction for programming key activities and projects in all functional areas.

When corporate resources are scarce and corporate strengths are limited, it is fatal to spread them across too many markets. Rather, these critical resources should be concentrated on those key markets (key in terms of type of market, geographic location, time of entry, and commitment) that are decisive for the business's success. Merely allocating resources in the same way that other firms do yields no competitive differential. If, however, it can be discovered which markets really hold potential, the business will be able to lever itself into a position of relative competitive superiority.

This chapter will identify different aspects of market strategies that companies commonly pursue and will analyze their impact on performance vis-à-vis SBU objectives. The use of these strategies will be illustrated with examples from the marketing literature. The appendix at the end of this chapter will summarize each strategy in terms of definition, objectives, requirements, and expected results.

DIMENSIONS OF MARKET STRATEGIES

Market strategies deal with the perspectives of markets to be served. These perspectives can be determined in different ways. For example, a company may serve an entire market or dissect it into key segments on which to concentrate its major effort. Thus, market scope is one aspect of market strategy. The geographic dimensions of a market constitute another aspect: a company may focus on a local, regional, national, or international market. Another strategic variable is the time of entry into a market. A company may be the first, among the first few, or among the last to enter a market. Commitment to a market is still another aspect of market strategy. This commitment can be to achieve market dominance, to become a major factor in the market, or merely to play a minor role in it. Finally, a company may intentionally decide to dilute a part of its market as a matter of strategy. Briefly, then, the following constitute the major market strategies that a company may pursue:

- Market-scope strategy
- Market-geography strategy
- Market-entry strategy
- Market-commitment strategy
- Market-dilution strategy

MARKET-SCOPE STRATEGY

Market-scope strategy deals with the coverage of the market. A business unit may serve an entire market or concentrate on one or more of its parts. Three major alternatives in market-scope strategy are single-market strategy, multimarket strategy, and total-market strategy.

Single-Market Strategy

A variety of reasons may lead a company to concentrate its efforts on a single segment of a market. For example, in order to avoid confrontation with large competitors, a small company may find a unique niche in a market and devote its energies to serving this niche. Design and Manufacturing Corporation (D&M) is a classic example of a successful single-market strategy. In the late 1950s, Samuel Regenstrief studied the dishwasher market and found (a) high growth potential; (b) market domination by GE; and (c) absence of a manufacturer to supply large retailers, such as Sears, with their own private brand. These conclusions led him to enter the dishwasher market and to concentrate his efforts on a single segment: national retailers. The company has emerged as the largest producer of dishwashers in the world with over 25 percent of the U.S. market. A D&M executive describes the company's strategy in the following words: "Sam knew precisely what segment of the market he was going after; he hit it at exactly the right time; and he has set up a tightly run organization to take full advantage of these opportunities."[1]

The story of Tampax also illustrates the success of the single-market strategy. Tampax had a minimal share of a market dominated by Kimberly-Clark's Kotex and Personal Product's Modess. Tampax could not afford to compete head-on with these major brands. To sell its different concept of sanitary protection—internal protection—the company found that newer, younger users were more open-minded and very brand loyal. Starting from a premise that had great appeal for the young user, that internal protection offers greater freedom of action, Tampax concentrated on reaching young women. Its single-market strategy has proved to be highly beneficial.[2] Even today the company's advertising is scarcely distinguishable from the firm's first efforts.

In the competitive field of cosmetics, Noxell Corporation (a division of Procter & Gamble), marketer of the popular Noxzema and Cover Girl brands of makeup and skin cream, found success in a single segment of the $15-billion cosmetics industry that its rivals disdain: the mass market. Noxell's products are aimed primarily at teenagers and evoke the image of fresh-faced natural beauty. Widely distributed and heavily advertised, Noxell's brands are easily recognizable by their low price. Content to sell its products in chains such as Kmart and

Wal-Mart, the company avoids more prestigious, but cutthroat, department and specialty store businesses. The determination to sell exclusively through mass merchandisers is based on Noxell's belief that distribution through department stores is unattractive: it requires leasing counter space, keeping large inventories on hand, and paying commissions to salespeople. Noxell's continued sales growth and healthy profit performance attest to the viability of concentrating on a single segment of the market.[3]

There is no magic formula for choosing a segment. A business should analyze the market carefully to find a segment that is currently being ignored or served inadequately. Then it should concentrate on the chosen segment wholeheartedly, despite initial difficulties, and avoid competition from the established firms.

New market segments often emerge as a result of changes in the environment. For example, the women's movement motivated Smith and Wesson Corp. to launch Lady Smith in 1989, a line of guns specifically designed for women. The result: sales to women jumped from 5 percent of the company's total to nearly 20 percent.[4] Despite the cutthroat competition from mass merchandisers such as Toys "R" Us, FAO Scharz continues to successfully operate by targeting upscale children.

The single-market strategy consists of seeking out a market segment that larger competitors consider too small, too risky, or just plain unappealing. The strategy will not work in areas where the market power of big companies is important in realizing economies of scale, as in the extractive and process industries, for example. Companies concentrating on a single market have the advantage of being able to make quick responses to market opportunities and threats through appropriate changes in policies. The single-market, or niche, strategy is often born of necessity. Lacking the resources to fight head-to-head battles across the board with larger entrenched competitors, winners typically seek out niches that are too small to interest the giants or that can be captured and protected by sheer perseverance and by serving customers surpassingly well.

As far as the impact of the single-market strategy is concerned, it affects profitability in a positive direction. When effort is concentrated on a single market, particularly when competition is minimal, it is feasible to keep costs down while prices are kept high, thus earning substantially higher profits. Although its growth objective may not be achieved when this strategy is followed, a company may be able to increase its market share if the chosen segment is large enough vis-à-vis the overall market.

Multimarket Strategy

Instead of limiting business to one segment and thus putting all its eggs in one basket, a company may opt to serve several distinct segments. To implement a multimarket strategy successfully, it is necessary to choose those segments with which the company feels most comfortable and in which the company is able to avoid confronting companies that serve the entire market. This point may be illustrated with reference to Crown Cork and Seal Company. The company is a major producer of metal cans, crowns (bottle caps), closures (screw caps and bottle lids), and filling machinery for beer and soft drink cans. The industry is characterized by a really dynamic environment: technological breakthroughs, new concepts of packaging, new materials, and threats of self-manufacture by large users are common. Crown Cork and Seal, as a matter of strategy, decided to concentrate on two segments: (a) cans for such "hard-to-hold" products as beer and soft drinks and (b) aerosol containers. Its new strategy paid off. The company outperformed its competitors both in sales growth and in return on sales in the 1980s and 1990s. As it should with any strategic choice, the company fully committed itself to its strategy despite the lure of serving other segments. For example, in spite of its 50 percent share in the motor oil can business, Crown Cork decided not to continue to compete aggressively in that market.[5]

The multimarket strategy can be executed in one of two ways: either by selling different products in different segments or by distributing the same product in a number of segments. Toyota Motor Corporation, for example, introduced its Lexus line of cars in 1989. The car was directed toward luxury car buyers who traditionally had looked to BMW and Mercedes-Benz. Toyota entered a different segment with a different product. In contrast, the Green Giant Company expanded into another segment by distributing an existing product more widely; that is, by supplying its frozen vegetables, corn on the cob, for example, to all Church's Fried Chicken and Kentucky Fried Chicken fast-food outlets.[6]

Total-Market Strategy

A company using the total-market strategy serves an entire spectrum of a market by selling different products directed toward different segments of the market. The strategy evolves over a great number of years of operation. A company may start with a single product. As the market grows and as different segments emerge, leading competitors may attempt to compete in all segments by employing different combinations of product, price, promotion, and distribution strategies. These dominant companies may also attempt to enter new segments as they emerge. As a matter of fact, the leading companies may themselves create new segments and try to control them from the outset.

A number of companies in different industries have followed this strategy. General Motors, for one, has traditionally directed its effort to securing an entire market: "A car for every pocket and taste." With its five auto lines (Chevrolet, Pontiac, Oldsmobile, Buick, and Cadillac), along with a variety of small trucks, the company attempts to compete in all conceivable segments.

IBM now also follows an across-the-board strategy. It has a system for meeting the requirements of all types of customers. In the mid-1980s, as the personal computer segment emerged, IBM was somewhat slow to respond but finally developed a personal computer of its own. Similarly, in the consumer products area, the Coca-Cola Company has Coca-Cola, Diet Coke, Tab, Sprite, Fresca, and Fanta to satisfy different drinking tastes. The company even has a brand of orange juice, Minute Maid, for the segment of consumers who drink juice rather than carbonated beverages.

The total-market strategy is highly risky. For this reason, only a very small number of companies in an industry may follow it. Embracing an entire market requires top management commitment. In addition, a company needs ample resources to implement it. Finally, only companies in a strong financial position may find this strategy attractive. As a matter of fact, a deteriorating financial position may force a company to move backward from an across-the-board market strategy. Chrysler Corporation's financial woes in the 1990s led it to reduce the scope of its markets overseas at a time when experts were anticipating the emergence of a single global market. The total-market strategy can be highly rewarding in terms of achieving growth and market share, but it may or may not lead to increased profitability.

Seeking Changes in Market Scope

There are only limited periods during which the fit between the key requirements of a market and the particular competencies of a firm competing in that market is at an optimum. Companies should not, therefore, tie themselves to a particular market strategy permanently. Environmental shifts may necessitate a change in perspective from one period to another. Consider the American Express credit card. At one time, it had potent snob appeal meant for upscale customers. But as competition in the credit card business intensified, many American Express card holders exchanged their cards for others that required no annual fee and provided revolving credit at modest interest rates. This forced American Express to redefine its market. In 1994, it began offering a number of new cards, each one targeted at a different segment of the consumer market. Some cards bore the exclusive imprimatur of AmEx with annual fee waived, others shared billing with other companies that offered a range of enticements, such as frequent-flyer miles and car discounts. All offered revolving credit at competitive rates. Where business travelers were once AmEx's preferred clientele, every creditworthy American was now being wooed.[7] Similarly, Gerber Products long dominated the U.S. baby food market, but declining birth rates forced it to seek growth elsewhere. The company has been planning to introduce foods for older people.[8]

The J.C. Penney Company, after 75 years of being identified as a retailer of private-label soft goods to price-conscious customers, decided in the 1980s to change the scope of its market. The company transformed itself so that it occupied a position between a traditional department store and a discount store (something along the lines of a moderately priced department store with emphasis on higher-priced fashion) in hard goods, housewares, and especially apparel. The company continued to upgrade throughout the 1980s and 1990s and has successfully been able to attract more upscale customers.

Disney's emphasis on the 5- to 13-year-old age market has been a phenomenon in itself. During the 1960s, this segment continued to grow, providing the company with opportunities for expansion. In the 1970s, however, this segment shrank; it declined further in the 1980s, leading the company to change its strategic perspectives. It began serving the over-25 age group by making changes in its current offerings and by undertaking new projects: Epcot Center, Disney MGM Studios theme park, and a water park are all attached to Disney World in Florida.[9]

Briefly, then, markets are moving targets, and a company's strategic perspectives must change accordingly.

MARKET-GEOGRAPHY STRATEGY

Geography has long been used as a strategic variable in shaping market strategy. History provides many examples of how businesses started locally and gradually expanded nationally, even internationally. Automobiles, telephones, televisions, and jet aircraft have brought all parts of the country together so that distance ceases to be important, thus making geographic expansion an attractive choice when seeking growth.

Consider the case of Ponderosa System, a fast-food chain of steak houses (a division of Metromedia Steak Houses, Inc.). The company started in 1969 with four restaurants in Indiana. By 1970 it had added 10 more restaurants in Indiana and southern Ohio. At the end of 1994, there were almost 800 Ponderosa Steak Houses all over the country.

There are a variety of reasons for seeking geographic expansion: to achieve growth, reduce dependence on a small geographic base, use national advertising media, realize experience (i.e., economies of scale), utilize excess capacity, and guard against competitive inroads by moving into more distant regional markets. This section examines various alternatives of market-geography strategy. The purpose here is to highlight strategic issues that may dictate the choice of a geographic dimension in the context of market strategy.

Local-Market Strategy

In modern days, the relevance of local-market strategy may be limited to (a) retailers and (b) service organizations, such as airlines, banks, and medical centers. In many cases, the geographic dimensions of doing business are decided by law. For example, until recently, an airline needed permission from the Civil Aeronautics Board (which was dissolved in 1983 after the airline industry deregulation) to change the areas it could cover. By the same token, banks traditionally could only operate locally.

Of the 2 million retailers in the United States, about half have annual sales of less than $100,000. Presumably, these are all local operations. Even manufacturers may initially limit the distribution of new products to a local market. Local-market strategy enables a firm to prosper by serving customers in a narrow geographic area well. The strategy emphasizes personal service, which bigger rivals may shun.

Regional-Market Strategy

The regional scope of a business may vary from operations in two or three states to those spread over larger sections of the country: New England, the Southwest, the Midwest, or the West, for example. Regional expansion provides a good compromise between doing business locally and going national.

Regional expansion ensures that, if business in one city is depressed, favorable conditions prevailing in other regions allow the overall business to remain satisfactory. In the 1980s, Marshall Field, the Chicago-based department store (now a division of Dayton-Hudson Company), found itself pummeled by recent demographic and competitive trends in that city. Therefore, it decided to expand into new regions in the South and West. This way it could lessen its concentration in the Midwest and expand into areas where growth was expected.

Further, it is culturally easier to handle a region than an entire country. The logistics of conducting business regionally are also much simpler. As a matter of fact, many companies prefer to limit themselves to a region in order to avoid competition and to keep control centralized. Regional-market strategy allows companies to address America's diversity by dividing the country into well-defined geographic areas, choosing one or more areas to serve, and formulating a unique marketing mix to serve each region.

Many businesses continue to operate successfully on a regional scale. The following large grocery chains, for example, are regional in character: Safeway in the West, Kroger in the Midwest, and Stop & Shop in the East. Regional expansion of a business helps achieve growth and, to an extent, gains market share. Simply expanding a business regionally, however, may or may not affect profitability.

Geographic expansion of a business to a region may become necessary either to achieve growth or to keep up with a competitor. For example, a small pizza chain with about 30 restaurants in an Ohio metropolitan area had to expand its territory when Pizza Hut started to compete aggressively with it.

At times, a regional strategy is much more desirable than going national. A company operating nationally may do a major portion of its business in one region, with the remainder spread over the rest of the country, or it may find it much more profitable to concentrate its effort in a region where it is most successful and divest itself of its business elsewhere.

National-Market Strategy

Going from a regional to a national market presumably opens up opportunities for growth. This may be illustrated with reference to Borden, Inc. A dairy business by tradition, in the 1980s Borden decided to become a major player in the snack food arena. It acquired seven regional companies, among them Snacktime, Jays, and Laura Scudder's, to compete nationally, to grow, and to provide stiffer competition for PepsiCo's Frito-Lay division.

It was the prospect of growth that influenced the Radisson Hotel Corporation of Minneapolis to go national and to become a major competitor in the hotel business. Radisson decided to move into prime "gateway" markets—New York, Los Angeles, Boston, Chicago, and San Francisco—where it could compete against such giants as Marriott and Hyatt.

In some cases, the profit economics of an industry requires going national. For example, success in the beer industry today demands huge advertising outlays, new product introductions (e.g., light beer), production efficiencies, and wide distribution. These characteristics forced Adolph Coors to go national.

Going national, however, is far from easy. Each year a number of products enter the market, hoping eventually to become national brands. Ultimately, however, only a small percentage of them hit the national market; a still smaller percentage succeed.

A national-market strategy requires top management commitment because a large initial investment is needed for promotion and distribution. This requirement makes it easier for large companies to introduce new brands nationally, partly because they have the resources and are in the position to take the risk and partly because a new brand can be sheltered under the umbrella of a successful brand. For example, a new product introduced under GE's name has a better chance of succeeding than one introduced by an unknown company.

To implement a national-market strategy successfully, a company needs to institute proper controls to make sure that things are satisfactory in different regions. Where controls are lacking, competitors, especially regional ones, may find it easy to break in. If that situation comes about, the company may find itself losing business in region after region. Still, a properly implemented national-market strategy can go a long way in providing growth, market share, and profitability.

International-Market Strategy

A number of corporations have adopted international-market postures. The Singer Company, for example, has been operating overseas for a long time. The international-market strategy became a popular method for achieving growth objectives among large corporations in the post-World War II period.

In its attempts to reconstruct war-torn economies, the U.S. government provided financial assistance to European countries through the Marshall Plan. Because the postwar American economy emerged as the strongest in the world, its economic assistance programs, in the absence of competition, stimulated extensive corporate development of international strategies.

At the end of 1993, according to a U.S. Department of Commerce report, U.S. direct investment abroad was estimated at $798 billion, up from $314 billion in 1987. About 75 percent of U.S. investment overseas has traditionally been in developed countries. However, as many developing countries gained political freedom after World War II, their governments also sought U.S. help to modernize their economies and to improve their living standards. Thus, developing countries have provided additional investment opportunities for U.S. corporations, especially in more politically stable countries. It is interesting, however, that although for cultural, political, and economic reasons more viable opportunities were found in Western Europe, Canada, and, to a lesser extent, Japan, developing countries provided a better return on direct U.S. investment. For example, in 1992 developing countries accounted for about 32 percent of income but less than 25 percent of investment.[10]

In recent years, overseas business has become a matter of necessity from the viewpoint of both U.S. corporations and the U.S. government. The increased competition facing many industries, resulting from the saturation of markets and competitive threats from overseas corporations doing business domestically, has forced U.S. corporations to look to overseas markets. At the same time, the unfavorable balance of trade, partly due to increasing energy imports, has made the need to expand exports a matter of vital national interest. Thus, although in the 1950s and 1960s international business was considered a means of capitalizing on a new opportunity, in today's changing economic environment it has become a matter of survival.

Generally speaking, international markets provide additional opportunities over and above domestic markets. In some cases, however, a company may find the international market an alternative to the domestic market. Massey-Ferguson decided long ago to concentrate on sales outside of North America rather than compete with powerful U.S. farm equipment producers. Massey's entire organization, including engineering, research, and production, is geared to market changes overseas. It has learned to live with the instability of foreign markets and to put millions of dollars into building its worldwide manufacturing and marketing networks. The payoff for the company from its emphasis on the international market has been encouraging. In the 1990s, the company outperformed both Deere and International Harvester.[11]

With the world's biggest private inventory of commercial softwood, Weyerhaeuser has been able to build an enviable export business—a market its competitors have virtually ignored until recently. This focus has given Weyerhaeuser a unique advantage in a rapidly changing world market. Consumption of forest products overseas in the 1990s has been increasing at double the domestic rate of 2 to 3 percent annually. Future prospects overseas continue to be attractive. Particularly dramatic growth is expected in the Pacific Basin, which Weyer-haeuser is ideally located to serve. Moreover, dwindling timber supplies and high oil costs are putting European and Japanese producers at an increasing disadvantage even in their own markets, creating a vacuum that North American producers are now rushing to fill. With a product mix already heavily weighted toward export commodities and with unmatched access to deep-water ports, Weyerhaeuser is far ahead of its competitors in what is shaping up to be an export boom in U.S. forest products. Exports, which in 1988 accounted for 25 percent of Weyerhaeuser's sales and an even higher percentage of its profits, could account for fully half of the company's total revenues by the year 2000.[12]

Other Dimensions of Market-Geography Strategy

A company may be regional or national in character, yet it may not cover its entire trading area. These gaps in the market provide another opportunity for growth. For example, the Southland Corporation has traditionally avoided putting its 7-Eleven stores (now a division of the Yokado Group of Japan) in downtown areas. About 6,500 of these stores in suburban areas provide it with more than $2 billion in sales. A few years ago, the company opened a store at 34th and Lexington in New York City, signaling the beginning of a major drive into the last of the U.S. markets that 7-Eleven had not yet tapped. Similarly, Hyatt Corp. has hotels in all major cities but not in all resort and suburban areas. To continue to grow, this is the gap the company plans to fill in the 1990s.[13]

Gaps in the market are left unfilled either because certain markets do not initially promise sufficient potential or because local competition appears too strong to confront. However, a corporation may later find that these markets are easy to tap if it consolidates its position in other markets or if changes in the environment create favorable conditions.

MARKET-ENTRY STRATEGY

Market-entry strategy refers to the timing of market entry. Basically, there are three market-entry options from which a company can choose: (a) be first in the market, (b) be <u>among the early entrants</u>, or (c) be <u>a laggard</u>. The importance of the time of entry can be illustrated with reference to computers. Experience has shown that if new product lines are acceptable to users and if their impact is properly controlled through pricing and contractual arrangements, sales of an older line can be stimulated. Customers are more content to upgrade within the current product line if they know that a more advanced machine is available whenever they need it. A successful introduction, therefore, requires that the right product is announced at the right time. If it is announced too early, the manufacturer will suffer a drop in revenues and will lose customers to the competition.

First-In Strategy

Handwritten margin notes:
1) It can create a lead for itself
2) Costs go down as experience ↑, so, provide lower prices that competitors cannot match
3) If patented, enjoy virtual monopoly for the life of patent

To be the first in the market with a product provides definite advantages. The company can create a lead for itself that others will find difficult to match. Following the experience curve concept, if the <u>first entrant</u> gains a respectable share of the market, across-the-board costs should go down by a fixed percentage every time experience doubles. This cost advantage can be passed on to customers in the form of lower prices. Thus, competitors will find it difficult to challenge the first entrant in a market because, in the absence of experience, their costs and hence their prices for a similar product will be higher. If the new introduction is protected by a patent, the first entrant has an additional advantage because it will have a virtual monopoly for the life of the patent.

The success story of Kinder-Care Learning Centers illustrates the significance of being first in the market. In 1968 a real estate developer, Perry Mendel, had an idea that many people thought was outrageous, impractical, and probably immoral. He wanted to create a chain of child care centers, and he wanted to use the same techniques of standardization that he had seen work for motels and fast-food chains. Convinced that the number of women working outside the home would continue to increase, Mendel started Kinder-Care Learning Centers. In its brief history, the company has become a dominant force in the commercial child care industry.

The strategy to be the first, however, is not without <u>risks</u>. The first entrant must stay ahead of technology or risk being dethroned by competitors. Docutel Corporation provides an interesting case. This Dallas-based company was the first to introduce automated teller machines (ATMs) in the late 1960s. These machines made it possible for customers to withdraw cash from and make deposits to their savings and checking accounts at any time by pushing a few buttons. Docutel had virtually no competition until 1975, and as recently as 1976, the company had a 60 percent share of the market for ATMs. Then the downfall began. Market share fell to 20 percent in 1977 and to 8 percent in 1978. Docutel's fortunes changed because the company failed to maintain its technological lead. Its second-generation ATM failed miserably and thus made room for competitors. Diebold was the major beneficiary of Docutel's troubles: its share of the market jumped to 70 percent in 1978 from barely 15 percent in 1976. Although Docutel's comeback efforts have been encouraging, the company may never again occupy a dominant position in the ATM industry.

A company whose strategy is to be the first in the market must stay ahead no matter what happens because the cost of yielding the first position to someone else later can be very high. Through heavy investment in promotion, the first entrant must create a primary demand for a product where none exists. Competitors will find it convenient to piggyback because by the time they enter the market, primary demand is already established. Thus, even if a company has been able to develop a new product for an entirely new need, it should carefully evaluate whether it has sufficient technological and marketing strength to command the market for a long time. Competitors will make every effort to break in, and if the first company is unsure of itself, it should wait. Apple Computer, for example, was the first company in the personal computer field. Despite its best efforts, it could not compete against IBM. The upstart company that always talked confrontation with IBM finally decided to play second fiddle. If properly implemented, however, the strategy to be first can be highly rewarding in terms of growth, market share, and profitability.

Early-Entry Strategy

Several firms may be working on the same track to develop a new product. When one introduces the product first, the remaining firms are forced into an early-entry strategy, whether they had planned to be first or had purposely waited for someone else to take the lead. If the early entry takes place on the heels of the first entry, there is usually a dogfight between the firms involved. By and large, the fight is between two firms, the leader and a strong follower (even though there may be several other followers). The reason for the fight is that both firms have worked hard on the new product, both aspire to be the first in the market, both have made a strong commitment to the product in terms of resources. In the final phases of their new-product development, if one of the firms introduces the product first, the other one must rush to the market right away to prevent the first company from creating a stronghold. Ultimately, the competitor with a superior marketing strategy in terms of positioning, product, price, promotion, and distribution comes out ahead.

After the first two firms find their natural positions in the market and the market launches itself on a growth course, other entrants may follow. These firms exist on the growth wave of the market and exit as the market matures.

When Sara Lee Corp. introduced its new Wonderbra in the U.S. in 1994, the rival VF Corp. watched closely. Only after American shoppers began buying it in large numbers did VF offer up its own It Must Be Magic version. But once VF decided to enter the market, it moved swiftly using state-of-the-art distribution, surging ahead with nationwide distribution ahead of Sara Lee. VF's "second-to-the-market" approach, and bringing high technology to the nitty-gritty details of distribution, have helped it avoid the financial risk that beset clothing makers.[14]

Early entry on the heels of a leader is desirable if a company has an across-the-board superior marketing strategy and the resources to fight the leader. As a matter of fact, the later entrant may get an additional boost from the groundwork laid by the leader (in the form of the creation of primary demand). A weak early entrant, however, will be conveniently swallowed by the leader. The Docutel case discussed above illustrates the point. Docutel was the leader in the ATM market. However, being a weak leader, it paved the way for a later entrant, Diebold, to take over the market it had developed.

As the market reaches the growth phase, a number of other firms may enter it. Depending on the length of the growth phase and the point at which firms enter the market, some could be labeled as early entrants. Most of these early entrants prefer to operate in specific market niches rather than compete against major firms. For example, a firm may concentrate on doing private branding for a major retailer. Many of these firms, particularly marginal operations, may be forced out of the market as growth slows down. In summary, an early-entry strategy is justifiable in the following circumstances:

1. When the firm can develop strong customer loyalty based on perceived product quality and retain this loyalty as the market evolves.
2. When the firm can develop a broad product line to help discourage entries and combat competitors who choose a single-market niche.
3. When either current investment is not substantial or when technological change is not anticipated to be so rapid and abrupt as to create obsolescence problems.
4. When an early entrant can initiate the experience curve and when the amount of learning is closely associated with accumulated experience that cannot readily be acquired by later entrants.
5. When absolute cost advantages can be achieved by early commitment to raw materials, component manufacture, distribution channels, and so forth.
6. When the initial price structure is likely to be high because the product offers superior value to products being displaced.
7. When prospective competitors can be discouraged as the market is not strategically crucial to them and existing competitors are willing to see their market shares erode.

Early entry, therefore, can be a rewarding experience if the entry is made with a really strong thrust directed against the leader's market or if it is carefully planned to serve an untapped market. Early entry can contribute significantly to profitability and growth. For the firm that takes on the leader, the early entry may also help in gaining market share.

Laggard-Entry Strategy

The laggard-entry strategy refers to entering the market toward the tail end of the growth phase or in the maturity phase of the market. There are two principal alternatives to choose from in making an entry in the market as a laggard: to enter as imitator or as initiator. An imitator enters the market as a me-too competitor; that is, imitators develop a product that, for all intents and purposes, is similar to one already on the market. An initiator, on the other hand, questions the status quo and, after doing some innovative thinking, enters the market with a new product. Between these two extremes are companies that enter stagnant markets with modified products.

Entry into a market as an imitator is short-lived. A company may be able to tap a portion of a market initially by capitalizing on the customer base of the major competitor(s). In the long run, however, as the leader discards the product in favor of a new or improved one, the imitator is left with nowhere to go. In the early 1970s, Honeywell was faced with a decision: Which type of advanced computer system should it develop, an imitation of the IBM 360 or its own new version? The company favored the second alternative:

> [Although] the copy might make it easier to tap IBM's huge customer base, it was rejected on several counts. First, it relegated Honeywell to the status of a "me too" company. Secondly, even if a high performance/low cost system were developed, there was no assurance that customers would want an imitation. "After all, if you are looking for a Ford, you go to a Ford dealer." It was agreed that the Task Force would develop its own state-of-the-art system.[15]

This strategy worked well for Honeywell. The company developed a new series of computers especially suited to manufacturing operations and made strong inroads into European markets.

Imitators have many inherent advantages that make it possible to run a profitable business. These advantages include availability of the latest technological improvements; feasibility of achieving greater economies of scale; ability to obtain better terms from suppliers, employees, or customers; and ability to offer lower prices. Thus, even without superior skills and resources, an imitator may perform well.

The initiator starts by seeking ways to dislodge the established competitor(s) in some way. Consider the following examples:

> The blankets produced by an electrical appliance manufacturer carried the warning: "Do not fold or lie on this blanket." One of the company's engineers wondered why no one had designed a blanket that was safe to sleep on while in operation. His questioning resulted in the production of an electric underblanket that was not only safe to sleep on while in operation, but was much more efficient: being insulated by the other bed clothes, it wasted far less energy than conventional electric blankets, which dissipate most of their heat directly into the air.
>
> A camera manufacturer wondered why a camera couldn't have a built-in flash that would spare users the trouble of finding and fixing an attachment. To ask the question was to answer it. The company proceeded to design a 35mm camera with built-in flash, which has met with enormous success and swept the Japanese medium-priced single-lens market.[16]

These two examples illustrate how a latecomer may be able to make a mark in the market through creativity and initiative. In other words, by exploiting technological change, avoiding direct competition, or changing the accepted business structure (e.g., a new form of distribution), the initiator has an opportunity to establish itself in the market successfully.

The Wilmington Corporation adopted the middle course when entering the pressed glass-ceramic cookware market in 1977. Until that time, Corning Glass Works was the sole producer of this product. Corning held a patent that expired in January 1977. The Wilmington Corporation opted not to enter the market with a me-too product. It sought entry into the market with a modified product line: round containers in solid colors. Corning's product was square-shaped and white, with a cornflower design. The company felt that its product would enlarge the market by appealing to a broader range of consumer tastes.[17]

Whatever course a company may pursue to enter the market, as a laggard, it cannot expect much in terms of profitability, growth, or market share. When laggards enter the market, it is already saturated; only established firms can operate profitably. As a matter of fact, their built-in experience affords the established competitors an even greater advantage. An initiator, however, may be able to make a profitable entry, at least until an established firm adds innovation to its own line.

MARKET-COMMITMENT STRATEGY

The **market-commitment strategy** refers to the degree of involvement a company seeks in a particular market. It is widely held that not all customers are equally important to a company. Often, such statements as "17 percent of our customers account for 60 percent of our sales" and "56 percent of our customers provide 11 percent of our sales" are made, which indicate that a company should make varying commitments to different customer groups. The commitment can be in the form of financial or managerial resources or both. Presumably, the results from any venture are commensurate with the commitment made, which explains the importance of the commitment strategy.

Commitment to a market may be categorized as strong, average, or light. Whatever the nature of the commitment, it must be honored: a company that fails to regard its commitment can get into trouble. In 1946, the Liggett and Myers Tobacco Company had a 22 percent share of the U.S. cigarette market. In 1978, its share of the market was less than 3.5 percent; in 1989, slightly less than 3 percent.[18] A variety of reasons has been given for the company's declining fortunes, all amounting to a lack of commitment to a market that at one time it had commanded with an imposing market share. These reasons included responding too slowly to changing market conditions, using poor judgment in positioning brands, and failing to attract new and younger customers. The company lagged behind when filters were introduced and missed industry moves to both king-size and extra-long cigarettes. It also missed the market move toward low-tar cigarettes. Its major entry in that category, Decade, was not introduced until 1977, well after competitors had established similar brands. Liggett and Myers illustrates that a company can lose a comfortable position in any market if it fails to commit itself adequately to it.

Strong-Commitment Strategy | The strong-commitment strategy requires a company to operate in a market optimally by realizing economies of scale in promotion, distribution, manufacturing, and so on. If a competitor challenges a company's position in the market, the latter must fight back aggressively by employing different forms of product, price, promotion, and distribution strategies. In other words, because the company has a high stake in the market, it should do all it can do to defend its position.

A company with a strong commitment to a market should refuse to be content with the status quo. It should foresee its own obsolescence by developing new products, improving product quality, and increasing expenditures for sales force, advertising, and sales promotion relative to the market's growth rate.[19]

This point may be illustrated with reference to the Polaroid Corporation. The company continues to do research and development to stay ahead of the field. The original Land camera, introduced in 1948, produced brown-and-white pictures. Thereafter, the company developed film that took truly black-and-white pictures with different ASA speeds. Also, the time involved in the development of film was reduced from the original 60 seconds to 10 seconds. In 1963 the company introduced color-print film with a development time of 60 seconds; in the early 1970s, the company introduced the SX-70 camera, which made earlier Polaroid cameras obsolete. Since its introduction, a variety of changes and improvements have been made both in the SX-70 camera and in the film that goes into it. A few years later, the company introduced yet another much-improved camera, Spectra. In 1976 Kodak introduced its own version of the instant camera. Polaroid charged Kodak with violating seven Polaroid patents and legally forced Kodak out of the instant photography business.[20] The result: Polaroid has retained its supremacy in the instant photography field, a field to which it has been solely committed.

The nature of a company's commitment to a market may, of course, change with time. Until 1971, Procter & Gamble had a weak commitment to the coffee market, especially in the East. Its Folgers coffee was almost unknown east of the Mississippi. In the early 1970s, however, the company made a strong commitment to the coffee market in the East, city by city. At that time, a small company called Breakfast Cheer Coffee Company made $12 million a year in sales and had an 18 percent share of the coffee market in Pittsburgh. By 1974, because of Procter & Gamble's strength, Breakfast Cheer's sales had plummeted to $2.3 million and its market share had dwindled to under 1 percent. Procter & Gamble had become a major factor in coffee in the Pittsburgh market.[21]

Strong commitment to a market can be highly rewarding in terms of achieving growth, market share, and profitability. A warning is in order, however. The commitment made to a market should be based on a company's resources, its strengths, and its willingness to take risks to live up to its commitment. For example, Procter & Gamble could afford to implement its commitment to the Pittsburgh market because it had a good rapport with distributors and dealers and the resources to launch an effective promotional campaign. A small company could not have afforded to do all of that.

Average-Commitment Strategy

When a company has a stable interest in a market, it must stress the maintenance of the status quo, leading to an only average commitment to the market. Adoption of the average-commitment strategy may be triggered by the fact that a strong-commitment strategy is not feasible. The company may lack the resources to make a strong commitment; a strong commitment may be in conflict with top management's value orientation; or the market in question may not constitute a major thrust of the business in, for example, a diversified company.

In April 1976, when the Eastman Kodak Company announced its entry into the instant photography field, the company most worried about this move was Polaroid. Because Polaroid had a strong commitment to the instant photography market, it did not like Kodak being there just for the sake of competition. As Polaroid's president commented, "This is our very soul that we are involved with. This is our whole life. For them it's just another field."[22] Similarly, when Frito-Lay (a division of PepsiCo) entered the cookie business in 1982, the industry leader, Nabisco, had to adopt a new strategy to defend its title in the business. As an executive of the company noted, "We aren't going to sit on our haunches and let 82 years of business go down the drain."[23]

A company with an average commitment to a market can afford to make occasional mistakes because it has other businesses to compensate for them. Essentially, the average-commitment strategy requires keeping customers happy by providing them with what they are accustomed to. This can be accomplished by making appropriate changes in a marketing program as required by environmental shifts, thus making it difficult for competitors to lure customers away. Where commitment is average, however, the company becomes vulnerable to the lead company as well as the underdog. The leader may wipe out the average-commitment company by price cutting, a feasible strategy because of the experience effect. The underdog may challenge the average-commitment company by introducing new products, focusing on new segments within the market, trying out new forms of distribution, or launching new types of promotional thrusts. The best defense for a company with an average commitment to a market is to keep customers satisfied by being vigilant about developments in its market.

An average commitment may be adequate, as far as profitability is concerned, if the market is growing. In a slow-growth market, an average commitment is not conducive to achieving either growth or profitability.

Light-Commitment
Strategy

A company may have only a passing interest in a market; consequently, it may make only a light commitment to it. The passing interest may be explained by the fact that the market is stagnant, its potential is limited, it is overcrowded with many large companies, and so on. In addition, a company may opt for light commitment to a market to avoid antitrust difficulties. GE maintained a light commitment in the color television market because the field was overcrowded, particularly by Japanese companies. (In 1988, GE sold its television business to Thomson, a French company.) In the early 1970s, Procter & Gamble adopted the light-commitment strategy in the shampoo market, presumably to avoid antitrust difficulties such as those it had encountered with Clorox several years previously; Procter & Gamble let its share of the shampoo market slip from around 50 percent to a little over 20 percent, delayed reformulating its established brands (Prell and Head & Shoulders), introduced only one new brand in many years, and substantially cut its promotional efforts.[24]

A company with a light commitment to a market operates passively and does not make any new moves. It is satisfied as long as the business continues to be in the black and thus seeks very few changes in its marketing perspectives. Overall, this strategy is not of much significance for a company pursuing increasing profitability, greater market share, or growth.

MARKET-DILUTION STRATEGY

In many situations, a company may find reducing a part of its business strategically more useful than expanding it. The **market-dilution strategy** works out well when the overall benefit that a company derives from a market, either currently or potentially, is less than it could achieve elsewhere. Unsatisfactory profit performance, desire for concentration in fewer markets, lack of top management knowledge of the market, negative synergy vis-à-vis other markets that the company serves, and lack of resources to develop the market fully are other reasons for diluting market position.

There was a time when dilution of a market was considered an admission of failure. In the 1970s, however, dilution came to be accepted purely as a matter of strategy. Different ways of diluting a market include demarketing, pruning marginal markets, key account strategy, and harvesting strategy.

Demarketing Strategy

Demarketing, in a nutshell, is the reverse of marketing. This term became popular in the early 1970s when, as a result of the Arab oil embargo, the supply of a variety of products became short. **Demarketing** is the attempt to discourage customers in general or a certain class of customers in particular on either a temporary or permanent basis.

The demarketing strategy may be implemented in different ways. One way involves keeping close track of time requirements of different customers. Thus, if one customer needs the product in July and another in September, the former's order is filled first even though the latter confirmed the order first. A second way of demarketing is rationing supplies to different customers on an equitable basis. Shell Oil followed this route toward the end of 1978 when a gasoline shortage occurred. Each customer was sold a maximum of 10 gallons of gasoline at each filling. Third, recommending that customers use a substitute product temporarily is a form of demarketing. The fourth demarketing method is to divert a customer with an immediate need for a product to another customer to whom the product was recently supplied and who is unlikely to use it immediately. The company becomes an intermediary between two customers, providing supplies of the product to one customer whenever they are needed if present supplies are transferred to the customer in need.

The demarketing strategy is directed toward maintaining customer goodwill during times when customer demands cannot be adequately met. By helping customers in the different ways discussed above, the company hopes that the situation requiring demarketing is temporary and that, when conditions are normal again, customers will be inclined favorably toward the company. In the long run, the demarketing strategy should lead to increased profitability.

Pruning-of-Marginal Markets Strategy

Reasons for using:
① Results in a much higher growth rate
② Provides cash for investment in faster-growing higher-return markets
③ Helps to restore balance
④ Enables the company to limit its operations to growth markets only

A company must undertake a conscious search for those markets that do not provide rates of return comparable to those rates that could be attained if it were to shift its resources to other markets. These markets potentially become candidates for pruning. The pruning of marginal markets may result in a much higher growth rate for the company as a whole. Consider two markets, one providing 10 percent and the other 20 percent on original investments of $1 million. After 15 years, the first market will show an equity value of $4 million, as opposed to $16 million for the second one. Pruning can improve return on investment and growth rate by ridding the company of markets that are growing more slowly than the rest of its markets and by providing cash for investment in faster-growing, higher-return markets. Several years ago, A&P closed more than 100 stores in markets where its competitive position was weak. This pruning effort helped the company to fortify its position and to concentrate on markets where it felt strong.

Pruning also helps to restore balance. A company may be out of balance when it has too many diverse and difficult markets to serve. By pruning, the company may limit its operations to growth markets only. Because growth markets require heavy doses of investment (in the form of price reductions, promotion, and market development) and because the company may have limited resources, the pruning strategy can be very beneficial. Chrysler Corporation, for example, decided in 1978 to quit the European market so that it could use its limited resources to restore its position in the U.S. market. The pruning strategy is especially helpful in achieving market share and profitability. / ROI

Key-Markets Strategy

In most industries, a few customers account for a major portion of volume. This characteristic may be extended to markets. If the breakdown of markets is properly done, a company may find that a few markets account for a very large share of its revenues. Strategically, these key markets may call for extra emphasis in terms of selling effort, after-sales service, product availability, and so on. As a matter of fact, the company may decide to limit its business to these key markets alone.

The key-markets strategy requires:

1. A strong focus tailored to environmental differences (i.e., don't try to do everything; rather, compete in carefully selected ways with the competitive emphasis differing according to the market environment).
2. A reputation for high quality (i.e., turn out high-quality products with superior performance potential and reliability).
3. Medium to low relative prices complimenting high quality.
4. Low total cost to permit offering high-quality products at low prices and still show high profits.

Harvesting Strategy

The harvesting strategy refers to a situation where a company may decide to let its market share slide deliberately. The harvesting strategy may be pursued for a variety of reasons: to increase badly needed cash flow, to increase short-term earnings, or to avoid antitrust action. Usually, only companies with high market share can expect to harvest successfully.

If a product reaches the stage where continued support can no longer be justified, it may be desirable to realize a short-term gain by raising the price or by lowering quality and cutting advertising to turn an active brand into a passive one. In any event, the momentum of the product may continue for years with sales declining but with useful revenues still coming in.

Because they reduce a firm's strategic flexibility, exit barriers may prevent a company from implementing a harvesting strategy. Exit barriers refer to circumstances within an industry that discourage the exit of competitors whose performance in that particular business may be marginal. Three types of exit barriers are (a) a thin resale market for the business's assets, (b) intangible strategic barriers as deterrents to timely exit (e.g., value of distribution networks, customer goodwill for the other products of the company, or strong corporate identification with the product), and (c) management's reluctance to terminate a sick line. When exit barriers disappear or when their effect ceases to be of concern, a harvesting strategy may be pursued.

SUMMARY

This chapter illustrated various types of market strategies that a company may pursue. Market strategies rest on a company's perspective of the customer. Customer focus is a very important factor in market strategy. By diligently delineating the markets to be served, a company can effectively compete in an industry even with established firms.

The five different types of market strategies and the various alternatives under each strategy that were examined in this chapter are outlined below:

1. Market-scope strategy
   a. Single-market strategy
   b. Multimarket strategy
   c. Total-market strategy

2. Market-geography strategy
   a. Local-market strategy
   b. Regional-market strategy
   c. National-market strategy
   d. International-market strategy

3. Market-entry strategy
   a. First-in strategy
   b. Early-entry strategy
   c. Laggard-entry strategy

4. Market-commitment strategy
   a. Strong-commitment strategy
   b. Average-commitment strategy
   c. Light-commitment strategy

5. Market-dilution strategy
   a. Demarketing strategy

b. Pruning-of-marginal-markets strategy
c. Key-markets strategy
d. Harvesting strategy

Application of each strategy was illustrated with examples from marketing literature. The impact of each strategy was considered in terms of its effect on marketing objectives (i.e., profitability, growth, and market share).

DISCUSSION QUESTIONS

1. What circumstances may lead a business unit to change the scope of its market?
2. Under what conditions may a company adopt across-the-board market strategy?
3. Can a company operating only locally go international? Discuss and give examples.
4. Examine the pros and cons of being the first in a market.
5. What underlying conditions must be present before a company can make a strong commitment to a market?
6. Define the term *demarketing*. What circumstances dictate the choice of demarketing strategy?
7. List exit barriers that may prevent a company from implementing a harvesting strategy.

NOTES

1 "Design and Manufacturing Corporation," a case copyrighted in 1972 by the President and Fellows of Harvard College, 4.
2 "They're More Single-Minded at Tambrands," *Business Week* (28 August 1989): 28.
3 "Why Noxell Is Touching Up Its Latest Creation," *Business Week* (11 July 1988): 92.
4 "This Bud's For You, No Not You—Her," *Business Week* (4 November 1991): 86.
5 "Crowning Achievement," *Forbes* (29 October 1990): 178.
6 "Green Giant's Growth Ho-Ho-Hopes," *Advertising Age* (28 May 1990): 20.
7 "Do You Still Know Me?," *Time* (12 September 1994): 60.
8 "Gerber's New Chief Doesn't Take Baby Steps," *Business Week* (7 November 1988): 30. See also *Fortune* (13 March 1989): 140.
9 John Huey, "Eisner Explains Everything," *Fortune* (17 April 1995): 44.
10 *Statistical Abstract of the United States*, 1995, p. 788.
11 See *Masey-Ferfuson's Annual Report for 1994*.
12 Marc Beauchamp, "Lost in the Woods," *Forbes* (16 October 1989): 22; see also *Weyerhaeuser Company's Annual Report for 1994*.
13 "Glitzy Resorts and Suburban Hotels: Hyatt Breaks New Ground," Business Week (4 May 1987): 100. See also company's Annual Report for 1994.
14 "Just Get It to the Stores on Time," *Business Week* (6 March 1995): 66.
15 "Honeywell Inc. EDP Division," a case copyrighted in 1975 by the President and Fellows of Harvard College, 10.
16 Kenichi Ohmae, "Effective Strategies for Competitive Success," *McKinsey Quarterly* (Winter 1978): 55.
17 "Wilmington Corporation," a case copyrighted in 1976 by the President and Fellows of Harvard College.

[18] John Koten, "Liggett's Cigarette Unit Lags, and Some Believe It May Be Snuffed Out," *Wall Street Journal* (27 November 1978): 1.

[19] Robert D. Buzzell and Frederick D. Wiersema, "Successful Share-Building Strategies," Harvard Business Review (January–February 1981), 135–44.

[20] Alex Taylor III, "Kodak Scrambles to Refocus," *Fortune* (3 March 1986): 34.

[21] Bill Henderickson, "Tiny Firms Are Losers in Coffee War Fought by Two Big Marketers," *Wall Street Journal* (3 November 1977): 1.

[22] *New York Times* (28 April 1976): 23.

[23] Ann M. Morrison, "Cookies Are Frito-Lay's New Bag," *Fortune* (9 August 1982): 64.

[24] Nancy Giges, "Shampoo Rivals Wonder When P&G Will Seek Old Dominance," *Advertising Age* (23 September 1974): 3.

APPENDIX | *Perspectives of Market Strategies*

I.
Market-Scope Strategy

A. Single-Market Strategy

Definition: Concentration of efforts in a single segment.

Objective: To find a segment currently being ignored or served inadequately and meet its needs.

Requirements: (a) Serve the market wholeheartedly despite initial difficulties. (b) Avoid competition with established firms.

Expected Results: (a) Low costs. (b) Higher profits.

B. Multimarket Strategy

Definition: Serving several distinct markets.

Objective: To diversify the risk of serving only one market.

Requirements: (a) Careful selection of segments to serve. (b) Avoid confrontation with companies serving the entire market.

Expected Results: (a) Higher sales. (b) Higher market share.

C. Total-Market Strategy

Definition: Serving the entire spectrum of the market by selling differentiated products to different segments in the market.

Objective: To compete across the board in the entire market.

Requirements: (a) Employ different combinations of price, product, promotion, and distribution strategies in different segments. (b) Top management commitment to embrace entire market. (c) Strong financial position.

Expected Results: (a) Increased growth. (b) Higher market share.

II.
Market-Geography Strategy

A. Local-Market Strategy

Definition: Concentration of efforts in the immediate vicinity.

Objective: To maintain control of the business.

Requirements: (a) Good reputation in the geographic area. (b) Good hold on requirements of the market.

Expected Results: Short-term success; ultimately must expand to other areas.

B. **Regional-Market Strategy**

Definition: Operating in two or three states or over a region of the country (e.g., New England).

Objectives: (a) To diversify risk of dependence on one part of a region. (b) To keep control centralized.

Requirements: (a) Management commitment to expansion. (b) Adequate resources. (c) Logistical ability to serve a regional area.

Expected Results: (a) Increased growth. (b) Increased market share. (c) Keep up with competitors.

C. **National-Market Strategy**

Definition: Operating nationally.

Objective: To seek growth.

Requirements: (a) Top management commitment. (b) Capital resources. (c) Willingness to take risks.

Expected Results: (a) Increased growth. (b) Increased market share. (c) Increased profitability.

D. **International-Market Strategy**

Definition: Operating outside national boundaries.

Objective: To seek opportunities beyond domestic business.

Requirements: (a) Top management commitment. (b) Capital resources. (c) Understanding of international markets.

Expected Results: (a) Increased growth. (b) Increased market share. (c) Increased profits.

III.
Market-Entry
Strategy

A. **First-In Strategy**

Definition: Entering the market before all others.

Objective: To create a lead over competition that will be difficult for them to match.

Requirements: (a) Willingness and ability to take risks. (b) Technological competence. (c) Strive to stay ahead. (d) Heavy promotion. (e) Create primary demand. (f) Carefully evaluate strengths.

Expected Results: (a) Reduced costs via experience. (b) Increased growth. (c) Increased market share. (d) Increased profits.

B. **Early-Entry Strategy**

Definition: Entering the market in quick succession after the leader.

Objective: To prevent the first entrant from creating a stronghold in the market.

Requirements: (a) Superior marketing strategy. (b) Ample resources. (c) Strong commitment to challenge the market leader.

Expected Results: (a) Increased profits. (b) Increased growth. (c) Increased market share.

C. Laggard-Entry Strategy

Definition: Entering the market toward the tail end of growth phase or during maturity phase. Two modes of entry are feasible: (a) Imitator—Entering market with me-too product; (b) Initiator—Entering market with unconventional marketing strategies.

Objectives: Imitator—To capture that part of the market that is not brand loyal. Initiator—To serve the needs of the market better than present firms.

Requirements: Imitator—(a) Market research ability. (b) Production capability. Initiator—(a) Market research ability. (b) Ability to generate creative marketing strategies.

Expected Results: Imitator—Increased short-term profits. Initiator—(a) Put market on a new growth path. (b) Increased profits. (c) Some growth opportunities.

IV.
Market-
Commitment
Strategy

A. Strong-Commitment Strategy

Definition: Fighting off challenges aggressively by employing different forms of product, price, promotion, and distribution strategies.

Objective: To defend position at all costs.

Requirements: (a) Operate optimally by realizing economies of scale in promotion, distribution, manufacturing, etc. (b) Refuse to be content with present situation or position. (c) Ample resources. (d) Willingness and ability to take risks.

Expected Results: (a) Increased growth. (b) Increased profits. (c) Increased market share.

B. Average-Commitment Strategy

Definition: Maintaining stable interest in the market.

Objective: To maintain the status quo.

Requirements: Keep customers satisfied and happy.

Expected Results: Acceptable profitability.

C. Light-Commitment Strategy

Definition: Having only a passing interest in the market.

Objective: To operate in the black.

Requirements: Avoid investing for any long-run benefit.

Expected Results: Maintenance of status quo (no increase in growth, profits, or market share).

V.
Market-Dilution
Strategy

A. Demarketing Strategy

Definition: Discouraging customers in general or a certain class of customers in particular, either temporarily or permanently, from seeking the product.

Objective: To maintain customer goodwill during periods of shortages.

Requirements: (a) Monitor customer time requirements. (b) Ration product supplies. (c) Divert customers with immediate needs to customers who have a supply of the product but no immediate need for it. (d) Find out and suggest alternative products for meeting customer needs.

Expected Results: (a) Increased profits. (b) Strong customer goodwill and loyalty.

B. Pruning-of-Marginal-Markets Strategy

Definition: Weeding out markets that do not provide acceptable rates of return.

Objective: To divert investments in growth markets.

Requirements: (a) Gain good knowledge of the chosen markets. (b) Concentrate all energies on these markets. (c) Develop unique strategies to serve the chosen markets.

Expected Results: (a) Long-term growth. (b) Improved return on investment. (c) Decrease in market share.

C. Key-Markets Strategy

Definition: Focusing efforts on selected markets.

Objective: To serve the selected markets extremely well.

Requirements: (a) Gain good knowledge of the chosen markets. (b) Concentrate all energies on these markets. (c) Develop unique strategies to serve the chosen markets.

Expected Results: (a) Increased profits. (b) Increased market share in the selected markets.

D. Harvesting Strategy

Definition: Deliberate effort to let market share slide.

Objectives: (a) To generate additional cash flow. (b) To increase short-term earnings. (c) To avoid antitrust action.

Requirements: High-market share.

Expected Results: Sales decline but useful revenues still come in.

Product Strategies

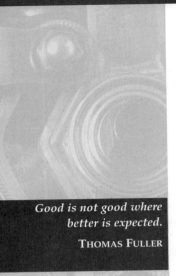

Product strategies specify market needs that may be served by different product offerings. It is a company's product strategies, duly related to market strategies, that eventually come to dominate both overall strategy and the spirit of the company. Product strategies deal with such matters as number and diversity of products, product innovations, product scope, and product design. In this chapter, different dimensions of product strategies are examined for their essence, their significance, their limitations, if any, and their contributions to objectives and goals. Each strategy will be exemplified with illustrations from marketing literature.

DIMENSIONS OF PRODUCT STRATEGIES

The implementation of product strategies requires cooperation among different groups: finance, research and development, the corporate staff, and marketing. This level of integration makes product strategies difficult to develop and implement. In many companies, to achieve proper coordination among diverse business units, product strategy decisions are made by top management. At Gould, for example, the top management decides what kind of business Gould is and what type it wants to be. The company pursues products in the areas of electromechanics, electrochemistry, metallurgy, and electronics. The company works to dispose of products that do not fall strictly into its areas of interest.[1]

In some companies, the overall scope of product strategy is laid out at the corporate level, whereas actual design is left to business units. These companies contend that this alternative is more desirable than other arrangements because it is difficult for top management to deal with the details of product strategy in a diverse company. In this chapter, the following product strategies are recognized:

- Product-positioning strategy
- Product-repositioning strategy
- Product-overlap strategy
- Product-scope strategy
- Product-design strategy
- Product-elimination strategy
- New-product strategy
- Diversification strategy
- Value-marketing strategy

Each strategy is examined from the point of view of an SBU. The appendix at the end of this chapter summarizes each strategy, giving its definition, objectives, requirements, and expected results.

PRODUCT-POSITIONING STRATEGY

The term *positioning* refers to placing a brand in that part of the market where it will receive a favorable reception compared to competing products. Because the market is heterogeneous, one brand cannot make an impact on the entire market. As a matter of strategy, therefore, a product should be matched with that segment of the market in which it is most likely to succeed. The product should be positioned so that it stands apart from competing brands. Positioning tells what the product stands for, what it is, and how customers should evaluate it.

Positioning is achieved by using marketing mix variables, especially design and communication. Although differentiation through positioning is more visible in consumer goods, it is equally true of industrial goods. With some products, positioning can be achieved on the basis of tangible differences (e.g., product features); with many others, intangibles are used to differentiate and position products. As Levitt has observed:

> Fabricators of consumer and industrial goods seek competitive distinction via product features—some visually or measurably identifiable, some cosmetically implied, and some rhetorically claimed by reference to real or suggested hidden attributes that promise results or values different from those of competitors' products.
>
> So too with consumer and industrial services—what I call, to be accurate, "intangibles." On the commodities exchanges, for example, dealers in metals, grains, and pork bellies trade in totally undifferentiated generic products. But what they "sell" is the claimed distinction of their execution—the efficiency of their transactions in their client's behalf, their responsiveness to inquiries, the clarity and speed of their confirmations, and the like. In short, the offered product is differentiated, though the generic product is identical.[2]

The desired position for a product may be determined using the following procedure:

1. Analyze product attributes that are salient to customers.
2. Examine the distribution of these attributes among different market segments.
3. Determine the optimal position for the product in regard to each attribute, taking into consideration the positions occupied by existing brands.
4. Choose an overall position for the product (based on the overall match between product attributes and their distribution in the population and the positions of existing brands).

For example, cosmetics for the career woman may be positioned as "natural," cosmetics that supposedly make the user appear as if she were wearing no makeup at all. An alternate position could be "fast" cosmetics, cosmetics to give the user a mysterious aura in the evenings. A third position might be "light" cosmetics, cosmetics to be worn for tennis and other leisure activities.

Consider the positioning of beer. Two positioning decisions for beer are light versus heavy and bitter versus mild. The desired position for a new brand of beer can be determined by discovering its rating on these attributes and by considering the size of the beer market. The beer market is divided into segments according to these attributes and the positions of other brands. It may be found that the heavy and mild beer market is large and that Schlitz and Budweiser compete in it. In the light and mild beer market, another big segment, Miller may be the dominant competitor. Management may decide to position a new brand in competition with Miller.

Disney stores demonstrate how adequate positioning can lead to instant success.[3] Disney stores earn more than three times what other specialty stores earn per every square foot of floor space. Disney has created retail environments with entertainment as their chief motif. As a customer enters the store, he/she sees the Magic Kingdom, a land of bright lights and merry sounds packed full of Mickey Mouse merchandise. From a phone at the front of each store, a customer can get the Disney channel or book a room in a Disney World hotel. Disney designers got down on their hands and knees when they laid out the stores to be sure that their sight lines would work for a three-year-old. The back wall, normally a prime display area, is given over to a large video screen that continuously plays clips from Disney's animated movies and cartoons. Below the screen, at kid level, sit tiers of stuffed animals that toddlers are encouraged to play with. Adult apparel hangs at the front of the stores to announce that they are for shoppers of all ages. Floor fixtures that hold the merchandise angle inward to steer shoppers deeper into this flashy money trap. Managers spend six weeks in intensive preparatory classes and training before being assigned to a store. Garnished with theatrical lighting and elaborate ceiling displays, the stores have relatively high start-up and fixed costs, but once up and running, they earn high margins.

Six different approaches to positioning may be distinguished:

1. Positioning by attribute (i.e., associating a product with an attribute, feature, or customer benefit).
2. Positioning by price/quality (i.e., the price/quality attribute is so pervasive that it can be considered a separate approach to promotion).
3. Positioning with respect to use or application (i.e., associating the product with a use or application).
4. Positioning by the product user (i.e., associating a product with a user or a class of users).
5. Positioning with respect to a product class (e.g., positioning Caress soap as a bath oil product rather than as soap).
6. Positioning with respect to a competitor (i.e., making a reference to competition as in Avis's now-famous campaign: "We're number two, so we try harder.").

Two types of positioning strategy are discussed here: single-brand strategy and multiple-brand strategy. A company may have just one brand that it may place in one or more chosen market segments, or, alternatively, it may have several brands positioned in different segments.

Positioning a Single Brand

To maximize its benefits with a single brand, a company must try to associate itself with a core segment in a market where it can play a dominant role. In addition, it may attract customers from other segments outside its core as a fringe benefit. BMW does very well, for example, positioning its cars mainly in a limited segment to high-income young professionals.

An alternative single-brand strategy is to consider the market undifferentiated and to cover it with a single brand. Several years ago, for example, the Coca-Cola Company followed a strategy that proclaimed that Coke quenched the thirst of the total market. Such a policy, however, can work only in the short run. To seek entry into a market, competitors segment and challenge the dominance of the single brands by positioning themselves in small, viable niches. Even the Coca-Cola Company now has a number of brands to serve different segments: Classic Coke, New Coke, Diet Coke, Fanta, Sprite, Tab, Fresca, and even orange juice.

Consider the case of beer. Traditionally, brewers operated as if there were one homogeneous market for beer that could be served by one product in one package. Miller, in order to seek growth, took the initiative to segment the market and positioned its High Life brand to younger customers. Thereafter, it introduced a seven-ounce pony bottle that turned out to be a favorite among women and older people who thought that the standard twelve-ounce size was simply too much beer to drink. But Miller's big success came in 1975 with the introduction of another brand, low-calorie Lite. Lite now stands to become the most successful new beer introduced in the United States in this century.

To protect the position of a single brand, sometimes a company may be forced to introduce other brands. Kotler reports that Heublein's Smirnoff brand had a 23 percent share of the vodka market when its position was challenged by Wolfschmidt, priced at $1 less a bottle. Instead of cutting the price of its Smirnoff brand to meet the competition, Heublein raised the price by one dollar and used the increased revenues for advertising. At the same time, it introduced a new brand, Relska, positioning it against Wolfschmidt, and also marketed Popov, a low-price vodka. This strategy effectively met Wolfschmidt's challenge and gave Smirnoff an even higher status. Heublein resorted to multiple brands to protect a single brand that had been challenged by a competitor.[4]

Anheuser-Busch has been dependent on Bud and Bud Light for more than two-thirds of its brewery volume and for over half of its sales revenues. It was this dependence on a single brand that led the company to introduce Michelob. This brand, however, is not doing as well as expected, and at the same time, rivals are showing signs of fresh energy and determination, making it urgent for the company to diversify.[5]

Whether a single brand should be positioned in direct competition with a dominant brand already on the market or be placed in a secondary position is another strategic issue. The head-on route is usually risky, but some variation of this type of strategy is quite common. Avis seemingly accepted a number-two position in the market next to Hertz. Gillette, on the other hand, positioned Silkience shampoo directly against Johnson's Baby Shampoo and Procter & Gamble's Prell. Generally, a single-brand strategy is a desirable choice in the short run, particularly when the task of managing multiple brands is beyond the managerial and financial capability of a company. Supposedly, this strategy is more conducive to achieving higher profitability because a single brand permits better control of operations than do multiple brands.

There are two requisites to managing a single brand successfully: a single brand must be so positioned that it can stand competition from the toughest rival, and its unique position should be maintained by creating an aura of a distinctive product. Consider the case of Cover Girl. The cosmetics field is a crowded and highly competitive industry. The segment Cover Girl picked out—sales in supermarkets and discount stores—is one that large companies, such as Revlon, Avon, and Max Factor, have not tapped. Cover Girl products are sold at a freestanding display without sales help or demonstration. As far as the second requisite is concerned, creating an aura of a distinctive product, an example is Perrier. It continues to protect its position through the mystique attached to its name. In other words, a single brand must have some advantage to protect it from competitive inroads.

Positioning Multiple Brands

Business units introduce multiple brands to a market for two major reasons: (a) to seek growth by offering varied products in different segments of the market and (b) to avoid competitive threats to a single brand. General Motors has a car to sell in all conceivable segments of the market. Coca-Cola has a soft drink for each different taste. IBM sells computers for different customer needs. Procter & Gamble offers a laundry detergent for each laundering need. Offering multiple brands to different segments of the same market is an accepted route to growth.

To realize desired growth, multiple brands should be diligently positioned in the market so that they do not compete with each other and create cannibalism. For example, 20 to 25 percent of sales of Anheuser-Busch's Michelob Light are to customers who previously bought regular Michelob but switched because of the Light brand's low-calorie appeal.[6] The introduction of Maxim by General Foods took sales away from its established Maxwell House brand. About 20 percent of sales of Miller's Genuine Draft beer come from Miller High Life.[7] Thus, it is necessary to be careful in segmenting the market and to position the product, through design and promotion, as uniquely suited to a particular segment.

Of course, some cannibalism is unavoidable. But the question is how much cannibalism is acceptable when introducing another brand. It has been said that 70 percent of Mustang sales in its introductory year were to buyers who would have purchased another Ford had the Mustang not been introduced; the remaining 30 percent of its sales came from new customers. Cadbury's experience with the introduction of a chocolate bar in England indicates that more than 50 percent of its volume came from market expansion, with the remaining volume coming from the company's existing products. Both the Mustang and the chocolate bar were rated as successful introductions by their companies. The apparent difference in cannibalism rates shows that cost structure, degree of market maturity, and the competitive appeal of alternative offerings affect cannibalism sales and their importance to the sales and profitability of a product line and to individual items.[8]

An additional factor to consider in determining actual cannibalism is the vulnerability of an existing brand to a competitor's entry into a presumably open spot in the market. For example, suppose that a company's new brand derives 50 percent of its sales from customers who would have bought its existing brand. However, if 20 percent of the sales of this existing brand were susceptible to a competitor's entry (assuming a fairly high probability that the competitor would have indeed positioned its new brand in that open spot), the actual level of cannibalism should be set at 30 percent. This is because 20 percent of the revenue from sales of the existing brand would have been lost to a competitive brand had there been no new brand.

Multiple brands can be positioned in the market either head-on with the leading brand or with an idea. The relative strengths of the new entry and the established brand dictate which of the two positioning routes is more desirable. Although head-on positioning usually appears risky, some companies have successfully carried it out. IBM's personal computer was positioned in head-on competition with Apple's. Datril, a Bristol-Myers painkiller, was introduced to compete directly with Tylenol.

Positioning with an idea, however, can prove to be a better alternative, especially when the leading brand is well established. Positioning with an idea was attempted by Kraft when it positioned three brands (Breyers and Sealtest ice cream and Light 'n' Lively ice milk) as complements rather than as competitors. Vick Chemical positioned Nyquil, a cold remedy, with the idea that Nyquil assured a good night's sleep. Seagram successfully introduced its line of cocktail mixes, Party Tyme, against heavy odds in favor of Holland House, a National Distillers brand, by promoting it with the Snowbird winter drink.[9]

Positioning of multiple brands and their management in a dynamic environment call for ample managerial and financial resources. When these resources are lacking, a company is better off with a single brand. In addition, if a company already has a dominant position, its attempt to increase its share of the market by introducing an additional brand may invite antitrust action. Such an eventuality should be guarded against. On the other hand, there is also a defensive, or share-maintenance, issue to be considered here even if one has the dominant entry. A product with high market share may not remain in this position forever if competitors are permitted to chip away at its lead with unchallenged positions.

As a strategy, the positioning of multiple brands, if properly implemented, can lead to increases in growth, market share, and profitability.

PRODUCT-REPOSITIONING STRATEGY

Often, a product may require repositioning. This can happen if (a) a competitive entry is positioned next to the brand, creating an adverse effect on its share of the market; (b) consumer preferences change; (c) new customer preference clusters with promising opportunities are discovered; or (d) a mistake is made in the original positioning.

Citations from the marketing literature serve to illustrate how repositioning becomes desirable under different circumstances. When A & W went national in 1989 with its cream soda, it failed to clearly articulate the position. As a result, research showed that consumers perceived cream soda as an extension of the root beer family. To correct this, the company repositioned the brand as a separate soda category by emphasizing the vanilla flavor through advertising and packaging. Following the repositioning, cream soda's sales increased rapidly.[10]

Over the years, Coca-Cola's position has shifted to keep up with the changing mood of the market. In recent years, the theme of Coca-Cola's advertising has evolved from "Things go better with Coke" to "It's the real thing" to "Coke is it" to "Can't beat the feeling" to "Catch the Wave" to "Always new, always real, always you, always Coke." The current perspective of Coca-Cola's positioning is to reach a generation of young people and those young at heart.

The risks involved in positioning or repositioning a product or service are high. The technique of perceptual mapping may be used gainfully to substantially reduce those risks. Perceptual mapping helps in examining the position of a product relative to competing products. It helps marketing strategists

- Understand how competing products or services are perceived by various consumer groups in terms of strengths and weaknesses.
- Understand the similarities and dissimilarities between competing products and services.
- Understand how to reposition a current product in the perceptual space of consumer segments.
- Position a new product or service in an established marketplace.
- Track the progress of a promotional or marketing campaign on the perceptions of targeted consumer segments.

The use of perceptual mapping may be illustrated with reference to the automobile industry. Exhibit 14-1 shows how different cars are positioned on a perceptual map. The map helps the marketing strategist in calculating whether a company's cars are on target. The concentration of dots, which represent competing models, shows how much opposition there is likely to be in a specific territory on the map. Presumably, cars higher up on the graph fetch a higher price than models ranked toward the bottom where the stress is on economy and practicality. After looking at the map, General Motors might find that its Chevrolet division, traditionally geared to entry-level buyers, ought to move down in practicality and more to the right in youthfulness. Another problem for General Motors, which the map so clearly demonstrates, is the close proximity of its Buick and Oldsmobile divisions. This close proximity suggests that the two divisions are waging a marketing war more against each other than against the competition.

Basically, there are three ways to reposition a product: among existing users, among new users, and for new uses. The discussion that follows will elaborate on these repositioning alternatives.

diff uses

Repositioning among Existing Customers

Repositioning a product among existing customers can be accomplished by promoting alternative uses for it. To revitalize its stocking business, Du Pont adopted a repositioning strategy by promoting the "fashion smartness" of tinted hose. Efforts were directed toward expanding women's collections of hosiery by creating a new fashion image for hosiery: hosiery was not simply a neutral accessory;

EXHIBIT 14-1
Perceptual Map of Brand Images

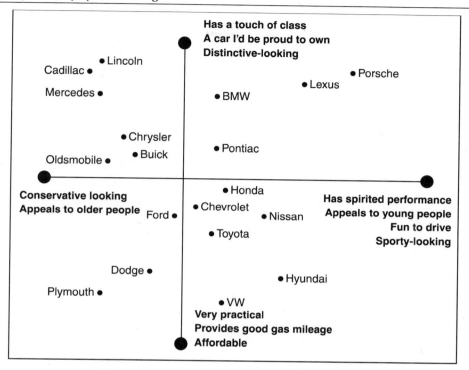

rather, a suitable tint and pattern could complement each garment in a woman's wardrobe.

General Foods Corporation repositioned Jell-O to boost its sales by promoting it as a base for salads. To encourage this usage, the company introduced a variety of vegetable-flavored Jell-Os. A similar strategy was adopted by 3M Company, which introduced a line of colored, patterned, waterproof, invisible, and write-on Scotch tapes for different types of gift wrapping.

The purpose of repositioning among current users is to revitalize a product's life by giving it a new character as something needed not merely as a staple product but as a product able to keep up with new trends and new ideas. Repositioning among users should help the brand in its sales growth as well as increasing its profitability.

Repositioning among New Users

Repositioning among new users requires that the product be presented with a different twist to people who have not hitherto been favorably inclined toward it. In so doing, care must be taken to see that, in the process of enticing new customers, current customers are not alienated. Miller's attempts to win over new customers for Miller High Life beer are noteworthy. Approximately 15 percent of the population consumes 85 percent of all the beer sold in the United States. Miller's slogan "the champagne of bottled beer" had more appeal for light users than for heavy users. Also, the image projected too much elegance for a product like beer. Miller decided to reposition the product slightly to appeal to a wider range of beer drinkers without weakening its current franchise: "Put another way, the need was to take Miller High Life out of the champagne bucket, but not to put it in the bathtub." After conducting a variety of studies, Miller came up with a new promotional campaign built around this slogan: "If you've got the time, we've got the beer." The campaign proved to be highly successful. Through its new slogan, the brand communicated three things: that it was a quality product worth taking time out for; that it was friendly, low-key, and informal; and that it offered relaxation and reward after the pressures of the workday.

At Du Pont, new users of stockings were created by legitimizing the wearing of hosiery among early teenagers and subteenagers. This was achieved by working out a new ad campaign with an emphasis on the merchandising of youthful products and styles to tempt young consumers. Similarly, Jell-O attempted to develop new users among consumers who did not perceive Jell-O as a dessert or salad product. Jell-O was advertised with a new concept—a fashion-oriented, weight-control appeal.

The addition of new users to a product's customer base helps enlarge the overall market and thus puts the product on a growth route. Repositioning among new users also helps increase profitability because very few new investments, except for promotional costs, need to be made.

Repositioning for New Uses

Repositioning for new uses requires searching for latent uses of the product. The case of Arm and Hammer's baking soda is a classic example of an unexplored use of a product. Today this product is popular as a deodorizer, yet deodorizing was not the use originally conceived for the product. Although new uses for a product can be discovered in a variety of ways, the best way to discover them is to gain insights into the customer's way of using a product. If it is found that a large number of customers are using the product for a purpose other than the one originally intended, this other use could be developed with whatever modifications are necessary.

Repositioning for new uses may be illustrated with reference to Disney World's efforts to expand its business. In 1991, it opened a Disney Fairy Tale Weddings Department, which puts on more than 200 full-service weddings a year, each costing about $10,000.[11]

At Du Pont, new uses for nylon sprang up in varied types of hosiery (stretch stockings and stretch socks), tires, bearings, etc. Its new uses have kept nylon on the growth path: wrap knits in 1945, tire cord in 1948, textured yarns in 1955, carpet yarns in 1959, and so on. Without these new uses, nylon would have hit the saturation level as far back as 1962.

General Foods found that women used powdered gelatin dissolved in liquid to strengthen their fingernails. Working on this clue, General Foods introduced a flavorless Jell-O as a nail-building agent.

The new-use strategy is directed toward revamping the sales of a product whose growth, based on its original conceived use, has slowed down. This strategy has the potential to increase sales growth, market share, and profitability.

PRODUCT-OVERLAP STRATEGY

The product-overlap strategy refers to a situation where a company decides to compete against its own brand. Many factors lead companies to adopt such a strategic posture. For example, A&P stores alone cannot keep the company's 42 manufacturing operations working at full capacity. Therefore, A&P decided to distribute many of its products through independent food retailers. A&P's Eight O'Clock coffee, for example, is sold through 7-Eleven stores. Procter & Gamble has different brands of detergents virtually competing in the same market. Each brand has its own organization for marketing research, product development, merchandising, and promotion. Although sharing the same sales force, each brand behaves aggressively to outdo others in the marketplace. Sears' large appliance brands are actually manufactured by the Whirlpool Corporation. Thus, Whirlpool's branded appliances compete against those that it sells to Sears.

There are alternative ways in which the product-overlap strategy may be operationalized. Principal among them are having competing lines, doing private labeling, and dealing with original-equipment manufacturers.

Competing Brands

In order to gain a larger share of the total market, many companies introduce competing products to the market. When a market is not neatly delineated, a single brand of a product may not be able to make an adequate impact. If a second brand is placed to compete with the first one, overall sales of the two brands should increase substantially, although there will be some cannibalism. In other words, two competing brands provide a more aggressive front against competitors.

Often the competing-brands strategy works out to be a short-term phenomenon. When a new version of a product is introduced, the previous version is allowed to continue until the new one has fully established itself. In this way, the competition is prevented from stealing sales during the time that the new product is coming into its own. In 1989, Gillette introduced the Sensor razor, a revolutionary new product that featured flexible blades that adjusted to follow the unique contours of the face. At the same time, its previous razor, Atra, continued to be promoted as before. It is claimed that together the two brands were very effective in the market. It is estimated that 36 percent of Sensor users converted from Atra. If Atra had not been promoted, this figure would have been much more, and Sensor would have been more vulnerable to the Schick Tracer and other rigid Atra lookalikes.[12]

To expand its overall coffee market, Procter & Gamble introduced a more economical form of ground coffee under the Folgers label. A more efficient milling process that refines coffee into flakes allows hot water to come into contact with more of each coffee particle when brewing, resulting in savings of up to 15 percent per cup. The new product, packaged in 13-, 26-, and 32-ounce cans, yielded the same number of cups of coffee as standard 16-, 32-, and 48-ounce cans, respectively. Both the new and the old formulations were promoted aggressively, competing with each other and, at the same time, providing a strong front against brands belonging to other manufacturers.

Reebok International products under the Reebok brand name directly compete with its subsidiary's brand, Avia. As noted earlier, the competing-brands strategy is useful in the short run only. Ultimately, each brand, Avia and Reebok, should find its special niche in the market. If that does not happen, they will create confusion among customers and sales will be hurt. Alternatively, in the long run, one of the brands may be withdrawn, thereby yielding its position to the other brand. This strategy is a useful device for achieving growth and for increasing market share.

Private Labeling | Private labeling refers to manufacturing a product under another company's brand name. In the case of goods whose intermediaries have significant control of the distribution sector, private labeling, or branding, has become quite common. For large food chains, items produced with their label by an outside manufacturer contribute significantly to sales. Sears, JCPenney, and other such companies merchandise many different types of goods—textile goods, electronic goods, large appliances, sporting goods, etc.—each carrying the company's brand name.

The private-label strategy from the viewpoint of the manufacturer is viable for the following reasons:

- Private labeling represents a large (and usually growing) market segment.
- Economies of scale at each step in the business system (manufacturing capacity, distribution, merchandising, and so on) justify the search for additional volume.
- Supplying private labeling will improve relationships with a powerful organized trade.
- Control over technology and raw materials reduces the risk.
- There is a clear consumer segmentation between branded and unbranded goods that supports providing private label.
- Private labeling helps eliminate small, local competitors.
- Private labeling offers an opportunity to compete on price against other branded products.
- Private labeling increases share of shelf space—a critical factor in motivating impulse purchases.

But here are also strong arguments against the private-label strategy:

- Market share growth through private-label supply always happens at the expense of profitability, as price sensitivity rises and margins fall.
- Disclosing cost information to the trade—usually essential for a private-label supplier—can threaten a firm's branded products.
- In order to displace existing private label suppliers, new entrants must undercut current prices, and thus risk starting a price war—in an environment where trade loyalty offers little protection.

- In young, growing markets, it is the brand leaders, not the private label suppliers, that influence whether the market will develop toward branded or commodity goods.
- Private labeling is inconsistent with a leader's global brand and product strategy—it raises questions about quality and standards, dilutes management attention, and affects consumers' perception of the main branded business.

Many large manufacturers deal in private brands while simultaneously offering their own brands. In this situation, they are competing against themselves. They do so, however, hoping that overall revenues will be higher with the offering of the private brand than without it. Coca-Cola, for example, supplies to A&P stores both its own brand of orange juice, Minute Maid, and the brand it produces with the A&P label. At one time, many companies equated supplying private brands with lowering their brands' images. But the business swings of the 1980s changed attitudes on this issue. Frigidaire appliances at one time were not offered under a private label. However, in the 1980s Frigidaire began offering them under Montgomery Ward's name.

A retailer's interest in selling goods under its own brand name is also motivated by economic considerations. The retailer buys goods with its brand name at low cost, then offers the goods to customers at a slightly lower price than the price of a manufacturer's brand (also referred to as a national brand). The assumption is that the customer, motivated by the lower price, will buy a private brand, assuming that its quality is on a par with that of the national brand. This assumption is, of course, based on the premise that a reputable retailer will not offer something under its name if it is not high quality.

Dealing with Original-Equipment Manufacturers (OEMs)

Following the strategy of dealing with an OEM, a company may sell to competitors the components used in its own product. This enables competitors to compete with the company in the market. For example, in the initial stages of color television, RCA was the only company that manufactured picture tubes. It sold these picture tubes to GE and to other competitors, enabling them to compete with RCA color television sets in the market.

The relevance of this strategy may be discussed from the viewpoint of both the seller and the OEM. The motivation for the seller comes from two sources: the desire to work at near-capacity level and the desire to have help in promoting primary demand. Working at full capacity is essential for capitalizing on the experience effect (see Chapter 12). Thus, by selling a component to competitors, a company may reduce the across-the-board costs of the component for itself, and it will have the price leverage to compete with those manufacturers to whom it sold the component. Besides, the company will always have the option of refusing to do business with a competitor who becomes a problem.

The second source of motivation is the support competitors can provide in stimulating primary demand for a new product. Many companies may be working on a new-product idea. When one of them successfully introduces the product, the others may be unable to do so because they lack an essential component or the technology that the former has. Since the product is new, the innovator may find the task of developing primary demand by itself tedious. It may make a strategic decision to share the essential-component technology with other competitors, thus encouraging them to enter the market and share the burden of stimulating primary demand.

A number of companies follow the OEM strategy. Auto manufacturers sell parts to each other. Texas Instruments sold electronic chips to its competitors during the initial stages of the calculator's development. In the 1950s, Polaroid bought certain essential ingredients from Kodak to manufacture film. IBM has shared a variety of technological components with other computer producers. In many situations, however, the OEM strategy may be forced upon companies by the Justice Department in its efforts to promote competition in an industry. Both Kodak and Xerox shared the products of their technology with competitors at the behest of the government. Thus, as a matter of strategy, when government interference may be expected, a company will gain more by sharing its components with others and assuming industry leadership. From the standpoint of results, this strategy is useful in seeking increased profitability, though it may not have much effect on market share or growth.

As far as the OEMs are concerned, the strategy of depending upon a competitor for an essential component only works in the short run because the supplier may at some point refuse entirely to sell the component or may make it difficult for the buyer to purchase it by delaying deliveries or by increasing prices enormously.

PRODUCT-SCOPE STRATEGY

The product-scope strategy deals with the perspective of the product mix of a company (i.e., the number of product lines and items in each line that the company may offer). The product-scope strategy is determined by making reference to the business unit mission. Presumably, the mission defines what sort of business it is going to be, which helps in selecting the products and services that are to become a part of the product mix.

The product-scope strategy must be finalized after a careful review of all facets of the business because it involves long-term commitment. In addition, the strategy must be reviewed from time to time to make any changes called for because of shifts in the environment. The point may be elaborated with reference to Eastman Kodak Company's decision to enter the instant photography market in the early 1970s. Traditionally, Polaroid bought negatives for its films, worth $50 million, from Kodak. In 1969, Polaroid built its own negative plant. This meant that Kodak would lose some $50 million of Polaroid's business and be left with idle machinery that had been dedicated to filling Polaroid's needs. Further, by producing its own film, Polaroid could lower its costs; if it then cut prices, instant photography might become more competitive with Kodak's business. Alternatively, if Polaroid held prices high, it would realize high margins and would soon be very rich indeed. Encouraged by such achievements, Polaroid could even develop a marketing organization rivaling Kodak's and threaten it in every sphere. In brief, Kodak was convinced that it would be shut out of the instant photography market forever if it delayed its entry any longer. Subsequently, however, a variety of reasons led Kodak to change its decision to go ahead with instant photography. Its pocket instamatic cameras turned out to be highly successful, and some of the machinery and equipment allocated to instant photography had to be switched over to pocket instamatics. A capital shortage also occurred, and Kodak, as a matter of financial policy, did not want to borrow to support the instant photography project. In 1976, Kodak again revised its position and did enter the field of instant photography.[13]

In brief, commitment to the product-scope strategy requires a thorough review of a large number of factors both inside and outside the organization. The three variants of product-scope strategy that will be discussed in this section are single-product strategy, multiple-products strategy, and system-of-products strategy. It will be recalled that in the previous chapter three alternatives were discussed under market-scope strategy: single-market strategy, multimarket strategy, and total-market strategy. These market strategies may be related to the three variants of product-scope strategy, providing nine different product/market-scope alternatives.

Single Product

A business unit may have just one product in its line and must try to live on the success of this one product. There are several advantages to this strategy. First, concentration on a single product leads to specialization, which helps achieve scale and productivity gains. Second, management of operations is much more efficient when a single product is the focus. Third, in today's environment, where growth leads most companies to offer multiple products, a single-product company may become so specialized in its field that it can stand any competition.

A narrow product focus, for example, cancer insurance, has given American Family Life Assurance Company of Columbus, Georgia, a fast track record. Cancer is probably more feared than any other disease in the United States today. Although it kills fewer people than heart ailments, suffering is often lingering and severe. Cashing in on this fear, American Family Life became the nation's first marketer of insurance policies that cover the expenses of treating cancer.

Despite its obvious advantages, the single-product company has two drawbacks: First, if changes in the environment make the product obsolete, the single-product company can be in deep trouble. American history is full of instances where entire industries were wiped out. The disposable diaper, initially introduced by Procter & Gamble via its brand Pampers, pushed the cloth diaper business out of the market. The Baldwin Locomotive Company's steam locomotives were made obsolete by General Motors' diesel locomotives.

Second, the single-product strategy is not conducive to growth or market share. Its main advantage is profitability. If a company with a single-product focus is not able to earn high margins, it is better to seek a new posture. Companies interested in growth or market share will find the single-product strategy of limited value.

Multiple Products

The multiple-products strategy amounts to offering two or more products. A variety of factors lead companies to choose this strategic posture. A company with a single product has nowhere to go if that product gets into trouble; with multiple products, however, poor performance by one product can be balanced out. In addition, it is essential for a company seeking growth to have multiple product offerings.

In 1970, when Philip Morris bought the Miller Brewing Company, it was a one-product business ranking seventh in beer sales. Growth prospects led the company to offer a number of other products. By 1978, Miller had acquired the number two position in the industry with 15 percent of the market. Miller continues to maintain its position (market share in 1994 was 16.8 percent), although Anheuser-Busch, the industry leader, has taken many steps to dislodge it.[14] As another example, consider Chicago-based Dean Foods Company, which traditionally has been a dairy concern. Over the years, diet-conscious and aging consumers have increasingly shunned high-fat dairy products in favor of low-calorie foods, and competition for the business that remains is increasingly fierce. In the early 1980s, to successfully operate in such an environment, the company decided to add other faster-growing, higher-margin refrigerated foods, such as party dips and cranberry drink, to the company's traditional dairy business. Dean's moves have been so successful that, although many milk processors were looking to sell out, Dean was concerned that it might be bought out. Similarly, Nike began with a shoe solely for serious athletes. Over the years, the company has added a number of new products to its line. It now makes shoes, for both males and females, for running, jogging, tennis, aerobics, soccer, basketball, and walking. Lately, it has expanded its offerings to include children.

Multiple products can be either related or unrelated. Unrelated products will be discussed later in the section on diversification. Related products consist of different product lines and items. A food company may have a frozen vegetable line, a yogurt line, a cheese line, and a pizza line. In each line, the company may produce different items (e.g., strawberry, pineapple, apricot, peach, plain, and blueberry yogurt). Note, in this example, the consistency among the different food lines: (a) they are sold through grocery stores, (b) they must be refrigerated, and (c) they are meant for the same target market. These underpinnings make them related products.

Although not all products may be fast moving, they must complement each other in a portfolio of products. The subject of product portfolios was examined in Chapter 10. Suffice it to say, the multiple-products strategy is directed toward achieving growth, market share, and profitability. Not all companies get rich simply by having multiple products: growth, market share, and profitability are functions of a large number of variables, only one of which is having multiple products.

System of Products

The word *system*, as applied to products, is a post-World War II phenomenon. Two related forces were responsible for the emergence of this phenomenon: (a) the popularity of the marketing concept that businesses sell satisfaction, not products; and (b) the complexities of products themselves often call for the use of complementary products and after-sale services. A cosmetics company does not sell lipstick, it sells the hope of looking pretty; an airline should not sell plane tickets, it should sell pleasurable vacations. However, vacationers need more than an airline ticket. Vacationers also need hotel accommodations, ground transportation, and sightseeing arrangements. Following the systems concept, an airline may define itself as a vacation packager that sells air transportation, hotel reservations, meals, sightseeing, and so on. IBM is a single source for hardware, operating systems, packaged software, maintenance, emergency repairs, and consulting services. Thus, IBM offers its customers a system of different products and services to solve data management problems. Likewise, ADT Ltd. is a company whose product is security systems. Beginning with consulting on the type of security systems needed, ADT also provides the sales, installation, service, updating on new technologies to existing systems, and the actual monitoring of these alarm systems either by computer, or with patrol services and security watchman.

Offering a system of products rather than a single product is a viable strategy for a number of reasons. It makes the customer fully dependent, thus allowing the company to gain monopolistic control over the market. The system-of-products strategy also blocks the way for the competition to move in. With such benefits, this strategy is extremely useful in meeting growth, profitability, and market share objectives. If this strategy is stretched beyond its limits, however, a company can get into legal problems. Several years ago, IBM was charged by the Justice Department with monopolizing the computer market. In the aftermath of this charge, IBM has had to make changes in its strategy.

The successful implementation of the system-of-products strategy requires a thorough understanding of customer requirements, including the processes and functions the consumer must perform when using the product. Effective implementation of this strategy broadens both the company's concept of its product and market opportunities for it, which in turn support product/market objectives of growth, profitability, and market share.

PRODUCT-DESIGN STRATEGY

A business unit may offer a standard or a custom-designed product to each individual customer. The decision about whether to offer a standard or a customized product can be simplified by asking these questions, among others: What are our capabilities? What business are we in? With respect to the first question, there is a danger of overidentification of capabilities for a specific product. If capabilities are overidentified, the business unit may be in trouble. When the need for the product declines, the business unit will have difficulty in relating its product's capabilities to other products. It is, therefore, desirable for a business unit to have a clear perspective about its capabilities. The answer to the second question determines the limits within which customizing may be pursued.

Between the two extremes of standard and custom products, a business unit may also offer standard products with modifications. These three strategic alternatives, which come under the product-design strategy, are discussed below.

Standard Products

Offering standard products leads to two benefits. First, standard products are more amenable to the experience effect than are customized products; consequently, they yield cost benefits. Second, standard products can be merchandised nationally much more efficiently. Ford's Model T is a classic example of a successful standard product. The standard product has one major problem, however. It orients management thinking toward the realization of per-unit cost savings to such an extent that even the need for small changes in product design may be ignored.

There is considerable evidence to suggest that larger firms derive greater profits from standardization by taking advantage of economies of scale and long production runs to produce at a low price. Small companies, on the other hand, must use the major advantage they have over the giants, that is, flexibility. Hence, the standard-product strategy is generally more suitable for large companies. Small companies are better off as job shops, doing customized work at a higher margin.

A standard product is usually offered in different grades and styles with varying prices. In this manner, even though a product is standard, customers have broader choices. Likewise, distribution channels get the product in different price ranges. The result: standard-product strategy helps achieve the product/market objectives for growth, market share, and profitability.

Customized Products

Customized products are sold on the basis of the quality of the finished product, that is, on the extent to which the product meets the customer's specifications. The producer usually works closely with the customer, reviewing the progress of the product until completion. Unlike standard products, price is not a factor for customized products. A customer expects to pay a premium for a customized product. As mentioned above, a customized product is more suitable for small companies to offer. This broad statement should not be interpreted to mean that large companies cannot successfully offer customized products. The ability to sell customized products successfully actually depends on the nature of the product. A small men's clothing outlet is in a better position to offer custom suits than a large men's suit manufacturer. On the other hand, GE is better suited to manufacture a custom-designed engine for military aircraft than a smaller business.

Over and above price flexibility, dealing in customized products provides a company with useful experience in developing new standard products. A number of companies have been able to develop mass market products out of their custom work for NASA projects. The microwave oven, for example, is an offshoot of the experience gained from government contracts. Customized products also provide opportunities for inventing new products to meet other specific needs. In terms of results, this strategy is directed more toward realizing higher profitability than are other product-design strategies.

Standard Products with Modifications

The strategy of modifying standard products represents a compromise between the two strategies already discussed. With this strategy, a customer may be given the option to specify a limited number of desired modifications to a standard product. A familiar example of this strategy derives from the auto industry. The buyer of a new car can choose type of shift (standard or automatic), air conditioning, power brakes, power steering, size of engine, type of tires, and color. Although some modifications may be free, for the most part the customer is expected to pay extra for modifications.

This strategy is directed toward realizing the benefits of both a standard and a customized product. By manufacturing a standard product, the business unit seeks economies of scale; at the same time, by offering modifications, the product is individualized to meet the specific requirements of the customer. The experience of a small water pump manufacturer that sold its products nationally through distributors provides some insights into this phenomenon. The company manufactured the basic pump in its facilities in Ohio and then shipped it to its four branches in different parts of the country. At each branch, the pumps were finished according to specifications requested by distributors. Following this strategy, the company lowered its transportation costs (because the standard pump could be shipped in quantity) even while it provided customized pumps to its distributors.

Among other benefits, this strategy permits the business unit to keep in close contact with market needs that may be satisfied through product improvements and modifications. It also enhances the organization's reputation for flexibility in meeting customer requirements. It may also encourage new uses of existing products. Other things being equal, this strategy can be useful in achieving growth, market share, and profitability.

PRODUCT-ELIMINATION STRATEGY

Marketers have believed for a long time that sick products should be eliminated. It is only in recent years that this belief has become a matter of strategy. A business unit's various products represent a portfolio, with each product playing a unique role in making the business viable. If a product's role diminishes or if it does not fit into the portfolio, it ceases to be important.

When a product reaches the stage where continued support is no longer justified because performance is falling short of expectations, it is desirable to pull the product out of the marketplace. Poor performance is easy to spot. It may be characterized by any of the following:

1. Low profitability.
2. Stagnant or declining sales volume or market share that is too costly to rebuild.
3. Risk of technological obsolescence.
4. Entry into a mature or declining phase of the product life cycle.
5. Poor fit with the business unit's strengths or declared mission.

Products that are not able to limp along must be eliminated. They drain a business unit's financial and managerial resources, resources that could be used more profitably elsewhere. Hise, Parasuraman, and Viswanathan cite examples of a number of companies, among them Hunt Foods, Standard Brands, and Crown Zellerbach, that have reported substantial positive results from eliminating products.[15] The three alternatives in the product-elimination strategy are harvesting, line simplification, and total-line divestment.

Harvesting

Harvesting refers to getting the most from a product while it lasts. It is a controlled divestment whereby the business unit seeks to get the most cash flow it can from the product. The harvesting strategy is usually applied to a product or business whose sales volume or market share is slowly declining. An effort is made to cut the costs associated with the business to improve cash flow. Alternatively, price is increased without simultaneous increase in costs. Harvesting leads to a slow decline in sales. When the business ceases to provide a positive cash flow, it is divested.

Du Pont followed the harvesting strategy in the case of its rayon business. Similarly, BASF Wyandotte applied harvesting to soda ash. As another example, GE harvested its artillery business a few years ago. Even without making any investments or raising prices, the business continued to provide GE with positive cash flow and substantial profits. Lever Brothers applied this strategy to its Lifebuoy soap. The company continued to distribute this product for a long time because, despite higher price and virtually no promotional support, it continued to be in popular demand.

Implementation of the harvesting strategy requires severely curtailing new investment, reducing maintenance of facilities, slicing advertising and research budgets, reducing the number of models produced, curtailing the number of distribution channels, eliminating small customers, and cutting service in terms of delivery time, speed of repair, and sales assistance. Ideally, harvesting strategy should be pursued when the following conditions are present:

1. The business entity is in a stable or declining market.
2. The business entity has a small market share, but building it up would be too costly; or it has a respectable market share that is becoming increasingly costly to defend or maintain.
3. The business entity is not producing especially good profits or may even be producing losses.
4. Sales would not decline too rapidly as a result of reduced investment.
5. The company has better uses for the freed-up resources.
6. The business entity is not a major component of the company's business portfolio.
7. The business entity does not contribute other desired features to the business portfolio, such as sales stability or prestige.

Line Simplification

Line-simplification strategy refers to a situation where a product line is trimmed to a manageable size by pruning the number and variety of products or services offered. This is a defensive strategy that is adopted to keep a falling line stable. It is hoped that the simplification effort will restore the health of the line. This strategy becomes especially relevant during times of rising costs and resource shortages.

The application of this strategy in practice may be illustrated with an example from GE's housewares business. In the early 1970s, the housewares industry faced soaring costs and stiff competition from Japan. GE took a hard look at its housewares business and raised such questions as: Is this product segment mature? Is it one we should be harvesting? Is it one we should be investing money in and expanding? Analysis showed that there was a demand for housewares, but demand was just not attractive enough for GE at that time. The company ended production of blenders, fans, heaters, and vacuum cleaners because they were found to be on the downside of the growth curve and did not fit in with GE's strategy for growth.

Similarly, Sears, Roebuck & Co. overhauled its retail business in 1993, dropping its famous catalog business, which contributed over $3 billion in annual sales. Sears' huge catalog operations had been losing money for nearly a decade (about $175 million in 1992), as specialty catalogs and specialty stores grabbed market share from the country's once-supreme mail-order house.[16]

The implementation of a line-simplification strategy can lead to a variety of benefits: potential cost savings from longer production runs; reduced inventories; and a more forceful concentration of marketing, research and development, and other efforts behind a shorter list of products.

However, despite obvious merits, simplification efforts may sometimes be sabotaged. Those who have been closely involved with a product may sincerely feel either that the line as it is will revive when appropriate changes are made in the marketing mix or that sales and profits will turn up once temporary conditions in the marketplace turn around. Thus, careful maneuvering is needed on the part of management to simplify a line unhindered by corporate rivalries and intergroup pressures.

The decision to drop a product is more difficult if it is a core product that has served as a foundation for the company. Such a product achieves the status of motherhood, and a company may like to keep it for nostalgic reasons. For example, the decision by General Motors to drop the Cadillac convertible was probably a difficult one to make in light of the prestige attached to the vehicle. Despite the emotional aspects of a product-deletion decision, the need to be objective in this matter cannot be overemphasized. Companies establish their own criteria to screen different products for elimination.

In finalizing the decision, attention should be given to honoring prior commitments. For example, replacement parts must be provided even though an item is dropped. A well-implemented program of product simplification can lead to both growth and profitability. It may, however, be done at the cost of market share.

Total-Line Divestment   Divestment is a situation of reverse acquisition. It may also be a dimension of market strategy. But to the extent that the decision is approached from the product's perspective (i.e., to get rid of a product that is not doing well even in a growing market), it is an aspect of product strategy. Traditionally, companies resisted divestment for the following reasons, which are principally either economic or psychological in nature:

1. Divestment means negative growth in sales and assets, which runs counter to the business ethic of expansion.
2. Divestment suggests defeat.
3. Divestment requires changes in personnel, which can be painful and can result in perceived or real changes in status or have an adverse effect on the entire organization.
4. Divestment may need to be effected at a price below book and thus may have an adverse effect on the year's earnings.
5. The candidate for divestment may be carrying overhead, buying from other business units of the company, or contributing to earnings.

With the advent of strategic planning in the 1970s, divestment became an accepted option for seeking faster growth. More and more companies are now willing to sell a business if the company will be better off strategically. These companies feel that divestment should not be regarded solely as a means of ridding the company of an unprofitable division or plan; rather, there are some persuasive reasons supporting the divestment of even a profitable and growing business. Businesses that no longer fit the corporate strategic plan can be divested for a number of reasons:

- There is no longer a strategic connection between the base business and the part to be divested.
- The business experiences a permanent downturn, resulting in excess capacity for which no profitable alternative use can be identified.
- There may be inadequate capital to support the natural growth and development of the business.
- It may be dictated in the estate planning of the owner that a business is not to remain in the family.
- Selling a part of the business may release assets for use in other parts of the business where opportunities are growing.
- Divestment can improve the return on investment and growth rate both by ridding the company of units growing more slowly than the basic business and by providing cash for investment in faster-growing, higher-return operations.

Whatever the reason, a business that may have once fit well into the overall corporate plan can suddenly find itself in an environment that causes it to become a drain on the corporation, either financially, managerially, or opportunistically. Such circumstances suggest divestment.

Divestment helps restore balance to a business portfolio. If the company has too many high-growth businesses, particularly those at an early stage of development, its resources may be inadequate to fund growth. On the other hand, if a company has too many low-growth businesses, it will often generate more cash than is required for investment and will build up redundant equity. For a business to grow evenly over time while showing regular increments in earnings, a portfolio of fast- and slow-growth businesses is necessary. Divestment can help achieve this kind of balance. Finally, divestment helps restore a business to a size that will not lead to an antitrust action.

The use of this strategy is reflected in GE's decision to divest its consumer electronics business in the early 1980s. In order to realize a return that GE considered adequate, the company would have had to make additional heavy investments in this business. GE figured that it could use the money to greater advantage in an area other than consumer electronics. Hence, it divested the business by selling it to Thomson, a French company.

Essentially following the same reasoning, Olin Corporation divested its aluminum business on the grounds that maintaining its small 4 percent share required big capital expenditures that could be employed more usefully elsewhere in the company. Westinghouse sold its major appliance line because it needed at least an additional 3 percent beyond the 5 percent share it held before it could compete effectively against industry leaders GE and Whirlpool. GE and Whirlpool divided about half the total market between them. Between 1986 and 1988, Beatrice sold two-thirds of its business, including such well-known names as Playtex, Avis, Tropicana, and Meadow Gold. The company considered these divestments necessary to transform itself into a manageable organization.[17]

It is difficult to prescribe generalized criteria to determine whether to divest a business. However, the following questions may be raised, the answers to which should provide a starting point for considering divestment:

1. **What is the earnings pattern of the unit?** A key question is whether the unit is acting as a drag on corporate growth. If so, then management must determine whether there are any offsetting values. For example, are earnings stable compared to the fluctuation in other parts of the company? If so, is the low-growth unit a substantial contributor to the overall debt capacity of the business? Management should also ask a whole series of "what-if" questions relating to earnings: What if we borrowed additional funds? What if we brought in new management? What if we made a change in location? etc.

2. **Does the business generate any cash?** In many situations, a part of a company may be showing a profit but may not be generating any discretionary cash. That is, every dime of cash flow must be pumped right back into the operation just to keep it going at existing levels. Does this operation make any real contribution to the company? Will it eventually? What could the unit be sold for? What would be done with the cash from this sale?

3. **Is there any tie-in value—financial or operating—with existing business?** Are there any synergies in marketing, production, or research and development? Is the business countercyclical? Does it represent a platform for growth internally based or through acquisitions?

4. **Will selling the unit help or hurt the acquisitions effort?** What will be the immediate impact on earnings (write-offs, operating expenses)? What effect, if any, will the sale have on the company's image in the stock market? Will the sale have any effect on potential acquisitions? (Will I, too, be sold down the river?) Will the divestment be functional in terms of the new size achieved? Will a smaller size facilitate acquisitions by broadening the "market" of acceptable candidates, or, by contrast, will the company become less credible because of the smaller size?

In conclusion, a company should undertake continual in-depth analysis of the market share, growth prospects, profitability, and cash-generating power of each business. As a result of such reviews, a business may need to be divested to maintain balance in the company's total business. This, however, is feasible only when the company develops enough self-discipline to avoid increasing sales volume beyond a desirable size and instead buys and sells businesses with the sole objective of enhancing overall corporate performance.

NEW-PRODUCT STRATEGY

New-product development is an essential activity for companies seeking growth. By adopting the new-product strategy as their posture, companies are better able to sustain competitive pressures on their existing products and make headway. The implementation of this strategy has become easier because of technological innovations and the willingness of customers to accept new ways of doing things.

Despite their importance in strategy determination, however, implementation of new-product programs is far from easy. Too many products never make it in the marketplace. The risks and penalties of product failure require that companies move judiciously in adopting new-product strategies.

Interestingly, however, the mortality rate of new product ideas has declined considerably since the 1960s. In 1968, on average, 58 new product ideas were considered for every successful new product. In 1981, only seven ideas were required to generate one successful new product. However, these statistics vary by industry. Consumer nondurable companies consider more than twice as many new product ideas in order to generate one successful new product, compared to industrial or consumer durable manufacturers.[18]

Top management can affect the implementation of new-product strategy; first, by establishing policies and broad strategic directions for the kinds of new products the company should seek; second, by providing the kind of leadership that creates the environmental climate needed to stimulate innovation in the organization; and third, by instituting review and monitoring procedures so that managers are involved at the right decision points and can know whether or not work schedules are being met in ways that are consistent with broad policy directions.

The term *new product* is used in different senses. For our purposes, the new-product strategy will be split into three alternatives: (a) product improvment/ modification, (b) product imitation, and (c) product innovation.

Product improvement/modification is the introduction of a new version or an improved model of an existing product, such as "new, improved Crest." Improvements and modifications are usually achieved by adding new features or styles, changing processing requirements, or altering product ingredients. When a company introduces a product that is already on the market but new to the company, it is following a product-imitation strategy. For example, Schick was imitating when it introduced its Tracer razor to compete with Gillette's Sensor. For our purposes, a product innovation will be defined as a strategy with a completely new approach in fulfilling customer desires (e.g., Polaroid camera, television, typewriter) or one that replaces existing ways of satisfying customer desires (e.g., the replacement of slide rules by pocket calculators).

New-product development follows the experience curve concept; that is, the more you do something, the more efficient you become at doing it (for additional details, see Chapter 12). Experience in introducing products enables companies to improve new-product performance. Specifically, with increased new-product experience, companies improve new-product profitability by reducing the cost per introduction. More precisely, with each doubling of the number of new-product introductions, the cost of each introduction declines at a predictable and constant rate. For example, among the 13,000 new products introduced by 700 companies surveyed by Booz, Allen, and Hamilton between 1976 and 1981, the experience effect yielded a 71 percent cost curve. At each doubling of the number of new products introduced, the cost of each introduction declined by 29 percent.[19]

Product Improvement/ Modification

An existing product may reach a stage that requires that something be done to keep it viable. The product may have reached the maturity stage of the product life cycle because of shifts in the environment and thus has ceased to provide an adequate return. Or product, pricing, distribution, and promotion strategies employed by competitors may have reduced the product to the me-too category. At this stage, management has two options: either eliminate the product or revitalize it by making improvements or modifications. Improvements or modifications are achieved by redesigning, remodeling, or reformulating the product so that it satisfies customer needs more fully. This strategy seeks not only to restore the health of the product but sometimes seeks to help distinguish it from competitors' products as well. For example, it has become fashionable these days to target an upscale, or premium, version of a product at the upper end of the price performance pyramid.[20] *Fortune's* description of Kodak's strategy is relevant here:

> On the one hand, the longer a particular generation of cameras can be sold, the more profitable it will become. On the other hand, amateur photographers tend to use less film as their cameras age and lose their novelty; hence, it is critical that Kodak keep the camera population eternally young by bringing on new generations from time to time. In each successive generation, Kodak tries to increase convenience and reliability in order to encourage even greater film consumption per camera—a high "burn rate," as the company calls it. In general, the idea is to introduce as few major new models as possible while ringing in frequent minor changes powerful enough to stimulate new purchases.
>
> Kodak has become a master of this marketing strategy. Amateur film sales took off with a rush after 1963. That year the company brought out the first cartridge-loading, easy-to-use instamatic, which converted many people to photography and doubled film usage per camera. A succession of new features and variously priced models followed to help stimulate film consumption for a decade. Then Kodak introduced the pocket instamatic, which once again boosted film use both because of its novelty and because of its convenience. Seven models of that generation have since appeared.[21]

Kodak's strategy points out that it is never enough just to introduce a new product. The real payoff comes if the product is managed in such a way that it continues to flourish year after year in a changing and competitive marketplace.

In the 1990s, the company continued to pursue the strategy with yet another new product, the throwaway camera. Fun, cheap, and easy to use are the features that have turned the disposable camera (basically a roll of film with a cheap plastic case and lens) into a substantial business. In 1992, the sales at retail reached over $200 million with Kodak holding over 65% of the market.[22]

There is no magic formula for restoring the health of a product. Occasionally, it is the ingenuity of the manager that may bring to light a desired cure. Generally, however, a complete review of the product from marketing perspectives is needed to analyze underlying causes and to come up with the modifications and improvements necessary to restore the product to health. For example, General Mills continues to realize greater profits by rejuvenating its old products—cake mixes, Cheerios, and Hamburger Helper. The company successfully builds excitement for old products better than anyone else in the food business by periodically improving them. Compared with Kellogg, which tends not to fiddle with its core products, General Mills takes much greater risks with established brands. For instance, the company introduced two varieties of Cheerios—Honey Nut in 1979 and Apple Cinnamon in 1988—and successfully created a megabrand.[23]

To identify options for restoring a damaged product to health, it may be necessary to tear down competing products and make detailed comparative analyses of quality and price. One framework for such an analysis is illustrated in Exhibit 14-2.

The basic premise of Exhibit 14-2 is that by comparing its product with that of its competitors, a company is able to identify unique product strengths on which to pursue modifications and improvements. The use of the analysis suggested by Exhibit 14-2 may be illustrated with reference to a Japanese manufacturer. In 1978, Japan's amateur color film market was dominated by Kodak, Fuji, and Sakura, the last two being Japanese companies. For the previous 15 years, Fuji had been gaining market share, whereas Sakura, the market leader in the early 1950s with over half the market, was losing ground to both its competitors. By 1976, Sakura had only about a 16 percent market share. Marketing research showed that, more than anything else, Sakura was the victim of an unfortunate word association. Its name in Japanese means "cherry blossom," suggesting a soft, blurry, pinkish image. The name Fuji, however, was associated with the blue skies and white snow of Japan's sacred mountain. Being in no position to change perceptions, the company decided to analyze the market from structural, economic, and customer points of view. Sakura found a growing cost consciousness among film customers: to wit, amateur photographers commonly left one or two frames unexposed in a 36-exposure roll, but they almost invariably tried to squeeze extra exposures onto 20-exposure rolls. Here Sakura saw an opportunity. It decided to introduce a 24-exposure film. Its marginal costs would be trivial, but its big competitors would face significant penalties in following suit. Sakura was

EXHIBIT 14-2
Product-Change Options after Competitive Teardown

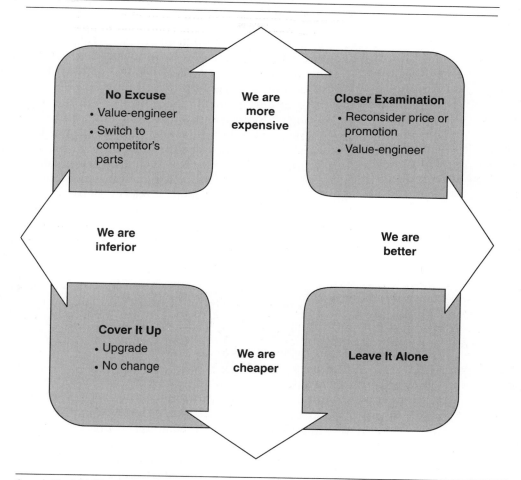

Source: Kenichi Ohmae, "Effective Strategies for Competitive Success", *McKinsey Quarterly*, (Winter 1978): 57. Reprinted by permission of the publisher.

prepared to cut its price if the competition lowered the price of their 20-frame rolls. Its aim was twofold. First, it would exploit the growing number of cost-minded users. Second, and more important, it would be drawing attention to the issue of economics, where it had a relative advantage, and away from the image issue, where it could not win. Sakura's strategy paid off. Its market share increased from 16 percent to more than 30 percent.[24] Overall, the product-improvement strategy is conducive to achieving growth, market share, and profitability alike.

Product Imitation | Not all companies like to be first in the market with a new product. Some let others take the initiative. If the innovation is successful, they ride the bandwagon of the successful innovation by imitating it. In the case of innovations protected by patents, imitators must wait until patents expire. In the absence of a patent, however, the imitators work diligently to design and produce products not very different from the innovator's product to compete vigorously with the innovator.

The imitation strategy can be justified in that it transfers the risk of introducing an unproven idea/product to someone else. It also saves investment in research and development. This strategy particularly suits companies with limited resources. Many companies, as a matter of fact, develop such talent that they can imitate any product, no matter how complicated. With a limited investment in research and development, the imitator may sometimes have a lower cost, giving it a price advantage in the market over the leader.

Another important reason for pursuing an imitation strategy may be to gainfully transfer the special talent a company may have for one product to other similar products. For example, the Bic Pen Corporation decided to enter the razor business because it thought it could successfully use its aggressive marketing posture in that market. In the early 1970s, Hanes Corporation gained resounding success with L'eggs, an inexpensive pantyhose that it sold from freestanding racks in food and drugstore outlets.

The imitation strategy may also be adopted on defensive grounds. Being sure of its existing product(s), a company may initially ignore new developments in the field. If new developments become overbearing, however, they may cut into the share held by an existing product. In this situation, a company may be forced to imitate the new development as a matter of survival. Colorado's Adolph Coors Company conveniently ignored the introduction of light beer and dismissed Miller Lite as a fad. Many years later, however, the company was getting bludgeoned by Miller Lite. Also, Anheuser-Busch began to challenge the supremacy of Coors in the California market with its light beer. The matter became so serious that Coors decided to abandon its one-product tradition and introduced a low-calorie light beer.

Another example of product imitation is provided by Anheuser-Busch. It took direct aim at Miller Brewing Company's Miller Genuine Draft by using similar market imagery to introduce Michelob Golden Draft. The new Michelob came in clear bottles like Genuine Draft and had a similar black and gold label. It was claimed to be cold filtered like the Genuine Draft.

Imitation also works well for companies that want to enter new markets without resorting to expensive acquisitions or special new-product development programs. For example, Owens-Illinois adapted heavy-duty laboratory glassware into novelty drinking glasses for home use.

Although imitation does avoid the risks involved in innovation, it is wrong to assume that every imitation of a successful product will succeed. The marketing program of an imitation should be as carefully chalked out and implemented as that of an innovation. Imitation strategy is most useful for achieving increases in market share and growth.

Product Innovation | Product-innovation strategy includes <u>introducing a new product to replace</u> an <u>existing product</u> in order to satisfy a need in an <u>entirely different</u> way or to provide a new approach to satisfy an existing or latent need. This strategy suggests that the entrant is the first firm to develop and introduce the product. The ballpoint pen is an example of a new product; it replaced the fountain pen. The VCR was a new product introduced to answer home entertainment needs.

Product innovation is an important characteristic of U.S. industry. Year after year companies spend billions of dollars on research and development to innovate. In 1993, for example, American industry spent about $83.5 billion on research and development. Research and development expenditures are expected to continue rising at an average of 10 percent annually throughout the rest of the 1990s.[25] This shows that industry takes a purposeful attitude toward new-product and new-process development.

Product innovation, however, does not come easy. Besides involving major financial commitments, it requires heavy doses of managerial time to cut across organizational lines. And still the innovation may fail to make a mark in the market. A number of companies have discovered the risks of this game. Among them is Texas Instruments, which lost $660 million before withdrawing from the home computer market. RCA lost $500 million on ill-fated videodisc players. RCA, GE, and Sylvania, leaders in vacuum-tube technology, lost out when transistor technology revolutionized the radio business. RJR Nabisco abandoned the "smokeless" cigarette, Premier, after a 10-year struggle and after spending over $500 million.[26]

Most innovative products are produced by large organizations. Initially, an individual or a group of individuals may be behind it, but a stage is eventually reached where individual efforts require corporate support to finally develop and launch the product. To encourage innovation and creativity, many large companies are spinning off companies. For example, Colgate-Palmolive Co. launched Colgate Venture Co. to support entrepreneurship and risk taking. In this way, a congenial environment within the large corporation is maintained for generating and following creative pursuits.[27]

In essence, innovation flourishes where divisions are kept small (permitting better interaction among managers and staffers), where there is willingness to tolerate failure (encouraging plenty of experimentation and risk taking), where champions are motivated (through encouragement, salaries, and promotions), where close liaison is maintained with the customer (visiting customers routinely; inviting them to brainstorm product ideas), where technology is shared corporate wide (technology, wherever it is developed, belongs to everyone), and where projects are sustained, even if initial results are discouraging.

The development of a product innovation typically passes through various stages: idea generation, screening, business analysis, development of a prototype, test market, and commercialization. The idea may emerge from different sources: customers, private researchers, university researchers, employees, or research labs. An idea may be generated by recognizing a consumer need or just by pursuing a scientific endeavor, hoping that it may lead to a viable product.

Companies follow different procedures to screen ideas and to choose a few for further study. If an idea appears promising, it may be carried to the stage of business analysis, which may consist of investment requirements, revenue and expenditure projections, and financial analysis of return on investment, pay-back period, and cash flow. Thereafter, a few prototype products may be produced to examine engineering and manufacturing aspects of the product. A few sample products based on the prototype may be produced for market testing. After changes suggested in market testing have been incorporated, the innovation may be commercially launched.

Procter & Gamble's development of Pringles is a classic case of recognizing a need in a consumer market and then painstakingly hammering away to meet it.[28] Americans consume about one billion dollars' worth of potato chips annually, but manufacturers of potato chips face a variety of problems. Chips made in the traditional way are so fragile that they can rarely be shipped for more than 200 miles; even then, a quarter of the chips get broken. They also spoil quickly; their shelf life is barely two months. These characteristics have kept potato chip manufacturers split into many small regional operations. Nobody, before Procter & Gamble, had applied much technology to the product since it was invented in 1853.

Procter & Gamble knew these problems because it sold edible oils to the potato chip industry, and it set out to solve them. Instead of slicing potatoes and frying them in the traditional way, Procter & Gamble's engineers developed a process somewhat akin to paper making. They dehydrated and mashed potatoes and pressed them for frying into a precise shape, which permitted the chips to be stacked neatly on top of one another in hermetically sealed containers that resemble tennis ball cans. Pringles potato chips stay whole and have a shelf life of at least a year.

After a new product is screened through the lab, the division that will manufacture it takes over and finances all further development and testing. In some companies, division managers show little interest in taking on new products because the costs of introduction are heavy and hold down short-term profits. At Procter & Gamble, executives ensure that a manager's short-term record is not marred by the cost of a new introduction.

Before a new Procter & Gamble product is actually introduced to the market, it must prove that it has a demonstrable margin of superiority over its prospective competitors. A development team begins refining the product by trying variations of the basic formula, testing its performance under almost any conceivable condition, and altering its appearance. Eventually, a few alternative versions of the product are produced and tested among a large number of Procter & Gamble employees. If the product gets the approval of employees, the company presents it to panels of consumers for further testing. Procter & Gamble feels satisfied if a proposed product is chosen by fifty-five out of one hundred consumers tested. Though Pringles potato chips passed all these tests, they only recently started showing any profits for Procter & Gamble.

There is hardly any doubt that, if an innovation is successful, it pays off lavishly. For example, nylon still makes so much money for Du Pont that the company would qualify for the Fortune 500 list even if it made nothing else.[29] However, developing a new product is a high-risk strategy requiring heavy commitment and having a low probability of achieving a breakthrough. Thus, the choice of this strategy should be dictated by a company's financial and managerial strengths and by its willingness to take risks. Consider the case of Kevlar, a super-tough fiber (lightweight but five times stronger than steel) invented by Du Pont. It took the company 25 years and $900 million to come out with this product, more time and money than the company had ever spent on a single product. Starting in 1985, however, the payoff began: annual sales reached $300 million. Du Pont forecasts Kevlar's annual sales growth at 10 percent during the 1990s. Meanwhile, the company continues its quest for new applications that it hopes will make Kevlar a blockbuster.[30]

Exhibit 14-3 suggests an approach that may be used to manage innovations successfully. As a company grows more complex and decentralized, its new-product development efforts may fail to keep pace with change, weakening vital lines between marketing and technical people and leaving key decisions to be made by default. The possible result is the ultimate loss of competitive edge. To solve the problem, as shown in Exhibit 14-3a, both technical and market opportunity may be plotted on a grid. From this grid, innovations may be grouped into three classes: heavy emphasis (deserving full support, including basic research and development); selective opportunistic development (i.e., may be good or may be bad; may require a careful approach and top management attention); and limited defense support (i.e., merits only minimum support). Exhibit 14-3b lists the relevant kinds of programs for each area. This approach helps gear research efforts to priority strategic projects.

DIVERSIFICATION STRATEGY

Diversification refers to seeking unfamiliar products or markets or both in the pursuit of growth. Every company is best at certain products; diversification requires substantially different knowledge, thinking, skills, and processes. Thus, diversification is at best a risky strategy, and a company should choose this path only when current product/market orientation does not seem to provide further opportunities for growth. A few examples will illustrate the point that diversification does not automatically bring success. CNA Financial Corporation faced catastrophe when it expanded the scope of its business from insurance to real estate and mutual funds: it ended up being acquired by Loews Corporation. Schrafft's restaurants did little for Pet Incorporated. Pacific Southwest Airlines acquired rental cars and hotels, only to see its stock decline quickly. Diversification into the wine business (by acquiring Taylor Wines) did not work for the Coca-Cola Company.[31]

The diversification decision is a major step that must be taken carefully. On the basis of a sample from 200 Fortune 500 firms and the PIMS database (see Chapter 12), Biggadike notes that it takes an average of 10 to 12 years before the return on investment from diversification equals that of mature businesses.[32]

EXHIBIT 14-3
Managing Innovations

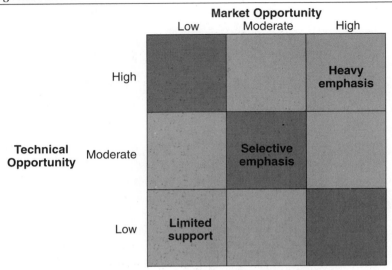

(a) The R&D Effort Portfolio

R&D Program Elements						
R&D Emphasis	*Primary Level of Funding*	*Focus of Work*	*Level of Basic Research*	*Technical Risk*	*Acceptable Time for Payoff*	*Projects to Exceed or Maintain Competitive Parity*
Heavy	High	Balance between new and existing products	High	High	Long	Many
Selective	Medium	Mainly existing products	Low	Medium	Medium	Few
Limited	Low	Existing processes	Very low	Low	Short	Very few

(b) Implied Nature of R&D Effort

Source: Richard N. Foster, "Linking R&D to Strategy," *Business Horizons,* December 1980. Copyright 1980, by the Foundation for the School of Business at Indiana University. Reprinted by permission.

The term *diversification* must be distinguished from integration and merger. *Integration* refers to the accumulation of additional business in a field through participation in more of the stages between raw materials and the ultimate market or through more intensive coverage of a single stage. *Merger* implies a combination of corporate entities that may or may not result in integration. Diversification is a strategic alternative that implies deriving revenues and profits from different products and markets. The following factors usually lead companies to seek diversification:

1. Firms diversify when their objectives can no longer be met within the product/market scope defined by expansion.
2. A firm may diversify because retained cash exceeds total expansion needs.
3. A firm may diversify when diversification opportunities promise greater profitability than expansion opportunities.
4. Firms may continue to explore diversification when the available information is not reliable enough to permit a conclusive comparison between expansion and diversification.

Diversification can take place at either the corporate or the business unit level. At the corporate level, it typically entails entering a promising business outside the scope of existing business units. At the business unit level, it is most likely to involve expanding into a new segment of the industry in which the business presently participates. The problems encountered at both levels are similar and may differ only in magnitude.

Diversification strategies include internal development of new products or markets (including development of international markets for current products), acquisition of an appropriate firm or firms, a strategic alliance with a complementary organization, licensing of new product technologies, and importing or distributing a line of products manufactured by another company. The final choice of an entry strategy involves a combination of these alternatives in most cases. This combination is determined on the basis of available opportunities and of consistency with the company's objectives and available resources.

Caterpillar Tractor Company's entry into the field of diesel engines is a case of internal diversification. Since 1972, the company has poured more than $1 billion into developing new diesel engines "in what must rank as one of the largest internal diversifications by a U.S. corporation."[33] Hershey Foods ventured into the restaurant business by buying the Friendly Ice Cream Corporation, illustrating diversification by acquisition. Hershey adopted the diversification strategy for growth because its traditional business, chocolate and candy, was stagnant because of a decline in candy consumption, sharp increases in cocoa prices, and changes in customer habits. Hershey subsequently sold Friendly in 1988 to a private company, Tennessee Restaurant Co.[34]

An empirical study of entry strategy shows that higher barriers are more likely to be associated with acquisition than with entry through internal development. Thus, in choosing between these two entry modes, business unit managers should take into account, among other factors, the entry barriers surrounding the market and the cost of breaching them. Despite high apparent barriers, the entrant's relatedness to the new entry may make entry financially more desirable.[35]

Essentially, there are three different forms of diversification a company may pursue: concentric diversification, horizontal diversification, and conglomerate diversification. No matter what kind of diversification a company seeks, the three essential tests of success are

1. **The attractiveness test**—The industries chosen for diversification must be structurally attractive or capable of being made attractive.

2. **The cost-of-entry test**—The cost of entry must not capitalize all future profits.
3. **The better-off test**—The new unit must either gain competitive advantage from its link with the corporation or vice versa.[36]

Concentric Diversification

Concentric diversification bears a close synergistic relationship to either the company's marketing or its technology, or both. Thus, new products that are introduced share a common thread with the firm's existing products, either through marketing or production. Usually, the new products are directed to a new group of customers. Texas Instrument's venture into pocket calculators illustrates this type of diversification. Using its expertise in integrated circuits, the company developed a new product that appealed to a new set of customers. On the other hand, PepsiCo's venture into the fast-food business through the acquisition of Pizza Hut is a case of concentric diversification in which the new product bears a synergistic relationship to the company's existing marketing experience.

Toys "R" Us branched into children's clothing on the ground that its marketing as well as technological skills (purchasing power, brand name, storage facilities, retail outlets, and sophisticated information systems) would give it an edge in the new business. Similar logic persuaded Honda to diversify from motorcycles to lawn mowers and cars; and Black & Decker from power tools to home appliances.[37]

Although a diversification move per se is risky, concentric diversification does not lead a company into an entirely new world because in one of two major fields (technology or marketing), the company will operate in familiar territory. The relationship of the new product to the firm's existing product(s), however, may or may not mean much. All that the realization of synergy does is make the task easier; it does not necessarily make it successful. For example, Gillette entered the market for pocket calculators in 1974 and for digital watches in 1976. Later it abandoned both businesses. Both pocket calculators and digital watches were sold to mass markets where Gillette had expertise and experience. Despite this marketing synergy, it failed to sell either calculators or digital watches successfully. Gillette found that these lines of business called for strategies totally different from those it followed in selling its existing products.[38] Two lessons can be drawn from Gillette's experience. One, there may be other strategic reasons for successfully launching a new product in the market besides commonality of markets or technology. Two, the commonality should be analyzed in breadth and depth before drawing conclusions about the transferability of current strengths to the new product.

Philip Morris's acquisition of Miller Brewing Company illustrates how a company may achieve marketing synergies through concentric diversification. Cigarettes and beer are distributed through many of the same retail outlets, and Philip Morris had been dealing with them for years. In addition, both products serve hedonistic consumer markets. Small wonder, therefore, that the marketing research techniques and emotional promotion appeals of cigarette merchandising worked equally well for beer. Miller moved from seventh to second place in the beer industry in the short span of six years.

Horizontal
Diversification

Horizontal diversification refers to new products that technologically are unrelated to a company's existing products but that can be sold to the same group of customers to whom existing products are sold. A classic case of this form of diversification is Procter & Gamble's entry into potato chips (Pringles), toothpaste (Crest and Gleem), coffee (Folgers), and orange juice (Citrus Hill). Traditionally a soap company, Procter & Gamble diversified into these products, which were aimed at the same customers who bought soap. Similarly, Maytag's entry into the medium-priced mass market to sell refrigerators and ranges, in addition to selling its traditional line of premium-priced dishwashers, washers, and dryers, is a form of horizontal diversification.

Note that in the case of concentric diversification, the new product may have certain common ties with the marketing of a company's existing product except that it is sold to a new set of customers. In horizontal diversification, by contrast, the customers for the new product are drawn from the same ranks as those for an existing product.

Other things being equal, in a competitive environment horizontal diversification is more desirable if present customers are favorably disposed toward the company and if one can expect this loyalty to carry over to the new product; in the long run, however, a new product must stand on its own. For example, if product quality is lacking, if promotion is not effective, or if the price is not right, a new product will flop despite customer loyalty to the company's other products. Thus, while Crest and Folgers made it for Procter & Gamble, Citrus Hill has been struggling, and Pringles has been disappointing, even though all these products are sold to the same "loyal" customers. In other words, horizontal diversification should not be regarded as a route to success in all cases. An important limitation of horizontal diversification is that the new product is introduced and marketed in the same economic environment as the existing products, which can lead to rigidity and instability. Stated differently, horizontal diversification tends to increase the company's dependence on a few market segments.

Conglomerate
Diversification

In conglomerate diversification, the new product bears no relationship to either the marketing or the technology of the existing product(s). In other words, through conglomerate diversification, a company launches itself into an entirely new product/market arena. ITT's ventures into bakery products (Continental Baking Company), insurance (Hartford Insurance Group), car rentals (Avis Rent-A-Car System, Inc.), and the hotel business (Sheraton Corporation) illustrate the implementation of conglomerate diversification. (ITT divested its car rental business a few years ago.)

Dover Corp. provides another example of conglomerate diversification. The company with annual sales of over $3 billion is a manufacturer with 54 operating companies engaged in more than 70 diverse businesses, from elevators and garbage trucks to valves and welding torches.[39]

It is necessary to remember here that companies do not flirt with unknown products in unknown markets without having some hidden strengths to handle conglomerate diversification. For example, the managerial style required for a new product to prosper may be just the same as the style the company already has. Thus, managerial style becomes the basis of synergy between the new product and an existing product. By the same token, another single element may serve as a dominant factor in making a business attractive for diversification.

Inasmuch as conglomerate diversification does not bear an obvious relationship to a company's existing business, there is some question as to why companies adopt it. There are two major advantages of conglomerate diversification. One, it can improve the profitability and flexibility of a firm by venturing into businesses that have better economic prospects than those of the firm's existing businesses. Two, a conglomerate firm, because of its size, gets a better reception in capital markets.

Overall, this type of diversification, if successful, has the potential of providing increased growth and profitability.

VALUE-MARKETING STRATEGY

In the 1990s, *value* has become the marketer's watchword. Today, customers are demanding something different than they did in the 1980s. They want the right combination of product quality, good service, and timely delivery. These are the keys to performing well in the next decade. It is for this reason that we examine this new strategic focus.

Value marketing strategy stresses real product performance and delivering on promises. Value marketing doesn't mean high quality if it is only available at ever-higher prices. It doesn't necessarily mean cheap, if cheap means bare bones or low-grade. It doesn't mean high prestige, if the prestige is viewed as snobbish or self-indulgent. At the same time, value is not about positioning and image mongering. It simply means providing a product that works as claimed, is accompanied by decent service, and is delivered on time.

The emphasis on value is part atmospherics, part economics, and part demographics. Consumers are repudiating the wretched excesses of the 1980s and are searching for more traditional rewards of home and family. They are concerned about the seemingly nonending economic ups and down. The growing focus on value also stems from profound changes in the American consumer marketplace.

For example, real income growth for families got a boost when women entered the work force. But now, with many women already working and many baby boomers assuming new family responsibilities, the growth in disposable income is scarily slow. Aging baby boomers whose debt burden is already high realize that they must worry about their children's college tuitions and their own retirement. At the same time, the new generation of consumers is both savvier and more cynical than were its predecessors. Briefly, consumers want products that perform, sold by advertising that informs. They are concerned about intrinsic value, not simply buying to impress others.

Quality Strategy   Traditionally, quality has been viewed as a manufacturing concern. Strategically, however, the idea of total quality is perceived in the market; that is, quality must exude from the offering itself and from all the services that come with it. The important point is that quality perspectives should be based on customer preferences, not on internal evaluations. The ultimate objective of quality should be to delight the customer in every way possible, providing levels of service, product quality, product performance, and support that are beyond his/her expectations. Ultimately, quality may mean striving for excellence throughout the entire organization.[40] For assessing perceived quality, the step-by-step procedure used by the Strategic Planning Institute may be followed:

1. A meeting is held, in which a multifunctional team of managers and staff specialists identify the non-price product and service attributes that affect customer buying decisions. For an office equipment product, these might include durability, maintenance costs, flexibility, credit terms, and appearance.

2. The team is then asked to assign "importance weights" for each attribute representing their relative decisions. These relative importance weights sum to 100. (For markets in which there are important segments with different importance weights, separate weights are assigned to each segment.)

3. The management team creates its business unit's product line, and those of leading competitors, on each of the performance dimensions identified in Step 1. From these attribute-by-attribute ratings, each weighted by its respective importance weight, an overall relative quality score is constructed.

4. The overall relative quality score and other measures of competitive position (relative price and market share) and financial performance (ROI, ROS, and ROE) are validated against benchmarks based on the experience of "look-alike" businesses in similar strategic positions in order to check the internal consistency of strategic and financial data and confirm the business and market definition.

5. Finally, the management team tests its plans and budgets for reality, develops a blueprint for improving market perceived quality, relative to competitors', and calibrates the financial payoff.

   In many cases, the judgmental ratings assigned by the management team are tested (and, when appropriate, modified) by collecting ratings from customers via field interviews.[41]

This approach to assessing relative quality is similar to the multiattribute methods used in marketing research. These research methods are, however, employed primarily for evaluating or comparing individual products (actual or prospective), whereas the scores here apply to a business unit's entire product line.

Attaining adequate levels of excellence and customer satisfaction often requires significant cultural change; that is, change in decision-making processes, interfunctional relationships, and the attitudes of each member of the company. In other words, achieving total quality objectives requires teamwork and cooperation. People are encouraged and rewarded for doing their jobs right the first time rather than for their success in resolving crises. People are empowered to make decisions and instilled with the feeling that quality is everyone's responsibility.

The following are the keys to success in achieving world-class total quality. First, the program requires unequivocal support of top management. The second key to success is understanding customer need. The third key is to fix the business process, if there are gaps in meeting customer needs. The fourth key is to compress cycle time to avoid bureaucratic hassles and delays. The next is empowering people so that they are able to exert their best talents. Further, measurement and reward systems must be reassessed and revamped to recognize people. Finally, the total quality program should be a continuous concern, a constant focus on identifying and eliminating waste and inefficiency throughout the organization.

Organizationally, the single most important aspect of implementing a quality strategy is to maintain a close liaison with the customer. Honda's experience in this matter in designing the new Accord is noteworthy:

> When Honda's engineers began to design the third-generation (or 1986) Accord in the early 1980s, they did not start with a sketch of a car. The engineers started with a concept—"man maximum, machine minimum" that captured in a short, evocative phrase the way they wanted customers to feel about the car. The concept and the car have been remarkably successful: since 1982, the Accord has been one of the best-selling cars in the United States; in 1989, it was the top-selling car. Yet when it was time to design the 1990 Accord, Honda listened to the market, not to its own success. Market trends were indicating a shift away from sporty sedans toward family models. To satisfy future customers' expectations and to reposition the Accord, moving it up-market just a bit, the 1990 model would have to send a new set of product messages—"an adult sense of reliability." The ideal family car would allow the driver to transport family and friends with confidence, whatever the weather or road conditions; passengers would always feel safe and secure.
>
> This message was still too abstract to guide the engineers who would later be making concrete choices about the new Accord's specifications, parts, and manufacturing processes. So the next step was finding an image that would personify the car's message to consumers. The image that managers emerged with was "a rugby player in a business suit." It evoked rugged, physical contact, sportsmanship, and gentlemanly behavior—disparate qualities the new car would have to convey. The image was also concrete enough to translate clearly into design details. The decision to replace the old Accord's retractable head lamps with headlights made with a pioneering technology developed by Honda's supplier, Stanley, is a good example. To the designers and engineers, the new lights' totally transparent cover glass symbolized the will of a rugby player looking into the future calmly, with clear eyes.
>
> The next and last step in creating the Accord's product concept was to break down the rugby player image into specific attributes the new car would have to possess. Five sets of key words captured what the product leader envisioned: "open minded," "friendly communication," "tough spirit," "stress-free," and "love forever." Individually and as a whole, these key words reinforced the car's message to consumers. "Tough spirit" in the car, for example, meant maneuverability, power, and sure handling in extreme driving conditions, while "love forever" translated into long-term reliability and customer satisfaction. Throughout the course of the project, these phrases provided a kind of shorthand to help people make coherent design and hardware choices in the face of competing demands.[42]

There are three generic approaches to improving quality performance: catching up, pulling ahead, and leapfrogging.[43] Catching up involves restoring those aspects about which the firm has been behind to standard. Catching up is a defensive strategy where the emphasis is either to be as good as the competition or to barely meet market requirements. Pulling ahead, going further than the customer asks or achieving superiority over the competition, provides a firm competitive advantage that may lead to greater profitability. Thus, it makes sense to resist the temptation to focus on just catching up and to find a way to make a sustainable move to pull ahead. Finally, leapfrogging involves negating competitive disadvantage, that is, creating a sustainable competitive advantage through differentiation. In other words, leapfrogging comprises coming from behind and getting ahead of the competition through providing a quality product in keeping with customer demands. For example, by leapfrogging Detroit on several key attributes, Japanese companies rolled further up the "quality-for-price curve"; that is, they shifted into better value positions.

Several benefits accrue to businesses that offer superior perceived quality, including stronger customer loyalty, more repeat purchases, less vulnerability to price wars, ability to command higher relative price without affecting share, lower marketing costs, and share improvements.

Customer-Service Strategy

Customer service has come to occupy an important place in today's competitive market. Invariably, customers want personal service, the kind of service delivered by live bodies behind a sales counter, a human voice at the other end of a telephone, or people in the teller's cage at the bank. Paying attention to the customer is not a new concept. In the 1950s, General Motors went all the way toward consumer satisfaction by designing cars for every lifestyle and pocketbook, a breakthrough for an industry that had been largely driven by production needs ever since Henry Ford promised to deliver any color car as long as it was black. General Motors rode its insights into customers' needs to a 52 percent share of the U.S. car market in 1962.[44] But with a booming economy, a rising population, and virtually no foreign competition, many U.S. companies had it too easy. Through the 1960s and into the 1970s, many U.S. car makers could sell just about anything they could produce. With customers seemingly satisfied, management concentrated on cutting production costs and making splashy acquisitions. To manage these growing behemoths, CEOs turned to strategic planning, which focused on winning market share, not on getting in touch with remote customers. Markets came to be defined as aggregations of competitors, not as customers.

In recent times, Japanese companies were the first to recognize a problem. They started to rescue customers from the limbo of so-so merchandise and take-it-or-leave-it service. They built loyalty among U.S. car buyers by assiduously uncovering and accommodating customer needs. The growing influence of Japanese firms as well as demographics and hard economic times have forced American companies to realize the need to listen to customers.

Creative changes in service can make the difference. For example, companies offering better service can charge 10 percent more for their products than competitors.[45] Even smaller companies with fewer management layers are finding that personal relationships between senior executives and customers can help in various ways. Many companies attach so much importance to service that they require their senior managers to put in time at the front lines. For example, Xerox requires that its executives spend one day a month taking complaints from customers about machines, bills, and service. Similarly, at Hyatt Hotels, senior executives put in time as bellhops.[46]

Briefly, a company must decide who it wants to serve, discover what those customers want, and set a strategy that single-mindedly provides that service to those customers. With such clearly articulated goals, top management can give front line employees responsibility for responding instantly to customer needs in those crucial moments that determine the company's success or failure. The following episode, which underlines Scandinavian Airlines' emphasis on service, shows how far a company can go to stand by the customer.

> Rudy Peterson was an American businessman staying at the Grand Hotel in Stockholm. Arriving at Stockholm's Arlanda airport for an important day trip with a colleague to Copenhagen on a Scandinavian Airlines (SAS) flight, he realized he'd left his ticket in his hotel room.
>
> Everyone knows you can't board an airplane without a ticket, so Rudy Peterson resigned himself to missing the flight and his business meeting in Copenhagen. But when he explained his dilemma to the ticket agent, he got a pleasant surprise. "Don't worry, Mr. Peterson," she said with a smile. "Here's your boarding card. I'll insert a temporary ticket in here. If you just tell me your room number at the Grand Hotel and your destination in Copenhagen, I'll take care of the rest."
>
> While Rudy and his colleague waited in the passenger lounge, the ticket agent dialed the hotel. A bellhop checked the room and found the ticket. The ticket agent then sent an SAS limo to retrieve it from the hotel and bring it directly to her. They moved so quickly that the ticket arrived before the Copenhagen flight departed. No one was more surprised than Rudy Peterson when the flight attendant approached him and said calmly, "Mr. Peterson? Here's your ticket."
>
> What would have happened at a more traditional airline? Most airline manuals are clear: "No ticket, no flight." At best, the ticket agent would have informed her supervisor of the problem, but Rudy Peterson almost certainly would have missed his flight. Instead, because of the way SAS handled his situation, he was both impressed and on time for his meeting.[47]

The SAS experience shows how far a business must be willing to go to become a truly customer-driven company, a company that recognizes that its only true assets are satisfied customers, all of whom expect to be treated as individuals.

Many firms argue that service by definition is difficult to guarantee. Services are generally delivered by human beings, who are less predictable than machines. Services are also usually produced at the same time that they are consumed. Although there can be exceptions to the rule, service can be guaranteed in any field. Consider the guarantee offered by "Bugs" Burger Bug Killers (BBBK), a Miami-based pest extermination company, a division of S.C. Johnson and Sons:

> Most of BBBK's competitors claim that they will reduce pests to "acceptable levels"; BBBK promises to eliminate them entirely. Its service guarantee to hotel and restaurant clients promises:
> - You don't owe one penny until all pests on your premises have been eradicated.

- If you are ever dissatisfied with BBBK's service, you will receive a refund for up to 12 months of the company's services plus fees for another exterminator of your choice for the next year.
- If a guest spots a pest on your premises, BBBK will pay for the guest's meal or room, send a letter of apology, and pay for a future meal or stay.
- If your facility is closed down due to the presence of roaches or rodents, BBBK will pay any fines, as well as all lost profits, plus $5,000. In short, BBBK says, "If we don't satisfy you 100%, we don't take your money."[48]

The company's service program has been extremely successful. It charges up to 10 times more than its competitors and yet has a disproportionately high market share in its operating areas.

In designing a good service program, a company should be conversant with a number of important trends. First, customers don't read (e.g., customers don't read assembly and operation instructions). Second, customers don't understand ownership responsibilities (e.g., some hotels require customers to program their own wake-up calls into a confusing computerized system). Third, high technology and product complexity make product differentiation difficult (i.e., with like products, better service can become an important differentiating factor). Fourth, consumers have lower confidence and expectations for products and services (i.e., customer service can have an enormous impact on consumer confidence). Fifth, high-quality service has become a product attribute (i.e., consumers rate qualitative service factors as more important than product cost and features). Sixth, consumer attention is drawn to negative publicity (i.e., negative word of mouth is extremely detrimental). Seventh, consumers believe they are not getting their money's worth.

Improved customer service can play a major role in changing customer perceptions about a product and its value and can directly affect a company's success and profitability. The quality of service a company provides depends largely on people, not only those with direct customer responsibility but also with managers, supervisors, and support staff. Thus, success in providing adequate service largely depends on preparing employees for it.

Time-Based Strategy

When a product market changes quickly, companies must respond quickly if they want to preserve their positions. In today's changing markets, time-based strategy that aims to beat the competition has assumed new dimensions.

GE has cut the time to deliver a custom-made industrial circuit breaker box from three weeks to three days. In the past, AT&T needed two years to design a new phone; now it needs only one year. Motorola used to take three weeks to turn out electronic pagers after the factory received the order; now it takes two hours.[49]

Time-based strategy brings about important competitive benefits. Market share grows because customers love getting their orders now. Inventories of finished goods shrink because they are not necessary to ensure quick delivery; the fastest manufacturers can make and ship an order the day it is received. For this and other reasons, costs fall. Many employees become satisfied because they are working for a more responsive, more successful company and because speeding operations requires giving them more flexibility and responsibility. Quality also improves. Briefly, doing it fast forces a firm to do it right the first time.

Speed can also pay off in product development even if it means going over budget by as much as 50 percent. For example, a model developed by McKinsey and Co. shows that high-tech products that come to market on budget but six months late earn 33 percent less profit over five years. In contrast, coming out 50 percent over budget but on time cuts profits only by 4 percent.[50]

To implement a time-based strategy, the entire production process must be redesigned for speed. GE's experience is relevant here. Its circuit breaker business was old and stagnant. Market growth was slow and Siemens and Westinghouse were strong competitors. GE assembled a team of manufacturing, design, and marketing experts to focus on overhauling the entire process. The goal was to cut the time between order and delivery from three weeks to three days. Six plants around the United States were producing circuit breaker boxes. The team consolidated production into one plant and automated its facilities. But the team did not automate operations as they were. In the old system, engineers custom-designed each box, a task that took about a week. Engineers chose from 28,000 unique parts to create a box. To set up an automated system to handle that many parts would have been a nightmare. The design team reduced the number of parts to 1,275, making most parts interchangeable. Even with this drastic reduction in parts, customers were still given 40,000 different sizes, shapes, and configurations from which to choose.

The team also devised a way to phase out the engineers, by replacing them with computers. Now a salesperson enters the specifications for a circuit breaker into a computer at GE's main office and the order flows to a computer at the plant, which automatically programs factory machines to custom-make the order with minimum waste.

Although these advances are indeed impressive, the team still had to conquer another source of delay—solving problems and making decisions on the factory floor. The solution was to eliminate all line supervisors and quality inspectors, reducing the organizational layers between worker and plant manager from three to one. Everything middle managers used to handle—vacation scheduling, quality, work rules—became the responsibility of the 129 workers on the floor, who were divided into teams of 15 to 20. It worked. The more responsibility GE gave the workers, the faster problems were solved and decisions were made.

The results: The plant that used to have a two-month backlog of orders now works with a two-day backlog. Productivity has increased 20 percent over the past year. Manufacturing costs have dropped 30 percent, or $5.5 million a year, and return on investment is running at over 20 percent. The speed of delivery for a higher-quality product with more features has shrunk from three weeks to three days. And GE is gaining share in a flat market.[51]

Another area ripe for time-based strategy is the administrative/approval area. According to the Thomas Group, a Dallas-based consulting firm specializing in speed, manufacturing typically takes only 5 to 20 percent of the total time that is needed to get an order for a given product to market; the rest is administrative.[52]

For example, at Adca Bank, a subsidiary of West Germany's Reebobank (with assets of $90 billion), an application for a loan used to go through numerous layers of bureaucracy. A branch would send a loan application to a loan officer at headquarters, who would look at it and change it. Then the loan officer's manager would look at the application and change it, and so on. The bank eventually got rid of five layers of management and gave officers in all branches more authority to make loans. It used to take 24 managers to approve a loan. Now it takes 12.

Teamwork seems to be the key ingredient among the fastest companies. Nearly all of them form multidepartment teams. AT&T formed teams of six to twelve members, including engineers, manufacturers, and marketers, with complete authority to make every decision about how a product would look, work, be made, and cost. At AT&T the key was setting rigid speed requirements, such as six weeks, and leaving the rest to the team. Teams could meet these strict deadlines because they did not need to send each decision up the line for approval. With this new approach, AT&T cut development time for its new 4200 phone from two years to just a year while lowering costs and increasing quality.

Application of time-based strategy to distribution is equally important. Even the world's fastest factory cannot provide much of a competitive advantage if everything it produces gets snagged in the distribution chain. For example, Benetton takes its distribution very seriously and has created an electronic loop that links sales agent, factory, and warehouse. If a saleswoman in one of Benetton's Los Angeles shops finds that she is starting to run out of a best-selling sweater, she calls one of Benetton's 80 sales agents, who enters the order in a personal computer, which sends it to a mainframe in Italy. The mainframe computer, which has all of the measurements for the sweater, sets the knitting machines in motion. Once the sweaters are finished, workers box them up and label the box with a bar code containing the Los Angeles address. The box then goes into the warehouse. The computer next sends a robot flying. The robot finds the box and any others going to Los Angeles, picks them up, and loads them onto a truck. Including manufacturing time, Benetton can get an order to Los Angeles in four weeks.

Implementation of time-based strategy requires a number of steps. First, start from scratch (set a time goal and revamp entire operations to meet this goal rather than simply improving efficiency in current operations). Second, wipe out approvals (i.e., cut down bureaucratic layers of control and let people make decisions on the spot). Third, emphasize teamwork (i.e., establish multidepartment teams to handle the work). Fourth, worship the schedule (i.e., nothing short of disaster should be a valid excuse for delay). Fifth, develop time-effective distribution (i.e., snags in distribution must be simultaneously worked out). Sixth, put speed in the culture (i.e., train people in the company at all levels to understand and appreciate the significance of speed).

The advantages of speed are undeniably impressive. Although it is a common precept that time is money, in practice, companies have paid only lip service to it. The time it took to do a job, whatever the amount, was considered a necessity to meet organizational requirements, systems, procedures, and hierarchical relationships. Now, however, there is a new realization that time saved is a strategic factor for gaining competitive advantage. Companies that grasp and appreciate the unprecedented advantages of getting new products to market sooner and orders to customers faster hold the key for achieving competitive preeminence in the 1990s and beyond.

SUMMARY

Product strategies reflect the mission of the business unit and the business it is in. Following the marketing concept, the choice of product strategy should bear a close relationship to the market strategy of the company. The various product strategies and the alternatives under each strategy that were discussed in this chapter are outlined below:

1. Product-positioning strategy
   a. Positioning a single brand
   b. Positioning multiple brands

2. Product-repositioning strategy
   a. Repositioning among existing customers
   b. Repositioning among new users
   c. Repositioning for new uses

3. Product-overlap strategy
   a. Competing brands
   b. Private labeling
   c. Dealing with original-equipment manufacturers (OEMs)

4. Product-scope strategy
   a. Single product
   b. Multiple products
   c. System of products

5. Product-design strategy
   a. Standard products
   b. Customized products
   c. Standard product with modifications

6. Product-elimination strategy
   a. Harvesting
   b. Line simplification
   c. Total-line divestment

7. New-product strategy
   a. Product improvement/modification
   b. Product imitation
   c. Product innovation

8. Diversification strategy
   a. Concentric diversification
   b. Horizontal diversification
   c. Conglomerate diversification

9. Value-marketing strategy
   a. Quality strategy
   b. Customer-service strategy
   c. Time-based strategy

The nature of different strategies was discussed, and their relevance for different types of companies was examined. Adaptations of different strategies in practice were illustrated with citations from published sources.

DISCUSSION QUESTIONS

1. Discuss how a business unit may avoid problems of cannibalism among competing brands.
2. Conceptualize how a lagging brand (assume a grocery product) may be repositioned for new uses.
3. What criteria may be employed to determine the viable position for a brand in the market?
4. What conditions justify a company's dealing in multiple products?
5. Are there reasons other than profitability for eliminating a product? Discuss.
6. What factors must be weighed to determine the viability of divesting an entire product line?
7. Under what circumstances is it desirable to adopt a product-imitation strategy?

NOTES

[1] Edward H. Kolcum, "Gould Will Use Same Market Strategy under Encore Ownership," *Aviation Week and Space Technology* (17 April 1989): 53.
[2] Theodore Levitt, "Marketing Success through Differentiation of Anything," *Harvard Business Review* (January–February 1980): 82.
[3] Christopher Knowlton, "How Disney Keeps the Magic Going," *Fortune* (4 December 1989): 11.
[4] Philip Kotler, *Marketing Management*, 5th ed. (Englewood Cliffs, NJ: Prentice-Hall, 1994), 310.
[5] Subhash C. Jain, "Global Competitiveness in the Beer Industry: A Case Study," Food Marketing Policy Center, University of Connecticut, Research Report No. 28, November, 1994.
[6] Prudential Securities Incorporated, *Anheuser-Busch Company Update*, June 1993.
[7] Ira Teinowitz, "Beer Battle Heats Up: New Brands Score," *Advertising Age* (13 August 1990): 21.
[8] Roger A. Kerin, Michael G. Harvey, and James T. Rothe, "Cannibalism and New Product Development," *Business Horizons* (October 1978): 31.
[9] John P. Maggard, "Positioning Revisited," *Journal of Marketing* (January 1976): 63–66.
[10] Alison Fahey, "A&W Aims Younger," *Advertising Age* (27 January 1992): 12.
[11] Eric Morgenthaler, "People Are So Goofy About Disney World, They Marry There," *Wall Street Journal* (28 October 1992): A1.
[12] Based on an interview with a Gillette executive. See also Lawrence Ingrassia, "Schick Razor to Try for Edge against Gillette," *Wall Street Journal* (9 October 1990): B1.
[13] Alex Taylor III, "Kodak Scrambles to Reforms," *Fortune* (3 March 1986): 34.

[14] Alix M. Freedman, "Upstart Miller Brew Stirs Up Beer Market," *Wall Street Journal* (5 October 1988): B1. Also see Patricia Sellers, "Busch Fights to Have It All," *Fortune* (15 January 1990): 87.

[15] Richard T. Hise, A. Parasuraman, and Ramaswamy Viswanathan, "Product Elimination: The Neglected Management Responsibility," *Journal of Business Strategy* (Spring 1984): 56–63.

[16] Gregory A. Patterson and Christina Duff, "Sears Trims Operations, Ending an Era," *Wall Street Journal* (26 January 1993): B1.

[17] "How Sweet It Is to Be out from under Beatrice's Thumb," *Business Week* (9 May 1988): 98.

[18] *New Products Management for the 1980s* (New York: Booz, Allen, & Hamilton Inc., 1982), 14.

[19] *New Products Management for the 1980s*, 18.

[20] John A. Quelch, "Marketing the Premium Product," *Business Horizons* (May–June 1987): 38–45. See also David A. Garvin, "Competing on the Eight Dimensions of Quality," *Harvard Business Review* (November–December 1987): 101–09.

[21] Bro Uttal, "Eastman Kodak's Orderly Two-Front War," *Fortune* (September 1976): 123.

[22] "The Hottest Thing Since the Flashbulb," *Business Week* (7 September 1992): 72. Also see *Eastman Kodak Company's Annual Report for 1993.*

[23] Patricia Sellers, "A Boring Brand Can Be Beautiful," *Fortune* (18 November 1991): 48.

[24] Kenichi Ohmae, "Effective Strategies for Competitive Success," *McKinsey Quarterly* (Winter 1978): 56–57.

[25] "Could America Afford the Transistor Today?" *Business Week* (7 March 1994): 80.

[26] "Flops," *Business Week* (16 August 1993): 76.

[27] Ronald Alsop, "Consumer-Product Giants Relying on 'Intrapreneurs' in New Ventures," *Wall Street Journal* (22 April 1988): 35.

[28] Peter Vanderwicken, "P&G's Secret Ingredient," *Fortune* (July 1974): 75. See also "The Miracle Company," *Business Week* (19 October 1987): 84.

[29] *The Economist* (23 January 1988): 75.

[30] Laurie Hays, "Du Pont's Difficulties in Selling Kevlar Show Hurdles of Innovation," *Wall Street Journal* (29 September 1987): 1. See also *E. I. du Pont de Nemours and Company, Annual Report for 1990.*

[31] "Coke's Man on the Spot," *Business Week* (25 July 1985): 56.

[32] E. Ralph Biggadike, "The Risky Business of Diversification," *Harvard Business Review* (May–June 1979): 103–11. See also E. Ralph Biggadike, *Corporate Diversification: Entry Strategy and Performance* (Boston: Division of Research, Harvard Business School, 1979).

[33] "A Revved-up Market for Diesel Engine Makers," *Business Week* (5 February 1979): 76.

[34] Richard Gibson, "Restaurant Rescuer Don Smith Hopes for More Than Potluck at Friendly's," *Wall Street Journal* (11 August 1988): 34.

[35] George S. Yip, "Diversification Entry: Internal Development Versus Acquisition," *Strategic Management Journal* (October–December 1982): 331–46. See also Malcolm S. Salter and Wolf A. Weinhold, "Choosing Compatible Acquisitions," *Harvard Business Review* (January–February 1981): 117–27.

[36] Michael E. Porter, "From Competitive Advantage to Corporate Strategy," *McKinsey Quarterly* (Spring 1988): 43.

[37] "Hopelessly Seeking Synergy," *The Economist* (20 August 1994): 53

[38] "Gillette: After Diversification That Failed," *Business Week* (28 February 1977): 58–62.

[39] "Who Says the Conglomerate Is Dead?" *Business Week* (23 January 1995): 92.

[40] Robert Jacobson and David A. Aaker, "The Strategic Role of Product Quality," *Journal of Marketing* (October 1987): 31–44.

[41] Bradley T. Grale and Robert D. Buzzell, "Market Perceived Quality: Key Strategic Concept," *Planning Review* (March–April 1989): 11.

[42] Kim B. Clark and Takahiro Fujimoto, "The Power of Product Integrity," *Harvard Business Review* (November–December 1990): 110.

[43] Gale and Buzzell, "Market Perceived Quality," 7–8 and 14–16.

[44] Frank Rose, "Now Quality Means Service Too," *Fortune* (22 April 1991): 98.

[45] "King Customer," *Business Week* (12 March 1990): 90.

[46] Rose, "Now Quality Means Service Too," 100.

[47] Jan Carlzon, "Putting the Customer First: The Key to Service Strategy," *McKinsey Quarterly* (Summer 1987): 38–39.

[48] Christopher W. L. Hart, "The Power of Unconditional Service Guarantees," *Harvard Business Review* (July–August 1988): 54.

[49] Brian Dumaine, "How Managers Can Succeed through Speed," *Fortune* (13 February 1989): 54. See also Warren B. Brown and Necmi Karagozoglu, "Leading the Product Development," *Academy of Management Executive* (1993): 36–47.

[50] Edward G. Krubasik, "Customize Your Product Development," *Harvard Business Review* (November-December 1988): 46–52.

[51] Dumaine, "How Managers Can Succeed through Speed," 57–58. See also "Mattel's Wild Race to Market," *Business Week* (12 February 1994): 62.

[52] This example and the ones that follow are based on Dumaine, "How Managers Can Succeed through Speed."

APPENDIX | *Perspectives on Product Strategies*

I. Product-Positioning Strategy

Definition: Placing a brand in that part of the market where it will have a favorable reception compared with competing brands.

Objectives: (a) To position the product in the market so that it stands apart from competing brands. (b) To position the product so that it tells customers what you stand for, what you are, and how you would like customers to evaluate you. In the case of positioning multiple brands: (a) To seek growth by offering varied products in differing segments of the market. (b) To avoid competitive threats to a single brand.

Requirements: Use of marketing mix variables, especially design and communication efforts. (a) Successful management of a single brand requires positioning the brand in the market so that it can stand competition from the toughest rival and maintaining its unique position by creating the aura of a distinctive product. (b) Successful management of multiple brands requires careful positioning in the market so that multiple brands do not compete with nor cannibalize each other. Thus it is important to be careful in segmenting the market and to position an individual product as uniquely suited to a particular segment through design and promotion.

Expected Results: (a) Meet as much as possible the needs of specific segments of the market. (b) Limit sudden changes in sales. (c) Make customers faithful to the brands.

II. Product- Repositioning Strategy	*Definition:* Reviewing the current positioning of the product and its marketing mix and seeking a new position for it that seems more appropriate. *Objectives:* (a) To increase the life of the product. (b) To correct an original positioning mistake. *Requirements:* (a) If this strategy is directed toward existing customers, repositioning is sought through promotion of more varied uses of the product. (b) If the business unit wants to reach new users, this strategy requires that the product be presented with a different twist to the people who have not been favorably inclined toward it. In doing so, care should be taken to see that, in the process of enticing new customers, current ones are not alienated. (c) If this strategy aims at presenting new uses of the product, it requires searching for latent uses of the product, if any. Although all products may not have latent uses, there are products that may be used for purposes not originally intended. *Expected Results:* (a) Among existing customers: increase in sales growth and profitability. (b) Among new users: enlargement of the overall market, thus putting the product on a growth route, and increased profitability. (c) New product uses: increased sales, market share, and profitability.
III. Product-Overlap Strategy	*Definition:* Competing against one's own brand through introduction of competing products, use of private labeling, and selling to original-equipment manufacturers. *Objectives:* (a) To attract more customers to the product and thereby increase the overall market. (b) To work at full capacity and spread overhead. (c) To sell to competitors; to realize economies of scale and cost reduction. *Requirements:* (a) Each competing product must have its own marketing organization to compete in the market. (b) Private brands should not become profit drains. (c) Each brand should find its special niche in the market. If that doesn't happen, it will create confusion among customers and sales will be hurt. (d) In the long run, one of the brands may be withdrawn, yielding its position to the other brand. *Expected Results:* (a) Increased market share. (b) Increased growth.
IV. Product-Scope Strategy	*Definition:* The product-scope strategy deals with the perspectives of the product mix of a company. The product-scope strategy is determined by taking into account the overall mission of the business unit. The company may adopt a single-product strategy, a multiple-product strategy, or a system-of-products strategy. *Objectives:* (a) Single product: to increase economies of scale by developing specialization. (b) Multiple products: to cover the risk of potential obsolescence of the single product by adding additional products. (c) System of products: to increase the dependence of the customer on the company's products as well as to prevent competitors from moving into the market. *Requirements:* (a) Single product: company must stay up-to-date on the product and even become the technology leader to avoid obsolescence. (b) Multiple

products: products must complement one another in a portfolio of products. (c) System of products: company must have a close understanding of customer needs and uses of the products.

Expected Results: Increased growth, market share, and profits with all three strategies. With system-of-products strategy, the company achieves monopolistic control over the market, which may lead to some problems with the Justice Department, and enlarges the concept of its product/market opportunities.

V. Product-Design Strategy

Definition: The product-design strategy deals with the degree of standardization of a product. The company has a choice among the following strategic options: standard product, customized product, and standard product with modifications.

Objectives: (a) Standard product: to increase economies of scale of the company. (b) Customized product: to compete against mass producers of standardized products through product-design flexibility. (c) Standard product with modifications: to combine the benefits of the two previous strategies.

Requirements: Close analysis of product/market perspectives and environmental changes, especially technological changes.

Expected Results: Increase in growth, market share, and profits. In addition, the third strategy allows the company to keep close contacts with the market and gain experience in developing new standard products.

VI. Product-Elimination Strategy

Definition: Cuts in the composition of a company's business unit product portfolio by pruning the number of products within a line or by totally divesting a division or business.

Objectives: To eliminate undesirable products because their contribution to fixed cost and profit is too low, because their future performance looks grim, or because they do not fit in the business's overall strategy. The product-elimination strategy aims at shaping the best possible mix of products and balancing the total business.

Requirements: No special resources are required to eliminate a product or a division. However, because it is impossible to reverse the decision once the elimination has been achieved, an in-depth analysis must be done to determine (a) the causes of current problems; (b) the possible alternatives, other than elimination, that may solve problems (e.g., Are any improvements in the marketing mix possible?); and (c) the repercussions that elimination may have on remaining products or units (e.g., Is the product being considered for elimination complementary to another product in the portfolio? What are the side effects on the company's image? What are the social costs of an elimination?).

Expected Results: In the short run, cost savings from production runs, reduced inventories, and in some cases an improved return on investment can be expected. In the long run, the sales of the remaining products may increase because more efforts are now concentrated on them.

VII. New-Product Strategy

Definition: A set of operations that introduces (a) within the business, a product new to its previous line of products; (b) on the market, a product that provides a new type of satisfaction. Three alternatives emerge from the above: product improvement/modification, product imitation, and product innovation.

Objectives: To meet new needs and to sustain competitive pressures on existing products. In the first case, the new-product strategy is an offensive one; in the second case, it is a defensive one.

Requirements: A new-product strategy is difficult to implement if a "new product development system" does not exist within a company. Five components of this system should be assessed: (a) corporate aspirations toward new products, (b) organizational openness to creativity, (c) environmental favor toward creativity, (d) screening method for new ideas, and (e) evaluation process.

Expected Results: Increased market share and profitability.

VIII. Diversification Strategy

Definition: Developing unfamiliar products and markets through (a) concentric diversification (products introduced are related to existing ones in terms of marketing or technology), (b) horizontal diversification (new products are unrelated to existing ones but are sold to the same customers), and (c) conglomerate diversification (products are entirely new).

Objectives: Diversification strategies respond to the desire for (a) growth when current products/markets have reached maturity, (b) stability by spreading the risks of fluctuations in earnings, (c) security when the company may fear backward integration from one of its major customers, and (d) credibility to have more weight in capital markets.

Requirements: In order to reduce the risks inherent in a diversification strategy, a business unit should (a) diversify its activities only if current product/market opportunities are limited, (b) have good knowledge of the area in which it diversifies, (c) provide the products introduced with adequate support, and (d) forecast the effects of diversification on existing lines of products.

Expected Results: (a) Increase in sales. (b) Greater profitability and flexibility.

IX. Value-Marketing Strategy

Definition: The value-marketing strategy concerns delivering on promises made for the product or service. These promises involve product quality, customer service, and meeting time commitments.

Objectives: Value-marketing strategies are directed toward seeking total customer satisfaction. It means striving for excellence to meet customer expectations.

Requirements: (a) Examine customer value perspectives. (b) Design programs to meet customer quality, service, and time requirements. (c) Train employees and distributors to deliver on promises.

Expected Results: This strategy enhances customer satisfaction, which leads to customer loyalty and, hence, to higher market share. This strategy makes the firm less vulnerable to price wars, permitting the firm to charge higher prices and, thus, earn higher profits.

Pricing Strategies

Pricing has traditionally been considered a me-too variable in marketing strategy. The stable economic conditions that prevailed during the 1960s may be particularly responsible for the low status now ascribed to the pricing variable. Strategically, the function of pricing has been to provide adequate return on investment. Thus, the timeworn cost-plus method of pricing and its sophisticated version, return-on-investment pricing, have historically been the basis for arriving at price.

In the 1970s, however, a variety of events gave a new twist to the task of making pricing decisions. Double-digit inflation, material shortages, the high cost of money, consumerism, and post-price controls behavior all contributed to making pricing an important part of marketing strategy.

Despite the importance attached to it, effective pricing is not an easy task, even under the most favorable conditions. A large number of internal and external variables must be studied systematically before price can be set. For example, the reactions of a competitor often stand out as an important consideration in developing pricing strategy. Simply knowing that a competitor has a lower price is insufficient; a price strategist must know how much flexibility a competitor has in further lowering price. This presupposes a knowledge of the competitor's cost structure. In the dynamics of today's environment, however, where unexpected economic changes can render cost and revenue projections obsolete as soon as they are developed, pricing strategy is much more difficult to formulate.

This chapter provides a composite of pricing strategies. Each strategy is examined for its underlying assumptions and relevance in specific situations. The application of different strategies is illustrated with examples from pricing literature. The appendix at the end of this chapter summarizes each strategy by giving its definition, objectives, requirements, and expected results.

REVIEW OF PRICING FACTORS

Basically, a pricer needs to review four factors to arrive at a price: pricing objectives, cost, competition, and demand. This section briefly reviews these factors, which underlie every pricing strategy alternative.

Pricing Objectives

*profit oriented → net profit %.
or target ROI*

*volume oriented → % market
share*

Broadly speaking, pricing objectives can be either profit oriented or volume oriented. The profit-oriented objective may be defined either in terms of desired net profit percentage or as a target return on investment. The latter objective has been more popular among large corporations. The volume-oriented objective may be stated as the percentage of market share that the firm would like to achieve. Alternatively, it may simply be stated as the desired sales growth rate. Many firms also consider the maintenance of a stable price as a pricing goal. Particularly in cyclical industries, price stability helps to sustain the confidence of customers and thus keeps operations running smoothly through peaks and valleys.

For many firms, there can be pricing objectives other than those of profitability and volume, as shown in Exhibit 15-1. Each firm should evaluate different objectives and choose its own priorities in the context of the pricing problems that it may be facing. The following list contains illustrations of typical pricing problems:

1. Decline in sales.
2. Higher or lower prices than competitors.
3. Excessive pressure on middlemen to generate sales.
4. Imbalance in product line prices.
5. Distortion vis-à-vis the offering in the customer's perceptions of the firm's price.
6. Frequent changes in price without any relationship to environmental realities.

EXHIBIT 15-1
Potential Pricing Objectives

1. Maximum long-run profits.
2. Maximum short-run profits.
3. Growth.
4. Stabilize market.
5. Desensitize customers to price.
6. Maintain price-leadership arrangement.
7. Discourage entrants.
8. Speed exit of marginal firms.
9. Avoid government investigation and control.
10. Maintain loyalty of middlemen and get their sales support.
11. Avoid demands for "more" from suppliers.
12. Enhance image of firm and its offerings.
13. Be regarded as "fair" by customers (ultimate).
14. Create interest and excitement about the item.
15. Be considered trustworthy and reliable by rivals.
16. Help in the sale of weak items in the line.
17. Discourage others from cutting prices.
18. Make a product "visible."
19. "Spoil market" to obtain high price for sale of business.
20. Build traffic.

Source: Alfred R. Oxenfeldt, "A Decision-Making Structure for Price Decisions," *Journal of Marketing* (January 1973): 50. Reprinted by permission of the American Marketing Association.

These problems suggest that a firm may have more than one pricing objective, even though these objectives may not be articulated as such. Essentially, pricing objectives deal directly or indirectly with three areas: profit (setting a high enough price to enable the company to earn an adequate margin for profit and reinvestment), competition (setting a low enough price to discourage competitors from adding capacity), and market share (setting a price below competition to gain market share).

As an example of pricing objectives, consider the goals that Apple Computer set for Macintosh:[1]

1. To make the product affordable and a good value for most college students.
2. To get certain target market segments to see the Macintosh as a better value than the IBM PC.
3. To encourage at least 90 percent of all Apple retailers to carry the Macintosh while providing a strong selling effort.
4. To accomplish all this within 18 months.

Cost

Fixed and variable costs are the major concerns of a pricer. In addition, the pricer may sometimes need to consider other types of costs, such as out-of-pocket costs, incremental costs, opportunity costs, controllable costs, and replacement costs.

To study the impact of costs on pricing strategy, the following three relationships may be considered: (a) the ratio of fixed costs to variable costs, (b) the economies of scale available to a firm, and (c) the cost structure of a firm vis-à-vis competitors. If the fixed costs of a company in comparison to its variable costs form a high proportion of its total costs, adding sales volume will be a great help in increasing earnings. Consider, for example, the case of the airlines, whose fixed costs are as high as 60 to 70 percent of total costs. Once fixed costs are recovered, any additional tickets sold add greatly to earnings. Such an industry is called volume sensitive. There are some industries, such as the consumer electronics industry, where variable costs constitute a higher proportion of total costs than do fixed costs. Such industries are price sensitive because even a small increase in price adds much to earnings.

If the economies of scale obtainable from a company's operations are substantial, the firm should plan to expand market share and, with respect to long-term prices, take expected declines in costs into account. Alternatively, if operations are expected to produce a decline in costs, then prices may be lowered in the long run to gain higher market share.

If a manufacturer is a low-cost producer relative to its competitors, it will earn additional profits by maintaining prices at competitive levels. The additional profits can be used to promote the product aggressively and increase the overall market share of the business. If, however, the costs of a manufacturer are high compared to those of its competitors, the manufacturer is in no position to reduce prices because that tactic may lead to a price war that it would most likely lose.

Different elements of cost must be differently related in setting price. Exhibit 15-2 shows, for example, how computations of full cost, incremental cost, and

EXHIBIT 15-2
Effect of Costs on Pricing

Cost Pricing

Costs	Product A	Product B
Labor (L)	$ 80	$120
Material (M)	160	80
Overhead (O)	40	80
Full cost (L + M + O)	280	280
Incremental cost (L + M)	240	200
Conversion cost (L + O)	120	200

Product Line Pricing

	Markup (M')	Product A	Product B
Full-Cost Pricing			
P = FC + (M')FC	20%	$336	$336
Incremental-Cost Pricing			
P = (L + M) + M'(L + M)	40%	336	280
Conversion-Cost Pricing			
P = (L + O) + M'(L + O)	180%	336	560

conversion cost may vary and how these costs affect product line prices. Exhibit 15-3 shows the procedure followed for setting target-return pricing.

Competition   Exhibit 15-4 shows the competitive information needed to formulate a pricing strategy. The information may be analyzed with reference to these competitive characteristics: number of firms in the industry, relative size of different members of the industry, product differentiation, and ease of entry.

EXHIBIT 15-3
Computation of Target-Return Pricing

Manufacturing capacity	200,000
Standard volume (80%)	160,000
Standard full cost before profit	$100/unit
Target profit	
Investment	$20,000,000
ROI target	20%
ROI target	$4,000,000
Profit per unit at standard ($4,000,000 ÷ 160,000)	$25/unit
Price	$125/unit

EXHIBIT 15-4
Competitive Information Needed for Pricing Strategy

1. Published competitive price lists and advertising.
2. Competitive reaction to price moves in the past.
3. Timing of competitors' price changes and initiating factors.
4. Information on competitors' special campaigns.
5. Competitive product line comparison.
6. Assumptions about competitors' pricing/marketing objectives.
7. Competitors' reported financial performance.
8. Estimates of competitors' costs—fixed and variable.
9. Expected pricing retaliation.
10. Analysis of competitors' capacity to retaliate.
11. Financial viability of engaging in price war.
12. Strategic posture of competitors.
13. Overall competitive aggressiveness.

In an industry where there is only one firm, there is no competitive activity. The firm is free to set any price, subject to constraints imposed by law. As an Illinois Bell executive said about pricing (before the AT&T split): "All we had to do was determine our costs, and then we would go to the commission—the Illinois Commerce Commission, and they would give us the allowable rate of return."[2] Conversely, in an industry comprising a large number of active firms, competition is fierce. Fierce competition limits the discretion of a firm in setting price. Where there are a few firms manufacturing an undifferentiated product (such as in the steel industry), only the industry leader may have the discretion to change prices. Other industry members will tend to follow the leader in setting price.

The firm with a large market share is in a position to initiate price changes without worrying about competitors' reactions. Presumably, a competitor with a large market share has the lowest costs. The firm can, therefore, keep its prices low, thus discouraging other members of the industry from adding capacity, and further its cost advantage in a growing market.

If a firm operates in an industry that has opportunities for product differentiation, it can exert some control over pricing even if the firm is small and competitors are many. This latitude concerning price may occur if customers perceive one brand to be different from competing brands: whether the difference is real or imaginary, customers do not object to paying a higher price for preferred brands. To establish product differentiation of a brand in the minds of consumers, companies spend heavily for promotion. Product differentiation, however, offers an opportunity to control prices only within a certain range.

In an industry that is easy to enter, the price setter has less discretion in establishing prices; if there are barriers to market entry, however, a firm already in the industry has greater control over prices. Barriers to entry may take any of the following forms:

1. Capital investment.
2. Technological requirements.
3. Nonavailability of essential materials.
4. Economies of scale that existing firms enjoy and that would be difficult for a new-comer to achieve.
5. Control over natural resources by existing firms.
6. Marketing expertise.

In an industry where barriers to entry are relatively easy to surmount, a new entrant will follow what can be called *keep-away pricing*. This pricing strategy is necessarily on the lower side of the pricing spectrum.

Demand | Exhibit 15-5 contains the information required for analyzing demand. Demand is based on a variety of considerations, of which price is just one. Some of these considerations are

1. Ability of customers to buy.
2. Willingness of customers to buy.
3. Place of the product in the customer's lifestyle (whether a status symbol or a product used daily).
4. Benefits that the product provides to customers.
5. Prices of substitute products.
6. Potential market for the product (is demand unfulfilled or is the market saturated).

EXHIBIT 15-5
Customer Information Needed for Pricing Strategy

1. The customer's value analysis of the product: performance, utility, profit-rendering potential, quality, etc.
2. Market acceptance level: the price level of acceptance in each major market, including the influence of substitutes.
3. The price the market expects and the differences in different markets.
4. Price stability.
5. The product's S curve and its present position on it.
6. Seasonal and cyclical characteristics of the industry.
7. The economic conditions now and during the next few periods.
8. The anticipated effect of recessions; the effect of price change on demand in a declining market (e.g., very little with luxury items).
9. Customer relations.
10. Channel relations and channel costs to figure in calculations.
11. The markup at each channel level (company versus intermediary costs).
12. Advertising and promotion requirements and costs.
13. Trade-in, replacement parts, service, delivery, installation, maintenance, preorder and postorder engineering, inventory, obsolescence, and spoilage problems and costs.
14. The product differentiation that is necessary.
15. Existing industry customs and reaction of the industry.
16. Stockholder, government, labor, employee, and community relations.

7. Nature of nonprice competition.
8. Customer behavior in general.
9. Segments in the market.

All these factors are interdependent, and it may not be easy to estimate their relationship to each other precisely.

Demand analysis involves predicting the relationship between price level and demand while considering the effects of other variables on demand. The relationship between price and demand is called elasticity of demand or sensitivity of price. **Elasticity of demand** refers to the number of units of a product that would be demanded at different prices. Price sensitivity should be considered at two different levels: total industry price sensitivity and price sensitivity for a particular firm.

Industry demand for a product is considered to be elastic if, by lowering prices, demand can be substantially increased. If lowering price has little effect on demand, demand is considered inelastic. The environmental factors previously mentioned have a definite influence on demand elasticity. Let us illustrate with a few examples. During the energy crisis, the price of gasoline went up, leading consumers to reduce gasoline usage. By the same token, since gasoline prices have gone down, people have again started using gas more freely. Thus, demand for gasoline can be considered somewhat elastic.

A case of inelastic demand is provided by salt. No matter how much the price fluctuates, people are not going to change the amount of salt that they consume. Similarly, the demand for luxury goods, yachts, for example, is inelastic because only a small proportion of the total population can afford to buy yachts.

Sometimes the market for a product is segmented so that demand elasticity in each segment must be studied. The demand for certain types of beverages by senior citizens might be inelastic, though demand for the same products among a younger audience may be especially elastic. If the price of a product goes up, customers have the option of switching to another product. Thus, availability of substitute products is another factor that should be considered.

When the total demand of an industry is highly elastic, the industry leader may take the initiative to lower prices. The loss in revenue due to decreased prices will be more than compensated for by the additional demand expected to be generated; therefore, the total dollar market expands. Such a strategy is highly attractive in an industry where economies of scale are achievable. Where demand is inelastic and there are no conceivable substitutes, price may be increased, at least in the short run. In the long run, however, the government may impose controls, or substitutes may be developed.

The demand for the products of an individual firm derives from total industry demand. An individual firm is interested in finding out how much market share it can command by changing its own prices. In the case of undifferentiated standardized products, lower prices should help a firm increase its market share as long as competitors do not retaliate by matching the firm's prices. Similarly, when business is sought through bidding prices, lower prices should help achieve the firm's objectives. In the case of differentiated products, however, market share can be improved even when higher prices are maintained (within a certain range). Products may be differentiated in various real and imaginary ways. For example, by providing adequate guarantees and after-sale service, an appliance manufacturer may maintain higher prices and still increase market share. Brand name, an image of prestige, and the perception of high quality are other factors that may help to differentiate a product in the marketplace and thus create an opportunity for the firm to increase prices and not lose market share. Of course, other elements of the marketing mix should reinforce the product's image suggested by its price. In brief, a firm's best opportunity lies in differentiating the product and then communicating this fact to the customer. A differentiated product offers more opportunity for increasing earnings through price increases.

The sensitivity of price can be measured by taking into account historical data, consumer surveys, and experimentation. Historical data can either be studied intuitively or analyzed through quantitative tools, such as regression, to see how demand goes up or down based on price. A consumer survey to study the sensitivity of prices is no different from any other market research study. Experiments to judge what level of price generates what level of demand can be conducted either in a laboratory situation or in the real world. For example, a company interested in studying the sensitivity of prices may introduce a newly developed grocery product in a few selected markets for a short period at different prices. Information obtained from this experiment should provide insights into the elasticity of demand for the product. In one study, the prices of 17 food products were varied in 30 food stores. It was found that the product sales generally followed the law of demand: when prices were raised 10 percent, sales decreased about 25 percent; a price increase of 5 percent led to a decrease in sales of about 13 percent; a lowering of prices by 5 percent increased sales by 12 percent; and a 10 percent decrease in price improved sales by 26 percent. In another study, a new deodorant that was priced at 63 cents and at 85 cents in different markets resulted in the same volume of sales. Thus, price elasticity was found to be absent, and the manufacturer set the product price at 85 cents.[3]

To conclude this discussion on pricing factors, it would not be out of place to say that, while everybody thinks businesses go about setting prices scientifically, very often the process is incredibly arbitrary. Although businesses of all types devote a great deal of time and study to determine the prices to put on their products, pricing is often more art than science. In some cases, setting prices does involve the use of a straightforward equation: material and labor costs + overhead and other expenses + profit = price. But in many other cases, the equation includes psychological and other such subtle subjective factors that the pricing decision may essentially rest on gut feeling. Exhibit 15-6 suggests one way of combining information on different pricing factors to make an objective pricing decision in industrial marketing. For example, price sensitivity, visibility to competition, and strength of supplier relationships are used to rank various customers, allowing a different pricing strategy to be adopted for each customer to effectively achieve profit, share, and communication objectives.

EXHIBIT 15-6
Pricing Guide

Company Relationship with Customer (Leverage)	Visibility of Price to Competition (Knowledge)	Customer's Price Sensitivity	
		Low	High
Strong	High	To gain profit and communicate high price	To maintain share and communicate willingness to fight
	Low	To gain profit	
Weak	High	To communicate high price	
	Low	To gain share	

Source: Robert A. Garda, "Industrial Pricing: Strategy vs. Tactics." Reprinted by permission of publisher, from *Management Review*, November 1983, © 1983. American Management Association, New York. All rights reserved.

PRICING STRATEGY FOR NEW PRODUCTS

The pricing strategy for a new product should be developed so that the desired impact on the market is achieved while the emergence of competition is discouraged. Two basic strategies that may be used in pricing a new product are skimming pricing and penetration pricing.

Skimming Pricing

Skimming pricing is the strategy of establishing a high initial price for a product with a view to "skimming the cream off the market" at the upper end of the demand curve. It is accompanied by heavy expenditure on promotion. A skimming strategy may be recommended when the nature of demand is uncertain, when a company has expended large sums of money on research and development for a new product, when the competition is expected to develop and market a similar product in the near future, or when the product is so innovative that the market is expected to mature very slowly. Under these circumstances, a skimming strategy has several advantages. At the top of the demand curve, price elasticity is low. Besides, in the absence of any close substitute, cross-elasticity is also low. These factors, along with heavy emphasis on promotion, tend to help the product make significant inroads into the market. The high price also helps segment the market. Only nonprice-conscious customers will buy a new product during its initial stage. Later on, the mass market can be tapped by lowering the price.

If there are doubts about the shape of the demand curve for a given product and the initial price is found to be too high, price may be slashed. However, it is very difficult to start low and then raise the price. Raising a low price may annoy potential customers, and anticipated drops in price may retard demand at a particular price. For a financially weak company, a skimming strategy may provide immediate relief. This model depends on selling enough units at the higher price to cover promotion and development costs. If price elasticity is higher than anticipated, a lower price will be more profitable and "relief giving."

Modern patented drugs provide a good example of skimming pricing. At the time of its introduction in 1978, Smithkline Beecham's anti-ulcer drug, Tagamet, was priced as high as $10 per unit. By 1990, the price came down to less than $2; it was sold for about 60 cents in 1994. (Tagamet was to lose patent protection in the U.S. in 1995, unleashing a flood of cheaper generics onto the American market.)[4] Many new products are priced following this policy. Videocassette recorders (VCRs), frozen foods, and instant coffee were all priced very high at the time of their initial appearance in the market. But different versions of these products are now available at prices ranging from very high to very low. No conclusive research has yet been done to indicate how high an initial price should be in relation to cost. As a rule of thumb, the final price to the consumer should be at least three or four times the factory door cost.

The decision about how high a skimming price should be depends on two factors: (a) the probability of competitors entering the market and (b) price elasticity at the upper end of the demand curve. If competitors are expected to introduce their own brands quickly, it may be safe to price rather high. On the other hand, if competitors are years behind in product development and a low rate of return to the firm would slow the pace of research at competing firms, a low skimming price can be useful. However, price skimming in the face of impending competition may not be wise if a larger market share makes entry more difficult. If limiting the sale of a new product to a few selected individuals produces sufficient sales, a very high price may be desirable.

Determining the duration of time for keeping prices high depends entirely on the competition's activities. In the absence of patent protection, skimming prices may be forced down as soon as competitors join the race. However, in the case of products that are protected through patents (e.g., drugs), the manufacturer slowly brings down the price as the patent period draws near an end; then, a year or so before the expiration of the patent period, the manufacturer saturates the market with a very low price. This strategy establishes a foothold for the manufacturer in the mass market before competitors enter it, thereby frustrating their expectations.

So far, skimming prices have been discussed as high prices in the initial stage of a product's life. Premium and umbrella prices are two other forms of price skimming. Some products carry premium prices (high prices) permanently and build an image of superiority for themselves. When a mass market cannot be developed and upper-end demand seems adequate, manufacturers will not risk tarnishing the prestigious image of their products by lowering prices, thereby offering the product to everybody. Estee Lauder cosmetics, Olga intimate apparel, Brooks Brothers clothes, and Johnston and Murphy shoes are products that fall into this category.

Sometimes, higher prices are maintained in order to provide an umbrella for small high-cost competitors. Umbrella prices have been aided by limitation laws that specify minimum prices for a variety of products, such as milk.

Du Pont provides an interesting example of skimming pricing. The company tends to focus on high-margin specialty products. Initially, it prices its products high; it then gradually lowers price as the market builds and as competition grows.[5] Polaroid also pursues a skimming pricing strategy. The company introduces an expensive model of a new camera and follows up the introduction with simpler lower-priced versions to attract new segments.[6]

Penetration Pricing

Penetration pricing is the strategy of entering the market with a low initial price so that a greater share of the market can be captured. The penetration strategy is used when an elite market does not exist and demand seems to be elastic over the entire demand curve, even during early stages of product introduction. High price elasticity of demand is probably the most important reason for adopting a penetration strategy. The penetration strategy is also used to discourage competitors from entering the market. When competitors seem to be encroaching on a market, an attempt is made to lure them away by means of penetration pricing, which yields lower margins. A competitor's costs play a decisive role in this pricing strategy because a cost advantage over the existing manufacturer might persuade another firm to enter the market, regardless of how low the margin of the former may be.

One may also turn to a penetration strategy with a view to achieving economies of scale. Savings in production costs alone may not be an important factor in setting low prices because, in the absence of price elasticity, it is difficult to generate sufficient sales. Finally, before adopting penetration pricing, one must make sure that the product fits the lifestyles of the mass market. For example, although it might not be difficult for people to accept imitation milk, cereals made from petroleum products would probably have difficulty in becoming popular.

How low the penetration price should be differs from case to case. There are several different types of prices used in penetration strategies: restrained prices, elimination prices, promotional prices, and keep-out prices. Restraint is applied so that prices can be maintained at a certain point during inflationary periods. In this case, environmental circumstances serve as a guide to what the price level should be. Elimination prices are fixed at a point that threatens the survival of a competitor. A large, multiproduct company can lower prices to a level where a smaller competitor might be wiped out of the market. The pricing of suits at factory outlets illustrates promotional prices. Factory outlets constantly stress low prices for comparable department store-quality suits. Keep-out prices are fixed at a level that prevents competitors from entering the market. Here the objective is to keep the market to oneself at the highest chargeable price.

A low price acts as the sole selling point under penetration strategy, but the market should be broad enough to justify low prices. Thus, price elasticity of demand is probably the most important factor in determining how low prices can go. This point can be easily illustrated.[7] Convinced that shoppers would willingly sacrifice convenience for price savings, an entrepreneur in 1981 introduced a concentrated cleaner called 4 + 1. Unlike such higher-priced cleaners as Windex, Fantastik, and Formula 409, this product did not come in a spray bottle. It also needed to be diluted with water before use. The entrepreneur hoped for 10 percent of the $200 million market. But the product did not sell well. The product was not as price elastic as the entrepreneur had assumed. Though the consumer tends to talk a lot about economy, the lure of convenience is apparently stronger than the desire to save a few cents. Ultimately, 4 + 1 had to be withdrawn from most markets.

Unlike Du Pont, Dow Chemical Company stresses penetration pricing. It concentrates on lower-margin commodity products and low prices, builds a dominant market share, and holds on for the long haul. Texas Instruments also practices penetration pricing. Texas Instruments starts by building a large plant capacity. By setting the price as low as possible, it hopes to penetrate the market fast and gain a large market share.

Penetration pricing reflects a long-term perspective in which short-term profits are sacrificed in order to establish sustainable competitive advantage. Penetration policy usually leads to above-average long-run returns that fall in a relatively narrow range. Price skimming, on the other hand, yields a wider range of lower average returns.[8]

PRICING STRATEGIES FOR ESTABLISHED PRODUCTS

Changes in the marketing environment may require a review of the prices of products already on the market. For example, an announcement by a large firm that it is going to lower its prices makes it necessary for other firms in the industry to examine their prices. In 1976, Texas Instruments announced that it would soon sell a digital watch for about $20. The announcement jolted the entire industry because only 15 months earlier the lowest-priced digital was selling for $125. It forced a change in everyone's strategy and gave some producers real problems. Fairchild Camera and Instrument Corporation reacted with its own version of a $20 plastic-cased digital watch. So did National Semiconductor Corporation. American Microsystems, however, decided to get completely out of the finished watch business.[9]

A review of pricing strategy may also become necessary because of shifts in demand. In the late 1960s, for example, it seemed that, with the popularity of miniskirts, the pantyhose market would continue to boom. But its growth slowed when the fashion emphasis shifted from skirts to pants. Pants hid runs, or tears, making it unnecessary to buy as many pairs of pantyhose. The popularity of pants also led to a preference for knee-high hose over pantyhose. Knee-high hose, which cost less, meant lower profits for manufacturers. Although the pantyhose market was dwindling, two new entrants, Bic Pen Corporation and Playtex Corporation, were readying their brands for introduction. Their participation made it necessary for the big three hosiery manufacturers—Hanes, Burlington, and Kayser-Roth—to review their prices and protect their market shares. An examination of existing prices may lead to one of three strategic alternatives: maintaining the price, reducing the price, or increasing the price.

Maintaining the Price | If the market segment from which the company derives a big portion of its sales is not affected by changes in the environment, the company may decide not to initiate any change in its pricing strategy. The gasoline shortage in the aftermath of

① Market segment is not affected by changes in environment
② magnitude of change is indeterminable·

the fall of the Shah of Iran did not affect the luxury car market because buyers of Cadillac, Mercedes-Benz, and Rolls-Royce were not concerned about higher gas prices. Thus, General Motors did not need to redesign the Cadillac to reduce its gas consumption or lower its price to make it attractive to the average customer.

The strategy of maintaining price is appropriate in circumstances where a price change may be desirable, but the magnitude of change is indeterminable. If the reaction of customers and competitors to a price change cannot be predicted, maintaining the present price level may be appropriate. Alternatively, a price change may have an impact on product image or sales of other products in a company's line that it is not practical to assess. Several years ago, when Magnavox and Sylvania cut the prices of their color television sets, Zenith maintained prices at current levels. Because the industry appeared to be in good shape, Zenith could not determine why its competitors adopted such a strategic posture. Zenith continued to maintain prices and earned higher profits.

Politics may be another reason for maintaining prices. During the year from 1978 to 1979, President Carter urged voluntary control of wages and prices. Many companies restrained themselves from seeking price changes in order to align themselves behind the government's efforts to control inflation.

Concern for the welfare of society may be another reason for maintaining prices at current levels. Even when supply is temporarily short of demand, some businesses may adopt a socially responsible posture and continue to charge current prices. For example, taxi drivers may choose not to hike fares when subway and bus service operators are on strike.

Reducing the Price

There are three main reasons for lowering prices. First, as a defensive strategy, prices may be cut in response to competition. For example, in October 1978, Congress authorized the deregulation of the airline industry. Deregulation gave airlines almost total freedom to set ticket prices. Thus, in spring of 1995, in response to Continental Airline's $198 round-trip fare on its New York–Los Angeles route, United Airlines acted to meet this competitive fare. United's regular round-trip coach fare at the time was about $750. Similarly, other carriers were forced to reduce their fares on different routes to match these prices. In addition, to successfully compete in mature industries, many companies reduce prices, following a strategy that is often called value pricing. For example, in light of slipping profit margins and lower customer counts, McDonald's cut prices under pressure from major rivals Taco Bell and Wendy's.[10]

A second reason for lowering prices is offensive in nature. Following the experience curve concept (see Chapter 12), costs across the board go down by a fixed percentage every time experience doubles. Consequently, a company with greater experience has lower costs than one whose experience is limited. Lower costs have a favorable impact on profits. Thus, as a matter of strategy, it behooves a company to shoot for higher market share and to secure as much experience as possible in order to gain a cost and, hence, a profit advantage. A company that successfully follows this strategy is Home Depot, the largest home repair chain in the country. The policy of everyday low prices has enabled the company to grow into a $2.8 billion chain of 118 stores, mostly in the sunbelt. Home Depot's goal is to go national with $10 billion in sales at more than 350 locations by 1996.[11]

Technological advances have made possible the low-cost production of high-quality electronics gear. Many companies have translated these advances into low retail prices to gain competitive leverage. For example, in 1978 a Sony clock radio, with no power backup and a face that showed nothing more than the current time, sold for $80. In 1988, a Sony clock radio priced at about $40 had auxiliary power and showed the time at which the alarm was set as well as the current time. In 1995, the same radio was available for less than $25.

Texas Instruments has followed the experience curve concept in achieving cost reductions in the manufacture of integrated circuits. This achievement is duly reflected in its strategy to slowly lower prices of such products as electronic calculators. Compaq Computer Corp. followed a similar strategy to make a dramatic comeback in the PC market. Even in other businesses where technological advances have a less critical role to play in the success of the business, a price reduction strategy may work out. Consider the case of Metpath, a clinical laboratory. In the late 1960s, at about the time Metpath was formed, the industry leader, Damon Corporation, was acquiring local labs all around the country; by the early 1970s, other large corporations in the business—Revlon, Bristol-Myers, Diamond Shamrock, and W.R. Grace—began doing the same. Metpath, however, adopted a price-cutting strategy. In order to implement this strategy, it took a variety of measures to achieve economies of scale. Figuring that there were not many economies of scale involved in simply putting together a chain of local labs that operated mostly as separate entities, to reduce costs, Metpath focused on centralizing its testing. A super lab that did have those economies of scale was created, along with a nationwide network to collect specimens and distribute test results. Metpath's strategy paid off well. It emerged as the industry leader in the clinical lab-testing field. Heavy price competition, much of it attributed to Metpath, led some of the big diversified companies, including W.R. Grace and Diamond Shamrock, to pull out of the business.[12]

The recession in early 1990s caused consumers to tighten belts and to be more sensitive to prices. Sears, therefore, adopted a new pricing policy whereby prices on practically all products were permanently lowered. The company closed its 824 stores for two days to remark price tags and to implement its "everyday low pricing" strategy. A number of other companies, such as Wal-Mart, Toys "R" Us, and Circuit City, also pursue this strategy by keeping prices low year-round, avoiding the practice of marking them up and down. Consumers like year-round low prices because constantly changing sale prices makes it hard to recognize a fair deal.[13] Similarly, fast-food chains have started offering "value" menus of higher-priced items.

The third and final reason for price cutting may be a response to customer need. If low prices are a prerequisite for inducing the market to grow, customer need may then become the pivot of a marketing strategy, all other aspects of the marketing mix being developed accordingly.

As an example, in 1993 Philip Morris used price as an aggressive marketing tactic to seek growth for its Marlboro brand of cigarette. Its 40 cents-per-pack cut grabbed consumers' attention, narrowed the gap with discount brands, and squeezed competitors. In less than a year, Marlboro's share of the U.S. cigarette market increased from 20 percent to 25 percent, higher than it has been before.[14]

In adopting a low-price strategy for an existing product, a variety of considerations must be taken into account. The long-term impact of a price cut against a major competitor is a factor to be reckoned with. For example, a regional pizza chain can cut prices to prevent Pizza Hut from gaining a foothold in its market only in the short run. Eventually, Pizza Hut (a division of PepsiCo) will prevail over the local chain through price competition. Pizza Hut may lower prices to such an extent that the local chain may find it difficult even to recover its costs. Thus, competitive strength should be duly evaluated in opting for low-price strategy.

In a highly competitive situation, a product may command a higher price than other brands if it is marketed as a "different" product—for example, as one of deluxe quality. If the price of a deluxe product is reduced, the likely impact on its position should be looked into. Sony television sets have traditionally sold at premium prices because they have been promoted as quality products. Sony's higher-price strategy paid off: the Sony television rose to prominence as a quality product and captured a respectable share of the market. A few years later, however, consumer pressures led Sony dealers to reduce prices. This action not only hurt Sony's overall prestige, it made some retailers stop selling Sony because it had now become just one of the many brands they carried. In other words, the price cut, though partly initiated by its dealers, cost Sony its distinction. Even if its sales increased in the short run, the price cut did not prove to be a viable strategy in the long run because it went against the perception consumers had of Sony's being a distinctive brand. Ultimately, consumers may perceive Sony as just another brand, which will affect both sales and profits.

It is also necessary to examine thoroughly the impact of a price cut of one product on other products in the line.

Finally, the impact of a price cut on a product's financial performance must be reviewed before the strategy is implemented. If a company is so positioned financially that a price cut will weaken its profitability, it may decide not to lower the price even if lowering price may be in all other ways the best course to follow. For instance, a mere 1 percent price decrease for an average company would destroy over 11 percent of the company's operating profit dollars.[15]

Increasing the Price | An increase in price may be implemented for various reasons. First, in an inflationary economy, prices may need to be adjusted upward in order to maintain profitability. During periods of inflation, all types of costs go up, and to maintain adequate profits, an increase in price becomes necessary. How much the price should be increased is a matter of strategy that varies from case to case. Conceptually, however, price should be increased to such a level that the profits before and after inflation are approximately equal. An increase in price should also take into account any decline in revenue caused by shifts in demand due to price increases. Strategically, the decision to minimize the effects of inflationary pressures on the company through price increases should be based on the long-term implications of achieving a short-run vantage.

It must also be mentioned that it is not always necessary for a company to increase prices to offset inflationary pressures. A company can take nonprice measures as well to reduce the effects of inflation. For example, many fast-food chains expanded menus and seating capacity to partially offset rising costs. Similarly, a firm may substantially increase prices, much more than justified by inflation alone, by improving product quality or by raising the level of accompanying services. High quality should help keep prices and profits up because inflation-weary customers search for value in the marketplace. Improved product quality and additional services should provide such value.

Price may also be increased by downsizing (i.e., decreasing) package size while maintaining price. In a recession, downsizing helps hold the line on prices despite rising costs. Under inflationary conditions, downsizing provides a way of keeping prices from rising beyond psychological barriers. Downsizing is commonly practiced by packaged-goods companies. For example, recently Procter & Gamble cut the number of diapers in a package from 88 to 80 while leaving the price the same. In this example, downsizing effectively resulted in a price increase of 9.1 percent. Similarly, H. J. Heinz reduced the contents of its 6.5-ounce StarKist Seafood (tuna) can by three-eighths of an ounce. By keeping exactly the same price as before, the company gained an invisible 5.8 percent price increase.[16]

Prices may also be increased when a brand has a monopolistic control over the market segments it serves. In other words, when a brand has a differential advantage over competing brands in the market, it may take advantage of its unique position, increasing its price to maximize its benefits. Such a differential advantage may be real or may exist just in the mind of the consumer. In seeking a price increase in a monopolistic situation, the increase should be such that customers will absorb it and still remain loyal to the brand. If the price increase is abnormal, differential advantage may be lost, and the customer will choose a brand based on price.

The downside of increasing price may be illustrated with reference to coffee. Let us say that there is a segment of customers who ardently drink Maxwell House coffee. In their minds, Maxwell House has something special. If the price of Maxwell House goes up (assuming that the prices of other brands remain unchanged), these coffee drinkers may continue to purchase it because the brand has a virtual monopoly over their coffee-drinking behavior. There is a limit, however, to what these Maxwell House loyalists will pay for their favorite brand of coffee. Thus, if the price of Maxwell House is increased too much, these customers may shift their preference.

From the perspective of strategy, this example indicates that, in monopolistic situations, the price of a brand may be set high to increase revenues and profits. The extent of the increase, however, depends on many factors. Each competitor has a different optimum price level for a given end product for a given customer group. It is rare that such optimum prices are the same for any two competitors. Each competitor has different options based on different cost components, capacity constraints, financial structure, product mix, customer mix, logistics, culture, and growth rate. The competitor with the lowest optimum price has the option of setting the common price; all others must follow or retreat. However, the continued existence of competitors depends on each firm retreating from competition when it is at a disadvantage until each competes primarily in a "competitive segment," a monopolistic situation where it has an advantage compared to all others. This unique combination of characteristics, matched with differentials in the competitive environment, enables each firm to coexist and prosper in its chosen area (i.e., where it has monopolistic control).

Sometimes prices must be increased to adhere to an industry situation. Of the few firms in an industry, one (usually the largest) emerges as a leader. If the leader raises its price, other members of the industry must follow suit, if only to maintain the balance of strength in the industry. If they refuse to do so, they are liable to be challenged by the leader. Usually, no firm likes to fight the industry leader because it has more at stake than the leader.

In the U.S. auto industry, there are three domestic firms: General Motors, Ford, and Chrysler. General Motors is the industry leader in terms of market share. If General Motors increases its prices, all other members of the industry increase prices. Thus, a firm may be compelled to increase price in response to a similar increase by the industry leader. The leader also sets a limit on price increases, with followers frequently setting their prices very close to those of the leader. Although an increase is forced on a firm in this situation, it is a good strategic move to set a price that, without being obviously different, is higher than the leader's price.

Prices may also be increased to segment the market. For example, a soft drink company may come out with a new brand and direct it toward busy executives/professionals. This brand may be differentiated as one that provides stamina and invigoration without adding calories. To substantiate the brand's worth and make it appear different, the price may be set at double the price of existing soft drinks. Similarly, the market may be segmented by geography, with varying prices serving different segments. For example, in New York City, a 6.4-ounce tube of Crest toothpaste may sell for $3.89 on Park Avenue, for $3.29 on the Upper East Side, and for $2.39 on the Lower East Side.

Hewlett-Packard Company operates in the highly competitive pocket calculator industry, where the practice of price cutting is quite common. Nonetheless, Hewlett-Packard thrives by offering high-priced products to a select segment of the market. It seems to appeal to a market segment that is highly inelastic with respect to price but highly elastic with respect to quality. The company equips its calculators with special features and then offers them at a price that is much higher than the industry average. In other words, rather than running the business on the basis of overall volume, Hewlett-Packard realizes high prices by being a specialist that serves a narrow segment. In cosmetics or automobiles, for example, there may be a tenfold cost difference between mass market products and those designed, produced, packaged, distributed, and promoted for small high-quality niches. Up-market products are often produced by specialists, companies such as Daimler-Benz or BMW, that can compete successfully around far-larger producers of standard products.

Many airlines have successfully used price structure to differentiate market segments and objectives based on customer price sensitivity. Business travelers are relatively price insensitive, whereas tourists are very sensitive to the price of tickets. In order to increase the volume of tourist traffic without forgoing bread-and-butter revenues from business customers, airlines have developed price structures based on characteristics that differentiate these two customer segments.

For example, tourists generally spend a weekend at their destination; business travelers do not. By changing the structure from pricing flights to pricing itineraries, the airlines can discount itineraries that include a Saturday night stay. Most business customers cannot take advantage of such discounts without incurring substantial inconvenience. This enables the airline to increase tourist volume while maintaining high prices among the business customer segment. Such pricing policies have led to as much as 10 times the difference in fares paid for the same seat. Thus, a flexible pricing strategy permits a company to realize high prices from customers who are willing to pay them without sacrificing volume from customers who are not.[17]

Increase in price is seductive in nature. After all, improvements in price typically have three to four times the effect on profitability as proportionate increases in volume. But the increase should be considered for its effect on long-term profitability, demand elasticity, and competitive moves. Although a higher price may mean higher profits in the short run, the long-run effect of a price increase may be disastrous. The increase may encourage new entrants to flock to the industry and competition from substitutes. Thus, before a price increase strategy is implemented, its long-term effect should be thoroughly examined. Further, an increase in price may lead to shifts in demand that could be detrimental. Likewise, the increase may negatively affect market share if the competition decides not to seek similar increases in price. Thus, competitive posture must be studied and predicted. In addition, a company should review its own ability to live with higher prices. A price increase may mean a decline in revenues but an increase in profits. Whether such a situation will create any problem needs to be looked into. Will laying off people or reassigning sales territories be problematic? Is a limit to price increases called for as a matter of social responsibility? In 1979, President Carter asked businesses to adhere to 7 percent increases in prices and wages voluntarily. In a similar situation, should a company that otherwise finds a 10 percent increase in price strategically sound go ahead with it? Finally, the price increase should be duly reinforced by other factors in the marketing mix. A Chevy cannot be sold at a Cadillac price. A man's suit bearing a Kmart label cannot be sold on a par with one manufactured by Brooks Brothers. Chanel No. 5 cannot be promoted by placing an ad in *TV Guide*. The increased price must be evaluated before being finalized to see whether the posture of other market mix variables will substantiate it.

Finally, the timing of a price increase can be nearly as important as the increase itself. For example, a simple tactic of lagging competitors in announcing price increases can produce the perception among customers that you are the most customer-responsive supplier. The extent of the lag can also be important.

PRICE-FLEXIBILITY STRATEGY

A price-flexibility strategy usually consists of two alternatives: a one-price policy and a flexible-pricing policy. Influenced by a variety of changes in the environment, such as saturation of markets, slow growth, global competition, and the consumer movement, more and more companies have been adhering in recent years to flexibility in pricing of different forms. Pricing flexibility may consist of setting different prices in different markets based on geographic location, varying prices depending on the time of delivery, or customizing prices based on the complexity of the product desired.

One-Price Strategy | A one-price strategy means that the same price is set for all customers who purchase goods under essentially the same conditions and in the same quantities. The one-price strategy is fairly typical in situations where mass distribution and mass selling are employed. There are several advantages and disadvantages that may be attributed to a one-price strategy. One advantage of this pricing strategy is administrative convenience. It also makes the pricing process easier and contributes to the maintenance of goodwill among customers because no single customer receives special pricing favors over another.

A general disadvantage of a one-price strategy is that the firm usually ends up broadcasting its prices to competitors who may be capable of undercutting the price. Total inflexibility in pricing may undermine the product in the marketplace. Total inflexibility in pricing may also have highly adverse effects on corporate growth and profits in certain situations. It is very important that a company remain responsive to general trends in economic, social, technological, political/legal, and competitive environments. Realistically, then, a pricing strategy should be periodically reviewed to incorporate environmental changes as they become pronounced. Any review of this type would need to include a close look at a company's position relative to the actions of other firms operating within its industry. As an example, it is generally believed that one reason for the success of discount houses is that conventional retailers have rigidly held to traditional prices and margins.

Flexible-Pricing Strategy | A flexible-pricing strategy refers to situations where the same products or quantities are offered to different customers at different prices. A flexible-pricing strategy is more common in industrial markets than in consumer markets. An advantage of a flexible-pricing strategy is the freedom allowed to sales representatives to make adjustments for competitive conditions rather than refuse an order. Also, a firm is able to charge a higher price to customers who are willing to pay it and a lower price to those who are unwilling, although legal difficulties may be encountered if price discrimination becomes an issue. Besides, other customers may become upset upon learning that they have been charged more than their competitors. In addition, bargaining tends to increase the cost of selling, and some sales representatives may let price cutting become a habit.

Recently, many large U.S. companies have added new dimensions of flexibility to their pricing strategies. Although companies have always shown some willingness to adjust prices or profit margins on specific products when market conditions have varied, this kind of flexibility is now being carried to the state of high art. The concept of price flexibility can be implemented in four different ways: by market, by product, by timing, and by technology.

Price flexibility with reference to the market can be achieved either from one geographic area to another or from one segment to another. Both Ford and General Motors charge less for their compact cars marketed on the West Coast than for those marketed anywhere else in the country. Different segments make different uses of a product: many companies, therefore, consider customer usage in setting price. For example, a plastic sold to industry might command only 30 cents a pound; sold to a dentist, it might bring $25 a pound. Here again, the flexible-pricing strategy calls for different prices in the two segments.[18]

Price flexibility with reference to the product is implemented by considering the value that a product provides to the customer. Careful analysis may show that some products are underpriced and can stand an upgrading in the marketplace. Others, competitively priced to begin with, may not support any additional margin because the matchup between value and cost would be lost.

Costs of all transactions from raw material to delivery may be analyzed, and if some costs are unnecessary in a particular case, adjustments may be made in pricing a product to sell to a particular customer. Such cost optimization is very effective from the customer's point of view because he or she does not pay for those costs for which no value is received.

Price flexibility can also be practiced by adding to the price an escalation clause based on cost fluctuations. Escalation clauses are especially relevant in situations where there is a substantial time gap between confirmation of an order and delivery of the finished product. In the case of products susceptible to technological obsolescence, price is set to recover all sunken costs within a reasonable period.

The flexible-pricing strategy has two main characteristics: an emphasis on profit or margins rather than simply on volume and a willingness to change price with reference to the existing climate. Caution is in order here. In many instances, building market share may be essential to cutting costs and, hence, to increasing profits. Thus, where the experience curve concept makes sense, companies may find it advantageous to reduce prices to hold or increase market share. However, a reduction in price simply as a reactionary measure to win a contract is discounted. Implementation of this strategy requires that the pricing decision be instituted by someone high up in the organization away from salespeople in the field. In some companies, the pricing executive may report directly to the CEO.

In addition, a systematic procedure for reviewing price at quarterly or semi-annual intervals must be established. Finally, an adequate information system is required to help the pricing executive examine different pricing factors.

PRODUCT LINE-PRICING STRATEGY

A modern business enterprise manufactures and markets a number of product items in a line with differences in quality, design, size, and style. Products in a line may be complementary to or competitive with each other. The relationships among products in a given product line influence the cross-elasticities of demand between competing products and the package-deal buying of products complementary to each other. For example, instant coffee prices must bear some relationship to the prices of a company's regular coffee because these items are substitutes for one another; therefore, this represents a case of cross-elasticity. Similarly, the price of a pesticide must be related to that of a fertilizer if customers are to use both. In other words, a multiproduct company cannot afford to price one product without giving due consideration to the effect its price produces on other products in its line.[19]

The pricing strategy of a multiproduct firm should be developed to maximize the profits of the entire organization rather than the profitability of a single product. For products already in the line, pricing strategy may be formulated by classifying them according to their contribution as follows:

1. Products that contribute more than their pro rata share toward overhead after direct costs are covered.
2. Products that just cover their pro rata share.
3. Products that contribute more than incremental costs but do not cover their pro rata share.
4. Products that fail to cover the costs savable by their elimination.

With such a classification in mind, management is in a better position to study ways of strengthening the performance of its total product line. Pricing decisions on individual products in the four categories listed here are made in the light of demand and competitive conditions facing each product in the line. Consequently, some products (new products) may be priced to yield a very high margin of profit; others (highly competitive standard products) may need to show an actual loss. By retaining these marginal products to "keep the machines running" and to help absorb fixed overhead costs, management may be able to maximize total profit from all of its lines combined. A few items that make no contribution may need to be kept to round out the line offered.

General Motors' pricing structure provides a good illustration of this procedure. To offset lower profit margins on lower-priced small cars, the company raises the prices of its large cars. The prices of its luxury cars are raised much more than those of its standard cars. For example, in 1991 a Cadillac Seville sold for more than $55,000, four times the price of the company's lowest-priced car. Ten years ago, the top of the line was three times as costly as the lowest-priced car. The gap is widening, however, because the growing market for small cars with low markups makes it necessary for the company to generate high profits on luxury cars to meet its profit goals. Thus, it is expected that toward the end of the 1990s, General Motors will be selling a Cadillac for $80,000.

For a new product being considered for addition to the line, strategy development proceeds with an evaluation of the role assigned to it. The following questions could be asked:

1. What would the effect be on the company's competing products at different prices?
2. What would be the best new-product price (or range), considering its impact on the total company offerings as a whole? Should other prices be adjusted? What, therefore, would be the incremental gain or loss (volumes and profits of existing lines plus volumes and profits of the new line at different prices)?
3. Is the new product necessary for staying ahead of or catching up with the competition?
4. Can it enhance the corporate image, and if so, how much is the enhancement worth?

If product/market strategy has been adequately worked out, it will be obvious whether the new product can profitably cater to a particular segment. If so, the pricing decision will be considerably easier to make; costs, profit goals, marketing goals, experience, and external competition will be the factors around which price will be determined.

Where there is no specific product/market match, pricing strategy for a new product considered for the line will vary depending on whether the product is complementary or competitive vis-à-vis other products in the line. For the complementary product, examination of the industry price schedule, which is the primary guide for the bottom price, top price, and conventional spread between product prices in a given industry, may be necessary. There are three particularly significant factors in product line-pricing strategy. The lowest price in the market is always the most remembered and unquestionably generates the most interest, if not the most traffic; the top market price implies the ability to manufacture quality products; and a well-planned schedule structure (one that optimizes profit and, at the same time, is logical to customers) is usually carefully studied and eventually followed by the competition regardless of who initiated it. In addition, however, there can be a product in the line with the objective of pricing to obtain the principal profit from a product's supplies or supplementary components.

If the anticipated product is competitive, a start will need to be made with the following market analysis:

1. Knowledge of the industry's pricing history and characteristics regarding the line.
2. Comparison of company and competitor products and volumes, showing gaps and areas of popularity.
3. Volume and profit potentials of the company line as is.

4. Volume and profit potentials with the new internally competitive product.
5. Effect on company volume and profit if competition introduced the proposed product and the company did not.
6. Impact of a possible introduction delay or speedup.

With this information on hand, computations for cost-plus markup should be undertaken. Thereafter, the pricer has three alternatives to set price: (a) add a uniform or individual markup rate to the total cost of the product, (b) add a markup rate that covers all the constant costs of the line, and (c) add the rate necessary for achieving the profit goal. These three alternatives have different characteristics. The first one hides the contribution margin opportunities. The second alternative, although revealing the minimum feasible price, tends to spread constant-cost coverage in such a manner that the product absorbing the most overhead is made the most price attractive. The third alternative assigns the burden to the product with the highest material cost, an action that may be competitively necessary. No matter which alternative is pursued, however, the final price should be arrived at only after it has been duly examined with reference to the market and the competition.

LEASING STRATEGY

The major emphasis of a pricing strategy is on buying a product outright rather than leasing it. Except in housing, leasing is more common in the marketing of industrial goods than among consumer goods, though in recent years there has been a growing trend toward the leasing of consumer goods. For example, some people lease cars. Usually, by paying a specified sum of money every month, similar to a rental on an apartment, one can lease a new car. Again, as in the case of housing, a lease is binding for a minimum period, such as two years. Thus, the consumer can lease a new car every other year. Because repairs in the first two years of a car's life may not amount to much, one is saved the bother of such problems.

Although there may be different alternatives for setting the lease price, the lessor usually likes to recover the investment within a few years. Thereafter, a very large portion of the lease price (or rent) is profit. A lessor may set the monthly rental on a car so that within a few months, say 30, the entire cost of the car can be recovered. For example, the monthly rental on a Toyota Corolla, based on its 1994 price (assuming no extras), may be about $179 a month (the sticker price is $13,948). With the term set at 30 months, the dealer gets all his or her money back in about 27 months. (It should be noted that a dealer gets a car at the wholesale price, not the sticker price, which is the suggested retail price.) The important thing is to set the monthly lease rate and the minimum period for which the lease is binding in such proportions that the total amount that the lessee pays for the duration of the lease is less than what he or she would pay in monthly installments on a new car. As a matter of fact, the lease rate must be substantially less than that in order for the buyer to opt to lease.

Automobile renting is transforming the market perspectives of the industry. One-fourth of all cars and trucks sold in 1993 went out under lease. By the year

2000, it is predicted, half of all cars and trucks will be leased. The reason for this shift in automobile buying is easy to understand. About 75 percent of car buyers need some sort of financing, and with interest on car loans no longer deductible, leasing's relatively low monthly payments are enticing. For the auto companies, leasing camouflages price increases, and restores brand loyalty. It offers companies an opportunity to strike up a relationship with the customers. Further, it attracts younger buyers to luxury brands and smoothes industry sales throughout the year.[20]

Leasing works out to be a viable strategy for other products as well. For example, furniture renting may be attractive to young adults, people of high mobility (e.g., executives, airline stewards), and senior citizens who may need appropriate furnishings only temporarily when their children's families come to visit. In addition, apartment owners may rent furniture to provide furnished units to tenants.

In industrial markets, the leasing strategy is employed by essentially all capital goods and equipment manufacturers. Traditionally, shoe machinery, postage meters, packaging machinery, textile machinery, and other heavy equipment have been leased. Recent applications of the strategy include the leasing of computers, copiers, cars, and trucks. As a matter of fact, just about any item of capital machinery and equipment can be leased. From the customer's point of view, the leasing strategy makes sense for a variety of reasons. First, it reduces the capital required to enter a business. Second, it protects the customer against technological obsolescence. Third, the entire lease price, or rental, may be written off as an expense for income tax purposes. This advantage, of course, may or may not be relevant depending on the source of funds the customer would have used for the outright purchase (i.e., his or her own money or borrowed funds). Finally, leasing gives the customer the freedom not to get stuck with a product that may later prove not to be useful.

From the viewpoint of the manufacturer, the leasing strategy is advantageous in many ways. First, income is smoothed out over a period of years, which is very helpful in the case of equipment of high unit value in a cyclical business. Second, market growth can be boosted because more customers can afford to lease a product than can afford to buy. Third, revenues are usually higher when a product is leased than when it is sold.

BUNDLING-PRICING STRATEGY

Bundling, also called **iceberg pricing**, refers to the inclusion of an extra margin (for support services) in the price over and above the price of the product as such. This type of pricing strategy has been popular with companies that lease rather than sell their products. Thus, the rental price, when using a bundling strategy, includes an extra charge to cover a variety of support functions and services needed to maintain the product throughout its useful life. Because unit profit increases sharply after a product completes its planned amortization, it is desirable for firms that lease their products to keep the product in good condition, thus enhancing its working life for high resale or re-leasing value. The bundling strategy permits a company to do so because a charge for upkeep, or iceberg, services is included in the price.

IBM once followed a bundling strategy, whereby it charged one fee for hardware, service, software, and consultancy. In 1969, however, the Justice Department charged IBM with monopolizing the computer market. Subsequently, the company unbundled its price and started selling computers, software, service, and technical input separately.

Under the bundling strategy, not only are costs of hardware and profits covered, anticipated expenses for extra technical sales assistance, design and engineering of the system concept, software and applications to be used on the system, training of personnel, and maintenance are also included. Although the bundling strategy can be criticized for tending to discourage competition, one must consider the complexities involved in delivering and maintaining a fault-free sophisticated system. Without the manufacturer taking the lead in adequately keeping the system in working condition, customers would have to deal with a variety of people to make use of such products as computers.[21] At least in the initial stages of a technologically oriented product, a bundling strategy is highly useful from the customer's point of view.

For the company, this strategy (a) covers the anticipated expenses of providing services and maintaining the product, (b) provides revenues for supporting after-sales service personnel, (c) provides contingency funds to meet unanticipated happenings, and (d) ensures the proper care and maintenance of the leased products. The bundling strategy also permits an ongoing relationship with the customer. In this way the company gains firsthand knowledge of the customer's needs that may help to shift the customer to a new generation of the product. Needless to say, the very nature of the bundling strategy makes it most relevant to technologically sophisticated products, particularly those marked by rapid technological obsolescence.

On the negative side, the bundling strategy tends to inflate costs and distort prices and profitability. For this reason, during unfavorable economic conditions, it may not be an appropriate strategy to pursue. Grocery wholesalers, for instance, may pass through a straight invoice cost and then charge separately for delivery, packaging, and so on. A growing number of department stores now charge extra for home delivery, gift wrapping, and shopping bags. Thus, people who don't want a service need not pay for it.

PRICE-LEADERSHIP STRATEGY

The price-leadership strategy prevails in oligopolistic situations. One member of an industry, because of its size or command over the market, emerges as the leader of an entire industry. The leading firm then makes pricing moves that are duly acknowledged by other members of the industry. Thus, this strategy places the burden of making critical pricing decisions on the leading firm; others simply follow the leader. The leader is expected to be careful in making pricing decisions.

A faulty decision could cost the firm its leadership because other members of the industry would then stop following in its footsteps. For example, if, in increasing prices, the leader is motivated only by self-interest, its price leadership will not be emulated. Ultimately the leader will be forced to withdraw the increase in price.

The price-leadership strategy is a static concept. In an environment where growth opportunities are adequate, companies would rather maintain stability than fight each other by means of price wars. Thus, the leadership concept works out well in this case. In the auto industry, General Motors is the leader, based on market share. The other two domestic members of the industry adjust their prices to come very close to any price increase by General Motors.

Usually, the leader is the company with the largest market share. The leadership strategy is designed to stave off price wars and "predatory" competition that tend to force down prices and hurt all parties. Companies that deviate from this form are chastised through discounting or shaving by the leaders. Price deviation is quickly disciplined.

Successful price leaders are characterized by the following:

1. Large share of the industry's production capacity.
2. Large market share.
3. Commitment to a particular product class or grade.
4. New cost-efficient plants.
5. Strong distribution system, perhaps including captive wholesale outlets.
6. Good customer relations, such as technical assistance for industrial buyers, programs directed at end users, and special attention to important customers during shortages.
7. An effective market information system that provides analysis of the realities of supply and demand.
8. Sensitivity to the price and profit needs of the rest of the industry.
9. A sense of timing to know when price changes should be made.
10. Sound management organization for pricing.
11. Effective product line financial controls, which are needed to make sound price-leadership decisions.
12. Attention to legal issues.[22]

In an unfavorable business environment, it may not be feasible to implement a leadership strategy because firms may be placed differently to interact with the environment. Thus, the leader hesitates to make decisions on behalf of an entire industry because other firms may not always find its decisions to their advantage. For this reason, the price leader/follower pattern may be violated.

In order to survive during unfavorable conditions, even smaller firms may take the initiative to undercut the price leader. For example, during 1988 when the list prices of steel were similar, companies freely discounted their prices. In the chemical industry, with increasing competition from overseas, the price-leadership strategy does not work. Companies thus plan a variety of temporary allowances to generate business. The following quote highlights the erosion of the leadership strategy in the glass container industry:

Traditional patterns of price leadership also are breaking down in the glass container industry, with smaller companies moving to the fore in pricing. Last year, for example, Owens-Illinois, Inc.—which is larger than its next five competitors combined—increased its list prices by 4½ percent. Fearing that the increase would hurt sales to brewing companies that were just beginning to switch to glass bottles, the smaller companies broke ranks and offered huge discounts. The action not only negated O-I's increase but served notice that the smaller companies were after O-I's market share.[23]

An automatic response to a leader's price adjustment assumes that all firms are more or less similarly positioned vis-à-vis different price variables (i.e., cost, competition, and demand) and that different firms have common pricing objectives. Such an assumption, however, is far from being justified. The leadership strategy is an artificial way to enforce similar pricing responses throughout an industry. Strategically, it is a mistake for a company to price in a manner identical to that of its competitors. It should price either above or below the competition to set itself apart.

PRICING STRATEGY TO BUILD MARKET SHARE

Recent work in the area of marketing strategy has delineated the importance of market share as a key variable in strategy formulation. Although market share has been discussed earlier with reference to other matters, this section examines the impact of market share on pricing strategy.

Time and again it has been noted that higher market share and experience lead to lower costs. Thus, a new product should be priced to improve experience and market share. The combination of enhanced market share and experience gives a company such a cost advantage that it cannot ever profitably be overcome by any competitor of normal performance. Competitors are prevented from entering the market and must learn to live in a subordinate position.

Assuming the market is price sensitive, it is desirable to develop the market as early as possible. One way of achieving this is to reduce price. Unit costs are necessarily very high in the early stages of any product; if price is set to recover all costs, there may be no market for the product at its initial price in competition with existing alternatives. Following the impact of market share and experience on prices, it may be worthwhile to set price at a level that will move the product. During the early stages of a product introduction, operations may need to be conducted even at a loss. As volume is gained, costs go down, and even at an initial low price the company makes money, implying that future competitive cost differentials should be of greater concern than current profitability. Of course, such a strategic posture makes sense only in a competitive situation. In the absence of competition there is every reason to set prices as high as possible, to be lowered only when total revenue will not be affected by such an action.

The lower the initial price set by the first producer, the more rapidly that producer builds up volume and a differential cost advantage over succeeding competitors and the faster the market develops. In a sense, employing a pricing strategy that builds market share is a purchase of time advantage. However, the lower the initial price, the greater the investment required before the progressive reduction of cost results in a profit. This in turn means that the comparative investment resources of competitors can become a significant or even the critical determinant of competitive survival.

Two limitations, however, make the implementation of this type of strategy difficult. First, the resources required to institute this strategy are more than those normally available to a firm. Second, the price, once set, must not be raised and should be maintained until costs fall below price; therefore, the lower the price, the longer the time needed to realize any returns and the larger the investment required. When a future return is discounted to present value, there is obviously a limit.

It is these difficulties that lead many firms to set initial price to cover all costs. This policy is particularly likely to be adopted when there is no clear competitive threat. As volume builds and costs decline, visible profitability results, which in turn induces new competitors to enter the field. As competitors make their moves, the innovating firm has the problem of choosing between current profitability and market share. Strategically, however, the pricing of a new product, following the relationship between market share and cost, should be dictated by a product's projected future growth.

SUMMARY

Pricing strategy is of interest to the very highest management levels of a company. Yet few management decisions are more subject to intuition than pricing. There is a reason for this. Pricing decisions are primarily affected by factors, such as pricing objectives, cost, competition, and demand, that are difficult to articulate and analyze. For example, assumptions must be made about what a competitor will do under certain hypothetical circumstances. There is no way to know that for certain; hence the characteristic reliance on intuition.

This chapter reviewed the pricing factors mentioned above and examines important strategies that a pricer may pursue. The following strategies were discussed:

1. Pricing strategies for new products.
2. Pricing strategies for established products.
3. Price-flexibility strategy.
4. Product line-pricing strategy.
5. Leasing strategy.
6. Bundling-pricing strategy.
7. Price-leadership strategy.
8. Pricing strategy to build market share.

There are two principal pricing strategies for new products, skimming and penetration. Skimming is a high-price strategy; penetration strategy sets a low initial price to generate volume. Three strategies for established products were discussed: maintaining the price, reducing the price, and increasing the price. A flexible-pricing strategy provides leverage to the pricer in terms of duration of commitment both from market to market and from product to product. Product line-pricing strategy is directed toward maintaining a balance among different products offered by a company. The leasing strategy constitutes an alternative to outright sale of the product. The bundling strategy is concerned with packaging products and associated services together for the purposes of pricing. Price-leadership strategy is a characteristic of an oligopoly, where one firm in an industry emerges as a leader and sets the pricing strategy to build market share. Setting price to build market share emphasizes the strategic significance of setting an initially low price to gain volume and market share, thereby enabling the firm to achieve additional cost reductions in the future.

DISCUSSION QUESTIONS

1. Is the maintenance of a stable price a viable objective? Why?
2. Is there a conflict between profit and volume objectives? Doesn't one lead to the other? Discuss.
3. What are the advantages of using incremental costs instead of full costs for pricing? Are there any negative implications of using incremental costs that a pricing strategist needs to be aware of?
4. What assumptions need to be made about competitive behavior for formulating pricing strategy?
5. "Short-term price increases tend to depress industry profits in the long run by accelerating the introduction of new capacity and depressing market demand." Discuss.
6. Following the experience curve concept, the initial price of a new product should be set rather low; as a matter of fact, it may be set below cost. Taking into account the popularity of this thesis, discuss the relevance of the skimming strategy.
7. What factors are ascribed to the decline in popularity of the price-leadership strategy?

NOTES

[1] Thomas T. Nagle, *The Strategy and Tactics of Pricing* (Englewood Cliffs, NJ: Prentice-Hall, 1987), 8.

[2] Heywood Klein, "Illinois Bell Faces New Environment as Era of Competitive Pricing Nears," *Wall Street Journal* (31 December 1981): 9.

[3] Mark I. Alpert, *Pricing Decisions* (Glenview, IL: Scott, Foresman, 1971), 96.

[4] "Having an Ulcer is Getting a Lot Cheaper," *Business Week* (9 May 1994): 30.

[5] "Pricing Strategy in an Inflation Economy," *Business Week* (6 April 1974): 43.

[6] Philip Kotler, *Marketing Management,* 7th ed. (Englewood Cliffs, NJ: Prentice-Hall, 1991), 478.

[7] *Wall Street Journal* (31 December 1981): 9.

[8] William H. Redmond, "Innovation, Price Strategy and Long Term Performance," *Working Paper* (Waltham, MA: Bentley College, 1987).

[9] "How T.I. Beat the Clock on Its $20 Digital Watch," *Business Week* (31 May 1976): 62–63. (For different reasons, T.I. quit the digital watch business itself a few years later. But the point made here with reference to pricing is still relevant.)

[10] Richard Gibson, "Discount Menu Is Coming to McDonald's as Chain Tries to Win Back Customers," *Wall Street Journal* (30 November 1990): B1. See also "Grocery Price Wars Squeeze Marketers" *Wall Street Journal* (7 November 1991): B1.

[11] "Will Home Depot Be the 'Wal-Mart of the '90s?'" *Business Week* (19 March 1990): 124.

[12] Ignatics Chitbebhen, "Clinical Case," *Forbes* (20 May 1989): 178.

[13] "Looking Downscale Without Looking Down," *Business Week* (8 October 1990): 62.

[14] "The Smoke Clears at Marlboro," *Business Week* (31 January 1994): 76.

[15] Michael V. Marn and Robert L. Rosiello, "Managing Price, Gaining Profit," *Harvard Business Review* (September–October 1992): 48.

[16] John B. Hinge, "Critics Call Cuts in Package Size Deceptive Move," *Wall Street Journal* (February 5 1991): B1.

[17] Andrew A. Stern, "Pricing and Differentiation Strategies," *Planning Review* (September–October 1989): 30–34.

[18] Thomas Nagle, "Pricing as Creative Marketing," *Business Horizons* (July–August 1983): 14–19

[19] See Andrew A. Stern, "The Strategic Value of Price Structure," *Journal of Business Strategy* (Fall 1986): 22–31. See also Gerard J. Tellis, "Beyond the Many Faces of Price: An Integration of Pricing Strategies," *Journal of Marketing* (October 1986): 146–60.

[20] "Leasing Fever," *Business Week* (7 February 1994): 92.

[21] Tellis, "Beyond the Many Faces of Price," 146–60.

[22] Stuart U. Rich, "Price Leaders: Large, Strong, but Cautious about Conspiracy," *Marketing News* (25 June 1982): 11.

[23] "Flexible Pricing," *Business Week* (12 December 1981): 81.

APPENDIX | *Perspectives on Pricing Strategies*

I.
Price Strategies for
New Products

A. Skimming Pricing

Definition: Setting a relatively high price during the initial stage of a product's life.

Objectives: (a) To serve customers who are not price conscious while the market is at the upper end of the demand curve and competition has not yet entered the market. (b) To recover a significant portion of promotional and research and development costs through a high margin.

Requirements: (a) Heavy promotional expenditure to introduce product, educate consumers, and induce early buying. (b) Relatively inelastic demand at the upper end of the demand curve. (c) Lack of direct competition and substitutes.

Expected Results: (a) Market segmented by price-conscious and not so price-conscious customers. (b) High margin on sales that will cover promotion and research and development costs. (c) Opportunity for the firm to lower its price and sell to the mass market before competition enters.

B. Penetration Pricing

Definition: Setting a relatively low price during the initial stages of a product's life.

Objective: To discourage competition from entering the market by quickly taking a large market share and by gaining a cost advantage through realizing economies of scale.

Requirements: (a) Product must appeal to a market large enough to support the cost advantage. (b) Demand must be highly elastic in order for the firm to guard its cost advantage.

Expected Results: (a) High sales volume and large market share. (b) Low margin on sales. (c) Lower unit costs relative to competition due to economies of scale.

II.
Pricing Strategies
for Established
Products

A. Maintaining the Price

Objectives: (a) To maintain position in the marketplace (i.e., market share, profitability, etc.). (b) To enhance public image.

Requirements: (a) Firm's served market is not significantly affected by changes in the environment. (b) Uncertainty exists concerning the need for or result of a price change. (c) Firm's public image could be enhanced by responding to government requests or public opinion to maintain price.

Expected Results: (a) Status quo for the firm's market position. (b) Enhancement of the firm's public image.

B. Reducing the Price

Objectives: (a) To act defensively and cut price to meet the competition. (b) To act offensively and attempt to beat the competition. (c) To respond to a customer need created by a change in the environment.

Requirements: (a) Firm must be financially and competitively strong to fight in a price war if that becomes necessary. (b) Must have a good understanding of the demand function of its product.

Expected Results: Lower profit margins (assuming costs are held constant). Higher market share might be expected, but this will depend upon the price change relative to competitive prices and upon price elasticity.

C. Increasing the Price

Objectives: (a) To maintain profitability during an inflationary period. (b) To take advantage of product differences, real or perceived. (c) To segment the current served market.

Requirements: (a) Relatively low price elasticity but relatively high elasticity with respect to some other factor such as quality or distribution. (b) Reinforcement from other ingredients of the marketing mix; for example, if a firm decides to increase price and differentiate its product by quality, then promotion and distribution must address product quality.

Expected Results: (a) Higher sales margin. (b) Segmented market (price conscious, quality conscious, etc.). (c) Possibly higher unit sales, if differentiation is effective.

III.
Price-Flexibility
Strategy

A. One-Price Strategy

Definition: Charging the same price to all customers under similar conditions and for the same quantities.

Objectives: (a) To simplify pricing decisions. (b) To maintain goodwill among customers.

Requirements: (a) Detailed analysis of the firm's position and cost structure as compared with the rest of the industry. (b) Information concerning the cost variability of offering the same price to everyone. (c) Knowledge of the economies of scale available to the firm. (d) Information on competitive prices; information on the price that customers are ready to pay.

Expected Results: (a) Decreased administrative and selling costs. (b) Constant profit margins. (c) Favorable and fair image among customers. (d) Stable market.

B. Flexible-Pricing Strategy

Definition: Charging different prices to different customers for the same product and quantity.

Objective: To maximize short-term profits and build traffic by allowing upward and downward adjustments in price depending on competitive conditions and how much the customer is willing to pay for the product.

Requirements: Have the information needed to implement the strategy. Usually this strategy is implemented in one of four ways: (a) by market, (b) by product, (c) by timing, (d) by technology. Other requirements include (a) a customer-value analysis of the product, (b) an emphasis on profit margin rather than just volume, and (c) a record of competitive reactions to price moves in the past.

Expected Results: (a) Increased sales, leading to greater market share. (b) Increased short-term profits. (c) Increased selling and administrative costs. (d) Legal difficulties stemming from price discrimination.

IV.
Product Line-Pricing
Strategy

Definition: Pricing a product line according to each product's effect on and relationship with other products in that line, whether competitive or complementary.

Objective: To maximize profits from the whole line, not just certain members of it.

Requirements: (a) For a product already in the line, strategy is developed according to the product's contributions to its pro rata share of overhead and direct costs. (b) For a new product, a product/market analysis determines whether the product will be profitable. Pricing is then a function of costs, profit goals, experience, and external competition.

Expected Results: (a) Well-balanced and consistent pricing schedule across the product line. (b) Greater profits in the long term. (c) Better performance of the line as a whole.

V. Leasing Strategy

Definition: An agreement by which an owner (lessor) of an asset rents that asset to a second party (lessee). The lessee pays a specified sum of money, which includes principal and interest, each month as a rental payment.

Objectives: (a) To enhance market growth by attracting customers who cannot buy outright. (b) To realize greater long-term profits; once the production costs are fully amortized, the rental fee is mainly profit. (c) To increase cash flow. (d) To have a stable flow of earnings. (e) To have protection against losing revenue because of technological obsolescence.

Requirements: (a) Necessary financial resources to continue production of subsequent products for future sales or leases. (b) Adequate computation of lease rate and minimum period for which lease is binding such that the total amount the lessee pays for the duration of the lease is less than would be paid in monthly installments on an outright purchase. (c) Customers who are restrained by large capital requirements necessary for outright purchase or need write-offs for income tax purposes. (d) The capability to match competitors' product improvements that may make the lessor's product obsolete.

Expected Results: (a) Increased market share because customers include those who would have forgone purchase of product. (b) Consistent earnings over a period of years. (c) Greater cash flow due to lower income tax expense from depreciation write-offs. (d) Increased sales as customers exercise their purchase options.

VI. Bundling-Pricing Strategy

Definition: Inclusion of an extra margin in the price to cover a variety of support functions and services needed to sell and maintain the product throughout its useful life.

Objectives: (a) In a leasing arrangement, to have assurance that the asset will be properly maintained and kept in good working condition so that it can be resold or re-leased. (b) To generate extra revenues to cover the anticipated expenses of providing services and maintaining the product. (c) To generate revenues for supporting after-sales service personnel. (d) To establish a contingency fund for unanticipated happenings. (e) To develop an ongoing relationship with the customer. (f) To discourage competition with "free" after-sales support and service.

Requirements: This strategy is ideally suited for technologically sophisticated products that are susceptible to rapid technological obsolescence because these products are generally sold in systems and usually require the following: (a) extra technical sales assistance, (b) custom design and engineering concept for the customer, (c) peripheral equipment and applications, (d) training of the customer's personnel, and (e) a strong service/maintenance department offering prompt responses and solutions to customer problems.

Expected Results: (a) Asset is kept in an acceptable condition for resale or re-lease. (b) Positive cash flow. (c) Instant information on changing customer needs. (d) Increased sales due to "total package" concept of selling because customers feel they are getting their money's worth.

VII.
Price-Leadership Strategy

Definition: This strategy is used by the leading firm in an industry in making major pricing moves, which are followed by other firms in the industry.

Objective: To gain control of pricing decisions within an industry in order to support the leading firm's own marketing strategy (i.e., create barriers to entry, increase profit margin, etc.).

Requirements: (a) An oligopolistic situation. (b) An industry in which all firms are affected by the same price variables (i.e., cost, competition, demand). (c) An industry in which all firms have common pricing objectives. (d) Perfect knowledge of industry conditions; an error in pricing means losing control.

Expected Results: (a) Prevention of price wars, which are liable to hurt all parties involved. (b) Stable pricing moves. (c) Stable market share.

VIII.
Pricing Strategy to Build Market Share

Definition: Setting the lowest price possible for a new product.

Objective: To seek such a cost advantage that it cannot ever be profitably overcome by any competitor.

Requirements: (a) Enough resources to withstand initial operating losses that will be recovered later through economies of scale. (b) Price-sensitive market. (c) Large market. (d) High elasticity of demand.

Expected Results: (a) Start-up losses to build market share. (b) Creation of a barrier to entry to the industry. (c) Ultimately, cost leadership within the industry.

Distribution Strategies

Distribution strategies are concerned with the channels a firm may employ to make its goods and services available to customers. **Channels** are organized structures of buyers and sellers that bridge the gap of time and space between the manufacturer and the customer.

Marketing is defined as an exchange process. In relation to distribution, exchange poses two problems. First, goods must be moved to a central location from the warehouses of producers who make heterogeneous goods and who are geographically widespread. Second, the goods that are accumulated from diversified sources should represent a desired assortment from the viewpoint of customers. These two problems can be solved by the process of sorting, which combines concentration (i.e., bringing the goods from different sources to a central location) and dispersion (i.e., picking an assortment of goods from different points of concentration). Two basic questions need to be answered here. Who should perform the concentration and dispersion tasks—the manufacturer or intermediaries? Which intermediary should the manufacturer select to bring goods close to the customer? These questions are central to distribution strategies.

Other strategy-related matters discussed in this chapter include scope of distribution (i.e., how widespread distribution may be), use of multiple channels to serve different segments, modification of channels to accommodate environmental shifts, resolution of conflict among channels, and use of vertical systems to institute control over channels. Each strategic issue is examined for its relevance in different circumstances. The application of each strategy is illustrated with examples from marketing literature.

CHANNEL-STRUCTURE STRATEGY

The **channel-structure strategy** refers to the number of intermediaries that may be employed in moving goods from manufacturers to customers. A company may undertake to distribute its goods to customers or retailers without involving any intermediary. This strategy constitutes the shortest channel and may be labeled a *direct distribution strategy*. Alternatively, goods may pass through one or more intermediaries, such as wholesalers or agents. This is an *indirect distribution strategy*. Exhibit 16-1 shows alternative channel structures for consumer and industrial products.

EXHIBIT 16-1
Typical Channel Structures

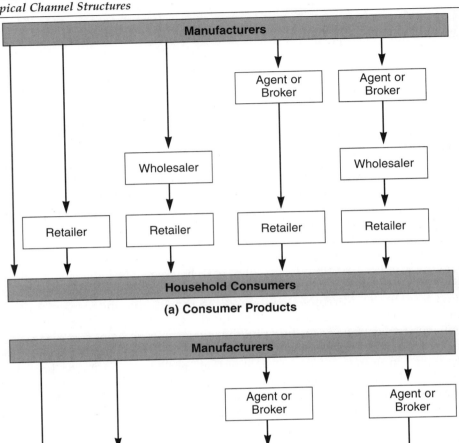

(a) Consumer Products

(b) Industrial Products

Decisions about channel structure are based on a variety of factors. To a significant extent, channel structure is determined by where inventories should be maintained to offer adequate customer service, fulfill required sorting processes, and still deliver a satisfactory return to channel members.

An underlying factor in determining channel-structure strategy is the use of intermediaries. The importance of using intermediaries is illustrated with reference to an example of a primitive economy used by Alderson.[1] In a primitive economy, five producers produce one type of item each: hats, hoes, knives, baskets, or pots. Because each producer needs all the other producers' products, a total of 10 exchanges are required to accomplish trade. However, with a market (or middlemen), once the economy reaches equilibrium (i.e., each producer-consumer has visited the market once), only five exchanges need to take place to meet everyone's needs. Let n denote the number of producer-consumers. Then the total number of transactions (T) without a market is given by:

$$T_{\text{without}} = \frac{n(n-1)}{2}$$

and the total number of transactions with a market is given by:

$$T_{\text{with}} = n$$

The efficiency created in distribution by using an intermediary may be viewed using this equation:

$$\text{Efficiency} = \frac{T_{\text{without}}}{T_{\text{with}}} = \frac{n(n-1)}{2} \times \frac{1}{n} = \frac{n-1}{2}$$

In the example of five producer-consumers, the efficiency of having a middleman is 2. The efficiency increases as n increases. Thus, in many cases, intermediaries may perform the task of distribution more efficiently than manufacturers alone.

Postponement-Speculation Theory

Conceptually, the selection of channel structure may be explained with reference to Bucklin's postponement-speculation framework.[2] The framework is based on risk, uncertainty, and costs involved in facilitating exchanges. Postponement seeks to eliminate risk by matching production/distribution with actual customer demand. Presumably, postponement should produce efficiency in marketing channels. For example, the manufacturer may produce and ship goods only on confirmed orders. Speculation, on the other hand, requires undertaking risk through changes in form and movement of goods within channels. Speculation leads to economies of scale in manufacturing, reduces costs of frequent ordering, and eliminates opportunity cost.

Exhibit 16-2 shows the behavior of variables involved in the postponement-speculation framework. The vertical axis shows the average cost of undertaking a function for one unit of any given commodity; the horizontal axis shows the time involved in delivering a confirmed order. Together, the average cost and the delivery time measure the cost of marketing tasks performed in a channel with reference to delivery time. The nature of the three curves depicted in Exhibit 16-2 should be understood: C represents costs to the buyer for holding an inventory; AD', costs involved in supplying goods directly from a manufacturer to a buyer; and DB, costs involved in shipping and maintaining speculative inventories (i.e., in anticipation of demand).

EXHIBIT 16-2
Using the Postponement-Speculation Concept to Determine Channel Structure

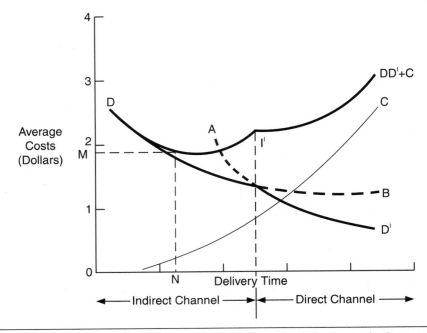

Source: Louis P. Bucklin and Leslie Halpert, "Exploring Channels of Distribution for Cement with the Principle of Postponement-Speculation," in *Marketing and Economic Development*, ed. Peter D. Bennett (Chicago: American Marketing Association, 1965), 698. Reprinted by permission of the American Marketing Association.

Following Bucklin's framework, one determines the channel structure by examining the behavior of the C, AD', and DB curves:

1. The minimal cost of supplying the buyer for every possible delivery time is derived from curves AD' and DB. As may be seen in [Exhibit 16-2], especially fast delivery service can be provided only by the indirect channel (i.e., by using a stocking intermediary). However, at some delivery time, I', the cost of serving the consumer directly from the producer will intersect and fall below the cost of indirect shipment. The minimal costs derived from both curves are designated DD'. From the perspective of channel cost, it will be cheaper to service the buyer from a speculative inventory if delivery times shorter than I' are demanded. If the consumer is willing to accept delivery times longer than I', then direct shipment will be the least expensive.
2. The minimal total cost curve for the channel with respect to delivery time is derived by summing the cost of moving goods to the buyer, DD', and the buyer's costs of holding inventory, C. The curve is represented in [Exhibit 16-2] by DD' + C. Total channel costs initially fall as delivery time lengthens because increased buyer expenses are more than made up for by savings in other parts of the channel. Gradually, however, the savings from these sources diminish and buyer costs

begin to rise more rapidly. A minimal cost point is reached, and expenses for the channel rise thereafter. Channel structure is controlled by the location of this minimum point. If, as in the present case, it falls to the left of I', then goods would be expected to flow through the speculative inventory (i.e., an intermediary). If, on the other hand, the savings of the buyer from postponement had not been as great as those depicted, the minimum point would have fallen to the right of I' and shipments would have been made directly from the producer to the consumer.[3]

Benetton, an Italian apparel maker, offers an excellent example of a distribution strategy that combines speculation with postponement in an effort to optimize both service and cost. Speculation involves commitment by retailers to specific inventory items months before the start of the selling season. It leads to such advantages for Benetton as low-cost production (via use of subcontractors) and good quality control (via centralized warehousing and assembly of orders). Postponement of orders requires last-minute dyeing of woolen items at an added cost. The advantages of speculation are flexibility in meeting market needs and reduced inventory levels.[4]

Additional Consideration in Determining Channel Structure

The postponement-speculation theory provides an economic explanation of the way the channels are structured. Examined in this section are a variety of environmental influences on channel-structure strategy formulation. These influences may be technological, social and ethical, governmental, geographical, or cultural.

Many aspects of channel structure are affected by technological advances. For example, mass retailing in food has become feasible because of the development of automobiles, highways, refrigerated cars, cash registers, packaging improvements, and mass communications (television). In the coming years, television shopping with household computer terminals should have a far-reaching impact on distribution structures.[5] Technological advances permitted Sony to become dominant in the U.S. market for low-priced CD players. Sony developed prepackaged players that could be sold through mass retailers so that even sales clerks without technical know-how could handle customers.

How technology may be used to revamp the operations of a wholesaler, making it worthwhile to adopt indirect channels, is illustrated by the case of Foremost-McKesson, the nation's largest wholesale distributor. A few years ago, the company found itself in a precarious position. Distribution, though one of the company's most pervasive business functions, did not pay. Foremost-McKesson merely took manufacturers' goods and resold them to small retailers through a routine process of warehousing, transportation, and simple marketing that offered thin profits. As a matter of fact, at one time the company came close to selling off drug wholesaling, its biggest business. Instead, however, its new chief executive decided to add sophisticated technology to its operations in order to make the company so efficient at distribution that manufacturers could not possibly do as well on their own. It virtually redefined the function of the intermediary. Having used the computer to make its own operations efficient, it devised ways to make its data processing useful to suppliers and customers, in essence making Foremost part of their marketing teams. Since the company computerized its operations, Foremost has turned around dramatically. Here are the highlights of Foremost's steps in reshaping its role:

- Acting as middleman between drugstores and insurance offices by processing medical insurance claims.
- Creating a massive "rack jobbing" service by providing crews to set up racks of goods inside retail stores, offering what amounts to a temporary labor force that brings both marketing know-how and Foremost merchandise along with it.
- Taking waste products as well as finished goods from chemical manufacturers, and recycling the wastes through its own plants—its first entry into chemical waste management.
- Designing, as well as supplying, drugstores.
- Researching new uses for products it receives from manufacturers. Foremost found new customers, for example, for a Monsanto Co. food preservative from among its contacts in the cosmetics industry.[6]

Social taboos and ethical standards may also affect the channel-structure decision. For example, Mallen reports that *Viva*, a woman's magazine, had achieved a high circulation in supermarkets and drugstores in Canada. When *Viva* responded to readers' insistence and to competition from *Playgirl* by introducing nude male photos, most supermarkets banned the magazine. Because supermarkets accounted for more than half of *Viva's* circulation, *Viva* dropped the photos so that it could continue to be sold through this channel.[7]

The channel-structure strategy can also be influenced by local, state, and federal laws in a variety of ways. For example, door-to-door selling of certain goods may be prohibited by local laws. In many states (e.g., California and Ohio) wine can be sold through supermarkets, but other states (e.g., Connecticut) do not permit this.

Geographic size, population patterns, and typology also influence the channel-structure strategy. In urban areas, direct distribution to large retailers may make sense. Rural areas, however, may be covered only by wholesalers.

With the inception of large grocery chains, it may often appear that independent grocery stores are dying. The truth is, however, that independent grocery stores as recently as 1988 accounted for 46 percent of all grocery sales in the country—over $148 billion. Thus, a manufacturer can ill afford not to deal with independents and to reach them it must go through wholesalers. Wetterau, for example, is a grocery wholesale firm in Hazelwood, Missouri, which did over $6 billion worth of business serving almost 3,000 retail grocery stores. It does not do any business with chain stores. But because of Wetterau's determination to offer its customers relatively low prices, a wide selection of brands, service programs carefully designed to make brands more profitable, and a personal interest in their success, its customers are almost fanatically loyal. The company offers its customers—small independent retail stores—a variety of services, including lease arrangements, store design, financing packages, training, and computerized inventory systems. These services tend to enhance customers' competitiveness by reducing their operating costs and by simplifying their bookkeeping, which in turn helps Wetterau to earn profits.[8] The Wetterau example shows that to reach smaller retailers, particularly in areas far removed from large metropolises, the indirect distribution strategy is appropriate. The wholesaler provides services to small retailers that a large manufacturer can never match on its own.

Finally, cultural traits may require the adoption of a certain channel structure in a setting that otherwise might seem an odd place for it. For example, in many parts of Switzerland, fruits and vegetables are sold in a central marketplace in the morning by small vendors, even though there are modern supermarkets all over. This practice continues because it gives customers a chance to socialize while shopping. Similarly, changing lifestyles among average American consumers and their desire to have more discretionary income for life-fulfillment activities appear to be making warehouse retailing (e.g., Sam's Club) more popular. This is so because prices at warehouse outlets—grocery warehouses, for example—are substantially lower than at traditional stores.

Channel Design Model

Presented below is a channel design model that can be used to make the direct/indirect distribution decision. The model involves six basic steps.

1. List the factors that could potentially influence the direct/indirect decision. Each factor must be evaluated carefully in terms of the firm's industry position and competitive strategy.
2. Pick out the factors that will have the most impact on the channel design decision. No factor with a dominant impact should be left out. For example, assume that the following four factors have been identified as having particular significance: market concentration, customer service level, asset specificity, and availability of working capital.
3. Decide how each factor identified is related to the attractiveness of a direct or an indirect channel. For example, market concentration reflects the size distribution of the firm's customers as well as their geographical dispersion. Therefore, the more concentrated the market, the more desirable the direct channel because of the lower costs of serving that market (high = direct; low = indirect). Customer service level is made up of at least three factors: delivery time, lot size, and product availability. The more customer service required by customers, the less desirable is the direct channel (high = indirect; low = direct). The direct channel is more desirable, at least under conditions of high uncertainty in the environment, with a high level of asset specificity (high = direct; low = indirect). Finally, the greater the availability of working capital, the more likely it is that a manufacturer can afford and consider a direct channel (high = direct; low = indirect). Note that a high level on a factor does not always correspond to a direct channel.
4. Create a matrix based on the key factors to consider the interactions among key factors. If only two factors are being considered, a two-by-two matrix of four cells would result. For three factors, a three-by-three matrix of nine cells would result. For four factors, a four-by-four matrix of sixteen cells would result, and so on. If more than five or six factors are involved, a series of smaller models could be constructed to make this fourth step more manageable. Exhibit 16-3 presents a four-by-four matrix developed for this example.
5. Decide (for each cell in the matrix) whether a direct channel, an indirect channel, or a combination of both a direct and an indirect channel is most appropriate,

considering the factors involved. Combination channels are becoming more common in business practice, especially in industrial markets.

For some cells in the matrix, deciding which channel design is best is rather easy to do. For example, Cell 1 in Exhibit 16-3 has all four factors in agreement that an indirect channel is best. This is also true for Cell 16: a direct channel is the obvious choice. For other cells, choosing between a direct channel and an indirect channel is not as easy because factors conflict with each other to some extent. For example, in Cell 14, asset specificity is low, suggesting that an indirect channel is best. The other three factors suggest otherwise, however; the market is concentrated, customer service requirements are low, and the availability of capital to the manufacturer is high. Taken together, the factors in Cell 14 reveal that a direct channel would be most attractive. In the cells that have factors that conflict with one another, the strategist must make trade-offs among them to decide whether a direct channel, indirect channel, or combination of channels is best.

6. For each product or service in question, locate the corresponding cell in the box model. The prediction in this cell is the one that should be followed or at least the one that should be most seriously considered by the firm.

The accuracy of the model generated by this method depends totally on the expertise and skills of the person who builds and uses it. If carefully constructed, such a model can be invaluable in designing more efficient and effective channels of distribution.[9]

EXHIBIT 16-3
Designing a Distribution Channel Matrix

				Asset Specificity			
				Low		High	
				Capital Availability		Capital Availability	
				Low	High	Low	High
Market Concentration	Low	Customer Service Level	High	cell 1 indirect	cell 3 indirect	cell 2 indirect	cell 4 combination
			Low	cell 5 indirect	cell 7 combination	cell 6 combination	cell 8 direct
	High	Customer Service Level	High	cell 9 indirect	cell 11 combination	cell 10 direct	cell 12 direct
			Low	cell 13 combination	cell 15 combination	cell 14 direct	cell 16 direct

Source: Gary L. Frazier, "Designing Channels of Distribution," *The Channel for Communication* (Seattle, Wash.: Center for Retail Distribution Management, University of Washington, 1987): 3–7.

DISTRIBUTION-SCOPE STRATEGY

For an efficient channel network, the manufacturer should clearly define the target customers it intends to reach. Implicit in the definition of target customers is a decision about the scope of distribution the manufacturer wants to pursue. The strategic alternatives here are exclusive distribution, selective distribution, and intensive distribution.

Exclusive Distribution

Exclusive distribution means that one particular retailer serving a given area is granted sole rights to carry a product. For example, Hart, Schaffner, and Marx suits are distributed exclusively through select stores in an area. Several advantages may be gained by the use of exclusive distribution. It promotes tremendous dealer loyalty, greater sales support, a higher degree of control over the retail market, better forecasting, and better inventory and merchandising control. The impact of dealer loyalty can be helpful when a manufacturer has seasonal or other kinds of fluctuating sales. An exclusive dealership is more willing to finance inventories and thus bear a higher degree of risk than a more extensive dealership. Having a smaller number of dealers gives a manufacturer or wholesaler greater opportunity to provide each dealer with promotional support. And with fewer outlets, it is easier to control such aspects as margin, price, and inventory. Dealers are also more willing to provide data that may be used for marketing research and forecasts. Exclusive distribution is especially relevant for products that customers seek out. Examples of such products include Rolex watches, Gucci bags, Regal shoes, Celine neckties, and Mark Cross wallets.

On the other hand, there are several obvious disadvantages to exclusive distribution. First, sales volume may be lost. Second, the manufacturer places all its fortunes in a geographic area in the hands of one dealer. Exclusive distribution brings with it the characteristics of high price, high margin, and low volume. If the product is highly price elastic in nature, this combination of characteristics can mean significantly less than optimal performance. Relying on one retailer can mean that if sales are depressed for any reason, the retailer is then likely to be in a position to dictate terms to other channel members (i.e., the retailer becomes the channel captain).

For example, assume that a company manufacturing traditional toys deals exclusively with JCPenney. For a variety of reasons, its line of toys may not do well. These reasons may be a continuing decline in the birthrate, an economic recession, the emerging popularity of electronic toys, higher prices of the company's toys compared to competitive brands, a poor promotional effort by JCPenney, and so on. Because it is the exclusive distributor, however, JCPenney may put the blame on the manufacturer's prices, and it may demand a reduction in prices from the manufacturer. Inasmuch as the manufacturer has no other reasons to give that could explain its poor performance, it must depend on JCPenney's analysis.

The last disadvantage of exclusive distribution is one that is easy to overlook. In certain circumstances, exclusive distribution has been found to be in violation of antitrust laws because of its restraint on trade. The legality of an exclusive contract varies from case to case. As long as an exclusive contract does not undermine competition and create a monopoly, it is acceptable. The courts appear to use the following criteria to determine if indeed an exclusive distribution lessens competition:

1. Whether the volume of the product in question is a substantial part of the total volume for that product type.
2. Whether the exclusive dealership excludes competitive products from a substantial share of the market.

Thus, a company considering an exclusive distribution strategy should review its decision in the light of these two ground rules.

Intensive Distribution

The inverse of exclusive distribution is intensive distribution. **Intensive distribution** makes a product available at all possible retail outlets. This may mean that the product is carried at a wide variety of different and also competing retail institutions in a given area. The distribution of convenience goods is most consistent with this strategy. If the nature of a product is such that a consumer generally does not bother to seek out the product but will buy it on sight if available, then it is to the seller's advantage to have the product visible in as many places as possible. The Bic Pen Corporation is an example of a firm that uses this type of strategy. Bic makes its products available in a wide variety of retail establishments, ranging from drugstores, to "the corner grocery store," to large supermarkets. In all, Bic sells through 250,000 retail outlets, which represent competing as well as noncompeting stores. The advantages to be gained from this strategy are increased sales, wider customer recognition, and impulse buying. All of these qualities are desirable for convenience goods.

There are two main disadvantages associated with intensive distribution. First, intensively distributed goods are characteristically low-priced and low-margin products that require a fast turnover. Second, it is difficult to provide any degree of control over a large number of retailers. In the short run, uncontrolled distribution may not pose any problem if the intensive distribution leads to increased sales. In the long run, however, it may have a variety of devastating effects. For example, if durable products such as Sony television sets were to be intensively distributed (i.e., through drugstores, discount stores, variety stores, etc.), Sony's sales would probably increase. But such intensive distribution could lead to the problems of price discounting, inadequate customer service, and noncooperation among traditional channels (e.g., department stores). Not only might these problems affect sales revenues in the long run, but the manufacturer might also lose some of its established channels. For example, a department store might decide to drop the Sony line for another brand of television sets. In addition, Sony's distinctive brand image could suffer. In other words, the advantages furnished by intensive distribution should be related carefully to product type to decide if this form of distribution is suitable. It is because of the problems outlined above that one finds intensive distribution limited to such products as candy, newspapers, cigarettes, aspirin, and soft drinks. For these types of products, turnover is usually high and channel control is usually not as strategic as it would be, say, for television sets.

Selective Distribution

Between exclusive and intensive distribution, there is selective distribution. **Selective distribution** is the strategy in which several but not all retail outlets in a given area distribute a product. **Shopping goods**—goods that consumers seek on the basis of the most attractive price or quality characteristics—are frequently distributed through selective distribution. Because of this, competition among retailers is far greater for shopping goods than for convenience goods. Naturally, retailers wish to reduce competition as much as possible. This causes them to pressure manufacturers to reduce the number of retail outlets in their area distributing a given product in order to reduce competition.

The number of retailers under a selective distribution strategy should be limited by criteria that allow the manufacturer to choose only those retailers who will make a contribution to the firm's overall distribution objectives. For example, some firms may choose retail outlets that can provide acceptable repair and maintenance service to consumers who purchase their products. In the automotive industry, selective criteria are used by manufacturers in granting dealerships. These criteria consist of such considerations as showroom space, service facilities, and inventory levels.

The point may be illustrated with reference to Pennsylvania House, a furniture company. The company used to have 800 retail accounts, but it cut this number to 500. This planned cut obviously limited the number of stores in which the company's product line was exposed. More limited distribution provided the company with much stronger support among surviving dealers. Among these 500 dealers, there was a higher average amount of floor space devoted to Pennsylvania House merchandise, better customer service, better supplier relations, and most important for the company, it increased sales per account by a factor of three.[10]

Selective distribution is best applied under circumstances in which high sales volume can be generated by a relatively small number of retailers or, in other words, in which the manufacturer would not appreciably increase its coverage by adding additional dealers. Selective distribution can also be used effectively in situations in which a manufacturer requires a high-caliber firm to carry a full product line and provide necessary services. A dealer in this position is likely to require promotional and technical assistance. The technical assistance is needed not only in conjunction with the sale but also after the sale in the form of repair and maintenance service. Again, by limiting the number of retail outlets to a select few capable of covering the market, the manufacturer can avoid unnecessary costs associated with signing on additional dealers.

Obviously, the greatest danger associated with a strategy of selective distribution is the risk of not adequately covering the market. The consequences of this error are greater than the consequences of initially having one or two extra dealers. Therefore, when in doubt, it is better to have too much coverage than not enough.

In selective distribution, it is extremely important for a manufacturer to choose dealers (retailers) who most closely match the marketing goals and image intended for the product. There can be segments within retail markets; therefore, identifying the right retailers can be the key to penetrating a chosen market. Every department store cannot be considered the same. Among them there can be price, age, and image segmentation. One does not need to be very accurate in distinguishing among stores of the same type in the case of products that have no special image (i.e., those that lend themselves to unsegmented market strategies and mass distribution). But for products with any degree of fashion or style content or with highly segmented customer groups, a selective distribution strategy requires a careful choice of outlets.

To appraise what type of product is suitable for what form of distribution, refer to Exhibit 16-4. This exhibit combines the traditional threefold classification of consumer goods (convenience, shopping, and specialty goods) with a threefold classification of retail stores (convenience, shopping, and specialty stores) to determine the appropriate form of distribution. This initial selection may then be examined in the light of other considerations to make a final decision on the scope of distribution.

MULTIPLE-CHANNEL STRATEGY

The multiple-channel strategy refers to a situation in which two or more different channels are employed to distribute goods and services. The market must be segmented so that each segment gets the services it needs and pays only for them, not for services it does not need. This type of segmentation usually cannot be done effectively by direct selling alone or by exclusive reliance upon distributors. The Robinson-Patman Act makes the use of price for segmentation almost impossible when selling to the same kind of customer through the same distribution channel. Market segmentation, however, may be possible when selling directly to one class of customer and to another only through distributors, which usually requires different services, prices, and support. Thus, a multiple-channel strategy permits optimal access to each individual segment.

Basically, there are two types of multiple channels of distribution, complementary and competitive.

Complementary Channels

Complementary channels exist when each channel handles a different noncompeting product or noncompeting market segment. An important reason to promote complementary channels is to reach market segments that cannot otherwise be served. For example, Avon Products, which had sold directly to consumers for 100 years, broke the tradition in 1986 and began selling some perfumes (e.g., Deneuve fragrance, which sells for as much as $165 an ounce) through department stores. The rationale behind this move was to serve customer segments that the company could not reach through direct selling.[11] Samsonite Corporation sells the same type of luggage to discount stores that it distributes through department stores, with some cosmetic changes in design. In this way the company is able to

EXHIBIT 16-4

Selection of Suitable Distribution Policies Based on the Relationship between Type of Product and Type of Store

Classification	Consumer Behavior	Most Likely Form of Distribution
Convenience store/ convenience good	The consumer prefers to buy the most readily available brand of a product at the most accessible store.	Intensive
Convenience store/shopping good	The consumer selects his or her purchase from among the assortment carried by the most accessible store.	Intensive
Convenience store/specialty good	The consumer purchases his or her favorite brand from the most accessible store carrying the item in stock.	Selective/ exclusive
Shopping store/ convenience good	The consumer is indifferent to the brand of product he or she buys but shops different stores to secure better retail service and/or retail price.	Intensive
Shopping store/shopping good	The consumer makes comparisons among both retail-controlled factors and factors associated with the product (brand).	Intensive
Shopping store/specialty good	The consumer has a strong preference as to product brand but shops a number of stores to secure the best retail service and/or price for this brand.	Selective/ exclusive
Specialty store/convenience good	The consumer prefers to trade at a specific store but is indifferent to the brand of product purchased.	Selective/ exclusive
Specialty store/shopping good	The consumer prefers to trade at a certain store but is uncertain as to which product he or she wishes to buy and examines the store's assortment for the best purchase.	Selective/ exclusive
Specialty store/specialty good	The consumer has both a preference for a particular store and for a specific brand.	Selective/ exclusive

Source: Louis P. Bucklin, "Retail Strategy and the Classification of Consumer Goods," *Journal of Marketing* (January 1963): 50–55; published by the American Marketing Association.

reach middle- and low-income segments that may never shop for luggage in department stores. Similarly, magazines use newsstand distribution as a complementary channel to subscriptions. Catalogs serve as complementary channels for large retailers such as JCPenney.

The simplest way to create complementary channels is through private branding. This permits entry into markets that would otherwise be lost. The Coca-Cola Company sells its Minute Maid frozen orange juice to A&P to be sold under the A&P name. At the same time, the Minute Maid brand is available in A&P stores. Presumably, there are customers who perceive the private brand to be no different in quality from the manufacturer's brand. Inasmuch as the private brand is always a little less expensive than a manufacturer's brand, such customers prefer the lower-priced private brand. Thus, private branding helps broaden the market base.

There is another reason that may lead a manufacturer to choose this strategy. In instances where other firms in an industry have saturated traditional distribution channels for a product, a new entry may be distributed through a different channel. This new channel may then in turn be different from the traditional channel used for the rest of the manufacturer's product line. Hanes, for example, decided to develop a new channel for L'eggs (supermarkets and drugstores) because traditional channels were already crowded with competing brands. Likewise, R. Dakin developed nontraditional complementary channels to distribute its toys. Although most toy manufacturers sell their wares through toy shops and department stores, Dakin distributes more than 60 percent of its products through a variety of previously ignored outlets such as airports, hospital gift shops, restaurants, amusement parks, stationery stores, and drugstores. This strategy lets Dakin avoid direct competition.[12] In recent years, many companies have developed new channels in the form of direct mail sales for such diverse products as men's suits, shoes, insurance, records, newly published books, and jewelry.

A company may also develop complementary channels to broaden the market when its traditional channel happens to be a large account. For example, Easco Corporation, the nation's second-largest maker of hand tools, had for years tied itself to Sears, Roebuck and Company, the world's largest retailer, supplying wrenches, sockets, and other tools for the retailer's Craftsman line. Sears accounted for about 47 percent of Easco's sales and about 62 percent of its pretax earnings in the mid-1980s. But as Sears's growth slowed, Easco had a critical strategic dilemma: What do you do when one dominant customer stops growing and starts to slip? The company decided to lessen its dependence on Sears by adding some 500 new hardware and home-center stores for its hand tools.[13]

To broaden their markets in recent years, many clothing manufacturers, including Ralph Lauren, Liz Claiborne, Calvin Klein, Anne Klein, and Adrienne Vittadini, have opened their own stores to sell a full array of their clothes and accessories.[14]

Complementary channels may also be necessitated by geography. Many industrial companies undertake direct distribution of their products in such large metropolitan areas as New York, Chicago, Detroit, and Cleveland. Because the market is dense and because of the proximity of customers to each other, a salesperson can make more than 10 calls a day. The same company that sells directly to its customers in urban environments, however, may use manufacturer's representatives or some other type of intermediary in the hinterlands because the market there is too thin to support full-time salespeople.

Another reason to promote complementary channels is to enhance the distribution of noncompeting items. For example, many food processors package fruits and vegetables for institutional customers in giant cans that have little market among household customers. These products, therefore, are distributed through different channels. Procter & Gamble manufactures toiletries for hotels, motels, hospitals, airlines, and so on, which are distributed through different channel arrangements. The volume of business may also require the use of different channels. Many appliance manufacturers sell directly to builders but use distributors and dealers for selling to household consumers.

The basis for employing complementary channels is to enlist customers and segments that cannot be served when distribution is limited to a single channel. Thus, the addition of a complementary channel may be the result of simple cost-benefit analysis. If by employing an additional channel the overall business can be increased without jeopardizing quality or service and without any negative impact on long-term profitability, it may be worthwhile to do so. However, care is needed to ensure that the enhancement of the market through multiple channels does not lead the Justice Department to charge the company with monopolizing the market.

Competitive The second type of multiple-channel strategy is the competitive channel.
Channels **Competitive channels** exist when the same product is sold through two different and competing channels. This distribution posture may be illustrated with reference to a boat manufacturer, the Luhrs Company. Luhrs sells and ships boats directly to dealers, using one franchise to sell Ulrichsen wood boats and Alura fiberglass boats and another franchise to sell Luhrs wood and fiberglass/wood boats. The two franchises could be issued to the same dealer, but they are normally issued to separate dealers. Competition between dealers holding separate franchises is both possible and encouraged. The two dealers compete against each other to the extent that their products satisfy similar consumer needs in the same segment.

The reason for choosing this competitive strategy is the hope that it will increase sales. It is thought that if dealers must compete against themselves as well as against other manufacturers' dealers, the extra effort will benefit overall sales. The effectiveness of this strategy is debatable. It could be argued that a program using different incentives, such as special discounts for attaining certain levels of sales, could be just as effective as this type of competition. It could be even more effective because the company would eliminate costs associated with developing additional channels.

Sometimes a company may be forced into developing competing channels in response to changing environments. For example, nonprescription drugs were traditionally sold through drugstores. But as the merchandising perspectives of supermarkets underwent a change during the post-World War II period, grocery stores became a viable channel for such products because shoppers expected to find convenience drug products there. This made it necessary for drug companies to deal with grocery wholesalers and retail grocery stores along with drug wholesalers and drugstores. In the 1980s, Capital Holding Corp. (a life insurance company located in Louisville, Kentucky) adopted a variety of marketing innovations. For example, in 1985 it began selling life insurance in novel ways, notably through supermarkets. Impressed by Capital Holding's steady growth and strong financial performance, many other insurance companies were forced to develop new channels to sell their insurance products.[15]

The argument behind the competitive channel strategy is that, although two brands of the same manufacturer may be essentially the same, they may appeal to different sets of customers. Thus, General Motors engages different dealers for its Buick, Cadillac, Chevrolet, Oldsmobile, and Pontiac cars. These dealers vigorously compete with one another. A more interesting example of competing multiple channels adopted by automobile manufacturers is provided by their dealings with car rental companies. Carmakers sell cars directly to car rental agencies. Hertz, for example, buys from an assembly plant and regularly resells some of its slightly used cars in competition with new cars through its more than 100 offices across the United States. Many of these offices are located in close proximity to dealers of new cars. Despite such competition, a manufacturer undertakes distribution through multiple channels to come off, on the whole, with increased business.

In adopting multiple competing channels, a company needs to make sure that it does not overextend itself; otherwise it may spread itself too thin and face competition to such an extent that ultimate results are disastrous. McCammon cites the case of a wholesaler who adopted multiple channels and thus exposed itself to a grave situation:

> Consider, for example, the competitive milieu of Stratton & Terstegge, a large hardware wholesaler in Louisville. At the present time, the company sells to independent retailers, sponsors a voluntary group program, and operates its own stores. In these multiple capacities, it competes against conventional wholesalers (Belknap), cash and carry wholesalers (Atlas), specialty wholesalers (Garcia), corporate chains (Wiches), voluntary groups (Western Auto), cooperative groups (Colter), free-form corporations (Interco), and others. Given the complexity of its competitive environment, it is not surprising to observe that Stratton & Terstegge generates a relatively modest rate of return on net worth.[16]

One of the dangers involved in setting up multiple channels is dealer resentment. This is particularly true when competitive channels are established. When this happens, it obviously means that an otherwise exclusive retailer will now suffer a loss in sales. Such a policy can result in the retailer electing to carry a different manufacturer's product line, if a comparable product line is available. For example, if a major department store such as Lord & Taylor is upset with a manufacturer such as the Hathaway Shirt Company for doing business with discounters (i.e., for adopting competing channels), it can very easily give its business to another shirt manufacturer.

Multiple channels also create control problems. National Distillers and Chemical Corporation had a wholly owned New York distributor, Peel Richards, that strictly enforced manufacturer-stipulated retail prices and refused to do business with price cutters. Since R.H. Macy discounted National Distiller's products, Peel Richards stopped selling to them. R.H. Macy retaliated by placing an order with an upstate New York distributor of National Distillers.[17] National Distillers had no legal recourse against either R.H. Macy or the upstate New York distributor, who was an independent businessperson.

These problems do not diminish the importance of multiple distribution: they only suggest the difficulties that may arise with multiple channels and the difficulties with which management must contend. A manufacturer's failure to use multiple channels gives competitors an opportunity to segment the market by concentrating on one or the other end of the market spectrum. This is particularly disastrous for a leading manufacturer because it must automatically forgo access to a large portion of market potential for not being able to use the economies of multiple distribution.

CHANNEL-MODIFICATION STRATEGY

The **channel-modification strategy** is the introduction of a change in existing distribution arrangements based on evaluation and critical review. Channels should be evaluated on an ongoing basis so that appropriate modification may be made as necessary.[18] A shift in existing channels may become desirable for any of the following reasons:

1. Changes in consumer markets and buying habits.
2. Development of new needs in relation to service, parts, or technical help.
3. Changes in competitors' perspectives.
4. Changes in relative importance of outlet types.
5. Changes in a manufacturer's financial strength.
6. Changes in the sales volume level of existing products.
7. Changes in product (addition of new products), price (substantial reduction in price to gain dominant position), or promotion (greater emphasis on advertising) strategies.

Channel Evaluation | Channels of distribution may be evaluated on such primary criteria as cost of distribution, coverage of market (penetration), customer service, communication with the market, and control of distribution networks. Occasionally, such secondary factors as support of channels in the successful introduction of a new product and cooperation with the company's promotional effort also become evaluative criteria. To arrive at a distribution channel that satisfies all these criteria requires simultaneous optimization of every facet of distribution, something that is usually not operationally possible. Consequently, a piecemeal approach may be followed.

Cost of Distribution. A detailed cost analysis of distribution is the first step in evaluating various channel alternatives on a sales-cost basis. This requires classification of total distribution costs under various heads and subheads. Exhibit 16-5 illustrates such a cost classification based on general accounting practices; information about each item should be conveniently available from the controller's office.

The question of evaluation comes up only when the company has been following a particular channel strategy for a number of years. Presumably, the company has pertinent information to undertake distribution cost analysis by customer segment and product line. This sort of data allows the analyzer to find out how cost under each head varies with sales volume; for example, how warehousing expenses vary with sales volume, how packaging and delivery expenses are related to sales, and so on. In other words, the purpose here is to establish a relationship between annual sales and different types of cost. These relationships are useful in predicting the future cost behavior for established dollar-sales objectives, assuming present channel arrangements are continued.

To find out the cost of distribution for alternative channels, estimates should be made of all relevant costs under various sales estimates. Cost information can be obtained from published sources and interviews with selected informants. For example, assume that a company has been selling through wholesalers for a number of years and is now considering distribution through its own branches. To follow the latter course, the company needs to rent a number of offices in important markets. Estimates of the cost of renting or purchasing an office can be furnished by real estate agents. Similarly, the cost of recruiting and hiring additional help to staff the offices should be available through the personnel office. With the relevant information gathered, simple break-even analysis can be used to compute the attractiveness of the alternative channel.

Assume that a company has 20,000 potential customers and, on an average, that each of them must be contacted every two weeks. A salesperson who makes 10 calls a day and who works five days a week can contact 100 customers every two weeks. Thus, the company needs $20,000 \div 100 = 200$ salespeople. If each salesperson receives $30,000 in salary and $20,000 in expenses, the annual cost of its salespeople is $10,000,000. Further, assume that 10 sales managers are required for control and supervision and that each one is paid, say, $50,000 a year. The cost of supervision would then be $500,000. Let $9,500,000 be the cost of other overhead, such as office and warehouse expenses. The total cost of direct distribution will then be $10,000,000 + $500,000 + $9,500,000, or $20 million. Assume that distribution through wholesalers (the arrangement currently being pursued) costs the company 25 percent of sales. Assuming sales to be x, we can set up an equation, $0.25x + \$20$ million, and solve for x ($x + \$80$ million). If the company decides to go to direct distribution, it must generate a sales volume of $80 million before it can break even on costs. Thus, if sales potential is well above the $80 million mark, direct distribution is worth considering.

One problem with break-even analysis is that distribution alternatives that are considered equally effective may not always be so. It is a pervasive belief that

EXHIBIT 16-5
Representative List of Distribution Costs by Function

1.   Direct Selling

Salaries: administrative and supervisory
Clerical
Salespeople
Commission
Travel and entertainment
Training
Insurance: real and property; liability; workmen's comp
Taxes: personal property; social security; unemployment insurance
Returned-goods expense chargeable to salespeople
Pension
Rent
Utilities
Repair and maintenance
Depreciation
Postage and office supplies

2.   Advertising and Sales Promotion

Salaries: administrative and supervisory; clerical; advertising production
Publication space: trade journals; newspapers
Product promotion: advertising supplier; advertising agency fees; direct-mail expenses; contests; catalogs and price list
Cooperative advertising: dealers; retail stores; billboards

3.   Product and Package Design

Salaries: administrative and supervisory
Wages
Materials
Depreciation

4.   Sales Discounts and Allowances

Cash discounts on sales
Quantity discounts
Sales allowances

5.   Credit Extension

Salaries: administrative and supervisory; credit representatives; clerical
Bad debt losses
Forms and postage
Credit rating services
Legal fees: collection efforts
Travel

Financial cost of accounts receivable

6.   Market Research

Salaries: administrative; clerical
Surveys: distributors; consumers
Industry trade data
Travel

7.   Warehousing and Handling

Salaries: administrative
Wages: warehouse services
Depreciation: furniture; fixtures
Insurance
Taxes
Repair and maintenance
Unsalable merchandise
Warehouse responsibility
Supplies
Utilities

8.   Inventory Levels

Obsolescence markdown
Financial cost of carrying inventories

9.   Packing, Shipping, and Delivery

Salaries: administrative; clerical
Wages: truck drivers; truck maintenance persons; packers
Shipping clerks
Truck operators
Truck repairs
Depreciation: furniture; fixtures; trucks
Insurance
Taxes
Utilities
Packing supplies
Postage and forms
Freight: factory to warehouse; warehouse to customer; factory to customer
Outside trucking service

10.   Order Processing

Order forms
Salaries: administrative
Wages: order review clerks; order processing clerks; equipment operators
Depreciation: Order processing equipment

EXHIBIT 16-5 (continued)
Representative List of Distribution Costs by Function

11.   Customer Service

Salaries: administrative; customer service representatives; clerical
Stationery and supplies

12.   Printing and Recording of Accounts Receivable

Sales invoice forms
Salaries: clerical; administrative; accounts receivable clerks; sales invoicing equipment operators
Depreciation: sales invoicing equipment

13.   Returned Merchandise

Freight
Salaries: administrative; clerical; returned-goods clerical
Returned-goods processing: material labor
Forms and supplies

the choice of a distribution channel affects total sales revenue just as the selection of an advertising strategy does. For example, a retailer may receive the same number of calls under either of two channel alternatives: from the company's salesperson or from a wholesaler's salesperson. The question, however, is whether the effect of these calls is the same. The best way to handle this problem is to calculate the changes that would be necessary in order to make channel alternatives equally effective. To an extent, this can be achieved either intuitively or by using one of the mathematical models reported in the marketing literature.

Coverage of the Market. An important aspect of predicting future sales response is the penetration that will eventually be achieved in the market. For example, in the case of a drug company, customers can be divided into three groups: (a) drugstores, (b) doctors, and (c) hospitals.

One measure of the coverage of the market (or penetration of the market) is the number of customers in a group contacted or sold, divided by the total number of customers in that group. Another measure may be penetration in terms of geographical coverage of territory. But these measures are too general. Using just the ratio of customers contacted to the total number of customers does not give a proper indication of coverage because not all types of customers are equally important. Therefore, customers may be further classified, as shown in the accompanying display:

Customer Group	Classification	Basis of Classification
Drugstores	Large, medium, and small	Annual turnover
Hospitals	Large, medium, and small	Number of beds
Doctors	Large, medium, and small	Number of patients attended

Then the desired level of penetration for each subgroup should be specified (e.g., penetrate 90 percent of the large, 75 percent of the medium, and 50 percent of the small drugstores). These percentages can be used for examining the effectiveness of an alternative channel.

An advanced analysis is possible, however, by building a penetration model. The basis of the model is that increments in penetration for equal periods are proportional to the remaining distance to the aimed penetration. The increments in penetration in a period t will be: $t = rp(1 - r)t - 1$, where p = targeted or aimed penetration and r = penetration ratio. This ratio signifies how rapidly the cumulative penetration approaches aimed penetration. For example, if aimed penetration is 80 percent and if r = 0.3, then first-year penetration is $80 \times 0.3 = 24$ percent. Next year, the increment in penetration will be $80 \times 0.3 \times 0.7 = 16.8$ percent. Hence, cumulative penetration at the end of the second year will be 24 + 16.8 = 40.8. The value of p for each subgroup is a matter of policy decision on the part of the company. The value of r depends on the period during which aimed penetration is to be achieved and on sales efforts in terms of the number of medical representatives/salespeople and their call pattern for each subgroup. For the existing channel (selling through the wholesalers), the value of r can be determined from past records. For the alternate channel (direct distribution), the approximate value of r can be computed in one of two ways:

1. Company executives should know how many salespeople would be kept on the rolls if the alternate channel were used. The executives can also estimate the average number of calls a day a salesperson can make and hence the average number of customers in a subgroup he or she can contact. With this information, the value of r can be determined as follows:

$$\frac{\text{Number of customers in a subgroup contacted under existing channel}}{\text{Number of customers in a subgroup that would be contacted in alternate channel}} = \frac{\text{Value of } r \text{ for existing channel}}{\text{Value of } r \text{ for alternate channel}}$$

2. A second approach may be to find out (or estimate) the penetration that would be possible after one year if the alternate channel is used, then to substitute this in the penetration equation to find r when p and t are known.

The penetration model makes it easier to predict the exact coverage in each subgroup of customers over a planning period (say, five years hence). The marketing strategist should determine the ultimate desired penetration p and the time period in which it is to be achieved. Then the model would be able to predict which channel would take the penetration closer to the objective.

Customer Service. The level of customer service differs from customer to customer for each business. Generally speaking, the sales department, with feedback from the field force, should be able to designate the various services that the company should offer to different consumer segments. If this is not feasible, a sample survey may be planned to find out which services customers expect and which services are currently being offered by competitors. This information can be used to develop a viable service package. Then the capability and willingness of each channel alternative to provide these services may be matched to single out the most desirable channel. This can be done intuitively. A more scientific approach would be to list and assign weights to each type of service, then rate different channels according to their ability to handle these services. Cumulative scores can be used for the service ranking of channel alternatives. Conjoint measurement can be used to determine which services are most important to a particular segment of customers.

Communication and Control. **Control** may be defined as the process of taking steps to bring actual results and desired results closer together. **Communication** refers to the information flow between the company and its customers. To evaluate alternate channels on these two criteria, communication and control objectives should be defined. With reference to communication, for example, information may be desired on the activities of competitors, new products from competitors, the special promotional efforts of competitors, the attitudes of customers toward the company's and toward competitors' services, and the reasons for success of a particular product line of the company.[19] Each channel alternative may then be evaluated in terms of its willingness, capabilities, and interest in providing the required information. In the case of wholesalers, the communication perspective may also depend on the terms of the contract. But the mere fact that they are legally bound by a contract may not motivate wholesalers to cooperate willingly. Finally, the information should be judged for accuracy, timeliness, and relevance.

Channel Modification

Environmental shifts, internal or external, may require a company to modify existing channel arrangements. A shift in trade practice, for instance, may render distribution through a manufacturer's representative obsolete. Similarly, technological changes in product design may require frequent service calls on customers that wholesalers may not be able to make, thus leading the company to opt for direct distribution.

To illustrate the point, consider jewelry distribution. For centuries, jewelry was distributed through jewelry shops that relied on uniqueness, craftsmanship, and mystique to reap fat margins on very small volumes. Traditionally, big retailers shunned jewelry as a highly specialized, slow-moving business that tied up too much money in inventory. But this attitude has changed in the last few years. For example, between 1978 and 1982, jewelry stores' share of the jewelry market declined from 65 percent to less than 50 percent. On the other hand, relying on hefty advertising and deep discounting, mass merchandisers (e.g., JCPenney, Sears, Montgomery Ward, Target, and others) have been making fast inroads into the jewelry business. For example, in 1983 JCPenney became the fourth-largest retail jewelry merchant in the United States behind Zale, Gordon Jewelry, and Best Products, the catalog showroom chain. Such a shift in trade practice requires that jewelry manufacturers modify their distribution arrangements.[20]

Similarly, as computer makers try to reach ever-broadening audiences with lower-priced machines, they need new distribution channels. Many of them, IBM and Apple, for example, are turning to retail stores. In the 1970s, people would have laughed at the idea of selling computers over the counter; now it is a preferred way of doing business. The tantalizing opportunity to sell computers to consumers has also given birth to specialty chains specializing in computer and related items.

Generally speaking, a new company in the market starts distribution through intermediaries. This is necessary because, during the initial period, technical and manufacturing problems are big enough to keep management busy. Besides, at this stage, the company has neither the insight nor the capabilities needed to deal successfully with the vagaries of the market. Therefore, intermediaries are used. With their knowledge of the market, they play an important role in establishing a demand for a company's product. But once the company establishes a foothold in the market, it may discover that it does not have the control of distribution it needs to make further headway. At this time, channel modification becomes necessary.

Managerial astuteness requires that the company do a thorough study before deciding to change existing channel arrangements. Taking a few halfhearted measures could create insurmountable problems resulting in loose control and poor communication.[21] Further, the intermediaries affected should be duly taken into confidence about a company's plans and compensated for any breach of terms. Any modification of channels should match the perspectives of the total marketing strategy. This means that the effect of a modified plan on other ingredients of the marketing mix (such as product, price, and promotion) should be considered. The managers of different departments (as well as the customers) should be informed so that the change does not come as a surprise. In other words, care needs to be taken to ensure that a modification in channel arrangements does not cause any distortion in the overall distribution system.

CHANNEL-CONTROL STRATEGY

Channel arrangements traditionally consisted of loosely aligned manufacturers, wholesalers, and retailers, all of whom were trying to serve their own ends regardless of what went on elsewhere in the channel structure. In such arrangements, channel control was generally missing. Each member of the channel negotiated aggressively with others and performed a conventionally defined set of marketing functions.

Importance of Channel Control

For a variety of reasons, control is a necessary ingredient in running a successful system. Having control is likely to have a positive impact on profits because inefficiencies are caught and corrected in time. This is evidenced by the success of voluntary and cooperative chains, corporate chains, franchise alignments, manufacturers' dealer organizations, and sales branches and offices. Control also helps to realize cost effectiveness vis-à-vis experience curves. For example, centralized organization of warehousing, data processing, and other facilities provide scale efficiencies. Through a planned perspective of the total system, effort is directed to achieving common goals in an integrated fashion.

Channel Controller

The focus of channel control may be on any member of a channel system: the manufacturer, wholesaler, or retailer. Unfortunately, there is no established theory to indicate whether any one of them makes a better channel controller than the others.[22] For example, one appliance retailer in Philadelphia with a 10 percent market share, Silo Incorporated, served as the channel controller there. This firm had no special relationship with any manufacturer, but if a supplier's line did not do well, Silo immediately contacted the supplier to ask that something be done about it.[23] Wal-Mart (in addition to JCPenney and Sears) can be expected to be the channel controller for a variety of products. Among manufacturers, Kraft ought to be the channel controller for refrigerated goods in supermarkets. Likewise, Procter & Gamble is a channel controller for detergents and related items. Ethan Allen decided to control the distribution channels for its line of Early American furniture by establishing a network of 200 dealer outlets. Sherwin-Williams decided to take over channel control to guide its own destiny because traditional channels were not showing enough aggressiveness. The company established its own chain of 2,000 retail outlets.

These examples underscore the importance of someone taking over channel leadership in order to establish control. Conventionally, market leadership and the size of a firm determine its suitability for channel control. Strategically, a firm should attempt to control the channel for a product if it can make a commitment to fulfill its leadership obligations and if such a move is likely to be economically beneficial in the long run for the entire channel system.

Vertical Marketing Systems

Vertical marketing systems may be defined as:

professionally managed and centrally programmed networks [that] are pre-engineered to achieve operating economies and maximum market impact. Stated alternatively, vertical marketing systems are rationalized and capital-intensive networks designed to achieve technological, managerial, and promotional economies through the integration, coordination, and synchronization of marketing flows from points of production to points of ultimate use.[24]

The vertical marketing system is an emerging trend in the American economy. It seems to be replacing all conventional marketing channels as the mainstay of distribution. As a matter of fact, according to one estimate, vertical marketing systems in the consumer-goods sector account for about 70 to 80 percent of the available market.[25] In brief, vertical marketing systems (sometimes also referred to as centrally coordinated systems) have emerged as the dominant ingredient in the competitive process and thus play a strategic role in the formulation of distribution strategy.

Vertical marketing systems may be classified into three types: corporate, administered, and contractual. Under the corporate vertical marketing system, successive stages of production and distribution are owned by a single entity.[26] This is achieved through forward and backward integration. Sherwin-Williams owns and operates its 2,000 retail outlets in a corporate vertical marketing system (a case of forward integration). Other examples of such systems are Hart,

Schaffner, and Marx (operating more than 275 stores), International Harvester, Goodyear, and Sohio. Not only a manufacturer but also a corporate vertical system might be owned and operated by a retailer (a case of backward integration). Sears, like many other large retailers, has financial interests in many of its suppliers' businesses. For example, about one-third of DeSoto (a furniture and home furnishings manufacturer) stock is owned by Sears. Finally, W. W. Grainger provides an example of a wholesaler-run vertical marketing system. This firm, an electrical distributor with 1987 sales of $590 million, has seven manufacturing facilities.

Another outstanding example of a vertical marketing system is provided by Gallo, the wine company.

> The [Gallo] brothers own Fairbanks Trucking company, one of the largest intrastate truckers in California. Its 200 semis and 500 trailers are constantly hauling wine out of Modesto and raw materials back in including . . . lime from Gallo's quarry east of Sacramento. Alone among wine producers, Gallo makes bottles—two million a day— and its Midcal Aluminum Co. spews out screw tops as fast as the bottles are filled. Most of the country's 1,300 or so wineries concentrate on production to the neglect of marketing. Gallo, by contrast, participates in every aspect of selling short of whispering in the ear of each imbiber. The company owns its distributors in about a dozen markets and probably would buy many . . . more . . . if the laws in most states did not prohibit doing so.[27]

In an **administered vertical marketing system,** a dominant firm within the channel system, such as the manufacturer, wholesaler, or retailer, coordinates the flow of goods by virtue of its market power. For example, the firm may exert influence to achieve economies in transportation, order processing, warehousing, advertising, or merchandising. As can be expected, it is large organizations like Wal-Mart, Safeway, JCPenney, General Motors, Kraft, GE, Procter & Gamble, Lever Brothers, Nabisco, and General Foods that emerge as channel captains to guide their channel networks, while not actually owning them, to achieve economies and efficiencies.

In a **contractual vertical marketing system,** independent firms within the channel structure integrate their programs on a contractual basis to realize economies and market impact. Primarily, there are three types of contractual vertical marketing systems: wholesaler-sponsored voluntary groups, retailer-sponsored cooperative groups, and franchise systems. Independent Grocers Alliance (IGA) is an example of a wholesaler-sponsored voluntary group. At the initiative of the wholesaler, small grocery stores agree to form a chain to achieve economies with which to compete against corporate chains. The joining members agree to adhere to a variety of contractual terms, such as the use of a common name, to help realize economies on large order. Except for these terms, each store continues to operate independently. A retailer-sponsored cooperative group is essentially the same. Retailers form their own association (cooperative) to compete against corporate chains by undertaking wholesaler functions (and possibly even a limited amount of production); that is, they operate their own wholesale companies to serve member retailers. This type of contractual vertical marketing system is operated primarily, though not exclusively, in the food line. Associated Grocers Co-op and Certified Grocers are examples of retailer-sponsored food cooperative groups. Value-Rite, a group of 2,298 stores, is a drugstore cooperative.[28]

A **franchise system** is an arrangement whereby a firm licenses others to market a product or service using its trade name in a defined geographic area under specified terms and conditions. In 1984, there were more than 2,000 franchisers in the United States, twice as many as in 1973. Practically any business that can be taught to someone is being franchised. In 1985, sales of goods and services by all franchising companies (manufacturing, wholesaling, and retailing) exceeded $500 billion. Approximately one-third of all U.S. retail sales flow through franchise and company-owned units in franchise chains.[29]

In addition to traditional franchising businesses (e.g., fast food), banks are doing it, as are accountants, dating services, skin care centers, tub and tile refinishers, tutors, funeral homes, bookkeepers, dentists, nurses, bird seed shops, gift wrappers, wedding consultants, cookie bakers, popcorn poppers, beauty shops, baby-sitters, and suppliers of maid service, lawn care, and solar greenhouses. The Commerce Department forecasts that by the year 2000 franchising will account for half of all retail sales. Four different types of franchise systems can be distinguished:

1. The manufacturer-retailer franchise is exemplified by franchised automobile dealers and franchised service stations.
2. The manufacturer-wholesaler franchise is exemplified by Coca-Cola and Pepsi-Cola, who sell the soft drink syrups they manufacture to franchised wholesalers who, in turn, bottle and distribute soft drinks to retailers.
3. The wholesaler-retailer franchise is exemplified by Rexall Drug Stores, Sentry Drug Centers, and ComputerLand.
4. The service sponsor-retailer franchise is exemplified by Avis, Hertz, and National in the car rental business; McDonald's, Chicken Delight, Kentucky Fried Chicken, and Taco Bell in the prepared foods industry; Howard Johnson's and Holiday Inn in the lodging and food industry; Midas and AAMCO in the auto repair business; and Kelly Girl and Manpower in the employment service business.

Vertical marketing systems help achieve economies that cannot be realized through the use of conventional marketing channels. In strategic terms, vertical marketing systems provide opportunities for building experience, thus allowing even small firms to derive the benefits of market power. If present trends are any indication, in the 1990s vertical marketing systems should account for almost 90 percent of total retail sales. Considering their growing importance, conventional channels will need to adopt new distribution strategies to compete against vertical marketing systems. For example, they may

1. Develop programs to strengthen customers' competitive capabilities. This alternative involves manufacturers and wholesalers in such activities as sponsoring centralized accounting and management reporting services, formulating cooperative promotional programs, and cosigning shopping center leases.

2. Enter new markets. For example, building supply distributors have initiated cash-and-carry outlets. Steel warehouses have added glass and plastic product lines to their traditional product lines. Industrial distributors have initiated stockless buying plans and blanket order contracts so that they may compete effectively for customers who buy on a direct basis.
3. Effect economies of operation by developing management information systems. For example, some middlemen in conventional channels have installed the IBM IMPACT program to improve their control over inventory.
4. Determine through research the focus of power in the channel and urge the channel member designated to undertake a reorganization of marketing flows.[30]

Despite the growing trend toward vertical integration, it would be naive to consider it an unmixed blessing. Vertical integration has both pluses and minuses—more of the latter, according to one empirical study on the subject.[31] For example, vertical integration requires a huge commitment of resources: in mid-1981, Du Pont acquired Conoco in a $7.3 billion transaction. The strategy may not be worthwhile unless the company gains needed insurance as well as cost savings. As a matter of fact, some observers have blamed the U.S. automobile industry's woes, in part, on excessive vertical integration: "In deciding to integrate backward because of apparent short-term rewards, managers often restrict their ability to strike out in innovative directions in the future."[32]

CONFLICT-MANAGEMENT STRATEGY

It is quite conceivable that the independent firms that constitute a channel of distribution (i.e., manufacturer, wholesaler, retailer) may sometimes find themselves in conflict with each other. The underlying causes of conflict are the divergent goals that different firms may pursue. If the goals of one firm are being challenged because of the strategies followed by another channel member, conflict is the natural outcome. Thus, channel conflict may be defined as a situation in which one channel member perceives another channel member or members to be engaged in behavior that is preventing or impeding it from achieving its goals.

Disagreement between channel members may arise from incompatible desires and needs. Weigand and Wasson give four examples of the kinds of conflict that may arise:

A manufacturer promises an exclusive territory to a retailer in return for the retailer's "majority effort" to generate business in the area. Sales increase nicely, but the manufacturer believes it is due more to population growth in the area than to the effort of the store owner, who is spending too much time on the golf course.

A fast-food franchiser promises "expert promotional assistance" to his retailers as partial explanation for the franchise fee. One of the retailers believes that the help he is getting is anything but expert and that the benefits do not correspond with what he was promised.

Another franchiser agrees to furnish accounting services and financial analysis as a regular part of his service. The franchisee believes that the accountant is nothing more than a "glorified bookkeeper" and that the financial analysis consists of several pages of ratios that are incomprehensible.

A third franchiser insists that his franchisees should maintain a minimum stock of certain items that are regularly promoted throughout the area. Arguments arise as to whether the franchiser's recommendations constitute a threat, while the franchisee is particularly concerned about protecting his trade name.[33]

The four strategic alternatives available for resolving conflicts between channel members are bargaining, boundary, interpenetration, and superorganizational strategies.[34] Under the **bargaining strategy**, one member of the channel takes the lead in activating the bargaining process by being willing to concede something, with the expectation that the other party will reciprocate. For example, a manufacturer may agree to provide interest-free loans for up to 90 days to a distributor if the distributor will carry twice the level of inventory that it previously did and will furnish warehousing for the purpose. Or a retailer may propose to continue to carry the television line of a manufacturer if the manufacturer will supply television sets under the retailer's own name (i.e., the retailer's private brand). The bargaining strategy works out only if both parties are willing to adopt the attitude of give-and-take and if bottom-line results for both are favorable enough to induce them to accept the terms of the bargain.

The **boundary strategy** handles the conflict through diplomacy; that is, by nominating the employee most familiar with the perspectives of the other party to take up the matter with his or her counterpart. For example, a manufacturer may nominate a veteran salesperson to communicate with the purchasing agent of the customer to see if some basis can be established to resolve the conflict. A department store manager may be upset with a manufacturer's decision to start supplying the product to a mass retailer, such as JCPenney. To resolve such a conflict, the manufacturer's salesperson may meet with the purchasing agent to talk over business in general, and in between the talks, the salesperson may indicate in a subtle way that the company's decision to supply the product to JCPenney for sale through catalogs is motivated by its desire to help the department store: in the long run, the department store will reap the benefits of the brand name popularity triggered by the deal with JCPenney. Besides, the salesperson may be authorized to propose that his or her company will agree not to sell the top of the line to JCPenney, thus ensuring that it will continue to be available only through major department stores. In order for this strategy to succeed, it is necessary that the diplomat (the salesperson in the example) be fully briefed on the situation and provided leverage with which to negotiate.

The **interpenetration strategy** is directed toward resolving conflict through frequent informal interactions with the other party to gain a proper appreciation of each other's perspectives. One of the easiest ways to develop interaction is for one party to invite the other to join its trade association. For example, several years ago television dealers were concerned because they felt that the manufacturers of television sets did not understand their problems. To help correct the situation, the dealers invited the manufacturers to become members of the National Appliance and Radio-TV Dealers Association (NARDA). Currently, manufacturers take an active interest in NARDA conventions and seminars.

Finally, the focus of **superorganizational strategy** is to employ conciliation, mediation, and arbitration to resolve conflict. Essentially, a neutral third party is brought into the conflict to resolve the matter. **Conciliation** is an informal attempt by a third party to bring two conflicting organizations together and make them come to an agreement amicably. For example, an independent wholesaler may serve as a conciliator between a manufacturer and its customers. Under **mediation,** the third party plays a more active role. If the parties in conflict fail to come to an agreement, they may be willing to consider the procedural or substantive recommendations of the mediator.

Arbitration may also be applied to resolve channel conflict. Arbitration may be compulsory or voluntary. Under compulsory arbitration, the dispute must by law be submitted to a third party, the decision being final and binding on both conflicting parties. For example, the courts may arbitrate between two parties in dispute. Years ago, when automobile manufacturers and their dealers had problems relative to distribution policies, the court arbitrated. Voluntary arbitration is a process whereby the parties in conflict submit their disputes for resolution to a third party on their own. For example, in 1955 the Federal Trade Commission arbitrated between television set manufacturers, distributors, and dealers by setting up 32 industry rules to protect the consumer and to reduce conflicts over distribution. The conflict areas involved were tie-in sales; price fixing; mass shipments used to clog outlets and foreclose competitors; discriminatory billing; and special rebates, bribes, refunds, and discounts.[35]

Of all the methods of resolving conflict, arbitration is the fastest.[36] In addition, under arbitration, secrecy is preserved and less expense is incurred. Inasmuch as industry experts serve as arbitrators, one can expect a fairer decision. Thus, as a matter of strategy, arbitration may be more desirable than other methods for managing conflict.

SUMMARY

Distribution strategies are concerned with the flow of goods and services from manufacturers to customers. The discussion in this chapter was conducted from the manufacturer's viewpoint. Six major distribution strategies were distinguished: channel-structure strategy, distribution-scope strategy, multiple-channel strategy, channel-modification strategy, channel-control strategy, and conflict-management strategy.

Channel-structure strategy determines whether the goods should be distributed directly from manufacturer to customer or indirectly through one or more intermediaries. Formulation of this strategy was discussed with reference to Bucklin's postponement-speculation theory. Distribution-scope strategy specifies whether exclusive, selective, or intensive distribution should be pursued. The question of simultaneously employing more than one channel was discussed under multiple-channel strategy. Channel-modification strategy involves evaluating current channels and making necessary changes in distribution perspectives to accommodate environmental shifts. Channel-control strategy focuses on vertical marketing systems to institute control. Finally, resolution of conflict among channel members was examined under conflict-management strategy.

The merits and drawbacks of each strategy were discussed. Examples from marketing literature were given to illustrate the practical applications of different strategies.

DISCUSSION QUESTIONS

1. What factors may a manufacturer consider to determine whether to distribute products directly to customers? Can automobiles be distributed directly to customers?
2. Is intensive distribution a prerequisite for gaining experience? Discuss.
3. What precautions are necessary to ensure that exclusive distribution is not liable to challenge as a restraint of trade?
4. What strategic factor makes the multiple-channel strategy a necessity for a multiproduct company?
5. What criteria may a food processor adopt to evaluate its channels of distribution?
6. What kinds of environmental shifts require a change in channel arrangements?
7. What reasons may be ascribed to the emergence of vertical marketing systems?
8. What strategies may conventional channels adopt to meet the threat of vertical marketing systems?
9. What are the underlying sources of conflict in distribution channel relations? Give examples.
10. What is the most appropriate strategy for resolving a channel conflict?

NOTES

[1] Wroe Alderson, "Factors Governing the Development of Marketing Channels," in *Marketing Channels for Manufactured Products*, ed. Richard M. Clewett (Homewood, IL: Richard D. Irwin, 1964), 7.

[2] Louis P. Bucklin, *A Theory of Distribution Channel Structure* (Berkeley: IBER Special Publications, University of California, 1966); and "Postponement, Speculation and Structure of Distribution Channels," in *The Marketing Channel: A Conceptual Viewpoint*, ed. Bruce E. Mallen (New York: John Wiley & Sons, 1967), 67–74.

[3] Louis P. Bucklin and Leslie Halpert, "Exploring Channel of Distribution for Cement with the Principle of Postponement-Speculation," in *Marketing and Economic Development*, ed. Peter D. Bennett (Chicago: American Marketing Association, 1965), 699.

[4] See "Benetton," in Robert D. Buzzell and John A. Quelch, *Multinational Marketing Management* (Reading, MA: Addison-Wesley Publishing Co., 1988), 47–76.

[5] See Louis W. Stern and Patrick J. Kaufmann, "Electronic Data Interchange in Selected Consumer Goods Industries: An Interorganizational Perspective," in *Marketing in an Electronic Age*, ed. Robert D. Buzzell (Boston: Harvard Business School Press, 1985), 52–73.

[6] Leslie Easton, "Distributing Value: A Revamped McKesson Corporation Is Producing Surprises," *Barron's* (3 August 1987): 13, 41–42.

[7] Bruce Mallen, *Principles of Marketing Channel Management* (Lexington, MA: Lexington Books, 1977), 179.

[8] *Wetterau, Inc., Annual Report for 1993.*

[9] V. Kasturi Rangan, Melvyn A. J. Menezes, and E.P. Maier, "Channel Selection for New Industrial products: A Framework, Method and Application," *Journal of Marketing* (July 1992): 69–82.

[10] Ronald L. Ernst, "Distribution Channel Detente Benefits Suppliers, Retailers and Consumers," *Marketing News* (7 March 1980): 19.

[11] "Avon Will Offer Perfumes through Department Stores." *Wall Street Journal* (21 August 1986): 16.

[12] "R. Dakin: Marketing Old-Style Toys through Offbeat Outlets," *Business Week* (24 December 1979): 94.

[13] "Easco: Turning to New Customers While Helping Sears Promote Tools," *Business Week* (6 October 1980): 62.

[14] Terry Agins, "Clothing Makers Don Retailers' Garb," *Wall Street Journal* (13 July 1989): B1.

[15] "Even Star Insurers Are Feeling the Heat," *Business Week* (14 January 1985): 119.

[16] Bert C. McCammon, Jr., "Future Shock and the Practice of Management" (Paper presented at the Fifth Annual Research Conference of the American Marketing Association, Madrid, Spain, 1973), 9.

[17] Robert E. Weigand, "Fit Products and Channels to Your Market," *Harvard Business Review* (January–February 1977): 95–105.

[18] Glenn A. Mercer, "Don't Just Optimize—Unbundle," *The McKinsey Quarterly* 3 (1994): 103–16.

[19] See Jakki Mohr and John R. Nevin, "Communication Strategies in Marketing Channels: A Theoretical Perspective," *Journal of Marketing* (October 1990): 36–51.

[20] "Chain Stores Strike Gold in Jewelry Sales," *Business Week* (6 February 1984): 56.

[21] See Howard Sulton, *Rethinking the Company's Selling and Distribution Channels* (New York: Conference Board, 1986), Research Report 885.

[22] Gul Butaney and Lawrence H. Wortzell, "Distributor Power versus Manufacturer Power: The Customer Role," *Journal of Marketing* (January 1988): 52–63.

[23] "An Appliance Dealer with a Real Clout," *Business Week* (6 November 1971): 76.

[24] Bert C. McCammon, Jr., "Perspectives for Distribution Programming," in *Vertical Marketing Systems,* ed. Louis P. Bucklin (Glenview, IL: Scott, Foresman, 1970), 43.

[25] Philip Kotler, *Marketing Management,* 7th ed. (Englewood Cliffs, NJ: Prentice-Hall, 1994), 519.

[26] See John Stuckey and David White, "When and When Not to Vertically Integrate," *The McKinsey Quarterly* 3, (1993): 3–27.

[27] Jaclyn Fireman, "How Gallo Crushes the Competition," *Fortune* (1 September 1986): 27.

[28] *Wall Street Journal* (2 October 1986): 1.

[29] *Franchising in the Economy: 1983–85* (Washington, DC: Department of Commerce, 1985).

[30] Louis W. Stern, Adel I. El-Ansary, and James R. Brown, *Management in Marketing Channels* (Englewood Cliffs, NJ: Prentice-Hall, 1989), 299.

[31] Robert D. Buzzell, "Is Vertical Integration Profitable?" *Harvard Business Review* (January–February 1983): 92–102.

[32] Robert H. Hayes and William J. Abernathy, "Managing Our Way to Economic Decline," *Harvard Business Review* (July–August 1980): 72.

[33] Robert Weigand and Hilda C. Wasson, "Arbitration in the Marketing Channel," *Business Horizons* (October 1974): 40.

[34] See Louis W. Stern and Adel I. El-Ansary, *Marketing Channels,* 3rd ed. (Englewood Cliffs, NJ: Prentice-Hall, 1988), 290–98.

35 Stern and El-Ansary, *Marketing Channels.*
36 Rajiv P. Dant and Patrick L. Schul, "Conflict Resolution Processes in Contractual Channels of Distribution," *Journal of Marketing* (January 1992): 38–54.

APPENDIX | *Perspectives on Distribution Strategies*

I.
Channel-Structure Strategy

Definition: Using perspectives of intermediaries in the flow of goods from manufacturers to customers. Distribution may be either direct (from manufacturer to retailer or from manufacturer to customer) or indirect (involving the use of one or more intermediaries, such as wholesalers or agents, to reach the customer).

Objective: To reach the optimal number of customers in a timely manner at the lowest possible cost while maintaining the desired degree of control.

Requirements: Comparison of direct versus indirect distribution on the basis of (a) cost, (b) product characteristics, (c) degree of control, and (d) other factors.

Costs: (a) Distribution costs. (b) Opportunity costs incurred because product not available. (c) Inventory holding and shipping costs.

Product Characteristics: (a) Replacement rate. (b) Gross margin. (c) Service requirements. (d) Search time.

Degree of Control: Greater when direct distribution used.

Other Factors: (a) Adaptability. (b) Technological changes (e.g., computer technology). (c) Social/cultural values.

Expected Results: (a) Direct distribution: (i) high marketing costs, (ii) large degree of control, (iii) informed customers, and (iv) strong image. (b) Indirect distribution: (i) lower marketing costs, (ii) less control, and (iii) reduced channel management responsibilities.

II.
Distribution-Scope Strategy

Definition: Establishing the scope of distribution, that is, the target customers. Choices are exclusive distribution (one retailer is granted sole rights in serving a given area), intensive distribution (a product is made available at all possible retail outlets), and selective distribution (many but not all retail outlets in a given area distribute a product).

Objective: To serve chosen markets at a minimal cost while maintaining desired product image.

Requirements: Assessment of (a) customer buying habits, (b) gross margin/turnover rate, (c) capability of dealer to provide service, (d) capability of dealer to carry full product line, and (e) product styling.

Expected Results: (a) Exclusive distribution: (i) strong dealer loyalty, (ii) high degree of control, (iii) good forecasting capability, (iv) sales promotion assistance from manufacturer, (v) possible loss in sales volume, and (vi) possible antitrust violation. (b) Selective distribution: (i) extreme competition in marketplace, (ii) price discounting, and (iii) pressure from channel members to reduce number of outlets. (c) Intensive distribution: (i) low degree of control, (ii) higher sales volume, (iii) wide customer recognition, (iv) high turnover, and (v) price discounting.

III. *Multiple-Channel Strategy*	*Definition:* Employing two or more different channels for distribution of goods and services. Multiple-channel distribution is of two basic types: complementary (each channel handles a different noncompeting product or market segment) and competitive (two different and competing channels sell the same product).
	Objective: To achieve optimal access to each individual market segment to increase business. Complementary channels are used to reach market segments otherwise left unserved; competitive channels are used with the hope of increasing sales.
	Requirements: (a) Market segmentation. (b) Cost/benefit analysis. Use of complementary channels prompted by (i) geographic considerations, (ii) volume of business, (iii) need to distribute noncompeting items, and (iv) saturation of traditional distribution channels. Use of competitive channels can be a response to environmental changes.
	Expected Results: (a) Different services, prices, and support provided to different segments. (b) Broader market base. (c) Increased sales. (d) Possible dealer resentment. (e) Control problems. (f) Possible over-extension. Over-extension can result in (i) decrease in quality/service and (ii) negative effects on long-run profitability.
IV. *Channel-Modification Strategy*	*Definition:* Introducing a change in the existing distribution arrangements on the basis of evaluation and critical review.
	Objective: To maintain an optimal distribution system given a changing environment.
	Requirements: (a) Evaluation of internal/external environmental shifts: (i) changes in consumer markets and buying habits, (ii) changes in the retail life cycle, (iii) changes in the manufacturer's financial strength, and (iv) changes in the product life cycle. (b) Continuous evaluation of existing channels. (c) Cost/benefit analysis. (d) Consideration of the effect of the modified channels on other aspects of the marketing mix. (e) Ability of management to adapt to modified plan.
	Expected Results: (a) Maintenance of an optimal distribution system given environmental changes. (b) Disgruntled dealers and customers (in the short run).
V. *Channel-Control Strategy*	*Definition:* Takeover by a member of the channel structure in order to establish control of the channel and provide a centrally organized effort to achieve common goals.

Objectives: (a) To increase control. (b) To correct inefficiencies. (c) To realize cost-effectiveness through experience curves. (d) To gain efficiencies of scale.

Requirements: Commitment and resources to fulfill leadership obligations. Typically, though not always, the channel controller is a large firm with market leadership/influence.

Expected Results (Vertical Marketing System): (a) Increased control. (b) Professional management. (c) Central programming. (d) Achievement of operating economies. (e) Maximum market impact. (f) Increased profitability. (g) Elimination of inefficiencies.

**VI.
Conflict-
Management
Strategy**

Definition: Resolving conflict among channel members.

Objective: To devise a solution acceptable to the conflicting members so that they will cooperate to make it work.

Requirements: Choice of a strategy for solving the conflict. (a) Bargaining: (i) both parties adopt give-and-take attitude and (ii) bottom line is favorable enough to both parties to induce them to accept the terms of the bargain. (b) Boundary: (i) nomination of an employee to act as diplomat, (ii) diplomat is fully briefed on the situation and provided with leverages with which to negotiate, and (iii) both parties are willing to negotiate. (c) Interpenetration: (i) frequent formal interactions with the other party to develop an appreciation of each other's perspectives and (ii) willingness to interact to solve problems. (d) Superorganizational: A neutral third party is brought into the conflict to resolve the matter by means of (i) conciliation, (ii) mediation, or (iii) arbitration (compulsory or voluntary).

Expected Results: (a) Elimination of snags in the channel. (b) Results that are mutually beneficial to the parties involved. (c) Need for management time and effort. (d) Increased costs. (e) Costs incurred by both parties in the form of concessions.

Promotion Strategies

Promotion strategies are concerned with the planning, implementation, and control of persuasive communication with customers. These strategies may be designed around advertising, personal selling, sales promotion, or any combination of these. The first strategic issue involved here is how much money may be spent on the promotion of a specific product/market. The distribution of the total promotional budget among advertising, personal selling, and sales promotion is another strategic matter. The formulation of strategies dealing with these two issues determines the role that each type of promotion plays in a particular situation.

Clear-cut objectives and a sharp focus on target customers are necessary for an effective promotional program. In other words, merely undertaking an advertising campaign or hiring a few salespeople to call on customers may not suffice. Rather, an integrated communication plan consisting of various promotion methods should be designed to ensure that customers in a product/market cluster get the right message and maintain a long-term cordial relationship with the company. Promotional perspectives must also be properly matched with product, price, and distribution perspectives.

In addition to the strategic issues mentioned above, this chapter discusses strategies in advertising and personal selling. The advertising strategies examined are media strategy and copy strategy. Strategic matters explored in the area of personal selling are those concerned with designing a selling program and supervising salespeople. The formulation of each strategy is illustrated with reference to examples from the literature.

STRATEGIES FOR DEVELOPING PROMOTIONAL PERSPECTIVES

The amount that a company may spend on its total promotional effort, which consists of advertising, personal selling, and sales promotion, is not easy to determine. There are no unvarying standards to indicate how much should be spent on promotion in a given product/market situation. This is so because decisions about promotion expenditure are influenced by a complex set of circumstances.

Promotion-
Expenditure Strategy

Promotion expenditure makes up one part of the total marketing budget. Thus, the allocation of funds to one department, such as advertising, affects the level of expenditure elsewhere within the marketing function. For example, a company may need to choose between additional expenditures on advertising or a new package design. In addition, the perspectives of promotion expenditure must be examined in the context of pricing strategy. A higher price obviously provides more funds for promotion than does a lower price. The amount set aside for promotion is also affected by the sales response to the product, which is very difficult to estimate accurately. A related matter is the question of the cumulative effect of promotion. The major emphasis of research in this area, even where the issue is far from being resolved, has been on the duration of advertising effects. Although it is generally accepted that the effects of advertising and maybe the effects of other forms of promotion as well may last over a long period, there is no certainty about the duration of these benefits. The cumulative effect depends on the loyalty of customers, frequency of purchase, and competitive efforts, each of which may be influenced in turn by a different set of variables.

Promotion expenditures vary from one product/market situation to another. Consider the case of McDonald's. It spent $185.9 million on television advertising in 1983, over twice as much as its rival Burger King. Yet the research showed that viewers remembered and liked Burger King's ads better than McDonald's. There is no way to be sure if McDonald's advertising budget was more than optimum. Similarly, the best-known and best-liked television ad in 1983 was for Miller Lite, a commercial showing people arguing whether Miller tasted great or was less filling. This campaign performed better than all other beer commercials even though several companies spent more money on their campaigns than Miller did.[1] Again, despite the ad's success, it is difficult to say if Miller's budget was optimum.

Promotion, however, is the key to success in many businesses. To illustrate this point, take the case of Isordil, a brand of nitrate prescribed to heart patients to prevent severe chest pains. Made by the Ives Laboratories division of the American Home Products Corporation, it was introduced in 1959 and has since grown to claim almost 50 percent of a $200-million-a-year market. Ives claims that Isordil is longer acting and in certain ways more effective than other nitrate drugs on the market. No matter that the Food and Drug Administration has not yet approved all of the manufacturer's claims, nor that some doctors think that Isordil differs little from competing drugs—Ives has promoted its nitrate so aggressively for so long that many doctors think only of Isordil when they think of nitrates. The success of Isordil illustrates the key importance of promotion: "Indeed, the very survival of a drug in today's highly competitive marketplace often depends as much on a company's promotion talents as it does on the quality of its medicine."[2]

Promotion induces competitors to react, but there is no way to anticipate competitive response accurately, thus making it difficult to decide on a budget. For example, during the decade from 1980 to 1990, the promotional costs of Anheuser-Busch rose by $6 a barrel of beer (from $3 in 1980 to $9 in 1990).[3]

Although the company has been able to prevent Miller's inroads into its markets, the question remains if continuing to increase ad budgets is the best strategy.

Despite the difficulties involved, practitioners have developed rules of thumb for determining promotion expenditures that are strategically sound. These rules of thumb are of two types: they either take the form of a breakdown method or they employ the buildup method.

Breakdown Methods.   There are a number of breakdown methods that can be helpful in determining promotion expenditures. Under the *percentage-of-sales approach*, promotion expenditure is a specified percentage of the previous year's or predicted future sales. Initially, this percentage is arrived at by hunch. Later, historical information is used to decide what percentage of sales should be allocated for promotion expenditure. The rationale behind the use of this approach is that expenditure on promotion must be justified by sales. This approach is followed by many companies because it is simple, it is easy to understand, and it gives managers the flexibility to cut corners during periods of economic slowdown. Among its flaws is the fact that basing promotion appropriation on sales puts the cart before the horse. Further, the logic of this approach fails to consider the cumulative effect of promotion. In brief, this approach considers promotion a necessary expenditure that must be apportioned from sales revenue without considering the relationship of promotion to competitor's activities or its influence on sales revenues.

Another approach for allocating promotion expenditure is to spend as much as can be afforded. In this approach, the availability of funds or liquid resources is the main consideration in making a decision about promotion expenditure. In other words, even if a company's sales expectations are high, the level of promotion is kept low if its cash position is tight. This approach can be questioned on several grounds. It makes promotion expenditures dependent on a company's liquid resources when the best move for a cash-short company may be to spend more on promotion with the hope of improving sales. Further, this approach involves an element of risk. At a time when the market is tight and sales are slow, a company may spend more on promotion if it happens to have resources available. This approach does, however, consider the fact that promotion outlays have long-term value; that is, advertising has a cumulative effect. Also, under conditions of complete uncertainty, this approach is a cautious one.

Under the *return-on-investment approach*, promotion expenditures are considered as an investment, the benefits of which are derived over the years. Thus, as in the case of any other investment, the appropriate level of promotion expenditure is determined by comparing the expected return with the desired return. The expected return on promotion may be computed by using present values of future returns. Inasmuch as some promotion is likely to produce immediate results, the total promotion expenditure may be partitioned between current expense and investment. Alternatively, the entire promotion expenditure can be considered an investment, in which case the immediate effect of promotion can be conceived as a return in period zero. The basic validity and soundness of the return-on-investment approach cannot be disputed. But there are several problems in its application. First, it may be difficult to determine the outcomes of different forms of promotion over time. Second, what is the appropriate return to be expected from an advertising investment? These limitations put severe constraints on the practical use of this approach.

The *competitive-parity approach* assumes that promotion expenditure is directly related to market share. The promotion expenditure of a firm should, therefore, be in proportion to that of competitors in order to maintain its position in the market. Thus, if the leader in the industry allocates 2 percent of its sales revenue for advertising, other members of the industry should spend about the same percentage of their sales on advertising. Considering the competitive nature of our economy, this seems a reasonable approach. It has, however, a number of limitations. First, the approach requires a knowledge of competitors' perspectives on promotion, and this information may not always be available. For example, the market leader may have decided to put its emphasis not on promotion per se but on reducing prices. Following this firm's lead in advertising expenditures without reference to its prices would be an unreliable guide. Second, one firm may get more for its promotion dollar through judicious selection of media, timing of advertising, skillful preparation of ads, a good sales supervision program, and so on. Thus, it could realize the same results as another firm that has twice as much to spend. Because promotion is just one of the variables affecting market performance, simply maintaining promotional parity with competitors may not be enough for a firm to preserve its market share.

Buildup Method. Many companies have advertising, sales, and sales promotion (merchandising) managers who report to the marketing manager. The marketing manager specifies the objectives of promotion separately for the advertising, personal selling, and sales promotion of each product line. Ideally, the spadework of defining objectives should be done by a committee consisting of executives concerned with product development, pricing distribution, and promotion. Committee work helps incorporate inputs from different areas; thus, a decision about promotion expenditure is made in the context of the total marketing mix. For example, the committee may decide that promotion should be undertaken to expose at least 100,000 households to the product; institutional customers may be sought through reductions in price.

In practice, it may not always be easy to pinpoint the separate roles of advertising, personal selling, and sales promotion because these three methods of promotion usually overlap to some degree. Each company must work out its own rules for a promotion mix. Once the tasks to be performed by each method of promotion have been designated, they may be defined formally as objectives and communicated to the respective managers. On the basis of these objectives, each promotion manager probably redefines his or her own goals in more operational terms. These redefined objectives then become the modus operandi of each department.

Once departmental objectives have been defined, each area works out a detailed budget, costing each item required to accomplish the objectives of the program. As each department prepares its own budget, the marketing manager may also prepare a summary budget for each of them, simply listing the major expenditures in light of the overall marketing strategy. A marketing manager's budget is primarily a control device.

When individual departments have arrived at their estimates of necessary allocation, the marketing manager meets with each of them to approve budgets. At that time, the marketing manager's own estimates help assess department budgets. Finally, an appropriation is made to each department. Needless to say, the emphasis on different tasks is revised and the total budget refigured several times before an acceptable program emerges. A committee instead of just the marketing manager may approve the final appropriation for each department.

The buildup method forces managers to analyze scientifically the role they expect promotion to play and the contribution it can make toward achieving marketing objectives. It also helps maintain control over promotion expenditure and avoid the frustrations often faced by promotion managers as a result of cuts in promotion appropriations due to economic slowdown. On the other hand, this approach can become overly scientific. Sometimes profit opportunities that require additional promotion expenditure may appear unannounced. Involvement with the objective and task exercise to decide how much more should be spent on promotion takes time, perhaps leading to the loss of an unexpected opportunity.

Promotion Mix Strategy

Another strategic decision in the area of promotion concerns the allocation of effort among the three different methods of promotion. **Advertising** refers to non-personal communication transmitted through the mass media (radio, television, print, outdoors, and mail). The communication is identified with a sponsor who compensates the media for the transmission. **Personal selling** refers to face-to-face interaction with the customer. Unlike advertising, personal selling involves communication in both directions, from the source to the destination and back. All other forms of communication with the customer other than those included in advertising and personal selling constitute **sales promotion**. Thus, coupons, samples, demonstrations, exhibits, premiums, sweepstakes, trade allowances, sales and dealer incentives, cents-off packs, rebates, and point-of-purchase material are all sales promotion devices.

A variety of new ways have been developed to communicate with customers. These include telemarketing (i.e., telephone selling) and demonstration centers (i.e., specially designed showrooms to allow customers to observe and try out complex industrial equipment). The discussion in this chapter will be limited to the three traditional methods of promotion. In some cases, the three types of promotion may be largely interchangeable; however, they should be blended judiciously to complement each other for a balanced promotional perspective. Illustrated below is the manner in which a chemical company mixed advertising with personal selling and sales promotion to achieve optimum promotional performance:

An advertising campaign aimed at customer industries, employees, and plant communities carried the theme, "The little chemical giant." It appeared in *Adhesive Age*,

American Paint & Coating Journal, Chemical & Engineering News, Chemical Marketing Reporter, Chemical Purchasing, Chemical Week, Modern Plastics, and *Plastics World*.

Sales promotion and personal selling were supported by publicity. Editorial tours of the company's new plants, programs to develop employee understanding and involvement in the expansion, and briefings for local people in towns and cities where USIC [the company] had facilities provided a catalyst for publicity.

Personal selling was aggressive and provided direct communication about the firm's continued service. USIC reassured producers of ethyl alcohol, vinyl acetate monomer, and polyethylene that "we will not lose personal touch with our customers."[4]

Development of an optimum promotion mix is by no means easy. Companies often use haphazard, seat-of-the-pants procedures to determine the respective roles of advertising, personal selling, and sales promotion in a product/market situation.

Decisions about the promotional mix are often diffused among many decision makers, impeding the formation of a unified promotion strategy. Personal selling plans are sometimes divorced from the planning of advertising and sales promotion. Frequently, decision makers are not adequately aware of the objectives and broad strategies of the overall product program that the promotion plan is designed to implement. Sales and market share goals tend to be constant, regardless of decreases or increases in promotional expenditures. Thus they are unrealistic as guides and directives for planning, as criteria for promotional effectiveness, or even as a fair basis for application of the judgment of decision makers. Briefly, the present state of the art in the administration of the promotion function is such that cause-and-effect relationships as well as other basic insights are not sufficiently understood to permit knowledgeable forecasts of what to expect from alternate courses of action. Even identifying feasible alternatives can prove difficult.

A variety of factors should be considered to determine the appropriate promotion mix in a particular product/market situation. These factors may be categorized as product factors, market factors, customer factors, budget factors, and marketing mix factors, as outlined in Exhibit 17-1.

Product Factors. Factors in this category relate principally to the way in which a product is bought, consumed, and perceived by the customer. For industrial goods, especially technical products, personal selling is more significant than advertising because these goods usually need to be inspected and compared before being bought. Salespeople can explain the workings of a product and provide on-the-spot answers to customer queries. For customer goods such as cosmetics and processed foods, advertising is of primary importance. In addition, advertising plays a dominant role for products that provide an opportunity for differentiation and for those being purchased with emotional motives.

The perceived risk of a purchase decision is another variable here. Generally speaking, the more risk a buyer perceives to be associated with buying a particular product, the higher the importance of personal selling over advertising. A buyer generally desires specific information on a product when the perceived risk

EXHIBIT 17-1
Criteria for Determining Promotion Mix

Product Factors
1. Nature of product
2. Perceived risk
3. Durable versus nondurable
4. Typical purchase amount

Market Factors
1. Position in its life cycle
2. Market share
3. Industry concentration
4. Intensity of competition
5. Demand perspectives

Customer Factors
1. Household versus business customers
2. Number of customers
3. Concentration of customers

Budget Factors
1. Financial resources of the organization
2. Traditional promotional perspectives

Marketing Mix Factors
1. Relative price/relative quality
2. Distribution strategy
3. Brand life cycle
4. Geographic scope of market

is high. This necessitates an emphasis on personal selling. Durable goods are bought less frequently than nondurables and usually require a heavy commitment of resources. These characteristics make personal selling of greater significance for durable goods than advertising. However, because many durable goods are sold through franchised dealerships, the influence of each type of promotion should be determined in light of the additional push it would provide in moving the product. Finally, products purchased in small quantities are presumably purchased frequently and require routine decision making. For these products, advertising should be preferable to personal selling. Such products are often of low value; therefore, a profitable business in these products can only be conducted on volume. This underlines the importance of advertising in this case.

Market Factors. The first market factor is the position of a product in its life cycle. The creation of primary demand, hitherto nonexistent, is the primary task during the introductory stage; therefore, a great promotion effort is needed to explain a new product to potential customers. For consumer goods in the introductory stage, the major thrust is on heavy advertising supported by missionary selling to help distributors move the product. In addition, different devices of sales promotion (e.g., sampling, couponing, free demonstrations) are employed to entice the customer to try the product. In the case of industrial products, personal selling alone is useful during this period. During the growth phase, there is increasing demand, which means enough business for all competitors. In the case of consumer goods, however, the promotional effort shifts to reliance on advertising. Industrial goods, on the other hand, begin to be advertised as the market broadens. However, they continue to require a personal selling effort. In the maturity phase, competition becomes intense, and advertising, along with sales promotion, is required to differentiate the product (a consumer good) from competitive brands and to provide an incentive to the customer to buy a particular product. Industrial goods during maturity call for intensive personal selling. During the decline phase, the promotional effort does not vary much initially from that during the maturity phase except that the intensity of promotion declines. Later, as price competition becomes keen and demand continues to decline, overall promotional perspectives are reduced.

For a given product class, if market share is high, both advertising and personal selling are used. If the market share is low, the emphasis is placed on either personal selling or advertising. This is because high market share seems to indicate that the company does business in more than one segment and uses multiple channels of distribution. Thus, both personal selling and advertising are used to promote the product. Where market share is low, the perspectives of the business are limited, and either advertising or personal selling will suffice, depending on the nature of the product.

If the industry is concentrated among a few firms, advertising has additional significance for two reasons: (a) heavy advertising may help discourage other firms from entering the field, and (b) heavy advertising sustains a desired position for the product in the market. Heavy advertising constitutes an implied warranty of product performance and perhaps decreases the uncertainty consumers associate with new products. In this way, new competition is discouraged and existing positions are reinforced.

Intensity of competition tends to affect promotional blending in the same way that market share does. When competition is keen, all three types of promotion are needed to sustain a product's position in the market. This is because promotion is needed to inform, remind, and persuade customers to buy the product. On the other hand, if competitive activity is limited, the major function of promotion is to inform and perhaps remind customers about the product. Thus, either advertising or personal selling is emphasized.

Hypothetically, advertising is more suited for products that have relatively latent demand. This is because advertising investment should open up new opportunities in the long run, and if the carryover effect is counted, expenditure per sales dollar would be more beneficial. If demand is limited and new demand is not expected to be created, advertising outlay would be uneconomical. Thus, future potential becomes a significant factor in determining the role of advertising.

Customer Factors. One of the major dimensions used to differentiate businesses is whether products are marketed for household consumption or for organizational use. There are several significant differences in the way products are marketed to these two customer groups, and these differences exert considerable influence on the type of promotion that should be used. In the case of household customers, it is relatively easy to identify the decision maker for a particular product; therefore, advertising is more desirable. Also, the self-service nature of many consumer-product sales makes personal selling relatively unimportant. Finally, household customers do not ordinarily go through a formal buying process using objective criteria as organizational customers do. This again makes advertising more useful for reaching household customers. Essentially the same reasons make personal selling more relevant in promoting a product among organizational customers.

The number of customers and their geographic concentration also influence promotional blending. For a small customer base, especially if it is geographically concentrated, advertising does not make as much sense as it does in cases where customers are widely scattered and represent a significant mass. Caution is needed here because some advertising may always be necessary for consumer goods, no matter what the market perspectives are. Thus, these statements provide only a conceptual framework and should not be interpreted as exact yes/no criteria.

Budget Factors.   Ideally, the budget should be based on the promotional tasks to be performed. However, intuitively and traditionally, companies place an upper limit on the amount that they spend on promotion. Such limits may influence the type of promotion that may be undertaken in two ways. First, a financially weak company is constrained in undertaking certain types of promotion. For example, television advertising necessitates a heavy commitment of resources. Second, in many companies the advertising budget is, by tradition, linked to revenues as a percentage. This method of allocation continues to be used so that expected revenues indicate how much may be spent on advertising in the future. The allocated funds, then, automatically determine the role of advertising.

Marketing Mix Factors.   The promotion decision should be made in the context of other aspects of the marketing mix. The price and quality of a product relative to competition affect the nature of its promotional perspectives. Higher prices must be justified to the consumer by actual or presumed product superiority. Thus, in the case of a product that is priced substantially higher than competing goods, advertising achieves significance in communicating and establishing the product's superior quality in the minds of customers.

The promotion mix is also influenced by the distribution structure employed for the product. If the product is distributed directly, the sales force can largely be counted on to promote the product. Indirect distribution, on the other hand, requires greater emphasis on advertising because the push of a sales force is limited. As a matter of fact, the further the manufacturer is from the ultimate user, the greater the need for the advertising effort to stimulate and maintain demand. The influence of the distribution strategy may be illustrated with reference to two cosmetics companies that deal in similar products, Revlon and Avon. Revlon distributes its products through different types of intermediaries and advertises them heavily. Avon, on the other hand, distributes primarily directly to end users in their homes and spends less on advertising relative to Revlon.

Earlier we examined the effect on the promotion mix of a product's position in its life cycle. The position of a brand in its life cycle also influences promotional perspectives. Positioning a new brand in the desired slot in the market during its introduction phase requires a higher degree of advertising. As a product enters the growth phase, advertising should be blended with personal selling. In the growth phase, the overall level of promotion declines in scope. When an existing brand reaches the maturity phase in its life cycle, the marketer has three options: to employ life-extension strategies, to harvest the brand for profits, and/or to introduce a new brand that may be targeted at a more specific segment of the market. The first two options were discussed in Chapter 13. As far as the third option is concerned, for promotional purposes, the new brand will need to be treated like a new product.

Finally, the geographic scope of the market to be served is another consideration. Advertising, relatively speaking, is more significant for products marketed nationally than for those marketed locally or regionally. When the market is geographically limited, one study showed that even spot television advertising proved to be more expensive vis-à-vis the target group exposures gained.[5] Thus, because advertising is an expensive proposition, regional marketers should rely less on advertising and more on other forms of promotion, or they should substitute another element of the marketing mix for it. For example, a regional marketer may manufacture private label brands.

Conclusion | Although these factors are helpful in establishing roles for different methods of promotion, actual appropriation among them should take into consideration the effect of any changes in the environment. For example, in the 1970s soft drink companies frequently used sales promotion (mainly cents off) to vie for customers. In the 1980s, however, the markers of soft drinks changed their promotion mix strategy to concentrate more on advertising. This is evidenced by the fact that the five largest soft drink makers spent about $250 million on advertising in 1984, 40 percent more than they spent in 1979. One reason for this change in promotional perspective was the realization that price discounting hurt brand loyalties; because Coke and Pepsi had turned their colas into commodities by means of cents-off promotion, the consumer now shopped for price.[6]

In addition, the promotion mix may also be affected by a desire to be innovative. For example, Puritan Fashions Corporation, an apparel company, traditionally spent little on advertising. In the late 1970s, the company was continually losing money. Then, in 1977, the company introduced a new product, body-hugging jeans, and employed an unconventional promotion strategy. It placed Calvin Klein's label on its jeans, sold them as a prestige trouser priced at $35 (double the price of nonlabeled styles), and advertised them heavily. This promotion mix provided the company with instant success. Although Puritan had no previous experience with jeans, the company's production soared to 125,000 pairs a week within one year, giving Puritan a 25 percent share of a $1 billion retail market.[7] Although promotional innovation may not last long because competitors may soon copy it, it does provide the innovator with a head start.

Promotional blending requires consideration of a large number of variables, as outlined above. Unfortunately, it is difficult to assign quantitative values to the effect that these variables have on promotion. Thus, decisions about promotional blending must necessarily be made subjectively. These factors, however, provide a checklist for reviewing the soundness and viability of subjective decisions.

Recent research conducted by the Strategic Planning Institute for Cahners Publishing Co. identified the following decision rules that can be used in formulating ad budgets. These rules may be helpful in finalizing promotion mix decisions.[8]

1. **Market share**—A company that has a higher market share must generally spend more on advertising to maintain its share.
2. **Sales from new products**—If a company has a high percentage of its sales resulting from new products, it must spend more on advertising compared to companies that have well-established products.
3. **Market growth**—Companies competing in fast-growing markets should spend comparatively more on advertising.
4. **Plant capacity**—If a company has a lot of unused plant capacity, it should spend more on advertising to stimulate sales and production.
5. **Unit price (per sales transaction)**—The lower the unit price of a company's products, the more it should spend on advertising because of the greater likelihood of brand switching.
6. **Importance of product to customers (in relation to their total purchases)**—Products that constitute a lower proportion of customers' purchases generally require higher advertising expenditures.
7. **Product price**—Both very high-priced (or premium) products and very low-priced (or discount) products require higher ad expenditures because, in both cases, price is an important factor in the buying decision and the buyer must be convinced (through advertising) that the product is a good value.
8. **Product quality**—Higher-quality products require a greater advertising effort because of the need to convince the consumer that the product is unique.
9. **Breadth of product line**—Companies with a broad line of products must spend more on advertising compared to companies with specialized product lines.
10. **Degree of standardization**—Standardized products produced in large quantities should be backed by higher advertising outlays because they are likely to have more competition in the market.

ADVERTISING STRATEGIES

Companies typically plan and execute their advertising through five stages: developing the budget, planning the advertising, copy development and approval, execution, and monitoring response.[9] Exhibit 17-2 summarizes who participates in each stage and the end product.

Media-Selection Strategy | **Media** may be defined as those channels through which messages concerning a product or service are transmitted to targets. The following media are available to

EXHIBIT 17-2
The Advertising Planning Process

Stage	Preliminary players	End product
Developing the marketing plan and budget	Product manager	Budget Spending guidelines Profit projections
Planning the advertising	Product manager Advertising manager Ad agency Corporate advertising department	Identification of the target market Allocating of spending Statement of advertising strategy and message
Copy development and approval	Ad agency Copy research company Product manager Advertising manager Senior management	Finished copy Media plan (with reach and frequency projections)
Execution	Ad agency or media buying company	Actual placement
Monitoring response	Market research manager Product manager Ad agency (research)	Awareness, recognition, and perception tracking Perceptual maps Sales/share tracking

advertisers: newspapers, magazines, television, radio, outdoor advertising, transit advertising, and direct mail.

Selection of an advertising medium is influenced by such factors as the product or service itself, the target market, the extent and type of distribution, the type of message to be communicated, the budget, and competitors' advertising strategies. Except for the advertising perspectives employed by the competition, information on most of these factors is presumably available inside the company. It may be necessary to undertake a marketing research project to find out what sorts of advertising strategies competitors have used in the past and what might be expected of them in the future. In addition, selection of a medium also depends on the advertising objectives for the product/market concerned. With this information in place, different methods may be used to select a medium.

Advertising Objectives. To build a good advertising program, it is necessary first to pinpoint the objectives of the ad campaign. It would be wrong to assume that all advertising leads directly to sales. A sale is a multiphase phenomenon, and advertising can be used to transfer the customer from one phase to the next: from unawareness of a product or service, to awareness, to comprehension, to conviction, to action. Thus, the advertiser must specify at what stage or stages he or she wants advertising to work. The objectives of advertising may be defined by any one of the following approaches: inventory approach, hierarchy approach, or attitudinal approach.

Inventory Approach. A number of scholars have articulated inventories of functions performed by advertising. The objectives of an ad campaign may be defined from an inventory based on a firm's overall marketing perspective. For example, the following inventory may be used to develop a firm's advertising objectives:

A. Increase sales by

1. Encouraging potential purchasers to visit the company or its dealers.
2. Obtaining leads for salespeople or dealers.
3. Inducing professional people (e.g., doctors, architects) to recommend the product.
4. Securing new distributors.
5. Prompting immediate purchases through announcements of special sales and contests.

B. Create an awareness about a company's product or service by

1. Informing potential customers about product features.
2 Announcing new models.
3. Highlighting the unique features of the product.
4. Informing customers as to where the product may be bought.
5. Announcing price changes.
6. Demonstrating the product in use.

The inventory approach is helpful in highlighting the fact that different objectives can be emphasized in advertising and that these objectives cannot be selected without reference to the overall marketing plan. Thus, this approach helps the advertiser avoid operating in a vacuum. However, inherent in this approach is the danger that the decision maker may choose nonfeasible and conflicting objectives if everything listed in an inventory seems worth pursuing.

Hierarchy Approach. Following this approach, the objectives of advertising should be stated in an action-oriented psychological form. Thus, the objectives of advertising may be defined as (a) gaining customers' initial attention, perception, continued favorable attention, and interest; or (b) affecting customers' comprehension, feeling, emotion, motivation, belief, intentions, decision, imagery, association, recall, and recognition. The thesis behind this approach is that customers move from one psychological state to another before actually buying a product. Thus, the purpose of advertising should be to move customers from state to state and ultimately toward purchasing the product. Although it makes sense to define the purpose of an individual ad in hierarchical terms, it may be difficult to relate the purpose so defined to marketing goals. Besides, measurement of psychological states that form the basis of this approach is difficult and subjective compared to the measurement of goals such as market share.

Attitudinal Approach. According to this approach, advertising is instrumental in producing changes in attitudes; therefore, advertising goals should be defined to influence attitudinal structures. Thus, advertising may be undertaken to accomplish any of the following goals:

1. Affect those forces that influence strongly the choice of criteria used for evaluating brands belonging to the product class.
2. Add characteristic(s) to those considered salient for the product class.
3. Increase/decrease the rating for a salient product class characteristic.
4. Change the perception of the company's brand with regard to some particular salient product characteristic.
5. Change the perception of competitive brands with regard to some particular salient product characteristic.

The attitudinal approach is an improvement over the hierarchical approach because it attempts to relate advertising objectives to product/market objectives. This approach indicates not only the functions advertising performs, it also targets the specific results it can achieve.

Advertising objectives should be defined by a person completely familiar with all product/market perspectives. A good definition of objectives aids in the writing of appropriate ad copy and in selecting the right media. It should be recognized that different ad campaigns for the same product can have varied objectives. But all ad campaigns should be complementary to each other to maximize total advertising impact.

Product/market advertising objectives may be used to derive media objectives. Media objectives should be defined so as to answer such questions as: Are we trying to reach everybody? Are we aiming to be selective? If housewives under 30 with children under 10 are really our target, what media objectives should we develop? Are we national or regional? Do we need to concentrate in selected counties? Do we need reach or frequency or both? Are there creative considerations to control our thinking? Do we need color or permanence (which might mean magazines and supplements), personalities and demonstration (which might mean television), the best reminder for the least money (which might mean radio or outdoor), superselectivity (which might mean direct mail), or going all the way up and down in the market (which could mean newspapers)? The following is a list of sample media objectives based on these questions:

1. We need a national audience of women.
2. We want them between 18 and 34.
3. Because the product is a considered purchase, we need room to explain it thoroughly.
4. We need color to show the product to best advantage.
5. We must keep after these women more than once, so we need frequency.
6. There's no way to demonstrate the product except in a store.

Media-Selection Procedure. Media selection calls for two decisions: (a) which particular medium to use and (b) which specific vehicles to choose within a given medium. For example, if magazines are to be used, in which particular magazines should ads be placed? The following two approaches can be used in media selection: cost-per-thousand-contacts comparison and matching of audience and medium characteristics.

Cost-per-Thousand-Contacts Comparison. The cost-per-thousand-contacts comparison has traditionally been the most popular method of media selection.

Although simple to apply, the cost-per-thousand method leaves much to be desired. Basing media selection entirely on the number of contacts to be reached ignores the quality of contacts made. For example, an advertisement for a women's dress line appearing in *Vogue* would make a greater impact on those exposed to it than would the same ad appearing in *True Confessions*. Similarly, *Esquire* would perhaps be more appropriate than many less-specialized magazines for introducing men's fashions.

Further, the cost-per-thousand method can be highly misleading if one considers the way in which advertisers define the term *exposure*. According to the media definition, exposure occurs as soon as an ad is inserted in the magazine. Whether the exposure actually occurs is never considered. This method also fails to consider editorial images and the impact power of different channels of a medium.

Matching of Audience and Media Characteristics. An alternative approach to media selection is to specify the target audience and match its characteristics to a particular medium. A step-by-step procedure for using this method is described below:

1. Build a profile of customers, detailing who they are, where they are located, when they can be reached, and what their demographic characteristics are. Setting media objectives (discussed earlier) is helpful in building customer profiles.
2. Study media profiles in terms of audience coverage. Implicit in this step is the study of the audience's media habits (i.e., an examination of who constitutes a particular medium's audience).
3. Match customer profiles to media profiles. The customer characteristics for a product should be matched to the audience characteristics of different media. This comparison should lead to the preliminary selection of a medium, based primarily on the grounds of coverage.
4. The preliminary selection should be examined further in regard to product and cost considerations. For some products, other things being equal, one medium is superior to another. For example, in the case of beauty aids, a product demonstration is helpful; hence, television would be a better choice than radio. Cost is another concern in media selection; information on cost is available from the media themselves. Cost should be balanced against the benefit expected from the campaign under consideration.
5. Finally, the total budget should be allocated to different media and to various media vehicles. The final selection of a medium should maximize the achievement of media objectives. For example, if the objective is to make people aware of a product, then the medium selected should be the one that reaches a wide audience.

Basically, two types of information are required for media selection: customer profile and audience characteristics. The advertiser should build a customer profile for his or her product/market. Information about various media is usually available from media owners. Practically all media owners have complete information available to them concerning their audiences (demographics and circulation figures). Each medium, however, presents the information in a way that makes it look best. It is desirable, therefore, to validate the audience information supplied by media owners with data from bureaus that audit various media. The Audit Bureau of Circulations, the Traffic Audit Bureau, and the Business Publications Audit of Circulation are examples of such audit bureaus.

Evaluation Criteria. Before money is committed to a selected medium, it is desirable to review the medium's viability against evaluation criteria. Is the decision maker being thorough, progressive (imaginative), measure-minded, practical, and optimistic? Thoroughness requires that all aspects of media selection be given full consideration. For maximum impact, the chosen medium should be progressive: it should have a unique way of doing the job. An example of progressiveness is putting a sample envelope of Sanka coffee in millions of copies of TV Guide. Because of postal regulations, this sampling could not be done in a magazine that is purchased primarily through subscriptions. But TV Guide is mainly a newsstand magazine. Measure-mindedness refers to more than just the number of exposures. It refers not only to frequency and timing in reaching the target audience but also to the quality of the audience; that is, to the proportion of heavy to light television viewers reached, proportion of men to women, working to nonworking women, and so on. Practicality requires choosing a medium on factual, not emotional, grounds. For example, it is not desirable to substitute a weak newspaper for a strong one just because the top management of the company does not agree with the editorial policy of the latter. Finally, the overall media plan should be optimistic in that it takes advantage of lessons learned from experience.

| *Advertising-Copy Strategy* | **Copy** refers to the content of an advertisement. In the advertising industry, the term is sometimes used in a broad sense to include the words, pictures, symbols, colors, layout, and other ingredients of an ad. Copywriting is a creative job, and its quality depends to a large extent on the creative ability of writers in the advertising agency or in the company. However, creativity alone may not produce good ad copy. A marketing strategist needs to have his or her own perspectives incorporated in the copy (what to say, how to say it, and to whom to say it) and needs to furnish information on ad objectives, product, target customers, competitive activity, and ethical and legal considerations. The creative person carries on from there. In brief, although copywriting may be the outcome of a flash of inspiration on the part of an advertising genius, it must rest on a systematic, logical, step-by-step presentation of ideas. |

This point may be illustrated with reference to Perrier, a brand of bottled water that comes from mineral springs located in southern France. In Europe, this product has been quite popular for some years; in the United States, however, it used to be available in gourmet shops only. In 1977, the company introduced the product to the U.S. market as a soft drink by tapping the adult user market with heavy advertising. Perrier's major product distinction is that its water is naturally carbonated spring water. The product was aimed at the affluent adult population, particularly those concerned with diet and health, as a status symbol and a sign of maturity. Perrier faced competition from two sources: regular soft drink makers and potential makers of mineral water. The company took care of its soft drink competition by segmenting the market on the basis of price (Perrier was priced 50 percent above the average soft drink) and thus avoided direct confrontation. In regard to competition from new brands of mineral water, Perrier's association with France and the fact that it is constituted of naturally carbonated spring water were expected to continue as viable strengths. This information was used to develop ad copy for placement in high-fashion women's magazines and in television commercials narrated by Orson Welles. The results were astonishing. In less than five years, Perrier became a major liquid drink in the U.S. market.[10]

Essentially, ad copy constitutes an advertiser's message to the customer. To ensure that the proper message gets across, it is important that there is no distortion of the message because of what in communication theory is called noise. Noise may emerge from three sources: (a) dearth of facts (e.g., the company is unaware of the unique distinctions of its product), (b) competitors (e.g., competitors make changes in their marketing mix to counter the company's claims or position), and (c) behavior traits of the customers or audience. Failure to take into account the last source of noise is often the missing link in developing ad copy. It is not safe to assume that one's own perspectives on what appeals to the audience are accurate. It is desirable, therefore, to gain, through some sort of marketing research, insights into behavior patterns of the audience and to make this information available to the copywriter. For example, a 1993 Research International Organization (RIO) study of teenagers in 26 countries provides the following clues for making an effective appeal to young customers.

1. Never talk down to a teenager. While "hip" phraseology and the generally flippant tone observed in the teenager's conversation may be coin of the realm from one youngster to another, it comes across as phony, foolish, and condescending when directed at him or her by an advertiser. Sincerity is infinitely more effective than cuteness. Entertainment and attention-getting approaches by themselves do little to attract a teenager to the merits of a product. In fact, they often dissuade the youngster from making a purchase decision.

2. Be totally, absolutely, and unswervingly straightforward. Teenagers may act cocky and confident in front of adults, but most of them are still rather unsure of themselves and are wary of being misled. They are not sure they know enough to avoid being taken advantage of, and they do not like to risk looking foolish by falling for a commercial gimmick. Moreover, teenagers as a group are far more suspicious of things commercial than adults are. Advertising must not only be noticed; it must be believed.

3. Give the teenager credit for being motivated by rational values. When making a buying selection, adults like to think they are doing so on the basis of the benefits the product or service offers. Teenagers instinctively perceive what's "really there" in an offering. Advertising must clearly expose for their consideration the value a product or service claims to represent.

4. Be as personal as possible. Derived from the adult world of marketing, this rule has an exaggerated importance with teenagers. In this automated age, with so many complaining of being reduced en masse to anonymity, people are becoming

progressively more aware of their own individuality. The desire to be personally known and recognized is particularly strong with young people, who are urgently searching for a clear sense of their own identity.[11]

Findings from communications research are helpful in further refining the attributes of ad copy that an advertising strategist needs to spell out for the copy-writer.

Source Credibility. An ad may show a celebrity recommending the use of a product. It is hoped that this endorsement will help give the ad additional credibility, credibility that will be reflected in higher sales.

Research on the subject has shown that an initially credible source, such as Miss America claiming to use a certain brand of hair spray, is more effective in changing the opinion of an audience than if a similar claim is made by a lesser-known source, such as an unknown homemaker. However, as time passes, the audience tends to forget the source or to dissociate the source from the message.[12] Some consumers who might have been swayed in favor of a particular brand because it was recommended by Miss America may revert to their original choice, whereas those who did not initially accept the homemaker's word may later become favorably inclined toward the product she is recommending. The decreasing importance of the source behind a message over time has been called the **sleeper effect.**[13]

Several conclusions can be drawn from the sleeper effect. In some cases, it may be helpful if the advertiser is disassociated as much as possible from the ad, particularly when the audience may perceive that a manufacturer is trying to push something.[14] On the other hand, when source credibility is important, advertisements should be scheduled so that the source may reappear to reinforce the message.

Balance of Argument. When preparing copy, there is a question of whether only the good and distinctive features of a brand should be highlighted or whether its demerits should be mentioned as well. Traditionally, the argument has been, "Put your best foot forward." In other words, messages should be designed to emphasize only the favorable aspects of a product. Recent research in the field of communication has questioned the validity of indiscriminately detailing the favorable side. It has been found that

1. Presenting both sides of an issue is more effective than giving only one side among individuals who are initially opposed to the point of view being presented.
2. Better-educated people are more favorably affected by presentation of both sides; poorly educated persons are more favorably affected by communication that gives only supporting arguments.
3. For those already convinced of the point of view presented, the presentation of both sides is less effective than a presentation featuring only those items favoring the general position being advanced.
4. Presentation of both sides is least effective among the poorly educated who are already convinced of the position advocated.

5. Leaving out a relevant argument is more noticeable and detracts more from effectiveness when both sides are presented than when only the side favorable to the proposition is being advanced.[15]

These findings have important implications for developing copy. If one is trying to reach executive customers through an ad in the *Harvard Business Review*, it probably is better to present both favorable and unfavorable qualities of a product. On the other hand, for such status products and services as Rolex diamond watches and Chanel No. 5 perfume, emphasis on both pros and cons can distort the image. Thus, when status is already established, a simple message is more desirable.

Message Repetition. Should the same message be repeated time and again? According to learning theory, reinforcement over time from different directions increases learning. It has been said that a good slogan never dies and that repetition is the surest way of getting the message across. However, some feel that, although the central theme should be maintained, a message should be presented with variations.

Communication research questions the value of wholesale repetition. Repetition, it has been found, leads to increased learning up to a certain point. Thereafter, learning levels off and may, in fact, change to boredom and loss of attention. Continuous repetition may even counteract the good effect created earlier. Thus, advertisers must keep track of the shape of the learning curve and develop a new product theme when the curve appears to be flattening out. The Coca-Cola Company, for example, regularly changes its message to maintain audience interest.[16]

1886—Coca-Cola
1905—Coca-Cola revives and sustains
1906—The Great National Temperance Beverage
1922—Thirst knows no season
1925—Six million a day
1927—Around the corner from everywhere
1929—The pause that refreshes
1938—The best friend thirst ever had
1948—Where there's Coke there's hospitality
1949—Along the highway to anywhere
1952—What you want is a Coke
1956—Makes good things taste better
1957—Sign of good taste
1958—The cold, crisp taste of Coke
1963—Things go better with Coke
1970—It's the real thing
1971—I'd like to buy the world a Coke
1975—Look up, America
1976—Coke adds life
1979—Have a Coke and a smile
1982—Coke is it

1985—We've got a taste for you
1986—Catch the wave
1987—When Coca-Cola is a part of your life, you can't beat the feeling
1988—Can't beat the feeling
1990—Always new, always real
1992—Always you, always coke
1995—Always spring, always coke

Rational versus Emotional Appeals. Results of studies on the effect of rational and emotional appeals presented in advertisements are not conclusive. Some studies show that emotional appeals have definite positive results.[17] However, arousing emotions may not be sufficient unless the ad can rationally convince the subject that the product in question will fulfill a need. It appears that emphasis on one type of appeal—rational or emotional—is not enough. The advertiser must strike a balance between emotional and rational appeals. For example, Procter & Gamble's Crest toothpaste ad, "Crest has been recommended by the American Dental Association," has a rational content; but its reference to cavity prevention also excites emotions. Similarly, a Close-up toothpaste ad produced for Lever Brothers is primarily emotional in nature: "Put your money where your mouth is." However, it also has an economic aspect: "Use Close-up both as a toothpaste and mouthwash."

An example of how emotional appeal complemented by service created a market niche for an unknown company is provided by Singapore Airlines. Singapore is a Southeast Asian nation barely larger than Cleveland. Many airlines have tried to sell the notion that they have something unique to offer, but not many have succeeded. Singapore Airlines, however, thrives mainly on the charm of its cabin attendants, who serve passengers with warm smiles and copious attention. A gently persuasive advertising campaign glamorizes the attendants and tries to convey the idea of in-flight pleasure of a lyrical quality. Most of the airline's ads are essentially large, soft-focus color photographs of various attendants. A commercial announces: "Singapore girl, you look so good I want to stay up here with you forever." Of course, its emotional appeals are duly supported by excellent service (rational appeals to complement emotional ones). The airline provides gifts, free cocktails, and free French wines and brandy even to economy-class passengers. Small wonder that it flies with an above-average load factor higher than that of any other major international carrier. In brief, emotional appeal can go a long way in the development of an effective ad campaign, but it must have rational underpinnings to support it.

Comparison Advertising. Comparison advertising refers to the comparison of one brand with one or more competitive brands by explicitly naming them on a variety of specific product or service attributes. Comparison advertising became popular in the early 1970s; today one finds comparison ads for all forms of goods and services. Although it is debatable whether comparative ads are more or less effective than individual ads, limited research on the subject indicates that in some cases comparative ads are more useful.

Many companies have successfully used comparison advertising. One that stands out is Helene Curtis Industries. The company used comparison ads on television for its Suave brand of shampoo. The ads said: "We do what theirs does for less than half the price." Competitors were either named or their labels were clearly shown. The message that Suave is comparable to top-ranking shampoos was designed to allay public suspicion that low-priced merchandise is somehow shoddy. The campaign was so successful that within a few years Suave's sales surpassed those of both Procter & Gamble's Head & Shoulders and Johnson & Johnson's Baby Shampoo in volume. The company continues to use the same approach in its advertising today. Comparison advertising clearly provides an underdog with the chance to catch up with the leader.[18]

In using comparison advertising, a company should make sure that its claim of superiority will hold up in a court of law. More businesses today are counter-attacking by suing when rivals mention their products in ads or promotions. For example, MCI has sought to stop an AT&T ad campaign (aimed at MCI) that claims that AT&T's long-distance and other services are better and cheaper.[19]

PERSONAL SELLING STRATEGIES

Selling Strategy | There was a time when the problems of selling were simpler than they are today. Recent years have produced a variety of changes in the selling strategies of businesses. The complexities involved in selling in the 1990s are different from those in the 1980s. As an example, today a high-principled style of selling that favors a close, trusting, long-term relationship over a quick sell is recommended. The philosophy is to serve the customer as a consultant, not as a peddler. Discussed below are objectives and strategic matters pertaining to selling strategies.

Objectives. Selling objectives should be derived from overall marketing objectives and should be properly linked with promotional objectives. For example, if the marketing goal is to raise the current 35 percent market share in a product line to 40 percent, the sales manager may stipulate the objective to increase sales of specific products by different percentage points in various sales regions under his or her control.

Selling objectives are usually defined in terms of sales volume. Objectives, however, may also be defined for (a) gross margin targets, (b) maximum expenditure levels, and (c) fulfillment of specific activities, such as converting a stated number of competitors' customers into company customers.

The sales strategist should also specify the role of selling in terms of personal selling push (vis-à-vis advertising pull). Selling strategies depend on the consumer decision process, the influence of different communication alternatives, and the cost of these alternatives. The flexibility associated with personal selling allows sales presentations to be tailored to individual customers. Further, personal selling offers an opportunity to develop a tangible personal rapport with customers that can go far toward building long-term relationships. Finally, personal selling is the only method that secures immediate feedback. Feedback helps in taking timely corrective action and in avoiding mistakes. The benefits of personal selling, however, must be considered in relation to its costs. For example, according to the research department of the McGraw-Hill Publications Company, per call personal selling expenditures for all types of personal selling in 1983 came to $205.40, up 15.4 percent from 1981.[20] Thus, the high impact of personal selling should be considered in light of its high cost.

Strategic Matters. As a part of selling strategy, several strategic matters should be resolved. A decision must be made on whether greater emphasis should be put on maintaining existing accounts or on converting customers. Retention and conversion of customers are related to the time salespeople spend with them. Thus, before salespeople can make the best use of their efforts, they must know how much importance is to be attached to each of these two functions. The decision is influenced by such factors as the growth status of the industry, the company's strengths and weaknesses, competitors' strengths, and marketing goals. For example, a manufacturer of laundry detergent will think twice before attempting to convert customers from Tide (Procter & Gamble's brand) to its own brand. On the other hand, some factors may make a company challenge the leader. For example, Bic Pen Corporation aggressively promotes its disposable razor to Gillette customers. The decision to maintain or convert customers cannot be made in isolation and must be considered in the context of total marketing strategy.[21]

An important strategic concern is how to make productive use of the sales force. In recent years, high expenses (i.e., cost of keeping a salesperson on the road), affordable technological advances (e.g., prices of technology used in telemarketing, teleconferencing, and computerized sales have gone down substantially), and innovative sales techniques (e.g., video presentations) have made it feasible for marketers to turn to electronic marketing to make the most productive use of sales force resources. For example, Gould's medical products division in Oxnard, California, uses video to support sales efforts for one of its new products, a disposable transducer that translates blood pressure into readable electronic impulses. Gould produced two videotapes—a six-minute sales presentation and a nine-minute training film—costing $200,000. Salespeople were equipped with videorecorders an additional $75,000 investment—to take on calls. According to Gould executives, video gives a concise, clear version of the intended communication and adds professionalism to their sales effort. Gould targeted its competitors' customers and maintains that it captured 45 percent of the $75 million transducer market in less than a year. At the end of nine months, the company had achieved sales of more than 25,000 units per month, achieving significant penetration in markets that it had not been able to get into before.[22]

Another aspect of selling strategy deals with the question of who should be contacted in the customer organization. The buying process may be divided into four phases: consideration, acceptance, selection, and evaluation. Different executives in the customer organization may exert influence on any of the four phases. The sales strategist may work out a plan specifying which salesperson should call upon various individuals in the customer organization and when. On occasion, a person other than the salesperson may be asked to call on a customer. Sometimes, as a matter of selling strategy, a team of people may visit the customer. For example, Northrop Corporation, an aerospace contractor, assigns aircraft designers and technicians—not salespeople—to call on potential customers. When Singapore indicated interest in Northrop's F-5 fighter, Northrop dispatched a team to Singapore that included an engineer, a lawyer, a pricing expert, a test pilot, and a maintenance specialist.

A manufacturer of vinyl acetate latex (used as a base for latex paint) built its sales volume by having its people call on the "right people" in the customer organization. The manufacturer recognized that its product was used by the customer to produce paint sold through its marketing department, not the purchasing agent or the manager of research. So the manufacturer planned for its people to meet with the customer's sales and marketing personnel to find out what their problems were, what kept them from selling more latex paint, and what role the manufacturer could play in helping the customer. It was only after the marketing personnel had been sold on the product that the purchasing department was contacted. Thus, a good selling strategy requires a careful analysis of the situation to determine the key people to contact in the customer organization. A routine call on a purchasing agent may not suffice.

The selling strategy should also determine the size of the sales force needed to perform an effective job. This decision is usually made intuitively. A company starts with a few salespeople, adding more as it gains experience. Some companies may go a step beyond the intuitive approach to determine how many salespeople should be recruited. For instance, consideration may be given to factors such as the number of customers who must be visited, the amount of market potential in a territory, and so on. But all these factors are weighed subjectively. This work load approach requires the following steps:

1. Customers are grouped into size classes according to their annual sales volume.
2. Desirable call frequencies (number of sales calls on an account per year) are established for each class.
3. The number of accounts in each size class is multiplied by the corresponding call frequency to arrive at the total work load for the country in sales calls per year.
4. The average number of calls a sales representative can make per year is determined.
5. The number of sales representatives needed is determined by dividing the total annual calls required by the average annual calls made by a sales representative.

Sales Motivation and Supervision Strategy

To ensure that salespersons perform to their utmost capacity, they must be motivated adequately and properly supervised. It has often been found that salespeople fail to do well because management fails to carry out its part of the job, especially in the areas of motivation and supervision. Although motivation and supervision may appear to be mundane day-to-day matters, they have far-reaching implications for marketing strategy. The purpose of this section is to provide insights into the strategic aspects of motivation and supervision.

Motivation. Salespeople may be motivated through financial and nonfinancial means. Financial motivation is provided by monetary compensation. Nonfinancial motivation is usually tied in with evaluation programs.[23]

Compensation. Most people work to earn a living; their motivation to work is deeply affected by the remuneration they receive. A well-designed compensation plan keeps turnover low and helps to increase an employee's productivity. A compensation plan should be simple, understandable, flexible (cognizant of the differences between individuals), and economically equitable. It should also provide incentive and build morale. It should not penalize salespeople for conditions beyond their control, and it should help develop new business, provide stable income, and meet the objectives of the corporation. Above all, compensation should be in line with the market price for salespeople. Because some of these requisites may conflict with each other, there can be no one perfect plan. All that can be done is to try to balance each variable properly and design a custom-made plan for each sales force.

Different methods of compensating salespeople are the salary plan, the commission plan, and the combination plan. Exhibit 17-3 shows the relative advantages and disadvantages of each plan.

The greatest virtue of the straight-salary method is the guaranteed income and security that it provides. However, it fails to provide any incentive for the ambitious salesperson and therefore may adversely affect productivity. Most companies work on a combination plan, which means that salespeople receive a percentage of sales as a commission for exceeding periodic quotas. Conceptually, the first step in designing a compensation plan is to define the objective. Objectives may focus on rewarding extraordinary performance, providing security, and so on. Every company probably prefers to grant some security to its people and, at the same time, distinguish top employees through incentive schemes. In designing such a plan, the company may first determine the going salary rate for the type of sales staff it is interested in hiring. The company should match the market rate to retain people of caliber. The total wage should be fixed somewhere near the market rate after making adjustments for the company's overall wage policy, environment, and fringe benefits. A study of the spending habits of those in the salary range of salespeople should be made. Based on this study, the percentage of nondiscretionary spending may be linked to an incentive income scheme whereby extra income could be paid as a commission on sales, as a bonus, or both. Care must be taken in constructing a compensation plan. In addition to being equitable, the plan should be simple enough to be comprehensible to the salespeople.

Once compensation has been established for an individual, it is difficult to reduce it. It is desirable, therefore, for management to consider all the pros and cons of fixed compensation for a salesperson before finalizing a salary agreement.

Evaluation. Evaluation is the measurement of a salesperson's contribution to corporate goals. For any evaluation, one needs standards. Establishment of standards, however, is a difficult task, particularly when salespeople are asked to perform different types of jobs. In pure selling jobs, quotas can be set for minimal

EXHIBIT 17-3

Advantages and Disadvantages of Various Sales Compensation Alternatives

Salary Plan

Advantages

1. Assures a regular income.
2. Develops a high degree of loyalty.
3. Makes it simple to switch territories or quotas or to reassign salespeople.
4. Ensures that nonselling activities will be performed.
5. Facilitates administration.
6. Provides relatively fixed sales costs.

Disadvantages

1. Fails to give balanced sales mix because salespeople would concentrate on products with greatest customer appeal.
2. Provides little, if any, financial incentive for the salesperson.
3. Offers few reasons for putting forth extra effort.
4. Favors salespeople who are the least productive.
5. Tends to increase direct selling costs over other types of plans.
6. Creates the possibility of salary compression where new trainees may earn almost as much as experienced salespeople.

Commission Plan

Advantages

1. Pay relates directly to performance and results achieved.
2. System is easy to understand and compute.
3. Salespeople have the greatest possible incentive.
4. Unit sales costs are proportional to net sales.
5. Company's selling investment is reduced.

Disadvantages

1. Emphasis is more likely to be on volume than on profits.
2. Little or no loyalty to the company is generated.
3. Wide variances in income between salespeople may occur.
4. Salespeople are encouraged to neglect nonselling duties.
5. Some salespeople may be tempted to "skim" their territories.
6. Service aspect of selling may be slighted.
7. Problems arise in cutting territories or shifting people or accounts.
8. Pay is often excessive in boom times and very low in recession periods.
9. Salespeople may sell themselves rather than the company and stress short-term rather than long-term relationships.
10. Highly paid salespeople may be reluctant to move into supervisory or managerial positions.
11. Excessive turnover of sales personnel occurs when business turns bad.

EXHIBIT 17-3 (continued)
Advantages and Disadvantages of Various Sales Compensation Alternatives

Combination Plan

Advantages

1. Offers participants the advantage of both salary and commission.
2. Provides greater range of earnings possibilities.
3. Gives salespeople greater security because of steady base income.
4. Makes possible a favorable ratio of selling expense to sales.
5. Compensates salespeople for all activities.
6. Allows a greater latitude of motivation possibilities so that goals and objectives can be achieved on schedule

Disadvantages

1. Is often complex and difficult to understand.
2. Can, where low salary and high bonus or commission exist, develop a bonus that is too high a percentage of earnings; when sales fall, salary is too low to retain salespeople.
3. Is sometimes costly to administer.
4. Unless a decreasing commission rate for increasing sales volume exists, can result in a "windfall" of new accounts and a runaway of earnings.
5. Has a tendency to offer too many objectives at one time so that really important ones can be neglected, forgotten, or overlooked.

performance, and salespeople achieving these quotas can be considered as doing satisfactory work. Achievement of quotas can be classified as follows: salespeople exceeding quotas between 1 to 15 percent may be designated as average; those between 16 and 30 percent as well-performing; finally, those over 30 percent can be considered extraordinary salespeople. Sales contests and awards, both financial and nonfinancial, may be instituted to give recognition to salespeople in various categories.

Supervision. Despite the best efforts in selecting, training, and compensating salespeople, they may not perform as expected. Supervision is important to ensure that salespeople provide the services expected of them. Supervision of salespeople is defined in a broader sense to include the assignment of a territory to a salesperson, control over his or her activities, and communication with the salesperson in the field.

Salespeople are assigned to different geographic territories. An assignment requires solving two problems: (a) forming territories so that they are as much alike as possible in business potential and (b) assigning territories so that each salesperson is able to realize his or her full potential. Territories may be formed by analyzing customers' locations and the potential business they represent. Customers can be categorized as having high, average, or low potential. Further, probabilities in terms of sales can be assigned to indicate how much potential is realizable. Thus, a territory with a large number of high-potential customers with a high probability of buying may be smaller in size (geographically) than a territory with a large number of low-potential customers with a low probability of buying.

Matching salespeople to territories should not be difficult once the territories have been laid out. Regional preferences and the individual affiliations of salespeople require that employees be placed where they will be happiest. It may be difficult to attract salespeople to some territories, whereas other places may be in great demand. Living in big metropolitan areas is expensive and not always comfortable. Similarly, people may avoid places with poor weather. It may become necessary to provide extra compensation to salespeople assigned to unpopular places.

Although salespeople are their own bosses in the field, the manager must keep informed of their activities. To achieve an adequate level of control, a system must be created for maintaining communication with employees in the field, for guiding their work, and for employing remedial methods if performance slackens. Firms use different types of control devices. Some companies require salespeople to fill in a call form that gives all particulars about each visit to each customer. Some require salespeople to submit weekly reports on work performed during the previous week. Salespeople may be asked to complete several forms about sales generated, special problems they face, market information collected, and so on. Using a good reporting system to control the sales force should have a positive influence on performance. In recent years, more and more companies have begun to use computer-assisted techniques to maintain control of the activities of their sales forces.

Management communicates with salespeople through periodic mailings, regional and national conferences, and telephone calls. Two areas of communication in which management needs to be extra careful to maintain the morale of good salespeople are (a) in representing the problems of the field force to people at headquarters and (b) in giving patient consideration to the salesperson's complaints. A sales manager serves as the link between the people in the field and the company and must try to bring their problems and difficulties to the attention of top management. Top management, not being fully aware of operations in the field, may fail to appreciate problems. It is, therefore, the duty of the sales manager to keep top management fully posted about field activities and to secure for salespeople its favor. For example, a salesperson in a mountainous area may not be able to maintain his or her work tempo during the winter because of weather conditions. Management must consider this factor in reviewing the salesperson's work. It is the manager's duty to stand by and help with occupational or personal problems bothering salespeople.

Close rapport with salespeople and patient listening can be very helpful in recognizing and solving sales force problems. More often than not, a salesperson's problem is something that the company can take care of with a little effort and expenditure if it is only willing to accept such responsibility. The primary thing, however, is to know the salesperson's mind. This is where the role of the supervisor comes in. It is said that the sales manager should be as much a therapist in solving the problems of his or her salespeople as the latter should be in handling customers' problems.

SUMMARY

Promotion strategies are directed toward establishing communication with customers. Three types of promotion strategies may be distinguished. Advertising strategies are concerned with communication transmitted through the mass media. Personal selling strategies refer to face-to-face interactions with the customer. All other forms of communication, such as sampling, demonstration, cents off, contests, etc., are known as sales promotion strategies. Two main promotion strategies were examined in this chapter: promotion-expenditure strategy, which deals with the question of how much may be spent on overall promotion, and promotion mix strategy, which specifies the roles that the three ingredients of promotion (i.e., advertising, personal selling, and sales promotion) play in promoting a product.

Discussed also were two advertising strategies. The first, media-selection strategy, focuses on the choice of different media to launch an ad campaign. The second, advertising-copy strategy, deals with the development of appropriate ad copy to convey intended messages. Two personal selling strategies were examined: selling strategy and sales motivation and supervision strategy. Selling strategy emphasizes the approach that is adopted to interact with the customer (i.e., who may call on the customer, whom to call on in the customer organization, when, and how frequently). Sales motivation and supervision strategy is concerned with the management of the sales force and refers to such issues as sales compensation, nonfinancial incentives, territory formation, territory assignments, control, and communication.

DISCUSSION QUESTIONS

1. Outline promotion objectives for a packaged food product in an assumed market segment.
2. Develop a promotion-expenditure strategy for a household computer to be marketed through a large retail chain.
3. Will promotion-expenditure strategy for a product in the growth stage of the product life cycle be different from that for a product in the maturity stage? Discuss.
4. How may a promotion budget be allocated among advertising, personal selling, and sales promotion? Can a simulation model be developed to figure out an optimum promotion mix?
5. Is comparison advertising socially desirable? Comment.
6. Should the media decision be made before or after the copy is first developed?
7. Which is more effective, an emotional appeal or a rational appeal? Are emotional appeals relevant for all consumer products?

NOTES

[1] John Koten, "Creativity, Not Budget Size, Is Vital to TV-Ad Popularity," *Wall Street Journal* (1 March 1984): 25.

[2] Michael Waldholz, "Marketing Is the Key to Success of Prescription Drugs," *Wall Street Journal* (24 January 1982): 1.

[3] Richard Gibson, "Marketers' Mantra: Reap More with Less," *Wall Street Journal* (22 March 1991): B1.

[4] "USIC Chem. Ads Start to Support Effort to Double Sales in 5 Years," *Industrial Marketing* (June 1986): 1–4.

[5] Michael E. Porter, "Interbrand Choice: Media Mix and Market Performance," *American Economic Review* (6 May 1976): 190–203.

[6] Trish Hall, "In Soft-Drink Wars, Brand Loyalty Can Last as Long as a Few Minutes," *Wall Street Journal* (13 May 1985): 25.

[7] "Puritan Fashions: Trying to Protect a Bonanza Built on Designer Jeans," *Business Week* (13 August 1979): 56.

[8] See *Workbook for Estimating Your Advertising Budget* (Boston: Cahners Publishing Co., 1984).

[9] Naras V. Eechambadi, "Does Advertising Work?" *The McKinsey Quarterly* 3 (1994): 117–129.

[10] E. S. Browning, "Perrier's Vincent Plans Wave of Change as a Fresh Regime Displaces the Old?" *Wall Street Journal* (14 February 1991): B1.

[11] "The Generation Gap in Point Form: Some Recent Reflections on the Vital Signs and Values of the Youth Market," *Marketing* (U.K.) (14 February 1994): 21. Also see Jeanne Whalen, "Market Trends: Retailers Aim Straight at Teens," *Advertising Age* (5 September 1994): 1.

[12] See Stratford P. Sherman, "When You Wish upon a Star," *Fortune* (19 August 1985): 66.

[13] See Carl I. Hoveland, Irving L. Janis, and Harold H. Kelley, *Communication and Persuasion* (New Haven: Yale University Press, 1953), 225.

[14] Thomas R. King, "Credibility Gap: More Consumers Find Celebrity Ads Unpersuasive," *Wall Street Journal* (5 July 1985): B5.

[15] Carl I. Hoveland, Arthur A. Lumsdaine, and Fred D. Sheffield, "The Effect of Presenting 'One Side' versus 'Both Sides' in Changing Opinions on a Controversial Subject," in *The Process and Effect of Mass Communication*, ed. Wilbur Schramm (Urbana: University of Illinois Press, 1960), 274.

[16] Based on information supplied by the Coca-Cola Company.

[17] Hoveland, Janis, and Kelley, *Communication and Persuasion*, 57.

[18] Joanne Lipman, "Amex Card Takes on Visa Over Olympics," *Wall Street Journal* (3 February 1992): B1.

[19] "A Comeback May Be Ahead For Brand X," *Business Week* (4 December 1989): 35.

[20] "Average Cost Shatters $200 Mark for Industrial Sales Calls, but Moderation Seen in 1984 Hikes," *Marketing News* (17 August 1987): 16. The study also showed that the larger the sales force, the lower the cost. For instance, companies with fewer than 10 salespeople spent more than $290.70 per call; companies with more than 100 spent $147.10. This underscores the significance of the experience effect (see Chapter 12).

[21] Jaclyn Fireman, "The Death and Rebirth of the Salesman," *Fortune* (25 July 1994): 80.

[22] "Rebirth of a Salesman: Willy Loman Goes Electronic," *Business Week* (27 February 1984): 103.

[23] Alan Farnham, "Mary Kay's Lessons in Leadership," *Fortune* (20 September 1993): 68.

APPENDIX | *Perspectives on Promotion Strategies*

I.
Promotion-
Expenditure Strategy

Definition: Determination of the amount that a company may spend on its total promotional effort, which includes advertising, personal selling, and sales promotion.

Objective: To allocate enough funds to each promotional task so that each is utilized to its fullest potential.

Requirements: (a) Adequate resources to finance the promotion expenditure. (b) Understanding of the products/services sales response. (c) Estimate of the duration of the advertising effect. (d) Understanding of each product/market situation relative to different forms of promotion. (e) Understanding of competitive response to promotion.

Expected Results: Allocation of sufficient funds to the promotional tasks to accomplish overall marketing objectives.

II.
Promotion Mix Strategy

Definition: Determination of a judicious mix of different types of promotion.

Objective: To adequately blend the three types of promotion to complement each other for a balanced promotional perspective.

Requirements: (a) Product factors: (i) nature of product, (ii) perceived risk, (iii) durable versus nondurable, and (iv) typical purchase amount. (b) Market factors: (i) position in the life cycle, (ii) market share, (iii) industry concentration, (iv) intensity of competition, and (v) demand perspectives. (c) Customers factors: (i) household versus business customers, (ii) number of customers, and (iii) concentration of customers. (d) Budget factors: (i) financial resources of the organization and (ii) traditional promotional perspectives. (e) Marketing mix factors: (i) relative price/relative quality, (ii) distribution strategy, (iii) brand life cycle, and (iv) geographic scope of the market. (f) Environmental factors.

Expected Results: The three types of promotion are assigned roles in a way that provides the best communication.

III.
Media-Selection Strategy

Definition: Choosing the channels (newspapers, magazines, television, radio, outdoor advertising, transit advertising, and direct mail) through which messages concerning a product/service are transmitted to the targets.

Objective: To move customers from unawareness of a product/service, to awareness, to comprehension, to conviction, to the buying action.

Requirements: (a) Relate media-selection objectives to product/market objectives. (b) Media chosen should have a unique way of promoting the business. (c) Media should be measure-minded not only in frequency, in timing, and in reaching the target audience but also in evaluating the quality of the audience. (d) Base media selection on factual not connotational grounds. (e) Media plan should be optimistic in that it takes advantage of the lessons learned from experience. (f) Seek information on customer profiles and audience characteristics.

Expected Results: Customers are moved along the desired path of the purchase process.

IV. *Advertising-Copy* *Strategy*	*Definition:* Designing the content of an advertisement. *Objective:* To transmit a particular product/service message to a particular target. *Requirements:* (a) Eliminate "noise" for a clear transmission of message. (b) Consider importance of (i) source credibility, (ii) balance of argument, (iii) message repetition, (iv) rational versus emotional appeals, (v) humor appeals, (vi) presentation of model's eyes in pictorial ads, and (vii) comparison advertising. *Expected Results:* The intended message is adequately transmitted to the target audience.
V. *Selling Strategy*	*Definition:* Moving customers to the purchase phase of the decision-making process through the use of face-to-face contact. *Objective:* Achievement of stated sales volume and gross margin targets and the fulfillment of specific activities. *Requirements:* (a) The selling strategy should be derived from overall marketing objectives and properly linked with promotional objectives. (b) Decision on maintenance of existing accounts versus lining up new customers. (c) Decision on who should be contacted in customer's organization. (d) Determine optimal size of sales force. *Expected Results:* (a) Sales and profit targets are met at minimum expense. (b) Overall marketing goals are achieved.
VI. *Sales Motivation* *and Supervision* *Strategy*	*Definition:* Achieving superior sales force performance. *Objective:* To ensure optimal performance of the sales force. *Requirements:* (a) Motivation financial and nonfinancial. (b) Adequate compensation package. (c) Evaluation standards. (d) Appropriate territory assignment, activity control, and communication. *Expected Results:* Business objectives are met adequately at minimum expense.

Global Market
Strategies

One of the most significant developments in recent years has been the emergence of global markets. Today's market provides not only a multiplicity of goods but goods from many places. It would not be surprising to discover that your shirt comes from Taiwan, your jeans from Mexico, and your shoes from Italy. You may drive a Japanese car equipped with tires manufactured in France, with nuts and bolts produced in India, and with paint from a U.S. company. Gucci bags, Sony Walkmans, and McDonald's golden arches are seen on the streets of Tokyo, London, Paris, and New York. Thai goods wind up on U.S. grocery shelves as Dole canned pineapple and on French farms as livestock feed. Millions of consumers worldwide want all the things that they have heard about, seen, or experienced via new communication technologies. Firms today are enmeshed in world competition to serve these consumers, no matter where they live.

A number of broad forces have led to growing globalization of markets.[1] These include

1. **Growing similarity of countries**—Because of growing commonality of infrastructure, distribution channels, and marketing approaches, more and more products and brands are available everywhere. Similar buyer needs thus manifest themselves in different countries. Large retail chains, television advertising, and credit cards are just a few examples of once-isolated phenomena that are rapidly becoming universal.
2. **Falling tariff barriers**—Successive rounds of bilateral and multilateral agreements have lowered tariffs markedly since World War II. At the same time, regional economic agreements, such as the European Union (EU), have facilitated trade relations.
3. **Strategic role of technology**—Technology is not only reshaping industries but contributing toward market homogenization. For example, electronic innovations have permitted the development of more compact, lighter products that are less costly to ship. Transportation costs themselves have fallen with the use of containerization and larger-capacity ships. Increasing ease of communication and data transfer make it feasible to link operations in different countries. At the same time, technology leads to an easy flow of information among buyers, making them aware of new and quality products and thus creating demand for them.

The impact of these forces on the globalization of markets may be illustrated with reference to a few examples. Kids everywhere are playing Nintendo and bounding along the streets to the sound of Sony Walkmans. The videocassette recorder market took off simultaneously in Japan, Europe, and the United States, but the most extensive use of videocassette recorders today is probably in places like Riyadh and Caracas. Shopping centers from Dusseldorf to Rio sell Gucci shoes, Yves St. Laurent suits, and Gloria Vanderbilt jeans. Siemens and ITT telephones can be found almost everywhere in the world. The Mercedes-Benz 190E and the Toyota Corolla are as much objects of passion in Manila as in California.

Just about every gas turbine sold in the world has some GE technology or component in it, and what country doesn't need gas turbines? How many airlines around the world could survive without Boeing or Airbus? Third World markets for high-voltage transmission equipment and diesel-electric locomotives are bigger than those in developed countries. And today's new industries— robotics, videodisks, fiber optics, satellite networks, high-technology plastics, artificial diamonds—seem global from birth.

Briefly, these forces have homogenized worldwide markets, triggering opportunities for firms to seek business across national borders. For U.S. corporations, the real impetus to overseas expansion occurred after World War II. Attempting to reconstruct war-torn economies, the U.S. government, through the Marshall Plan, provided financial assistance to European countries. As the postwar American economy emerged as the strongest in the world, its economic assistance programs, in the absence of competition, stimulated extensive corporate development of international strategies. Since then, many new players, not only from Europe but from Southeast Asia as well, have entered the arena to serve global markets. Asian competitors have been particularly quick to exploit new international competitive conditions as well as cross-cutting technologies to leapfrog well-established rivals.

Global markets offer unlimited opportunities. But competition in these markets is intense. To be globally successful, companies must learn to operate and compete as if the world were one large market, ignoring superficial regional and national differences. Corporations geared to this new reality can benefit from enormous economies of scale in production, distribution, marketing, and management. By translating these benefits into reduced world prices, they can dislodge competitors who still operate under the perspectives of the 1970s and 1980s. Companies willing to change their perspectives and become global can attain sustainable competitive advantage.

IDENTIFYING TARGET MARKETS

The World Bank lists 132 countries. Different countries represent varying market potential due to economic, cultural, and political contrasts. These contrasts mean that a global marketer cannot select target customers randomly but must employ workable criteria to choose countries where the company's product/service has the best opportunity for success.

Major Markets   The most basic information needed to identify markets concerns population because people, of course, constitute a market. The population of the world reached an estimated 5.4 billion in 1993. According to the latest estimates from the United Nations, this total is expected to increase to 6.2 billion by the year 2000 and to almost 8.5 billion by 2025. Current world population is growing at about 1.7 percent per year. This is a slight decline from the peak rate of 1.9 percent, but the absolute number of people being added to the world's population each year is still increasing. This figure is expected to peak at the turn of the century at about 90 million additional people per year.

Population growth rates vary significantly by region. Europe has the lowest rate of population growth at only about 0.3 percent per year. Several European countries, including Austria, Denmark, West Germany, Luxembourg and Sweden, are experiencing declining populations. Growth rates are also below 1 percent per year in North America.

The regions with the highest population growth rates are Africa (3 percent per year), Latin America (2 percent per year) and South Asia (1.9 percent per year). China, the world's most populous country, is growing at only about 1.2 percent per year. Even so, it means that China's population increases by over 12 million people each year. The world's second most populous country, India, is growing at over 1.7 percent per year. India's population is expected to grow from 900 million today to 1 billion by about 2003.

One striking aspect of population growth in developing countries is the rapid rate of urbanization. The urban population is growing at less than 1 percent in Europe and in North America, but it is growing at almost 3.5 percent in the developing world. Today 15 of the 20 largest urban agglomerations are in the developing world. By the year 2000, 17 of the 20 will be in the developing world. The only cities in the top 20 located in developed countries will be Tokyo, New York, and Los Angeles. The world's largest cities will be Mexico City (27 million) and Sao Paulo (25 million).

The above information shows that the total market in Europe and North America will not be increasing; the population of these two continents will not add much to total market size. Of course, these populations are growing older, so certain segments will increase in number. For example, the total population of Europe will increase only 2.8 percent from 1990 to 2000, but the over-65 population in Europe will increase by 14 percent during the same period.

In the developing world, the increase in numbers does not necessarily mean increased markets for U.S. business. The fastest-growing region in the world, Africa, is also experiencing low or negative rates of economic growth per capita. Many Latin American countries, Mexico in particular, are hampered by huge external debts that force them to try to limit imports while using their resources to generate foreign exchange for debt service. In most of these cases, the problem of foreign debt will need to be solved before the growing populations in the developing world will translate into large markets for U.S. business.

Obviously, population figures alone provide little information about market potential because people must have the means in terms of income to become viable customers. In Exhibit 18-1, population combined with per capita GNP provides an estimate of consuming capacity. An index of consuming capacity depicts absolute, or aggregate, consumption, both in the entire world and in individual economies. Consumption rates can be satisfied either domestically or through imports.

The information in Exhibit 18-1 should be interpreted cautiously because it makes no allowances for difference in the purchasing power among different countries. Two conclusions are obvious, however: (a) aggregate consuming

EXHIBIT 18-1
Consuming Capacities of Selected Countries

Country	Population *	Per Capita GNP †	Index of Consuming Capacity ‡
United States	255.4	23,240	5,935.5
Japan	124.5	28,190	3,509.7
Germany	80.6	23,030	1,856.2
France	57.4	22,260	1,277.7
Italy	57.8	20,460	1,182.6
United Kingdom	57.8	17,790	1,028.3
Canada	27.4	20,710	567.5
Brazil	153.9	2,770	426.3
Netherlands	15.2	20,480	311.3
Australia	17.5	17,260	302.1
Mexico	85.0	3,470	295.0
India	883.6	310	273.9
Switzerland	6.9	36,080	249.0
Belgium	10.0	20,880	208.8
Argentina	33.1	6,050	200.3
Denmark	5.2	26,000	135.2
Turkey	58.5	1,980	115.8
South Africa	39.8	2,670	106.3
Thailand	55.8	1,260	70.3
Israel	5.1	13,220	67.4
Philippines	64.3	770	49.5
New Zealand	3.4	12,300	41.8
Peru	22.4	950	21.3
Ecuador	11.0	1,070	11.8
Paraguay	4.5	1,380	6.2
Honduras	5.4	580	3.1
Uganda	17.5	170	3.0

* *World Bank Report*, 1994. Figures in millions.

† *Statistical Abstract of the United States: 1994* (Washington, D.C.: U.S. Department of Commerce). Figures in U.S. dollars.

‡ Per capita GNP (gross national product) multiplied by total population in billions.

capacity depends upon total population as well as per capital income and (b) advanced countries dominate as potential customers.

Although population and income variables provide a snapshot of the market opportunity in a given country, a variety of other factors must be considered to identify viable markets. These factors are urbanization, consumption patterns, infrastructure, and overall industrialization. Taking these factors into account, *Business International* has identified twelve countries as major global markets (see Exhibit 18-2).[2] Interestingly, three of these twelve countries—China, Brazil, and India—are developing countries.

Although these twelve countries have been identified as the principal global markets by *Business International*, they may not all be viable markets from the viewpoint of U.S. firms. A variety of environmental factors (political, legal, cultural) affect market opportunity in a nation. For example, Brazil is burdened with

EXHIBIT 18-2
Size, Growth, and Intensity of World's 12 Largest Markets

	Market Size (% of World Market)			Market Intensity (World = 1.00)			Five Year Market Growth (%)
	1982	1987	1992	1982	1987	1992	1992
Major Markets							
United States	21.39	19.41	20.27	4.56	4.21	5.41	5.47
Japan	9.42	8.07	10.04	3.56	3.17	5.30	21.02
China	4.70	12.24	9.98	0.19	0.48	0.26	22.73
Russia	13.62	12.86	5.71	2.11	1.99	1.72	− 9.29
India	1.49	2.31	4.91	0.09	0.13	0.13	29.83
Germany	4.79	4.21	4.86	3.81	3.56	5.04	9.43
Italy	4.04	3.58	3.69	3.36	3.22	4.46	9.05
France	3.81	3.34	3.62	3.44	3.15	4.30	15.16
United Kingdom	3.23	2.81	3.15	2.78	2.67	3.75	2.47
Brazil	2.46	3.00	2.56	0.88	1.01	0.85	− 4.65
Mexico	1.28[1]	1.49	2.47	0.85[1]	0.80	1.44	94.71
Canada	2.07	1.99	1.96	3.98	3.89	4.66	1.66

Source: Crossborder Monitor, August 31, 1994, p. 4.
Notes: **Market Size** shows the relative dimension of each national or regional market as a percentage of the total world market. The percentages for each market are derived by averaging the corresponding data on total population (double-weighted), urban population, private consumption expenditure, steel consumption, electricity production, and ownership of telephones, passenger automobiles, and televisions.

Market Intensity measures the richness of the market, or the degree of concentrated purchasing power it represents. Taking the world's market intensity as 1, the EIU has calculated the intensity of each country or region as it relates to this base. The intensity figure is derived from an average of per-capita ownership, production, and consumption indicators. Specifically, it is calculated by averaging per-capita figures for automobiles in use (double-weighted), telephones in use, televisions in use, steel consumption, electricity production, private consumption expenditure (double-weighted), and the percentage of population that is urban (double-weighted).

Market Growth is an average of cumulative growth in several key economic market indicators: population, steel consumption, electricity production, and ownership of passenger automobiles, trucks, buses, and televisions.

debt, which limits the amount of export potential in that country; China's political control limits freedom of choice; India's regulations make it difficult for foreign corporations to conduct business there. Thus, many countries may not have large market potential, yet they may constitute important markets for U.S. business.

Exhibit 18-3 lists the top 25 U.S. export markets. Also shown is the dollar amount of exports to each country in 1993. It should be noted that, globally speaking, although Canada ranks as the 12th largest market in the world (see Exhibit 18-2), it represents the single largest market for the United States, accounting for over one-fifth of its trade.

Emerging Markets   Traditionally, a major proportion of international business activities of U.S. corporations has been limited to developed countries. For example, at the end of 1992, total U.S. direct investment was estimated to be $776 billion, of which almost 75 percent was in developed countries. Slowly, however, new markets are unfolding. Consider the newly industrializing countries. During the decade of the

EXHIBIT 18-3
Top 25 U.S. Markets: U.S. Domestic and Foreign Goods Exports, 1993 (f.a.s. Value)

	$ billions
1. Canada	100.2
2. Japan	48.0
3. Mexico	41.6
4. United Kingdom	26.4
5. Germany	19.0
6. Taiwan	16.3
7. South Korea	14.8
8. France	13.3
9. Netherlands	12.8
10. Singapore	11.7
11. Hong Kong	9.9
12. Belgium-Luxembourg	9.4
13. China	8.8
14. Australia	8.3
15. Switzerland	6.8
16. Saudi Arabia	6.7
17. Italy	6.5
18. Malaysia	6.1
19. Brazil	6.0
20. Venezuela	4.6
21. Israel	4.4
22. Spain	4.2
23. Argentina	3.8
24. Thailand	3.8
25. Philippines	3.5

Source: Business America, April 19, 1994, p. 10.

1980s, South Korea, Singapore, Taiwan, and Hong Kong were the world's fastest-growing economies and consequently offered new opportunities for U.S. firms.

In recent years, even developing countries, at least the more politically stable ones, have begun to show viable market potential. A number of developing countries are achieving higher and higher growth rates every year.[3] Although an individual country may not provide adequate potential for U.S. corporations, developing countries as a group constitute a major market. In 1993, over one-fourth of U.S. trade was with developing countries. In future years, the flow of U.S. trade with developing countries should increase. An Organization of Economic Cooperation and Development (OECD) study showed that, in 1970, OECD countries, with just 20 percent of the world's people, had 83 percent of the world's trade in manufactures; whereas developing countries, with 70 percent of the world's people, captured just 11 percent of the trade. In the year 2000, however, it is estimated that OECD countries, with 15 percent of the population, will have 63 percent of the world's trade in manufactures; developing countries, with 78 percent of the population, will account for 28 percent of world trade.[4] Interestingly, although for cultural, political, and economic reasons, Western Europe, Canada, and to a lesser extent Japan have always been predominantly important for business, many developing countries provide a better return on U.S. investment.

The relevance of emerging markets for the United States can be illustrated with reference to Pacific basin countries. Over the last quarter century, streams of food, fuels, textiles, cameras, cars, and videocassette recorders flowing from countries all across Asia exerted heavy pressure on Western economies. Since 1962, this outpouring of exports has increased the Asian/Pacific share of world trade from less than 10 percent in the 1970s to over 25 percent in the 1990s and has pushed one Asian economy after another out of the Dark Ages and into the global marketplace.

For U.S. marketers, rising Pacific power holds both a threat and a promise. The threat is dramatically increased competition for sales and market share, both at home and abroad. In 1993 alone, Asian/Pacific countries supplied 40 percent of all U.S. merchandise imports and contributed some $68 billion to the U.S. trade deficit, 70 percent of the total. As for the promise, there is the emergence of a market of more than two billion potential consumers. In the last 25 years, as the Pacific region began its time-bending leap into the twentieth century, millions of Asians began an equally rapid transition from rural to urban, from agrarian to industrial, and from feudal to contemporary society. With more of the Pacific region's rural population traveling to cities to shop every day, the demand for goods and services—from the most basic household commodities to sophisticated technical devices—is soaring. In coming years, as rising incomes continue to bolster the spending power of Asia's new consumer population, the opportunities for shrewd marketers will be unparalleled.

Barriers to conducting business in the region are beginning to fall, too. Increasingly, throughout the region English is the language of commerce, and an allegiance to free market economics is widespread. And, as companies such as

McDonald's, General Foods, Unilever, and Coca-Cola have already discovered, from Penang to Taipei, this is a region where well-made and well-marketed products and services are witnessing increasing acceptance.

As modern influences exert greater pressure on traditional Asian cultures, two trends with important implications for marketers are starting to take shape:

- Although each Asian nation is culturally distinct, consumers throughout the Pacific region are gradually sharing more of the same wants and needs. As Asian homogenization progresses, sophisticated strategies and considerable economies of scale in regional and global marketing and advertising will become increasingly relevant.[5]
- Many Western marketers misinterpret the nature of current changes in the Pacific region. Despite the Big Macs, the Levi's, the Nikes, and all the other familiar trappings, Asia is not Westernizing—it's modernizing. Asian consumers are buying Western goods and services, not Western values and cultures.

Elsewhere in the East, India and China are two large markets that should provide unprecedented opportunities for U.S. corporations in the remainder of the 1990s and beyond as their economies become fully market oriented. A growing number of U.S. consumer-goods companies have begun to make inroads in China. In November 1987, Kentucky Fried Chicken Corp. opened the first Western fast-food restaurant in China. Coca-Cola and PepsiCo are aggressively expanding distribution. Kodak and other foreign film suppliers have attained a 70 percent share of the color film market. Nescafé and Maxwell House are waging coffee combat in a land of tea.[6]

A number of U.S. companies—Pepsi, Timex, General Foods, Kellogg—have entered India to serve its emerging middle class.[7] Thus, the developing countries provide new opportunities for U.S. corporations to expand business overseas: as their wealth grows, U.S. marketing possibilities expand.

It has been observed that early in the next century Latin American countries, too, will emerge as modern, Northern-styled marketplaces with improved transportation systems, subsidized credit to native businesses, and marketing education programs. All of these changes should result in more efficient channels of distribution, more local marketing support services, and fewer bottlenecks that hamper exchanges. All of these indications point toward a variety of emerging opportunities for U.S. corporations in Latin America.

For example, a few years ago, the Gillette Co., discovered that only 8 percent of Mexican men who shave used shaving cream. Sensing an opportunity, Gillette in 1975 introduced plastic tubes of shaving cream in Guadalajara, Mexico, that sold for half the price of its aerosol. In a year's time, 13 percent of Guadalajaran men began to use shaving cream. Gillette has been selling its new product, Prestobarba (Spanish for "quick shave"), in the rest of Mexico, in Colombia, and in Brazil.[8]

These emerging markets in less-developed countries can help many U.S. corporations to counter the results of demographic changes in Western nations examined above.[9] As mentioned above, in most advanced nations of the world, birthrates are declining while population in the developing countries is growing. This increasing population holds the future growth potential for U.S. business.

With the fall of the Berlin Wall and the lifting of the Iron Curtain, new opportunities await Western managers in Eastern Europe, previously a forbidden region. In many ways, the opening of Eastern Europe could prove even more important than the drive for a single market in Western Europe. Take, for example, Poland, Hungary, and Czechoslovakia. Their combined GNP is larger than that of China. These three countries also have relatively well-trained and reliable workers who work for less than a quarter of what Western Europeans are paid.[10] Giving them access to their developed neighbors' markets and hefty injections of Western capital, they could become the tigers of Europe. As their economies grow, they should develop into viable markets for a variety of goods and services.

Developments in Eastern Europe will benefit American companies in two ways. First, as Eastern Europe's backward economies finally integrate into the global economy and take off, new market opportunities should emerge. Second, sales to Western Europe by U.S. firms, made even more dynamic by its expanding Eastern frontier, will increase. Just as markets in the 1980s were developed by Reaganomics and Thatcherism, markets in the 1990s and beyond will be developed by the shifting of the ideological plates that have separated the world's geopolitical land masses. Companies that aim for global market and remain competitive will be the winners.

The Triad Market

From a global perspective, the United States, Canada, Japan, and Western Europe, often referred to as *triad countries*, constitute the major market. Although elsewhere opportunities are emerging, in the foreseeable future these countries continue to be the leading markets. They account for approximately 14 percent of the world's population, but they represent over 70 percent of world gross product. As such, these countries absorb a major proportion of capital and consumer products and, thus, are the most advanced consuming societies in the world. Not only do most product innovations take place in these countries, but they also serve as the opinion leaders and mold the purchasing and consumption behavior of the remaining 86 percent of the world's population.

For example, over 90 percent of the world's computers are used by triad countries. In the case of numerically controlled machine tools, almost 100 percent are distributed in the triad market. The same pattern follows in consumer products. The triad accounts for 92 percent of the demand for electronic consumer goods. What these statistics point to is that a company that ignores the market potential of the triad does so at its own peril.[11]

An interesting characteristic of the triad market is the universalization of needs. For example, not too long ago manufacturers of capital equipment produced machinery that reflected strong cultural distinctions. West German machines reflected that nation's penchant for craftsmanship; American equipment was often extravagant in its use of raw materials. But these distinctions have disappeared. The best-selling factory machines have lost the "art" element that once distinguished them and have become both in appearance and in the level of skill that they require much more similar. The current revolution in production engineering has brought about ever-increasing global standards of performance. In an era when productivity improvements can quickly determine life or death on a global scale, companies cannot afford to indulge in a metallic piece of art that will last 30 years.

At the same time, consumer markets have become fairly homogeneous. Ohmae notes that

> Triad consumption patterns, which is both a cause and an effect of cultural patterns, has its roots to a large extent in the educational system. As educational systems enable more people to use technology, they tend to become more similar to each other. It follows, therefore, that education leading to higher levels of technological achievement also tends to eradicate differences in lifestyles. Penetration of television, which enables everyone possessing a television set to share sophisticated behavioral information instantaneously throughout the world, has also accelerated this trend. There are, for example, 750 million consumers in all three parts of the Triad (Japan, the United States and Canada, the nations of Western Europe) with strikingly similar needs and preferences. . . . A new generation worships the universal "now" gods— ABBA, Levi's and Arpege. . . . Youngsters in Denmark, West Germany, Japan, and California are all growing up with ketchup, jeans, and guitars. Their lifestyles, aspirations, and desires are so similar that you might call them "OECDites" or Triadians, rather than by names denoting their national identity.[12]

There are many reasons for the similarities and commonalities in the triad's consumer demand and lifestyle patterns. First, the purchasing power of triad residents, as expressed in discretionary income per individual, is more than 10 times greater than that of residents of developing countries. For example, television penetration in triad countries is greater than 94 percent, whereas in newly industrialized countries it is 25 percent; for the developing countries, it is less than 10 percent. Second, their technological infrastructure is more advanced. For example, over 70 percent of triadian households have a telephone. This makes it feasible to use such products as facsimile, teletext, and digital data transmission/ processing equipment. Third, the educational level is much higher in triad nations than in other parts of the world. Fourth, the number of physicians per 10,000 in triad countries, which creates demand for pharmaceuticals and medical electronics, exceeds 30. Fifth, better infrastructure in the triad leads to opportunities not feasible in less-developed markets. For example, paved roads have made rapid penetration of radial tires and sports cars possible.

ENTRY STRATEGIES

Four different modes of business offer a company entry into foreign markets: (a) exporting, (b) contractual agreement, (c) joint venture, and (d) manufacturing.

Exporting | A company may minimize the risk of dealing internationally by exporting domestically manufactured products either by minimal response to inquiries or by systematic development of demand in foreign markets. Exporting requires minimal capital and is easy to initiate. Exporting is also a good way to gain international experience. A major part of overseas involvement among large U.S. firms is through export trade.

Contractual Agreements

There are several types of contractual agreements:

- **Patent licensing agreements**—These agreements are based on either a fixed-fee or a royalty basis and include managerial training.
- **Turnkey operations**—These operations are based on a fixed-fee or cost-plus arrangement and include plant construction, personnel training, and initial production runs.
- **Coproduction agreements**—These agreements are most common in socialist countries, where plants are built and then paid for with part of the output.
- **Management contracts**—Currently widely used in the Middle East, these contracts require that a multinational corporation provide key personnel to operate a foreign enterprise for a fee until local people acquire the ability to manage the business independently. For example, Whittaker Corp. of Los Angeles operates government-owned hospitals in several cities in Saudi Arabia.
- **Licensing**—Licensing works as a viable alternative in some contractual agreement situations where risk of expropriation and resistance to foreign investments create uncertainty. *Licensing* encompasses a variety of contractual agreements whereby a multinational marketer makes available intangible assets—such as patents, trade secrets, know-how, trademarks, and company name—to foreign companies in return for royalties or other forms of payment. Transfer of these assets usually is accompanied by technical services to ensure proper use. Licensing, however, has some advantages and disadvantages as summarized below.[13]

Advantages of Licensing

1. Licensing requires little capital and serves as a quick and easy entry to foreign markets.
2. In some countries, licensing is the only way to tap the market.
3. Licensing provides life extension for products in the maturity stage of their life cycles.
4. Licensing is a good alternative to foreign production and marketing in an environment where there is worldwide inflation, shortages of skilled labor, increasing domestic and foreign governmental regulation and restriction, and tough international competition.
5. Licensing royalties are guaranteed and periodic, whereas shared income from investment fluctuates and is risky.
6. Domestically based firms can benefit from product development abroad without incurring research expense through technical feedback arrangements.
7. When exports no longer are profitable because of intense competition, licensing provides an alternative.
8. Licensing can overcome high transportation costs, which make some exports noncompetitive in target markets.
9. Licensing is also immune to expropriation.
10. In some countries, manufacturers of military equipment or any product deemed critical to the national interest (including communications equipment) may be compelled to enter licensing agreements.

Disadvantages of Licensing

1. To attract licensees, a firm must possess distinctive technology, a trademark, and a company or brand name that is attractive to potential foreign users.

2. The licensor has no control over production and marketing by the licensee.
3. Licensing royalties are negligible compared with equity investment potential. Royalty rates seldom exceed 5 percent of gross sales because of government restrictions in the host country.
4. The licensee may lose interest in renewing the contract unless the licensor holds interest through innovation and new technology.
5. There is a danger of creating competition in third, or even home, markets if the licensee violates territorial agreements. Going to court in these situations is expensive and time-consuming, and no international adjudicatory body exists.

Joint Ventures

Joint venture represents a higher-risk alternative than exporting or contractual agreements because it requires various levels of direct investment. A joint venture between a U.S. firm and a native operation abroad involves sharing risks to accomplish mutual enterprise. Once a firm moves beyond the exporting stage, joint ventures, incidentally, are the next most common form of entry. One example of a joint venture is General Motors Corporation's partnership with Egypt's state-owned Nasar Car Company, a joint venture for the assembly of trucks and diesel engines. Another example of a joint venture is between Matsushita of Japan and IBM, a joint venture established to manufacture small computers. Joint ventures normally are designed to take advantage of the strong functions of the partners and to supplement their weak functions, be they management, research, or marketing.

Joint ventures provide a mutually beneficial arrangement for domestic and foreign businesses to join forces. For both parties, the venture is a means to share capital and risk and make use of each other's technical strength. Japanese companies, for example, prefer entering into joint ventures with U.S. firms because such arrangements help ensure against possible American trade barriers. American firms, on the other hand, like the opportunity to enter a previously forbidden market, to utilize established channels, to link American product innovation with low-cost Japanese manufacturing technology, and to curb a potentially tough competitor.

As a case in point, General Foods Corporation tried for more than a decade to succeed in Japan on its own but watched the market share of its instant coffee (Maxwell House) drop from 20 to 14 percent. Then, in 1975, the firm established a joint venture with Ajinomoto, a food manufacturer, to use the full power of Ajinomoto's product distribution system and personnel and managerial capabilities. Within two years, Maxwell House's share of the Japanese instant coffee market recovered.[14]

Joint ventures, however, are not an unmixed blessing. The major problem in managing joint ventures stems from one cause: there is more than one partner and one of the partners must play a key dominant role to steer the business to success.

Joint ventures should be designed to supplement each partner's shortcomings, not to exploit each other's strengths and weaknesses. It takes as much effort to make a joint venture a success as to start a grass roots operation and eventually bring it up to a successful level. In both cases, each partner must be fully prepared to expend the effort necessary to understand customers, competitors, and itself. A joint venture is a means of resource appropriation and of easing a foreign business's entry into a new terrain. It should not be viewed as a handy vehicle to reap money without effort, interest, and/or additional resources.

Joint ventures are a wave of the future. There is hardly a Fortune 500 company active overseas that does not have at least one joint venture. Widespread interest in joint ventures is related to the following:

1. **Seeing market opportunities**—Companies in mature industries in the United States find joint venture a desirable entry mode to enter attractive new markets overseas.
2. **Dealing with rising economic nationalism**—Host governments are often more receptive to or require joint ventures.
3. **Preempting raw materials**—Countries with raw materials, such as petroleum or extractable material, usually do not allow foreign firms to be active there other than through joint venture.
4. **Sharing risk**—Rather than taking the entire risk, a joint venture allows the risk to be shared with a partner, which can be especially important in politically sensitive areas.
5. **Developing an export base**—In areas where economic blocs play a significant role, joint venture with a local firm smooths the entry into the entire region, such as entry into the European Union through a joint venture with an English company.
6. **Selling technology**—Selling technology to developing countries becomes easier through a joint venture.

Even a joint venture with a well-qualified majority foreign partner may provide significant advantages:

1. **Participation in income and growth**—The minority partner shares in the earnings and growth of the venture even if its own technology becomes obsolete.
2. **Low cash requirements**—Know-how and patents or both can be considered as partial capital contribution.
3. **Preferred treatment**—Because it is locally controlled, the venture is treated with preference by government.
4. **Easier access to a market and to market information**—A locally controlled firm can seek market access and information much more easily than can a firm controlled by foreigners.
5. **Less drain on managerial resources**—The local partner takes care of most managerial responsibilities.
6. **U.S. income tax deferral**—Income to the U.S. minority partner is not subject to U.S. taxation until distribution.[15]

Manufacturing

A multinational corporation may also establish itself in an overseas market by direct investment in a manufacturing and/or assembly subsidiary. Because of the volatility of worldwide economic, social, and political conditions, this form of involvement is most risky. An example of a direct investment situation is Chesebrough-Pond's operation of overseas manufacturing plants in Japan, England, and Monte Carlo.

Manufacturing around the world is riskier, as illustrated by Union Carbide's disaster in Bhopal, India: in the worst industrial accident that has ever occurred, a poisonous gas leak killed over 2,000 people and permanently disabled thousands. It is suggested that multinational corporations should not manufacture overseas where the risk of a mishap may jeopardize the survival of the whole company. As a matter of fact, in the wake of the Bhopal accident, many host countries tightened safety and environmental regulations. For example, Brazil, the world's fourth-largest user of agricultural chemicals, restricted the use of the deadly methyl isocyanate.[16]

Conclusion | A firm interested in entering the international market must evaluate the risk and commitment involved with each entry and choose the entry mode that best fits the company's objectives and resources.[17] Entry risk and commitment can be examined by considering five factors:

1. Characteristics of the product.
2. The market's external macroenvironment, particularly economic and political factors, and the demand and buying patterns of potential customers.
3. The firm's competitive position, especially the product's life-cycle stage, as well as various corporate strengths and weaknesses.
4. Dynamic capital budgeting considerations, including resource costs and availabilities.
5. Internal corporate perceptions that affect corporate selection of information and the psychic distance between a firm's decision makers and its target customers as well as control and risk-taking preferences.

These five factors combined indicate that risk should be reviewed vis-à-vis a company's resources before determining a mode of entry.

Computerized simulation models can be employed to determine the desired entry route by simultaneously evaluating such factors as environmental opportunity, risk index, competitive risk index, corporate strength index, product channel direction index, comparative cost index, and corporate policy and perception index.[18]

GLOBAL MARKET ENVIRONMENT

Not only are the risk factors underlying the mode of entry largely contingent on the nature of the foreign environment, but these environmental forces also influence the development of marketing strategies. Decision making for expansion into global markets is strategically similar to the decision-making process guiding domestic marketing endeavors. More specifically, four marketing strategy variables—product, price, distribution, and promotion—need to be as systematically addressed in the context of international marketing as they are in formulating domestic marketing strategies. What is different about international marketing, however, is the environment in which marketing decisions must be made and the influence that environment has in shaping marketing strategies. The principal components of the international marketing environment include cultural, political, legal, commercial, and economic forces. Each of these forces represents informational inputs that must enter into the strategy formulation process.

⟲✓Culture | **Culture** refers to learned behavior over time, passed on from generation to generation. This behavior manifests itself in the form of social structure, habits, faith, customs, rituals, and religion, each of which tends to affect individual lifestyles, which in turn shape consumption patterns in the marketplace. Thus, what people of a particular country buy, why they buy, when they buy, where they buy, and how they buy are largely culturally determined. There are five elements of culture: material culture, social institutions, man and universe, aesthetics, and language. Each of these elements varies from country to country. The importance to marketers of understanding these often subtle variations has been illustrated by Dichter:

> In puritanical cultures it is customary to think of cleanliness as being next to godliness. The body and its functions are covered up as much as possible.
>
> But in Catholic and Latin countries, to fool too much with one's body, to overindulge in bathing or toiletries, has opposite meaning. Accordingly, an advertising approach based on puritanical principles, threatening Frenchmen that if they didn't brush their teeth regularly, they would develop cavities or would not find a lover, failed to impress. To fit the accepted concept of morality, the French advertising agency changed this approach to a permissive one.[19]

Similarly, language differences from one country to another could lead to problems because literal translations of words often connote different meanings. Two classic examples of marketing blunders include "Body by Fisher," which when literally translated into Flemish meant "Corpse by Fisher," and "Let Hertz Put You in the Driver's Seat," which when literally translated into Spanish meant "Let Hertz Make You a Chauffeur."[20] Even the choice of color for packaging and advertising may influence marketing decisions. For example, in the United States, white is equated with purity. In most Asian countries, however, white is associated with death in the same way that black is a symbol of mourning in American culture. In short, culture could have and has had far-reaching effects on the success of overseas marketing strategies.

Politics | The laissez-faire era when governments had little if anything to do with the conduct of business is past history. Today, even in democratic societies, governments exercise a pervasive influence on business decisions. In fact, it is not uncommon to find that the governments of many overseas countries actually own and operate certain businesses. One example of a government-owned and -operated business is Air France, the French airline company.

Although the degree of intervention varies across countries, developments in developing countries perhaps represent situations where government policies are most extreme. Therefore, to be successful overseas, a global marketer should determine the most favorable political climates and exploit those opportunities first. Robinson suggests that the degree of political vulnerability in a given overseas market can be ascertained by researching certain key issues. Positive answers to the following questions signal political troubles for a foreign marketer:

1. Is the supply of the product ever subject to important political debates? (sugar, salt, gasoline, public utilities, medicines, foodstuffs)

2. Do other industries depend upon the production of the product? (cement, power, machine tools, construction machinery, steel)
3. Is the product considered socially or economically essential? (key drugs, laboratory equipment, medicines)
4. Is the product essential to agricultural industries? (farm tools and machinery, crops, fertilizers, seed)
5. Does the product affect national defense capabilities? (transportation industry, communications)
6. Does the product require important components that would be available from local sources and that otherwise would not be used as effectively? (labor, skill, materials)
7. Is there competition or is it likely from local manufacturers in the near future? (small, low-investment manufacturing)
8. Does the product relate to channels of mass communication media? (newsprint, radio equipment)
9. Is the product primarily a service?
10. Does the use of the product, or its design, rest upon some legal requirements?
11. Is the product potentially dangerous to the user? (explosives, drugs)
12. Does the product induce a net drain on scarce foreign exchange?[21]

Legal Aspects

Despite the best intentions, differences may reasonably arise between parties doing business. What recourse exists for the resolution of differences and whose laws will apply are of vital concern to global marketers. Although there is no simple solution to such a complex problem, it is important that marketers anticipate areas where disputes are likely to arise and establish beforehand agreements on the means to use and which country will have jurisdiction in the resolution of differences. Legal difficulties in marketing are most prevalent regarding the following issues:

1. Rules of competition about
   a. collusion
   b. discrimination against certain buyers
   c. promotional methods
   d. variable pricing
   e. exclusive territory agreement.
2. Retail price maintenance laws.
3. Cancellation of distributor or wholesaler agreements.
4. Product quality laws and controls.
5. Packaging laws.
6. Warranty and after-sales exposure.
7. Price controls and limitations on markups or markdowns.
8. Patents, trademarks, and copyright laws and practices.

Needless to say, the marketer in conjunction with legal counsel should probe these areas and establish with the buyer various contingencies prior to the making of commitments.

Commercial Practices

An international marketer must be thoroughly familiar with the business customs and practices in effect in overseas markets. Although some evidence suggests that business traditions in a country may undergo a change as a result of dealing with foreign corporations, such transformations are long-term processes. Thus, local customs and practices must be researched and adhered to in order to gain the confidence and support of local buyers, channel intermediaries, and other business operatives. The specific customs and practices of a country may be studied with reference to the following factors:

Business Structure

Size
Ownership
Various business publics
Sources and level of authority
    Top management decision making
    Decentralized decision making
    Committee decision making

Management Attitudes and Behavior

Personal background
Business status
Objectives and aspirations
    Security and mobility
    Personal life
    Social acceptance
    Advancement
    Power

Patterns of Competition

Mode of Doing Business

Level of contact
Communications emphasis
Formality and tempo
Business ethics
Negotiation emphasis

Economic Climate

Only a small percentage of people in the world approach the standard of living experienced in the United States and in other advanced industrialized countries. The level of economic development in various countries can be explained and described through a number of measures. One common measure used to rank nations economically is per capita GNP.

According to Rostow, the countries of the world can be grouped into the following stages of economic development: (a) the traditional, (b) the precondition for take-off, (c) the take-off, (d) the drive to maturity, and (e) mass consumption.[22] Most African, Asian, and Latin American countries would be categorized as underdeveloped, having lower living standards and limited discretionary income. The amount of work required to earn enough to purchase a product varies greatly among different countries. For example, to buy one kilogram of sugar, a person in the United States needs to work a little over five minutes; in

Greece it takes 53 minutes of labor to earn an equivalent amount. In many African and Asian countries, the effort needed to buy a kilogram of sugar and, for that matter, other similar products is even higher.

STRATEGY FOR GLOBAL MARKETING PROGRAMS

Two opposite viewpoints for developing global marketing strategy are commonly expounded. According to one school of thought, marketing is an inherently local problem. Due to cultural and other differences among countries, marketing programs should be tailor-made for each country. The opposing view treats marketing as know-how that can be transferred from country to country. It has been argued that the worldwide marketplace has become so homogenized that multinational corporations can market standardized products and services all over the world with identical strategies, thus lowering their costs and earning higher margins.

Localized Strategy

The proponents of localized marketing strategies support their viewpoint based on four differences across countries:[23] (a) buyer behavior characteristics, (b) socioeconomic condition, (c) marketing infrastructure, and (d) competitive environment. A review of the marketing literature shows how companies often experience difficulties in foreign markets because they did not fully understand differences in buyer behavior. For example, Campbell's canned soups—mostly vegetable and beef combinations packed in extra-large cans—did not catch on in soup-loving Brazil. A postmortem study showed that most Brazilian housewives felt they were not fulfilling their roles if they served soup that they could not call their own. Brazilian housewives had no problems using dehydrated competitive products, such as Knorr and Maggi, which they could use as soup starters and still add their own ingredients and flair.[24] Also, Johnson & Johnson's baby powder did not sell well in Japan until its original package was changed to a flat box with a powder puff. Japanese mothers feared that powder would fly around their small homes and enter their spotlessly clean kitchens when sprinkled from a plastic bottle. Powder puffs allowed them to apply powder sparingly.[25] Similarly, advertisers have encountered difficulty when using colors in certain foreign countries. For example, purple is a death color in Brazil, white is for funerals in Hong Kong, and yellow signifies jealousy in Thailand. In Egypt the use of green, which is the national color, is frowned upon for packaging.[26]

Socioeconomic differences (i.e., per capita income, level of education, level of unemployment) among countries also call for a localized approach toward international marketing. For example, limited economic means may prevent masses in developing countries from buying the variety of products that U.S. consumers consider essential. To bring such products as automobiles and appliances within the reach of the middle class in developing countries, for example, the products must be appropriately modified to cut costs without reducing functional quality.

Differences in the character of local marketing infrastructure across countries may suggest pursuing country-specific marketing strategies. The marketing infrastructure consists of the institutions and functions necessary to create, develop, and service demand, including retailers, wholesalers, sales agents, warehousing, transportation, credit, media, and more. Consider the case of media. Commercial television is not available in many countries. Sweden, for example, lacks this element of the marketing infrastructure. In many countries, for example, Switzerland, commercials on television are allowed on a limited scale. Suntory (a Japanese liquor company) considers the ban on advertising liquor on U.S. television as a main deterrent for not entering the U.S. market in a big way.[27] Similarly, the physical conditions of a country (i.e., climate, topography, and resources) may require localized strategies. In hot climates, as in the Middle East, such products as cars and air conditioners must have additional features. Differences in telephone systems, road networks, postal practices, and the like may require modifications in marketing practices. For example, mail-order retailing is popular in the United States but is virtually nonexistent in Italy because of differences in its mail system.[28]

Finally, differences in the competitive environment among countries may require following localized marketing strategies. Nestlé, for example, achieved more than a 60 percent market share in the instant coffee market in Japan but less than 30 percent in the United States. Nestlé had to contend with two strong domestic competitors in the United States, namely General Foods, which markets the Maxwell House, Yuban, and Brim brands, and more recently Procter & Gamble, which markets Folgers and High Point. Nestlé faced relatively weak domestic competitors in Japan. IBM, which is the leading computer company in the world, slipped to third place in the Japanese market in 1984 behind Fujitsu Ltd. and NEC Corporation in terms of total revenue. Nestlé and IBM must reflect differences in their competitive environments in such marketing choices as pricing, sales force behavior, and advertising.[29]

Standardized Strategy

In contrast to the view that marketing strategies must be localized, many scholars and practitioners argue that significant benefits can be achieved through standardization of marketing strategies on a global basis. As a matter of fact, some people recommend an extreme strategy: offering identical products at identical prices through identical distribution channels and supporting these identical products by identical sales and promotional programs throughout the world. Levitt asserts that "commercially, nothing confirms this as much as the success of McDonald's from the Champs Elysees to the Ginza, of Coca-Cola in Bahrain and Pepsi-Cola in Moscow, and of rock music, Greek salad, Hollywood movies, Revlon cosmetics, Sony televisions, and Levi's jeans everywhere."[30] Although across-the-board standardization, as proposed by Levitt, may be difficult, it is commonly accepted that the marketplace is becoming increasingly global, and indeed standardized strategies have been successfully pursued in many cases.[31] Among consumer durable goods, Mercedes-Benz sells its cars by following a universal marketing program. Among nondurable goods, Coca-Cola is ubiquitous. Among industrial goods, Boeing jets are sold worldwide based on common marketing perspectives.

Past research shows that, other things being equal, companies usually opt for standardization. A recent study on the subject lends support to the high propensity to standardize all or parts of marketing strategy in foreign markets. For example, an extremely high degree of standardization appears to exist in brand names, physical characteristics of products, and packaging.[32] More than half of the products that multinational corporations sell in less-developed countries originate in the parent companies' home markets. Of the 2,200 products sold by the 61 subsidiaries in the sample, 1,200 had originated in the United States or the United Kingdom.[33]

The arguments in favor of standardization are realization of cost savings, development of worldwide products, and achievement of better marketing performance. Standardization of products across national borders eliminates duplication of such costs as research and development, product design, and packaging. Further, standardization permits realization of economies of scale. Also, standardization makes it feasible to achieve consistency in dealing with customers and in product design. Consistency in product style—features, design, brand name, packaging—should establish a common image of the product worldwide and help increase overall sales. For example, a person accustomed to a particular brand is likely to buy the same brand overseas if it is available. The global exposure that brands receive these days as a result of extensive world travel and mass media requires the consistency that is feasible through standardization. Finally, standardization may be urged on the grounds that a product that has proved to be successful in one country should do equally well in other countries that present more or less similar markets and similar competitive conditions.[34]

Conclusion

Although standardization offers benefits, too much attachment to standardization can be counterproductive. Marketing environments vary from country to country, and thus a standard product originally conceived and developed in the United States may not really match the conditions in each and every market. In other words, standardization can lead to substantial opportunity loss.

Pond's cold cream, Coca-Cola, and Colgate toothpaste have been cited as evidence that a universal product and marketing strategy for consumer goods can win worldwide success. However, the applicability of a universal approach for consumer goods appears to be limited to products that have certain characteristics, among them universal brand name recognition (generally earned by huge financial outlays), minimal product knowledge requirements for consumer use, and product advertisements that demand low information content. Clearly, Coca-Cola, Colgate toothpaste, McDonald's, Levi's jeans, and Pond's cold cream display these traits. Thus, whereas a universal strategy can be effective for some consumer products, it is clearly an exception rather than the general rule. Those who argue that consumer products no longer require market tailoring due to the globalization of markets brought about by today's advanced technology are not always correct.

A multinational corporation that intends to launch a new product into a foreign market should consider the nature of its products, its organizational capabilities, and the level of adaptation required to accommodate cultural differences between the home and the host country. A multinational corporation should also analyze such factors as market structures, competitors' strategic orientations, and host government demands.

The international marketplace is far more competitive today than in the 1980s and most likely will remain so in the rest of 1990s and beyond. Thus, to enhance competitive advantage some sort of adaptation might provide a better match between a product and local marketing conditions. Ohmae's charges against American companies for not adapting their products to Japanese needs are revealing:

> Yet, American merchandisers push such products as oversize cars with left-wheel drive, devices measuring in inches, appliances not adapted to lower voltage and frequencies, office equipment without kanji capabilities and clothes not cut to smaller dimensions. Most Japanese like sweet oranges and sour cherries, not visa versa. That is because they compare imported oranges with domestic mikans (very sweet tangerines) and cherries with plums (somewhat tangy and sour).[35]

There are several patterns and various degrees of differentiation that firms can adopt to do business on an international scale. The most common of these are obligatory and discretionary product adaptation. An **obligatory**, or **minimal**, **product adaptation** implies that a manufacturer is forced to introduce minor changes or modifications in product design for either of two reasons. First, adaptation is mandatory in order to seek entry into particular foreign markets. Second, adaptation is imposed on a firm by external environmental factors, including the special needs of a foreign market. In brief, obligatory adaptation is related to safety regulations, trademark registration, quality standards, and media standards. An obligatory adaptation requires mostly physical changes in a product. **Discretionary**, or **voluntary**, **product adaptation** reflects a sort of self-imposed discipline and a deliberate move on the part of an exporter to build stable foreign markets through a better alignment of product with market needs and/or cultural preferences.

Swiss-based pharmaceutical maker Ciba-Geigy's efforts in adapting its products to local conditions are noteworthy. Basic to the company's adaptation program are quality circles. These circles include local executives with line responsibilities for packaging, labeling, advertising, and manufacturing. They are responsible for determining (a) if Ciba-Geigy's products are appropriate for the cultures in which they are sold and meet users' needs, (b) if products are promoted in such a way that they can be used correctly for purposes intended, and (c) if, when used properly, products present no unresponsible hazards to human health and safety.[36]

MARKETING IN GLOBAL BUSINESS STRATEGY

International marketing strategy is significant in formulating global business strategy in three different ways.[37] First, what should be the global *configuration* of marketing activities? That is, where should such activities as new product development advertising, sales promotion, channel selection, marketing research, etc., be performed? Second, how should global marketing activities performed in different countries be *coordinated*? Third, how should marketing activities be *linked* with other activities of the firm? Each of these aspects is examined below.

Configuration of Marketing Activities

Marketing activities, unlike those in other functional areas of a business, must be dispersed in each host country to make an adequate response to local environments. Although this configuration is valuable in being customer oriented, not all marketing activities need to be performed on a dispersed basis. In many cases, competitive advantage is gained in the form of lower cost or enhanced differentiation if selected activities are performed centrally as a result of technological changes, buyer shifts, and evolution of marketing media. These activities comprise production of promotional materials, sales force, service support organization, training, and advertising.

The centralized production of advertisements, sales promotion materials, and user manuals can lead to a variety of benefits. Economies of scale can be reaped in both development and production. For example, experienced art directors and producers can be hired to create better ads at a greater speed or lower cost. The use of centralized printing permits the latest technology to be adopted. On the other hand, excessive transportation costs and cultural differences among nations may make the production of some materials (e.g., user manuals) impractical.

Sales force, at least for some businesses, can be centralized in one location. Alternatively, highly skilled sales specialists can be stationed at the headquarters or in a regional office to provide sales support in different countries. Centralization of the sales force is most effective when the complexity of the selling task is very high, and the products being sold are high-ticket items purchased infrequently.

Like sales force, high-skilled service specialists can be located at world or regional headquarters. They can visit different subsidiaries to provide nonroutine service. Along the same lines, service facilities (service center, repair shop) can be regionalized at a few locations, especially for complex jobs. Such centralization should permit the use of state-of-the-art facilities and qualified service people, resulting in better service at lower cost.

Training of marketing personnel can be effectively centralized and lead to economies of scale in production and delivery of training programs, faster accumulated learning (brought by people with varied experiences assembled in one place), and increased uniformity around the world in implementing marketing programs. Training centralization, however, must be weighed against travel time and cost.

Although cultural differences between nations require advertising to be tailored to each country, in many ways global advertising is gaining acceptance. First, a company may select one ad agency to handle its global campaign, economizing in campaign development, seeking better coordination between the parent and subsidiaries, and facilitating a consistent advertising approach worldwide. For example, British Airways uses one agency, Saatchi and Saatchi, worldwide. Second, many companies advertise in the global media, for example, in *The Economist*, in certain trade magazines, or at international sports events seen by viewers around the world, such as at U.S. Open tennis matches. Finally, many media (e.g., airport billboards, airline and hotel magazines) have a decidedly international reach. For these reasons, centralization of advertising makes sense. Yet government rules and regulations relative to advertising, distinct national habits, language differences, and lack of media outlets may require dispersion of advertising to different countries.

International Marketing Coordination

International marketing activities dispersed in different countries should be properly coordinated to gain competitive advantage. Such coordination can be achieved in the following ways:

1. **Performing marketing activities using similar methods across countries**—This form of coordination implies standardizing activities across nations. Some strategies, including brand name, product positioning, service standards, warranties, and advertising theme, are easier to coordinate than are other marketing strategies. On the other hand, distribution, personal selling, sales training, pricing, and media selection are difficult to coordinate across nations.
2. **Transferring marketing know-how and skills from country to country**—For example, a market entry strategy successfully tried in one country can be transferred and applied in another country. Likewise, customer and market information can be transferred for use by other subsidiaries. Such information may relate to shifts in buyer purchasing patterns, recent trends in technology, lifestyle changes, successful new product or feature introductions, new promotion ideas, and early market signals by competitors.
3. **Sequencing of marketing programs across countries**—For example, new products or new marketing practices may be introduced in various countries in a planned sequence. In this way, programs developed by one subsidiary can be shared by others to their mutual advantage and, thus, should result in substantial cost savings. To reap the benefits of sequencing, a company must create organizational mechanisms to manage the product line from a worldwide perspective and to overcome manager resistance to change in all participating countries.
4. **Integrating the efforts of various marketing groups in different countries**—Perhaps the most common form of such integration is managing relationships with important multinational customers, often called *international account management*. International account management systems are commonly used in service firms. For example, Citibank handles some accounts on a worldwide basis. It has account officers responsible for coordinating services to its large corporate customers anywhere in the world.

Competitive advantage can result from international account management systems in a variety of ways. They can lead to economies in the utilization of the sales force if duplication of selling effort is avoided. They can allow a company to differentiate itself from its competitors by offering a single contact for international buyers. They can also leverage the skills of top salespersons by giving them more influence over the entire relationship with major customers. Some of the potential impediments to using international account management include increased travel time, language barriers, and cultural differences in how business is conducted. Dealing with a major customer through a single coordinator may also heighten the customer's awareness of its bargaining power.

Integration of effort across countries can lead to competitive advantage in other areas as well; for example, after-sale service. Some international companies have come to realize that the availability of after-sale service is often as important as the product itself, especially when a multinational customer has operations in remote areas of the world or when the customer moves from country to country.

Marketing's Linkage to Nonmarketing Activities

A global view of international marketing permits linking marketing functions to upstream and support activities of the firm, which can lead to advantage in various ways. For example, marketing can unlock economies of scale and learning in production and/or research and development by (a) supporting the development of universal products by providing the information necessary to develop a physical product design that can be sold worldwide; (b) creating demand for more universal products even if historical demand has been for more varied products in different countries; (c) identifying and penetrating segments in many countries to allow the sale of universal products; and (d) providing services and/or local accessories that effectively tailor the standard physical product.

DEVELOPING GLOBAL MARKET STRATEGY: AN EXAMPLE

Decisions related to foreign market entry, expansion, and conversion as well as to phasing out of foreign markets call for systematic effort. Illustrated here is one method of developing a global market strategy. The method consists of three phases:

1. Appropriate national markets are selected by quickly screening the full range of options without regard to any preconceived notions.
2. Specific strategic approaches are devised for each country or group of countries based on the company's specific product technologies.
3. Marketing plans for each country or group of countries are developed, reviewed, revised, and incorporated into the overall corporate concept without regard to conventional wisdom or stereotypes.

Phase 1: Selecting National Markets

There are over 132 countries in the world; of these, the majority may appear to present entry opportunities. Many countries go out of their way to attract foreign investment by offering lures ranging from tax exemptions to low-paid, amply skilled labor. These inducements, valid as they may be in individual cases, have repeatedly led to hasty foreign market entry.

A good basis for selecting national markets is arrived at through a comparative analysis of different countries, with long-term economic environment having the greatest weight. First, certain countries, because of their political situations (e.g., Libya under Qaddafi), should be considered unsuitable for market entry. It might help to consult a political index that rates different countries for business attractiveness. The final choice should be based on the company's own assessment and risk preference. Further, markets that are either too small in terms of population and per capita income or that are economically too weak should be eliminated. For example, a number of countries with populations of less than

20 million and with annual per capita incomes below $2,000 are of little interest to many companies because of limited demand potential.

The markets surviving this screening should then be assessed for strategic attractiveness. A battery of criteria should be developed to fit the specific requirements of the corporation. Basically, the criteria should focus on the following five factors (industry/product characteristics may require slight modification):

1. Future demand and economic potential.
2. Distribution of purchasing power by population groups or market segments.
3. Country-specific technical product standards.
4. Spillover from the national market (e.g., the Andes Pact provides for low-duty exports from Colombia to Peru).
5. Access to vital resources (qualified labor force, raw materials sources, suppliers).

There is no reason to expand the list because additional criteria are rarely significant enough to result in useful new insights. Rather, management should concentrate on developing truly meaningful and practical parameters for each of the five criteria listed above so that the selection process does not become unnecessarily costly and the results are fully relevant to the company concerned. For example, a German flooring manufacturer, selling principally to the building industry, selected the following yardsticks:

1. **Economic potential**—New housing needs and GNP growth.
2. **Wealth**—Per capita income, per capita market size for institutional building or private dwellings (the higher the per captia income, market volume, and share of institutional buildings, the more attractive the market).
3. **Technical product standards**—Price level of similar products, for example, price per square meter for floor coverings (the higher the price level, the more attractive the market tends to be for a technically advanced producer).
4. **Spillover**—Area in which the same building standards (especially fire safety standards) apply (e.g., the U.S. National Electrical Manufacturers' Association standards are widely applicable in Latin America; British standards apply in most Commonwealth countries).
5. **Resource availability**—Annual production volume of PVC (an important raw material for the company).

Through these criteria, the analysis of economic potential was based on two factors: housing needs and economic base (see Exhibit 18-4). In specifying these criteria, the company deliberately confined itself to measures that (a) could readily be developed from existing sources of macroeconomic data, (b) would show trends as well as current positions, and (c) matched the company's particular characteristics as closely as possible.

Since German producers of floor covering employ a highly sophisticated technology, it would have been senseless to give a high ranking to a country with only rudimentary production technology in this particular facet. Companies in other industries, of course, would consider other factors—auto registrations per 1,000 population, percentage of households with telephones, density of household appliance installations, and the like.

EXHIBIT 18-4

Assessing Country Economic Potential: The Case of a Building Industry Flooring Supplier

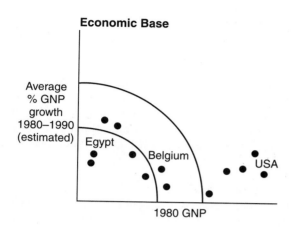

Economic Base

Average % GNP growth 1980–1990 (estimated)

Egypt

Belgium

USA

1980 GNP

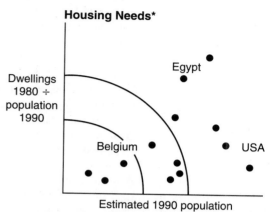

Housing Needs*

Dwellings 1980 ÷ population 1990

Egypt

Belgium

USA

Estimated 1990 population

* Assumes 1990 target = 2.5 persons per dwelling (catch-up and new demand).

Economic Base

		Weak	Medium	Strong
Housing Needs	High	Egypt Pakistan	Korea Nigeria	USA Japan
	Medium	Yugoslavia	United Kingdom	Germany France
	Low	Denmark	Belgium	Sweden

Examples: Sweden—needs only in replacement sector; Pakistan—economically too weak to meet needs.

The resulting values are rated for each criterion on a scale of one to five so that, by weighting the criteria on a percentage basis, each country can be assigned an index number indicating its overall attractiveness. In this particular case, the result was that, out of the 49 countries surviving the initial screening, 16 were ultimately judged attractive enough on the basis of market potential, per capita market size, level of technical sophistication, prevailing regulations, and resource availability to warrant serious attention.

Interestingly, the traditionally German-favored markets of Austria and Belgium emerged with low rankings from this strategically based assessment because the level of potential demand was judged to be insufficient. Some new markets, Egypt and Pakistan, for example, were also downgraded because of inadequate economic base. Likewise, even such high-potential markets as Italy and Indonesia were eliminated for objective reasons (in the latter case, the low technical standard of most products).

Phase 2: Determining Marketing Strategy

After a short list of attractive foreign markets has been compiled, the next step is to group these countries according to their respective stages of economic development. Here the criterion of classification is not per capita income but the degree of market penetration by the generic product in question. For example, the floor covering manufacturer grouped countries into three categories—developing, takeoff, and mature—as defined by these factors (see Exhibit 18-5):

1. **Accessibility of markets**—Crucial for the choice between export and import production.
2. **Local competitive situation**—Crucial for the choice between independent construction, joint venture, and acquisition.
3. **Customer structure**—Crucial for sales and distribution strategy.
4. **Re-import potential**—Crucial for international product/market strategy.

The established development phases and their defining criteria must be very closely geared to the company situation because it is these factors, not the apparent attractiveness of markets, that will make or break the company's strategic thrust into a given country.

This being the case, for each country or group of countries on the short list, management should formulate a generic marketing strategy with respect to investment, risk, product, and pricing policies; that is, a unified strategic framework applicable to all the countries in each stage of development should be prepared. This step should yield a clear understanding of what the respective stages of economic development of each country entail for the company's marketing strategies (see Exhibit 18-6 on page 520).

Companies are too often inclined to regard "overseas" as a single market or at least to differentiate very little among individual overseas markets. Another common error is the assumption that product or service concepts suited to a highly developed consumer economy work as well in any foreign market. This is rarely true: different markets demand different approaches.

Across-the-board strategic approaches typically result in ill-advised and inappropriate allocation of resources. In less-developed markets that could be

EXHIBIT 18-5
Grouping Countries by Phase of Development

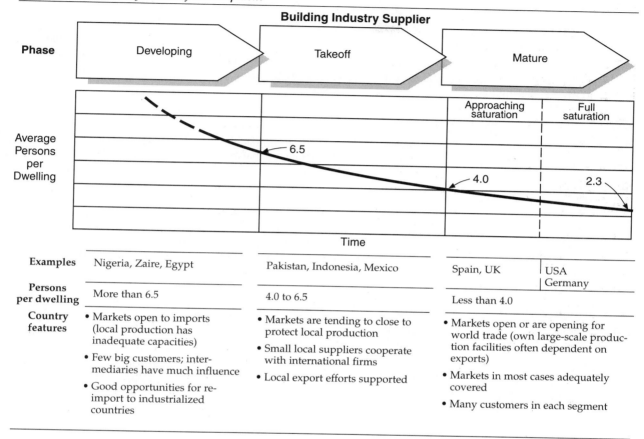

| | Nigeria, Zaire, Egypt | Pakistan, Indonesia, Mexico | Spain, UK | USA Germany |

Examples	Nigeria, Zaire, Egypt	Pakistan, Indonesia, Mexico	Spain, UK	USA
				Germany
Persons per dwelling	More than 6.5	4.0 to 6.5	Less than 4.0	
Country features	• Markets open to imports (local production has inadequate capacities) • Few big customers; intermediaries have much influence • Good opportunities for re-import to industrialized countries	• Markets are tending to close to protect local production • Small local suppliers cooperate with international firms • Local export efforts supported	• Markets open or are opening for world trade (own large-scale production facilities often dependent on exports) • Markets in most cases adequately covered • Many customers in each segment	

perfectly well served by a few distributors, companies have in some cases established production facilities that are doomed to permanent unprofitability. In markets already at the takeoff point, companies have failed to build the necessary local plants and instead have complained about declining exports only to finally abandon the field to competitors. In markets already approaching saturation, companies have often sought to impose domestic technical standards where adequate standards and knowledge already exist or have tried to operate like mini replicas of parent corporations, marketing too many product lines with too few salespeople. Again and again, product line offerings are weighted toward either cheaper- or higher-quality products than the local market will accept. Clearly, the best insurance against such errors is to select strategies appropriate to the country.

Phase 3: Developing Marketing Plans

In developing detailed marketing plans, it is first necessary to determine which product lines fit which local markets as well as the appropriate allocation of

EXHIBIT 18-6
Developing Standard Strategies

Phase	Developing	Takeoff	Mature
Basic Strategy	**Test Market**	**Build Base**	**Expand/Round Off Operations**
	Pursue profitable individual projects and/or export activities	Allocate substantial resources to establish leading position in market	Allocate resources selectively to develop market niches

Elements of Strategy

Investment	Minimize (distribution and services)	Invest to expand capacity (relatively long payback)	Expand selectively in R&D, production, and distribution (relatively short payback)
Risk	Avoid	Accept	Limit
Know-how transfer (R&D)	Document know-how on reference projects	Use local know-how in • Product technology • Production engineering	Transfer know-how in special product lines; acquire local know-how to round off own base
Market share objective	Concentrate on key projects; possibly build position in profitable businesses with local support	Extend base with • New products • New outlets • New applications	Expand/defend
Cost leadership objective	Minimum acceptable (especially reduction of guarantee risks)	Economies of scale; reduction of fixed costs	Rationalize; optimize resources
Product	Standard technology; simple products	Aim for wide range; "innovator" role	Full product line in selected areas; products of high technical quality
Price	Price high	Aim for price leadership (at both ends)	Back stable market price level
Distribution	Use select local distributors (exclusive distribution)	Use a large number of small distributors (intensive distribution)	Use company sales force (selective distribution)
Promotion	Selective advertising • With typical high prestige products • Aiming at decision makers	Active utilization of selective marketing resources	Selected product advertising

resources. A rough analysis of potential international business, global sales, and profit targets based on the estimates worked out in Phase 1 help in assigning product lines. A framework for resource allocation can then be mapped according to rough comparative figures for investment quotas, management needs, and skilled labor requirements. This framework should be supplemented by company-specific examples of standard marketing strategies for each group of countries.

Exhibit 18-7 illustrates the resource allocation process. Different product lines are assigned to different country groups, and for each country category, different strategic approaches—for example, support on large-scale products, establishment of local production facilities, cooperation with local manufacturers—are specified.

EXHIBIT 18-7
A Specimen Framework for Resource Allocation

Phase	Specimen Countries	Resource Allocation by Product Division					
		PVC Floor Coverings	Carpeting	Suspended Ceilings	Wall Paneling	PVC Tubes	Plastic-Coated Roof Insulation
Developing "Test market"	Nigeria	Intensive	No operations	Moderate	No operations	Intensive	Intensive
(Share of total resources: 20%)	Specific plans • Develop own plastics-processing facilities. • Acquire plastics processors.						
Takeoff "Build base"	Indonesia	Moderate	No operations	No operations	No operations	Moderate	Moderate
(Share of total resources: 50%)	Specific plans • Give support in key projects. • Cooperative with state-owned construction organization.						
Mature "Expand/round off operations"	Spain	Moderate	Moderate	Intensive	Intensive	No operations	No operations
(Share of total resources: 30%)	Specific plans • Develop local facilities for tufting and paneling. • Acquire/cooperate with suppliers using unique product and production technology. • Develop own distribution channel. • Extend range to provide complete interior equipment program (system concept).						

No operations.
Moderate.
Intensive.

The level of detail in this resource allocation decision framework depends on a number of factors: company history and philosophy, business policy objectives, scope and variety of product lines, and the number of countries to be served. Working within this decision framework, each product division should analyze its own market in terms of size, growth, and competitive situations; assess its profitability prospects, opportunities, and risks; and identify its own current strategic position on the basis of market share, profit situation, and vulnerability to local risks. Each product division is then in a position to develop country-specific marketing alternatives for servicing each national market. Top management's role throughout is to coordinate marketing strategy development efforts of various divisions and continually to monitor the strategic decision framework.

The three-phase approach illustrated above exhibits a number of advantages:

- It allows management to set up, with a minimum of planning effort, a strategic framework that gives clear priority to market selection decisions, thus making it much easier for divisions to work out effective product line strategies unhampered by the usual chicken-or-egg problem.
- Division managers can foresee at a fairly early stage what reallocations of management, labor, and capital resources are needed and what adjustments may need to be imposed from the top due to inadequate resources.
- The company's future risk profile can be worked out in terms of resource commitment by country group and type of investment.
- The usual plethora of "exceptional" (and mostly opportunistic) product/market situations is sharply reduced. Only the really unique opportunities pass through the filter; exceptions are no longer the rule.
- The dazzling-in-theory but unrealistic-in-practice concept of establishing production bases in low-wage countries, buying from the world's lowest-cost sources, and selling products wherever best prices can be had is replaced by a realistic country-by-country market evaluation.
- Issues of organization, personnel assignment, and integration of overseas operations into corporate planning and control systems reach management's attention only after the fundamental strategic aspects of the company's overseas involvement have been thoroughly prepared.

In brief, the three-phase approach enables management to profitably concentrate resources and attention on a handful of really attractive countries instead of dissipating its efforts in vain attempts to serve the entire world.

SUMMARY | Internationalization of business has become a fact of life. Company after company finds that decisions made elsewhere in the world have a deep impact on its business. Although many firms have long been engaged in foreign business ventures, the real impetus to overseas expansion came after World War II. The globalization of business is accounted by such forces as (a) growing similarity of countries (e.g., commonality of infrastructure and channels of distribution); (b) falling tariff barriers; and (c) technological developments that, for example, permit the development of compact, easy-to-ship products.

Traditionally, major U.S. business activities overseas have been concentrated in developed countries. In recent years, developing countries have provided additional opportunities for U.S. corporations, especially in more politically stable countries. Yet although an individual developing country may not provide adequate potential for U.S. companies, developing countries as a group constitute a major market. The emerging markets in developing countries can help many U.S. corporations counter the results of matured markets in Western nations.

A firm aspiring to enter the international market may choose among various entry modes—exporting, contractual agreement, joint venture, or manufacturing. Each entry mode provides different opportunities and risks. The differentiation of global and domestic marketing largely revolves around the nature of environmental forces impinging on the formulation of strategy. International marketers must be sensitive to the environmental influences operating in overseas markets. The principal components of the international marketing environment include cultural, political, legal, commercial, and economic forces. Each of these forces represents informational inputs that must be factored into the decision-making process.

An important question that global marketers need to answer is whether the same product, price, distribution and promotion approach is adequate in foreign markets. In other words, a decision must be made about which is the more appropriate of two marketing strategies: localization or standardization. On the one hand, environmental differences between nations suggest using localization. On the other hand, there are potential gains to consider in standardizing market strategy. International marketers must examine all criteria in order to decide the extent to which marketing perspectives should vary from country to country.

International marketing plays three important roles in global business strategy. These are *configuration* of marketing activities (i.e., where different marketing activities should be performed), *coordination* (i.e., how international marketing activities dispersed in different countries should be coordinated), and the *linkage* of international marketing with other functions of the business.

The chapter ended with a framework for designing global market strategy. The framework consists of three steps: (a) selecting national markets, (b) determining marketing strategy, and (c) developing marketing plans.

DISCUSSION QUESTIONS

1. What forces are responsible for the globalization of markets? 492
2. How does culture affect international marketing decisions? Explain with examples. 506
3. Given their low per capita income, why should companies be interested in developing countries? 508
4. What are the different modes of entry into the international market? What are the relative advantages and disadvantages of each mode? 501
5. What are the advantages of international marketing strategy standardization?

6. Under what circumstances should marketing be adapted to local conditions?

7. What role does marketing play in global business strategy?

NOTES

[1] George S. Yip, "Global Strategy in a World of Nations?" *Sloan Management Review* (Fall 1991): 29–39. Also see Thomas A. Stewart, "Welcome to the Revolution," *Fortune* (13 December 1993): 66.

[2] *Crossborder Monitor* (31 August 1994): 4.

[3] Tom Martin, "The World Economy in Charts," *Fortune* (25 July 1994): 118.

[4] "Leap Forward or Sink Back," *Development Forum* (March 1982): 3.

[5] See Richard N. Farmer, "Would You Want Your Granddaughter to Marry a Taiwanese Marketing Man?" *Journal of Marketing* (October 1987): 111–16.

[6] "Laying Foundation for the Great Mall of China," *Business Week* (25 January 1988): 68.

[7] Subhash C. Jain, *Market Evolution in Developing Countries: Unfolding of the Indian Market* (Binghamton N.Y.: The Haworth Press, Inc., 1993).

[8] David Wessel, "Gillette Keys Sales to Third World Tastes," *Wall Street Journal* (23 January 1986): 35.

[9] See Anthony J. O'Reilly, "Establishing Successful Joint Ventures in Developing Nations: A CEO's Perspective," *Columbia Journal of World Business* (Spring 1988): 3–9.

[10] Richard I. Kirkland, Jr., "Who Gains from the New Europe," *Fortune* (18 December 1989): 83.

[11] Kenichi Ohmae, *Triad Power* (New York: The Free Press, 1985), Chapter 4.

[12] Ohmae, *Triad Power*, 23.

[13] Allan C. Reddy, "International Licensing May Be Best Bet for Companies Seeking Foreign Markets," *Marketing News* (12 November 1982): 6. Also see Farok J. Contractor, "Technology Licensing Practice in U.S. Companies: Corporate and Public Policy Implications," *Columbia Journal of World Business* (Fall 1983): 80–88

[14] Ohmae, *Triad Power*, 116.

[15] F. Kingston Berlew, "The Joint Venture: A Way into Foreign Markets," *Harvard Business Review* (July–August 1984): 48. Also see Farok Contractor, "A Generalized Theorem of Joint-Venture and Licensing Negotiations," *Journal of International Business Studies* (Summer 1985): 23–49.

[16] "For Multinationals It Will Never Be the Same," *Business Week* (24 December 1984): 57.

[17] See M. Krishna Erramilli and C. P. Rao, "Choice of Foreign Market Entry Modes by Service Firms," *1988 Educators' Conference Proceedings* (Chicago: American Marketing Association, 1988), 20.

[18] James D. Goodnow, "Development of Personal Computer Software for International Mode of Entry Decisions" (Paper presented at the 1985 Annual Meeting of the Academy of International Business, New York, October 1985).

[19] Ernest Dichter, "The World Customer," *Harvard Business Review* (July–August 1962): 116.

[20] David A. Ricks, *Big Business Blunders* (Homewood, IL: Dow Jones-Irwin, 1983), 83–85.

[21] Richard D. Robinson, "Background Concepts and Philosophy of International Business from World War II to the Present," *Journal of International Business Studies* (Spring–Summer 1981): 13–21.

[22] Walt W. Rostow, *The Stages of Economic Growth* (London: Cambridge University Press, 1960), 10.

[23] Subhash C. Jain, "Standardization of International Marketing Strategy," *Journal of Marketing* (January 1989): 70–79.

[24] "Brazil: Campbell Soup Fails to Make It to the Table," *Business Week* (21 October 1981): 66.

[25] Louis Kraar, "Inside Japan's 'Open' Market," *Fortune* (5 October 1981): 122.

[26] C. L. Lapp, "Marketing Goofs in International Trade," *The Diary of Alpha Kappa Psi* (February 1983): 4.

[27] Hirotaka Takeuchi and Michael E. Porter, "Three Roles of International Marketing in Global Strategy," in *Competition in Global Industries*, ed. Michael Porter (Boston: Harvard Business School Press, 1986), 113.

[28] Takeuchi and Porter, "Three Roles of International Marketing," 114.

[29] Ralph Z. Sorenson and Ulrich E. Wiechmann, "How Multinationals View Marketing Standardization," *Harvard Business Review* (May–June 1975): 38.

[30] Ted Levitt, "The Globalization of Markets," *Harvard Business Review* (May–June 1983): 92–102.

[31] Eugene H. Fram and Riad Ajami, "Globalization of Markets and Shopping Stress: Cross Country Comparisons," *Business Horizons* (January–February, 1994): 17–23.

[32] Sorenson and Wiechmann, "How Multinationals View Marketing Standardization," 38–56.

[33] John S. Hill and Richard R. Still, "Adapting Products to LDC Tastes," *Harvard Business Review* (March–April 1984): 93–94.

[34] William W. Lewis and Marvin Harris, "Why Globalization Must Prevail," *The McKinsey Quarterly* 2 (1992): 114–31.

[35] Ohmae, *Triad Power*, 101–02.

[36] W. Chan Kim and R. A. Manborgue, "Cross-cultural Strategies," *Journal of Business Strategy* (Spring 1987): 30–31.

[37] See Takeuchi and Porter, "Three Roles of International Marketing," 111–46.

Cases

The Gillette Company

In the spring of 1986, Joseph A. Marino, vice president of marketing in Gillette's shaving division, was concerned about the future prospects of his business. With sales of $2.4 billion, Gillette is the world's largest blade and razor manufacturer and claims a remarkable 62 percent share of the $700-million U.S. shaving market.

Growth in razors and blades has been slowing down, however, and competitors were putting a few nicks in Gillette's performance. Revenues had increased just 3 percent over the previous three years (i.e., 1982–85), and during 1985, profits had risen only 1 percent to $160 million. Gillette had to produce a steady stream of new shaving products just to hold its ground in the United States.

More disturbing was that cheap disposable razors—unknown 12 years ago—now accounted for more than half of U.S. sales. That figure has been growing, and even though Gillette dominated the disposable market, cheaper razors meant lower profits. For a company that received one-third of its sales and two-thirds of its earnings from blades and razors, that was bad news. Foreign business, which accounted for about 57 percent of corporate sales and 61 percent of profits, was a sore spot, too. Although a weaker dollar was expected to boost Gillette's overseas earnings, a weaker dollar would help Gillette only in the short term. Foreign razor and blade markets were also mature.

RAZOR TECHNOLOGY

Ever since an ambitious inventor named King C. Gillette introduced the first safety razor in 1903, men have been accustomed to continual, extensively advertised advances from Gillette in the state of the art of shaving. The company spends more than $20 million a year on shaving research and development. With the aid of the latest scientific instruments, a staff of 200 explores the fringes of metallurgical technology and biochemical research. They subject the processes of beard growth and shaving to the most rigorous scrutiny.

Every day some 10,000 men carefully record the results of their shaves for Gillette on data processing cards, including the precise number of their nicks and cuts. Five hundred of those men shave in 32 special in-plant cubicles under carefully controlled and monitored conditions, including observation by two-way mirrors and videotape cameras. In certain cases, sheared whiskers are collected, weighed, and measured. The results of the tests are fed into a computer and processed by sophisticated statistical programs.

Gillette scientists know, for instance, that a man's beard grows an average of 15/1000 of an inch a day, or 5½ inches a year; that it covers about a third of a square foot of his face and contains 15,500 hairs; that shaving removes about 65 milligrams of whiskers daily, which amounts to a pound of hair every 16 years; that during an average lifetime a man will spend 3,350 hours scraping 27½ feet of whiskers from his face.

Occasionally other companies have obtained a technological jump on Gillette. In the early 1960s, a new longer-life stainless steel blade from Wilkinson Sword of Great Britain temporarily stole a big share of the market from Gillette's carbon steel Super Blue Blade. But Gillette, as it always does, soon introduced its own longer-life version and recaptured much of the lost market.

To fully comprehend Gillette's research and development inroads, one must visit its research facilities in South Boston. Displayed there are pictures taken through a field emission scanning electron microscope that can magnify objects 50,000 times. The photographs showed tiny sections—1/10,000 of an inch—of the edges of razor blades

---

This case was prepared as a basis for class discussion rather than to illustrate either effective or ineffective handling of an administrative situation.

made by Gillette and some of its competitors. The edges of the competitors' blades looked rough and jagged. Although not exactly Iowa farmland, the edges of the Gillette blade resembled softly rolling hills, like the Berkshires in Connecticut. The reason for Gillette's less formidable topography was the new "microsmooth" process invented by Gillette, whereby blades are given extra smooth edges by particles of aluminum oxide energized by ultrasonic waves.

COMPETITION

Probably no company in this country has so thoroughly dominated one consumer market as long as Gillette. A huge concern with $2.4 billion in annual sales (1985 figure), it controls over 62 percent of the shaving market. Electric razors in their initial years appeared to pose a big challenge to Gillette's wet-shaving products. But today, they are used by only a quarter of all shavers, and most owners shave with them only occasionally. As a matter of fact, due to continual advances in wet shaving and the inability of electrics to deliver a comparably close shave, their use is slowly declining. Gillette's few competitors, such as Schick (22 percent of the market), American Safety Razor, and Wilkinson, have been reduced mainly to manufacturing knockoff versions of and refill blades for Gillette razors.

Just when its competitors adjusted to one shaving system, Gillette unleashed yet another advance. In 1971 it was Trac II, a razor system that featured two parallel blades mounted in a cartridge 60/1000 of an inch apart. Gillette said the idea arose from a phenomenon called *hysteresis* discovered by its research and development people through slow motion microphotography. When a razor blade cuts through a whisker, the whisker is pulled slightly out of the follicle. A second blade, arranged in tandem, can thus take a second, closer slice off the whisker before it retracts and can thus provide a cleaner shave. In 1977, after research and development expenditures of over $8 million, Gillette made another "quantum leap forward," as the

company termed it, with Atra, a razor featuring a twin-blade cartridge that swivels during shaving and thus follows the face's contours. Gillette said its tests showed that, whereas the twin Trac II blades are in contact with the face an average of only 77 percent of the time, the Atra can raise the figure to 89 percent.

The $7.95 Atra razor is the apotheosis of Gillette technology, engineering, and design. Weighing a hefty 1½ ounces, it is a luxurious, elaborately crafted machine with a thick, beautifully tooled aluminum handle. Refill blades retail for 56 cents each. The Atra is available in expensive gift versions: one ($19.95) is goldplated with a rosewood handle; another ($49.95) features a sterling silver handle designed by Reed and Barton that resembles an antique table knife.

Recently, the company rolled out a new version of Atra called Atra Plus, a razor with a lubricating strip above the blade for smoother shaves.

A relatively recent entrant into the shaving business is the Bic Pen Corporation, maker of the familiar ballpoint pen. The company, which has $200 million in annual sales, is located in modest quarters in Milford, Connecticut. It does not have anyone regularly assigned to explore the fringes of shaving technology. It does not have a field emission scanning electron microscope. It does not do any ultrasonic honing. It maintains only a small shave-testing panel of about a hundred people who do not fill out data processing cards. It does not know and does not care how many hairs are in the average man's beard or how fast they grow.

The apotheosis of Bic technology, engineering, and design is the Bic Shaver. Weighing only a quarter of an ounce, it is a diminutive, characterless object made of white plastic that looks like something used in hospitals. In fact, a version of it *is* used in hospitals. It has only one blade mounted on a short, hollow handle and sells for about 99 cents for four or for 25 cents each. When the blade wears out, you throw the whole thing away. The Bic Shaver is not available in gold or silver plate or aluminum or anything else but plastic. It does not come in gift versions.

Bic Pen Corporation, though, is selling 200 million shavers a year in the United States, nearly twice as many as the number of Atra blades that Gillette is selling. The Bic Shaver, in fact, is the most serious challenge Gillette has faced since the early days of King Gillette.

Though Bic and Gillette came to purvey disposability from different perspectives, it was inevitable that sooner or later they would clash. The first clash between Gillette and Bic was in pens. Beginning in the 1950s, the pen market rapidly became commoditized as inexpensive but high-quality ballpoints gained at the expense of high-priced, high-status pens. When Bic's throwaway "stick" pen began selling for 19 cents in the U.S. market in 1958, its major competitor was a 98-cent refillable pen made by Paper Mate, which Gillette had acquired in 1955. Paper Mate fought back with its low-priced Write Brothers line of stick pens. But Gillette's mass market advertising and promotion skills were no match for those of Baron Bich. Bic now has 60 percent of the ballpoint market versus Paper Mate's 20 percent.

The next clash involved butane cigarette lighters. Gillette initially went the cachet route with the 1971 purchase of S.T. Dupont, a prestigious French concern that produces luxury lighters selling for several hundred dollars. According to an ad, 500 separate steps and six months are required to manufacture Dupont lighters. Bic and Gillette, though, recognized that the lighter market was ripe for commoditization. By 1974, both were selling disposable lighters for $1.49, which were later reduced to 89 cents. These disposable lighters quickly stole market share from status brands.

"Dupont lighters are in a class by themselves, and people are willing to pay a premium for them." It was said that the click of a Dupont was so distinctive that, if you lit up in a restaurant, people knew you were using a Dupont. Now you can buy a disposable—a light at the end of a piece of plastic—for 89 cents. Why do people want a disposable lighter? They're utilitarian. They work. You can lose them and not care because you have no investment in them, no loyalty toward them.

Gillette has done only slightly better with disposable lighters than with disposable pens. Bic's lighter now has a 52 percent share of the market; Gillette's disposable Cricket has 30 percent. Bic's feel for the mass market, it should be noted, is not unerring. Its felt-tip Bic Banana pen, though lower priced, has solidly been bested by Gillette's Flair. "In all honesty, the Banana just wasn't a very good product," concedes a Bic marketing manager.

The shaving market is the most recent and most crucial clash. Bic introduced its disposable shaver to Europe in 1975 and moved into Canada the following year. Aware that the United States would be next, Gillette came out with its own blue plastic disposable called Good News!, which has a Trac II twin-blade head, in 1976. Gillette, which knows a lot more about selling shavers than lighters and pens, has been no pushover for Bic. Each company now has about half of the disposable market.

Good News!, though, is really bad news for Gillette. One must appreciate that the razor blade business is a fixed-sum game: sales in this country are relatively static at about two billion blades a year. Since Gillette is the dominant manufacturer, every new razor and blade it introduces in effect cannibalizes its older products. Atra takes business away from Trac II, which took business away from double-edge blades. But Gillette has never bothered much about this because its new products are invariably higher priced than its old products.

The problem is that Good News! sells for a lot less than any of Gillette's older products. Price is the key to commodity competition, and to stay competitive with the 25-cent Bic Shaver and with disposables from a few other producers, Gillette has had to sell Good News! for much less than the retail price of an Atra or Trac II cartridge. As many Trac II and Atra users have figured out, although you have to pay as much as 56 cents for a twin-blade refill cartridge from Gillette, you can get precisely the same cartridge mounted on a plastic handle for as little as 25 cents. Good News! not only produces fewer revenues per blade sale for Gillette but creates higher costs because Gillette must supply a handle as well as a cartridge. Every time

Good News! gains a couple of points of market share, Gillette loses millions of dollars in sales and profits.

CORPORATE CULTURE

To fully grasp the intensity of Bic Pen Corporation's challenge, it is necessary to flash back briefly to the early days of Bic and Gillette. The founders of the two companies were strong-willed men who single-mindedly pursued powerful and remarkably similar visions. King Gillette's vision came one morning in 1895 when he started shaving with his old straight-edged razor. It was not only dull, he realized, but beyond the help of his leather strop. To reestablish its edge, it would have to be honed by the local barber or cutler. At the time, Gillette was working for a company that made a great deal of money manufacturing bottle caps. The inventor of the bottle cap had often regaled Gillette with the bountiful proceeds derived from putting out an inexpensive item that people repeatedly use and throw away. In a flash, as he looked at his spent straight-edged razor, Gillette conceived of the idea of a safety razor with a disposable blade.

Less is known of the early vision of Marcel L. Bich, the reclusive Italian-born businessman and yachtsman who founded Société Bic in Paris, which controls the U.S.-based Bic Pen Corporation. But it is said that, in the late 1940s, "Baron" Bich, as he calls himself, hit upon the idea of a low-priced, reliable, disposable ballpoint pen. Existing ballpoints, which not only were expensive and required refills, frequently malfunctioned.

Gillette and Bich went on to make fortunes from disposability. But over a period of time, the philosophies of their companies diverged. Particularly after the death of King Gillette in 1932, his company sought to give its blades, and especially its handsome razor handles, an aura of not only superior performance but class and cachet. Each new technological leap could thus be more easily accompanied by a liberal leap in price and profit margin. Gillette's chief marketing strategy became the promotion of new captive "systems," or blade-handle combinations. Just as Kodak makes most of its money not on its cameras but on its film, profits in shaving are not in razor handles but in blades. Yet if a man could become convinced to trade up to a new, more expensive handle, such as Atra, he would then have to buy new, more expensive blades designed to fit only that handle.

Gillette was never concerned about what its people call "the low end of the market," that is, cheap private label blades. If you put out a class product, Gillette believed, the major portion of the always-status-seeking masses would buy it. Shaving being serious business and the way one's face appears to other people all day being a matter of some importance, most men, Gillette knew, didn't want to skimp and settle for an ordinary shave when for a little more money they could feel secure that they were getting the "best" shave from Gillette.

In recent years, as the vision of its founder faded, Gillette conglomerated into nondisposability. It acquired other companies and began marketing such class durables as cameras and hi-fi equipment. Durables, though, have never been as profitable for Gillette as razors and blades. In 1985, although the company's shaving division produced only 33 percent of its sales, it yielded 67 percent of the year's profits.

Baron Bich, whose first business venture was making parts for pen makers in Paris, eschewed class and pursued mass with a vengeance. He was taken with the potential of what Bic people call "commoditization," the devolution in recent years of certain expensive, high-status durables, including watches and cigarette lighters, into inexpensive, nonstatus, more or less disposable items. Commoditization has several basic causes. One is a shift in taste: different eras accord cachet to different products. More important is the technology of mass production. An item often has status because it is difficult and time-consuming to make and must sell at a high price. But if production techniques are developed that allow the item to be spewed out by automated assembly lines at a cost of pennies with little if any loss in functional quality, its status and allure will abate. People will not feel embarrassed to buy and to be seen using the new, cheap version of the item.

A final cause of commoditization is consumers' growing resistance to what is called market "segmentation," the proliferation of new brands, flavors, and other diverse variants of common consumer goods. Although 35 years ago, according to a *Los Angeles Times* article, a retailer could satisfy 88 percent of his or her customers by stocking only five brands of cigarettes, now, to supply the same percentage of smokers, 58 different cigarette brands with a bewildering variety of lengths, filters, packages, flavors, and tar and nicotine contents must be carried. Large conglomerate consumer goods firms compete, not on the basis of who can sell for the lowest price, but on the basis of who can churn out and most aggressively market the largest number of new products.

Though all of this adds heavily to cost, consumers have generally been willing to pay premium prices for cosmetic differentiation. This allows companies to recoup their extra costs and to earn extra profits. But now, according to a recent *Harvard Business Review* study, consumers have become more price- and value-conscious and are beginning to rebel. In growing numbers, they are refusing to pay extra for individualized frills. They are bypassing national brands in favor of heavily discounted brandless products.

Baron Bich put a brand on his products. But to sell them as cheaply as possible and make them appeal to as many people as possible, he stripped them of all traces of cachet, glamour, and nonfunctional frills. He reduced them to pure generic utility and simplicity. He made them commodities. His marketing strategy was just as simple: high value at a low price. It was a strategy that would have won the admiration of King C. Gillette.

PSYCHOLOGY OF SHAVING

The battle between Bic and Gillette is more than a conventional contest over which kind of razor people want to use. It is a battle over one of the most enduring male rituals of daily American life.

Those of us who are old enough remember how the ritual used to be conducted because many of us watched it every morning. Like a chemist with mortar and pestle, our fathers would whip up a rich lather by stirring their shaving brushes around in their large ceramic mugs. Like an orchestra conductor during a brisk allegro, they would strop their gleaming straight-edge razors on long strips of leather. Writer Richard Armour once recalled the scene: "I loved to watch him grimace and pull the skin taut with his fingers preparatory to a daring swipe from cheekbone to chin. I held my breath while he shaved his upper lip, coming perilously close to his nose, and when he started his hazardous course along his jawbone, risking an ear lobe. When he scraped around his Adam's apple, with a good chance of cutting his throat, I had to turn away until I thought the danger was past."

Armour lamented that safety razors and aerosol lathers had taken the "skill, fun, and danger" out of shaving. Though the audience, if there is an audience, may be less apt, the morning ritual continues to occupy a very special place in most men's lives. Face shaving is one of the few remaining exclusively male prerogatives. It is a daily affirmation of masculinity. One study indicated that beard growth is actually stimulated by the prospect of sexual relations. A survey by New York psychologists reported that, although men complain about the bother of shaving, 97 percent of the sample would not want to use a cream, were one to be developed, that would permanently rid them of all facial hair. Gillette once introduced a new razor that came in versions for heavy, regular, and light beards. Almost nobody bought the light version because nobody wanted to acknowledge lackluster beard production. (Later Gillette brought out an adjustable razor that enabled men with sparse whiskers to cope with their insufficiency in private.)

The first shave remains a rite of passage into manhood that is often celebrated with the gift of a handsome new razor (or the handing down of a venerable old razor) and a demonstration of its use from the father. Though shaving may now require less skill and involve less danger than it once did, most men still want the razor they use to reflect their belief that shaving remains serious business. They regard their razor as an important personal tool, a kind of extension of self, like an expensive pen, cigarette lighter, attaché case, or golf club set. Gillette has labored hard, with success, to maintain the razor's masculine look, heft, and feel as well as its status as an item of personal identification worthy of, for instance, a Christmas gift.

For over 80 years, Gillette's perception of the shaving market and the psychology of shaving has been unerring. Though its products formally have only a 62 percent share, its technology and marketing philosophy have held sway over the entire market.

Now, however, millions of men—about 12 million, to be more precise—are scraping their faces with small, asexual, nondescript pieces of plastic costing 25 cents, an act that would seem to be the ultimate deromanticization, even negation, of the shaving ritual, thus relegating shaving to a pedestrian, trivial daily task.

NEW SEGMENTS

Good News! is a defensive product for Gillette. Though distributing it widely, the company is spending negligible money advertising it. Gillette knows, though, that it must do more than counter the Bic threat. It must keep the whole disposable market contained. That means, most immediately, luring from disposables two chief categories of users: teenagers and women.

According to Marino, shaving is just not a high-interest category to a lot of kids in high school: "They don't have to have a Gillette razor or their father's razor to prove they're old enough to shave. They don't need life-style reflection in a razor. They want a good shave, but they don't want to pay a lot of money." One might venture several explanations for kids' indifference to the traditional aura of shaving. According to some people, there has been a progressive emasculation of the American male. Given this hypothesis, the unisex plastic disposable

is a predictable response. Another view is that boys today are more secure in their sexual identities than the previous generation and thus don't need the old symbols of masculinity.

Whatever the case, as far as Gillette is concerned, use of disposables is an ephemeral adolescent affection. As kids grow up, Gillette expects that promotion, advertising, and sampling will convince them that captive systems, such as Atra and Trac II, are a better and more mature way to shave.

Women are a more complex problem. Despite the fact that as many adult women shave as men, though much less often, Gillette and the other U.S. razor manufacturers are so male oriented that until quite recently they never sold a razor designed for women. Women had no choice but to pay for such masculine features as hefty metal handles. One Gillette marketing man contends with a leer that "women seem to like a longer handle for some unknown reason." Yet already nearly 40 percent of women who shave have switched to disposables. Bic is now selling the Bic Lady Shaver, a slightly modified version of its regular disposables. Gillette, Schick, and other producers are trying to find ways to entice women away from disposables with feminine versions of their male products.

So far, Gillette's contain-and-switch strategy has not been very successful. In 1976, Gillette said disposables would never get more than 7 percent of the market. Marino said at the time, "You know, we considered it for trips and locker rooms, for the guy who forgets his razor." The disposable market, though, soon soared past 7 percent, forcing Gillette into continual upward revisions of its estimates. In terms of units sold, disposables have now reached 50 percent of the market.

Bic is predicting that disposables will ultimately capture 60 percent of the market. Indeed, Bic has been investing so much money advertising its shaver—$15 million in 1985—that it lost $5 million on the product. Baron Bich is known for his willingness to run a deficit promoting a product as long as it keeps gaining market share. As evidence that gains will continue, Bic people point to the huge disposable market share in many European countries: 75 percent in Greece, 50 percent in Austria, 45 percent in Switzerland, 40 percent in France. According to Bic, mass products tend to follow the population curve. If 40 percent of one segment of the population uses disposables, eventually everybody will.

PRODUCT IMPROVEMENTS

When it got into a war in the old days, Gillette could always win by unleashing its ultimate weapon: superior technological strength. Shaving technology, though, has come a long way since 1903. Further innovations are not easy. It is awfully hard to make the next dramatic improvement.

One potential leap would be a blade so tough that you would not have to wash your face to soften your beard. But few experts see such a blade as technically feasible. Dry beard hair is extremely abrasive and about as strong as copper wire of the same thickness. Even though today's blades are made of very durable steel, their precision-honed edges are quickly destroyed by dry whiskers.

Another potential improvement is a much longer-lasting blade. Yet such an advance may not be worth the effort. The only technology that matters now is that of assembly lines, which can reduce manufacturing costs.

Whatever the likelihood of future quantum leaps, the fact remains: despite the topographical differences discernable by high-powered microscopes, today all brands of razor blades deliver an extremely good shave. Gillette studies show that over 93 percent of shavers rate the shaves they are receiving as very good or excellent. Asked about the quality of Schick's blades, a Gillette executive conceded that it is much the same as that of his company's blades. "They have the same steel, the same coatings. Schick has copied us very well and done a hell of a good job. I think our quality is more consistent, but as far as giving you a good shave, their blades are damn good."

Gillette's chief selling point against Bic is the alleged superiority of twin blades against a single blade. But to what degree this advantage can be capitalized on is debatable. As a Bic executive put it, "We don't really know what happens when two blades shave the skin, but our tests show that a large percentage of customers can't tell the difference. I give Gillette a lot of credit for coming up with the two-blade concept. It's a magnificent marketing idea. Two blades are better than one. It has a surface sense of logic to it. But on a perceptual level, which is the level most of us deal on, there isn't any difference."

OPPORTUNITIES IN THIRD WORLD MARKETS

Gillette discovered a while back that only 8 percent of Mexican men who shave use shaving cream. The rest soften their beards with soapy water or—ouch!—plain water, neither of which Gillette sells.

Sensing an opportunity, Gillette introduced plastic tubes of shaving cream that sold for half the price of its aerosol in Guadalajara (Mexico) in 1985. After a year, 13 percent of Guadalajaran men used shaving cream. Gillette is now planning to sell its new product, Prestobarba (Spanish for "quick shave"), in the rest of Mexico, Colombia, and Brazil.

Tailoring its marketing to Third World budgets and tastes—from packaging blades so they can be sold one at a time to educating the unshaven about the joys of a smooth face—has become an important part of Gillette's growth strategy. The company sells its pens, toiletries, toothbrushes, and other products in developing countries. But despite Gillette's efforts to diversify, razor blades still produce one-third of the company's revenue and two-thirds of its pre-tax profit.

The market for blades in developed countries is stagnant. On the other hand, in the Third World a very high proportion of the population is under 15 years old. All those young men are going to be in the shaving population in a very short time.

Few U.S. consumer-products companies that compete in the Third World have devoted as much energy or made as many inroads as Gillette, which draws more than half its sales from abroad. Since the company targeted the developing world in 1969, the proportion of its sales that come from Latin America, Asia, Africa, and the Middle East has doubled to 20 percent; dollar volume has risen sevenfold.

Gillette has had a strong business in Latin America since it began building plants there in the 1940s. Fidel Castro once told television interviewer Barbara Walters that he grew a beard because he couldn't get Gillette blades while fighting in the mountains.

The company's push into Asia, Africa, and the Middle East dates to 1969 when Gillette dropped a policy of investing only where it could have 100 percent-owned subsidiaries. That year, it formed a joint venture in Malaysia, which was threatening to bar imports of Gillette products. The company has added one foreign plant nearly every year in such countries as China, Egypt, Thailand, and India and is now looking at Pakistan, Nigeria, and Turkey.

The company always starts with a factory that makes double-edged blades—still popular in the Third World—and, if all goes well, expands later into production of pens, deodorants, shampoo, or toothbrushes. Only a few ventures have gone sour: a Yugoslav project never got off the ground and Gillette had to sell its interest in Iran to its local partners.

In a few markets, Gillette has developed products exclusively for the Third World. Low-cost shaving cream is one. Another is Black Silk, a hair relaxer developed for sale to blacks in South Africa that is now being introduced in Kenya.

Gillette often sells familiar products in different packages or smaller sizes. Because many Latin American consumers cannot afford a seven-ounce bottle of Silkience shampoo, for instance, Gillette sells it in half-ounce plastic bubbles. In Brazil, Gillette sells Right Guard deodorant in plastic squeeze bottles instead of metal cans.

But the toughest task for Gillette is convincing Third World men to shave. The company recently began dispatching portable theaters to remote villages—Gillette calls them "mobile propaganda units"—to show movies and commercials that teach daily shaving. In South African and Indonesian versions, a bewildered bearded man enters a locker room where clean-shaven friends show him how to shave. In the Mexican one, a handsome sheriff, tracking bandits who have kidnapped a woman, pauses on the trail to shave every morning. The camera lingers as he snaps a double-edged blade into his razor, lathers his face, and strokes it carefully. In the end, of course, the smooth-faced sheriff gets the woman.

In other commercials, Gillette agents with an oversized shaving brush and a mug of shaving cream lather up and shave a villager while others watch. Plastic razors are then distributed free and blades, which of course must be bought, are left with the local storekeeper.

Such campaigns may not win immediate converts, but in the long run, they should establish the company's name in the market.

GILLETTE'S OTHER PRODUCTS

The outlook is even dimmer in toiletries, Gillette's second most important market. The company has lost market share in each of its major product categories since 1981. Consider Right Guard, Gillette's leading brand. In 1970 it claimed 30 percent of the $1.2 billion deodorant business; now it gets a mere 7 percent. Right Guard's positioning as a "family deodorant" was undercut when rivals successfully split the market into men's and women's products. Gillette's current $30 million advertising campaign, reasserting the brand as a man's deodorant, hasn't stopped the slide.

Because of the limited prospects in blades and toiletries, Gillette is searching for other opportunities in personal health care products. Given Gillette's track record and cautious nature, that won't be easy. Sales of writing and office products, such as Paper Mate and Flair pens, peaked at $304 million in 1981. In 1985, profits fell 12 percent, to $10 million. The writing and office products division now accounts for 11 percent of company revenues but just 2 percent of earnings. In another recent attempt to diversify, Gillette bought small stakes in a half-dozen tiny companies in such diverse fields as hearing aids, biotechnology, and personal computer software. But these "greenhouse projects" have yet to bloom.

Why hasn't the company done better? Critics say Gillette has become risk-averse, partly because of a civil service mentality among employees. Middle management is considered weak because the company has a history of promoting people who've been there the longest. That tendency has kept Gillette from moving aggressively.

Gillette's plan for creating a new line of branded low-price personal care products is an example. For 18 months it has been testing a line of unisex toiletries under its Good News! label, which now appears only on disposable razors. Gillette plans to sell 12 products, from shaving cream to shampoo, all for the same price in nearly identical packages. It hopes these "branded generics" will rack up $100 million in sales when available nationally.

Unfortunately, that date keeps being postponed. Test marketing took six months longer than planned, and a national rollout was still more than a year off. Part of the delay resulted from a change in advertising. Initial ads, which had a patriotic theme, failed to emphasize quality and low price. Gillette has also cut the wholesale price on the generics from $1.25 to $1.09.

A second new venture also had problems. Gillette's German subsidiary, Braun, introduced an electric shaver in the United States. Backed by a relatively small $7 million budget, it started running national advertising in the fall of 1985. But success is not easy. Braun has been entering a declining U.S. electric shaver market where rigid consumer loyalties have generated a phenomenal 90 percent repurchase rate for market leaders Norelco and Remington.

GILLETTE'S STRATEGY

In the final analysis, Gillette's strategy is to keep as much pressure as possible on Bic's profits with the hope that its rival will be forced out of the razor

market. To increase that pressure, Gillette has been putting the squeeze on Bic's other businesses.

The competition between the Boston-based giant and the French-owned upstart has begun to take on the characteristics of a vicious street fight in which price slashing is the main weapon and market share the main prize. In terms of size, the match is uneven. Gillette weighs in at about $24 billion in sales; Bic tips the scales at around $750 million, some $225 million of which comes from its American offshoot, Bic Pen Corporation. Even so, the smaller company has managed to cut up its competitor first with disposable ballpoint pens, then disposable lighters, and most recently with disposable razors.

Take the seesaw battle over lighters. Gillette was the first of the two companies to go after the U.S. market. In 1972 it brought out its Cricket brand. By the time Bic introduced its own lighter the following year, Gillette had cornered 40 percent of the market. Demand was growing so rapidly, however, that at first Bic had no trouble gaining on Gillette. But when supply began to catch up with demand, Bic recognized it had a problem. Despite what it claimed was a better product and despite its flashy "Flick My Bic" ad campaign, sales of the two lighters ran neck and neck.

At the time Bic had to decide what it wanted to achieve. As a company executive recalls: "We had to decide whether we wanted to just sit back and enjoy substantial short-term profits or go after market share." Bic opted for market share and in mid-1977 slashed the wholesale price of its lighter by 32 percent.

Gillette did not follow suit immediately, largely because its per unit manufacturing costs were higher than Bic's and its management was reluctant to accept such a low return. When Gillette finally did retaliate with a price cut, Bic reduced its price still further and a ferocious price war ensued. By the end of 1978, it was apparent that Bic's "big play" was successful. Bic had taken over nearly 50 percent of the market; Gillette's share had slumped to 30 percent. Moreover, in 1978 Bic reported $9.2 million on pre-tax profits for its lighter division, while Gillette suffered an estimated loss of almost the same amount.

In 1981, despite continuing losses, Gillette turned the tables and started selling its Cricket lighters at a 10 percent discount off the Bic price. The counterattack hasn't substantially hurt Bic's market share, but it has effectively limited profits and thus the amount of money Bic can keep pouring into razors.

The big question is whether such pressure on profits will force Bic to abandon the razor market before Gillette's own business is radically altered or even irreparably harmed. According to one observer, the competition between the rivals is no longer just a matter of one pen or one lighter or one razor against another. It is a war on all fronts.

Becton Dickinson and Company: Multidivisional Marketing Programs

In January 1990, Robert Jones, vice president of Sales for Becton Dickinson Division (BDD), received a phone call from John Kmetz, a BDD sales representative. Kmetz explained that Health Medical Center (HMC), a 435-bed teaching hospital, was evaluating the hypodermic products of a competitor, and was preparing to convert to that line based on cost savings potential. Kmetz also informed Jones of the following:

- HMC purchased BDD syringes and needles from a contract established with Allied Purchasing Group (APG), a large hospital buying group. However, HMC was experiencing financial problems, and the competitor had offered a 15 percent discount off the price charged to HMC for hypodermics via BDD's contract with APG.
- HMC also purchased products sold by other BD divisions besides BDD.
- After consulting with his district and regional sales managers, Kmetz was recommending a 10 percent price reduction for HMC. However, he also noted that Ed Haire, BDD's director of Contract Sales, was concerned that this would undermine BDD's pricing structure with APG-member hospitals. Haire's initial reaction was to let HMC convert to the competitor whose unproven product might not withstand conversion among end users. Haire indicated that, if the competing product did fail, BDD could protect its pricing structure within a large buying group and demonstrate the competitor's liabilities to other accounts.
- HMC expected a formal proposal from BDD in 10 days.

Jones contacted Robert Flaherty, president of BDD, and noted that the size, prestige, and influence of HMC required a carefully planned response from BDD. Flaherty agreed, and noted that BD was currently running a program intended to develop multidivisional marketing efforts. He wondered if such an approach might help in dealing with HMC. Jones considered this a potentially attractive alternative to a price response, but was concerned that, with only 10 days available, time for preparing a multidivisional response was scarce. In addition, Jones was unsure of the support he could expect from other BD divisions involved with HMC. Jones agreed to gather more information and make a recommendation to Flaherty about the HMC situation.

COMPANY BACKGROUND

Becton Dickinson (BD) manufactured products for health care professionals, medical institutions, industry, and the general public. The company was organized into two sectors—Medical (59 percent of 1989 sales) and Diagnostic (41 percent)—and 19 operating divisions. (See Exhibit 1.)

Each division was a profit center with its own marketing and sales organization, national accounts program, distribution network, customer service department, billing and accounts receivables procedures, and warehousing facilities. One executive noted that "interaction between divisions has, historically, been minimal; and that has probably meant some inefficiencies and duplication. But there has also been responsibility, accountability, and a clear product-market focus with this decentralized approach. Increasingly, however, we must respond to customers seeking more efficient and effective approaches to their operating and service needs."

Professor Frank V. Cespedes and Research Associate Laura Goode prepared this case as the basis for class discussion rather than to illustrate either effective or ineffective handling of an administrative situation. Printed by permission of the Harvard Business School.

EXHIBIT 1
Operation Structure—Becton Dickinson Medical and Diagnostic Sectors

Medical Sector

- BD Acute Care
- BD Canada
- BD Consumer Products
- BD Critical Care Monitoring
- BD Division
- BD Infusion Systems

- BD Pharmaceutical Systems
- BD Polymer Research
- BD Medical Gloves
- Deseret Medical
- Ivers Lee

Diagnostic Sector

- BD ACCU-GLASS
- BD Advanced Diagnostics
- BD Diagnostic Instrument Systems
- BD Immunocytometry Systems

- BD Labware
- MD Microbiology Systems
- BD Primary Care Diagnostics
- BD VACUTAINER Systems

Note: "BD" is used above to abbreviate Becton Dickinson.

Market Trends

Among the most important trends in the hospital market during the 1980s was the growth of buying groups, or group purchasing organizations (GPOs). One impact was that primary decision-making authority for many major medical supply items gradually shifted (in part or in whole, depending upon the product and application) away from end-users of medical supplies to nonusers (purchasing administrators or materials management), and often away from individual institutions to centralized GPOs. As a result, BD operating divisions that previously dealt with distinct decision makers in separate hospital departments often experienced "overlap" in purchasing processes for their products at the group level. A single individual or committee within a GPO often became the primary decision maker for a range of BD core products.

Not all in the industry agreed on the value and future role of GPOs. Groups varied considerably in the benefits offered to their member hospitals and in the contractual compliance they could obtain from members. Indeed, as one BD manager noted, "an important marketing and sales task in this business is judging which groups will succeed, to what extent, and how to relate to the differences among groups. Especially in our product cate-gories, there are large volumes at stake, and in these competitive sales situations you soon learn what the sports announcers mean when they talk about 'the thrill of victory and the agony of defeat.'"

Competitive Developments

BD competed with various suppliers of medical and diagnostic products, including Terumo Corporation, a Japanese firm that sold over 1,000 health care products worldwide. In the United States, Terumo competed directly against BD in several businesses including hypodermics, diabetes care products, I.V. catheters, and specimen collection. Although it offered prices significantly below established market levels, Terumo had achieved limited success in the U.S. market against individual BD divisions.

Terumo's recent activities were more significant in scope than anything attempted earlier. In 1988, Terumo completed construction of a $70 million hypodermic plant in Maryland, with capacity to supply a significant portion of the hypodermic products used in the United States. Trade reports indicated that Terumo planned this to be the first of three major U.S. manufacturing plants, and that

EXHIBIT 1 *(continued)*

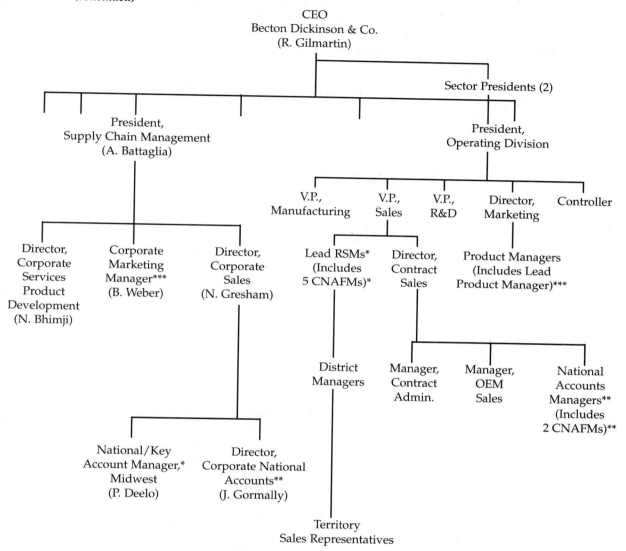

Legend: Asterisks indicate liaison activities between corporate headquarters and operating divisions for multidivisional sales and marketing efforts.

  * = Deelo (NAM, Midwest); corporate national account field managers (CNAFMs); lead regional sales managers

  ** = Gormally (Director, corporate national accounts); divisional national account managers (NAMs)

  *** = Weber (Corporate Marketing Manager); divisional lead product managers

Terumo regarded hypodermics as especially "visible" products that could be used as lead items to establish stronger brand identity and distribution capabilities for other products slated to be manufactured at Terumo's other planned U.S. manufacturing facilities. In the months before opening its U.S. plant, Terumo dramatically increased its promotional spending, efforts to expand its distribution network, and its field sales organization (which increased to about 30 salespeople for hypodermic products and I.V. catheters by 1989).

While Terumo established plants in the United States, BD was completing a major hypodermic manufacturing facility in Singapore to better service the Far Eastern market. Worldwide in 1989, BD generated about 2.5 times the sales revenue generated by Terumo, and also held about double the unit share position for syringes and needles (both companies' largest single product category in terms of sales volume).

DEVELOPMENT OF MULTIDIVISIONAL MARKETING PROGRAMS

While BD management continued to regard a divisionalized organization as the best approach for maintaining competitive position and financial performance, the company also began investigating in 1988 a multidivisional response to market developments. One executive explained that, implemented properly, such an approach could produce many benefits:

First, we can better demonstrate BD's importance within an account. In many instances, our total sales with a hospital or GPO are large but "hidden" because those sales are spread across product lines sold by different divisions.

Second, the appropriate approach can help to promote the many services that, as a corporation, we already provide to accounts. BD products are typically positioned as the top-quality brands supported by the broadest product line in the category (which facilitates ordering and usage by the customer), an intensive distribution network (which makes inventory-management tasks easier to handle and plan), end-

user training by our sales forces, and other services. But many accounts focus on price and ignore these services unless there's a coordinated effort among divisions that sell to the same account.

Third, this approach can also mean effective use of resources to develop additional value-added services and programs. This can be done through product bundling agreements and/or through the provision of order-processing systems or other services that might be prohibitive on the scale of any one division's business with an account, but feasible and attractive from a multidivisional perspective.

In early 1989, therefore, BD's CEO, Raymond Gilmartin, established a new operating group, Supply Chain Management (SCM), reporting to the CEO and charged with helping to better service customers who contract with several BD divisions. The head of the new SCM group was Alfred J. Battaglia, who had previously been president of the specimen collection division. Battaglia described the group's mission:

Supply chain management refers to activities which transport information and materials from our suppliers to our end users. At each step, modifications to the product and various services are what finally constitute the total value package a company offers to customers. SCM essentially provides leadership to an association of functional disciplines that, in total, manage these activities. The disciplines include corporate logistics, information systems, purchasing, EDI Service Products of various sorts, and corporate sales and marketing efforts.

SCM serves both internal and external customer groups. We try to coordinate different functional disciplines across divisions in dealing with external groups that work with a number of BD operating units; this would include many distributors, GPOs, individual hospitals, warehouse operations, and materials suppliers. Consolidated purchasing probably represents the greatest single short-term opportunity we have; but coordinated MIS and corporate marketing efforts are probably the biggest longer-term opportunities.

A key premise in our approach is that health care players at all levels of the supply chain are vitally interested in asset-management techniques and systems that can lower their total costs of obtaining and using needed products and services. Our ability to manage these activities across divisions can further differentiate our offerings and strengthen our relationships with end users, distributors, and suppliers.

Reporting to Battaglia were several managers responsible for aspects of multidivisional efforts. (See Exhibit 1.) In explaining the evolution of the SCM organization over the past year, Battaglia emphasized that the following concepts and issues had proven to be particularly important: the development and dissemination of market-segmentation and account-selection criteria for multidivisional efforts; a distinction between value-added and basic services; the continuing development of common information and communication systems; and the delineation of organizational roles and incentives for multidivisional marketing and sales efforts.

Market Segmentation

Identifying potential multidivisional-program accounts was a necessary first step. Mark Throdahl, BD's director of corporate planning, helped to develop many of the segmentation and account-selection criteria that informed SCM efforts. He explained that:

> Traditionally, we categorized customers by products and amounts bought from various BD divisions. That's the way we think, but not the way markets act. For multidivisional-marketing purposes, effective segmentation revolves around customer demographics (the account's size, location, and type of funding—for example, not-for-profit or for-profit hospitals); operating variables (the brands used in a product category and usage frequency); purchasing approaches (centralized or decentralized by department, channels utilized for various purchases, the frequency of purchase); and the technologies used (disposable vs. reusables). Without using such criteria to tailor our product and service offering to select accounts, we risk "averaging" our capabilities.

Using these criteria, the SCM group with marketing and sales managers from various divisions established a four-part "Profiling and Plan Development Process." Part one, account selection, involved identifying "important, susceptible, and/or vulnerable accounts" where a multidivisional effort was appropriate. At this stage, the goal was to distinguish between national accounts and key accounts, with the latter as the target for multidivisional efforts.

A *national account* was typically a hospital buying group with membership spanning several states; the group negotiated contracts in individual BD product categories. For such accounts, each division had national account managers (NAMs) responsible for sales of their division's products to these accounts, including negotiation of prices and terms with the account. NAMs reported to a divisional director of contract sales, responsible for administering contracts to the division's national accounts and reporting divisional sales to such accounts to corporate headquarters. Corporate then aggregated this data and might offer such accounts financial incentives, depending upon the total volume purchased by the account.

Allied Purchasing Group, the GPO through which BDD sold its hypodermic products to HMC, was a national account purchasing products from BD under a volume-based discount known as a Z contract.

A *key account* was an individual hospital that might belong to a GPO but that chose to seek an agreement directly with BD. These accounts were of sufficient size or importance to merit the additional time and effort required to generate, negotiate, and administer a multidivisional agreement. Throdahl noted that, "unlike a national account, these key-account programs do depend upon a high level of cooperation and communication among divisions. Often, key accounts are selected because of a competitive threat or opportunity best addressed by assembling different value-added services, rather than a price discount."

Part two of the Plan Development Process involved divisional input concerning the key account. An important step at this stage was development of a key account profile by regional sales managers (RSMs) from relevant divisions. One

RSM described this as "a working document that captures information most pertinent to our position and the decision process at the account. It helps to define the framework within which an effective interdivisional action plan can develop."

The key account profile included a listing of important contacts in each department at the account, current product usage, individual RSMs' judgments about product potential at the account, the account's current group affiliation(s), distributors utilized, and preferred distributors (if any), as well as an assessment designed (as one RSM described it) "simply to generate discussion and some consensus about current risks and opportunities at the account. This assessment is made in terms of product categories, but it can generate suggestions about services that can help to minimize a given risk or maximize an opportunity."

The next parts of the account-planning process involved development of a multidivisional action plan for the account. The goal, as one RSM noted, was to "translate the account profile into a specific tactical plan that spells out individual division and salesperson responsibilities with target dates for completion. You need that specificity in order to make the process real for our people in the field, who respond more to tactical moves than grand strategy plans at accounts." Another RSM noted:

First, the key account profile must clearly specify our objectives via coordinated efforts. Second, the action plan must focus on resources and opportunities not available through individual divisional approaches: what can we accomplish more effectively together, rather than separately? I'm busy, and not a big believer in teamwork for its own sake; so I think it's important that synergy possibilities be spelled out and not assumed.

Value-Added vs. Basic Services

An important goal of multidivisional efforts was achieving competitive advantage for BD through superior customer service. The SCM group distinguished between basic or expected services, and value-added or unexpected services. Basic services included fulfillment accuracy, on-time delivery,

damage-free goods, efficient order-inquiry routines, effective sales representation, accurate invoicing, and efficient in-servicing of end users. Value-added services included custom-designed product labeling, customized quality-control recommendations for customers, deferred billing, priority order processing through dedicated order-entry specialists, JIT inventory management, extended warranty plans, and perhaps new services in areas such as waste disposal and risk management. Effective provision of the latter services often required multidivisional coordination.

Throdahl explained that "the ultimate rationale for these efforts is to focus our sales efforts, and the customer's purchase criteria, on total cost-in-use and away from price." He noted that BD field salespeople had traditionally sold to purchasing and end users rather than the administrative personnel likely to be most cognizant of total cost-in-use. "This represents an important training issue for us," he noted. Battaglia added:

All the value-added programs in the world won't mean anything if our reps don't understand them, don't want to understand them, or can't use them. So this thrust must be supported by effective sales management, especially by the RSMs who are a key link in field motivation. Then, for the individual field sales rep, it means (among other things) knowing your account well enough so that you can operationalize the impact of cutting delivery time or order-transaction costs or the amount of product held in inventory. However, salespeople who have grown up in a different selling environment are not immediately comfortable with this type of selling effort. That's another reason we need closer coordination between sales and marketing people in multidivisional efforts.

Information Systems

Developing common information systems was cited as a key in multidivisional efforts. "Many of the initiatives," noted Battaglia, "are increasingly information-based. MIS developments are creating opportunities for cost savings and services that differentiate traditional product offerings and supplier-distributor-buyer relationships."

At BD, each division had its own information systems with different product numbering schemes, order placement protocols, inventory tracking, billing, and financial systems. In 1989, SCM began a multiyear project aimed at instituting common product, customer, and vendor identifiers across divisions. "We need a common corporate database for account and product information," said one BD manager. "With this data, our position in contract negotiations is stronger; without it, field people in various divisions must spend lots of time in meetings, and that in turn can discourage efforts on multidivisional opportunities."

Naz Bhimji, director of Corporate Service Product Development, was responsible for computerized aspects of service development. He noted that, "My current focus is primarily the distributors: in this industry, they are a critical link in the supply chain." According to one industry report, "As much as 25%–30% of the cost in the [hospital supply] channel is redundant and could be eliminated if one were to start with a clean slate. But this requires a great deal of trust—a true 'partnership'—between distributor, manufacturer, and hospital . . . [and] a heavy dose of technology to accomplish the exchange of data efficiently."[1] The same report, based on a survey of 950 hospitals and 150 distributors, estimated that reducing materials-related costs by $250,000 "can have the same bottom line impact for hospitals as $8.3 million in increased revenues because of the associated costs (in storage, handling, financing, etc.) and fixed reimbursement programs." But the report also noted:

> Materials management has not been a priority for hospital executives, who do not understand the costs involved or how large they are. Hospital management believes its costs are 15% of the total operating budget, whereas the range is realistically 25%–33%. (Meanwhile) product price is an important factor in a hospital's decision to look at value-added services. For instance, lower product acquisition cost was overwhelmingly selected as the top desired benefit [ahead

of (2) better productivity, (3) better service, (4) increased revenue, and (5) better supplier relationships] . . . which may indicate that the hospital is not yet focusing on total delivered cost. This could trigger additional costs for the distributor or manufacturer in the investor stage.

Bhimji was developing a new electronic link (known as the Speed-Com® system) between BD and many of its distributors, which he described as "the first phase of a longer-range program." Phase one focused on electronic ordering and billing procedures. Suppliers of such systems claimed that vendors saved $.50 to $1.00 per purchase order line when the order was entered electronically versus by mail or phone. Phase two sought to replace increasingly time-consuming rebate mechanics with a net-billing approach (i.e., any rebates or volume-discounts already included in the billing on the basis of distributors notifying BD of product shipments). Bhimji noted:

> One impact is to minimize quarterly buy-ins (i.e., distributors buying higher volumes of a product that is being promoted in a given quarter and then stocking that product in various shipping locations). This will lower distributors' warehousing costs and working capital requirements, and improve their cash flow. It lowers our shipping costs and helps to smooth-out costly surges in our warehousing and manufacturing; it also lowers our administrative and order-transaction costs by providing a single order point for different divisions' products. And it enables the end customer to select a distributor of choice—i.e., one who, via this link, can lower the hospital's inventory levels and operating costs.

Speed-Com, by providing data on dealer inventory status and end-customer demand across product categories, also built the foundation for Phase 3, an automatic replenishment system among BD, distributor, and user-customer. The goal was to provide, based on dealer forecasts of end-user demand and inventory targets needed for reaching agreed-upon service levels, an "orderless" system that would replenish dealer inventory on a regularly scheduled basis. "Such a system can lower total

---

[1] Arthur Andersen & Co., *Stockless Materials Management* (Health Industry Distributors Association, 1989).

cost-in-use," noted Bhimji, "at equal or improved service levels for all the players involved. For distributors, it minimizes intermediate inventory levels, improves order-entry accuracy, and waives order-minimum requirements; for users, it means better, guaranteed levels of service at lower administrative costs; and for BD, it can mean the ability to use our increasingly automated manufacturing capabilities to respond quickly and economically to changes in demand patterns." He added that these initiatives were both "necessary infrastructure *and* motivation for multidivisional efforts."

Sales and Marketing Organization

By January 1990, the sales and marketing structure for multidivisional efforts had evolved to include managers at both the corporate and divisional levels. This structure, noted Battaglia, reflected both resource constraints and "a philosophy that the key account program will ultimately be driven by the divisions with coordination help from corporate."

At corporate headquarters, Noah Gresham was appointed corporate director of sales with responsibility for both national account and multidivisional key account efforts. Gresham had been in BD sales positions for nearly two decades. Reporting to Gresham were Phil Deelo, corporate national accounts manager Midwest (a new position created in September 1989), and John Gormally, director of corporate national accounts (a position Gormally assumed in November 1989).

Deelo's responsibilities were to assist divisions in developing multidivisional agreements and providing corporate support, when possible. He participated in key account profiling sessions, assisted on sales calls, and served as a liaison between divisional sales personnel and corporate sales management. He noted that "I've worked as an RSM in two BD divisions and I believe in decentralization: competitive positions differ, and good salespeople come in different shapes, sizes, and approaches. But I also believe in corporate sales efforts, because we often don't maximize our opportunities across divisions."

When Deelo's position was created, it was also decided to establish a new sales office in Chicago which, in addition to Deelo, would house the midwest RSMs from seven divisions: BDD, Acute Care, Deseret Medical Systems, Microbiology, BDVS, Labware, and Diagnostic Instrument Systems. Each RSM had previously been located in a separate divisional sales office. "The shared office," he explained, "makes busy field people think in multidivisional terms and deal with one another on a daily basis."

As director of corporate national accounts, Gormally worked with division NAMs that called on GPOs. Each division's vice president of sales set goals for his or her NAMs in terms of annual sales volumes, margins, and allowable incentives. Gormally had no authority over such decisions but did have some input via meetings with the NAMs and divisional sales management. Gormally also had direct responsibility for seven national accounts.

Gormally had worked in various sales positions for over 11 years in four different BD divisions. He noted:

[I]n my current position, my primary customers are the NAMs in various divisions, and that's as it should be: the account manager ultimately has real knowledge of what an account wants, not corporate. In my position, you 'win' when you get various NAMs to buy into decisions that affect cross-divisional positions at their accounts. My job is to keep this big-picture perspective in front of them and, when possible, coordinate efforts.

At the division level, multidivisional sales efforts focused on two positions: the lead regional sales manager (lead RSM), and the corporate national accounts field manager.

The lead RSM served as the central coordinator for multidivisional agreements. He or she organized the account-profile and account-planning sessions, led the effort toward successful implementation of the plan, and typically served as the primary account contact for matters concerning a multidivisional agreement. (See Exhibit 2.) A multidivisional agreement (or contract) was defined as a customized offering by two or more divisions to designated key accounts with an emphasis on value-added service programs rather than financial incentives (although the latter were not excluded from these agreements). Any financial incentives in a multidivisional agreement were to be funded pro-rata by the participating divisions and paid to the account by the division represented by the lead RSM. Pricing and terms for products were negotiated by the participating divisions.

The lead RSM might come from corporate, but was typically expected to be a divisional RSM and to perform multidivisional activities in addition to his or her ongoing sales management responsibilities. Gresham explained that the lead RSM was "typically the person from the division with the most to gain or the most to lose at a key account. That provides the incentive to assume the role and make the required efforts as team facilitator and coordinator with the account." This approach was

EXHIBIT 2
"Lead RSM" Role in Multidivisional Key Account Program

1. *Identification of Key Account*

    - A potential account is usually identified by a division or divisions that are under competitive pressure *or* see new business opportunities *or* we wish to solidify a strong position.
    - The lead RSM may come from the initiating division *or* may be the corporate national account field manager *or* the corporate national account manager—midwest region.
    - Lead RSM polls all appropriate divisions for level of interest.
    - Lead RSM review survey of responses and communicates "go or no go" decisions to all RSMs.

2. *Developing the Key Account Profile, Plan, and Proposal*

    - Lead RSM schedules an RSM team meeting.
    - Team completes key account profile, action plan, and preliminary proposal, including appropriate input from marketing.
    - Team members secure value-added offering and pricing approvals from their division management.
    - Corporate national accounts is consulted prior to finalizing the proposal. This requirement is satisfied if either the corporate national account field manager or corporate national account manager—midwest region is involved because they are expected to communicate routinely with corporate sales.

3. *Interfacing and Negotiating with Key Accounts*

    - Lead RSM sets up meeting between customer and selected team members.
    - Proposal is submitted to customer, discussed, and customized to meet the customer's needs.
    - An additional RSM meeting may be needed to address customer modifications.
    - The modified proposal, in the form of an agreement or contract, is submitted to the customer for signature by lead RSM.

4. *Managing Key Accounts after the Multidivisional Agreement Is Signed*

    - Schedule an implementation planning meeting with customer management and our participating divisions. Agree on contract implementation plan.
    - Each divisional RSM team member should submit divisional implementation plan to lead RSM.
    - Lead RSM to review contract progress quarterly with the customer.
    - Quarterly implementation status report sent to RSM team by lead RSM.

initiated at sales meetings in March 1989 where RSMs from different divisions were organized into teams to discuss and plan for multidivisional efforts. RSMs who participated in these sessions and subsequent efforts had a variety of opinions about the process:

The account-planning sessions are very important because they force people into thinking specifically about the role of our various contacts in an account, segmentation issues, and risk/opportunity assessments. Initially, each divisional RSM had its own divisional agenda primarily in mind. But continued meetings tend to promote a healthy give-and-take among RSMs.

* * * * *

Each session involves a full day and typically a two-month lead time to get a date on the schedules of four to six busy sales managers. Also, different divisions have different conceptions of marketing and sales, and some divisions seem to think that multidivisional marketing is great if *they* define the rules.

* * * * *

In our company, interdivisional communication was not perceived as important. Few RSMs had common past experiences on which to build, despite selling to many of the same accounts. Back at the division, moreover, the lead RSM can be perceived as an ambivalent figure. Especially when a product has a high share position with an account, there's a feeling in some divisions that the lead RSM may sacrifice too much for multidivisional efforts.

* * * * *

This new process creates expectations about working together and a system of informal debits and credits among RSMs. Still, in many accounts, I have spent years sweating for business in an increasingly tough marketplace. Now, somebody from another division, with less at stake than I have, has influence over my plans and contact with my account. You wonder if they're as committed as you are to making things happen at that account.

The lead RSM was eligible for a $200 cash award when he or she successfully signed a key account agreement. The incentive was increased to $250 for the second agreement, and $300 each for the third and any subsequent agreements. In addition, any sales or marketing managers that played an "active role" on the key-account team were eligible for a cash award of one-half that awarded to the lead RSM. The determination of "active participation" was made by the lead RSM, while the incentive awards were funded by corporate.

The position of corporate national accounts field manager (CNAFM) was created in October 1989 to formalize multidivisional responsibilities performed by certain senior sales executives in addition to their normal divisional sales activities. The initial appointees to this position were five RSMs and two NAMs from different divisions and geographical regions. They were expected to devote approximately 10 percent of their time to the CNAFM role, which included participation in key-account sales and marketing training programs and participating as lead RSM for at least one key account. Those appointed as CNAFMs were nominated by their respective divisional presidents, given a $1,500 salary increase, and were eligible for the incentives available to lead RSMs and key-account team members described above. Gresham noted that "externally, some customers simply want to deal with someone whose business card indicates that he or she is a corporate representative. This is especially important at the levels where multidivisional agreements get signed. Internally, the position is a way of developing a cadre of people who have this experience and formal responsibility for thinking about corporate objectives."

These sales positions were complemented by a number of marketing positions focused on multidivisional efforts. In 1989, Bette Weber was appointed corporate marketing manager, a new position whose responsibilities included working with divisional sales and marketing personnel on programs supporting key account activities; conducting training sessions intended to enhance divisional understanding of BD's key account programs; and providing corporate marketing analyses and support in specific account situations. Weber identified four "tiers" of buyers at accounts—CFO, materials management, purchasing, and end users—and noted that much of her work is aimed at "moving our presence up to CFO and materials management levels." She noted that both sales and marketing input were important in such efforts because "sales and marketing hear with different ears; each has ongoing access to information and experience not immediately visible to the other."

During the past year, Battaglia and others in the SCM group had spoken at a number of divisional sales meetings throughout BD. Exhibit 3 provides a graphic that SCM managers had found useful in general explanations of how the value-added services concept related to BD's various sales efforts and its ultimate offering to customers.

HEALTH MEDICAL CENTER

HMC was a leading teaching hospital in the southeastern United States. Most other health care providers in the area regarded HMC as an innovator in

EXHIBIT 3
Overview

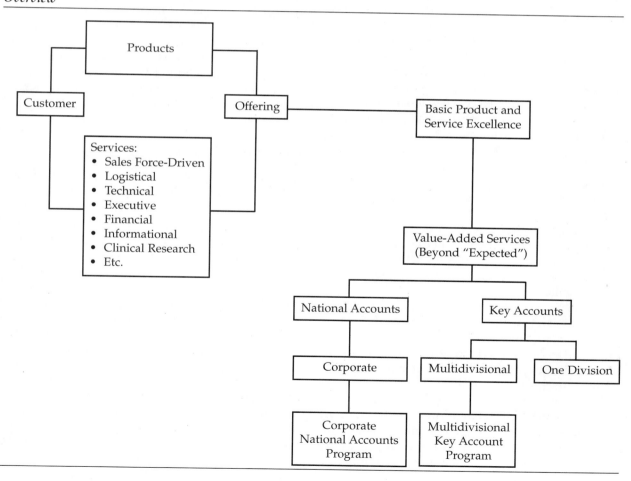

health care training, medical procedures, and use of medical devices. As a customer, HMC also had a reputation as a "renegade" institution: it was a member of two other GPOs in addition to APG, and continually shopped among these GPOs for the best price and terms in a product category. In 1989, HMC had begun purchasing BDD syringes and needles via the BDD-APG national account contract, after previously purchasing these products via an individual contract signed directly with BDD.

In addition to BDD, four other BD divisions sold significant amounts of product to HMC, through separate sales and distribution efforts and a variety of separate contracts. However, BDD had the most substantial presence in the account, with previous year's sales of $252,000, of which $216,000 was needles and syringes. Exhibit 4 provides a brief description of the five BD divisions that sold to HMC, their major product lines, primary contacts at hospitals, and contracting mechanisms with accounts such as HMC. Exhibit 5 outlines current BD product usage at HMC as well as estimates of potential sales volume represented by HMC in a product category. Exhibit 6 indicates the BD sales personnel responsible for HMC; consistent with BD's decentralized operations, there were five sales representatives (and five different sales management organizations) responsible for sales and service to HMC.

HMC was facing a severe budget deficit. State funding had been slashed, and HMC had instituted expense reduction measures, including the indefinite layoff of over 100 hospital personnel. Overall responsibility for expense reductions rested with Stan Delaney, vice president of financial services (see Exhibit 7), whose plan included $175,000 in expense reductions from materials management. He asked Phil Robinson (administrator of financial services) to implement this reduction with Judy Koski (director of materials management). Of the $175,000 required reduction, Robinson recommended that $100,000 come from medical supply costs. Koski agreed, and gave Joanne Wilson (purchasing manager) the responsibility for determining how to save $100,000 on medical supplies.

According to John Kmetz (the BDD sales rep at the HMC account), Wilson accepted the assignment with reservations:

> Wilson felt that Koski (her boss) underestimated the difficulty of saving this much money. Koski had never really gotten involved in any activities related to purchasing medical supplies, and Wilson was also somewhat peeved that she, as the purchasing expert, was not consulted earlier about this decision. Nevertheless, Wilson recognized the pressures being placed on Koski and, knowing that she had little choice, accepted the assignment without mentioning her doubts.

Wilson first analyzed the hospital's usage rates and costs for its top ten supply products. To do this, she solicited the help of Ted Barber, general manager of City Surgical, HMC's largest distributor, which supplied 80 percent of its medical supplies. Barber had previously been HMC's director of purchasing, and Wilson had reported to him. According to the BDD salesperson, City Surgical had "a very strong lock" on the supplies business at HMC.

Competitor's Response

In conducting her analysis, Wilson noted that syringes and needles were the second-largest medical supply expense item at HMC. Not long before, moreover, she had been visited by a Terumo salesperson (along with a distributor sales rep from one of City Surgical's local competitors), who encouraged her to evaluate Terumo's new hypodermics line. HMC had used Terumo's IV catheters, blood collection needles, and arterial blood gas kits for a number of years. At the time, however, Wilson was not ready to undergo the end user turmoil required for a hypodermics product evaluation. Such a process typically took three to four months and involved testing at nursing stations, the filling out of numerous forms by various hospital personnel, and meetings among the hospital committees involved in a major evaluation. But given her recent expense-reduction task, she decided an evaluation might now be warranted.

EXHIBIT 4
Description of Five BD Operating Divisions

Division	Major Products	Primary End Users	Primary Decision Influencers	Distribution System	Contracting Mechanism	# Sales Reps
BDAC	• Blades • Surgeons' gloves • Scrubs • Preps • Suction	• Scrub nurses • Surgeons • Circulating nurses	• Purchasing groups • Purchasing managers • OR supervisor	• Broad (except for Beaver line)	• Direct sell, contract with customer	98
BDD	• Hypodermic syringes/needles • Insulin syringes • Disposal products • Exam gloves • Thermometers	• Nurses • Doctors • Pharmacists	• Purchasing groups • Purchasing managers • Evaluating committees • Distributors (nonhospital)	• Very broad	• Hospital—direct sell, contract (Z)	100
BDMS	• Prepared plated media • Dried culture media • Manual sensitivity disks • Anaerobic systems • Rapid manual tests	• Microbiologists	• Microbiology dept. • Pathologists • Purchasing groups (limited)	• Select	• Direct sell, contract (Z)	75
BDVS	• B.C. tubes • B.C. needles • SST tubes	• Hospital labs • Commercial labs	• Purchasing groups • Lab managers • Department supervisors • Phlebotomists	• Broad/focused	• Direct sell, contract (Z)	54
DM	• IV catheters	• Nurses	• Purchasing groups • Head critical care nurse • Anesthesiologist • IV therapist	• Broad	• Direct sell, contract (not Z)	72

BDAC = *Becton Dickinson Acute Care Division*
BDD   = *Becton Dickinson Division*
BDMS = *Becton Dickinson Microbiology Systems*
BDVS = *Becton Dickinson VACUTAINER Systems*
DM   = *Deseret Medical Division*

EXHIBIT 5
Health Medical Center—Becton Dickinson Product Usage

Division	Product	BD Product Used in Medical Center?	Annualized Current or Potential $ Sales (000)
Becton Dickinson Acute Care	• Arterial Blood Gas Syringes/Kits	No	$31
	• BARD-PARKER Surgical Blades/Scalpels	Yes	17
	• E-Z SCRUBS	No	50
	• EUDERMIC and SPECTRA Surgeons' Gloves	Yes	40
	• Suction Canisters	No	40
	• Suction Catheters and Kits	No	34
Becton Dickinson Division	• BD Brand Fever Thermometers	Yes	$22
	• BD Brand Pharmacy Products	Yes	7
	• BD Brand Syringes and Needles	Yes	216
	• BD Brand Technique Needles	Yes	7
	• TRU-TOUCH Vinyl Examination Gloves	No	40
Becton Dickinson Microbiology Systems	• Prepared Plated Media	Yes	$53
Becton Dickinson VACUTAINER Systems	• MICROTAINER Brand Microcollection Tubes	Yes	$ 5
	• SST Brand Serum Separation Tubes	Yes	4
	• VACUTAINER Brand Blood Collection Needles	No	11
	• VACUTAINER Brand Blood Collection Tubes	Yes	21
Deseret Medical	• ANGIOCATH IV Catheter	Yes	$40
	• E-Z Sets	No	15
	• Epidural Tray	No	30
	• INSYTE IV Catheter	No	45
	• PRN	No	15

In considering an evaluation, Wilson first asked Barber if City Surgical could supply Terumo syringes and needles to HMC. Barber said he could. Kmetz noted that:

City Surgical is a Terumo distributor. However, City Surgical is also part of BDD's Advantage Distributor Program, where it's eligible for financial incentives if it surpasses previous year's unit sales of BDD's products and agrees not to "actively" convert a BDD account to a different brand. Also, Terumo's hypodermics line was introduced to Wilson via a competing distributor. So, my perception is that Barber was definitely interested in the prospect of supplying their line, but was cautious in voicing support of Terumo at the account.

Barber then arranged a meeting among Wilson, himself, and Terumo personnel. Along with Terumo's local sales rep, Terumo's northeastern sales manager and national sales director flew in to attend. At the meeting, Terumo personnel demonstrated the "special" features of Terumo's new syringe, but Wilson noted that she had seen similar features on samples of BDD's new syringe. When the discussion turned to price, Terumo guaranteed a 15 percent discount off HMC's current pricing for BDD hypodermics. (Terumo managers knew that HMC purchased these products off the APG contract, and set their prices 15 percent below the contract price. At current volumes, this meant a $32,000 savings in hypodermics expenses for

EXHIBIT 6
Divisional BD Sales Structure Responsible for Health Medical Center

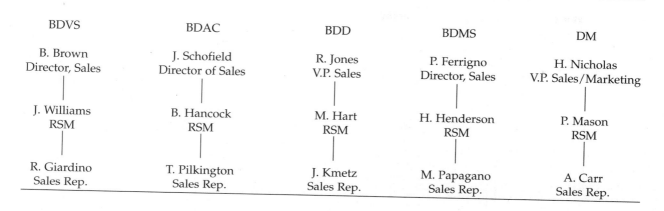

BDVS	BDAC	BDD	BDMS	DM
B. Brown Director, Sales	J. Schofield Director of Sales	R. Jones V.P. Sales	P. Ferrigno Director, Sales	H. Nicholas V.P. Sales/Marketing
J. Williams RSM	B. Hancock RSM	M. Hart RSM	H. Henderson RSM	P. Mason RSM
R. Giardino Sales Rep.	T. Pilkington Sales Rep.	J. Kmetz Sales Rep.	M. Papagano Sales Rep.	A. Carr Sales Rep.

HMC.) The meeting ended with Terumo personnel inviting Wilson to tour Terumo's new U.S. manufacturing plant. Wilson declined, but expressed her pleasure at the invitation and their "attentive recognition of HMC's importance and current financial difficulties."

Wilson agreed to set up a Terumo hypodermics evaluation at HMC. She knew that, if successful, a switch would mean that she had attained one-third of her expense-reduction goal. She also knew that BDD hypodermics commanded strong loyalty among end users at HMC, and that conversion to a new brand would be a major undertaking. But she felt that, given the hospital's financial situation, purchasing had more power to implement this type of change.

Wilson's next action was to present Terumo's hypodermics line to HMC's evaluation committee (composed of managers from different administrative and clinical departments) in order to determine which departments would conduct the evaluation. It was decided that anesthesiology, pediatrics, and pharmacy would participate.

BDD Response

When the evaluation was initiated, Kmetz detailed for Wilson BDD's product line breadth, in-service support, and unblemished record of high product quality in hypodermics. However, Wilson explained her expense-reduction goals and indicated that HMC would convert to Terumo if the evaluation were successful. But Wilson did agree to give Kmetz access to the evaluating departments and to give BDD an opportunity to retain the hypodermics business if equal cost savings could be offered.

During the final stages of the evaluation process, Kmetz intensified his efforts to retain the business. He demonstrated that Terumo could not supply all the needle and syringe items offered by BDD, and that buying these items off the APG contract would increase HMC's costs by $7,000 (thus reducing the purported cost savings to $25,000). Kmetz also explained BDD's inability to undercut the APG contract. Wilson said she understood the situation, but stated that only an equivalent price discount would suffice, and repeated her plans to complete the evaluation and convert to Terumo's line if necessary.

By January 1990, the evaluation was completed: HMC's evaluation committee approved Terumo for use and then turned the decision over to the standards committee which, after a review of the product, also approved Terumo's hypodermics line for use at HMC.

EXHIBIT 7
Health Medical Center Organizational Chart

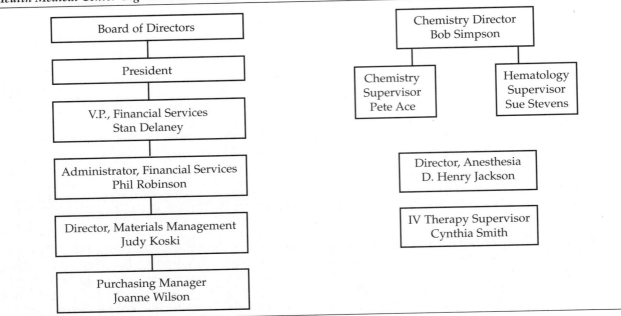

Kmetz then consulted with Ed Haire (BDD's director of contract sales) and Wally Joyce (the BDD district manager to whom Kmetz reported). Both emphasized the dangers and potential consequences of undermining a contract with a large GPO, but also felt that HMC was too important an account to lose, especially at a time when Terumo was aggressively seeking sales for its new hypodermics line at prestigious teaching institutions. Kmetz noted that, "I see an opportunity to save this account: we have a good relationship there with end users, and it may be possible to retain the business with a 10 percent price reduction."

Current Situation

After speaking with Flaherty (president of BDD), Jones (BDD's vice president of sales) contacted Kmetz and Joyce about the possibility of a multidivisional approach to the HMC situation. He explained that HMC could become a key account and that interdivisional programs and services could provide cost savings equivalent to, or more than, that represented by Terumo's lower price, while maintaining BDD's pricing on its APG contract and perhaps solidifying its position with purchasing influences at levels higher than Wilson. He found that both Kmetz and Joyce were concerned about what they termed this "change in direction." "Wilson expects a formal proposal from us in 10 days," noted one. "This account has clearly expressed its desire for a straight discount," said the other, "and we risk any chance of saving the business by introducing a new, unproven approach in such a tight time period."

Concurrently, Jones and Marty Hart (BDD's RSM in the southeastern region) contacted relevant personnel at the other BD divisions involved at HMC. The following summarizes the reactions and information they received from those divisions:

BD's *Acute Care* division (BDAC) had a strong field relationship with Wilson and others in purchasing.

Their primary products at the account were surgical blades/scalpels and surgeons' gloves. This represented two of BDAC's eight major product lines, and thus the potential existed for significant sales increases at HMC. David Pulsifer, BDAC's president, also indicated that he had long known Barber (City Surgical's president) and agreed to call Barber in order to clarify the distributor's position. After a phone conversation, Pulsifer reported that Barber said, "I've done business with BD for years and would prefer to keep them as the primary hypodermics supplier to HMC. But I've also got to protect myself if that account decides to switch to another brand." Pulsifer expressed his division's willingness to participate in a multidivisional effort at HMC.

Deseret Medical (DM) division had been acquired by BD in 1986. Pam Mason, Deseret RSM, explained that the division only had the IV catheter business in the anesthesia department at HMC. "We have a good relationship with key anesthesia personnel, including the department director," Ms. Mason noted. "But we do not have a strong overall presence in the account and my field rep reports that at least one important decision influencer there—the IV therapy supervisor—has been difficult to deal with."

Mason also explained that, six months earlier, she had tried to get HMC to adopt Deseret's new Insyte catheter product, which was proprietary and had features that significantly reduced usage complications in many applications. HMC had evaluated Insyte and found it acceptable in all areas except neonatal and pediatrics, where end users preferred current products. "Without usage in these key departments," she noted, "Deseret can't demonstrate a significant cost savings to HMC. In addition, this account currently doesn't measure certain usage costs where Insyte is particularly cost effective." Mason stated that she welcomed the opportunity to work on a multidivisional agreement with HMC, "especially if it contains incentives helpful in placing this new product there."

BD VACUTAINER Systems (BDVS) sold blood collection tubes and needles. Jeff Williams, BDVS's RSM, explained that this division had long had "a solid, well-entrenched position at HMC with tubes, but we don't service their blood-collection needle business. Our relations with key lab personnel are very strong, and purchasing has historically had little involvement with blood-collection products. In fact, our divisional sales strategy is to solidify end user brand preference for BDVS products and keep purchasing out of this process." Williams expressed the concern that a multidivisional effort at HMC would increase purchasing's involvement in blood-collection buying decisions, and said his position was "noncommittal" with respect to BDVS involvement in such an approach.

BD's *Microbiology Division* (BDMS) sold products used by various hospital and commercial labs to diagnose infectious diseases and determine proper therapy. Harry Henderson, an RSM at BDMS, noted that the division had a strong position at HMC for one of its major product lines, prepared plate media. He further noted that, in recent years, BDMS had been able to raise its prices on these products with little impact on sales volumes or buyer resistance:

> First, we have an outstanding product whose quality is widely recognized; second, our salespeople deal exclusively with end users who view product quality as the paramount issue in this medical application. This is especially true at a research and teaching institution like HMC. By contrast, most other BD divisions must work, at least in part, with purchasing personnel for whom price is a priority.

In light of these differences, Henderson reported that BDMS was "concerned" about a multidivisional program at HMC.

Jones and Hart also spoke with sales and marketing personnel in other divisions, and found a variety of opinions. A district manager commented: "HMC is not worth the time and effort of an interdivisional approach. They have historically shopped among buying groups and vendors; they're interested in price, not service." A sales representative said: "I'm concerned about which distributor gets the benefit of any multidivisional agreement we might reach. City Surgical hasn't been important, or particularly supportive, for sales of my product line. There are other distributors to HMC that I'd want to see rewarded by any multidivisional approach."

An RSM (who was not involved with the HMC account) described the proposed approach as "a too-little-too-late attempt to rescue BDD from a tough situation." Another RSM noted that "for years, I've worked to solidify our division's position at that account. Then, with a multidivisional approach, people from other divisions are formatting my plans and programs. Those RSMs don't know much about my previous efforts, and I'm uncomfortable when other people are dealing with my contacts and customers."

A product manager from one division involved with HMC strongly supported a multidivisional approach: "There are many opportunities there for cross-divisional services, especially in logistics, order entry, and waste disposal." At corporate headquarters, Gresham expressed his willingness to become actively involved at corporate and divisional levels to help secure needed resources and support. Similarly, Deelo, while not responsible for accounts in the southeastern region, also volunteered to help where appropriate and to provide information concerning previous multidivisional agreements that might be useful in thinking about the HMC situation.

After these meetings, Jones requested Kmetz to contact HMC in order to gauge possible receptiveness to a multidivisional proposal that would emphasize a product and service package intended to deliver cost savings in excess of those represented by Terumo's hypodermics discount. Kmetz then spoke with Wilson and reported that "Joanne seemed apathetic about the possibility, but did not reject the idea outright. She reiterated her request for a price equivalent to Terumo's offer, and said she still expected a BD proposal by the following week."

Conclusion

Jones spoke again with Flaherty. Both agreed to set up a day's meeting with personnel from the various divisions involved with the HMC account. Attendees would include the five division presidents, sales directors, relevant RSMs and sales reps, as well as Gresham and Deelo. "Bob," said Flaherty to Jones,

> I'd like to use that meeting as a way to fashion a multidivisional proposal for HMC, and I'd like you to think about what's involved in getting required support from other divisions. As far as expenses are concerned, I'm happy to have BDD act as the lead division and accept the incremental expenses in this situation. However, if you think that a multidivisional approach is not feasible in this situation, and that BDD's best bet is a price response, then let me know that as well.

Mr. Jax Fashion Inc.

It was 6:30 A.M., Monday, January 16, 1989; dawn had not yet broken on the Vancouver skyline and Louis Eisman, President of Mr. Jax Fashion Inc., was sitting at his desk pondering opportunities for future growth. Growth had been an important objective for Eisman and the other principal shareholder, Joseph Segal. Initially, the company had focused on the professional/career women's dresses, suits, and coordinates market, but by 1986 it had virtually saturated its ability to grow in this Canadian market segment. Growth was then sought through the acquisition of four companies: a woolen textile mill and three apparel manufacturing companies. The result of this decade-long growth was that the company had become the sixth-largest apparel manufacturer in Canada.

In the future, Eisman felt continued growth would require a modified approach. A particularly good growth option appeared to be expansion into the U.S. market. The window for U.S. growth seemed very favorable for Mr. Jax over the next several years. Good growth was forecast in the women's career/professional market, Mr. Jax's principal market segment, and the recently ratified Free Trade Agreement (FTA) would provide an excellent low tariff environment for expansion into the U.S. Yet, Eisman wanted to ensure that the appropriate growth strategy was selected because he was certain that, if the right approach were taken, Mr. Jax could be a major international apparel company by the end of the next decade.

THE INDUSTRY

The apparel industry was divided into a variety of market segments based upon gender, type of garment, and price points. Based on price points, the women's segments ranged from low-priced unex-ceptional to runway fashion segments. Low-priced segments competed on a low-cost manufacturing capability, while the higher-quality segments competed on design and marketing capabilities. In fact, companies in the higher-priced segments often subcontracted out manufacturing because it required a different skill base.

The professional/career women's segment ranged from the medium to medium-high price points. During the late 1970s and early 1980s, this segment had experienced strong growth due to the demographic growth in career-oriented, professional women. In the U.S., it had grown by 50 percent annually during the first half of the 1980s, but had slowed to about 20 percent in 1988, and experts predicted that by the mid-1990s growth would drop to the rate of GNP growth. The U.S. professional/career women's segment was estimated to be $2 billion in 1988. The Canadian market was estimated to be one-tenth this size and growth was expected to emulate that in the U.S. market. Yet, the exact timing of the slowing of growth was difficult to predict because of the extreme cyclicality in the fashion industry.

Competition

Some of the more prominent Canada-based companies competing in the professional/career women's segment included:

- *Jones New York of Canada*, a marketing subsidiary of a U.S.-based fashion company, was thought to share the leadership position with Mr. Jax in the Canadian professional/career women's market. The company focused exclusively on marketing clothes to this market segment. Manufacturing was contracted out to Asian companies.

This case was written by Professors C. Patrick Woodcock and J. Michael Geringer, with the assistance of Professor H. Crookell as a basis for class discussion only. Some of the data and figures presented represent estimations by the authors rather than by management or the company. Figures are in Canadian dollars unless otherwise stated. Copyright © 1989 by The University of Western Ontario.

- *The Monaco Group* had become a major Canadian designer and retailer of men's and women's fashions during the 1980s. By 1988, the company had sales of $21 million and a rate of return on capital of over 20 percent. It designed its own fashion lines and merchandised them through its own retail outlets as well as major department stores. Manufacturing was contracted to Asian companies. Recently, the company had been purchased by Dylex Inc., a large Canada-based retail conglomerate with 2,000 retail apparel stores located in both Canada and the U.S.

- *Nygard International Ltd.*, with revenues of over $200 million, was Canada's largest apparel manufacturer. Approximately one-third of its sales and production were located in the U.S. This company had historically focused on lower-priced clothing, but it had hired away Mr. Jax's former designer to create the Peter Nygard Signature Collection, a fashion line aimed at the professional/career women's market. This new line had been out for only six months and sales were rumored to be moderate.

Additional competition in this Canadian segment included a wide variety of U.S. and European imports. These companies generally manufactured garments in Asia and marketed them in Canada through independent Canadian sales agents. Historically, most had concentrated their marketing resources on the rapidly growing U.S. market, yet many had captured a significant share of the Canadian market based upon strong international brand recognition.

Prominent U.S.-based competition included the following companies:

- *Liz Claiborne* was the originator of the professional/career women's fashion look. This company, started in 1976, grew tremendously during the late 1970s and early 1980s, and by 1988 it had sales in excess of $1.2 billion (U.S.). Claiborne generally competed on price and brand recognition, a strategy copied by many of the larger companies in this segment. To keep prices low, Claiborne contracted out manufacturing to low-cost manufacturers, 85 percent of which were Asian. The company's large size allowed it to wield considerable influence over these manufacturing relationships. Recently, the company had diversified into retailing.

- *J.H. Collectibles*, a Milwaukee-based company, had one of the more unique strategies in this segment. It produced slightly upscale products emphasizing quality and delivery. It owned manufacturing facilities in Wisconsin and Missouri and had sales of $200 million (U.S.).

- *Jones of New York*, the parent company of Jones New York of Canada, was a major competitor in the U.S. market. In fact, the majority of its $200 million (U.S.) in sales was derived from this market.

- *Evan-Picone* was a U.S.-based apparel designer and marketer that had become very successful in the slightly older professional/career women's market. This company also contracted out its manufacturing function and had annual sales in excess of $200 million (U.S.).

In addition, there were a myriad of other apparel designers, marketers, and manufacturers competing in this segment. They included such companies as Christian Dior, Kasper, Pendleton, Carole Little, Susan Bristol, J.G. Hooke, Ellen Tracy, Anne Klein II, Perry Ellis, Adrienne Vittadini, Tahari, Harv, Bernard, Norma Kamali, Philippe Adec, Gianni Sport, Regina Porter, and Herman Geist.

Profitability in this segment had been excellent. Liz Claiborne led profitability in the apparel industry with a 5-year average return on equity of 56 percent and a 12-month return of 45 percent. J.H. Collectibles had averaged over 40 percent return on equity during the last 5 years. This compared to an average return on equity in the overall apparel industry of 12.5 percent in the U.S. and 16 percent in Canada during the past five years.

Distribution

The selection and maintenance of retail distribution channels had become a very important consideration for apparel manufacturers in the 1980s. The retail industry had gone through a particularly bad year in 1988, although the professional/career women's segment had been relatively profitable. Overall demand had declined and retail analysts were predicting revenue increases of only 1–2 percent in 1989, which paled beside the 6–7 percent growth experienced in the mid-1980s. The consensus was that high interest rates and inflation as well as somewhat stagnant demand levels were suppressing overall profitability in this industry. In addition, the industry appeared to be moving into a period of consolidation, resulting in a shift in power from the designers to the retailers.

To counter the retailers' increasing power, some apparel designers had been vertically integrating into retailing. The attractiveness of this option was based on controlling the downstream distribution channel activities and thus enabling an apparel company to aggressively pursue increased market share. The principal components for success in the retail apparel industry were location, brand awareness, and superior purchasing skills. The apparel companies that had integrated successfully into retailing were the more market-oriented firms such as Benetton and Esprit.

The Free Trade Agreement

Historically, developed nations had protected their textile and clothing industries through the imposition of relatively high tariffs and import quotas. Tariffs for apparel imported into Canada averaged 24.5 percent and 22.5 percent into the U.S. while tariffs for worsted woolen fabrics, one of the principal ingredients for Mr. Jax's products, were 22.5 percent into Canada and 40 percent into the U.S. Import quotas were used to further limit the ability of developing country manufacturers to import into either country. Despite these obstacles, Canadian apparel imports had grown from 20 percent to 30 percent of total shipments during the 1980s, most of which came from developing countries. Shipments from the U.S. represented an estimated $200 million in 1988, while Canadian manufacturers exported approximately $70 million to the U.S.

The Free Trade Agreement (FTA) would alter trade restrictions in North America considerably. Over the next 10 years, all clothing and textile tariffs would be eliminated between Canada and the U.S., but stringent "rules of origin" would apply. To qualify, goods not only had to be manufactured in North America, but they also had to utilize raw materials (i.e., yarn, in the case of textiles, and fabric, in the case of apparel) manufactured in North America. Unfortunately, these "rules of origin" favored U.S. apparel manufacturers as 85 percent of the textiles they used were sourced in the U.S., while Canadian manufacturers utilized mostly imported textiles. To ameliorate this disadvantage, a clause was appended to the agreement that allowed Canadians to export $500 million worth of apparel annually into the U.S., which was exempt from the "rules of origin" but would have a 50 percent Canadian value-added content. There was much speculation as to how this exemption would be allocated in approximately five years when demand was projected to exceed the exemption limit. Experts expected that companies that successfully demonstrated the competitive ability to export into the U.S. would have first rights to these exceptions.

Many industry experts had contemplated the consequences of the FTA and there was some agreement that in the short-term the FTA would most severely impact the lower-priced apparel segments in Canada because of the economies of scale that existed in the U.S. market (i.e., the average U.S. apparel manufacturer was 10 times larger than its Canadian counterpart). Yet, long-term prospects for all segments were restrained because most experts agreed that the industry was slowly being pressured by the Canadian government to become internationally competitive. The question was when international negotiations would eliminate more of the protection afforded to the industry. It was with this concern that Eisman had been continuously pushing the company to become a major international fashion designer and manufacturer.

Overall, Eisman considered the FTA a mixed blessing. Competition in Canada would increase moderately over time, but he felt that the lower tariff rates and the company's high-quality, in-house woolen mill presented a wonderful competitive advantage and opportunity for potential expansion into the U.S. market.

MR. JAX FASHIONS

In 1979, a venture capital company owned by Joseph Segal acquired a sleepy Vancouver-based apparel manufacturer having $3 million in sales, 70 percent of which was in men's wear. Segal immediately recruited Mr. Louis Eisman, a well-known women's fashion executive, who proceeded to drop the men's clothing line and aggressively refocus the company on the career/professional women's market segment.

Eisman appreciated the importance of design and for the first three years he designed all of the new fashion lines. In 1982, he recruited an up-and-coming young Canadian fashion designer, yet he continued to influence the direction of designs considerably. He traveled to Europe for approximately two months annually to review European fashion design trends and procure quality fabrics appropriate for the upcoming fashion season. He personally reviewed all designs. The combined women's fashion knowledge and designing abilities provided Mr. Jax with a high-quality, classically designed product that differentiated it from most other Canadian competition. In 1989, the designer resigned and Eisman recruited a New York-based fashion designer, Ron Leal. Leal had excellent design experience in several large U.S.-based design houses and, unlike the previous designer, he brought considerable U.S. market experience and presence.

Eisman's energy and drive were also critical in establishing the merchandising and distribution network. He personally developed relationships with many of the major retailers. He hired and developed sales agents, in-house sales staff, and in 1983, recruited Jackie Clabon who subsequently became VP-Marketing and Sales. The sales staff were considered to be some of the best in the industry. Clabon's extensive Canadian sales and merchandising experience combined with Eisman's design and marketing strength provided Mr. Jax with considerable managerial depth in these critical activities.

Initially, acceptance by Eastern fashion buyers was cool. The fashion "establishment" was highly skeptical of this Vancouver-based apparel designer and manufacturer. Thus, Eisman focused on smaller independent retail stores, which were more easily swayed in their purchasing decisions; as Mr. Jax gained a reputation for high-quality, classical design, and excellent service, larger retail chains started to place orders. By 1988, Mr. Jax's products were sold in over 400 department and specialty stores across Canada. Major customers included The Bay, Eaton's, Holt Renfrew, and Simpson's and, although initial marketing efforts were aimed at the smaller retailer, the majority of Mr. Jax's sales were now to the larger retail chains. The apparel lines were sold through a combination of sales agents and in-house salespersons. Ontario and Quebec accounted for 72 percent of its sales. In addition, two retail stores had recently been established in Vancouver and Seattle; the Vancouver store was very profitable but the Seattle store was very unprofitable.

Many industry experts felt that Mr. Jax's product line success could be attributed directly to Eisman. He was known for his energy and brashness, as well as his creativity and knowledge of the women's fashion market. In his prior merchandising and marketing experience, he had developed an intuitive skill for the capricious women's apparel market. This industry was often considered to be one of instinct rather than rationality. Eisman was particularly good at design, merchandising, and marketing. He worked very closely with these departments, often getting involved in the smallest details. As Eisman said, "It is the details that make the difference in our business." Although Eisman concentrated a great deal of his effort and time on these functions, he also attempted to provide guidance to production. The production function had been important in providing the service advantage

Mr. Jax held over imports. By 1988, Mr. Jax's professional/career women's fashion lines accounted for $25 million in revenues and $3 million in net income (see Exhibit 1).

Diversification through Acquisitions

In 1986, Segal and Eisman took Mr. Jax public, raising in excess of $17 million although they both retained one-third equity ownership. The newly raised capital was used to diversify growth through the acquisition of four semi-related companies.

In 1986, Surrey Classics Manufacturing Ltd., a family owned Vancouver-based firm, was purchased for $2 million. This company was principally a manufacturer of lower-priced women's apparel and coats. The acquisition was initially made with the objective of keeping the company an autonomous unit. However, the previous owner and his management team adapted poorly to their subordinated position within the Mr. Jax organization and, upon expiration of their non-competition clauses, they resigned and started a competing company. Unfortunately, sales began to decline rapidly because of this new competition and the absence of managerial talent. To stem the losses, a variety of designers was hired under contract. However, Surrey's poor cash flow could not support the required promotional campaigns and the new fashion lines fared poorly, resulting in mounting operating losses.

In late 1988, Eisman reassigned Mr. Jax's VP-Finance as interim manager of Surrey Classics. As Eisman stated, "The company needed a manager who knew the financial priorities in the industry and could maximize the effectiveness of the company's productive capacity." Several administrative functions were transferred to Mr. Jax, including design, pattern making, sizing, and scaling operations. Marketing and production continued to be independent operations housed in a leased facility just outside of Vancouver. Surrey Classics now produced a diversified product line that included Highland Queen, a licensed older women's line of

woolen apparel, and Jaki Petite, a Mr. Jax fashion line patterned for smaller women. During this turn-around, Eisman himself provided the required industry-specific management skills, which demanded a considerable amount of his time and attention. Presently, Eisman kept in daily contact and was involved in most major decisions. During this time Surrey's revenues had declined from $12 million in 1986 to $10.8 million in 1988 and net income had dropped from $100 thousand in 1986 to a loss of approximately $2 million in 1988. Eisman felt that in the next two years Surrey's operations would need to be rationalized into Mr. Jax's to save on overhead costs.

West Coast Woolen Mills Ltd. was a 40-year-old family-owned and Vancouver-based worsted woolen mill. Mr. Jax acquired the company for $2.2 million in 1987. Eisman was able to retain most of the previous management, all of whom had skills quite unique to the industry. West Coast marketed fabric to customers across Canada. In 1986, its sales were $5 million, profits were nil, and its estimated capacity was $10 million annually. The company was the smallest of three worsted woolen mills in Canada, and in the U.S. there were about 18 worsted woolen manufacturers, several of which involved divisions of some of the largest textile manufacturing companies in the world.

Both Mr. Jax and West Coast had mutually benefited from this acquisition. The affiliation allowed Mr. Jax to obtain control of fabric production scheduling, design, and quality. In particular, Mr. Jax had been able to significantly reduce order lead times for fabric produced at this subsidiary, although the effects of this on West Coast had not been studied. West Coast benefited from increased capital funding, which had allowed it to invest in new equipment and technology, both important attributes in such a capital-intensive industry. These investments supported the company's long-term strategic objective of becoming the highest quality, most design-conscious worsted woolen mill in North America. This objective had already been reached in Canada.

EXHIBIT 1
Mr. Jax Fashion Inc.

Income Statement (000's)

Year	1981	1982	1983	1984	1985	1986	1987 (9 months)	1988
Sales	4,592	4,315	5,472	7,666	13,018	24,705	53,391	72,027
Cost of sales	2,875	2,803	3,404	4,797	7,885	14,667	38,165	49,558
Gross profit	1,717	1,512	2,068	2,869	5,133	10,038	15,226	22,469
Selling & gen. admin.	1,172	1,117	1,458	1,898	2,434	4,530	9,071	18,175
Income from operations	545	395	610	971	2,699	5,508	6,155	4,294
Other income	22	25	25	10	16	564	418	117
Loss from discontinued operation								(554)
Income before taxes	567	420	635	981	2,715	6,072	6,573	3,857
Income Taxes								
Current	150	194	285	432	1,251	2,874	2,746	1,825
Deferred	47	2	(5)	28	24	57	245	(195)
Net income	370	224	355	521	1,440	3,141	3,582	2,227
Share price range						$7.5–$11	$8–$18	$7.5–$14

Balance Sheet (000's)

Year	1981	1982	1983	1984	1985	1986	1987	1988
Current Assets								
Short-term investments	—	—	—	—	—	5,027	1,794	495
Accounts receivable	709	874	961	1,697	2,974	6,430	16,133	14,923
Inventories	464	474	684	736	1,431	3,026	15,431	16,914
Prepaid expenses	11	15	20	22	201	398	404	293
Income taxes recoverable	—	—	—	—	—	—	—	1,074
Prop., plant & equip.	318	349	424	572	795	4,042	7,789	13,645
Other assets	—	—	—	—	—	273	526	513
Total assets	1,502	1,712	2,089	3,027	5,401	22,196	42,077	47,857
Current Liabilities								
Bank indebtedness	129	356	114	351	579	575	1,788	4,729
Accounts payable	490	435	678	963	1,494	3,100	4,893	6,934
Income taxes payable	126	58	86	153	809	1,047	546	
Deferred taxes	84	86	81	109	133	217	462	267
Shareholder Equity								
Share equity	127	7	13	5	4	12,252	26,577	26,577
Retained earnings	546	770	1,125	1,446	2,347	5,005	7,811	9,350
Total liabilities	1,502	1,712	2,097	3,027	5,401	22,196	42,077	47,857

Note: In 1987, the accounting year end was changed from February 1988 to November 1987. This made the 1987 accounting year nine months in duration.

Years 1981 to 1984 were estimated from Change in Financial Position Statements.

Mr. Jax was presently fulfilling 30 to 40 percent of its textile demands through West Coast. The remainder was being sourced in Europe. By 1988, West Coast's revenues were $6.5 million and profitability was at the break-even point.

In 1987, Mr. Jax acquired Olympic Pant and Sportswear Co. Ltd. and Canadian Sportswear Co. Ltd., both privately owned companies, for $18.3 million. The former management, excluding owners, was retained in both of these Winnipeg-based companies.

Olympic manufactured lower-priced men's and boys pants and outerwear as well as some women's sportswear. Canadian Sportswear manufactured low-priced women's and girls outerwear and coats. Canadian Sportswear was also a certified apparel supplier to the Canadian Armed Forces and, although these types of sales made up a minority of its revenue base, such a certification provided the company with a small but protected market niche. The disparity in target markets and locations between these companies and Mr. Jax dictated that they operate largely independently. The expected synergies were limited to a few corporate administrative functions such as finance and systems management.

Combined revenues for these companies had declined from $35 million in 1986 to $30 million in 1988. Both of these companies had remained profitable during this period, although profits had declined. In 1988, combined net income was $1.2 million. Management blamed declining revenues on increased competition and a shortage of management because of the previous owner's retirement.

The Corporation's Present Situation

Diversification had provided the company with excellent growth, but it had also created problems. The most serious was the lack of management control over the now-diversified structure (Exhibit 2). By 1988, it had become quite clear that without the entrepreneurial control and drive of the previous owners, the companies were not as competitive as they had been prior to their acquisition. Therefore, in late 1988, Eisman recruited a new CFO, Judith Madill, to coordinate a corporate control consolidation program. Madill had extensive accounting and corporate reorganization experience, but had limited operating experience in an entrepreneurial environment such as the fashion industry. Madill suggested that corporate personnel, financial, and systems management departments be established to integrate and aid in the management of the subsidiaries. Eisman was not completely convinced this was the right approach. He had always maintained that one of Mr. Jax's competitive strengths was its flexibility and rapid response time. He thought that increased administrative overhead would restrict this entrepreneurial characteristic in the company and that extra costs would severely restrict future expansion opportunities. Thus, he had limited the overhead expansion to two industrial accountants for the next year.

Consolidation was also occurring in the existing organization. Eisman was presently trying to recruit a vice president of production. Mr. Jax had never officially had such a position and, unfortunately, recruiting a suitable candidate was proving to be difficult. The problem was that there were relatively few experienced apparel manufacturing executives in North America. Furthermore, Vancouver was not an attractive place for fashion executives because it, not being a fashion center, would isolate them from future employment opportunities, and higher salaries as well as lower taxes tended to keep them in the U.S. Yet, a manager of production was badly needed to coordinate the internal production consolidation program. Originally, production had been located in an old 22,000 square foot facility. By 1986, it had grown to 48,000 square feet located in four buildings throughout Vancouver. Production flow encompassed the typical apparel industry operational tasks (see Exhibit 3). However, the division of tasks between buildings made production planning and scheduling very difficult. Production problems slowly accumulated between 1986 and 1988. The

EXHIBIT 2
Mr. Jax Organizational Chart

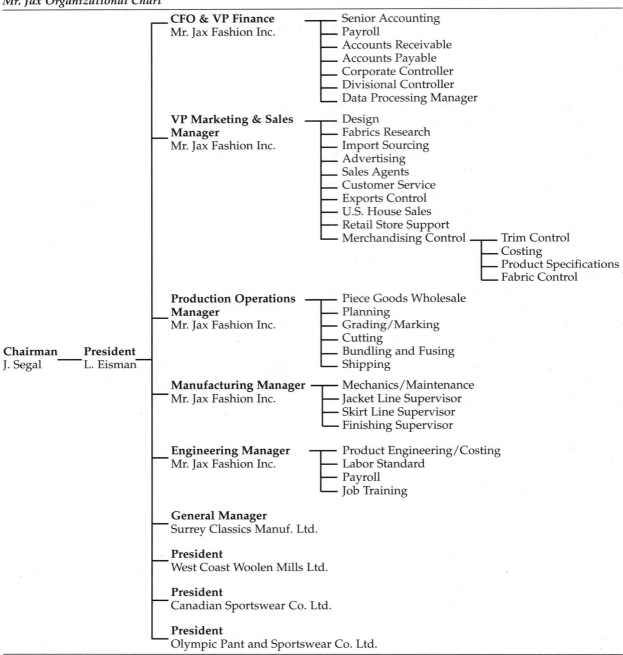

Chairman — **President**
J. Segal — L. Eisman

CFO & VP Finance
Mr. Jax Fashion Inc.
- Senior Accounting
- Payroll
- Accounts Receivable
- Accounts Payable
- Corporate Controller
- Divisional Controller
- Data Processing Manager

VP Marketing & Sales Manager
Mr. Jax Fashion Inc.
- Design
- Fabrics Research
- Import Sourcing
- Advertising
- Sales Agents
- Customer Service
- Exports Control
- U.S. House Sales
- Retail Store Support
- Merchandising Control
  - Trim Control
  - Costing
  - Product Specifications
  - Fabric Control

Production Operations Manager
Mr. Jax Fashion Inc.
- Piece Goods Wholesale
- Planning
- Grading/Marking
- Cutting
- Bundling and Fusing
- Shipping

Manufacturing Manager
Mr. Jax Fashion Inc.
- Mechanics/Maintenance
- Jacket Line Supervisor
- Skirt Line Supervisor
- Finishing Supervisor

Engineering Manager
Mr. Jax Fashion Inc.
- Product Engineering/Costing
- Labor Standard
- Payroll
- Job Training

General Manager
Surrey Classics Manuf. Ltd.

President
West Coast Woolen Mills Ltd.

President
Canadian Sportswear Co. Ltd.

President
Olympic Pant and Sportswear Co. Ltd.

EXHIBIT 3
Production Flowchart

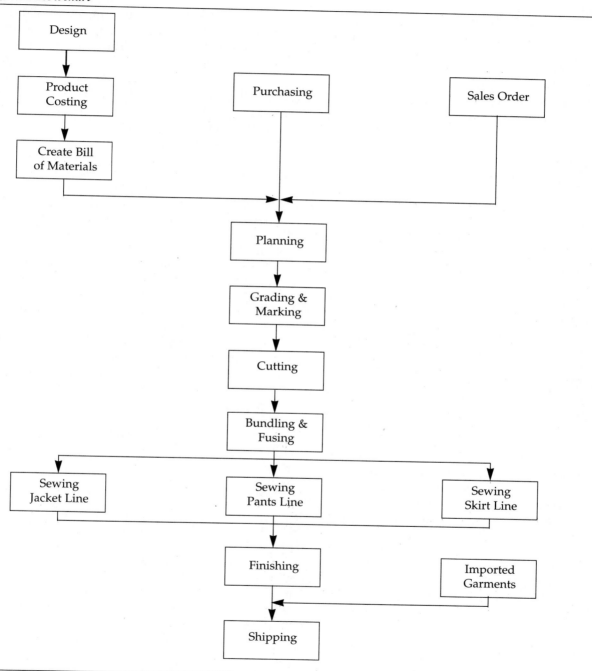

problems not only restricted capacity, but also caused customer service to deteriorate from an excellent shipment rate of approximately 95 percent of orders to recently being sometimes below the industry average of 75 percent. Mr. Jax's ability to ship had been a key to its growth strategy in Canada. Normally, apparel manufacturers met between 70 to 80 percent of their orders, but Mr. Jax had built a reputation for shipping more than 90 percent of orders.

Consolidation had begun in the latter part of 1987. An old building in downtown Vancouver was acquired and renovated. The facility incorporated some of the most modern production equipment available. In total, the company had spent approximately $3.5 million on upgrading production technology. Equipment in the new facility included a $220,000 Gerber automatic cloth cutting machine to improve efficiency and reduce waste; $300,000 of modern sewing equipment to improve productivity and production capacity; a $200,000 Gerber production moving system to automatically move work to appropriate work stations as required; and a computerized design assistance system to integrate the above equipment (i.e., tracking in-process inventory, scheduling, planning and arranging, and sizing cloth patterns for cutting). The objectives of these investments were to lower labor content, improve production capacity, and reduce the time required to produce a garment.

In the last quarter of 1988, Mr. Jax had moved into this newly renovated head office facility. The building, which was renovated by one of Italy's leading architects, represented an architectural marvel with its skylights and soaring atriums. The production department had just recently settled into its expansive space. However, the move had not gone without incident. The equipment operators had difficulties adapting to the new machines. Most of the workers had become accustomed to the repetitive tasks required of the old technology. The new equipment was forcing them to retrain themselves and required additional effort; something that was not appreciated by many of the workers. In addition, the largely Asian work force had difficulty understanding retraining instructions because English was their second language.

To further facilitate the implementation of the consolidation program, an apparel production consultant had been hired. The consultant was using time-motion studies to reorganize and improve task efficiency and effectiveness. An example of a problem that had resulted from the move was the need for integration between the overall production planning, task assignment, worker remuneration, and the new Gerber production moving system, if effective operation was desired. If these elements were not integrated, the new system would in fact slow production. Unfortunately, this integration had not been considered until after the move and the machine subsequently had to be removed until adjustments were made. The adjustments required converting workers from a salary base to a piece rate pay scale. The consultants were training all the workers to convert to piece rate work and to operate the necessary equipment in the most efficient manner. Three workers were being trained per week. The conversion was expected to take two years.

Despite these ongoing problems, production appeared to be improving and operational activities were now organized and coordinated with some degree of efficiency. Eisman was hopeful that production would gain the upper hand in the fight to remedy scheduling problems within the next six months.

Opportunities For Future Growth

Despite problems such as those detailed above, Mr. Jax's revenues and profits had grown by 1,500 percent and 500 percent, respectively, over the past eight years. Furthermore, Eisman was extremely positive about further growth opportunities in the U.S. market. During the past two years, Eisman had tested the Dallas and New York markets. Local sales agents had carried the Mr. Jax fashion line and 1988 revenues had grown to $1 million (U.S.), the majority of which had come from Dallas. Follow-up research revealed that retail purchasers liked the "classical European styling combined with the North American flair."

This initial success had been inspiring, but it had also exposed Eisman to the difficulties of entering the highly competitive U.S. market. In particular, attaining good sales representation and excellent service, both of which were demanded by U.S. retailers, would be difficult to achieve. Securing first-class sales representation required having either a strong market presence or a promising promotional program. In addition, Mr. Jax had found U.S. retailers to be extremely onerous in their service demands. These demands were generally a result of the more competitive retail environment. Demands were particularly stringent for smaller apparel suppliers because of their nominal selling power. These demands ranged from very low wholesale prices to extremely fast order-filling and re-stocking requirements. Eisman recognized that Mr. Jax would need to establish a focused, coordinated, and aggressive marketing campaign to achieve its desired objectives in this market.

Eisman had studied two alternate approaches to entering the U.S. market. One approach involved establishing a retailing chain, while the other involved starting a U.S.-based wholesale distribution subsidiary responsible for managing the aggressive promotional and sales campaign required.

Establishing a retail chain would require both new capital and skills. Capital costs, including leasehold improvements and inventory, would be initially very high and an administrative infrastructure as well as a distribution and product inventorying system would need to be established. Yet, starting a retail chain did have benefits. The retail approach would provide controllability, visibility, and rapid market penetration. It was the approach taken by many of the aggressive apparel companies in the women's professional/career market segment, such as Liz Claiborne, Benetton, and Esprit. Furthermore, Mr. Jax's marketing strength fit well with this strategic approach. Experts estimated that the initial capital required would be about $10 mil-

lion to open up the first 30 stores, and then cost $300,000 per outlet thereafter. Sales revenues would grow to between $300,000 and $750,000 per outlet, depending upon the location, after two to five years. Operating margins on apparel stores were slightly less than 10 percent. Experts felt that within five years the company could possibly open 45 outlets; five the first year and ten each year thereafter. In summary, this option would entail the greatest financial risk, but it would also have the greatest potential return.

The alternative approach was to establish a U.S. distribution subsidiary. This alternative would require capital and more of the same skills the company had developed in Canada. In general, the company would need to set up one or more showrooms throughout the U.S. The location of the showrooms would be critical to the approach eventually implemented. Exhibit 4 illustrates regional apparel buying habits in North America.

A wholesale distribution approach could be carried out in one of two ways: either on a regional or national basis. A regional approach would involve focusing on the smaller regional retail stores. These stores tended to attract less competitive attention because of the higher sales expense-to-revenue ratio inherent in servicing these accounts. The approach required the new distributor to provide good-quality fashion lines and service the accounts in a better manner than established suppliers. An advantage to this approach was that regional retailers demanded fewer and smaller price concessions compared to the larger national chains. The obstacles to this approach included the large sales force required and the superior service capability. Even though Mr. Jax had utilized this strategy successfully in Canada, success was not assured in the U.S. because of the very competitive environment. These factors made this approach both difficult to implement and slow relative to other approaches. Experts estimated fixed costs to average $1 million annually per region, of which 75 percent would be advertising and 25 percent other promotional costs. Additional operating costs would consist of sales commissions (7 percent of sales) and administrative

EXHIBIT 4
North American Apparel Consumption by Region

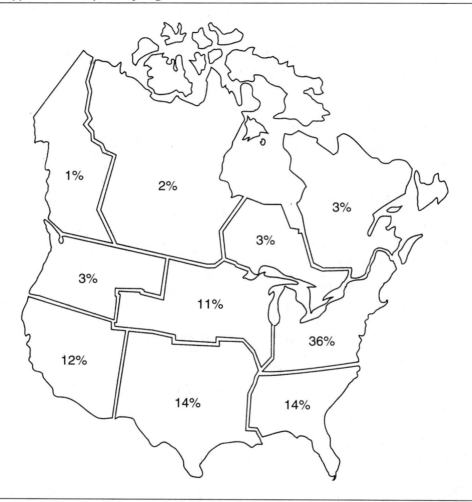

Source: U.S. & Canadian Governments.

overhead costs. Revenues would be dependent upon many factors, but an initial annual growth rate of $1 million annually within each region was considered attainable over the next five years. In summary, this approach would minimize Mr. Jax's risk exposure, but it would also minimize the short-term opportunities.

The national approach was also a viable option. The greatest challenge in a national strategy would be the difficulty in penetrating well-established buyer/seller relationships. Floor space was expensive and national chains and department stores tended to buy conservatively, sticking with the more reputable suppliers who they knew could produce a salable product and service large orders. They also tended to demand low prices and rapid re-order terms. In summary, the national approach provided significant entry barriers, but it also provided the greatest potential for market share growth. Clearly, if economies of scale and competitive advantage in the larger North American context was the desired goal, this had to be the eventual strategy.

The principal costs of this approach would be the advertising and promotional expenses. National apparel companies had advertising expenditures of many millions of dollars. In discussions with Eisman, industry advertising executives had recommended an advertising expenditure of between $3 and $5 million annually in the first three years and then, if successful, increasing it by $1 million annually in the next two successive years. Additional operating costs would be required for sales commissions (7 percent of sales) and administrative overhead. The results of this approach were very uncertain and two outcomes were possible. If the approach was successful, Eisman expected that one or two accounts grossing $1 to $2 million annually could be captured in the first two years. Eisman then felt the sales would expand to about $5 million in the third year and increase by $5 million annually for the next two successive years. However, if the expected quality, design, or service requirements were not sustained, sales would probably decline in the third year to that of the first year and then virtually disappear thereafter.

Both the national and regional approaches would require an infrastructure. Depending upon the approach taken, the head office could be located in a number of places. If a national approach were taken, Mr. Jax would need to locate in one of the major U.S. apparel centers (e.g., New York or California). Eisman estimated that the national approach would require a full-time Director of U.S. Operations immediately, while the regional approach could delay this hiring until required. Such a managing director would require extensive previous experience in the industry and be both capable and compatible with Mr. Jax's marketing, operating, and strategic approach. To ensure top-quality candidates, Eisman felt that a signing bonus of at least $100,000 would need to be offered. The remuneration would be tied to sales growth and volume, but a continued minimum salary guarantee might be necessary until the sales reached some minimum volume. In addition, a full-time sales manager would be required. Eisman estimated that the subsidiary's administrative expense would be $500,000 if a regional approach were taken, versus $1 million for a national approach in both cases. Overhead costs would then escalate by approximately $0.5 million annually for the first five years.

Eisman had now studied the U.S. growth options for over six months. He felt a decision had to be made very soon, otherwise the company would forfeit the time window over which market growth opportunities clearly existed. The new FTA environment and the growth in the professional/career women's market segment were strong incentives, and delaying the decision would only increase the costs as well as the possibility of failure. Eisman realized the decision was critical to the company's evolution toward its ultimate goal of becoming a major international fashion company. The challenge was deciding which approach to take, as well as the sequencing and timing of the subsequent actions.

"We've got some important decisions to make on Arctic Power for 1988," said Linda Barton, Senior Product Manager for the brand. "As I see it, we can continue to develop our strong markets in Quebec, the Maritimes, and British Columbia or we can try to build market share in the rest of Canada." Ms. Barton was discussing the future of Arctic Power, one of Colgate-Palmolive Canada's leading laundry detergents, with Gary Parsons, the Assistant Product Manager on the brand.

"Not only do we have to consider our strategic direction," replied Mr. Parsons, "but we also have to think about our positioning strategy for Arctic Power. I'm for running the Quebec approach in all our markets." Mr. Parsons was referring to the Quebec advertising campaign, which positioned Arctic Power as the superior detergent for cold water cleaning.

"I'm not sure, given the mixed results achieved with our 1986 Western campaign," said Linda. "However, we are making great progress with our current advertising in British Columbia. It might be more effective outside of Quebec. Remember, cold water washing is a newer concept for the Western provinces. We have to overcome that obstacle before we can get people to buy Arctic Power. Let's go over the data again, then make our decisions."

THE COMPANY

Colgate-Palmolive Canada is a wholly owned subsidiary of Colgate-Palmolive, a large multinational with divisions in 58 countries. Worldwide company sales in 1986 were $4.9 billion with profits of $178 million. The Canadian subsidiary sales exceeded $250 million annually. Colgate-Palmolive Canada (CPC) manufactures a range of household, health, and personal care products. Among CPC's major brands are ABC, Arctic Power, and Fab (laundry detergents), Palmolive (dish washing liquid), Ajax (cleanser), Irish Spring (bar soap), Ultra Brite and Colgate (toothpastes), Halo (shampoo), and Baggies (food wrap).

Under the product management system at CPC, product managers are assigned responsibility for specific brands, such as Arctic Power. Their overall goals are to increase the sales and profitability of their brand. To meet these goals, the product manager supervises all marketing functions including planning, advertising, selling, promotion, and market research. In planning and executing programs for a brand, the product manager usually is assigned an assistant product manager and they work closely together to accomplish the brand goals.

Prior to the late 1970s, CPC essentially followed the strategy of nationally supporting most of its brands. The result was that CPC was spread too thin with too many brands. There were insufficient resources to properly promote and develop all of the CPC line and profits and market share were less than satisfactory. Beginning in the late 1970s and continuing to the early 1980s, the Canadian division altered its strategy. An extensive review of the entire product line was conducted and CPC moved to what was referred to as a regional brand strategy. Where a brand had regional strength, resources were focused on that area with the objective of building a strong and profitable brand in that region. For example, Arctic Power had a relatively strong market share in Quebec and the Maritimes, where the proportion of consumers

This case was prepared by Professor Gordon McDougall, Wilfrid Laurier University, and Professor Douglas Snetsinger, University of Toronto, as the basis for classroom discussion rather than to illustrate either effective or ineffective handling of an administrative situation. Names and proprietary data have been disguised but all essential relationships have been preserved. It is reproduced here by permission of the North American Case Research Association and the authors. Copyright © 1989.

using cold water to wash clothes was considerably higher than the national average. Promotional support was withdrawn from the rest of Canada and those resources were focused on Quebec and the Maritimes.[1] Arctic Power was still distributed nationally but by the end of 1981, national market share was 4 percent, consisting of an 11 percent share in Quebec, a 5 percent share in the Maritimes, and a 2 percent share in the rest of Canada. Over the next four years, marketing efforts were concentrated primarily on Quebec, and to a lesser extent on the Maritimes. This approach worked well for Arctic Power. By the end of 1985, Arctic Power's national share had increased to 6.4 percent; share in Quebec had risen to 18 percent, share in the Maritimes was 6 percent, and share was less than 2 percent in the rest of Canada. With the increase in sales and profitability, the decision was made to target Alberta and British Columbia for 1986. The results of these efforts exceeded expectations in British Columbia but were less than satisfactory in Alberta.

THE LAUNDRY DETERGENT MARKET

The laundry detergent market was mature, with unit sales increasing by approximately 1 percent annually and dollar sales increasing by about 5 percent each year between 1983 and 1986 (Exhibit 1). Three large consumer packaged goods companies, Procter & Gamble, Lever Detergents, and CPC, dominated the market. All three were subsidiaries of multinational firms and sold a wide range of household and personal care products in Canada. Procter & Gamble Canada had annual sales exceeding $1 billion and some of its major brands included Crest (toothpaste), Ivory and Zest (bar soaps), Secret (deodorant), Pampers and Luvs

(disposable diapers), and Head & Shoulders (shampoo). P&G held a 44 percent share of the laundry detergent market in 1986, due primarily to the large share (34 percent) held by Tide, the leading brand in Canada.

Lever Detergents, with annual Canadian sales in excess of $400 million, operated primarily in the detergent, soap, and toiletry categories. Major brands included Close-up (toothpaste) and Dove and Lux (bar soaps). Lever held a 24 percent share of the laundry detergent market; its leading brand was Sunlight, with a 13 percent share.

CPC was the only one of the three companies to gain market share in the laundry detergent market between 1983 and 1986. In 1986, CPC's total share was 23 percent, up from 16 percent in 1983. ABC, a value brand, positioned to attract consumers interested in "value for less money," more than doubled its share between 1983 and 1986 and was the second leading brand with a 14 percent share.

COMPETITIVE RIVALRY

Intense competitive activity was a way of life in the laundry detergent business. Not only did the three major firms have talented and experienced marketers, but they competed in a low-growth market where increased sales could only be achieved by taking share from competitive brands. A difficult task facing any product manager in this business was to identify the marketing mix that would maximize share while maintaining or increasing brand profitability; a task that had both long- and short-term implications. In the long term, competitors strove for permanent share gains by building a solid franchise of loyal users based on a quality product and a strong brand image or position. These positioning strategies were primarily executed through product formulation and advertising campaigns. However, companies also competed through consumer and trade promotions (e.g., coupons, feature specials in newspaper ads), tactics that were more short-term in nature. Trade and consumer promotions were critical to maintain prominent shelf display and to attract competitors' customers. In

[1] The Maritimes contained the four Eastern provinces: Newfoundland, Nova Scotia, Prince Edward Island, and New Brunswick. In 1988, the population of Canada was estimated at 25.8 million people: Maritimes (2.3 million), Quebec (6.6 million), Ontario (9.4 million), Manitoba and Saskatchewan (2.1 million), Alberta (2.4 million), and British Columbia (3.0 million).

EXHIBIT 1
Laundry Detergent Market

	1983	1984	1985	1986
Colgate				
ABC	6.0	9.8	11.8	13.9
Arctic Power	4.7	5.6	6.4	6.5
Fab	2.1	1.3	1.6	1.4
Punch	2.0	.7	.4	.3
Dynamo	1.0	.8	.6	.5
Total Colgate	15.8	18.2	20.8	22.6
Procter & Gamble				
Tide	34.1	35.1	32.6	34.1
Oxydol	4.9	4.2	4.0	3.3
Bold	4.8	4.2	3.2	2.3
Other P&G brands	4.7	4.8	4.4	4.3
Total P&G	48.5	48.3	44.2	44.0
Lever				
Sunlight	13.9	12.2	14.2	13.4
All	4.1	3.7	3.8	3.2
Surf	2.6	2.6	2.7	2.2
Wisk	3.8	4.1	4.1	4.4
Other Lever brands	.9	.8	.6	.4
Total Lever	25.3	23.4	25.4	23.6
All *other* brands	10.4	10.1	9.6	9.8
Grand total	100.0	100.0	100.0	100.0
Total Market				
• Metric Tonnes ('000)	171.9	171.9	173.6	175.3
(% change)	2.0	0.0	1.0	1.0
• Factory Sales ('000,000)	$265.8	$279.1	$288.5	$304.7
(% change)	6.2	5.0	3.0	6.0

Source: Company records.

virtually every week of the year, at least one brand of detergent would be "on special" in any given supermarket. The product manager's task was to find the best balance between these elements in making brand decisions.

Reformulating brands, the changing of the brand ingredients, was a frequent activity in the laundry detergent business. Reformulating a brand involved altering the amount and kind of active chemical ingredients in the detergents. These active ingredients cleaned the clothes. Each of these cleaning ingredients was efficacious for particular cleaning tasks. Some of these ingredients were good for cleaning clay and mud from cotton and other natural fibers, while others would clean oily soils from polyesters, and yet others were good for other cleaning problems. Most detergents were formulated with a variety of active ingredients to clean in a wide range of conditions. As well, bleaches, fabric softeners, and fragrances could be included.

Thus, laundry detergents contained different *levels* and *mixes* of active ingredients. The major decision was the *amount* of active ingredients that would be used in a particular brand. In simple terms, the greater the proportion of active ingredients, the better the detergent was at cleaning clothes. However, all detergents would get clothes clean. For example, in a recent test of 42 laundry detergents, *Consumer Reports* concluded: "Yes, some detergents get clothes whiter and brighter than others, but the scale is clean to cleanest, not dirty to clean."

The Canadian brands of laundry detergent contained various amounts of active ingredients. As shown in the following table, Tide and Arctic Power had more active ingredients than any other brand.

Level of Active Ingredients of Laundry Detergents

1	2	3	4	5
Some private labels	Bold III Oxydol Surf All	ABC Fab Cheer 2 Sunlight	—	Arctic Power Tide

Source: Company records.

Note: The scale of active ingredients increases from (1) to (5).

In fact, Tide and Arctic Power were equivalent brands in terms of the level of active ingredients. These two brands, referred to as the "Cadillacs" of detergents, had considerably higher levels of active ingredients than all other detergents. While the actual mix of active ingredients differed between the two brands (with Arctic Power having a greater mix of ingredients that were more suited to cold water washing), the cleaning power of Tide and Arctic Power were equal.

As the amount of active ingredients in a brand increased, so did the cost. Manufacturers were constantly facing the trade-off between cost and level of active ingredients. At times, they had the opportunity to reduce unit costs by switching one type of active ingredient (a basic chemical) for another, depending on the relative costs of the ingredients.

In this way, the level of ingredients remained the same, only the mixture changed. Manufacturers changed the physical ingredients of a brand in order to achieve an efficient per unit cost, to provide a basis for the repositioning or restaging of the brand, and to continue to deliver better consumer value.

Maintaining or increasing share through repositioning or other means was critical because of the profits involved. One share point was worth approximately $3 million in factory sales and the cost and profit structures of the leading brands were believed to be similar. While some economies of scale accrued to the largest brands, the average cost of goods sold was estimated at 54 percent of sales, leaving a gross profit of 46 percent. Marketing expenditures include trade promotions (16 percent), consumer promotions (5 percent), and advertising expenditures (7 percent), leaving a contribution margin of 18 percent. Not included in these estimates were management overheads and expenses (e.g., product management salaries, market research expenses, sales salaries, and factory overheads), which were primarily fixed. In some instances, lower share brands were likely to spend higher amounts on trade promotions to achieve their marketing objectives.

One indication of competitive activity was reflected in advertising expenditures between 1982 and 1986. Total category media advertising increased by 12 percent to $14.4 million (Exhibit 2). As well, substantial increases in trade promotions had occurred during that period. While actual expenditure data were not available, some managers felt that twice as much was being spent on trade promotions versus advertising. As one example in Montreal, in a nine-month period in 1986, Tide was featured in weekly supermarket advertisements 80 times and Arctic Power was featured 60 times. Typically, the advertisement cost for a feature was shared by the manufacturer and the retailer. At times during 1986, consumers could have purchased six litres of Arctic Power or Tide for $3.49 (regular price of $5.79). There was also a strong indication that the frequency and size of price specials on detergents was increasing. The

EXHIBIT 2
Share of National Media Expenditures (1982–1986)

	Percentages				
	1982	*1983*	*1984*	*1985*	*1986*
ABC	6.4	8.9	12.3	14.0	13.6
Arctic Power	6.1	6.1	6.7	7.2	9.3
Tide	21.0	17.8	19.1	16.4	29.77
Oxydol	5.1	4.5	5.9	6.6	6.4
Sunlight	14.1	10.8	10.5	9.1	11.3
All	10.3	5.5	6.9	7.7	4.0
Wisk	9.9	12.8	10.3	10.4	14.6
All *other* brands	27.1	33.6	28.3	28.6	12.1
Total	100.0	100.0	100.0	100.0	100.0
Total spending ('000)	$12,909	$13,338	$14,420	$13,718	$14,429
% Change	29.2	3.3	8.1	-4.9	5.2

Source: Company records.

average retail price of laundry detergents (based on the volume sold of all detergents at regular and special prices) had only increased by 4 percent in the last three years, whereas cost of goods sold had increased by 15 percent during the same period.

One final observation was warranted. Between 1983 and 1986, the four leading brands—Tide, ABC, Sunlight, and Arctic Power—had increased their share from 58.7 percent to 67.9 percent of the total market. The three manufacturers appeared to be focusing their efforts primarily on their leading brands and letting the lesser brands decline in share.

POSITIONING STRATEGIES

While positioning strategies were executed through all aspects of the marketing mix, the strategy was most clearly seen in the advertising execution.

Tide was the dominant brand in terms of share of market and share of media expenditures. Tide's strategy was to sustain this dominance through positioning the brand as superior to any other brand on generic cleaning benefits. In 1986, four national and four regional commercials were aired

to support this strategy. These commercials conveyed that Tide provided the benefits of being the most effective detergent for "tough" situations such as for ground-in dirt, stains, and bad odors. Tide also aired copy in Quebec claiming effectiveness in all temperatures. Most of Tide's copy was usually developed around a "slice of life" or testimonial format.

Other brands in the market faced the situation of going head-to-head with Tide's position or competing on a benefit Tide did not claim. Most had chosen the latter route. CPC's ABC brand had made strong gains in the past four years, moving from sixth to second place in market share based on its value position. ABC was positioned as the low-priced, good-quality cleaning detergent. Recent copy for ABC utilized a demonstration format where the shirts for twins were as clean when washed in ABC versus a leading higher-priced detergent with the statement: "Why pay more, I can't see the difference." Sunlight, a Lever's brand, had for several years attempted to compete directly with Tide and build its consumer franchise based on efficacy and lemon-scent freshness. Advertising execution had been of the up-beat, up-scale lifestyle approach and less of the straight-forward problem solution or straight-talking approaches seen in other detergent advertising. More recently, Sunlight had been moving toward ABC's value position while retaining the lemon freshness heritage. Sunlight was positioned in 1986 as the detergent that gave a very clean, fresh wash at a sensible price. The final brand that attempted to compete for the value position was All. The advertising for All also claimed that the brand particularly whitened white clothes and had a pleasant fragrance.

Arctic Power had been positioned as the superior-cleaning laundry detergent especially formulated for cold water washing. For the Eastern market, Arctic Power advertising had utilized a humorous background to communicate brand superiority and its efficacy in cold water. For the Western market, a nontraditional, up-beat execution was used to develop the cold water market.

Wisk, which had received much attention for its "ring around the collar" advertising, competed directly with Tide on generic cleaning qualities and provided the additional benefit of a liquid formulation. Tide Liquid was introduced in 1985 but received little advertising support in 1986.

Fab and Bold 3 competed for the "softergents" market. Both products, which had fabric softeners in the formulation, were positioned to clean effectively while softening clothes and reducing static cling. Another detergent with laundry product additives was Oxydol, which was formulated with a mild bleach. Oxydol was positioned as the detergent that kept colors bright while whitening whites.

The other two nationally advertised brands were Cheer 2 and Ivory Snow. Cheer 2 was positioned as the detergent that got clothes clean and fresh. Ivory Snow, which was a soap and not a detergent, was positioned as the laundry cleaning product for infants' clothes that provided superior softness and comfort.

The positioning strategies of these brands reflected the benefit segmentation approach used to market laundry detergents. Most brands attempted to appeal to a wide target (primarily women in the 18 to 49 age group) based on benefits rather than specific demographic segments.

THE COLD WATER MARKET

Every February, CPC commissioned an extensive market research study to identify trends in the laundry detergent market. Referred to as the tracking study, approximately 1,800 personal interviews were conducted with female heads-of-households across Canada each year. Among the wealth of data provided by the tracking study was information on cold water usage in Canada. Regular cold water usage was growing in Canada and, by 1986, 29 percent of households were classified as regular (five or more times out of ten) cold water users (Exhibit 3). Due to cultural and marketing differences, Quebec (55 percent) and the Maritimes (33 percent) had more cold water users than the national average.[2] A further 25 percent of all Canadian households occasionally (one to four times out of ten) used cold water for washing.

For households that washed regularly or occasionally with cold water, the most important benefits of using cold water fell into two broad categories (Exhibit 4). First, it was easier on or better for clothes in that cold water stopped shrinkage, prevented colors from running, and colors stayed bright. Second, it was more economical in that it saved energy, was cheaper, saved hot water, and saved on electricity. Households in Quebec, the Maritimes, and British Columbia mentioned the "economy" benefit more frequently, whereas households in the rest of Canada mentioned the "easier/better" benefit more often.

[2] Canada has two major cultural groups, the English (who emigrated primarily from the British Isles) and the French (who emigrated from France). Of the 6.2 million French-speaking Canadians, most reside in Quebec (5.3 million) and the Maritimes (264,000). Historically, many French-speaking Canadians had washed clothes in cold water.

EXHIBIT 3
Proportion of Households Washing with Cold Water (1981–1986)

	Percentages					
	1981	*1982*	*1983*	*1984*	*1985*	*1986*
National	20[a]	22	26	26	26	29
Maritimes	23	25	32	40	32	33
Quebec	35	41	49	48	53	55
Ontario	14	13	18	16	11	17
Prairies	12	12	13	11	10	17
B.C.	13	19	20	17	22	21

Source: Tracking study.

[a]20 percent of respondents did 5 or more out of 10 wash loads in cool or cold water.

$N = 1800$.

ARCTIC POWER

Having achieved reasonable success in Eastern Canada and returned the brand to profitability, Linda Barton decided to increase the brand's share in Alberta and British Columbia for 1986. That brand plan is reported below.

The 1986 Brand Plan for Arctic Power

Objectives. Arctic Power's overall objective is to continue profit development by maintaining modest unit volume growth in Quebec and the Maritimes while developing the Alberta and B.C. regions.

EXHIBIT 4
Most Important Benefit of Cold Water Washing, 1986

Reason	*National*	*Maritimes*	*Quebec*	*Ontario*	*Man./Sask.*	*Alta.*	*B.C.*
• Stops shrinkage	22.7[a]	19.4	5.2	32.7	35.4	35.4	30.2
• Saves energy	16.5	12.5	32.1	8.2	2.1	9.9	12.9
• Prevents colors from running	11.6	17.4	0.0	21.8	21.3	9.9	2.9
• Cheaper	11.1	19.4	10.4	10.2	2.8	9.3	16.5
• Saves hot water	9.7	9.7	15.5	6.8	11.3	3.1	3.6
• Colors stay bright	8.8	4.2	7.8	11.6	9.2	6.8	7.9
• Saves on electricity	8.7	19.4	0.5	8.2	5.7	16.1	25.9
• Easier on clothes	8.5	11.1	6.7	8.8	10.6	13.7	5.0

Source: Tracking study.

[a]When asked what they felt was the most important benefit of cold water washing, 22.7 percent of all respondents said "stops shrinking."

Sample includes all households that washed one or more times out of last 10 washes in cold water.

$N = 956$.

Only the eight most frequent responses are reported.

Long Term (by 1996). The long-term objective is to become the number three brand in the category with market share of 12 percent. Arctic Power will continue to deliver a minimum 18 percent contribution margin. This will require (1) maintenance of effective creative/media support; (2) superior display prominence, particularly in the key Quebec market; (3) continued investigation of development opportunities; and (4) cost of goods savings programs where possible.

Short Term. The short-term objective is to sustain unit growth while building cold water washing dominance. This will require current user reinforcement and continued conversion of warm water washing users. Specifically, in fiscal 1986, Arctic Power will achieve a market share of 6.5 percent on factory sales of $22.0 million and a contribution margin of 18 percent. Regional share objectives are Maritimes—6.3 percent; Quebec—17.2 percent; Alberta—5 percent; and B.C.—5 percent.

Marketing Strategy. Arctic Power will be positioned as the most effective laundry detergent especially formulated for cold water washing. The primary target for Arctic Power is women 18 to 49 and skewed towards the 25 to 34 segment. The secondary market is all adults.

Arctic Power will defend its franchise by allocating regional effort commensurate with brand development in order to maintain current users. In line with the Western expansion strategy, support will be directed to Alberta and B.C. to enhance the acceptance of cold water washing and thereby broaden the appeal among occasional and nonusers of Arctic Power.

Media Strategy. The media strategy objective is to achieve high levels of message registration against the target group, through high message continuity and frequency/reach. Media spending behind regional television will be allocated 75 percent to brand maintenance and 25 percent to investment spending for brand and cold water market

development. Arctic Power will have the number five share of media expenditure position nationally while being the number three detergent advertiser in Quebec.

	T.V. Spending	*GRP's Week*
1985 Plan	$1,010,000	92
Actual	$990,000	88
1986 Plan	$1,350,000	95

GRP (Gross Rating Points) is a measurement of advertising impact derived by multiplying the percentage of the target population exposed to an advertisement by the average number of exposures per person.

Arctic Power's 1986 media spending of $1.35 million is a 36 percent increase over 1985. This returns Arctic Power to its reach objective of 90 percent in Quebec, five points ahead of a year ago. In addition, two new television markets have been added with enhanced support in B.C. and Alberta. Reach objectives will be achieved by skewing more of Arctic Power's spending into efficient daytime spots, which cost less than nightime network spots and are more flexible in light of regional reach objectives.

Scheduling will maintain continuous flighting established in 1985 with concentrations at peak dealing time representing 40 weeks on-air in the east and 32 weeks in the west.

Copy Strategy: Quebec/Maritimes. The creative objective is to convince consumers that Arctic Power is the superior detergent for cold water washing. The consumer benefit is that when they are washing in cold water, Arctic Power will clean clothes and remove stains more effectively than other detergents. The support for this claim is based on the special formulation of Arctic Power. The executional tone will be humorous but with a clear, rational explanation.

Copy Strategy: B.C./Alberta. The creative objective is to convince consumers that cold water washing is better than hot and when washing in cold water to use Arctic Power. The consumer benefit is that cold water washing reduces shrinkage, color run, and energy costs. The executional tone needs to be distinct from other detergent advertising to break-through traditional washing attitudes and will be young-adult oriented, light, "cool," and up-beat.

Consumer Promotions. The objective of consumer promotions in Quebec/Maritimes is to increase the rate of usage by building frequency of purchase among existing users. The objective in B.C./Alberta is to increase the rate of trial of Arctic Power. In total, $856,000 will be spent on consumer promotions.

1. **January:** $.50 In-pack Coupon—To support trade inventory increases and retain current customers in the face of strong competitive activity, 400,000 coupons will be placed in all sizes in the Quebec/ Maritimes distribution region. The coupon is for 6L or 12L sizes and expected redemption is 18 percent at a cost of $50,000.

2. **April:** To generate a 17 percent recent trial of regular-sized boxes of Arctic Power in B.C. and Alberta, a 500 ml saleable sample prepriced at $.49 will be distributed through food and drug stores. In addition, a $.50 coupon for the 6L or 12L size will be placed on the pack of all samples. The offer will penetrate 44 percent of households in the region at a total cost of $382,000.

3. **June:** $.40 Coupon through Free-Standing Insert— To sustain interest and foster trial, a $.40 coupon will be delivered to 30 percent of homes in Alberta/B.C. The coupon is redeemable on the 3L size and expected redemption is 4.5 percent at a cost of $28,000.

4. **April/July:** Game (Cool-by-the-Pool)—Five in-ground pools and patio accessories will be given away through spelling POWER by letters dropped in boxes of Arctic Power. Two letters will be placed in each box through national distribution and will coincide with high trade activity and the period in which the desirability of the prizes is highest, at a cost of $184,000.

5. **September:** $.75 Direct Mail National Coupon Pack (excluding Ontario)—To maximize swing buyer volume (from competition) in Quebec and encourage trial in the west, a $.75 coupon for the 6L or 12L size will be mailed to 70 percent of households in the primary market areas, generating a 3 percent redemption rate at a cost of $212,000.

Trade Promotions. The objectives of the trade promotions is to maintain regular and feature pricing equal to Tide and encourage prominent shelf facing. An advertising feature is expected from each key account during every promotion event run in Quebec and the Maritimes. Distribution for any size is expected to increase to 95 percent. In the West, maximum effort will be directed at establishing display for the 6L size and four feature events will be expected from each key account. Distribution should be developed to 71 percent in B.C. and 56 percent in Alberta. Average deal size will be 14 percent off regular price or $5.00 per 6L case. In addition, most trade events will include a $1.00 per case allowance for co-op advertising and merchandising support. The total trade budget is $3.46 million, which includes $1 million investment spending in the West. The promotion schedule is presented below.

Arctic Power 1986 Promotional Schedule												
Trade Promotions	J	F	M	A	M	J	J	A	S	O	N	D
Maritimes	X			X		X			X		X	
Quebec	X	X		X			X	X		X		X X
Alberta/B.C.	X				X		X		X X			
Consumer Promotions												
East $.50 coupon	X	X										
West sample/coupon				X								
West $.40 coupon						X						
National game				X	X	X						
National $.75 coupon									X			

Results of the Western Campaign

In August of 1986, during the middle of the Western campaign, a "minitracking" study was conducted in the two provinces to monitor the program. The results of the August study were compared with the February study and reported in Exhibit 5. Market share for Arctic Power was also measured on a bi-monthly basis and the figures are shown at the top of the next page.

The campaign clearly had an impact as brand and advertising awareness had increased, particularly

					1986					
	1983	1984	1985	D/J	F/M	A/M	J/J	A/S	O/N	Total 1986
Alberta	0.7	2.3	1.7	1.4	1.1	2.8	2.8	2.4	1.9	2.1
B.C.	3.2	4.0	3.9	4.0	4.0	6.1	6.1	7.3	5.4	5.5

Arctic Power Market Share

in Alberta (Exhibit 5). Brand trial within the previous six months had more than doubled in Alberta and was up over 25 percent in B.C. However, market share had peaked at 2.8 percent in Alberta and by the end of the year had declined to 1.9 percent. Market share in B.C. had reached a high of 7.3 percent and averaged 5.5 percent for the year.

In attempting to explain the different results in the two provinces, Linda Barton and Gary Parsons isolated two factors. First, B.C. had always been a

EXHIBIT 5
Results of Western Campaign

	Prelaunch (February 1986)		Postlaunch (August 1986)	
	Alberta	*B.C.*	*Alberta*	*B.C.*
Unaided Brand Awareness[a]				
Brand mentioned total (%)	13.3	20.3	18.1	24.2
Advertising Awareness				
1. Advertising mentioned (unaided)[b] (%)	1.9	7.9	20.3	11.5
2. Advertising mentioned (aided)[c] (%)	18.5	27.9	31.4	34.6
Brand Trial				
1. Ever tried[d] (%)	25.0	43.0	36.3	48.0
2. Used (last six months)[e] (%)	6.8	15.1	17.1	19.4
Image Measure[f]				
• Cleaning and removing dirt	1.0	1.2	1.2	1.5
• Removing tough stains	.7	.9	0.9	1.4
• Being good value for the price	.5	.9	1.0	1.4
• Cleaning well in cold water	1.2	1.3	1.7	1.8
Conversion to Cold Water				
• Average number of loads out of 10 washed in cold water	1.8	2.2	2.0	2.3

Source: Tracking study.

[a]Question: When you think of laundry detergents, what three brands first come to mind? Can you name three more for me? *Brand mentioned total* is if the brand was mentioned at all. On average, respondents mentioned 4.5 brands.

[b]Question: What brand or brands of laundry detergent have you seen or heard advertised? *Advertising mentioned (unaided)* is any mention of brand advertising mentioned.

[c]Question: Have you recently seen or heard any advertising for brand? *Advertising mentioned (aided)* is if respondent said yes when asked.

[d]Question: Have you ever tried *brand*?

[e]Question: Have you used *brand* in the past six months?

[f]Respondents rated the brand on the four image measures. The rating scale ranged from –5 (doesn't perform well) to +5 (performs well).

"good" market for Arctic Power with share figures around 4 percent, whereas Alberta was less than half that amount. Second, there had been a considerable amount of competitive activity in Alberta during the year. Each of the three major firms had increased trade and consumer promotions to maintain existing brand shares.

ARCTIC POWER—1987

The 1987 brand plan for Arctic Power was similar in thrust and expenditure levels to the 1986 plan. Expenditure levels in Alberta were reduced until the full implications of the 1986 campaign could be examined. Market share in 1987 was expected to be 6.7 percent, up marginally from the 6.5 percent share achieved in 1986 (Exhibit 6).

Each year, every product manager at CPC conducted an extensive brand review. The review for Arctic Power included a detailed competitive analysis of the four leading brands on a regional basis and was based primarily on the tracking study. In July 1987, Linda Barton and Gary Parsons were examining the tracking information that summarized regional information on four critical aspects of the market—brand image

(Exhibit 7), brand and advertising awareness (Exhibit 8), brand trial and usage in last six months (Exhibit 9), and market share and share of media expenditures (Exhibit 10). Future decisions for Arctic Power would be based, in large part, on this information.

THE DECISION

Prior to deciding on the strategic direction for Arctic Power, Ms. Barton and Mr. Parsons met to discuss the situation. It was a hot Toronto day in early July 1987. Ms. Barton began the discussion. "I've got some estimates on what our shares are likely to be for 1987. It looks like we'll have a national share of 6.7 percent, broken down as follows: Maritimes (6.3 percent), Quebec (18 percent), Ontario (1 percent), Manitoba/Saskatchewan (0.1 percent), Alberta (2 percent), B.C. (6 percent)."

Mr. Parsons responded, "I think our problem in Alberta was all the competitive activity. Under normal conditions we'd have achieved 5 percent of that market. But the Alberta objective is small when you think about what we could do in our other undeveloped markets. I've been giving it a lot of

EXHIBIT 6
Arctic Power
Market Share and Total Volume by Region (1983-1987E)

| | Market Share | | | | | |
Region	1983	1984	1985	1986	1987E	*1986 Total Volume[a] ('000 litres)*
National	4.7	5.6	6.4	6.5	6.7	406,512
Maritimes	5.3	5.7	6.3	6.3	6.3	32,616
Quebec	12.3	13.8	17.7	17.5	18.0	113,796
Ontario	.9	1.1	1.1	.8	1.0	158,508
Manitoba/Saskatchewan	.2	.2	.1	.1	.1	28,440
Alberta	.7	2.3	1.7	2.1	2.0	40,644
British Columbia	3.2	4.0	3.9	5.5	6.0	32,508

Source: Company records.
   [a]All laundry detergent.
   1987E = Estimated.

EXHIBIT 7
Brand Images by Region, 1986

Image Measure[a]	National	Maritimes	Quebec	Ontario	Man./Sask.	Alberta	B.C.
Arctic Power							
• Cleaning and removing dirt	1.4	2.0	2.5	.8	.4	1.0	1.2
• Removing tough stains	1.1	1.6	1.9	.7	3.0	.7	.9
• Being good value for the price	1.1	1.4	2.6	.3	.2	.5	.9
• Cleaning well in cold water	1.6	2.1	2.8	1.0	.4	1.2	1.3
ABC							
• Cleaning and removing dirt	1.0	1.9	.5	.9	1.1	1.2	1.6
• Removing tough stains	.5	1.1	.0	.6	.8	.7	.9
• Being good value for the price	1.5	2.4	.8	1.5	1.3	1.7	2.1
• Cleaning well in cold water	.6	1.0	.1	.7	.7	.7	.7
Sunlight							
• Cleaning and removing dirt	2.0	1.9	1.8	2.4	1.9	1.6	1.6
• Removing tough stains	1.6	1.6	1.5	1.9	1.4	1.2	1.2
• Being good value for the price	2.0	1.7	1.9	2.4	1.8	1.7	1.5
• Cleaning well in cold water	1.4	1.1	1.5	1.7	1.2	1.1	.7
Tide							
• Cleaning and removing dirt	3.4	3.7	3.2	3.6	3.5	3.3	3.2
• Removing tough stains	3.0	3.1	2.8	3.3	3.0	2.7	2.7
• Being good value for the price	3.1	3.1	3.3	3.1	2.8	3.0	2.7
• Cleaning well in cold water	2.4	2.3	2.6	2.5	2.4	2.3	1.9

Source: Tracking study.

[a]Respondents rated each brand on the four image measures. The rating scale ranged from –5 (doesn't perform well) to +5 (performs well).

N = 1816.

A difference of .2 is likely to be significant in statistical terms.

thought and we should go national with Arctic Power. We've got a brand that is equal to Tide and we've got to stop keeping it a secret from the rest of Canada. If we can duplicate the success we had in B.C., we'll turn this market on its ear."

"Wait a minute, Gary," said Linda. "In 1986 we spent almost $2,000,000 on advertising and consumer and trade promotions in the West. Even though spending returned to normal levels this year, that was a big investment to get the business going and it will be at least four years before we get that money back. If we go after the national market, you can well expect Tide to fight back with trade spending, which will make your share or margin objectives even harder to achieve. On a per capita basis we'd have to spend at least as much in our underdeveloped markets as we spent in the West. We've got a real problem here. Our brand may be as good as Tide, but I don't think we can change a lot of consumers' minds, particularly the loyal Tide users. I hate to say it, but for many Canadians, when they think about washing clothes, Tide is the brand they think will clean their clothes better than any other brand. I agree that the size of the undeveloped market warrants another look. But remember, any decision will have to be backed up with a solid analysis and a plan that senior management will buy."

Gary replied, "I know that even if I am right it will be a tough sell. I haven't got it completed yet, but I'm working out the share level we will need to break even if we expanded nationally."

EXHIBIT 8
Brand and Advertising Awareness by Region, 1986

	Percentages						
	National	*Maritimes*	*Quebec*	*Ontario*	*Man/Sask*	*Alberta*	*B.C.*
Unaided Brand Awareness[a]							
1. Brand Mentioned First							
Arctic Power	4.4	7.0	12.5	.0	0.0	1.0	2.6
ABC	8.1	18.4	4.6	7.3	4.7	8.4	12.8
Sunlight	9.3	8.4	9.6	9.3	12.0	9.1	7.9
Tide	57.9	55.5	41.9	69.7	63.1	59.7	54.4
2. Brand Mentioned Total							
Arctic Power	23.0	43.5	49.8	5.0	3.0	13.3	20.3
ABC	61.3	82.6	47.9	64.0	56.1	67.5	64.9
Sunlight	58.1	60.2	50.8	65.0	58.5	62.0	46.6
Tide	94.8	95.7	88.8	98.0	97.3	97.4	94.4
Advertising Awareness							
1. Advertising Mentioned (Unaided)[b]							
Arctic Power	7.0	10.7	17.5	.7	.0	1.9	7.9
ABC	25.2	32.8	20.8	27.0	17.3	30.5	24.9
Sunlight	8.6	4.7	5.9	13.0	5.0	6.8	8.2
Tide	44.0	40.1	32.7	55.0	46.2	48.4	35.4
2. Advertising Mentioned (Aided)[c]							
Arctic Power	29.2	38.8	55.1	15.3	5.6	18.5	27.9
ABC	56.1	61.5	55.1	56.0	51.5	60.4	53.4
Sunlight	29.9	20.1	26.4	40.3	21.3	21.1	24.9
Tide	65.3	60.9	54.8	78.0	68.1	65.3	48.4

Source: Tracking study.

[a]Question: When you think of laundry detergents, what three brands first come to mind? Can you name three more for me? *Brand mentioned first* is the first brand mentioned. *Brand mentioned total* is if the brand was mentioned at all. On average, respondents mentioned 4.5 brands.

[b]Question: What brand or brands of laundry detergent have you seen or heard advertised? *Advertising mentioned (unaided)* is any mention of brand advertising mentioned.

[c]Question: Have you recently seen or heard any advertising for *brand*? *Advertising mentioned (aided)* is if respondent said yes when asked.

N = 1816.

Linda responded, "Well, when you get that done, we will talk about national expansion again. For the moment, we have to resolve this positioning dilemma. I don't like a two-country approach, but it does seem to make sense in this case. I think we might still want to focus on the brand in the East and continue to develop the cold water washing market in the West."

Gary would have preferred to continue the discussion of national expansion, but realized he would have to do some work and at least produce the share estimate before he raised the subject again. Therefore, he replied, "I agree that Canada is not one homogeneous market, but that perspective can be taken to extremes. I worry that all of this data we get on the regional markets is getting in the

EXHIBIT 9

Brand Trial in Last Six Months by Region, 1986

Brand Trial	National	Maritimes	Quebec	Ontario	Man./Sask.	Alberta	B.C.
1. Ever Tried[a]							
Arctic Power	42.4	67.9	75.6	19.7	20.3	25.0	43.0
ABC	60.4	83.9	50.8	60.0	53.5	62.7	67.9
Sunlight	66.3	65.6	59.4	75.0	67.1	58.1	58.7
Tide	93.6	91.0	90.1	97.3	95.0	91.9	92.1
2. Used (Last Six Months)[b]							
Arctic Power	19.4	29.8	46.5	4.3	2.3	6.8	15.1
ABC	37.2	56.2	34.7	32.3	29.2	39.3	47.5
Sunlight	38.3	29.8	38.0	44.3	36.2	36.7	28.5
Tide	68.1	66.6	66.0	73.3	67.8	69.5	54.8

Source: Tracking study.

[a]Question: Have you ever tried *brand*?

[b]Question: Have you used *brand* in the past six months?

Note: On average, respondents had 1.3 brands of laundry detergents in the home.

N = 1816.

EXHIBIT 10

Market Share and Share of Media Expenditures by Region, 1986

	Percentages						
	National	Maritimes	Quebec	Ontario	Man./Sask.	Alberta	B.C.
Market Share							
Arctic Power	6.5	6.3	17.5	.8	.1	2.1	5.5
ABC	13.9	27.8	8.6	13.8	11.6	16.1	21.5
Sunlight	13.4	7.7	12.1	16.4	14.2	10.4	11.3
Tide	34.1	24.5	28.3	39.3	40.0	36.9	28.5
All *other* brands	32.1	33.7	33.5	29.7	34.1	34.5	33.2
Total	100.0	100.0	100.0	100.0	100.0	100.0	100.0
Share of Media Expenditures[a]							
Arctic Power	9.3	13.1	16.1	.5	1.4	16.0	13.1
ABC	13.6	14.7	9.1	18.4	17.3	12.1	12.1
Sunlight	11.3	11.1	11.1	12.6	10.2	10.1	9.8
Tide	29.7	27.8	25.1	33.1	38.1	30.2	28.7
All *other* brands	36.1	33.3	38.6	35.4	33.0	31.6	36.3
Total	100.0	100.0	100.0	100.0	100.0	100.0	100.0
Total $ ('000)	14,429	695	4,915	4,758	928	1,646	1,487

Source: Company records.

[a]The total amount of advertising spent by all brands was determined. The amount spent by each brand as a percentage of total spending was calculated.

way of good marketing judgment. I prefer a unified strategy and the Quebec campaign has a proven track record."

Linda concluded, "Let's go over the data again, then start making our decisions. Remember, our goal is to develop a solid brand name for 1988 for Arctic Power."

Kortec and Wrenware Architectural Hardware

It was the spring of 1991. Tim McDern was just getting in from his weekly tennis match. The match, a victory, had provided a short but much-needed break from the problem he was facing as Director of International Sales of Kortec and Wrenware Architectural Hardware.

Kortec and Wrenware Architectural Hardware were two separate and distinct companies in the architectural hardware business operating as a single division of a Fortune 100 company (The Lock Company) in central Connecticut. Each company operated separately, each with its own brand names, product lines, and distribution channels. Due to changes in the architectural hardware industry, it was no longer a perceived benefit, nor was it cost-effective, to support two separate brand names.

Reorganizations of sorts had already taken place to combine the separate support areas for the two brand names. Consideration was now being given to coming up with a new brand name for the two companies. McDern's assignment was to determine the alternate approaches The Lock Company could follow in trying to come up with a new brand name, along with the positive and negative factors that should be considered with each approach (specifically, as they related to their international markets) when it came time to actually decide on a new brand name.

COMPANY BACKGROUND

Kortec and Wrenware Architectural Hardware both manufactured commercial locksets, exit devices, closers, and key systems. Each company was started independently in the mid-1800s as a diversified manufacturer of products that ranged from locks to furniture hardware to mailboxes. They were strong competitors with each other in the area of locks. Over time, both of their product lines phased out the furniture hardware and mailboxes and concentrated on commercial locks. The companies went on to expand their product lines to include exit devices and door closers.

As the companies continued to evolve separately, they developed their own unique product lines, distribution channels, and markets.

In the early 1900s, these two staunch competitors took a step that shocked the hardware industry. They decided to merge at the corporate level, but they continued to run their operations separately, with separate product lines, distribution channels, and markets.

In the 1930s and 1940s, the companies experienced some economic gains by using the same screws in the manufacture of the two separate and distinct locks sold by each of the divisions. This marked the first significant step to further economies of scale by the two companies.

In the 1950s and 1960s, the synergy continued. The companies began using the same components in the manufacture of their locksets, with the exception of the key systems. By this time, each company was producing very similar lockset designs, with the primary differences being in the key systems used. They also continued to maintain separate brand names, distribution channels, geographic markets (international only), sales forces, and management.

In the late 1960s, a Fortune 500 company acquired both companies and began to operate them as a single division. At this time, the companies were

---

This case was prepared as a basis for class discussion rather than to illustrate either effective or ineffective handling of an administrative situation.

brought under a single roof for the first time—an 800,000 square-foot facility. Because they now shared the same physical location, the companies were able to combine their manufacturing processes, engineering support, and new product development. However, they continued to maintain different brand names, sales organizations, distribution channels, and geographic markets.

In the late 1980s, the Fortune 500 corporation was acquired by a Fortune 100 corporation (The Lock Company). It was at this time that senior management decided to merge its sales and marketing organizations to support the two different brand names. Due to various considerations, which will be discussed in the next several sections, it was felt to be no longer cost-effective, nor were there any perceived benefits, to maintain separate sales and marketing organizations.

Product Description

The product lines of Kortec and Wrenware had evolved so that they were built with identical components except for the key system. The key system is the part of the lockset that is referred to as the *cylinder.* The key system is the major element of the product that keeps the two brands different. Once set up, the key system controls who has access through any particular lock in the system. This is an important concept for two reasons:

1. When an order is received, it is very important to get the precise specifications about the key systems needed (how many and on which doors each system will be installed). An example would be the security needs of a hospital. Each key system in the hospital must be individually set up to provide or restrict access to the locks in the system. In setting up a hospital's key system, the purchaser (installer) of the system needs to know who should have access to what rooms. The hospital would not want the janitor's key to fit the narcotics room lock, yet the janitor must have access to a number of other rooms for maintenance. Thus, it is very important to identify up front precisely who needs access to what areas to avoid future re-works for the installer and unforseen breaches in security for the customer.

2. Because the key systems of Kortec and Wrenware are designed differently, purchasers must consider these differences carefully before choosing the company from which to purchase key systems. It is probable that, in the lifetime of a key system, additions or changes will be made to the system. Purchasers need assurances that they will be able to acquire locksets compatible with their existing key systems when they are needed.

Market

Kortec and Wrenware's products were primarily sold for new commercial construction and for the aftermarket (i.e., for replacement on buildings such as offices, schools, hospitals, and hotels). Both companies had sales in the U.S., Canada, and in 65 countries overseas. Both companies had been selling overseas since the late 1800s and had been exerting a strong emphasis on international sales over the last 15–20 years. Each brand name had its regional strength. Kortec's strength was largely in North America and Asia while Wrenware's strength was in Europe and the Middle East.

Distribution Channels

(Manufacturer → Distributor → End User). Distribution of the products for both Kortec and Wrenware was primarily through small, privately-owned family businesses, which would frequently act as subcontractors on new and after-market projects. Distribution through this channel was referred to as *one-step distribution* because the product went to one middleman before going to the end user. For the most part, these distributors supported either the Kortec or Wrenware name. Within a given city, there were as few as one or as many as three distributors.

(Manufacturer → Wholesaler → Distributor → End User). Wholesalers were also used to some extent. This was referred to as *two-step distribution.* The wholesalers in the architectural hardware industry had actually helped bring the two brand names closer together. The distributors and end users had gradually become aware that the Kortec and Wrenware products were essentially the same. As a result, the end user would frequently go to a distributor and ask for either brand. For example, if an end user went to a Kortec distributor and asked for a Wrenware product, the distributor was forced to seek out a wholesaler to obtain the product because the distributor was forbidden by agreement with Kortec from going to Wrenware directly.

Distributors had historically been brand loyal, but this had been changing over time. New competition was offering new alternatives. In addition, senior management at The Lock Company no longer saw any "perceived benefit" to having two unique brand names in the marketplace because the end users and people in the architectural hardware industry were aware of the product similarities and differences in the key systems. Experience was showing that distributors were able to get both products from wholesalers. It made sense to reduce the total number of distributors. Therefore, senior management reduced the number of distributors from approximately 900 in the 1970s to approximately 400 in the late 1980s (200 for Kortec and 200 for Wrenware).

Support for Distribution

Operating two separate sales and marketing organizations required The Lock Company to maintain two separate channels of support for their salespeople, for literature (catalogues, price books, and technical manuals), for promotions (they needed two separate booths at trade shows and any promotional items ordered had to be brand specific), and for advertisements (the ads had to be brand specific). Maintaining two separate channels had become very expensive, especially in light of increased competition and the fact that the industry was becoming more and more aware of how similar Kortec and Wrenware products were to each other. The economic benefits of operating these areas separately no longer exceeded the economic costs. Senior managers at The Lock Company decided that the company would be in a better position by combining the monies spent on sales and marketing—they'd get more bang for their buck.

PERCEIVED STRENGTHS AND WEAKNESSES IN THE MARKET

The Lock Company perceived various strengths and weaknesses in Kortec's and Wrenware's positions in the architectural hardware market. This information would be relevant to any decision made regarding changing the individual brand names.

Strengths in the Market

Brand Awareness. Both Kortec's and Wren-ware's names were easily recognized by the domestic commercial hardware industry, which consisted of the architects who drew the building designs as well as the end users. This was not the case in the international markets, where each company had a regional presence. In international markets, either the Kortec or Wrenware name was known, but not both.

Market Coverage. Both Kortec and Wrenware had domestic and international sales (North America, Canada, and 65 countries overseas).

Full Line Product Strength. Both companies carried a full assortment of products for commercial doors consisting of locksets, key systems, closers, and exit devices. Because of this, buyers were able to obtain everything they needed from either company (some competitors carried less than a full product line).

Breadth of Product Line. Both Kortec's and Wrenware's product lines consisted of locksets, key systems, closers, and exit devices in a broad range of price ranges and grade levels.

Regional Sales Office Presence in International Markets. Between the two companies, the major markets of the world were covered. The international offices were responsible for their own sales and marketing efforts (i.e., they prepared their own brochures). Thus, they were able to "think globally, yet act locally." The international offices were also free to take what they could use from the home office and either use it "as is" or enhance the design to meet their own local needs. In addition, the brochures were designed with an international flavor (e.g., they were written in the local language and included such things as metric conversions).

Weaknesses

Reduction in Distribution Loyalty. Kortec and Wrenware faced reduction in distributor loyalty due to increased competition. Hardware products were becoming more and more generic.

Reduced Visibility of Brand Names. Economic constraints combined with the need to split the advertising and promotion dollars to cover two separate brand names tended to reduce the overall visibility of each brand.

Delivery and Quality of Products. Delivery and quality of products, especially in the international markets, had taken a downturn within the past five years. As a result, competitors had picked up some of their markets. Kortec and Wrenware were in the process of addressing these issues through new manufacturing processes; however, the benefits would not be felt immediately.

Promotional and Technical Support Materials in Disrepair. Both Kortec and Wrenware were in need of new promotional and technical support literature. However, due to the pending brand name decision, managers did not want to develop new materials. A complete product catalogue alone would cost each company $200,000 to develop, design, print, and deliver for worldwide distribution. Managers decided to live with the existing materials for the time being.

New '92 Sales Brochures Needed. New brochures were needed for the upcoming year at a cost of approximately $80,000 for each company. Management was uncertain about whether or not to combine them.

Expertise in Distribution. As stated earlier, it is very important for vendors selling key systems to get accurate key-system specifications with each order. In addition, there must be a thorough understanding of the *application of the products.* The purchasers/architects must be careful to comply with various fire codes, handicap codes, UL (Underwriters Laboratory) codes, as well as other laws.

Kortec's and Wrenware's distribution networks, now seen as a strength, could become a weakness due to the recent reduction in distributors around the world.

DECISIONS...DECISIONS...

Tim McDern settled back in his favorite recliner to ponder his assignment. He needed to develop the alternative approaches The Lock Company should consider when determining a new brand name. In addition, he needed to determine the various positive and negative factors that should be considered (specifically, those related to their international markets) when it came time to determine a new brand name.

McDern took a sip of his Gatorade and thought to himself: "In coming up with the various alternative approaches, there will be certain factors that may pertain to more than one alternative." He decided to call these "generic factors." He would list other factors under each alternative approach separately.

So, relying on his knowledge of Kortec's and Wrenware's backgrounds and their perceived strengths and weaknesses, McDern pulled out a notebook and began to write.

GENERIC FACTORS

McDern considered generic factors to be such basic factors as language differences, possibility of brand piracy, and local laws in the markets served by both companies that would affect the new brand name, no matter what approach was followed.

Language

Because Kortec and Wrenware had sales in 65 foreign countries, marketing would take place in a variety of foreign languages. A number of questions had to be answered before a brand name could be chosen. Would the brand name be easily *translatable* to the various languages? Could the brand name be easily *pronounced* in all of the languages? (For example, if *Wrenware* were chosen as the brand name, Asian customers would have difficulty pronouncing the name because of their trouble in pronouncing the 'R' and 'W' sounds of the English language. Could or would this have an effect on sales?) Would the brand name inadvertently insult a particular culture because of what that name might mean when translated to the language of that culture (or even standing on its own untranslated)? McDern realized the need to be sensitive to the various *cultures* in which Kortec and Wrenware operated.

In addition, two other factors that needed to be considered were the length of the name and the image that the name would project. The Lock Company would not want a name that was too long to print when preparing written materials in many different languages. The length might also affect customers' ability to remember the name, especially if a totally new brand name were chosen. And, depending upon the name chosen, certain negative images might be implied in one or more of the various cultures in which the companies did business. An example would be a name that might imply a weak company or a shoddy product in any of the markets, depending upon how the brand name were translated or interpreted. Another example might be that the name chosen is acceptable but very similar to the name of another company in any of the markets that has a shoddy reputation; The Lock Company would not want its name inadvertently confused with or associated with the shoddy company or product.

Any one or more of these factors could adversely affect The Lock Company's market in the foreign countries.

Brand Piracy

In selecting a brand name, laws of the various countries regarding brand name piracy must be considered. There are three general forms of piracy:

1. *Imitation*—A company may copy your established brand name or logo.
2. *Faking*—A company may identify its product with a symbol or logo very similar to your established brand/logo.
3. *Pre-emption*—A company may register your brand name in its country before you and then possibly try to sell it back to you to make money.

Between them, Kortec and Wrenware were already established in 65 foreign countries and did not have any piracy problems with their current names.

Local Laws

The names currently used in foreign countries complied with the laws of those countries, but The Lock Company needed to consider the various laws and procedures to register its new brand name when the time came. In addition, The Lock Company needed to be cognizant of the fact that, if it were to choose a new brand name, it would need to ensure that the new name did not infringe upon any other companies already doing business in any of the foreign markets under that name.

Once McDern had finished listing his generic factors, he turned his attention to some alternatives The Lock Company should consider before determining a new brand name. He listed these, along with various international factors, both positive and negative, that should also be considered before choosing the brand name.

ALTERNATIVE 1—LITERALLY DO NOTHING

The Lock Company could literally do nothing and continue to do business under the two separate company names. McDern listed this alternative, although he knew it would not be considered. The Lock Company had already made the decision to combine the various parts of the company operations and look for a new brand name. As stated above, there were no more economies of scale operating under separate names.

Still, it was an alternative in the event that no new brand name could be agreed upon. A positive factor in this case was the fact that the Kortec and Wrenware names were already established overseas; on the negative side, The Lock Company would need to maintain two separate sets of support materials (determined as not cost-effective).

ALTERNATIVE 2—KEEP SAME NAMES BUT DIFFERENTIATE THE PRODUCTS

McDern felt that under this alternative The Lock Company could continue to operate the companies under the same two separate names but somehow differentiate the products. By differentiating the products, The Lock Company might substantiate the costs that would be necessary to support two brand names.

The differentiation between the names could come by way of *product quality*. For example, Kortec might be marketed as a high quality, high cost product while Wrenware could be the lesser quality, lower cost product.

An alternative differentiation could come by way of *product market*. For example, Kortec might be targeted toward the hotel and hospital market while Wrenware would be targeted toward the school and prison market.

A third alternative differentiation could be by *geographic market*. For example, Kortec might be targeted at North America and Asia while Wrenware might be targeted at Europe and the Middle East. Their current regional strengths were already located in these markets.

The positive and negative factors to be considered in differentiating the products were:

Product Quality

Negative. The two companies were in predominantly separate market concentrations overseas. For example, it could potentially cost The Lock Company a great deal of money to introduce the Wrenware name to the Asian market, where it is currently not readily recognized.

Negative. The existing distributors of the Wrenware product might become upset if their product began being marketed as one of lesser quality. This could affect future sales as well as relationships with existing customers, to whom distributors had previously marketed Wrenware as a high quality product. Thus, relationships with distributors as well as existing and future customers could be affected.

Negative. The overlap in the markets might create confusion both on the part of purchasers and on the part of those providing the support and necessary technical expertise.

Positive. Differentiating by product quality, if successful, would substantiate the need to continue to support two brand names. It might also help expand the market share of both lines. The Lock Company may be able to pick up some of their competitors' market share by marketing both a high quality product and one of lesser quality.

Product Market

Positive. Again, if successful, keeping the same names but differentiating the products might cause The Lock Company to focus on more specific types of markets.

Negative. Again, this might have a negative impact on distributors and existing customers. Distributors with contacts in a particular industry (e.g., schools) might suddenly find their product targeted toward hotels, which could affect their sales. Existing customers might also be confused. For example, if school customers needed additional locks that had originally been bought from Kortec, they would be confused to find that Wrenware was now being targeted toward their school—especially since the key systems from the two companies originally were not compatible. McDern made a note that, if this option were to be pursued, The Lock Company would need to be careful how it introduced and promoted the change.

Geographic Market

Positive. The products were already primarily established and concentrated in different geographic markets. The Lock Company would not need to worry about introducing a new brand name. In a sense, the brand name may already be widely recognized in the geographic markets, or it may be the leading seller—no need, then, to interrupt this process.

Negative. This, in a sense, was The Lock Company's current situation, which it hoped to change.

Product Quality and Market

Negative. The architects in the foreign countries were not as familiar with the similarities between the existing brands. This could have an adverse effect on their recommendations if the companies suddenly began being targeted toward different markets. The architects might be confused or unfamiliar with the specifications of the alternative brand name.

ALTERNATIVE 3—COMBINE THE EXISTING NAMES

Under this alternative, the two company names could be combined in a form such as "Kortec & Wrenware Architectural Hardware."

Positive. This would enable The Lock Company to keep both names. Architects and end users would then not be totally confused by the change. They would still see a name they recognized.

Positive. It would result in fewer costs than having to introduce a "new" or "different" brand name to the markets served.

Negative. The name of the company would become very long. This is important when preparing written literature (catalogues, brochures, advertising—too long is *not good*). For example, the name is put in every "environment" possible, such as letterheads, business cards, trade show booths, etc. A longer name would make it more costly and difficult to prepare these materials. A longer name would also be harder for customers to remember.

Negative. Confusion might be created in existing markets. For example, in Hong Kong the name Wrenware means nothing because the product is currently not distributed there.

Major Negative. In those countries where both products were offered, and given the fact that (a) the distribution channels were recently reduced to approximately 200 for each brand name and (b) most distributors were selling either one or the other brand name, The Lock Company is now conceivably going to be asking distributors to sell a product that they had considered to be a competitive brand name. These distributors, for example, may have promoted Kortec while criticizing Wrenware because they carried only the Kortec product. The previous separate sales forces selling to the distributors had also promoted in this manner. Now they will be asked to sell a product that includes a name they may have previously "badmouthed." This could have an adverse effect on the distributors' existing relationships with their customers.

Negative. The existing names may have meant something special to the architects. The Lock Company wouldn't want to lose their association with the existing brand name.

ALTERNATIVE 4—USE EITHER ONE NAME OR THE OTHER

Positive. Consideration should be given to language, culture, and local brand name laws, as previously discussed. In light of these considerations, The Lock Company would want to choose the name that gave off the stronger image (e.g., Kortec sounds like a stronger company) or be more easily pronounced, (e.g., Kortec may be more easily pronounced, depending on the culture).

Positive. A distribution system is already established in those countries served by the company that would lose its name. Additional work in the form of well-prepared advertising, support, and promotional materials could help overcome the recognition problem faster than if The Lock Company attempted to go in without an established distribution channel and support materials.

Negative. Using one name only, The Lock Company runs the risk of loss of name recognition in the countries served by the company that would lose its name. Additional costs of introduction and promotion would also result. There is a risk of losing sales in these areas, at least until name recognition for the new name is established.

ALTERNATIVE 5—NEW NAME

Alternative 5 would involve coming out with an entirely new brand name.

Positive. The opportunity would exist here for a clever, descriptive brand name and/or trademark or logo. The name chosen might enable The Lock Company to tie the brand name more closely to the product it is offering.

Positive. A new name would enable The Lock Company to update its technical manuals, etc., that were in a state of disrepair. In addition, it would offer The Lock Company the opportunity to develop new and better materials.

Positive. The Lock Company could also continue to sub-label whatever brand name was chosen with "A Fortune 100 Company: The Lock Company," to help maintain the customers' identification with its products. This might help alleviate some anxieties arising from a brand name change.

Positive. Given that various cultural factors are taken into consideration in arriving at a new

name, it will be very important how The Lock Company then uses and effectively markets that name in the future. For example, "Coke" doesn't mean anything by itself as a word but it has been so effectively marketed that it has become synonymous with the soft drink.

Negative. A new name would require The Lock Company to scrap its existing support materials that contained the old name and develop new materials. This would be more expensive up front. Using any one of the other alternatives would have enabled the company to use its existing materials for a while longer.

Negative. Finding a new name would most likely require hiring an expert consultant. The consultant would be responsible for determining if the name was already being used, whether it infringed upon existing trademarks or logos, and the impact the new name would have in existing foreign markets with respect to language, culture, and existing local laws, etc.

McDern looked up at the clock as it struck 1 A.M. Before he retired for the night, he reflected on what he had been doing.

In preparing the alternative courses of action that The Lock Company would consider when determining a new brand name for its international markets, he found there was much more to renaming a company than simply coming up with a new name and figuring the associated costs. For instance, the language, culture, and laws of each foreign market had to be considered. Nor could established relationships with distributors and customers be neglected. All in all, there were many associated issues to consider, not just a name change. Arriving at a new brand name would require expert consultants, brand awareness studies (both nationally and internationally), studies on the distribution networks used by both Kortec and Wrenware, and a significant amount of related analysis. The Lock Company would need hard facts to back up any decision it would make.

This was not a short-term but a long-term decision that would affect the long-term positioning of the company. Key strategic decisions would need to be made in order to position The Lock Company to capture a worldwide market share. These decisions should only be made after considering the various international implications and factors.

In early 1986, Christie Hefner, president and chief operating officer, Playboy Enterprises, Inc., had been reviewing the company's strategies to face the changing world. Once considered a trendsetter for urban sophisticates, the adult leisure company in recent years has increasingly found its offerings out of step with the times.

As a writer on social issues put it, "The image of the playboy in a smoking jacket is obsolete. People today are more interested in their cars and their careers than they are in sex." Although that claim may be open to dispute, Playboy has reason to be alarmed. The circulation of its flagship magazine has dwindled to just over four million a month from more than seven million in 1972. The number of Playboy Club key holders has fallen steadily. The cable television Playboy Channel, once seen as crucial to the company's future, loses money and has yet to prove that it can survive in its highly competitive field.

Between 1983 and 1985, *Playboy's* revenue fell by nearly 50 percent. It earned a profit on operations in only one of four years between 1982 and 1985, when it was forced by old legal problems to give up its lucrative casinos. The company was in the black (by $6.7 million) in its 1985 fiscal year only because of returns on $60 million in investments. And its auditors qualified their opinion on the financial statement for that year because of uncertainty over whether Playboy can collect all it is owed on one casino sale.

COMPANY HISTORY

Initially, Playboy Enterprises, Inc. was established as HMH Publishing Company in 1953 to publish *Playboy*. The present name was adopted in 1971.

Today the company's businesses, in addition to *Playboy* and *Games* magazines, include the development and production of programming principally for pay television and videocassettes and products for direct sale and licensing that feature the Playboy name and trademarks for worldwide distribution. In addition, the company owns and franchises Playboy Clubs. In the 1970s, the company entered the resort hotel and casino business in different places, including London, Miami, the Bahamas, and Atlantic City. However, in 1982 the company discontinued its resort hotel and casino operations.

ENVIRONMENTAL CHANGES

Playboy is a victim of the social changes it helped promote. Attitudes toward sex have evolved rapidly since the days when the magazine could shock millions by publishing two photographs of an undraped Marilyn Monroe. Today, *Playboy* must compete, not only with countless far more lurid "skin books," but also against the popular media. Rock songs may have X-rated lyrics and an episode of "Dynasty" may be nearly as titillating as a centerfold.

As Ms. Hefner puts it, "We no longer can contrast ourselves to a gray-flannel Eisenhower society. It's now a lot more difficult for us to offer something unique."

Yet Playboy also finds itself considerably vexed these days by those who consider its business immoral or sexist or both. Although its cable television fare isn't hard-core, for instance, it has repeatedly been challenged in court (so far unsuccessfully) by communities that want it banned.

After ABC recently broadcast a film based on Gloria Steinem's critical account of her 1963 stint as a bunny, Playboy President Christie Hefner fired off a memo asking her staff to "ponder what it is Playboy and all of its resources can and should be

---

This case was prepared as a basis for class discussion rather than to illustrate either effective or ineffective handling of an administrative situation.

doing to counter the . . . misimpression out there that we are not good guys."

Perhaps a tougher problem for Hefner, though, is finding a clear mission for Playboy in the 1990s, one as potent as her father's former vision for the company. In an era of aggressive careerism among both sexes, the company no longer gets much mileage out of the so-called Playboy philosophy, Mr. Hefner's concept of the lifestyle of a man of leisure.

THE REAL PROBLEM

Some company officials believe that one of Playboy's biggest handicaps may be its association with the public image of its founder, now 59 years old. As a Playboy executive put it, "Pajamas just aren't as fashionable as they used to be."

Though still the best-selling magazine for men, Playboy has fallen far behind arch-rival Penthouse in lucrative newsstand sales. According to Penthouse publisher Bob Guccione, "Playboy's market is older and its readers are passing into oblivion." Playboy executives say that the readership age difference is minimal. However, there are other worrisome signs. A Chicago newsstand operator who has sold many copies of Playboy speaks of the typical buyer as "a guy who thinks he's up-to-date but isn't." One woman who posed for a pictorial was surprised when she saw the letters the feature generated: "A whole bunch of them were from guys in prison." A former public relations executive for Playboy contends that the company "doesn't want to face reality—that time has passed it by."

NEW STRATEGY

Against this background, Playboy Enterprises is undertaking what Hefner calls a "repositioning." The strategy, she says, is to go after a more upscale audience by being more in tune with current tastes and values. "I think we should be on the cutting edge of how people who have changed their behavior to reflect a more liberal lifestyle are going to live."

The October 1985 issue of Playboy, marked "Collector's Edition," began what the company calls the magazine's next generation. This included greater coverage of such "life style" subjects as personal finance and home electronics. An ad in that issue asked, "What sort of man reads Playboy?" and offered as an example race car driver Danny Sullivan. Posing in a black silk evening jacket, he explained that he "grew with the magazine," learning, for instance, to care about clothes. Curiously, elsewhere in the issue was a piece satirizing the consumer society.

Sensitive to criticism that it portrays women as sex objects, Playboy intends to feature some who are more mature or more accomplished. The lead feature in the November 1985 issue was a nod in this direction, but it hardly seemed likely to defuse the moral issue. Picturing members of Mensa, the club people can join only if they have high IQs, the feature was entitled "America's Smartest Girls Pose Nude."

Nevertheless, Hefner says Playboy's effort to move upscale is working. As evidence, she notes that the October 1985 issue carried advertising for Campbell Soup's Le Menu frozen dinners.

Covers of the new generation Playboy are to have a glitzier look. They are planned in long meetings by a committee of fashion and art experts who try to base their designs as much on the latest fashions as on erotic content.

The graphics also are slicker and a different printing process binds pages with glue instead of staples, giving a more finished look. According to Playboy's art director, "The magazine is supposed to look a lot more like the kind of thing you'd put on a coffee table." That goal may be a bit optimistic, however; newsstands say that half of the buyers of Playboy still ask for a paper bag to carry it home in.

The new magazine retains many standard features, like the Playboy Advisor, which intersperses advice about sex with answers to questions about stereos or turbochargers. Some editors complain about the uneven quality and occasionally questionable taste of color cartoons. Mr. Hefner himself is said to have rejected an editor's plea to eliminate the Party Jokes feature, which in the October 1985 issue regaled readers with one-liners like, "What's boffo box office among milkmaids? *Pail Rider*."

The "repositioning" also applies to the Playboy Clubs, which haven't had a major updating since they were started a quarter-century ago. Even with a recent redecorating, the club in Chicago, with its plush red carpeting and black leather bar stools, looks a little like a museum for the jazz age. A gift shop upfront peddling Playboy T-shirts, cigarette lighters, and golf putters lends a touristy atmosphere to the place.

Rather than confront the deteriorating image of its big-city clubs, Playboy several years ago headed for the hinterlands, franchising clubs in places like Lansing, Michigan, and Des Moines, Iowa, where they might still have novelty value. But without a strong big-city base, the whole chain lost its urban gleam. The Lansing club began resorting to such decidedly unglamorous promotions as lip-sync contests and valet parking for farm tractors.

THE NEW YORK EXPERIMENT

In the fall of 1985, the company reopened its newly done New York club. It was a bold experiment. The cottontailed bunnies were replaced by hostesses greeting guests wearing long, glittering Jean Harlow-style gowns. Some of the waiters were men. Absent were the traditional pool table, party balloons, and Leroy Neiman paintings. Instead, video effects, stage acts, and music by a 10-piece house orchestra were offered.

The New York club's new look was sculpted by Richard Melman, who is noted for elaborate concept restaurants that are as much show-biz productions as eateries. He selected bunnies with talent as bodybuilders, astrologists, and jugglers. Costumes ranged from a sequined one called the Michael Jackson outfit, to sweater dresses, to a take-off of the current cottontail suit. The idea of male waiters (called rabbits) was to help women feel more comfortable in the club.

It remains to be seen if the company will convert other clubs to the New York style. The company has 12 other Playboy Clubs, ten of which are franchised rather than company owned. A section of the club called Cafe Playboy may be tested as a prototype for a chain of franchised bars open to the public. (A Playboy key still is needed for admittance to the clubs, though temporary memberships are readily available.)

STRATEGY FOR OTHER BUSINESSES

Playboy's products division, too, is working to bolster the company's image—or at least to stop endangering it. The division has sold countless key chains, air fresheners, and the like, even though doing so risked cheapening the company's trademark. Now Playboy is moving away from novelty items and into fashion apparel and branded consumer products. One success is Playboy's men's underwear, the second-best-selling brand.

Playboy still has some hard thinking to do about its video operation. The division, which launched the first sex-oriented cable channel for a mass audience five years ago, had identity problems from the start. Unable to decide how racy to be, the channel wound up alienating viewers at both ends of the spectrum.

Earlier in 1985, for instance, the channel stopped offering erotic programming during prime time and switched to mainstream movies and quasi-journalistic specials such as "Omar Sharif Hosts the Prostitutes of Paris." Viewership dropped and Playboy soon reverted to prime-time prurience.

Partly because of its turnabouts, the Playboy Channel has had the highest disconnect rate in the industry, 13 percent of viewers each month. Its current level of about 762,000 subscribers isn't enough to pay for the quality programming that might attract a larger audience. At $20 million, the channel's yearly budget is less than a network might spend during a season on a single series.

As a result, Playboy is de-emphasizing the channel as its main outlet for programming and will focus more on cassette sales and a recently launched pay-per-view service. It also is weighing a return to producing a late-night variety show or hour-long specials, either of which it would try to sell to one of the networks.

Still, Playboy's video operations, like the rest of its empire, is continuing to grope for the right formula for today's audience. As Ms. Hefner sums up, "We have to reflect a modern, sophisticated image."

In August 1988, the sales and marketing executives of Aldus Corporation met at a Massachusetts resort to begin their strategic marketing planning for 1989. At the meeting, Richard Strong, Marketing Manager for Aldus Europe, proposed that Aldus split its product family into two distinct product lines: the Aldus Executive Series, which would include PageMaker, Persuasion, and additional new products that would be aimed at the business market, and the Aldus Professional Series, which would include a professional version of PageMaker, Aldus Freehand, Aldus Snapshot, and additional new products that would be aimed at the creative graphics professional market. Richard Strong argued that his proposal would allow Aldus to develop two separate, focused product and market strategies for these two major market segments.

The initial response to Richard's proposal was cautiously favorable. On the surface, it would solve a lot of problems. It would allow Aldus to clarify the positioning of each of its major products, while helping the company establish a strong and unique company identity in each of its two major market segments. However, the company has based its success to date on offering a single product line that bridged the gap between business and creative professionals. Furthermore, it was not at all clear how the multibranding decision would be implemented at the sales and distribution levels, either domestically or internationally.

The Aldus corporate marketing staff was given the challenge of evaluating Richard Strong's proposal and developing a detailed implementation plan if the multibranding decision was recommended for adoption.

ALDUS CORPORATION

Aldus Corporation was founded in February 1984 to develop a cost-effective and easy-to-use software tool that would perform on a microcomputer many of the page layout and design functions of a workstation-, minicomputer- or mainframe-based publishing system. The result was PageMaker, which allowed people to design, edit, and produce printed communications electronically, thereby reducing the time and expense associated with traditional publishing techniques. This new microcomputer-based publishing soon became known as "desktop publishing," a term coined by Aldus's founder and president, Paul Brainerd.

Before founding Aldus, Paul Brainerd had been a vice president with a company that manufactured dedicated publishing systems for newspapers and magazines. Prior to that, Brainerd was editor-in-chief of the *Minnesota Daily* and assistant to the operations director for the Minneapolis Star and Tribune Company.

Aldus Corporation shipped its first copies of PageMaker for the Apple Macintosh in July 1985, and by 1988 it had become the international standard for desktop publishing software. Both the Macintosh version of PageMaker and the PC version, which was first shipped in January 1987, had been translated into more than ten languages. A Japanese Kanji version of PageMaker for the Macintosh was scheduled for introduction in September 1988. This would be the first Asian language desktop publishing software product from a U.S. company.

In June 1987, Aldus completed a successful public offering of 2,240,000 shares of common stock, raising approximately $31 million to support future

---

growth. Later in 1987, Aldus became a multi-product company with the acquisition of the marketing and distribution rights to two new products: Aldus FreeHand, a drawing tool for the Apple Macintosh, and Aldus SnapShot, an electronic photography program for the PC. In July 1988, the company announced its fourth major product, Aldus Persuasion, a desktop presentation software program for the Macintosh, scheduled to be released late in 1988. While the new products gave Aldus a more diversified portfolio, PageMaker was still accounting for about 80 percent of Aldus's sales in mid-1988. The financial highlights of Aldus's first five years of operations are shown in Exhibit 1.

Aldus Corporation derived its name from Aldus Manutius, a fifteenth century Venetian scholar who founded the Aldine Press, the first modern publishing house. He was also known for having invented italic type and for standardizing the rules of pronunciation.

BUSINESS STRATEGY

Paul Brainerd attributed a great deal of Aldus's early success to its effective use of strategic alliances, the development of a motivated and educated network of resellers, and a highly successful public relations campaign.

From the beginning, one of Aldus Corporation's basic business strategies had been to forge strategic alliances with other vendors for both technical and marketing purposes. The strategic alliance with Apple was particularly important. In 1985 Aldus, which was then working on its first version of PageMaker, employed a total of 15 people. The marketing function was composed of one salesperson, a part-time marketing consultant, and Paul Brainerd. As Paul Brainerd later commented: "The name of the game was clearly leverage—how could we at Aldus leverage off our very limited resource base?" The initial version of PageMaker was designed to run on an Apple Macintosh computer. In 1984, Apple had about 2,000 dealers in the United States and Canada. It was clear to the man-

agement team at Aldus that, if PageMaker were successful, one sale of the software package could result in several thousands of dollars of hardware sales (in computers, printers, and other peripheral equipment). If Apple could be convinced of the potential value of PageMaker as a means of generating hardware sales, it had the financial and organizational resources to be of great assistance to Aldus.

At the same time that Aldus was looking at Apple, Apple was facing some significant problems of its own. Apple had been developing a laser printer, the LaserWriter, to complement the Macintosh computer. This project was running into considerable opposition within Apple. The organization was still smarting from the demise of the expensive Lisa computer, and some Apple managers were questioning the wisdom of marketing a printer selling for $7,000. At this price, it would cost twice as much as the basic computer. In addition, there were no applications that fully utilized its capabilities. However, Steve Jobs continued to support the laser printer project and Apple was already working with Adobe Systems and its PostScript graphics language that would be a crucial element in taking full advantage of the LaserWriter's capabilities. In July 1984, Aldus demonstrated a prototype of PageMaker to the Apple project manager for the LaserWriter. An informal alliance was formed. Apple would provide the work-station and the laser printer, Adobe the PostScript language, and Aldus the business application.

Over the next year, Paul Brainerd visited Apple at least once every four to six weeks. Bruce Blumberg, the Apple project manager for the LaserWriter, informally introduced Paul to many Apple employees, and through corridor and office conversations Paul developed an understanding of their needs. Aldus played the lead role in developing marketing materials that would demonstrate to potential users the possible applications of desktop publishing. Apple often played the lead role in advertising and promoting these applications to potential users, featuring desktop publishing applications in its business media advertising for the

EXHIBIT 1

Aldus Corporation—Selected Financial Highlights

Consolidated Condensed Balance Sheet	July 1, 1988	Dec. 31, 1987	Dec. 31, 1986	Dec. 31, 1985
Assets				
Current Assets				
Cash and marketable securities	$ 33,429,006	$31,736,569	$ 3,159,937	$ 903,039
Other current assets	18,790,193	10,266,49	22,051,494	594,966
Total current assets	52,219,199	42,003,061	5,211,431	1,498,005
Equipment and leasehold improvements, net	4,833,736	4,004,413	791,443	174,186
Capitalized software development costs	2,986,854	2,387,685	377,960	–
Other assets, substantially all intangible assets	570,237	592,283	–	1,620
	$ 60,610,026	$48,987,442	$ 6,380,834	$1,673,811
Liabilities and Shareholders' Equity				
Current Liabilities				
Accounts payable and accrued liabilities	$ 5,944,218	$ 3,929,736	$ 1,071,546	$ 185,335
Deferred technical support revenue	672,392	334,874	116,722	62,062
Income taxes payable	1,012,000	–	1,433,000	167,000
Total current liabilities	7,628,610	4,264,610	2,621,268	414,397
Lease obligations	127,325	218,783	–	–
Deferred income taxes	1,157,000	1,168,000	144,000	6,000
Shareholders' equity	51,697,091	43,336,049	3,615,566	1,253,414
	$ 60,610,026	$48,987,442	$ 6,380,834	$1,673,811
Working capital	$ 44,590,589	$37,738,451	$ 2,590,163	$1,083,608

Consolidated Condensed Statement of Income

	6 months ending July 1, 1988	Year ending			
		Dec. 31, 1987	Dec. 31, 1986	Dec. 31, 1985	Dec. 31, 1984
Net sales	$35,075,105	$39,542,200	$11,135,688	$2,234,424	$ –
Operating expenses					
Cost of sales	7,494,841	8,600,441	1,066,417	161,890	
Selling, general, and administrative	14,700,460	16,597,433	5,518,519	1,120,948	121,590
Research and development	3,798,793	2,502,337	590,401	297,637	117,750
Income from operations	9,081,011	11,841,989	3,960,351	653,949	(239,340)
Interest income, net	810,746	972,483	151,801	37,138	21,854
Other expenses	(474,549)	(253,377)	–	–	–
Income before provision for income taxes	9,417,208	12,561,095	4,112,152	691,087	(217,486)
Extraordinary credit	–	–	–	80,000	–
Provision for income taxes	2,982,000	4,755,500	1,750,000	253,000	–
Net income	$ 6,435,208	$ 7,805,595	$ 2,362,152	$ 518,087	$ (217,486)
Net income per share of common stock	$.50	$.66	$.21	$.05	$(.02)

Macintosh. Together, Apple and Aldus wrote Apple's marketing plan for penetrating the publishing market.

The project took on a new urgency within Apple with the increased emphasis John Sculley, the new president of Apple Computer, was placing on the penetration of the business market. The only "solutions-oriented" application with a detailed marketing plan ready for implementation was desktop publishing. Some people within Apple were skeptical about the size of the segment, but both Sculley and Jobs felt instinctively that desktop publishing could be very successful with businesses. Potentially, it could revolutionize the printing business within organizations by eliminating the need for having documents typeset, "pasted-up," and printed. It promised to bring centralized electronic publishing to the desktop. As the marketing of desktop publishing gained momentum, it became apparent that it was the perfect "Trojan horse" for Apple. Desktop publishing provided Apple with an entry into businesses. As it became established in an organization, individuals recognized the "user-friendliness" of the Macintosh's graphical interface and began using the Macintosh for new applications, and in some organizations the Macintosh began spreading from department to department.

The strategic alliance with Apple resulted in Aldus gaining access to Apple's 2,000 dealer reseller network in North America. In order to develop this dealer network into an effective marketing organization for desktop publishing, Aldus and Apple jointly determined the tasks that needed to be done, prioritized them, and then allocated each of the high-priority tasks to one of the two partners. One outcome of this process was a very successful series of seminars that provided dealer personnel with a "hands-on" experience with desktop publishing. Apple promoted the seminars within its dealer network and provided facilities and hardware. Aldus provided the software and two teams of people to mount the seminars across North America. Each of the teams visited 10 cities over a two-week period. Thus, by leveraging off the resources and facilities of Apple, Aldus was quickly able to gain visibility with key dealers and in the marketplace.

The third key element that Paul Brainerd felt had contributed to the early success of Aldus Page-Maker was an extensive public relations effort. Given his experience in the publishing business as an editor, Paul knew the potential influence of people in the media. Paul identified the top ten computer press people and contacted them about the potential of desktop publishing. He explained to them the product concept and demonstrated the product to them. Fortunately, most of them were familiar with the difficulties of the traditional printing process and many, seeing the potential of desktop publishing, became excited about the product and wrote extensively about it.

Looking back on the first couple of years of Aldus's history, Paul attributed a great deal of the company's success to having a very clear plan, having a set of priorities, and having focused the company's very limited resources on these priorities.

THE DESKTOP PUBLISHING BUSINESS

Businesses, which produced a wide variety of printed material for internal and external distribution, had generally utilized in-house publication departments or commercial printers to perform design, paste-up, proofing, and typesetting of high-quality printed communications. Historically, typographic-quality publications had been produced by large commercial printers utilizing typesetters and software pagination systems based on mainframes or minicomputers. Such systems required users to have considerable skill and training in page layout and makeup and were expensive, with prices ranging from $30,000 to over $200,000. Consequently, such systems had been sold primarily to large newspapers, magazines, corporate communication departments, and commercial typesetters.

Advances in microcomputers and graphics technology, combined with the availability of low-cost laser printers and the development of page composition software, had facilitated the advent of relatively low-cost microcomputer-based publishing solutions. These systems allowed the integration of text and graphics and the production of typeset-quality printed communications. A typical desktop publishing system, consisting of a microcomputer, a laser printer, and the PageMaker software, cost approximately $8,000 to $12,000 in 1988. Desktop publishing solutions offered users increased control over the printing process and improved quality and timeliness of printed material. Because desktop publishing systems were affordable and easy to use, they had significantly expanded the market for publishing systems and were becoming increasingly popular with a broad range of small businesses, large corporations, government agencies, educational institutions, graphic designers, and business professionals. Typical applications included business communications, such as newsletters, reports to shareholders, and in-house magazines; advertising materials, including ads, brochures, and other promotional materials; sales and marketing materials, such as catalogues, price lists, and directories; manuals and other forms of documentation; and presentation graphics. Industry analysts expected the market (in $ terms) for desktop publishing systems based on microcomputers to more than double by 1992.

MARKET SEGMENTATION AND CUSTOMERS

Aldus management viewed the desktop publishing market as being divided into four major segments based on the computer operating system used (Apple Macintosh or IBM PC AT or compatible) and whether or not the user was a business person or a creative graphics professional. A creative graphics professional was defined as anybody who bought typesetting services or physically prepared documents for publication. The four segments are shown in Exhibit 2.

Aldus first introduced PageMaker into Segment 1 in 1985. PageMaker offered this segment of users a substitute technology for manual ways of working or for buying outside typesetting services. The second segment (Segment 2 in Exhibit 2) attracted to PageMaker was a group of Macintosh technology enthusiasts in the business market, who were graphically-oriented and who wished to incorporate graphics into their documents, or who simply wanted their documents to look more attractive. This segment began to develop in 1986, and its growth accelerated with the increasing availability of laser printers in the office environment. The innovators and early adopters in both Segments 1 and 2 had a high degree of technical competence and were prepared to invest the time and effort to learn how to use the relatively complex desktop publishing software. The third segment PageMaker began to penetrate in 1987, after the release of the PC version of the product, was the PC business segment (Segment 3 in Exhibit 2). Part of this segment's growth was due to some business people being impressed with the attractiveness of documents developed with a desktop publishing system on the Macintosh and wanting to be able to produce similar documents on their IBM AT or compatible. The fourth segment was the PC creative graphics professional. Some industry observers wondered why this segment continued to exist, since the ease-of-use of the

EXHIBIT 2
Segmentation of the Desktop Publishing Market

	Type of Operating System	
Type of User	PC (MS-DOS)	*Macintosh*
Business	Segment 3	Segment 2
Graphics Professional	Segment 4	Segment 1

graphically-oriented Macintosh suggested that they would be better served by a Macintosh-based desktop publishing system. However, there were a number of reasons for the segment's continued existence: some companies were totally committed to IBM or IBM-compatible computers, other companies were attracted to IBM-compatible desktop publishing systems because they could be cheaper than Macintosh systems, and still other companies because the choice of the computer had been made on the basis of the availability of other software packages. The OS/2 system, which had been announced by IBM and Microsoft, promised to make IBM or compatible systems more attractive systems for desktop publishing.

In Segment 1, PageMaker dominated the market with about a 70 percent market share. Quark's Xpress and Letraset's Ready-Set-Go owned much of the rest of the market and Quark's market share was increasing. Market research conducted by Aldus suggested that less than 20 percent of the potential graphics art market had "come down" to desktop publishing by the summer of 1988. One Aldus marketing executive suggested that the potential creative graphics professional market might be fully tapped in three to five years.

PageMaker was also the market share leader in Segment 2. By 1988, Aldus's sales into this segment were increasingly tied to new Macintosh installations, since most of the Macintosh-installed base that had a use for PageMaker had already bought desktop publishing software. Future sales of PageMaker in this segment were highly dependent on Apple's continued ability to develop new customers and to increase its penetration of its existing customer base.

Segment 3 was believed to be a huge potential market given the large PC-installed base and the increasing availability of laser printers. Aldus believed that the real competition in this segment was advanced word processors, or low-end desktop publishing software. Ventura Publishing and PageMaker had roughly equal shares of the high-end desktop publishing market in this segment.

PageMaker had a strong market share position in Segment 4, but, for the reasons suggested above,

this was not a large segment. The aggregate market shares for Aldus and the other major players in the Macintosh and MS-DOS desktop page layout markets in 1987 are shown in Exhibit 3.

In small- and medium-sized organizations, the decision to move to desktop publishing was often made by high-level managers. The decision about which software package to purchase was often left to the judgment of the individuals that would be directly using the software. In large organizations, a variety of different buying processes was evident with major differences between organizations being attributable to the degree of centralization in the information systems function. Perhaps the most common buying pattern observed, for a niche application such as desktop publishing, was for the individual department or function using desktop publishing to select one of the available packages. However, the organization would only provide support for one, or perhaps two packages.

MARKETING

Product Line

In addition to PageMaker, Aldus had a number of other software products in its product line or under development. However, PageMaker still accounted for over 80 percent of Aldus Corporation's sales.

In July 1987, Aldus had acquired the marketing rights to a PostScript-based Macintosh drawing program that was introduced into the market in November 1987 as Aldus FreeHand. Aldus Free-Hand was launched as a direct competitor to Adobe System's Illustrator product and it enjoyed substantial early market success by offering the "power of Illustrator with the ease of use of MacDraw." By the late summer of 1988, version 2.0 of FreeHand was engaged in a highly competitive battle with Adobe Illustrator 88 for market dominance in the PostScript drawing program category. At the same time, Aldus was attempting to expand the market for FreeHand beyond that category by also positioning its offering against MacDraw II, a

EXHIBIT 3
World Desktop Page Layout Market, 1987

Software Vendor	MS-DOS Units Value			
	Units	*Unit Share*	*Value (millions)*	*Dollar Share*
Aldus	69,062	30.5%	$30.87	42.4%
Ventura	60,090	26.6%	$32.87	45.2%
Software Publishing Corp.	39,521	17.5%	$2.98	4.1%
DRI	7,667	3.4%	$2.35	3.2%
Unison World	27,278	12.1%	$1.29	1.8%
Springboard	16,201	7.2%	$0.77	1.1%
AT	2,951	1.3%	$0.53	0.7%
Other	3,355	1.5%	$1.08	1.5%
Total	226,145		$72.74	

Software Vendor	Macintosh Units Value			
	Units	*Unit Share*	*Value (millions)*	*Dollar Share*
Aldus	38,148	53.9%	$12.37	54.0%
Letraset	14,504	20.5%	$4.37	19.1%
Quark	9,612	13.6%	$3.46	15.1%
Orange Micro	8,466	12.0%	$2.73	11.9%
Total	70,729		$22.93	

Source: International Data Corporation

higher-priced and more sophisticated version of the original MacDraw program.

In September 1987, the company acquired both the marketing and development rights to a personal computer-based "electronic photography" application that was introduced to the market in November 1987. Aldus SnapShot was a more troubled software product due to the restricted availability of the hardware required to run it on its MS-DOS platform. The concept of "electronic photography" had failed to capture the market's imagination in the way that "desktop publishing" had done, and Aldus had been unable to forge the strategic alliances with hardware vendors that would be required to make the product an unqualified market success.

In February 1988, Aldus acquired both the marketing and development rights to a desktop presentation product that was introduced in August 1988 as Aldus Persuasion, and was scheduled to be shipped in the fourth quarter of 1988. This acquisition was particularly important to Aldus for several reasons. First, the product itself was believed to be superior to any other desktop presentation product on the market, capable of "setting the standard" for desktop presentation products in much the same way that PageMaker had done for desktop publishing products. Second, the desktop presentation market was believed to meet or exceed the market opportunity represented by desktop publishing—and was significantly larger that the potential market for FreeHand or

SnapShot. Third, the desktop presentation market was clearly perceived as a "business market." Thus, it was hoped that Aldus Persuasion would help to position Aldus Corporation as a player in the mainstream business software market rather than the smaller graphic arts niche.

In August 1988, Aldus was actively seeking additional acquisitions and was also engaged in the internal development of new software products for the business market.

Pricing

One of the crucial early marketing decisions made by Aldus was the pricing of PageMaker for the Macintosh. In 1984, the most expensive piece of Macintosh software was Excel, a spreadsheet program, which had a list price of $395. After some debate, Aldus management decided to price Page-Maker at $495, feeling that any lower price would result in it not being viewed as a serious business tool. There was no visible resistance in the market to the price. Subsequently, when Aldus introduced Version 3.0 of PageMaker for the Macintosh in 1987, the price was raised to $595.

The PC version of PageMaker was expensive to develop and Aldus's management believed it would be more expensive to sell and service in the market. With some trepidation, they priced this version of PageMaker at $695, a $200 premium over the then-current Macintosh version price. Xerox's Ventura Publisher for the PC was announced almost simultaneously and was priced at $895, although Xerox's higher channel discounts resulted in its retail price being $795, a $100 premium over PageMaker. Aldus moved the price of the PC version of the product to $795 when Version 3.0 was introduced.

DISTRIBUTION AND SALES

Aldus distributed its products primarily through retail dealers and original equipment manufacturers (OEMs). OEMs and large retailers paid about 50 percent of the suggested retail price. The company had been selective in both authorizing and retaining dealers who were committed to supporting its products. No single dealer, chain, or OEM accounted for more than 10 percent of sales.

Domestic Retail Distribution

When Aldus first began marketing PageMaker, the desktop publishing product category did not exist. Aldus knew that there were some graphic arts customers with a need for the product, but that it would need to play the major role in developing dealers to sell desktop publishing solutions. The Aldus sales force began working directly with the dealers to educate them on the benefits of desktop publishing and to help them develop sales materials and sales programs for desktop publishing. In choosing dealers for PageMaker, Aldus used three major criteria: the dealer must have a storefront, must sell hardware and software in order to provide a total solution, and must be focused on a vertical market. The company marketed PageMaker through independent dealers and large-volume chains such as Businessland, ComputerLand, Entre, Sears Business Centers, Inacomp, Computer Factory, Nynex, and others. More recently, Aldus had begun marketing PageMaker through value-added resellers (VARs), who distributed Aldus's products with other hardware and software products in various configurations designed to best meet specific end-user needs.

By late 1986, the dealer network in North America had grown to 1,200 dealers for the Apple Macintosh version of PageMaker. With the introduction of the PC version, Aldus authorized an additional, largely new, set of dealers for the product. With almost 3,000 dealers by early 1987, it became increasingly difficult for the small Aldus sales force to maintain all these relationships. Therefore, in March 1987 Aldus signed an agreement with Microamerica to serve as its primary third-party distributor of PageMaker to authorized dealers in the domestic retail market. PageMaker was the first software product carried by Microamerica. Aldus selected Microamerica because it did carry hardware and because it had invested in developing training facilities around the United States. Although Aldus continued to sell directly to retail dealers, this arrangement permitted small independent authorized dealers to purchase directly from Aldus or from Microamerica. Micro-america offered delivery within 24 hours of an order, minimizing the inventory carrying costs for small dealers. By August 1988, the company had over 3,100 separate authorized dealer locations.

Domestic Sales Force

By the summer of 1988, Aldus had a seven-person corporate sales force in the United States to do missionary selling, but these individuals did not make any direct sales. This corporate sales force was devoting a lot of its energies on trying to persuade major corporations to standardize on PageMaker. In addition, a sales force of about 40 dealer account managers and associate sales representatives was deployed throughout the country to stimulate dealer and VAR sales and to assist dealers and

VARs with market education and development. The full cost of an Aldus salesperson in the United States, including salary, commissions, benefits, and office costs, was about $100,000 in 1988. The sales organization in the United States was divided into three regions, with the regional sales managers reporting to the Director of Sales (see Exhibit 4).

International Distribution

Aldus made an early commitment to marketing its products globally. Even before the first product was shipped in the United States, the first distributor was signed up in Europe. Distribution developed differently in the international market than it had in the United States. In Europe, the typical Aldus approach in a country was to appoint a lead distributor, who was typically one of the top five distributors in the country and who had a network of resellers. In early 1987, Aldus established a marketing, distribution, and support joint venture corporation in Scotland. Aldus U.K. was 50 percent owned by Aldus and 50 percent owned by the two

EXHIBIT 4
Organization Chart

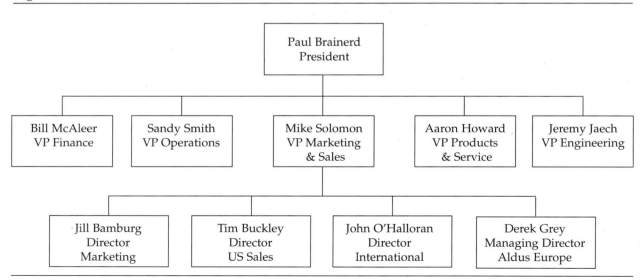

individuals who held the exclusive license to distribute Aldus's products in the United Kingdom and Ireland. Later, in 1987, Aldus bought the other 50 percent of the joint venture and this became Aldus Europe. Aldus Europe provided a coordinating function for all of Aldus's activities in Europe. In the next two years, subsidiaries were set up in the United Kingdom, Sweden, and West Germany. The subsidiaries were established to provide the marketing function for Aldus that the distributors were not providing and to allow Aldus to build real cooperative relationships with the IBM and Apple organizations in the major countries. By mid-1988, Aldus was supporting 10 localized versions of PageMaker[1] and 5 translations of Aldus FreeHand in close to 40 countries. For calendar 1988, it was estimated that about 40 percent of Aldus's sales would come from its international operations.

OEM Distribution

The company had entered into OEM distribution agreements with Hewlett-Packard, DEC, Wang, Olivetti, and IBM. The OEM agreements typically granted the right to distribute the company's prepackaged products with the OEM's microcomputers and, in some cases, related peripheral hardware, such as printers. The products were distributed under Aldus's trademarks.

In October 1986, Aldus entered into a cooperative marketing agreement with Hewlett-Packard and Microsoft. The three companies agreed to jointly market and promote a desktop publishing solution based on the Hewlett-Packard Vectra microcomputer and its LaserJet printer family, Microsoft Windows graphical operating environment and Microsoft Word word processing software, and the PC version of PageMaker. The three companies planned to promote their products through a one-year advertising campaign, dealer

training programs, trade show exhibits, seminars, and other activities.

MARKETING BUDGETS

The total marketing and sales budget for Aldus amounted to about 20 percent of sales. In 1988, the company expected to spend about $1.5 million on media advertising. New product launches and launches of major new releases of a current product were becoming increasingly expensive. Aldus management believed that by 1988 a major launch or relaunch cost about $750,000 in the Macintosh market and $1.5–2.0 million in the PC market. These figures included advertising, dealer rollout expenses, public relations, collateral materials, demonstration materials (such as diskettes or videos), and third-party marketing programs (such as joint promotions with vendors of complementary hardware or supplies).

TECHNICAL SUPPORT AND SERVICE

Aldus provided technical support, service, and training to the market through several channels, including the use of an "800" telephone support center. It offered direct technical support to individuals and corporations through several different programs. In addition, it had developed a U.S. network of over 70 Authorized Trainers to offer training and consulting in major U.S. markets. Finally, an additional informal network of over 200 "service bureaus" had sprung up in the United States to offer typeset-quality desktop publishing output using Linotronic imagesetters.

COMPETITION

The desktop publishing market was highly competitive and had been subject to rapid change, which was expected to continue in the future. The company believed that the principal competitive factors in the desktop publishing market included product features and functions, ease of understanding and operating the software, product

---

[1]For example, the Italian version of PageMaker had all user messages and documentation in Italian, and all measurement references were in millimeters.

reliability, price/performance characteristics, brand recognition, and availability and quality of support and training services. Aldus competed within the desktop publishing software industry with small independent software vendors and large corporations. Some of Aldus's actual and potential competitors had financial, marketing, and technological resources greater than those of Aldus.

To date, price competition had not been a major factor among producers of desktop publishing software. However, suppliers of word processing, database, and spreadsheet applications software programs had experienced significant price reductions through the use of "site licenses" (permitting copying of the program and documentation) and discount pricing for large-volume corporate customers.

The Macintosh version of PageMaker competed with software from a variety of independent vendors. Partly as a result of Aldus's close alliance with Apple, PageMaker soon gained ascendancy over its early competitors: Boston Software's MacPublisher and a product called Scoop, which was marketed by Tangent. By mid-1988, Ready-Set-Go from Letraset, a company well-known to the graphics market as a supplier of press type, had been relegated to the position of a well-financed also-ran. The major competitive threat in 1988 was Quark Xpress priced at $795, which had become a strong contender in the high end of the market. Quark had a similar distribution system to Aldus, relying heavily on retailers and VARs, but its network was not as extensive as Aldus's. Quark Xpress had a somewhat higher level of typographic sophistication than PageMaker. The software design was more modular than PageMaker's and it was possible for VARs to customize the software to meet the specific needs of particular end use markets. For example, a VAR that was targeting weekly newspapers might use the standard Quark Xpress page composition software but add a software module that would allow the newspaper to quickly "dummy" in advertisements. At the corporate level, Quark was not believed to provide the same level of customer support as Aldus. By August 1988, Quark enjoyed more than a 15 percent share of the total Macintosh market for desktop publishing, and a much higher share in the creative graphics professional segment. Some Aldus executives attributed part of its success to its exclusive focus on this segment, while both PageMaker and Aldus Corporation attempted to appeal to a much broader market.

The PC version of PageMaker competed primarily with the software offered by several vendors including the Xerox Corporation, which held exclusive marketing and distribution rights to Ventura Publisher. Ventura had beaten the PC version of PageMaker to the market by about three months. Ventura Publisher targeted customers who prepared long structural documents that incorporated both text and graphics. Training materials, such as manuals, reference materials, and certain types of proposals were typical applications. This was in contrast to PageMaker, which was better suited to applications with a higher design content. While Ventura focused largely on the product development task, Xerox handled the marketing. Ventura benefitted from its association with the Xerox name and Xerox's existing retail presence due to its typewriter, copiers, and printer product lines. Xerox viewed Ventura Publisher as an opportunity to leverage hardware sales into the desktop publishing market. Prior to the introduction of Ventura Publisher there was no MS-DOS desktop publishing product. Xerox had set up a separate business unit, Xerox Desktop Software (XDS), to market Ventura Publisher and other similar products. From Aldus's perspective, the relationship between Xerox and Ventura had not lived up to its full potential. XDS seemed to have some difficulty getting top management support and attention and Xerox had not been as successful as it had hoped in developing personal computers and low-cost printers that would benefit from XDS's efforts. In fact, Xerox had withdrawn from the personal computer market. Nevertheless, the Ventura product was selling well against the MS-DOS version of PageMaker and was making unchallenged claims of "market leadership on the PC platform," which ran the risk of becoming a self-fulfilling prophecy.

In addition to competition within the desktop publishing category, Aldus faced competition from three other sources: low-end competitors, led by Software Publishing's First Publisher; dedicated large-scale electronic publishing systems; and a variety of word processing software programs, which were increasingly incorporating low-end desktop publishing features. The dedicated electronic publishing systems, provided by companies such as Interleaf Corporation and Atex, were designed for publication and engineering departments and other groups requiring additional composition and pagination features. In general, the cost of a stand-alone workstation or a centralized minicomputer or mainframe-based publishing system was substantially higher than for microcomputer-based desktop publishing systems. Of these indirect competitors for PageMaker, Aldus executives believed that the word processors represented the most significant threat because of their ability to address the needs of the business market, which had by now eclipsed the creative graphics professional segment as the dominant portion of the market. Word processing programs were generally less expensive than desktop publishing software and were easier to use. However, word processing programs generally lacked the flexibility and features of PageMaker, such as the ability to set up elaborate layouts including mixed columns and to integrate text and graphics from other software programs.

Aldus also competed with other companies in the microcomputer software market for dealers and distributors, and for alliances with other hardware and software vendors. The principal considerations for distributors and dealers in determining which products to offer include profit margins, product support and service, and credit terms.

THE PROPOSAL

By the summer of 1988, Richard Strong and others believed they were witnessing some troubling trends. As PageMaker became a more sophisticated product that met the evolving needs of the high-end user, the product became less attractive to the less sophisticated business segment of the market. Unfortunately, the primary distribution channels, the retail dealers, lacked the sophistication to support the high-end user. Thus, Richard Strong believed that Aldus was in danger of serving neither segment of the market well. The situation was exacerbated in Europe by the weaker position of the Apple Macintosh, which made Aldus's sales in Europe much more heavily dependent on the MS-DOS version of PageMaker and the other products. Given the relatively small size of the MS-DOS graphic arts professional segment of the market, Aldus Europe was particularly dependent on the business segment of the market for growth.

As he looked to the future, Richard saw the needs of the business user and the creative graphics professional continuing to diverge. The creative graphics professionals would demand increasing sophistication (including more control over typography), more features and greater power, access to more sophisticated support and technical assistance, and greater compatibility with the other software and hardware (such as sophisticated scanners and image setters) they used in their businesses. As the business segment of the market for desktop publishing continued to expand, attracting less technically sophisticated users, the demand for greater ease of use, greater automation, and reduced training periods for new users to become proficient would be key needs. With user-friendly and well-documented software, the need for technical assistance for this segment of the market would probably diminish.

Richard Strong believed that trying to meet the divergent needs of these segments with PageMaker and one product line was placing huge demands on the software development people. The program code required for a program like PageMaker was huge (over 1 million lines of code). The complexity of the product would complicate the program upgrade task and probably delay upgrade schedules. Internally, there was conflict in the organization. Some of the software development people were oriented to the business market and some were oriented to the graphics market, but both groups could only respond to their markets' needs through one product.

Richard Strong proposed that Aldus be split into two divisions focused on the business and the professional segments of the market. Given the relative size of the two markets, the business division would probably be three times the size of the graphics division in terms of staff. In particular, he suggested that the professional product line be anchored around a version of PageMaker priced around $2,000. This sophisticated, powerful desktop publishing product would be complemented by a number of other software tools for the graphic arts professional. The effective sales, distribution, and other sales service and support for this product line would require a new high-end distribution channel.

The business product line would be anchored around a $500 version of PageMaker. The product line would contain a range of easy-to-use software tools for the office worker, and would be distributed through a broad distribution network.

These product line and organizational decisions were being made in the context of what many industry executives saw as increasing polarization of the software distribution industry. The "mass market" was increasingly being served by superstores, software-only retailers, mail order firms, and telemarketers. The high-end was served increasingly by VARs and other boutiques that could provide needs assessments, consulting, training, and after-sales service and support. Traditional independent hardware dealers, who also sold software, seemed to be becoming a much less viable channel for software.

While others at the meeting saw merit in Richard's proposal, they pointed out a number of areas of concern. From a technical perspective, a brand split would be difficult to do given the way the computer code had been written for PageMaker. The code was not split into distinct modules, which meant that a brand split would require a major software development effort. The software engineering resources were already being strained with new product development efforts and the work on the development of the next release of PageMaker (Release 4.0), which was due in less than eighteen months. While a divisional structure had merit, several executives felt such a dramatic move was premature given Aldus's financial and human resources. In addition, the marketing costs of launching and supporting two product lines would not be trivial. There was also the question of whether the creative graphics professional market was large enough to support a separate division.

At the conclusion of the sales and marketing meeting, the Aldus corporate marketing staff were asked to evaluate the proposal and to develop a specific set of recommendations. If the decision were made to split the product line, a plan would need to be developed to address some of the concerns raised by Richard Strong. In particular, how could the marketing communications mix (advertising, direct mail, collateral materials, and personal selling) be developed to address the two market segments most effectively? If the decision were made to split the product line, then the marketing strategies for the two markets would need to be specified. In addition, in the latter case, a communications strategy would be required to explain the split to Aldus's current resellers, the industry infrastructure, the trade press, and the financial community.

Millipore New Product Commercialization: A Tale of Two New Products

In 1993, Millipore was poised to launch several innovative product lines. Company executives had particularly high hopes for the LC/MS product line in the Water Chromatography Division and Viresolve in the Process Division. Much of the potential success of these products rested on commercialization decisions made in the past three years by their respective protagonists: Dave Strand, V.P. for new business development at Waters, and Paul Sekhri, product manager for Viresolve at the Process Division.

In early 1990, Dave Strand was given the task of commercializing Millipore's innovative liquid chromatography/mass spectrometry (LC/MS) product line. Strand had come to Waters a few years earlier, when the software firm he helped found was purchased by Waters. A rising star in the Waters Chromatography Division, he hoped that successful introduction of these products would reestablish Waters' claim to technological leadership in the liquid chromatography (LC) marketplace. That title had been challenged for the first time in 1983 when Hewlett-Packard—until then a small player in the LC market—had beaten Waters to market with the photodiode array (PDA) detector for liquid chromatography systems. Waters still dominated the LC market that it gave birth to in 1958 with 40–45 percent of the global LC market (to HP's 22–23 percent). With the introduction of new technologies like LC/MS, Waters sought to place a lock on the LC market that would make it unprofitable for any firm to challenge its position. As Dave Strand put it, "We want to make the view not worth the climb."

In October 1990, Paul Sekhri, a young marketing manager with several years of experience working for start-ups in the biotech industry, was hired to commercialize a newly developed membrane system capable of removing viruses from protein drugs developed using biotechnology. Over the last few years, Millipore had been struggling to better serve the rapidly growing biotechnology industry, and the virus removal product was one of the most promising biotechnology products that Millipore had yet developed. While "market characterization" and beta tests had been a central part of the development process, when Sekhri arrived he was met with many remaining commercialization issues:

> When I started, my boss, Tim Leahy, said "Your job is to commercialize this product." So I asked, "What's the name of it?" He said, "That's up to you." I asked, "What are you charging for it?" He said, "That's up to you." I asked, "How are you distributing it?" He said "That's up to you." There was just a big, clean slate.

Millipore's leading competitor in virus removal was Asahi, a small Japanese company. Asahi's membrane products, except for the virus removal membrane, were distributed in the United States by Pall. Worldwide, Pall was Millipore's leading competitor with 13 percent share. Millipore (with $174 million in sales) had 22 percent.

MILLIPORE CORPORATE BACKGROUND

With worldwide sales of $750 million in 1991, Millipore was the market leader in the $3.4 billion

---

Research Associate Kevin Bartus prepared this case under the supervision of Professor V. Kasturi Rangan as the basis for class discussion rather than to illustrate either effective or ineffective handling of an administrative situation. Printed by permission of the Harvard Business School.

separations industry. Millipore's products were primarily based on two separations technologies: membrane technology and chromatography.

Membrane technology separated the components of a substance primarily according to the size of those components. A substance, such as water, air, or chemicals, was filtered through thin screens called membranes, which were made of various materials and had small holes of different sizes. The pores allowed components (molecules, ions, or particles) of certain sizes to pass through, while others were trapped on the surface of the membrane. Millipore offered a wide range of membrane types, sizes, and configurations.

In a typical chromatographic separation, the substance or sample to be separated was injected into a fluid such as water. This solution was then pumped through a tube called a column, which was packed with chemical materials. As the sample traveled through the column, the chemical packing separated the sample into its individual chemical molecules or components. As each component left the column, it was sensed by a detector, which transmitted a signal to a recording device. Information about each component was then depicted on a chart called a chromatogram. The total system consisted of an injector, a pump, a column, a detector, and a recorder. Millipore participated in a wide range of liquid chromatography applications.

The membrane separation and chromatography technologies were used in two types of customer applications: analysis and purification. Products for analytical applications were used to gain knowledge about a sample by detecting, identifying, and/or quantifying its chemical, physical, or biological components. Products for purification applications were used to help manufacture or process a customer's product by removing contaminants or by isolating and purifying specific components from complex mixtures.

Exhibit 1 provides an overview of the corporation's sales by customer application, customer segment, and geography. As can be seen from Exhibit 1, while chromatography technology was used predominantly in analytical applications, membrane

technology was used for both analytical and purification applications. Millipore grouped its customers into eight major markets: pharmaceutical (e.g., Pfizer), biotechnology (e.g., Genentech), life-sciences (e.g., Massachusetts Institute of Technology), food-and-beverage (e.g., Coca-Cola), microelectronics (e.g., IBM), chemical (e.g., Dow), environmental (e.g., U.S. Environmental Protection Agency), and patient-care (e.g., Massachusetts General Hospital). Its customers included corporations of all types and sizes, government agencies, hospitals, universities, and research institutions.

Profit-and-loss responsibility at Millipore Corporation was organized by three major product divisions:

1. Chromatography Division (also called Waters chromatography, after Jim Waters, its founder). The LC/MS project was being developed under this division.
2. Process Systems Group (purification applications of membrane technology). The Virus Removal project was being developed under this division.
3. Analytical Systems Division (analytical applications of membrane technology).

A separate division called Intertech handled operations in Latin America, Eastern Europe, Africa, and Asia (except Japan, which was handled by Nihon Millipore).

Table 1 shows an approximation of sales by each product division as constructed from Exhibit 1.

TABLE 1
Five-Year Sales History by Product Division ($ millions)

	1991	1990	1989	1988	1987
Waters	291	287	267	260	228
Process	267	238	194	177	142
Analytical	188	178	154	142	118
Intertech	67	68	62	59	46

Each of the first three divisions had profit-and-loss responsibility with independent marketing, sales, R&D, and manufacturing operations. Because of common membrane technology, Analytical and

EXHIBIT 1

Five-Year Revenue Review by Technology/Market/Geography ($ in thousands)

	1991	1990	1989	1988	1987	5-Year Growth Rate
Sales by Product Line and Technology						
Analytical						
Membranes	$145,909	$139,358	$124,612	$123,241	$110,773	9%
Chromatograph	265,412	259,693	242,574	230,741	207,944	8%
Other	42,429	38,638	29,698	18,824	6,392	96%
Sub-Total	453,750	437,689	396,884	372,806	325,109	11%
Purification						
Membranes	257,476	226,156	186,981	170,307	130,084	19%
Chromatography	26,454	26,669	24,739	29,059	20,884	10%
Other	10,299	12,648	7,726	6,751	12,405	—
Sub-Total	294,229	265,473	219,446	206,117	163,373	17%
Total	$747,979	$703,162	$616,330	$578,923	$488,482	13%
Sales by Market						
Industrial[a]	$512,219	$476,104	$427,617	$399,406	$329,015	14%
University/Government	178,016	172,504	139,568	133,195	110,810	15%
Patient Care/Medical Research	57,744	54,554	49,145	46,322	48,657	3%
Total	$747,979	$703,162	$616,330	$578,923	$488,482	13%
Sales by Geographic Area						
United States	$274,718	$267,627	$250,218	$230,010	$203,827	9%
Western Europe	234,201	230,391	183,824	176,077	152,085	14%
Japan	171,279	136,205	120,123	112,838	86,206	18%
Other[b]	67,781	68,939	62,165	59,998	46,364	11%
Total	$747,979	$703,162	$616,330	$578,923	$488,482	13%

[a] Under Industrial was included industries such as pharmaceutical, biotechnology, chemical, and microelectronics.

[b] This included sales to Latin America, Africa, Eastern Europe, and other countries in Asia except Japan.

Process Systems shared manufacturing facilities. The company as a whole operated in 70 countries worldwide, with its world headquarters for Process Systems and Analytical Systems at Bedford, Massachusetts, and its Waters Chromatography division at Milford, Massachusetts. (See Exhibit 2 for a corporate organization chart.)

As can be seen from Exhibit 2, core R&D, under Jack Johansen, was a key corporate function. Core R&D supplied divisions with short-term and long-term research support for product development as well as conducting some research of its own on core technologies with potential long-term payoffs. Approximately 80 percent of the corporation's $66 million R&D budget was spent on divisional product development projects and the rest on core R&D. The divisional R&D budgets were allocated more or less in proportion to their sales revenues. According to Millipore's technology V.P., roughly 50 percent of the R&D budget was spent on incremental new products and the other half on "change the name of the game" kind of innovations.

EXHIBIT 2
Millipore Organization Chart, March 1992

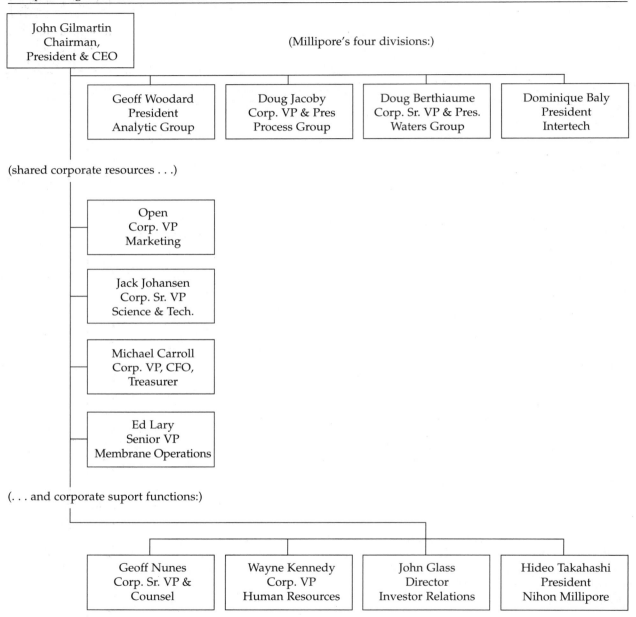

(Millipore's four divisions:)

John Gilmartin Chairman, President & CEO

Geoff Woodard President Analytic Group	Doug Jacoby Corp. VP & Pres Process Group	Doug Berthiaume Corp. Sr. VP & Pres. Waters Group	Dominique Baly President Intertech

(shared corporate resources . . .)

Open Corp. VP Marketing

Jack Johansen Corp. Sr. VP Science & Tech.

Michael Carroll Corp. VP, CFO, Treasurer

Ed Lary Senior VP Membrane Operations

(. . . and corporate suport functions:)

Geoff Nunes Corp. Sr. VP & Counsel	Wayne Kennedy Corp. VP Human Resources	John Glass Director Investor Relations	Hideo Takahashi President Nihon Millipore

Source: Casewriter's depiction of organization from company data.

Sales and marketing functions at Millipore were organized under each division (see Exhibit 3). In each country, one of the divisional sales managers also acted as country manager, a position that included responsibility for administrative functions such as order-entry, shipment, and invoicing. For example, Art Caputo acted both as the North American sales manager for Waters and as the

EXHIBIT 3
Organization of Sales and Marketing Functions at Millipore

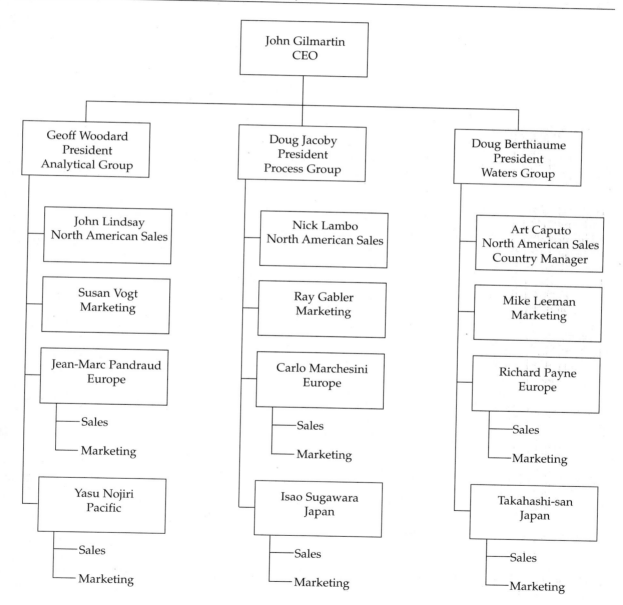

country manager for North America. The three major Millipore divisions shared common distribution warehouses and logistics facilities worldwide. The North American sales operation was headquartered at Marlborough, Massachusetts.

New Product Development

Core R&D supplied divisions with short-term and long-term research for product development in addition to conducting some research of its own on core technologies with potential long-term payoffs.

The initiative for division product development came up from the division. Each of the three divisions had its own unique new product development system. The Analytical and Process Groups were decentralized into market-focused Business Units. Project ideas were submitted by marketing, sales, and R&D people, and allocation of resources was made by the general managers of the Business Units and divisional presidents. Resources for new membrane development to support divisional projects were allocated by the Core Membrane V.P. for R&D, who was also responsible for allocating resources to core research projects. The process was iterative, often involving ranking of projects based on their market potential and strategic importance with the final cut being made by budgetary constraints. (See Exhibit 4 for the evaluation framework used at the Analytical Group.) At the Process Systems group, the procedure was more informal, but addressed similar issues. At Waters, the procedure was somewhat different. Top managers from each functional area constituted a New Product Committee. Marketing, Sales, R&D, Manufacturing, and overseas country heads were all part of this committee. They each brought in ideas supplied to them by their constituencies, and the committee as a whole then decided on how to allocate its resources.

John Gilmartin, the CEO of Millipore Corporation, had set a goal of 15 percent growth in sales accompanied by a 10 percent return on sales and assets. This had to be achieved in an environment where the industry was growing at only about 8 percent. The corporation, therefore, was focused on exploiting niche marketing opportunities with new products. John Gilmartin had set a target of achieving 40 percent of annual sales from products introduced in the recent three years. Figures compiled by the corporate planning department indicated that such a target had not been achieved in the last five years.

Table 2 provides a brief description of the 11 key new product introductions in 1991.

THE LC/MS PROJECT AT THE WATERS DIVISION

The LC/MS project at Waters had a checkered history. In 1990, Dave Strand inherited a program in tatters. No working mass spectrometer prototypes had been developed. Little systematic marketing research had been done, and there were no agreements with component vendors. (See Exhibit 5 for a brief history of the previous product development effort.)

As can be seen from Exhibit 5, the LC/MS effort first originated with a desire to build an interface to feed into the mass spectrometer. A liquid chromatography system could separate different chemicals from a compound solution, and the typical chromatography detector could tell the analyst how much of each chemical was present. But identification of each chemical could be done only on the basis of comparison to a standard; if it was known that caffeine took 30 minutes to travel through a chromatography column made of silica gel, then the analyst had reason to believe that an unknown chemical taking 30 minutes to pass through silica gel was in fact caffeine. Mass spectrometry took identification a significant step further. A chemical like caffeine was broken into ionic components and flung against a screen (an electromagnetic field was used, thus differentiating between components on the basis of mass and charge). The pattern on the screen formed a unique "fingerprint" for each chemical, identifying the chemical with certainty. While conventional LC detectors were adequate for identifying a spectrum

EXHIBIT 4
New Product Evaluation Criteria at Analytical Group

	Return Analysis	Weights	0	1	2
S	Market Size (potential market–current year)	7	<$5M	$5M-$20M	$20M>
S	Market Growth (5 years out)	9	<15%	15% – 30%	30%>
S	Market Share (3rd year after K.O.)	5	<15%	15% – 40%	40%>
S	Strategic Importance to Base Business	15	Base <$5M	Base = $5M – $20M	Base $20M>
S	Potential for New Market Segment	10	All business pertains to base	Some potential for new cust. base	Totally new customer base
F	3rd Year Sales (net of cannibalization)	9	<$1M	$1M – $4M	$4M>
F	Total 5 Years Sales (net of cannibalization)	12	<$4M	$4M – $15M	$15M>
F	Net Present Value	14	<$0M	$0M – $1.5M	$1.5M>
M	Potential Geographies for Sales	4	One geography	Two geographies	Worldwide
M	Potential for Product Differentiation	9	Comp. has similar and superior	Similar, but ours superior	We are only one in market
M	Potential Patent Protection	6	No patent position	Weak patent position	Strong patent position
		100			

	Risk Analysis				
C	Total R&D Cost (5 years–only MAG)	6	<$.75M	$.75M-$3M	>$3M
C	Total Capital Cost (5 years–only MAG)	3	<$.5M	$.5M-$2.5M	>$2.5M
C	Market Development Cost (5 yrs. Mktg. & Prom.)	4	<$.25M	$.25M-$1.5M	>$1.5M
R	Technology Risk	9	We already own technology	Technology exists	Technology requires invention
R	Strength of Technology Skills	7	Have skills and necessary quantity	Have skills, not nec. quantity	Do not have nec. skills or quantity
R	Product/Engineering Development Risk	4	We do it every day	Others do it, we have to acquire	No one has done it
R	Strength of Development Skills	4	Have skills and necessary quantity	Have skills, not nec. quantity	Do not have nec. skills or quantity
R	Manufacturing Technology Risk	4	We do it every day	Others do it, we have to acquire	Requires Mfg. invention
R	Strength of Manufacturing Skills	4	Have skills and necessary quantity	Have skills, not nec. quantity	Do not have nec. skills or quantity
R	Sales and Service Skills	4	Sales force well trained	Significant training & redirection	Add specialists
R	Regulatory Impact	3	Not regulated	Regulated, we're in	Regulated, we're not in
Cmp	Presence of Dominant Competitor	3	Competitor has <15% share	Competitor has 15% – 40% share	Competitor has >40% share
Cmp	Number of Competitors	2	<3	3 – 5	>5
Cmp	Risk of Existing Competitive Technology	4	No existing competitive technology	Exists, but not fully developed	Comp. tech already commercialized
Cmp	Risk of Alternative New Technology	4	No existing alternative new tech.	Exists, but not fully developed	Alternative new tech. commercialized
		65			

Weighing Breakdown

Return

Strategic (S)	46%	Risk – Cost (C)	20%
Financial (F)	35%	Risk (R)	60%
Miscellaneous (M)	19%	Competition (Cmp)	20%

TABLE 2
New Product Introduction in 1991

Waters Chromatography Division

1. *717 Auto Sampler*: Upgrade of existing Waters auto sampler line, redesigned and repositioned to address recurring reliability problems.

2. *996 Photo Diode Array (PDA) Detector*: An in-house redesign of a product originally sourced from a Japanese vendor.

3. *Millennium Software*: First chromatography software to integrate essentially all data collection and analysis functions required by liquid chromatographers. First Waters product to run on Windows. Required for use on 996 PDA. Useful only with other Waters products.

Analytical Division

4. *Analyzer Feed System (AFS)*: Water purifier for laboratory systems. Redesign of a previously failed product launch. 1992 revenues of $700,000.

5. *Base Station—Automated DNA Sequencer*: Developed by a now defunct division as part of a broad effort to exploit the growing biotech market. Effort undermined by early field problems and a dominant competitor.

6. *ConSep/1*: A liquid chromatography system developed at Analytical to allow customers to take advantage of Memsep—a technology recently purchased by Millipore, which incorporates a membrane (versus the more typical gel or treated beads) in a chromatographic column. Memsep's recent sales had been flagging, presumably because existing chromatography systems were not capable of utilizing the new technology to its full potential. Consep/1 was developed to address this need.

7. *Expedite*: An automated DNA synthesizing station. Developed in part to promote sales of specialty chemicals used to manufacture DNA, which are manufactured by a wholly owned subsidiary.

Process Division

8. *Viresolve:* Novel virus removal system developed for the biopharmaceutical market.

9. *Opti-Seal*: Replacement for existing product.

10. *Opti-Cap*: Replacement for existing product.

11. *IntegriTest:* Novel method for testing the integrity of membranes. Launch challenged by design problems and demanding training requirements.

of 25 compounds or less, mass-specific detectors were enormously cost efficient over a larger range, exceeding 75 compounds.

In order for the output of an LC system to be fed directly into a mass spec, an "interface" had to drastically reduce the amount of liquid flow and turn the remaining liquid molecules into gaseous ions. Interfaces such as thermospray and particle beam had been developed for use with "small" molecules such as caffeine, but these interfaces often destroyed the "big" molecules, such as proteins, typically analyzed by the biotechnology industry. At the close of the 1980s, the electrospray interface became commercially available for the biotechnology market. By 1993, the most common LC/MS interfaces for "small" molecules were

EXHIBIT 5
History of the LC/MS Project

1985:	A marketing manager and a scientist at Waters collaborated to develop liquid chromatography systems tailored specifically for use with the mass spectrometers and interfaces offered by mass spectrometry firms.
1986:	Sales of "tailored LCs" begin.
1987:	Sales of "tailored LCs" hit $500,000. Funding officially assigned to development program. Waters begins a series of meetings with component vendors with the aim of eventually building mass spectrometers in-house using purchased components. A favorite idea involves developing a smaller version of the full-scale mass spectrometer offered by other firms. Scientists at Waters also begin to develop proprietary LC/MS interfaces.
1988:	Newly hired project manager from outside builds a team of scientists capable of developing a full-scale mass spectrometer in-house. Interface development scaled back. New strategy is to aim for the high end of the analytic market with a full-scale machine, eventually offering a smaller mass spectrometer in addition. Vendor agreements are pursued, some as a temporary measure until component manufacture can be brought in-house.
1989:	Project manager is dismissed amidst financial and strategic concerns. Much of the scientific team he assembled disperses.
1990:	Dave Strand inherits the LC/MS program.
1992:	Extrel acquired.

particle beam and thermospray, and electrospray for "large" molecules.[1]

There were approximately 10,000 mass spectrometrists in the United States, most of whom had a Ph.D. There were 100,000 chromatographers in the United States, most of whom did not have a Ph.D.

The two types of scientists usually worked for the same companies and often worked on the same development project. A large pharmaceutical company trying to discover a new drug, for example, might have a chromatography lab work on the more "routine" analysis and have the mass spectrometrists work on the more difficult problems. The mass spectrometrists might use their own chromatography equipment, but "to them it's just another input to their MS." Should the chromatographers require mass spectrometry, they would take a tray of samples up a floor or across the hall to the mass spectrometrists, who might charge a few hundred dollars per sample.

An integrated LC/MS system offered advantages to both mass spectrometrists and chromatographers. Mass spectrometrists, generally considered the more "elite" of the two groups due to more rigorous education and training requirements, already used liquid chromatography to separate compounds into pure samples prior to analysis by mass spectrometry. To them, an integrated system offered greater efficiency. Chromatographers often asked mass spectrometrists to positively identify chemicals for them on a mass spectrometer. To them, an integrated system, especially one that was easy enough for a chromatographer to run, offered the advantages of mass spectrometry without having to bother mass spectrometrists.

Customer Perceptions

One of the first tasks that Dave Strand concentrated on when he took over the job in 1990 was better understanding customer interest in LC/MS systems. Two focus sessions were conducted.

---

[1]Molecules were characterized by their molecular weight as small or big. Amino acids, drug conjugates, neurotransmitters, carbohydrates, surfactants, peptides, proteins, and DNA represent a range of molecules from small to big.

The first focus session, held in February of 1991, involved a group of chromatographers from the pharmaceutical, industrial chemical, and consumer products industries. These potential LC/MS customers were asked what they wanted in an LC/MS and how purchasing decisions might be made. Attributes of an ideal system included something "easy, straightforward, and rugged," and several chromatographers expressed a desire for a "tabletop model." There was general agreement that the lower the price was, the more input the chromatographer would have on the purchasing decision, and the more widely used the unit would be. "On a benchtop for $50,000," said one chromatographer, "we'd have one for each of our development chemists." Others cited $100,000 as the price point that would allow chromatographers, not mass spectrometrists, to make the ultimate decision.

The second session, held in December of 1991, was conducted individually with scientists (predominantly Ph.D's) in pharmaceutical and biotechnology industries. Participants were questioned on their desire for alternative LC and MS technologies, on their perception of Waters, and on their perceptions of potential LC/MS vendors. Several scientists voiced a desire for a smaller-scale LC system. "It fills a niche for biomolecules, small samples for research," said one participant (later market research indicated that in fact about 9 percent of the LC market was interested in smaller-scale LC). When asked to give their perceptions of Waters, reactions were mixed. "They're people who know HPLC," said one scientist. "Waters has a good reputation with us," said another.

Situation at the Start of 1993

With these concerns of focus-session participants in mind, and given the difficulty Waters continued to have in making arrangements for sourcing mass spec components, in 1992 Waters purchased Extrel, a $12 million manufacturer of laboratory analysis equipment. Extrel had built a credible reputation in mass spectrometry, with sales of about 30 research-grade, full-function mass spectrometers per year. As 1993 began, Waters and Extrel engineers were working hard to develop the lower-tier, mass-specific detector that Waters managers had sought for so many years. Meanwhile, sales of tailored LCs continued.

COMMERCIALIZATION OF LC/MS

Market Definition: Chromatographers versus Mass Spectrometrists

By offering a "mass spec adapted for LC utilization," Waters planned to take advantage of its dominance in the LC marketplace. Although the centerpiece of Strand's launch, a scaled-down mass spectrometer, was aimed at chromatographers and not the mass spectrometrists, there was an important relationship of influence between the two customers. Mass spectrometrists were in a sense the "prima donnas" of the analytical laboratory, generally more highly educated and more highly paid than the chromatographers. Because of this status and because of their knowledge of the science of mass spectrometry, the purchase of a scaled-down mass spectrometer was likely to require their blessing, if not their official approval.

Although Strand's "detector-level" mass spectrometer (so called because of its intended similarity to the other detectors used by chromatographers) was clearly aimed at lowering the dependence of chromatographers on mass spectrometrists, the latter were expected to feel no threat. Strand recalled the reaction of mass spectrometrists to the introduction of detector-level mass spectrometers for gas chromatography in the mid-'80s. Mass spectrometrists "looked at them as helpful, because they filtered out the mundane problems and allowed them to work on the more interesting problems." Far from feeling threatened, Strand expected mass spectrometrists to help chromatographers choose a good detector-level mass spectrometer. "There's a feeling," suggested Strand, "that you have to have their tacit blessing, that this is a good product. It may not be as powerful as my million-dollar machine, but for $100,000, this is a good beginner's tool and an acceptable adjunct to an LC system."

Strand felt that he had a good sense of what customers expected and desired. "I've attended probably every scientific conference there is and talked to a lot of people. We've done three rounds of focus sessions which have been very helpful in understanding what the product issues were. We think we know based on focus-session work what it would take to get customers to buy from us, and what price range and technology tradeoffs they would be willing to accept."

Although the detector-level mass spectrometer (called MSD or mass specific detector) had not yet been tested at any customer site, in late 1992 Waters conducted a focus session with mock-ups of the product to get feedback on size, serviceability, accessibility, and integration. The feedback was quite positive.

Segmentation

In 1991, the market for MSD integrated with LC systems was estimated to be $50 million. Although no one firm currently sold "detector-level" mass spectrometers for liquid chromatography, the market for these products was expected to be $110 million by 1996. The research-grade, full-function mass spectrometer integrated with gas or liquid chromatography sold for about $250,000 to $500,000. Competitors like Finnigan, VG, Sciex, and Hewlett-Packard occupied this $300 million market. HP and Varian also made a MSD integrated with gas chromatography. This, however, was a smaller $150 million market.

Dave Strand divided the potential market for LC/MS in two ways, both largely derived from Waters' experience with liquid chromatography. One approach segmented users into four groups, each comprising about a quarter of the existing LC/MS market: Pharmaceutical, Industrial Chemical, Biopharmaceutical, and Environmental. This segmentation was not based so much on SIC-type classifications as it was on the application that the LC was used for; for example, many traditional

pharmaceutical companies had begun to use biotechnology to develop biopharmaceutical drugs.

Waters was already strong in both the pharmaceutical and the industrial chemical segments of the chromatography market. In 1989, the size of pharmaceutical segment of the chromatography market was $319 million, of which Waters held 27 percent. The industrial chemical segment was $438 million, of which Waters held 19 percent. Strand felt that LC/MS products would do particularly well in industrial chemicals, because "industrial is sort of mundane; often those sales for us are unopposed. But if you go into the pharmaceutical or any of the biopharmaceutical companies, there's brisk competition to get in there."

Strand also divided the market according to how research-oriented the chromatographer was. Sixty percent of all chromatographers were involved in quality control or quality assurance (QC/QA), involving tasks such as ensuring that each production batch had a desired level of a certain chemical. More research oriented were the methods developers (30 percent), who designed procedures for QC/QA. Most research oriented were the researchers (10 percent), who were involved in developing new chemicals or drugs. Many Waters managers saw a rough progression of influence from the researchers down to the methods developers and then to QA/QC, but no vendor had actively exploited that progression. Eighty-eight percent of current LC/MS sales were to researchers and methods developers, but Strand hoped that eventually his detector-level mass spectrometer would appeal to the much larger but much more conservative QC/QA market.

Comparable Introductions in the Past

Waters' managers expected sales for the detector-level mass spectrometer market to grow from $0 to $110 million in four years. This estimate was based on two similar introductions in the past: GC-MSD and PDA detectors. HP had introduced GC-MSD, a detector-level mass spectrometer (MSD, or "mass-specific detector") for gas chromatography in 1983, and later introduced PDA detectors. As illustrated in Exhibit 6, the GC-MSD market grew from zero to over 1,200 units in five years, an annualized growth of over 400 percent. Recalling these historic market growth rates played a larger role in helping Strand estimate sales of the detector-level mass spectrometer. The estimate was also based on the expectation that 10–12 percent of all LC systems would include a mass spec detector within four years, since in 1992 10–12 percent of all LC systems had PDAs.

Launch

Strand had received several suggestions for the LC/MS introduction, though specific launch dates and details were yet to be finalized. One suggestion was to stage the launch. That is, the company would first tailor the Extrel mass spectrometer (named Benchmark) to capillary-scale liquid chromatography. This would be particularly appealing to biopharmaceutical researchers who worked with small sample sizes. Building on this experience, Waters could then launch the conventional scale LC tailored to the mass-specific detector (code-named "Mercury"). This would appeal to the industrial chemicals segment. This detector was expected to measure only 20″ × 20″ × 15″ and weigh 150 lbs., compared with Benchmark at 3′ × 2′ × 2′ and 350 lbs. It was considered ambitious, but not impossible, to introduce Benchmark at the 1993 Pittcon trade show for chromatographers, followed by the Mercury launch about six to nine months later at the American Society of Mass Spectrometrists.

Art Caputo, the Waters sales manager, was involved in virtually all of the major decisions on LC/MS development. His plan was to initially rely on Extrel salespeople and a handful of specialists, but slowly train his entire sales team of nearly 200

EXHIBIT 6
Growth Rates of Two Similar Products: GC-MSD and LC-PDA

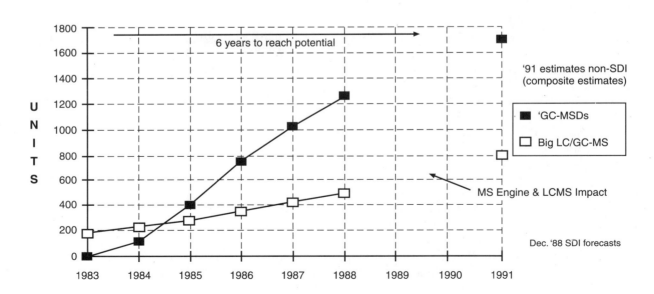

GC-MS Historical WW Unit Growth

salespeople. "That is the only way we can ramp up Mercury sales from 50 units in 1991 to nearly 300 units by 1996," concluded Caputo.

REMAINING COMMERCIALIZATION ISSUES

Waters managers believed that where chromatographers had the authority to purchase their own equipment, it was generally only for instruments costing $100,000 or less. While Benchmark was priced at $180,000 to $200,000, Mercury had to be priced below the $100,000 point. HP typically sold their GC/MSD for under $75,000, and although a detector-level mass spectrometer for LC systems was likely to sell for more, Waters took the GC/MSD as a starting point for calculating target cost. "We took the pieces apart on an HP GC/MSD and estimated that it could be built for about $20,000. We have set for ourselves a manufacturing target somewhat more than that, and achieving that would be very important for our success in this marketplace," reasoned Dave Strand. "It is an interesting industry," he added. "Competition is based on value-added and technology and participants usually respect each other's market position.

There's been a little disruption throughout the last decade. That's why we are keen to have that technological lead in Mercury," he concluded.

VIRUS REMOVAL COMMERCIALIZATION AT THE PROCESS GROUP

When Paul Sekhri inherited the virus removal project in 1990, several working beta sites were already installed, and the original developers of the product idea were still involved in assisting him in the launch phase. (See Exhibit 7 for a brief history of the virus removal product development.)

In 1985, Tony DiLeo, an R&D manager, knew that Millipore had only begun to exploit the tangential flow membrane technology that his team had developed. In tangential flow filtration, fluid circulated across the membrane surface and was slowly pulled through the membrane by suction. Because of their more sophisticated designs, tangential flow systems were not as simple for users to operate as conventional "dead-end" filters, such as coffee filters. Tangential flow did, however, offer less clogging and thus better performance when used to discriminate between particles of similar size.

EXHIBIT 7
History of the Viresolve Project

1985:   Tangential flow expert at Millipore searches for additional applications of tangential flow technology. A top marketing manager generates a short list of potential applications. Technical teams test feasibility of potential applications.

1986:   Promising virus removal trials are presented to top management. Proponents of virus removal gather further customer information, and a major Millipore customer makes a presentation to top management requesting development of a virus removal product.

1987:   Project is officially funded, and development work begins. Membrane manufacturing process is altered to enable production of membranes with fewer defects in pore size.

1988:   Development work continues. Decision made to focus on membrane development before firming designs for a device to deploy the membrane.

1989:   Formal project plan constructed by project leader, allowing different sections of project team to more effectively work in parallel.

1990:   Working membrane developed. In all, six tests at customer sites are conducted between 1987 and 1990. Paul Sekhri hired to commercialize product.

At DiLeo's request, Ray Gabler, a top marketing manager, spoke with many of Millipore's key bio-tech and pharmaceutical customers to identify a list of 11 promising applications for this technology. Running preliminary experiments and investigating each application's complexity and probable length of development time, DiLeo and his group narrowed the list to three promising applications. One of these applications was virus removal.

Virus removal had always been a problem in the development of biotechnology drugs. Some drugs were derived directly from mammalian blood plasma or cells. When these substances were extracted from the body, viruses often came along for the ride. In 1985, for example, human growth hormone extracted from the pituitary glands of cadavers contained undetected Creutzfeldt-Jakob viruses, which infected and killed several treated patients. Another class of biotech drugs, such as Genetech's tPA for heart attacks, were developed using recombinant DNA, in which gene fragments from a mammalian cell were spliced into rapidly reproducing organisms. Monoclonal antibodies such as Centacor's Centoxin for septic shock were also developed using mammalian cells, but instead of using only a gene fragment, the entire cell was used. In the development of both recombinant DNA drugs and monoclonal antibodies, viruses were often unintentionally removed from the mammal along with the original source cells. In addition, viruses sometimes inhabited the media used to grow cell cultures. Finally, viral contamination was a potential result of careless laboratory procedure.

When DiLeo and Gabler spoke with customers about this problem, it became apparent that these "biopharmaceutical" customers were highly dissatisfied with current methods of virus removal, and were very interested in more effective solutions to this problem. Indeed, two key customers were instrumental in convincing top management at Millipore to put resources into developing a membrane system capable of removing viruses in a consistent and validatable fashion. Validation, or proof of virus removal, was expected to become an increasingly important part of the FDA approval process.

The virus removal project was established with division funds in 1987. Day-to-day project management was handled by DiLeo, with Gabler handling customer contacts and negotiation of a total of six test sites. A detailed Program Plan that DiLeo developed in 1989 played a critical part in ensuring that development went smoothly. The plan included PERT charts developed by the scientist in charge of each facet of development, as well as estimates of performance parameters that enabled each of the sub-project teams to work in parallel. Although the original completion target was missed by about six months, the relative smoothness of the development project could be attributed to an accurate early product definition, continual contact with the market, and access to development resources.

Industry

At least half of all of Millipore's business was directly or indirectly tied to the pharmaceutical market. Viresolve was one of several new products specifically designed to tap into a fast-growing segment of that market: "biopharmaceuticals." Biopharmaceuticals were therapeutics produced through genetic engineering, and both traditional pharmaceutical companies and recently founded biotech companies were taking part in the research. In 1992, the biopharmaceutical market was about $3 billion, expected to grow to $30 billion by the year 2000.

COMPETITION

Inactivation of Viruses

The most prevalent ways of dealing with harmful viruses involved inactivating them instead of actually removing them. Viruses exhibited many of the characteristics of living organisms, and so inactivating a virus was tantamount to rendering it lifeless, and hence harmless. Methods of inactivation included physical techniques such as heat and ultraviolet radiation, but these methods could also harm or destroy the proteins that drug manufacturers wanted to process.

Chemical inactivation techniques were much more prevalent. The "solvent detergent" method, developed by the New York Blood Center, broke down the lipid (fat) coat that enveloped many viruses (in a manner very similar to soap breaking down oils). "I'd say every blood product company, and most pharmaceutical companies, use the solvent detergent method," said Paul Sekhri. "They have a very nice track record. In the three million units of product that have used solvent detergent, they have never had one incident of infection. But there's a drawback to that. You have to know the virus you're removing. Many viruses had no lipid coats, for example, and were thus unaffected by solvent detergent."

Millipore emphasized that any virus unaffected by inactivation methods such as solvent detergent represented an accident waiting to happen. "My approach to marketing Viresolve is that we can remove even unknown viruses," said Paul Sekhri. "That sounds really strange. But it's been interesting to see how the market is slowly embracing that thought. Every single major virological accident in the past ten years has been because of a virus that the manufacturer didn't know was there. We can address that with this system. With an inactivation method you can't."

Physical Removal of Viruses

Membranes were generally considered the most effective manner of physically removing viruses. Size exclusion membranes, like Viresolve, worked by allowing smaller molecules, like proteins, to pass. Larger particles, like viruses, were retained. Exhibit 8 shows the virus removal properties of Viresolve/70.) The size of a virus is characterized by its diameter in a nanometers (one billionth of a meter). Viresolve's effectiveness is measured in terms of Log Reduction Value (i.e., 7 log removal meant that the membrane would miss one virus particle out of every 10 to the seventh power, or 10 million virus particles). Providing validation of virus removal was the competitive advantage that Millipore had chosen to emphasize in Viresolve over other membranes. There were two important types of validation. One involved providing published proof that a specific virus had been removed to a specific degree using the membrane product in the manufacturer's test facilities. This type of validation was instrumental in helping Millipore compete against conventional multi-use membranes. A second type of validation involved providing a method for the customer to test each purchased membrane to assure that it would

EXHIBIT 8
Virus Removal Properties of Viresolve/70

VIRESOLVE/70 QUALIFICATION
PREDICTED MINIMUM SYSTEM PERFORMANCE
• Virus removal in PBS

	Virus Diameter (nm)	1-Stage (log removal)	2-Stage (log removal)
Parvovirus	22	1.5–1.8	2.7–3.0
Hepatitis C	40	3.3–3.4	6.5–6.7
BVD	40	3.3–3.4	6.5–6.7
HBV	42	3.5–3.8	6.8–7.1
Adenovirus	70	6.0–6.3	
HIV	100	7.4–7.7	
Herpesvirus	100	7.4–7.7	

remove viruses as advertised. Millipore had developed a "correlating integrity test" to meet this latter need, which appeared to be a substantial asset.

Some manufacturers of conventional filtration membranes had recently repositioned their existing membrane lines to take advantage of the growing interest in virus removal. While their advertising emphasized the familiarity of their approach to virus removal, their technical documentation conceded less-effective performance than the newer Viresolve technology. For example, their 1990 literature claimed to remove the Murine (Mouse) Leukemia Virus to about 4 logs, while the Viresolve/70's 1992 literature claimed removal of the same virus to about 7 logs. This was far more virus particles than most drug raw materials contained. Moreover, the Pall membrane admittedly was not effective against the smallest known virus, polio, which Viresolve/70 could remove to 3.5 logs. Exhibit 9 illustrates the performance of Viresolve against competitors, including Pall's Nylon 66 membrane. The exhibit plots virus size against removal rate by Viresolve. For example, Viresolve removed the Sindbis virus, a particle about 54.1 nanometers (billionths of a meter) in size, to 6 logs, while Pall's membrane was effective to only 3 logs.

Millipore managers were much more concerned about the new product developed by Asahi. Laboratory tests appeared to indicate that Asahi's "Planova" was effective in virus removal. Moreover, their membrane used the more familiar "dead-end" filtration technology, which worked in a manner similar to a coffee filter. In Viresolve's "tangential flow" technology, liquid flowed perpendicular to the surface and was drawn through the filter using suction. Because tangential flow systems were still relatively unfamiliar and because there were more process variables involved, they were generally more challenging for the customer to properly install.

A key advantage that tangential flow provided, however, was that it allowed Millipore to use membranes which held viruses back on the surface of the membrane. Asahi used a "hollow fiber" approach, which captured viruses within the membrane's depth. Taking advantage of their simpler membrane design, Millipore scientists developed a "correlating integrity test" to verify (or "validate") that a given Viresolve membrane would actually work as promised. The test was "nondestructive," and so the tested membrane could later be put to use with absolute confidence in its performance.

Asahi also had an integrity test that customers could use, but the test was "destructive" and so the membrane could be tested only after it had been used. Hence the customer could never be certain of the membrane's performance until after it had been used. "We won a major battle for a contract with a major British pharmaceutical company about three months ago," recalled Sekhri. "We went head to head with Asahi. They liked a lot of things about Asahi, but it came down to the integrity test. They didn't feel comfortable without absolutely knowing what their log values were. They thought of our test as being something really new, really special in the marketplace, and they went with Viresolve."

COMMERCIALIZATION ISSUES

Market Segmentation and the Viresolve Product Line

The pores in the Viresolve membrane were small enough to prevent viruses from passing but large enough to allow most proteins through. The smaller the protein, the more likely that a size exclusion approach would work for removing viruses. One type of market segmentation, therefore, was based on the size of the protein. There were three broad segments of the protein purification market.

First were the makers of proteins using recombinant DNA technology, in which genes were "spliced" into a host cell to enable that cell to manufacture the desired protein. These proteins tended to be small, generally under 70,000 daltons (unit of molecular weight). The Viresolve/70 was targeted at these customers—makers of interferons,

EXHIBIT 9
Viresolve's Performance Against Competitors

New Membrane Provides Validatable Performance

Millipore, the world leader in membrane technology, has developed the Viresolve virus removal module, the first technology to deliver validatable viral clearance.

Viresolve modules consist of unique nanoselective membranes that can remove 4–6 logs of 40 nm sized viruses and 8+ logs of retroviruses, while recovering greater than 90 percent of proteins the size of human albumin and smaller. In fact, log reduction values can be almost doubled by running Viresolve modules in series.

Mammalian Virus Retention by Viresolve Is Predictable

Particle LRV as a Function of Particle Diameter
(Includes Mammalian Viruses)

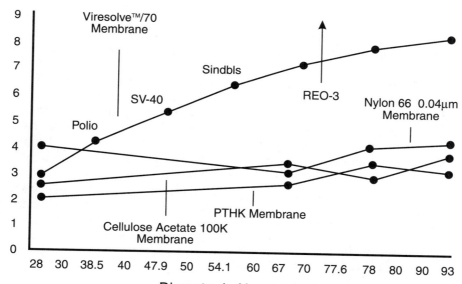

Diameter in Nanometers
Minimum virus removal using Viresolve/70 system.

Note: "LRV" = Log Reduction Value = $\dfrac{C\ feed}{C\ filtrate}$

---

growth factors, clotting stimulating factors, interleukins, and hormones.

A second segment was the makers of proteins using monoclonal antibodies, in which a cell which produced a desirable protein was fused with a cancerous ("immortal") cell to produce a hybrid cell capable of producing the desired protein and multiplying spontaneously to produce many more identical hybrids cells. These proteins were of moderate size, typically under 180,000 daltons. The Viresolve/180 was targeted at these customers—makers of Monoclonal antibodies and Ig fragments.

The third segment was blood processors, and Millipore had not yet developed a Viresolve-type product to meet this need. "It's probably the bigger part of the market," Sekhri conceded. "I get at least one call every week from a major blood company." The problem was that the principle of size exclusion, the method by which the Viresolve membrane operated, could not be readily applied to blood processing. Blood contains proteins that are as large, or larger, than the largest commonly found viruses. Techniques other than size exclusion had certainly been used in virus removal, but not as reliably. "We are working on that. It's kind of the next phase, maybe *Viresolve 3.*"

Naming the Product

Soon after arriving at Millipore, Sekhri distributed a companywide memo requesting a name for a "new technology capable of removing viruses from proteins." Names like Virex, Viratain, and Virecut were submitted. Some, like Virex, were already used; Virex was a software program to remove computer viruses. At the conclusion of a meeting with about 20 Millipore people, Sekhri made the final choice to go with Viresolve.

Understanding Customer Needs—Installing "Specials"

Sekhri personally handled the first few sales. During 1991 and 1992, Sekhri and three applications engineers, trained to ensure that Viresolve performed optimally, helped the first 50 or 60 customers worldwide install pre-launch versions of Viresolve. These early versions of the product were known internally as "specials." Sekhri sought to ensure that the first industry impressions of Viresolve would be positive ones.

> It's a brand new technology in a very conservative market. We could not afford to have any failures in the marketplace. If a customer just got one of these things and ran it and then said, "It doesn't work," it could very well be because the customer didn't know what he or she was doing. If that customer started telling the

very small, close-knit biotech market that Viresolve doesn't work, that would be the death blow to us.

The novel tangential-flow technology that Viresolve employed was a bit trickier to run than the traditional dead-end flow technology used by competitors. Explained Sekhri:

> You don't just press a button. There's optimization involved. So we thought that we would actually go out to every customer in the field ourselves, and do the trials, and write them up a full report, and then say, "Great, now you know how to do it and you're on your own."

This approach seemed to be succeeding in building appreciation for Viresolve, and for tangential-flow technology. Sekhri added, "If there is an existing perception on the part of customers, it may be that dead-end filtration is easiest, but our educated customers know that tangential-flow filtration makes a lot of sense for this application."

The list of customers targeted for "specials" was developed by Sekhri with help from Nick Lambo, the Process Division sales manager. "We identified customers that had the highest potential for Viresolve products," Lambo recalled. But the actual sales calls were done by Paul Sekhri, with three applications engineers (one each in the United States, Europe, and Japan) handling installation. "We didn't really want to get our salespeople turned on to a product that was in alpha stages."

Costs and Pricing

Sekhri calculated a price for Viresolve by looking at what Millipore charged for its ultrafiltration membranes and calculating a premium based on what advantages Viresolve offered over ultrafiltration and the other membranes that competitors used to remove viruses. These filters often had relatively inconsistent pore sizes and had typically been designed nearly a decade earlier for other applications. Stated Sekhri:

> I knew that we had a three-part package. We had a membrane that was dedicated to the removal of

viruses from proteins, and could do that reproducibly and predictably. We had validation data, which I have found to be almost as valuable as the membrane itself. Our competitors are running into problems with that right now. Their customers are saying, "It's great, we're using your membrane, so give us all of the validation data." But they don't have the data. And the third part was that we could verify the membrane's use through what's called a "correlating integrity test." So in thinking of what we charge for standard ultrafiltration membranes, I figured we could charge a premium.

Another pricing consideration was whether or not to sell the membrane modules as disposable. Sekhri asked a number of customers, "Would you rather spend more money for a single-use disposable, or spend less money for a reusable," although reusing a membrane meant having to prove that all of the previously retrieved viruses had been cleaned off. Acceptable tests for this were not reliable enough for some customers. According to Sekhri, customers said, "We'd rather have a single-use disposable, even if we have to pay a little bit more money for it." Viresolve modules were sold as single-use plastic devices and membranes, although the metal housing was permanent. One exception to this indifference to prices was the 10-square-foot module, which was considered by some customers to be too expensive for such frequent disposal. Added Sekhri: "So we compromised by validating five-time reuse."

The prices for Viresolve were as follows: 1/3-square-foot module: $500; 1-square-foot module: $1,200; 10-square-foot module: $2,000. For the 1-square-foot module, the comparable price for an ultrafiltration membrane (the technology that Viresolve replaced for this application) was $500–$600. For the 10-square-foot module, it was $1,000–$1,200. Ultrafiltration membranes could be reused 10 to 20 times. The 1-square-foot module processed 20 to 30 liters, and the 10-square-foot module about 100 liters, with times varying by process. Prices on both of the smaller units had been raised once since initial introduction.

For many customers, the price of a Viresolve unit was a trivial part of their production costs.

Interferon, for example, was worth $1.5 million a liter by the time it reached the Viresolve membrane in the process. Millipore recommended that Viresolve be installed in the downstream processing of biopharmaceuticals after steps like filtration, chromatography, centrifugation, extraction, flocculation, and electrokinetic separation had been completed.

LAUNCH

"We define a launch as: product is on the shelf, with a full complement of training and literature in place," said Nick Lambo. To Paul Sekhri, this translated into two chief tasks: "preparing the customer to buy, and preparing applications specialists [the salesforce] to sell."

Preparing Customers to Buy

Preparing customers to buy was done largely through word-of-mouth advertising and promotion. Sekhri had seeded the word-of-mouth process by ensuring that the first customers had favorable experiences. Promotion was done through the scientific press, conferences, and the trade press. Several of the product's developers wrote technical papers for prestigious scientific journals. Sekhri traveled extensively to attend trade conferences and make presentations, and he also hired a public relations firm. "We hired a PR firm because this is what I would consider really exciting news, a really good story. They helped us conduct a number of press conferences, and because of the press conferences we had a number of articles written into some pretty reputable journals. From reading these articles, people have called me up directly."

Viresolve Module Size

Millipore planned to introduce three different sizes of Viresolve: 1/3 square foot, 1 square foot, and 10 square foot. The smallest size was primarily for research work, the largest primarily for production work. Although tests at customer sites had taken place exclusively in R&D labs with small Viresolve modules, sales to production facilities were traditionally the Process Division's strength. The forthcoming 10-square-foot module would also allow Millipore salespeople to address the full life cycle of customer needs—from development of a new therapeutic to production of it.

Preparing the Sales Force to Sell

Training the sales force ("applications specialists") to sell Viresolve consisted chiefly of preparing training materials, conducting a two-day training seminar, and responding to follow-up questions from the field. During 1992, Sekhri prepared a "Launch Manual" and "Reference Materials" for each salesperson involved. The material included a description of the product line, prices, detailed answers to commonly asked questions, copies of Viresolve and competitive advertisements, published validation studies for Viresolve versus its competitors, and a step-by-step guide through the sales cycle. "I've launched the product in Europe and Japan, and they're kind of running by themselves," said Paul Sekhri. "I get maybe three to five FAXes a day" from salespeople around the world with questions.

The U.S. launch was originally scheduled for the fourth quarter of 1992, but was delayed until spring of 1993. In October of 1992, a "scaled back" version was conducted. One representative from each of four to six regions was brought in and given specialized training in Viresolve. These representatives had "the best and most concentrated opportunities for the product initially," according to Nick Lambo, who had a total of around 20 sales representatives dedicated to pharmaceuticals.

"The next step is to train the full U.S. sales force, and that's going to happen in April 1993. We're going to do this whole dog-and-pony show that we did in Europe for two days again." The training included presentations and teaching sessions, as well as "wet work" with actual Viresolve modules.

A crucial part of the sales cycle was the conducting of a feasibility study using actual customer samples. The launch package described how the salesperson was to go about arranging these studies. Once the initial contact was made, customers filled out a form explaining their virus removal needs. The salesperson faxed the form to Millipore application engineers, who let the salesperson know within 48 hours whether or not the application appeared to make sense. Once a mutually convenient date was set, the application engineer, customer, and salesperson all met to conduct the feasibility study at the customer site, using a sample of the material to be purified. Within two weeks, application engineers completed a report and Federal Expressed it to the customer, who then made the decision whether or not to purchase Viresolve. From this point on, the salesperson kept in touch with the application engineers for any further technical assistance.

Launch Strategy

Two elements of the launch strategy were considered particularly crucial. First, Lambo and Sekhri wanted biopharmaceutical firms to use Viresolve in the R&D process, so that there was a natural progression to using it in production. This would happen both because of familiarity with the product and because of the product's inclusion in the FDA approval process. "What you want to do ideally is work with the customer as they develop the processes for drugs, to educate and inform them of our technology, to prove it on small scale so that it carries through into the process step," said Nick Lambo. "If you miss that opportunity to get it inserted early, there's a lot more work to be done."

The historic strength of Lambo's sales force made this particularly challenging. "My organization tends to focus on the production scale end," which was where the 10-square-foot version might be used. "But products like Viresolve have to be inserted in the R&D stages, early on. By the time production has begun, getting them retroactively inserted is difficult." To improve his organization's ability to handle this challenge, Lambo had hired an R&D engineer in California to concentrate strictly on "R&D insertion" of Millipore products, including Viresolve. "If that's successful, and we think it will be, then I'll rapidly apply for another headcount in other parts of the world."

The other crucial element of the launch strategy was to push the Viresolve/70 hardest in the initial stages of the launch. Because the disparity between protein and virus sizes was greatest for the applications that Viresolve/70 was targeted at, Sekhri felt that the chances for dramatic success were best with this product. Such dramatic success, it was felt, could help set the stage for the commercial success of later products in the Viresolve line.

Forecasting Sales

Sekhri had forecast sales of $200,000 in 1992. Viresolve had achieved $300,000 in sales by the middle of the fourth quarter.

Many managers at Millipore couldn't help but contrast Viresolve with launches of product line extensions, many of which began with sales in the millions of dollars. Nick Lambo expressed these sentiments: "Viresolve is an exciting product because it is a major leap of faith. It's something no one else has on the market. The frustrating part is, you're not going to see a rapid sales ramp."

REMAINING COMMERCIALIZATION ISSUES

Repeating Viresolve's European Successes in the United States

To date, interest in Europe had been particularly strong. Explained Sekhri:

> In Europe, the government has already published guidelines for virus removal. The United States has not yet published guidelines. That's why some U.S. customers say, "We'll use it when we're told we need to use it." Well, in Europe they're being told to use it. All of the early adopters came out of Europe.

The absence of U.S. regulations made the U.S. launch of Viresolve all the more challenging.

Millipore was working on the development of the 10-square-foot module which could be sold to manufacturing facilities. The smaller Viresolve modules were more suited to R&D facilities. "We've got to have the 10-square-foot module," insisted Nick Lambo. "This is not an R&D tool, and unless you can show a clear path to production scale, the product will have short-term interest." The 10-square-foot Viresolve module was one of the top development priorities of the R&D manager in the Pharmaceutical group of the Process Division.

Millipore was already looking into several promising extensions of the Viresolve product line. A similar system might be designed to remove nucleic acids or pyrogens. "Any time you have a product stream that could be contaminated by a biological agent you need a membrane to filter it out," explained Sekhri. Millipore was also very interested in designing a system to provide virus removal to blood processing companies, using a technology different from size exclusion.

While Viresolve would undoubtedly meet with a measure of success, some managers at Millipore were concerned that the product might have a limited window of opportunity. "There are some people in my organization who think that this product may have a short life cycle," noted Nick Lambo. "You're talking about mammalian cell technology and the viruses present in that. As technology moves away from that, as more products are being built through other kinds of technology, it may not be an issue." As genetic engineers gained the ability to chemically synthesize more proteins instead of modifying mammalian cells to produce them, these managers felt that there would be correspondingly less risk of viral infection. Other managers, however, argued that research on new biotechnology drugs would probably always involve the use of mammalian cells, and thus the need for virus removal products would continue.

"It's been a year since we introduced green products at Loblaws and the decisions still are not getting any easier." In early July 1990, Scott Lindsay was reflecting upon his decision as to which, if any, of three possible products he would recommend for the G·R·E·E·N line: an energy-efficient light bulb, toilet tissue made from recycled paper, or a high-fiber cereal.

As Director of International Trade for Intersave Buying & Merchandising Services (a buying division for Loblaws), it was Scott's job to source and manage about 400 corporate brands (No Name, President's Choice, G·R·E·E·N)[1] for Loblaws in Canada. In four days, Scott would have to make his recommendations to the buyers' meeting.

The "green line" for which Scott was sourcing products was a new concept for Loblaws and its customers. Launched in 1989 as part of the corporate President's Choice brands, green products had characteristics that were less hazardous to the environment and/or contributed to a more healthy lifestyle. At issue for Scott was deciding what was "green" and balancing the financial requirements of the company with the socially responsible initiative of the green line.

As well, his most pressing concern was his ability to convince the president, Dave Nichol, of the merits of his recommendations. Mr. Nichol was the driving force behind the corporate brands, and he maintained involvement and final authority on these important product decisions.

In preparation for the buyers' meeting, Scott had to have his written recommendations on Dave Nichol's desk that day. Dave Nichol required that recommendations include retail price and cost data, projected annual sales in units and dollars, as well as total gross margin expected. In addition to the expected results, best and worst case scenarios were also required. As well, primary reasons for and against the proposal needed to be given. Typically, the recommendations were made based on the Ontario market as it was the proving ground for new products.

The first product Scott was considering was a new energy-efficient light bulb, which had been successfully marketed in Germany. The bulb lasted at least ten times longer than a regular light bulb but was substantially more expensive. There was no question in Scott's mind that the energy-efficient bulb had strong "green" characteristics and would enhance Loblaws' green image. However, a potential consumer price of $20 and low retail margins were a troubling combination. He knew that store managers, who were measured on sales volume and profits, would not be enthusiastic about a product that would not deliver sales or profits. These store managers controlled the individual products and brands that were carried in their stores.

The second new product was, in fact, not a new product at all. Loblaws had been selling a toilet tissue manufactured with 100% recycled material under its No Name corporate label. The existing product could be repackaged under the G·R·E·E·N label and sold beside the No Name line of products. The green packaging might alert consumers sensitive to the recycled feature, thereby generating greater volumes for the product. Further, Scott realized there was an opportunity to price the "green" toilet tissue at a higher price than the No Name, providing a higher profit margin.

---

[1] No Name, President's Choice, and G·R·E·E·N are all trademarks, owned by Loblaws Companies Limited.

This case was written by Professor Gordon H. G. McDougall and Professor Douglas Snetsinger of Wilfrid Laurier University as a basis of classroom discussion rather than to illustrate either effective or ineffective handling of an administrative situation. Reprinted by permission of the authors.

Copyright © 1991. Some data are disguised.

The final product under consideration was a new corn flake product for the very "crowded" breakfast cereal category. The new cereal had an unusually high fiber content. The "body friendly" nature of the cereal was the basis for considering it for the green line. Its additional feature was that it could be sourced at a cost much lower than the national brands.

LOBLAWS COMPANIES LIMITED

Loblaw Companies Limited is part of George Weston Ltd., a conglomerate of companies that operate in three basic areas: food processing, food distribution, and natural resources. George Weston is the sixth largest company in Canada with sales of $10.5 billion and net income of $988 million in 1989. The Loblaw Companies, an integrated group of food wholesaling and retailing companies, had total sales and net earnings in 1989 of $7,934 million and $70 million respectively.

THE GREEN IDEA

The G·R·E·E·N line launch had its origins in one of Dave Nichol's buying trips to Germany in 1988, where he was struck by the number of grocery products that were being promoted as "environmentally friendly." He discovered that *The Green Consumer Guide,* a "how-to" book for consumers to become environmentally responsible, had become a best-seller in England. In late 1988, Loblaws began collecting information on Canadian attitudes about the environment. The results suggested that an increasing number of Canadians were concerned about environmental issues, and some expressed a willingness to pay extra to purchase environmentally safe products. Further, many said they were willing to change supermarkets to acquire these products (see Exhibit 1).

THE G·R·E·E·N LAUNCH

Armed with this supportive data, in late January 1989, Loblaws management decided to launch by July 1989 a line of 100 products that were either environmentally friendly or healthy for the body. These products would be added to the family of the corporate line and called G·R·E·E·N. Although the task was considered ambitious, the corporation believed it had the requisite size, strength, influence, network, imagination, and courage to be successful. Loblaws contacted a number of prominent environmental groups to assist in the choice of products. These groups were requested to make a "wish list" of environmentally safe products. Using this as a guide, Loblaws began to source the products for the G·R·E·E·N launch.

A few products, such as baking soda, simply required repackaging to advertise the already existing environmentally friendly qualities of the product. Intersave Buying and Merchandising Services were able to source some products through foreign suppliers, such as the Ecover line of household cleaning products, to be marketed under the G·R·E·E·N umbrella. All G·R·E·E·N products were rigorously tested as well as screened by environmental groups such as Pollution Probe and Friends of the Earth. This collaboration was developed to such an extent that a few of the products were endorsed by Pollution Probe.

The G·R·E·E·N product line, consisting of about 60 products, was launched on June 3, 1989. Initial G·R·E·E·N products included phosphate-free laundry detergent, low-acid coffee, pet foods, and biodegradable garbage bags (see Exhibit 2). A holistic approach was taken in selecting these initial products; for example, the pet food products were included because they provided a more healthful blend of ingredients for cats and dogs. The G·R·E·E·N products were offered in a distinctively designed package with vivid green coloring. When the package design decisions were being made, it was learned that 20 percent of the Canadian population is functionally illiterate. Management felt that the distinct design would give these consumers a chance to readily identify these brands.

The G·R·E·E·N launch was supported with a $3 million television and print campaign. Consumers were informed of the new product line using the

EXHIBIT 1
Consumer Attitudes on Environment

1. National survey on issues.

What is the most important issue facing Canada today?

Issues	1985	1986	1987	1988	1989
Environment	*	*	2	10	18
Goods and services tax	*	*	*	*	15
Inflation/Economy	16	12	12	5	10
Deficit/Government	6	10	10	6	10
National unity	*	*	*	*	7
Free trade	2	5	26	42	7
Abortion	*	*	*	*	6
Employment	45	39	20	10	6

Source: Maclean's/Decima Research
*Not cited by a significant number of poll respondents.
Note: Survey conducted in early January of each year.

2. Loblaws customers surveys.

How concerned are you about the environment? (%)
Extremely (32), Quite (37), Somewhat (24), Not Very (5), Don't Care (2)

How likely is it that you would purchase environmentally friendly products?
Very (49), Somewhat (43), Not too (2), Not at all (4)

How likely is it that you would switch supermarkets to purchase environmentally friendly products?
Very (2), Somewhat (45), Not too (24), Not at all (10)

Note: Survey conducted in early 1989.

June 1989 issue of the *Insider's Report*. In an open letter to consumers, Mr. Nichol addressed Loblaws motivation for the G·R·E·E·N launch (see Exhibit 3). Part of the motivation was also to offer consumers a choice that could, in the longer term, provide educational benefits for consumers on specific green issues. As well, by offering the choice, consumers could "vote at the cash register" and, in a sense, tell Loblaws what they were willing to buy and what green products they would accept. The G·R·E·E·N line was to be typically priced below national brand products.

The G·R·E·E·N introduction was not without its problems. Shortly after the launch, members of the Pollution Probe rejected their previous endorsement of the G·R·E·E·N disposable diaper. These members felt that the group should not support a less than perfect product. The G·R·E·E·N diaper was more environmentally friendly than any other disposable brand. However, it was not, in Pollution Probe's opinion, environmentally pure. Further, it was felt that endorsing such products compromised the integrity and independence of the organization. This prompted the resignation of Colin Issac, the director of Pollution Probe. The group subsequently discontinued its endorsement of the diaper, but continued its support of six other G·R·E·E·N products.

Controversy also arose around the introduction of the G·R·E·E·N fertilizer. Greenpeace, a prominent environmental group, rejected Loblaws' claims that the fertilizer had no toxic elements and therefore was environmentally pure. The group did not know that Loblaws had spent substantial funds to determine that the product was free of toxic chemicals.

EXHIBIT 2
The Initial G·R·E·E·N Products

Food
Just Peanuts Peanut Butter
Smart Snack Popcorn
"The Virtuous" Soda Cracker
Cox's Orange Pippin Apple Juice
White Hull-less Popcorn
Reduced Acid Coffee
Boneless and Skinless Sardines
"Green" Natural Oat Bran
Naturally Flavoured Raisins: Lemon, Cherry,
    Strawberry
"Green" Turkey Frankfurters
100% Natural Rose Food
Norwegian Crackers
Turkey Whole Frozen
Gourmet Frozen Foods (low-fat)
"If the World Were PERFECT" Water

Cleaning/Detergent Products
All-Purpose Liquid Cleaner with Bitrex
"Green" Automatic Dishwasher Detergent
Ecover 100% Biodegradable Laundry Powder*
Ecover Dishwasher Detergent
Laundry Soil and Stain Remover with Bitrex
Drain Opener with Bitrex
Ecover Fabric Softener
Ecover 100% Biodegradable Toilet Cleaner
Ecover 100% Biodegradable Wool Wash
Ecover Floor Soap
"Green" 100% Phosphate-Free Laundry Detergent

Pet Food
Low Ash Cat Food
Slim & Trim Cat Food
All Natural Dog Biscuits

Cooking Products
"The Virtuous" Canola Oil
"The Virtuous" Cooking Spray
Baking Soda

Paper-Based Products
Bathroom Tissue
"Green" Ultra Diapers
"Green" Foam Plates
Swedish 100% Chlorine-Free Coffee Filters
"Green" Baby Wipes
"Green" Maxi Pads

Oil-Based Products
Biodegradable Garbage Bags
Hi-Performance Motor Oil
Natural Fertilizer
Lawn and Garden Soil

Other Products
Green T-Shirt/Sweatshirt
Green Panda Stuffed Toy
Green Polar Bear Stuffed Toy
Cedar Balls

*The Ecover brands are a line of cleaning products made by Ecover of Belgium. These products are vegetable oil based and are rapidly biodegradable. Loblaws marketed these products under the G·R·E·E·N umbrella.

Both incidents, although unfortunate, focused the attention of Canadians on the G·R·E·E·N product line. The media highlighted Loblaws as the only North American retailer to offer a line of environmentally friendly products. The publicity also prompted letters of encouragement from the public who supported Loblaws' initiative. Surveys conducted four weeks after the line introduction revealed an 82 percent awareness of the G·R·E·E·N line with 27 percent of the consumers actually purchasing at least one of the G·R·E·E·N products. In Ontario alone, the G·R·E·E·N line doubled its projected sales and sold $5 million in June 1989.

THE FIRST YEAR OF G·R·E·E·N

The launch of G·R·E·E·N was soon followed by a virtual avalanche of "environmentally friendly" products. Major consumer goods companies such as Procter & Gamble, Lever Brothers, and Colgate-Palmolive introduced Enviro-Paks, phosphate-free detergents, and biodegradable cleaning products. Competing supermarket chains had varied

EXHIBIT 3
The Insider's Report—Open Letter

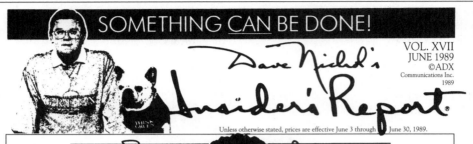

SOMETHING CAN BE DONE!

Dave Nichol's Insider's Report

VOL. XVII
JUNE 1989
©ADX
Communications Inc.
1989

Unless otherwise stated, prices are effective June 3 through June 30, 1989.

President's Choice G·R·E·E·N™

An Open Letter To Canadian Consumers about President's Choice G•R•E•E•N Products

Over the last year, while travelling the world looking for new products, I was astounded at the level of consumer interest in environmentally friendly products. For example, the best-selling book in England last year was an environmental handbook ranking retailers and their products.

Back in Canada, I noticed that every public opinion poll indicated that the environment was the number one concern of Canadian consumers—confirming what my mail had been telling me for at least a year.

Convinced that this concern was genuine, the Insider's Report team met with executives of many of Canada's leading environmental groups and asked them what products they would like to see us create that would in some way help to reduce pollution. The guidance was the genesis of the G·R·E·E·N "Environment Friendly™" product program and in many cases we actually worked with these groups to develop specific products which they then felt confident in endorsing.

At the same time we also began development of "Body Friendly™" (low calorie, high fibre, low fat, low cholesterol, etc.) products under the G·R·E·E·N label. This Insider's Report highlights the first wave of our new President's Choice G·R·E·E·N product program.

Here are a few points of clarification about the program.

1. With few exceptions, President's Choice G·R·E·E·N products are priced at, or below the price of the national brand to which they are an alternative.

2. We do not intend to censor products that some may feel are "environmentally-unfriendly." We see our role as providing a choice so you may decide for yourself.

3. Protecting the environment is a young and therefore, imprecise science. As a result, not all groups agree on what the best products are to help control pollution. For example, some advise us to use paper

pulp trays for all eggs while others say recyclable, ozone-friendly foam tray made with pentane instead of chlorofluorocarbons (C.F.C's) are a better solution. We accept the fact that it is inevitable that not all environmental groups will agree with all of our President's Choice G·R·E·E·N products.

4. Some may accuse us of being "environmental opportunists." WE SEE OUR ROLE AS PROVIDING PRODUCTS THAT PEOPLE WANT. That's why we created No Name products when Canada's food inflation was running at 16%. That's why we created President's Choice products when a demand for superior-quality products arose. And that's why we've created G·R·E·E·N products when the overwhelming concern of Canadians is the environment.

We invite you to read about our new President's Choice G·R·E·E·N products in this Insider's Report and decide for yourself whether or not they fill a real need in our society.

5. A number of our G·R·E·E·N products are products that we've carried for years (such as baking soda). Putting them under the G·R·E·E·N label was in response to environmental groups who chided us by saying, "You have a number of products in your stores right now that could help fight pollution but you have to bring them to your customer's attention and then explain how to use them."

We acknowledge that we are not environmental experts and we readily admit that we do not have all the answers. However, we feel strongly that these products are a step in the long journey toward the solution of our enormous environmental problems. If G·R·E·E·N products do nothing more than help raise awareness of the need to address environmental issues NOW, and give Canadians hope that SOMETHING CAN BE DONE, then in the end, they will have made a positive contribution.

Dave Nichol

David Nichol, President
Loblaw International Merchants

Loblaws   **super**centre   **zehrs**   **no frills**

Selected products also available at
Mr. Grocer, valu-mart®, freshmart™
and Your Independent Grocer®.

PRINTED ON RECYCLED NEWSPRINT

responses from launching their own "green" line (Miracle Mart introduced three "Green Circle" products, Oshawa Foods introduced about 10 "Greencare" products) to highlighting environmentally sensitive products in their stores (Safeway) to improving its internal practices through recycling and other activities (Provigo).

During the year, Loblaws continued to develop and promote the G·R·E·E·N product line. In the first year of G·R·E·E·N, Loblaws sold approximately $60 million worth of G·R·E·E·N products and "broke even" on the line.

THE DECISIONS

As Scott began to make his decisions on the three products, he reflected on the past year. He thought that $60 million in sales for the G·R·E·E·N line was reasonable, but he had hoped the line would do better. He remembered some of the products that just didn't fit in the line, such as "green" sardines. "I don't think we sold 20 cans of that stuff." Scott and the other buyers at Intersave were very concerned when a product didn't sell. Individual store managers, who were held accountable for the sales and profits of their stores, did not have to list (that is, stock in the store that he or she managed) any product, including any in the G·R·E·E·N line. If a store manager thought the product was unsuitable for the store, it wasn't listed. As well, if a buyer got a product listed and it didn't sell, his or her reputation with the store managers would suffer.

Light Bulb

The proposal by Osram, a well-known German manufacturer, was a true green product. The Osram light bulb was a compact fluorescent bulb that could replace the traditional incandescent light bulb in specific applications. The unique aspect of this product was that while fluorescent light technology was commonplace (these long-tube lights were common in office buildings), only recently had the product been modified for use as a replacement for traditional light bulbs. The major benefits of fluo-

rescent light bulbs were that they used considerably less energy than incandescent light bulbs (for example, a 9 watt fluorescent bulb could replace a 40 watt incandescent bulb and still provide the same lighting level, while using only 22.5 percent of the energy) and it lasted at least 10 times longer (an estimated 2,000 hours versus 200 hours for the incandescent bulb). To date, the major application for compact fluorescents had been in apartment buildings in stairwells where lights remained on 24 hours a day. Apartment building owners purchased them because the bulbs lowered both energy costs and maintenance costs (less frequent replacement).

The compact fluorescent had limited applications in the home. Because of its unique shape, it could not be used with a typical lampshade. The main application was likely to be in hallways where it was difficult to replace a burned-out bulb. Even in these situations, a new fixture (that is, an enclosure) might be required so that the compact fluorescent would fit.

The bulb's energy efficiency and long-lasting features were well tested and had been sold for specialized industrial use for several years. The bulb was making satisfactory inroads in Germany even though it was priced at the equivalent of $40 Canadian.

Loblaws sold a variety of 60 and 100 watt No Name and Phillips light bulbs in packages of four. In total, the light bulb category generated over $1 million in gross margin for Loblaws in 1989 (see Exhibit 4).

The initial Osram proposal was to sell the product to Loblaws at $19.00 per bulb. Even if the markup were set at 5 percent, Loblaw's retail price would be $19.99. Scott talked this over with a number of people at Loblaws and concluded that the price was too high to be accepted by Canadian consumers. At this time, Ontario Hydro entered the picture. Ontario Hydro was extremely concerned about its ability to meet the power demands of its customers in the next decade and was engaged in aggressive energy conservation programs. Ontario Hydro was prepared to offer a $5 rebate for every light bulb that was sold in Ontario in the three

EXHIBIT 4
Light Bulbs (1989)

	Average Retail Price* ($)	Average Cost ($)	Annual Sales ($000)	Total Gross Margin ($000)	Market Share (%)
Loblaws					
60 Watt	2.25	1.25	470	209	18
60 Watt Soft	2.75	1.50	426	193	16
100 Watt	2.25	1.25	294	130	11
100 Watt Soft	2.75	1.50	279	127	11
Total Loblaws			1,468	659	56
Phillips					
60 Watt	2.40	1.50	367	138	14
60 Watt Soft	3.20	1.65	341	165	13
100 Watt	2.40	1.50	236	88	9
100 Watt Soft	3.20	1.65	102	102	8
Total Phillips			1,153	493	44
Total			2,621	1,152	100

*Based on four-packs (that is, four light bulbs in a package). Total unit sales were 1,019,000 (four-packs).

months following the launch. Although it meant customers would need to request the rebate by mail, it reduced the effective price of the bulb to the consumer to $14.99.

Scott felt that the combination of the rebate, a retail price at only half that paid by German consumers, and a strong environmental message had strong merchandising appeal that could be exploited in the launch of the bulb. Nevertheless, the sales potential was still unclear. Loblaws' annual sales in Ontario were nearly four million bulbs, or $2.7 million. Because this product was unique and new, Scott had difficulty estimating its sales potential. His best guess was that Loblaws might sell anywhere from 10,000 to 50,000 Osram bulbs in one year. Scott thought that half the sales would come from regular customers and the other half from customers coming to Loblaws specifically to buy the bulb. Scott also felt that after three months, the price should be raised to

$24.99 retail to generate a reasonable margin for Loblaws.

Scott thought that if half the volume were generated at the higher price, it would certainly be easier to maintain the support of the store managers. At the $24.99 price, the margin would be $5.99 per bulb. Even considering the cannibalization issue, the margin on the higher priced Osram would be about four times higher than the margin for a four-pack of regular bulbs. However, it would be necessary to calculate the contribution for the year to see what the net effect would be for the line. The shelf space required for these bulbs would be minimal and could be handled by some minor changes to the layout of the existing bulbs.

BATHROOM TISSUE

The bathroom tissue category was a highly competitive, price-sensitive market. The category was one of the largest in the Loblaws lineup, generating over $31 million in retail sales in Ontario and $7 million in contribution (see Exhibit 5). Bathroom tissue was more important to Loblaws than just a volume generator. It was one of the few product categories that would draw price-conscious buyers into the store. Loblaws listed 40 different sizes and colors from various manufacturers. There were six Loblaws brands in the category. Loblaws was aggressive at delisting any competitive or corporate brand that did not meet turnover or profitability goals. Manufacturers were just as aggressive at providing allowance and merchandising incentives to ensure satisfactory margins for Loblaws and to facilitate retail price reductions that in turn would enhance turnover and maintain volume goals. Two national brands—Royale and Cottonelle—held shares of 46 percent and 30 percent respectively.

For 1989, Loblaws' brands held 16 percent of the market with No Name White providing a total gross margin of over $1 million. Loblaws' No Name White was sourced for an average cost of $1.15 for a 4-roll package. These lower costs were largely based on the fact that the tissue was manufactured with totally recycled material. This product feature made it a candidate for G·R·E·E·N line consideration. The existing product could simply be repackaged with the distinctive G·R·E·E·N labeling and an emphasis placed on the recycled character of the product. No development or testing costs would be required, and art work and new labeling costs would be minimal.

Several decisions needed to be considered with respect to the repackaging of the No Name product. Should the new product replace the old or simply be added to an already crowded category? Should the price of the new product be set higher than that set for the old? Should the product be launched at all?

READY-TO-EAT CEREAL

Loblaws sold more than $14 million worth of family cereals (that is, cereals targeted at the "family" market) in Ontario in 1989 (see Exhibit 6). Loblaws corporate brand share of the family cereal segment, at 14 percent, was lower than corporate objectives for this category. One of Scott Lindsay's goals was to increase Loblaws' share for this category. The brand leaders, such as Kellogg's Corn Flakes, Nabisco Shreddies, and General Mills' Cheerios, were as familiar to shoppers as any other product or brand in a store. With decades of advertising and promotional support, these brands had become thoroughly entrenched in the minds and pantries of generations of Canadians.

The brand names of these market leaders provided the manufacturers with strong protection against competitors. However, the manufacturing process did not. The manufacturing processes were well known in the industry, and many firms could produce identical products at favorable costs. Loblaws had found several products from domestic sources that appeared to be as good if not better than the national brands. One such product was a corn flake product that had a very high fiber content. The new product would appeal to those customers who had been primed by the health claims of high fiber diets. In sensory tests, it had proven to have an excellent taste and texture profile and was equal to or preferred in blind taste tests to some of the market leaders. Moreover, the product could be obtained for $1.40 per 500g package.

The President's Choice brands were beginning to make inroads in this market, and this new product could increase the share. However, it was not clear how to position the high-fiber corn flake product. Should it go in the regular President's Choice line as a line extension of the current corn flake product, or should it be packaged as a G·R·E·E·N product? As a regular President's Choice product, it would be positioned directly against Kellogg's as an all-around cereal with extra value. As a G·R·E·E·N product, it would be positioned less against Kellogg's and much more towards a health/"good-for-you claim." G·R·E·E·N positioning might also minimize any cannibalization of the President's Choice corn flakes. The lower sourcing costs provided some flexibility on pricing. It could be priced as low as $1.75, like the current President's Choice corn flakes, and still

EXHIBIT 5
Bathroom Tissue (1989)

	Average Retail Price [1] ($)	Average Cost ($)	Annual Sales ($000)	Total Gross Margin ($000)	Market Share (%)
Loblaws [2]					
President's Choice	2.50	1.95	1,542	339	5
No Name White	1.75	1.15	3,084	1,052	10
No Name Coloured	1.80	1.35	386	96	1
Loblaws Total			5,012	1,487	16
Royale					
White	1.85	1.55	10,795	1,751	34
Coloured	2.00	1.60	3,855	771	12
Royale Total			14,650	2,522	46
Cottonelle					
White	1.85	1.45	4,627	1,000	15
Coloured	1.95	1.50	4,627	1,068	15
Cottonelle Total			9,254	2,068	30
Other Brands					
Capri	1.50	0.90	945	378	3
April Soft	1.40	0.95	721	232	2
Jubilee	1.35	0.70	386	186	1
Dunet	2.45	1.60	405	140	1
White Swan	1.55	1.00	463	164	1
Other Brands Total			2,920	1,100	8
Total			31,836	7,177	100

[1] Statistics for the prices, costs, and sales have been collapsed over the various sizes and reported in equivalent four-roll packs. Total unit sales were 17,125,000 (four-roll packs).

[2] With respect to colors and sizes, Loblaws offered six varieties, Royale (eight varieties), Cottonelle (eight varieties), Capri (four varieties), April Soft (three varieties), Jubilee (two varieties), Dunet (one variety), and White Swan (eight varieties).

maintain good margins; or it could be priced as high as Kellogg's Corn Flakes at $2.30 and generate superior margins.

Having reviewed the three proposals, Scott began the process of preparing his recommenda-tions. "I'll start with the financial projections," thought Scott, "then consider the pros and cons of each proposal. Then it's decision time."

EXHIBIT 6
Family Cereals (1989)

	Average Retail Price* ($)	Average Cost ($)	Annual Sales ($000)	Total Gross Margin ($000)	Market Share (%)
President's Choice					
Bran with Raisins	2.35	1.50	1,051	380	7.4
Honey Nut Cereal	3.00	1.40	324	173	2.3
Toasted Oats	3.00	1.45	221	114	1.5
Corn Flakes	1.75	1.20	193	60	1.4
Crispy Rice	3.20	1.50	263	139	1.8
Loblaws Total			2,052	866	14.3
Kellogg's					
Corn Flakes	2.30	1.80	1,436	312	10.1
Raisin Bran	2.75	2.00	1,236	324	8.7
Honey Nut Corn Flakes	3.95	2.70	460	141	3.2
Rice Krispies	3.95	2.52	899	315	6.3
Common Sense	4.40	2.70	433	167	3.0
Mini-Wheat	3.30	2.00	326	129	2.3
Variety Pack	5.90	3.90	309	105	2.2
Other Kellogg's	3.41	2.26	258	87	1.8
Kellogg's Total			5,357	1,580	37.5
Nabisco					
Shreddies	2.35	1.70	2,725	754	19.1
Apple/Cinnamon	2.25	1.50	169	57	1.2
Raisin Wheat	3.30	2.10	139	50	1.0
Nabisco Total			3,033	861	21.2
General Mills					
Cheerios	3.80	2.60	1,171	370	8.2
Cheerios/Honey Nut	3.90	2.60	1,017	339	7.1
General Mills Total			2,188	709	15.3
Quaker					
Corn Bran	3.50	2.25	389	139	2.7
Life	3.15	2.10	358	119	2.5
Oat Bran	4.10	2.80	281	89	2.0
Muffets	2.65	1.60	92	36	0.6
Quaker Total			1,120	383	7.8
Others	2.40	1.45	573	227	4.0
Total			14,323	4,626	100.0

*Based on 500-gram size. Total unit sales were 4,950,000 (500-gram size).

Cereals are packaged in several different sizes. Some brands, such as Kellogg's Corn Flakes, could have four different sizes (e.g., 350g, 425g, 675g, 800g) on the shelf at one time. To facilitate comparisons, all figures have been converted to a standard 500g size; where brands had multiple sizes, the figures are reported as averages, weighted by the sales volume of the size.

Lever Brothers'Introduction of Snuggle Fabric Softener

It was early May 1990 and Lever Brothers Eastern Regional Sales Manager, Mr. David Lewis, was pondering his assignment. Mr. Lewis needed to devise a strategy to introduce into his region Snuggle, Lever Brothers' newest entry into the fast-growing liquid fabric softener market.

The product had already been successfully introduced into the Milwaukee Test Market, the Midwest, West, Central, Southeast, and Southwest regions. Only the Eastern region remained. The company believed it had the right combination of ingredients for unprecedented success—a quality product, a lower price, and a magical "spokesbear." Snuggle had broken all records since its introduction, and it was Mr. Lewis's job to continue its success.

HISTORY

Lever Brothers Company is one of the United States' best-known manufacturers and marketers of soaps, detergents, toiletries, and food products. It is a member of the worldwide Unilever corporation, which includes more than 500 companies and offers one of the widest varieties of products and services in the world.

The name Unilever was coined in 1929, when the Margarine Union merged with Lever Brothers and changed its name to Unilever Limited. At the same time, the Margarine Union in the Netherlands became Unilever N.V. Unilever Limited has its head offices in London; the offices of Unilever N.V. are in Rotterdam.

Each Unilever director is on the board of both parent companies and, as much as possible, both companies work as one company—Unilever.

Today's Unilever traces its roots to nineteenth century Europe. The company is a direct result of the ingenuity and hard work of three European families, the Lever and Jurgens families of England and the Van den Burgh family of the Netherlands.

In 1885, William and James Lever founded their soap company. Through innovative marketing and packaging, their soap, known as Sunlight, became the world's biggest selling soap by 1887.

Years earlier, Anton Jurgens and his three sons became engaged in the butter trade. Unfortunately, as time went on, they found it increasingly difficult to obtain their raw materials. Luckily, in 1869 they found a way to overcome their supply problem. They simply bought the rights to a French chemist's latest product, margarine.

Finally, Simon Van den Burgh and his sons, rival exporters of cheap butter from the Netherlands, also heard about the new invention, and they also began to make margarine.

All three firms grew at great rates. Each firm expanded its product line, with Jurgens and Van den Burgh even entering the business of manufacturing soap.

All three firms shared a great deal in common. All relied on the same basic raw materials of oils and fats and the same refining processes. Their production was on a large scale and their distribution channels were alike. Their products also tended to be ordinary necessities intended to be consumed or used in millions of homes.

With such similarities, it was logical that these companies would someday come together. Through a series of mergers and acquisitions, the three grew into today's Unilever.

This case was prepared as a basis for classroom discussion rather than to illustrate either effective or ineffective handling of an administrative situation.

In 1989, Unilever operated over 500 companies in more than 70 countries, employed over 330,000 people, and had sales of over $24 billion. One of its most important companies is the Lever Brothers Company in the United States.

Lever Brothers started in 1895, with a small sales office in New York. Slowly the company grew with such products as Lifebuoy, Sunlight, and Welcome. For its first 25 years, the company concentrated on the New England market. Then in 1919, with the introduction of Rinso, the first granulated packaged soap, the company went national. In 1924, Lux, the first white milled perfumed soap to be made in America and sold at a popular price, was introduced. By 1929, Lever Brothers became the third largest producer of soap and glycerine in the United States.

Through the 1930s and '40s, Lever Brothers grew. It expanded its manufacturing capacity time and again. It built or acquired plants in Hammond, Indiana; Edgewater, New Jersey; Baltimore, Maryland; Chicago, Illinois; and St. Louis, Missouri. The company diversified into shortening, margarine, and toothpaste (Pepsodent).

In the 1950s, Lever Brothers introduced a procession of new products. Such products as Lux liquid detergent—the first liquid detergent to be packaged in cans; Wisk, the first liquid heavy-duty laundry detergent; Imperial, the first premium margarine; Dove, the new type of toilet bar containing one-quarter cleansing cream; and Mrs. Butterworth's syrup, the first syrup blended with butter, were all introduced.

Through the 1960s and '70s, Lever Brothers introduced more notable new products such as a Pepsodent denture brush, Soft Imperial margarine, Drive detergent, Close-up and Aim toothpastes, Caress body bar, Promise margarine, and Signal mouthwash.

Finally, the 1980s brought us Shield deodorant soap, Aim Mint toothpaste, Sunlight dishwashing liquid, Impulse body spray, Sunlight automatic dishwashing detergent, Snuggle fabric softener sheets, Surf high suds detergent, and now Snuggle Liquid Fabric Softener.

From its modest start in 1895, Lever Brothers has grown to be one of the largest soap, detergent, and toiletry producers in the country.

LEVER BROTHERS ORGANIZATION: HOUSEHOLD PRODUCTS

Lever Brothers was a decentralized company that had three operating divisions. These were Household Products (HHP), Personal Products (PPD), and Foods. Each division had its own president and officers, and each was responsible, as far as is practical, for all resources and services necessary for its operation. This organizational structure was completed in 1981.

The sales force sold Lever's household products throughout the United States. To facilitate this selling activity, the sales force was divided into six regions. Each region was divided into districts, and each district was divided into areas/units. Finally, each area/unit was divided into sales territories. These were, in turn, headed by Regional Sales Managers, District Sales Managers, Area Assistants, and District Field Sales Managers, who were assigned to assist District Sales Managers in managing some districts.

This organization allowed for maximum flexibility when making decisions to best serve the requirements of different market zones throughout the country. For example, local promotions were determined by buying preferences and competitive approaches in a particular market, and these could be different from those in another district.

The six regions and 22 districts are listed in Exhibit 1.

HOUSEHOLD PRODUCTS DIVISION: CHANNELS OF DISTRIBUTION

Lever Brothers used two different channels of distribution. They were as follows:

1. Manufacturer (Lever Brothers) who sold to **wholesalers** and **chain headquarters** who supplied to **retailers** or **chain stores** who sold directly to **consumers**.

EXHIBIT 1
Lever Brothers Household Products Division Field Sales Organization

Eastern Region	Central Region	Southeastern Region
Boston	Detroit	Charlotte
New York	Syracuse	Atlanta
Philadelphia	Cincinnati	Orlando
	Cleveland/Pittsburgh	Baltimore

Southwestern Region	Midwestern Region	Western Region
New Orleans	Chicago	Los Angeles
Dallas	Kansas City	San Francisco
Houston	Minneapolis	Portland
Denver	St. Louis	

2. Manufacturer (Lever Brothers) who sold directly to **retailers** who sold to **consumers**.

HOUSEHOLD PRODUCTS DIVISION: CATEGORIES OF MERCHANDISE

The Household Products division sold four types of products: laundry detergents, dishwashing detergents, fabric softeners, and toilet bars. In the fabric softener field, Lever offered three products: Final Touch and two types of Snuggle, which came in liquids or sheets.

Final Touch was introduced in 1964 and was marketed as a premium fabric softener, while Snuggle Liquid and Sheets were both priced approximately 10 percent below the premium market.

PRODUCT/MARKET INFORMATION

Product

Snuggle was a premium quality liquid fabric softener that softened the whole wash, controlled static cling, and gave clothes a fresh smell at a price that was really less expensive than other premium fabric softeners. It would be available in the normal variety of sizes—17 oz., 33 oz., 64 oz., 96 oz., and 128 oz.

Market

The liquid fabric softener category was large and growing. In 1989, sales were $398 million, an in-crease of 22 percent since 1985. The liquid softener market could be expanded because 30 percent of all households still did not use a fabric softener. The liquid fabric softener category was dominated by premium-priced products. Each of the nationally supported brands (i.e., Downy, manufactured by Procter & Gamble, and Final Touch, manufactured by Lever Brothers) had one thing in common—a premium price. An opportunity existed to expand the choice consumers had by offering a quality liquid fabric softener at a price that was really less expensive.

I. Category Structure. Fabric softeners are primarily used by consumers to soften clothes, control static cling, and provide a fresh scent. The fabric softener market can be segmented by form into two groups—liquid softeners and dryer sheets.

- Liquid softeners are usually added to the washer during the rinse cycle. They tend to provide superior softening.
- Dryer sheets are pre-cut or come in tear-off fabric sheets that are tossed into the dryer along with the wash. Dryer sheets provide superior static cling control and convenience.

1989 Fabric Softener Category Share by Segment

	Unit Share	Dollar Share
Liquids	56%	59%
Dryer Sheets	44%	41%

II. Competitive Environment.

A. Liquids. The liquid fabric softener category was divided into three distinct segments: dilutes, concentrates, and super concentrates (see Exhibit 2). Concentrates, which were the preferred form, currently represented 77 percent of the total liquid market. The three liquid forms were differentiated by recommended usage amounts and cost per ounce and generally competed only within their segment.

Nationally, Regular Downy was the leading brand with a 43.6 percent share of the liquid category, followed by Final Touch with 14.1 percent and Snuggle with 11.3 percent of the market. In the Midwest, Snuggle currently had a 31.2 percent share, and in the West, the product had a 23.7 percent share.

Liquid Shares—1989

Brand	National	Midwest	West
Downy Total	54.5	48.2	57.7
Regular	43.6	36.9	47.3
Super Conc.	10.9	11.3	10.4
Snuggle	11.3	31.2	23.7
Final Touch	14.1	9.8	4.6
Sta-Puf	4.8	2.5	3.1
All Others	15.3	8.3	10.9

Only Final Touch and Downy received national advertising support. Both were premium-priced products but were differentiated by the whitening ability of Final Touch.

Product	Advertising Claim
Final Touch	Softness, Fragrance, Static Cling, and Whiteness
Downy	Softness, Fragrance, Static Cling

The following is market share data from three major cities in the Eastern Region:

SAMI Rankings—Liquid Fabric Softeners*
12 Week–Physical Case Share, Period Ending 4/26/90

Boston/Providence

Brand	Share
Downy	36.7
Final Touch	17.9
Downy T. C.	10.4
Lavender Sachet	5.2
Sta-Puf	1.1

Brand	Size	Share
Downy	64 oz.	14.3
Downy	96 oz.	12.2
Final Touch	64 oz.	8.0
Downy	33 oz.	7.4
Downy T. C.	21.5 oz.	6.7
Final Touch	33 oz.	6.2
Lavender Sachet	46 oz.	4.3
Downy T. C.	32 oz.	3.8
Final Touch	96 oz.	3.7
Downy	17 oz.	2.8

*Private labels and generics not included.

EXHIBIT 2
Liquid Softener Segmentation

Segment	Recommended Usage Amount	Price Per Ounce	Cost Per Use
Dilutes	6–8 ounces	1.4 cents	9.7 cents
Concentrates	3 ounces	3.5 cents	10.5 cents
Super Concentrates	1 ounce	10.2 cents	10.2 cents

New York

Brand	Share
Downy	35.0
Final Touch	19.3
Downy T. C.	9.1
Lavender Sachet	6.8
Sta-Puf Concentrate	5.1

Brand	Size	Share
Downy	96 oz.	15.4
Downy	64 oz.	10.7
Final Touch	64 oz.	8.5
Downy	33 oz.	7.4
Final Touch	33 oz.	6.4
Downy T. C.	32 oz.	4.7
Lavender Sachet	46 oz.	4.6
Final Touch	96 oz.	4.5
Downy T. C.	21.5 oz.	3.9
Sta-Puf Concentrate	64 oz.	2.6

Philadelphia

Brand	Share
Downy	30.6
Final Touch	20.4
Downy T. C.	9.8
Sta-Puf Concentrate	7.8
Lavender Sachet	6.1

Brand	Size	Share
Downy	64 oz.	13.2
Final Touch	64 oz.	8.9
Downy	96 oz.	8.8
Final Touch	33 oz.	7.6
Downy	33 oz.	5.9
Downy T. C.	32 oz.	5.5
Sta-Puf Concentrate	64 oz.	4.8
Downy T. C.	21.5 oz.	4.3
Lavender Sachet	46 oz.	4.3
Final Touch	96 oz.	3.9

B. Dryer. In the dryer segment, Bounce was the dominant brand with 50.3 percent share.

Dryer Shares*—1989

Brand	Share of Dryer Segment
Bounce Total	50.3
Regular	43.1
Unscented	7.2
Cling Free	12.1
All Others	37.7

*Excludes Snuggle Sheet Test Market

III. Category Pricing. Final Touch and Downy were both premium-priced and at parity to each other. Sta-Puf, which did not receive national advertising support and had a national share of only 4.8 percent, was priced at an average 10.8 percent discount to the premium brands. In general, dryer products were priced 50 percent below comparable liquid products on a per-use basis (see Exhibit 3).

IV. Category Spending. More than half of the total marketing support in the fabric softener category was placed behind promotion, while the balance was spent on advertising.

Category Spending*—1989		Percent
Promotion	$ 6,500M	57%
Advertising	46,900M	43
	$109,400M	100%

Fabric Softener Category 1989 Advertising Spending*		
Brand	$MM	Share of Spending
Liquids		
Downy**	$20.4	69%
Final Touch	9.0	31
Total Liquids	$29.4MM	100%
Dryer		
Bounce	$ 9.7	55%
Cling Free	6.8	39
Toss N Soft	1.0	6
Total Dryer	$17.5MM	100%

*Excludes Snuggle
**Includes Triple Concentrated

EXHIBIT 3
Category Pricing

	Pack	Pkg. Wt.	$/Case	$/Unit	$Cost/Use*
Final Touch	12's	33 oz.	14.04	1.17	.106
	6's	64 oz.	13.30	2.22	.104
	4's	96 oz.	13.09	3.27	.012
Downy	12's	33 oz.	14.04	1.17	.106
	6's	64 oz.	17.73	2.22	.104
	4's	96 oz.	19.64	3.27	.012
Bounce	12's	20 use	12.34	1.03	.051
	12's	40 use	24.03	2.00	.050
	8's	60 use	22.41	2.80	.047
Cling Free	10's	24 use	12.24	1.22	.051
	6's	36 use	10.77	1.80	.050
	4's	54 use	10.04	2.51	.047

*Liquids: 3 oz./use; Dryer: 1 sheet/use

All the major fabric softener brands placed the majority of their advertising weight in network television (see Exhibit 4).

V. 1989 Promotional Summaries. Final Touch offered the highest off-label values in the category. Sta-Puf was currently on a pre-price strategy.

	Off Label		Pre-Price
	Final Touch	Downy	Sta-Puf
Size			
32 oz.	25 cents	20 cents	$0.99
64 oz.	50 cents	40/45 cents	1.89
96 oz.	75 cents	60 cents	2.79
Couponing	20 cents	20 cents	–

EXHIBIT 4
% Dollars Spending by Daypart—1989

	Network TV				Spot TV	Print	Radio
	Total	Prime	Day	Fringe			
Liquid							
Downy	82%	37%	45%	–	18%	–	–
Final Touch	59%	32%	27%	–	41%	–	–
Sta-Puf	–	–	–	–	–	–	100%
Dryer							
Bounce	71%	26%	45%	–	29%	–	–
Cling Free	84%	46%	36%	2%	16%	–	–

VI. Seasonality. Overall, category sales were relatively constant throughout the year with a slight increase in total fabric softener sales in the winter months caused by increased dryer product sales. The Eastern region did not deviate from this pattern.

VII. Miscellaneous Data.

Liquid Fabric Softeners Five-Year Volume Trends

	1985	1986	1987	1988	1989
Case volume (MM)	25.7	24.9	24.9	26.0	28.8
% Change vs. Year Ago	–1	–3	–	+4	+11
Dollar Volume ($MM)	$325	$336	$359	$373	$398
% Change vs. Year Ago	+7	+3	+7	+4	+7

Liquid Fabric Softeners
Five-Year Share Trends—By Size

	1985	1986	1987	1988	1989
17 oz.	8%	7%	7%	6%	4%
33 oz.	26%	26%	25%	24%	21%
64 oz.	39%	40%	41%	42%	45%
96 oz.	26%	26%	27%	28%	30%
128 oz.	1%	1%	–	–	–

Eastern Region Liquid Fabric Softeners
1989 Share By Brand

	Boston	New York	Philadelphia
Downy Regular	48.6	43.5	38.2
Downy Triple Conc.	5.9	5.3	5.1
Final Touch	17.2	21.0	23.1
Sta-Puf	3.9	5.4	6.7
All Other	24.4	24.8	26.9

SNUGGLE ADVERTISING

To date, Snuggle's advertising strategy had been to convince consumers that new Snuggle was a quality liquid fabric softener that softened the whole wash, controlled static cling, gave clothes a fresh smell, and was really less expensive than premium liquid fabric softeners.

Snuggle was being positioned among the other premium liquid softeners—Downy and Final Touch. However, Snuggle was priced less than these brands. Consumers would be able to get all the quality softener benefits they desired, but at a lower price.

Snuggle was being supported with unique and memorable advertising. The brand's advertising featured Snuggle the teddy bear—a character who represented the essence of softness.

Snuggle spent all of its advertising budget on television, the most effective medium for reaching large numbers of the target audience, women 25–54 years of age. Snuggle advertising reached over 90 percent of the target audience and had twice as many prime-time announcements as Downy. In 1989, Lever Brothers spent $17 million on advertising Snuggle while Downy spent $15 million.

SNUGGLE PROMOTION

Snuggle's introductory program was the strongest in the history of the fabric softener category. On a national basis, Lever spent $60 million on trade and consumer promotions to support the brand during its introductory year. The promotional program was designed to:

1. Secure 3 size distribution.
2. Maximize trade feature and display support.
3. Generate consumer trial and repeat purchase.
4. Accelerate product movement.
5. Obtain a significant on-shelf price advantage vs. Downy.

The following methods could be employed in attaining the above goals:

1. Discounts off invoice price—Budgeted up to $1.50.
2. Special promotional allowances—Budgeted up to $1.50.
3. Extended dating—variable.
4. Carload pricing—40,000 lbs./carload—variable.
5. Mailing of free samples—70 percent of homes would receive a free 6 oz. sample via direct mail. This would

be the first sampling effort in the liquid fabric softener category in over 20 years. Research showed that 75 percent of consumers who tried a free Snuggle sample would buy it.

6. Couponing—Industry norm is 20 cents per coupon. Budgeted to spend up to 50 cents per coupon.

SNUGGLE PRICING

Snuggle fabric softener would be priced between 11 to 14 percent less than the premium brands in the liquid fabric softener category—Final Touch and Downy.

Snuggle was not a price brand. It was positioned in the premium segment of the liquid fabric softener market. Price brands did not provide the same quality softener benefits that Snuggle delivered.

The trade price of Snuggle should be close to the same margin as Downy so that Snuggle would offer a meaningful price differential to consumers at the retail level.

A primary part of Snuggle's positioning was a price benefit that provided consumers a better value for their dollar.

Upon introduction, if Downy reduced its price in a defensive move, Snuggle would reduce its price accordingly so as to maintain the correct price differential. (See Exhibit 5.)

The following is a listing of all material available to each sales representative for the Snuggle introduction:

Flip Flop Presentation
Stencil
Ad Slicks
Combination Card
Display Banner (18" x 49")
Plastic Shelf Talker
Spanish Plastic Shelf Talker

Shelf Strip
4-page Brochure
2-page Sell Sheet
MPO Cassette
Planograms
Spanish Combination Card

SNUGGLE'S POTENTIAL SOURCES OF BUSINESS

Category growth was one potential source of new business for Snuggle. In the Milwaukee test market, liquid softener sales had increased over 20 percent since the introduction of Snuggle.

In every area where Snuggle had been introduced, the smaller brands such as Sta-Puf and Rain Barrel experienced the largest percentage share decline. Downy and Final Touch lost a proportionately smaller percentage of their business.

Snuggle would have some impact on Final Touch, but primarily the business would come from the "all other" brands. Final Touch's whiteness benefit would still provide it with a unique positioning in the category.

Additionally, Final Touch had instituted consumer and trade defense plans. Snuggle was not meant to replace Final Touch. Lever Brothers wanted to use Snuggle and Final Touch to enhance its market position so it could overtake P&G as the number one liquid fabric softener manufacturer.

EXHIBIT 5
Retail Price and Profit Margin Guide—Snuggle vs. Downy

Profit Margin	33 oz.		64 oz.		96 oz.	
	Snuggle	*Downy*	*Snuggle*	*Downy*	*Snuggle*	*Downy*
1%	$1.03	$1.18	$1.95	$2.23	$2.89	$3.31
2%	$1.04	$1.19	$1.97	$2.26	$2.92	$3.34
3%	$1.05	$1.21	$1.99	$2.29	$2.95	$3.37
4%	$1.06	$1.22	$2.01	$2.30	$3.98	$3.40
5%	$1.08	$1.23	$2.04	$2.33	$3.01	$3.44
6%	$1.09	$1.24	$2.06	$2.36	$3.03	$3.48
7%	$1.10	$1.26	$2.08	$2.38	$3.07	$3.51
8%	$1.11	$1.27	$2.10	$2.41	$3.11	$3.56
9%	$1.12	$1.29	$2.13	$2.44	$3.14	$3.60
10%	$1.14	$1.30	$2.15	$2.46	$3.18	$3.64
11%	$1.15	$1.31	$2.17	$2.49	$3.21	$3.68
12%	$1.16	$1.33	$2.20	$2.52	$3.24	$3.72
13%	$1.17	$1.34	$2.22	$2.55	$3.28	$3.76
14%	$1.19	$1.36	$2.25	$2.58	$3.32	$3.81
15%	$1.20	$1.38	$2.28	$2.61	$3.36	$3.85
16%	$1.22	$1.39	$2.30	$2.64	$3.40	$3.90
17%	$1.23	$1.41	$2.33	$2.67	$3.44	$3.94
18%	$1.25	$1.43	$2.36	$2.70	$3.48	$3.99
19%	$1.26	$1.44	$2.39	$2.74	$3.53	$4.04
20%	$1.28	$1.46	$2.42	$2.77	$3.57	$4.09
21%	$1.29	$1.48	$2.45	$2.80	$3.62	$4.14
22%	$1.31	$1.50	$2.48	$2.84	$3.67	$4.20
23%	$1.33	$1.52	$2.51	$2.87	$3.71	$4.25
24%	$1.34	$1.54	$2.55	$2.92	$3.76	$4.31
25%	$1.36	$1.56	$2.58	$2.96	$3.81	$4.36

Fike's European Strategies

In November 1992, Mr. Heikki Gronlund, Senior Vice president, International Operations received a detailed report on the European operations of the Fike Corporation from Mr. Bob Michelson, the Managing Director of the company's European subsidiary, Fike Europe NV, Antwerp, Belgium. After carefully reviewing the contents of the report, Mr. Gronlund was wondering whether Fike Europe NV should continue its current strategies and practices or whether the company should make any changes, especially in the light of the 1992 greater integration of the Western European markets. Mr. Gronlund was concerned about strategic planning for the 1990s and beyond in Europe, which would enable Fike Europe NV to face up to the new business challenges of post "Europe 1992."

FIKE CORPORATION

The Fike Corporation was started in 1945 by the Fike family. It continues to be a family-held company. Over the past four decades, the company has expanded its operations both in the U.S. and abroad. Currently, the Fike Corporation consists of Fike Metal Products, New York; Fike Europe NV, Antwerp, Belgium; Fike Japan, Tokyo, Japan; Fike Southeast Asia, Singapore; Fike Canada, Burlington, Ontario, Canada; Fike United Kingdom, Kaidstone, Kent, England; and Fike France, Cergy-Pontoise, France.

Fike Metal Products is a leading developer and manufacturer of pressure-relieving devices commonly known as rupture disc assemblies. Having recognized the need for this type of technology in the protection of dust and vapor-handling equipment, Fike Metal Products developed the Fike Explosion Venting Assembly (U.S. Pat. No. 4,067,154). Fike Explosion Vents represent the latest advancements in low-pressure relief techniques.

Industries utilizing dust- or vapor-handling equipment are faced with a continuous explosion potential. The versatility and reliability of the Fike Explosion Vent has opened new frontiers for protecting every type and configuration of dust- or vapor-handling equipment. The types of equipment that need to be protected consist of crushers, pulverizers, ducts, screw feed conveyors, dryers, furnaces, blenders, pipes, silos, coating machines, grain elevators, grinders, dust collectors, conveyors, bucket elevators, ovens, spray dryers, mixers, bins, spreaders, and air scrubbers.

According to a sales brochure offering Fike's explosion testing services:

> A 1991 study by Industrial Risk Insurers (IRI) shows that explosions resulted in more damage than all other losses combined. The study places the average loss due to a combustion explosion within equipment at $961,268.

The Explosion Protection Group of Fike Corporation offers a wide range of explosibility tests designed to assist industry in mitigating explosion hazards. The Testing Center at Fike is staffed with testing technicians under the direction of a combustion phenomena research scientist. Among the many services offered are explosibility testing in both small- and large-scale explosion chambers. Fike's test vessels are designed and constructed to provide accurate data that can be projected to full-scale processes.

Tests are conducted according to ASTM (American Society for Testing and Materials) and ISO (International Standards Organization) standards. A confidential report describing the procedures used and results obtained is provided to the customer.

According to another sales brochure on the company's explosion isolation valve:

This case was prepared by Professor C. P. Rao of Old Dominion University. It is intended as a basis for class discussion and student analysis. Printed by permission of the author.

For over 40 years we have been solving overpressure and explosion protection problems and continuously challenge ourselves to develop innovative solutions to our customers' process safety needs. This commitment is illustrated by the development of the Fike Explosion Isolation Valve by our Explosion Protection Group. This development greatly extends the process designer's and plant safety personnel's ability to limit damage from process deflagrations. Explosion isolation is compatible with other explosion protection methods you may be considering or currently have in place. Explosion venting, explosion suppression or pressure containment may be combined with isolation to best meet your overall explosion protection needs.

The above descriptions provide a brief overview of the industrial products and services marketed by the Fike Corporation. While a full range of explosion protection products and services are marketed in the United States, the overseas sales are limited to only some of the products and services.

FIKE'S OVERSEAS BUSINESS OPERATIONS

In the mid-1960s, Fike started exploring overseas business opportunities. Contacts were established with a business firm in Philadelphia that was an importer into many European countries. Exclusive national distributorships were contracted with this Philadelphia firm. The Philadelphia firm used to buy the products from Fike and paid in U.S. dollars. Fike provided technical support and sales-oriented support activities in the form of technical seminars. By the late 1970s, European sales accounted for hundreds of thousands of U.S. dollars.

In 1982, Fike participated in a world exhibition of chemical products in Europe. In the same year, Mr. Gronlund was appointed as manager in charge of the company's international business operations. Since Mr. Gronlund's appointment, Fike's commitment to the international dimension of its business has greatly increased. International business operations are not merely limited to exports but are also involved in substantial investments wherever it is felt feasible and necessary. The growth and evolution of the company's international business is outlined in the following account from the "Fortieth Year Report" of the company published in 1984.

In the early years of the company, the traditional rupture disc product line was brought to the international marketplace through conventional export arrangements with national importers. Many of these agents, especially in Europe, have been associated with us for twenty years and more and enjoy considerable success.

With a Europe-wide network of specialized distributors knowledgeable in technical sales, we have been able to win customers in fields as demanding as both the nuclear and aerospace programs. We have also introduced the use of rupture discs as cost-effective, fail-safe devices into markets where they have been largely unknown in the past.

These efforts have gained us a corporate reputation for quality and the best service and support in the industry. Despite national competitors in some countries, there is a large acceptance of Fike and Fike rupture discs as the ultimate in reliability.

Outside Europe the activity was very low indeed. Japan had long been considered a good export opportunity, but the usual problems of dealing with a complex and vastly different system had hindered real penetration. The creation of Fike Japan Corporation as a joint venture effort in 1980 proved to be the making of a Far Eastern success story, one of which we are very proud.

Too often today we hear complaints by otherwise well-informed people decrying the lack of opportunities in Japan. At Fike we emphatically wish to state the contrary. With the proper approach and dedication to the market, the Japanese will accept quality products regardless of their origin.

Fike Japan looks forward to continued growth. Current plans call for an expansion into other Far Eastern markets and the installation of further manufacturing capabilities in Japan.

Heartened by the solid growth and success in Japan as well as in Europe, the company decided to formally recognize the importance of overseas business by establishing an International Operations center in the home office in 1982. Dedicated to seeking opportunities in foreign markets, it is the task of this group to make recommendations and manage the corporation's involvement in all foreign ventures.

The European countries presented an immediate prospect for added sales. An evaluation of the various national markets showed room for a strong entry by a reputable manufacturer of top quality safety relief products. Germany and Switzerland, in particular, have pioneered work in industrial explosion safety from both a scientific and practical view, and created a strong demand for our type of products. At the same time it was recognized that further penetration in Europe would have to be as an EEC manufacturer to regain our cost-competitiveness against the various local producers, and to give our customers the security of local services and support.

In the spring of 1984 a site near Antwerp, Belgium was purchased, and Fike Europe NV was established as a wholly-owned subsidiary of Fike Metal Products. We are pleased to say that our customers have responded very favorably to this move and 1985 will be a year of great development as we swing into full in-house production of a large number of products.

We view the creating of a European company as a major step in our international marketing, and as a sign of our belief in the great importance of Western Europe in all our corporate activities. Fike Europe is, furthermore, the vehicle responsible for serving the emerging markets of Africa and the Middle East, where we see ever-increasing activity in the "downstream" products of the petrochemical industries.

There is a definite long-term trend towards the transfer of technology from the developed to the developing nations of the world. In the core chemical and petrochemical markets of the rupture disc product line this means a higher rate of market growth overseas than here at home. In the United States we are blessed with the world's largest domestic market, but we cannot ignore the increasing internationalization of all business.

We are gearing our operations accordingly. With a multinational ability to exchange technical know-how and information and productive capacity, we can meet the needs of the world's markets now and in the future.

Most of the other product areas have yet to test international waters, but as we see opportunities for bringing the specialties to foreign markets we intend to develop them aggressively.

With so many different possibilities for tackling complex markets worldwide, we remain guided by some very basic beliefs instilled in the company by two generations of family leadership.

First and foremost we shall stay true to the task of being a manufacturer of our own products. By keeping control of all the quality control and production operations, we will make a better product and serve our customers more faithfully than our competition.

Investment in selected overseas manufacturing sites is a must for continued growth. The days of pure exporting are long gone, even for advanced high technology products. By producing locally we demonstrate our desire to become totally involved in the market, and accept the necessity of modifying our products to meet local needs.

Because we manufacture many items that are ultimate safety devices protecting peoples' lives, we will always be conscious of the tremendous responsibility we have to make sure every product performs every time. We will not take the risk of letting other people produce our rupture discs and related safety devices for us. And we will remain firm in our stand of retaining full control over products carrying the trusted Fike name.

FIKE'S EUROPEAN OPERATIONS

As is evident from the above account of the company's evolution and its approach toward its international business operations, the Western European markets form the major part of the total international business operations. Historically, Fike has had longer involvement in these markets and, outside the U.S., the Western European markets collectively represent the largest market for the company's products. The overall importance of the Western European markets is expected to increase with the full integration of these markets in 1992. Consistent with the overall importance of the Western European markets for the international business segment of the company, Fike's involvement in these markets has grown through expanded manufacturing and marketing activities in various European markets. As mentioned earlier, a fully owned manufacturing subsidiary was established in 1984 at Antwerp, Belgium. Following this move, the marketing of the company's products has been progressively changed from dependence on distributors to a company-managed sales force. These intensified manufacturing and marketing investments in Western Europe required a total investment of about U.S. $3 million. This investment represented about one-tenth of Fike's total investment in the company operations. The European operations mainly consisted of manufacturing and marketing of 12 different rupture discs and vents. The rupture disc is the major product line of Fike's European operations. The competitive standing of Fike for discs and vents in seven Western European markets, which account for a major part of the company's European operations, is provided in Exhibits 1 and 2.

In order to strengthen its market position in the Western European markets, Fike Europe progressively eliminated the distributors in various European markets. In 1992, the company sales force marketed Fike's products and services in Belgium,

France, Germany, Italy, and the U.K. However, Fike Europe still continues to utilize the services of distributors in Denmark, the Netherlands, Spain, Sweden, and Switzerland. Currently, the company is in the process of establishing direct sales offices in Spain and the Netherlands. However, the transition from indirect distribution through distributors to direct distribution through a company-managed sales force has not always been a smooth process. For example, in the U.K., the transition from indirect to direct distribution has been quite smooth. The distributors readily agreed to the new arrangement without any resistance to the change. As a result of the shift to a direct company-managed sales force, the U.K. sales have increased by eleven times.

The problems experienced in other Western European countries in bringing about the shift from indirect distribution to direct distribution has varied from country to country. In Germany, the

EXHIBIT 1
Composition of European Market for Rupture Discs: Estimated Market Shares of Competitors in 1992

				Competitors						
Rank	Country	Total	Fike	A	B	C	D	E	F	Other
6	Belgium (S)	100	20	40	20	5	5	2	2	6
3	France (S)	100	20	25	20	20	2	10	3	–
1	Germany (S)	100	5	30	12	7	11	6	6	23
4	Italy (S)	100	10	23	6	20	2	–	–	39
2	U.K. (S)	100	6	28	4	38	–	23	1	–
10	Denmark (D)	100	35	40	10	5	5	–	–	5
5	Holland (D)	100	26	18	32	9	–	–	5	10
8	Spain (D)	100	14	–	71	10	–	5	–	–
9	Sweden (D)	100	38	25	10	3	10	2	3	9
7	Switzerland (D)	100	20	15	–	–	5	10	–	50

Notes: RANK—Market size rank for the ten European countries covered.

All numbers except under column *Rank* are percentages.

For some countries the percentage of market shares of various competitors do not add up to 100 due to non-availability of data.

(S) — Company direct sales to customers

(D) — Sales through distributors to customers

Source: Fike Europe company records, 1992.

EXHIBIT 2

Composition of European Market for Vents: Estimated Market Shares of Competitors in 1992

| Rank | Country | Total | Fike | Competitors | | | | | | |
				A	B	C	D	E	F	Other
2	Belgium (S)	100	40	–	–	10	40	–	–	10
3	France (S)	100	35	2	2	35	5	20	1	–
1	Germany (S)	100	9	5	1	3	80	–	2	–
5	Italy (S)	100	25	–	–	14	61	–	–	–
6	U.K. (S)	100	27	12	–	32	2	27	–	–
8	Denmark (D)	100	33	10	–	10	5	–	–	–
4	Holland (D)	100	41	3	5	10	39	–	2	–
7	Spain (D)	100	12	–	2	10	76	–	–	–
9	Sweden (D)	100	40	15	–	7	30	8	–	–
10	Switzerland (D)	100	10	–	–	–	90	–	–	–

Notes: RANK—Market size rank for the ten European countries covered.

All numbers except under column *Rank* are percentages.

For some countries the percentage of market shares of various competitors do not add up to 100 due to non-availability of data.

(S) — Company direct sales to customers

(D) — Sales through distributors to customers

Source: Fike Europe company records, 1992.

company had good relations with the distributor, but felt that it was not getting its fair share of the market. Through negotiations, it was agreed that the distributors would give their best shot, but this arrangement did not work and expected sales did not take place. Hence, a phasing-out program over a period of 18 months has been implemented without much of a problem. An ex-employee of the distributor joined Fike's German office and no significant sales dislocation was experienced. On the other hand, in France, the distributor fought tooth and nail. A court case initiated in 1986 is still continuing. This dispute initially caused considerable discontinuity in the company's business. The Managing Director of Fike Europe would prefer to resolve this situation amicably through negotiations, but the company's legal counsel believes that the longer the court case drags on, the more the issue becomes dormant without any adverse effects on the company's operations in France.

Fike Europe is in the process of establishing direct offices in Spain and the Netherlands. In both countries, Fike has had long-standing relationships with the respective distributors. Direct distribution is used for different reasons in each of these countries. In Spain, it was observed that sales were growing very slowly; it was also felt by Fike Europe that the management of the distributor was somewhat old-fashioned and not aggressive enough. In any case, company management believed that its products were not getting proper sales attention and hence it was decided to establish a direct sales office in Spain. In contrast, different factors in the Netherlands precipitated the move for establishing a direct sales office. The relations between the company and its distributor have been long established and quite satisfactory. Fike personnel have been in constant touch with the distributor salespersons and overall sales performance has been found to be satisfactory. However, the distributor was taken over by a Swedish company that emphasizes its own company-manufactured products rather than traded products. Hence, it was decided to get out of this relationship. Fike Europe expects that the transition will be quite smooth.

According to Mr. Gronlund, Fike Europe operations possessed the following key characteristics:

1. Country managements are highly diversified. Hence, each European country management is localized.
2. Management in each country enjoys considerable autonomy with overall control on financial performance exercised by Fike Europe and the Senior Vice President, International Operations at the U.S. head office.
3. Management in each country decides which products and services will be offered in its own markets. This policy is based on the fact that the country managements have the pertinent knowledge, beliefs, and values that are relevant for each of their own markets.
4. Although management in each country is considered a sales office of Fike Europe, each acts as if it is independent and autonomous. While the basic technical service components are the same in all the European countries, management in each country sets its own prices, specific services, and other aspects of dealing with customers and competitors.
5. Fike management does not believe in molding one uniform approach and does not force a single way of doing business on its individual Western European markets.

Fike's business in Europe is also characterized by significant levels of competition in all the European markets. In terms of country-of-origin there are two U.K. competitors, one German, one Italian, and two U.S. competitors in the European markets. At present there are no Japanese competitors.

As far as Fike's European business operations are concerned, Mr. Gronlund thinks that EC-1992 is a non-event because Fike Europe is already a European company. Currently, 60 percent of Fike Europe's total business is met by its own manufacturing facilities in Antwerp, Belgium. The remaining 40 percent of Fike Europe's business needs are supplied by Fike USA. Recently, Fike Europe obtained ISO 9000 certification, which further strengthens its competitive position in the European markets. The only major effect of the EC-92 phenomenon on Fike's European operations is the effect of the changed VAT (value added tax) rules on the company's computerized accounting system.

The company is currently exploring business possibilities in Eastern Europe. Some limited sales have been achieved in East European countries. According to Mr. Gronlund, the major hurdle for further sales growth in the former communist countries is the lack of foreign exchange experienced by most of these countries. However, in anticipation of future growth prospects in the Russian market, a Fike Russia sales office was recently opened in St. Petersburg, Russia.

The following assessment of the European markets, both west and east, is included in the 1992 annual report of Fike Europe:

> The economic recession which started in 1991 has continued in 1992, and so far no signs of improvement are noticed. Most of the projects that have been put on ice in 1991 are still on ice or cancelled. An increasing number of companies are laying off people or are going bankrupt. It seems the recession is also hurting the chemical industry. Big companies, like Bayer and BASF, are cutting cost and production personnel and even Monsanto is closing down part of its operation. All in all it seems that Fike Europe is still doing OK as we will end up with an increase in consolidated turnover.
>
> On January 1st, 1993, the united European market is a fact. The only immediate change that will happen is the difference in VAT administration (which will make things more complicated). On rupture discs a European standard has been finalized and this standard will be in effect somewhere mid 1995. However, the differences with today's requirements are minimal.
>
> The only change we can feel is that all countries of the EC have to comply with the safety and environmental requirements as laid down in European standards. The result will be that countries which used to have less stringent requirements on safety and environment will need to comply now. Therefore, countries such as Greece, Spain, Portugal, etc. will be more receptive to Fike products.

In Eastern Europe most of the currencies now are convertible. The only problem is exponential inflation. On top of this is the internal political situation, which is very uncertain. Most of the Eastern Europe political leaders are struggling to survive. It is clear that the priorities do not include safety and environment. Their major concern is food, clothing, and consumer products. However, Eastern Europe is still a market for the future and Fike needs to be present there to capitalize on opportunities as they emerge.

In the 1992 annual report of Fike Europe, Mr. Bob Michelson concluded with the following thought:

It seems to me that in the past Fike has always put the emphasis on marketing the products. I believe that the time is right for Fike to actually market the company. We are truly a different company from the competition as we have the complete line of products, including expertise and test facilities. We need to market ourselves as the leader in this field. Such marketing can only be done in an organized and global way, so that the same image is presented worldwide. Therefore, I believe it would be right if Fike Corporation could set up a marketing group to determine international image-building advertising and product introduction.

John Pollock hung up the phone and walked out of the office and into the prep area of the small Charlotte, North Carolina, wholesale bakery. He smiled at his wife Terri and exclaimed, "It looks like we have a chance to become The Brownie Factory!" The call, from an airline supplier, brought back to life a proposal that John and Terri had all but dismissed. The only catch was that the firm wanted John to indicate his level of interest in the alternative they were offering by July 18, 1988, and that was only 48 hours away. "It's really a blessing," thought John. "We've needed to make a decision on the brownie and this will force us to do just that."

In the last two months, the goal of transforming the small, wholesale bakery operation from one of producing limited quantities of a relatively large number of products to the exclusive production of a gourmet brownie had become a passion of the couple. As a result, John had gathered information on several marketing options for the brownie. John and Terri were both extremely excited about the product. In fact, they had tentatively decided to change the name of their wholesale bakery to The Brownie Factory. Their excitement notwithstanding, the couple had been hesitant to take any action because they were not totally comfortable with any of the alternatives.

When John finished telling Terri about the call, she suggested that they take the information on all their options home that night and reconsider them at the same time that they were evaluating the latest alternative. "That's a good idea," agreed John. "It could be that the best strategy would be a combination of options." Regardless of the result, John wanted to be certain they considered every angle—particularly since this new option would commit the bakery under a production contract.

THE POLLOCK'S BAKERY

In the 20 months that the bakery had been in operation, the business had enjoyed a steady, if unspectacular, increase in business. "We started with no commercial baking experience, but with a commitment to quality. I approached a number of restaurants and specialty shops in Charlotte and convinced them to add some of our dessert items to their product line on a trial basis. Almost every one turned into a regular customer," noted John. The couple attributed this success to the consistently high quality of their products. "If we're not completely satisfied with a product, then it will never be delivered to a customer," explained John. "Yes," added Terri, "we've given a lot of 'rejected' products to our family and friends."

The couple felt that a key to the success of their products was the quality of the ingredients that they used. Terri's most important contribution to the operation was development of the recipes that the bakery used. She insisted on using only the highest-quality ingredients and on mixing by hand rather than using the commercial mixer when possible, as well as limiting or eliminating the use of preservatives. While these decisions almost certainly contributed to the products' quality, they also increased costs. John justified their approach by saying, "I couldn't look my customers in the eye if I left them a shoddy product."

Making bakery products with all natural ingredients generally carries with it two disadvantages. In addition to the higher cost of ingredients, products with all natural ingredients are usually higher in calories. "None of our customers have raised either of these concerns," noted John. "The quality of our products has seemed to justify the higher

This case was prepared by Professor D. Michael Fields and Professor Neil C. Herndon, Jr. of Southwest Missouri State University solely for the purpose of stimulating student discussion. It is reproduced here by permission of the North American Case Research Association and the authors.

Copyright © 1992.

price. And as far as buying a premium dessert goes, it appears that people either don't care how many calories a product has or they just don't want to know."

Another indication of the couple's level of personal pride was the manner in which they maintained the bakery. Even with the powdery nature of many of the ingredients, the bakery was consistently in spotless condition. This was particularly significant, since few of their customers ever saw the wholesale bakery and they really didn't have to maintain such high standards. "Both our products and our place of business are reflections of the kind of people we are," noted Terri.

Both John and Terri were comfortable with the bakery's manufacturing/supplier role. Neither

desired their business to become a retail operation. "We're working enough as it is now. We just don't have the time to handle single-item sales," explained Terri. "And besides," she added, "our bakery's main entrance is from an alley—it just wouldn't work." It also opens another can of worms," interjected John, "when you produce for retail, the sale of your production run is no longer guaranteed."

The present product line had grown to eighteen items in five different categories (see Exhibit 1). Although not all products were produced daily, all were being produced at least once a week and some were being baked several times a week. "We spend a lot of time shifting from product to product," admitted Terri.

EXHIBIT 1
Bakery Product Line, May 1988

Item	Unit price	Ingredient cost	Margin	Quantity sold 1/1/88–4/1/88
Cheesecake (14.5%)*				
Plain	$12.00	$4.35	$7.65	95
Chocolate	13.00	6.47	6.53	60
New York	15.50	8.75	6.75	65
Amaretto	13.00	6.72	6.28	9
Coffee cake (1.0%)				
Plain	11.00	5.24	5.76	15
Chocolate Chip	6.50	3.99	2.51	2
Other cakes (8.3%)				
Spice	6.50	3.74	2.76	4
Carrot	12.00	7.35	4.65	12
Truffle	8.25	4.93	3.32	36
Pound	10.00	5.13	4.87	80
Muffins (20.1%)				
Bran	6.00 (doz.)	2.68	3.32	275
Blueberry	6.60 (doz.)	3.25	3.35	80
Pumpkin	6.60 (doz.)	3.25	3.35	80
Applenut	6.60 (doz.)	3.25	3.35	40
Miscellaneous snacks (56.1%)				
Chocolate Oatmeal Bars	7.20 (pan)	4.01	3.19	300
Lemon Bars	6.00 (doz.)	3.68	2.32	35
Blonde Brownies	10.00 (pan)	5.13	4.87	120
Cupcakes	4.80 (pan)	2.94	1.86	40

*The numbers in parentheses indicate the estimated percentage of actual production time spent on each category.

Some of the growth in the product line had been the result of the couple's effort to be responsive to the requests of their customers. On several occasions, customers had asked the bakery to develop new items for them. Typically, these requested items found their way into the regular product line. Unfortunately, many of them were low-volume items (see Exhibit 1), and John admitted that they were unprofitable to produce. "Some of these were bad business decisions," explained John, "but it's hard to say 'no' to the requests of regular customers."

John and Terri were the only two employees of the bakery, and the demands of the broad product line had lengthened both total production time and their work week. "Most weeks, we work at least 55 hours over five and a half days," noted Terri. "On an average day we will be involved in production of the various products for 8 hours. It usually takes John about 2 hours to make deliveries and while he's doing that, I clean the bakery up. It can get tiring. There are some friends we could call on in case of emergency, but we just can't allow ourselves to get sick." In fact, in the last fiscal year, the couple had only used 25 to 30 hours of additional labor.

As in the case with most new businesses, the bakery did not make a profit in its first year of operation (see the firm's income statement for fiscal 1987 in Exhibit 2). Although the loss was not unexpected, John was concerned about the prospects for reaching profitability in the near term. "I know it's normal, but it's still awfully frustrating to put in the kind of hours we are working and still lose money," explained John. John felt that increased volume would help the bakery achieve profitability.

Both John and Terri were apprehensive about the potential impact on product quality if another production shift were added. Their decisions on the product line had been complicated by the fact that the bakery had continued to increase sales in the first quarter of 1988 with its present product line. Although sales for many retailers are traditionally slowest in the first quarter, John had noticed in the bakery's first full year of operation that demand from the firm's customers had remained relatively constant, making the first quarter proportionally representative for the year.

John felt that the key to long-term profitability was trimming the product line. Clearly, the optimal solution in terms of efficiency would be to dedicate the entire production to a single product that would support an acceptable contribution margin. "I think our brownie holds the key to the future success of our business," noted John. "But

EXHIBIT 2
Income Statement, 1987

Sales		$35,710.66
Cost of goods sold		
Ingredients	$13,352.48	
Bakery supplies	770.90	
Labor	123.00	
Samples	16.00	
Total cost of goods sold		14,262.38
Gross margin		$21,448.28
Operating expenses		
Kitchen equipment	$ 1,968.39	
Delivery expense	1,917.52	
Salaries—officers	9,450.00	
Rent	3,250.00	
Utilities	2,091.00	
Interest expense	2,267.62	
Depreciation expense	2,978.35	
Amortization expense	857.94	
Insurance	1,384.13	
Advertising	291.50	
Bank charges	113.06	
Maintenance and repairs	308.03	
Office supplies	300.72	
Payroll taxes	878.86	
Taxes and licenses	240.00	
Telephone	799.99	
Miscellaneous	52.98	
Total operating expenses		29,150.09
Net income (loss)		($ 7,701.81)

the problem is figuring out how to transform 'the bakery' into The Brownie Factory."

THE BROWNIE

The present brownie was the result of several months of hard work by Terri. She had started with what she considered to be an excellent family recipe and incorporated the bakery's philosophy of using all-natural ingredients. Terri enlisted the help of a series of the couple's friends to evaluate the results as she varied the brownie recipe. The present, and what John and Terri considered to be the final, recipe had drawn the most enthusiastic support of the testers. Terri had made two changes that the couple felt significantly differentiated their product from anything on the market. Terri explained, "The first thing I did was to give our brownie a more cake-like texture—rather than making it soft and gooey. The second difference was the use of pure chocolate instead of cocoa, which gives it a distinctive flavor."

John had decided that the most appropriate unit size for the brownie would be a $2 \times 3 \times \frac{3}{4}$ inch serving. The cost of the ingredients for a brownie of these dimensions would be $0.20 per unit. Individual packaging would add an additional 3 cents to the cost. The bakery had traditionally targeted a markup of 50 percent (twice the cost) to reach a selling price for each of the categories of products (see Exhibit 1), and John saw no reason to alter the pricing philosophy. Given these price parameters, John had set the bakery's selling price for the brownie at $0.40 each in the tray or $0.46 each if they were individually wrapped.

With the present equipment, John estimated that the small bakery's production potential was 5,000 brownies per week. The capacity could be doubled with the addition of another oven. John felt that a used oven could be purchased for $2,000.

THE LOCAL BROWNIE MARKET

The Charlotte market, like most, offered consumers a wide range of choices in their selection of brownies. John felt the overall market could be broken down into two major segments, based on how the brownies were sold. The "tray" market consisted of retailers who offered full-service counters for bakery products. These were typically limited to retail bakery operations, supermarkets that had a bakery department, and a few convenience stores that sold individual products from a display case. John did not consider the tray market to be a lucrative segment, since most of these outlets had facilities on hand to produce their own brownies. However, four of the bakery's present customers had expressed interest in selling John and Terri's brownie from the tray (see Exhibit 3), and the projected quantities were substantial.

The market for individually wrapped brownies appeared to John to hold the greatest promise. It also attracted a large number of established competitors. A list of the major companies selling individually wrapped brownies to supermarkets and convenience stores in the Charlotte market can be found in Exhibit 4. As shown, the per brownie prices ranged from a low of $0.99 for a dozen 1-ounce Little Debbie brownies to a high of $0.79 for a 3-ounce Sara Lee brownie.

To give him a better idea of how the new brownies stacked up against the competition, John had dimensioned the brownies on the familiar basis of texture and sweetness. John was pleased with the results (see Exhibit 5). The couple's brownie had a position that distinguished it from the existing competitors' offerings.

John was also encouraged by the interest expressed in the projected new brownie by the bakery's present customers. John had mentioned that the couple was considering adding a gourmet brownie to their product line and, in some cases, had left a sample of their brownie. Customers had estimated that they could sell 82 dozen of the individually wrapped new brownies each week (see Exhibit 3).

The possibility of an additional competitor in the Charlotte market had gained John's attention. Two months before, John had heard a rumor that Rachel's Brownies was close to signing an

EXHIBIT 3
Brownie Purchase Estimates of Existing Customers

Customer	Brownies per week (in dozens)	Trays of 6 dozen brownies per week
1. Out to Lunch (3 locations)	30	
2. Treats	8	
3. Reed's Supermarket	6	12
4. Wine Shop	2	
5. Eat Out	5	
6. Phil's Deli	9	
7. Berry Brook	2	
8. The Home Economist	4	
9. The Mill	3	12
10. Selwyn's	2	24
11. People's	3	12
12. The Fresh Market	8	—
Totals	82 doz.	60 trays

agreement with a local distributor to begin selling Rachel's own gourmet brownie in the Charlotte market. Rachel's was a firm that started selling its brownies in a produce shop and in an ice cream store in Philadelphia in 1975. In less than 10 years the firm had grown to the point that they were producing more than 5 million brownies annually. Rachel's typically marketed brownies in 1-pound tins to supermarkets (retailing at $3.79) and individually wrapped units to convenience stores (retailing at $0.75).

John was clearly concerned. "If they do enter the market," noted John, "they'll be difficult to compete with. Their gourmet brownie and ours will be competing for the same customers, and I am sure distributors would prefer to handle Rachel's product because of their proven history." Although John had heard nothing more about Rachel's entering the market, he felt there was a 75 percent likelihood that Rachel's would be in the Charlotte market in the next 6 months.

EXHIBIT 4
Sample of Individually Wrapped Brownies Sold in Area Stores

Brownie name	Weight (oz.)	Price
Bebo	3.00	$0.49
Claey's	1.75	0.49
Hostess	3.00	0.69
Little Debbie*	12.00	0.99
Moore's	1.60	0.49
Sara Lee	3.00	0.79

*Packaged and sold in boxes of 12 1-oz. brownies.

THE OPTIONS

John had initially considered four alternative ways to market the brownie: selling to distributors, retailing from carts on the street, selling to existing customers, and selling to airline food suppliers. His listing of the advantages and disadvantages of each is shown in Exhibit 6.

EXHIBIT 5
Local Brownie Market Dimensioned by Sweetness and Texture

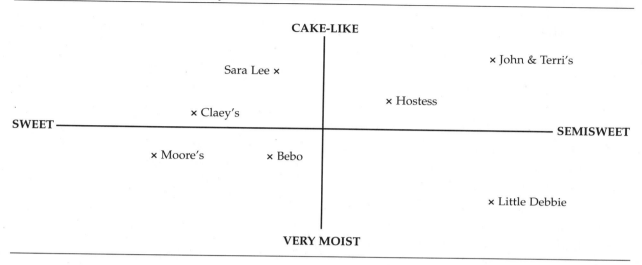

Selling the brownie to distributors had initially been John's first choice. This method would allow the brownie to quickly be exposed to a wide range of customers through the distributors' established networks of retailers. John had made presentations to two local distributors and had received a cool reception in both instances. "I was surprised," noted John. "The volume that both required was much larger than I had anticipated. One distributor said that he would not touch a new product that wouldn't produce $6,000 per week in sales. The other, although less specific, indicated that any new product he added to his product line would have to be accompanied with 'substantial' advertising to the ultimate consumer to help assure product movement. Also, both indicated their markup would be in the 15 to 20 percent range because of the risk of adding a product which had not previously been on the market."

Another option that John had pursued was selling brownies from a vending cart in the downtown section of Charlotte. Charlotte had become a regional banking center, and it was estimated that over 40,000 people worked in the immediate downtown area. The city had approved and encouraged organized street vending. Presently, ten vendors had licenses and were selling their products from carts on downtown streets (see Exhibit 7). John estimated that it would take approximately $1,200 to put a cart on the street. As John explained it:

> I know that the downtown area is filled with upscale customers, but the thing that bothers me here is that I've just never been involved with retail. Also, I don't know how difficult it will be to find and keep a salesperson. Are we going to be able to find someone who will be willing to work only when the weather's good? What are we going to do if the product is already baked and the person doesn't show up? These uncertainties concern me.

An additional option that John had considered was the addition of the brownie to the bakery's existing product line. Periodically, customers asked John if he had started baking the gourmet brownie yet. As could be expected, the customers that were particularly interested were those who had projected the highest level of sales for the brownie (see Exhibit 3). John admitted:

> This would clearly be the easiest way to introduce our brownie, but the exposure to the total Charlotte

EXHIBIT 6
Advantages and Disadvantages of Options to Market Brownies

Advantages	Disadvantages
Distributors	
Wide distribution	Prohibitively high sales minimums
Maximum consumer exposure	Accompanying advertising expected
Opportunity to establish brand name	Pushes retail price higher
Guaranteed sales	
Retail on street	
Active downtown area	Startup costs of $1,200
Accepted mode of sale	Widely fluctuating (weather-dependent) sales
Begin to establish brand name	Must find, train, and retain salespersons
Sell to existing customers	
Little resistance	Limited market exposure
Brownie would receive favorable placement	Lengthening of product line
	Cannibalization of blonde brownies
Sell to airline food supplier	
Guaranteed sales	Cost exceeds stated maximum price
Known quantities	Limited contract time
Exposure to consumers	
Begin to establish brand name	

market would be limited and I have so little time to go out and try to find new accounts. Our customers are excited about it, but I think our new brownie would cannibalize about half of the sales of our blond brownie. Besides, if we add the brownie, where is the time to produce it going to come from? Does it mean we will need to get to the bakery at 4 a.m. instead of 5 a.m.? We want the brownie to shorten our product line, not to lengthen it.

The final option was the sale of the brownie to Food Service Professionals (FSP), an airline food supplier. John had made the proposal about 3 months earlier. At that time, he had taken samples of the brownie in its standard 2 x 3 x ¾ inch serving and had suggested that the individually wrapped brownie be the dessert portion of the in-flight meal. John described the negotiation this way:

It seemed that this might be a good way to get some brand recognition. That's why I suggested the individually wrapped brownie. I remember that the first Eagle snacks I ever had were on an airplane. Then when I later saw them in the store, I had already sampled them and knew how good they were. I wanted to do this on a smaller scale with our brownie. If we sold the brownies by the tray (unwrapped), then I can't see any long-term benefits for us. FSP didn't think long-term, either; their standard supply contract was for about 90 days. Anyway, the proposal died when we talked about the price. When I gave them our $0.46 unit price, Ms. Abrams, the FSP rep, indicated that they targeted their dessert cost at $ 0.30 and that their absolute cost ceiling for dessert portions was $0.35. That essentially ended the discussion; they clearly weren't going to budge from that figure and I didn't feel we could come down that much on our price either.

EXHIBIT 7
Presently Licensed Street Vendors,
Charlotte, North Carolina

Vendor	Products sold
1. Halfpenny	Nachos, baked potatoes
2. TCBY	Yogurt
3. Zackebobs	Shish kebob
4. LaLamas	Hot dogs, drinks
5. Purple Shop	Sundry items
6. John C's	German hot dogs
7. Kwik Way	Hot dogs
8. Larry's	Ice cream
9. Lemon Quench	Drink products
10. Jerry's	Ice cream

The couple realized that most options for the brownies would require at least some additional capital to implement. "We've got a family member who has indicated a willingness to invest $10,000 to help us. If that's not enough, then I'll go to the bank and take out a loan for more. I'll do whatever is necessary," explained John.

THE CALL

The call that July morning had been from Jan Abrams at Food Service Professionals. After sum-marizing the results of their previous meeting, she indicated that the firm had a counterproposal for John to consider. Rather than the 2 × 3 × ¾ inch portion that had been initially presented, she proposed that the size of the individually wrapped brownies be reduced to 2 × 2 × ¾ inch and, since the size of the brownie was being reduced by one-third, that the price be reduced to $0.30 per unit. Jan also indicated that FSP needed to determine in the next two days whether John had any interest in the alternative proposal. "I apologize for our sense of urgency, but we are going to make a change in our dessert offerings and we want to get our fourth quarter menus resolved. Using a reduced portion of your brownie was a last-minute suggestion from a member of my staff," explained Jan. She concluded the call by indicating that she felt that acceptance of her counterproposal would likely lead to a contract for a guaranteed order for at least 4,000 units per week for a period of 13 weeks—beginning October 1. FSP would also require an option to renew the contract. Jan indicated that in instances where firms maintained expected quality, the renewal option was usually exercised.

As John reflected on the call, he was excited, but realized that he would have to weigh the decision carefully. He had to make sure that every issue was considered. The option could contractually bind the small bakery for as long as six months. Still, he was smiling as he walked out of the office to tell Terri.

As CEO Morry Weiss looked at the corporate rose logo of the world's largest publicly owned manufacturer of greeting cards and related social-expression merchandise, American Greetings (AG), he reflected upon the decade of the 1980s. In 1981, he had announced the formulation of a corporate growth objective to achieve $1 billion in annual sales by 1985, which would represent a 60 percent increase over 1982 sales of $623.6 million.

It was 1986 before AG reached that goal with sales of $1.035 billion. The profit margin, however, was 5.75, the lowest in five years and down from its high of 8.090 percent in 1984. In its fiscal year ending February 28, 1990, AG reported sales of $1.286 billion with a profit margin of 5.51 percent. He looked at the ten-year sales, net income and selling, distribution, and marketing costs summary prepared by his corporate staff (see Exhibit 1). Weiss realized its increase in sales had come at a high price with an escalated and intensified battle for market share dominance among the three industry leaders, Hallmark, Gibson, and AG. In the final analysis, market shares had not really changed that much among the big three. Now each was determined to defend its respective market shares. The nature of the greeting card industry changed dramatically. Previously, the two leading firms, Hallmark and AG, peacefully coexisted by having mutually exclusive niches. Hallmark offered higher-priced, quality cards in department stores and card shops, and AG offered inexpensive cards in mass-merchandise outlets. However, AG's growth strategy to attack the industry leader and its niche followed by Gibson's growth strategy and Hallmark's defensive moves changed the industry. AG was now in the position of defending its competitive position.

THE GREETING CARD INDUSTRY

According to *GM News*, Americans exchanged more that 7.1 billion cards in 1988—around 29 per person, which is down from the highest per capita card consumption of 30 in 1985. And with the average retail price per card of $1.10, that made "social expression" a $4 billion business. According to the Greeting Card Association, card senders sent the following cards:

Holiday	Units Sold	Percent
Christmas	2.2 B	30.99
Valentine's Day	850 M	11.97
Easter	180 M	2.54
Mother's Day	140 M	1.97
Father's Day	85 M	1.20
Graduation	80 M	1.13
Thanksgiving	40 M	.56
Halloween	25 M	.35
St. Patrick's Day	16 M	
Grandparent's Day	10 M	
Chanukah	9 M	
Other Seasons	5 M	

Half of the total greeting cards purchased in 1988 were seasonal cards. The remainder were in the category of everyday cards. Everyday cards, especially non-occasion cards or alternative cards, are on the increase. According to *Forbes* and

This case was prepared by Professor Dan Kopp and Professor Lois Shufeldt, Southwest Missouri State University, as a basis for class discussion rather than to illustrate either effective or ineffective administrative practices. It is reprinted here by permission of the North American Case Research Association and the authors.

American Demographics, the alternative card market is the fastest-growing segment at 25 percent per year, and the card industry as a whole grew at 5 percent per year. Alternative cards are not geared to any holiday, but can be inspirational, satirical, or ethnic in nature. This segment is directed toward the estimated 76 million baby boomers. Formerly, it was the focus strategy of the many small card makers who had 70 percent of the market. Now, however, the big three have captured 87 percent of the market.

Most industry analysts consider the greeting card industry to be in or near the maturity stage. According to Prudential-Bache, the industry unit growth rate was 2–4 percent from 1946–1985. The greeting card industry is comprised of from 500–900 firms, which range from three major corporations to many small family organizations. The industry is dominated by the big three: Hallmark, American Greetings, and Gibson. The estimated market shares are:

Company	1989	1985	1977
Hallmark	40–42%	42%	50%
AG	32–33	33	24
Gibson	8–10	9	5

(Estimates vary according to the source.)

During the 1980s, the big three engaged in market share battles through intense price, product, promotion, and place competition. The primary

EXHIBIT 1

Ten-Year Sales, Net Income and Selling, Distribution, and Marketing Costs Summary

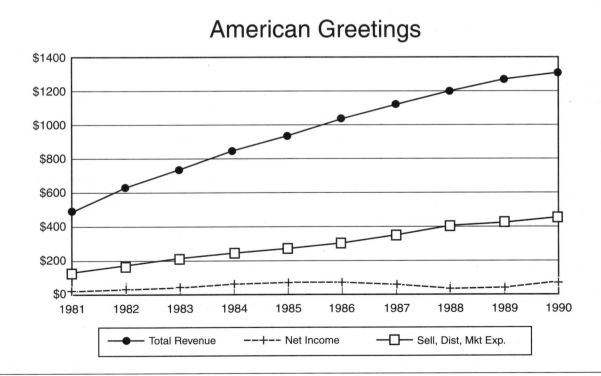

price competition (through discounts to retailers) was during the period 1985 through 1987, although it still continues at a lesser rate today. According to *Value Line*, the end result was the reduction of profits with little change in market shares. In fact, retailer concessions made to gain accounts are difficult to remove; retailers are reluctant to give them up. However, according to Prudential-Bache, price competition may again emerge in selective target markets, such as large chains, as the card firms try to hold or steal accounts.

Market niches were also attacked. According to the *Insider's Chronicle*, the biggest battlefields were the gift and specialty card shops, which once were the exclusive domain of Hallmark and alternative cards. A 1989 comparison of the three firms reveals the following:

Firm	Sales	NI	#Employ	#Products	#Outlet
Hallmark	$ 2.0B	NA	28,000	20,300	37,000
AG	$ 1.3B	$44.2M	29,000	20,000	90,000
Gibson	$ .4B	$35.0M	7,900	NA	50,000

Source: 10-K

OBJECTIVES

When asked about AG's 1989 performance, Morry Weiss replied,

Our goal was to improve competitiveness and enhance future earnings prospects in order to maximize shareholder value. AG refocused its world wide business operating strategies. While we have not reached the upper levels of that goal, substantial progress was made in 1989. We are reducing seasonal product returns, accounts receivable, and inventories. These are indicators how well a business is being operated, and the results show that our people have made substantial progress. We are committed to making even further improvement in these areas. (1989 Annual Report)

Weiss further explained,

1989 sales increased despite the loss of revenue caused by the divestiture during the year of the Company's AmToy and Plymouth divisions and several foreign subsidiaries.

. . . net income was affected by restructuring costs which included the cost of relocating Carlton Cards/US to Cleveland, Ohio; consolidating certain manufacturing operations; and selling, consolidating or downsizing several unprofitable businesses. (1989 Annual Report)

His assessment of AG's 1990 performance was:

It was the kind of year you have to feel good about. Our performance demonstrated our ability to produce outstanding earnings, even in a year when the revenue gain was modest. To accomplish this required enormous effort in every department. It required a diligent watch over expenses, while increasing productivity. (1990 Annual Report)

Morry Weiss also commented about AG's growth:

We are building a more synergistic relationship between our core business and our subsidiary operations in order to increase our value to our retailers.

Our goal is to be a full-service provider to our retailer accounts. The more we represent a single source for a variety of consumer products, the more important a resource we become. (1990 Annual Report)

. . . growth is expected to continue as we accelerate new product development for the everyday cards. (1989 Annual Report)

To reach this aim of providing retailers not only greeting cards, but complementary products, AG has made the following acquisitions:

Company	Products
Acme Frame Products	Picture Frames
Wilhold Hair Care Products	Hair Care Products
Plus Mark	Promotional Christmas Products
A.G. Industries	Greeting Card Cabinets/ Displays

MARKETING STRATEGIES

Product

AG produces a wide product line, including greeting cards, gift wrap, party goods, toys, and gift items. Greeting cards accounted for 65 percent of the company's 1990 fiscal sales. The breakdown of sales by major product categories follows:

Category	1990	1986	1984	1980
Everyday greeting cards	41%	37%	36%	34%
Holiday greeting cards	24	29	27	27
Gift wrap and party goods	17	18	21	21
Consumer products (toys, etc.)	9	7	7	9
Stationery	9	9	9	9

Source: AG's Annual Report.

The essence of AG's product strategy is identifying consumer needs, creating responses that sell, and pre-testing to determine the winners. AG believes in identifying consumer needs and responding to them with creative products. Research is a key ingredient. Over 12,000 North American households are surveyed annually to obtain information about every greeting card purchased and received. AG utilizes focus group sessions, simulated shopping surveys, and shopping mall interviews. Especially important is ongoing life-style research to identify changing tastes and consumer needs for product development.

Research efforts have resulted in new products. Couples, an everyday card line that answers the trend back to more sincere romantic relationships, and Kid Zone, which responds to the need for more effective communication with children, were introduced during fiscal 1990. 1960's popular Holly Hobbies designs were reintroduced when research indicated a trend toward more traditional values.

Morry Weiss commented on the Couples line:

> We've proven our ability to meet the challenge of the marketplace. Couples takes its place alongside a pantheon of our major greeting card innovations. (1989 Annual Report)

AG has one of the largest creative staffs in the world with over 550 artists, stylists, writers, designers, photographers, and planners. They create more than 20,000 new greeting card designs each year.

AG also engages in retail pre-testing to determine which product ideas have the greatest chance of sales. This is extremely important, due to the competitiveness of the market and retailers' need to have a fast turnover. A network of retail test stores is used. New cards are rated based upon actual sales performance, and those with the best sales ratings are distributed worldwide.

AG is trying to take advantage of the alternative card segment. Alternative cards now command 20 percent of the everyday greeting card market, and the double digit annual growth rate is expected to continue. Carlton Cards is AG's specialty card subsidiary and has been recently moved from Dallas to AG's Cleveland headquarters. Carlton will concentrate on "swiftly developing products unique to the more avant-garde tastes of the specialty store consumer."

AG pioneered licensing and is an industry leader in character licensing. Its strategy has been to maximize the potential of its creative and marketing expertise. The following identifies some of AG's character licenses.

Character	Year
Holly Hobbie	1968/1989
Ziggy	1971
Strawberry Shortcake	1980
Care Bears	1983
Herself the Elf	1983
Popples	1983

Most of AG's licensed characters have been successful. Strawberry Shortcake has been one of the most popular licensed characters. According to Forbes, however, all of AG licensed characters have not been successful. One flop, Herself the Elf, was perceived by retailers as being too much like Strawberry Shortcake; it also missed the Christmas season because of production problems. Another failure was Get Along Gang, which tried to appeal to both little girls and boys. AG's licensing income is shown in the following table.

Year	Income
1984	$17.5
1985	$20.9
1986	$17.6
1988	$16.5
1989	$13.3
1990	$11.8

Source: AG's Annual Reports.

Distribution

AG distributes its products through 90,000 retail outlets throughout the world in 50 countries and 12 languages. AG's major channels of distribution, in order of importance, include drug stores, mass merchandisers, supermarkets, stationery and gift shops, combo stores (stores combining food, general merchandise, and drug items), variety stores, military post exchanges, and department stores (AG's 1989 10-K).

AG's primary channels of distribution (which include supermarkets, chain drug stores, and mass retail merchandisers) have experienced growth due to demographic and life-style changes. The increase of working women has caused consumers to purchase more cards in convenient locations. Today, 55 percent of all everyday greeting cards are purchased in convenient locations.

AG's five largest customers accounted for about 17.4 percent of net sales. These customers included mass merchandisers, major drug stores, and military exchanges.

AG has 26 regional and 58 district sales offices in the U.S., Canada, United Kingdom, France, and Mexico.

Promotion

Service is a key value to AG's marketing effort, as reflected in the following:

One of our cornerstone values is service to the customer. While we are a leader in marketing innovation, we earned our reputation for superior customer service by clinging to old-fashioned ideas. We get to know our customers—and their customers—and learn how their businesses operate. (1990 Annual Report)

The services that AG provides its retailers are based upon three key ingredients: knowledgeable sales force, large force of in-store service personnel, and quick response to needs. AG offers the following:

- Largest full-time sales force in the industry, which is composed of highly trained experts.
- National force of 12,000 part-time in-store merchandising representatives who visit mass retail stores to restock goods, realign products, set up new displays and point-of-purchase materials, generate reorders, and process returns.
- Provide computerized network that allows AG to more quickly and consistently ship complete and accurate orders to retailers. (1990 Annual Report)

According to Weiss,

AG is focusing on building a strong partnership with retailers and consumers. We will expand distribution of our products in the global marketplace. We will "partner" with retail accounts by making greeting card departments more profitable. And we will improve our response to consumers' needs for appropriate products and attractive, easy to shop departments. (1990 Annual Report)

AG tries to achieve more sales and profits from the space allocated by retailers by making them more productive. This is accomplished by sophisticated merchandising that makes greeting card displays more "consumer friendly." Since women purchase approximately 90 percent of all greeting cards, AG has redesigned greeting card cabinets to respond to the fact that women spend less time in stores than previously. Redesigned greeting card cabinets display 40 percent more cards in the same amount of space. Point of purchase signs and new caption locators ("Mother," "Stepdaughter," and the like) have also been produced.

Themes are becoming more important in merchandising. These are used for "particular seasons or occasions that project a strong message to consumers and evoke an immediate awareness of the occasion." Related to this is a new concept called "occasion merchandising which groups various products for everyday occasions such as cards, gift wrap, candles, invitations, party goods, and so on."

AG tries to design its marketing programs to increase customer traffic and profitability of the greeting card department. Realizing the need for retailers to differentiate themselves and their products, AG attempts to work on an individual basis to customize the greeting card department for each retailer. This is accomplished via market research and technology. This is especially important to large chains that must contend with regional differences. Greeting card departments can be customized to reflect a specific area's demographics. If, for example, the demographic profile is comprised of a large number of elderly individuals or "yuppies," specific products would be featured to target that segment.

A summary of AG's selling, distribution, and marketing expenses is displayed below:

Year	Percent
1981	28.2
1982	28.7
1983	29.2
1984	29.3
1985	29.0
1986	29.8
1987	31.6
1988	33.4
1989	32.6
1990	32.9

Source: AG's Annual Report.

PRODUCTION STRATEGIES

AG has 34 plants and facilities in the United States, Canada, the United Kingdom, France, and Mexico. This is down from the 49 plants and facilities in 1986. The company owns approximately 4.8 million square feet and leases 11.3 million square feet of plant, warehouse, store, and office space. It meets its space needs in the U.S. through long-term leases of properties constructed and financed by community development corporations and municipalities.

AG had taken steps in 1987 through 1990 to cut production costs. It has tried to improve its production efficiency by cutting costs and reducing work-in-process inventories. AG also invested heavily in automated production equipment to cut labor costs in 1988. AG has also benefited from lower cost for raw materials and fewer product returns because of better inventory control. AG's material, labor, and other production costs are as follows:

Year	% of Sales
1981	44.7
1982	44.3
1983	41.3
1984	40.5
1985	39.9
1986	40.2
1987	42.3
1988	45.1
1989	42.8
1990	41.5

PERSONNEL STRATEGIES

In 1989, American Greetings employed over 15,000 full-time and 14,000 part-time people in the United States, Canada, Mexico, and Europe. This equates to approximately 20,500 full-time employees.

Hourly plant employees at Cleveland, Ohio; Bardstown and Corbin, Kentucky; Greeneville, Tennessee; Chicago, Illinois; and in the United Kingdom and Canada are union. All other office and manufacturing employees are not union. Labor relations are considered to be satisfactory.

When asked about AG employees, Morry Weiss commented:

But perhaps our greatest strength is the men and women who create, manufacture, distribute, sell, and support our products. They are committed to knowing our customers, meeting their needs with quality products and providing service before and after the sale. (1990 Annual Report)

AG has a non-contributing profit-sharing plan for most of its U.S. employees, as well as a retirement income guarantee plan. It also has several pension plans covering certain employees in foreign countries (1990 Annual Report).

FINANCE STRATEGIES

Exhibits 2 through 4 contain relevant financial information for American Greetings. The financial condition of AG has been fluctuating over the years. In the early- to mid-1980s, AG profit margins increased from 5.42 percent in 1981 to its high of 8.09 percent in 1984. ROI was 6.14 percent in 1981; its high was 9.94 percent in 1985. However, AG's financial performance in the mid- to late-1980s was disappointing, with the profit margin falling to 2.84 percent in 1988 with an ROI of 2.90 percent. In 1990, AG's profit margin had risen to 5.51 percent with a ROI of 6.33 percent.

Irving Stone commented about AG's 1990 performance:

> Fiscal 1990 revenues were a record $1.31 billion. This marks the 84th consecutive year that revenues have increased since the Company's founding in 1906.
>
> And, . . . revenue was driven by higher sales of everyday greeting cards, our low-cost high margin core products. Fourth quarter sales were particularly strong. We expect to continue reporting good sales results.
>
> The market value of our common stock rose 47 percent, from $21.25 on February 28, 1989 to $31.25 at the fiscal year close on February 28, 1990. This compares favorably to 27 percent increases for both the Dow Jones Industrial Average and the Standard and Poor's 500 Stock Index. Total returns to stockholders—share price appreciation plus dividends—was 50 percent in Fiscal 1990. (1990 Annual Report)

AG's stock price has ranged from a low of 9 1/2 in 1981 to a high of 37 1/8 in 1990.

MANAGEMENT

AG is organized via a divisional profit center basis. Each division has its own budget committee, while an executive management committee composed of five senior executives approves the strategic plans for all the divisions. Strategic plans are established in one, three, ten, and twenty year time frames. Corporate AG maintains strict budgetary and accounting controls.

The basic domestic greeting card business is placed under the U.S. Greeting Card Division. Domestic and International Subsidiary Operations, including the licensing division, are a second unit, with corporate management a third. AG decentralized its structure in 1983.

American Greetings is composed of the following divisions:

U.S. Greeting Card Division. Encompasses core business of greeting cards and related products, including manufacturing, sales, merchandising, research, and administrative services. Produces and distributes greeting cards and related products domestically. Same products are distributed throughout the world by international subsidiaries and licensees.

Domestic and International Subsidiaries. AG's domestic and international subsidiary operations include the following:

Domestic
Acme Frame Products
A.G. Industries, Inc.
Plus Mark, Inc.
Wilhold Hair Care Products
Summit Corporation/Summit Collection
Those Characters from Cleveland, Inc.

International
Carlton Cards, Ltd.—Canada
Rust Craft Canada
Carlton Cards, Ltd.—England
Carlton Cards France
Felicitaciones Nacionales S.A. de C.V.—Mexico

EXHIBIT 2

Consolidated Statements of Financial Position 1981–1990 (Thousands of Dollars)

Assets	1990	1989	1988	1987	1986	1985	1984	1983	1982	1981
Current Assets										
Cash and equivalents	$ 122,669	$ 94,292	$ 36,534	$ 17,225	$ 26,853	$ 66,363	$ 62,551	$ 19,950	$ 3,367	$ 2,522
Trade accounts receivable, less allowances for sales returns and doubtful accounts	254,285	242,582	278,559	284,135	240,471	173,637	146,896	148,018	131,996	114,051
Inventories:										
Raw material	51,075	48,478	56,122	56,057	59,343	59,197	48,738	47,636	53,515	39,329
Work in process	42,139	51,625	61,406	69,668	60,179	53,728	43,929	54,756	52,214	37,506
Finished products	208,918	197,618	245,801	202,412	181,237	152,543	139,275	122,167	97,221	88,759
	302,132	297,721	363,329	328,137	300,759	265,468	231,942	224,559	202,950	165,594
Less LIFO reserve	85,226	83,017	77,274	75,392	76,552	71,828	63,455	59,345	55,051	46,287
	216,906	214,704	286,055	252,745	224,207	193,640	168,487	165,214	147,899	119,307
Display material and factory supplies	25,408	25,192	30,299	29,770	26,826	20,809	11,532	12,245	11,724	14,529
Total Inventories	242,314	239,896	316,354	282,515	251,033	214,449	180,019	177,459	159,623	133,836
Deferred income taxes	51,315	49,542	39,935	26,593	36,669	33,016	26,517	24,847	18,014	17,685
Prepaid expenses and other	10,362	11,020	8,672	9,679	6,228	4,795	4,187	3,524	2,057	1,985
Total current assets	680,945	637,332	680,054	620,147	561,254	492,260	420,170	373,798	315,057	270,079
Other Assets	107,788	92,285	95,752	89,488	47,085	31,634	34,820	32,866	22,063	17,054
Property, Plant and Equipment										
Land	6,229	6,471	7,548	7,956	7,523	6,822	6,621	5,427	3,380	2,590
Buildings	215,458	216,545	223,491	183,481	165,241	143,671	133,868	118,398	110,479	101,781
Equipment and fixtures	354,979	340,233	319,353	269,644	222,718	182,101	158,507	133,731	115,927	108,463
	576,666	563,249	550,392	461,081	395,482	332,594	298,996	257,756	229,786	212,834
Less accumulated depreciation and amortization	224,383	205,246	175,917	148,097	130,519	108,591	95,092	83,745	75,052	66,763
Property, plant and equipment—net	352,283	358,003	374,475	312,984	264,963	224,003	203,904	174,011	154,734	146,071
	$1,141,016	$1,087,620	$1,150,281	$1,022,619	$873,302	$747,897	$658,894	$580,675	$491,854	$433,204
Liabilities and Shareholders' Equity										
Current Liabilities										
Notes payable to banks	36,524	17,201	13,956	25,092	15,921	4,574	4,647	29,836	4,564	14,087
Accounts payable	75,146	79,591	98,270	69,175	66,685	56,840	52,302	40,568	39,016	34,479
Payrolls and payroll taxes	45,315	38,839	33,759	31,230	28,675	26,761	23,160	16,914	17,224	14,191
Retirement plans	10,878	8,573	4,148	10,966	11,697	12,612	10,362	7,405	5,696	4,990
State and local taxes	3,056	2,763	2,796	2,811	2,448	3,278	2,920			
Dividends payable	5,281	5,311	5,338	5,343	5,317	4,622	3,304	2,641	1,918	1,776
Income taxes	6,430	6,693	13,782	—	18,988	27,465	23,672	8,841	12,177	12,079
Sales returns	21,182	24,543	28,273	29,964	23,889	21,822	17,795	16,423	9,241	10,752
Current maturities of long-term debt		3,740	54,150	10,894	4,786	4,359	6,432	6,998	6,531	7,033
Total current liabilities	200,756	184,491	251,676	185,720	178,721	161,851	144,485	132,074	99,645	102,307
Long-Term Debt	235,497	246,732	273,492	235,005	147,592	112,876	119,941	111,066	148,895	113,486
Deferred Income Taxes	100,159	91,409	86,426	77,451	64,025	47,422	28,972	21,167	15,530	11,861

EXHIBIT 2
(continued)

	1990	1989	1988	1987	1986	1985	1984	1983	1982	1981
Shareholders' Equity										
Common shares-par value $1										
Class A	29,946	29,692	29,628	29,552	29,203	28,835	28,397	27,996	12,293	12,227
Class B	2,063	2,497	2,528	2,588	2,982	3,046	3,070	3,080	1,413	1,434
Capital in excess of par value	110,234	105,245	104,209	102,718	94,744	87,545	80,428	76,851	37,690	37,124
Shares held in Treasury	(26,692)	(14,767)	(14,199)	(15,409)	(16,801)	(13,688)	(9,158)	(7,179)	(3,829)	
Cumulative translation adjustment	(8,186)	(4,790)	(7,564)	(11,604)						
Retained earnings	497,239	447,111	424,085	416,598	374,525	320,010	262,759	215,620	180,217	154,765
	604,604	564,988	538,687	524,443	482,964	425,748	365,496	316,368	227,784	205,550
Total shareholders' equity	$1,141,016	$1,087,620	$1,150,281	$1,022,619	$873,302	$747,897	$658,894	$580,675	$491,854	$423,204

EXHIBIT 3
Consolidated Statement of Income 1981–1990 (Thousands of Dollars)

	1990	1989	1988	1987	1986	1985	1984	1983	1982	1981
Net sales	$1,286,853	$1,252,793	$1,174,817	$1,102,532	$1,012,451	$919,371	$817,329	$722,431	$605,970	$489,213
Other income	22,131	22,566	24,155	23,463	23,200	26,287	22,585	20,252	17,634	9,059
Total Revenue	1,308,984	1,275,359	1,198,972	1,125,995	1,035,651	945,658	839,914	742,683	623,604	498,272
Costs and expenses:										
Material, labor, other production costs	543,602	546,214	540,143	476,725	416,322	377,755	339,988	310,022	276,071	222,993
Selling, distribution and marketing	431,254	415,597	400,033	355,363	308,745	274,095	246,456	217,022	179,021	140,733
Administrative and general	149,771	148,095	135,224	125,407	131,928	123,750	112,363	96,012	76,494	61,033
Depreciation and amortization	40,251	39,527	34,191	29,059	23,471	18,799	15,507	13,890	12,752	10,863
Interest	27,691	33,479	32,787	24,875	19,125	15,556	16,135	24,086	21,647	13,548
Restructuring charge	—	23,591	—	12,371	—	—	—	—	—	—
	1,192,569	1,206,503	1,142,378	1,023,800	899,591	809,955	730,449	661,032	565,985	449,170
Income Before Income Taxes	116,415	68,856	56,594	102,195	136,060	135,703	109,465	81,651	57,619	49,102
Income Taxes	44,238	24,582	23,203	38,834	61,635	61,338	49,807	37,069	24,776	22,587
Net Income	$72,177	$44,274	$33,391	$63,361	$74,425	$74,365	$59,658	$44,582	$32,843	$26,515
Net Income Per Share	$2.25	$1.38	$1.04	$1.97	$2.32	$2.35	$1.91	$1.54	$1.20	$.97

EXHIBIT 4

Selected Financial Data, Years Ended February 28 or 29, 1985–1981

Summary of Operations	1985	1984	1983	1982	1981
Total Revenue	$ 945,658	$ 839,914	$ 742,683	$ 623,604	$ 498,272
Materials, labor and other products	382,205	344,313	313,769	278,866	225,356
Depreciation & amortization	18,799	15,507	13,890	12,752	10,863
Interest expense	15,556	16,135	24,086	21,647	13,548
Net income	74,365	59,658	44,582	32,843	26,515
Net income per share	2.35	1.91	1.54	1.20	.97
Cash dividends per share	.54	.40	.31	.27	.26
Fiscal year end market price/share	33.06	23.69	18.69	9.63	5.50
Average number shares outstanding	31,629,418	31,240,455	28,967,092	27,352,342	27,314,594

Financial Position					
Accounts Receivables	$ 173,637	$ 146,896	$ 148,018	$ 131,996	$ 114,051
Inventories	214,449	180,019	177,459	159,623	133,836
Working capital	330,409	275,685	241,724	215,412	167,772
Total assets	747,897	685,894	580,675	491,854	433,204
Capital additions	43,575	46,418	33,967	26,720	22,768
Long-term debt	112,876	119,941	111,066	148,895	113,486
Shareholder's equity	425,748	365,496	316,368	227,784	205,550
Shareholder's equity/share	13.35	11.62	10.18	8.31	7.52
Net return average shhld equity	19.2 %	17.8 %	17.1 %	15.4 %	13.7 %
Pre-tax return on TR	14.4 %	13.0 %	11.0 %	9.2 %	9.9 %

Selected Financial Data, Years Ended February 28 or 29, 1990–1986

Summary of Operations	1990	1989	1988	1987	1986
Total Revenue	$1,308,984	$1,275,359	$1,198,972	$1,125,995	$1,035,651
Materials, labor and other products	543,602	546,214	540,143	476,725	420,747
Depreciation & amortization	40,251	39,527	34,191	20,059	23,471
Interest expense	27,691	33,479	32,787	24,875	19,125
Net income	72,177	44,274	33,391	63,361	74,425
Net income per share	2.25	1.38	1.04	1.97	2.32
Cash dividends per share	.66	.66	.66	.66	.62
Fiscal year end market price/share	31.25	21.25	17.63	28.75	35.62
Average number shares outstanding	32,029,533	32,146,971	32,068,752	32,212,556	32,059,851

Financial Position					
Accounts Receivables	$ 254,285	$ 242,582	$ 278,559	$ 284,135	$ 240,471
Inventories	243,314	239,896	316,354	282,515	251,033
Working capital	480,189	452,841	428,378	434,427	382,533
Total assets	1,141,016	1,087,620	1,150,281	1,022,619	873.302
Capital additions	42,869	41,938	96,682	68,740	61,799
Long-term debt	235,497	246,732	273,492	235,005	147,592
Shareholder's equity	604,604	564,988	538,687	524,443	482,964
Shareholder's equity/share	18.89	17.55	16.75	16.32	15.01
Net return average shhld equity	12.3 %	8.0 %	6.3 %	12.7 %	16.5 %
Pre-tax return on TR	8.9 %	5.4 %	4.7 %	9.1 %	13.1 %

The number of domestic operations in 1986 included seven versus six in 1990. Firms divested included AmToy, Inc., Drawing Board Greeting Cards, Inc., and Tower Products, Inc.

The number of international operations in 1986 was thirteen versus five in 1990. Among the international operations consolidated included one in Canada, four in Continental Europe, one in Monaco, and four in the United Kingdom.

Exhibit 5 provides a corporate directory of management personnel and their divisional assignments.

EXHIBIT 5
Corporate Directory

Board of Directors	Corporate Officers

Board of Directors

Irving I. Stone[1]
Chairman

Morry Weiss[1]
President
Chief Executive Officer

Scott S. Cowen[2]
Dean, Weatherhead School of Management
Case Western Reserve University

Edward Fruchtenbaum[1]
President, U.S. Greeting Card Division

Herbert H. Jacobs
(personal investments and consultant)

Frank E. Joseph[2]
Retired Attorney

Millard B. Opper
Retired Chairman of Canadian Operations

Albert B. Ratner[1]
President and CEO
Forest City Enterprises, Inc.
(real estate development and operation)

Harry H. Stone[2]
President
The Courtland Group (personal investments)

Milton A. Wolf[2]
Former United States Ambassador to Austria
(personal investments)

Morton Wyman[1]
Retired Executive Vice President

Abraham Zaleznik
Professor, Harvard Business School
(consultant to business and government)

Corporate Officers

Irving I. Stone
Chairman

Morry Weiss
President, Chief Executive Officer

Edward Fruchtenbaum
President, U.S. Greeting Card Division

Ronald E. Clouse
Senior Vice President

Rubin Feldman
Senior Vice President

Henry Lowenthal
Senior Vice President, Chief Financial Officer

Packy Nespeca
Senior Vice President, Corporate Trade Development

James R. Van Arsdale
Senior Vice President

John M. Klipfell
Senior Vice President

Harvey Levin
Senior Vice President, Human Resources

Jon Groetzinger, Jr.
General Counsel & Secretary

William S. Meyer
Controller

Eugene B. Scherry
Treasurer

[1]Member of Executive Committee
[2]Member of Audit Committee

EXHIBIT 5
Corporate Directory (continued)

U.S. Greeting Card Division

Edward Fruchtenbaum
President

Sales and Marketing

Mary Ann Corrigan-Davis
Vice President, Product Management

Gary E. Johnston
Vice President, Creative

Raymond P. Kenny
Vice President, Planning & Research

William R. Mason
Vice President, General Sales Manager

> **Dan Moraczewski**
> Vice President, Sales—Zone 1

> **William R. Parsons**
> Vice President, Sales—Zone II

> **Donovan R. McKee**
> Vice President, Sales—Carlton Cards

George Wenz
Vice President, Sales—National Accounts

Operations

James R. Van Arsdale
Senior Vice President

> **James H. Edler**
> Vice President, Materials Management

> **Dean D. Trilling**
> Vice President, Information Services

> **John T. Fortner**
> Vice President, Manufacturing

>> **Thomas O. Davis**
>> Vice President, Manufacturing
>> Everyday Division

>> **Robert C. Swilik**
>> Vice President, Manufacturing
>> Seasonal Division

Domestic and International Subsidiary Operations

Ronald E. Clouse
Senior Vice President

> **Acme Frame Products, Inc.**
> Cleveland, Ohio
> Howard Reese, President

> **A.G. Industries, Inc.**
> Cleveland, Ohio
> Charles H. Nervig, President

> **Plus Mark, Inc.**
> Cleveland, Ohio
> Erwin Weiss, President

> **Wilhold Hair Care Products**
> Cleveland, Ohio
> Ronald J. Peer, President

> **Dale J. Beinker**
> Vice President, International

> **Carlton Cards, Ltd.**
> Dewsbury, England
> Alistair Mackay, Chairman

>> **Carlton Cards France**
>> Paris, France
>> Raphael Barda, Managing Director

> **Felicitaciones Nacionales S.A. de C.V.**
> Mexico City, Mexico
> Felix G Antonio, President

John M. Kilpfell
Senior Vice President

> **Carlton Cards, Ltd.**
> Toronto, Ontario
> James E. Semon, President

>> **Rust Craft Canada**
>> Brampton, Ontario
>> Mike Johnson, General Manager

> **The Summit Corporation**
> Cleveland, Ohio
> Alan Vilensky, Vice President

>> **Summit Collection**
>> Cleveland, Ohio
>> Joy Sweeney, Vice President

> **Those Characters**
> **From Cleveland, Inc.**
> Cleveland, Ohio
> Jack S. Chojnacki, Ralph E. Shaffer, Co-Presidents

Source: 1990 Annual Report

AG's domestic and international sales are listed in Exhibit 6.

FUTURE OF AG

When asked about the future of AG, Morry Weiss responded,

We are poised for perhaps the most successful period in our history.

We are prepared to strengthen our core business and improve our position in the greeting card industry; to provide a greater return to our shareholders; and to afford our employees even greater opportunities for growth and career advancement.

The strategies we will employ to achieve our goals for the new year and beyond are clear. We have well defined corporate strengths which we will target to build even stronger partnerships with retailers and consumers. (1990 Annual Report)

Irving Stone's view of the future included:

We are optimistic about the future. We are confident that we can achieve even more exciting results . . . in the future.

We face the future confident that our commitment to help people build and maintain relationships will produce even more innovative products like Couples. (1989 Annual Report)

According to the *U.S. Industrial Outlook Handbook*, industry sales should grow between 3 to 4 percent annually through 1992. Moderate growth is predicted due to forecasted moderate growth in the GNP, real disposable personal income, and personal consumption expenditures. For continued growth and profitability, the *U.S. Industrial Outlook Handbook* recommends diversification into related product lines, institution of more cost cutting strategies, monitoring of demand for current lines, divesting of unprofitable lines, and better matching of demand with supply to avoid after-holiday returns.

The unit growth rate for the greeting card industry between 1987 and 2015 is estimated to be between 1 to 3 percent. Exhibit 7 provides the forecast according to Prudential-Bache Securities. The primary reason for the slowing of unit growth is due to the postwar baby boomers who have already entered their high card-consumption years. With the declining birth rate of the 1970s and 1980s, consumption of cards is expected to decline.

EXHIBIT 6
Sales Recap

Year	Domestic Sales	GPM*	Foreign Sales	GPM*	US%	INT%
1990	1,088,438	11.86	220,546	6.79	83.15	16.85
1989	1,039,464	7.75	235,895	9.22	81.50	18.50
1988	996,628	7.79	202,344	5.80	83.12	16.88
1987	940,565	13.28	185,430	1.19	83.53	16.47
1986	874,255	15.38	161,396	12.82	84.42	15.58
1985	799,805	16.51	145,853	13.18	84.58	15.42
1984	717,057	15.18	122,857	13.61	85.37	15.63
1983	631,143	14.29	111,549	13.94	85.00	15.00
1982	523,467	12.54	100,137	13.61	85.40	14.60
1981	440,516	12.27	57,756	14.87	88.41	11.59

*Gross Profit Margin
Source: AG Annual Reports.

EXHIBIT 7
The Greeting Card Industry Consumption Forecast

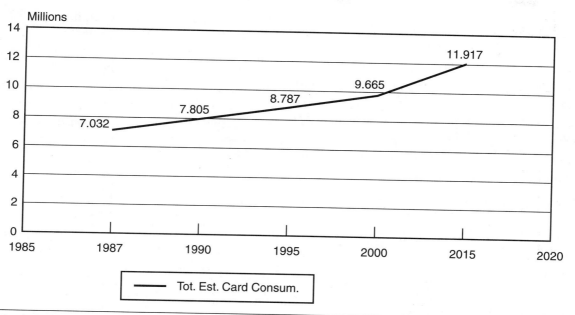

Source: Prudential-Bache Securities Inc.

However, greeting card officials optimistically project that the rate of consumption will increase moderately from the current per-capita rate of 29 cards to 44 cards per-capita by 2015. Greeting card sources also report that consumers are upgrading their purchases to higher-priced cards, thus generating more profits per sale. The aging population, those over 55, also tend to send more cards than do younger persons.

Prudential-Bache's expectations for the future of the greeting card industry include:

Price competition will remain a concern because of the maturity of the industry and the limited number of large players.

At least 5 to 10 percent of the industry's current sales are to retail outlets that the industry leaders will never serve due to the small size of these outlets, which makes it too expensive to reach.

The greeting card industry is an area ripe for potential acquisition.

AG is and will continue to experience increased competition in its promotional gift-wrap area.

The big three can be challenged by any small well-run company.

It is unlikely that the big three with combined market share of 80 to 85 percent will continue to expand to "own the market." The dynamic competitive nature of the industry prohibits this.

There is not much room for the big three to grow by capturing more of the remaining market they are not reaching. (Prudential-Bache Greeting Cards Industry Update, August 9, 1989)

As CEO Morry Weiss thought about the future, he wondered what directions he would give his Strategic Planning committee as they formulated AG's strategies for the 1990s. Looking again at the ten-year summary, he pondered what changes AG should make in its competitive strategies.

ENDNOTES

American Greetings Annual Reports 1981–1990.

American Greetings Form 10-K, 1988–1989.

"American Greetings," *Insider's Chronicle,* February 8, 1988. p. 3.

"American Greetings Corporation," *Moody's Industrial Manual,* 1989, p. 1428.

"American Greetings," *Value Line,* April 27, 1990.

"Flounder," *Forbes,* April 25, 1988, p. 352.

"Funny Valentines," *American Demographics,* February 1989, p. 7.

"Greeting Cards, Industry Update," *Prudential-Bache Securities,* December 30, 1988.

"Greeting Cards, Industry Update," *Prudential-Bache Securities,* August 9, 1989.

"Greeting Cards, Industry Update," *Prudential-Bache Securities,* September 27, 1989.

"Greeting Cards Departments . . . Mass Retail Outlets," *GM News,* 1989, pp. 10+.

U.S. Industrial Outlook, *Department of Commerce,* 1988, pp. 29–16 to 29–17.

Middlesex Mutual Assurance Company

Middlesex Mutual Assurance Company (MMA) was a small 150-year-old property casualty insurer that did 95 percent of its business in Connecticut. It sold insurance strictly through the independent agency system. Currently, about 25 percent of the agents in Connecticut represented MMA. MMA's forte was homeowners' insurance; it was the market leader in this line of insurance with approximately 10 percent of the market.

The key success factor for MMA had been excellent rapport with its independent agency force: agents enjoyed personalized service from company personnel who knew the Connecticut market quite well. MMA's main weakness was that it essentially offered only homeowners' insurance; it did not participate in any life or health insurance. However, these markets were of crucial importance to independent agents.

Recently, the coverage line for homeowners' insurance had been aggressively sought after by other insurance companies, and MMA was not confident that it could maintain market leadership in this line. Competition was becoming intense from sectors within and outside the independent agency system.

In the fall of 1990, Mr. Roger Smith, executive vice president of marketing at MMA, wondered what changes (if any) MMA could make in its distribution system to help ensure continued market leadership in the homeowners' insurance line.

INDUSTRY BACKGROUND

Financial

Property casualty insurance has characteristically been a good, healthy business to be in. Premium growth has been improving steadily since the 1950s, as shown in Exhibit 1.

The industry has been very profitable for most participants, particularly during the 1983–1987 period. The average ROE for the property casualty insurance industry during this period was 18.5 percent versus 14 percent for Standard and Poor's Top 500. The tremendous profitability in the industry for this time period can be explained as follows. Operations for 1980 and 1981 produced an underwriting loss; that is, companies paid out more in claims and operating expenses than they received in premium dollars. Because of this underwriting loss, companies sought and received large rate increases, which greatly increased premium income. At about the same time, interest rates on investable funds rose dramatically as a result of the general economic conditions that prevailed at the time. Thus, insurers not only received a large increase in premiums but were able to earn very attractive rates of return on the premiums they collected. Insurers could earn investment dollars on premiums until the premiums were actually paid out in claims. Often, claims were not paid until many years after premiums had been paid. This was particularly true in commercial lines where claims were not realized for many years (consider products liability where faulty parts cause an airplane to crash five years after they have been installed).

Naturally, the increase in premium levels and windfall investment income greatly increased insurers' profits. Increased profits led to increased capacity in the industry for two reasons:

1. Insurers, who were making high profits, wanted to provide more insurance coverage.
2. High profits attracted new entrants into the business.

Adequate insuring capacity to support society's needs was surpassed by an overcapacity, a "glut," in effect, of available insurance, as shown in Exhibit 2.

This case was prepared as a basis for class discussion rather than to illustrate either effective or ineffective handling of an administrative situation.

EXHIBIT 1
Middlesex Mutual Assurance Company
Property Casualty Insurance Premium Growth, 1972 to 1988

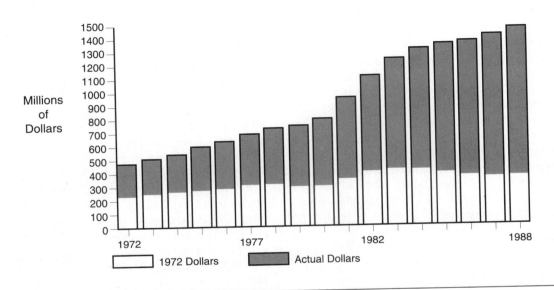

Source: Best's Aggregates and Averages.

At first, companies could sustain an underwriting loss but still make a profit because of investment income on premium dollars. However, price cutting continued to a point where investment income could no longer offset huge underwriting losses, and companies began to lose money. Worse, interest rates began to decline rapidly with the improving overall economy. By early 1990, many insurers were on the verge of becoming financially insolvent. In order to remain solvent, many insurers began to raise premium rates; others were forced to cancel many policies or provide more restrictive coverage.

In general, the commercial lines market was most subject to the volatility described above—risks in commercial lines generated larger premiums and more investment income. Personal lines pricing, profitability, and availability were much more stable during this time.

Distribution

The insurance industry employed two basic means of distribution: independent agents and direct writers. Independent agency companies essentially acted as wholesalers—their insurance was marketed by agents who represented their companies as well as competitors. Direct writers, on the other hand, employed their own sales forces, or marketed their products through print or television media. (Note: Insurance for very large corporations is typically supplied by brokers who operate in much the same way as independent agents except that, unlike an agent, a broker represents the client rather than the insurer.)

Agency companies have been in business since before the turn of the century, whereas most direct writers gained prominence after World War II. In their traditional roles, agents, who were thought of

EXHIBIT 2
Middlesex Mutual Assurance Company
Growth in Policyholders' Surplus, 1972 to 1988

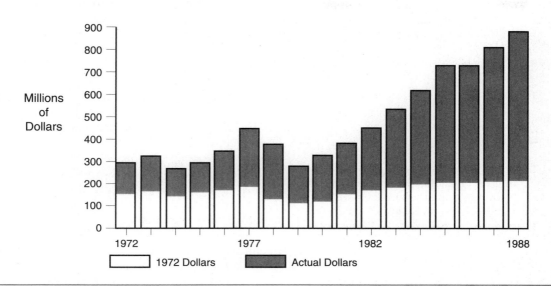

Source: Best's Aggregates and Averages.

as professionals similar to lawyers or accountants, would tailor programs of insurance to the needs of their clients. Direct writers approached insurance as more of a commodity; personal service was sacrificed for low price. Direct writing lent itself well to the personal lines business (i.e., auto and homeowners' insurance) because personal lines coverages are less complex and the personal lines customer generally does not require the degree of service that a commercial customer requires. During the past 20 years, agents tended toward commercial lines business—an area they continued to dominate. Direct writers had advanced dramatically in the personal lines. To illustrate the point, Exhibit 3 shows the direct writers' share in the homeowners' business.

Direct writers did not generally fare well in commercial lines. Their market shares remained low, and they were much less profitable in this area than agency companies. Most of their growth in commercial lines came from very small, unsophisti-

cated accounts. However, the traditional roles of the direct writer and agency company had been somewhat changed, mainly for these reasons:

1. Agency companies were placing less emphasis on commercial lines. The chief factor was the terrible financial results they recently experienced in commercial lines. Their managements were under pressure to improve operating results, and emphasis on personal lines was the easiest way to accomplish the same. Further, as shown in Exhibit 4, the commercial lines market available to the independent agent was shrinking. On the other hand, the personal lines represented an area of potential growth.

2. Direct writers had come a long way in improving their level of service to the client. Direct writers had invested a great deal of time and effort in streamlining their operations. In some cases, direct writers provided service equal to or better than the level provided by agency companies.

3. Direct writers had begun to pursue commercial lines, especially small businesses. Many small business owners viewed insurance as a commodity; indeed,

EXHIBIT 3

Middlesex Mutual Assurance Company
Market Share Trends in Homeowners' Insurance

	Market Share	
Year	Agency	Direct
1972	72%	28%
1978	59%	41%
1982	54%	46%
1983	53%	47%
1985	50%	50%

Source: Best Executive Data Service.

there was little coverage difference in small business insurance, and the required service level was similar to personal lines (i.e., relatively low). Further, the small business was becoming highly important to the U.S. economy: over 600,000 new businesses were started each year. According to Naisbitt, author of *Megatrends,* the United States would be in an "entrepreneurial explosion" to the end of this decade. The implication was that there will be no shortage of small commercial lines prospects for some time to come. In order to preserve their dominance in the commercial lines, agency companies would need to become adept at handling small businesses that required commodity-oriented insurance.

It was generally conceded that the direct writers enjoyed a 10 percent distribution cost advantage over the agency companies. This advantage was due to the fact that the direct writers, owing to lack of a "middleman," were able to save on business distribution costs because their business systems were more streamlined. Further, they enjoyed a more efficient allocation of tasks: the producer spent time selling, while the company's wholesale function was to support the salesperson. With agency companies, the agent performed a great many activities (other than selling) that could be performed more efficiently at the company level, albeit at a less personalized level (e.g., claims handling, billing, etc.).

The agency companies realized that they would have a tough task invading the personal lines market and protecting their dominance in the small business commercial lines market. Significant portions of each of these markets demonstrated the belief that insurance is a commodity. Of necessity, the winner in a commodity market is the contestant who can offer the lowest price and still make a profit, and the direct writers generally had a 10 percent cost advantage with which to work.

Agency companies were observed taking the following actions in the personal lines and small business commercial lines markets:

1. Agency companies had halted the rapid advance of the direct writers by pricing under costs. Such action could not be sustained indefinitely.

EXHIBIT 4

Middlesex Mutual Assurance Company
Market Shares by Distribution Channel in the Commercial Lines Market

	Market Share				
Year	Risk Retention	Captive	Brokers	Independent Agents	Direct Writers
1980	10.2%	2.3%	26.4%	44.5%	16.6%
1982	12.1%	4.6%	21.9%	45.0%	16.4%
1985	13.9%	7.2%	23.0%	40.2%	15.7%
1995*	15.0%	11.0%	24.0%	35.0%	15.0%

Source: Best Executive Data Service.
*Data for 1995 are projections.

2. Efforts were made to improve efficiency of independent agency distribution channel by

a. **Increasing emphasis on automation.** Many companies pursued electronic interface with their agencies; however, agents represent several companies, and they must interface with each one separately, which drastically decreases efficiency and increases agents' expenses. Lately, consulting firms have emerged, whose purpose is to standardize company/agency interface so that an agency can interface with all the companies it represents. This would substantially lower costs and enable companies to more effectively compete with direct writers. However, at the time of writing this case, the standardized system had not enjoyed widespread use.

b. **Experimenting with alternative distribution systems.** Hartford Insurance Group began marketing auto insurance directly to the consumer; they directly solicited consumers who were members of the American Association of Retired Persons. Other companies actively pursued relationships or joint ventures with banks.

c. **Beginning to pay agents lower commissions.** In return for accepting lower commissions, agents would need to perform fewer administrative and service tasks. The company would largely assume these tasks. Agents would spend more time selling rather than servicing.

d. **Dealing with fewer agents.** Economies of scale could be realized if companies could deal with fewer agencies, with each agency producing higher amounts of premium.

e. **Introducing product innovations.** Several insurers developed combination auto-homeowners' policies with broadened coverage. The slightly broadened coverage altered the commodity nature of the product. Further, an account with both auto and homeowners in one policy was less expensive to sell and service. Direct writers had yet to mimic this product. Other innovations included premium payment by credit cards.

f. **Using sophisticated marketing techniques.** Agency companies woke up and realized that consumers would not beat a path to their door to buy insurance. Companies started to mimic and improve some of the direct writers' effective promotion and pricing strategies.

As if the threat from existing direct writers wasn't enough, a significant threat was posed from new entrants, chiefly banks. Banks have intimate contact with all homeowners and automobile owners, not only because most people have checking and savings accounts, but because people utilize the bank for auto and homeowner mortgages and loans. Attitude surveys have shown that the average consumer places more credibility in a banker's advice than in an insurance agent's advice. Banks would possess an enormous competitive advantage because they see a large audience of insurance prospects on a daily basis. Further, as Exhibit 5 shows, the public as a whole would be predisposed to buy insurance from a banker if the purchase of insurance would enhance the likelihood of obtaining a loan.

Further trends affecting the industry were (a) the public's perception that it understood more about insurance than previously and (b) the increased level of information available to consumers.

According to the *Public Attitude Monitor*, people are more aware of what insurance is and does (see Exhibit 6). More-informed people might rely less on the advice of an agent and be attracted to commodity-like pricing.

In regard to level of information, the day is not far off when people will have access to insurance pricing over personal computers at home.

To the extent that people are familiar with insurance and view it as a commodity, pricing will play a more important role in determining where insurance is purchased.

MMA PERSPECTIVES

MMA had been extremely profitable, although industry performance as a whole had deteriorated markedly during the last few years. The homeowners' insurance business (MMA's forte) had been much more stable than commercial lines. Further, MMA had been operating in an unusually favorable competitive environment for these reasons:

1. Direct writers were not as strong in Connecticut (the main geographic area in which MMA operated) as they were on a countrywide basis (see Exhibit 7).

EXHIBIT 5
Middlesex Mutual Assurance Company
Public Perceptions Regarding Relationships between Financial Transactions by Banks and Insurance Companies

Situation	All Respondents						
	Strongly Agree	*Agree*	*Probably Agree*	*Probably Disagree*	*Disagree*	*Strongly Disagree*	*No Answer*
If banks sold auto insurance, people would be expected to buy auto insurance there in order to get an auto loan.	6%	25%	24%	14%	23%	6%	1%
If auto insurance companies owned banks, people would be expected to finance cars there in order to get or keep auto insurance coverage.	5	28	26	15	20	5	1
If banks sold home insurance, people would be expected to buy homeowners' insurance there in order to get a mortgage loan.	5	26	27	16	20	5	1
If home insurance companies offered mortgage loans, people would be expected to get mortgages there in order to get homeowners' insurance.	5	24	29	16	20	5	1

Number = 1.516

Source: Public Attitude Monitor, December, 1989.

Clearly, MMA's homeowners' insurance business had yet to be subjected to the degree of direct writer erosion exhibited in other areas of the country.

2. Despite the agency companies' dominance in the Connecticut personal lines market, most of their marketing thrust was directed toward commercial lines. Agency companies were not particularly aggressive in personal lines; they had really been asleep in regard to personal lines and were merely resting on their laurels.

Due to the relative weakness of direct writers in Connecticut and apathy on the part of agency companies, MMA had thrived and had become the market leader in the homeowners' insurance business, with a 10 percent market share. However, the favorable competitive environment enjoyed by MMA could deteriorate for the following reasons:

1. **Increased competition**—In addition to the growing threat posed by direct writers and new entrants, agency companies could begin to emphasize personal lines coverage instead of commercial lines coverages. Agency companies were awakened from their slumber and were using sophisticated and aggressive marketing techniques to obtain homeowners' insurance. Profitability in the homeowners' insurance line was expected to deteriorate rapidly as competition intensified.

Of special concern to MMA was the degree of leverage that the large agency companies had over MMA agents (keep in mind that agents are independent and represent several companies). Large companies usually offer a full line of insurance services to their agents: personal lines (including personal auto), commercial lines, life and health insurance, and financial planning services. In order for independent

EXHIBIT 6
Middlesex Mutual Assurance Company
Percentage of Men and Women Saying They Consider
Themselves Well Informed about Auto Insurance

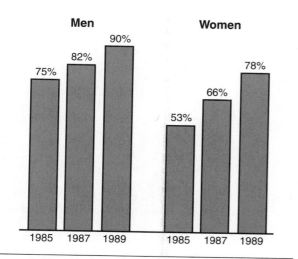

Source: Public Attitude Monitor, March 1990.

agents to survive, they needed to have all of these services available to their clients. Large agency companies realized how important they were to agents, and they also realized that their agents were giving much homeowners' insurance business to MMA. Homeowners' insurance was now recognized as a profitable line, and companies became upset when agents were placing homeowners' insurance with MMA, only to place the less desirable lines of business with them. Many companies offered MMA agents lucrative deals for books of MMA homeowners' insurance business. Others threatened to terminate their relationship with MMA agents unless the companies targeted their agents who were also MMA agents with promotional policyholders (many of whom presumably had homeowners' insurance with MMA) indicating they would receive a 10 percent discount on both the auto and homeowners' policies if they would place both coverages with their company.

The "strong-arm tactics" referred to above were usually resisted by independent agents because they wished to retain their independence as to what company they placed their clients with. True to their

name, most agents were highly independent in nature, and did not take kindly to insurance companies dictating business practice to them. However, agents were under a great deal of competitive pressure, and many had no choice but to submit to the demands of large full-service companies.
2. **Consumer trends**—There was increasing evidence that personal lines coverages were becoming viewed as more and more of a commodity, especially among the middle and lower socioeconomic classes. These people could be expected to seek out the lowest available price. As mentioned earlier, those persons wanting low price would be aided in the future by increasing access to information, probably by way of computer terminals.
3. **Distribution**—MMA did business exclusively through independent agents. The viability of the agency system, especially in personal lines, was being severely challenged by direct writers and new entrants. As previously mentioned, many companies weren't tying themselves directly to the fate of the independent agency system; many were beginning to develop alternative distribution mechanisms.

MMA corporate culture strongly opposed any experimentation with an alternative distribution system. The reasoning was simple. MMA was not a full-service company; it essentially offered only homeowners' insurance. MMA was viewed by agents as a nice company to represent but most often wasn't perceived as a bread-and-butter company. Other companies would be very happy to write an agent's homeowners' insurance book of business, albeit at a slightly lower service level. Because MMA was not an essential company to represent, agents could cease doing business with MMA without jeopardizing the viability of their own operations. Further, one of MMA's key success factors was its excellent rapport with agents. To damage this rapport was viewed as a serious mistake.

As previously mentioned, larger companies were actively reducing the number of agents through which they wrote business and were demanding that their remaining agents place higher amounts of premium with them. MMA executives believed that large companies, with their large overheads, could not economically service the small agent. MMA, on

EXHIBIT 7
Middlesex Mutual Assurance Company
Competitive Position of Agency Companies versus Direct Writers

Personal Auto Insurance

	1988 U.S. Market Share	1988 CT Market Share
Agency companies	38.2%	58.0%
Direct writers	61.8%	42.0%

Homeowners' Insurance

Agency companies	53.7%	74.3%
Direct writers	46.3%	25.7%

Source: A.M. Best Company, A7 reports, 1989.

the other hand, had a strong local presence in Connecticut and could economically service smaller agents that larger companies could not. Industry data indicated that there were plenty of small agents in existence, with new agencies being created every day. These small agencies may not generate enough premium to quench the appetite of large companies, but MMA believed that enough small agents would survive and prosper to warrant consideration as a viable target market for MMA.

In short, Mr. Smith realized that the distribution of homeowners' insurance could change rapidly, and this was of great concern to him. After much deliberation, he felt that MMA should consider the following alternative courses of action:

1. Do nothing; just continue to sell homeowners' insurance through independent agents.
2. Continue selling just homeowners' insurance through agents but streamline the distribution system by using automation and more efficient allocation of tasks between company and agency.

3. Become a more important market to the agents by adding automobile insurance coverage. Otherwise, business as usual.
4. Become a more important market to the agent by adding automobile insurance, while adding the efficiency measures mentioned in Step 2.
5. Develop direct writing capabilities that would bypass the agent.

Mr. Smith decided on the following criteria to evaluate potential alternative actions:

1. Action must be of benefit to independent agents; agent alienation must be avoided.
2. Action must be within reasonable current capabilities of MMA.
3. Action must ensure short-term growth and viability of MMA in the homeowners' insurance market.
4. Action must ensure long-term growth and viability of MMA in the homeowners' insurance market.

The alternative courses of action and the criteria by which they were evaluated are summarized in a decision matrix in Exhibit 8.

EXHIBIT 8
Middlesex Mutual Assurance Company—Evaluation of Alternative Actions

Alternatives	Action must benefit independent agents; alienation must be minimized or avoided	Action must complement and be compatible with MMA internal operations	*Criteria* Action must ensure short-term growth and viability of MMA homeowners' insurance product	Action must ensure long-term growth and viability of MMA homeowners' insurance product	Total
1. Do nothing; continue to sell just homeowners' insurance coverage through independent agents.	3	2	2	0	7
2. Continue selling homeowners' insurance coverage through independent agents but streamline distribution process by use of automation and more efficient allocation of tasks between agent and company.	2	2	3	2	9
3. Become a more important market to the agent by offering personal auto insurance; otherwise, business as usual.	4	3	3	2	12
4. Become a more important market to the agent by offering personal auto insurance; also increase efficiency by taking actions outlined in alternative (2).	4	3	3	4	14
5. Develop direct writing capabilities that bypass the agent.	0	2	0	3	5

Values

0—Very negative effect	1—Somewhat negative effect	2—Neutral effect	3—Somewhat beneficial effect	4—Very beneficial effect

Source: Company records.
MMA executives selected alternative 4; it had the highest score of 14.

In 1993 Anheuser-Busch (A-B) controlled 46 percent of the U.S. beer market and had clearly established itself as the ruler in the industry. The self-proclaimed "King of Beers" had successfully fought off a challenge by Miller, the second-largest brewer in the industry, to take over the throne. Several of the other top 10 companies in the industry were in trouble and seeking merger partners. They, therefore, presented no threat to the firmly placed crown of A-B, and A-B began seeking to capitalize on its competitor's turmoil.

August Busch III, chairman of A-B, felt very smug about his company's strong leadership position within the industry. He was confident that the company could "continue to dominate its rivals simply by redoubling its efforts—building huge and efficient breweries, spending heavily on advertising and promotion, maintaining price leadership where it holds commanding share, and cutting prices where needed to gain business." According to Dennis Long, president of A-B's Beer Division, "If you segment this country geographically, demographically, and by competitors, it gives you great confidence that there is still considerable room for us to grow."

A-B intended to increase its market share to 55 percent by the year 2000. It was seeking to increase its capacity 27 percent by means of a five-year capital expansion plan. This involved an investment of approximately $2 billion. A previous five-year expansion program costing $1.8 billion had increased the capacity of A-B by 50 percent. The major question facing A-B and its chairman was whether A-B would be able to achieve its objectives of increased market share and capacity in light of the decrease in beer consumption growth from 5 percent annually in the 1970s to less than 3 percent in 1992. This decrease was a direct result of the increased popularity of other beverages and a decrease in the number of 18- to 34-year-olds.

INDUSTRY BACKGROUND

Small-scale brewing in the United States began in 1633, when the first commercial brewery was founded in the Dutch colonial town of New Amsterdam, now New York City. It was not until the 1840s that large-scale brewing began to take place as a result of the introduction of a different type of yeast from Germany. The 1870s saw the continued evolution of the beer industry when Louis Pasteur developed the process for controlling fermentation. This made the bottling of beer commercially feasible. During the 1900s, two events had a serious impact on the industry. These events were the results of regulatory and technological changes. The first, Prohibition, occurred in 1920, at a time when the industry consisted almost exclusively of local and regional brewers, numbering approximately 1,500 brewers. When Prohibition was repealed in 1933, fewer than 800 of these brewers had survived. The second event, the introduction of commercial television, occurred in 1946. National advertising began to play an important role in determining market leadership. Television had given a definite edge to those brewers who could afford to advertise by placing their brand first in the consumer's mind.

Consolidation of the Industry

Over the past decade, the $10.5 billion beer industry had undergone considerable change. Consolidation had occurred as a result of the absorption by large brewers of many regional brewers. There were 92 breweries in 1970, and in 1992 that number

---

This case was prepared as a basis for class discussion rather than to illustrate either effective or ineffective handling of an administrative situation.

had decreased to 18. In 1992, 79 percent of all the beer sold came from only three of these brewers, and 69 percent was accounted for by A-B and Miller (see Exhibit 1).

This market dominance by A-B and Miller had drastically altered the industry. A-B and Miller paid their unionized employees more than the average wage in the industry, took advantage of economies of scale, and spent more than their competitors for advertising. They gained considerable control over the market as a result of their marketing expertise, an avalanche of money, and a great deal of animosity toward each other. The remaining brewers (except perhaps Coors) provided little challenge for the two leaders. The smaller brewers were suffering from such nightmares as ineffective production and pricing decisions, poor marketing, and continuous management turnover. As a result of their weak position, the smaller brewers had banded together. It had been necessary for several of them to merge in order to survive. The long-run outlook for the industry was even greater consolidation.

It appeared that the beer industry was headed toward a controlled oligopoly, similar to that of the tobacco industry. Companies were dissuaded from entering the industry because of high entry costs and low-growth prospects. High entry costs involved two separate considerations: (a) the expense required to build marketing and production groups able to compete with A-B and Miller

and (b) the expense and difficulty involved in competing, based on product differentiation. Product differentiation was necessary since price competition alone was not sufficient. However, small brewers were resorting to price cutting in an effort to simply maintain current market shares. This made the low-growth prospects of the industry very apparent. The only small brewer that could possibly compete with A-B and Miller was G. Heileman, because of its low-cost production facilities.

Along with a reduction in the number of brewers over the long run, it was expected that the number of brands would also decrease. However, this could be offset by new types of beer being offered to new market segments. If greater industry consolidation and stronger competition were to occur in the future, A-B and Miller could potentially benefit from it. A more stable industry would result in an end to the vicious price cutting of the past, and profits would be more easily achieved for the few firms remaining in the industry.

Market Shifts

The existing brewers sold different types of beer in all segments of the market. In order to continue expansion, new types of beer were continually being produced. The most recent opportunity for growth had come from the light segment. In the 1970s, only 3 percent of the total market was attributed to light beer. By 1992, light beer accounted for almost one-fourth of the total market. Three factors had contributed to the growth in this segment. First, the 25- to 34-year old age group drank the greatest amount of diet soft drinks, and their health-conscious attitudes had had an effect on their beer-drinking habits. Although the total population was growing at a rate of 1 percent annually, this age segment was forecast to grow at a 2 percent annual rate over the next five years. The second factor involved the increased importance of women in the light beer market. As a group, women appeared to prefer light beer. The third factor contributing to the growth of the light beer segment was advertising. In 1992, Miller held 40 percent of the light beer market; it

EXHIBIT 1
Market Share in the Beer Industry

Company	Share in 1981	Share in 1992
Anheuser-Busch	30.3 %	46.2 %
Miller	22.4	22.4
Heileman	7.8	5.3
Coors	7.4	10.4
Stroh	5.0	7.6
Genesee	2.0	1.2
Other	4.7	6.9
Total	100.0 %	100.0 %

had achieved its market leadership by appealing to the more weight-conscious drinker, such as the older male beer drinker.

Imports were another area in which the possibility for growth existed. In 1992, imported beer represented only 4.3 percent of total beer consumption. This market segment was expected to increase by 50 percent in size by the year 2000. Competition in this area is a matter of taste and image. The leading imports were marketed by companies that were not involved with domestic beer products, but most of the larger domestic brewers sold at least one import. Major brewers obviously considered it important to be represented in all segments and regions of the beer market (see Exhibit 2).

Market Segmentation

To be successful in the national market, three types of strengths were required: marketing skill, product mix, and distribution. The current leaders in the national beer market, A-B and Miller, were strong in all three areas (see Exhibit 3). They possessed marketing expertise, powerful wholesaler networks, and broad product lines. The strength of their product lines was their focus on the high-margin and high-growth light, premium, and super-premium beer segments. In 1992, A-B and Miller held 68.6 percent of the market, and it was projected that by the end of the decade they would hold 80 percent. Consolidation had accelerated because many small competitors were unable to execute effective marketing programs. It was obvious from this that marketing prowess was necessary for success. Product mix was important because the value of the product mix must be greater than the summed values of the individual products, otherwise referred to as *synergy*. If this is not the case, it would be cost prohibitive to introduce a brand. Effective distribution was also a necessary ingredient to success. There was a tendency among consumers to purchase the brand sold in their neighborhood tavern. In order to capture these on-premise sales, effective distribution was essential. Although distribution strength varied from segment to segment, A-B was strongest in distribution overall.

As mentioned above, imported beer represented a mere 4.3 percent of the market in 1992. This market segment had grown slowly over the preceding five years but was expected to grow to 5 percent by 1995. Importers continued to expand their markets by introducing new types of beers to appeal to different segments of the drinking-age population (e.g., Amstel Light). Heineken controlled 30 percent of the imported beer market and Molson controlled 20 percent, but recently these brewers had been losing part of their market share to Beck, Moosehead, and Labatt. The major U.S. producers had only recently begun to market one or more types of imported beers. Imported beers had a distinctive taste and were marketed to appeal to consumers who were inner-directed, upscale, and urban. The imported segment was the sole segment

EXHIBIT 2

Principal Brands of Major Brewers

Company	Premium	Super	Light	Imported
Anheuser-Busch	Budweiser	Michelob	Budweiser Light	Carlesberg
Miller	Miller High Life	Lowenbrau	Lite	Molson
Stroh	Stroh	Signature	Stroh Light	–
S&P Industries	Pabst Blue Ribbon	–	Pabst Lite	–
Coors	Coors	George Killian's Special Ale	Coors Light	–
Heileman	Old Style	Special Export	Several entries	Beck's

EXHIBIT 3

Strengths of Major Competitors in the Beer Industry in Three Key Areas

Company	Distribution	Marketing Strength	Product Mix
Anheuser-Busch	• Strongest in the industry. • Excellent unit volume increases.	• Superior—after the expenditure of considerable money, time, and effort. • Benefits to both unit volume and productivity.	• The best in the industry. • Something for everyone, but unit volume predominantly in the most profitable segment. • A plus for productivity.
Miller (Philip Morris)	• Far superior to the industry average. • Promotes good unit volume growth.	• Deepest pockets in the industry. • Proven skill. • Benefits to both unit volume and productivity.	• Limited but concentrated in the most profitable segment. • A plus for productivity.
Heileman	• Very strong in some areas and weak in most others. • Unit growth at industry average or slightly better.	• Limited financial strength but very efficient with the dollars it spends. • Makes it a viable competitor in the industry.	• Limited in the most profitable; very strong in the least profitable. • No impact on productivity.
Coors	• Deteriorating in traditional markets; weak in new markets. • Continuing declines in unit volume.	• Thus far, underwhelming. • Both unit volume and productivity declining.	• Limited but concentrated in the most profitable segments. • A potential but unrealizable plus for productivity.
S&P Industries	• Weak and getting weaker. • Continuing declines in unit volume.	• Ineffective and low budget. • Effecting declines in both unit volume and productivity.	• Concentrated in the least profitable segments. • No impact on productivity.

Source: Prudential-Bache's *Brewery Industry Outlook,* March 13, 1993.

of the total beer market that could experience a sales slowdown when the economy decelerated.

The small brewers also marketed beer that had a distinctive taste. These brewers tended to sell on a regional basis, staying in well-defined areas close to home. They specialized in lower-priced beers and controlled less than 5 percent of the total beer market in 1992. The number of small, local, family-owned breweries had decreased, and it was expected that this trend would continue. Between 1980 and 1990 this market declined substantially in size. As a result of increased fixed costs, many of

these brewers had been unable to afford to continue in business on their own. With those that were able to survive, one of the key factors had been community pride and interest in the local brewery.

Competition

There are three areas in which brewers compete with one another: packaging, advertising, and price. Packaging provides brewers with a method of segmentation. Packaging choices include the traditional 12-ounce six-pack in bottles or cans;

20-ounce cans; 40-ounce bottles; 7-ounce eight-pack in bottles or cans; 12-ounce twelve pack in bottles or cans; and various keg sizes. During 1991, 59 percent of the total beer consumed was from cans, 32 percent was from returnable bottles, and 9 percent was from nonreturnable bottles. The use of returnable bottles had increased significantly since 1991 as a result of the passage of deposit laws in 43 states.

Over the past decade, advertising had become the major marketing tool. Since 1987, the advertising expenditures of the major brewers had been growing by more than 12 percent annually. Effective advertising had increased brand loyalties. There was an understanding among brewers to advertise in a legal and morally responsible manner. In order to promote the image of being socially responsible, brewers sponsored many public service commercials involving the subjects of teenage pregnancy and drunk driving. They did not show minors, intoxicated people, or the actual consumption of beer in their advertising. There were several market segments that were important targets of advertising campaigns. These included college students, sports fans, and ethnic groups. The brewers attempted to instill brand loyalty in college students by sending representatives to the campuses (Miller) or by sponsoring activities with promotional samples (Budweiser). The Hispanic market was large and important. To appeal to this market segment, Coors used actors of Hispanic background in its advertising, and A-B used a Spanish advertising agency to promote Michelob.

As new products were introduced, they were being targeted directly toward certain market segments. This was achieved mainly through advertising campaigns. Miller Lite was targeted toward older men; Michelob 7-ounce bottles were targeted toward 24- to 35-year-old women. In all the advertisements, focus was placed on identification with males, females, or couples. Beer is an extremely image-oriented product, and advertising campaigns were using a new emphasis. Instead of promoting beer just as a beverage that goes with a simple, relaxed lifestyle, the focus was on beer

as a reward for a job well done. In these commercials, beer was the reward after a hard day's work or for winning at a sport. Humor was often injected into the commercials. Advertising played an important role in the beer industry, and it gave those brewers who could afford it a definite competitive advantage.

Price was no longer the important marketing tool it once was. It had lost its competitive importance. The emphasis had shifted to media. Pricing policies now depended upon product positioning. Brewers sold a number of price-sensitive brands, including super-premium, premium, popular-priced, light, and generic beer. It was expected that the premium, super-premium, and light brands would seek annual price increases of 6–7 percent compared with the smaller increases of 3–5 percent sought by the popular-priced brands.

Environmental Factors Affecting the Beer Industry

There were certain economic and demographic factors that affected the beer industry. Two of these factors were the unpredictability of changes in consumer tastes and preferences, and the effect of extended recessionary forces. If the demand for beer were to weaken substantially, this could result in an overcapacity in the industry. Other factors were increased beer consumption by women and the health-conscious attitude regarding lightness and moderation. The potential impact of these factors would be a favoring of beer over distilled spirits that would provide opportunity for enlargement and further segmentation of the beer market. A final factor encompassed all future movements in consumer economics and demographics. One of these forecasted trends was an increase of 20 percent in the 25- to 44-year-old age group by 1997. This age group had a greater amount of discretionary income, tended to eat out more frequently, and was more likely to entertain at home. Another forecasted trend involved the primary beer drinking age segment. The 18- to 24-year-old age group was expected to decrease in size. These projected trends would not be beneficial to the beer industry.

There were also regulatory factors that affected the beer industry. These included stricter litter control requirements, additional legislation requiring bottle deposits, the raising of the drinking age, and increases in the excise tax. If brewers were required to make alterations in their packaging and methods of distribution, the possible result would be increased costs and, therefore, lower profit margins. This also might result if additional legislation were passed requiring bottle deposits. Raising the drinking age would result in a shrinking of the number of 18- to 24-year-olds who could legally drink, which would also negatively affect brewers' profits. If there were a flat increase in the excise tax, this could lead to a re-distribution of profits. The hardest hit by the increase, on a percentage basis, would be popular-priced and generic beers. This could lead consumers to believe that the price differential among brands was narrowing and, therefore, cause them to change to more expensive beers. This might prove devastating to the small regional brewers who specialized in lower-priced beers. The granting of permission for territorial agreements between wholesalers would also affect the beer industry. The provision of exclusive regional rights would widen the gap between the strong and the weak wholesalers.

Industry Financial and Operating Performance

In the past, the financial success of brewers had paralleled their performance in marketing, distribution, and product mix. The brewers who had displayed strength in these three areas had gained increasing control over the beer market, whereas the weaker performers had been losing market share.

Even though the gap between the strong and weak brewers had been widening, most brewers' profit margins had been hurt by the price wars of the past. This had somewhat limited flexibility in pricing. As a result, several other components of profitability had become important. These were productivity, unit volume, and gross margin. Productivity could be increased through changes to more favorable product mixes. There had been a shift to brands that had growth opportunities and/or appealing gross profit margins. The gross profit margin of each beer segment and its three-to five-year growth within each segment are shown in Exhibit 4.

Both A-B and Miller had focused their product lines on the fast-growing and high-margin light, premium, and super-premium market segments. Light beer was a good brand to market since it was usually less costly to produce, sold at a premium, had a high profit margin, and was, therefore, more profitable than other brands. In 1992, another factor of productivity, operating rate, did not look good for most of the producers in the industry. The average operating rate for the industry was 75 percent of capacity, far below the optimum rate of 90 to 95 percent. A-B was the only brewer with strength in this area; its plants were operating at approximately 98 percent of capacity.

The second important component of profitability was unit volume; the higher the unit volume, the greater the profitability. Since a flattening of beer consumption trends was forecast, the ability of individual brewers to increase their unit volume would depend upon several factors. These included their capacity to finance strong marketing programs and the presence of strong distribution systems.

The third component of profitability was gross margin, which is equal to sales minus cost of goods sold. This figure represented the maximum amount that could be spent on marketing and administrative expenditures without incurring an operating loss. Past and projected industry gross profit is shown in Exhibit 5. The industry gross profit per barrel, excluding A-B and Miller, equaled only two-thirds that of A-B. It was not within the financial means of most brewers to reach a competitive level of marketing since this would necessitate a substantial increase in spending. There was apparently a dichotomy in the industry that could be expressed as "The rich get richer and the not-so-rich are lucky to keep running in place." In summation, higher gross

EXHIBIT 4
Gross Margins in Different Beer Segments

Beer Segment	Gross Margin For Brewer	Gross Margin For Wholesaler	% of Industry Volume
Popular-priced	10% – 16%	20% – 22%	22%
Premium-priced	28% – 30%	25% – 27%	40%
Light beer	30% – 32%	25% – 27%	28%
Super premium-priced	37% – 39%	25% – 27%	2%

Sources: Beverage Industry, Prudential Securities estimates, March 13, 1993.

margins represented more available funds for marketing expenditures. This in turn led to increased market share and sales, the results of which were greater volume and productivity, and, therefore, increased profitability.

The factors that would affect the future performance of the industry were a slow-growth environment, recession, and the cost outlook. The first factor, a slow-growth environment, would necessitate that even more emphasis be placed on increasing productivity and unit volume. Recession, the second factor, would have an impact upon certain

brands of beer, the brands marketed to the people most affected by a recession. A good example of this is Miller High Life, which is strongly marketed toward blue-collar workers. Lastly, the outlook for costs was that (a) the costs of raw materials and packaging would increase at a rate lower than that of inflation and that (b) advertising would not exceed an annual growth rate of 12 percent. Such a favorable cost outlook would enable brewers to keep operating margins within a 3 to 5 percent increase. Exhibit 6 presents a breakdown of the costs of the major brewers.

EXHIBIT 5
Past and Estimated Future Changes in Industry Gross Profit (Profit and Barrelage in Millions)

	1972	1977	1982	1992
Industry				
Total barrelage	131.8	156.9	180.0	209.0
Total gross profit	$1,479.5	$1,915.5	$2,454.5	$3,224.2
Gross profit/barrel	$11.23	$12.21	$13.64	$15.43
Anheuser-Busch				
Total barrelage	26.5	36.6	59.1	86.6
Total gross profit	$392.6	$571.1	$976.1	$1,555.7
Gross profit/barrel	$14.82	$15.60	$16.52	$17.96
Miller				
Total barrelage	5.3	24.2	39.3	54.5
Total gross profit	$71.6	$368.2	$580.7	$865.7
Gross profit/barrel	$13.51	$15.21	$14.78	$15.88
Industry—Less Bud and Miller				
Total barrelage	100.0	96.1	81.6	67.9
Total gross profit	$1,015.3	$976.2	$897.7	$802.8
Gross profit/barrel	$10.15	$10.96	$11.00	$11.82

Source: Prudential-Bache's *Brewery Industry Outlook*, March 13, 1993.

EXHIBIT 6
Estimated Cost Breakdown for Major Brewers

Packaging	45 %
Raw materials	15
Labor	12
Marketing	20
All other	8
Total	100 %

Source: Prudential-Bache's *Brewery Industry Outlook*, March 13, 1993.

ANHEUSER-BUSCH PERSPECTIVES

Company Background

A-B was founded in 1852. Its corporate headquarters are in St. Louis, Missouri. The present chairman is August Busch III, a fourth-generation brewer. In 1957, A-B took the industry leadership away from Schlitz and has held this leadership position ever since. During that period, A-B has had to fend off challenges from both Schlitz and Miller. By the 1970s, A-B had grown so contented that even a challenge by Schlitz did not elicit any response. The brewer was running out of beer every summer and saw no need to market aggressively. The challenge by Schlitz failed only as a result of several marketing blunders that cost Schlitz many loyal customers. It was a challenge by Miller, acquired in 1969–70 by Philip Morris, Inc., that posed a definite threat to the leadership position of A-B and prompted it to act. A-B was in the middle of an awkward transition of management when Miller attacked, but what made matters considerably worse was a strike the summer of 1976 that kept its beer off the shelves that summer. In retaliation, A-B made an all-out effort to defeat Miller and successfully retained its leadership position. The war between A-B and Miller badly crippled the rest of the brewers in the industry, who were constantly struggling to survive.

Since 1976, A-B has increased its number of brands from three to fifteen to target all market segments. Busch and Natural Pilsner are marketed as popular-priced brands, Budweiser and Budweiser Light as premium brands, and Michelob, Michelob Light, Michelob Classic Dark, and an import as super-premium brands. All of its brands are backed by heavy advertising and promotion expenditures. The amount spent by A-B on media rose 180 percent, to $643 million, between 1981 and 1990. A-B was outspending all other brewers in the sponsoring of sporting events. In 1992 it sponsored 98 professional and 310 college sports events.

Brewers have used "image" advertising to position their products ever since advertising was first employed, but its use has been on the rise in the past few years. The original targeted beer segment of Budweiser had a strong, rugged image and, therefore, from the beginning, Budweiser had been associated with the Clydesdale horses. A team of these horses pulled the original Budweiser wagon, but their use had become primarily ceremonial. The type of people now drinking Budweiser were higher-income, middle-aged individuals, more likely to be men and less likely to be minorities. In order to attract a broader market, including women, minorities, and older and younger people, A-B established a new campaign to promote Budweiser based on the slogan "This Bud's for you." The overall consumption of Budweiser tended to be evenly distributed geographically. As a result, it did not face the same problem as Miller High Life, which tended to be skewed geographically toward the economically depressed areas of the country. Exhibit 7 presents the estimated media costs of major competitors.

A-B marketed three light beers, Budweiser Light, Michelob Light, and Natural Light. These three brands were marketed toward the premium, super-premium, and mid-price market segments, respectively. When Budweiser Light was introduced in 1982, it met with unexpected success. This brand emphasized sports and was marketed with a sport-oriented theme, "Bring out your best. . . ." Budweiser Light was targeted toward the heavy beer drinker who was athletic and active, whereas

EXHIBIT 7
Comparison of Advertising Expenditures in the Beer Industry

Advertising Expenditures	1981	1982	1983	1984	1985	1986	1987	1988	1989	1990
Total Beer Industry	$351.8	$406.5	$494.7	$575.8	$602.5	$688.8	$684.5	$720.4	$677.2	$643.2
% Change		-15.5%	21.5%	16.4%	4.6%	14.3%	-0.6%	5.2%	-6.0%	-3.5%
Anheuser-Busch	$117.2	$164.3	$197.8	$245.8	$270.0	$337.4	$339.0	$369.7	$346.0	$301.1
% Change		40.1%	20.4%	24.3%	9.8%	25.0%	0.5%	9.1%	-6.4%	-13.0%
% of Total Industry	33.3%	40.4%	40.0%	42.7%	44.8%	49.0%	49.5%	51.3%	51.1%	46.1%
Market Share	30.0%	32.4%	32.9%	35.0%	37.1%	38.6%	40.6%	41.9%	43.0%	44.6%
Miller	$91.1	$115.5	$133.9	$163.7	$163.5	$201.2	$170.9	$168.4	$149.5	$188.6
% Change		26.8%	15.9%	22.3%	-0.1%	23.1%	-15.1%	-1.5%	-11.2%	26.2%
% of Total Industry	25.9%	28.4%	27.1%	28.4%	27.1%	29.2%	25.0%	23.4%	22.1%	28.9%
Market Share	22.2%	21.5%	20.4%	20.5%	20.2%	20.5%	20.8%	21.5%	22.2%	22.7%
Coors	$23.0	$22.1	$30.4	$38.1	$58.4	$77.7	$84.7	$111.1	$114.3	$122.4
% Change		-3.5%	37.3%	25.2%	53.3%	33.2%	9.0%	31.2%	2.9%	7.1%
% of Total Industry	6.5%	5.4%	6.1%	6.6%	9.7%	11.3%	12.4%	15.4%	16.9%	18.7%
Market Share	7.3%	6.5%	7.5%	7.2%	8.0%	8.1%	8.4%	8.8%	9.5%	9.9%

Source: Beverage Industry and Leading National Advertisers.

Miller Lite was targeted toward the older male beer drinker who was weight conscious.

Busch, a popular-priced beer, was targeted toward the free-spirited man. Promotional campaigns for this brand were geared toward the hard-working blue-collar employee who headed to the mountains for relaxation. The super-premium market segment was dominated by Michelob, an A-B brand, and close behind was Lowenbrau, a Miller brand. There had been a slowing in the growth of this market segment. The new promotional campaign for Michelob Light targeted white-collar men and women who entertained, belonged to country clubs, and could afford to spend a little more for a special occasion beer. This campaign centered on heritage, tradition, quality, and distinctiveness. A-B, with its many expenditures on advertising, closely followed by Miller, was the leader of the industry.

Wholesalers have high fixed expenses as a result of the large capital outlays required to purchase trucks, etc. Therefore, a wholesaler depends on volume sales for profit and concentrates effort upon the brands that offer the greatest volume. It can be seen in Exhibit 8 that A-B and Miller had greater volume than competing brewers. A-B achieved product distribution through a network of 950 wholesalers and was reputed to have the most effective network of wholesalers in the industry. A-B had provided considerable support to its wholesalers, including the establishment of in-depth training seminars on financial management and warehousing. Wholesaler performance was evaluated on the basis of the frequency with which calls were made upon accounts, the weekly and monthly sales of all beers, and several other factors. It was normal for an A-B wholesaler to hold from 12 to more than 20 days' inventory, depending on the season. With a high inventory turnover rate, a wholesaler was able to generate profits much more quickly. The effective wholesaler system of A-B proved invaluable since it was forecast that, in the future, the fight between the brewers would be focused at the wholesaler level.

Company Financial and Operating Performance

A-B's many interests include baking operations, snack foods, transportation services, a baseball franchise, and real estate development. Despite these other interests, A-B's beer operations dominate its revenue base. The beer operations accounted for approximately 85 percent of revenue in 1992. As of June 1992, A-B controlled 46 percent of the U.S. beer market. It controlled 31.4 percent in 1982, 28.2 percent in 1980, and 23 percent in 1977. This was an increase in market share of 44 percent between 1982–1992. The volume of beer sold by A-B also increased significantly over these ten years. In 1982 A-B had total sales of $5.3 billion, and its profit for the year was $287.3 million. In 1992, A-B's sales amounted to more than $13 billion, while the net income was $917 million. Exhibit 9 presents the financial and operating performance of A-B.

Over this ten-year period, A-B had experienced an increase in sales and profits of 150 percent and 220 percent, respectively (see Exhibit 10). It had a unit profitability of approximately $3.59 per barrel of beer sold, greater than that of the rest of the industry. Although it was forecast that total market earnings would increase by 15 to 20 percent in 1993, it was projected that A-B earnings would increase by 30 to 40 percent. As a result of its profit leadership in the industry, A-B had price elasticity.

EXHIBIT 8

Average Case Volume per Brand
per Distributor for Different Brewers

AnheuserBusch	859,000
Miller	637,000
Heileman	108,000
Coors	438,000
Stroh	280,000
S&P Industries	154,000
Industry average	541,000
Industry average less A-B	405,000

Source: Prudential-Bache's *Brewery Industry Outlook,* March 13, 1993.

EXHIBIT 9
Consolidated Balance Sheet—Anheuser-Busch Companies, Inc., and Subsidiaries

Assets (In millions) December 31,	1992	1991
Current Assets:		
Cash and marketable securities	$ 215.0	$ 97.3
Accounts and notes receivable, less allowance for doubtful accounts of $4.9 in 1992 and $5.5 in 1991	649.8	654.8
Inventories—		
Raw materials and supplies	417.7	397.2
Work in process	88.7	92.5
Finished goods	154.3	145.9
Total inventories	660.7	635.6
Other current assets	290.3	240.0
Total current assets	1,815.8	1,627.7
Investments and Other Assets:		
Investments in and advances to affiliated companies	171.6	116.9
Investment properties	164.8	159.9
Deferred charges and other non-current assets	356.3	365.6
Excess of cost over net assets of acquired businesses, net	505.7	519.9
	1,198.4	1,162.3
Plant and Equipment:		
Land	273.3	308.9
Buildings	3,295.2	3,027.8
Machinery and equipment	7,086.9	6,583.9
Construction in progress	729.7	669.0
	11,385.1	10,589.6
Accumulated depreciation	(3,861.4)	(3,393.1)
	7,523.7	7,196.5
	$10,537.9	$ 9,986.5

A-B had experienced operating and financial success as a result of both productivity gains and unit volume increases. It had spent more than $2 billion over the past five years on a program to increase capacity. This had both expanded and upgraded the cost-effectiveness of the A-B plants. Over the next five years, A-B intended to invest another $2 billion in order to increase capacity from 62 million barrels to over 75 million. A significant portion of these funds was likely to be internally generated. A-B acquired the second-largest domestic baker, Campbell-Taggert, which should result in an increase in the amount of funds generated internally.

A-B had successfully positioned its products in the high-margin and fast-growing beer segments. It had also employed an aggressive marketing strategy. As a result, A-B had achieved increases in unit volume that were greater than the growth in industry sales. Over the next five years, it was projected that annual unit growth for A-B would be 8 to 10 percent. In order to obtain operating flexibility, A-B

EXHIBIT 9 *(continued)*

Consolidated Statement of Income—Anheuser-Busch Companies, Inc., and Subsidiaries

(In millions, except per share data) Year Ended December 31,	1992	1991	1990
Sales	$13,062.3	$12,634.2	$11,611.7
Less federal and state excise taxes	1,668.6	1,637.9	868.1
Net sales	11,393.7	10,996.3	10,743.6
Cost of products and services	7,309.1	7,148.7	7,093.5
Gross profit	4,084.6	3,847.6	3,650.1
Marketing, distribution and administrative expenses	2,308.9	2,126.1	2,051.1
Operating income	1,775.7	1,721.5	1,599.0
Other income and expenses:			
Interest expense	(199.6)	(238.5)	(283.0)
Interest capitalized	47.7	46.5	54.6
Interest income	7.1	9.2	7.0
Other income/(expense), net	(15.7)	(18.1)	(25.5)
Income before income taxes	1,615.2	1,520.6	1,352.1
Provision for income taxes:			
Current	561.9	479.1	429.9
Deferred	59.1	101.7	79.8
	621.0	580.8	509.7
Net income, before cumulative effect of accounting changes	994.2	939.8	842.4
Cumulative effect of changes in the method of accounting for postretirement benefits (FAS 106) and income taxes (FAS 109), net of tax benefit of $186.4 million	(76.7)	–	–
Net Income	$ 917.5	$ 939.8	$ 842.4
Primary Earnings per Share:			
Net income, before cumulative effect	$ 3.48	$ 3.26	$ 2.96
Cumulative effect of accounting changes	(.26)	–	–
Net income	$ 3.22	$ 3.26	$ 2.96
Fully Diluted Earnings per Share:			
Net income, before cumulative effect	$ 3.46	$ 3.25	$ 2.95
Cumulative effect of accounting changes	(.26)	–	–
Net income	$ 3.20	$ 3.25	$ 2.95

Note: During 1992 the company elected to early adopt the new Financial Accounting Standards pertaining to Postretirement Benefits (FAS 106) and Income Taxes (FAS 109). This decision affects the comparability of 1992 reported results with those of prior years. Management believes that readers of the company's financial statements need to be fully aware of the impact the adoption of these Standards has on 1992 operating results and earnings per share. Excluding the financial impact of these Standards, 1992 operating income, income before income taxes, net income and fully diluted earnings per share would have been $1,830.8 million, $1,676.0 million, $1,029.2 million and $3.58, respectively.

EXHIBIT 10

Financial Summary—Operations, Anheuser-Busch Companies, Inc., and Subsidiaries

(In millions, except per share data)	1992	1991	1990
Consolidated Summary of Operations			
Barrels sold	86.8	86.0	86.5
Sales	$13,062.3	$12,634.2	$11,611.7
Federal and state excise taxes	1,668.6	1,637.9	868.1
Net sales	11,393.7	10,996.3	10,743.6
Cost of products and services	7,309.1	7,148.7	7,093.5
Gross profit	4,084.6	3,847.6	3,650.1
Marketing, distribution and administrative expenses	2,308.9	2,126.1	2,051.1
Operating income	1,775.7(1)	1,721.5	1,599.0
Interest expense	(199.6)	(238.5)	(283.0)
Interest capitalized	47.7	46.5	54.6
Interest income	7.1	9.2	7.0
Other income/(expense), net	(15.7)	(18.1)	(25.5)
Gain on sale of Lafayette plant	–	–	–
Income before income taxes	1,615.2(1)	1,520.6	1,352.1
Income taxes	621.0	580.8	509.7
Net income, before cumulative effect of accounting changes	994.2(1)	939.8	842.4
Cumulative effect of changes in the method of accounting for postretirement benefits (FAS 106) and income taxes (FAS 109), net of tax benefit of $186.4 million	(76.7)	–	–
Net Income	$ 917.5	$ 939.8	$ 842.4

Source: Annual Report of the Company.

had also employed vertical integration. Many of the processes involved in the manufacturing of beer were carried on in-house at the A-B facilities. These included barley malting, metalized paper printing, and can manufacturing. Although A-B was putting considerable effort into expansion, other brewers were attempting to increase their return on investment by restricting capacity.

Expansion

In the 1970s, A-B was unsuccessful in its efforts to market root beer and a low-alcohol lemon-lime drink. As a result of these past failures, the company was moving into new areas more cautiously. Also, A-B had teamed up with partners for certain

ventures. It had moved into the rapidly expanding "wine on tap" business with a partner, LaMont Winery, Inc. In this business, A-B was marketing larger kegs that distributed white, red, and rosé wines under the Master Cellars brand name. A-B had also expanded through diversification into the snack food business. Its Eagle Snacks were being distributed nationwide through bars and convenience stores. The company's latest offering in the beer market was O'Doul's, a non-alcoholic beer. It was hoped that this brand would succeed well in the new, emerging non-alcoholic segment.

In planning the future expansion of A-B, August Busch III had several strategic alternatives to consider. These could be divided into two categories: those involving beer operations and those

EXHIBIT 10
(continued)

1989	1988	1987	1986	1985	1984	1983	1982
80.7	78.5	76.1	72.3	68.0	64.0	60.5	59.1
$10,283.6	$ 9,705.1	$ 9,110.4	$ 8,478.8	$ 7,756.7	$ 7,218.8	$ 6,714.7	$ 5,251.2
802.3	781.0	760.7	724.5	683.0	657.0	624.3	609.1
9,481.3	8,924.1	8,349.7	7,754.3	7,073.7	6,561.8	6,090.4	4,642.1
6,275.8	5,825.5	5,374.3	5,026.5	4,729.8	4,464.6	4,161.0	3,384.3
3,205.5	3,098.6	2,975.4	2,727.8	2,343.9	2,097.2	1,929.4	1,257.8
1,876.8	1,834.5	1,826.8	1,709.8	1,498.2	1,338.5	1,226.4	758.8
1,328.7	1,264.1	1,148.6	1,018.0	845.7	758.7	703.0	499.0
(177.9)	(141.6)	(127.5)	(99.9)	(96.5)	(106.0)	(115.4)	(93.2)
51.5	44.2	40.3	33.2	37.2	46.8	32.9	41.2
12.6	9.8	12.8	9.6	21.3	22.8	12.5	17.0
11.8	(16.4)	(9.9)	(13.6)	(23.3)	(29.6)	(14.8)	(5.8)
–	–	–	–	–	–	–	20.4
1,226.7	1,160.1	1,064.3	947.3(2)	784.4	692.7	618.2	478.6
459.5	444.2	449.6	429.3	340.7	301.2	270.2	191.3
767.2	715.9	614.7	518.0(2)	443.7	391.5	348.0	287.3(3)
–	–	–	–	–	–	–	–
$ 767.2	$ 715.9	$ 614.7	$ 518.0(2)	$ 443.7	$ 391.5	$ 348.0	$ 287.3(3)

involving nonbeer operations. Within the beer operations category there were several possible alternatives for expansion, including the light beer segment, acquisitions, European markets, divestitures, the Eastern bloc, and the 3.2 beer segment. There was definitely opportunity for expansion through the light beer segment because it was estimated that the potential for market penetration was at least 40 percent and currently penetration was only 25 percent. It would also be possible for A-B to expand through the acquisition of smaller brewers. The disadvantage of A-B of acquiring smaller brewers would be that most of these brewers tended to concentrate on unique market segments that would be too small or uneconomical for A-B to serve. Therefore, these acquisitions might offer few advantages. However, it might prove nec-

essary to acquire some smaller brewers in order to stop them from banding together and establishing a third power in the industry.

Another way in which A-B could promote expansion was through European markets. It would be beneficial for A-B to explore and evaluate untapped European markets. The question mark in this alternative was whether A-B brands would be able to compete successfully against the heavier, fuller European brands. It could also prove beneficial to A-B to divest its Natural Light brand of beer, which had proved to be unsuccessful. In 1992 this brand was lowered in price when selling to supermarket accounts, since this was where consumers were extremely price sensitive. It appeared that the consumer was not attracted to A-B's idea of a "natural" beer as A-B had expected. There was potential for further expansion if A-B divested its Natural Light brand and used these brewing facilities for the production of Budweiser Light.

Another possible alternative for A-B was to put a vigorous effort into pursuing "Eastern" markets. It appeared that the Japanese were extremely attracted to products that project "Western" culture. The Japanese company that marketed Suntory whiskey was promoting the product in California to encourage its projection of a "Western" image so that it would be accepted in Japan. An aggressive marketing effort in this area of the world should promote the expansion of A-B. Expansion could also be promoted through pursuit of the 3.2 beer market segment. This variety of beer has half the alcohol, and thus half the calories, of regular beer. The only problem with pursuing this market segment was that it could affect the sales of light beer, which also has fewer calories than regular beer.

The other category of alternatives through which expansion could be achieved involved non-beer operations. The major questions concerning Eagle Snacks and their potential for expansion involved the growth of the snack food market, how the product could be differentiated, and whether or not the product could obtain a significant part of the retail business, considering Frito-Lay's market domination. A-B could potentially expand through growth in the snack food business.

The other area through which A-B could expand was wine and spirits. Exhibit 11 compares the 1992 consumption of various liquids, such as beer, wine, spirits, etc. A-B had already moved into the "wine on tap" business with a partner. There were a number of other possibilities in this area it could explore. One of these possibilities involved determining the feasibility of acquiring a winery and taking advantage of A-B's strengths in distribution and marketing. Another possibility involved

exploring the potential for developing a product to compete with "Club Cocktails," currently being marketed by Heublein, Inc. A-B has great potential for further expansion since its strengths allow it to diversify. It has many possibilities to consider for future expansion.

To sum up, the future outlook for A-B is good. Its facilities were operating at 98 percent of capacity, and the brewer was confident that it could maintain its dominance in the industry. August Busch III was not fazed by slowing beer consumption and was confident that A-B could achieve its objectives of increased market share and capacity. If the company continued its aggressive marketing strategy and capitalized upon its ability to diversify and expand in other areas, there appeared to be no reason why it would not achieve its objectives.

EXHIBIT 11
1992 Liquid Consumption in the U.S. (Gallons per Capita)

Soft drinks	40.1
Coffee	26.1
Beer	24.4
Milk	20.5
Tea	6.3
Powdered drinks	NA
Juices	6.6
Spirits	1.9
Wines	2.3
Bottled water	2.2
Water	46.1
Total	176.5

Source: Beverage Industry, May 14, 1993.

Lonetown Press

Lonetown Press was opened in January 1992 to provide a highly personalized contract printing service to artists and others devoted to hand-printed lithography as a fine art medium. Founded by Randy Folkman, a master printer with eight years of experience, the company was capitalized for about $30,000 of Randy's money, which was used for the purchase of a Griffen Press and printing materials and supplies. Lonetown was located about 40 miles north of New York City in Fairfield County of southwestern Connecticut.

Randy planned to operate as a one-man shop at least for the first year. As a master printer and occasional artist in his own right, he had worked at Redvale Press, a private printing studio, for the two years prior to founding Lonetown. Before that he was employed for two years at a studio, in New York City and for four years at a print shop in Houston, Texas. While in Texas he completed his hand printing apprenticeship under the supervision of a Tamarind-trained master printer.

Randy wanted to work primarily at his printing and was especially interested in working with up-and-coming artists. Over the long term he wanted Lonetown to become recognized as a quality, highly personalized shop. At the same time, Randy hoped to pay himself fairly and make some profits as well as learn more about how prints are distributed. Otherwise, he did not want to become overly involved in what he saw as the business or "financial" side of Lonetown.

With the founding of Lonetown Press, Randy realized he would need to determine what price to charge and how to quote prices. He contacted an accountant with whom he shared his background and knowledge of the business.

HAND-PRINTED LITHOGRAPHY

Artists are attracted to hand-printed lithography because of its mystique, the quantity of images that are produced, and the technical results the medium offers. Lithographs are created by drawing on a stone or plate with pencils, crayons, or other materials with which artists are familiar. With a variety of surfaces and materials available, the medium is versatile for artists who can easily visualize from the drawing the resulting prints or graphics, as they are called in the trade. The development of hand-printed lithography in the United States is described by Antreasian and Adams:

> Although the principles of lithography are in essence simple, the technical processes involved in the printing of fine lithographs are exceptionally complex. For this reason, artists wishing to make lithographs have, since the early years of the nineteenth century, worked in collaboration with master lithographic printers: Gericault with Hullmandel and Villain, Redon with Blanchard and Clot, Picasso and Braque with Mourlot and Desjobert.
>
> Any lithograph printed from a stone or plate conceived and executed by the artist is an original lithograph, whether it is printed by the artist himself or by a collaborating printer. Until late in the nineteenth century, lithographs were rarely signed in pencil, and individual impressions were seldom numbered. Since that time, however, it has become customary for artists to sign and number each impression, attesting in this way both to the authenticity of the print and to its quality. Often, prints made in a lithographic workshop also bear the printer's bindstamp or chop. Like the artist's signature, this mark attests to the quality of the work.
>
> Original lithographs are normally printed in limited editions, although the size of the edition may vary

This case was prepared by Professor Fred W. Kniffin of the University of Connecticut, with the assistance of Amy Erlanger, as a basis for class discussion rather than to illustrate either effective or ineffective handling of an administrative situation.

over a wide range. In the United States, artists' editions characteristically range from ten to one hundred; in Europe, editions of two hundred or more are not uncommon. The limiting of editions is due not so much to technical considerations as to intention. The artist may wish as a matter of principle to limit editions of his work, or he may wish to avoid an undue commitment of time or money to a single edition. . . .

By 1960, lithographic workshops had all but disappeared in this country. There were few master printers, and it was only with the greatest difficulty that an artist might engage himself in lithography. As a result, few of the major artists working in the United States made lithographs during the 1940s and 1950s.

In 1960, Tamarind Lithography Workshop was established in Los Angeles under a grant from the Ford Foundation for the primary purpose of providing a new stimulus to the art of the lithograph in the United States. Since 1960, a number of professional lithographic workshops have opened throughout the country, many of them staffed by artisans trained at Tamarind. The lithographic workshops maintained at art schools and university art departments have likewise increased in number and, under the influence of the Tamarind program, have greatly improved in quality. Now, in the United States as well as in Europe, the artist again finds it possible to work in collaboration with skilled printers, and in these circumstances American Lithography has enjoyed a notable renaissance.

While hand-printed graphics drawn by an artist were considered original art, they were priced lower than original canvasses and were therefore generally more affordable. With lower prices than canvasses, the sales of hand-printed lithographs held up well in periods of recession when sales of the total art market were predictably slower.

Prices for hand-printed lithographs varied from $30 to $10,000 for modern prints; older prints of old masters were even higher. An artist whose canvasses commanded $20,000 might sell his hand-printed graphics for $1,000 each. Typical prices for 22 × 30 inch prints ranged anywhere from $150 to $500 depending upon the artist, printer, and where the prints were purchased.

Consumers acquired prints from art galleries, publishing houses, and auctions and from other individuals such as dealers, interior decorators, artists, and printers. Corporate art buyers often purchased graphics for their headquarters and other executive office buildings.

The publisher of a print is anyone who pays for the printing costs of an edition. Publishers may be galleries or publishing houses, or individuals such as dealers, artists, or printers. When not the artist, the publisher pays the artist a flat fee and after paying the printing costs owns all the prints except those few retained by the printer and the artist.

In response to an inquiry from Lonetown's accountant, a master printer stated that in his experience graphics or print galleries operated on a 50 percent markup from their selling price to the consumer. Of the costs that galleries paid publishers for prints, he estimated that artists' fees accounted for 25 percent and printing costs another 25 percent with the balance going to publishers. On this basis, a print offered by a gallery to retail at $2,000 to the buyer entailed total printing costs of $250.

THE INDUSTRY AND LONETOWN PRESS

The hand-printed lithography business in the United States had perhaps a half dozen major print shops that generally did their own publishing. These major shops usually employed four or more printers, while the balance of the industry of 50 or so shops were one- or two-printer operations. There were probably fewer than sixty print shops in the U.S. accepting hand-printed lithography work in 1992. Recent price schedules of the Tamarind Institute and two printing companies are shown in Exhibits 1, 2, and 3.

For at least some of their business, most shops copublished. This involved a negotiation of charges in which the printer accepted some number of copies of the artist's edition in exchange for the printer's services. For example, Lonetown Press might retain 10 to 25 copies of a 50-print edition in lieu of the costs for printing services rendered. In this situation, the artist would not incur an outlay for printing and Lonetown would assume responsibility for selling the graphics to compensate for the printing.

EXHIBIT 1
Typical Prices for Lithographic Printing

Effective 1 January 1992
The total cost of an edition is the *base charge,* plus the *impression charge,* plus *surcharges* (if any), plus the *cost of paper.* Paper will be billed at the most recent price paid by Tamarind with an allowance for care and shipping. The dimensions of a lithograph (paper size) are also a factor in determination of price. Tamarind's prices for printing are established in four groups, according to dimensions, and show the *maximum size* allowed for that price category. Prices for lithographs larger than 30 by 40 inches will be estimated upon request.

Base Charges
The *base charges* (per edition) include the services of Tamarind's professional staff, all costs related to graining of stones or plates, lithographic materials used in making drawings, materials and papers used in proofing, such proofing as is reasonable and necessary to arrive at a *bon à tirer* impression, the printing of the first ten proofs and/or impressions (however they may be designated), curating services, tissues, and wrapping materials (packing for shipment, if desired, is billed separately).

	Size 15 by 22 in. 38 by 56 cm.	Size 19 by 25 in. 49 by 64 cm.	Size 22 by 30 in. 56 by 76 cm.	Size 30 by 40 in. 76 by 102 cm.
One color	$140.00	$200.00	$240.00	$ 340.00
Two colors	320.00	390.00	450.00	580.00
Three colors	450.00	530.00	600.00	750.00
Four colors	560.00	640.00	710.00	900.00
Five colors	660.00	740.00	820.00	1,050.00
Six colors	760.00	880.00	930.00	1,200.00

Impression Charges
The first ten proofs and/or impressions are included in the base charge; no charge is made for proofs and/or impressions rejected because of technical imperfections, or for proofs or impressions that become the property of the collaborating printers or of Tamarind. The following charges apply to all other impressions, however they may be designated:

	Size 15 by 22 in. 38 by 56 cm.	Size 19 by 25 in. 49 by 64 cm.	Size 22 by 30 in. 56 by 76 cm.	Size 30 by 40 in. 76 by 102 cm.
One color	$ 6.00	$ 7.00	$ 8.00	$10.00
Two colors	12.00	14.00	16.00	20.00
Three colors	18.00	21.00	24.00	30.00
Four colors	23.00	25.00	27.00	33.00
Five colors	27.00	29.00	31.00	36.00
Six colors	31.00	33.00	35.00	39.00

EXHIBIT 1 *(continued)*

Surcharges

Stone charges: Technical processes: At sizes below 22 by 30 there is no price differential for work on stone. Surcharges for stone begin at 22 by 30 inches ($40.00) and increase proportional to size; the surcharge for use of our largest stone (36 by 52 inches) is $165.00.

Blended inking: A surcharge will be added for use of blended or split inking. The charge is determined by the complexity of the blend; it will never be less than 10 percent and may be up to double the impression charge.

Curatorial services: When the design of a print requires special curatorial services (as examples, tearing to a template, cutting to irregular shapes, applying metallic leaf, etc.), surcharges will be added proportional to the time required.

Technical processes: Use of all standard lithographic drawing materials and processes is included in the base charge, including direct drawing on stones or plates or through transfer methods. For use of photographic processes and such special techniques as image reversal, printing on chine colle, etc., surcharges will be added proportional to the time required.

Examples

The cost of editions of 50 impressions of single-color lithographs at sizes 19 by 25 inches and 22 by 30 inches printed from stone on Rives BFK, would be calculated as follows:

	19 by 25 in.	22 by 30 in.
Base charge	$200.00	$240.00
Surcharge for stone	0	40.00
Impression charge (50%*)	350.00*	400.00*
Paper charges	50.00	50.00
Total:	$600.00	$730.00

*This figure may be adjusted depending upon the number of trial and/or color trial proofs.

Abandoned Projects

On occasion, an artist reaches a decision to abandon a project without printing an edition. In that event, Tamarind will refund a portion of the base charges, as follows:

1. If the project is abandoned prior to processing and proofing of the plates and/or stones, Tamarind's total charge will be the sum of $100.00, plus any surcharges for stone, plus $25 for each metal plate (or small stone) used. The remainder will be refunded or applied to another project.

2. If the project is abandoned during or at the end of a first proofing session (a session in which all of the printing elements are proofed, one upon another), Tamarind's total charge will be the sum of the surcharges for stone, and 75 percent of the base charge. The remainder will be refunded or applied to another project.

3. If a project is abandoned at any point beyond the end of the first proofing session (as defined above), the full base charge will be paid.

PAYMENT OF ONE-HALF THE TOTAL ESTIMATED CHARGES
IS DUE BEFORE WORK IS BEGUN.
THE BALANCE IS DUE UPON DELIVERY OF THE EDITION.

EXHIBIT 2
Vermont Graphics, Inc.*

Price List
September 1990
Proofing Charges (price including all materials)

Colors/Runs	15 × 22	22 × 30	29 × 41
One	$ 78.25	$ 117.20	$ 156.25
Two	148.50	219.00	281.25
Three	219.00	320.25	406.25
Four	289.00	422.00	531.25
Five	359.00	535.50	656.25
Six	516.00	750.00	937.50
Seven	600.00	872.00	1,087.50
Eight	684.50	828.00	1,237.50
Nine	768.75	1,015.65	1,387.50
Ten	853.00	1,237.50	1,537.50

Printing Charges per Impression

Colors/Runs	15 × 22	22 × 30	29 × 41
One	$ 7.75	$ 10.25	$ 13.30
Two	14.50	18.50	23.70
Three	21.00	27.00	34.30
Four	27.75	35.50	44.80
Five	34.50	52.75	55.30
Six	49.00	62.70	79.00
Seven	57.00	72.75	91.50
Eight	65.18	82.80	103.25
Nine	73.20	93.00	116.75
Ten	81.00	103.00	129.50

*Disguised name.

EXHIBIT 3
Oklahoma Print Shop*

Price List
For 22" x 30" Size
50 Prints
June 1992
Proofing Charges

Colors/Runs	
One	$120.00
Two	170.00
Three	235.00
Four	285.00
Five	350.00
Six	420.00
Seven	495.00
Eight	575.00
Nine	665.00
Ten	735.00

Printing Charges per Impression

Colors/Runs	
One	$ 7.20
Two	10.80
Three	16.80
Four	21.60
Five	25.20
Six	28.80
Seven	32.40
Eight	36.00
Nine	39.60
Ten	43.20

A variation on co-publishing occurred when printers gave discounts in exchange for a part of the edition. These types of agreements were believed to be particularly appealing to up-and-coming artists to whom Randy wished to cater.

Lonetown's accountant had developed estimates of both annual and per job costs for the shop, since she was thinking of adding a markup to labor and/or material costs as the basis for creating a price schedule. Randy, however, was somewhat skeptical of this approach because he had concerns about pricing too high or too low in relation to competition. He wanted to price high enough to be taken seriously, but low enough to attract initial business. The accountant figured business expenses would run $11,000 annually, not including Randy's salary needs of $30,000 per year.

Lonetown Press Annual Expenses

Public relations (personal entertainment)	$ 3,000
Advertising	2,000
Travel expenses	2,000
Depreciation	1,300
Lawyer & accountant fees	1,000
Insurance, electricity, heat	1,000
Property taxes	700
Total	$11,000

In addition to the master printer's labor hours, cost estimates that could be directly traced to each job were:

5-Color—50 Print Edition

Item	Cost
Standard paper	$ 175
Ink	10
Printing plates	95
Various chemicals	20
Total costs per job	$ 300

The most comfortable edition size for Lonetown Press was 50 prints; and editions over 200 prints were definitely less desirable. With editions of 150 and over, the master printer in a one-person shop often encountered some tedium, which could adversely affect the quality of his work.

At Lonetown, the largest acceptable print was 30 × 40 inches since this was the maximum size that the Griffen Press could accommodate. Smaller paper sizes presented no problems.

Although four to five colors appealed most to Randy, the number of colors in a print was not of great importance. However, since each color in a print must be printed separately, printing additional colors required additional printing time.

A typical or average job for Lonetown might be a 5-color 22″ × 30″ edition of 50 prints. Randy felt that he could produce 25 such editions per year, or about one such edition every two weeks. Working at this rate would leave him barely sufficient time left over to consult with artists and galleries and do his bookkeeping and purchasing.

Randy felt confident about the long-term success of Lonetown; however, his immediate concern was quoting prices on several pending inquiries. He had decided that his price schedule should have separate prices for proofing and printing, prices for three sizes (18″ × 24″, 22″ × 30″, 30″ × 40″) and prices for one to ten colors. In addition, he wanted his price schedule to in some way reflect his preference for printing smaller editions.

Springboard Software, Inc.

Springboard produces and markets high quality, high value software products to satisfy the educational and productivity needs of consumers and students in the home and educational marketplaces.

The company has traditionally produced and continues to produce educational products characterized as aids to help children learn specific curriculums. We are now emphasizing, however, products which help people access data, organize data, understand data and make wonderful, effective presentations of data.

These remarks, made by John Paulson, Chairman and Chief Executive Officer of Springboard Software, Inc., in January 1986, summarized his company's primary activities. Springboard had undergone many changes since its founding over three years earlier, as had the industry as a whole. The company had produced several educational products that had been or were currently on the industry's best-seller lists. Substantial growth did not begin for the company, however, until the February 1985 release of THE NEWSROOM, software that made possible the creation of a small newspaper with a personal computer. The success of this product dramatically expanded the options available to Springboard's management. The most intriguing choice facing John Paulson and Springboard Software early in January 1986 was whether to enter the business segment and, if so, how.

COMPANY BACKGROUND

Springboard Software, Inc. (formerly Counterpoint Software, Inc.) was engaged in the business of developing, marketing, and selling high-quality educational and productivity software products for the home and school marketplaces. Prior to founding the company, John Paulson had been a music teacher in the Wayzata Public School system. Paulson taught himself computer programming while still a teacher. His first computer program was written for his own children and was designed to help them learn basic skills through a series of nine activities. Paulson was careful to design the product so that it would not frustrate children, but would give them a feeling of satisfaction and accomplishment:

> Young children are seldom in control of anything. A well designed software program, however, can put them in charge of their computer activities. This helps them develop confidence in themselves and their ability to participate in the world.

The user interface and sound pedagogical principles of this first program made it very effective and popular with children. Paulson decided to market it under the name EARLY GAMES FOR YOUNG CHILDREN and assigned it a retail price of $29.95. His first customer was Dayton's, Minneapolis' largest department store. Although the product was not professionally packaged, Dayton's made an initial purchase of twelve units. Sales to consumers were brisk and Dayton's began a cycle of reordering.

Encouraged by similar experiences with other retail stores, Paulson decided to quit teaching, seek funding, and start an educational software company. The company was incorporated on August 24, 1982, with an initial capitalization of $40,000. Using a color photo of his daughter on the front, Paulson repackaged EARLY GAMES, hired two telephone salesmen, and got a list of all the registered Apple

This case was prepared by Professor Natalie Tabb Taylor, Babson College, as a basis for classroom discussion rather than to illustrate either effective or ineffective handling of a managerial situation. It is reproduced here by permission of the North American Case Research Association.

dealers in America. In September 1982 he mailed free sample products to every Apple dealer and had the salesmen follow up with telephone calls a few days later. Even though initial orders were small—between one and ten units—the company began shipping product in October. By December, EARLY GAMES was the number-two Apple educational software product in the country. The company broke even in 1982 with sales of $87,000.

In 1983, Springboard added IBM, Atari, Tandy, and Commodore versions of EARLY GAMES to its product line. Four new titles with translations for various machine formats were also added. New packaging was developed and the company began a small advertising campaign. Sales for this first full year in operation reached $750,000.

In August of 1983, Cherry Tree Ventures, a Minneapolis venture firm, invested approximately $250,000 in Springboard to help it with cash flow problems and to position it for additional venture capital investments in 1984. At this time, the company's board of directors decided to hire a professional, experienced manager to function as CEO so that Paulson could focus his efforts on product development. An executive search was undertaken and an individual with a strong marketing background was found who became CEO in 1984.

The results of 1984 were not good, however. The company focused its efforts on developing relationships with the mass merchants at the expense of its established channels of distribution, the computer specialty stores. As part of this plan, a considerable amount of money was spent on advertising, packaging, and promoting the growing Springboard line of products to consumers. These expenditures were funded by an additional $2 million of venture capital. Even though five new programs were added to the company's product line in 1984, Springboard lost $1.6 million on roughly $1 million in sales. The company began to experience severe problems with cash flow.

In February of 1985, Paulson's product development team released THE NEWSROOM. It was an immediate and unqualified success, even though it was launched without a single consumer ad or any promotion. Shortly thereafter, John Paulson resumed his position as Chief Executive Officer.

INDUSTRY AND COMPETITION

The microcomputer software industry had experienced dramatic growth in its less than ten years in existence. However, during 1985, the rate of growth slowed. Software sales tended to track the activity of related hardware. Personal computer hardware sales had been in a slump throughout 1985. Industry experts attributed the slowdown to a number of factors, including:

- A glut in hardware suppliers and products.
- Saturation in the business and home market segments.
- Potential buyers waiting for new generations of machines.
- The need for new applications software.

The market for micro software was subject to rapid changes in technology. In order to succeed, a firm had to be able to create innovative new products reflecting technological changes in hardware and software as well as customer needs and to translate current products into newly accepted hardware formats in order to gain and maintain market share. By 1986, the supply of software products exceeded demand. Retail shelf space was limited; hence, competition intensified as increased emphasis was placed on price concessions, brand recognition, advertising, and dealer merchandising.

Rapid sales growth attracted a number of different players into the software industry. Hardware manufacturers such as IBM, Apple, Commodore, and Atari had integrated backward into software development. As hardware prices decreased and equipment became increasingly indistinguishable to consumers, software was becoming the primary means of adding value. Apple, for example, bundled a word processing program and graphics program with every Macintosh it sold. Software helped manufacturers differentiate their hardware from competitors' offerings.

Certain companies whose primary activities were in other industries had diversified into the software industry as well. Book publishers, for example, had entered the education market in order to capitalize on their established contacts and channels of distribution.

A separate group of companies competed in software only and were referred to as independents or third-party software houses. Independent software companies tended to be privately held and functioned either as developers or publishers. Developers wrote programs that they licensed to publishers. Most publishers licensed programs and provided whatever expertise and resources were required to bring programs to market. Few were involved in both development and publishing. Most began as publishers, but increased competition forced them into development only or else drove them out of business altogether. The industry was currently undergoing a shakeout. Management believed more casualties would occur in the near future, creating potential opportunities for the surviving publishers.

While there were approximately 3,500 companies competing in the software industry, Springboard had roughly fifty direct competitors in the home and school market. No single company competed directly with Springboard's product line on a title-by-title basis. Sales figures for competitors were difficult to get, since the majority of these companies were privately owned. Competitor profiles, prepared by Springboard personnel, can be found in Appendix A. Additional information about the industry can be found in the report, Microcomputer Applications Software Industry—1986.[1]

PRODUCTS

In the first two years of its history, Springboard produced educational products for children. By 1986, the emphasis had shifted to products designed to help people of all ages become more productive in their lives at home and at school.

The cornerstone of Springboard's product development philosophy was product usefulness. As John Paulson explained:

Many of our competitors have entered this marketplace with a callous disregard for the consumer's wants and needs. They have often underestimated both the intelligence of the consumer and the importance of the technology. Humans are tool users, after all, and the computer is the most important, versatile tool ever created. To market products which exploit consumers' naiveté and superficial curiosity is counterproductive indeed. The quick sale may be made, but eventually the consumer will realize that money has been spent on something that is not useful. It will be some time before that consumer considers buying software again.

Furthermore, the growth of computer penetration is slowed considerably by those who market poorly conceptualized software that does not represent a real value to the consumer. When a potential computer buyer investigates the available software, he or she is often reassured that there is no persuasive reason to own a computer. It may be months, even years before that consumer bothers to investigate a computer purchase again. And when the consumer does return to the computer store, the first question will still be "Why do I need a computer?" It is up to the software developers and marketers to provide compelling reasons.

That is why each and every product Springboard produces is, first and foremost, very useful. Each product takes advantage of the computer's unique capabilities to help people do things they want to do in ways more efficient, more effective and more satisfying than they could possibly do without the computer. Every Springboard program provides an excellent reason for having a computer.

By year end 1985, Springboard had a total of thirteen program titles, most of which were available in different machine formats. Exhibit 1 provides information about Springboard's product line. Three of the titles listed were about to be discontinued because they did not represent the level of sophistication exhibited by the other products in terms of concept, design, or execution.

---

[1] *Case Research Journal*, Spring 1988, p. 25.

EXHIBIT 1
Springboard Product Series and Titles as of November 1985

Series/Titles	Date of Introduction	Suggested Age Group	Suggested Retail
Early Games Series			
Early Games for Young Children	Sept. 1982	2½–6	$34.95
Stickers	March 1984	4–12	$34.95
Easy as ABC	June 1984	3–6	$39.95
*Music Maestro	May 1983	4–10	$34.95
*Make a Match	Sept. 1983	2½–6	$29.95
Skill Builders Series			
Piece of Cake Math	Sept. 1983	7–13	$34.95
Fraction Factory	Sept. 1983	8–14	$29.95
Creative Path Series			
Rainbow Painter	June 1984	4 and up	$34.95
The Newsroom	Feb. 1985		$59.95
Clip Art Collection, Vol. I	June 1985		$29.95
Puzzle Master	Sept. 1984	4 and up	$34.95
Mask Parade	Sept. 1984	4–12	$39.95
Family Series			
*Quizagon	June 1984	Teens and adults	$44.95

Source: Company.
*Soon to be discontinued.

By September 1985, THE NEWSROOM had become the best-selling home computer program in the U.S., according to the Softsel Hot List, the industry's guide to best-selling software programs at the wholesale level. In October, this program tied for places nine through fourteen at 2 percent in terms of unit market share of leading titles, regardless of category, as shown in the third graph in Exhibit 2. By 1985 year end, THE NEWSROOM and related programs accounted for roughly three-quarters of Springboard's unit sales.

The second-largest contributor to sales was EARLY GAMES FOR YOUNG CHILDREN, Paulson's first program. Sold primarily into the home market for use by preschoolers, EARLY GAMES had been identified in 1985 by the *Wall Street Journal* as the nation's fourth best seller in microcomputer educational software.

The company stood behind every title it sold with a guarantee that was rarely found in the industry: If a consumer was not satisfied for any reason, the product could be returned directly to Springboard for a full refund. To date, returns totaled less than 1 percent of sales.

CUSTOMER MARKETS

Roughly 75 percent of Springboard's sales were made to the home market, primarily through computer specialty stores. Most of the remainder were to schools, either through educational distributors or local retail outlets. Approximately 5 percent of sales were through exclusive distribution agreements in different countries of the world.

During 1985, management determined that Springboard did not have the resources to effectively penetrate the education market. As a result, the company entered into a licensing agreement with Scholastic Software, Inc. to distribute a special school edition of THE NEWSROOM in the U.S. and

EXHIBIT 2
Springboard Software, Inc.
October 1985 Market Share by Publisher and by Title

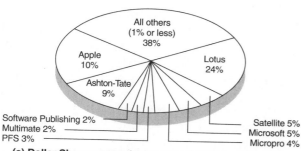

(a) Dollar Share among the Leading Publishers—October
(9 publishers with shares higher than one percent)

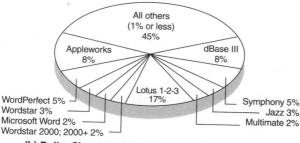

(b) Dollar Share among the Leading Titles—October
(10 titles with shares higher than one percent)

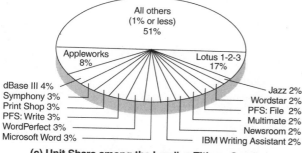

(c) Unit Share among the Leading Titles—October
(14 titles with shares higher than one percent)

Canada. Under this arrangement, Scholastic would produce a school package containing a teacher's guide and backup disks, capabilities that Springboard did not possess. Packaged in a Scholastic box, the title of the program and the name Springboard would be prominently displayed. Scholastic would sell the school edition for $75.

Scholastic had an excellent reputation in the industry. Other noted companies had entered into similar arrangements with them. Intentional Educations, for instance, had licensed a Scholasticized version of its hit program BANK STREET WRITER. Additionally, Scholastic had a large direct sales force that was already selling a variety of products to schools.

A potential drawback to this arrangement was that Springboard could not prevent Scholastic from selling the school edition to their educational distributors. Those distributors might eventually sell the school edition to retailers, where it would compete with Springboard's consumer version of THE NEWSROOM. Management felt that this represented a minor threat.

PRODUCT DEVELOPMENT

Springboard was unusual in the industry in that it developed its products in-house. Management believed that internal development facilitated control of product quality, expense, and schedule. The firm's recent experience with translations for THE NEWSROOM had brought this point home clearly. When demand developed for an IBM version of the program, the translation had to be subcontracted because Springboard had no IBM programmers. Commissioned in February for March delivery, the translation was not completed until late July. Bringing this translation to market had taken much longer and had cost much more than anticipated.

This experience coupled with the rapid growth in the IBM PC's installed base, shown in Exhibit 3, prompted management to augment its in-house programming staff with a team of IBM programmers. Management continued to explore outside sources for certain new products in order to:

1. Expand its product line more rapidly.
2. Reduce product development risk.
3. Encourage cross-fertilization of ideas.

EXHIBIT 3
Springboard Software, Inc.
Home and Personal Computer Year-end
Installed Base, 1982–1984 (000 Units)

	1982	1982	1984
Apple II/IIe/IIc	500	900	2,000
Apple Macintosh	—	—	265
IBM PC/XT/AT	700	1,300	2,200
IBM PCjr	—	275	175
Commodore 64	1,100	1,500	3,100
Commodore 128	—	—	—
All others*	800	1,200	2,700
Total	3,100	5,175	10,540

Source: Marketing Technology, January 1985.
*Includes Radio Shack TRS 80, Tandy 1000/1200/2000, Atari.

4. Develop specific expertise within certain organizations.

Springboard was also unusual in the industry in that it had proprietary code that allowed for the electronic transfer of graphics between incompatible IBM, Apple II, Macintosh, and Commodore computers. Since educational products tended to be graphics oriented, this capability dramatically reduced the resources required to translate programs from one machine to another. As Paulson explained:

> Springboard has this unusual capability because it has an extraordinarily skilled and dedicated product development team. State-of-the-art programmers are supported by a staff of experienced computer artists and child development specialists. The programmers have displayed a remarkable ability to adapt to different machines as required by the marketplace.

All Springboard products were written in assembly code. Although use of higher-level languages reduced product development time, Springboard products tended to require assembly code in order to maximize the limited capabilities of popular computers. A program as advanced as THE NEWSROOM, for instance, could not be developed for the 64K Apple II computer in Pascal, C, Forth, or any other compiled language. While use of assembly language increased product development time, it also made it more difficult for competitors to imitate Springboard's programs.

Another characteristic of the code developed for Springboard products was its evolutionary nature. Each product under development presented programming challenges that, when solved, provided a stepping stone to the next product. The programmers had methodically developed a library of software tools that could easily be adapted to specific program needs, thereby reducing product development time for future products. As a result, Springboard's existing product line represented a progression in programming capabilities that was marked by what was referred to internally as *generations*. In addition, current programs provided revenues to help fund programs under development.

In program development, Paulson placed top priority on developing families of products with the same relationship as a razor to razor blades:

> THE NEWSROOM, for example, is a powerful graphics/text presentation program that comes with over 600 wonderful, useful pieces of clip art. The number 600 is an interesting one in that it represents a real value to the consumer. Yet, after using THE NEWSROOM for a while, the consumer realized that this amount of clip art has only whetted his or her appetite. That's why we are developing the CLIP ART COLLECTION. To date, we have released CLIP ART COLLECTION VOLUME I and are thinking about releasing a VOLUME II featuring business clip art. VOLUME I sells very well, second only to THE NEWSROOM.
>
> Our ability to transfer graphics between incompatible computers electronically makes our razor blades very attractive. Once the art has been created, it takes only hours to make it available on all machine formats. Furthermore, as we continue to market high quality applications programs which use clip art, a larger and larger installed base of users will be purchasing the CLIP ART COLLECTION.

Springboard created products for proven hardware only. New computer brands and models had to establish a significant user base before management would allocate resources to support them.

PRODUCTION

Springboard subcontracted disk duplication and product packaging. The company currently had several suppliers. Management preferred to pay a slight premium for duplication and packaging in order to work with local suppliers.

Management had evaluated and expected to continue to evaluate the benefits of integrating backward into disk duplication. Disk duplication was not considered to be technically difficult, but experienced individuals were required to oversee this kind of operation. Bulk disks, for instance, required special handling. Duplication had to take place in a climate-controlled room, equipped with special air purifiers. Although prices were dropping, duplication equipment was still very expensive. Packaging was a separate operation, requiring specialized equipment, and tended to be labor intensive.

There appeared to be a trend toward in-house duplication among the larger software companies. Most of Springboard's direct competitors, however, did not perform their own disk duplication. Springboard's management felt that the economies of scale were not yet available to make backward integration superior to present supplier arrangements.

The company leased approximately 5,000 square feet of office space in a Minneapolis suburb for an annual rental of approximately $96,000. The lease was to expire in 1988. The company's executive, marketing, product development, and operations were located at these facilities.

MARKETING AND DISTRIBUTION

A key conclusion of the early 1984 business plan was that Springboard should shift emphasis to the mass volume retailer (MVR) channel of distribution. As a result, a mass marketing strategy was developed. This strategy was fashioned after Spinnaker Software's, the industry's fastest growing educational software company at the time. Spinnaker was the first company to apply sophisticated consumer marketing techniques in selling micro software. This approach bought them a considerable amount of shelf space in such major U.S. MVR's as Sears, Kmart, and Toys "R" Us.

As a result of adopting a similar strategy, Springboard began to neglect its traditional distributor and computer specialty store channels of distribution. An example of this neglect was the manner in which the company changed its name from Counterpoint to Springboard. Communication with retailers was not effective enough to be able to make the connection between the two names. Retailers mistakenly thought Counterpoint had gone out of business. Springboard was simply a new company they had never heard of. The result was a dramatic decrease in shelf space for Springboard's existing products and minimal access for its new products.

Financial results for 1984 did not meet expectations. Gross sales of well over $3 million were forecast for the year; actual sales barely reached $1 million. Paulson believed the shortfall was created primarily by the unwise and unsuccessful shift to the MVR channel of distribution as well as callous handling of existing accounts and ineffective use of resources. Springboard had considerably less distribution in the fourth quarter (the peak season) of 1984 than it had enjoyed in 1983.

Springboard's disappointing performance was masked somewhat by the problems suffered by the industry as a whole. Research firms had predicted a 100 percent increase in 1984 educational software sales whereas only 60 percent growth actually occurred. Spinnaker, for example, posted $15 million in sales, a fraction of the $50+ million its management had projected for the year. As a result, the ability of mass merchants to sell software and the effectiveness of large ad budgets and mass marketing techniques in general became topics of debate in the industry.

When Paulson took over again as CEO in 1985, he steered the company back to its original distribution channels. The computer specialty store, which purchased from the company's wholesale distributor customers, was once again the focus of

Springboard's marketing and sales team efforts. Paulson had not ruled out the Spinnaker strategy entirely, however. As he explained:

> At this time, the big dollar marketing approach to consumer software is not leading to success. It can achieve moderate sales levels, but only at the sacrifice of profitability. Word of mouth from an army of satisfied customers is far more effective than a large ad budget. This may change in the future, however. It is important that we continue to evaluate just exactly what marketing techniques are effective and how much capital they require.

The company continued to support its dominant mode of distribution, wholesale distributors, as it attempted to expand into large chains of computer specialty stores. Management was cautiously testing distribution through certain MVRs as well as new forms of distribution such as electronic distribution and direct marketing. Springboard's international distribution strategy was to expand through the use of agents and licensing agreements. The company's top four customers accounted for 18 percent, 15 percent, 14 percent and 12 percent respectively of total gross sales volume during 1985.

FINANCE

Springboard had net sales of $889,750 and a $1.6 million net loss in 1984, the most recent year for which information was available. Unaudited financial results for the first nine months of fiscal 1985 indicated that the company was profitable on $3.1 million in net sales. See Exhibits 4 and 5 for historical and recent financial information for the company. While final results were not yet in, year-end 1985 sales were expected to approach the six million dollar mark.

Springboard made a small public offering in Minnesota in 1983, which was exempt from SEC requirements for public financial reporting under Regulation A because of its small size and the limited number of shares sold. Roughly 8 percent of the 1.6 million shares currently outstanding were traded publicly through a second-tier Minneapolis broker who made a market in the stock. Shares had traded in the $2 to $3 range over the last year. As of January 1986, the company's major shareholders with their respective holdings were as follows:

Cherry Tree Venture Capital	30%
Former Chairman and CEO	15%
V. Suarez, private investor	10%
John Paulson	4%

The company currently had a $1.0 million total credit line, composed of a $150,000 term loan on fixed assets and a $850,000 formula-based working capital loan. Springboard had paid no dividends to date.

ORGANIZATIONAL STRUCTURE AND MANAGEMENT PHILOSOPHY

During 1985, three full-time employees were added to the company—two for the newly created Customer Support group and one for the Marketing Department. By January 1986, Springboard had 24 employees in total as shown in Exhibit 6. Contractors were hired to augment certain capabilities in advertising, public relations, and production. Although the company had experienced a lot of change in its short history, Paulson felt confident about the personnel and Springboard's outlook:

> The most important, wonderful asset of Springboard is the people. The management team is experienced, competent and dedicated. This is critical since Springboard is in a constant state of change. The growth rate of the company and of the industry in general requires that management respond appropriately to a variety of problems and opportunities.
>
> All of the employees are capable and share a common commitment. It is not unusual to hear people talking at lunch about ways they can improve efficiency or solve a problem. They know they can freely discuss their feelings about what the company is doing and share their ideas and suggestions with management.
>
> It is my job to make certain that everyone understands and appreciates the importance of their unique roles within the company, how their responsibilities

EXHIBIT 4
Springboard Software, Inc.
Balance Sheet 1982–1984

	1984	1983	1982
Assets			
Current assets			
Cash and cash equivalents	$ 408,469	$ 73,206	$14,372
Accounts receivable, less allowance for doubtful accounts: 1984–$23,953; 1983–$10,000	354,455	273,252	35,561
Inventories	153,605	112,505	7,387
Prepaid expenses	74,882	1,286	478
Total current assets	991,411	460,249	54,798
Certificate of deposit	150,000	–	–
Property and equipment at cost	227,849	30,737	1,333
Less: accumulated depreciation	(39,635)	(4,904)	(45)
	188,214	25,833	1,288
Product rights	–	1,229	2,364
	$1,329,625	$487,311	$58,450
Liabilities and Shareholders' Equity			
Current liabilities			
Accounts payable	$ 221,293	$154,438	$ 1,048
Working capital bank loan	154,608	–	–
Current portion of long-term debt	37,500	–	–
Accrued liabilities			
Payroll and taxes withheld	12,857	31,162	9,762
Vacation pay	10,372	2,515	–
Other	56,230	2,423	–
Total current liabilities	493,220	190,538	10,810
Long-term debt less current portion	103,125	–	–
Total liabilities	596,345	190,538	10,810
Commitments			
Shareholders' equity			
Convertible preferred	83,737	14,000	–
Common stock	7,850	5,350	4,100
Additional paid-in capital	2,363,490	384,654	43,400
Retained earnings (deficit)	(1,721,797)	(107,231)	140
Total equity	733,280	296,773	47,640
	$1,329,625	$487,311	$58,450

Source: Company annual report.

EXHIBIT 5

Springboard Software, Inc.
Statement of Operations Years Ended December 31, 1984,
1983 and from August 24, 1982, through December 31, 1982

	1984	1983	1982
Gross revenue	$ 1,017,773	$ 766,100	$87,062
Less: sales returns*	128,123	42,452	–
Net revenue	889,650	723,648	87,062
Cost of sales	471,874	232,337	20,589
Gross profit*	417,874	491,311	66,473
Percent to net sales	47.0%	67.9%	76.4%
Operating Expenses			
Marketing	816,967	–	–
Sales	264,631	282,062	31,565
General and administrative	490,628	231,665	18,358
Research and development	411,967	92,290	16,645
Interest expense	35,473	–	–
Other	12,774	(7,335)	(235)
Total operating expenses	2,032,440	598,682	66,333
Net profit (loss) before income tax	(1,614,566)	(107,371)	140
Income tax expense	–	–	–
Net profit (loss)	$(1,614,566)	$(107,371)	$ 140
Net loss per common share	$ (2.92)	$ (.22)	$ .00
Weighted average common shares outstanding	552,077	493,333	400,833

1985 Press Release

Minneapolis, October 18, 1985—Springboard Software, Inc. announced net sales figures for the first three quarters of this year to be $3,066,000. Net sales for the same period last year were $501,000.

Unaudited financial results for the first nine months indicate the company is profitable.

Source: Company.

interrelate and how much the company values their participation. From the very beginning I have insisted that all employees participate in the company's Incentive Stock Option Plan. I want all of our goals and hopes to be harmonious. I will work hard to ensure that everyone who is contributing to our success will share fairly in its rewards.

Springboard is not, after all, a factory. It is not buildings or disks or cash flow. Our most important asset is our people. We depend upon them for the expertise, insight and creativity that success demands. And they deliver. They are determined to transform programs into best-selling products, problems into worthwhile opportunities, and Springboard into one of the most respected leaders of this fascinating industry.

FUTURE EXPANSION PLANS

By January 1986 although home and school remained Springboard's primary markets, management was considering creating business editions for certain titles. Paulson described the situation in this way:

EXHIBIT 6
Springboard Organizational Chart, January 1986

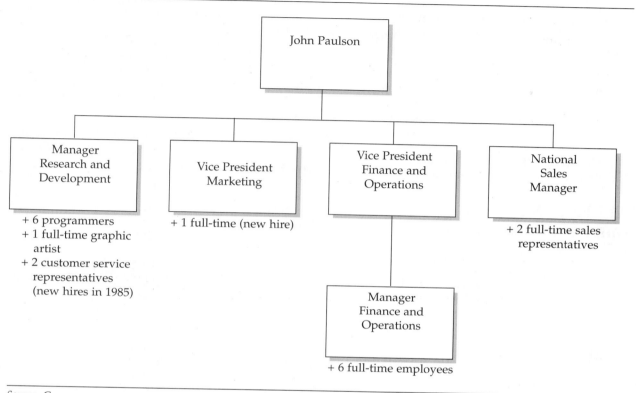

Source: Company.

Because productivity titles are more useful to a wide variety of people, they have the potential of being sold into the business marketplace. THE NEWSROOM, for instance, is the most popular program currently being sold in schools in America, as well as being a best-seller to the home market. We anticipated sales into each of these markets when we developed the program. The interest of the business world in THE NEWSROOM, however, came as a surprise. It has many capabilities business people want to have.

Paulson felt that sales of this program into the business market would be inhibited by the following factors:

1. The packaging featured a picture of a high school newspaper.

2. The clip art included was not business oriented.
3. The price point was too low to get the support of business retail outlets.
4. The program copy protection would be considered to be inconvenient.

This situation required careful consideration, however, for it was likely to be repeated with other productivity programs currently under development, which, when completed, would represent a new generation of Springboard products.

A separate issue to be addressed was the disappointing sales performance of some of the company's other programs, which Paulson perceived to be of superior quality to competitive offerings. In Paulson's words:

Although EARLY GAMES continues to sell well and THE NEWSROOM is a tremendous success, other titles are not reaching their sales potential. MASK PARADE, RAINBOW PAINTER, STICKERS and PUZZLE MASTER are all outstanding products but they do not sell as well as they should. EASY AS ABC, for instance, is often cited by dealers, teachers and parents as the best alphabet program on the market, but it is consistently outsold by competing products which are nowhere near as good. Increasing the sales of these particular titles is one of the important challenges facing Springboard management.

Our overall challenge is how to best use limited dollars to sell Springboard products. Is it possible to promote the company brand or is it safer to promote specific titles? How can management protect the strong growth of THE NEWSROOM and related products and still develop sales for the titles which are not achieving their potential? What is the best way to release the new products? What role does trade advertising play? How should it be balanced with consumer ads? What monies should be dedicated to promotions, point of purchase displays and other related tactics?

With these thoughts in mind, Paulson turned his attention to the 1986 report on the Microcomputer Applications Software Industry.

APPENDIX A

Springboard Software, Inc.: Competitor Profiling

Name	Spinnaker	Broderbind
Generic strategy	• Low-cost producer—branding • Breadth of line/access to shelf • 60 percent in mass retail—first on the scene • Price sensitive • Preemptive shelf space managers	• Focused on basic needs of less sophisticated users • 30% MVR (C64 version of Print Shop), 70% specialty
Strengths	• First mover/shelf control • Strong marketing management • Strong financing • Diverse line • Many offerings • Bid ad dollars = reviews • Continuity in marketplace • Slick marketers • Have executed a plan • Videotape concept supports MVR strength	• "Hot" products—item merchants • Product strategy = Apple hit to C64 • Royalty strategy (reduced royalty % of revenues from 33% to 28%) • Reduced administrative costs from 21% to 13%—Talent spotters • Probably attract free-lance authors • Not promotional or price oriented • International dealings, good connection with Japan and MSX • First mover in "genres"—"Good enough" product/user accessible • 20 percent tech ⟶ 80% need of consumer
Weaknesses	• Defective disks and programs • Lost First Software • MVR want hits, not full line • Dependent on MVR—working capital in channel (no controls) • Weak quality image, especially in schools • Dependent on C64 base • Inconsistent quality/appeal due to unrelated authors/sources—not highly thought of in traditional channels of distribution	• Marketing not POS • Milk products • Need items • Lack of franchise on names • Second-rate packaging • Apple is 60% of sales, IBM only 16%

Name	*Spinnaker*	*Broderbind*
General information		• 1984 sales of $11M, net income of $500K • Discount (55 percent); terms (30 days); freight (FOB headquarters; no coop; defective [return for replacement only]); stock bal (10 percent of purchases over last 120 days) • Policies set in stone, they do not bargain and are tough to work with • Sales management left 3/85; company run by finance people • Order fulfillment good but takes 3-4 weeks • Support distributors, do not sell direct • Produce home and personal productivity programs under $100 • Games account for 20 percent of sales • Planning product line based on hobbies and pursuits • Bought Synapse in 1984 for $450K, may be looking for others

Name	*Random House*	*CBS Software*
Generic strategy	• Differentiated • Educational (mostly), some productivity and entertainment • High price	• Differentiated • Entertainment, education
Strengths	• Strong financing • Great licenses: Peanuts, Garfield, Potato Head • Both in-house programming as well as external licensing • Eight new programs in 1984; expect 18 new titles in 1985 • Division for school market: internal sales staff and packaging • Sell Handleman two titles . . . is this a strength?	• Financial strength • Offers extremely good terms • Ability to market to the consumer (entertainment business) • Name recognition • @ 37 titles—breadth of line • Strong distribution (retail service reps—good or bad?) • Licensed famous characters like Big Bird • Ads in *Time, Newsweek, People* • Promotions: Buy Felony and get another title free plus $5 refund • Parent and associated companies
Weaknesses	• No major hits • Not currently selling Softsel • Heavy reliance on education (starting to do utilities/entertainment) • Me-too packaging • Me-too marketing • Weak in IBM format	• Trying to be all things to all people • Maybe too big, not in tune with pulse of the industry • Service • No big winners in product line • Small presence at CES—are they getting out of business? • Rumored to be losing money • High return rate, low satisfaction • MVR is 50% of business, schools 10% • Specialty stores declining (40%)

Name	Random House	CBS Software
General information	• Division formed in 1982 • Dominant format is Apple, some C64, weak in IBM PC	• Me-too packaging • Focus on C64 and Atari—changing to IBM, Apple • Licenses are costly • Main sales team has been fired • Planning ad shift towards schools • Changing to S.A.T. types and home productivity • Outside sales reps may start calling on large school districts

Name	Davidson and Associates	EPYX
Generic strategy	• Focused	• Differentiated • Entertainment and utility products
Strengths	• Focused on basic skills (utility) • All five products sell well (3 on charts) • Weak marketing works • Little known about them	• Profitable in April and May • Licenses: Barbie Dolls, G.I. Joe, Hotwheels, Olympics, etc. • Have been able to choose their distribution channels • Hot product (Fastload for C64)
Weaknesses	• Only five products • Original product is cash cow (3 yrs. old) • Questionable product development capability • Packaging/marketing *appears* weak	• Lost $500,000 in 1984 • Computer specialty stores generate only 40% of revenue • Mass merchants generate 60% • Heavy reliance on entertainment software (starting to do utilities) • Packaging (me-too) • Marketing (me-too) • Primarily C64 revenues (trying to change to Apple/IBM) • Probably pay heavy fees for licenses and royalties • Uphill battle to change image from entertainment to anything better
General information	• Founded 1982 • 1983 sales = $750,000 • 1984 sales = $2,500,000	• Founded in 1978 as Automated Simulations Inc. • Name change to EPYX in 1983 • Product philosophy, according to Bob Botch, marketing director, is to slow down new product intros because of slower growth rate of home computer market: • new products require more planning • increased support for products • used to sell entertainment but now concentrating on utility products • expanding line to include high-end machines • Used to intro 25 titles per year, now down to 10-15. They will only support the best-selling titles.

Name	Davidson and Associates	EPYX
		• Botch thinks Apple and IBM computers have more active users and longer life cycles • Most successful product is Fastload for C64 (retail of $30-$40): initially represented 50% of sales, now represents 15%. Thus they plan to release more hardware/software utilities as well as home productivity.

Name	Houghton Mifflin	Hayden
Generic strategy	• Focused • "The 150 year old software company" . . . selling as an old established school book publisher (American Heritage Dictionary & Iowa Test of Basic Skills)	• "Throw a lot of titles at the wall and see what sticks" (50+ titles in a wide range of software categories; education, business, entertainment, and productivity)
Strengths	• Well recognized and highly regarded by its market (schools) • Money • Solid and deep penetration of the school market • Good, consistent image in the product line . . . packaged by well-defined series • Reasonable and stable pricing (c. $39.95) • Established line of reps to schools • Relatively alone in an unusual niche . . . business education (DO MORE Series; instructional aids to PFS, Lotus & Multiplan)	• Diverse line going in the largest segments of the market (education, business, entertainment and productivity) • Strong representation in the MAC world with five bestsellers "out of the chute": Ensemble, I Know It's Here Somewhere, Hayden Speller (all MAC only, business and productivity bestsellers), Sargon III , and Music Works (MAC conversion from Apple) • 7 bestsellers in all of the categories mentioned: Ensemble, I Know It's Here Somewhere, Hayden Speller, Sargon III, Music Works, Score Improvement System (MAC), Holy Grail • Company name recognition • Established channel through reps to retailers
Weaknesses	• Limited distribution . . . almost 100% to schools through reps . . . SoftKat is an exclusive and their only access to the consumer market via retail . . . very weak distribution at the retail level • No bestsellers • Software such a nominal part of their business . . . may account for the relatively low profile in the industry and to the consumer • Depends entirely on outside sources for software development and conversion • Very limited promotional material . . . advertising restricted to school magazines • Drill and practice type software uninspired	• Rely almost entirely on reps • Lack of branding or consistent image throughout product line . . . confusing and weak packaging • Maybe cash poor (Consumer Electronics Show [CES] was financially hard on them and a "complete bust") • Dependent on outside for virtually all software development/conversion • Educational line is graphically dry and not at all their best performer . . . emphasizing the productivity and business software

Name	*Grolier Electronic Publishing, Inc.*

Generic strategy	• Differentiated . . . GEP's goal is to utilize electronic media to deliver information and educational programs in a timely, unique manner in ways that have never before been possible
	• Currently participates in several market niches:
	  • productivity (spreadsheets, database, graphs)
	  • interactive adult computer adventure programs
	  • educational (pre/elem levels) NEW 6-85

Strengths	• GEP is a subsidiary of Grolier, Inc. (the world's leading publisher of encyclopedias) • Good management team with emphasis in publishing and microcomputer software sales and marketing • Strong financial backing from parent company • Product line has 20 titles (Apple/IBM/Comm 64) • Retail pricing mostly $30-$40 range • Has comprehensive advertising plan to support sales • Introduced "Miss Mouse" and "Ryme Land" reading readiness software for kids (4-7) • Can leverage "Grolier" name and reputation for quality educational materials
Weaknesses	• GEP was started in 1982 . . . just entered the software field in 1984 • Majority of the programs were just released and many are scheduled for release in next few months • No products on the hit lists yet

ISG Technologies, Inc.

Mike Hopkinson, Director of North American Sales for ISG Technologies, Inc. (ISG) of Mississauga, Ontario, paced his office and considered what he should do about the deteriorating relationship between ISG and its North American distributor, Precision Medical Instruments Ltd. (Precision).[1] ISG was a Canadian company that sold medical imaging computers in North America and Europe; 1991 sales had been $11.4 million.

It was January 1992 and Hopkinson was furious after receiving a telephone message from Precision's sales manager telling Hopkinson that Precision had set a new sales record in December with orders for 40 magnetic resonance imaging systems. Although Hopkinson would have expected sales of 10 to 15 of ISG's add-on imaging computer systems with that many orders, Precision had sold only one. Most of ISG's U.S. sales were being made either through ISG's own efforts, or from a contract with Philips Medical Systems Nederland B.V. to supply a similar computer workstation product that was sold under the Philips brand name.

Despite recent overtures from Precision offering to rebuild the increasingly strained relationship with ISG and Precision's promises of better sales performance in the months ahead, Hopkinson felt that the time had come to consider other alternatives. He knew that any recommendation he made would be critically important to ISG since 90 percent of its sales were in the United States. Hopkinson had to make a decision soon because his recommendation could affect planned product launches and negotiations with other distributors in Europe and the Far East.

ISG'S PRODUCTS

Radiologists used Computed Tomography (CT or CAT) scanners and Magnetic Resonance Imaging (MRI or MR) scanners to examine the internal anatomy of patients. CT and MRI scanners were essentially x-ray machines capable of producing a cross-sectional image through a patient's anatomy. CT scanners were used to examine bony structures and MRI scanners were used to create similar images of soft tissues. MRI images were very effective in detecting cancer, such as brain tumors, that would otherwise be difficult, if not impossible, to detect.

Both of these imaging systems gave radiologists and surgeons a series of images, each a "slice" through the patient's anatomy. A single examination might yield as many as 150 individual "slices" through the relevant anatomy. The surgeons and radiologists then had to visualize a three-dimensional picture of the patient's anatomy based on these individual frames.

ISG designed products that took these individual images and combined them in a computer to build a two-dimensional or three-dimensional model of the anatomy. The surgeon or radiologist could then view the model on a computer screen, rotate it, remove portions of it, make it transparent, color-code tissue types, or perform a multitude of other manipulations. For example, a surgeon could examine the interior of someone's brain to locate a tumor, determine the tumor's exact position relative to other tissues, measure its volume, and plan a surgical approach. The hospital could realize

---

This case was based upon material developed by Kathryn Robertson and Joseph Lombardo and prepared by John O'Sullivan under the supervision of Professor C.B. Johnston for the sole purpose of providing material for class discussion at the Western Business School. Certain names and other identifying information may have been disguised to protect confidentiality. It is not intended to illustrate either effective or ineffective handling of a managerial situation.

[1] Disguised name.

significant time savings in the operating room because of less time taken in exploration. In the radiology department, these images were a great aid in diagnosis.

Allegro

The Allegro was ISG's primary product. It comprised a computer workstation and a software package for data processing and image manipulation. A radiologist transferred scanner data on computer tape to the Allegro where it was processed into a two-dimensional or three-dimensional model. A radiologist or surgeon could then manipulate the image on the workstation screen and then save it or print it out.

ISG modified off-the-shelf workstations[2] by adding proprietary graphics accelerators.[3] The Allegro was a stand-alone device that competed with several other similar products and with workstations sold by original equipment manufacturers (OEMs) with CT and MRI scanners. It had several advantages over both of these competing product groups. Unlike many other third-party workstations, the Allegro was compatible with several major scanners. Also, unlike most other third-party manufacturers, ISG was aggressive in upgrading the Allegro to avoid obsolescence as new ISG software or scanning capabilities became available. The Allegro had much more power and flexibility than workstations provided by manufacturers of scanning equipment. Additionally, while other manufacturers' workstations were being used for image manipulation, the scanner had, in some cases, to remain idle. Because the Allegro was not directly connected to the scanner, it decoupled image manipulation from the scan-

---

[2] A workstation is the industry term for a very fast microcomputer.

[3] Graphics accelerators were add-on circuit boards that greatly increased a computer's speed in processing complex graphics images. Such accelerators were widely used in Computer-Aided Design applications, for example.

ning process, allowing institutions to obtain greater capacity utilization from their expensive scanning equipment.

The Allegro was priced at $140,000 to $200,000 depending upon options requested. Despite being more expensive (competitive products were priced from $70,000 to $300,000) than most of its competitors, the Allegro sold well because radiologists considered it superior in terms of image quality. The Allegro had faster hardware and more sophisticated software that resulted in better, more usable images. Between the Allegro and Gyroview (see below) products, ISG held 45 percent of the independent medical imaging market in 1991. From early 1988 until December 1991, ISG had sold 106 Allegros and Mike Hopkinson was forecasting sales of 80 units in calendar 1992.

ISG was, at that time, developing several Allegro spin-off products called Plan View Stations. Surgeons and other specialists would use these workstations to view and further manipulate images previously processed by the Allegro. Because a Plan Station would not need to process scanner input, it would require less computing capacity and would be lower priced than the Allegro.

Gyroview

This product was similar to an Allegro workstation but sold under the Philips brand name as an add-on to Philips MRI scanners. Philips shipped its own workstations to ISG, who then installed graphics accelerators and software that had been developed exclusively for Philips, but functioned in a similar manner to the Allegro's software. ISG had recently finished a new software package that allowed the Gyroview to operate with Philips CT scanners as well. The agreement between Philips and ISG required that ISG ensure that the software used to run the Gyroview remained exclusive to the Philips product and that Philips would pay a fixed unit price. By December 1991, 141 Gyroview workstations had been sold, an average of one Gyroview for every two Philips MRI sales.

ISG's contract with Philips had expired in October 1991 and had been extended for successive one-month periods since. The parties were negotiating a new, more flexible contract during the winter of 1992. Because Philips provided the hardware, ISG charged a much lower price than it did to retail customers of the Allegro. The usual invoice price on a Gyroview unit was $46,000, which provided a 66 percent gross margin for ISG.

Viewing Wand

The Viewing Wand was an articulated arm that connected to a modified Allegro workstation. It had several joints and culminated in a thin metal probe about six inches long. When the patient's anatomy was displayed in an image on the screen, the surgeon could, during an operation, place the probe into an incision in the patient's head, for example, and an image of the probe would appear on the screen in the image of the interior structures of the patient's head. The image on the monitor could be rotated, sliced, sectioned, or manipulated in different ways. The surgeon was then able to know exactly where he or she was at that stage in relation to the interior structures of the brain, thus potentially reducing the size of the skull incision, the amount of collateral damage to sensitive brain tissue, and the total surgery time. Clinical trials had indicated that the average time spent establishing tumor location was reduced from hours to minutes with use of the Wand. This product represented the first successful attempt to bring computer-based real-time three-dimensional imaging into the operating room and was believed to have the potential to expand ISG's potential market dramatically.

Although it was still in clinical trials and awaiting regulatory approval in the U.S., the Wand had generated significant interest among neurosurgeons. ISG expected to expand its application to other medical specialties soon after introduction. The wand and its accompanying workstation were to be priced at around $200,000.

Other Products

ISG also marketed several other products. There was a series of add-on software packages designed for specific medical applications such as knee surgery. These products were collectively called Clinical Application Packages (CAP). ISG also licensed its basic software architecture to GE, who used it as a base for the software sold with GE workstations. ISG was hoping that this software architecture (called IAP) would become an industry standard and would generate significant license fees. ISG also gained revenue from service contracts and from providing hardware and software upgrades to existing customers. For the last six months of 1991, the breakdown of sales by product was: Allegro – 46%, Gyroview – 37%, Viewing Wand – 4%, CAP – 4%, Upgrades – 4%, IAP – 3%, Service – 2%.

THE MEDICAL IMAGING MARKET

The Customers

CT and MR scanners were in different phases of product life cycle. CT scanners had been available since the early 1970s and there were approximately 5,000 in operation in the U.S., with sales estimated at 600 per year and prices ranging from $0.5 million to $1.0 million. CT scanners were nearing the saturation level. The rate of sales growth was flat and the price had been dropping steadily. MR scanners, on the other hand, were newer and more sophisticated. This market was in a growth phase with sales of 400 units per year with unit prices ranging from $1.0 million to $2.0 million. By 1991, approximately 2,500 MR scanners had been installed in the U.S. Sales in Canada were forecast to total 40–50 units in 1992 for both types of scanner. Patients usually were sent through a CT scan first and then sent to the MR scanner only if additional information was needed. Some managers at ISG maintained that MR scanners would eventually entirely replace CT scanners as the price came down. If true, ISG would benefit greatly as the management believed that their products were superior to all others in the interpretation of MR images.

There were two kinds of institutional customers for medical imaging systems: (a) hospitals, which accounted for 70 percent of ISG sales, and (b) imaging centers, which accounted for 30 percent. In the United States, there were about 1,000 free-standing imaging centers. These were private companies that owned and operated expensive imaging equipment and functioned much like private labs doing medical tests. Centers such as these obtained reimbursement from private and public medical insurers for the procedures performed. In early 1992, however, the future status of these centers was in question. Many were owned or partly owned by physicians. Activists and medical insurers had uncovered evidence of physicians prescribing self-referred tests that had been carried out at clinics in which they had financial interests. As a result of these charges, several politicians had introduced legislation that would force massive divestitures by physicians. The actual implications of the legislation were still unclear and confusion reigned about the status of many of these clinics. As a result, few clinics were prepared to make major equipment purchases and sales to this segment had almost stopped.

The other major segment was hospitals, of which there were about 6,000 in the United States and 600 in Canada. The key hospital decision maker was typically the director of radiology. The Radiology Department usually encompassed most kinds of imaging used by the hospital including ultrasound, nuclear medicine, X-rays, and scanning. Its services were provided to different physicians such as general practitioners, cardiologists, surgeons, and other specialists.

The director of radiology controlled a large personnel and equipment budget and made decisions about how that money should be spent. These directors were subject to pressure for equipment acquisitions from several different divisions within the Radiology Department. For example, the chief of nuclear medicine might make a case to replace outdated equipment, while the head of ultrasound might argue that extra capacity was needed in her area. Surgeons and other physicians, through the kind of procedures they requested, also had an influence upon equipment purchases. This was because surgeons were responsible for bringing patients into the hospitals, thereby creating revenue.

A director would decide that a certain piece of equipment was needed on medical grounds and initiate the first phase of product investigation. The chief radiology technician would research product offerings, invite bids, and structure alternatives. If the purchase were routine, the director would make a decision and pass it on to the administration for a "rubber stamp" approval. If the purchase were outside the normal budget or risky in some way, the director might form a committee of two or three qualified persons, from within and beyond the hospital, to examine the options and make recommendations. Large purchase recommendations were often reviewed by the hospital board of directors. In past years, administrators had traditionally stayed clear of involvement in the evaluation of equipment acquisition decisions. However, by the early 1990s, hospital administrators had become more involved in the decision process in response to the funding crisis that was overtaking many institutions.

The economics of medical technology markets were driven by health insurance. Hospital and imaging center revenues were derived from reimbursement by public and private medical insurers. A case for a new piece of equipment and the resulting new procedure could be made on the grounds of a medical case, a business case, or both. As medical insurance costs were under constant review by these insurers, it was always possible that reimbursement for these procedures could be reduced or eliminated. There were two schools of thought about how the realities of rising health care costs might affect ISG. The first opinion held that expensive imaging tests might someday be eliminated or restricted by insurers that needed to drastically cut reimbursements. The second held that products such as ISG's that improved efficiency were unlikely to suffer from future cost reductions.

The Competitive Environment

The medical imaging market was highly competitive and characterized by rapid technological advances. For a manufacturer, success depended on technological superiority, price and performance measures, and equipment upgrades that kept installed equipment current with the increasingly sophisticated needs of medical practitioners. Additionally, product reliability, effective service, and customer support played significant roles in developing and maintaining customer preferences.

ISG currently had four independent workstation competitors who shared roughly equal market shares. Some of these competitors had links to important major scanner manufacturers. Independently manufactured workstations accounted for 30 percent of the overall image processing market. While these products were integral to the scanner systems they interpreted, all were either more expensive and/or inferior in performance to the Allegro. (See Exhibits 1 and 2 for scanner market share.) The major X-ray manufacturers dominated the imaging workstation market with a combined total of 75 percent of all workstation sales. The independent manufacturers accounted for the rest. ISG was the most important of these with an overall market share of 11.25 percent. ISG's four other third-party competitors had roughly equal market shares of approximately 3.5 percent each.

ISG managers worried little about the independent competition. Competing products were not as sophisticated either in software or hardware, as those of ISG. These third-party manufacturers had salesforces of 3-5 people. The major scanner manufacturers were a different matter. Despite similar product shortfalls, they had a competitive edge when it came to making sales. The scanner salespeople argued that the hospital and clinics should not risk the problems that might come from trying to add an independently manufactured workstation to their expensive new scanner. It would be much safer, they suggested, to stay with the workstation provided by the company that made the scanner in the first place. The scanner companies could also offer deep discounts on workstations that were, to them, relatively low-cost add-ons to the more lucrative scanner sales. The major manufacturers' salesforces totaled over 500 persons in the U.S.

The Regulatory Environment

Governmental agencies regulated the marketing and sale of ISG's products in most jurisdictions. In the United States, the products were regulated under two different acts, both administered by the Food and Drug Administration (FDA). The FDA had required all medical devices introduced into the market to obtain either (a) a Premarket Notification Clearance—known as a 510(K)—or (b) a Premarket Approval (PMA). If the FDA accepted that a product was similar to a product that had already been approved, then the manufacturer could apply for a 510(K) clearance. If, on the other hand, the FDA felt that this was an entirely new product, or a product that required special scrutiny, the manufacturer would have to apply for a PMA. The process of obtaining a 510(K) typically took several months and involved the submission of limited clinical data and supporting information, while PMA approval usually took more than a year and required the submission of significant quantities of clinical data and manufacturing information. All of ISG's previous clearances had taken place through the 510(K) process. In requesting clearance for its Viewing Wand, ISG had argued that it was merely a new application of the previously approved Allegro and should, therefore, qualify for the 510(K) process. In January 1992, the FDA had yet to rule on this request.

ISG HISTORY

ISG was founded in 1982 as an imaging technology contract research and development firm. The company's initial success had been the "Tour of the Universal," a space flight simulator installed at Toronto's CN Tower in 1986. Thereafter, ISG concentrated on the development of imaging products

EXHIBIT 1
North American Workstation Imaging Market Share—1990

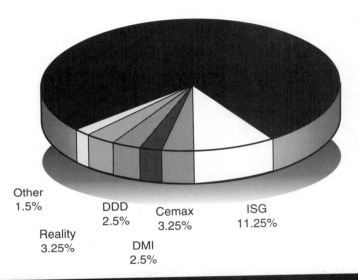

NORTH AMERICAN OVERALL WORKSTATION IMAGING MARKET SHARE 1990

Other
1.5%

DDD
2.5%

Cemax
3.25%

ISG
11.25%

Reality
3.25%

DMI
2.5%

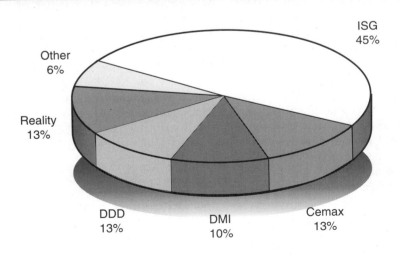

NORTH AMERICAN INDEPENDENT WORKSTATION IMAGING MARKET SHARE 1990

ISG
45%

Other
6%

Reality
13%

DDD
13%

DMI
10%

Cemax
13%

EXHIBIT 2
North American Magnetic Resonance Imaging (MRI) Market Share—1990

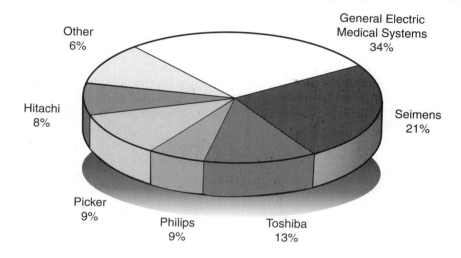

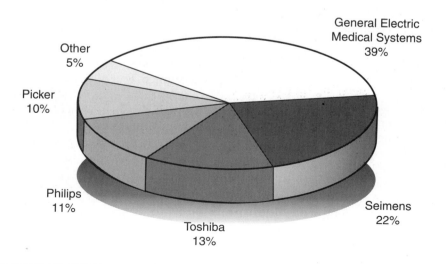

for the aerospace industry but found little success due to an "unpolished" product and the skepticism of potential customers about ISG's capabilities. Some of the managers thought that they might adapt ISG's technology to the new and less crowded field of medical imaging. The company hired Dr. Michael Greenberg, a Toronto neurosurgeon, as a consultant to examine the possibility. Dr. Greenberg's study was encouraging and he joined ISG full time in 1987 to help develop a medical imaging product.

In early 1988, the company had expended the funds raised in earlier years and, with a negative cash flow and no successful products, was experiencing great difficulty in raising more capital. Dr. Greenberg, however, was able to arrange new venture capital financing on the strength of the medical imaging product's market potential. Conditions imposed by the new financiers included concentration of company resources on the development of a medical product and the elevation of Dr. Greenberg to president. Some of the founders of the firm became displeased with their resulting demotions and loss of control, and within a year of the refinancing, most of the original employees had departed, leaving Dr. Greenberg in effective control.

Dr. Greenberg proved to be an energetic president. The company vigorously pursued product development and constructed a prototype. Key improvements were made in image quality and MRI scanner compatibility. Marketing plans were developed and implemented. Dr. Greenberg had established a relationship with a U.S. distributor (Precision) and was personally involved in the sale of units to the more important and prestigious customers such as Johns Hopkins of Baltimore, Maryland, Yale University, and The University of California—Los Angeles. During fiscal 1991, ISG had turned a small profit (see Exhibits 3 and 4 for financial statements and Exhibit 4 for sales data) and achieved a 10 percent share in the U.S. workstation market for its chief product, the Allegro workstation.

ISG'S MARKETING STRATEGY

ISG's overall plan was straightforward. It sought to translate high R&D expenditures into innovative, leading-edge products supported by superior customer service. The Viewing Wand was an example of this strategy; from the R&D on the Allegro, ISG had developed an entirely new product for an as-yet untapped market: real-time three-dimensional computer imaging for the operating room.

Sales efforts were concentrated on directors of radiology and the physicians who might generate demand for procedures the Allegro could provide. ISG, in concert with Precision, used several sales tools. It commissioned peer-reviewed medical research papers from physicians using its system to make a medical case to others. Videos, brochures, and other sales material were generated for the Precision salesforce and salespeople used customized profit analyses to make the business case for the Allegro (see Exhibit 5 for a typical business case). ISG also participated in trade shows to build brand awareness and preference. The premier sales tool, however, was the "roadshow," staged by ISG for qualified prospects.[4] A salesperson and a technician would visit the customer's premises with an Allegro workstation and process the customer's own clinical data. By applying the technology to the physician's own cases, ISG found that it could make a more persuasive case for the product to be purchased.

ISG's key market was the United States, which accounted for 90 percent of sales.[5] Outside North America, ISG was targeting Europe and Japan for immediate development. ISG's efforts in Europe were complicated by several factors. Europe was Philips' main market and ISG's policy was to avoid direct competition with Philips whenever possible.

---

[4] A qualified prospect was one that (a) had the budget, (b) was planning a decision within 90 days, and (c) had a champion in the prospect's organization who would drum up interest in the roadshow.

[5] ISG's sales were divided between the U.S. (90%), Canada (2%), and Europe (8%).

EXHIBIT 3
ISG Financial Statements—ISG Technologies Inc.

Consolidated Balance Sheets

	June 30, 1990	June 30, 1991	December 31, 1991 (Unaudited)
Assets			
Current assets:			
Accounts receivable (note 2)	$ 2,109,307	$ 5,975,249	$ 8,402,449
Inventory (note 3)	1,145,413	1,489,488	1,175,394
Prepaid expenses	168,884	160,497	256,404
	3,423,604	7,625,234	9,834,247
Fixed assets (note 4)	511,907	569,623	670,240
Other assets (note 5)	50,000	129,766	1,014,954
	$ 3,985,511	$ 8,324,623	$11,519,441
Liabilities and Shareholders' Equity			
Current liabilities:			
Bank indebtedness (note 6)	$ 569,905	$ 1,611,390	$ 1,086,555
Accounts payable and accrued liabilities (note 7)	1,974,060	2,999,424	2,719,109
Current portion of capital lease payments	27,182	43,774	38,718
Convertible debenture (note 8)	–	1,100,001	–
	2,571,147	5,754,589	3,844,382
Long-term debt:			
Capitalized leases (note 9)	49,078	56,539	39,847
Shareholders' equity:			
Capital stock (note 10)	14,146,952	15,295,366	21,151,156
Deficit	(12,781,666)	(12,781,871)	(13,515,944)
	1,365,286	2,513,495	7,635,212
Contingency (note 11)			
Subsequent events (note 16)	$ 3,985,511	$ 8,324,623	$11,519,441
On behalf of the Board:			

(Signed) MICHAEL M. GREENBERG	(Signed) RICHARD L. LOCKIE
Director	Director

In early 1992, ISG had a two-person direct sales-force based in the UK. The company had inherited these salespeople from its former European distributor, who had gone bankrupt. ISG had a month-to-month contract with these salespeople. This arrangement gave ISG some European coverage while allowing time to develop an overall strategy for the European market.

Europe was an agglomeration of many totally distinct national markets, each with its own ethnic, cultural, economic, and political characteristics. For example, the British National Health Service had been in a state of crisis for some years due to health care cutbacks by the Thatcher government. Germany was preoccupied with raising the former East Germany's health care standards to western levels.

EXHIBIT 3 (continued)
ISG TECHNOLOGIES, INC.—Consolidated Statements of Income

	1987	1988	1989	1990	1991	1990	1991
			Years ended June 30,			Six months ended December 31, (Unaudited)	
Sales	$ –	$ 862,427	$ 1,784,240	$ 6,338,678	$11,394,952	$4,745,532	$6,265,398
Cost of goods sold	–	358,000	862,960	2,926,712	4,738,535	2,091,754	3,032,069
Gross profit	–	504,427	921,280	3,411,966	6,656,417	2,653,778	3,233,329
Other income:							
Contract revenue	56,447	172,494	212,692	278,480	924,111	345,753	624,091
Service and other revenue	82,635	60,902	62,266	116,819	57,922	116,751	444,308
	139,082	233,396	274,958	395,299	982,033	462,504	1,068,399
	139,082	737,823	1,196,238	3,807,265	7,638,450	3,116,282	4,301,728
Expenses:							
Research and development	1,114,000	997,000	1,535,520	1,903,104	2,368,169	1,074,573	1,511,186
Marketing	671,942	1,882,131	1,426,606	2,098,615	2,415,933	1,015,046	1,850,699
Sales commissions	–	–	134,299	1,043,733	1,242,044	546,234	386,549
General and administrative	402,752	767,914	1,564,405	1,555,572	1,710,957	818,127	1,053,138
Interest:							
Long-term (note 8)	–	90,555	35,258	13,647	78,143	11,412	(45,443)
Other	24,474	38,749	111,460	36,609	105,953	44,138	110,409
Depreciation	206,337	309,959	189,659	224,438	281,848	135,728	176,209
	2,419,505	4,086,308	4,997,207	6,875,718	8,203,047	3,645,258	5,042,747
Less expenditures recovered (note 2)	141,597	–	361,288	570,069	580,466	336,022	92,097
	2,277,908	4,086,308	4,635,919	6,305,649	7,622,581	3,309,236	4,950,650
Income (loss) before extraordinary item	(2,138,826)	(3,348,485)	(3,439,681)	(2,498,384)	15,869	(192,954)	(648,922)
Extraordinary item—write off of note receivable net of deferred taxes of $2,082,500 (note 12)	(2,417,500)	–	–	–	–	–	–
Net income (loss)	$(4,556,326)	$(3,348,485)	$(3,439,681)	$(2,498,384)	$15,869	$192,954	$(648,922)
Earnings (loss) per share before extraordinary item	$ (1.16)	$ (1.81)	$ (1.00)	$ (.44)	$ 0.00	$ (0.03)	$ (0.10)
Earnings (loss) per share after extraordinary item	$ (2.46)	$ (1.81)	$ (1.00)	$ (.44)	$ 0.00	$ (0.03)	$ (0.10)

ISG recognized that it would need to develop a strategy for each of these distinct markets, or find someone who could do it for them.

Japan, on the other hand, was a relatively homogeneous market, similar to Canada and other countries where medical expenditures were centralized in government health ministries. Japanese doctors were more technically oriented than those in other countries and liked to know the technical details of products they used. The Japanese manufactured their own scanners, so that the price was comparatively low and they were in wide use. ISG's main

EXHIBIT 4
ISG Sales Data—1989–1991

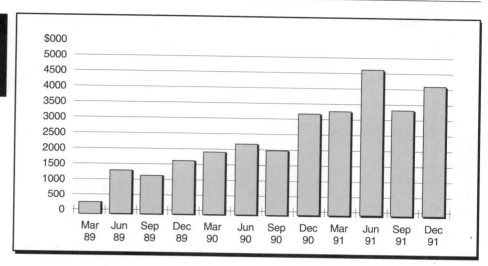

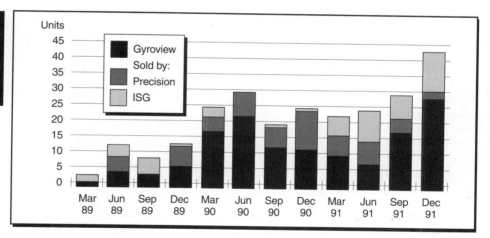

Units sold by:	Mar 89	Jun 89	Sep 89	Dec 89	Mar 90	Jun 90	Sep 90	Dec 90	Mar 91	Jun 91	Sep 91	Dec 91
Philips (Gyroview)	1	4	3	5	17	22	12	11	9	6	17	28
ISG	2	4	0	1	3	0	1	1	5	10	8	13
Precision	0	3	5	7	4	7	6	12	8	8	4	2
Total	3	12	8	13	24	29	19	24	22	24	29	43

EXHIBIT 5
Typical ISG Supplied Business Case

ISG Technologies, Inc. Profitability Analysis

Lessee:
Equipment: Allegro
Price: $175,000
Lease Term: 60 mos.
Lease Rate Factor: 0.0254
Monthly Payment: $4,445

	Year 1	Year 2	Year 3	Year 4	Year 5
	2	3	4	5	6
Studies per day	2	3	4	5	6
Studies per month	40	60	80	100	120
Studies per year	480	720	960	1,200	1,440
Charges per study	$ 350	$ 364	$ 379	$ 394	$ 409
Revenue	$168,000	$ 262,080	$363,418	$472,443	$589,609
Less bad debt	20%	20%	20%	20%	20%
Less supplies per study	$ 15	$ 15	$ 15	$ 15	$ 15
Net Revenue	$127,200	$ 209,664	$290,734	$377,394	$471,687
Expenses:					
Lease payment	$ 53,340	$ 53,340	$ 53,340	$ 53,340	$ 53,340
Personnel (1/2 time)	$ 15,000	$ 15,750	$ 16,538	$ 17,364	$ 18,233
Maintenance/service	$ 0	$ 14,000	$ 14,700	$ 15,435	$ 16,207
Rent/overhead	$ 1,000	$ 1,050	$ 1,103	$ 1,158	$ 1,216
Operating Profit	$ 57,860	$ 125,524	$205,054	$290,657	$382,692
Break-even:					
Studies per day	1.1	1.3	1.2	1.2	1.2
Studies per month	22	25	25	24	24
Studies per year	262	305	298	291	285
Charge per study	$ 265	$ 276	$ 288	$ 300	$ 313

problem was in developing the sort of cultural understanding and personal ties needed to do business in an environment where it was difficult for non-Japanese products to develop credibility. In the winter of 1992, ISG was actively seeking allies who would be able to help overcome these barriers. Despite its negative experience with Precision, it had considered establishing a dealer relationship in Japan.

History of Relationship With Precision

When Greenberg took over the company in the spring of 1988, ISG found itself with only one salesperson to cover 5,000 hospitals in the United States. With Dr. Greenberg and some of the engineering staff working part-time on sales, ISG was able to field four salespeople. This sales team was too small to provide the company with the kind of growth desired by ISG's management. The management team realized that with a 1988 loss of $3 million on revenues of $1 million, ISG could ill afford the expense of hiring its own salesforce. To build an effective team, ISG thought that it would need to train new salespeople for six months, and support them with the resources needed to compete with the salespeople fielded by major manufacturers and independent suppliers.

Because of the difficulty of financing such a strategy, ISG sought a distributor for North America. Although many distributors were considered, few had the industry experience that ISG sought and most were regionally, rather than nationally, focused. After several months, ISG opened negotiations with Precision, a large nationwide distributor of medical imaging equipment with sales of $70 million. Precision had a salesforce of 25 persons across North America and an effective service and support organization.

Precision's corporate strategy and the key to its success had been the aggressive selling of less expensive products than those available from the big U.S.-based scanning companies. For example, Precision marketed Hitachi MRI scanners, which sold for 30 percent less than a similar machine from GE. Its market focus was exclusively on the radiology departments to whom they sold CT and MRI scanners, specialized cameras, ultrasound equipment, and other products. Both ISG and Precision reasoned that when Precision found a buyer for a scanner, it could promote an ISG workstation along with the scanner, with little extra selling effort.

A one-year contract between ISG and Precision was signed on June 1, 1989. The contract stated that Precision would be the exclusive agent for the sale of ISG's CAMRA S2000 (the predecessor of the Allegro) throughout Canada and the continental United States. Certain clients with whom ISG preferred to deal directly were exempted.[6] ISG agreed to train all Precision sales personnel, provide sales

kits and promotional material, engage in customer training, and promote the product at industry trade shows. Precision promised to pursue sales leads, achieve stated quarterly quotas, participate in trade shows and roadshows in conjunction with ISG, and participate in monthly sales meetings at ISG's head office. Termination of the contract could be accomplished with 30 days' notice in writing by either party if one felt that the other had violated or failed to comply with any of the terms of the agreement. The contract could be extended by mutual agreement.

ISG projected sales of 60 CAMRA S2000 units in North America for the first year of the agreement and expected Precision to sell 54 of these systems, with ISG selling the remainder. No formal quotas were set, however, for complete workstation systems, spare parts, or accessories. Instead, Precision sales forecasts were used as informal quotas. The chronology of a typical sale was as follows:

1. Precision salespeople would identify potential leads through client visits for scanners or related equipment sales.
2. Precision would make an initial sales pitch.
3. Likely leads would be qualified by Precision and ISG.
4. Precision would arrange a "roadshow" for qualified prospects; ISG personnel would participate.
5. Precision would close the sale with help from ISG representative.
6. ISG would install the unit and train the client personnel.
7. Precision would invoice ISG for the commission.
8. ISG would receive payment from the client and pay the Precision invoice.

ISG determined commissions by using a complicated schedule that plotted the list price of the product against the actual sale price. Under this system, commissions varied from 23 to 27 percent of the actual customer-paid price for products discounted 0 to 12 percent. This meant that commissions usually ranged from $20,000 to $35,000 on a $150,000 workstation.

ISG began training the Precision salesforce in Toronto immediately following the verbal

---

[6] ISG reserved the area surrounding New York City and a number of "house accounts" that ISG had previously established for the purpose of new product testing and collaborative research. These accounts were:

Sunnybrook Hospital, Toronto, Ontario, Canada

The Toronto General Hospital, Toronto, Ontario, Canada

Buffalo Children's Hospital, Buffalo, NY, USA

Johns Hopkins Memorial Hospital, Baltimore, Maryland, USA

Boston Children's Hospital, Boston, Massachusetts, USA

Massachusetts General Hospital, Boston, Massachusetts, USA

agreement in March 1989. The newly trained salesforce began selling in April 1989. Despite Precision's sale of three systems compared to a target of six in the first full quarter, ISG thought the results promising in light of the dramatic increase in sales prospects turned up by the Precision salesforce. By March 1990, however, orders began to decline. When asked by ISG, Precision was vague about the causes. Despite Precision's contention that it was not quite the end of the quarter and that sales were still forthcoming, there was no improvement in April or May.

In June, an ISG technician who had been on a field installation was told that Precision was in the process of changing its sales strategy and completely reorganizing its sales organization. Precision confirmed this and informed ISG that its current structure was ill suited to the quickly changing marketplace and unable to compete effectively. Precision told ISG that the salespeople often found that it took more time to sell the workstation than it did to sell the scanner. Precision promised ISG a new, dedicated salesforce. To ISG's chagrin, the new salesforce was to be composed of approximately 20 new college graduates with little or no previous sales experience. In addition to the Allegro (which had replaced the CAMRA S2000), this salesforce would also be responsible for a new Hitachi cardiac ultrasound product.

ISG stockholders became restive in the next six months as sales languished while the new sales team was trained. By January 1991, however, the new salesforce was showing progress and it appeared that sales would reach a level satisfactory to ISG. Unfortunately, it soon became apparent that one of the tools Precision was using to drive sales was deep discounting. Large discounts seriously eroded ISG's profits as well as Precision's salespersons' commissions. Discounting in the form of including extra options at no extra charge had always been a tactic that both companies had agreed with in the past. ISG now began to question the practice, thinking that a lower list price might make more sense. In response to a request made by Precision, ISG set minimum commissions of $25,000 for orders not exceeding a total discount of $60,000 and a minimum of $20,000 for orders that did exceed a $60,000 total discount. This plan was put in place for February and March. ISG considered setting these minimums even lower to discourage the practice of deep discounting.[7]

In March, sales started to slip again, but because of reporting lags, ISG did not become aware of this until June. Pressed by ISG, Precision explained that the problem stemmed from another realignment of salesforce responsibilities. Sales of the Hitachi cardiac ultrasound product were booming and Precision had transferred sales staff previously dedicated to ISG back to the original Hitachi MRI salesforce. This was the same salesforce that Precision had taken the Allegro away from the year before. This salesforce would then theoretically represent ISG products with 20 representatives. ISG management had doubts about how effective that representation would be.

Managers at ISG were extremely upset with these developments. They felt that ISG was losing control of sales, and that Precision might never develop ISG products to their full market potential. Serious consideration was given to forming a dedicated ISG sales organization. The company already had three technical sales managers[8] who could form the nucleus of a direct sales organization. Before a firm decision was made, however, the vice president of sales, marketing, and service left the company.

---

[7] On an average sale of $150,000 U.S., ISG made a gross profit of $84,000 to $85,000 before commissions. The accounting system did not assign any fixed cost on a per unit basis, but costs such as R&D and other overheads were allocated on a product-by-product basis at the end of the fiscal year. During the six months ending on December 31, 1991, ISG paid sales commissions to Precision of $330,000 and commissions of $54,000 to ISG personnel.

[8] The technical sales managers provided technical and sales support to Precision.

The Decision

Mike Hopkinson joined ISG as Director of North American Sales in October 1991. He had 20 years of experience in the computerized medical imaging equipment sales field and had previously been National Sales Manager at Dornier Medical Systems (Canada) of Toronto and North American Sales Manager at Quantified Signal Imaging Inc., also of Toronto.

Hopkinson felt that there were several options open to ISG. First: Stay with Precision, re-educate the new salesforce, and specify minimum quotas in the contract. Second: Change direction and develop relationships with other major scanner companies, similar to the Philips arrangement, while dropping direct sales altogether. Third: Focus on a single exclusive alliance with a major scanner company. Fourth: Develop an ISG direct salesforce.

Several issues would affect Hopkinson's choice. One outside analyst projected total ISG sales for 1992 at almost $17 million in North America. (See Exhibit 6 for geographic breakdown of ISG sales.) Half of this revenue was expected to come from sales of the Allegro, 40 percent from Gyroview, 7 percent from sales of the Viewing Wand, and the rest from licensing proprietary software to GE.

Hopkinson thought that this goal could be met by the Precision salesforce if they made sales of ISG products a high priority. He was uncertain whether an ISG salesforce, which would need six months of training, could meet these goals within the fiscal reporting period.

Preliminary investigations showed that a salesperson would cost ISG about $60,000 per annum in salary, $5,000 per month in travel and administration expenses, and $5,000 in commissions per sale. This would be offset by the elimination of the commissions now being paid to Precision. The other marketing expenses, amounting to $2.4 million in 1991, would remain unchanged whether the products were sold by ISG or by Precision. If he chose any other option besides staying with Precision, Hopkinson would need to consider the best time to break the contract, how much preparation should be done before it was broken, and what impact such a move would have on ISG's revenues.

Hopkinson also knew that his decision about Precision would have an effect upon ISG's negotiations with other distributors in Europe and Japan. With the imminent introduction of the Viewing Wand and the year-end in sight, Hopkinson had to make a speedy decision.

EXHIBIT 6
Geographic Breakdown of ISG Sales

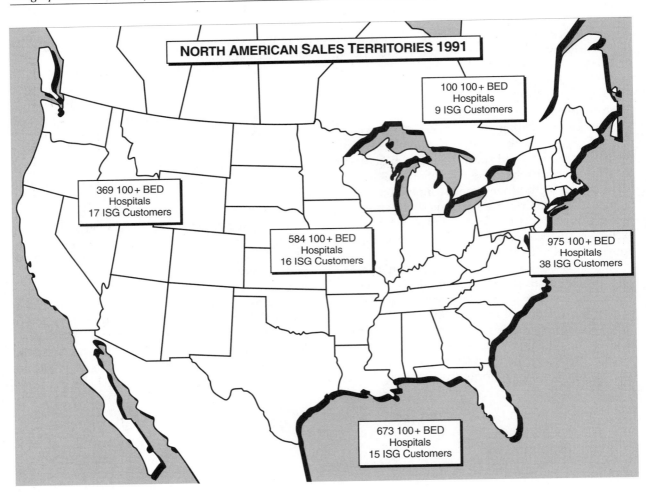

NORTH AMERICAN SALES TERRITORIES 1991

100 100+ BED
Hospitals
9 ISG Customers

369 100+ BED
Hospitals
17 ISG Customers

584 100+ BED
Hospitals
16 ISG Customers

975 100+ BED
Hospitals
38 ISG Customers

673 100+ BED
Hospitals
15 ISG Customers

The North Face

CASE 19

The North Face was a privately owned company that designed, manufactured, and sold high-quality outdoor equipment and clothing. It began as a specialty mountain shop in San Francisco in 1966 and started manufacturing in Berkeley in 1968. Since that time, the company had emphasized quality backpacking and mountaineering equipment featuring state-of-the-art design and functional detail. The North Face soon dominated this market and became the market leader in three of the four product categories it manufactured—tents, sleeping bags, backpacks, and clothing. Sales in 1980 were in excess of $20 million (see Exhibits 1 and 2 for historical financial statements). All items were produced domestically at the company's manufacturing facility in Berkeley. In the early 1980s, The North Face operated five well-located retail stores and two factory outlets in the San Francisco Bay area and Seattle. In addition, it employed fourteen independent sales representatives who covered ten sales territories in the U.S. Its dealer structure consisted of about 700 specialty shops throughout the U.S. as well as representation in 20 foreign countries.

The company's desire for continued growth in the face of a maturing backpacking market prompted Hap Klopp, President of The North Face and the driving force behind its success to date, to investigate expansion into new products related to the current backpacking business. One avenue of growth that appeared to have significant potential was that of Alpine (downhill) ski clothing. This opportunity was pursued, with the result that The North Face skiwear line was being readied for formal introduction in Fall 1981.

The uppermost question in management minds at this point was: What was the most effective way to distribute the new skiwear line?

EARLY HISTORY

Hap Klopp, 39-year-old President of The North Face and a graduate of the Stanford MBA program, purchased the original company in 1968, following a brief period as manager of another backpacking retail outlet in the San Francisco Bay area. At that time, the operation consisted of three retail stores and a small mail-order business. The firm sold a line of private-label backpacking and brand-name downhill ski equipment. Klopp closed two stores, brought in equity, and opened a small manufacturing facility for the production of down-filled sleeping bags in the back of the main store in Berkeley, California. Sales in 1969 were just under $500,000.

Prior to 1971, most of the retail sales were in Alpine (downhill) ski equipment, where competition had depressed the margins. To gain relief, management decided to concentrate on the backpacking and ski-touring (cross-country) markets, where margins were higher and such adverse influences as seasonality, fashion cycles, and weather conditions were less damaging.

THE NORTH FACE PRODUCTS

The North Face manufactured four key lines for the backpacking market: sleeping bags, packs, outdoor clothing, and tents. All products stressed quality, design, and durability and were priced for the high-end of the market. All products carried a full lifetime warranty.

Sleeping Bags

North Face sleeping bags ranged from "Expeditionary" models (designed to provide protection to −40° F) to bags offering various combinations of

This case was prepared by Gary Mezzatesta and Valorie Cook, Stanford Graduate School of Business, under the supervision of Professor Robert T. Davis. Reprinted with permission of Stanford University Graduate School of Business, copyright © 1983 by the Board of Trustees of the Leland Stanford Junior University.

EXHIBIT 1
Profit and Loss Comparisons (in 000's)

	1977	1978	1979	1980
Sales				
Manufacturing	$11,437	$13,273	$15,153	$17,827
Retail	2,254	2,570	2,879	3,368
Total	$13,691	$15,843	$18,032	$21,195
Cost of sales	9,337	11,188	12,443	13,964
Gross margin	4,354	4,655	5,589	7,231
Selling and operating expense	2,186	2,320	2,646	3,306
Contributing to overhead	2,168	2,335	2,943	3,925
Corporate G&A expense	686	685	777	924
Interest expense	242	268	438	658
Incentive compensation and ESOP	235	204	253	330
Total	$ 1,163	$ 1,157	$ 1,468	$ 1,912
Total pre-tax profits	$ 1,005	$ 1,178	$ 1,475	$ 2,013
Total after-tax profits	$ 498	$ 609	$ 776	$ 1,019

lightness and warmth (aimed at satisfying the needs of the vacationing, leisure-oriented backpacker). The North Face bags were considered superior to competitive products in construction and durability and offered the optimal trade-off between warmth and weight. As the company grew, TNF expanded the variety of sleeping bags offered to meet virtually every environmental condition that a backpacker could expect in the U.S. The quality of down used, the nylon fabric thread count, the unique coil zippers, and the stitching were key points of differentiation. Goose down bags retailed from $162 to $400, with the price escalating as the warmth of the bag increased. Initially, the bags were only down-filled, but in recent years, a complete line of synthetic-filled models were introduced. Synthetic fills were preferred by some for damp weather environments and where weight and compressibility were of lesser importance. Synthetic bags ranged in retail price from $75 to $205—also at the top end of the competitive market.

From the start, the company had manufactured only two sizes of sleeping bags instead of the usual three found in the industry. This policy not only simplified production but also reduced retailers' stocking needs and retail stock outs. When TNF began, sleeping bags had been the fastest-growing segment of the backpacking industry, but this growth had begun to slow during the early '70s.

Parkas and Other Outdoor Clothing

Parkas and functional outerwear were the growth leaders for The North Face in 1981. Its line included a range of parkas designed to appeal to the serious backpacker. Design stressed maximum comfort over a wide temperature range and contained convenient adjustments for ventilation control. Other features, such as pocket design, snap-closed flaps over zippers, and large overstuffed collars, further enhanced the line. As the industry grew and fashion became more of an element, a much wider range of colors and surface fabrics were incorporated into the line. Materials such as Gore-Tex (a breathable yet waterproof material) had been introduced, which offered a functional advantage over existing products on the market. Two types of parkas were offered: those that afforded primary protection from cold, damp conditions (generally of synthetic material); and those that were intended to withstand cold, dry conditions (primarily of

EXHIBIT 2

Comparative Balance Sheets (Year Ended September 30—in 000's)

	1977	1978	1979	1980
Assets				
Current				
Cash	$ 110	$ 149	$ 201	$ 370
Accounts receivable	2,765	3,765	3,910	4,573
Inventories	4,496	4,494	4,452	5,947
Other	319	329	229	196
Long-term	803	1,012	1,256	1,437
Other assets	65	68	100	104
Total assets	$8,558	$9,817	$10,148	$12,627
Liabilities				
Current				
Notes payable to bank	$2,624	$3,180	$ 2,563	$ 2,613
Accounts payable	2,019	2,186	2,109	2,231
Accrued liabilities	693	589	627	783
Income taxes payable	318	339	360	568
Current portion LT debt	141	159	222	316
Other				
Long-term debt	351	302	360	1,103
Deferred income taxes	33	73	143	230
Stockholders' Equity				
Common stock—A	1,687	1,687	1,687	1,687
Common stock—B	0	2	2	2
Retained earnings	692	1,300	2,075	3,094
Total liabilities	$8,558	$9,817	$10,148	$12,627

down). As in fabrics, a number of new, strongly promoted synthetics, such as Thinsulate, Polarguard, and Hollofill, had been incorporated into the line to meet expanding consumer base and desires. Parkas varied in price from approximately $50 for a synthetic-filled multipurpose vest to $265 for a deluxe expeditionary model. The company was in the process of trying to sell a system of clothing called "layering," which utilized multiple layers of clothing confined in a variety of ways to meet climatic conditions.

Tents

In 1981, The North Face had revolutionized the world market for lightweight backpacking tents with its geodesic designs. With assistance from well-known design engineer R. Buckminster Fuller, the company's employees had created and patented geodesic tents. These tents provided the greatest volume of internal space with the least material and the highest strength-to-weight ratio of any tent design. They also had more headroom, better use of floor space, and better weather shedding. Because geodesics were freestanding, they also required less anchoring to the earth. Competitors throughout the world were beginning to copy the products; but to date, the company had not legally pursued its patent protection. Other special tent features included reinforced seams and polymer-coated waterproof fabric that management believed provided three times the tear strength and superior performance at subfreezing temperatures. The company had helped develop unique tent poles that were available nowhere else in the world. The North Face still carried two A-frame tents for the purpose of price and continuity of line at $200 and $240 price points, while the geodesic line had eight tents ranging from $220 to $600. As with the other North Face products, these were at the high end of the price spectrum; but management was convinced that consumers were getting very good value for their money.

The market for tents had accelerated recently with the introduction of the geodesics, which met new customers' needs better than did A-frame tents. Management felt that two to four years of rapid growth in geodesic tent sales would continue while A-frames were becoming obsolete, and then the market would return to its former modest levels of growth.

Backpacks

The North Face divided the pack market into three segments:

- Soft packs/day packs
- Internal frame packs
- External frame packs

The North Face introduced the first domestically made internal frame pack, which created a market niche and produced extremely good sales for the company. Retail price ranges from $45 to $115 were at the high end of the scale, but management was sure that the quality details (including extra-strength nylon, bartack stitching, extra loops and straps, high-strength aluminum, etc.) made these good values for the money.

In the soft-pack area, there were fewer features to distinguish the company's products from its competitors'. Price competition—with competitors' prices from $16 to $37—was much more noticeable.

In the external frame market, historically dominated by Kelty, the company had introduced a remarkably different patented product called the Back Magic. It was an articulated pack with independent shoulder and hip suspension that placed the weight of the pack closer to the backpacker's center of gravity than other packs had done. Although offering an expensive product ($150 to $160) and encountering some bothersome contractor delays, the company was significantly increasing its market share in this category.

Additionally, to expand this category of the company's sales and to open up a whole new market for its dealers, The North Face introduced a complete line of soft luggage in 1981. The company was attempting to capitalize upon the peripatetic nature of its customers and its belief that customers wanted the much higher quality traditionally found in luggage shops. Features such as binding in all seams, leather handles on nylon webbing, shoulder straps with leather handles, and numerous zippered internal pockets were incorporated. Prices ranged from $40 to $65.

MARKETING PHILOSOPHY

The North Face promoted more than just a product, it fostered a way of life. Throughout the ranks of management one found a cadre of outdoor enthusiasts.

It is important to note how Hap Klopp viewed his company's business:

> [The North Face] may be selling bags, tents, packs, boots, or parkas, but I suggest that people are buying better health, social contact, sunshine, adventure, self-confidence, youth, exercise, romance, a change of pace, or a chance to blow off steam and escape from the urban degeneration of pollution, economic collapse, and congestion.

One central theme served as the foundation for The North Face's corporate strategy. It was best summarized by Hap Klopp: "Make the best product possible, price it at the level needed to earn a fair return, and guarantee it forever." Hap contended that profits were not made from the first sale to a customer. After all, it took considerable effort and money to attract that purchase in the first place. Rather, the customer had to be treated well once he or she had been attracted. Repeat sales were the key to this business's profitability. Hence, there was the need to provide a product that would always satisfy.

A key conceptual tool that North Face used to analyze the backpacking market and similar specialty markets is what Klopp called "the pyramid of influence":

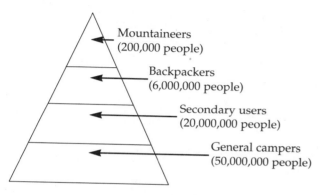

Mountaineers (200,000 people)

Backpackers (6,000,000 people)

Secondary users (20,000,000 people)

General campers (50,000,000 people)

Within this hierarchy, management believed that word-of-mouth communication flowed down a chain of expertise from the mountaineer, to the backpacker, to the secondary user, and finally to the general camping public. Those at the high end of the chain, the "technocrats," tended to influence the buying decisions of the average outdoorsman, who relied upon recommendations and brand image rather than personal research. The North Face characterized the market pyramid as shown in Exhibit 3.

The company believed that a number of its competitors had made serious marketing blunders in changing their distribution and products to meet the needs of the larger, lower strata, thereby ignoring the pattern of influence of the pyramid and the foundation of the business. This led to the erosion of their name and franchise in all of the strata. In contrast, The North Face's long-term strategy was to maintain an orientation toward the top of the pyramid and quietly broaden the line so that its existing dealers would be able to meet the needs of both the peak of the pyramid and the emerging customers.

The North Face adamantly declared that the pattern of influence in specialty markets only worked one way—downward. By designing and selling high-quality functional items focused at the top of the pyramid, a firm could systematically build a strong market image hinging on credibility. Klopp discounted the integrity and wisdom of the switch from a "top down" to a "bottom up" strategy. Many companies shortsightedly looked at the financials associated with each segment and changed their distribution network and products to meet the larger, lower strata. This process, Klopp claimed, eventually led to failure, since ignoring the foundations of the business eventually caused a "franchise erosion" at all levels of the pyramid. In short, lowering the quality of product and service to maintain sales growth was a no-win game that would inevitably lead to erosion of market and image and to the advancement of someone who was at the top of the cone. If a company wanted to maintain its commitment to a market and customer group for the long term, it had to stick to the "top down" approach.

EXHIBIT 3
Market Pyramid Characteristics

Segment	Use	Price	Preferred Product Characteristics
Mountaineer	Frequent, hard	No object	Durable, functional, perfect workmanship
Backpacker	Frequent, careful	Value conscious	Lightweight, repairable, comfortable, brand more important
Secondary user	Inconsistent, careful	Value conscious	Durable, multipurpose, comfortable, brand name
General camper	Inconsistent, careless	Price sensitive	Simple, sturdy, multipurpose, brand name

Because of its strict adherence to this philosophy, The North Face approached the marketplace with the following strategy: enter specialty markets; nurture them carefully; focus R&D at the top of the pyramid; use specialty shops to skim the market; target promo efforts for trendsetters. Once a dominant position in a market was established, growth was sought via two paths:

1. Finding new geographical or new use markets.
2. Introducing new quality products.

The company led the backpacking industry with the following market shares (estimated from available data) in 1980:

	Market Share	Industry Ranking
Outerwear/clothing	47%	1
Sleeping bags	48%	1
Tents	28%	1
Packs	20%	3

The North Face accounted for 21.9 percent of the sales of backpacking products to specialty stores in 1980, while its closest competitor achieved a 13.5 percent market share. In summary, the company's distinctive competence, which distinguished it from its competition, was the manufacture of high-quality functional products of classic design, which sold at a premium price and carried a lifetime warranty. The key success factors were thought to be the company's reputation as a specialty supplier of quality products, its strong relationship with its distribution network, and its high-caliber management team. The North Face was generally recognized as having the best management team in the industry, due to its depth of industry knowledge and length of time in the business.

While the backpacking industry had enjoyed substantial growth over the past decade, from total U.S. industry specialty store sales of $15,400,000 in 1971 to $81,700,000 in 1980, the backpacking market appeared to be maturing, with total sales forecasted to grow to $95,100,000 by 1985. (See Exhibit 4 for historical and projected market size.) Klopp believed that the industry was out of the high-growth stage of the product life cycle, heading

EXHIBIT 4

U.S. Industry Specialty Store Sales* of Backpacking Products (Wholesale Prices in 000's)

	Total Sales
1971	$15,400
1972	$21,600
1973	$27,400
1974	$40,700
1975	$44,800
1976	$57,050
1977	$65,850
1978	$70,400
1979	$77,500
1980	$81,700
1981 (est.)	$84,300
1982 (est.)	$86,900
1983 (est.)	$90,100
1984 (est.)	$92,400
1985 (est.)	$95,100

*Domestic only.

toward the maturity stages; the increasing difficulty the company reported in achieving product differentiation seemed to validate this observation.

Channels of Distribution

The North Face's reliance on the "pyramid of influence" also dictated its handling of distribution channels. Since they were in specialized markets, The North Face preferred to build its brand name carefully by using specialty stores as a foundation. Once this foundation was established, The North Face attempted to nurture it carefully by providing the dealers with new products and techniques (via training classes) to attract new customers. The company only used the more general sporting goods stores (e.g., Herman's, EMS) when it needed geographic coverage in a particular area, and even then tried to limit distribution to certain outlets of the chain. The firm avoided mass merchandising stores as much as possible. TNF felt that specialty shops developed brand awareness and consumer franchise for their products, while the general shops exploited their brand name. Thus, it relied heavily upon the prosperity of these specialty outlets. Careful control of the channels lay at the cornerstone of The North Face's marketing strategy.

Wholesaling. Backpacking industry sales were distributed among retail stores in the following proportions:

	Dollar Value	Number of Outlets
Backpacking specialty stores	50%	40%
Sports specialty stores	25%	30%
General sporting goods stores	10%	5%
Ski shops, department stores, etc.	15%	25%

Sales were fairly evenly distributed among the Pacific, North Central, and Northeast regions of the U.S., with lesser proportions falling in the Mountain and Southern states.

The North Face sold primarily to approximately 700 retail stores, 75 percent of which specialized in backpacking and mountaineering equipment and the rest in general sporting goods. Wholesale distribution by The North Face was handled by 14 independent sales representatives who carried hiking, mountaineering, and cross-country skiing lines. These representatives covered 10 sales territories in the U.S. and were paid on commission. The North Face products were their major source of income. Management felt that this network was especially valuable as a conduit for information about market conditions, product knowledge, retail management programs, and competition. It was estimated that 55–60 percent of all consumer purchases resulted from word-of-mouth endorsement from a satisfied friend or from a sales presentation in the store. Thus, the primary marketing thrust of The North Face was to

1. Sell dealers on the company's products and markets.
2. Provide information and point-of-sale aids to help floor salespeople.

The representatives were crucial to this effort and all were carefully chosen by the Sales and Marketing Vice President and co-founder, Jack Gilbert. As a group, the reps had an average of seven to eight years' experience in the industry, were avid backpackers and lovers of the outdoors, and had been with The North Face since its inception. The reps were highly successful and had been well treated by the company through the years. Over that time, the nature of their responsibilities had evolved from pioneering or prospecting for new accounts to training existing accounts in industry and management techniques, having established The North Face as the authority in the backpacking field.

The company long pursued a policy of building stable, ongoing relationships with carefully selected dealers. It followed a limited distribution policy, seeking to maintain a balance of dealers and market demand in any geographic area. The company individually reviewed and approved all potential dealer locations, including new locations of existing accounts, and was committed to maintaining and strengthening its dealers. In seeking new product areas in which to expand, it was considered important for The North Face to evaluate the potential of its current dealers to sell the products under consideration.

Retailing. The North Face's retailing objective was to use its own retail stores to attain its desired market share and profit objectives only where wholesaling was unable to achieve satisfactory market penetration and where the policy had no adverse impact on wholesale distribution. To meet this objective, the strategy was to expand existing outlets and introduce new outlets in an orderly fashion, locating only where conflict with the wholesale division was minimized. This strategy was reinforced in the following policy statement:

> The Retail Division will continue to examine expansion possibilities on a local basis. The Retail Division will not expand into any domestic geographic area which will have a significant adverse effect on the wholesale sales of The North Face. The focus of expansion efforts will only be around those areas where The North Face presently has established stores.

The North Face currently owned and operated five well-located retail stores and two factory outlets in the San Francisco Bay area and Seattle. In 1980, the mail-order operation was closed down due both to its lack of profitability and its perceived conflict with the wholesaling operations. In recent years, the Retail Division had enjoyed considerable increases in sales and profits, significantly above the industry average:

Company Stores (in 000's)

	1977	1978	1979	1980
Sales	$2,189	$2,574	$2,884	$3,368
Gross margins	N/A	974	1,156	1,446
Profits/contribution	N/A	104	220	364
Inventory turns1.	6X	1.7X	2.1X	2.1X
Transfers to stores*	$ 918	$ 908	$ 770	$1,120

*Sales from company wholesale to company retail.

It should be noted that the "transfer" figures represented sales from company wholesale to company retail. Management felt that not all of these sales would have gone to independents if the company stores had not existed. This is important to consider in looking at The North Face's total profitability. The significance of these figures was underscored by the comparison that the average North Face store bought $200,000 from wholesaling, while the average wholesale account bought slightly over $30,000 annually. Additionally, the Retail Division test-marketed some promotional programs and products and, through its factory outlets, took nearly $500,000 of seconds—which otherwise would have created image problems if sold through wholesale channels—as well as products that were made out of overstocked materials supplies. While the exact impact on corporate profit of these activities was hard, if not impossible, to calculate, it was thought to be considerable.

Conflict between Retailing and Wholesaling. A continual conflict existed between retail and wholesale because of the feeling that retail might expand into an area that was beyond its domain. In part to alleviate this problem, the Retail Division closed down its mail-order operation. The retail expansion into Seattle caused the loss of some wholesale business and was used as a lever by some competitive reps; but since The North Face did not terminate any existing dealers, the issue died. Although there were a number of good wholesale accounts left, The North Face did not sell to them because of the geographical protection it had granted its dealers. The company felt it received increased loyalty and purchases because of this protection and would lose them if its accounts were increased randomly.

Differing opinions on the subject of further retail expansion existed even at the highest levels of the company. At one point, at least, Klopp felt that retail expansion was the most effective means of generating market share and promoting brand-name allegiance, while Jack Gilbert, the Sales and Marketing Vice President, had serious reservations in three areas:

1 *The impact on the dealers*—Gilbert felt that retailers in this industry were "very paranoid" that manufacturers would expand their retail operations. Indeed, competitive reps in the industry were known to advise dealers not to "give too much of your business to The North Face because they are out there gathering information about your market area in order to expand their retail operation." He believed that a North Face retail expansion would damage the company's excellent relationship with its dealers.
2. *The profit implications*—While the going margin at retail was 40 percent compared to a target margin at wholesale of 30 percent, entry into expanded retail operations was not a profitable strategy in the short run. The initial investment for a store was $40,000 in fixtures and capital improvements, plus $100,000 of inventory at retail prices. It took three years for an individual store to make the contribution management wanted—12 percent contribution to overhead and 8 percent to pretax profits.
3. *Growth*—Finally, Gilbert was concerned about whether The North Face could meet its growth objectives by going both the wholesale and retail routes, particularly given the company's limited financial resources.

Additional concerns regarding inventory control and the development of capable store managers via a training program were voiced by John McLaughlin, Financial Vice President for The North Face.

Outlook toward Growth

Maintaining a healthy rate of growth was also a major goal of management. The style of the company was aggressive and entrepreneurial. Klopp and his management team did not want to risk frustrating the young, energetic staff they had gathered. As mentioned earlier, the backpacking industry seemed to be entering the maturity phase of the product life cycle. Over the past few years, the total market was growing only at a 5 percent compound annual growth rate. The North Face had grown at a faster rate than the overall market, consistently gaining market share, but it was evident that this situation could not last forever, especially given the company's reliance on the "pyramid of influence" theory.

In evaluating potential new markets, management looked for opportunities that could fulfill the following objectives:

- An overlap with current customer base.
- A product compatible with current machinery capabilities.
- A line that would complement seasonal production peaks.
- A market in which "top down" strategy would work.
- A line that matched with the interests and expertise of the existing management team.
- A line that would maintain and strengthen The North Face's current dealer network.
- A line that would not threaten or cannibalize the base business.

TNF's decision-making style added further complexity to the situation. The firm espoused a collaborative style of strategy formation and implementation. Employee input and consensus were essential. Klopp fostered this environment by utilizing a paternalistic management style. In fact, each individual felt as if he or she had influence on the direction of TNF. In the context of the approaching decision, this meant that marketing needed to receive a general approval before entering a new business.

The Skiwear Line

The company's desire for continued growth in the face of this maturation of the backpacking market spurred management to investigate expansion into new products. In looking at manufacturing and marketing growth opportunities, the company analyzed its own sales, those of its dealers, and the markets highlighted to see what opportunities were not being completely exploited. Interestingly, the company found that, although it never manufactured or marketed its products specifically for skiing, it held nearly 2 percent of the skiwear market; in some categories, such as down vests, it had nearly 5 percent. It was also discovered that over two-thirds of all dealers handling The North Face products also sold skiwear. Most appealing was the fact that the market appeared to be highly fragmented. As pointed out in an industry study published in May 1980: "Most skiwear categories have one or two market leaders, but in all areas no one brand dominates the market. In fact, in all categories studied, it required between 9 and 12 brands to make up 70 percent of the market share in dollars."

Market Size (1980—in 000's)

Adult down parkas/vests	$ 30,000
Adult non-down parkas/vests	54,000
Adult bibs and pants	21,000
Shell pants	1,600
X-country ski clothing	2,600
	$ 109,200

Exhibits 5 and 6 contain details on the skiwear market.

These factors, coupled with an increasing number of requests for uniforms "that work" (i.e., functional, durable, and warm) from ski instructors, ski patrollers, and other professional users thought to influence the market, led The North Face to introduce its skiwear line. The company's strategy in skiwear was predicated on the same strategy as its backpacking business—functionally designed, classically styled clothing. The skiwear was targeted to the "professional skier" (not the racer),

EXHIBIT 5
Skiwear* Market Sales 1979–1980 (in millions)

	Dollars	Market Share
1. White Stag	$ 27.0	12.5%
2. Roffee	19.0	8.8
3. Skyr	13.5	6.3
4. Head Ski & Sportswear	13.0	6.0
5. Aspen	12.5	5.8
6. Gerry	12.0	5.5
7. Swing West (Raven)	10.0	4.6
8. Alpine Designs	9.0	4.2
9. Obermeyer	8.0	3.7
10. Sportscaster	7.5	3.5
11. Beconta	7.0	3.3
12. Bogner America	7.0	3.3
13. C.B. Sports	6.0	2.8
14. Serac	5.0	2.3
15. Profile	5.0	2.3
16. Demetre	5.0	2.3
17. Woolrich	4.5	2.0
18. The North Face	4.0	1.9
19. Other	41.0	18.9
	$216.0	100.0%

*Excluding underwear.

since management felt that a Trendsetter and Uniform Program targeted to ski patrollers and lift operators would serve to trigger sales in the same manner that using mountaineers impacted the backpacking pyramid of influence.

Issues with Skiwear

The decision to introduce skiwear was also not without some problems. Although a majority of the dealers carried skiwear, some did not. The latter might oppose "The North Face" trade name going into another local store, even if it was part of a product line they didn't carry. Further, the current dealers were not always the most influential top-end shops required to build a market, and their ski departments might not take The North Face's ski-oriented products as seriously as they did the company's backpacking offerings. Similarly, some of the

best ski shops that influenced the entire market were not presently The North Face outlets. Out of a total market size of over 3,000 Alpine ski dealers, only about 475 were currently carrying The North Face products. Moreover, the sales reps already had a very extensive line and it was a concern of management that they might have difficulty pushing the ski items during the critical start-up phase. Further, this expansion into a new area in effect required the established sales reps to "start over" again with prospecting for new accounts, a task that might tax their capabilities and desires.

Different complications arose in each of TNF's markets. The following example from a metropolitan center in California highlights some critical issues.

At the time of the skiwear decision, TNF distributed its backpacking products primarily through one large specialty backpacking/skiing shop in the city. Suburban neighborhood stores were utilized for additional coverage. The city store ranked among the top 20 percent of TNF dealers. In the past, TNF had rewarded this supplier by witholding merchandise from direct competitors.

TNF serviced this account with regular visits of the local sales representative, frequent visits by sales managers, an annual dealer seminar, and periodic information-gathering visits by top management. The store's annual sales topped $1 million, with 65–70 percent of this deriving from backpacking products. Sales of TNF items accounted for the majority of backpacking revenue. TNF management felt that this shop, as the largest specialty shop in the area, "made" the area backpacking market. TNF developed consumer awareness via close association with this outlet and by regular coop advertisements. In short, if a serious local backpacker needed equipment, he or she would most likely shop at this store.

In backpacking, this shop had little formidable competition. Some second tier specialty shops existed, but they offered less ease of access and a narrower product range. A wide variety of general sporting goods shops also competed in the territory. These stores each had backpacking sections

EXHIBIT 6

Estimated Market Share by Segments of Skiwear Market

Down Parkas				Non-Down Parkas				Bibs			
Men's		Women's		Men's		Women's		Men's		Women's	
1. Gerry	21.7%	1. Gerry	15.0%	1. Roffee	14.6%	1. Roffee	12.4%	1. Skyr	13.7%	1. Roffee	15.0%
2. Roffee	8.6%	2. Slalom	9.8%	2. White Stag	8.7%	2. White Stag	12.3%	2. Roffee	12.4%	2. Skyr	14.6%
3. Alpine Designs	7.4%	3. Roffee	8.7%	3. Skyr	8.0%	3. Skyr	10.6%	3. White Stag	11.0%	3. White Stag	9.1%
4. Powderhorn	5.4%	4. Head	7.8%	4. Head	7.7%	4. Head	10.2%	4. Head	7.2%	4. Head	6.6%
5. Head	5.3%	5. Mountain Goat*	6.1%	5. C.B. Sports	7.2%	5. Slalom	6.2%	5. Beconta	5.2%	5. Slalom	6.5%
6. White Stag	4.7%	6. White Stag	4.7%	6. Serac	5.9%	6. Swing West	5.0%	6. Swing West	4.9%	6. Swing West	4.6%
7. Mountain Goat*	3.6%	7. Tempco	4.2%	7. Cevas	4.6%	7. Bogner	4.4%	7. Gerry	4.1%	7. No. 1 Sun**	4.6%
8. C.B. Sports	3.3%	8. Sportscaster	3.9%	8. Slalom	4.2%	8. Cevas	3.2%	8. Slalom	3.9%	8. Beconta	4.4%
9. Obermeyer	3.1%	9. No. 1 Sun**	3.4%	9. Swing West	4.2%	9. No. 1 Sun**	3.0%	9. No. 1 Sun**	3.8%	9. Gerry	3.8%
10. Sportscaster	3.1%	10. C.B. Sports	2.8%	10. No. 1 Sun**	3.8%	10. C.B. Sports	2.6%	10. Alpine Designs	3.7%	10. Bogner	3.1%
11. All other	33.8%	11. All other	33.6%	11. All other	31.1%	11. All other	30.1%	11. All other	30.1%	11. All other	27.7%

*Second brand name of White Stag.

**Second brand name of Head.

but did not emphasize service. TNF did not associate with these stores.

Unfortunately, the skiing market was much more fragmented in this territory. Although TNF's key backpacking account also sold skiing products, it did not have a dominant position. The store was one of the handful of large dealers that handled skiwear. It did not "make the market." Instead, it often reacted to the environment in setting pricing, merchandising, and product selection policies. In addition, five comparably sized ski specialty shops (no backpacking gear at all) competed in this territory. Each shop carried roughly the same product line, frequently featuring loss leadership on hardware (Rossignol, Nodica, Lange, etc.). Soft goods were the primary profit maker. The offerings emphasized aesthetics and functionality.

TNF management obviously faced a serious problem in introducing the skiwear line in this market. On the one hand, they owed special consideration to their key backpacking account. But they also realized that this account alone would not develop sufficient brand awareness as a pioneer for the skiwear line. The key account's owner was concerned about losing backpacking sales if TNF decided to offer its products to other area shops. In this territory, as in others, TNF needed to act quickly and carefully.

EXHIBIT 7
Partial Organization Chart

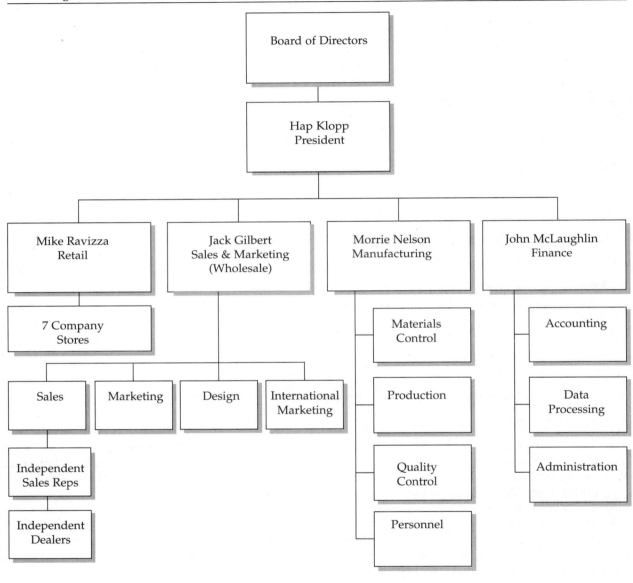

Backgrounds

Mike Ravizza, Retail—Joined The North Face in 1969; Stanford undergraduate.

Jack Gilbert, Sales & Marketing—Co-founder of The North Face in 1968; Stanford undergraduate.

Morrie Nelson, Manufacturing—Joined The North Face in 1975; University of Washington undergraduate, Santa Clara MBA.

John McLaughlin, Finance—Joined The North Face in 1970; Dartmouth undergraduate, Stanford MBA.

Owatonna Tool Company: Timing Product Modifications

It was August of 1984, and Mr. Steve Fergusson, the product manager of Owatonna Tool Company's (OTC) electronics division, was pondering the report of his development engineers. Clearly, his technical experts had opened up some very novel and creative possibilities for design modifications in the division's leading product—the automotive computer monitor. However, Fergusson wondered if some of the ideas contained in the report were a little ahead of their time. He was not sure what would be the appropriate timing to introduce the design advancements into the market, especially since there was no external pressure on the company to do so at the present time. He realized that in September the automobile industry would begin its 1985 model year (September 1984–August 1985). Therefore, he must make his decision immediately without any further delay.

COMPANY BACKGROUND

OTC was established in 1922 in a small industrial town in the upper Midwest to manufacture manual and hydraulic pullers required in automotive repairs and maintenance work. By the 1980s, the company had grown to become one of the major manufacturers and marketers of automotive tools and equipment in the United States.

The company had adopted a matrix organization structure consisting of line and staff functions that formed a grid. Under this setup, purchasing, finance, production, and marketing consisting of advertising, distribution, and sales were organized as line functions serving all products of the company. The sales department was further divided into several divisions based on various market segments served by the company. On the other hand, under the vice president of product management, six product managers carried out the staff function of coordinating the activities of all line departments concerning their respective product groups. Mr. Fergusson was the product manager of the electronics division. Exhibit 1 presents the organization structure of the company.

As of 1984, the electronics division's sales of $10 million accounted for 15 percent of the company sales. The division earned a profit before tax of 12 percent on sales. Sales were growing at 15 percent per year.

DEVELOPMENT OF AUTOMOTIVE COMPUTERS AND MONITORS PRIOR TO 1980

Prelude

In 1969, the Environmental Protection Agency (EPA) started tightening the emission requirements for the automobile industry. The international oil crisis had also taken its worst turn at that time. The automobile industry responded to these changes by developing automotive computers that could monitor all systems in an automobile and adjust ignition timing, air-fuel mixture, and fuel flow into the carburetor to keep the engine running at optimal performance conditions. However, these computers were far from user-friendly. Accessing their self-diagnostic feedback required the use of the tedious breakout box diagnosis traditionally used by auto mechanics (more popularly known as service technicians in the 1980s) to check the electrical

This case was prepared by Professor Shreekant G. Joag, St. John's University, as the basis for class discussion rather than to illustrate either effective or ineffective handling of a managerial situation. All proper names have been disguised.

It is reproduced here by permission of the North American Case Research Association and the author. Copyright © 1991.

EXHIBIT 1
The Organization Structure of OTC

OTC's Matrix Organization Structure			OTC's Staff Division (Based on Product Groups)					
			Electronics & Diagnostics	Special Tools	Pullers	Hydraulics	Equipment	Miscellaneous
OTC's Line Departments (Based on Functions)								
1. Purchasing								
2. Finance								
3. Production								
4. Marketing	Advertising							
	Distribution							
	Sales	Original Equipment Manufacturers (OEMs)						
		Automobiles and Heavy Duty Users						
		Industrial Buyers						
		International Sales						
		Canada						
		Special Projects						
		Job Order Business						
		Intercompany Business						

Source: Owatonna Tool Company.

systems of the cars. Therefore, major American automakers encouraged OTC and another company named Mega Systems Inc. (MSI), located in the Northeast, to develop the scanner or monitor.

The Automotive Computer Monitor

A typical monitor was a calculator-like instrument with several alphanumeric keys. It could be connected to the vehicle computer by inserting its power plug into the cigarette lighter outlet and its input-output plug into the underdash assembly line communications link (ALCL) provided in the vehicle. Once connected, certain parameters specifying the maker of the car, model name, year, and the computer system code had to be input to the monitor using the keyboard. Once programmed in this manner, the monitor provided unprecedented access to all information available in the onboard computer. With appropriate commands, it could display the value of different input variables used by the computer to control various functions of the automobile. The performance characteristics of the vehicle could also be read directly on the monitor display. The monitor could also point out inconsistencies in the performance of various subsystems through different trouble codes. Thus, the monitor could be used to quiz the computer system and obtain all-around information about the total performance of the car. A simple manual accompanying the monitor provided all necessary instructions, which could be mastered within a short time by any technician with a good basic knowledge of automobiles. Exhibit 2 presents an illustration of the monitor.

Design Characteristics of the Monitor

Initially, separate monitors were developed for each make of car, treating them as products designed for totally separate applications. Perhaps the limited experience with the product and limitations of available memory in the monitors were among the important reasons that favored such design. At that time, it was realized that with every passing year, automakers would introduce new computer systems with changed designs and enhanced control capabilities in their new car models. Further, since a vehicle had an expected physical life of 10 to 15 years, the first batch of cars with computers would be around and must be maintained that long. As such, the pool of cars requiring monitors for diagnosis would build up over the first 10 to 15 years. Thereafter, every year the oldest cars would drop out of the pool and the new cars would be added.

Thus, in the first year of their introduction, monitors would only need to have the ability to diagnose computerized cars manufactured in that year. However, in the following year, their capabilities would need to be enhanced to diagnose the newer and more advanced computers in new model cars in addition to the first-year cars. Thus, every year monitors would need to build in an enhanced cumulative capability of diagnosing an ever-increasing variety of automotive computer systems.

The problem of such upgrading had two aspects. First, all new monitors would need to be manufactured as per the upgraded design specifications. However, it would also be necessary to upgrade the capabilities of monitors sold in the past that were

EXHIBIT 2
The Automotive Computer Monitor

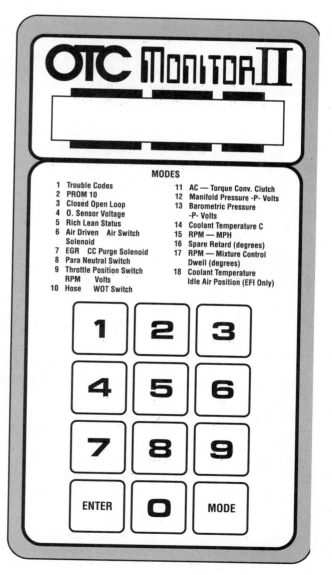

presently with customers. This would be especially important to those customers whose business was to maintain their clients' cars.

These considerations led to the development of the erasable or reprogrammable memory. An erasable memory was a small and replaceable component of the monitor that could be reprogrammed and/or redesigned to enhance the cumulative diagnostic capability of the monitor. Such upgrading would enable the monitor to handle the new computer system introduced by an automaker in addition to those used in the past. This approach made it possible for monitor manufacturers to standardize the design of the rest of the monitor. Only the erasable memory program would be changed every year to create a new and upgraded version of the monitor. This also simplified the problem of upgrading monitors sold to customers in the past. Every year, all customers who had purchased monitors in the past would be asked to send their monitors back to the manufacturer, where the erasable memory would be replaced by a new reprogrammed and upgraded memory and the monitors returned to the customers.

MONITOR INDUSTRY AT THE BEGINNING OF THE 1981 MODEL YEAR

At the beginning of the 1981 model year, all major automakers had big plans to introduce their own versions of automotive computers in their cars. There were two leading manufacturers that wanted to introduce their automotive computer monitors in the market: OTC and MSI. Each had developed three types of monitors meant for General Motors, Ford, and Chrysler cars, respectively. The monitor prices were to be in the $300 to $400 range. Monitors were expected to have a physical life of five to ten years with 6.67 as the average. However, in any year, there was always the possibility that significant technological changes would render older monitors completely unupgradable to handle future automotive computers. Since the automotive computer and the monitor were both at very early stages of their life cycles, and since the development of a monitor required full cooperation of automakers, monitors were initially developed only for American-made passenger cars.

MARKET FOR AUTOMOTIVE COMPUTER MONITORS

The market for the automotive computer monitors could be conceptualized as consisting of three major segments. The first segment comprised new car dealers of major automakers. Every year, new car dealers would purchase automotive tools and equipment to maintain and upgrade their ability to service the cars sold during the last 10 to 15 years. A major part of these purchases was initiated by principal automakers. Whenever a new model car was ready for introduction, automakers developed a standard set of essential tools and equipment necessary for effective troubleshooting, repair, and maintenance of the new model cars. Further, they appointed specific suppliers to produce the essential tools and make them available to dealers. Automakers required their dealers to participate in the essential service tools programs by buying the tool sets from the appointed suppliers. In 1981, the cost to a dealer of a typical tool set was $400–$500. Such programs were considered essential to ensure the proper infrastructure of repair and maintenance services necessary to service new model cars. However, dealers were free to and, in fact, did purchase additional tools and equipment of their own accord if that would enhance their efficiency and profitability.

Thus, the inclusion of an item into the essential service tools program of an automaker was the easiest—though not the only—way to tap this segment since that created a captive market for the item in the dealership network. In view of the functional superiority of the monitor over the traditional breakout box diagnosis using several electrical instruments, OTC felt that the rightful place for the monitor was in the essential service tools programs of major automakers.

The second aftermarket segment consisted of three subsegments: service stations, independent repair shops, and fleet service locations that serviced their clients' cars. Traditionally, this segment looked up to new car dealers as the opinion leaders with the latest know-how in the field. However, in many other respects, its needs were quite distinct from those of dealers. The third ultimate user segment consisted of consumer car owners. While only a few car owners preferred to repair their own cars, it was conceivable that a much larger number of car owners would be interested in a monitor-like product. It would help them to conduct a preliminary diagnosis when a car needed repairs. It would also serve as a cross-check on the diagnosis made by the service technician. Experts in the field felt that a monitor providing only a limited function feedback would be adequate for this segment. However, the consumer segment may require the monitor to be priced under $100 if a sizable market penetration was to be achieved.

Each customer in any of the three market segments could be considered to represent a one-time purchase potential for at least one monitor. Customers dealing with a larger number and variety of vehicles and employing several technicians, such as a large dealer or service station, may require more than one monitor. Further, all customers represented a potential for replacement demand when their monitors wore out. In addition, depending on the nature of their need, customers in some of the segments may require an annual upgrading of their older monitors. Exhibit 3 presents statistical data on the size of the three market segments at the end of calendar years 1980–1983, and projected data for year 1984 and 1985. Even though the automobile industry operated on the basis of a September–August model year, all quantitative information presented in the exhibits of this case is for a January–December calendar year.

NEW PRODUCT INTRODUCTION STRATEGIES OF MONITOR MANUFACTURERS: 1981–1984

Early Failures of OTC and MSI

At the beginning of model year 1981, both OTC and MSI felt that marketing the monitor to new car

dealers through major automakers was the best way to introduce the product in the market. First, this involved dealing with only a handful of customers. Second, once the monitor was included in the essential service tools programs, it would enjoy an instant captive market in the dealership network. Finally, new car dealers were the opinion leaders for the other two market segments. Therefore, logically, the dealers segment had to be the first choice. However, both OTC and MSI failed to convince the three major American automakers to include the monitor in their essential service tools programs and their essential tools continued to include only the traditional breakout box procedure instead.

There were two reasons behind this outcome. First, the monitor failed to meet the criterion of a "widely available tool" required by the EPA for its inclusion in the essential service tools programs. Second, due to the monitors' relatively high prices, automakers feared dealer resistance and did not want to be involved in promoting monitors actively.

There were only two exceptions, both short-lived. In the 1981 model year, American Motors included an OTC monitor in its essential service tools program. Similarly, in the 1982 model year, the Buick division of General Motors included an MSI monitor in its essential service tools program. The monitor was dropped from each program in the following year due to dealer resistance.

OTC's Revised Marketing Strategy

Even though OTC failed to win the support of automakers in introducing the monitor to the new car dealers segment, that did not in any way diminish the importance of that segment in its overall strategy. In 1981, OTC approached dealers directly to introduce its monitor. However, as was expected, it experienced only a slow and limited success in winning that segment. During 1981–1984, 20 percent of OTC's monitor sales came from the dealers segment.

In 1982, OTC directly introduced its GM monitors in aftermarket segments of service stations,

EXHIBIT 3

The U.S. Market for Automotive Computer Monitors

(A) NEW CAR DEALERS AS OF DECEMBER 31

	Number of Dealers					
Automaker	1980	1981	1982*	1983*	1984*P	1985*P
General Motors	10,635	10,590	10,160	10,040	9,965	9,830
Ford	5,667	5,643	5,414	5,508	5,564	5,517
Chrysler	3,807	3,791	3,637	3,864	3,988	4,003
American Motors	1,663	1,656	1,589	1,526	1,465	1,421
Other U.S.	978	975	934	906	899	877
Total U.S.	22,750	22,655	21,734	21,844	21,881	21,648
Intercorporate Duals	979	975	935	1,003	979	975
Net U.S.	21,772	21,680	20,799	20,841	20,902	20,673

*Source: Automotive News, Market Data Books, 1983–1986, Detroit, Michigan: Crain Communications. All other figures estimated by extrapolation.

(B) AFTERMARKET CUSTOMERS AS OF DECEMBER 31

Subsegment
Number of Customers (in 000's)

	1980	1981*	1982	1983	1984*P	1985P
Service Stations	119	120	119	118	115	120
Independent Repair Shops	135	136	140	143	150	155
Fleet Service Locations	38	39	39	39	39	40
Total	292	295	298	301	304	315

*Source: Service Job Analysis, 1984, Des Plaines, Illinois: Hunter Publishing Company. All other figures estimated by extrapolation.

(C) NEW CAR REGISTRATIONS BY CONSUMER CAR OWNERS DURING CALENDAR YEAR

Auto Make
Number of New Car Registrations (in 000's)

	1980	1981	1982	1983	1984P	1985P
General Motors	4,066	3,758	3,413	3,928	4,501	4,583
Ford	1,466	1,378	1,294	1,527	1,951	2,045
Chrysler	625	740	668	820	963	1,121
American Motors	151	133	109	191	189	128
Other U.S.	4	4	3	1	1	1
Total	8,761	8,444	7,754	8,924	10,129	10,889*

P: Projections as available to Fergusson in August 1985.

Source: Automotive News, Market Data Books, 1983–1986, Detroit, Michigan: Crain Communications..

independent repair shops, and fleet service locations. Thus, in effect, OTC took its product directly to the technicians who would actually use it. OTC sales representatives met with technicians to teach them the fundamentals of computer diagnostics.

Traditionally, automobile technicians viewed the automobile as an assembly of several independent systems. Consequently, their fault detection procedures were based on the process of elimination to identify the faulty system. It was not very easy for them to visualize that the onboard computer transformed the automobile into one integrated system where anything could affect everything else. For example, improper fuel delivery could be caused not only by a faulty carburetor but also by a defective sensor wrongly reading the coolant temperature and, thereby, leading the computer to wrongly conclude that the engine was overheated. Thus, OTC sales representatives had to train the technicians to think about a computerized automobile in a totally new manner. In addition, the training involved actual use of a monitor in measuring the vehicle's inputs and outputs of the automotive computer to identify discrepancies and diagnose performance problems.

However, once trained, technicians quickly realized that the handheld monitor was a much faster diagnostic tool compared to the traditional procedure using several electrical instruments, as prescribed by the vehicle manufacturers. Thus, the direct training program became the cornerstone of OTC's eventual success in gaining a leading position in aftermarket segments. During 1981–1984, 80 percent of OTC's monitor sales came from aftermarket segments. Until August 1984, OTC had still not introduced its monitors in the consumer car owners segment.

Marketing Strategies of the Competitors

MSI was able to begin its marketing operations only in 1982. It adopted similar strategies to introduce its monitors in the early years. Being the only other marketer of monitors, it was also able to gain a sizable share of the market.

In 1984, MSI licensed Electra Corporation to manufacture and market its GM monitors in aftermarket segments. Electra introduced its monitors at substantially lower prices compared to OTC and MSI and quickly became a major force in the market. However, the impact of Electra on OTC was, to some extent, dampened as well as masked by two reasons. First, Electra monitors were much more difficult to use than OTC monitors, which somewhat limited their quick acceptance in the market.

Second, the market for the industry as a whole was growing and offered enough room for all competitors to maintain their sales growth. Therefore, it was some time before OTC realized that it had actually lost its market share and that Electra's penetration strategy had succeeded in carving out a sizable share of the market.

Both the Ford Motor Company and Chrysler Corporation also developed monitors for their own cars and started marketing them in 1984. However, these products were of only average quality and lacked the intensive marketing backup enjoyed by OTC, MSI, and Electra monitors. As such, they had only a tiny share of the market. None of the five monitor manufacturers had introduced the monitor in the consumer segment of automobile owners until late 1984.

MONITOR MARKET SEGMENTS BY AUTO MAKE

As stated earlier, separate monitors were initially developed for each make of car. Therefore, the monitor market could also be segmented by the make of the car for which the monitors were designed: GM, Ford, and Chrysler. One major factor determining the sales volume in each segment was the computer protocol policy adopted by the respective automaker. As early as 1981, GM had made a policy decision to disclose its computer protocol, making it possible for monitor manufacturers to develop a full-function monitor. Chrysler made a similar decision in model year 1983. However, Chrysler had developed a communications link (ALCL) only for its fuel injected cars. Such cars represented only a small proportion of the total cars produced by the company at that time. Moreover, in view of its smaller market share, there were fewer Chrysler cars in the market that could use monitors. Ford did not develop a communications capability for its automotive computers in view of the complexities of diagnosis. Instead, it chose to have the computer perform a self-test and produce coded messages called service codes. This delayed the development of monitors for Ford cars.

Further, Ford monitors remained limited function monitors that, in turn, limited their usefulness and their sales.

As of 1984, practically all monitors sold by OTC were for GM cars, only a very few were for Chrysler cars, and none were for Ford cars. The same was true of MSI and Electra. All monitors sold by the Ford Motor Company and Chrysler Corporation were only for their own cars. In spite of this, OTC felt that the sales of monitors for Ford, Chrysler, and American Motors cars would gain momentum in the future. Therefore, future marketing plans and sales forecasts must consider all American-made cars as the potential market and not focus on GM cars alone.

Exhibit 4 traces the history of the development of various automotive computer systems by the three leading American automakers. Exhibit 5 presents the developments in diagnostic information available from the computer monitors. Exhibit 6 presents various competing monitor brands, years of their introduction, product features (limited or

EXHIBIT 4
History of Development of Automotive Computer Systems

System Code	System Name	Model Year of Introduction (X)				
		1981	1982	1983	1984	1985P
(A) General Motors						
1	1981	X				
2	EFI/TBI		X	X	X	X
3	FULL		X	X		
4	OLDS LC		X	X		
5	Min-T		X	X	X	X
6	CFI 2BL TBI			X	X	X
7	PONT 4 PFI				X	X
8	BUI 6 PFI				X	X
9	ISUZU			X	X	
10	CHEV TRK			X	X	
11	PONT EFI				X	X
12	OLDS FULL				X	X
13	CHEV PFI					X
14	PONT 6 PFI					X
15	6.2L DSL					X
	TOTAL	1	4	7	10	11
(B) Ford Motor Company						
1	MCU	X	X	X	X	X
2	EEC IV			X	X	X
	TOTAL	1	1	2	2	2
(C) Chrysler Corporation						
1	EFI/TBI			X	X	X
2	TURBO				X	X
3	FBC					X
4	MEX				X	X
	TOTAL	–	–	1	3	4

P: Projected
Source: Owatonna Tool Company.

EXHIBIT 5
Developments in the Diagnostic
Information Available from the Monitors

	Number of Diagnostic Functions Available in Monitors for Fuel Injected Cars of Automaker (Computer System Name)		
Model Year	GM (EFI)	Ford (MCU)	Chrysler (EFI)
1981	28 (1981)	3	–
1982	35	3	–
1983	38	3	2
1984	37	3	13
1985P	38	3	15

P: Projected

Source: Owatonna Tool Company.

full function), and prices. Exhibit 7 presents some basic financial information about major monitor manufacturers as of December 1984. Exhibit 8 presents OTC's unit sales of monitors for each make of automobile for the period 1981–1984.

Exhibit 9 presents overall market shares of monitor manufacturers based on unit sales for the period 1981–1984. It was believed that by 1984, the relative market shares had reached a steady state and would not change dramatically unless due to some unforeseen reasons. During 1980–1984, the dependence of other monitor manufacturers on new car dealers and aftermarket segments was similar to that of OTC.

RIGHT TIME FOR PRODUCT MODIFICATIONS?

During 1981–1984, OTC's electronics division had been busy perfecting its monitor technology. Many interesting technical innovations had been made during this process. It was OTC's practice to consider new innovations and product modifications only after prototypes of new designs were produced and tested. This made it possible for the company to actually start production and shipments within two months of a final decision to launch a new design. In an August 1984 product development report, OTC's engineers presented

three design modification alternatives for Fergusson's consideration. Clearly, the designs presented were novel and creative. However, Fergusson was not sure if some of the ideas were a little ahead of their time. He was concerned that product modifications may in fact harm the company's competitive position if introduced prematurely.

Two conflicting reasons confounded these concerns. First, all three major manufacturers were vigorously pursuing their research and development efforts. Even though OTC was much ahead of its competitors, Fergusson believed that, given the time, all monitor manufacturers would be able to develop similar technologies in their laboratories. This was a good reason to introduce innovations as soon as they were made and enjoy the benefit of being the first in the market. Second, the electronics industry was famous for imitative competition, and monitors were no exception. Therefore, it was felt that the company that was the first to introduce important design modifications in the market would enjoy only a short-term advantage over its competitors—for a year at the most. Thereafter, other competitors would also introduce similar or even better products, bringing the average relative market shares back to their steady state. This was a good reason not to rush product changes unless there were other compelling reasons.

Therefore, it was necessary to evaluate the proposed product modifications primarily on the basis of their long-term impact. Criteria such as enhanced contribution margins would benefit OTC alone, whereas other effects such as proportion of total market potential tapped and expansion of the total market would benefit the monitor industry as a whole. The three monitor design modification alternatives before Fergusson in August 1984 are described below.

Alternative 1: Status Quo

The first alternative was to maintain the status quo. The company's present products were technically equivalent, operationally superior, and easier to use than competing products. Further, the present

EXHIBIT 6

Competing Monitor Brands, Features, and Prices for Different Auto Makes

Model Year	Auto Make	Monitor Manufacturer OTC	MSI	Electra	Ford	Chrysler
1981	GM	Monitor	–	–	–	–
	Ford	–	–	–	–	–
	Chrysler	–	–	–	–	–
	AMC*	MT 501 (Discontinued)				
1982	GM	Monitor 2 $399	Meg $440	–	–	–
	Ford	–	–	–	–	–
	Chrysler	–	–	–	–	–
	AMC	–	–	–	–	–
1983	GM	Monitor 2 $399	Meg and Minimeg $440 and $275			
	Ford	–	–	–	–	–
	Chrysler	–	–	–	–	–
	AMC	–	–	–	–	–
1984	GM	Monitor 4 $399	Minimeg only $275	Electra $349		
	Ford	–	–	–	Scat Limited Function $185	–
	Chrysler	Data Scan Full Function $349	–	–	–	Digital Readout Box Limited Function $185
	AMC	–	–	–	–	–
1985 Expected	GM	Monitor 85 $299	Minimeg $275	Electra $249	-	–
	Ford	Unnamed Limited Function $179	–	–	Scat Limited Function $185	–
	Chrysler	Data Scan Full Function $349	–	–	–	Digital Readout Box Limited Function $185
	AMC	–	–	–	–	–

*AMC = American Motor Company

Source: Owatonna Tool Company.

system of separate designs for each make of car fragmented the market three ways and made it less economical for new manufacturers to enter the market. Therefore, this alternative would be pursued until either the demand situation changed or competition became a major threat. While this alternative appeared safe enough, Fergusson felt that such reactive strategy would be incompatible

EXHIBIT 7

Comparative Financial Information about Major Monitor Manufacturers as of December 1984 (Projected)

	Monitor Manufacturer				
	OTC Electronics	*MSI*	*Electra*	*Ford Motor Company*	*Chrysler Corporation*
Total Sales M$	10.000	7.000	5.000	N.A.	N.A.
% Sales Growth Per Year	15	10	10	N.A.	N.A.
Profits as % of Sales	10	15	13	N.A.	N.A.
Product Lines	OEM Projects Electronic Instruments	Electronic Instruments	Electronic Instruments	Automobiles Accessories	Automobiles Accessories

N.A. = Not Available. Specific figures for monitor sales were not available for these companies. Since Ford and Chrysler are very large corporations, their overall sales were irrelevant to give any understanding of their monitor sales.
Source: Owatonna Tool Company.

with OTC's aggressive and proactive strategies of the past.

1985 would be the fifth year since the introduction of computerized cars in the market. By now, new car dealers and aftermarket segments had gained some valuable experience in repairing these cars and had started appreciating the value of the monitor as a diagnostic tool. The marketing efforts of OTC, MSI, and Electra had further accelerated this process. Further, it was expected that in 1985 Electra would reduce its monitor prices by $100 each and, in that case, OTC would have to do the same for its GM and Chrysler monitors to retain its market share. MSI was not expected to reduce prices in view of its smaller market share and already very low prices. Collectively, these factors would give a major boost to overall monitor sales. Therefore, it was estimated that the industry as a whole would be able to sell at least one new monitor each to 45 percent of the new car dealers and at least an average of three monitors (designed for different auto makes) each to 5 percent of the aftermarket customers. OTC would retain its overall market share at its 1984 level. In addition, there would be replacement sales for monitors sold in the past that had worn out (whose physical life would expire) during the year. Under this alternative, one new monitor would replace each expired monitor.

The present design required customers who wanted to upgrade their monitors to return them to OTC for upgrading. The cost of this service would be $75 per monitor. The sales of the upgrading service would amount to half the total population of monitors with new car dealers and aftermarket customers as at the end of the previous year. No specific estimates of new monitor and upgrading service sales were available for the consumer segment since none of the monitor manufacturers had yet introduced the product to this segment. However, it was felt that most consumers may not have any need for upgrading services. Under this alternative, OTC would earn a contribution of 20 percent on its sales revenue.

Alternative 2: Three-in-One Design

The second alternative was to physically merge the GM, Ford, and Chrysler monitors into one unit, keeping the basic design concept unchanged. The recent expansions in memory capacity had made it possible to design a single monitor with the ability to access the automotive computer systems manufactured by all three major American automakers. The new monitor would be identical to the existing ones except that a single machine would be able to diagnose GM, Ford, and Chrysler cars.

EXHIBIT 8
OTC's Unit Sales of Monitors 1981–1984

	Number of Monitors Sold in Calendar Year			
Make of the Automobile	*1981*	*1982*	*1983*	*1984*
General Motors	500	7,200	11,273	7,720
Ford Motor Company	Negligible	Negligible	Negligible	Negligible
Chrysler Corporation	Negligible	Negligible	Negligible	Negligible
American Motor Company	3,500*	–	–	–
Other U.S. Cars	–	–	–	–
Total	4,000	7,200	11,273	7,720

*Discontinued, already obsolete, and would not be upgraded any longer.

Source: Owatonna Tool Company.

Purely from the technical and customer convenience viewpoints, this alternative appeared superior to the existing design of separate monitors for the three auto makes. Furthers, it would offer economies of scale through product simplification, standardization, and reduced variety of models for production and inventory. The total cost of making one three-in-one monitor would be substantially lower than the cost of making three separate monitors. The monitor would be priced at $420. Estimating demand for such a design would be complex. The reaction of each of the three market segments would depend upon its basic needs and what the new design offered it in turn. The product would increase the monitor industry's penetration of segments reacting favorably by 5 percent and reduce its penetration of segments reacting unfavorably by 10 percent as compared to the first alternative of status quo. In view of the comprehensive design, only one monitor would be sufficient to service all makes of cars. Therefore, a conservative estimate of the market could be made by assuming the sale of only one monitor per customer. In addition, there would be replacement sales for monitors sold in the past that wear out during a given year. Once again, one new three-in-one monitor would replace one expired monitor.

If the three-in-one design were introduced in 1985, the older designs would be discontinued, as would the upgrading services for them. Thus, in

EXHIBIT 9
Market Shares of Major Monitor Manufacturers

	% Market Share by Unit Sales in Calendar Year			
Monitor Manufacturer	*1981*	*1982*	*1983*	*1984*
OTC	100	60	60	40
MSI	–	40	40	20
Electra	–	–	–	35
Ford Motor Co.	–	–	–	3
Chrysler Corp.	–	–	–	2

Source: Owatonna Tool Company.

1985 there would be no demand for upgrading services. The new design also required all customers who wanted to upgrade their monitors to return them to OTC. The cost of this service would be $100 per monitor. However, such demand would materialize only from year 1986 onwards. As in the case of the first alternative, the sales of the upgrading service would amount to half the total population of three-in-one monitors with new car dealers and aftermarket customers. The consumer segment may not have any need for the upgrading service since a typical consumer would need to diagnose just one car. Under this alternative, OTC's contribution would increase to 25 percent of its sales revenue. The higher contribution could also serve as an added cushion to face future competition.

Fergusson was concerned about another matter. In the past, the competition was kept at bay due to the heavy research and financial inputs needed to develop and market the three separate computer monitors with small individual markets. However, the economies of scale offered by the three-in-one design may make the industry more attractive to potential competitors desirous of entering the field.

Alternative 3: Cartridge Design

Technically, the third alternative was the most innovative of all. OTC engineers had developed a new monitor with a standard base unit that could be used with any make of car. The erasable memory was taken out of the base unit and put into a plug-in memory cartridge. Separate cartridges were designed for each make of car. Thus, using two adapter cables and a memory cartridge of the right type, the base unit could be used for GM, Ford, or Chrysler cars. The cost of the monitor with three cartridges would be lower than three separate monitors but higher than one three-in-one monitor. It would still offer the advantages of economies of scale and increased profitability.

The biggest advantage of this monitor was the manner in which customers may perceive it. To a customer, it would offer a unique flexibility. It could be adapted to any customer's needs simply by buying appropriate cartridges. Moreover, there would be no need to return the monitor every year for upgrading. Instead, the customer would only have to buy new upgraded memory cartridges. Past surveys had shown that the customers viewed the returning of monitors for annual upgrading very negatively. They associated it with lack of quality and permanency in the product. The cartridge design would be able to overcome these negative connotations and convince customers that a monitor was, in fact, a durable product with long life.

This monitor would be sold at a price of $400 for the basic set (a base unit plus one free cartridge of choice). Additional cartridges would be sold at $50 each. Thus, a full set (a base unit plus three cartridges) would cost the customer $500.

Estimating demand for this design would also be complex. The reaction of each of the three market segments would depend upon its basic needs and what the new design had to offer as compared to the existing one. The product could increase the monitor industry's penetration of segments reacting favorably by 10 percent and reduce its penetration of segments reacting unfavorably by 5 percent as compared to the first alternative of status quo. It was expected that the monitor industry would be able to sell at least one basic set to a new car dealer and at least one full set to an aftermarket customer. There would also be additional replacement sales for monitors sold in the past that wear out during a given year. The expired monitors with new car dealers would be replaced by basic sets, whereas those with aftermarket customers would be replaced by full sets.

With the introduction of the cartridge design, the older monitors and upgrading services for them would be discontinued. Moreover, the new design would not need any upgrading services. Thus, the concept of annual upgrading would cease to exist beginning in 1985. Instead, beginning in 1986, there would be sales of upgraded replacement cartridges to past customers. Every year, about 80 percent of the total population of cartridge design monitors with new car dealers would generate a demand for one replacement cartridge each. Similarly, 80 percent of the population of monitors with aftermarket customers would generate a demand for an average of three replacement cartridges each. There may be no demand for replacement cartridges in the consumer segment. Under this alternative, OTC's contribution would be 20 percent of its sales revenue.

IMPORTANT CONSIDERATIONS FOR THE DECISION

What concerned Fergusson the most about these ideas was the uncertainty about the ideal timing of their introduction. He was not sure that such major innovations should be marketed so early in the life cycle of a product. First of all, the product was still in its infancy. Therefore, the attention of the industry should be focused more on convincing the customers of the basic usefulness of the product concept. Such effort needed a technically stable product to back it up. Instead, if the product design kept changing frequently, new customers may decide to wait until the product line stabilized. That may be very harmful to the momentum of sales. Moreover, Fergusson felt that such innovations had not become necessary for the continued success of the product. He also felt that the present fragmented market had kept the potential competition at bay. He was not certain how that would change with the adoption of the newer designs.

Fergusson realized that one way or the other, he would need to make up his mind soon so that the marketing plans for 1985 could be finalized in time.

Discount Retailing Battlefield: Kmart vs. Wal-Mart

In June 1995, Floyd Hall took over as the CEO of Kmart Corporation. His predecessor, Joseph Antonini, who ran the company for seven years, was forced to resign three months earlier due to continued lukewarm performance of the company vis-à-vis its archrival Wal-Mart. A winning strategy for the company must now be chalked out.

DISCOUNT RETAILING ARENA

For seven years, Joseph Antonini led a discount store to battle against what appeared to be its twin. The two chains looked alike, sold the same products, sought each other's customers. The competition, however, was over: Sam Walton's Wal-Mart Stores Inc. had won.

So bleak were the prospects for Kmart Corp. that in February 1995 an advertising agency bidding for its business, N.W. Ayer & Partners, recommended that it stop competing against Wal-Mart and transform itself into a big convenience chain where customers could go for milk and cigarettes. "It seems that the only way for [Kmart] to survive is to find a different niche," summarized the N.W. Ayer's presentation. Kmart, of course, rejected the idea.

Though the new leader could spark high hopes for ringing cash registers, Kmart still had major operational and managerial issues to deal with.

While an air of inevitable defeat had recently settled over Kmart, a short look back found many observers believing deeply in Kmart and Mr. Antonini. In fact, many of the investors who demanded his ouster as president and chief executive officer had gambled on him to outfox his counterparts at Wal-Mart not so long ago. They questioned some of the strategies of Mr. Walton, Wal-Mart's founder. They also thought Mr. Antonini had more pizazz, better locations, and a solid turnaround plan.

"He's taken a tired, dispirited company and revived it," declared a prominent retail analyst in a 1991 *Forbes* magazine article that described Wal-Mart's stock as overpriced and Kmart as a good bet.

Considering the similarity of their stores and missions, analysts attributed the different fates of Kmart and Wal-Mart primarily to management. Sam Walton, they said, was smarter than Mr. Antonini.

When Mr. Antonini took the reigns of Kmart in 1987, he had his hands full. He inherited some stores that were as old as 17 years, with water-warped floors, broken light fixtures, shelves placed too close together, and cheap displays set in the middle of aisles. Also, his predecessors had neglected to implement the sophisticated computer systems that were helping Wal-Mart track and replenish its merchandise swiftly and efficiently.

Overall, however, Kmart was way ahead. It had nearly twice as many discount stores, 2,223 to 1,198. The Troy, Michigan, chain also had sales of $25.63 billion, compared with $15.96 billion for Wal-Mart. Thanks to advertising and its large urban presence, Kmart and its red "K" logo also had greater visibility.

Although Wal-Mart had a more consistent record of earnings and revenue growth, in the eyes of many experts it had never played in the major leagues. Unlike Kmart, whose stores sat on expensive urban real estate and competed against other big discounters, Wal-Mart sat in pastures outside

---

This case was prepared by Juan M. Florin, doctoral student at the University of Connecticut, and the author as a basis for class discussion rather than to illustrate either effective or ineffective handling of an administrative situation.

small towns and picked off the customers from aging mom-and-pop shops.

Like the minor leaguer admiring a star in the bigs, Mr. Walton regarded Kmart with awe. "So much about their stores was superior to ours," Mr. Walton said in his autobiography, "that sometimes I felt like we couldn't compete." On the other hand, Mr. Antonini was heard by company insiders to dismiss Wal-Mart executives as "snake-oil salesmen."

So rapidly was Wal-Mart multiplying across the rural landscape that an invasion of urban America—and a confrontation with Kmart—became inevitable. To prepare for the encounter, Mr. Antonini focused on his own strength: marketing and merchandising. A self-promoter with a boisterous voice and a wide smile, Mr. Antonini invested heavily in national television campaigns and glamorous representatives such as Jaclyn Smith, a former "Charlie's Angels" television star who had her own line of clothes for Kmart.

That effort only widened a public-awareness gap between the two retailers. Even before the successful campaign with Ms. Smith, Kmart's "blue-light special" was famous around the country. Meanwhile, as recently as the late 1980s, most Americans had never seen a Wal-Mart advertisement, not to mention a store.

Mr. Walton did little to change that. He avoided publicity. And instead of marketing, he became obsessed with operations. He invested tens of millions of dollars in a companywide computer system linking cash registers to headquarters, enabling him to quickly restock goods selling off the shelves. He also invested heavily in trucks and distribution centers, around which he located his stores. Besides enhancing his control, these moves sharply reduced costs.

That was a gamble. While Kmart tried to improve its image and cultivated store loyalty, Mr. Walton kept lowering costs, betting that price would prove more important than any other factor.

As discounting fever deepened across America, analysts and shareholders came to expect huge growth from these retailers. In trying to meet these expectations, Messrs. Antonini and Walton once again trod different paths. Mr. Antonini tried bolstering growth by overseeing the purchase of other types of retailers: the Sports Authority sporting-goods chain, OfficeMax office-supply stores, Borders bookstores, and Pace Membership Warehouse clubs. Besides additional revenue, these chains would decrease dependence on profits from discounting. "It's the way of the future," Mr. Antonini declared of such diversification.

In Bentonville, Arkansas, meanwhile, Mr. Walton was taking precisely the opposite tack—betting everything on discount retailing. He started Sam's Club, a deep-discount, members-only retailer that was modeled after California-based Price Club, which devised the concept. Then Mr. Walton tried a brand of discounting that Kmart had already tried and abandoned in the 1960s—groceries. His first experiment, a massive Hyper-mart more than 230,000 square feet in size, suffered. Customers complained that the produce wasn't fresh or well-presented—and that they were having trouble finding things in stores so big that stockers wore roller skates. The Hypermart, Mr. Walton conceded, didn't work. Undaunted, he launched a revised concept: the Supercenter, a combination discount store and grocery that was smaller than the Hypermart.

By 1991, three years after Mr. Antonini took charge of Kmart, Wal-Mart surpassed it. For the retail year that ended in January 1991, Wal-Mart had sales of $32.6 billion, compared with Kmart's $29.7 billion (see Exhibit 1). For Kmart, the scary part was that Wal-Mart still had fewer stores—1,721 to Kmart's 2,330.

But Mr. Antonini and other Kmart supporters took comfort in knowing that Wal-Mart was running out of small towns to conquer. To continue growing, it would need to invade Kmart's turf: the more expensive and competitive big city. To prepare for that invasion, Mr. Antonini launched a $3.5 billion, five-year plan to renovate, enlarge, or replace Kmart's oldest and shabbiest stores. Analysts called him a "visionary," and often joined him on tours of prototype stores.

EXHIBIT 1
Changing Fortune

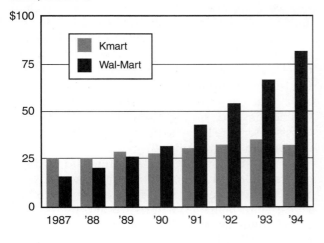

Sales, in billions

Source: Company annual reports.

But the least visible difference between Wal-Mart and Kmart was beginning to matter a lot. Wal-Mart's incredibly sophisticated distribution, inventory, and scanner systems meant that customers almost never encountered depleted shelves or price-check delays at the cash register. The halls of Kmart, meanwhile, were filed with distribution horror stories. Joseph R. Thomas, who oversaw distribution, said that, in retrospect, he should have smelled trouble when he found warehouses stuffed full of merchandise on Dec. 15, the height of the Christmas season.

Although Mr. Antonini poured a fortune into a frantic attempt to catch up, Kmart was so far behind that a November 1993 internal company report found that Kmart employees woefully lacked the training and skill to plan and control inventory. Kmart's cash registers often didn't have up-to-date information and would enter wrong prices. That led to a lawsuit by the Riverside County district attorney's office, claiming that 72 California Kmart stores had overcharged customers. In May 1994, Kmart settled for $985,000.

Consider the case of Anita Joy Winter. She went to a Naperville, Illinois, Kmart with three items on her list: underwear for her husband, contact-lens cleaner, and dish towels. The store was out of everything but the towels, and even then didn't have the beige color she wanted. After that, the register rang up a price more than 70 cents above what the shelf advertised, which took 10 minutes to straighten out. The consequence? "It's been 'Thank God for Wal-Mart' ever since," says Ms. Winter, who shops at a suburban Chicago Wal-Mart at least twice a week.

To the surprise of many, the higher cost and greater competitiveness of big cities hardly registered at Wal-Mart, now under the leadership of David Glass, the successor to Mr. Walton, who died in 1992 at age 74. The company had pared costs so aggressively in so many areas that it was passing on the high cost of, say, Long Island, New York, real estate and still easily under pricing Kmart. Moreover, its stores were often twice as large as older Kmarts. The effect, when Wal-Mart put in a 125,000 square-foot, slick new store across from an old 60,000 square-foot competitor, was just devastating.

Of the two retailers' diversification efforts, Kmart again proved the least successful. Mr. Antonini's plan to make Kmart a combination discount and specialty-retailing empire began to unravel at the end of 1993. While the specialty stores—those offering books, office supplies, or sporting goods—had contributed 30 percent of sales the year before, they only made up 15 percent of operating profit. And Kmart's discount stores were quickly losing market share to Wal-Mart. Shareholders demanded Mr. Antonini get rid of his prize jewels and focus on the discount stores. At the insistence of shareholders and against Mr. Antonini's wishes, Kmart announced at the end of 1994 a plan to sell majority stakes in three of its specialty retail chains.

Wal-Mart, meanwhile, couldn't roll out its new Supercenters fast enough. The concept of buying general merchandise and groceries in one store—at a discount—was proving successful around the country, prompting Kmart to start a similar chain. But the cost of opening Super Kmarts only detracted from the continuing, and largely disappointing, effort to renovate general-merchandise Kmarts. Though the stores were all supposed to have a new look by 1996—with wider aisles, gleaming floors and expanded departments—a third of them remained untouched. And those that had been renovated weren't producing the sales gains that had been expected.

As a result, even after $1.8 billion in asset sales in 1994, Kmart's operating profit was so disappointing that the company could barely cover its 96-cents-a-share annual dividend and had to scale back capital spending to about $800 million from at least $1 billion (see Exhibit 2).

The most telling statistic: Kmart's market share of total discount sales in 1995 had dropped to 22.7

percent from 34.5 percent in 1987, when Mr. Antonini took over as chairman, president, and chief executive officer. Wal-Mart had soared to 41.6 percent from 20.1 percent.

In the end, attitude may have made a bigger difference than strategy. In Bentonville, Mr. Walton and Mr. Glass asked subordinates what wasn't working, and chided them for failing to deliver any bad news. Executives were expected to spend much of their week visiting stores, actively soliciting proposals from subordinates. And Mr. Walton always acted as if a fierce competitor was just behind him and gaining. Even publicly, he and Mr. Glass were more likely to discuss Wal-Mart's weaknesses than its strengths.

In Troy, by contrast, Mr. Antonini didn't think others could tell him much about the business. A Kmart employee since 1964, when he started as an assistant manager, he bristled at criticism and was known as a "Teflon-coated" boss because

EXHIBIT 2
Diverging Paths: Wal-Mart vs. Kmart

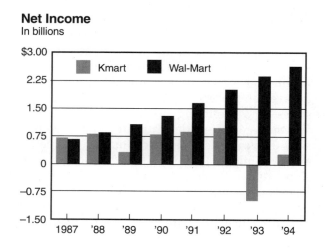

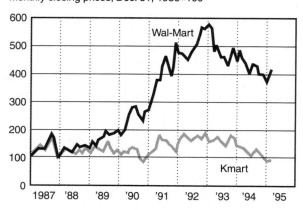

Sources: Company annual reports, *Baseline.*

suggestions for change slid right off. Insiders say he didn't do much hiring of managers from outside the company who might challenge him, and he flayed or fired consultants who recommended everything from management changes to targeting a narrower consumer market.

In fall of 1993, munching a sandwich in a shiny new Super Kmart store, Mr. Antonini expressed the possibility of following the lead of Mr. Walton and writing a book detailing a retail success.

KMART CORPORATION

Company History

A new concept in merchandising backed by thousands of dedicated men and women changed the S.S. Kresge Company from a fledgling newcomer in the variety store field to a multi-billion-dollar chain of general merchandise and specialty retail stores.

In 1899, Sebastian Spering Kresge opened his first store in downtown Detroit. By 1912, Kresge had 85 stores with annual sales of more than $10 million. Kresge stores appealed to shoppers with the stores' low prices, open displays, and convenient locations. Inflation in the World War I era forced Kresge to raise prices to 25¢, and in the mid-'20s, Kresge opened "green-front stores" to sell items at a dollar or less, often next to the red-front dime stores. Kresge went into the first suburban shopping center—Country Club Plaza in Kansas City, Missouri—in 1929. By 1930, variety-store chains had become commonplace because they provided a wide array of goods at low prices. Meanwhile, supermarket chains were introducing the public to self-service shopping. The Kresge Company launched its newspaper advertising program in the early 1930s. Radio promotions followed 20 years later, and television was added in 1968. Today, print ads still dominate Kmart's advertising program, with 72 million circulars weekly for insertion in 1,500 newspapers nationwide.

With the opening of America's first discount stores in 1953, a new era in retailing had dawned.

The Ann and Hope Mill Outlet in Rhode Island, which manufactured tinsel and corsage ribbons, sold discounted ribbons and greeting cards as well as women's house dresses for $2.19 each. Several other discount houses emerged in the 1950s, leading Kresge President Harry B. Cunningham to study a similar strategy for his organization. The result was the opening of the first Kmart discount department store, in Garden City, Michigan, in 1962. In Kmart's first year of operation, corporate sales topped $483 million. By 1966, Kresge registered its first billion-dollar year with 162 Kmart stores in operation. The name of the company was changed to Kmart Corporation in 1977 to reflect the fact that more than 95 percent of sales were generated by Kmart stores. By 1994, Kmart was the nation's second-largest general merchandise retailer with $34 billion in sales. Today, there are more than 2,400 Kmart stores in the United States, Puerto Rico, Canada, the Czech Republic, Slovakia, Mexico, Singapore, and Australia. Kmart employs some 300,000 individuals worldwide. Loyalty and long service are common; thousands of Kmart associates have worked for the company for 25 years or longer. Store management teams are responsible for the profitability of their own units and have the authority to make certain independent decisions about their operations.

In the early '70s, the company pursued an aggressive expansion plan that included opening 271 stores in 1976. In 1981, the company shifted toward refurbishing existing stores. For almost 80 percent of the American public, Kmart is the nearly complete one-stop shopping center. Still, the company is working to prompt customers to think of Kmart for even more of their shopping needs. In the 1980s, Kmart had the highest shopper traffic in the nation.

Today's Kmart differs greatly from its forerunner of the '60s. Kmart emphasizes top brands and a strong program of private-label products for the value-conscious customer. These merchandise lines include the Jaclyn Smith apparel line, Fuzzy Zoeller golf apparel, designer jeans for men and women, name-brand athletic shoes, Martha Stewart fashions for the home, prestige cosmetics and fragrances, and many respected names in home improvement and health and beauty care. The company adheres to a "satisfaction always" policy, which means that customers receive refunds and exchanges with ease. The Kmart Price Promise gives each store manager and associate the power to match competitor's prices. This policy ensures Kmart remains America's price leader. The company has made strides towards more efficient operations. Kmart Information Network (KIN) is an electronic system that connects all stores, distribution centers, and headquarters and streamlines various office procedures. Point-of-sale equipment is in all 2,400 stores. In 1986, Kmart and GTE established a satellite-based communications network. Thirteen distribution centers supply stores with a substantial amount of their basic stock; most stores are less than one day's drive from a distribution center.

Diversification and Modernization

The acquisition of the nation's largest retail bookstore chain, Walden Book Company, Inc., was completed on August 9, 1984. In addition to books, Waldenbooks stores also carry video and music selections and computer software. Average stores occupy 3,000 square feet and are located primarily in regional shopping malls and strip shopping centers. Kmart Corporation completed the acquisition of Builders Square, Inc. (formerly Home Centers of America) on September 27, 1984. A typical Builders Square store occupies approximately 80,000 square feet and features name-brand merchandise at discount prices. Assortments include lumber, building materials, hardware, paint, plumbing and electrical supplies, and garden and home improvement goods. In 1987, the company celebrated the 25th anniversary of Kmart stores and announced a partnership with Bruno's, Inc., of Birmingham, Alabama to develop American Fare, combination concept stores, in the United States. The company also moved to streamline operations, closing its Central Regional Office in Plymouth, Michigan and

realigning its five remaining regional offices. The company also established a Marketing Department to strengthen communication to its customers about the Kmart store.

In 1988, Kmart announced two new retailing concepts to be developed by its Builders Square subsidiary—Sports Giant, a chain of sporting goods superstores, and Office Square, a warehouse-type office supply store. In February 1990, Kmart announced an accelerated five-year, $3.5 billion new store opening, enlargement, and modernization program. This aggressive program involved building approximately 280 new full-size Kmart stores, enlarging 700 existing stores, relocating 300 others, and refurbishing 670 to bring their fixturing and layout up to the new store standards. The early 1990 acquisition of The Sports Authority allowed the company to move forward in the sporting goods mega-store arena. The company's Sports Giant stores were converted to The Sports Authority stores. In September 1990, Kmart acquired 22 percent ownership interest in OfficeMax, an office supply superstore chain. OfficeMax agreed to acquire the Office Square business of Kmart's subsidiary Builders Square. Kmart acquired the remaining interest in OfficeMax in November 1991.

A new, bold Kmart logo was unveiled in September 1990, signaling change and innovation for the chain. The new symbol keeps Kmart in step with the times and reflects the dynamism and excitement of the company's commitment to renewal. In 1991, Kmart raised $1 billion dollars in equity through a Preferred Equity Redemption Cumulative Stock offering (PERCS), ensuring the completion of its modernization program in 1996. At year end 1991, approximately 30 percent of the chain's Kmart stores sported the updated look.

Kmart's subsidiary operations, which in 1992 included Builders Square, OfficeMax, The Sports Authority, Waldenbooks, and Borders, were under the Specialty Retail Group. By year-end 1993, Kmart had completed more than half of its comprehensive store renewal program. Kmart also stepped up the roll-out of combination stores called

Super Kmart Centers. In 1993, Kmart sold its Pace Membership Warehouse subsidiary. Kmart also announced the sale of Payless Drugstore Northwest to Thrifty Drugs. By the end of 1994, there were 67 Super Kmart Centers nationwide. Borders-Walden, Inc. announced a corporate restructuring, renaming the entity Borders Group, Inc. Kmart sold its 21.5 percent interest in Coles Myer Ltd. and announced plans for Initial Public Offerings (IPOs) in Sports Authority, OfficeMax, and Borders Group, Inc.

Kmart initiated a productivity improvement process to reduce expenses by $600 to $800 million by the end of 1996. This process included the review of all aspects of the business to ensure growth in sales and earnings. A merchandise flow task force also was formed to focus on inventory flow, especially high-velocity consumable items. Financial information on the company is summarized in Exhibit 3.

International Expansion

Kmart made its initial entry into the European market when it purchased its first store in the Czech Republic in May 1992. Later that year, Kmart finalized the purchase of 12 additional stores in the Czech Republic and Slovakia. Kmart also announced plans to expand global operations, through joint ventures, in Mexico and Singapore. In 1994, Kmart opened its thirteenth distribution center in Brighton, Colorado, and stores in Mexico and Singapore.

Corporate Culture

The Thirtieth Anniversary of Kmart in 1992 marked the celebration of an institution deeply ingrained in the fabric of American life. Since its beginnings as Kresge, Kmart has successfully met the challenge of serving the changing needs of the American family.

Three savvy merchants, leaders of their generations, have played significant roles in the history of Kmart. The first was the founder, Sebastian Spering

(S.S.) Kresge, who built not only a successful retailing chain, but more important for its future, a flexible and responsive organization; the second, Harry Cunningham, emerged from the ranks to transform Kresge into Kmart; and until June 1995, Joe Antonini, the president and CEO who spearheaded Kmart's renewal for today's customer. Of all the great variety stores founded at the time of Kresge, only Kmart has maintained its leadership of American retailing.

Kmart was founded by a traveling salesman from Pennsylvania, Sebastian Spering Kresge. Kresge's variety stores spread throughout urbanizing America. Later there were larger stores expanding the product lines and broadening the customer base. Through all this, S.S. Kresge was a man of vision deeply in tune with the dynamics of a growing America. Despite his personal frugality—and to the shock of his colleagues and associates—he borrowed heavily to invest in store expansion to go where his customers were.

Kresge believed that one should both entice and listen to the customer; he ran specials in his stores on a weekly basis so that each week there would be a new reason to shop at Kresge. He also left Kresge employees free to exercise their judgment and do their jobs—all who worked for him said that he never looked over their shoulders (in an age of heavy employee supervision)—an early example of the empowerment of employees.

Harry Cunningham, the next great Kresge/ Kmart leader, also was known for listening to his customers. As a young manager, he asked the sales clerks to record all customer requests on little blue cards. Cunningham read the blue cards daily, ordering the merchandise requested. Within a year, Cunningham increased his store sales by 100 percent. Before he took over as president in 1959, Cunningham toured the country. He looked at his and other people's stores, he listened to the people, and he thought about the emergence of the new suburban lifestyle. He saw a sea of young families needing to furnish their homes, but, like all young families strapped by cash, they desired high quality at a low price. This post-war generation, newly

EXHIBIT 3

Kmart Corporation Consolidated Statements of Income (Dollars in millions, except per-share data)

	Fiscal Year Ended		
	Jan. 25, 1995	Jan. 26, 1994	Jan. 27, 1993
Sales	$34,025	$36,694	$33,366
Licensee fees and other income	288	296	292
	34,313	36,990	33,658
Cost of merchandise sold (includes buying and occupancy costs)	25,992	27,520	24,516
Selling, general and administrative expenses	7,701	8,217	7,393
Gain on subsidiary public offerings	(168)	–	–
Store restructuring and other charges	–	1,348	–
Interest expense:			
Debt—net	258	303	243
Capital lease obligations and other	236	192	185
	34,019	37,580	32,337
Income (loss) from continuing retail operations before income taxes and equity income	294	(590)	1,321
Equity in net income of unconsolidated companies	80	52	54
Income taxes	114	(191)	474
Net income (loss) from continuing retail operations before extraordinary item and the effect of accounting changes	260	(347)	901
Discontinued operations including the effect of accounting changes, net of income taxes of $7, $(61) and $11, respectively	20	(77)	40
Gain (loss) on disposal of discontinued operations, net of income taxes of $215 and $(248), respectively	16	(521)	–
Extraordinary item, net of income taxes of $(6)	–	(10)	–
Effect of accounting changes, net of income taxes of $(37)	–	(19)	–
Net income (loss)	$ 296	$ (974)	$ 941
Earnings per common and common equivalent share:			
Net income (loss) from continuing retail operations before extraordinary item and the effect of accounting changes	$ .55	$ (.78)	$ 1.97
Discontinued operations including the effect of accounting changes, net of income taxes	.04	(.17)	.09
Gain (loss) on disposal of discontinued operations, net of income taxes	.04	(1.14)	–
Extraordinary item, net of income taxes	–	(.02)	–
Effect of accounting changes, net of income taxes	–	(.04)	–
	$ .63	$ (2.15)	$ 2.06
Weighted average shares (millions)	456.6	456.7	455.6

EXHIBIT 3 (continued)
Kmart Corporation Consolidated Statements (Dollars in millions)

	Jan. 25, 1995	Jan. 26, 1994
Assets		
Current assets:		
Cash (includes temporary investments of $93 and $32, respectively)	$ 480	$ 449
Merchandise inventories	7,382	7,252
Accounts receivable and other current assets	1,325	1,816
Total current assets	9,187	9,517
Investments in affiliated retail companies	368	606
Property and equipment—net	6,280	5,886
Other assets and deferred charges	910	799
Goodwill—net of accumulated amortization of $45 and $59, respectively	284	696
	$17,029	$17,504
Liabilities and Shareholders' Equity		
Current liabilities:		
Long-term debt due within one year	$ 236	$ 390
Notes payable	638	918
Accounts payable — trade	2,910	2,763
Accrued payrolls and other liabilities	1,313	1,347
Taxes other than income taxes	272	271
Income taxes	257	35
Total current liabilities	5,626	5,724
Capital lease obligations	1,777	1,720
Long-term debt	2,011	2,227
Other long-term liabilities (includes store restructuring obligations)	1,583	1,740
Shareholders' equity:		
Preferred stock, 10,000,000 shares authorized;		
Series A, 5,750,000 shares authorized and issued at January 26, 1994	–	986
Series C, 790,287 shares authorized; shares issued 658,315 and 784,938, respectively	132	157
Common stock 1,500,000,000 shares authorized; shares issued 464,549,561 and 416,546,780, respectively	465	417
Capital in excess of par value	1,505	538
Performance restricted stock deferred compensation	–	(3)
Retained earnings	4,074	4,237
Treasury shares	(86)	(109)
Foreign currency translation adjustment	(58)	(130)
Total shareholders' equity	6,032	6,093
	$17,029	$17,504

Source: Kmart Corporation 1994 Annual Report.

affluent, produced the baby boomers and was the first generation to make shopping a vocation.

In his travels, Cunningham visited a new kind of store—the discount store. While the stores themselves were badly managed, he saw the beauty of the concept and understood how the professional Kresge organization could do better. Initially, the Kresge Board was skeptical because of the unproven success of those initial discounters, but Cunningham was persuasive in his belief that Kresge could provide value to the customer while maintaining high quality standards. Investing for the future, they spent more than $80 million. By the time the first Kmart opened in March 1962, there were 32 more locations ready to go.

Cunningham's blue index cards and S.S. Kresge's special promotions were transformed into a unique American experience—the blue light special. Its origins were humble but the blue light special has entered the vernacular and is a registered trademark.

In the spirit of Harry Cunningham and S.S. Kresge, Joe Antonini has had the vision to address the needs of today's woman, the core Kmart customer. As head of apparel in 1983, he began the transformation of the Kmart organization and the Kmart shopping experience. The women's apparel section was totally revamped and the Jaclyn Smith Collection was created. He followed with many lines designed for today's "busy, budget-conscious mom," the woman who plays many roles in the life of her family and community.

Antonini's understanding of that special woman, the Kmart customer, spurred him to examine her entire shopping experience. Just as other great retailers have entered the psyche of their customers, Kmart understands theirs—the time pressures and the multiple roles, the need for convenience, the requirement of value, and the desire to translate the new fashion and home trends to enrich her life and that of her family. Respect for the customer and a desire to make the shopping experience both fruitful and fun were the catalyst for the massive organizational redesign from the stores themselves to relationships with suppliers to the information systems necessary to bring the latest fashion to every shopper. Antonini's commitment to the Kmart customer led to an investment of $3.5 billion to refurbish and build the right kind of stores.

Super Kmart Center

Ranging in size from 160,000 to 190,000 square feet, Super Kmart Centers offer customers the ultimate experience in merchandise selection as well as an array of sensational groceries. Super Kmart Centers feature in-house bakeries, USDA fresh meats, fresh seafood (delivered daily), an array of hot and cold dishes from delicatessens, cookie kiosks, cappuccino bars, in-store eateries, fresh carry-out salad bars, and "Oriental-to-Go" menu items. To ensure grocery freshness, Kmart has developed its own grocery buying and operations division. Trained grocery personnel work closely with local suppliers to make regional fresh food available to shoppers. Cross merchandising offers added convenience at Super Kmart Centers. For example, toasters are above the fresh baked breads, kitchen gadgets are positioned across the aisle from produce, and infant centers feature everything for baby from food to clothing. In many locations, Super Kmart Centers provide customers with a selection of special services such as video rental, hair salon, florist, UPS shipping, banking and ATMs, lottery, money orders, as well as faxing and copy services with one-hour photo processing in the up-to-date image centers.

The first Super Kmart Center opened in Medina, Ohio on July 25, 1991. Its success and overwhelming acceptance by customers provided the foundation for Kmart's nationwide roll-out of 67 additional Super Kmart Centers over the last three years. More than 25 Super Kmart Centers are planned for 1995, bringing the total to about 100.

A company report noted:

The Super Kmart supercenter format is a dynamic new retail channel that builds on our core competencies and has strong potential for profitable growth. The Super Kmart format is based on a grocery-driven, high-frequency concept that, when executed properly, yields superior sales productivity and attracts a younger and more affluent family shopper than our traditional Kmart discount stores.

We are exploring ways to improve the Super Kmart "big box" concept by increasing the ease of shopping, providing more visual excitement and coherence within the store, creating better adjacencies of related merchandise, and reducing expenses. We may also develop a smaller Super Kmart format so we can expand into communities that cannot support the "big box."

The supercenter concept is a natural extension of our traditional business, which marries the need of our time-poor customers—who want convenience, value and one-stop shopping—with our desire for increased shopper frequency.

WAL-MART STORES

Samuel Moore Walton, the billionaire boy scout of Bentonville, Arkansas, built an empire on a fervid belief in value, pioneered by ideas like empowerment, and revolutionized retailing in the process. Dead at 74 after a long fight with cancer, he did not invent the discount department store, although it hardly seems possible that he didn't. He grabbed hold of the leading edge of retailing in 1962 and never let go, creating a value-powered merchandising machine that seems certain to outlive his memory.

In 1994, the still-young company earned $2.3 billion on sales of $67 billion. A $1,650 investment in 100 Wal-Mart shares in 1970, when they began trading, is worth $3 million today (see Exhibit 4 for financial information on the company). He taught American business that the vast amount of American people want value. He saw the future, and he helped make the future. According to a retail executive, while Walton was one of the great showmen of retailing, if he had been a television preacher he'd have become Pope. As a manager he applied such concepts as a flat organization, empowerment, and gain-sharing long before anyone gave them those names. In the 1950s he shared information and profits with all employees. He

ingested as much data as he could to get close to the customer and closer to the competition. He stressed flexibility and action over deliberation.

Wal-Mart is ultimately a monument to consumers: It has saved them billions. Sam Walton truly believed that nothing happens until a customer walks into a store with a purpose, buys something, and walks out. His philosophy was simple: satisfy the customer. Operating nearly 2,000 stores in 47 states, Wal-Mart remains the leader in the discount store industry. In addition, with over 400 Sam's Clubs, Wal-Mart is a major factor in the Warehouse Club industry. Combining general merchandise and groceries, Supercenters represent the company's fastest growing segment, with 65 to 70 stores planned in fiscal 1995 on a base of 68.

Walton long ago wanted manufacturers to see themselves, wholesalers, retailers, and consumers as parts of a single customer-focused process rather than as participants in a series of transactions. He personally and permanently altered the relationship between manufacturers and retailers, which has historically been, to put it politely, antagonistic. About five years ago he asked Procter & Gamble executives to view a focus group of Wal-Mart executives talking about their prickly relationship with the packaged-goods company. It was sobering. His strategy clearly was that we ought to be able to work together to lower the costs of both the manufacturer and the distributor and get lower costs for consumers. Walton got both sides to focus on distribution costs and how to cut them. Wal-Mart linked P&G with its computers to allow automatic reordering, thus avoiding bulges in order cycles. With better coordination of buying, P&G could plan more consistent manufacturing runs, rationalize distribution, and lower its costs, passing some of the savings on. This systematic approach is now in broad use throughout the industry. Walton has been described as a visionary, and he clearly was that. His vision was apparent in 1956 as a Ben Franklin variety store owner. To lure one of his first store managers, Bob Bogle, away from the state health department, Walton showed him the books

EXHIBIT 4
Wal-Mart Stores, Inc. Consolidated Statements of Income

(Amounts in thousands except per-share data.) Fiscal year ended January 31,	1994	1993	1992
Revenues:			
Net sales	$67,344,574	$55,483,771	$43,886,902
Rental from licensed departments	47,422	36,035	28,659
Other income—net	593,548	464,758	373,862
	67,985,544	55,984,564	44,289,423
Costs and Expenses:			
Cost of sales	53,443,743	44,174,685	34,786,119
Operating, selling, and general and administrative expenses	10,333,218	8,320,842	6,684,304
Interest Costs:			
Debt	331,308	142,649	113,305
Capital leases	185,697	180,049	152,558
	64,293,966	52,818,225	41,736,286
Income Before Income Taxes	3,691,578	3,166,339	2,553,137
Provision for Income Taxes:			
Current	1,324,777	1,136,918	906,183
Deferred	33,524	34,627	38,478
	1,358,301	1,171,545	944,661
Net Income	$ 2,333,277	$ 1,994,794	$ 1,608,476
Net Income Per Share	$ 1.02	$ .87	$ .70

Net Income (Millions of Dollars)

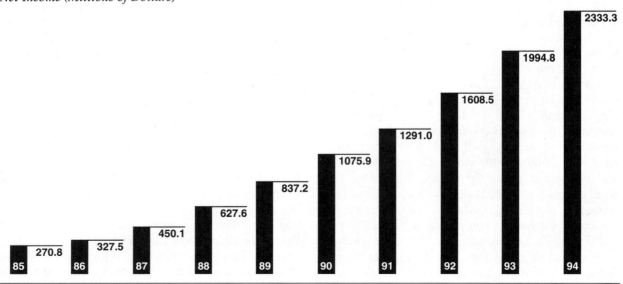

Source: Wal-Mart 1994 Annual Report.

EXHIBIT 4 (continued)

Wal-Mart Stores, Inc. Consolidated Balance Sheets

(Amounts in thousands.) January 31,	1994	1993
Assets:		
Current Assets:		
Cash and cash equivalents	$ 20,115	$ 12,363
Receivables	689,987	524,555
Recoverable costs from sale/leaseback	208,236	312,016
Inventories:		
At replacement cost	11,483,119	9,779,981
Less LIFO reserve	469,413	511,672
LIFO	11,013,706	9,268,309
Prepaid expenses and other	182,558	80,347
Total current assets	12,114,602	10,197,590
Property, Plant, and Equipment, at Cost:		
Land	2,740,883	1,692,510
Buildings and improvements	6,818,479	4,641,009
Fixtures and equipment	3,980,674	3,417,230
Transportation equipment	259,537	111,151
	13,799,573	9,861,900
Less accumulated depreciation	2,172,808	1,607,623
Net property, plant, and equipment	11,626,765	8,254,277
Property under capital leases	2,058,588	1,986,104
Less accumulated amortization	509,987	447,500
Net property under capital leases	1,548,601	1,538,604
Other Assets and Deferred Charges	1,150,796	574,616
Total assets	$26,440,764	$20,565,087
Liabilities and Shareholders' Equity		
Current Liabilities:		
Commercial paper	$ 1,575,029	$ 1,588,825
Accounts payable	4,103,878	3,873,331
Accrued liabilities	1,473,198	1,042,108
Accrued federal and state income taxes	183,031	190,620
Long-term debt due within one year	19,658	13,849
Obligations under capital leases due within one year	51,429	45,553
Total current liabilities	7,406,223	6,754,286
Long-Term Debt	6,155,894	3,072,835
Long-Term Obligations Under Capital Leases	1,804,300	1,772,152
Deferred Income Taxes	321,909	206,634
Shareholders' Equity:		
Preferred stock ($.10 par value; 100,000 shares authorized, none issued)		
Common stock ($.10 par value; 5,500,000 shares authorized, 2,298,769 and 2,299,638 issued and outstanding in 1994 and 1993, respectively)	229,877	229,964
Capital in excess of par value	535,639	526,647
Retained earnings	9,986,922	8,002,569
Total shareholders' equity	10,752,438	8,759,180
Total liabilities and shareholders' equity	$26,440,764	$20,565,087

Source: Wal-Mart 1994 Annual Report.

and offered to pay him 25 percent of the store's net profit in addition to salary.

STRATEGIC ANALYSIS OF WAL-MART'S SUCCESS

Wal-Mart's Competitive Capabilities

What accounts for Wal-Mart's remarkable success? Most explanations focus on a few familiar and highly visible factors: the genius of founder Sam Walton, who inspires his employees and has molded a culture of service excellence; the "greeters" who welcome customers at the door; the motivational power of allowing employees to own part of the business; the strategy of "everyday low prices," which offers the customer a better deal and saves on merchandising and advertising costs. Strategists also point to Wal-Mart's big stores, which offer economies of scale and a wider choice of merchandise.

But such explanations only redefine the question. *Why* is Wal-Mart able to justify building bigger stores? Why does Wal-Mart alone have a cost structure low enough to accommodate everyday low prices and greeters? And what has enabled the company to continue to grow far beyond the direct reach of Sam Walton's magnetic personality? The real secret of Wal-Mart's success lies deeper, in a set of strategic business decisions that transformed the company into a capabilities-based competitor.

The starting point was a relentless focus on satisfying customer needs. Wal-Mart's goals were simple to define but hard to execute: to provide customers access to quality goods, to make these goods available when and where customers want them, to develop a cost structure that enables competitive pricing, and to build and maintain a reputation for absolute trustworthiness. The key to achieving these goals was to make the way the company replenished inventory the centerpiece of its competitive strategy.

This strategic vision reached its fullest expression in a largely invisible logistics technique known as "cross-docking." In this system, goods are continuously delivered to Wal-Mart's warehouses, where they are selected, repacked, and then dispatched to stores, often without ever sitting in inventory. Instead of spending valuable time in the warehouse, goods just cross from one loading dock to another in 48 hours or less. Cross-docking enables Wal-Mart to achieve the economies that come from purchasing full truckloads of goods while avoiding the usual inventory and handling costs. Wal-Mart runs a full 85 percent of its goods through its warehouse system—as opposed to only 50 percent for Kmart. This reduces Wal-Mart's costs of sales by 2 percent to 3 percent compared with the industry average. That cost difference makes possible the everyday low prices.

But that's not all. Low prices in turn mean that Wal-Mart can save even more by eliminating the expense of frequent promotions. Stable prices also make sales more predictable, thus reducing stockouts and excess inventory. Finally, everyday low prices bring in the customers, which translates into higher sales per retail square foot. These advantages in basic economics make the greeters and the profit sharing easy to afford.

With such obvious benefits, why don't all retailers use cross-docking? The reason: it is extremely difficult to manage. To make cross-docking work, Wal-Mart has had to make strategic investments in a variety of interlocking support systems far beyond what could be justified by conventional ROI criteria. For example, cross-docking requires continuous contact among Wal-Mart's distribution centers, suppliers, and every point of sale in every store to ensure that orders can flow in and be consolidated and executed within a matter of hours. So Wal-Mart operates a private satellite-communication system that daily sends point-of-sale data directly to Wal-Mart's 4,000 vendors.

Another key component of Wal-Mart's logistics infrastructure is the company's fast and responsive transportation system. The company's 19 distribution centers are serviced by nearly 2,000 company-owned trucks. This dedicated truck fleet permits Wal-Mart to ship goods from warehouse to store in less than 48 hours and to replenish its store shelves twice a week on average. By contrast, the industry norm is once every two weeks.

To gain the full benefits of cross-docking, Wal-Mart has also had to make fundamental changes in its approach to managerial control. Traditionally in the retail industry, decisions about merchandising, pricing, and promotions have been highly centralized and made at the corporate level. Cross-docking, however, turns this command-and-control logic on its head. Instead of the retailer pushing products into the system, customers "pull" products when and where they need them. This approach places a premium on frequent, informal cooperation among stores, distribution centers, and suppliers—with far less centralized control.

The job of senior management at Wal-Mart, then, is not to tell individual store managers what to do but to create an environment where they can learn from the market—and from each other. The company's information systems, for example, provide store managers with detailed information about customer behavior, while a fleet of airplanes regularly ferries store managers to Bentonville, Arkansas headquarters for meetings on market trends and merchandising.

As the company has grown and its stores have multiplied, even Wal-Mart's own private air force hasn't been enough to maintain the necessary contacts among store managers. So Wal-Mart has installed a video link connecting all its stores to corporate headquarters and to each other. Store managers frequently hold video conferences to exchange information on what's happening in the field, such as which products are selling and which ones aren't, which promotions work and which don't.

The final piece of this capabilities mosaic is Wal-Mart's human resources system. The company realizes that its frontline employees play a significant role in satisfying customer needs. So it attempts to enhance its organizational capability with programs such as stock ownership and profit sharing geared toward making its personnel more responsive to customers. Even the way Wal-Mart stores

are organized contributes to this goal. Where Kmart has 5 separate merchandise departments in each store, Wal-Mart has 36. This means that training can be more focused and more effective, and employees can be more attuned to customers.

Kmart/Wal-Mart Contrasts

Kmart did not see its business this way. While Wal-Mart was fine-tuning its business processes and organizational practices, Kmart was following the classic textbook approach that had accounted for its original success. Kmart managed its business by focusing on a few product-centered strategic business units, each a profit center under strong centralized line management. Each SBU made strategy—selecting merchandise, setting prices, and deciding which products to promote. Senior management spend most of its time and resources making line decisions rather than investing in a support infrastructure.

Similarly, Kmart evaluated its competitive advantage at each stage along a value chain and subcontracted activities that managers concluded others could do better. While Wal-Mart was building its ground transportation fleet, Kmart was moving *out* of trucking because of a subcontracted fleet was cheaper. While Wal-Mart was building close relationships with its suppliers, Kmart was constantly switching suppliers in search of price improvements. While Wal-Mart was controlling all the departments in its stores, Kmart was leasing out many of its departments to other companies on the theory that it could make more per square foot in rent than through its own efforts.

This is not to say that the Kmart managers do not care about the business processes. After all, they have quality programs too. Nor is it that Wal-Mart managers ignore the structural dimension of strategy: They focus on the same consumer segments as Kmart and still need to make traditional strategic decisions such as where to open new stores. The difference is that Wal-Mart emphasizes behavior—the organizational practices and business processes in which capabilities are rooted—as the primary object of strategy and therefore focuses its managerial attention on the infrastructure that supports capabilities. This subtle distinction has made all the difference between exceptional and average performance.

Motorola, Inc.

Motorola is one of the world's leading diversified electronics manufacturers, providing wireless communications, semiconductor technology, and advanced electronics equipment and services for worldwide markets. Motorola has been an outstanding success in industries where many U.S. competitors have exited, and during a time when corporate America has been restructuring and retrenching in the face of recession. Motorola's revenues have grown from under $5 billion in 1983 to $16 billion in 1993, with an annual rate of 18 percent in the last two years, fueled by the proliferation of wireless communications in overseas markets. According to former CEO George Fisher, "I see no reason why we can't maintain that pace throughout the 1990's."[1] This tremendous growth has not come at the expense of profits or heavy borrowing: Profit margins and ROE have remained stable, with debt accounting for only 24 percent of capital, which is less than working capital. Moto-rola employs approximately 107,000 people worldwide, and ranks among the top 40 U.S. industrial companies in terms of total sales.

What makes Motorola's success even more impressive is the competitors that Motorola has gone up against. In its two main markets, semiconductors and communications, Motorola competes with the elite of Japanese industry in businesses that the Japanese government has targeted for nationally supported development. Yet Motorola is the worldwide leader in cellular phones, pagers, two-way radios, and advanced dispatch systems for commercial fleets. In telecommunications, Motorola has alternated between the number one and number two spots, while competing with AT&T and Ericsson. In microprocessors (MPUs),

Motorola is second only to Intel. Motorola does not just compete in these markets, it competes for the leadership position in these markets, with innovative products and the most advanced technology. In the words of one observer, "Its excellence lies in good part in a deeply bred ability to continually move out along the curve of innovation, to invent new, related applications of technology as fast as older ones become everyday, commodity type products."[2]

HISTORY

Paul V. Galvin established the Galvin Manufacturing Corp., in Chicago in 1928. The company first produced a "battery eliminator," which allowed customers to operate radios directly from household current instead of the batteries supplied with early models. Although this venture eventually failed, Galvin was more successful in the 1930s, when another venture successfully commercialized car radios under the brand "Motorola," a word that suggested sound in motion by combining "motor" with "Victrola." During this period, the company also established home radio and police radio departments, instituted pioneering personnel programs, and began national advertising. In the 1940s, the company started to do work for the government and opened a research laboratory in Phoenix, Arizona to explore solid-state electronics. The name of the company was changed to Motorola, Inc. in 1947.

By the time of Paul Galvin's death in 1959, Motorola was a leader in military, space, and commercial communications; had built its first semiconductor production facility; and was a growing

---

This case was prepared by Dean Aluzio, doctoral student, and Professor Michael Lubatkin, University of Connecticut, for class discussion. Printed by permission of the authors.

[1] DeYoung, H. Garret, "Motorola's strength comes from growth by renewal," *Electronic Business*, July 9, 1990, p. 30.

[2] Slutsker, Gary, "The company that likes to obsolete itself," *Forbes*, September 13, 1993, p. 140.

force in consumer electronics. Under the leadership of Paul Galvin's son, Robert W. Galvin, Motorola expanded into international markets in the 1960s, setting up sales and manufacturing operations around the world. In the 1970s, the company faced increasing Japanese competition, especially in consumer electronics. The company shifted its focus away from consumer electronics, selling off businesses such as color television. Faced with this stiff competition from overseas, Motorola's management staked the company's future on its ability to renew itself. The company instituted the Participative Management Program, which linked the needs and interests of employees more closely with the needs and interests of the company. In 1979, management began the journey toward total quality in all of Motorola's operations and products. This commitment to quality earned Motorola the coveted Malcolm Baldrige Quality Award in 1988, the first year the award was given.

George Fisher, appointed CEO in 1988, has continued to concentrate Motorola's energies on high-technology markets in commercial, industrial, and government fields, resulting in today's global customer base and strong position across a portfolio of related electronic product lines. Under Fisher's guidance, Motorola has experienced record sales growth in the last five years and has moved to the forefront of U.S. industry. Fisher left Motorola in October of 1993 to accept the CEO position at Eastman Kodak, leaving a company well positioned to exploit some of the future's most promising markets.

BUSINESS LINES

Motorola serves customers in four interdependent "arenas" of electronics—components, communications, computing, and control. Businesses within and across these arenas are managed as highly decentralized sectors, groups, or divisions, depending on size. There are currently three sectors (Semiconductor Products, Land Mobile Products, and General Systems) and four groups (Paging and Wireless Data Group, Government and Systems

Technology Group, Information Systems Group, and the Automotive and Industrial Electronics Group). There is also a New Enterprises unit, which serves as an incubator for new businesses. If a diversified corporation as large as Motorola can be said to have a single strategy, for Motorola the strategy has been to maintain, develop, and exploit expertise and technology to be the world's best manufacturer of products within its traditional arenas, while continually developing new products and technologies that expand, extend, and bridge these arenas.

The Semiconductor Products Sector designs and produces a broad line of discrete semiconductors and integrated circuits to serve the advanced systems needs of the computer, consumer, automotive, industrial, federal government/military, and telecommunications markets. The segment accounted for 32 percent of Motorola's 1992 sales and, in the third quarter of 1993, segment sales rose 31 percent to $1.51 billion, the 19th consecutive quarter of growth.[3] Motorola is the largest semiconductor manufacturer in North America, and ranks fourth in the world behind Hitachi, NEC, and Toshiba. While observers have pronounced doubts about Motorola's ability to keep pace in semiconductors while investing heavily in its other businesses, management has given its assurances that semiconductors will not be sacrificed. The company's portfolio of over 50,000 components is the broadest product line in the industry, and Motorola is particularly strong in eight-bit microcontrollers, digital signal processing, logic devices, discrete semiconductors, RISC microprocessors, and 16- and 32-bit microprocessors (see Appendix A for a list of sector and group products). Its MPUs have become the standard in products such as Apple Computers, Sega Game systems, and most new cars rolling out of Detroit. And in a joint venture with IBM and Apple, Motorola is developing the PowerPC family of MPUs, which could threaten Intel's dominant market position. IBM has started volume production of the PowerPC 601, and

---

[3] Motorola, 1993 Third Quarter Report.

the smaller, low-power portable computer design PowerPC 603 that Motorola will manufacture is being readied for introduction.[4] The company's MOS-11 fabrication plant in Austin, Texas is the world's first commercial semiconductor facility to manufacture eight-inch wafers, which allows a higher yield of chips per wafer.

The Semiconductor Products Sector, like other Motorola businesses, has been expanding overseas, particularly in Asia, which is the region with both the highest consumption of semiconductors and the fastest growth in consumption. Japan accounted for 10–15 percent of Motorola's semiconductor sales, and the Asia Pacific region led Motorola's 25 percent growth in orders in the third quarter of 1993.[5] In 1992, 52 percent of Motorola's sales were outside of the U.S. region. Asia accounted for 22 percent, including Japan, which accounted for 7 percent of total sales. Overall, the corporation's Asian sales are growing 2–3 times faster than sales to U.S. and Europe. According to Motorola's director of international operations, Rick Younts, Asia could be Motorola's largest source of revenue within a decade. Motorola's success in penetrating Asian markets is a result of a long-term commitment to the region. The company has been manufacturing for over 20 years in Korea, Taiwan, and Malaysia. According to Younts, Motorola was already moving into the emerging Asian markets just as the rest of the world was realizing their potential importance. This included doing business in China before it started to open up to Western business and competing with the Japanese in Japan and in their sphere of economic influence in Asia. Competing with the Japanese initiated the quality revolution and organizational renewal that transformed the company in the late 1970s and early 1980s. In the words of Younts, "the Japanese were the benchmark for quality." Competing with the Japanese in their domestic market meant that Motorola had to have comparable quality and service. In the opinion of Younts, "the Japanese customer is the most demanding in the world—he does not accept poor service or poor quality."

In businesses such as semiconductors, where volume is the key to success, Motorola had to compete with the Japanese everywhere in the world. Motorola's international strategy has been "to understand culture and market, to be an insider in the markets in which they operate, and to ultimately contribute to the betterment of the welfare and society of these markets." To become an insider has meant the distribution of activities throughout the world. The company has been opening design and manufacturing centers around the world to stay close to customers and competitors. Hong Kong has been chosen for development as a regional business center and semiconductor manufacturing site that might one day replicate Silicon Valley's mutually profitable alliance between industry and academia. In Japan, Motorola Nihon has succeeded in getting Motorola components designed into Japanese products. One example is how Motorola worked with Canon to develop the microprocessor controls for a new type of auto focus on Canon's 35mm cameras. Motorola has also teamed up with Toshiba, a leading producer of memory chips. Motorola did not participate in the development of the 256K generation of memory chips, and as a result has suffered from a weakness in memory chips ever since. The joint venture, Tohoku Semiconductor Corp., recently announced plans to build a $727 million plant in Sendai to produce 16K memory chips. The venture currently makes about 9 million components monthly, inclu-ding DRAMs, MPUs and microcontrollers, and has been used by the two companies to develop chips for HDTV applications and for Toyota car engines.[6]

The Land Mobile Products Sector designs, manufactures, and distributes two-way radios and other

---

[4] Ibid.
[5] Ibid.

[6] "Motorola, Toshiba Joint Venture Plans to Build Chip Plant," *Wall Street Journal*, June 24, 1993, p. B7.

forms of electronic communications systems for customers including agriculture, commercial, construction, education, state, government, health care, mining, petroleum, utilities, and transportation companies. The company's involvement in these products stems back to World War II, when Motorola made walkie-talkies for the U.S. Army. Motorola is the leading supplier in the largest segment of this industry, two-way private mobile radio, such as mobile radios used by taxicabs, police and fire departments, and trucking companies.

The General Systems Sector designs and manufactures computer-based cellular telephones and systems, personal communications systems, computers, microcomputer boards, and information processing and handling equipment. Motorola is the world's largest producer of mobile and portable cellular phones and has received more cellular system awards than any other company. More than half of the cellular revenues come from outside the United States, and Motorola has even succeeded in selling cellular equipment to Japan's NTT.

The cellular telephone is one of Motorola's greatest successes. Motorola spent 15 years and $150 million developing cellular technology before there was any significant demand.[7] This investment has paid off, for in the last two years cellular phones have outsold cord phones, and the customer base of 12 million continues to grow. Yet Motorola management is convinced that the company has barely scratched the surface of this market. Chris Galvin, Motorola assistant COO and son of retired CEO Bob Galvin, believes that "at some point during this decade, 20 percent of all POTS [plain old telephone services] will be portable. That's a tremendous market."[8] The company claims to be the only producer that offers cellular and portable phones as well as related infrastructure, test equipment, and reseller services. Since the average cellular subscriber requires about $1,500 in support equipment and services above the price of the phone, this market represents an incredible growth opportunity.

Motorola's entrance into cellular technology is a representative example of how the company spins off new technologies and businesses. In the early days of cellular, Edward Staiano saw that the emerging technology was being treated like a stepchild by the communications group, which back then was mainly involved in two-way radio systems. So Motorola gave Staiano free rein to develop the technology independently. Says Staiano, "So I moved out of the building with a few people, got a building down the road, and we ran basically like a startup. Motorola is one of the few big companies where you have a pretty good chance of starting up your own business and running it."[9] Staiano is now the president and general manager of the General Systems sector, and Motorola is now the dominant player in cellular technology.

Motorola not only pioneered cellular technology, but maintains leadership by continuously developing new products and markets ahead of the competition. One notable example is the MicroTac™ cellular phone Motorola introduced in 1989 as the world's smallest portable cellular phone. The phone was an instant success, and it took 18 months for competitors such as NEC, Fujitsu, Mitsubishi, and LM Ericsson to counterattack with competitive products. According to Motorola president Gary Tooker, the phone clearly illustrates how Motorola anticipates customer needs and introduces products that seem ahead of their time. "When we formed the MicroTac™ team, no one was demanding this product" says Tooker.[10]

Motorola not only anticipates customer needs with innovative products such as MicroTac™, but also creates demand by developing new markets. The General Systems Sector has been investing in

[7] Morone, Joseph G., "Technology and Competitive Advantage—The Role of General Management," *Research • Technology Management,* March–April 1993, p. 17.

[8] DeYoung, H. Garret, "Motorola's strength comes from growth by renewal," *Electronic Business,* July 9, 1990, p. 32.

[9] Slutsker, Gary, "The company that likes to obsolete itself," *Forbes,* September 13, 1993, p. 141.

[10] DeYoung, H. Garret, p. 33.

cellular network services to create cellular infrastructures in countries that have not yet developed them. Cellular networks may become the primary system in these countries because of the huge investments needed to connect a country through traditional wired phone lines. Motorola first got involved in network services in Hong Kong six years ago. According to Staiano, cellular did not exist in the colony, so he decided to jump-start it by taking a 30 percent equity position in a startup. Motorola originally decided not to compete with equipment customers, and thus did not invest in cellular networks in the U.S. Realizing what those missed opportunities cost them, Staiano now has bids to build cellular systems in six countries (with Motorola equipment), and the network ventures are among Motorola's most profitable and fastest-growing businesses.[11] Motorola also controls radio frequencies previously used for dispatch systems, and has the technology to convert these analog systems into high traffic digital networks that could compete with cellular networks. But according to some Motorola executives, these ventures are just vehicles to promote equipment sales, and the long-term strategy is to exit these businesses once the market is developed.

Motorola's involvement in the European and Japanese markets is especially important for cellular products, for it is expected that Japan and Europe will move more quickly to advanced digital systems than the U.S. Motorola has won several contracts from NTT, the Japanese communications authority, and for the Pan-European digital cellular network, or GSM. Motorola is already providing validation systems in several countries and has been chosen to supply operational systems in Sweden, Spain, and the U.K.

The Paging and Wireless Data Group designs, manufactures, and distributes products for paging and wireless data systems worldwide. Motorola is the world leader in pagers and paging systems. Pagers receive one-way messages that range from a simple beep to words and numbers that can be stored and displayed on a screen. Used traditionally to contact personnel in the field and prompt a phone call, customers are now finding more innovative uses for Motorola's pagers. Restaurants are using pagers to let waiters know when orders are ready. In China, where there is very limited telephone infrastructure, pagers are being used to send coded messages to field personnel, instructing them on their next task.

Motorola's paging operations were previously combined with land mobile products to form the Communications Sector, which accounted for 29 percent of 1992 sales. The sector was split in 1993, and paging and wireless data operations became its own group. The primary reason for the new organizational structure was to encourage the development of wireless data technology, which was being hindered by the dominant focus of the Communications Sector on land mobile products.

There are currently only about 200,000 users of wireless data systems, including the 50,000 UPS drivers who transmit package tracking data from Motorola equipment in their trucks. Revenues from wireless data services are still small, expected to be $192 million in 1993 and $303 million in 1994, according to Ira Brodsky of Datacomm Research in Wilmette, Illinois.[12] But Robert Growney, executive vice president and general manager of the Paging and Wireless Data Group, expects that the worldwide market will reach 26 million users by the year 2000.[13] At the forefront of this market is the development of personal digital assistants (PDAs), small palmtop computers that could revolutionize the way individuals organize and communicate information while on the go. Motorola has licensed two PDA formats: Apple Computer's Newton Operating System and General Magic's operating system. They have also established a joint venture with Samsung of Korea to manufacture portable palmtop computers. Motorola is also competing with a

---

[11] Slutsker, Gary, "The company that likes to obsolete itself," *Forbes*, September 13, 1993, p. 143.

[12] Collier, Andrew and Cray, Dan, "Wireless Data Market Still Up in the Air?" *Electronic News*, July 27, 1992, p. 19.

[13] Slutsker, Gary, p. 142.

GE-Ericsson joint venture and AT&T to supply the wireless modems that will make PDAs and the new generation of laptop computers feasible. The Hewlett-Packard 95LX palmtop was one of the first PDAs to be introduced, and Motorola furnished it with DataStream™, a nationwide broadcasting service supported by a miniature data transceiver.[14]

Like the General Systems Sector, the Paging and Wireless Data Group has also expanded into network development in order to create demand for equipment. The group has set up paging operations in countries such as Brazil, where they do not yet exist, and has been establishing wireless messaging networks in the U.S., such as Ardis™, a joint venture with IBM, and Embarc™, a receive-only e-mail network.

The Government and Systems Technology Group specializes in research, development, and production of electronic systems and equipment for the U.S. Department of Defense and other government agencies, commercial users, and international customers. Motorola has excelled in meeting the demands of complex military and aerospace markets, and its equipment has been on board virtually all U.S. space missions. The first words transmitted from the Moon to the earth came through a Motorola transponder. The 1988 photos of Neptune taken by the Voyager II were also sent back to earth by Motorola equipment.

This group is currently involved in the Iridium project, an ambitious attempt to make portable communication possible from any location in the world. The foundation of this global network will be 77 satellites in circular orbits around the earth. While the service will probably be considered too expensive for those accustomed to developed wire and cellular phone service, for travelers in uninhabited locations or in underdeveloped countries, the system will provide instant communication to anywhere in the world via portable phone. Motorola has spun off Iridium as an independent entity,

selling equity in the project to international consortiums, companies, and governments. But Motorola is expected to retain a 15 percent share and will supply the equipment necessary to make the system work. The $3.37 billion network is scheduled to begin operations in 1998.[15]

The Information Systems Group combines the capabilities of the Codex Corporation with those of Universal Data Systems to provide the elements for distributed data and voice networks for the communication of data through telephone lines, from basic modems to network management systems. Codex is helping to drive the analog-to-digital transformation within the industry by providing products that meet the need for analog services today while providing an easy path to meet future requirements for digital services. Motorola is also developing a wide range of products for the Integrated Services Digital Network (ISDN), including high-speed terminal adapters and products developed in conjunction with Northern Telecom.

The Automotive and Industrial Electronics Group serves the motor vehicle and industrial equipment industries through the development and production of a variety of electronic components, modules, and integrated electronic systems. High-technology automotive applications include power-train and chassis electronics, power controls, and sensors. Building on a dominant position in certain types of automotive sensors, the company hopes to develop new automotive applications, and then leverage the learning and production volume advantages to enter more lucrative markets in medical applications. Some of the newer product developments include engine management controls, anti-lock braking system controls, truck instrumentation, agricultural monitoring systems, and automotive theft alarms. Motorola is also positioned to develop electronics for the car of the future, such as voice-activated in-dash navigation systems and multiplex systems.

[14] Weber, Samuel, "Anatomy of Coopetition," *Electronics,* August 1991, p. 37.

[15] "Japanese Consortium to Take a 15 percent Stake in Motorola Project," *Wall Street Journal,* April 2, 1993, p. B3.

The New Enterprises organization manages Motorola's entry into emerging, high-growth, and high-technology areas. This outlet for entrepreneurial activity allows Motorola to exploit the initiative of its people in areas not directly related to existing operations. Two current ventures are Dascan and Emtek Health Care Systems. Dascan designs and produces supervisory control and data acquisition (SCADA) systems and cell controller systems for utility markets. Emtek provides clinical information management systems for hospital intensive care units. Successful start up operations are usually sold off, often to their management, or they are folded back into existing Motorola operations if the corporation sees a strategic fit.

MANAGEMENT PRACTICES

The heart of Motorola is the three-person office of the chief executive, previously made up of CEO George Fisher, President, and COO Gary Tooker, and Senior Executive Vice President and assistant COO Chris Galvin. George Fisher left unexpectedly in November 1993 to assume the position of CEO at Kodak, and a successor has not yet been confirmed. The three members of the Office of the Chief Executive share responsibility for operations, geographic areas, and focused concerns/initiatives. As of October 1993, George Fisher had responsibility for human resources, law, strategy, technology, and external relations. He also had regional ownership of Japanese operations. The focused corporate activities he oversaw included U.S. government relations, trade, corporate goals, women and minority development, trade policy committee, TQM, and product development. Gary Tooker had responsibility for Semiconductors, Land Mobile, and the Government Group, and also had finance, quality, and corporate manufacturing reporting to him. His geographic responsibilities encompassed the rest of Asia and the Americas. His focused activities included the Iridium project, cycle time, technology transfer, management incentive programs, product improvement, employee empowerment, and the environment. Chris Galvin is responsible for

General Systems, Paging and Wireless, Automotive, Information Systems, and New Enterprises. He takes geographic responsibility for Europe, the Middle East, and Africa, and directs acquisitions, consumer products, personal communications, and the premier employee program.

Despite the importance of the Office of the Chief Executive, Motorola is a highly decentralized company that keeps operating and strategic authority at the business level. Motorola uses financial controls to coordinate businesses, and finance departments report directly to corporate staff, with dotted line relations to the operating divisions. Finance, research, strategic planning, and quality are all small groups at the corporate level. Corporate staff takes responsibility for having expertise in functions whose development cannot be justified on an individual business level. Businesses draw on this expertise and ask corporate staff to be able to get up to speed quickly on new capabilities, such as competitor intelligence. But Motorola is not top-heavy; it maintains a good balance between corporate support staff and businesses. In the words of one executive, "It keeps staff small, running tight and in demand. They can't be running around with time on their hands looking for things to do. If they are, then they either over staffed or not staffed with the right people." According to a line manager, "there is not a lot of hands-on, day-to-day involvement by corporate staff. We look to the corporate staff for guidance, advice, and counseling on the future."

Corporate staff in legal, environmental, quality, human relations, and strategy departments develop and disseminate new ideas and set policy guidelines consistent with Motorola's mission, values, and history. Within these guidelines, Motorola businesses have the autonomy to develop their own strategies. But it is the corporation's mission that unifies and guides business strategy. Corporate headquarters has articulated the corporation's mission:

In each of our chosen areas of the electronics industry, we will grow rapidly by providing our world-wide customers what they want, when they want it, with Six-Sigma quality and best in class cycle time, as we strive to achieve our fundamental corporate objective of Total Customer Satisfaction, and to achieve our stated goals of increased global market share, best-in-class people, products, marketing, manufacturing, technology and service; and superior financial results."[16]

PARTICIPATIVE MANAGEMENT PROGRAM

The cornerstone of Motorola's informal, first-name-only culture is the company's Participative Management Program (PMP).[17] Building on the highly participative style of founder Paul Galvin, Motorola management created a system in the 1970s and 1980s in which employees have a greater stake in Motorola's future than Japanese workers have in their companies in Japan's best-run corporations.

The key building blocks of the PMP are work teams of 50 to 250 workers. Each employee shares in a common bonus pool with his or her team members. The idea is that the people in the pool will be responsible for their own performance—as measured by the production costs and materials used that are controllable by the team, by quality, by production levels, by inventory stock and finished goods, by housekeeping standards, and by safety records. Whenever an idea proposed by a team leads to a cost reduction or to production that exceeds target, all team members share in the gains through bonuses that can amount to 41 percent of base salary (the average varies between 8 and 12 percent).

An example of how the PMP program has increased worker productivity is the case of an assembly worker in a Fort Worth, Texas plant. She discovered that one of every ten screws she used to assemble a radio would break. Instead of just throwing the screws away, or reporting the problem to a supervisor, the employee called the vendor. After that initial conversation, her work team got together with the vendor and they collectively

solved the problem. It turned out that if the screws had proper heat treatment they wouldn't break. Another example of the trimming of waste is in the use of gold in the production of semiconductors. Before the PMP, something like 40 percent of the gold used was wasted. After two months of analysis, Motorola employees identified some fifty spots in the process where gold was being lost. Ultimately, they reduced waste to zero.

To make this system work at a large corporation, Motorola has established a communications network of hierarchical committees. Each team has one of its members on a steering committee at the next higher level in the company (which, in turn, has a member on another committee at the subsequent higher level). The steering committees perform several critical functions:

1. **Coordination**—A steering committee will act on ideas that come from a working group that require cooperation with one or more other working groups.
2. **Lateral Communication**—A steering committee will disseminate the ideas or practices of one working group to other groups, thus facilitating organizational learning.
3. **Downward Communication**—A steering committee will ensure that each work group has all the managerial information it requires to do its job.
4. **Upward Communication**—Since each steering committee is linked to the next level steering committee (which in turn reports to top management), shop floor issues reach Motorola executives after going through only four levels in the hierarchical chain.
5. **Control**—A steering committee negotiates output standards and measures performance with the work teams that report to it. This is a continuing process in which trust is built by clearly establishing the performance criteria by which work teams will be measured in advance of the evaluation process.
6. **Evaluation**—Based on the negotiated measures of performance, a steering committee evaluates the record of the work teams that report to it, and allocates rewards based on a pre-negotiated formula.

While originally intended for production workers, such as the quality and cycle time initiatives, Motorola has applied this idea across the entire organization. Professional, clerical, marketing,

---

[16] Motorola company brochure.

[17] Description of the Participative Management Program adapted, in part, from the book *Vanguard Management* by James O'Toole, Doubleday and Company, 1985.

research, and other staff people are also organized into teams and also partake in a PMP bonus program based on performance measures appropriate to their tasks. The PMP system is buttressed by Motorola's "I Recommend" plan. Every work area in the company has a bulletin board on which employees can post questions or recommendations. The questions and recommendations can either by signed or anonymous. Either way, the supervisor responsible for the area is required to post a reply within 72 hours. In those cases where it is impossible to obtain an answer that quickly, the supervisor must post the name of the person who is working on obtaining the information, along with the date by which a final answer will be posted.

The PMP has made participation the cornerstone of Motorola's culture. The reason why Motorola has institutionalized a level of participation formerly found only in smaller companies or Japanese companies is, according to former chief operating officer William Weisz, because "of our set of assumptions about human behavior." Significantly, in Motorola's employee handbook on PMP, the discussion begins with an elucidation of the company's assumptions about workers and work. (See Appendix B for James O'Toole's summary of Motorola's assumptions.)

QUALITY

Another distinction that sets Motorola apart from other U.S. firms is the commitment to quality and the importance of the corporate quality department. Motorola has adopted quality as the cornerstone of everything the company does. Its goal has been to achieve Six Sigma quality—3.4 defects per million. Motorola has actually achieved this condition in certain processes and products, and now aims for a doubling of quality improvement every two years, according to Paul Noakes, director of External Quality Programs. Although quality is the responsibility of line businesses, corporate staff play an important part in coordinating its development and maintenance across the organization. Their role within the company is to teach quality

and champion its cause, make sure material and techniques are up to date, and measure customer satisfaction and serve as the customer's advocate. Corporate quality staff are important participants in the semi-annual review meetings. Motorola has also taken on responsibility for converting others to the quality gospel. External programs champion TQM and the need for quality while showing other companies how Motorola does it.

Motorola's quality revolution started in 1979 at a meeting of corporate executives, when one of the attendees put it bluntly: "The real problem around here is that quality stinks." This started the dialogue on quality that would eventually force Motorola executives to face up to the fact that some of its products and operations did not make the grade.

According to Motorola president Gary Tooker, top executives faced a choice: Go back to the fundamentals or continue to lose customers to Japanese competitors with better quality.[18] Going back to the fundamentals meant assuming final responsibility for quality at corporate headquarters. "No one wants to do a lousy job," according to Richard Buetow, vice president and director of quality. "If a company has a quality problem, 95 percent of the fault is with management." So top management began to manage quality into Motorola's operations, aided by a participative management style that made quality everybody's responsibility. To help workers do their jobs better, Motorola now spends about $100 million a year on employee training and insists that every worker take a one-week company course in a job-related subject. The results of quality have not only been better products, more satisfied customers, and increasing market share; it has also eliminated the need for inspection and testing—a saving that Buetow estimates at 3 percent to 4 percent of the cost of sales.[19]

---

[18] DeYoung, H. Garret, "Motorola's strength comes from growth by renewal," *Electronic Business*, July 9, 1990, p. 32.

[19] Ibid., p. 32.

CYCLE TIME

Winning the ongoing corporate battle of constantly improving quality, Motorola's quality department has turned to new ways to help businesses reach their goal of total customer satisfaction. One important new initiative is the cycle time reduction program. The program was originally a response to customer dissatisfaction with Motorola's long lead time for product design and manufacturing. Through environmental scanning, contact with line businesses, and the constant attention to customer satisfaction, corporate staff recognized the need to improve in this area. After the idea had been approved by the CEO office, the corporate quality department took responsibility for an organization-wide program to reduce cycle time, first in manufacturing and product design, then eventually in all areas of the company's operations. It was not first executed as a pilot program, but instead was implemented across the whole organization simultaneously. In a two-day meeting, corporate staff introduced the problem and initiated discussion on how to reduce cycle times among the 180–200 corporate officers responsible for running line businesses. Eventually, corporate quality staff and line business personnel developed a methodology to attack the problem. First the process is mapped, then it is examined to determine which steps are critical and which are not. Non-value adding steps are eliminated, the process is simplified, and effort is directed only toward critical value adding activities.

INTRAORGANIZATIONAL RELATIONSHIPS

Although corporate headquarters staff may seek to proactively solve problems, they are not usually perceived as meddling in line affairs. Corporate staff expect problems to be solved at the business level, with expertise and information supplied as necessary. Proactive involvement often takes forms such as the cycle time initiative, or recommendations from the acquisitions office to make strategic investments in other companies. The corporation's ability to look at the company and the environment from a broader perspective than line managers sometimes makes involvement necessary and beneficial. An example is when a major Bell company had ordered some equipment from the cellular division for a major showcase in Baltimore. Due to the fact that the equipment was not in production yet and was still being assembled by engineers, the cellular division was not going to be able to supply by the deadline. The Bell company thought that the division was holding back on them in order to give priority to equipment Motorola was using to set up its own showcase. They complained to Executive Committee chairman and retired CEO Bob Galvin that the deck was being stacked against them. Galvin intervened by commandeering 15 engineers from each of the other operating divisions and temporarily putting them on the project so that the deadline could be honored.

Relationships between Motorola's independent businesses is like any vendor-customer relationship. While equipment divisions will buy from the components divisions when it is the best value, they do not hesitate to go outside the company for vendors. But according to one General Systems Sector executive, divisions are highly motivated to win internal orders. While having in-house customers is a valuable source of feedback, Motorola tries to be close to all of its customers, with semi-annual customer surveys and an emphasis on constant horizontal contact. Equipment divisions have their own liaisons with Semiconductors, but outside customers have the same access. There is some cooperative development, such as the Integrated Circuit Applications Research Lab (ICAR), which tried to develop future applications of integrated circuits through cooperation with internal users. But the real coordination of independent businesses comes from shared R & D resources and the Management Technology Review process.

RESEARCH AND DEVELOPMENT

As a corporation, Motorola spent $1.3 billion dollars on research and development activities in 1992. Research is a mix of centralized and decentralized facilities. Operating units buy R & D time from various research organizations throughout the organization to work on projects they are interested in. Relationships between businesses, projects, and R & D personnel may become semi-permanent. Divisions also have specific research and development activities on a decentralized basis. The corporation sponsors general research in the critical capabilities such as radio and systems, as well as developing new technologies, such as voice coding, that may one day be critical for multiple businesses. Corporate involvement in R & D means not only ensuring a steady stream of developments, but also imposing discipline: "We're like kids in a candy shop," Fisher acknowledges. "There are so many opportunities, but we know we can't pursue everything."[20]

MANAGEMENT TECHNOLOGY REVIEW

The Management Technology Review is a distinctive Motorola management practice that integrates the multiple streams of technology at the company. Semi-annually, corporate staff reviews each business in both a business management review and a technology management review. Although the issues are obviously intertwined, the two reviews are conducted separately so that conflicting issues do not obscure the review process. In the technology review process, Motorola charts out the expected evolution of products and technology in a technological road map, a forecast of future technological advancement with interim technological milestones, product destinations, and clearly delineated routes to these destinations. This is a very interactive process, and technical people at every level participate. All employees with technical knowledge are involved in generating the initial forecasts and in implementing the plan that will be based on these forecasts. The reviews are always attended by senior staff, such as a member of the

CEO office, the directors of quality, strategy and R & D, as well as senior people from other businesses. The participation of members of other Motorola businesses is important, for they may know where the required technology is within Motorola, possible outside sources, other possible applications for it, and opportunities to invest or license. During the review, these executives examine the road maps in light of the strength of competitors, experience curves, sales history, and Motorola's own distinctive competencies and interests. From this raw data, a long-term product plan is created, a map that indicates when and where to allocate corporate research resources, when to begin product development, when to introduce new products, and when to take existing products out of production.[21]

The review process explicates what each division expects in terms of technological breakthroughs. Since technical advancement of any division is partly dependent on the technical developments of other divisions and outside suppliers, this review/mapping process is a key coordinative mechanism between the different operating divisions. An example of how one division will anticipate technical breakthroughs in another might be when one of the communications equipment divisions calls for the development of a new kind of chip from the semiconductor division to make a new product feasible. By specifying future technological needs, the corporation can then make sure someone in the targeted division is given responsibility for meeting these needs. To demand breakthroughs from other divisions, managers have to make coherent arguments of why this breakthrough is important, and why it is possible. According to one General Systems Sector executive, technologists usually know where to expect the next breakthroughs, and this process stimulates those breakthroughs by having applications already demanding them.

[20] DeYoung, H. Garret, "Motorola's strength comes from growth by renewal," *Electronic Business,* July 9, 1990, p. 35.

[21] O'Toole, James, *Vanguard Management,* Doubleday and Company, 1985, p. 177.

The Management Technology Review is also an important opportunity for corporate management to realign businesses strategically. Products developed in one division may be transferred to another division or spun off on their own for a number of reasons. Usually it is because a business cannot fund the development of a certain type of technology that will play only a limited role in its current business domain. When the corporation finds a promising technology in danger of being cut, it might decide to accept responsibility for nurturing and developing that technology, giving it time to grow without the profit requirements that constrain the line businesses. Corporate headquarters staff learn about these opportunities through the network of reporting lines, the review process, and informal contact. Businesses are supposed to let it all hang out during the review, and this is encouraged by the Motorola culture of frank, forthright discussion and debate to resolve issues. Another hallmark of Motorola culture that aids in communication is informality, probably stemming from the fact that engineers tend to be informal people. If the CEO has a question, he is likely to talk to the engineer directly involved, not the engineer's boss. "I know technologists throughout the company," Fisher says. "We all understand how the company works, so that nobody's toes get stepped on when I call an engineer to find out how something really works or what his opinion is."[22]

SPINOFFS

Creating new products and technologies is the modus operandi of Motorola, according to one executive, and can be compared to the new business development process at 3M. As a result, employees are very conscious of the opportunities. There are big payoffs for success, and success is seen as a primary way to climb the corporate ladder. The corporation exploits this reservoir of entrepreneurial talent and initiative by giving financial support to initiatives outside of a particular business's mission, or by transferring responsibility for them to more suitable locations. Many managers have become senior VPs by growing a new business. Cellular and semiconductors are the spectacular examples.

Spinoffs come about for a number of reasons. Often, the autonomous initiatives of operating level engineers will result in products unrelated to the domain of the business where it was developed. When a breakthrough is made, it becomes a candidate for special organizational arrangements to facilitate further development. Pressure from customers who are not satisfied with service for specific products within a division is also a key motivating factor. And if outside consultants, analysts, or the press are pointing out a new technology as being a critical area in the future, Motorola might move to establish a strategic foothold in the area by establishing a spinoff. The process is usually straightforward, as divisions that do not want to use scarce resources to pursue something not directly related to current product lines either seek corporate help or let the technology be separated from the division.

Managers who fail to successfully develop a spinoff are not forced to leave the company. While there are no guarantees that such managers will get their old positions back, this is part of the risk/reward balance of the venture. A high percentage of success and the thrill of being on the cutting edge ensure that there are still plenty of entrepreneurial engineers willing to take this route.

---

[22] Slutsker, Gary, "The company that likes to obsolete itself," *Forbes*, September 13, 1993, p. 143.

APPENDIX A
Motorola's Products by Sector and Group

Semiconductor Products Sector Products

Bipolar, BiCMOS, and MOS Digital ICs
Bipolar, BiCMOS, CMOS, and Combined
   Technology Semi-custom Circuits
Custom and Semi-custom Semiconductors
Customer Defined Arrays
Data Conversion Circuits
Digital Signal Processing
Fiber Optic Active Components
Field Effect Transistors (FETs)
Industrial Control Circuits
Interface Circuits
Microcomputers and Peripherals
Microcontroller ICs
Microprocessors and Peripherals
Microcontroller ICs
Microprocessors and Peripherals
Microwave Transistors

MOS and Bipolar Memories
Motor Control Circuits
Open Architecture CAD Systems
Operational Amplifiers
Optoelectronics Components
Power Supply Circuits
Pressure and Temperature Sensors
Rectifiers
RF Modules
RF Power and Small Signal Transistors
SMARTMOS™ Products
Telecommunications Circuits
Thyristors and Triggers
TMOS and Bipolar Pager Products
Voltage Regulators Circuits
Zener and Tuning Diodes

Land Mobile Products Sector Products

Automatic Vehicle Locations Systems
Communications Control Centers
Communications System Installation and Maintenance
Emergency Medical Communications Systems
FM Two-Way Radio Products
   Base Station and Repeater Products
   Mobile Products
   Portable Products
   Signalling and Remote Control Systems

FM Two-Way Radio Systems
   Advanced Conventional Systems
Digital Voice Protection Systems
   Communication Systems
   Trunked Radio Systems
HF Single Sideband Communications Systems
Integrated Security and Access Control Systems

Paging and Wireless Data Group Products

Pagers and Components
CT2 (telepoint systems)
Radio Paging Systems

Mobile Data Systems
   Data Radio Networks
   Portable and Mobile Data Terminals
   RF Modems

General Systems Sector Products

Cellular Mobile, Portable, Transportable, and
   Personal Subscriber Products
Cellular Radiotelephone Systems
Multi-User Super Microcomputer Systems and
   Servers

Electronic Mobile Exchange (EMX) Series
HD, LD, and HDII Series Cellular Base Stations
Microcomputer (VME) Board Level Products
Software for Workgroup and Network
   Computing Communications
Wireless In-Building Network Products

APPENDIX A (continued)

Automotive and Industrial Electronics Group

Agricultural Vehicle Controls	Multiplex Systems
Anti-lock Braking Systems Controls	Power Modules
Automotive and Industrial Sensors	Solid State Relays
Automotive Body Computers	Steering Controls
Gasoline and Diesel Engine Controls	Suspension Controls
Ignition Modules	Transmission Controls
Instrumentation	Vehicle Navigation Systems
Keyless Entry Systems	Vehicle Theft Alarm Modules
Motor Controls	Voltage Regulators

Government Electronics Group Products

Fixed and Satellite Communications Systems	Video Processing Systems and Products
Space Communication Systems	Intelligent Display Terminals and Systems
Electronic Fuse Systems	Electronic Positioning and Tracking Systems
Missile Guidance Systems	Satellite Survey and Positioning Systems
Missile and Aircraft Instrumentation	Surveillance Radar Systems
Secure Telecommunications	Tracking and Command Transponder Systems
Drone and Target Command and Control Systems	Tactical Communications Transceivers

Information Systems Group

Codex Corporation Products

Network Management:
   Integrated network management that supports
   emerging international standards
   and complements key de facto industry
   standards
Digital Transmissions:
   DSU/CSUs, digital platforms, ISDN terminal
   adapters
Analog Transmission:
   V.32 and other dial modems, leased line
   modems
Data and Data/Voice Networking:
   T1 and subrate multiplexers, x.25 switches and

   PADs, statistical multiplexers
LAN internetworking:
   LAN/WAN bridges

UDS Products
Modems
Multiplexers
High Speed Digital Communication Products
ISDN Terminal Adapters
Micro-to-Mainframe Plug-in Boards
Network Management Services
Custom Data Comm Products

New Enterprises Organizations

EMTEK Health Care Systems
DASCAN

APPENDIX B
Summary of Motorola's Assumptions about Workers

1. Employee behavior is a consequence of how employees are treated.
2. Employees are intelligent, curious, and responsible.
3. Employees need a rational work world in which they know what is expected of them, and why.
4. Employees need to know how their jobs relate to the jobs of others and to company goals.
5. There is only one class of employee, not a creative management group and a group of others who carry out orders.
6. There is no one best way to manage.
7. No one knows how to do his or her job better than the person on the job.
8. Employees want to have pride in their work.
9. Employees want to be involved in decisions that affect their own work.
10. The responsibility of every manager is to draw out the ideas and abilities of workers in a shared effort of addressing business problems and opportunities.

APPENDIX C
Motorola Inc. Financial Information (Figures in billions of dollars)

	1992	1991	1990	1989	1988
Net Sales	13,303	11,341	10,885	9,620	8,250
Manufacturing and other costs of sales	8,508	7,245	6,882	5,905	5,040
Selling, general and administrative expenses	2,838	2,468	2,414	2,289	1,957
Depreciation expense	1,000	886	790	650	543
Interest expense, net	157	129	133	130	98
Total costs and expenses	12,503	10,728	10,219	8,974	7,638
Earnings before income taxes and cumulative effect of change in accounting principle	800	613	666	646	612
Income taxes on provided earnings	224	159	167	148	167
Net earnings before cumulative effect of change in accounting principle	576	454	499	498	445
Net earnings	453	454	499	498	445
Net earnings before cumulative effect of change in accounting principle as percent of sales	4.3%	4.0%	4.6%	5.2%	5.4%
Net earnings as a percent of sales	3.4%	4.0%	4.6%	5.2%	5.4%

Factory Direct Selling by Cironi's Sewing Center

"To do, or not to do, another factory warehouse sale. That is the question!" quipped Tony Cironi to himself as he pondered whether it was advisable to run another factory-direct-to-consumer (FDC) warehouse sale. A year earlier Tony had enthusiastically committed to doing his first, and so far only, FDC warehouse sale with Viking-White Sewing (VWS), a sewing machine manufacturer headquartered in Cleveland, Ohio. However, Tony's postsale evaluation had left him with mixed feelings about that type of sales promotion. Profits had been disappointing, and although he had protected his turf, he had concerns about the ethics of FDCs and their long-term effects on independent sewing machine dealers. Consequently, he had not pushed to do another one. But now he would need to sort through the facts and resolve his ambivalent feelings about FDCs because the Singer sales representative had just called to ask if Tony would be interested in putting on an FDC for Singer Sewing Machine Company (SSMC).

Tony had agreed to meet with the rep to discuss terms and arrangements. But even as he reached for his files on the previous year's Viking-White FDC, Tony felt vaguely upset. "I'm damned if I do and damned if I don't," he muttered to himself.

> Looks to me like the manufacturer has all the advantages and none of the grief in doing these FDCs. But if I don't do it, someone else will, and my Singer sewing machine sales will be down for a year!

FACTORY DIRECT SELLING

Factory direct selling can be implemented in a number of different formats and is prevalent in the household appliance industry. In the sewing machine industry, factory direct selling has taken the form of special promotions that are co-sponsored by manufacturers and dealers. It is typically presented to consumers as a factory-authorized inventory reduction sale or FDC warehouse sale. The typical format involves an off-premise warehouse or storefront location, exten-sive public-notice-type advertising, a short time period, and local dealer involvement for after-sale service.

In the sewing machine industry, Viking-White Sewing was the first sewing machine manufacturer to run FDCs. The idea had originated with Joe Fulmer, owner of a large sewing machine dealership in Dayton, Ohio, called The Stitching Post. Fulmer presented the idea to John Howitt, a VWS sales representative who convinced his firm to authorize such promotions. By 1988, Fulmer was running FDCs all over the country with cooperation from local dealers, and other sewing machine manufacturers were copying the VWS format.

Factory-direct-to-consumer warehouse sales have been and continue to be a heated and controversial issue in the sewing machine industry. Many dealers view the practice as predatory while others have profited greatly. Small dealers with nonexclusive franchises run the risk of outside dealers invading their areas and making the "easy" sales

This case was prepared by Professor J. B. Wilkinson, Youngstown State University, and Professor Gary B. Frank, University of Akron, with thanks to Bob Barnes of Barnes Sewing Center in Akron, Ohio, for his cooperation in the field research for this case. Originally presented at a workshop of the Decision Sciences Institute, November 1990. This case was written solely for the purpose of stimulating student discussion. All individuals and incidents are real, but names have been disguised at the organization's request.

through FDCs, leaving the local shops to cope with after-sale problems. Medium-to-large sewing machine dealers see FDCs as a means of competing with off-price retailers, factory outlets or malls, and large supermarket-type appliance dealers.

The Independent Sewing Machine Dealers Association (ISMDA) has taken a stand against the practice and has been seeking dealer support for a legal fund to pursue trial cases against dealers who run FDCs outside their own dealer territories. To this end, ISMDA has sponsored a number of full-page advocacy ads in the industry's trade journal (*Round Bobbin*) stating the association's objections to FDCs and other types of off-premise sales by dealers outside their dealer territories (see Exhibit 1). Typical of the FDCs that ISMDA objects to are the "motel sales" mounted by several large sewing machine dealers across the United States. Such sales are usually advertised in the local newspaper and held in a motel room for a day. Advertised products may or may not be immediately available to buyers depending on whether a truck with sufficient inventory is parked nearby.

ISMDA objects to off-premise sales done by dealers outside their dealer territories on two basic grounds: (a) they represent an unfair method of competition and (b) they often rely on practices that are deceptive to consumers. ISMDA contends that dealers who conduct FDC sales outside their own territories are invaders, "poaching" customers away from local dealers who cannot match the low prices that are advertised for selected brands and models. FDCs and motel sales can occur at any time and dealers have little if any warning that such a sale is about to occur in their territory. The first indication that a dealer may have of an upcoming FDC or motel sale is when the advertisement appears in the local newspaper. By then it is too late for any local dealer to retaliate.

Local dealers are faced with a number of frustrations. First, they are unable to offer loss leader prices on all brands and models on an everyday basis and unable to predict which brands and models might be the target of an FDC or motel sale. As a result, they are usually caught off-guard when such

EXHIBIT 1
ISMDA Advocacy Advertisement:
The Round Bobbin, *July 1990, p. 33.*

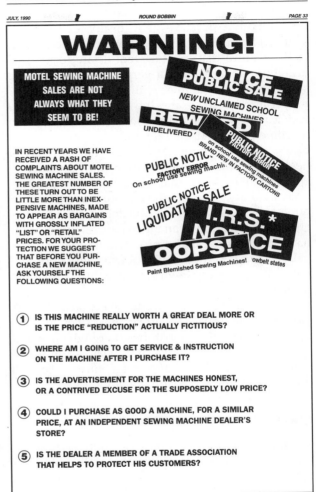

a sale occurs. Second, they are left with the after-sale service problems on the products that are sold to local customers at such sales. Their contracts with manufacturers require them to perform after-sale service on manufacturers' branded products for customers who reside in their market area. Products sold by FDCs or motel sales have a higher incidence of problems, since they are not checked or tested before delivery. Dealing with irate customers after such a sale creates a number of problems for local dealers, including loss of brand and dealer credibility if product problems cannot be resolved.

FDCs and motel sales also create opportunities for deceptive practices. For example, bait-and-switch is common. Sewing machine models that lack a feature that most sewers desire (e.g., "free arm") are advertised at a very low price. Because shoppers are not familiar with sewing machines by model number, they are drawn to the sale by the loss leader price on what looks to be a desirable machine model. At the sale, they are persuaded to buy a different model at a price that provides a healthy profit margin to the sponsor of the sale.

Another problem that often occurs is product unavailability. The products, purchased from a nonlocal source, may never be delivered, and buyers have no readily available recourse. Buyers also have no recourse if the products have been verbally misrepresented. Sale sponsor and salespeople are from "out of town" and are thus difficult to confront.

Despite these very serious objections, ISMDA has had little impact on off-premise sales held by dealers outside their territories. Large dealers and U.S. manufacturers have not been supportive. Some large dealers have even started to sell through toll-free 800 telephone numbers.

CIRONI'S VIKING-WHITE FDC

The initial proposal to sponsor a Viking-White factory warehouse sale was presented to Tony early in Spring 1988 by a VWS sales representative. Tony's immediate reaction was negative, but his subsequent investigation of other dealers' experiences caused him to decide in favor of the VWS proposal.

Tony's opportunity to observe a factory-direct-to-consumer warehouse sale firsthand was provided by Joe Fulmer, the dealer who had initiated FDCs in the sewing machine industry. Fulmer's FDC was conducted May 18–21, 1988, and Tony drove down to Dayton for the event. Based on observation of sales and his knowledge of dealer costs, Tony figured that Fulmer had to have cleared, *as a minimum,* $30,000 profit on approximately $120,000 in sales. As Tony observed to his wife afterward:

> That's pretty good for only several day's work! And the people who bought at that sale will be back to buy attachments, sewing accessories, cabinets, and other stuff!

In the end, the factor that loomed largest in Tony's mind was the possibility of a local competitor running a Viking-White FDC in his area—Akron, Ohio. He had added the Viking and White brands of sewing machines six months earlier, but his sales of those brands were disappointing. His share of Viking-White area sales was only 15 percent despite the fact that Cironi's Sewing Center was the largest (44 percent share of Akron area sewing machine sales) and fastest-growing sewing machine dealer in the Akron area.

Tony's addition of the Viking and White brands was part of a major strategic shift in the positioning of Cironi's Sewing Center. In searching for ways to expand volume, Tony had rejected the route taken by other independent sewing dealers, who had diversified into new merchandise areas including small appliances, ceiling fans, electronics, and stereo equipment. Instead, Tony had decided to position the store as a "category killer." He had seen the success other specialty retailers, such as Toys "R" Us, had when they focused on providing the entire range of available merchandise in a category. Tony had decided that he would make Cironi's Sewing Center the area superstore for sewing machines.

Part of Tony's problem was that VWS followed an intensive distribution policy. As a result, most sewing machine dealers in the Akron area carried the Viking and White brands, advertised them extensively, and offered frequent price reductions. In fact, the Akron market was considered to be highly price-competitive and overstored for sewing machines, primarily because the Singer brand was carried by all eight independent sewing machine dealers in the area, by Jo Ann Fabrics (a chain of fabric stores with four stores in the Akron area), and by Sears, Montgomery Ward, Zayre, and Best Products.

However, positioned as a category killer, Tony carried many additional brands of sewing machines (Baby Lock, Bernina, Pfaff, Elna, Singer, and Necchi), several of which (e.g., Bernina, Pfaff, and Elna) were distributed by him under exclusive territorial franchise agreements. Many local consumers were unfamiliar with these high-quality, high-priced European machines. However, shoppers who came into Cironi's Sewing Center to compare prices, model availability, and dealer assurances on well-known, inexpensive, lower-margin brands such as Viking-White or Singer often changed their minds and actually purchased a higher-priced Bernina, Pfaff, or Elna sewing machine. As a result, Tony consistently achieved a higher gross margin (40 percent) than other sewing machine dealers in the area, who struggled for gross margins of 30 to 35 percent.

Another factor contributing to Tony's impressive growth in sales—45 percent increase in dollar sales in 1988—was a heavy advertising and promotion campaign. This campaign had several components. Tony bought a quarter-page color ad in the yellow pages, 100 percent larger than the nearest competitors' ads, which were black and white. He advertised frequently in the metropolitan newspaper and in several suburban papers. Over a period of several years he had developed a computerized database of sewing customers, which was used for direct mailings of sales promotions. Finally, on a quarterly basis he included a discount coupon in a coupon book that was widely distributed by mail throughout the region.

In combination, the new sewing machine franchises and heavy promotion had spurred Cironi's unusual growth in a mature market. Tony's trading area expanded from local to regional. The added sewing machine lines had also opened up new markets. For example, Tony had been successful in winning major contracts for industrial sewing machines in two school districts—a success that was directly attributable to having exclusive territorial franchises for Bernina and Elna machines.

The addition of these higher-priced brands had fueled Tony's spectacular sales growth and market share performance. Their high prices acted to boost sales revenue, and their quality attracted shoppers from all over Northeast Ohio.

Yet, regardless of his strength in the premier brands, Tony was well aware of the need to establish himself as a Viking-White full-service dealer. Viking-White Sewing had high brand loyalty in the Akron area, and failure to carry the Viking and White brands would weaken his reputation as a full-line, full-service sewing center. But if a competitor ran a factory-direct-to-consumer warehouse sale for VWS, Tony's sales of Viking and White machines would be a "big zero" for the year, and he might even lose his franchise.

In the end, and in Tony's words:

> What the heck! I'll run the VWS FDC. Even if I break even, at least I will have protected my territory. As it stands now, some dealer in California might agree to sponsor a FDS with VWS *in my territory!* I can't allow that to happen. Competition is tough enough as it is!

Planning the Viking-White FDC warehouse sale was surprisingly simple. The VWS sales representative provided directions for time, location, promotion, and managing the event. Tony followed the recommended format and came up with the following plan:

Time. October 20–23, 1988.

Location. A commercial warehouse located on the opposite side of town, 10 miles away from Tony's store. Rental was $1,000 for 2,400 square feet of warehouse space for the period from October 18 to October 25, 1988 (two days prior to sale, four sale days, and two days after sale).

Product. Ninety percent of the White and Viking product lines (twenty models). VWS was to supply 1,000 machines on consignment; all shipping costs paid by the manufacturer. Sixty sewing machine cabinets from a cabinet company; all shipping costs paid by the dealer.

Price. Price leaders at near dealer cost (5 percent markup on retail) for Viking ($198), Sergers ($278), and White ($78) models prominently featured in advertisement. Average markup on retail of 40 percent on remainder (as opposed to 44 percent usual initial markup on retail). Markup of 20 percent on retail for cabinets (as opposed to 50 to 60 percent normal markup).

Advertising. Wednesday full-page, two-side, newspaper insert (Exhibits 2 and 3), Friday quarter-page ad, and Sunday quarter-page ad (Exhibit 4), for cost of $12,000, $2,500, and $3,500, respectively.

Sales. Five salespeople (area dealers) paid on commission (5 percent on sales) plus room and board ($40 per day each). VWS sales representative furnished by the manufacturer.

Evaluation of the Sale

Throughout the sale, Tony kept meticulous daily records of unit and dollar sales, shopper counts, and purchases (Exhibit 5). After the sale, he assessed the outcome as best he could (Exhibit 6), filed all the material related to the sale, and said to himself:

> This is crazy! I work myself into a frenzy over this sale, and what happens? I sell 278 machines and 22 cabinets for a grand total of $91,000. Cost of the merchandise alone was $56,550 for the machines and $3,200 for the cabinets—not to mention the shipping costs. I had to return most of the cabinets so my shipping cost for those suckers was $1,000! About the only reasonable cost in the whole mess was the telephone charges—only $150 for temporary phone installation and use during the sale.

Tony's problems didn't end when the sale was over. As he put it:

> I've had a steady stream of after-sale problems—people opening up cartons and finding the wrong machine inside, breaking machines in the setup process, or simply demanding service on a perfectly OK machine. And the lessons have been a real headache! More than 200 people so far have requested the free lessons that were part of the deal. At $5 to $6 an hour for two hours of instruction per class, with five to ten people in a class, I've spent at least $400 on those lessons.

The thing that really left a bad taste in Tony's mouth was the "repack" incident. (A "repack" is a product that has been returned to a manufacturer, repaired if necessary, and repackaged for sale as a new product.) When Tony examined a White overlock machine returned by a customer who had bought the machine on the first day of the sale, he found that the machine was filthy and definitely did not work properly. "Thank goodness," he said, "I was able to satisfy the customer with a new machine and identify the other repacks in the warehouse inventory. To think that White would do this to me. I can only hope that no other repacks were sold before I wised up to the situation!"

SINGER'S FDC PROPOSAL

Shortly after the initial contact from Singer, a factory sales representative met with Tony to explain Singer's format for an FDC warehouse sale. As Tony suspected, Singer's format differed little from that used by VWS. Singer would supply and deliver (without charge) a large number of machines on consignment to the warehouse sale site. A Singer sales representative would be on hand to assist with the sale. However, Tony would need to make all the arrangements for renting the warehouse, advertising the sale, finding area dealers who were willing to work the sale on commission, setting up and dismantling the sale, and so forth. Fixed costs for warehouse rent, advertising, telephone, and sales expense would be the same as for the VWS FDC. The FDC would be scheduled for September or October 1989, depending on warehouse and dealer availability.

Once again, Tony faced a dilemma. If he did not agree to do the Singer FDC, someone else probably would. The Singer brand accounted for close to 45 percent of all sewing machine sales in the Akron area ($960,000 in 1988, excluding mass merchandisers' house brands). Singer was distributed by all local sewing machine dealers. Competition was fierce; dealer margins for Singer were the

EXHIBIT 2
Newspaper Insert for Viking-White Warehouse Sale (Front)

PUBLIC NOTICE

FACTORY DIRECT SEWING MACHINE
WAREHOUSE SALE

ALL RESIDENTS OF NORTHEAST OHIO HAVE A UNIQUE OPPORTUNITY TO GET THE SEWING MACHINE OF THEIR CHOICE AT A REMARKABLE SAVINGS, DURING THE MILLION DOLLAR FACTORY AUTHORIZED STOCK REDUCTION SALE. MANY PRICES ARE BELOW OUR REGULAR WHOLESALE COST!!!

FREE ARMS-FLAT BEDS-PORTABLES-ZIG-ZAGS
AUTOMATICS-COMPUTERS-OVERLOCKS-CABINETS

VIKING

VIKING EUROPEAN QUALITY
A real value from Viking, all metal construction, automatic buttonhole, adjusting tension, 100% jam proof sewing, never needs oiling, suggested retail $449.00 LIMITED QUANTITIES.

WAREHOUSE PRICE $198

SERGERS

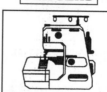

CUT YOUR SEWING TIME IN 1/2

FROM $278

WHITE

ALL METAL

HEAVY DUTY
White heavy duty zig-zag sews silk to leather, appliques, overcasts, darns and much more. Suggested retail $329.00.

WAREHOUSE PRICE $78

■ 4 DAYS ONLY!!! ■
THURS., OCT. 20; FRI., OCT. 21; SAT., OCT. 22; SUN., OCT. 23
9 AM - 9 PM

ONE THOUSAND MACHINES TO CHOOSE FROM. ALL ARE NEW IN FACTORY CARTONS. SOME OPEN STOCK DISPLAY MODELS, AND BUSINESS SCHOOL MACHINES. ALL IN FIRST CLASS OPERATING CONDITION, WITH FULL FACTORY WARRANTY. THIS LOCATION ONLY. HURRY, SOME QUANTITIES LIMITED.

─── OUR GUARANTEE ───
We will provide our full line of FREE SERVICES with all machines sold, even at these incredibly low prices.
• Up to 25-year factory parts warranty
• Up to 5 years free service
Complete training done to assure each individual full satisfaction with their new sewing machine. (Lessons and Service given by Barnes Sewing Center, State Rd. Shopping Center, Cuyahoga Falls, Ohio).

SALE HELD AT
VIKING/WHITE WAREHOUSE
3200 GILCHRIST RD.
MOGADORE
(Across from O'Neil's Dist. Center)
EXIT 27 OFF I-76

PHONE 784-5673
LIMITED QUANTITIES

MASTERCARD, VISA, DISCOVER, PERSONAL CHECKS, INSTANT CREDIT
& 90 DAYS SAME AS CASH

EXHIBIT 3
Newspaper Insert for Viking-White Warehouse Sale (Back)

EXHIBIT 4
*Quarter-Page Advertisement
for Viking-White Warehouse Sale*

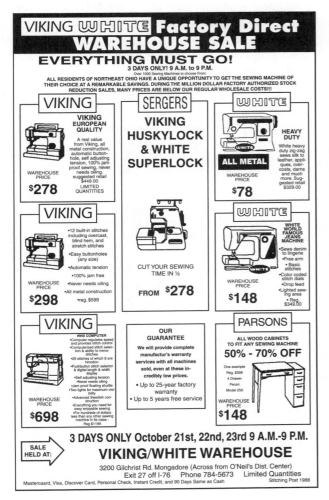

EXHIBIT 5
*Per Day Sewing Machine Sales and
Traffic Estimates for the Viking-White FDC*

Day	Dollar Sales	Unit Sales	Customer Traffic
Thursday, Oct. 20	$39,150	165	420
Friday, Oct. 21	23,490	70	270
Saturday, Oct. 22	17,660	50	150
Sunday, Oct. 23	6,700	15	60
Total	$87,000	300	900

Center had held nearly a 15 percent share of Viking-White's 12 percent share of Akron-area sewing machine sales prior to the VWS warehouse sale. Even though the VWS warehouse sale had been disappointing, Tony still considered the Viking and White brands to be essential to the merchandise offering of a full-service sewing machine dealer. VWS actively supported full-service sewing machine dealers through innovative merchandise/ promotion programs designed to improve dealer sales and profit performance. In return, sewing

EXHIBIT 6
*Sales, Expenses, and Profit,
Viking-White FDC, October 20–23, 1988*

	Sewing Machines	Cabinets	
Sales	$87,000	$4,000	
Cost of sales	56,550	3,200	
Gross margin	$30,450	$ 800	
Combined Gross Margin			$31,250
Expenses:			
Warehouse rent	$ 1,000		
Advertising	18,000		
Telephone	150		
Shipping (cabinets)	1,000		
Sales commission	4,550		
Sales expense	800		
Total			25,500
Profit			$ 5,750*

*Excludes after-sale service costs.

lowest in the industry (25 percent compared to 30 percent for Necchi, 37 percent for Viking-White or Elna, and 45 percent for Bernina or Pfaff). Moreover, Cironi's Sewing Center accounted for only 5 percent of all 1988 Singer sales in the Akron area.

Factors influencing whether or not to do a Singer FDC clearly differed from those that went into making the Viking-White decision. Cironi's Sewing machine dealers felt a commitment to the Viking and White brands.

Conversely, Singer seemed to be following price and distribution policies that were detrimental to the survival of full-service dealers. For example, Singer's decision to distribute the Singer brand of sewing machines through Sears had seriously hurt independent dealer sales. Independent dealers viewed Singer buyers as notorious price shoppers, and Sears could sell the volume necessary to support low markups. But when a Singer machine needed repair or after-sale service, independent dealers were expected to provide the necessary service *regardless of who sold the machine.* Although Singer reimbursed dealers for services covered under warranty, many dealers viewed this arrangement as a nuisance.

Tony wondered if he should lend his good name and reputation to a Singer warehouse sale. If Singer could not get a reputable local dealer to act as a sponsor and provide after-sale service, potential buyers might be "turned off." It would be more profitable for Tony to sell any other brand of sewing machine to a potential buyer. A successful Singer FDC might cannibalize potential sales of his other brands—brands that had higher profit margins. Following this train of thought, Tony reached for his files, saying to himself:

> I never really examined the issue of cannibalism. Do these factory warehouse sales cannibalize sales of other brands? Did my sales of Viking-White actually increase or merely shift from future time periods to the sale? Did I sacrifice future profits for current sales when I ran that FDC? If so, I'm not going to bite the Singer bait—margins on Singer are bad enough as it is. I could wind up with less profit than I did on the Viking-White deal. If I can't do at least as well as I did on the Viking-White warehouse sale, I shouldn't touch the Singer FDC!

Tony reached for his sales journal. The answer to his concern about cannibalism might be there—in those month-to-month dollar sales by brand (Exhibit 7). If the Viking-White warehouse sale had adverse effects on overall sales and profits, chances are that a Singer FDC would be the same—*or worse!*

EXHIBIT 7
Dollar Sales by Brand, June 1988–May 1989

				Brands			
Month	Baby Lock	Bernina	Elna	Pfaff	Necchi	Singer	Viking White
1988							
June	$ 3,695	$ 8,180	$ 965	$ 8,758	$ 1,180	$ 299	$ 1,270
July	5,293	12,400	1,250	3,950	1,000	1,310	2,800
Aug	4,958	14,560	1,400	11,400	2,026	3,315	965
Sept	2,395	11,500	1,350	11,833	395	290	2,750
Oct	3,550	7,950	680	4,800	750	500	87,770*
Nov	5,620	11,855	1,100	14,459	580	1,650	7,848
Dec	2,605	31,500	1,850	15,980	600	2,680	4,900
1989							
Jan	6,391	14,800	1,680	9,850	650	420	1,700
Feb	9,706	10,880	575	3,800	648	800	4,500
Mar	10,283	17,295	2,950	8,850	1,005	1,775	5,260
Apr	5,882	12,980	1,100	13,640	720	1,920	1,800
May	4,867	16,268	2,350	5,950	817	650	4,700

Total store sales, June 1988–May 1989 = $431,176

*Includes factory warehouse sales

Procter & Gamble—Scope

As Gwen Hearst looked at the year-end report, she was pleased to see that Scope held a 32 percent share of the mouthwash market for 1990. She had been concerned about the inroads that Plax, a prebrushing rinse, had made in the market. Since its introduction in 1988, Plax had gained a 10 percent share of the product category and posed a threat to Scope. As Brand Manager, Hearst planned, developed, and directed the total marketing effort for Scope, Procter & Gamble's (P&G) brand in the mouthwash market. She was responsible for maximizing the market share, volume, and profitability of the brand.

Until the entry of Plax, brands in the mouthwash market were positioned around two major benefits: fresh breath and killing germs. Plax was positioned around a new benefit—as a "plaque fighter"—and indications were that other brands, such as Listerine, were going to promote this benefit. The challenge for Hearst was to develop a strategy that would ensure the continued profitability of Scope in the face of these competitive threats. Her specific task was to prepare a marketing plan for P&G's mouthwash business for the next three years. It was early February 1991 and she would be presenting the plan to senior management in March.

COMPANY BACKGROUND

Based on the philosophy of providing products of superior quality and value that best fill the needs of consumers, Procter & Gamble is one of the most successful consumer goods companies in the world. The company markets its brands in more that 140 countries and had net earnings of $1.6 billion in 1990. The Canadian subsidiary contributed $1.4 billion in sales and $100 million in net earnings in 1990. It is recognized as a leader in the Canadian packaged goods industry, and its consumer brands lead in most of the categories in which the company competes.

Between 1987 and 1990, worldwide sales of P&G had increased by $8 billion and net earnings by $1.3 billion. P&G executives attributed the company's success to a variety of factors, including the ability to develop truly innovative products to meet consumers' needs. Exhibit 1 contains the statement of purpose and strategy of the Canadian subsidiary.

P&G Canada has five operating divisions, organized by product category. The divisions, and some of the major brands, are:

1. *Paper products:* Royale, Pampers, Luvs, Attends, Always
2. *Food and beverages:* Duncan Hines, Crisco, Pringles, Sunny Delight
3. *Beauty care:* Head & Shoulders, Pantene, Pert, Vidal Sassoon, Clearasil, Clarion, Cover Girl, Max Factor, Oil of Olay, Noxzema, Secret
4. *Health care:* Crest, Scope, Vicks, Pepto Bismol, Metamucil
5. *Laundry and cleaning:* Tide, Cheer, Bounce, Bold, Oxydol, Joy, Cascade, Comet, Mr. Clean

Each division has its own Brand Management, Sales, Finance, Product Development, and Operations line management groups and is evaluated as a profit center. Typically, within each division a brand manager is assigned to each brand (e.g., Scope). Hearst was in the Health Care Division and reported to the associate advertising manager for oral care, who, in turn, reported to the general manager of the division. After completing her business degree (B.B.A.) at a well-known Ontario business school in 1986, Hearst had joined P&G as a brand assistant. In 1987 she became the assistant brand manager for Scope and in 1988 she was

This case was written by Professor Gordon H. G. McDougall and Professor Franklin Ramsoomair of Wilfrid Laurier University as a basis of classroom discussion. Reprinted by permission of the authors.

EXHIBIT 1
*A Statement of Purpose and Strategy
Procter & Gamble, Canada*

We will provide products of superior quality and value that best fill the needs of consumers.

We will achieve that purpose through an organization and a working environment which attracts the finest people, fully develops and challenges our individual talents; encourages our free and spirited collaboration to drive the business ahead; and maintains the Company's historic principles of integrity, and doing the right thing.

We will build a profitable business in Canada. We will apply P&G worldwide learning and resources to maximize our success rate. We will concentrate our resources on the most profitable categories and on unique, important Canadian market opportunities. We will also contribute to the development of outstanding people and innovative business ideas for worldwide company use.

We will reach our business goals and achieve optimum cost efficiencies through continuing innovation, strategic planning and the continuous pursuit of excellence in everything we do.

We will continuously stay ahead of competition while aggressively defending our established profitable business against major competitive challenges despite short-term profit consequences.

Through the successful pursuit of our commitment, we expect our brands to achieve leadership share and profit positions and that, as a result, our business, our people, our shareholders, and the communities in which we live and work, will prosper.

Source: Company records.

promoted to brand manager. Hearst's rapid advancement at P&G reflected the confidence that her managers had in her abilities.

THE CANADIAN MOUTHWASH MARKET

Until 1987, on a unit basis the mouthwash market had grown at an average of 3 percent per year for the previous 12 years. In 1987, it experienced a 26 percent increase with the introduction of new flavors such as peppermint. Since then, the growth rate had declined to a level of 5 percent in 1990 (Exhibit 2).

The mouthwash market was initially developed by Warner-Lambert with its pioneer brand Listerine. Positioned as a therapeutic germ-killing mouthwash that eliminated bad breath, it dominated the market until the entry of Scope in 1967. Scope, a green, mint-tasting mouthwash, was positioned as a great tasting, mouth-refreshing brand that provided bad breath protection. It was the first brand that offered both effective protection against bad breath and a better taste than other mouthwashes. Its advertising focused, in part, on a perceived weakness of Listerine—a medicine breath (e.g., "Scope fights bad breath. Don't let the good taste fool you.")—and in 1976, Scope became the market leader in Canada.

In 1977, Warner-Lambert launched Listermint mouthwash as a direct competitor to Scope. Like Scope, it was a green, mint-tasting mouthwash and was positioned as a "good tasting mouthwash that fights bad breath." Within a year it had achieved a 12 percent market share, primarily at the expense of Listerine and smaller brands in the market.

In the 1970s Merrell Dow, a large pharmaceutical firm, launched Cepacol, which was positioned very close to Listerine. It achieved and held approximately 14 percent of the market in the early 1980s.

During the 1980s, the major competitive changes in the Canadian mouthwash market were:

- Listerine, which had been marketed primarily on a "bad breath" strategy, began shifting its position and in 1988 introduced the claim: "Fights plaque and helps prevent inflamed gums caused by plaque." In the U.S., Listerine gained the American Dental Association seal for fighting plaque but, as yet, did not have the seal in Canada.
- Listermint added fluoride during the early 1980s and added the Canadian Dental Association seal for preventing cavities in 1983. More recently, Listermint had downplayed fluoride and removed the seal.
- In early 1987, flavors were introduced by a number of brands including Scope, Listermint, and various store brands. This greatly expanded the market in 1987 but did not significantly change the market shares held by the major brands.

EXHIBIT 2
Mouthwash Market

	1986	1987	1988	1989	1990
Total Retail Sales (000,000)	$43.4	$54.6	$60.2	$65.4	$68.6
Total Factory Sales (000,000)	$34.8	$43.5	$48.1	$52.2	$54.4
Total Unit Sales (000)[a]	863	1,088	1,197	1,294	1,358
(% change)	3	26	10	8	5
(% change—"breath only)[b]	3	26	0	3	5
Penetration (%)[c]	65	70	75	73	75
Usage (# of times per week)[d]	2.0	2.2	2.3	2.4	3.0

Source: Company records.

[a] One unit or statistical case equals 10 litres or 352 fluid ounces of mouthwash.

[b] Excludes Plax and other prebrushing rinses.

[c] Percent of households having at least one brand in home.

[d] For each adult household member.

- Colgate Fluoride Rinse was launched in 1988. With the seal from the Canadian Dental Association for preventing cavities, it claimed that "Colgate's new fluoride rinse fights cavities. And, it has a mild taste that encourages children to rinse longer and more often." Colgate's share peaked at 2 percent and then declined. There were rumors that Colgate was planning to discontinue the brand.
- In 1988, Merrell Dow entered a licensing agreement with Strategic Brands to market Cepacol in Canada. Strategic Brands, a Canadian firm that markets a variety of consumer household products, had focused its efforts on gaining greater distribution for Cepacol and promoting it on the basis of price.
- In 1988, Plax was launched on a new and different platform. Its launch and immediate success caught many in the industry by surprise.

THE INTRODUCTION OF PLAX

Plax was launched in Canada in late 1988 on a platform quite different from the traditional mouthwashes. First, instead of the usual use occasion of "after brushing," it called itself a "prebrushing" rinse. The user rinses before brushing, and Plax's detergents are supposed to help loosen plaque to make brushing especially effective. Second, the

product benefits were not breath focused. Instead it claimed that "Rinsing with Plax, then brushing normally, removes up to three times more plaque than just brushing alone."

Pfizer Inc., a pharmaceutical firm, launched Plax in Canada with a promotional campaign budget that was estimated to be close to $4 million. The campaign, which covered the last three months of 1988 and all of 1989, consisted of advertising estimated at $3 million and extensive sales promotions including: (a) trial-size display in three drugstore chains ($60,000); (b) co-op mail couponing to 2.5 million households ($160,000); (c) instantly redeemable coupon offer ($110,000); (d) professional mailer to drug and supermarket chains ($30,000); and (e) a number of price reductions ($640,000). Plax continued to support the brand with advertising expenditures of approximately $1.2 million in 1990. In 1990, Plax held a 10 percent share of the total market.

When Plax was launched in the U.S., it claimed that using Plax "removed up to 300 percent more plaque than just brushing." This claim was challenged by mouthwash competitors and led to an investigation by the Better Business Bureau. The investigation found that the study on which Plax based its claim had panelists limit their toothbrushing to just 15 seconds—and didn't let them use toothpaste. A further study, where people were allowed to brush in their "usual manner" and with toothpaste, showed no overall difference in the level of plaque buildup between those using Plax and a control group that did not use Plax. Plax then revised its claim to "three times more plaque than just brushing alone." Information on plaque is contained in Appendix A.

THE CURRENT SITUATION

In preparing for the strategic plan, Gwen Hearst reviewed the available information for the mouthwash market and Scope. As shown in Exhibit 2, in 1990, 75 percent of Canadian households used one or more mouthwash brands and on average, usage was three times per week for each adult household member. Company market research revealed that users could be segmented on frequency of use; "heavy" users (once a day or more) comprised 40 percent of all users, "medium" users (two to six times a week) comprised 45 percent, and "light" users (less than once a week) comprised 15 percent. No information was available on the usage habits of prebrushing rinse users.

Non-users currently don't buy mouthwash because they either: (a) don't believe they get bad breath; (b) believe that brushing their teeth is adequate; and/or (c) find alternatives such as gums and mints more convenient.

The most important reasons why consumers use mouthwash follow:

Most important reason for using mouthwash:	%*
It is part of my basic oral hygiene	40
It gets rid of bad breath	40
It kills germs	30
It makes me feel more confident	20
To avoid offending others	25

*Multiple reasons allowed.

During 1990, a survey was conducted on the image mouthwash users had of the major brands

on the market (Exhibit 3). Respondents were asked to rate the brands on a number of attributes and the results showed that Plax had achieved a strong image on the "removes plaque/healthier teeth and gums" attributes.

Market share data revealed there was a substantial difference in the share held by Scope in food stores (e.g., supermarkets), 42 percent, versus drugstores, 27 percent (Exhibit 4). Approximately 65 percent of all mouthwash sales went through drugstores while 35 percent went through food stores. Recently, wholesale clubs, such as Price Club and Costco, had accounted for a greater share of mouthwash sales.[1] Typically, these clubs carried Cepacol, Scope, Listerine, and Plax.

Competitive data was also collected for advertising expenditures and retail prices. As shown in Exhibit 5, total media spending of all brands in 1990 was $5 million, with Scope, Listerine, and Plax accounting for 90 percent of all advertising. Retail prices were calculated based on a 750 mL bottle: both Listerine and Plax were priced at a higher level in food stores and Plax was priced at a premium in drugstores.

Information on the U.S. market for 1989 was also available (Exhibit 6). In contrast to Canada, Listerine held the dominant share in the U.S. market. Since early 1989, Listerine had been advertised heavily in the U.S. as "the only nonprescription mouthwash accepted by the American Dental Association for its significant help in preventing and reducing plaque and gingivitis." In clinical tests in the United States, Listerine significantly reduced plaque scores by roughly 20 to 35 percent, with a similar reduction in gingivitis. In Canada, the 1990 advertising campaign included the claim that Listerine has been clinically proven to "help prevent inflamed and irritated gums caused by plaque build-up." Listerine's formula relied on four essential oils—menthol, eucalyptol, thymol, and methyl salicylate—all derivatives of phenol, a powerful antiseptic.

---

[1] Wholesale clubs were included in food store sales.

EXHIBIT 3
Consumer Perceptions of Brand Images

All Users [a]

Attributes	Cepacol	Colgate	Listerine	Listermint	Plax	Scope
Reduces Bad Breath	...	...	...	...	—	...
Kills Germs	+	...	+	...	...	...
Removes Plaque	...	...	...	...	+	—
Healthier Teeth and Gums	...	...	...	...	+	—
Good for Preventing Colds	...	—	+	...	...	...
Recommended by Doctors/Dentists	...	...	...	...	+	...
Cleans Your Mouth Well	...	...	...	...	...	...

Brand Users [b]

Attributes	Cepacol	Colgate	Listerine	Listermint	Plax	Scope
Reduces Bad Breath	+	—	+	+	—	+
Kills Germs	+	...	+	+	—	...
Removes Plaque	—	+	+	—	+	...
Healthier Teeth and Gums	...	+	+	—	+	—
Good for Preventing Colds	+	—	+	—	+	—
Recommended by Doctors/Dentists	+	+	+	—	+	—

Source: Company records.

[a] Includes anyone who uses mouthwash. Respondents were asked to rate all brands (even those they hadn't used) on the attributes. A "+" means this brand scores *higher than average*. A "..." means this brand scored about average. A "—" means this brand scored *below average*. For example, Cepacol is perceived by those who use mouthwash as a brand that is good/better than most at "preventing germs."

[b] Includes only the users of that brand. For example, Cepacol is perceived by those whose "usual brand" is Cepacol as a brand that is good/better than most at "reducing bad breath."

Listerine had not received the consumer product seal given by the Canadian Dental Association (CDA) because the association was not convinced a mouthrinse could be of therapeutic value. The CDA was currently reviewing American tests for several products sold in Canada. In fact, any proposed changes to the formulation of mouthwashes or advertising claims could require approval from various regulatory agencies.

THE REGULATORY ENVIRONMENT

1. *Health Protection Branch (HPB):* This government body classifies products into "drug status" or "cosmetic status" based on both the product's action on bodily functions and its advertising claims. Drug products are those that affect a bodily function (e.g., prevent cavities or prevent plaque build-up). For "drug status" products, all product formulations, packaging, copy, and advertising must be precleared by the Health Protection Branch (HPB), with guidelines that are very stringent. Mouthwashes such as Scope that claim to only prevent bad breath are considered as "cosmetic status." However, if any claims regarding inhibition of plaque formation are made, the product reverts to "drug status" and all advertising is scrutinized.

2. *The Canadian Dental Association (CDA):* The CDA will, upon request of the manufacturer, place its seal of recognition on products that have demonstrated efficacy against cavities or against plaque/gingivitis. However, those products with the seal of recognition must submit their packaging and advertising to the CDA for approval. The CDA and the American Dental Association (ADA) are two separate bodies and are independent of one another, and don't always agree on issues. The CDA, for example,

EXHIBIT 4
Canadian Mouthwash Market Shares (%)

	Units			1990 Average	
	1988	1989	1990	Food	Drug
Scope	33.0	33.0	32.3	42.0	27.0
Listerine	15.2	16.1	16.6	12.0	19.0
Listermint	15.2	9.8	10.6	8.0	12.0
Cepacol	13.6	10.6	10.3	9.0	11.0
Colgate Oral Rinse	1.4	1.2	0.5	0.4	0.5
Plax	1.0	10.0	10.0	8.0	11.0
Store Brands	16.0	15.4	16.0	18.0	15.0
Miscellaneous Other	4.6	3.9	3.7	2.6	4.5
Total	100.0	100.0	100.0	100.0	100.0
Retail Sales (000,000)	$60.2	$65.4	$68.6	$24.0	$44.6

Source: Company records.

would not provide a "plaque/gingivitis" seal unless clinical studies demonstrating actual gum health improvements were done.

3. *Saccharin/Cyclamate Sweeteners:* All mouthwashes contain an artificial sweetener. In Canada, cyclamate is used as the sweetener as saccharin is considered a banned substance. In contrast, the U.S. uses saccharin because cyclamate is prohibited. Thus, despite the fact that many of the same brands competed in both Canada and the U.S., the formulas in each country were different.

THE THREE-YEAR PLAN

In preparing the three-year plan for Scope, a team had been formed within P&G to examine various options. The team included individuals from Product Development (PDD), Manufacturing, Sales, Market Research, Finance, Advertising, and Operations. Over the past year, the team had completed a variety of activities relating to Scope.

The key issue, in Hearst's mind, was how P&G should capitalize on the emerging market segment within the rinse category that focused more on "health-related benefits" than the traditional breath

strategy of Scope. Specifically with the launch of Plax, the mouthwash market had segmented itself along the "breath-only" brands (like Scope) and those promising other benefits. Plax, in positioning itself as a prebrushing rinse, was not seen as, nor did it taste like, a "breath refreshment" mouthwash like Scope.

Gwen Hearst believed that a line extension positioned against Plax, a recent entry into the market, made the most sense. If the mouthwash market became more segmented, and if these other brands grew, her fear was that P&G would be left with a large share of a segment that focused only on "breath" and hence might decline. However, she also knew that there were questions regarding both the strategic and financial implications of such a proposal. Exhibit 7 provides historical financials for Scope. In recent meetings, other ideas had been proposed, including "doing nothing" and looking at claims other than "breath" that might be used by Scope instead of adding a new product. Several team members questioned whether there was any real threat, as Plax was positioned very differently from Scope. As she

EXHIBIT 5
Competitive Market Data—1990

Advertising Expenditures (000)

Scope	$1,700
Listerine	1,600
Plax	1,200
Listermint	330
Cepacol	170

Media Plans

	No. of Weeks on Air	GRPs [a]
Scope	35	325
Listerine	25	450
Plax	20	325

Retail Price Indices

	Food Stores	Drugstores
Scope	98	84
Listerine	129	97
Listermint	103	84
Colgate	123	119
Plax	170	141
Store Brand	58	58
Cepacol	84	81
Total Market [b]	100	100

Source: Company records.

[a] GRP (Gross Rating Points) is a measurement of advertising impact derived by multiplying the number of persons exposed to an advertisement by the average number of exposures per person. The GRPs reported are monthly.

[b] An average weighted index of the retail prices of all mouthwash brands is calculated and indexed at 100 for both food stores and drugstores. Scope is priced slightly below this index in food stores and about 16% below in drugstores.

considered the alternatives, Hearst reviewed the activities of the team and the issues that had been raised by various team members.

PRODUCT DEVELOPMENT (PDD)

In product tests on Scope, PDD had demonstrated that Scope reduced plaque better than brushing alone because of antibacterial ingredients contained in Scope. However, as yet P&G did not have a clinical database to convince the HPB to allow

EXHIBIT 6
Canada–U.S. Market Share Comparison (1989) (% units)

Brands	Canada	United States
Scope	33.0	21.6
Listerine	16.1	28.7
Listermint	9.8	4.5
Cepacol	10.6	3.6
Plax	10.0	9.6

Source: Company records.

Scope to extend these claims into the prevention of inflamed gums (as Listerine does).

PDD had recently developed a new prebrushing rinse product that performed as well as Plax but did not work any better than Plax against plaque reduction. In fact, in their testing of Plax itself, PDD were actually unable to replicate the plaque reduction claim made by Pfizer that "rinsing with Plax, then brushing normally removes up to three times more plaque than brushing alone." The key benefit of P&G's prebrushing rinse was that it did taste better than Plax. Other than that, it had similar aesthetic qualities to Plax—qualities that made its "in mouth" experience quite different from that of Scope.

The Product Development people in particular were concerned about Hearst's idea of launching a line extension because it was a product that was only equal in efficacy to Plax for plaque reduction. Traditionally, P&G had only launched products that focused on unmet consumer needs—typically superior performing products. However, Hearst had pointed out, because the new product offered similar efficacy at a better taste, this was similar to the situation when Scope was originally launched. Some PDD members were also concerned that if they couldn't replicate Plax's clinical results with P&G's stringent test methodology, and if the product possibly didn't provide any greater benefit than rinsing with liquid, that P&G's image and credibility with dental professionals might be impacted. There was debate on this issue as others

EXHIBIT 7
Scope Historical Financials

Year	1988		1989		1990	
Total Market Size (units) (000)	1,197		1,294		1,358	
Scope Market Share	33.0%		33.0%		32.4%	
Scope Volume (units) (000)	395		427		440	
	$(000)	$/Unit	$(000)	$(Unit)	$(000)	$(Unit)
Sales	16,767	42.45	17,847	41.80	18,150	41.25
COGS	10,738	27.18	11,316	26.50	11,409	25.93
Gross Margin	6,029	15.27	7,299	15.30	6,741	15.32

Scope Marketing Plan Inputs

Scope "Going" Marketing Spending

Year	1990	1989	1988
Advertising (000)	$1,700	–	–
Promotion (000)	1,460	–	–
Total (000)	3,160	3,733	2,697

Marketing Input Costs

Advertising:		(See above.)
Promotion:	Samples	(Including Distribution): $0.45/piece
	Mailed Couponing	$10.00 per 1,000 for printing distribution $0.17 handling per redeemed coupon (beyond face value) redemption rates: 10% to 15%
	In-store Promotion	$200/store (fixed) $0.17 handling per redeemed coupon (beyond face value) redemption rates: 85% +

Source: Company records.

felt that as long as the product did encourage better oral hygiene, it did provide a benefit. As further support, they noted that many professionals did recommend Plax. Overall, PDD's preference was to not launch a new product but, instead, to add plaque reduction claims to Scope. The basic argument was that it was better to protect the business that P&G was already in than to launch a completely new entity. If a line extension was pursued, a product test costing $20,000 would be required.

SALES

The Sales people, who had seen the inroads Plax had been making in the marketplace, believed that Scope should respond quickly. They had one key concern—as stock-keeping units (SKUs) had begun to proliferate in many categories, the retail industry had become much more stringent regarding what it would accept. Now, to be listed on store shelves, a brand must be seen as unique enough from the competition to build incremental purchases—otherwise retailers argued that category sales volume would simply be spread over more units. When this happened, a retail outlet's profitability was reduced because inventory costs were higher but no additional sales revenue was generated. When a new brand was viewed as not generating more sales, retailers might still list the brand by replacing units within the existing line (e.g., drop shelf facings of Scope), or the manufacturer would pay approximately $50,000 per SKU in listing fees to add the new brand. This fee of $50,000 per SKU would enable a manufacturer to get national distribution with a retail chain such as Shopper's Drug Mart or Loblaws.

MARKET RESEARCH (MR)

Market Research had worked extensively with Hearst to test the options with consumers. Their work to date had shown:

1. A plaque reassurance on current Scope (i.e., "Now Scope fights plaque") did not seem to increase competitive users' desire to purchase Scope. This meant that it was unlikely to generate additional volume but it could prevent current users from switching.

   MR also cautioned that in adding "reassurances" to a product, it often takes time before the consumer accepts the idea and then acts on it. The issue in Hearst's mind was whether the reassurance would ever be enough. At best it might stabilize the business, she thought, but would it grow behind such a claim?

2. A "Better Tasting Prebrushing Dental Rinse" product did research well among Plax users, but did not increase purchase intent among people not currently using a dental rinse. MR's estimate was that a brand launched on this positioning, using the Scope name, would likely result in approximately a 6.5 percent share of the total mouthwash and "rinse" market on an ongoing basis. Historically, it has taken approximately two years to get to the ongoing level. However, there was no way for MR to accurately assess potential Scope cannibalization. "Use your judgment," MR had said. However, MR cautioned that although it was a product for a different usage occasion, it was unlikely to be 100 percent incremental business. Hearst's best rough guess was that this product might cannibalize somewhere between 2 to 9

percent of Scope's sales. An unresolved issue was the product's name—if it were launched, should it be under the Scope name or not? One fear was that if the Scope name was used it would either "turn off" loyal users who saw Scope as a breath refreshment product or confuse them.

MR had questioned Hearst as to whether she had really looked at all angles to meet her objective. Because much of this work had been done quickly, they wondered whether there weren't some other benefits Scope could talk about that would interest consumers and hence achieve the same objective. They suggested that Hearst look at other alternatives beyond just "a plaque reassurance on Scope" or a "line extension positioned as a 'Better Tasting Prebrushing Dental Rinse'."

FINANCE

The point of view from Finance was mixed. On the one hand, Plax commanded a higher $ price/litre and so it made sense that a new rinse might be a profitable option. On the other hand, they were concerned about the capital costs and the marketing costs that might be involved to launch a line extension. One option would be to source the product from a U.S. plant where the necessary equipment already existed. If the product were obtained from the U.S., delivery costs would increase by $1.00 per unit. Scope's current financial picture and an estimate of Plax's financial picture are provided in Exhibits 8 and 9.

PURCHASING

The purchasing manager had received the formula for the line extension and had estimated that the ingredients cost would increase by $2.55 per unit due to the addition of new ingredients. But, because one of the ingredients was very new, Finance felt that the actual ingredient change might vary by ± 50 percent. Packaging costs would be $0.30 per unit higher owing to the fact that the setup charges would be spread over a smaller base.

EXHIBIT 8
Scope 1990 Financials

	$(000)	$/Units
Net sales	18,150	41.25
Ingredients	3,590	8.16
Packaging	2,244	5.10
Manufacturing	3,080	7.00
Delivery	1,373	3.12
Miscellaneous	1,122	2.55
Cost of Goods Sold	11,409	25.93
Gross Margin	6,741	15.32

Source: Company records.

- Notes:
- Net Sales = P&G revenues.
- Manufacturing: 50% of manufacturing cost is fixed, of which $200M is depreciation. 20% of manufacturing cost is labor.
- Miscellaneous: 75% of miscellaneous cost is fixed.
- General office overheads are $1,366M.
- Taxes are 40%.
- Currently the plant operates on a five-day, one-shift operation.
- P&G's weighted average cost of capital is 12%.
- Total units sold in 1990 were 440,000.

ADVERTISING AGENCY

The advertising agency felt that making any new claims for Scope was a huge strategic shift for the brand. They favored a line extension. Scope's strategy had always been "breath refreshment and good tasting" focused, and they saw the plaque claims as very different, with potentially significant strategic implications. The one time they had focused advertising only on taste and didn't reinforce breath efficacy, market share fell. They were concerned that the current Scope consumer could be confused if plaque or any "nonbreath" claims were added and that Scope could actually lose market share if this occurred. They also pointed

EXHIBIT 9
Plax Financial Estimates (per unit)

Net sales	65.09
COGS	
Ingredients	6.50
Packaging	8.30
Manufacturing	6.50
Delivery	3.00
Miscellaneous	1.06
Total	25.36

Source: P&G estimates.

Notes: General overhead costs estimated at $5.88/unit.

out that trying to communicate two different ideas in one commercial was very difficult. They believed the line extension was a completely different product than Scope with a different benefit and use occasion. In their minds, a line extension would need to be supported on a going basis separately from Scope.

WHAT TO RECOMMEND?

Hearst knew the business team had thought long and hard about the issue. She knew that management was depending on the Scope business team to come up with the right long-term plan for P&G—even if that meant not introducing the new product. However, she felt there was too much risk associated with P&G's long-term position in oral rinses if nothing was done. There was no easy answer—and compounding the exigencies of the situation was the fact that the business team had differing points of view. She was faced with the dilemma of providing recommendations about Scope, but also needed to ensure that there was alignment and commitment from the business team or senior management would be unlikely to agree to the proposal.

APPENDIX A
Plaque

Plaque is a soft, sticky film that coats teeth within hours of brushing and may eventually harden into tartar. To curb gum disease—from which over 90 percent of Canadians suffer at some time—plaque must be curbed. Research has shown that, without brushing, within 24 hours a film (plaque) starts to spread over teeth and gums and, over days, becomes a sticky, gelatinous mat, which the plaque bacteria spin from sugars and starches. As the plaque grows, it becomes a home to yet more bacteria—dozens of strains. A mature plaque is about 75 percent bacteria; the remainder consists of organic solids from saliva, water, and other cells shed from soft oral tissues.

As plaque bacteria digest food, they also manufacture irritating malodorous by-products, all of which can harm a tooth's supporting tissues as they seep into the crevice below the gum line. Within 10 to 21 days, depending on the person, signs of gingivitis—the mildest gum disease—first appear; gums deepen in color, swell, and lose their normally tight, arching contour around teeth. Such gingivitis is entirely reversible. It can disappear within a week after regular brushing and flossing are resumed. But when plaque isn't kept under control, gingivitis can be the first step down toward periodontitis, the more advanced gum disease in which bone and other structures that support the teeth become damaged. Teeth can loosen and fall out, or require extraction.

The traditional and still best approach to plaque control is careful and thorough brushing and flossing to scrub teeth clean of plaque. Indeed, the anti-plaque claims that toothpastes carry are usually based on the product's ability to clean teeth mechanically, with brushing. Toothpastes contain abrasives, detergent, and foaming agents, all of which help the brush do its work.

Source: "The Plaque Debate," *Canadian Consumer,* 1990. No. 9, pp. 17–23.

Market, product, and organization dynamics can be explained in both quantitative and qualitative terms by a product life cycle graph. This analysis can provide an historical synopsis of important strategic decisions, including those of the competition. It can show how external factors lead to the success or failure of a specific strategy. And it can be used as a benchmark in determining future marketing actions and in monitoring success. Life cycle analysis gives an industrial company a very important record of marketing and strategy achievements and a very potent competitive weapon as well.

Product Life Cycle Theory (PLC) was introduced more than thirty years ago. Basically, it plots unit sales (or unit profits) against time to determine the evolutionary stages in the life cycle of a product (Exhibit 1). This information can prove invaluable in planning marketing and product strategies.

While there's an intuitive and logical appeal to this concept, as well as an elegant simplicity, not many industrial companies really understand how to develop and apply life cycle analysis because:

- PLC research has largely focused on consumer durable and nondurable applications, and very few industrial models have been developed.
- Many industrial companies lack the marketing resources to utilize and effectively implement PLC strategies.
- Managers need to make assessments of market conditions before making any predictions about product or market strategies.
- Most industries don't record the kind of information on product introductions and profitability that the PLC model requires.
- Industrial products tend to have extended life spans, and slower, more conservative markets. This makes monitoring PLC changes frustrating.

- The environment in which industrial products are sold is more difficult to manage than the consumer goods environment.

JOHNSON CONTROLS

Despite many of these difficulties, Johnson Controls, Inc., developed a successful life cycle process in order to study the product and market dynamics of building automation systems (BAS).

Established in 1885 by Warren Johnson, the inventor of the first electric room thermostat, Johnson Controls was first a leader in temperature control technology and in recent years in building control technology. The company is now a major multinational organization with nearly 30,000 employees. With net sales of over $1.4 billion in 1984, Johnson Controls ranks among the top 300 companies in the *Fortune* ratings. On the international level, Johnson Controls has participated in the construction of more buildings worldwide than any other company. Its Systems & Services Division is one of the three major influences in the building controls industry.

Johnson Controls' building automation system (BAS) products offer state-of-the-art technology to control and maximize energy use in the heating, cooling, ventilation, fire safety, security, lighting, communications, and maintenance of nonresidential buildings.

DEVELOPING A FRAMEWORK

Developing a PLC framework is a very creative endeavor. Many more factors than unit sales and time come into play. Although Johnson Controls' model worked well for their purposes, different

---

This case was prepared by Tracy K. Short, planning analyst, Systems and Services Division, Johnson Controls, Inc., Milwaukee, and appeared in "Industrial Product Life Cycle Analysis," *Planning Review,* November, 1985, pp. 18–23.

EXHIBIT 1
Classical Product Life Cycle Stages

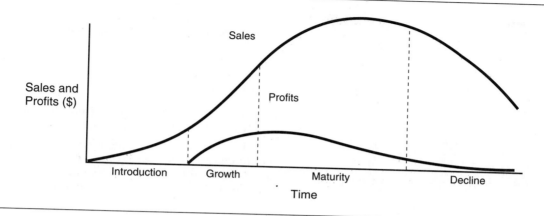

approaches may be more appropriate for other industrial firms. The key is flexibility. The process used in developing the life cycle scenario at Johnson Controls involved five steps:

- Building a quantitative model
- Identifying general product life cycle issues
- Generating solutions
- Determining the critical strategic issues
- Implementing the solutions

Building a Quantitative Model

Marketing research, sales reports, factory operations reports, pricing and financial data, and organizational charts were analyzed in great detail to develop a preliminary PLC model showing unit sales over time. Very often, past product sales information was difficult to obtain, especially in the desired form.

Classifying the various BAS products into manageable and meaningful life cycle groups was also difficult. A number of systems were introduced between 1965 and 1982, each one a functional or technological improvement on the one preceding it. Some systems were complex and handled large building energy and facility management, while others dealt with small buildings and were less involved.

We could have developed an analysis for each individual BAS product. However, the most practical solution seemed to lie in grouping the products on a technological basis:

- Three of the early systems were based on hardware technology. These systems constituted one product life cycle family called the T-6000 group.
- The next group of systems was based on the development of computerized centralization, providing not only basic energy management control but also increased building management capabilities. These products could be easily categorized into a second life cycle family, identified as the JC/80 group.
- The third life cycle family included systems based on further improvements in computer technology and, most importantly, in improved computer hierarchical design that permitted greater distributed processing, increased system functionality, and facility management capability. This family was labeled the JC/85 group.

Exhibit 2 shows the product life cycle for the T-6000 BAS family. Basic models such as these were also developed for the JC/80 and JC/85 families. A large model showing BAS unit sales from 1965 through 1984 was also mapped out to enable us to analyze the overlaps between the three families better.

EXHIBIT 2
T-6000 Series Product Life Cycle Stages

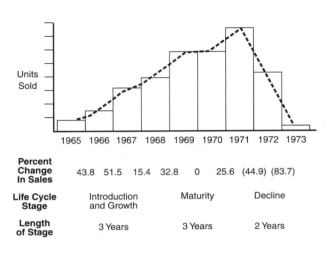

Percent Change In Sales	43.8 51.5 15.4 32.8	0	25.6 (44.9) (83.7)	
Life Cycle Stage	Introduction and Growth	Maturity	Decline	
Length of Stage	3 Years	3 Years	2 Years	

Life cycle stages were identified by studying the rate of change in units sold. Introductory and growth stages are theoretically identified by a fast increase in sales. A mature stage is indicated by slowing sales, and decline is shown by a negative growth rate. Determining the PLC stages of a product group were based largely on collective experience since it is rarely possible to be exact.

Identifying the Issues

Once we had the model, we could begin to ask the crucial questions that would pinpoint problem areas:

- Can we really establish the present and past life cycle positions of BAS products?
- What are the key environmental issues in the industry and how do they affect BAS markets and products (e.g., energy costs and nonresidential building construction)?
- How do the internal relationships between functional areas of the company (marketing, development, manufacturing) affect PLCs?
- Who are Johnson Controls' most important competitors? What products do they offer? What's their mar-

keting strategy? How does this influence building automation system PLCs?
- What are the reasons for the peaks and valleys in the PLC curve?
- What technological developments are influencing the BAS life cycle?
- How are the company's marketing strategies affecting sales—including pricing, promotion, and placement?

Because of their qualitative nature, the resolution of these issues was not clear. No sooner does one come to grips with a previously undefined parameter than one discovers even more hazy subissues lurking beneath it. After considerable study, we decided to use an interviewing process.

Generating Solutions

We conducted 19 individual interviews with management and staff professionals in research and development, marketing, manufacturing, finance, and sales to generate explanations of the life cycle trends. We selected these people on the basis of their tenure in the company and their experience, past and present, with BAS products. The interviews were open-ended, with no leading questions.

The interviewing process proved to be very effective. The respondents were presented with the three quantitative PLC models for each BAS product family and were asked to explain what they saw happening at various junctures on the curves. Specifically, they were asked to describe product developments, introductions, and transitions; pricing strategy; advertising strategy; planning efforts; organizational influences; and the impact of competition and external factors on sales over time.

We used the content analysis technique, popularized by John Naisbitt in *Megatrends*, to identify trends, issues, and key factors. Exhibit 3 shows one way the responses were grouped, analyzed, and related to changes in the U.S. economy from 1965 through 1978. Similar content analyses related Johnson Controls' BAS sales to changes in the competition, and in the construction and energy industries.

EXHIBIT 3

Comparison: Company X Sales to the Economy*

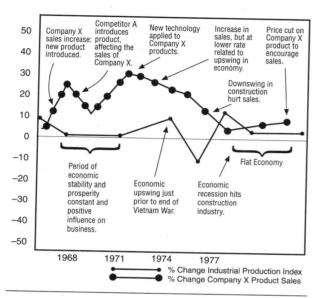

Company X sales increase: new product introduced.

Competitor A introduces product, affecting the sales of Company X.

New technology applied to Company X products.

Increase in sales, but at lower rate related to upswing in economy.

Price cut on Company X product to encourage sales.

Downswing in construction hurt sales.

Flat Economy

Period of economic stability and prosperity constant and positive influence on business.

Economic upswing just prior to end of Vietnam War.

Economic recession hits construction industry.

● — ● % Change Industrial Production Index
● — ● % Change Company X Product Sales

*Company X—fictitious data.

Determining Critical Strategic Issues

At this point, definite patterns in crucial life cycle issues began to emerge. These were issues that had had the most impact on BAS sales in the past and would probably continue to affect sales in the future. Basically, they involved:

- Products offered and technology used
- Prices
- Market position
- Overall marketing strategy
- Promotional emphasis
- Competitive influences

Exhibit 5 shows one analysis technique we used to relate critical issues to the product life cycle stages of the T-6000 family. A similar analysis was also done for the JC/80 and JC/85 families. The information in Exhibit 5 was based on the theoretical life cycle premises shown in Exhibit 4. Of course, in real life, not all products follow these guidelines. For example, at Johnson Controls the

introductory and growth stages of BAS products were often indiscernible and could be combined, leaving only three PLC stages to contend with instead of four.

Within each of the three product families, T-6000, JC/80, and JC/85, certain similarities in life cycle responses became apparent. There were also commonalities between each product family by life cycle stage.

Introductory Stage. Here, each new product family introduction had to consider the element of pent-up demand. The lesson here was for Johnson Controls to properly anticipate this demand—as well as the subsequent periods of decline—in order to minimize their effects on profits and return on investment.

Growth and Maturity Stage. At this point, the product life cycle study of the T-6000 and JC/80 families indicated that our major competitor seemed to market its new products just as ours were nearing their decline phase. Whether or not this was a planned strategy on the part of the competition, it indicated that we needed to develop a new strategy to protect our position, one that allowed us to introduce the industry's newest product ahead of the competition. This kind of forward planning will help us pin down the life cycle of our existing products more accurately, which will also allow us to maximize our profits without losing ground while simultaneously developing and introducing our new products.

The competition was very adept at using pricing and promotional weapons to their advantage. Although we viewed the competitive product as less capable from a technical standpoint, customers believed they were getting the best product. This was because the competition's advertising campaign leaned heavily on such emotional appeals as prestige—being first to install a system like this.

During the mid-1970s Johnson Controls successfully protected its maturing product position by developing a group of systems—part of the larger JC/80 family—that allowed our customers to upgrade as their needs dictated. We built our

EXHIBIT 4
Classical Strategies Associated with Product Life Cycle Stages

Effects and Responses	Product Life Cycle Stage			
	Introduction	Growth	Maturity	Decline
Competition	• None of importance (if leader).	• Some emulators (if leader).	• More rivals as profits increase for product/market.	• Fewer rivals due to shakeout of weak product offerings.
Overall strategy	• Market establishment; focus on early adopters.	• Market penetration; focus on followers and find new markets. • If follower, concentrate on segment that can be dominated.	• Defense of market/product position; check the inroads of competition. • Hold share by improving quality, increasing sales effort, and advertising.	• Prepare to remove product from market. • Achieve and secure any possible benefits. • Maximize cash flow by reducing investment, advertising, development.
Profits	• Negligible because of high production, development, and marketing costs.	• Reach peak levels as a result of high prices and growing demand.	• Increasing competition will cut into margins and ultimately reduce profits.	• Declining volume pushes costs up to levels that eliminate profits entirely.
Prices	• Set higher than in later stages because of development and introductory costs.	• Begin to reduce prices to discourage new competitors and to build share as growth matures. • If follower, keep prices below leader.	• Prices will decline and then stabilize as more substitute products become available and product differentiation diminishes.	• Further decline in prices.
Marketing and advertising	• Advertising and marketing expenditures should be high relative to sales compared with mature products.	• Expenditures remain high relative to expenditure rates of established products, but will start to decline in relation to sales because of rapid sales volume growth.	• Marketing and advertising expenditures to sales ratio will decline substantially because of reduced margins and demand.	• Further decline in expenditures.
Distribution	• To select customers who will buy and can refer product to others.	• Intensify efforts to gain share. • More broad-based application.	• Intensify efforts to defend share.	• Eliminate unprofitable efforts.

EXHIBIT 5

T-6000 Series Product Life Cycle Effects and Responses*

Effects and Responses	1965–1968		1969–1970	1970–1972
	Introduction	*Growth*	*Maturity*	*Decline*
Industry technology available	System format English language and control center capabilities available.		Coax cable expandability and digital transmission available.	• Fire and security applications developed for use with BAS. • Microprocessor technology available.
Competition	Competitor A not a threat.		Competitor A introduces new product using latest technology.	Competitor A threatens with a strong marketing and sales program.
JCI market strategy	T-6000 system introduced (first industry BAS).	T-6000 upgraded to increase market penetration.	T-6000 upgraded as defense to Competitor A.	Phased out T-6000s to introduce next generation system— JC/80.
JCI product distribution	Systems sold on a job-by-job basis—applications varied by job.			Branch distribution of BAS improved.
Pricing	Information unavailable.	Information unavailable.	Competitor A priced below JCI.	Competitor A priced below JCI.
JCI organization	Company building on computer and electronics experience.		• Select engineering group responsible for T-6000 sales and service. • Regions primarily responsible for design and operation.	

*Information is generalized to protect JCI confidentiality.

strategy on superior, user-friendly, upgradable products, a strong advertising campaign, and a well-thought-out market positioning strategy that allowed us to continue to generate profits from our maturing JC/80 product family.

Today, we're trying to be even more successful in managing our product lines to achieve maximum return on investment while guarding against competitive marketing initiatives and product campaigns.

Decline Stage. We noticed that the sales for each BAS product family decreased very rapidly to only a few units over a 24-month period at this stage. This always coincided with the introduction of a new JCI product. Although we could make up for lost sales with the increased earnings of the new product, we realized that had the decline of the old product been managed more slowly, overall sales might have been even better. We could be putting ourselves at risk by not avoiding the premature death of a successfully maturing product, especially in a rapidly growing, technically sophisticated market.

This information allowed us to develop a set of rules-of-thumb for marketing managers to use in future strategic planning efforts. Exhibit 6 shows possible strategies for the maturity and decline phases of the T-6000 family.

There's no one model that can be used by all businesses all the time in studying product life cycles. Even at Johnson Controls, the life cycle study approach for new products will be somewhat different. In some cases, such a study may simply prove too difficult. On the other hand, different lines of products that are related in function and technology can be grouped together. This turned out to be the most productive avenue to study BAS product life cycles at Johnson Controls.

IMPLEMENTING THE SOLUTIONS

The BAS product life cycle study took approximately six months to complete. One of its immediate benefits was that it paved the way for a related market study done soon after. According to William P. Lydon, Manager of Future Product Planning, "The study provided key information for a more comprehensive study of BAS products, which included further life cycle analysis, market segmentation analysis, market potential estimation, and a technology forecast."

Lee Fiegel, Director of Strategic Planning at the corporate level, felt that "the PLC study provided information that could aid marketing and product managers in setting cost and life cycle limitations on current products." Joel H. Richmond, now Manager of BAS Marketing Support Services, used the information in just that way. He developed a pricing scenario that allowed for recouping developing and marketing costs of existing software for the maturing DFMS product line without killing it with a new DFMS software introduction. According to Richmond, "Before we did the PLC analysis it was difficult to price existing software incrementally with newly developed software."

The PLC study reemphasized the importance of identifying the strategies appropriate to the different stages of a product's life span. Many manufacturers have a difficult time doing this, partly for reasons discussed above, but also because there's

EXHIBIT 6
T-6000 Possible Life Cycle Strategies

Maturity
1968–1971

- Increase market penetration.
- Defend established markets.
- Secure profits as soon as possible and cut costs.

Product
Selective addition of new features.

Price
High to take advantage of demand.

Placement
In key market segments.

Promotion
Create buyer preference.
Differentiate from competition.

Decline
1971–1973

- Milk all possible benefits.
- Prepare for removal or adaptation.
- Cut internal-support costs.

Product
No more features.

Price
Low to moderate to recover any possible profit.

Placement
Selective phase out of unprofitable segments.

Promotion
Minimal expense to cut costs.

often a tug of war between marketing and R&D.

Mike McLean, Manager of BAS Marketing, felt that "the PLC study helped marketing maintain a balance between the desires of the sales force and engineering development. Sales is always vying for the latest feature of product—the one they lost the last sale over—while engineering is always pushing to redesign, do it better, or make the product more sophisticated."

The PLC study helped give us perspective on such questions as:

- Does the product need a face lift?
- Should the product be discontinued? If so, when?
- Will advertising help?
- How long before we need to invest in a new design?

The PLC study was especially critical in identifying and establishing the historical opportunities and threats facing Johnson Controls, the prevailing competitive strategies, and how the company's strategies met these challenges.

Name Index

Subject Index